Development Economics

THEORY, EMPIRICAL RESEARCH, AND POLICY ANALYSIS

Development Economics

THEORY, EMPIRICAL RESEARCH, AND POLICY ANALYSIS

Julie Schaffner
Tufts University

WILEY

Vice President & Executive Publisher	George Hoffman
Executive Editor	Joel Hollenbeck
Content Editor	Jennifer Manias
Assistant Editor	Courtney Luzzi
Senior Editorial Assistant	Erica Horowitz
Director of Marketing	Amy Scholz
Assistant Marketing Manager	Puja Katariwala
Marketing Assistant	Mia Brady
Senior Production Manager	Janis Soo
Associate Production Manager	Joel Balbin
Production Editor	Yee Lyn Song
Cover Designer	Kenji Ngieng
Cover Photo Credit	© Evgeny Kuklev/iStockphoto

This book was set in Times Regular by MPS Limited and printed and bound by Quad/Graphics. The cover was printed by Quad/Graphics.

This book is printed on acid-free paper.

Founded in 1807, John Wiley & Sons, Inc., has been a valued source of knowledge and understanding for more than 200 years, helping people around the world meet their needs and fulfill their aspirations. Our company is built on a foundation of principles that include responsibility to the communities we serve and where we live and work. In 2008, we launched a Corporate Citizenship Initiative, a global effort to address the environmental, social, economic, and ethical challenges we face in our business. Among the issues we are addressing are carbon impact, paper specifications and procurement, ethical conduct within our business and among our vendors, and community and charitable support. For more information, please visit our website: www.wiley.com/go/citizenship.

Library of Congress Cataloging-in-Publication Data

Schaffner, Julie.
  Development economics : theory, empirical research, and policy analysis / Julie Schaffner, Tufts University.
    pages cm
  Includes index.
    ISBN 978-0-470-59939-6 (pbk. : alk. paper) 1. Economic development. 2. Economic policy. I. Title.
  HD77.S33 2014
  338.9—dc23
                                                                                      2013019193

Printed in the United States of America
VAEF27A57-6A42-4ABE-A441-BBC019A2AE13_121219

Brief Contents

Contents

3 Economic Growth   34

4 Economic Growth Theory in Historical Perspective   57

9   Labor Markets   208

10   Investment and Financial Markets   242

13 Policy, Governance, and Political Economy   346

Part IV   Policy Analysis Approach and Applications

14 Policy Analysis   377

15 Targeted Transfer Programs   391

16   Workfare   417

19 Education   496

20 Agricultural Research and Extension   523

Preface

Many students in development economics courses hope not only to learn *about* development, but also to become involved *in* development as researchers, policymakers, entrepreneurs, voters, program officers, or donors. If their involvement is to help make the world a better place, they must make good choices in their development activities. This means that they must acquire much more from their development courses than mere familiarity with development issues. They must acquire the skills and instincts necessary for rigorous, context-specific analysis of whatever development questions they might encounter. As I see it, they must learn how to think about development in a way that is disciplined by economic theory, informed by empirical research, and connected in a practical way to policy.

The relevant theory is not a single, grand theory that summarizes the entire socioeconomic system in several equations, nor is it a catalog of disjoint theories addressing miscellaneous development questions. Rather, it is a coherent framework built up from the foundations of microeconomic theory, which guides students in a logical fashion through the study of how people in developing countries make important decisions regarding consumption, time allocation, production, saving, and investment, and of what happens when many such decision makers interact with one another in market and nonmarket settings. The relevant theory relaxes assumptions that are maintained in basic microeconomics courses, acknowledging the potential importance in development studies of transaction and transportation costs, risk, imperfect information, institutional rules and norms, and insights from behavioral economics. While individual components of the theory focus on small subsets of socioeconomic outcomes—such as farm households' consumption and production choices or market prices—the framework also brings out the relationships among the many components, helping students build bridges from the micro study of choices and the meso study of markets and institutions to a coherent macro understanding of economic growth, poverty reduction, and development more generally. This text lays out such a theoretical framework.

Theory contributes the most to development when interacting with empirical research. Theories are sets of simplifying assumptions about how the world works that help analysts organize their study of development problems and policies. By working out the logical implications of a theory's assumptions, analysts can identify many forces that might improve a particular development outcome or many impacts that might follow from a particular policy. But only by bringing theory into contact with reality through empirical research can they learn which of the many *theoretically possible* causes or effects are likely to be *practically important* in a particular context. In addition, empirical research can reveal the inadequacy of current theories for explaining observed phenomena, thereby motivating construction of new theories with better predictive powers. Such new theories, in turn, raise new questions and open doors to new insights. This text helps readers understand the important interactions between theory and empirical research and reviews lessons learned from empirical research to date regarding many development questions.

Studying theory and empirical research is necessary but not sufficient preparation for development policy analysis. Students of development engage in policy analysis when they evaluate policies' benefits and costs, predict how changes in policies' designs or governance might alter their impacts, or identify how packages of policies might be used to achieve multiple goals with limited resources. Such information-gathering activities are vital to good decision making in development work. To perform such tasks well, students must learn: to identify in detail how a specific policy alters people's opportunities and constraints, to identify the groups directly affected by the policy, to study the policy's impacts on the behavior and well-being of those groups, to work out the implications of these behavioral changes for markets, institutions, and the environment, and to assess the resulting indirect impacts on the well-being of diverse groups throughout society. This text therefore presents a systematic approach to studying chains of policy impact and applies the approach in analyzing development policies of many types from around the world.

Intended Audience and Prerequisites

The book's primary audience includes upper-level economics undergraduates and master's-level students in public policy, international relations, economics, evaluation, and other social sciences. For Ph.D. students in economics, the text offers a broad and coherent perspective on development, which provides context and motivation for the narrow questions addressed in academic research. For development practitioners, it offers guidance for program design, policy advocacy, and evaluation.

The text is written for students who have taken intermediate microeconomics. It reviews basic concepts and builds standard theories from the ground up, but it does so quickly, in order to concentrate on application, extension, empirical testing, and interpretation.

The main body of the text requires no previous study of calculus, though some text boxes, footnotes, and end-of-chapter problems add interest for students who have studied calculus. The one exception is Chapter 4, on the historical evolution of growth theories, which employs calculus in the body of the text.

The text engages deeply with empirical research. It is accessible to students who have not yet taken econometrics, but it is also written to serve as a platform for courses with econometrics as a prerequisite. The text cites many important empirical research papers, and some text boxes examine the contributions of specific empirical papers in more detail. Appendix A provides a review of the basic statistical and econometric concepts that students require for interpreting empirical evidence and evaluating its quality. For students who have already taken introductory econometrics, it offers a focused review. For students who have not yet taken econometrics, it offers practical suggestions regarding the questions to ask when interpreting and evaluating statistical and econometric evidence.

Organization and Uses

The text is designed for multiple uses. Parts I through III (in order) could serve as the foundation for a **one-semester general introduction** to development. Part I offers a brief introduction to development and to the way economists approach the study of development. Part II examines the nature, underpinnings, and measurement of development success, first at the micro level of developing-country households, where development must raise well-being, and then at the macro level, where success requires some combination of economic growth and reductions in poverty, inequality, and vulnerability. In so doing, it builds the skeleton of the text's analytical framework, which emphasizes the many types of investment and innovation required for successful economic growth, and the more detailed changes in assets, markets, and institutions that must take place if economic growth is to bring improvements in well-being for many groups throughout society.

Part III fleshes out the analytical framework, presenting theories to guide study of the decisions, markets, and institutions that shape development outcomes, and demonstrating the theories' usefulness in policy-relevant empirical applications. At the heart of the framework are households with diverse assets and interests, who interact with one another in markets for goods, services, labor, credit, savings instruments, and insurance. They interact also in nonmarket settings, such as communities, where they might choose to cooperate in creating public goods, protecting common property resources, participating in informal insurance arrangements, or respecting one another's property rights. Their interactions in market and nonmarket settings are governed by institutional rules and norms, the quality of which differs greatly across countries and communities. The framework highlights that while markets and private institutions together encourage people to make many development-enhancing choices, they fail to deliver ideal development success for many reasons, creating the potential for governments, nongovernmental organizations (NGOs), and other actors to improve development outcomes by intervening in the socioeconomic system. Unfortunately, in practice, policy interventions sometimes fail to advance development, and in some cases even trap people in poverty. Policies enhance development only when leaders' policy choices are governed by healthy political institutions, when the policies are well-designed responses to correctly diagnosed market and institutional failures, when second-best problems do not give rise to large unintended costs, and when high-quality public sector institutions provide good governance for policy implementation.

Parts I through IV (in order) could serve as the foundation for a **two-semester sequence**, in which the first semester focuses on understanding development and the socioeconomic systems in which development takes place (highlighting the interaction between theory and empirical research, and using Parts I through III of the text), and the second semester focuses on policy analysis (using Part IV of the text). The first chapter in Part IV (Chapter 14) articulates an approach to systematic and comprehensive policy analysis in the form of seven questions. The questions formalize the instincts that well-trained economists bring to policy analysis. The approach calls on students to apply the analytical tools of Part III in working out all the theoretically possible direct and indirect impacts of a policy on diverse groups throughout society (and reasons why the impacts might be large or small) and then to seek out empirical evidence regarding the actual or likely sizes of the impacts in any particular context. It guides readers in studying how the nature, distribution, and sizes of policies' costs and benefits are shaped by the specifics of policy design, governance structure, and economic and institutional context.

The remainder of Part IV equips students more specifically to apply this approach in the analysis of eight classes of policies related to targeted transfers, workfare, agricultural markets, infrastructure, education, agricultural technology, microfinance, and health. The policy analysis application chapters offer many illustrations of three policy-analytic activities: evaluation of specific policies' overall benefits and costs, assessment of the tradeoffs associated with detailed policy design choices (e.g., choices regarding user fee levels or detailed eligibility requirements), and evaluation of governance structure reforms (e.g., reforms involving decentralization, increased community participation, increased use of performance contracting, or privatization).

Instructors may instead wish to draw on the chapters of Part IV in other ways. In one-semester **development economics courses highlighting policy applications**, instructors may follow some of the social science chapters of Part III with brief discussions of policy analysis application chapters from Part IV. Even though an important theme of the book is that comprehensive analysis of any one policy requires understanding of *all* the analytical tools of Part III (because a single policy can generate direct and indirect effects throughout the entire socioeconomic system), each policy analysis application chapter emphasizes some tools over others and may fruitfully be used in this way. For example, after setting the stage with Chapters 1, 2, 3, and 5, instructors might wish to interweave the application chapters with the tools chapters in the following way (though leaving some topics out to meet time constraints):

Social Science Chapters of Part III	Application Chapters from Part IV
Chapter 6: Consumption, time allocation, and production choices	Chapter 15: Targeted transfer programs
	Chapter 16: Workfare
Chapter 7: Households	Chapter 17: Agricultural market interventions and reforms
Chapter 8: Domestic markets for goods and services	Chapter 18: Infrastructure policies and programs
Chapter 11: International markets and general equilibrium	
Chapter 9: Labor markets	Chapter 19: Education

(Continued)

(Continued)

Social Science Chapters of Part III	Application Chapters from Part IV
Chapter 10: Investment and financial markets	Chapter 20: Agricultural research and extension Chapter 21: Microfinance Chapter 22: Public health, health care, and health insurance
Chapter 12: Institutions and cooperation Chapter 13: Policy, governance, and political economy	Revisit policy design and governance issues from Chapters 15 through 22

In courses aimed at equipping students for **development policy analysis or evaluation**, instructors could introduce development using Chapters 1, 2, 3, and 5; introduce policy, governance challenges, and policy analysis using Chapters 13 and 14; offer a brief review of econometric methods using Appendix A; and then organize the remainder of the course around the policy applications of Part IV, while providing students with references to prerequisite expositions of analytical tools from Part III as follows:

Policy Application Chapter of Part IV	Prerequisite Sections from Part III (in Addition to Chapter 13)
Chapter 15: Targeted transfer programs, and Chapter 16: Workfare	Section 6.2: Consumption choices Section 6.3: Labor supply choices Section 7.3: Non-unitary household theories Section 8.3: Market equilibrium in the presence of transfer costs Section 12.3C: Informal insurance institutions
Chapter 17: Agricultural market interventions and reforms	Section 6.4: Basic producer theory Section 7.2: Unitary household theories Section 8.3: Market equilibrium in the presence of transfer costs Section 9.3: Mobility in developing country labor markets Chapter 11: International markets and general equilibrium
Chapter 18: Infrastructure policies and programs	Section 8.3: Market equilibrium in the presence of transfer costs Section 8.4: The economics of market development Chapter 10: Investment and financial markets Section 12.2: Cooperation and institutions Section 12.3B: Institutions governing local common property resources
Chapter 19: Education	Section 9.4: Skill acquisition in developing country labor markets Chapter 10: Investment and financial markets
Chapter 20: Agricultural research and extension	Section 6.4: Basic producer theory Section 7.2: Unitary household theories Section 8.3: Market equilibrium in the presence of transfer costs Chapter 10: Investment and financial markets Section 12.3D: Land rights institutions
Chapter 21: Microfinance	Chapter 10: Investment and financial markets
Chapter 22: Public health, health care, and health insurance	Section 6.1: Choices, development, and development economics Chapter 10: Investment and financial markets Section 12.3C: Informal insurance institutions

Instructors might also wish to use Part IV to assist students working on policy papers as course assignments. Chapter 14 provides students with practical, general guidance for the relevant research. Once students have picked specific policy topics, instructors may offer additional guidance by pointing them to the most relevant of the policy analysis application chapters.

Pedagogical Features

The following features are included to facilitate learning:

- **Key terms** are rendered in boldface when first used in a chapter, signaling that students should be able to define and discuss the significance of these concepts. To facilitate the use of the book's chapters in diverse combinations and diverse order, some key terms are defined and bolded in more than one chapter.

- **Focal ideas** within the text are emphasized with shading, signaling that students should study the theoretical and empirical arguments leading up to these points and the elaborations and implications that follow from them.

- **Text boxes** illustrate and apply important concepts, while offering more detailed discussions of specific research projects and policy initiatives.

- **Questions for review** at the ends of chapters prompt students to identify and digest the main points of the chapters in the order in which the points are presented.

- **Questions for discussion** at the ends of chapters encourage students to synthesize the ideas and tools introduced in the chapters, to apply concepts in an open-ended way to new contexts, or to articulate their own position on value-laden questions. Instructors might wish to use some of these as springboards for class discussion.

- **Problems** guide students in a structured (and mostly closed-ended) way through the analysis of stylized models or policy problems, allowing students an opportunity to work with numbers, graphs, and the text's approach to policy analysis. Some problems offer a mathematical treatment of concepts treated only informally in the text or provide numerical examples to illuminate points made in the text.

- The **Glossary** defines key terms that are used in multiple chapters or that are especially important in contemporary development discussions.

Instructor Resources

The following resources can be found online at www.wiley.com/college/schaffner:

- The **Solutions Manual**, written by the author, contains answers for all problems and selected discussion questions.

- **PowerPoint Presentations**, created by the author, highlight the main points of each chapter and demonstrate the application of analytical tools. An **Image Gallery**, containing jpg files for all of the figures in the text, is also provided for instructor convenience.

- The **Test Bank**, written by Ting Levy of Florida Atlantic University, contains 25–30 questions per chapter. Multiple Choice, Short Answer, and Essay Questions vary in level of difficulty and are mapped to Learning Objectives of the text.

Acknowledgments

I can only begin to thank the countless teachers, colleagues, students, authors, interviewees, friends, and acquaintances from whom I have learned about development. Each one has helped shape this book in some way.

The colleagues and teachers to whom I am indebted include Jenny Aker, Steve Block, Bob Evenson, Michael Ferrantino, Paul Glewwe, Anjini Kochar, Patrick McEwan, Margaret McMillan, Jonathan Morduch, Eva Mueller, Paul Schultz, T.N. Srinivasan, Jee-Peng Tan, Shinsuke Tanaka, Chris Udry, Peter Uvin, Kim Wilson, Bruce Wydick, and especially Michael Klein, John Strauss, and Ann Velenchik, without whose encouragement and advice this book would not have been written.

So many students at Stanford, Boston University, and the Fletcher School at Tufts have kept me on my toes and shared their field and research experiences with me. With warm gratitude,

I especially acknowledge assistance and input from Xanthe Ackerman, Susan Banki, Maliheh Birjandi Feriz, Cara Carter Sechser, Farhan Charania, Susan Chun, John Floretta, Kathryn Griffin, Cornelia Jesse, Ines Kapphan, Georgia Kayser, Anthony Keats, Hye-Sung Kim, Ben Mazotta, Tammy McGavock, John Pollock, Ben Ratichek, Rob Reiling, Annika Rigole, Andrew Sargent, Katherine Scaife, Sarah Sitts, Vickie Slingerland, Gaurav Tiwari, Joanna Upton, Wei Yao, and Julie Zollman.

I am grateful for editorial contributions from Joel Hollenbeck, Erica Horowitz, Courtney Luzzi, Jennifer Manias, Emily McGee, Lacey Roberts, Yee Lyn Song, and especially George Lobell, whose tremendous enthusiasm and knowledge of the field gave this project momentum and direction.

For their helpful reviews, my editors and I would like to thank: Karna Basu, Hunter College; Kristie Briggs, Creighton University; Laura Ebert, State University of New York at New Paltz; Erwin Erhardt, University of Cincinnati; Sylvestre Gaudin, Oberlin College; Jonathan Haughton, Suffolk University; Shawn Knabb, Western Washington University; John McPeak, Syracuse University; Irfan Nooruddin, Ohio State University; Jonathan Robinson, University of California at Santa Cruz; Neslihan Uler, University of Michigan; Ann Velenchik, Wellesley College; Bruce Wydick, University of San Francisco; and Bassam Yousif, Indiana State University.

This project would have been impossible without the love and support of my husband and sons, the joys of my life, Steve, Thomas, and Matthew.

For opportunities to learn from people in many walks of life and for his call to practice justice and compassion, I give thanks to God. Anything of value here is by his grace.

What Is Development Economics Good For?

The average citizen of the United States is incredibly rich by world standards. She prospers on an income of $120 per day, while 90 percent of the world's population lives on than less than $10 per day, 40 percent get by on less than $2 per day, and 15 percent—nearly *one billion* human beings—live on less than $1 per day (Pritchett, 2006; Chen and Ravallion, 2010). In the world's poorest places, life expectancy is less than 50 years, and one baby in ten dies before reaching one year of age. Many families live in one-room shelters with few possessions, where drinking water is contaminated, roads are often impassable, and few children attend school.

The prevalence of poverty in a world where some people enjoy great prosperity raises big questions: Why are some people and countries so much poorer than others? How did some countries become prosperous? What can governments and philanthropic organizations do to reduce poverty and encourage the spread of prosperity? Such questions motivate interest in the subject of **development**, which encompasses the many ways material, physical, and social living standards might improve and the processes and policies that help bring those improvements about.

The discipline of economics offers a powerful framework for study of this complex subject. After describing the global patterns of poverty and prosperity that motivate interest in development, this chapter describes how economists approach three important tasks: defining the development objective, understanding the development process, and analyzing development policy.

1.1 Assessing Global Poverty and Prosperity
1.1A Lessons from international statistics

Global differences in income are vast, and the citizens of poor countries greatly outnumber the citizens of rich countries. The horizontal axis in Figure 1.1 measures countries' average income levels in 2010 as measured by gross domestic product (GDP) per capita in U.S. dollar equivalents (a measure of average annual income that we examine closely in Chapter 3), and the vertical axis measures the number of people living in countries with average incomes in the given ranges. Of the 189 countries for which data are available, the Democratic Republic of Congo (DRC) registers the lowest average annual income per person of $282. Average income in the United States, at $46,570, is 165 times greater than that! Eight small countries, together home to only one quarter of one percent of the world's population, are off the chart to the right, with average annual incomes greater than $50,000. Altogether, five percent of the world's people live in countries with average income at the U.S. level or higher, while almost half—well over three billion people— live in countries with average incomes one fifth of the U.S. level or less. Fivefold differences in average income mean large differences in the availability of resources for meeting needs and generating well-being!

Many of the world's poorest countries are in Africa. Figure 1.2 indicates the locations of the countries that the World Bank classifies as low-income (darkest shading), lower-middle income, upper-middle income, and high-income countries (lightest shading). Countries are defined as low income if their average incomes are less than $1,005 and as high income if their incomes are greater than $12,275. The dividing line between lower- and upper-middle income countries

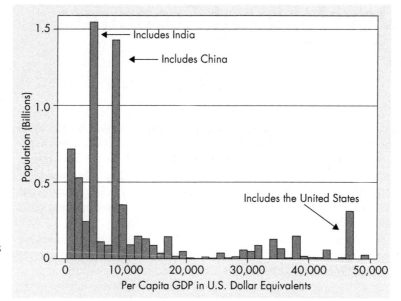

FIGURE 1.1
Distribution of the World's Population across Countries at Different Levels of Gross Domestic Product (GDP) Per Capita in 2010
Source: Heston et al. (2012).

is $3,975.[1] Many African and Asian countries qualify as low-income countries, and most Latin American countries qualify as middle-income countries.

The average income statistics employed in Figures 1.1 and 1.2, although useful and thought provoking, fall short of fully describing prosperity and deprivation for two reasons. First, average income figures tell us how much income each person in a country would have *if* all income were distributed equally, but in reality income is distributed unequally. Among countries with the same average income, rates of deep deprivation may be much higher where income is more unequally distributed. Second, income measures do not tell us everything we might wish to know about the quality of life. For example, even among people with the same income, some might have better access to clean water and good education or might face lower risk of going hungry. Hence it is useful to look beyond average income statistics to the broader range of statistics presented in Tables 1.1 and 1.2.

The **income poverty** statistics presented in Table 1.1 demonstrate that large fractions of the world's population live with very low incomes. As pointed out in Banerjee and Duflo (2008), the official poverty threshold in the United States is roughly $13 per person per day, so we should consider measures of poverty that use thresholds of $1.25 and $2 per day as conservative esti- mates of global poverty rates. Even so, nearly half the population of the developing world is poor by the $2 standard! If we were to employ a poverty threshold of $10 per day, Pritchett (2006) estimates that the vast majority of the world's population would qualify as poor, with only 0.8 billion people enjoying incomes above that level.

Income poverty differs greatly in breadth and depth across countries. In the bottom segment of Table 1.1, the regions of the developing world are listed in order from lowest to highest percentages of the population living on less than $1.25 per day. These percentages range from just 0.5 and 2.7 in Eastern Europe and the Middle East to 47.5 percent in sub-Saharan Africa. Per- centages of the population living on less than $2 per day range from 2.2 to 69.2.

Comparison of the $1.25- and $2-dollar-per-day poverty figures also reveals greater typical depth of poverty in sub-Saharan Africa, where 70 percent of those with incomes under $2 per day

---

[1] The average income figures used for the World Bank classification in Figure 1.2 differ from the average income figures used to construct Figure 1.1. The World Bank employs measures of per capita gross national income (GNI) in local currency converted to dollars using the Atlas Method. Figure 1.1 employs the more commonly used measure of per capita GDP converted to dollars using purchasing power parity exchange rates. Chapter 3 defines and discusses these different ways of measuring average income and converting into U.S. dollar equivalents.

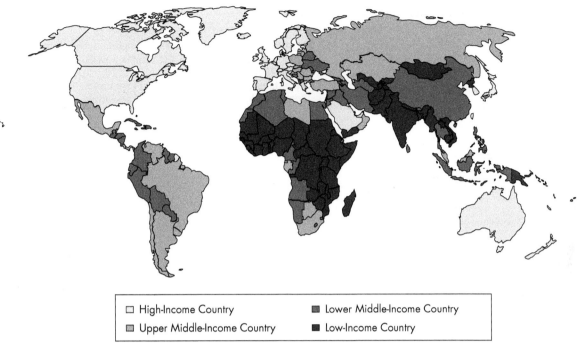

FIGURE 1.2
Geographic Distribution of Countries by Average Income Level
Source: World Bank (2012).

in fact have incomes lower than the more severe threshold of $1.25 per day. The comparable share in Eastern Europe and Central Asia is 20 percent, and the Middle East, East Asia, Latin America, and South Asia have shares ranging from 20 percent to 52 percent. Even though deep poverty is most prevalent in Africa, it is by no means a uniquely African problem. People live on less than $1.25 per day in all regions of the world. Many of the world's poorest people live in middle-income countries (Sumner, 2010).

Table 1.2 complements the income-based measures of poverty with more direct measures of deprivation, and it demonstrates that for many people, life is short, the death of

■ TABLE 1.1   Income Poverty Statistics for Low- and Middle-Income Countries by Region of the World, 2008

Region	Total Population of Region in 2008 (Millions)	Population Living on Less than $1.25 per Day		Population Living on Less than $2 per Day	
		Millions	Percent	Millions	Percent
Low- and middle-income countries	6,737.1	1,289	22.4	2,471	43.0
Eastern Europe and Central Asia	883.6	2	0.5	10	2.2
Middle East and North Africa	367.7	9	2.7	44	13.9
Latin America and the Caribbean	575.7	37	6.5	71	12.4
China	1,324.6	173	13.1	395	29.8
East Asia and the Pacific	2,173.0	284	14.3	659	33.2
South Asia	1,586.4	571	36.0	1,125	70.9
Sub-Saharan Africa	812.8	386	47.5	562	69.2

Source: World Bank (2012).

■ TABLE 1.2   Living Standards Indicators by Region of the World

Region	Life Expectancy at Birth, 2010 (Years)	Infant Mortality Rate, 2010 (Deaths per 1,000 Live Births)	Prevalence of Undernourishment, 2006–2008 (Percentage of Population)	Secondary School Gross Enrollment Rate, 2010 (Percent)	Access to Improved Water Source, 2010 (Percentage of Population)	Access to Improved Sanitation, 2010 (Percentage of Population)
High-income countries	80	5	<5	100	100	100
Low- and Middle-income Countries	68	45	14	64	86	56
Eastern Europe and Central Asia	71	19	6	89	96	84
Middle East and North Africa	72	27	7	72	89	88
East Asia and the Pacific	72	20	11	76	90	66
Latin America and the Caribbean	74	18	9	90	94	79
South Asia	65	52	20	55	90	38
Sub-Saharan Africa	54	76	22	36	61	31

Source: World Bank (2012).

children is commonplace, hunger is the norm, sending children to school is an insurmountable challenge, and even basic precautions against disease are lacking. Again, the aggregate statistics are particularly troubling for sub-Saharan Africa, where life expectancy is just 54 years, one out of every thirteen babies dies before age 5 years, more than one fifth of the population is malnourished, only one third of children attend secondary school, nearly 40 percent of the population lacks access to improved drinking water, and two thirds lack basic sanitation facilities.

1.1B Poverty in Ethiopia

Imagine living in rural Ethiopia, where most people live on less than $2 per day. You make your living by growing food on a small plot of land using only your own labor, the labor of your children and—if you are fortunate—a donkey or an ox. None of the adults in your village has ever been to school, and few of the children attend the nearest primary school, which lies several kilometers down a dusty, rutted track. You and your five children live in a one-room hut with a thatched roof and earth floor. You have no electricity and no running water, and your "bathroom" is the open field. You eat the same few foods at every meal—when you have food. You depend on rain to make your crops grow, and you know that every few years you and your neighbors will be struck by drought. You will do what you can, but your children will go hungry. Some children will die.

Household survey data suggest that most rural Ethiopian families indeed live in much the way you just imagined. Consider, for example, the statistics presented in Table 1.3, derived from Ethiopia's Welfare Monitoring Surveys of 2000 and 2004. Most Ethiopians (86 percent) live in rural areas, and the statistics in the first column tell us that 66 percent of rural households live in homes with thatched roofs and 77 percent use the field or forest as their toilet. The statistics in the second column suggest that life circumstances are somewhat better for the few Ethiopians who live in urban areas. Grass-roofed huts are replaced by shanties with corrugated tin roofs, and access to improved water, electricity, schools, and health centers is much better in urban areas, though certainly not guaranteed. But life is still uncomfortable and hard.

■ TABLE 1.3   **Ethiopian Living Standard Statistics**

	Rural	Urban
Number of households (millions)	11.3	2.1
Number of people (millions)	55.6	9.1
Share of total population (%)	86	14
Median number of:		
People in household	7	6
Rooms in dwelling	1	2
Percentage of households:		
With female head of household	18	34
With illiterate head of household	68	35
With grass roof	66	6
With corrugated iron roof	25	91
With electric lighting	1	74
Using collected firewood for fuel	81	19
Using field or forest for toilet	77	19
Using unprotected water source	77	9
Experiencing food shortage in last 12 months	35	16
Percentage of children 7 to 14 years old:		
Registered to attend school	39	84
Percent of households more than 5 kilometers from the nearest:		
Primary school	30	1
Secondary school	92	14
Health center	69	6
All-weather road	63	2

Source: Ethiopia's Welfare Monitoring Surveys of 2000 and 2004. All statistics refer to 2004 except those relating to shares of households living more than 5 km from nearest schools, health center, and all-weather road, which refer to 2000. The samples are representative only of the nonnomadic population.

Statistics like these help outsiders to imagine what poverty is like in Ethiopia, but for millions of Ethiopians no imagination is necessary. Listen to what some of them have to say about what life in poverty is like (Narayan et al., 2000):

"Living by scratching like a chicken."

"Life has made us ill."

"We are skinny."

"We are above the dead and below the living."

"We simply watch those who eat."

"Difficulties have made us crazy."

"From hand to mouth."

"A life that is like being flogged."

"Just a sip and no more drop is left."

"If one is full, the other will not be full."

"Always calf, never to be bull."

1.2 Defining the Development Objective

Many governments, intergovernmental organizations, nongovernmental organizations (NGOs), socially responsible enterprises, and even billionaires and rock stars have committed time and money to reducing poverty and promoting "development" in the world's poorer countries. Box 1.1 introduces the diverse array of **development actors** at work in the world today.

≡ Box 1.1 Diverse Development Actors

Country governments

Country governments bear central responsibility for creating development-friendly environments within developing countries. Many ministries and departments participate in a country's development work, but often a single government ministry shapes the overall development strategy. For example, the Kenyan Ministry of Planning and National Development (www.planning.go.ke) articulates its mission in this way: "To provide leadership in formulating, coordinating and implementing national policies for sustainable development," placing great emphasis on poverty-reduction programs.

Development-focused multilateral agencies

The development organizations most visible in the international press are multilateral development organizations, including affiliates of the World Bank and United Nations. The World Bank (www.worldbank.org), created in 1945, is a set of five international organizations, to which 188 countries belong and that operate together as a development bank. Initially created to support reconstruction in Europe after World War II, it is now devoted to promoting development in low- and middle-income countries with grants, loans, policy advice, technical assistance, and knowledge-sharing services. Central to the mandate of the United Nations (www.un.org), also created in 1945, is the promotion of higher living standards around the world. The pursuit of this objective, which constitutes 70 percent of its work, is carried out through many specialized agencies within the U.N. system, including the United Nations Development Program (UNDP), the U.N. Children's Fund (UNICEF), the World Food Program (WFP), the U.N. Industrial Development Organization (UNIDO), and the U.N. Educational, Scientific, and Cultural Organization (UNESCO), which have offices and field workers around the world.

Other multilateral organizations

The World Trade Organization (WTO) and the International Monetary Fund (IMF) serve developed as well as developing countries. The mission of the WTO, founded in 1995, is to provide "a forum for negotiating agreements aimed at reducing obstacles to international trade and ensuring a level playing field for all, thus contributing to economic growth and development" (www.wto.org). The IMF was created in 1944 for the purpose of promoting stability in the international financial system. Today the fundamental mission of the IMF is "to help ensure stability in the international system," by monitoring its members' economic conditions, policies, and financial regulations, lending to help countries cope with balance of payments difficulties, and offering policy advice (www.imf.org).

Bilateral organizations

Bilateral organizations are the agencies through which individual developed country governments promote development in low- and middle-income countries. For example, the U.S. Agency for International Development (USAID, www.usaid.gov), created in 1961, is a U.S. federal government agency that supports long-term growth and the achievement of U.S. foreign policy objectives in sub-Saharan Africa, Asia, Latin America, Europe, and Eurasia. Its counterpart in the United Kingdom is the Department for International Development (DFID, www.dfid.gov.uk) and in Sweden is the Swedish International Development Authority (SIDA, www.sida.org).

International NGOs

Nongovernmental organizations (NGOs) of many sorts are of great importance in day-to-day development efforts and are becoming increasingly involved in debates about development strategy. Some international NGOs have geographic reach similar to that of the large multilateral organizations. For example, CARE (www.care.org) works with women in over 80 countries to help communities escape poverty, by improving education, access to clean water, health, economic opportunity, and protection of natural resources. Alongside the large international NGOs work many smaller international NGOs, which might focus on development work in a single country or on providing solutions to specific problems (such as leprosy or low primary school enrollment) in just a few countries.

Local NGOs

Other NGOs of great vitality and creativity are home grown within developing countries. Most of these local NGOs never reach the newspapers in the developed countries, though a few have drawn attention for their economic and social innovations and achievements. One such organization is the Self Employed Women's Association (SEWA, www.sewa.org) in India. Established in 1972 as a trade union of self-employed women, it now promotes full employment and self-reliance among poor women not only through organizing campaigns but also through cooperative banking and the provision of health care, child care, and other services.

Alliances

Organizations working toward similar ends often form alliances or umbrella organizations to coordinate efforts, share knowledge, and partner in advocacy. For example, InterAction (www.interaction.org) is the largest alliance of U.S.-based international development and humanitarian organizations, and the British Overseas NGOs for Development (BOND, www.bond.org.uk) is the United Kingdom's largest network of voluntary development organizations.

Development consulting firms

Development consulting firms, such as Abt Associates (www.abtassociates.com) and Development Alternatives, Inc. (www.dai.com), are for-profit actors who contract with multilateral, bilateral, and other organizations to design, implement, or evaluate their programs.

Socially responsible enterprises and private foundations

Recent years have seen increased commitment to poverty reduction and development by the owners of for-profit corporations and enterprises who wish to use some or all of their business activities or profits in "socially responsible" ways. These actors include for-profit microfinance institutions that seek to help poor households by extending small loans to them, manufacturing enterprises that take an interest in the health and education of their developing country workers, and large and formal foundations funded by highly profitable businesses, such as the Bill and Melinda Gates Foundation (www.gatesfoundation.org).

Other civil society organizations

Within individual developing countries, increasing efforts are being made to bring together many development actors and other elements of civil society (such as religious organizations) to diagnose needs for poverty reduction and development, to debate development strategies, and to coordinate development efforts. A large number of prominent international development actors voiced support for such coordinating efforts in the 2005 Paris Declaration on Aid Effectiveness (http://www.oecd.org/dataoecd/11/41/34428351.pdf).

Academic researchers

A final set of actors whose behind-the-scenes efforts seek to facilitate poverty reduction and development are academic researchers at universities and other research organizations around the world. Through their teaching, academic economists equip development practitioners with ideas, knowledge, and analytical tools. Through their research, they enhance understanding of the constraints that shape the effects of development policies and programs. Increasingly academic economists—such as those associated with the Poverty Action Lab (www.povertyactionlab.org) and the Center for Global Development (www.cgdev.org)—are employing high-quality research tools in careful evaluation of the impacts of real-world programs, shedding new light on the relative merits of various poverty-reduction and development approaches.

The people who lead and work for the organizations described in Box 1.1 are motivated in great part by a desire to encourage and facilitate development. But what exactly is the "development objective" they pursue? Here we offer an umbrella definition, which captures the general concerns shared by most development actors, while leaving room for differences in their priorities:

The objective in development is sustained improvement in the well-being of a country's many people, with special emphasis on improvements for the poor.

This definition captures three sentiments shared by many development actors. First, the ultimate aim in development is to make people's lives better, and not merely to generate great economic statistics. Second, the hope in development is for improvements that are broadly shared by a country's diverse people, and especially by the poor. Third, development involves *sustained* improvement over many years. Even if incomes in the world's poor countries were to grow at the highest rates ever achieved, the growth would have to be sustained over decades to close the vast global gaps in living standards evident today.

The umbrella definition also allows for diversity in development actors' more specific definitions of their development objectives, along at least three dimensions. First, development actors differ in exactly how they define and measure well-being. Some treat income and well-being as nearly synonymous, while others place greater weight on nonincome features of living standards, such as access to health care.

Second, development actors differ in how, exactly, they weigh the experiences of diverse people against each other when evaluating overall development success. Some development actors value only improvements enjoyed by the poor, and they might consider periods of rising incomes among the poor as periods of development success, regardless of whether the incomes of the nonpoor are rising or falling. Others give more equal weight to changes for the nonpoor and the poor when assessing development success.

Third, development actors differ in the relative weights they place on immediate and longer-term improvements. Some development actors place great premium on meeting the immediate needs of today's poor, even if the assistance given to the poor provides them only temporary help. Other development actors, while maintaining concern about today's urgent needs, are more willing to postpone the enjoyment of some improvements, if by doing so they can produce larger and longer-lasting improvements in the future.

When measuring development success, development actors measure a variety of **development indicators**, or measures of the speed and nature of socioeconomic change, such as economic growth rates and changes in measures of poverty, inequality, and vulnerability, all of which we examine closely in Part II. Most development actors share interest in all these development outcomes, but they differ in how they define their priorities across the outcomes.

1.3 Understanding the Development Process

As an objective, development is widespread and sustained improvement in well-being. As a process, development is the web of economic and social change through which such widespread and sustained improvement comes about.

Within the framework that economists bring to the study of development, the accumulation of **assets** is central to the development process. Throughout this book we define the term assets very broadly to include any physical, mental, or social resources or attributes that expand in a long-lasting way an economy's capacity to provide the goods, services, security, and opportunities from which people derive their well-being. They include not only farm and business assets such as irrigation ditches, machines, and inventories but also infrastructure assets such as roads, telecommunications systems, and wells for safe drinking water; human assets such as education, job training, and health; and technological assets such as knowledge and use of improved methods for cultivating rice. We will see that:

> Development is most successful when an economy creates a healthy quantity and diverse array of assets, the assets are of high quality and durability, and the assets are distributed and employed in ways that channel their benefits broadly throughout society.

The quantity, quality, and types of assets that an economy creates in any period of time and the way the value generated by the assets is distributed across diverse groups are determined within a developing country's **socioeconomic system**. A country's socioeconomic system encompasses the many activities of its people, who seek the best for themselves and their families and who interact with each other in many market and nonmarket forums. They compete and transact with each other in goods, labor, and financial markets. They cooperate and bargain with each other, and interact in other ways, in nonmarket forums, such as the communities and larger societies in which they live and the networks and organizations to which they belong. Within these forums they might work together to create infrastructure or protect natural resources, respect each other's land rights, or provide each other with assistance when need and opportunity arise. They might also influence each other's preferences, beliefs, and knowledge. Their interactions in market and nonmarket forums are governed by **institutions**, which we define as sets of formal rules and informal norms, together with related enforcement mechanisms, that constrain people's choices in specific arenas. High-quality institutions discourage people from engaging in socially detrimental activities such as theft and fraud, and they encourage mutually beneficial trade and cooperation.

People determine the quantities and types of assets created within the socioeconomic system when they make choices regarding investments in irrigation ditches, use of new seed varieties, creation of new businesses, school attendance, health care use, saving, borrowing, cooperation in community projects, and fulfillment of contracts. They help determine how current assets are put to use and how the value generated is distributed when they make choices about what to produce, what to consume, what labor services to buy or sell, and how to interact with their neighbors in nonmarket forums. Owners of new assets help distribute benefits to others when they increase the demand for labor, increase the supply of basic consumer items, or give gifts to neighbors in need. Their many decisions are influenced by the quality of the markets to which they have access and the health of the institutions that govern their interactions in market and nonmarket settings.

We will learn that although people's initiative, creativity, and willingness to sacrifice are important driving forces in development, significant obstacles often prevent the residents of poor countries from undertaking key developmental activities. People living in remote locations remain cut off from markets by high transportation and communication costs when infrastructure is lacking. Weak legal and social institutions can combine with poor infrastructure to elevate the costs of market transactions more generally and to prohibit more sophisticated market exchanges. Barriers to labor mobility can inhibit workers from changing jobs or moving their families across country to take advantage of new job opportunities. The cost and difficulty of acquiring information and establishing trust limit the development of financial markets. Private institutions can fail to support cooperative investments in infrastructure and new technologies or to achieve desirable distributional outcomes through redistribution. Governments and NGOs have great potential to improve development outcomes by intervening in the socioeconomic system in ways that compensate for the failures of markets and private institutions. Unfortunately, their efforts can fail because designing and implementing successful policies is difficult. The public sector institutions they create can even slow development, whether intentionally or unintentionally, by fostering corruption, imposing bureaucratic barriers to private activity, or channeling benefits to the powerful rather than the poor. Where any of these obstacles remain severe, people remain poor. Thus:

> To understand the development process, and why development outcomes have been so much better in some places than others, we must understand the decisions, markets, and institutions that together determine what assets are created and who benefits from their creation.

Part III expounds the analytical framework and tools that economists bring to the study of decisions, markets, and institutions in developing countries. The framework reflects the basic proposition that we can gain important insight into the workings of the socioeconomic system by assuming that people seek to make themselves as well off as possible given the constraints they face, and then working hard to understand the way they evaluate their well-being and the nature of the constraints they face.

1.4 Analyzing Development Policy
1.4A Development policies and programs

Governments, NGOs, and other development actors implement a wide variety of policies, projects, and programs. Throughout the text we use **public sector** as a shorthand reference to governments, NGOs, and other development actors, and we use the term **policies** as a shorthand reference to the policies, projects, or programs they implement. We may distinguish three broad categories of policy.

Through **asset creation policies**, development organizations either invest directly in the creation of assets or encourage asset creation by private persons, families, and communities. The assets involved may be roads, machines, education, health, technological ideas, or other physical and human assets, and the policies may encourage their creation in diverse ways. Development actors might pay private sector contractors to undertake investments or may create grant schemes through which they finance investments by community groups. They might promote private business investment by improving access to credit, enhancing opportunities to save up for investments, allowing citizens of foreign countries to invest in local businesses, or increasing investor confidence by strengthening institutions for contract enforcement and protection of property. The design of asset creation policies influences not only the quantities and types of assets created but also who owns them, how they are employed and maintained, and who benefits from the value they generate.

Through **safety net policies**, development actors direct cash, goods, or services to households in pressing need. These policies aim to provide some combination of social assistance and social insurance. Social assistance offers long-term assistance to people who are chronically unable to engage in income-generating activities because, for example, they live in households left with few able-bodied workers as a result of disease or civil war. Social insurance provides short-term assistance to those who have been hit by shocks that leave them temporarily unable to generate income, perhaps because their crops have been hit by drought or disease or because they have lost jobs and must search for new ones. The primary function of safety net policies is to redistribute the income generated by the economy's assets. We will learn, however, that they may also generate secondary effects on the rate and nature of asset creation.

Finally, through policies of **intervention in markets for goods and services**, governments tax, subsidize, or regulate transactions in specific markets (such as the markets for rice or electronic goods) or involve themselves directly in buying and selling specific goods. Policies toward international trade, which discourage or encourage international import and export transactions, have figured prominently in development-policy debates for decades. We will examine the potential for such policies to alter the distribution of current income and the rate and nature of asset creation.

1.4B The need for good policy analysis and the role of economics

The history of the last five decades teaches that development success is possible. Many countries have doubled, tripled, or even quadrupled their average incomes over the last half century. The percentage of the developing world's population living on less than $1.25 per day fell from 52.2 percent in 1981 to 22.4 percent in 2008 (World Bank, 2012). Life expectancy in the developing world has risen from 40 to 65 years, and the share of newborns surviving to age 5 years has doubled. Besley and Cord (2007) document especially encouraging episodes of growth accompanied by significant poverty reduction, including the period of the 1960s through the mid-1990s in Indonesia and the 1990s in Vietnam.

We know not only that some countries have experienced episodes of successful development, but also that many *specific policies* of governments and other development actors have proved successful. Significant advances in health and life expectancy have arisen out of purposeful efforts to eradicate smallpox and polio, promote the use of oral rehydration therapy for children with diarrheal disease, control river blindness, and prevent HIV transmission, as well as efforts to expand access to clean drinking water and sanitation. In many countries where fewer than half the children attended primary school in the 1960s, efforts to draw more children into school have achieved nearly universal primary enrollment. Rural road construction has succeeded in expanding markets, raising incomes, and improving access to services (Khandker et al., 2009). Agricultural research and extension have helped farmers in some regions double or triple crop yields and have prevented new insect infestations and crop diseases from devastating staple food crops (Gabre-Madhin and Haggblade, 2004).

Unfortunately, history also teaches that development success is not guaranteed. Average incomes in some countries have risen little, and development policies have failed in many ways.

☰ Box 1.2 Resources for Development Efforts

Fully quantifying all of the resources (e.g., food, cement, time, talent, computers) committed to development work each year is an impossible task, but we may begin to understand the orders of magnitude involved by quantifying the money committed to this work by key actors.

One of the highest-profile sources of funds for development work is **official development assistance** (or **foreign aid**) from developed countries. The most comprehensive information regarding such assistance is collected by the Development Assistance Committee (DAC) of the Organisation for Economic Co-operation and Development (OECD) and is available at www.oecd.org/dac (see "Aid Statistics"). According to DAC statistics, in 2011 the 24 member countries of the DAC sent $94 billion through official bilateral channels. Non-DAC countries (primarily in Eastern Europe and the Middle East) accounted for another $8 billion. Donor nations also contributed another $34 billion to multilateral agencies like the World Bank. Altogether, this sums to $136 billion per year in external funding for poverty reduction and development in the developing world.

Although $136 billion is certainly a large sum of money, it would have to be stretched very thin to reach all 2.5 billion people living on less than $2 per day around the world. If it could be distributed directly to these people without having to spend any of the resources on identifying the poor or administering the programs (which we will discover in later chapters are costly and difficult tasks), ongoing funding at this level would increase their incomes by about 15 cents per day. An extra 15 cents would mean noticeable improvement for someone living on $2 a day or less, but it would fall far short of raising living standards to levels considered acceptable in developed countries.

Much poverty reduction and development work seeks not merely to prop up incomes with ongoing transfers but instead to create assets that raise incomes in longer-lasting ways. Thus it is useful to consider what would happen if all foreign aid could be invested in assets whose returns are distributed to the poor. If the $136 billion per year were invested in assets producing 10 percent per year dividends forever, and if the dividends could be costlessly and evenly distributed to the poor, then each year of funding at this level would add 1.5 cents per day to incomes on a permanent basis. Over several decades the cumulative effect might raise incomes by 50 cents per day. Though more substantial and more permanent than the effects associated with simply distributing the cash, such improvements are still rather modest. We must conclude that current foreign aid flows, although of great value, remain small in the face of great challenges.

Though official foreign assistance receives a great deal of attention in international discussions of development, it is by no means the only source of development funds. International NGOs channel substantial volumes of private donations from citizens of developed countries. In its annual *Index of Global Philanthropy and Remittances*, the Hudson Institute (2012) estimates that private philanthropy flows to development efforts from the United States and other OECD countries total $56 billion.

More important, developing country governments themselves raise revenues through taxation that may be put to work in a variety of activities, including poverty reduction and development efforts. A back-of-the-envelope calculation suggests that this is a substantially larger source of funding for development efforts than foreign aid. Using data on 70 developing countries for which the relevant information is available for 2009 in the *World Development Indicators Online* database, we find that government revenue (excluding foreign aid) ranges from 9 to 39 percent as a percentage of gross domestic product (GDP), with a GDP-weighted average of approximately 18 percent. If we apply this 18 percent to the entire GDP of the low- and middle-income countries, we estimate that government revenue in the developing countries is on the order of $2.5 trillion. Large fractions of this revenue are required for government activities that we probably would not classify as developmental (including military expenditures and government subsidies that primarily benefit the wealthy). Indeed, the fact that high-income countries collect an average of 24 percent of their higher GDPs in government revenue suggests that there are many things for governments to spend money on even outside of pressing poverty-reduction and development goals. Even if only one third of developing country government revenue is devoted to poverty-reduction and development purposes, however, this provides another $800 billion per year.

Casting the net more broadly, we might include in our accounts some spending by private enterprises that, though pursuing profits, also attempt to direct their energies in socially responsible ways, by providing good jobs, cheaper goods and services, or better technologies for low-income households. Even including these efforts, however, we would conclude that whereas the resources available for poverty reduction and development are sizeable enough to make a real difference, they are not in surplus. Good stewardship over these scarce resources is vital.

In some of the most disturbing cases, program funds have been diverted into the pockets of corrupt bureaucrats. Reinikka and Svensson (2004) estimate that prior to major governance reforms in Uganda, only 13 percent of central government transfers to schools in fact reached the schools, the rest being captured by government officials and politicians.

Even when funds are not pocketed, they sometimes achieve little good as a result of poor policy design or inadequate implementation. Sometimes the poor are excluded from water, power, education, health, or agricultural extension services because they cannot afford connection fees or because they live in remote villages beyond the reach of major programs. Even when the poor have access to services, the quality is often very low. For example, high rates of absenteeism among teachers in developing countries can shutter schools and reduce class time for students (Chaudhury et al., 2006), and when teachers do show up, inadequate training, poor facilities, and lack of textbooks often mean that children learn little.

Some programs create beneficial impacts in the short run, but their impacts fade away as tractors become idle for lack of spare parts, new irrigation systems are sabotaged as a result of conflict over the distribution of water, or roads crumble for lack of maintenance. For dismaying but insightful litanies of development failures, see Easterly (2001) and Easterly (2006).

Development policy's blemished track record is particularly troubling, because development efforts cost money, and the funds available for such work remain profoundly limited in the face of vast needs. Box 1.2 helps readers grasp some of the magnitudes involved. To make the most of scarce resources, development actors must search for ways to avoid policy failure and increase the rate of policy success.

To make the most of scarce resources, policymakers must ensure not only that each policy is well designed and implemented but also that the scarce resources are allocated carefully across policies of different types. Recall that the goal in development is *widely shared* improvement in well-being. Specific policies improve the welfare of specific groups of people, while leaving other groups largely untouched and imposing costs on yet other groups. For example, agricultural research and extension efforts to increase corn yields can raise corn farmers' incomes substantially and offer modest benefits to consumers who enjoy lower food prices, while *reducing* the incomes of wheat farmers (whose yields are unchanged but who might suffer falling crop prices). To achieve widespread improvements in well-being, policymakers must create *packages* of policies that together benefit *all* groups. This requires knowledge of how the distribution of impacts differs across policies of different types and designs.

Finally, making the most of the scarce resources available to governments and other development actors often means refraining from spending resources on activities that private individuals, firms, and communities would undertake even in the absence of intervention. To achieve greater success in complementing and encouraging private sector development activities, rather than merely duplicating or substituting for private sector accomplishments, policymakers require improved understanding of the decisions, markets and institutions that make up the socioeconomic system.

Making the most of scarce resources thus calls for good **policy analysis**, in which rigorous thinking and empirical research are employed in identifying needs, selecting policy approaches, making detailed policy design choices, monitoring program implementation, and evaluating policy impacts. The analytical framework and tools that economists bring to the study of development have many valuable uses in development policy analysis. More specifically, we will see that:

> Economic analysis offers valuable guidance for five important activities: (1) identifying the types of public sector intervention most likely to be complementary to the developmental activities of the private sector; (2) examining the differentiated and multidimensional impacts of specific policies; (3) examining how those impacts depend on details of design and implementation; (4) identifying ways to reduce corruption and improve policy implementation; and (5) learning from ongoing research, experimentation, monitoring, and evaluation.

The first activity helps avoid spending public resources on activities that the private sector is willing and able to undertake. The second and third help to identify combinations of policies that yield improvements in well-being for many groups and to inform choices regarding the details of policy design, while the fourth activity contributes to better policy implementation. The fifth activity is vital because our understanding of socioeconomic systems and development remains highly imperfect. Even when policymakers make the best possible use of all *current* knowledge as they select, design, and implement policies, they sometimes fail simply because the intelligent guesses they made about how the world works were incorrect. Monitoring and evaluation allow policymakers to catch mistakes and prevent continued waste of resources. More important, research, experimentation, monitoring, and evaluation add to knowledge and improve future policy choices.

1.5 This Text

The aim of this text is to equip readers for productive involvement in contemporary development efforts and debates, whether as policymakers, program managers, researchers, entrepreneurs, or well-informed voters and donors.

Part II takes a closer look at development objectives, first at the micro level of individuals and households, and then at the macro level of entire economies. We define important development outcomes (including well-being, economic growth, poverty, inequality, and vulnerability) and introduce the processes and forces capable of generating improvements in these outcomes. Part II also addresses the practical question of how to measure development outcomes when attempting to estimate the impacts of development policies and assess development success.

Part III then expounds in greater detail the analytical framework that economists bring to study of the socioeconomic systems in which development takes place. It presents tools for studying the many decisions, markets, and institutions important in development and for understanding how the various components of the socioeconomic system relate to one another. The discussion highlights potential obstacles to development and identifies ways policymakers might attempt to remove those obstacles. It also identifies reasons why policies might fail to improve development outcomes, thereby highlighting the need for ongoing research, experimentation, and policy evaluation.

The first chapter of Part IV describes a systematic approach to policy analysis. This approach helps students identify and apply the relevant analytical tools of Part III for rigorous and comprehensive analysis of specific policy questions. The remainder of Part IV employs the approach in analyzing policies of many types from around the world.

REFERENCES

Banerjee, Abhijit V., and Esther Duflo. "What is Middle Class About the Middle Classes Around the World?" *Journal of Economic Perspectives* 22(2): 3–28, 2008. doi:10.1257/jep.22.2.3

Besley, Tim, and Louise Cord (eds.). *Delivering on the Promise of Pro-Poor Growth: Insights and Lessons From Country Experiences.* Washington, DC: World Bank, 2007. doi:10.1596/978-0-8213-6515-1

Chaudhury, Nazmul, Jeffrey Hammer, Michael Kremer, Karthik Muralidharan, and F. Halsey Rogers. "Missing in Action: Teacher and Health Worker Absence in Developing Countries." *Journal of Economic Perspectives* 20(1): 91–116, 2006. doi:10.1257/089533006776526058

Chen, Shaohua, and Martin Ravallion. "The Developing World is Poorer Than We Thought, But No Less Successful in the Fight Against Poverty." *The Quarterly Journal of Economics* 125(4): 1577–625, 2010. doi:10.1162/qjec.2010.125.4.1577

Collier, Paul, and Stefan Dercon. "Review Article: The Complementarities of Poverty Reduction, Equity, and Growth: A Perspective on the World Development Report 2006." *Economic Development and Cultural Change* 55(1): 223–236, 2006. doi:10.1086/edcc.2006.55.issue-1

Easterly, William. *The Elusive Quest for Growth: Economists' Adventures and Misadventures in the Tropics.* Cambridge, Mass.: MIT Press, 2001.

Easterly, William. *The White Man's Burden: Why the West's Efforts to Aid the Rest Have Done So Much Ill and So Little Good.* New York: Penguin, 2006.

Gabre-Madhin, Eleni Z., and Steven Haggblade. "Successes in African Agriculture: Results of an Expert Survey." *World Development* 32(5): 745–766, 2004. doi:10.1016/j.worlddev.2003.11.004

Heston, Alan, Robert Summers, and Bettina Aten. "Penn World Table Version 7.1." Center for International Comparisons of Production, Income and Prices at the University of Pennsylvania, 2012. ttp://pwt.econ.upenn.edu/php_site/pwt_index.php

Hudson Institute Center for Global Prosperity. *The Index of Global Philanthropy and Remittances 2010.* Washington, DC: Hudson Institute, 2010. http://www.hudson.org/files/pdf_upload/Index_of_Global_Philanthropy_and_Remittances_2010.pdf

Khandker, Shahidur R., Zaid Bakht, and Gayatri B. Koolwal. "The Poverty Impact of Rural Roads: Evidence From Bangladesh." *Economic Development and Cultural Change* 57(4): 685–722, 2009. doi:10.1086/598605

Narayan, Deepa, Robert Chambers, Meera K. Shah, and Patti Petesch. "*Voices of the Poor: Crying Out for Change,*" 2000. http://go.worldbank.org/XMWSK7EMS0

Pritchett, Lant. "Who is Not Poor? Dreaming of a World Truly Free of Poverty." *The World Bank Research Observer* 21(1): 1–23, 2006. doi:10.1093/wbro/lkj002

Reinikka, R., and J. Svensson. "Local capture: Evidence from a Central Government Transfer Program in Uganda." *The Quarterly Journal of Economics* 119(2): 679–705, 2004. doi:10.1162/0033553041382120

Sumner, Andy. "*Global Poverty and the New Bottom Billion: What if Three-Quarters of the World's Poor Live in Middle-Income*

Countries?" IDS Working Paper 349. Brighton, UK: Institute of Development Studies, 2010. http://www.ids.ac.uk/files/dmfile /Wp349.pdf

World Bank. *World Development Indicators 2012*. Washington, DC: World Bank, 2012. http://data.worldbank.org/data-catalog/world-development-indicators

QUESTIONS FOR REVIEW

1. Figure 1.1 is constructed using data on average income and population for most countries of the world. Describe how this information is used to construct Figure 1.1. What facts do you take away from the figure regarding incomes around the world?

2. Using Figure 1.2, discuss the geographic distribution of countries with low average incomes.

3. What more do you learn from Tables 1.1 and 1.2 that is not evident in the average income data presented in Figure 1.1?

4. Read slowly through every row in Table 1.3 and discuss what you learn about life in Ethiopia.

5. Describe the range of actors involved in development work in the 21st century.

6. Discuss how development actors might define the development objectives they pursue. What do their development objective definitions share in common? How might they differ?

7. In broad terms, what is involved in the development process?

8. How is the term policy defined in this text?

9. What is involved in making the most of scarce development resources and how might the tools of economic analysis help in efforts to do this?

QUESTIONS FOR DISCUSSION

1. Many development actors have rallied around the United Nations' Millennium Development Goals (MDGs), which are listed in Table 1.4.

   a. What do the MDGs indicate about the relative emphasis placed by supporters on the following:
      • Income versus nonincome indicators of well-being

▓ TABLE 1.4   The Millennium Development Goals

Millennium Development Goals	Targets to Be Achieved between 1990 and 2015
Eradicate extreme poverty and hunger	• Reduce by half the proportion of people living on less than one dollar a day • Reduce by half the proportion of people who suffer from hunger
Achieve universal primary education	• Ensure that all boys and girls complete a full course of primary schooling
Promote gender equality and empower women	• Eliminate gender disparity in primary and secondary education preferably by 2005 and at all levels by 2015
Reduce child mortality	• Reduce by two thirds the mortality rate among children under five
Improve maternal health	• Reduce by three quarters the maternal mortality ratio
Combat HIV/AIDS, malaria, and other diseases	• Halt and begin to reverse the spread of HIV/AIDS • Halt and begin to reverse the incidence of malaria and other major diseases
Ensure environmental sustainability	• Integrate the principles of sustainable development into country policies and programs; reverse loss of environmental resources • Reduce by half the proportion of people without sustainable access to safe drinking water • Achieve significant improvement in lives of at least 100 million slum dwellers by 2020
Develop a global partnership for development	• Develop further an open trading and financial system that is rule based, predictable, and a nondiscriminatory trading and financial system • Address the special needs of the least developed countries • Address the special needs of landlocked countries and small island developing countries • Deal comprehensively with developing country debt problems • In cooperation with developing countries, develop and implement strategies for decent and productive work for youth • In cooperation with pharmaceutical companies, provide access to affordable essential drugs in developing countries • In cooperation with the private sector, make available the benefits of new technologies—especially information and communication technologies

Source: http://www.un.org/millenniumgoals/

- Well-being improvements for the poor versus the nonpoor
- Immediate versus longer-term improvements

b. What might explain the emphasis in the MDGs on defining measurable targets?

c. The MDGs have little to say about the process or policies through which the targets might be achieved. What are the potential benefits of remaining silent about the processes that will deliver MDG success and the policies development actors should employ in their efforts to achieve the MDGs? Do you see any potential costs? See Collier and Dercon (2006).

2. Describe a policy of a government, NGO, or other development actor. This may be a policy or program you have supported, studied, or heard about in the news.

a. Through what channels or in what ways do you think this policy might raise the well-being of some people?

b. For which types of people is this policy most likely to raise well-being?

c. For which types of people might this policy reduce well-being?

d. What are some reasons or ways the policy might fail to deliver many benefits?

2

Well-Being

The ultimate aim in development is to raise well-being for many people. This suggests two fundamental questions: First, what *is* well-being? Second, what kinds of change would raise well-being for people living in developing countries?

Basic economic principles suggest how to begin answering these questions. A critical premise in economic analysis is that people make choices with the aim of leaving themselves as well off as possible given the constraints they face. This suggests that we can learn about what people consider important for their well-being by observing what they choose to do, and we can identify the kinds of change that might raise their well-being by studying the constraints that limit success in these activities.

After first describing what life and the pursuit of well-being is like for 42 poor Bangladeshi households, this chapter offers a working definition of well-being. It then takes a more systematic look at what households around the developing world do in their pursuit of well-being: how they earn income, how they obtain the goods and services they value, how they cope with fluctuations and shocks, and how they build better futures through investment. Drawing on these observations, the chapter then identifies the many factors that limit households' success in their pursuit of well-being. We group these *determinants* of well-being into categories that will be important throughout the text: assets, needs, market conditions, and institutions. Finally, the chapter addresses the practical question of what data to collect when attempting to track well-being or measure policies' impacts on well-being.

We focus here on the pursuit of well-being by **households**, which are defined as groups of people sharing residences and meals. It is natural to think of household groups as pursuing well-being together, because household members share land, make joint choices about housing, and often jointly work out a division of labor within the household. In this chapter we treat the household as if it were a single, unified actor, pursuing a level of well-being that is shared by all members. In Chapter 7 we take a closer look at matters of cooperation, conflict, and power within households.

2.1 Life among the Poor in Bangladesh

Stuart Rutherford (2002) offers a vivid glimpse into the lives of 42 poor Bangladeshi households, whom he interviewed twice a month over the course of a year. All are very poor by developed country standards, though they are not unusually poor by local standards. Most live in one-room huts with mud floors and walls of mud or woven bamboo. The best off have a bed, one or two other pieces of furniture, and perhaps a fan and a television, but many have no furniture at all. Many eat just two meals a day. Most meals consist of boiled rice flavored with chilies and vegetables, with fish or meat once a week in good times. Food and the fuel to cook it together cost about 80 cents per day, which is a great burden given wages for tenuous employment on the order of just $1 or $1.20 per day.

Most households piece together income from diverse sources. The rural household headed by Saman and Hazara, one of the poorest households in the sample, combines income from four sources: Saman's earnings from casual farm labor, his earnings from fishing in the marsh (on the days he cannot find farm work), Hazara's income from egg sales, and her income from boiling and husking rice. In an urban household, old age and ill health prevent Abdur from contributing much to family income, but his wife Ranu has a job in a small soft drink factory, and their 14-year-old son Jahangir works in a garment factory at wages that are very low and paid irregularly. In another urban household Manzil rents out and repairs rickshaws. His 17-year-old son helps him in the workshop and has also saved up to buy a bicycle, which he now rents out. Other jobs represented in the sample include performing day labor on farms owned by others; cultivating rice or pineapples on the household's own land; raising chickens or cows; trading timber, fruit, saris, or sweets; or undertaking somewhat more formal employment as a maid-servant, factory worker, or night guard. Some households also beg or scavenge.

Some of the study households took steps to build a better future during the survey year. Manzil's household managed to fulfill its long-standing dream when it purchased an additional rickshaw for its rickshaw-rental business. Other households sent their children to school, despite the difficulty of paying school fees, hoping to improve their families' future prospects.

To buy a rickshaw or bicycle, or even to pay a school registration fee or buy clothing, households often must save over a period of time. Some make very small but frequent deposits of coins in mud banks (a type of piggy bank made out of clay, which must be broken to extract the savings), sew currency into their clothing, join savings clubs, or store cash with a local money guard (i.e., a neighbor who owns a good metal box with a lock and key). A few households finance investments by borrowing from microfinance institutions.

Many households also experienced the sorts of shocks that all households fear: unanticipated events that disrupt usual income or create sudden needs for expenditure, leading to dramatic reductions in living conditions. Such emergencies, which are often related to illness and injury, crop failures, or job loss, have the potential to wreak long-lasting havoc on a household's ability to meet its needs. Rutherford's study describes what happened to one family when the son, Kamrul, was injured.

> Some years back he had become involved in a business quarrel which turned violent, and had an arm and a leg broken. The medical bills were large, and this is how the household approached the task of settling them: first they used up business capital cash, then sold business assets. Next went home furnishings—a bed, a steel cupboard, a timber-and-glass sideboard. Only then did they start going the rounds of relatives and neighbours asking for howlats [informal interest-free loans], but with minimal success. So they offered to take loans on interest, but still very little was forthcoming. . . . Finally [the father] managed a big loan ($300) from a relative, at a nominal rate of 10% per month. To repay this, they put Sahana, their daughter, who was eleven years old at the time, into a garments factory job, and from her wage they've been paying down the loan intermittently ever since. (Rutherford, 2002, 50)

Networks of friends, relatives, and neighbors are clearly important in shaping the Bangladeshi households' opportunities and their abilities to cope with shocks. They frequently give or receive interest-free loans called *howlats* within these networks.

Unfortunately, not all social interactions are beneficial. One story demonstrates the burdens sometimes imposed by both social norms of dowry-giving and corruption in local government bureaucracies.

> First, because [Saman and Hazara] didn't pay enough dowry, their newly-married elder daughter's in-laws threatened to send her back home, and when Hazara failed to get Grameen Bank to give her a 'seasonal loan' to cover for the dowry, Saman had to borrow from his oldest son, something he was reluctant to do because the son forced him, in return, to transfer the homestead plot into his name. Second, Saman found he had to pay a bribe to get that land properly registered before he could transfer it, and he had to sell two trees ($5 each) to raise the cash for the bribe. (Rutherford, 2002, 10)

2.2 A Working Definition of Well-Being

The Bangladeshi households we just met devote much time and energy to earning income, because with income they can obtain important goods and services. They care about consuming not only food, clothing, and shelter but also health care, education, and other social services, and they care about the effectiveness of the services they obtain. Much of their work is arduous, suggesting that their well-being depends not only on what they are able to consume but also on how long and hard they have to work for it. They exert great effort in trying to avoid or cope with fluctuations in income and needs and in building better futures by acquiring equipment or education. The following definition of well-being captures this broad range of concerns:

> A person's **well-being** is a summary assessment of how good or bad her life circumstances are, paying attention at a minimum to the quantities and qualities of the goods and services she consumes, the activities to which she allocates her time, and her hopes and fears regarding the future.

Deep-thinking economists and philosophers raise two subtle questions about the nature of well-being that our practical definition does not seek to answer. First, what is the relationship between well-being and happiness? When people evaluate their own happiness, they take into account the diverse dimensions of their life circumstances, balance the various pleasures and pains against each other, and draw an overall conclusion regarding how happy they are. Equating well-being with happiness is attractive for the obvious reason that it takes very seriously peoples' own likes and dislikes.

Many development actors would refuse to equate well-being with happiness, however, for one of two reasons. First, some studies suggest that people living with very few material possessions and great insecurity adapt to their deprived situation, coming to accept it as natural or right. They lower their aspirations, thereby managing to achieve as high a psychological state of happiness as people who have more possessions and freedoms and are not similarly adapted (Sen, 1990; Clark, 2009). By the happiness criterion, those who are adapted to having few possessions, or to being sick and hungry, may be just as well off as those who have more possessions and are healthier and better fed. Many development observers and policymakers reject this judgment.

A second reason development actors might refuse to equate well-being with a person's own happiness arises because people sometimes lack knowledge about the ramifications of their choices. What leaves them happiest (in their ignorance) might not yield them the greatest well-being in a larger sense. For example, not knowing about the effects of vitamin consumption on health and life expectancy, people might think they are happiest spending their income on white rice (which might give them and their children the most calories per dollar), even though they would prefer to spend more on vitamin-rich vegetables if they fully understood the nutrition and health implications of their choices. (We return to these issues in Chapter 6.)

A second subtle question about the nature of well-being is this: Does well-being relate only to what people ultimately succeed in consuming, doing, and experiencing, or does it relate also to the rights and freedoms that shape their ability to attain these things? Much of standard economics is predicated on the narrow assumption that what matters to people is only what they ultimately consume and experience. The **utility** that people are assumed to maximize in economic models is usually a function only of these ultimate outcomes. Economist-philosophers like Amartya Sen, however, point out that such assumptions might lead to incomplete assessments of well-being. Suppose two people consume the exact same quantities of every consumption item, but for one person this pattern of consumption was the result of choice over how to spend his income, and for the other the consumption levels were dictated by the government. Sen argues that the well-being of the first is higher, precisely because he had the capability of making other consumption choices, whereas the second did not (Sen, 1999).

2.3 How Households in Developing Countries Pursue Well-Being

Economists think of well-being as an outcome determined in part by circumstances beyond peoples' control and in part by their choices. At any moment, people take as given the assets they already own or have access to, their needs, and the opportunities they face for interchange with others in market and nonmarket forums. They then make many choices about what to do with their time, money, and other assets, seeking to make the most of the opportunities they face. In this section we emphasize that:

> To identify the features of life circumstances that matter to developing country households, and then to identify the factors that constrain their pursuit of well-being, it is useful first to describe four sets of activities that are critical in their pursuit of well-being: earning income, acquiring goods and services, coping with fluctuations, and building better futures through investment.

In this section we simply *describe* the four sets of activities. In the next section we dig deeper to identify the features of life circumstances that *determine* the levels of well-being households are able to achieve.

2.3A How households in developing countries earn income

Figures 2.1 and 2.2 describe patterns of employment in four countries, which are located in diverse geographic regions and income brackets. With income per capita of $350, Malawi is classified as a low-income country by the World Bank. With incomes per capita of $2,500 and $8,890, Indonesia and Mexico are classed as lower-middle income and upper-middle income countries. Low- and middle-income countries are all considered "developing" countries, but they clearly span a tremendous range of economic conditions. With income per capita of $47,340, the United States is an example of a high-income country or "developed country" (World Bank, 2012).

Agriculture occupies a much larger share of the labor force in developing as compared to developed countries, though the shares also vary greatly among developing countries. We see this

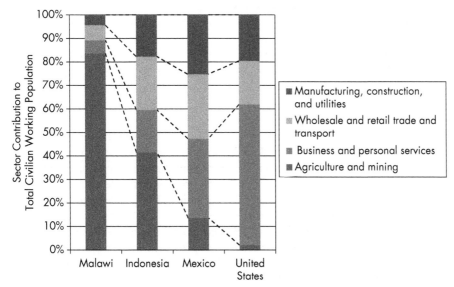

FIGURE 2.1
Percentage Distribution of Civilian Workers across Sectors in Countries at Different Income Levels
Source: ILO (2010). Based on data from national censuses and surveys in Malawi (1998), Indonesia (2008), Mexico (2008), and United States (2008).

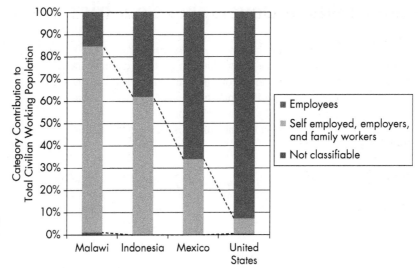

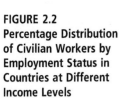

FIGURE 2.2
Percentage Distribution of Civilian Workers by Employment Status in Countries at Different Income Levels
Source: ILO (2010). Based on data from national censuses and surveys in Malawi (1998), Indonesia (2008), Mexico (2008), and United States (2008).

in Figure 2.1, which classifies households' main economic activities into sectors of economic activity and charts the percentages of households engaged in each sector. Notice that the decline in agriculture's employment share as we move from lower- to higher-income countries is associated with increases in the shares of most other sectors (and not just manufacturing), suggesting that economic development often involves the expansion of a web of interrelated activities in manufacturing, commerce, transportation, communication and a wide range of services.

The nature of employment arrangements, too, is different in developing as compared to developed countries. Figure 2.2 documents differences in the shares of workers by employment status in their main jobs. While the vast majority of workers in the United States are employees who work in businesses run by others, large percentages of workers in most developing countries work in small family enterprises run by themselves or other family members. Many of these family enterprises are family farms, but even in urban areas family enterprises are much more prevalent in developing than in developed countries. Nonagricultural family enterprises might sell saris door to door, run small sweet shops, or provide carpentry or taxi services.

Even among wage employees, the typical job tends to be quite different in developing and developed countries. Compared to the employment of typical households in the United States, the wage jobs obtained by members of the 42 Bangladeshi households were lower skilled, involved simpler production activities, and were probably located in smaller establishments. They were also profoundly less secure. For many in the Bangladesh sample, wage jobs lasted only a day at a time. Even in urban Colombia, where incomes are higher and agricultural work is much less important than in Bangladesh, employment arrangements also tend to differ in these same ways from typical employment arrangements in the United States (Schaffner, 2001). As compared to workers in the United States, workers in Colombia are less likely to be in white-collar (i.e., professional, technical, and managerial) occupations, more likely to be involved in industries with relatively simple technologies (such as food processing and textile production), more likely to be employed in very small establishments, and more likely to be in jobs that have lasted only a short time.

Table 2.1 employs household survey data to offer more detail regarding income-generating activities. The table compares four income groups among the "poor" and "middle class" (as defined by Banerjee and Duflo, 2008) and differentiates between rural and urban areas. For each country, the first row describes the percentage of all households falling into each income category. Together

■ TABLE 2.1 **Percentages of Households Earning Incomes from Various Sources by Income Level and Rural/Urban Location[a]**

	Less than $1/day		Less than $2/day		$2–$4/day		$6–$10/day	
	Rural	Urban	Rural	Urban	Rural	Urban	Rural	Urban
Malawi (2004–05)								
Share of all households	21%		63%		27%		3%	
Self-employed in agriculture	98.4	64.2	98.1	55.8	95.0	41.1	90.5	33.6
Self-employed in nonagriculture	25.6	24.1	28.3	34.8	34.3	39.7	32.1	36.6
Wage employed in agriculture	65.8	56.5	58.3	40.1	42.4	20.7	23.6	19.0
Wage employed in nonagriculture	22.1	37.0	23.3	47.9	27.5	60.4	31.7	67.6
Indonesia (2000)								
Share of all households	7%		55%		37%		3%	
Self-employed in agriculture	52.6	13.6	55.7	12.8	51.7	9.6	45.5	7.2
Self-employed in nonagriculture	35.7	50.1	35.1	48.7	43.2	52.0	51.8	52.4
Wage employed in agriculture	36.9	28.1	31.5	16.6	21.8	10.5	7.4	5.1
Wage employed in nonagriculture	33.4	74.1	36.2	71.4	40.5	72.1	46.3	71.6
Mexico (2002)								
Share of all households	14%		37%		31%		11%	
Self-employed in agriculture	27.2	1.8	25.4	6.4	21.2	6.1	16.3	7.5
Self-employed in nonagriculture	21.6	22.0	22.4	26.4	21.7	25.4	20.3	30.1
Wage employed in agriculture	23.6	2.1	18.3	1.6	7.8	1.2	5.6	0.5
Wage employed in nonagriculture	36.9	72.6	44.0	69.5	58.3	72.2	60.8	67.9

Sources: For Malawi data, author's calculations from the Malawi Second Integrated Household Survey, 2004–05. For Indonesia and Mexico, from Banerjee and Duflo (2008).
[a] Percentages indicate the shares of households within group (defined by income and rural/urban location) with at least one member in the indicated employment category.

the four income categories include the great majority of households in these countries; and households in all four categories earn incomes well below the official poverty lines of developed countries. The next four rows indicate the shares of households in each category that derive any income from four sources: self-employment and wage employment in agriculture and nonagriculture.

Table 2.1 yields several observations that are useful for future reference. First, agriculture is an important source of income for households in all income classes. Second, although agriculture is more important as a direct source of income in rural areas, it can serve as a source of income even in urban areas; some urban households cultivate small plots of land within city limits, own farms outside of town, or commute to work on farms owned by others. Third, self-employment is very common in agriculture and nonagriculture and in both rural and urban areas. Fourth, among agricultural income sources in rural areas, wage employment shows a sharp decline as income levels rise; a large fraction of wage labor employment in agriculture requires few skills and pays low wages. Fifth, the higher prevalence of nonagricultural wage employment among higher-income households suggests that nonagricultural wage-employment opportunities are more diverse than agricultural wage-employment opportunities, with a larger fraction requiring greater skills and offering greater rewards.

2.3B How households in developing countries spend income and acquire goods and services

Basic foods are very important in the budgets of low-income households. It is common for them to spend at least half, if not three quarters, of their total consumption budget on food (Banerjee and

Duflo, 2007). In rural northern Vietnam, even the better-off households devote from 25 to 60 percent of their consumption expenditure to a *single* food item: rice (Benjamin and Brandt, 2004).

As income levels rise, per-person food expenditure tends to rise, but its share in total consumption expenditure tends to fall, in an empirical pattern known as **Engel's Law**. Once income is sufficient to cover more than the basic foods required for survival, households use some additional income to purchase clothing, furniture, and eventually a more varied array of possessions. School fees and the purchase of medicines sometimes require large fractions of consumption expenditure (Banerjee and Duflo, 2007), and social customs at times require very large expenditures, even by the poor, on celebrations and rituals commemorating births, marriages, or deaths.

Acquiring goods and services often requires more than just paying out money. To acquire drinking water or fuel, for example, developing country households often spend hours each day walking to water sources or collecting firewood, and these burdens usually fall on women and children. Some women in rural Uganda spend two hours per day collecting water (United Nations Development Program, 2006).

To acquire health care services from public clinics, members of poor households might have to wait in line for long hours, and perhaps risk ill treatment by staff. Among women who had given birth in a rural health center in Zimbabwe and were asked to list the disadvantages of giving birth in such an institution, 22 percent reported being ridiculed for not having baby clothes, 16 percent reported being ordered by nurses to wash linen soon after delivery, and 13 percent reported being hit by a nurse during delivery (Filmer, et al., 2000)!

2.3C How households in developing countries cope with fluctuations and shocks

Households in developing countries face **fluctuations and shocks** of many sorts. Agriculture introduces seasonal fluctuations into the lives of many households. Farming households reap most of their income in harvest seasons and might generate very little income the rest of the year. During nonharvest seasons, as farmers demand less labor and supply less food, wages fall and food prices rise, spreading seasonal difficulties to nonfarm households as well. In countries like Gambia, seasonal fluctuations are so profound that the last months before the new harvest are called the "hungry season" (Lawrence et al., 1989).

Another fairly predictable source of variation in income and needs has to do with households' life cycles. As young families start out, they anticipate that income will soon rise, as the parents' time is freed up and children start contributing to family income, but then diminish in later years, as children leave home and parents become elderly. As parents look to the future they also foresee that needs for expenditure can rise rapidly first with childbirth and care for young children, later with the need to provide dowries for daughters or bride prices for sons, and yet later with increased needs for health care as the effects of age set in. Unfortunately, these life-cycle variations in income and needs tend not to match up. Income doesn't spike just when dowry payments are required, and incomes are often lowest just when health-related needs are highest in old age.

Recent research, including the Rutherford study for Bangladesh, highlights significant variation in income and needs over much shorter time scales that also create difficulties for households in developing countries. These variations arise out of the lumpiness of income receipts and consumption purchases. Even small-business owners with steady sales from month to month might experience only a few days of significant cash inflow during any given month. Similarly, workers with steady employment might receive their pay only once a month. The timing of these cash inflows might not match up well with the ideal timing of consumption purchases. Some foods must be purchased every day to prevent spoilage. Other basic goods are more cheaply obtained through bulk purchases, which can require payments larger than the income available on a typical payday.

Unpredictable shocks to agricultural productivity result from fluctuations in many factors beyond farmers' control: temperature, rainfall, size of insect populations, exposure to crop diseases, and more. Dercon (2002) reports that in a sample of rural Ethiopian households, 78 percent reported having been severely affected by a harvest failure in the last 20 years. Crop loss not only deprives farmers of most income, it also reduces wages for rural workers. During a drought in 1974 in Bangladesh, for example, real agricultural wages fell 50 percent (Jayachandran, 2006).

Another source of fluctuation in well-being is variation in market prices. Rising food prices help farmers who sell food and hurt the landless poor who buy food. An index of world food prices rose 83 percent over the three years prior to 2008, and the World Bank (2008) estimates that the net effect of this "global food price crisis" (which we examine more closely in Chapter 7) was to increase poverty significantly in many regions of the world.

Households face fluctuating returns in nonagricultural businesses as well. Small businesses selling handicrafts or carpentry services might suddenly find that their clients have run short of cash. Production and sales can suddenly stop because input supplies run short or workers become ill. Households working for wages face the risk of job loss.

Households in developing countries face many other potentially devastating shocks. High rates of illness and injury place households at risk of shocks that simultaneously reduce their income-generating capacity *and* increase their need for expenditures on medicine and health care (see Chapter 22). Where judicial systems offer only weak enforcement of contracts, households face the risk of losing assets through fraud or theft. Where governments are not committed to respecting private ownership, people also face the risk of losing assets to the government through expropriation. On top of this, many of the world's poor live in places where they cannot count on police to keep their neighborhoods safe and where they fear violence at the hands of warring militias.

The ebbs and flows of income, consumption needs, and prices matter because people would rather avoid great variation in their ability to meet needs. Many would prefer to eat two good meals every day rather than have several three-meal days followed by several one-meal days. When facing spikes in needs for expenditure when their daughters marry, they would rather be able to meet those needs without having to go hungry, even if it means consuming less at other times. In fact, people are generally willing to accept lower *average* consumption if this allows them to achieve fewer or smaller fluctuations, and thus fewer experiences of very low consumption. Economists often refer to this desire for steady consumption as an interest in **consumption smoothing**.

Households engage in many costly activities to smooth consumption in the face of fluctuations in income and needs. Consider first the activities households undertake *after* they have been hit by shocks to income or needs, which are referred to as **ex post responses to fluctuations**. To maintain their consumption in the face of a shock, households might take out a loan, promising to repay it with interest out of future income (when income and needs have returned to normal levels). They might attempt to borrow from many sources, including friends and neighbors, local moneylenders, pawn brokers, banks, or microfinance institutions. They might instead draw down past savings. If the shock reduces only the profitability of their farm or small business, they might also compensate by working more in wage labor markets (Kochar, 1999).

Knowing that they will be exposed to fluctuations in the future, households also take steps now that will help them avoid future fluctuations or cope with them better. These are referred to as **ex ante responses to fluctuations**. Households might save up, by spending less than their income on current consumption, so that they will have savings to draw down when needs rise relative to income. This saving can take many forms: placing currency in a mud bank, depositing savings in a bank account, buying durable goods like jewelry or household appliances, or lending to others against a promise of later repayment. In rare circumstances, households purchase formal insurance. They might also insure themselves informally through their participation in informal mutual assistance arrangements (as discussed in Chapter 12).

A final set of ex ante approaches to consumption smoothing falls under the label of **income smoothing**. Households engage in income smoothing when they choose income-generating strategies that are purposely designed either to reduce the magnitude of seasonal fluctuations in income or to reduce the probability of being hit by shocks (Morduch, 1995). For example, farmers might allocate some of their land to each of several crops that produce harvests in different seasons in order to spread out their cash inflows over the year. They might work several plots of land at different altitudes or with different soil qualities, rather than working with a comparable quantity of land in a single location, hoping to avoid the destruction of their entire crop by flood, drought, or disease. By working in off-farm employment as well as cultivating their land, they can shield themselves against the most devastating effects of either agricultural or nonagricultural downturns. They might also simply choose not to cultivate certain crops whose yields are particularly sensitive to weather conditions. Income smoothing is a constructive response to the fear of fluctuations, but it nonetheless raises concern among development analysts, because these efforts to avoid fluctuations can come at the cost of *reducing* households' *average* incomes, thereby increasing the average severity of their poverty (as we discuss in Chapter 10).

2.3D How households in developing countries build better futures through investment

Households in developing countries undertake investments of many sorts. Households **invest** when they undertake costly activities today that bear rewards only in the future. They might invest in the purchase or construction of physical assets such as farm land, irrigation ditches, wells for clean drinking water, or tools for repairing rickshaws. Sometimes families work together to create new roads or school buildings. Small-business owners invest in working capital when they purchase goods today that will be used to generate income a few weeks or months hence. For example, farmers invest in working capital when they purchase and apply fertilizer with a view to reaping a larger harvest several months later, and traders employ working capital when they purchase retail inventory with a view to selling the items in the coming days or weeks. People invest in human assets or **human capital** when they sacrifice money or time to acquire education or training for their families and when they obtain medical care that prevents a temporary illness or injury from turning into permanent disability or loss of life.

Sometimes the best route to increasing income is doing more of the same: cultivating the same crop on more land, running the same business with more rickshaws. But often the best route involves **innovation**, or adoption of new ways of doing work and life. Farmers might adopt a new technology by cultivating a newly developed seed variety. Small-business owners might find improved ways to organize their workplaces or might begin producing new, higher-quality products. Families might migrate, leaving behind familiar work and ways of life in order to take advantage of improved work opportunities in other places.

Households can undertake investment only if they have some way of **financing** it. That is, they must be able to cover the up-front costs. Households finance investment through **saving** when they abstain from consuming some of their income in the present in order to free up resources for buying or constructing assets. Savings may be explicit, as when they store up coins in a piggy bank. Sometimes the saving is implicit. For example, households might decide to allocate their children's time to attending school rather than to generating more household income on the family farm. They are saving implicitly, because they are consuming fewer goods and services in the present (relative to what they would consume if they were not sending their children to school) and they are using the implicit savings to finance investment in the creation of education assets. Households might instead borrow to undertake investment, in which case they may be able to invest without having to curtail near-term consumption.

2.4 Household-Level Determinants of Well-Being

The **determinants** of household-level well-being are the features of households' circumstances—such as how much land they own, how much education they have, what prices they must pay for food, what obligations they and their neighbors feel to share with each other—that they take as given in the present moment and that help to determine the level of well-being they achieve. Policymakers hoping to raise households' well-being must identify ways to alter these determinants in directions that allow households to achieve more in their pursuit of well-being.

In this section we identify the many possible determinants of well-being by identifying the factors that shape households' prospects for earning income, obtaining the goods and services that matter to them, coping with fluctuations, and building better futures through investment.

> The determinants of households' well-being may usefully be grouped into four categories of significance throughout the text: assets, needs, market conditions, and institutions.

2.4A Assets

A household's **assets** are its permanent or long-lasting attributes and resources that raise its effectiveness in pursuing well-being. Many household assets raise well-being by increasing households' productivity and income in wage employment or self-employment. In many households the most important productive assets are human assets: the time, energy, and skills of household members. The healthier a household's members are, and the more education, training, and experience they have, the more valuable its human assets.

Physical assets such as land, livestock, plows, and irrigation equipment raise productivity in farming, and assets such as stalls, shops, vehicles, machines, and inventory raise productivity in nonfarm family enterprises. Productivity also rises with households' knowledge of and access to technologies that raise the quantity or quality of goods and services their family farms and firms can produce for a given cost. Many farmers in Asia and Latin America, for example, were able to double their yields of rice, wheat, or corn by adopting higher-yielding seed varieties and related cultivation practices developed during the Green Revolution of the late 1960s and 1970s (Hazell and Ramaswamy, 1991).

Many additional assets that determine a household's productivity are owned by governments or groups, rather than by the household itself. Roads and electrical power generators often are owned by governments or private companies. Especially in small rural communities, some important assets are owned jointly by many households. For example, all households in a village might have the right to graze animals on common land or to fish and collect water from a lake or river.

A small number of households in developing countries own assets that produce income independently of the households' self- and wage-employment activities. These include savings deposits that produce interest income, and land, buildings, or equipment that are rented out to others and produce rental income. A very few households own insurance policies.

Some assets help determine the well-being a household achieves without necessarily affecting its productivity and income-generating options. Owning houses that are large and that offer good protection against the elements allow families to enjoy more valuable housing services. Owning or having access to a convenient source of clean drinking water brings benefits in taste, health, and time, and having access to a latrine or toilet brings benefits in reduced exposure to disease.

Policies that increase the quantity or quality of a household's assets raise its well-being in a long-lasting way. Knowing that people care about the future and are thus willing to invest, we recognize that such policies need not necessarily *give* people assets. Instead, they may encourage people to put some of their own resources into asset creation by strengthening their incentives to invest or by offering them new ways to borrow or save for financing the investment. After laying the groundwork in earlier chapters, we offer a general introduction to investment decisions in Chapter 10, and we examine a wide range of policies aimed at promoting asset creation in Chapters 15 through 22.

2.4B Needs

Levels of well-being are determined not only by the quantity and quality of households' assets but also by the nature and magnitude of their **needs**. Households' needs rise—and the level of well-being they can achieve on a given income falls—with the number of dependent mouths to feed. The number of dependents per family is often high in developing countries. Women in Germany give birth to an average of 1.4 children each, but women in Niger average 6.3 (World Bank, 2012). Numbers of dependents also increase when adult children take their parents into their households and when families take in orphans as foster children.

Needs are also shaped by the incidence of illness, injury, and disability. Households in developing countries face much higher risks of contracting debilitating and sometimes deadly infectious diseases, including malaria, tuberculosis, and AIDS. When they become ill or injured, their need to spend more on health care and medicine means they have less left over to spend on daily necessities. Households with disabled members, too, might have to spend more on special equipment and other assistance to achieve the same level of functioning and well-being as other households. We address efforts to improve well-being by reducing many of these needs in Chapter 22.

Households' needs are also influenced by cultural norms regarding dowries, bride prices, celebrations, and other required expenditures, and whether they are currently experiencing family births, marriages, or deaths. In South Asia the size of dowry payments ranges from one to seven times annual male wages, and payment of dowries can impoverish brides' families (Anderson, 2007). This motivates interest in efforts to improve well-being by altering burdensome social norms.

2.4C Market conditions

Economists are keenly aware of the critical role that markets play in determining a household's well-being. The markets with the most obvious implications for household well-being are goods markets and labor markets. Higher prices for outputs and lower prices for inputs raise potential profits from farms and nonfarm family enterprises, and higher wage levels raise potential earnings in wage employment. Access to a greater variety of consumer goods markets, and lower prices for consumer goods, raise the level of well-being households can achieve with a given (nominal) income.

Having taken a broad look at how households pursue well-being, we recognize also the critical role that financial markets play in facilitating households' efforts to cope with shocks and build better futures through investment. Households might benefit from new access to credit or to lower interest rates on credit, access to forms of saving that are more secure and pay interest, or ways of insuring their farm profits against catastrophic failure.

Policymakers interested in increasing a household's well-being might wish to raise prices for what the household sells, reduce prices for what it buys, or improve its financial options, and many policies affect market conditions (and thus household well-being) indirectly and even unintentionally. Thus, it is important to understand the forces that determine the spread of various markets, as well as the current levels of prices, interest rates, fees, and other important market conditions. Chapters 6 through 11 examine people's decisions regarding involvement in diverse markets and the forces that determine conditions in goods, labor, and financial markets. Chapter 17 examines policies of direct intervention in goods markets, Chapter 21 examines microfinance interventions in financial markets, Chapter 22 examines health insurance market interventions, and Chapters 15 through 22 point out many ways other policies may affect market conditions indirectly.

Unfortunately, changes in market conditions that benefit one set of households tend to reduce well-being for other households. For example, an increase in the price of corn raises well-being for farm households that sell corn but reduces well-being for households that purchase corn. Chapter 7 introduces a framework for systematic study of such differentiated effects across households of different types, which is employed in many subsequent chapters.

2.4D Institutions

Economists increasingly recognize that market transactions are not the only human interactions important in development. Market transactions involve buying, selling, lending, and borrowing. In **nonmarket interactions**, people cooperate, give gifts, share information, trust, steal, cheat, punish, reward, approve, or disapprove, and the quality of these nonmarket interactions can play an important role in determining well-being.

Economists also increasingly recognize that people's choices regarding market and non-market interactions are constrained not only by physical and technological limitations but also by "humanly devised constraints" called *institutions* (North, 1990). We define an **institution** as a set of formal rules and informal norms, together with related enforcement mechanisms, that constrain peoples' choices regarding a particular set of actions. Institutional rules and norms might prohibit theft or require people to share with less fortunate neighbors, while also dictating punishments for people caught flouting the rules.

At first glance it might seem that rules and norms that constrain peoples' choices must always reduce their well-being by reducing their range of options, but we will see that the discipline provided by institutions often *expands* opportunities by encouraging people to cooperate in mutually beneficial activities. For example, widely obeyed rules against theft restrict peoples' ability to benefit from stealing, but they create opportunities for beneficial market exchange by giving potential traders the confidence that they can set out wares for sale without risking loss to thieves. Similarly, rules and norms that limit the number of fish that village members may take from the village pond restrict the current income they can derive from fishing but also encourage discipline that protects the natural resource from destruction and prevents conflict. We might call such mutually beneficial institutions "healthy" or "high-quality" institutions.

Unfortunately, healthy institutions do not always arise, even when they would bring great value, and some institutional rules and norms are unhealthy, reducing the well-being of the people whose behavior they constrain. Institutions can be unhealthy when the institutional rules are imposed on members of less powerful groups by members of more powerful groups or when institutions that once supported beneficial cooperation grow anachronistic.

Some potentially important institutions are purely informal, involving social norms within neighborhoods, communities, kinship groups, or ethnic networks. Examples include informal insurance institutions that require neighbors to help one another cope with temporary cash shortages, and social norms requiring families to sacrifice animals to commemorate family deaths. Other institutions have more formal elements, involving laws relevant to all citizens of a state or country, or explicit rules relevant for all members of an organization such as an agricultural cooperative, labor union, or government bureaucracy. For example, laws might require people to fulfill contracts, and agricultural cooperatives might require members to pay dues and attend agricultural extension sessions. Even when formal rules are present, however, informal norms are often at work as well. For example, cultural norms of honesty sometimes help support compliance with formal contract law, and social customs of bribe-taking and opportunism sometimes direct government bureaucrats to disobey the formal rules that define their jobs.

A variety of institutions support the development of markets. Institutions preventing theft and promoting basic physical safety allow open air markets to emerge. Similarly, institutions encouraging people to fulfill formal or informal contractual promises allow more sophisticated markets to emerge. The quality of such institutions (which we examine more closely in Chapter 8) helps determine the market conditions that we have already identified as important for household well-being.

Many other institutions govern peoples' nonmarket interactions. Rules and norms guiding provision of services within public sector bureaucracies determine households' access to infrastructure, education, health care, and agricultural extension services. Formal tax and transfer programs help determine households' disposable incomes. Formal or informal community institutions can impose discipline on use of common land or fishing grounds and can facilitate cooperation in building roads and school buildings. The rules and norms associated with agricultural cooperatives might help farmers obtain discounts on fertilizer by coordinating bulk purchases. Informal gift-giving norms raise incomes for recipients, reduce incomes for givers, and can help everyone to cope better with fluctuations. Informal institutions governing communication within community, kinship, or professional networks affect households' access to valuable information about agricultural technologies or public health practices. Social norms favoring bribe-taking, the giving of dowries, and unhygienic practices create costly burdens.

We consider some social norms affecting individual and household choices in Chapters 6 and 7, institutions that support market expansion in Chapter 8, institutions that encourage or discourage labor mobility in Chapter 9, financial institutions in Chapter 10, institutions governing common property resources, informal insurance arrangements, and land rights in Chapter 12 (which also digs more deeply into the underpinnings of healthy institutions), and institutions through which policies are selected and implemented in Chapter 13. All the policy analysis chapters of Part IV wrestle with institutional questions as well.

Some economists and social scientists use the term **social capital** to capture the advantages that membership in various groups can create for people (Sobel, 2002). They characterize people and communities as possessing differing levels of social capital, in much the same way that they possess differing levels of physical or human capital. Although the concept of social capital is related to the concerns raised in the discussion of institutions, it is too blunt for our purposes and we avoid using it. We instead identify specifically the kinds of market and nonmarket interactions that matter in development and the institutions that govern them. This allows us to dig deeper into the building blocks of high-quality interactions and to appreciate better the multidimensional impacts—some good and some ill—that follow from institutional rules and norms.

2.5 Empirical Study of Well-Being

The ultimate objective in development policymaking is not merely to build roads or lend money to microenterprise owners. Roads and loans may be means to an end, but the ultimate objective is to raise well-being. Hence development professionals who wish to put scarce resources to best use need methods for assessing policies' impacts on well-being.

Assessing impacts on well-being is challenging, because we cannot measure well-being directly.[1] The best we can do is make educated guesses about well-being effects by examining what happens to **indicators** of well-being, which are imperfect measures or correlates of well-being. More specifically, we examine what happens to **living standards**, which are observable dimensions of life circumstances. Fortunately:

> Our knowledge of how households in developing countries pursue well-being equips us to identify the strengths and weaknesses of the living standard measures most commonly employed as indicators of well-being.

2.5A Real household income per capita

The most frequently used summary measure of a household's level of living is its real per capita household income. Ideally, the notion of **income** used in constructing the measure includes income

---

[1] Assessing impacts on well-being is also challenging because it is difficult to estimate true causal policy impacts rather than more general correlations in real world datasets. We discuss that challenge in Appendix A.

from all sources and in all forms, even the value of food a household produces for itself on its own farm.[2] The **nominal income measures** (i.e., measures reported in current currency units) that are constructed from households' responses to survey questions are divided by price indices, which describe variation across regions and over time in the price of a common basket of consumption items. This converts them into **real income measures**, which are good summary measures of households' abilities to purchase many of the goods and services that contribute directly to their well-being. Dividing total real household income by the number of household members is a simple (though imperfect) way of adjusting for differences in needs across households.

Though common and useful, per capita income measures can yield flawed inferences about how well-being varies across households or over time. Income measures shed no light on households' ability to obtain goods and services that are not acquired through well-functioning markets, such as rationed goods and services, health care, political liberties, or a healthy and pleasant environment. They are also insensitive to differences in the hours that households must work to obtain any given level of income. Furthermore, dividing by the number of household members (when constructing per capita measures) adjusts only imperfectly for differences in household needs. It fails, for example, to account for differences in needs associated with illness or disability.

Third, common measures of household income are derived from detailed questions regarding income receipts in the last 7, 14, or 30 days (because people tend not to remember very accurately over longer recall periods), and where incomes fluctuate from month to month, such short-term income measures can be misleading. For example, rural households interviewed in the harvest season (when income is high) might look much better off than households interviewed in the slack season (when income is low), even when their annual incomes are identical.

Fourth, current income measures at best describe the household's *current* ability to purchase goods and services. Among households with the same current income, some are enjoying a period of unusually high income but have few assets and expect to earn much less in the future. Others have more assets and expect to maintain their current level of income into the future. Yet others face tremendous investment opportunities and expect to earn much more in the future. Similarly, some households have strong reason to fear devastating future shocks to their income and others do not. Current income measures tell us nothing about these variations in expectations regarding the future.

2.5B **Real consumption expenditure per capita**

Another commonly used summary measure of a household's living standard is its real per capita **consumption expenditure**, or the total value of goods and services consumed by the household divided by the number of household members and adjusted for differences in prices. Ideally, good measures of consumption expenditure include not only the sums explicitly paid for the purchase of goods and services in markets but also the value of goods the household produces for its own consumption. Consumption expenditure and income (net of taxes) are closely related concepts, being equal for households that do not save, borrow, or draw down past savings. Consumption expenditure and income are measured in very different ways, however. Rather than attempting to identify every possible income source and asking detailed questions about each, the consumption expenditure approach identifies all possible sets of goods or services on which the household might make expenditures, and asks detailed questions about each of these.

---

[2] Accurate measurement of a household's total income is highly demanding of survey designers' care and of survey respondents' time and goodwill. For accurate measurement of total income, a survey questionnaire must contain detailed questions about all possible sources of income for all members who might be involved in generating income, and it must ask detailed series of questions regarding payments in cash, payments in kind, and production for own consumption for each possible income source. This is especially difficult in developing countries, where many household members work, where work is diverse and informal, and where pay takes many forms. Grosh and Glewwe (2000) provide a more detailed discussion of how to measure the components of income.

Consumption expenditure is thought to have two primary advantages over income as a summary indicator of living standards. First, though both concepts are difficult to measure, methods for measuring consumption expenditure inspire more confidence than income measurement methods, because it is easier to construct a complete list of questions about possible consumption items than it is to construct a complete list of questions about possible income sources. Second, if households are able to smooth consumption across months by saving some income in high-income seasons and later drawing down savings in low-income seasons, then measures of consumption expenditure in any one month are likely to provide more accurate descriptions of households' typical living standards than measures of income in the same short period.

Consumption expenditure measures share all the other weaknesses of income measures for drawing inferences about well-being, and arguably suffer an additional weakness. One way households might choose to enjoy an increase in income is to use it for financing investment. They might, for example, use additional income to purchase land or expand a small household enterprise. Consumption expenditure might thus remain steady even while income is increasing and household well-being is rising, because households use additional income to invest in asset creation rather than to increase current consumption.

2.5C Direct assessment

The well-being households pursue is a function of many dimensions of consumption and experience: consumption of diverse goods and services, enjoyment of leisure, health, sense of security and opportunity when looking to the future, political freedoms, and more. Income and consumption expenditure measures attempt to quantify enjoyment of these things only indirectly (and imperfectly). An obvious alternative or complementary approach is to measure directly many of the dimensions of enjoyment that households care about, such as food consumption, clothing purchases, housing quality, experience with illness and crime, access to health care and schooling, freedom to participate in local politics, and fears about the future.

As the primary approach to drawing inferences about well-being, the direct approach suffers an important practical weakness. It offers no obvious *summary* assessment of how overall well-being is changing over time or how it differs across households. If a household's consumption of clothing increases but its consumption of rice and the quality of its housing declines, has its well-being risen or fallen?

Specific direct measures also suffer from the weakness that the features of living conditions they measure are determined only in part by the household's ability to consume goods and services, and are determined also by household preferences. One family might have just as much purchasing power as another family, for example, but might prefer to eat a vegetarian diet and thus look poorer by a measure of chicken consumption.

Direct assessment, especially when focused on features of life circumstances for which income and consumption expenditure are not expected to be good gauges, is perhaps more useful as a supplement to (rather than a substitute for) income and consumption expenditure measures. It may be used to check, for example, what is happening to the time use of household members, to their access to rationed health care, and to the quality of their water and air. If income per capita is rising, the work hours of all members are holding constant or falling, and no deterioration is taking place in other key social and environmental circumstances, then the multiple measures taken together provide good evidence of improved well-being. Even if income per capita is only holding constant, these supplementary measures can reveal important improvements or deteriorations in well-being that should not be ignored.

2.5D Asset measures

Researchers increasingly recognize the significance of assets in the determination of household well-being. The quantity and nature of a household's assets are associated not only with current income and ability to consume but also with the level and potential variability of future income and consumption. Many assets with important implications for levels of well-being—the level of education of the household head, the quantity of agricultural land owned by the household—are also somewhat easier and less time consuming to measure than income itself. Thus asset measures are often employed as indirect indicators of well-being.

Asset-based measures have two drawbacks, however. First, assets take multiple forms (e.g., land, education, vehicles), and it can be difficult to create a summary measure of a household's assets for use in comparisons over time and across people. Second, income and well-being are determined not only by a household's assets but also by conditions in the markets and nonmarket institutions that determine the returns the household is able to derive from its assets. A household that has more assets but that lives in a region where prices in relevant markets are lower might be worse off than a household with fewer assets. Nonetheless, collecting data on assets is of great value for drawing inferences about households' well-being.

2.5E An example

Box 2.1 describes a study of the impacts of road improvement projects in Bangladesh. It demonstrates how estimating impacts on multiple indicators of living standards (and multiple indicators of local market conditions) allows researchers to construct an insightful and multidimensional description of project impacts on life and well-being.

≡ **Box 2.1** Drawing Inferences about the Impact of Road Improvements on Well-Being

The World Bank has financed construction or upgrading of many thousands of kilometers of road over the decades. Traditional evaluation studies measured the impacts of road projects in terms of kilometers of roads built or improved. Some evaluations went one step further and sought to estimate the reduction in transport costs enjoyed by road users. Researchers now point out the serious inadequacy of such evaluations. The objective in road construction projects is not merely to alter a region's physical landscape but to raise the well-being of the region's residents, and they aim to raise well-being not just by reducing transport costs but also by enhancing market and nonmarket connections and improving opportunities for investment. Good evaluations should assess project impacts on well-being and shed light on the channels through which these impacts come about.

Shahidur Khandker, Zaid Bakht, and Gavatri Koolwal set out to evaluate the impacts of two Bangladesh road improvement projects serving poor rural communities (Khandker et al., 2009). The projects upgraded road surfaces and added culverts and small bridges to roads that were already passable (not necessarily easily) by motorized vehicles before the project. Such upgrading potentially increases travel speed and safety and extends road use into rainy seasons. (The projects also upgraded some market infrastructure, but such efforts were minor compared to the road upgrading.) The authors collected wide-ranging information from nearly 2,000 households in two kinds of communities—some affected by the road improvement projects and some not—both before and after the project was implemented. This allowed them to estimate project impacts on many indicators using a variant of the difference-in-differences method for estimating impact (see Appendix A).

According to their estimates, the two road projects raised per capita consumption expenditure on average by 7.5 and 10.8 percent. They show, furthermore, that the projects raised consumption expenditure at the bottom of the income distribution by more than they raised incomes higher up the distribution and thus were useful for reducing poverty. In addition, estimates indicate that the road improvements greatly reduced the time it takes for people to get to market and increased enrollment in secondary schools (which tend to be located at some distance from many homes). The projects thus raised well-being along multiple dimensions.

The study also offers some insights into the channels through which the road improvements raised well-being. Transport costs for taking crops to market fell by about 25 percent, crop output prices rose by 3 percent, and fertilizer prices fell by 5 percent, indicating that the project increased the profitability of local farming. This motivated local farmers to expand crop production, leading to increases in harvest quantities of 8 percent in one project area and 22 percent in the other. Local wages also rose. As higher wages and greater returns to work on family farms rose, the quantity of labor supplied by households rose significantly. This indicates that the increases in consumption expenditure were not pure windfalls, because they were accompanied by increased work hours. This tempers our inferences about well-being somewhat, but it does not reverse our conclusion that well-being rose, because the labor supply increases were the result of choices by people for whom the benefits of the increased work presumably outweighed the costs.

In later chapters we will see how road improvements might have raised well-being in additional ways: reducing fluctuations in food prices and consumption, improving access to advanced agricultural technologies, improving opportunities for investment, and more. Thus we might like to see estimates of impacts on additional features of life circumstances and household assets. Nonetheless, by employing an array of indicators, this study offered valuable insight into the impacts of road improvements on peoples' well-being.

REFERENCES

Anderson, Siwan. "The Economics of Dowry and Brideprice." *Journal of Economic Perspectives* 21(4): 151–174, 2007. doi:10.1257/jep.21.4.151

Banerjee, Abhijit V, and Esther Duflo. "What is Middle Class About the Middle Classes Around the World?" *Journal of Economic Perspectives* 22(2): 3–28, 2008. doi:10.1257/jep.22.2.3

Banerjee, Abhijit V., and Esther Duflo. "The Economic Lives of the Poor." *Journal of Economic Perspectives* 21(1): 141–167, 2007. doi:10.1257/jep.21.1.141

Benjamin, Dwayne, and Loren Brandt. 2004. "*Agriculture and Income Distribution in Rural Vietnam Under Economic Reforms: A Tale of Two Regions.*" In Paul Glewwe, Agrawal Nisha, and David Dollar (eds.). *Economic Growth, Poverty, and Household Welfare in Vietnam.* Washington, DC: World Bank, 2004, pp. 133–186.

Block, Steven A. "Maternal Nutrition Knowledge and the Demand for Micronutrient-Rich Foods: Evidence From Indonesia." *Journal of Development Studies* 40(6): 82–105, 2004. doi:10.1080/0022038042000233812

Clark, David A. "Adaptation, Poverty and Well-Being: Some Issues and Observations With Special Reference to the Capability Approach and Development Studies." *Journal of Human Development and Capabilities* 10(1): 21–42, 2009. doi:10.1080/14649880802675051

Deaton, Angus. *The Analysis of Household Surveys: A Microeconometric Approach to Development Policy.* Washington, DC: World Bank, 1997. http://www-wds.worldbank.org/external/default/WDSContentServer/WDSP/IB/1997/07/01/000009265_3980420172958/Rendered/PDF/multi_page.pdf

Dercon, Stefan. "Income Risk, Coping Strategies, and Safety Nets." *The World Bank Research Observer* 17(2): 141–166, 2002. doi:10.1093/wbro/17.2.141

Filmer, Deon, Jeffrey S. Hammer, and Lant H. Pritchett. "Weak Links in the Chain: A Diagnosis of Health Policy in Poor Countries." *The World Bank Research Observer* 15(2): 199–224, 2000. doi:10.1093/wbro/15.2.199

Grosh, Margaret, and Paul Glewwe (eds.). *Designing Household Survey Questionnaires for Developing Countries: Lessons From 15 Years of the Living Standards Measurement Study* (Volume 1 of 3). Washington, D.C.: World Bank, 2000. http://go.worldbank.org/3FI67NHLV0

Hazell, Peter B. R., and C. Ramasamy. *The Green Revolution Reconsidered: The Impact of High-Yielding Rice Varieties in South India.* Baltimore: Johns Hopkins University Press, 1991. http://www.ifpri.org/sites/default/files/publications/hazell91.pdf

International Labour Organization (ILO). "LABORSTA Internet," 2010. http://laborsta.ilo.org/

Jayachandran, Seema. "Selling Labor Low: Wage Responses to Productivity Shocks in Developing Countries." *Journal of Political Economy* 114(3): 538–575, 2006. doi:10.1086/503579

Khandker, Shahidur R., Zaid Bakht, and Gayatri B. Koolwal. "The Poverty Impact of Rural Roads: Evidence From Bangladesh." *Economic Development and Cultural Change* 57(4): 685–722, 2009. doi:10.1086/598605

Kochar, Anjini. "Smoothing Consumption By Smoothing Income: Hours-of-Work Responses to Idiosyncratic Agricultural Shocks in Rural India." *Review of Economics and Statistics* 81(1): 50–61, 1999. doi:10.1162/003465399767923818

Lawrence, Mark, F. Lawrence, T. J. Cole, W. A. Coward, J. Singh, and R. G. Whitehead. "*Seasonal Pattern of Activity and Its Nutritional Consequence in Gambia.*" In David E. Sahn (ed.). *Seasonal Variability in Third World Agriculture: The Consequences for Food Security.* Baltimore: Johns Hopkins University Press, 1989, pp. 47–56.

Morduch, Jonathan. "Income Smoothing and Consumption Smoothing." *Journal of Economic Perspectives* 9(3): 103–114, 1995. doi:10.1257/jep.9.3.103

Munshi, Kaivan. "*Nonmarket Institutions.*" In Abhijit V. Banerjee, Roland Bénabou, and Dilip Mookherjee (eds.). *Understanding Poverty.* New York: Oxford University Press, 2006, pp. 389–400.

North, Douglas C. *Institutions, Institutional Change and Economic Performance.* New York: Cambridge University Press, 1990.

Rutherford, Stuart. "*Money Talks: Conversations With Poor Households in Bangladesh About Managing Money.*" Finance and Development Research Programme Working Paper No. 45. Manchester, UK: University of Manchester, 2002. http://www.sed.manchester.ac.uk/idpm/research/publications/archive/fd/fdwp45.pdf

Schaffner, Julie A. "Job Stability in Developing and Developed Countries: Evidence From Colombia and the United States." *Economic Development and Cultural Change* 49(3): 511–535, 2001. doi:10.1086/edcc.2001.49.issue-3

Sen, Amartya. "*Development as Capability Expansion.*" In Keith Griffin and John Knight (eds.). *Human Development and the International Development Strategy for the 1990s.* London: MacMillan, 1990, pp. 41–58.

Sen, Amartya. *Development as Freedom.* New York: Alfred A. Knopf, 1999.

Sobel, Joel. "Can We Trust Social Capital?" *Journal of Economic Literature* 40(1): 139–154, 2002. doi:10.1257/0022051027001

United Nations Development Programme (UNDP). *Human Development Report 2006: Beyond Scarcity: Power, Poverty and the Global Water Crisis.* New York: Palgrave Macmillan, 2006. http://hdr.undp.org/en/media/HDR06-complete.pdf

World Bank. *Rising Food Prices: Policy Options and World Bank Response.* Washington, DC: World Bank, 2008. http://siteresources.worldbank.org/NEWS/Resources/risingfoodprices_backgroundnote_apr08.pdf

World Bank. *World Development Indicators 2012.* Washington, DC: World Bank, 2012. http://data.worldbank.org/data-catalog/world-development-indicators

QUESTIONS FOR REVIEW

1. Discuss the significance of the working definition of well-being provided in the text.

2. Discuss the relationships between well-being and happiness, and between utility and capability.

3. What are some of the ways peoples' income-earning activities tend to differ between developing and developed countries?

4. On what do households in developing countries spend their incomes? What, other than money, might be required to obtain some goods and services?

5. To what kinds of fluctuation in income and need are developing country households exposed, and how might they try to ameliorate the impact of those fluctuations on their well-being?

6. How might developing country households invest in building better futures?

7. Describe the range of assets (broadly defined) that can figure as important determinants of households' well-being

8. What might cause the needs of one household to be greater than another's? What might cause a household's needs to rise from one year to another?

9. Give examples of how changing conditions in goods, labor, and financial markets might raise or lower a household's well-being.

10. Discuss the roles of nonmarket interactions and institutions in determining a household's well-being.

11. List some of the living standards measures most commonly employed in efforts to infer policy impacts on well-being, and discuss the strengths and weaknesses of each.

QUESTIONS FOR DISCUSSION

1. From what you were told about the 42 poor Bangladeshi households, what do you guess are some of the assets, markets and nonmarket institutions that play the most important roles in shaping their well-being?

2. If you have traveled in a poor region, whether in a developing country or an impoverished region within a richer country, discuss the following for those regions:
   - What are the most obvious (i.e., visible to a visitor) dimensions of living conditions that suggested low levels of well-being?
   - What would you guess are some of the difficult-to-observe dimensions of living standards that are also very poor in this region?

3. Consider two approaches for assessing household living standards and well-being. The first involves selecting a random sample of households within a region and using long, detailed questionnaires to elicit comprehensive information about income, consumption, and living standards more generally. The second involves a very short questionnaire that is administered to every household in a community, which includes only questions that are easy to answer and may be used to construct simple indices of households' living standards (e.g., questions about how many rooms respondents' homes have and whether the household head is literate). For what purposes is each method best suited? (Purposes might include identification of regions that merit priority in poverty reduction efforts, academic research on poverty, and assessment of eligibility for an emergency cash transfer program.) How could analysis of the results of the first approach be used to give practical guidance regarding the design of the second approach?

PROBLEMS

1. Suppose we know that a policy did not produce any change in a household's real per capita consumption expenditure. List at least five ways the policy might nonetheless have improved the household's well-being. That is, suggest at least five stories regarding how the household's circumstances might have changed, and how the household responded to those changes, that are consistent with the household's well-being rising even while its per capita consumption expenditure remains constant.

2. Suppose you are attempting to choose a measure of living standards for use in determining which households most need assistance. Discuss the relative merits of the following possible measures of living standards:

   - Real income per capita within the household over the last two weeks
   - Real income per capita within the household over the last 12 months
   - Real consumption expenditure per capita over the last month
   - Per capita meat consumption over the last month
   - Indicators of whether a household has a dirt floor, uses water from an improved source, and sends children to school
   - Individual measures of height (for age), weight (for age), and recent illness

chapter

3

Economic Growth

At the micro level of developing-country households, the objective in development is to raise well-being. At the macro level, the aim is to raise well-being not just for one household but for many and to raise well-being in a way that can be sustained and built upon over many years. Most development thinkers agree that widespread and sustained improvements in well-being are impossible without economic growth.

This chapter begins by defining economic growth, describing how it is measured, and examining how it relates to the larger development objective. It then demonstrates the tremendous variation in rates of economic growth across countries and raises the natural question: What causes rapid economic growth? We begin answering this question by describing the proximate sources of growth, which are the economic processes through which economic growth comes about. Digging deeper, the chapter then raises questions about the "determinants of economic growth," which are features of policy and of socioeconomic conditions that explain why growth rates are higher in some countries than others or why growth rates change over time within countries. We briefly review the large empirical literature employing aggregate-level cross-country data in the search for the determinants of growth, pointing out its lessons and limitations. We then argue the need for careful micro-level, context-specific analysis of barriers to growth and of the ways they might be overcome. Part III of the text equips readers for such analysis.

3.1 Meaning and Measurement of Economic Growth

3.1A The definition and developmental significance of economic growth

The rate of **economic growth** is the rate of increase in an economy's average income. In principle, average income is the total value of income earned in any form, from any source, by anyone in the country, divided by the number of people. Economic growth thus takes place when total income grows faster than the population.

Economic growth is also equal to growth in the per capita value of everything produced in the economy. An economy's total income equals the total value of its production because people derive their incomes from the production of goods or services, and all value created through production activities is paid out as income to someone in some form, whether as wages or as returns on capital and entrepreneurship.

Economic growth makes possible widely shared and sustained improvements in well-being. In the absence of growth, average income remains constant, and any effort to raise incomes or provide better health care services for some groups must come at the expense of others. Where average income is just $450 per year, as in Burundi, the best that can be achieved through such redistribution is widely shared poverty. Thus:

> Long-term development with the potential to raise well-being for all members of society, and to erase vast differences in living standards across countries, must involve economic growth.

Unfortunately, success in economic growth does not guarantee broader development success for two reasons. First, average income can grow rapidly even when the incomes of many individuals stagnate or decline. Thus, although high rates of economic growth make *possible* widespread improvements in material living standards, they do not *guarantee* that the improvements are widespread. Second, as discussed in Chapter 2, increases in a household's income do not guarantee that the household's well-being rises, because the improved income may be counterbalanced by deterioration in nonincome dimensions of living standards, such as health or fears regarding the future. Chapter 5 examines these potential differences between economic growth and development in more detail.

3.1B Measures of economic growth

The most common measures of economic growth are the average annual percentage growth rates in real per capita gross domestic product (GDP) and real per capita gross national product (GNP). **Gross domestic product** is defined as the total value of final goods and services produced within a country's borders over the course of a year. **Final goods** include both **consumption goods**, which are used up by consumers during the year, and **capital goods**, which are long-lived goods used in the production of other goods and services and not used up during the year. Final goods may be contrasted with **intermediate goods**, which are used up in the production of other goods and services during the year. For example, cotton thread is an intermediate good used up in the production of a final consumption good, clothing; steel is an intermediate good used up in the production of a capital good, factory equipment. The difference between the value of intermediate goods used in a production activity and the value of the final goods produced is called the activity's **value added**. Calculating the total value of all *final* goods and services produced during the year is equivalent to calculating the value added generated in *all* production activities.

In practice, obtaining accurate measures of GDP is difficult, especially in developing countries. A common approach to measuring the value of production is to observe goods and services as they pass through markets where transactions are recorded. In some developing countries, many goods and services never pass through monitored markets, because farm households consume their own produce and because many producers and consumers evade tax laws and regulation. Some developing-country statistics bureaus attempt to estimate these unmarketed and black-marketed components of national product, but estimates are often based on weak data and on estimation methods that differ across countries.

Incorporating the value of services and goods produced by government bureaucracies is also difficult, because they are often offered without charge or for fees that need not represent their full value. GDP accounting conventions call for valuing government goods and services at their cost of production.

Gross national product, also called **gross national income** (GNI), is the value of final goods and services produced by domestic factors of production, whether at home or abroad. The distinction between GDP and GNP can be significant when countries' labor or capital cross national borders to engage in production. The value of final goods and services produced by Brazilian labor and capital outside Brazil's borders (by Brazilian workers who have migrated to other countries for work, or by Brazilian capital invested outside Brazil) is counted in Brazil's GNP but not in its GDP. Similarly, the value of final goods and services produced by Japanese capital or labor within Brazil's borders is counted in Brazil's GDP but not in its GNP. In a few countries, large numbers of workers migrate temporarily to other countries for work, sending home large fractions of their earnings as international remittances. In such cases, GNP may be a better indicator of the income available to the domestic population than GDP.

For the purposes of comparing GDP or GNP across countries, income figures for all countries must be converted into identical currency units. The most common practice in development analysis is to convert into U.S. dollar equivalents using what are called **purchasing power parity (PPP) exchange rates**. To calculate these exchange rates, researchers in each country collect local price information that allows them to determine the cost in local currency of a basket of goods that costs one dollar in the United States. The PPP exchange rate between

Mexican pesos and U.S. dollars, for example, is the ratio of the peso price of a particular basket of goods and services to the dollar price of the same basket. This ratio indicates the number of pesos that have the same purchasing power as one dollar. Dividing a measure of GDP in local currency units (e.g., pesos) by the country's PPP exchange rate (in, e.g., pesos per dollar) yields a measure of GDP in U.S. dollar equivalents, allowing direct comparison of GDP magnitudes across countries. For more on PPP exchange rates, see Kravis (1986).

Sometimes GDP or GNP figures are converted into U.S. dollars using other exchange rates. For some statistics the World Bank uses Atlas conversion factors, which for most countries are three-year averages of countries' official market exchange rates; these are the actual rates at which people and firms in a given country can legally purchase dollars (expressed in units of local currency per dollar). When these conversion factors are employed in comparing GDP per capita across countries, the developing countries tend to look poorer relative to the developed countries than when the comparison employs PPP exchange rates.

Calculating GDP (or GNP) growth rates requires comparing the total value of goods and services produced in two different years. When the goods and services are valued using current prices (so that the goods produced in 2000 are valued using 2000 prices and the goods produced in 2010 are valued using 2010 prices), the resulting growth rate is a measure of **nominal GDP growth**. Nominal GDP might increase over time, either because the quantity of goods and services increases, or because the prices of the goods and services increase through inflation. **Real GDP growth** measures the portion of nominal GDP growth that can be attributed to increases in the quantity of goods and services produced rather than to price increases. The growth in real GDP from one year to the next is measured by using a single set of prices (often the prices in the first year) to value the quantities of goods and services produced in both years.

Economic growth rates measure growth in **per capita income**. Measures of per capita income are answers to the question: If we could redistribute all income until we achieve equality, without incurring any costs or losing any of the income in the process, what level of income would be enjoyed by everyone? Increases in per capita income thus indicate expansion of the level of material prosperity that everyone would share *if* income were distributed evenly.

Growth figures are usually reported as annual growth rates. This means that even when the period of interest is greater or less than one year, the average growth rate for that period is expressed as the growth that would occur over one full year at the observed pace. Growth rates are often expressed as **annually compounded** average rates. This means that the averages are calculated in a way that treats growth as a multiplicative process, in which growth in any one year increases the size of the base to which subsequent growth rates are applied. For example, the following table describes the evolution of GDP in an economy that starts with GDP of 100 and grows at a steady annually compounded rate of 3 percent for 10 years. We can see compounding in the calculation of Year 2 GDP, where the growth experienced from Year 1 to Year 2 (embodied in the final 1.03 factor) was applied not to the original 100 but to 100×1.03, which was the new level of GDP attained in Year 1, as a result of growth from Year 0 to Year 1.

Year	GDP
Year 0	100
Year 1	$100 \times 1.03 = 103$
Year 2	$100 \times 1.03 \times 1.03 = 106.09$
. . .	. . .
Year 10	$100 \times (1.03)^{10} \approx 134.39$

The average annually compounded growth rate over a 10-year period for a country that had GDP of *G0* in Year 0 and *G10* in Year 10 is the growth rate *r* (expressed, e.g., as $r = 0.03$ for a 3-percent growth rate) that solves the equation $G0(1 + r)^{10} = G10$.

3.2 Global Diversity in Growth Rates

Table 3.1 employs a commonly used source of data on economic growth, the Penn World Tables (Version 7.1, Heston et. al., 2012), and describes the range of average annually compounded growth rates over the period 1960–2010. Among the 110 countries for which adequate information was available, Taiwan achieved one of the highest annual growth rates, at 5.9 percent. The lowest growth rate was the Democratic Republic of Congo's *negative* 2.1 percent, and the most common growth rates were in the 1.0 to 1.5 percent and 1.5 to 2.0 percent ranges.

One way of understanding how large or small annually compounded growth rates are is to employ the **rule of 72**. This useful mathematical approximation tells us that to estimate roughly how many years it takes to double income per capita when the annually compounded growth rate is *g* percent, we simply divide *g* into the number 72. (See problem 1 for insight into why this works.) For example, at a growth rate of 3 percent per year, we can expect income per capita to double in roughly $72/3 = 24$ years. At a growth rate of 5 percent, we expect income per capita to double in less than 14½ years. With growth rates near 6 percent, the top performers in Table 3.1 doubled their average incomes more than four times in five decades! Growing at 1.99 percent, the United States doubled its average income just somewhat more than once during that period.

If lower-income countries consistently grew faster than higher-income countries, their average income levels would eventually catch up with developed country levels. Unfortunately, data on growth rates exhibit no strong tendency for poor countries to grow more rapidly. The horizontal axis in Figure 3.1 measures GDP per capita in 1960 (converted into U.S. dollar terms using PPP exchange rates), and the vertical axis measures the average rate of economic growth between 1960 and 2010. The scatter plot shows no strong tendency for poor countries to grow

■ **TABLE 3.1   Distribution of Countries by Average Annual Percentage Change in GDP Per Capita, 1960–2010**

Growth Rate Range	Number of Countries in Range	Example Countries
Over 5.5%	3	Korea, Taiwan
5.0 to 5.5%	3	Botswana, Singapore
4.5 to 5.0%	1	China
4.0 to 4.5%	2	Malaysia, Thailand
3.5 to 4.0%	5	Indonesia, Romania
3.0 to 3.5%	11	Egypt, India, Panama
2.5 to 3.0%	11	Israel, Pakistan, Spain
2.0 to 2.5%	12	Chile, France, Turkey
1.5 to 2.0%	16	Colombia, Nepal, United States
1.0 to 1.5%	18	Argentina, Malawi, South Africa
0.5 to 1.0%	10	Bangladesh, Rwanda, Venezuela
0.0 to 0.5%	11	Kenya, Senegal, Zimbabwe
−0.5 to 0.0%	3	Haiti, Nicaragua
−1.0 to −0.5%	3	Central African Republic, Madagascar
−1.5 to −1.0%	0	None
less than −1.5%	1	Democratic Republic of Congo

Source: Heston et al. (2012).

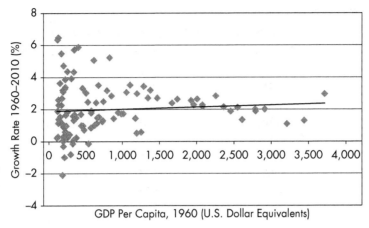

FIGURE 3.1
No Systematic Tendency for Poorer Countries to Catch Up
Source: Heston et al. (2012).

more rapidly than rich countries. Indeed, average growth rates appear even to rise slightly as the initial level of GDP per capita rises.

Figure 3.1 also demonstrates great diversity in growth rates among countries starting at low levels of average income. Some poorer countries grew very fast over this period, partially closing the gap in per capita incomes between them and the richer countries, but other poor countries stagnated and fell further behind.

Growth studies reaching farther back into history demonstrate an even stronger tendency for per capita incomes in richer countries to pull ahead of those in poorer countries. At the beginning of modern economic growth in about 1870, average incomes were much more similar across countries than they are today (Pritchett, 1997). The vast current differences in per capita income that we observed in Chapter 1—with GDP per capita more than 100 times greater in the richest countries compared to the poorest countries—are the result of "divergence, big time," as rapid economic growth in today's rich countries allowed them to pull away from the rest.

Economic growth rates also vary significantly across geographic regions of the world. Table 3.2 divides the 93 countries for which adequate data are available, and that had populations of at least 1 million in 1960, into geographic regions of the world. Within each region it gives equal weight to each country (regardless of the country's population size) when calculating medians across countries for various growth statistics. The table reports median average growth rates in the periods 1960 to 1980, 1980 to 2000, and 2000 to 2010. While growth rates in East Asia and the Pacific have often exceeded growth rates in the high-income countries, growth rates have been lower in many other parts of the developing world, especially in sub-Saharan Africa.

Table 3.2 demonstrates some tendency for growth rates to slow after 1980 all around the world. After 2000, average growth rates continued to slow in the high-income countries, but they picked up in many parts of the developing world.

3.3 The Proximate Sources of Economic Growth

Economic growth is necessary for sustained and broad-based development. To understand development, therefore, we must understand the ingredients of successful growth. In this section we examine the **proximate sources of economic growth**, which are the kinds of change in economic activity that give rise to growth.

Real per capita income rises when the total value of goods and services produced in the economy rises faster than the number of people available to produce it. Thus, to identify the proximate sources of growth we must identify the types of economic change that increase **aggregate labor productivity**, which is the average value of output produced per worker in the economy's farms, family enterprises, firms, and other production operations.

■ TABLE 3.2   **Growth Experience by Country Groups**

Region	Regional Median Average Annual Growth Rate		
	1960–1980	**1980–2000**	**2000–2010**
High-income countries	3.55	2.35	1.15
Low- and middle-income countries	2.21	0.66	3.28
Eastern Europe and Central Asia	5.58	0.64	5.29
East Asia and the Pacific	4.70	3.82	4.52
Middle East and North Africa	3.11	1.06	2.17
Latin America and the Caribbean	2.46	0.50	2.24
South Asia	1.66	1.24	4.92
Sub-Saharan Africa	0.92	−0.57	2.13

Source: Heston et al. (2012).

3.3A Theoretical framework for studying firm-level labor productivity

Production takes place when producers or entrepreneurs bring together the **factors of production**—labor, physical capital, and human capital—to create goods and services. Physical capital includes machines, tools, buildings, and other equipment and structures, and human capital encompasses the skills and abilities that workers bring into production as a result of past education, training, work experience, nutrition, and health care. We call each entrepreneur's production operation a "firm," even though in developing countries many operations are very small, informal, and embedded within households.

Producers use factors of production to produce **output**. When labor, physical capital, and human capital are the only inputs to production—as when, for example, a family enterprise uses its skilled labor and tools to produce carpentry services—the "output" is the entire value of services produced. When labor, physical capital, and human capital are combined with raw materials (such as raw cotton), intermediate goods (cotton thread), or services (electricity) to produce higher-value goods (woven cloth), the "output" produced by the basic factors of production (labor, physical capital, and human capital) is the value added embodied in the woven cloth.

Entrepreneurs' ability to turn labor, physical capital, and human capital into output is limited by the technology, or the array of technological options, at their disposal. The technological possibilities a firm faces can improve over time, whether through informal learning, purposeful invention, or technology purchase. Such **technical change** allows the firm to obtain more output, or higher-value output, from given quantities of the inputs.

Economists organize their thinking about technological possibilities and productivity around the concept of a **production function**, which describes how the maximum quantity of output achievable by a firm is related to the quantities of production factors employed. Here we keep things simple by assuming that output is just a function of the total number of workers L and the total value of physical and human capital K. Under these assumptions, we can write the production function this way

$$Y = F(L, K; A) \tag{3.1}$$

where Y is the maximum quantity of output that can be produced from given quantities of L and K, A is an index of the current level of technology, and $F(.)$ is the production function.

As you recall from earlier economics courses, it is standard to assume that the production function $F(.)$ is increasing in L, K, and A, and that it exhibits diminishing marginal products of L and K. The **marginal product of labor** (*MPL*) is the increase in output associated with a one-unit increase in labor while holding K and A constant.[1] A production function exhibits **diminishing marginal product of labor** when the *MPL* falls as the level of L rises while holding K (and A) constant. This captures the notion that as a producer adds workers, without increasing the total amount of capital, each new worker raises output by less than the one before. The **marginal product of capital** is defined in a symmetrical fashion. By assuming that the production function is increasing in A, we assume that technical change increases the maximum quantity of output derived from given levels of L and K.

We can evaluate whether a production function (at a given level of technology) has constant, increasing, or decreasing **returns to scale** by asking what happens to output when we double the amount of both inputs (K and L). If output just doubles, then the technology exhibits constant returns to scale. If output more than doubles (or less than doubles), it exhibits increasing returns to scale (or decreasing returns to scale).

The production functions just described imply some important relationships involving labor productivity that we will find useful at various points throughout the text. We graph these relationships in the two panels of Figure 3.2.

The left panel of Figure 3.2 graphs the marginal product of labor *MPL* and the average product of labor *APL* as functions of the quantity of labor employed by a firm (L) operating along its production function, while holding K constant. The *MPL* schedule is downward-sloping, reflecting our assumption of diminishing marginal products. The **average product of labor** (*APL*) is just total output ($Y = F(L, K; A)$) divided by the number of workers L. The *APL* schedule as a function of L is downward sloping for the same reason that the *MPL* schedule is downward sloping: each successive unit of labor adds less to output, reducing the average. It lies above the *MPL* schedule, however, because it averages the increments to output of all L units of labor currently employed, whereas the *MPL* is the increment to output associated only with the last unit of labor employed.

(a)   (b)

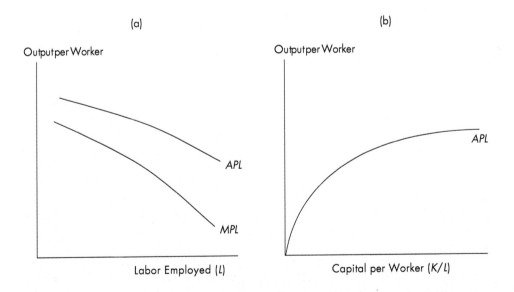

FIGURE 3.2
Labor Productivity Relationships within Firms

---

[1] When using calculus in the discussion of production relationships, we define the *MPL* as equal to the partial derivative of $F(.)$ with respect to L. This is the increase in output associated with an infinitesimally small increase in L, divided by that infinitesimally small quantity of labor. This is *approximately* equal to the increase in output associated with a *one-unit* increase in L.

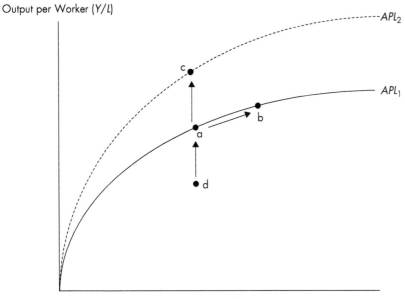

FIGURE 3.3
Sources of Productivity Growth within Firms

The right panel of Figure 3.2 graphs the average product of labor *APL* as a function of the quantity of capital employed by a firm operating along its production function. In this graph, rather than varying the labor input while holding capital and technology constant, we vary the capital input while holding the quantity of labor and technology constant. Because we are holding the quantity of labor constant, an increase in the capital input is also an increase in the quantity of **capital per worker**. Positive but diminishing marginal returns to capital imply that the slope of this graph is positive but declining as we move to the right.

Figure 3.3 illustrates the implications of technical change for a graph like Figure 3.2(b). By definition, if we increase *A* while holding both *L* and *K* constant, output per worker increases. An increase in *A* causes the *APL* schedule to shift up, as illustrated by the shift from schedule APL_1 to schedule APL_2.

Figure 3.3 offers a useful way of organizing thought about potential sources of productivity increase within individual firms. Consider first a firm facing the technology associated with curve APL_1 and operating at point a. This firm is *on its production function*, implying that it produces the maximum output possible given the labor and capital inputs it employs, and given the technological options available to it. Three sorts of change might increase labor productivity in this firm. It could move to the right along the APL_1 schedule to a point like b, either by *increasing the quantity of physical capital per worker* or by *increasing the quantity of human capital per worker*. It could instead shift up to point c by *acquiring or developing new technology* that allows it to get more output from the same quantities of labor, physical capital, and human capital. (It might, of course, also engage in more than one of these changes simultaneously.)

A fourth source of increase in labor productivity within a firm is possible for a firm facing the technology associated with schedule APL_1 and operating at point d. Such a firm is **technically inefficient**, meaning that it is failing to get as much output as is technologically possible given the input quantities and technology it employs. (We explore possible reasons for this in the following sections.) Such a firm could increase labor productivity by *increasing its* **technical efficiency**, moving from point d up toward point a.

3.3B Theoretical framework for studying aggregate labor productivity

Aggregate labor productivity is the ratio of GDP (i.e., the total value of production) to the total number of workers in the economy. Let $L_1, \ldots, L_n$ denote the quantities of labor devoted to all uses in the economy, where employment in diverse firms and unemployment are all distinct uses. Letting $Y_1, \ldots, Y_n$ denote the quantities of goods and services produced by labor devoted to each use and letting $p_1, \ldots, p_n$ denote the respective prices per units of output, we can write total GDP as the sum $p_1 Y_1 + \cdots + p_n Y_n$, and the total quantity of labor in the economy L as $L_1 + \cdots + L_n$. With a little algebra it is easy to show that aggregate labor productivity is equal to

$$\frac{GDP}{L} = \left(\frac{L_1}{L}\right) p_1 APL_1 + \cdots + \left(\frac{L_n}{L}\right) p_n APL_n \tag{3.2}$$

where (L_i/L) is the share of total labor devoted to activity i, and $p_i APL_i$ is the **value of the average product of labor** (*VAPL*) in activity i. This relationship tells us that we can calculate aggregate labor productivity by looking at how all labor in the country is allocated across diverse firms and other uses (including unemployment), observing the *VAPL* in each firm or use, and calculating the weighted average of all these *VAPLs*, where greater weights are given to the *VAPLs* associated with activities in which larger fractions of the country's labor are employed. This has important implications for thinking about sources of growth in aggregate labor productivity.

First, all four potential firm-level sources of productivity growth illustrated in Figure 3.3 remain relevant for thinking about productivity growth at the aggregate level. Aggregate labor productivity can rise as a result of increases in the economy-wide stocks of physical or human capital relative to the stock of labor and as a result of technical change and increases in efficiency within firms. Such changes must raise average labor productivity in at least some firms.

Second, aggregate productivity can also arise through the reallocation of labor across activities within the economy. Most obviously, if one of the current uses of labor is unemployment, then changes in economic performance that shift some labor out of unemployment (where labor productivity is zero) into productive firms (where labor productivity is greater than zero) will increase overall average labor productivity.

Similarly, if some labor is employed in wasteful activities, which use up productive resources but do not produce valuable output, then structural changes that shift labor away from wasteful activities into productive firms will again increase aggregate labor productivity. Examples of such wasteful activities involve efforts to appropriate income generated by someone else's production, through theft, some forms of litigation, extraction of bribes, and lobbying for preferential treatment by government. These activities are often labeled **rent seeking**, a term meant to contrast them with profit-seeking activities involving production (Krueger, 1974). Rent-seeking activities directly waste the resources devoted to them and induce additional waste indirectly, when they force producers to use labor and capital in protecting themselves against crime, fraud, and other rent-seeking practices.

Under certain circumstances, aggregate labor productivity may also be increased by shifting labor (or capital) from less-productive to more-productive sectors of the economy or by shifting labor from less-productive to more-productive firms within a sector. If $VMPL_i$ is less than $VMPL_j$ then shifting one unit of labor from firm i to firm j would raise the total value of production (because the *VMPL* is, by definition, the amount by which the value of production in a firm, and thus its contribution to GDP, rises or falls when one unit of labor is added to or removed from the firm).

If markets worked perfectly, there would be no scope for productivity improvements through reallocation of labor across sectors or firms. An important result in microeconomic theory is that if all markets in an economy work perfectly, then the *VMPL* (of a specific type of labor) should be equalized across uses throughout the economy, and there should be no scope for increasing productivity simply by shifting labor across uses. In Chapter 9, however, we consider possible labor market frictions that prevent *VMPLs* from being equated across uses.

Aggregate labor productivity can also increase through consolidation of production into larger firms in the presence of firm-level increasing returns to scale. If production of a good is characterized by increasing returns to scale, and its production currently takes place in many small firms, then, even though the *VMPL* may be equated across those firms, it may be possible to improve efficiency and raise aggregate labor productivity by pooling the inputs from the many small firms into a single larger firm. In Chapter 8, we examine how transportation costs and other factors might keep markets and production establishments small in early stages of development, and how reductions in those costs can allow increases in scale, possibly contributing to growth in average labor productivity.

The diverse sources of growth identified here differ in their potential for sustaining growth over the long run. Growth through reductions in inefficiency, reductions in unemployment, or reductions in rent-seeking activities can continue only until the inefficiency, underutilized resources, and rent-seeking activities disappear. Thus, while their elimination might generate a one-time episode of growth, it does not offer hope of indefinite growth. Even so, it is possible that such changes could increase growth rates by a significant amount for a decade or more.

Physical capital accumulation and human capital accumulation are freer of such obvious limitations. Such processes can keep going for a long time, though in the absence of accompanying changes in technology their growth impact would tend to diminish over time as diminishing marginal returns kick in. (The effect of diminishing marginal returns figures importantly into theoretical debates about sources of long-term economic growth, as described in Chapter 4.) Technical change is sometimes thought to have the greatest potential to generate growth that can be sustained at a steady pace indefinitely in the very long run.

We conclude that the following processes are capable of raising aggregate labor productivity and are thus potential proximate sources of economic growth:
- Increases in physical capital per worker
- Increases in human capital per worker
- Technical change
- Increases in technical efficiency within firms
- Increases in the efficiency of allocation of labor across firms
- Reductions in unemployment
- Reductions in rent-seeking and other wasteful activities

Of these processes, the first three are thought capable of generating economic growth over very long periods of time because they face no logical limits. The latter four are logically limited, because they are exhausted when all waste and inefficiency have been eliminated but can nonetheless contribute to growth over substantial periods of time.

3.3C Total factor productivity growth versus factor accumulation: growth and development accounting

Researchers have sought to determine the relative historical importance of two broad categories of proximate sources of economic growth: factor accumulation and increases in total factor productivity. **Factor accumulation** refers to growth in physical and human capital per worker. As you will learn in Chapter 4, physical capital accumulation was considered the key to economic growth in the 1940s and 1950s, and human capital accumulation began attracting attention in the 1960s.

Total factor productivity (TFP) growth is a catch-all category that includes all the other sources of productivity growth suggested above. It is defined as the portion of the rate of growth in aggregate labor productivity that cannot be explained as the result of increases in physical or human capital. When researchers first began studying TFP growth in the 1960s, they interpreted it primarily as the result of technical change, but researchers increasingly recognize that it also encompasses reductions in inefficiency and waste.

Over the last five decades, many researchers have employed the methods of growth accounting and development accounting in assessing the relative importance of factor accumulation and TFP growth. **Growth accounting studies**, which were first developed in the 1960s, seek to identify the shares of historical growth (in one or more countries) that can be attributed to factor accumulation versus TFP growth. They are based on highly simplified assumptions regarding the process through which a country's GDP is produced, which allow researchers to estimate how much of observed growth in GDP per capita may be explained by observed rates of growth in physical and human capital per worker and then to use the portion of growth that remains unexplained as an estimate of TFP growth. Box 3.1 offers an overview of growth accounting methods.

Early applications of growth accounting methods focused on the developed countries, where studies tended to find an even split between the portions of growth attributable to factor accumulation and the portions attributable to TFP growth. Subsequent studies have examined growth in a wider variety of countries. In a few countries in Latin America and East Asia, factor accumulation appears to play a significantly larger role (relative to TFP growth) than in developed countries, but many studies continue to find a nearly even split between factor accumulation and TFP growth for explaining historical growth (see Easterly and Levine, 2001).

Development accounting exercises are similar to growth accounting exercises. Rather than examining differences in GDP per capita over time within individual countries, they examine differences in average incomes across countries at the same time. Such differences in income levels shed light on the proximate sources of growth, because they are the result of differing growth rates over long periods of time. Such studies choose a base country (usually the United States) and measure for each country the percentage differences in average income, physical capital per worker, and human capital per worker relative to the U.S. levels. The studies then ask: How much of the overall variation in GDP per capita across countries at one point in time is attributable to differences in physical or human capital per worker and to differences in TFP? These studies tend to find that differences in physical and human capital per worker explain about half of the cross-country productivity differences, and differences in TFP explain the other half (Caselli, 2005). That is:

> The results of many growth accounting and development accounting exercises support the broad conclusion that both factor accumulation and total factor productivity growth have contributed significantly to historical economic growth.

Growth and development accounting exercises have been useful for drawing attention to TFP growth as well as factor accumulation as important proximate sources of economic growth, but they are subject to several profound limitations and should thus be interpreted with caution. First, they offer no insight into the relative importance of the highly diverse ways TFP might grow (as described earlier).

Second, they are based on simplified assumptions regarding the nature of production relations in the economy. If the underlying assumptions are incorrect, the methods can yield misleading results. Caselli (2005) finds that some of the standard results disappear when less-restrictive

≡ **Box 3.1** Growth Accounting Methods

Growth accounting exercises seek to decompose a country's overall growth rate during some period into a portion that can be attributed to factor accumulation and a portion that can be attributed to TFP growth. They are based on restrictive assumptions regarding the process through which a country's GDP is produced. Rather than acknowledging the existence of many firms and other possible uses of a country's capital and labor, the method essentially treats the entire economy as if it were a single firm, and it models total GDP (Y) as a simple function of the total quantities of physical capital K, labor L, and human capital per worker h. This production function is assumed to take a very simple form. For example, a study might posit that

$$Y = AK^{\alpha}(Lh)^{1-\alpha} \tag{1}$$

where Lh can be interpreted as "effective" or "quality-adjusted" labor and α is a technological parameter between 0 and 1 defining the exact way Y responds to changes in K and Lh. The higher is α, the greater is the importance of capital relative to labor in raising output. A is an index of total factor productivity (TFP). As long as α takes a value between zero and one, this production function exhibits diminishing marginal returns to both K and Lh, a property we would expect most production functions to satisfy. It also exhibits constant returns to scale.

Dividing through by L to turn this into a statement about GDP per worker y, we get

$$y = Ak^{\alpha}h^{1-\alpha} \tag{2}$$

where $k = K/L$ is physical capital per worker. This tells us that if the assumptions we have made are reasonable, then GDP per worker should be related to the levels of capital per worker and human capital per worker in this specific and simple way. Starting with equation 2, it is easy to show (see problem 4 at the end of the chapter) that

$$g_y = g_A + \alpha g_k + (1 - \alpha)g_h \tag{3}$$

where g_y, g_A, g_k, and g_h are the percentage growth rates in GDP per worker, TFP, physical capital per worker, and human capital per worker. Equation 3 indicates that under the assumptions made thus far, the rate of growth in GDP per capita should be equal to the rate of growth in TFP (g_A) plus a simple weighted sum of the growth rates in physical and human capital per worker (g_k and g_h), where the weight is the parameter describing the economy's simple production technology.

Growth accounting exercises involve choosing a value for α that is thought to give a good representation of technological realities; measuring g_y, g_k, and g_h; plugging all these numbers into equation 3; and then backing out a value for g_A, which is the only remaining unknown in the equation. For example, if researchers measure $g_y = 4$ (percent per annum), $g_k = 3$, and $g_h = 2$ and estimate $\alpha = 0.3$, then they would conclude that of the overall 4 percentage points of growth in GDP per capita, $0.3 \times 4 = 1.2$ percentage points are attributable to growth in physical capital per worker, $0.7 \times 2 = 1.4$ percentage points are attributable to growth in human capital per worker, and the remaining $4 - 1.2 - 1.4 = 1.4$ percentage points represent growth in TFP.

One critical challenge in carrying out a growth accounting exercise is to come up with an estimate of α. Two broad approaches have been taken to estimating this parameter. The first one is based on the observation that if the production function is well described by equation 1, then the marginal product of capital MPK is equal to $(\alpha Y)/K$ (the partial derivative of equation 1 with respect to K). Rearranging this expression, we find that α equals $(MPK \times K)/Y$. If we are willing to assume that rental markets for capital are perfectly competitive, then MPK should equal the rental rate earned per unit of capital (r). Substituting in r for the MPK, we find that α equals $(rK)/Y$, which is the ratio of total capital income in the economy to total GDP. It thus becomes possible to estimate α simply by observing the share of capital income in total income, a number that is close to 0.3 in the United States.

Another approach to estimating α employs econometric estimation. Equation 3 implies that the rate of economic growth g_y should be equal to a linear function of g_k and g_h, in which the intercept is the rate of TFP growth and the coefficients on g_k and g_h are estimates of α and $1-\alpha$. This suggests that the rate of TFP growth and the coefficients α and $1-\alpha$ can be estimated simultaneously by running regressions of per capita GDP growth on rates of growth in physical and human capital, employing observations from multiple years of growth experience.

Another challenge in carrying out a growth accounting exercise is in constructing good measures of the rates of growth in physical and human capital per worker (as well as in GDP per capita). For examples of how such measures might be constructed, see Caselli (2005).

assumptions about the functional form of the aggregate production function are employed. Third, these methods require estimates of critical quantities that are difficult to estimate, especially the growth rate of human capital per worker and the parameter describing the country's production technology.

Fourth, even if the assumptions on which these methods are based were valid, and the measures employed were accurate, the results would at best describe past growth or present income differences. They need not be good predictors of what *will* be the most important sources of growth in the future.

Finally, even if they accurately revealed the most promising proximate sources of future growth, growth accounting and development accounting exercises provide no insight into what sorts of *policies* might be required to achieve those promises. It might be the case, for example, that policies promoting technical change would be required to motivate investors to accumulate physical capital, or that policies promoting human capital accumulation would be required to facilitate adoption of new technologies and TFP growth.

Growth and development accounting exercises are not the only evidence used to argue the importance of TFP differences in explaining why aggregate labor productivity is so much lower in developing countries. Easterly and Levine (2001), among others, offer broad observations that imply lower TFP in developing countries as compared to developed countries. They point out that if there were no difference in TFP across countries, then by definition all differences in aggregate labor productivity must arise out of lower levels of physical and human capital per worker in the developing countries. In the terms of Figure 3.3, all countries would be on the same *APL* schedule, with capital per worker levels for developing countries lying to the left of those for developed countries. If the production technology is characterized by diminishing marginal returns to capital, then increases in capital per worker should raise output by more in developing countries than in developed countries. Physical and human capital should thus flow from the rich countries, where capital is abundant and returns to investment are lower, to poor countries, where capital is scarce and returns to investment are higher. But we do not observe such flows. Indeed, skilled laborers and capital tend to flow from poor countries, where they are scarce, to rich countries, where they are abundant! This suggests that returns to capital are not uniformly higher in poorer countries. Within our production function framework, it is most natural to conclude that lower levels of capital per worker in developing countries (which would tend to increase the marginal product, given diminishing returns) are more than compensated by lower levels of technology and efficiency (which can reduce marginal products and the level of productivity).

3.3D Room for improvement

In this section we observe that:

> Developing countries have significant scope for improvement in the levels of physical and human capital per worker, the use of improved technologies, and efficiency.

Cross-country data suggest that developing countries have plenty of room to increase their stocks of physical capital per worker. Standard measures of the value of the physical capital stock, expressed on a per-worker basis, are on the order of $1,900 per worker in Ethiopia, $16,000 in the Philippines, $38,000 in Brazil, and $223,000 in the United States.[2] The kinds of capital that come first to mind when analyzing productivity are tools, machines, and buildings employed in agricultural and manufacturing production. But physical infrastructure—including roads, ports, and communication and power networks—are also important and severely lacking in many developing countries (see Chapter 18).

Cross-country data also suggest plenty of room for increases in human capital per worker in the developing countries. According to Barro and Lee's (2001) calculations, in rich countries 71 percent of the population had at least some secondary education, and 28 percent had at least some postsecondary education. By contrast, in developing countries taken altogether, only 31 percent had at least some secondary education, only 7 percent had at least some postsecondary education, and 34 percent had no schooling at all! Education stocks are even lower in Africa, where only 2 percent of the population had any postsecondary education, 19 percent had at least some secondary education, and 43 percent had no schooling. On top of this, in countries where children get fewer years of schooling, the quality of schooling tends to be lower as well (see Chapter 19).

---

[2]These numbers are estimated using the perpetual inventory method described in Caselli (2005), employing the Penn World Tables data (Heston et al., 2012). They are reported in 2005 dollars per economically active member of the population.

Human capital differences across countries are further compounded by poorer nutrition and health in the developing countries. One of the most telling ways to describe cross-country difference in health is with statistics on average life expectancy, which in 2010 was 80 years in high-income countries but only 59 years in low-income countries, a difference of 21 years (World Bank, 2012).

According to the theoretical framework set out above, TFP can rise for many reasons: technical change, improvements in technical efficiency within firms, improved efficiency of labor allocation across firms, and reductions in unemployment and rent seeking. The potential for improvements in these areas is somewhat more difficult to quantify than the potential for increases in physical and human capital per worker, but fragmentary evidence suggests scope for future growth arising out of many of these processes.

Scope for technological improvement is suggested by the observation that many firms and farms in developing countries continue to use traditional, low-productivity methods of production, even when more modern methods are known to raise productivity. For example, many farmers in developing countries continue to use traditional seed varieties and traditional cultivation methods, even when evidence suggests that they could increase their productivity and profits by employing new seeds and modern fertilizers (Duflo et al., 2004). A report by the McKinsey Global Institute (cited in Banerjee and Duflo, 2004) similarly observed that many firms in the apparel industry continue to operate without spreading machines, despite the existence of other firms employing them profitably. This suggests that some growth in TFP is possible in developing countries through a process of technological catching up.

It is worth noting that despite widespread use of inferior technologies, some developing country producers also use state-of-the-art technologies. The McKinsey report also found that in the Indian dairy processing, steel, and software industries, the better firms were using current global best practices. Some farms in developing countries also cultivate crops with state-of-the-art cultivation methods. This suggests that greater adoption of improved technologies is a real possibility.

Even if the developing countries were to catch up technologically with the developed countries, they would have scope for further growth through technical change, simply by keeping pace with or contributing to advances in state-of-the-art technologies. Growth accounting exercises consistently demonstrate the importance of ongoing technical change in the developed countries.

Anecdotes and surveys indicate that firms in developing countries face many challenges that tend to reduce their technical efficiency, thus suggesting that scope exists for significant improvements in technical efficiency. Unreliable roads prevent timely delivery of raw materials, sometimes forcing firms' machines and workers to remain idle, and often causing firms to carry large precautionary inventories (see Box 8.1). Firms may also be idled periodically by unreliable delivery of inputs by suppliers, unreliable electricity supply, difficulties in obtaining spare parts, lack of skilled repair technicians, or lack of short-term credit for purchasing raw material (Fafchamps, 2004). Simple lack of training in basic business methods can render it difficult for producers to achieve as much as possible from the current technology. A dated but noteworthy study of clothing manufacturers employing the same technologies with comparably trained workers but located in different countries found that an operator working an 8-hour day produced 44 pairs of classic jeans in the United States, 28 to 30 pairs in East Asia, and 19 to 24 pairs in Colombia (Morawetz, 1981).

Whether significant scope exists for improvements in aggregate labor productivity simply through the reallocation of labor across sectors is less clear. The value of output per worker tends to be lower in agricultural sectors than in nonagricultural sectors, and these differences are greater in developing countries than in the developed countries (Caselli, 2005). Whether this implies that the *marginal* product of comparable labor is lower in agriculture than in nonagriculture is unclear, however (see problem 5). Theorists in the 1940s assumed that the marginal product of labor was virtually zero in some traditional sectors of the economy where standard economics simply did not apply (see the discussion of the Lewis model in Chapter 4). Subsequent research has cast doubt on the extreme assumptions of such models, but in Chapter 9 we will identify several reasons why marginal products of labor might differ across sectors and thus why reallocation across sectors could raise aggregate productivity. On the basis of a modified growth accounting study, Bosworth and Collins (2008) argue that productivity gains from moving labor out of agriculture into other sectors explain a significant portion of recent growth in China and India.

Scope also exists to increase typical firm size in developing countries. According to data assembled by Tybout (2000), the share of workers employed in establishments with only a few workers is much higher in most developing countries compared to the United States and other developed countries. The share of workers in establishments with one to four workers was 1.3 percent in the United States, 13.8 percent in Mexico, and 44.2 percent in Indonesia. The share of workers in establishments with one to nine workers was 3.9 percent in the United States but ranged from 40 to 90 percent across 16 developing countries. Whether strong economies of scale would cause increases in firm size to yield large increases in productivity is less clear. Tybout (2000) concludes that although one-person firms (of which there are many in developing countries) appear significantly less productive than the rest, there is no strong evidence of increasing returns to scale above that threshold.

If workers are unemployed, then structural changes that allow more workers to find jobs should increase aggregate labor productivity and GDP per capita. Some early theories of economic development assumed that such unemployment offered vast potential for growth throughout the developing world (see the discussion of the Harrod–Domar model in Chapter 4).

International Labor Organization (ILO) data reveal no uniform tendency for unemployment rates to be higher in poorer countries, but they do suggest that unemployment is a significant drag on aggregate labor productivity in some countries and time periods (ILO, 2011). The ILO defines people to be **unemployed** if they are without work, are currently available for work, and have engaged in some effort to seek work in the recent past. (This probably misses quite a few people who are not working and are willing to work but have given up on searching for work.) As of 2011 the average unemployment rate (as a percentage of the total number of people either employed or unemployed) in the developed economies and European Union was 8.5 percent, and it was as low as 4.2 percent in East Asia and as high as 11.2 percent in North Africa. Variation within regions is even greater. Within sub-Saharan Africa, for example, reported unemployment rates are more than 30 percent in Djibouti, Mauritania, and Namibia, and they are less than 1 percent in Benin, Burundi, Chad, and Rwanda. Thus, the absorption of unemployed workers into productive work appears not to offer an across-the-board source of potential economic growth throughout the developing world, though it may be important in countries experiencing macroeconomic crisis.

Scope seems also to exist to reduce waste associated with rent-seeking activities. Transparency International (2011) ranks countries on the basis of percentages of survey respondents who report they paid a bribe to obtain a service in the last year. This rate was less than 2 percent in rich countries like Denmark and the United Kingdom, but it was greater than 30 percent in Mexico and Bolivia and greater than 70 percent in Sierra Leone, Burundi, and Liberia.

The developing countries lag behind the developed countries in many areas important to aggregate labor productivity and GDP per capita. The developed countries' higher levels of physical and human capital per person, and of TFP, offer hope that improvement is possible in the developing countries. Unfortunately, it does not prove that improvement will be easy, nor does it prove that gains in any one of these areas will necessarily lead to rapid growth.

3.4 The Determinants of Growth

Identifying the proximate sources of growth alerts us to the kinds of improving change that deliver economic growth. But it does not answer the deeper, more policy-relevant questions: What *causes* economic growth to proceed more rapidly in some countries than others? And what could development actors do (or refrain from doing) to raise a country's rate of economic growth? These questions call us to identify the **determinants** of growth.

In what follows, we first describe an approach that many macroeconomists have taken to identifying growth determinants at the aggregate level. Unfortunately, we find that this literature has produced few practical and well justified policy conclusions. We then consider the micro-level underpinnings of successful growth and argue the need to search in a much more disaggregated and context-specific way for policies capable of speeding economic growth.

3.4A Cross-country growth regression studies

When comparable measures of economic growth rates became available for many countries in the late 1980s (Heston, 1991), macroeconomists began to search for empirically important growth determinants at the macro level by running cross-country growth regressions. (For an introduction to regression analysis, see Appendix A.) In the econometric models they estimate, the dependent variable is the rate of economic growth over a 10-, 20-, or 40-year interval. The regressors are measures of possible growth determinants measured at the country level.

Unlike the growth accounting literature, this cross-country growth regression literature has not been guided by a unifying theoretical framework, and it thus includes a wide range of studies that are difficult to compare. For example, researchers have made very different assumptions about the sets of potential determinants that must be included as regressors. Each study includes only a small number of regressors, because small sample sizes prevent the inclusion of more, but the range of potential determinants considered across all studies is very large. The comprehensive review in Durlauf et al. (2004) lists 145 potential determinants included in regressions by various authors (and provides examples of specific papers including each).

A first important set of regressors included in these studies are variables describing policies in place during the periods for which growth rates are measured. Inclusion of such variables reflects the hope that growth rates are determined in part by current policy choices and thus that cross-country growth regression research can help developing countries' policymakers identify policies that are good for growth. Examples of current policy variables considered in these studies are indicators of the extent to which trade policies discourage or encourage international trade, the ratio of government expenditures to overall GDP (as an indicator of how interventionist, redistributive, or undisciplined the government is), and levels or variability of inflation rates (as indicators of policymakers' seriousness in the pursuit of macroeconomic stability).

Cross-country growth regressions must include controls for more than current policies. Identical current policies are likely to result in higher growth rates where circumstances inherited from the past are more conducive to growth. This suggests that if cross-country regressions are to produce unbiased estimates of policy impacts on growth, they must include controls not only for policy but also for the conditions that policymakers inherit from the past. Researchers have included many categories of variables describing inherited conditions. They have included immutable physical country characteristics, such as the share of a country's territory in the tropics, whether the country is landlocked, and the value of the country's mineral deposits; and long-lasting social characteristics, such as the number and nature of languages spoken. They have also included indicators of institutional heritage, such as whether countries were colonized, who their colonizers were, and what legal institutions they inherited from colonial governments.

Among characteristics inherited from the more-recent past, researchers have included measures shaped by policies in recent decades (as well as by geography and institutions), such as beginning-of-period level of GDP per capita, education stocks or school enrollment rates, how long a country has been open to international trade, and income inequality. Increasingly, researchers include indicators of the quality of current government policy-implementing institutions, as reflected, for example, in indices of corruption, rule of law, and protection of property rights.[3,4]

Unfortunately, as we will see:

> It is difficult to draw strong and practical policy conclusions from cross-country growth regressions because they employ only very general measures of policy, they at best identify determinants that are important *on average* across diverse countries, and they suffer from a variety of econometric weaknesses.

Cross-country regressions employ measures of current or recent policy that are at best very crude, in that they are far removed from and only imperfectly correlated with the kinds of policy choices that policymakers face in practice. This limits their practical relevance to policymakers. For example, cross-country regressions might indicate that openness to international trade, high secondary school enrollment rates, or well-functioning bureaucracies are good for growth but do not indicate the details of how best to liberalize policies toward international trade, how to draw more children into secondary school, or how to improve bureaucracies.

Cross-country regressions must be formulated in ways that ignore most potential interactions among growth determinants. They often assume, for example, that if government spending has an impact on growth, then an increase in the government budget by one percentage point of GDP has the *same* impact on growth, regardless of whether the initial budget deficit is large or small, regardless of how the budget is allocated across such categories as infrastructure spending, social spending, and defense spending, and regardless of the quality of the government's bureaucracy. Similarly, they assume that opening to international trade would have the same impact on growth, regardless of whether the country's infrastructure and education stocks are adequate to support expansion of the export sector. It seems much more likely that the impacts of specific policy changes would differ from country to country. Thus, cross-country regressions at best identify policies that are good for growth on average throughout the world, but they do not reveal which policy changes would be the most important for speeding growth in any one country.

Cross-country regressions are also fraught with potential for biased estimation. Given the wide array of policies that might influence growth, and all the possible ways they might interact, it seems likely that most simple cross-country growth regressions omit some relevant growth determinants. Omission of relevant variables biases estimation, causing included variables to appear to affect growth rates to a greater or lesser degree than they actually do when (as seems likely) the omitted variables are correlated with the included variables, as discussed in Appendix A. In practice, estimated policy effects also tend to be highly fragile: Although they appear to have economically important and statistically significant effects in some regressions, their estimates are insignificant or even of opposite sign in regressions using different lists of regressors (Levine and Renelt, 1992; Durlauf et al., 2004). As a result of these weaknesses, many researchers are highly pessimistic about the potential to derive useful lessons from this literature.

Other authors are more optimistic, and argue that cross-country regressions do yield some robust results. Sala-i-martin, Doppelhofer, and Miller (2004), for example, assemble 67 regressors used by other authors and run regressions using subsets of these variables in many

---

[3]Early studies included an additional set of regressors suggested by an influential theoretical growth model: the neoclassical growth model. The assumptions of this model imply that a country's growth rate should be a function of its physical capital saving rate, human capital saving rate, and population growth rate, as well as its initial level of GDP per capita. The physical and human capital savings rates are usually controlled for in regressions using measures of the rates of physical and human capital investment. In the context of the neoclassical growth model these variables help determine growth through a somewhat subtle mechanism (see Chapter 4). In the context of practical policy-oriented growth determinants regressions, however, their role is unclear, because they are indicators of proximate sources of growth rather than deeper growth determinants.
[4]Many recent studies also probe the determinants of growth at a deeper level by examining the apparent impacts on growth of countries' political institutions, a subject to which we return in Chapter 13.

combinations. They argue that when estimates of a determinant's impact on growth are averaged across regressions, in a way that gives more weight to regressions that fit the data better, at least 18 growth determinants find robust support in the data. Some of the determinants they find to be robust, such as primary school enrollment rates and years of openness, are seen as confirming widespread beliefs that commitment to education and openness to international trade are important preconditions for economic growth.

Other determinants found to be robust in the Sala-i-martin et al. study point to important inherited differences across countries but yield no practical policy implications, because they are factors over which policymakers have little control. Such factors include the fraction of the country's area in the tropics, its population density in coastal areas, the fractions of the population that are Confucian, Muslim, and Buddhist, its degree of ethnolinguistic fractionalization (measured by the probability that two people randomly drawn from the population speak the same language), and whether the country was a Spanish colony.[5]

However, other determinants highlighted as robust in the Sala-i-Martin et al. study serve more to raise big questions than to explain growth performance. For example, the determinant they rank as the *most* robust is a dummy variable indicating whether or not the country is in East Asia. This just raises the question: What was it about countries in East Asia that allowed them to grow faster than the rest of world (after controlling for differences in other policy variables and socioeconomic conditions)?

3.4B The micro-level underpinnings of rapid economic growth

Cross-country regressions can offer some general insights into the determinants of growth, but they fall far short of identifying the practical steps that policymakers in any specific country should take to speed growth. Fortunately, when we use tools of economic analysis to identify the micro-level underpinnings of rapid economic growth, we discover a more promising way to search for context-specific policy recommendations. In this section we offer a brief sketch of the micro-level underpinnings of growth. Part III of the text offers a more thorough discussion of the micro-level underpinnings of development outcomes, including economic growth.

As discussed in Section 3.3, the proximate sources of economic growth are physical and human capital accumulation, technical change, improvements in efficiency, and reductions in waste. Thus we begin our search for insights regarding successful growth by identifying the *people* and *choices* that drive factor accumulation and TFP growth. After identifying them, we may begin studying the forces that strengthen or weaken people's *incentives* toward growth-enhancing choices.

Many people and organizations contribute to factor accumulation and TFP growth. Increases in physical capital are brought about by farmers, small business operators, formal firms (domestic or foreign), and community groups, when they construct or purchase buildings, equipment, inventories, roads, communication networks, and other physical assets. Human capital accumulates when families educate and provide good nutrition to their children, when adults enter literacy programs, and when workers and employers undertake job training. Technology advances when inventors develop and disseminate new ideas, and when farmers and entrepreneurs put new ideas into practice. Efficiency improves when entrepreneurs find better ways to avoid disruptions and when inefficient producers close up shop while new entrepreneurs open more productive enterprises.

---

[5]They also find that initial GDP per capita has a robustly negative effect on growth rates (in regressions that control appropriately for other important growth determinants like education variables). This means that after controlling for other critical socioeconomic conditions and policy variables, poorer countries do tend to grow faster, even though unconditional correlations like that in Figure 3.1 show no such tendency.

All this asset creation and TFP growth is possible only if the human beings who provide labor for production are willing to make big changes in their ways of life. Some must give up work on their families' farms to take up work in factories or call centers. Some must migrate from their small home communities to larger towns or cities. Some must take the risk of leaving jobs in old firms to find jobs in new ones.

Notice that the many growth-enhancing choices we have just described are precisely the choices through which people **invest** in building better futures for themselves and their families, as we described in Chapter 2. Knowing that people care about the future, we know they are *willing* to undertake such investments when they perceive that the benefits of improved future prospects are great enough to outweigh the costs, and they are *able* to make such investments when they have ways of financing the up-front costs. Thus:

> Digging deeper into the determination of growth rates requires close examination of the conditions under which people are willing and able to undertake the diverse investments required for successful economic growth.

In Part III we will learn that well-functioning markets can play important roles in motivating and facilitating investment. Goods markets provide entrepreneurs with opportunities to sell produce, thereby allowing them to reap returns on investments that expand their productive capacity. Rising demands for particular goods raise the goods' prices, signaling to entrepreneurs that investment in those sectors would be particularly valuable. Labor markets provide young people with incentives to invest in education and training when labor markets cause wages for scarce skilled labor to rise above wages for unskilled labor. Similarly, labor markets encourage workers to move into sectors and regions where rising demand raises wages. Through financial markets, potential investors who see lucrative investment opportunities, but who have no cash, may obtain financing for up-front investment costs.

Unfortunately, we will also learn in Part III that markets can fail to provide private individuals with adequate incentives or financing for some worthy investments. For example, as readers may have learned in earlier economics courses, markets fail to provide adequate incentive for private investment in **public goods**, which provide services that are valuable to many people and that cannot be denied to anyone wishing to use them. Private investors see little opportunity to gain from investment in rural roads (when it is impossible or uneconomical to charge tolls for road use) because they would enjoy only the benefits of their own road use while bearing the full cost of road construction. We will see that many important infrastructure assets, technological ideas, and legal institutions have such public goods qualities.

The public goods problem is just one of many diverse failures in goods, labor, or financial markets that can present obstacles to investment and that we will examine in Part III. Unfortunately, even if these problems affect only a few of the many kinds of investment necessary for growth, they can slow down the entire growth process, because lack of investment in one area can slow investment in others. For example, without investment in rural roads, markets in rural areas remain stunted, discouraging private investment in the expansion of farms and businesses (Chapter 8).

Private institutions (as defined in Chapter 2) sometimes arise to help circumvent market failures and facilitate beneficial investments. Community groups, for example, sometimes manage to undertake investment in community-level public goods by developing institutions that encourage cooperation. Sadly, nonmarket institutions, too, can fail for a variety of reasons (that we will examine in Chapter 12). When markets and private institutions fail, governments and NGOs may step in, hoping to improve growth and development performance by encouraging critical investments that private markets and institutions do not adequately support, but they succeed only when policies are well designed and the public institutions through which they are implemented provide good governance (challenges we examine in Chapter 13).

This highly abbreviated portrait of the decisions, markets and institutions that underlie growth suggests that:

> Growth is likely to be most successful where physical and institutional circumstances inherited from the past are the most propitious for the development of markets and for the development of current private institutions that encourage investment; where policies are well designed for encouraging critical investments not supported by markets and private institutions; and where policies are implemented through high-quality public sector institutions.

3.4C The need for micro-level, context-specific study

The discussion of the previous section suggests that practical and effective growth policy advice is likely to come out of empirical work that is more disaggregated, context-specific, and detailed than the cross-country growth regression research reviewed earlier.

Country-specific and disaggregated research is likely to be important in the search for effective growth-enhancing policies, because the sectors most likely to lead growth are likely to differ across countries, the types of investment most critical for growth are likely to differ across sectors, and the nature of the obstacles that might prevent private actors from undertaking investment differ across types of investment. Expanding commercial agriculture is likely to be more important to aggregate growth in countries with large agricultural frontiers than in small island economies. Improvements in rural road infrastructure and agricultural technologies are more important for expanding commercial agriculture, whereas private business investment and communication infrastructure may be more important for expanding export manufacturing or software-development sectors. Improving access to finance or reducing burdens imposed by dysfunctional government bureaucracy may be critical for encouraging private business investments, whereas the creation of high-quality institutions supporting collective provision of public goods may be more critical for encouraging expansion of rural road networks.

Research seeking to shed practical light on growth policy must also connect with policy at a more detailed level than has been the case in the cross-country growth-regression literature. Policy-relevant research must generate not just broad conclusions, such as "countries must invest in education to speed growth," but also more specific conclusions, such as recommendations about the school construction projects, scholarship programs, and school curriculum and management changes that are most likely to boost school attendance, school quality, and growth. Part III sets out the analytical tools and framework necessary for such disaggregated, context-specific, and policy-oriented research, and Part IV applies the tools in detailed study of development policies and programs.

REFERENCES

Acemoglu, Daron, Simon Johnson, and James A. Robinson. "Institutions as a Fundamental Cause of Long-Run Growth." In Philippe Aghion and Steven Durlauf (eds). *Handbook of Economic Growth*, Volume 1A. Amsterdam: Elsevier, pp. 385–472, 2005. doi:10.1016/S1574-0684(05)01006-3

Banerjee, Abhijit V., and Esther Duflo. "Growth Theory Through the Lens of Development Economics." In Philippe Aghion and Steven Durlauf (eds). *Handbook of Economic Growth*, Volume 1A. Amsterdam: Elsevier, 2005, pp. 473–552. doi:10.1016/S1574-0684(05)01007-5

Barro, Robert J., and Jong-Wha Lee. "International Data on Educational Attainment: Updates and Implications." *Oxford Economic Papers* 53 (3): 541–563, 2001. doi:10.1093/oep/53.3.541

Caselli, Francesco. "Accounting for Cross-Country Income Differences." In Philippe Aghion and Steven Durlauf (eds). *Handbook of Economic Growth*, Volume 1A. Amsterdam: Elsevier, 2005, pp. 679–741. doi:10.1016/S1574-0684(05)01009-9

Collier, P. *The Bottom Billion: Why the Poorest Countries Are Failing and What Can Be Done About It.* New York: Oxford University Press, 2007.

Duflo, Esther, Michael Kremer, and Jonathan Robinson. "Understanding Technology Adoption: Fertilizer in Western Kenya: Preliminary Results From Field Experiments." Working paper, Poverty Action Lab, MIT, 2004. http://sticerd.lse.ac.uk/dps/bpde2004/duflopaper.pdf

Durlauf, Steven N., Paul A. Johnson, and Jonathan R.W. Temple. "*Growth Econometrics*." In Philippe Aghion and Steven Durlauf (eds). *Handbook of Economic Growth*, Volume 1A. Amsterdam: Elsevier, 2005, pp. 555–677. doi:10.1016/S1574–0684(05)01008–7

Easterly, William, and Ross Levine. "What Have We Learned From a Decade of Empirical Research on Growth? It's Not Factor

Accumulation: Stylized Facts and Growth Models." *The World Bank Economic Review* 15(2): 177–219, 2001. doi:10.1093/wber/15.2.177

Fafchamps, Marcel. *Market Institutions in Sub-Saharan Africa: Theory and Evidence (Comparative Institutional Analysis)*. Cambridge, Mass.: MIT Press, 2004.

Heston, Alan, Robert Summers, and Bettina Aten. "Penn World Table Version 7.1." Center for International Comparisons of Production, Income and Prices at the University of Pennsylvania, 2012. http://pwt.econ.upenn.edu/php_site/pwt_index.php

International Labour Organization (ILO). *Key Indicators of the Labour Market (KILM)*, 7th Edition. Geneva: International Labour Office, 2011. http://kilm.ilo.org/kilmnet/

Krueger, Anne O. "The Political Economy of the Rent-Seeking Society." *American Economic Review* 64(3): 291–303, 1974. http://www.jstor.org/stable/1808883

Levine, Ross, and David Renelt. "A Sensitivity Analysis of Cross-Country Growth Regressions." *American Economic Review* 82(4): 942–963, 1992. http://www.jstor.org/stable/2117352

Murphy, Kevin M., Andrei Schleifer, and Robert W. Vishny. "Why is Rent-Seeking So Costly to Growth?" *American Economic Review* 83(2): 409–414, 1993. http://www.jstor.org/stable/2117699

Pritchett, Lant. "Divergence, Big Time." *Journal of Economic Perspectives* 11(3): 3–17, 1997. http://www.jstor.org/stable/2138181

Rodrik, Dani (ed). *In Search of Prosperity: Analytic Narratives on Economic Growth*. Princeton: Princeton University Press, 2003.

Temple, Jonathan. "The New Growth Evidence." *Journal of Economic Literature* 37(1): 112–156, 1999. doi:10.1257/jel.37.1.112

Transparency International. *Report on the Transparency International Global Corruption Barometer 2010/11*. Berlin: Transparency International, 2011. http://gcb.transparency.org/gcb201011/

Tybout, James R. "Manufacturing Firms in Developing Countries: How Well Do They Do, and Why?" *Journal of Economic Literature* 38(1): 11–44, 2000. doi:10.1257/jel.38.1.11

World Bank. *World Development Indicators 2012*. Washington, DC: World Bank, 2012. http://data.worldbank.org/data-catalog/world-development-indicators

QUESTIONS FOR REVIEW

1. What is economic growth and how does it relate to development? How is it measured?

2. What is GDP? What is GNP or GNI?

3. What constituted unusually high, unusually low, and common rates of average annually compounded growth rates in GDP per capita over the historical period 1960 to 2010?

4. What is the rule of 72?

5. What do we learn from Figure 3.1 about growth experiences in the 1960–2010 period?

6. What is meant by the term *proximate sources of economic growth*?

7. Why is understanding growth in aggregate labor productivity important for understanding economic growth?

8. Define every element in Figure 3.3. What is the relationship between the solid curve and the concept of a production function? Why does the curve start at the origin? Why is it concave?

9. Use Figure 3.3 to discuss the four sources of growth in average labor productivity within an individual firm.

10. Provide as comprehensive a list as possible of proximate sources of economic growth. Which of these would be defined as factor accumulation and which would be defined as growth in total factor productivity?

11. What is the purpose of growth accounting exercises? What is the purpose of development accounting exercises? In broad brush, what have we learned from these exercises?

12. What does it mean to seek out empirically important determinants of growth?

13. What are cross-country growth regressions and what are some of the broad patterns they reveal regarding the determinants of growth?

14. What are some weaknesses of cross-country growth regressions as tools for guiding growth policy?

15. Describe some of the people and choices that drive factor accumulation and TFP growth.

QUESTIONS FOR DISCUSSION

1. Read Collier (2007), Chapter 1. What does the author mean by "the bottom billion"? How does the author make his argument that achieving faster rates of economic growth must be the priority in development for the countries the world's "bottom billion" live? What do you think of this argument?

2. As poor economies grow, the share of production that passes through formal markets rises as subsistence farmers become more integrated into markets and improved law enforcement reduces black market activity. Would this process tend to raise or lower the measured rate of economic

growth? Would the measured rate of economic growth tend to understate or overstate the true rate of economic growth?

3. What is the intuition behind the assumption that production functions are characterized by diminishing marginal returns?

4. Read any chapter in Rodrik (2003) that provides a narrative of growth in a particular country. Which of the proximate sources of growth discussed in this chapter are emphasized in the narrative? What is said of the other proximate sources? What is said about the roles that markets, government policies, other institutions, and geography played in shaping growth performance? What lessons do you think this narrative yields regarding how to encourage good growth performance in other countries?

5. For each of the proximate sources of growth described in the text, describe the people and the choices that might be involved in driving that process.

6. Suppose that each of the following policies is successful in improving well-being for some particular set of households. Which of the policies would also contribute to economic growth? How?
   - Offer of subsidized primary education
   - Increase in the price of corn
   - Agricultural extension program
   - Distribution of cash in an emergency

PROBLEMS

1. If GDP per capita grows from an initial level of G_0 to the level G_t after t years have passed, then the average annually compounded rate of economic growth over the period is the growth rate r (expressed as a percentage) that solves the equation $G_0(1+r/100)^t = G_t$. Rearranging this expression, we find that

$$r = \left[\left(\frac{G_t}{G_0}\right)^{\frac{1}{t}} - 1\right]*100$$

The rule of 72 says that if a country grows at an annually compounded rate of r, then we can approximate the number of years it will take for the country's GDP per capita to double (D) using the calculation: $D = 72/r$. To calculate doubling time exactly, notice that the number of years D that it takes to double an initial income per capita of G_0 for a country growing at rate r solves the equation $G_0(1+r/100)^D = 2G_0$. Dividing both sides by G_0, taking the natural logarithm of both sides, and rearranging, we derive this formula for determining doubling time exactly:

$$D = \frac{\ln(2)}{\ln(1+r/100)}$$

It just so happens that for growth rates in the relevant ranges for studies of economic growth, the right-hand side of this equation is a function of r that is well approximated by the function $72/r$. The following table lists real per capita GDP for selected countries in 1960 and 2000 (in U.S. dollars).
   a. Calculate the average annually compounded rates of economic growth for each country to fill in column 3 in the table.
   b. Use the rule of 72 to calculate the approximate number of years it would take for GDP per capita to double in each country, assuming it continues to grow steadily at the rate you reported for part a. Record your answers in column 4.

c. Use the formula presented above to calculate more exactly the number of years it would take for GDP per capita to double in each country, assuming it continues to grow steadily at the rate you reported in part a. Record your answers in column 5.

Country	1 GDP per Capita 1960 (U.S. Dollars)	2 GDP per Capita 2000 (U.S. Dollars)	3 Average Annually Compounded Growth Rate 1960–2000 (Percent)	4 Doubling Time Using Rule of 72	5 Doubling Time Using Exact Calculation
Bolivia	2,431.39	2,929.19			
China	448.13	891.39			
Ghana	411.86	1,392.20			
Taiwan	1,443.61	1,9183.93			

2. Suppose a firm's production function is given by $F(L, H, K; A)$, where $L, H,$ and K are the current quantities of labor, human capital, and physical capital employed in production, and A is an index of the current level of technology. For each of the following changes, indicate whether it would raise, lower, or leave unchanged: (a) the average product of labor in the firm and (b) total factor productivity within the firm.
   - An increase in K, holding $L, H,$ and A constant, while the firm continues to operate on its production function
   - An increase in L, holding $H, K,$ and A constant, while the firm continues to operate on its production function
   - An increase in A, holding $L, H,$ and K constant, while the firm continues to operate on its production function
   - An increase in output that represents a movement toward operation on its production function, while holding $L, H, K,$ and A constant

3. According to the growth accounting equation discussed in Box 3.1, $g_y = g_A + \alpha g_k + (1 - \alpha)g_h$, where g_y, g_k, and g_h are growth rates of GDP per capita, capital per worker, and human capital per worker, and α is the share of capital income in total GDP. The first four columns of the following table give values for g_y, g_k, g_h, and α.

  a. Fill in the fifth and sixth columns of the table with the growth attributed to physical and human capital accumulation. These may be calculated as αg_k and $(1 - \alpha)g_h$, respectively.

  b. Fill in the seventh column of the table, plugging the values of g_y, g_k, g_h, and α into the growth accounting equation and backing out g_A.

  c. Fill in the final column of the table by calculating the fraction of overall growth (g_y) that is attributed to TFP by the growth accounting framework. (That is, divide g_A by g_y and multiply by 100.)

  d. Discuss the potential for inaccurate estimates of g_h and α to render misleading estimates of the importance of TFP growth.

				Growth Attributable to Physical Capital	Growth Attributable to Human Capital	TFP Growth	TFP Share in Growth
g_y	g_k	g_h	α				
5.2	4.0	2.0	0.3				
5.2	4.0	3.0	0.3				
5.2	4.0	2.0	0.4				

4. In this problem you will derive the growth accounting equation discussed in Box 3.1. Assume that the aggregate production function takes the form

$$y(t) = A(t)k(t)^\alpha h(t)^{1-\alpha}$$

where y, k, and h represent GDP per capita, physical capital per worker, and human capital per worker, and α is a technological parameter. We assume that A, k, and h are changing over time for unspecified reasons, and we use the functions $A(t)$, $k(t)$, and $h(t)$ to describe their levels at any point in time t. Derivatives of these functions with respect to time, $\frac{dy}{dt}$, $\frac{dk}{dt}$, and $\frac{dh}{dt}$, describe how fast they are growing (in absolute terms) at any point in time. Their growth rates (expressed as fractions) are equal to, $g_A = \frac{dA}{dt}/A$, $g_k = \frac{dk}{dt}/k$, and $g_h = \frac{dh}{dt}/h$. Because Y is a function of A, k, and h, it, too, is a function of time, with percentage growth rate $g_y = \frac{dy}{dt}/y$.

  a. Take the derivative with respect to time t of both sides of the aggregate production function equation.

  b. Divide both sides of this new equation by y, so that the left-hand side becomes g_y.

  c. Show how to transform the equation you just derived into the following: $g_y = g_A + \alpha g_k + (1 - \alpha)g_h$

5. Consider two firms that produce the same output. The marginal product of labor in each firm is a declining function of the quantity of labor employed there. In Firm 1, the marginal product of labor MPL_1 is described by the function $MPL_1 = 40 - 2L_1$, where L_1 is the quantity of labor employed in Firm 1. In Firm 2, the marginal product of labor is described by $MPL_2 = 30 - L_2$, where L_2 is the quantity of labor employed in Firm 2.

  a. Graph these functions in two graphs, side by side. Let your horizontal axes measure units of labor in the range of 0 to 20, and let your vertical axes measure the marginal product of labor in the range of 0 to 45 units of output.

  b. Suppose $L_1 = 6$ and $L_2 = 8$. What is the marginal product of labor in Firm 1? What is the marginal product of labor in Firm 2? Explain why the total quantity of output produced by the two firms together would rise if one unit of labor was moved from Firm 2 to Firm 1.

  c. At what levels of L_1 and L_2 do the marginal products of labor equal 20 in both firms? If these are in fact the quantities of labor employed in the two firms, what is the average product of labor in each firm? (*Hint:* The average product of labor is just the total product or total output divided by the quantity of labor employed. The total product is equal to the area under the marginal product of labor curve.) You have just shown that it is possible for the average products of labor to differ across firms (or sectors) even when the marginal products of labor are equal.

Economic Growth Theory in Historical Perspective

Growth has not always been understood in the broad terms described in Chapter 3. In the early years after World War II, when the field of economic development was born, physical capital accumulation was considered the main proximate source of growth and the world was thought to be filled with rigidities causing widespread market failure and necessitating heavy government involvement in development. Little thought was given to the role of institutions in the economy, and the prescriptions for good growth performance were thought to be largely the same throughout the developing world.

This chapter describes the evolution of economic thought regarding growth in developing countries from then until now, paying special attention to influential theoretical growth models. It offers an instructive example of how interactions between theoretical and empirical research can advance understanding of important processes.

4.1 Introduction to Theoretical Growth Models

A **theoretical growth model** is defined by a set of assumptions regarding the way economies work, which highlight the economic relationships that the model's builder considers most important for understanding economic growth. The purpose of the modeling exercise is to determine what the assumptions imply about how and why growth rates might change over time or differ across countries.

The assumptions on which growth models are based fall into two categories: technological and behavioral. **Technological assumptions** describe physical constraints on the maximum quantities of goods and services that an economy's firms can produce from various combinations of inputs. Simple growth models treat the entire economy as if it were a single firm and formalize the technological assumptions by writing down a single **aggregate production function**, which describes the maximum quantity of total GDP that may be achieved at any time as a function of the national aggregate quantities of various inputs and the current state of technical knowledge and expertise.

The technological assumptions underlying growth models have evolved over time in several important ways. First, early models assumed that GDP was a function of only two inputs: labor and physical capital. Only later did model builders recognize human capital as an additional important input to production. Second, whereas the earliest models assumed a very rigid technology in which producers faced only a single option for combining labor and capital to produce output, later models assumed that a wider array of technological options give producers flexibility to combine labor and other inputs in varying proportions. Third, whereas the earliest models assumed that production was characterized by constant returns to scale and constant marginal returns to capital, these were replaced in the 1960s by models assuming constant returns to scale but diminishing marginal returns to capital (as defined in Chapter 3), which were in turn replaced in the 1980s by models with increasing returns to scale and constant or increasing marginal returns to capital. We will see the significance of these changing assumptions for our understanding of economic growth below.

Growth models' **behavioral assumptions** describe how the inputs available at any point in time are allocated across activities (e.g., production of goods and services, research and development activities, or unemployment), and how the quantities of inputs available in the economy and the economy's technological options evolve over time. We call these behavioral assumptions, because they describe how the economy's firms choose what to produce, how to produce it, and what investments to make; how the economy's households choose where to work, what to consume, and what to save; and how markets work (or fail to work) when producers and consumers interact with each other. The simplest models assume that firms and households follow simple rules of thumb, such as the rule that households always save a certain percentage of their income, and assume that key features of the economy (such as the level of technology) always grow at exogenously fixed rates. More elaborate models build up assumptions from more detailed and thorough-going microeconomic foundations, describing producers and households as seeking to maximize profits or utility subject to the constraints they face.

Behavioral assumptions, too, have evolved over time in several important ways. First, the earliest models assumed that producers and households had little ability or inclination to modify their choices in response to economic conditions and that as a result, markets would fail to guide all the economy's inputs into their most productive uses. These were replaced by models making almost diametrically opposite assumptions, in which producers and households were assumed to face great flexibility and markets were assumed to function perfectly. More recently yet, these have been replaced by models staking out a more nuanced, intermediate position, in which producers and households are flexible and responsive to economic conditions but in which markets nonetheless might fail to direct all inputs into their best possible uses.

Second, the earliest models largely took technological conditions as fixed and unchanging. These were replaced by models in which technology was assumed to improve over time, for reasons that were unexplained within the model. More recently, model builders have tried to identify actors within their models who are responsible for generating technological improvements and to formulate assumptions about how these actors make the decisions that determine the rate of **technical change**.

Model builders make their assumptions specific and clear by writing them down as systems of mathematical equations. These equations involve **exogenous parameters**, whose values are taken as given from outside the model, and **endogenous variables**, whose values are determined (as functions of the exogenous parameters) by solving the system of equations. The most important endogenous variable in all these models is, of course, the rate of economic growth. Early models treated only the growth rate as endogenous, but later models have treated a growing array of variables—such as rates of investment and technical change—as jointly endogenous with the growth rate.

For each model we examine below, we describe the technological and behavioral assumptions, and their implications for how the growth rate would evolve over time if the parameters of the model remained constant and how a country's growth trajectory would change as a result of changes in key exogenous parameters. We embed this technical discussion of specific models into a larger description of the intellectual interplay between theoretical predictions and empirical observations that has driven the evolution of thought about economic growth.

4.2 The 1940s and 1950s: Capital Fundamentalism, Structuralism, and Dualism

4.2A Themes

Economic thought regarding growth in developing countries in the 1940s and 1950s was characterized by capital fundamentalism, structuralism, and dualism. **Capital fundamentalism** refers to the belief that the most important proximate source of economic growth is the accumulation of physical capital. The emphasis economists placed on capital accumulation in the

1940s is understandable, given the perception at the time that the Soviet Union's recent industrialization through rapid (and forced) saving and physical capital investment had been a great success.

Structuralism refers to the belief that the world is a rigid place, in which economic actors—especially the poor and tradition-bound peasants who were thought to populate developing countries—have little ability or inclination to alter what they do in response to economic incentives. When, for example, labor is plentiful and capital is scarce, the price of capital might rise, but such price increases would not set into motion self-equilibrating market processes, in which people decide to invest in the creation of more capital or to shift to production methods that make greater use of cheap labor and rely less on costly capital. In such a world, unemployment can remain rampant for long periods without markets showing any tendency to absorb the unemployed. This view was rendered compelling by the recent experience of the Great Depression.

Dualism refers to the belief that developing economies must be understood as having two sectors, traditional and modern, each with peculiar characteristics and very different growth prospects. The large traditional sector, often identified with agriculture, was assumed to be "backward," in the sense that production was overseen by poor, irrational peasants who were not driven by modern profit-maximizing motivations, who operated at very low levels of productivity, and who would have little prospect for improving their productivity even if they were inclined to try. The modern sector, often identified with manufacturing, was by contrast seen as a potentially dynamic sector, though still small in most developing countries. It was in modern manufacturing that physical capital accumulation was thought to hold tremendous promise of increasing productivity and incomes, and where producers were more inclined to plow growing profits back into saving and investment.

The predominant perspective on economic growth during this period had profound policy implications.

> In the 1940s and 1950s, capital fundamentalism motivated emphasis on raising rates of saving and physical capital accumulation. Structuralism motivated extensive government involvement in bringing those increases about. Dualism dictated that the new capital be concentrated in the modern manufacturing sector and that such "industrialization" be encouraged through subsidies and by protecting domestic manufacturing enterprises from international competition.

The following sections describe two influential theoretical growth models of the 1940s and 1950s. The Harrod–Domar model, which influenced thinking about growth in developed as well as developing countries, exhibits capital fundamentalist and structuralist thinking. The Lewis model incorporates dualism as well and was considered useful primarily for understanding developing countries.

4.2B The Harrod–Domar growth model

The ideas underlying what is now known as the Harrod–Domar growth model were introduced independently in papers by Roy Harrod (1939) and Evsey Domar (1946). At the center of the Harrod–Domar model is a very simple and extreme assumption regarding the economy's production technology: A fixed quantity u of labor and a fixed quantity v of physical capital are required to produce each unit of GDP. That is, the aggregate production function is assumed to take the following extreme form:

$$Y = min\left[\left(\frac{1}{u}\right)L, \left(\frac{1}{v}\right)K\right] \tag{4.1}$$

where Y is total GDP, L is the total quantity of labor, and K is the total quantity of physical capital. The $min[.,.]$ function indicates that total output is equal to the smaller of the two arguments. The parameters u and v are known as the *labor-output ratio* and the *capital-output ratio* and are fixed technological parameters defining an inflexible technology.

Notice several things about the technological assumptions embodied in equation 4.1. First, the production function assumes that capital and labor are the only important inputs to production. Second, it assumes that technological options are few and rigid. Indeed, labor and capital must always be combined in exactly the same proportion (u/v units of labor per unit of capital) to produce a unit of output; for this reason the technology is labeled a **fixed proportions production technology**. If the ratio of labor to capital in the economy is greater than u/v, then some labor has no use in production and will remain unemployed, and if the ratio of labor to capital is less than u/v, some capital will remain unemployed. Third, it assumes that production is characterized by constant returns to scale.

The model's behavioral assumptions offer simple descriptions of how K and L evolve over time and how given stocks of K and L are utilized at any point in time. The capital stock K is increased through investment. In an economy that is closed to international investment, increases in K must be financed by local saving. The critical behavioral assumption driving growth in K, then, is the assumption that people save a fixed proportion s of their total income. Capital accumulates when this saving is greater than the rate at which old capital depreciates. The labor force L is assumed to grow at an exogenously fixed rate n.[1] Significantly, the technological parameters u and v are taken as exogenously fixed, with no built-in tendency to evolve over time.

Labor is assumed (at most times) to be abundant relative to capital, in the sense that the current stock of capital is too small to provide productive employment for all workers. (This notion of labor abundance makes sense only as a result of the fixed proportions production technology, which implies that the current stock of capital K can provide productive employment for only $(u/v)K$ units of labor.) In practice, then, output can be treated as a function of K alone, because the economy's stock of labor never represents a constraint on production.

The assumptions of the previous several paragraphs may be summarized by a simple set of equations. Combining the technological assumptions with the assumption that labor never represents a constraint on production, we can state the economy's effective aggregate production function as

$$Y = \left(\frac{1}{v}\right)K \qquad (4.2)$$

This says that total GDP is just a constant multiple of the size of the capital stock. Denoting the derivative of a variable x with respect to time by $\dot{x}$, we can restate equation 4.2 in a way that illustrates the link between *increases* in Y and *increases* in K:

$$\dot{Y} = \left(\frac{1}{v}\right)\dot{K} \qquad (4.3)$$

That is, Y rises and falls strictly in proportion to K. Notice that as long as labor remains abundant relative to capital (so that this equation provides a good description of growth in aggregate production), the economy is characterized by constant marginal returns to capital: Each additional unit of capital increases Y by the same amount.

In light of equation 4.3, if we are to understand growth in Y, we must understand growth in K. Increases in the capital stock ($\dot{K}$) are achieved when the rate of investment exceeds the rate of

---

[1] Throughout this chapter we essentially treat the labor force as a fixed proportion of the total population, in which case the growth rate of the labor force is just the population growth rate, and growth in output per person is identical to growth in output per worker.

depreciation of the old capital stock. Invoking the assumption that people always save a fixed proportion s of their income and letting d represent the fraction of the old capital stock that decays or becomes obsolete each year, we can describe the change in size of the capital stock in a short interval of time as

$$\dot{K} = sY - dK \tag{4.4}$$

Equations 4.3 and 4.4 fully describe the assumptions of the model. We solve the model, seeking to understand its implications for growth, by solving this set of equations for a statement describing how the rate of economic growth $(\dot{Y}/Y)$ is determined as a function of the key exogenous parameters of the model (v, s, and d). Substituting equation 4.4 into equation 4.3, we find that

$$\dot{Y} = \left(\frac{1}{v}\right)(sY - dK) \tag{4.5}$$

or (dividing both sides by Y, and recognizing that $v = K/Y$)

$$\frac{\dot{Y}}{Y} = \frac{s}{v} - \left(\frac{d}{v}\right)\left(\frac{K}{Y}\right) = \frac{s}{v} - d \tag{4.6}$$

Equation 4.6 describes how the model's main endogenous variable, the growth rate of total GDP, is determined as a function of the model's parameters. (Later models focus on the growth rate in per capita rather than total GDP.) We conclude that as long as the parameters remain fixed, output growth proceeds at a constant rate. Differences in growth rates across countries must be attributed to differences in the saving rate s or the capital-output ratio v, and increasing a country's growth rate would require increasing s or reducing v (assuming the rate of depreciation is unalterable).

How might changes in s or v come about? In the model's world of rigidities and poorly functioning markets, increases in s are unlikely in the absence of intervention by developing country governments, and these governments might require assistance (i.e., foreign aid) from the world's rich countries. Reductions in the technological parameter v, which require improvements in efficiency or technology, were thought even more difficult to engineer even by government. The main conclusion of the model thus comes as little surprise given the assumptions on which it is built: To increase the GDP growth rate, a country's government must increase the rate of investment by the public sector, financing that investment through taxes and foreign aid.

The model has additional implications that are less obvious and that are less compelling in light of historical experience. In this model, the growth of K (and thus the rate of growth in the number of productive jobs) is governed by the saving rate, while growth in L (the number of workers) is governed by unrelated forces. It can be shown (see problem 1) that K (like Y) grows at the rate $(s/v) - d$, and the labor force grows at the rate n, which need not equal $(s/v) - d$. If K grows more rapidly than L then the number of jobs in the economy grows more rapidly than the number of workers, and unemployment falls. Under such circumstances, GDP per capita rises, even though the productivity of each employed worker remains fixed, simply because the share of workers who are in unproductive unemployment falls. If capital continues to grow more rapidly than the labor force, production might eventually use up all available labor. In this case, further capital accumulation bids up wages and prices, generating inflation without increasing output per capita, and growth in GDP per capita ceases. If, however, K grows less rapidly than L, then unemployment must rise and GDP per capita falls. Unless $s/v - d$ just happens to equal n, the economy will be marked by rising or falling unemployment. This **knife-edge** property of the model implies perpetual instability. Furthermore, if $s/v - d$ did just equal n, total GDP would rise but GDP per capita would remain constant. As we will see, the mismatch between these implications and real-world experience contributed to the eventual rejection of the Harrod–Domar model.

The basic ideas underlying the Harrod–Domar model have been built into a variety of more elaborate models over the years. The "two-gap model," like the Harrod–Domar model, pointed to the possibility of a gap between the amount of capital accumulation required to keep a growing population fully employed and the amount of finance for investment forthcoming through private savings. In addition, it raised the possibility of a second gap between the amount of foreign exchange required to purchase the required capital equipment from abroad and the amount of foreign exchange forthcoming from exports (Chenery and Strout, 1966). Multisector versions of these models, which distinguished multiple sectors by their requirements for capital, foreign exchange, and the outputs of other sectors, allowed policymakers to calculate the gaps that must be filled by policy on a sector-by-sector basis. For a provocative discussion of the genesis and ongoing legacy of these models in international development organizations, see Chapter 2 of Easterly (2001).

4.2C The Lewis model of labor-surplus dualistic development

In his famous article, "Economic Development with Unlimited Supplies of Labour," W. Arthur Lewis (1954) embedded capital fundamentalist notions in a model of an economy characterized by profound dualism and described economic growth as a process in which physical capital accumulation and structural change are intimately interrelated. The dualistic economy is composed of two sectors, the **subsistence sector** and the **capitalist sector**, which differ from each other in both production technology and behavioral relationships. The **structural change** that accompanies growth in this model is a shifting of labor out of the subsistence sector, where some labor is largely unproductive, into the modern sector, where that same labor can be brought into productive employment as physical capital accumulation creates new jobs.

In the large subsistence sector, which Lewis associated with traditional agriculture and some traditional handicrafts and services, production is a function only of labor and land. Physical capital plays no role, and thus the sector has no potential to grow through capital accumulation. While in principle subsistence sector producers can produce output with varying combinations of land and labor, in practice the ratio of labor to land is so high that the marginal product of labor is virtually zero. Labor is *in surplus* or *redundant*, in the sense that some workers can be withdrawn from the sector without reducing the sector's total output. Workers in agriculture are paid a wage that is fixed by tradition near the subsistence level, rather than by market forces, and this wage is greater than their marginal product of zero.

Neither producers nor workers in the Lewis model's subsistence sector save any of what they earn. Subsistence sector workers are willing to move into the modern sector if offered a wage equal to the subsistence wage plus some premium to compensate them for the difficulties and psychological costs of making such a move. Because their marginal product in the subsistence sector is zero, if they respond to such a premium and leave the sector, subsistence sector production remains the same. Thus, from a social perspective they are "free labor" (similar to the unemployed workers in the Harrod–Domar model) that can be moved into productive use in the modern sector without sacrificing any output or well-being elsewhere in the economy.

In the small capitalist sector, production is a function of labor and capital. Here is where capital accumulation has the potential to drive growth. Lewis associated this sector with commercial agriculture as well as modern manufacturing, but many of his followers associated the dynamism of this sector more exclusively with manufacturing.

The production function in the capitalist sector is of the sort described in Chapter 3, in which labor and capital may be combined in varying proportions to produce output, with each input subject to diminishing marginal returns. Capitalists (i.e., the owners of capital, who run firms in this sector) seek to maximize the profits they derive from their current holdings of capital and are motivated to save and reinvest those profits. In fact, they are assumed to save and reinvest *all* of their profits. They compete with one another and with the subsistence sector for workers, in equilibrium paying a wage equal to the subsistence wage plus the premium to compensate

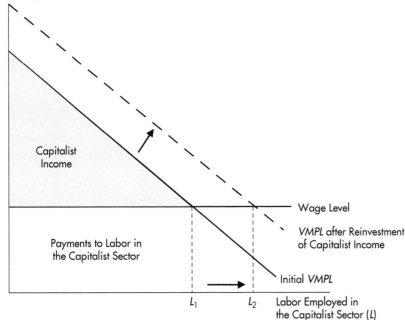

FIGURE 4.1
Growth and Structural Change under Labor Surplus Dualistic Development

workers for moving into capitalist sector work. Profit maximization requires that they hire the quantity of labor at which the value of the marginal product of labor (*VMPL*) equals this wage. (For a review of why this is the profit-maximizing quantity of labor, see section 6.4.)

Figure 4.1 summarizes these assumptions and illustrates their implications. The horizontal axis measures the quantity of labor employed in the capitalist sector. Any labor not employed in the capitalist sector remains in the subsistence sector. Thus a move to the right in this graph signifies a structural change, in which the share of labor employed in the subsistence sector declines and the share employed in the capitalist sector rises, as workers are drawn into capitalist sector employment. A move to the right also signifies an increase in the overall productivity of labor in the economy, as labor is drawn out of a sector in which its marginal product is zero and into a sector in which it has a positive marginal product.

The vertical axis in Figure 4.1 measures the *VMPL* in the capitalist sector. As described in Chapter 3, given any quantity of capital employed in the capitalist sector, we can trace out a downward-sloping *VMPL* schedule. The solid downward-sloping schedule is the *VMPL* schedule associated with an initial stock of capital. The horizontal line is drawn at the height of the wage that must be paid to draw workers out of the subsistence sector. What is important is that this wage is rigidly determined by tradition and does not increase as workers are drawn out of the subsistence sector. The intersection of the solid *VMPL* schedule with the horizontal wage line identifies the initial profit-maximizing level of employment in the capitalist sector (L_1).

The total value of production in this economy, and thus total income, is given by the total value of production in the capitalist sector plus the unchanging total value of production in the subsistence sector. The initial total value of production in the capitalist sector is the area under the solid *VMPL* schedule up to the point at which it intersects the wage line. Of this total area, the lower rectangle, which has width equal to the number of workers in the capitalist sector and height equal to the wage, has area equal to the total payments to labor in the capitalist sector. The remaining capitalist sector output, represented by the area of the shaded triangle, indicates the profits earned by capitalists.

This figure speaks to economic growth and structural change as a result of the assumption that capitalists save and reinvest their profits. Capitalists use their initial profits to increase the capital stock, causing an upward shift in the *VMPL* schedule, as illustrated by the shift to the dashed *VMPL* schedule in the figure. As the *VMPL* shifts, the profit-maximizing quantity of capitalist sector labor rises to L_2, and more workers are drawn out of the subsistence sector into the capitalist sector. The total value of output in the economy also grows.

The model associates structural change with accelerating investment and growth. When workers move from subsistence to capitalist sectors, their wages increase by the size of the premium paid in the capitalist sector, but the wage paid in each sector remains fixed, and total payments to labor throughout the economy rise little. Most of the increased value of production translates into increased capitalist income, leading to an increase in the capitalist share of income and an increase in the rate of saving and reinvestment. The existence of surplus labor, which causes the wage to remain low despite the pull of a rising capitalist sector, allows profits and the rate of saving and investment to increase. In labor-surplus economies, the rate of growth increases over time as the share of the capitalist sector in the total value of production rises. Countries that are further along in structural transformation grow more rapidly than others, until their labor surplus is exhausted, at which point wages begin to rise and the rate of increase in profits and investment falls.

Like the Harrod–Domar model, the Lewis model places great importance on saving and investment in physical capital as the route to economic growth. It differs, however, in its implications for the best way to promote that saving and investment. It describes a world in which capitalists are willing and able to undertake investment, provided they have profits to reinvest. From a social perspective, however, capitalists perceive too little incentive to produce and invest because they must pay a wage that is higher than their workers' marginal product in the subsistence sector. This means that at the private profit-maximizing level of capitalist sector employment (where the *VMPL* equals the wage), the *VMPL* is higher in the capitalist sector than in agriculture. If capitalists could be encouraged to draw even more workers out of the subsistence sector, the total value of production in the economy would rise. Thus, the model suggests that capitalists should be provided with added incentives to expand their production and profits. For analysts who took the capitalist sector to be synonymous with manufacturing and who observed that most manufactured goods sold in developing countries at the time were goods imported from the developed countries, the natural policy prescription of the model was to encourage the expansion of import-competing manufacturing enterprises by using tariff policies to protect them from international competition.

Notice that the model treats the large subsistence agricultural sector as playing a purely passive role in growth and development, that of releasing surplus workers to the modern manufacturing sector. Agriculture was assumed to have no growth potential of its own. Indeed, the model suggests that growth proceeds most successfully when agricultural productivity remains low, so that workers may be attracted out of agriculture at low wages that show no tendency to rise. If agricultural productivity and wages were to rise, the rate of profits in the manufacturing sector would fall, reducing the rate of saving and reinvestment. Thus, the worldview supported in the Lewis model encouraged a neglect of agriculture in the pursuit of growth and development.

As we will see in the next section, subsequent empirical research has led to rejection of most critical assumptions in the Lewis model and certainly to the model's growth policy implications. Some authors continue to argue the relevance of the model for understanding development (e.g., Knight, 2007), but their arguments suggest only superficial relevance. They point out that the Lewis model predicts very slow wage growth during early stages of economic growth and then more rapid increases in wages after growth has eliminated surplus labor and the Lewis model becomes irrelevant. They then present empirical evidence for several countries of early phases of economic growth accompanied by slow wage growth, followed by later phases of economic growth with rapid wage growth.

Such wage-growth patterns fall far short of confirming the Lewis model's assumptions or policy implications, because similar patterns of wage growth could be generated by very different models. For example, wage growth could follow this pattern even in models in which all sectors are capitalist and all workers and producers have equal propensities to save, as long as incipient wage increases lead to large increases in household labor supply at low levels of income and smaller increases in the hours of labor supplied at higher income levels. In such models, initial growth-induced increases in the demand for labor would lead to rapid increases in labor hours and slow increases in wages, whereas later growth and labor-demand expansion would induce more rapid wage growth and less expansion of labor hours. The models would thus explain wage growth patterns just as well as the Lewis model but would offer no justification for subsidizing modern sector expansion and would yield no prediction that expansion of a modern sector would raise rates of saving, investment, and growth.

Though we now reject the extreme assumptions of the Lewis model and many of its policy implications, contemporary development thinking continues to be shaped by Lewis's accurate observations that growth is almost always accompanied by structural change, that the elasticity of labor supply helps determine the extent to which the benefits of growth are shared by workers throughout the economy, and that wages sometimes tend to differ among identical workers in different sectors or geographic locations. All of these point to the need for careful study of labor markets in developing countries, as in Chapter 9.

4.3 The 1960s and 1970s: Neoclassical Perspectives, Technology, and Human Capital

4.3A Themes

Research in the 1960s and 1970s chipped away at the theoretical and empirical underpinnings of capital fundamentalism, structuralism, and dualism. Capital fundamentalism gave way to interest in the combined contributions of physical capital accumulation, technical change, and human capital accumulation. The introduction of a new theoretical growth model, the neoclassical growth model, raised theoretical questions about the potential for physical capital accumulation alone to explain the sustained growth observed in the United States and other countries and pointed toward technical change as an additional source of growth. Simultaneous developments in the study of labor markets and wage formation pointed to the importance of human capital accumulation. Growth accounting exercises (as discussed in Chapter 3) provided further reason to believe that human capital accumulation and technical change were at least as important as physical capital accumulation in explaining growth.

Structuralist views of developing country markets diminished as collection and analysis of data from farms and households in developing countries demonstrated that even poor rural families respond to economic incentives in ways predicted by models of rational economic behavior. The structuralist assumption that poorly functioning markets should be overridden by extensive government intervention was also called into question by highly disappointing experiences with government planning. Indeed, the intellectual pendulum swung to the opposite extreme in this period, as a growing number of development analysts argued for withdrawal of government intervention and greater reliance on markets for allocating resources and motivating growth.

Dualism of the sort exhibited in the Lewis model lost favor in this period, too, for a variety of reasons. Research suggested that the marginal product of labor is not zero in agriculture, that agriculture can be a dynamic source of saving and physical capital accumulation, and that investment in physical capital can induce productivity increases in agriculture as well as manufacturing. The experience of the Green Revolution (see Chapter 20), moreover, demonstrated the great potential for new technologies to increase agricultural productivity. On top of this, it was becoming apparent that many of the poor in developing countries earned their livelihoods in agriculture and would not begin to share in the benefits of growth and development for a very long time unless new efforts were made to increase agricultural productivity and income. For a more detailed discussion of changing economic thought regarding growth and development in this period, see Little (1982).

The policy implications of the new perspective on economic growth were very different from those of earlier years.

> In the 1960s and 1970s, new views of economic growth motivated greater interest in encouraging human capital investment and technical change, greater attention to agriculture, and reduced government involvement in the economy.

In what follows, we discuss three versions of the highly influential neoclassical growth model. The first is the "simple" model without technical change (or human capital accumulation) that Robert Solow used to demonstrate the inadequacy of physical capital accumulation alone to explain the real-world experience of sustained economic growth. The second is the model *with* technical change, in which Solow showed that introducing technical change solves the puzzle presented by the simpler model. The final version acknowledges that the accumulation of human as well as physical capital might be important in economic growth.

4.3B The simple neoclassical growth model

In his landmark paper "A Contribution to the Theory of Economic Growth" (1956), Robert Solow introduced what we now know as the neoclassical growth model, which served as the unifying framework for thought about economic growth for several decades. He motivated the new model by pointing out two reasons for dissatisfaction with the then-popular Harrod–Domar growth model. First, that model rests on stark technological assumptions that contemporary economists found implausible. Second, the knife-edge property of that model implies a perpetual macroeconomic instability that seemed counter to observed experience, at least in the United States.

Solow pointed out that the rigid assumptions and the unsatisfying implications of the Harrod–Domar model are closely interrelated. By assuming a production technology in which labor and capital can only be productively employed in exactly fixed proportions, the model assumes away any potential for producers to respond to capital scarcity by using more labor-intensive methods of production. If some workers are unemployed, we might expect them to offer to work at lower wages, rendering labor cheaper relative to capital. Producers who can choose from multiple production methods would be encouraged by the lower wages to switch to production methods that require more labor and less capital per unit of output. By so doing, they would increase the number of workers who can find employment with the fixed capital stock. If markets work perfectly, this process should continue until unemployment disappears. Such equilibrating changes were ruled out by the Harrod–Domar model's rigid technological assumptions.

Solow decided to examine what would happen to the predictions of the Harrod–Domar model as a result of just two changes in its assumption (one technological and one behavioral). First, he replaced the rigid fixed-proportions production technology by a **variable proportions** or **neoclassical production function**, in which output can be produced with varying combinations of labor and capital and each input is subject to diminishing marginal returns (assumptions that had long been employed in much economic analysis outside the areas of growth and development), Second, he replaced the assumption of extensive unemployed labor by the assumption that rational producers respond to signals in perfectly functioning markets in ways that drive the economy to full employment of both labor and capital at all times. Solow continued to assume, along with Harrod and Domar, that technology exhibits constant returns to scale, that saving is a fixed proportion of income, and that the labor force grows at an exogenously determined rate n.

Solow showed that introducing such changes to the model's assumptions eliminated its undesirable predictions of instability. Unemployment is eliminated from the model, and capital can accumulate relative to labor with no potential for a sudden deceleration of growth when unemployed labor is used up.

Solow also demonstrated, however, that making these changes leads to important changes in some of the model's predictions that had not previously been questioned. In the Harrod–Domar model, a constant saving rate can serve as the source of steady, sustained growth (as long as the economy doesn't run out of unemployed labor), and increases in the saving rate lead to sustained increases in the growth rate. We will see below that in Solow's neoclassical model, a constant rate of saving by itself cannot sustain growth in the long term, and permanent increases in the saving rate produce only temporary boosts in the rate of growth.

The source of this dramatic change in theoretical prediction is the assumption of neoclassical production technology, characterized by the diminishing marginal returns to capital. In the presence of such diminishing returns, a steady rate of saving implies steady additions to the capital stock as a proportion of output, but this translates into a *declining rate* of increase in capital per worker and a declining rate of economic growth, because as the quantity of capital per worker increases, diminishing returns dictate that additional units of capital lead to smaller and smaller increases in output per worker. In fact, growth in output per worker based entirely on saving and capital accumulation is bound eventually to grind to a halt in the simple neoclassical model. Increases in savings rates might boost growth in the short run and allow the economy to achieve a higher *level* of per capita GDP before economic growth halts, but such growth would ultimately cease. We demonstrate this formally below.

Solow did not stop there, however. He pointed out that the revised model, too, failed to match historical experience. The United States, for example, *had* experienced a nearly constant saving rate *and* steady growth over a very long period. He concluded that if growth based on steady capital accumulation alone is bound to diminish over time, then U.S. growth must have been based on something more than just steady capital accumulation. The something more to which he drew attention was technical change.

In this section, we describe what happens when we introduce Solow's neoclassical modifications of the Harrod–Domar model without introducing the possibility of technical change. We will examine this simple model's implications, including the puzzling prediction that growth must eventually grind to a halt.

We begin with the assumptions that the economy's aggregate production function is neoclassical and that the economy's stocks of labor and capital are fully employed at all times. These assumptions together underlie the assumption that

$$Y = F(K, L) \tag{4.7}$$

where Y is GDP and K and L are the economy's stocks of capital and labor inputs. The production function $F(.)$ is assumed to be characterized by diminishing marginal returns to either input. The production function furthermore exhibits constant returns to scale. The economy's many owners of capital and labor resources are assumed to sell capital and labor services to producers in perfect factor markets. In perfect markets, labor and capital are fully employed and are allocated across firms in ways that maximize their productivity. All this happens regardless of how ownership of the factors is distributed, and thus total production in the economy depends only on the total quantities of K and L and not on how their ownership is distributed. The rest of the model is the same as in Harrod–Domar: L is assumed to grow at a fixed rate n, K grows through capital accumulation financed by saving (in excess of the rate of depreciation d), and saving is a constant proportion s of income.

Notice that the only way for output per worker $(y = Y/L)$ to grow in this model is through increases in the capital-labor ratio $(k = K/L)$, which indicates the quantity of capital available per worker in the economy. Given our interest in the growth of per capita GDP, it will be useful to recast our technological assumptions in per-worker terms. Dividing both sides of equation 4.7 by L and invoking the assumption of constant returns to scale, we find that

$$y = \frac{Y}{L} = \left(\frac{1}{L}\right)F(K, L) = F\left(\frac{K}{L}, 1\right) = f(k) \tag{4.8}$$

where the last equality simply assigns a new name to the function describing the relationship between capital per worker and output per worker. This new function $f(.)$ relates the average product of labor y to the level of capital per worker k. As illustrated in Figure 3.3, y must increase with k, but it must increase at a decreasing rate as a result of diminishing marginal returns to capital.

Given the close link between the capital-labor ratio k and per capita production y, we can understand the model's implications for the rate of economic growth by understanding what governs the rate of change in k, which we denote by $\dot{k}/k$. It may be shown that the rate of growth of the capital-labor ratio is just the rate of growth of capital minus the rate of growth of labor, as in

$$\frac{\dot{k}}{k} = \frac{\dot{K}}{K} - \frac{\dot{L}}{L} \tag{4.9}$$

As in the Harrod–Domar model, $\dot{K}$ is equal to $sY - dK$, where Y now equals $F(K, L)$ and the rate of growth of the labor force is n. After making these substitutions, equation 4.9 becomes

$$\frac{\dot{k}}{k} = \frac{sF(K, L)}{K} - d - n \tag{4.10}$$

Noting that $F(K, L)$ may be written as $LF(k, 1) = Lf(k)$ (making use of the assumption of constant returns to scale), and multiplying both sides of the equation by k, we find the equation embodying the core implications for growth of the simple neoclassical model:

$$\dot{k} = sf(k) - k(n + d) \tag{4.11}$$

The left side is the change in k experienced in any period. If this is positive, k is rising; if it is negative, k is falling. The right side relates this change to current economic circumstances. The first term on the right side describes the saving and investment forthcoming per person at any current level of k. The second term indicates the investment per person required simply to maintain the entire labor force at the current level of k, given the need to replace depreciating capital and the need to equip additional workers entering the market through labor force growth. The equation tells us that if per-worker investment forthcoming is greater than the per-worker investment required to maintain a constant level of capital per worker, then the capital-labor ratio (and output per worker) will rise. If the per-worker investment forthcoming is less than $k(n + d)$, however, then the capital-labor ratio will fall.

One aim in analyzing a dynamic model like this is to determine the rates at which key variables (such as k and y) would grow in long-run **steady-state equilibrium**, which is achieved when the economy evolves to a point at which growth rates cease to change. To identify steady-state equilibrium in this model, it is useful to employ the diagram found in Figure 4.2a. The horizontal axis measures the capital-labor ratio k. The vertical axis is measured in units of output per worker, which are also the units in which we measure capital, saving, and investment. As indicated by the $f(k)$ graph, output per worker rises at a decreasing rate as k increases, because capital's marginal product is positive but diminishing. The figure describes what happens to the two components of the right side of equation 4.11 as k increases. Because $sf(k)$ is just a constant multiple (between zero and one) of $f(k)$, diminishing marginal returns to capital imply that the $sf(k)$ graph, too, has positive but decreasing slope. Since n and d are constants, $k(n + d)$ is a straight line out of the origin with slope $n + d$.

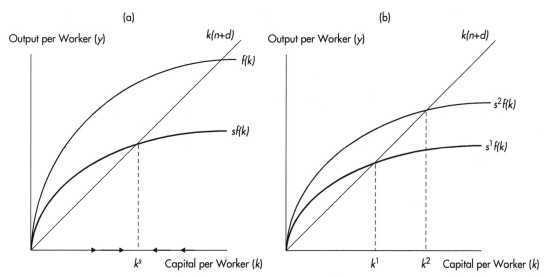

FIGURE 4.2
Steady-State Equilibrium in the Simple Neoclassical Growth Model

We can use Figure 4.2a to demonstrate a tendency for the economy to progress toward a steady-state equilibrium in which the capital-labor ratio and output per worker are unchanging.[2] That is, the economy will progress toward an equilibrium in which there is no (per capita) economic growth! To see this, notice first that if the economy ever reached the level of capital per worker k^s associated with the intersection of the $sf(k)$ and $k(n+d)$ graphs, the economy would remain at that level of k forever. At that level, the amount of investment forthcoming in the economy, $sf(k^s)$, is just enough $(k^s(n+d))$ to replace depreciated capital and to provide new workers with the same level of capital per person as the old workers already have. According to equation 4.11, $\dot{k}$ would be zero, and there would be no impetus for k (or y) to change.

Notice second that if we observe an economy at a level of k other than k^s, economic forces will be driving k toward k^s. For example, consider an economy with a level of k below k^s. For such an economy, $sf(k)$ would be greater than $k(n+d)$, and $\dot{k}$ would be positive. This means that k is growing and the economy is moving to the right in the diagram. k will continue to grow until it reaches the level k^s, at which point it ceases to grow. Similarly, if an economy started out with a level of k to the right of k^s the capital-labor ratio would be falling, and it would continue to fall until the economy finds itself in steady-state or long-run equilibrium at k^s.

Figure 4.2b demonstrates what would happen if we took an economy in initial steady-state equilibrium at k^1 and increased its saving rate of s^1 to s^2. The $sf(k)$ function would pivot up, remaining connected to the origin, as the unchanging $f(k)$ function is multiplied by a larger fraction. With an initial capital-labor ratio of k^1 and a new higher saving rate s^2, $s^2f(k^1)$ would exceed $k^1(n+d)$, and $\dot{k}$ (and the rate of growth in output per worker) would become positive, but this new growth in k and y would eventually die out as the economy tends toward a new long-run equilibrium with zero growth in per capita income. The increased frugality would not be without benefit, because the economy would eventually find itself in a new steady-state equilibrium characterized by a higher capital-labor ratio, k^2, and higher income per capita (at the intersection between the $k(n+d)$ line and the higher $s^2f(k)$ curve), but the sustained increase in s would produce a period of growth in output per worker that lasts only as long as it takes to achieve the new long-run equilibrium ratio of capital to labor k^2.

---

[2] This is true as long as the $sf(k)$ curve is not so low that it lies entirely beneath the $k(n+d)$ locus and that it is sufficiently curved that its slope does eventually fall below the slope of the $k(n+d)$ locus.

4.3C **The neoclassical growth model with technical change**

The implication that growth driven only by a constant saving rate should grind to a halt flies in the face of real-world experiences, such as that of the United States, which has managed to save and experience per capita income growth at fairly steady rates over long periods of time. Is this the sort of unfortunate theoretical implication that should lead us to discard the model? Solow's answer was that we should modify rather than discard the model. In particular, he suggested replacing the aggregate production function (equation 4.1) by the function

$$Y = F(K, AL) \tag{4.12}$$

where A is a parameter describing the level of technology. More specifically, A is a parameter whose increase signifies **labor augmenting technical change**. We can think of AL as the quantity of "effective labor" in the economy (i.e., the economy's capacity to fulfill labor tasks), and we can think of technical change (denoted by an increase in A) as change that allows each physical unit of labor to supply more effective labor. In the presence of labor-augmenting technical change, the ratio of capital to effective labor, and thus the marginal product of capital, can remain constant, even while the ratio of capital to physical labor is rising. Such technical change serves to counteract the diminishing returns to capital that caused growth to grind to a halt in the simplest neoclassical model.

To understand growth and long-run equilibrium in this economy, it is useful to define and understand the evolution over time of the ratio of capital to effective labor, K/AL, which we will call k^*. It can be shown that the growth rate of k^* is equal to

$$\frac{\dot{k}^*}{k^*} = \frac{\dot{K}}{K} - \frac{\dot{L}}{L} - \frac{\dot{A}}{A} \tag{4.13}$$

Making the same assumptions as before regarding the growth of K and L, assuming that A increases at the rate g, and multiplying both sides by k^*, this becomes

$$\dot{k}^* = sf(k^*) - k^*(n + d + g) \tag{4.14}$$

To understand the growth performance of the economy described by this equation, we turn to Figure 4.3. Here the horizontal axis measures the level of k^*, and the vertical axis measures output per effective worker ($y^* = Y/AL$) and investment per effective worker. Using the same logic as we applied to the previous diagram, we find that this economy will converge toward a steady-state equilibrium in which k^* is constant at the level k^{*s}, associated with the intersection of the two curves. Notice, however, that a steady state in which $k^* = K/AL$ is constant is a steady state in which K/L and GDP per capita must be rising! In fact, with A rising at the rate g, K/L must be rising at the constant rate g as well to hold k^* constant, and output per capita must be growing at the rate g, too. This model thus predicts that the economy will achieve a steady state in which output per worker grows at a constant rate, equal to the rate of labor-augmenting technical change, g. The introduction of technical change allows the model to explain sustained growth in the long run. While the rate of saving s does not influence the rate of growth in steady state, it continues to play a role in determining the steady-state level of k^* and thus the steady-state path of GDP per capita.

Solow's main purpose in constructing the neoclassical model with technical change was to construct a model that can explain the coexistence in a single country of a stable, positive growth rate and a stable rate of saving over a long period. But many subsequent researchers have pointed out the model's implications for differences across countries in rates of economic growth and have subjected these implications to empirical testing.

Output per Effective Worker (y*)

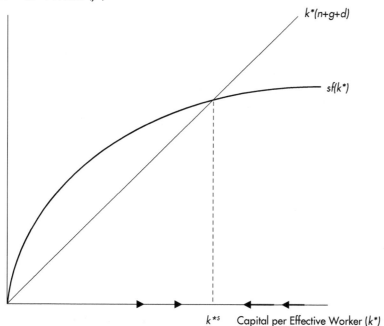

$k^*(n+g+d)$

$sf(k^*)$

k^{*s} Capital per Effective Worker (k^*)

FIGURE 4.3
Steady-State Equilibrium in the Neoclassical Growth Model with Technical Change

According to the model, if all countries were already in steady state and had access to the same technology, then all countries should be growing at the same rate, g. Observing that growth rates differ greatly across countries, we must conclude that if this model is a good representation of reality, then countries must not be in steady state.

Among countries that are out of steady state but heading toward the same steady state (because they are characterized by the same values for s and $n + g + d$), the countries that start out poorer grow faster in this model. Diagrams like Figure 4.3 would be identical for such countries, except that poorer countries would be starting out farther to the left of the steady-state level of k^*. Thus the model implies that if all countries were heading toward the same steady state, we should see evidence of **unconditional convergence**, in which poorer countries (i.e., countries starting at lower levels of k^* and GDP per capita) simply grow faster than richer countries. Though these countries start out poorer, the model predicts that they will ultimately catch up, erasing those initial differences and enjoying the same level of growth and per capita income in steady state.

Unfortunately, the data graphed in Figure 3.1 contradict this rather optimistic prediction. In the world as a whole there has been no systematic tendency for poorer countries to grow faster than richer countries. Indeed, some of the poorest countries have also experienced the worst growth performance.

If countries are out of steady state and are heading toward different steady states (because they differ in their values of s and $n + g + d$), then among countries starting at the same level of k^* and income per capita, those with lower s and higher $n + g + d$ should be heading toward lower steady-state levels of k^*. Because they are closer to their ultimate steady states, they should be growing slower. Once we allow for these differences in the steady states toward which countries are heading, the model predicts **conditional convergence**. This means that even though poor countries don't always grow faster than richer countries, it may still be the case that after controlling for differences across countries in s and $n + g + d$, poorer countries grow faster than richer countries. That is, if you ran a regression of growth rates on measures of s, $n + g + d$ and initial income per capita, the coefficient on income per capita would be negative (and the coefficient on s would be positive and the coefficient on $n + g + d$ would be negative).

Regressions employing data from the last four decades often reveal such patterns of conditional convergence. Such patterns have sometimes been taken as evidence in favor of the neoclassical model and against alternative models proposed later (which we discuss below), but it is now broadly recognized that empirical conditional convergence results can be reconciled with a wide range of theoretical models and thus do not, in fact, help establish the superiority of the neoclassical model (Romer, 1994; Durlauf et al., 2008).

More elaborate versions of the neoclassical growth model, which pay more explicit attention to the choices of the economy's many producers and owners of labor and capital, reveal that as long as the technologies faced by individual producers are characterized by constant returns to scale, and as long as producers operate in perfectly competitive output and input markets, then the economy will deliver optimal growth and continuous full employment without the need for government intervention. People who care about the future and who operate in perfect financial markets will correctly perceive the incentive to save and invest. There is thus no need to use government policy to encourage more investment or production. In fact, by distorting incentives for factor use and investment, government intervention is more likely to hurt growth than to help it. The model is thus consistent with a world view of rising importance in the 1960s and 1970s, in which the key to speeding growth was to pull government out of production, reduce government intervention in markets, and reduce government efforts to protect specific sectors of the economy from international competition.

4.3D Neoclassical growth with human capital

Though the notion of human capital is often traced back to Adam Smith, it was not until the 1960s that research into the role of human capital in determining productivity and incomes really took off, encouraged by the rising availability of large individual-level datasets on schooling and earnings (at least in the United States), as well as the introduction of computing power adequate for econometric analysis of those new datasets (Mincer, 1970). The emerging literature quickly demonstrated an important role for schooling and experience in raising people's incomes, presumably by increasing their productivity as workers. It was natural, then, for researchers whose interest in economic growth was revived by Solow's theoretical contribution to consider augmenting the model to incorporate human capital as an additional determinant of aggregate production. One example of how human capital may be introduced formally into the Solow framework is found in Mankiw et al. (1992), who replace Solow's aggregate production function by

$$Y = F(K, H, AL) \tag{4.15}$$

where H is total human capital, A continues to represent labor-augmenting technical change, and $F(.)$ exhibits diminishing marginal returns in each of its three arguments.[3] The authors assume that the creation of physical and human capital is financed by saving out of income, and they assume that a fraction s of income is devoted to physical capital investment and a fraction b is devoted to human capital investment. As the reader might guess, in this augmented Solow model, the economy converges to a steady state in which the values of physical capital per effective worker ($k^* = K/AL$) and human capital per effective worker ($h^* = H/AL$) are constant, the steady-state levels of these variables depend on the investment rates (s and b) as well as $n + g + d$, and steady-state income per worker grows at the rate of technical progress.

While interest in human capital introduced only minor modifications to economic growth theory in the 1960s and 1970s, it was associated with dramatic changes in the practice of

---

[3] In fact, they assumed a particular functional form, $Y = K^\alpha H^\beta (AL)^{1-\alpha-\beta}$, which allowed them to derive equations defining steady-state per capita income as an explicit function of $(n + g + d)$, s, b, α, and β, as well as a term capturing the fact that in steady state, income per capita is continuously rising at the rate of technical change, g. They show that this equation does a surprisingly good job of explaining differences across countries in per capita income.

development work by the large international organizations, for whom investment in education became the centerpiece of many efforts to promote growth and development. The popularity of investment in education can be explained in part by strong suspicions that such investments would be simultaneously beneficial for promoting growth, reducing inequality, and meeting the basic needs of the poor.

4.4 The 1980s to the Present: Market Imperfections, Increasing Returns, and Poverty Traps

4.4A Themes

The late 1980s brought a resurgence of interest in the theoretical study of economic growth as new data brought to light new patterns of growth experiences across countries and as developments in theoretical economics provided new analytical tools (Romer, 1994). While study of growth during the 1960s and 1970s was shaped by a single theoretical framework (the neoclassical model), theorists in more recent decades have developed a plethora of new models as they seek to wrestle with two sets of questions that were raised but not answered by the neoclassical model:

- What drives technical change?
- If investment in physical capital, human capital, and technical change is so important for growth and future well-being, and if people care about the future, then why don't we see more investment in poor countries? That is, why are some countries stagnating with low rates of saving, investment, and growth?

The new models of this period have brought thinking about economic growth even farther from capital fundamentalism. While still acknowledging the importance of physical capital, they reinforce interest in human capital, expand interest in the creation and adoption of improved technologies, and introduce new interest in reducing inefficiency and waste.

The new models also offer more nuanced alternatives to the structuralism and dualism of the 1940s and 1950s than was offered by the extreme neoclassical vision of perfect markets and perfectly integrated sectors. The models highlight various reasons why reasonably well-functioning markets might fail to deliver ideal investment, technical change, and growth. Some models raise the possibility of a new sort of dualism, in which entire poor countries, or poor populations within countries, might find themselves trapped in using traditional, low-productivity production methods, even while their higher-income neighbors pursue modern, higher-productivity methods and enjoy greater growth and prosperity. Under such circumstances policy and institutions might have roles to play in encouraging investment, innovation, and growth.

Altogether, the growth models of the 1980s to the present encourage careful micro study of the decisions, markets, and institutions affecting investment and TFP growth, and they point to a variety of reasons why markets and institutions can fail to deliver ideal growth outcomes.

4.4B Endogenizing technical change

The primary objective of a first subset of new growth theory was to endogenize technical change. Theorists in this literature agreed with Solow that technical change is important for long-run growth, but they were unsatisfied with the way Solow simply assumed a constant rate of technical change that was determined outside the model. **Endogenizing the rate of technical change** requires identifying specific choices people make that might give rise to technical change and then making assumptions about the ways current economic circumstances affect peoples' incentives toward these choices, thereby allowing the rate of technical change to be determined within the model.

Endogenizing technical change proved impossible to do within models that maintained the assumptions of constant returns to scale and perfect competition. These two assumptions together imply that payments to capital and labor must fully exhaust output, leaving nothing left over to serve as a reward for investments in technology improvements.[4] New growth theorists solved this problem in two quite different ways, both of which raised the possibility that markets might not lead the economy to ideal growth performance.

The first solution was to treat productivity advance as an unrewarded byproduct of decisions made without regard to their productivity impacts. That is, they treat technical change as an externality rather than an outcome that people seek to achieve on purpose. This eliminates the need to find any portion of total product left over after payments to capital and labor, which can be held out as a reward for purposeful efforts to improve technology. The second solution was to treat technical advance as the output of a purposeful, reward-seeking activity and to build rewards for these activities into the model by abandoning the assumption of perfect competition. The first solution seems more suited to explaining productivity advance that arises through informal learning by doing within production establishments, while the second solution seems more suited to understanding productivity advance that arises through formal, purposeful research and development activities.

Both solutions led to visions of economies that are characterized by increasing returns to scale. The models these efforts gave rise to are known as **endogenous growth models** because they sought to endogenize the rate of technical change, which was the sole determinant of the long-run rate of economic growth in the Solow framework.[5]

4.4C Productivity advance as a byproduct of investment in physical or human capital

The first approach to endogenizing productivity advance was to think of the productivity level A as an outcome that grew as an unintended byproduct of choices to invest in physical or human capital and thus to assume that the investments people make to increase their own physical or human capital have positive externalities on the productivity of other workers and producers throughout the economy. For example, in addition to raising their own productivity, workers' investments in their own human capital might help raise the productivity of their coworkers by creating an environment in which conversations among workers are more likely to lead to efficiency-enhancing experimentation and discovery. A seminal paper introducing such possibilities is Lucas (1988).

---

[4] We can demonstrate this formally as follows. Let $F(K, L; A)$ be a production function, w be the wage rate paid for a unit of labor, and r be the rental rate paid for a unit of capital. The production function exhibits constant returns to scale in K and L if and only if, for any value of λ, $F(\lambda K, \lambda L; A) = \lambda F(K, L; A)$. Taking derivatives of both sides of this equation with respect to λ, and letting F_K and F_L denote the partial derivatives of the production function with respect to its first and second arguments, we get $F_K(\lambda K, \lambda L; A)K + F_L(\lambda K, \lambda L, A)L = F(K, L; A)$. Since this must be true for any value of λ, it must be true for $\lambda = 1$, indicating that $F_K(K, L; A)K + F_L(K, L; A)L = F(K, L; A) = Y$. If producers behave in a perfectly competitive manner, then they should hire factors until the marginal product of capital (F_K) is equal to the rental rate paid per unit of capital, r, and the marginal product of labor (F_L) is equal to the wage paid per unit of capital, w. Thus, constant returns to scale and perfect competition together imply that $rK + wL = Y$. This tells us that with constant returns to scale (in K and L) and perfect competition, total payments to K and L indeed fully exhaust total output Y, leaving nothing left over to compensate anyone for purposeful efforts to increase A.

[5] Originally the label *endogenous growth model* also connoted that the model yielded a prediction that steady-state growth rates would be a function of policies shaping rates of investment in physical and human capital. This contrasted with the neoclassical model, in which such policies affect only the level of income per capita in steady state and rates of growth during the transition to steady state, while the rate of growth in steady state is fixed exogenously and unaltered by policy. This connotation has diminished in importance for reasons discussed in Jones (1998).

To introduce this notion formally into a model of economic growth, we might rewrite the aggregate production function this way:

$$Y = A(H) \, F(K, H, L) \tag{4.16}$$

The term $A(H)$ indicates that the level of productivity depends on the aggregate stock of human capital in the economy. Individual producers are assumed to be unaware of this link between their individual human capital decisions and the economy's level of productivity and simply take the current level of A as given. When holding A constant, the production function exhibits constant returns to scale in K, H, and L. From the perspective of the economy as a whole, however, investments in human capital not only add to the economy's human capital stock but also increase the level of productivity.

This might look like a very small change to the formal structure of a growth model, but it can in fact have profound implications. The key reason is this: If the production function exhibits constant returns to scale in K, H, and L while holding A constant, then when we acknowledge that increases in H also increase A, we discover that the economy as a whole is characterized by **increasing returns to scale**. That is, if we doubled K, H, and L we would more than double Y. More to the point, although H is (according to standard and sensible assumptions) subject to diminishing marginal returns when we hold A constant, it might be subject to constant or even increasing marginal returns when we acknowledge the externality.

In a diagram like Figure 4.3, the assumption of increasing returns to scale might imply that the $sf(k^*)$ curve is straight or even convex, rather than concave. Such modifications eliminate the Solow model's prediction that growth based on physical or human capital accumulation must evolve toward a steady state in which growth ceases. It also eliminates the implication that poor countries should grow faster than rich countries. Because the modification is built on the assumption of important externalities, it also raises the possibility that private human capital investors, who do not take the external benefits of their choices into account, will invest less than is socially desirable and that intervention by governments and other development actors might be useful for improving growth performance.

4.4D Productivity advance as the outcome of purposeful research, development, and technology transfer activities

The second approach to endogenizing A was to treat increases in A as the outcome of intentional efforts to develop or adopt new technologies and to make theoretical room for some of output to be used as reward for those activities by abandoning the assumption of perfect competition. These models distinguish between the currently developed countries that are **technology leaders**, in which the intentional activities of interest are the research and development activities that produce cutting-edge technologies, and the currently less-developed countries that are **technology followers**, in which the productivity-enhancing activities are efforts to acquire and adopt technologies already developed by the technology leaders.

These papers highlight a variety of reasons why private investment decisions might not deliver the socially optimal levels of investment in the creation and acquisition of new technology. The models also demonstrate how explicit attention to the peculiar features of technological ideas can lead to models characterized by increasing returns to scale, and thus by the possibility that poor countries will fail to catch up.

Growth in the technology leaders

Consider first the models, such as that in Romer's (1990) seminal paper, describing technical change and growth in the technology leaders. They point out that the purposeful research and development activities that often underlie technical change (and cause A to grow in formal models) require inputs of labor and other factors and thus are costly to undertake. They will be undertaken only if investors expect to receive at least enough future reward to cover their costs. When the new technological ideas produced through research and development may be freely copied, potential investors see no way to reap returns on their investments and do not invest because they would be unable to charge for the use of their ideas. Investment in research and development activities takes place only if a system of patent protection or effective trade secrets gives them temporary monopoly power over the use of the new ideas they generate. (We return to these concerns in Chapter 21.)

In Romer's (1990) model, the costliness of research and development activities is captured by assuming that some of the economy's labor resources must be allocated to research and development activities if technology is to advance. This creates a tradeoff between the two uses of labor in the economy: final goods production and efforts to improve technology. Total final goods production is shaped by the production function

$$Y = F(K, AL_Y) \tag{4.17}$$

where K represents physical and human capital and L_Y represents the quantity of labor devoted to final goods production. The level of technology A is now assumed to be the cumulative result of past research and development activity. More specifically, A is interpreted as the total number of *ideas* generated by research and development activities to date, and the ideas are blueprints for the production of new intermediate capital goods (such as new digital devices and software) that can be used in the production of final goods and services. Producers are assumed to achieve higher productivity (in their transformation of labor and capital into final goods) through the use of a richer array of intermediate capital goods. Some clever math, beyond the scope of this chapter, describes a more detailed production function involving multiple capital goods and shows that total output can ultimately be summarized, as in equation 4.17, as a function only of the total value of all the many capital goods K and the cumulative number of ideas A as well as the labor input L_Y.

Central to the Romer model are its assumptions regarding the production of new technological ideas. The production function for technological change is given by

$$\dot{A} = \nu(L_A, A)L_A \tag{4.18}$$

where $\dot{A}$ is the rate at which new ideas are created and L_A is the quantity of labor devoted to research and development activities (which must be equal to the difference between the total labor stock and L_Y).

The quantity $\nu(.)$ represents the productivity of labor in producing new ideas. It may be a declining function of L_A if larger numbers of researchers are more likely to duplicate one another's efforts, so that higher L_A results in a smaller output of ideas per research worker. Per-researcher productivity, $\nu(.)$, can rise or fall with the current level of technological attainment A. If researchers who start with a richer body of previous research are equipped to be more productive in their current research, then $\nu(.)$ is an increasing function of A. In principle, however, $\nu(.)$ might instead be a decreasing function of A, if the easiest-to-discover ideas tend to be discovered first, so that as A rises, additional research tends to produce fewer new ideas. In the model these effects of L_A and A on $\nu(.)$ are assumed to represent externalities, which are true at the level of the economy as a whole but are ignored by individual investors in research and development, who take the current level of $\nu(.)$ as unaffected by their choices.

Inventors are assumed to have exclusive rights to the use of their new ideas, which take the form of new designs for intermediate goods. They may either use the ideas to produce and sell the new intermediate goods themselves, or they may sell the use of the ideas to specialized intermediate goods producers. Exclusive use rights give producers of each intermediate good monopoly power and monopoly profits in their sales to producers of final goods. It is these monopoly profits that provide the motivation for investment in research.

The technology of final goods production is such that final producers always want to use some of every intermediate good that has ever been invented and that their demand for any one intermediate good weakens as the number of other intermediate goods rises. Thus, as the number of intermediate goods available in the economy rises, the profit earned by individual producers of intermediate goods falls. This implies that the more labor that is devoted to research, the lower is the expected return to additional investment in research. In equilibrium, researchers devote labor to research only up to the point at which the monopoly profit received from a new design is expected to just cover the cost of producing the design.

This model points to several reasons private individuals might fail to deliver the socially most desirable level of investment in new technology and thus offers additional reasons why well-designed government intervention might enhance growth behavior. First, it seems likely that today's research discoveries make tomorrow's research sector more productive, but unlikely that today's research investors take this positive future impact of their work into account when making their current investment decisions. This provides a reason to suspect that people underinvest in research.

Second, it is possible that when the number of current researchers rises (as the rate of investment in the research sector increases), the tendency for researchers to duplicate one another's efforts can rise, implying a reduction in the per-researcher production of distinct new ideas. Failing to take this effect into account, research investors might tend to overinvest in research.

Finally, it can be shown in these models that although monopoly profits are crucial as a source of return to research and development activities, they actually understate the benefits to society of the new ideas, suggesting another reason for private investors to underinvest in research. The net impact of all these imperfections is theoretically ambiguous, but they suggest the value of paying careful attention to the context-specific microeconomics of productivity advance.

Growth in the technology followers

Now consider models that analyze the rate of diffusion of new technologies to technology followers (see, for example, Jones, 1997, Chapter 6). The world technology frontier is assumed to grow through purposeful research and development efforts in the technology leaders, but the level of A in technology-follower countries is assumed to grow through efforts to adopt new technologies that are closer and closer to the technology frontier. The challenges of adopting new technologies can include the need to achieve high enough levels of human capital for operating the technologies successfully, the need to find funds to purchase the technology from a foreign inventor, and the need to convince the foreign inventor that its patent-based monopoly power over the idea will be protected within the technology follower country. Such models thus reinforce interest in human capital investments as a source of growth, and they raise questions about protection of intellectual property rights in developing countries. If technology acquisition is facilitated by relationships between domestic producers and foreign suppliers and buyers, then openness to international trade can also fuel rates of economic growth.

4.4E Investigating poverty traps

Endogenous growth theorists took as their starting point the apparent importance of technical change to long-term growth and sought to understand better what determines the rate of technical change. At the same time, other theorists took as their starting point the apparent failure of some poor countries to grow and sought to identify reasons poverty might be **self-reinforcing.** That is, they examined reasons why in poor economies, or for some poor groups within economies, poverty itself might in some sense be the barrier that prevents potential investors from investing (whether in physical capital, human capital, or modern technology).

Macro poverty traps

One class of models examined **macro poverty traps**. In simple versions of these models, economies are populated by large numbers of producers, each of whom faces a choice between two alternative actions: to continue producing with low-productivity methods or to undertake investment that allows them to produce using higher-productivity methods. For example, Murphy et al. (1989), who formalize an idea first suggested by Rosenstein-Rodan (1943), consider the choice between lower-productivity traditional handicraft production and modern manufacturing production. Macro poverty trap models seek to identify conditions under which economies end up in bad equilibria, in which all producers use low-productivity methods (dooming the economy to low per capita income) and in which no producer perceives any incentive to increase productivity by investing. Countries can end up in such equilibria even when good equilibria, in which everyone invests and achieves high productivity, are also possible.

Central to such models are relationships of the sort stylized in Figure 4.4. The horizontal axis measures the fraction of producers choosing to invest, ranging from 0 at the left end to 1 at the right. Movements to the right along this axis signify increases in the economy's level of investment and in the level of income per capita achieved after investment. The left end is thus associated with poverty and stagnation, while the right end is associated with prosperity and growth. The vertical axis measures the returns that individual producers anticipate receiving if they choose to invest in setting up a modern manufacturing enterprise. If they are to perceive an incentive to invest, this return must be greater than zero.

The economy faces the potential of falling into a macro poverty trap if the investment returns perceived by any one producer are related to the investment choices of other producers in the way illustrated in the diagram. The *slope* of the investment returns schedule is positive, indicating **complementarity** among investment decisions: As more producers decide to invest,

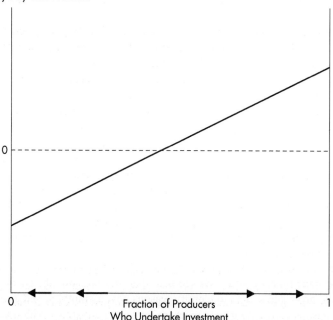

Expected Return to Investment as
Perceived by Any One Producer

Fraction of Producers
Who Undertake Investment

FIGURE 4.4
Dual Equilibria and a
Macro Poverty Trap

the return anticipated by any one producer rises. The *height* of the curve is such that when no one invests (at the left end of the diagram), the anticipated return on investment is negative, but if all producers invest (at the right end of the diagram), the anticipated return is positive. If this is the case, then the economy is characterized by **dual equilibria**. This means that the economy could settle down into two very different equilibrium levels of investment and prosperity, in which no forces create any tendency for change. The *good equilibrium* is found at the right end of the diagram. If all producers choose the high-productivity option, then all producers perceive strong incentives to continue doing so. Unfortunately, this economy also has the potential to end up in a *bad equilibrium* at the leftmost end of the diagram. If no producers invest, then no producer has any incentive to invest. Even if a few bold producers happen to invest, returns remain low enough to discourage investment, tending to return the economy to the bad equilibrium.

Whether the dual equilibrium vision of Figure 4.4 is relevant to the real world depends on whether the investment decisions of many producers really are interdependent in a way that causes the anticipated returns schedule to rise as it does in the figure. Authors of macro poverty trap models offer diverse reasons why this might be the case. Murphy et al. (1989) offer several reasons, all related to the role that individual investments play in increasing the size of the market for the goods produced by other investment projects. If, for example, producers must pay wage premiums to attract workers out of traditional handicraft activities into modern manufacturing, then when they set up a new modern enterprise they increase total wage income in the economy. If workers want to spend their income on the wide variety of goods produced by the economy's many potential investors, then this addition to wage income represents an increase in the demand for the outputs that might be produced by the economy's many other potential investors. This increase in the size of the market could mean that an investment by one producer increases the expected investment returns perceived by other investors, motivating the upward-sloping expected return schedule in Figure 4.4.

The authors point out that increases in market size only increase the potential return on investment (and yield the positive slope in the figure) if modern manufacturing production is subject to increasing returns to scale at the level of individual firms, so that unit costs of production fall as the scale of production increases, and costs thus fall below price only if the scale of production is sufficiently large. Thus, assumptions of increasing returns to scale at the micro level of individual investment projects are crucial for constructing macro poverty trap models of this sort.

As the literature has demonstrated, macro poverty traps can arise for quite different reasons. Rather than focusing on the choice between traditional and modern manufacturing production, Murphy et al. (1993) focus on choices between productive investment and rent-seeking. As defined in Chapter 3, *rent-seeking* is a label applied to activities in which actors attempt to acquire for themselves wealth produced by others, including theft and demands for bribes. The authors suggest that any one producer's incentive to engage in productive investment (rather than rent-seeking) will rise as more producers around them also choose investment over rent-seeking. Turning this around: The greater the share of potential investors who choose rent-seeking, the greater the incentive to become another rent-seeker. Why might this be? As larger fractions of the population engage in fraud and theft, the probability of being caught and punished for such activities might fall, and the social penalties for those who are caught might also fall, tending to reduce the costs relative to the benefits of rent-seeking. At the same time, as rates of fraud, theft, and other forms of rent-seeking rise, investors expect to enjoy fewer of the rewards of their investment. Thus it is possible for societies to become stuck in bad equilibria characterized by much rent-seeking and little investment.

Models of macro poverty traps construe poor economies' failure to grow as the result of a **coordination problem**. They are poor because no one potential investor has an incentive to undertake the kind of investment that can make the economy prosperous. Only if many potential investors could be encouraged to invest in more productive activities *simultaneously* would they find that their investments pay off, leading the economy to a better equilibrium. The models thus point to the importance of government or other institutions capable of coordinating profitable investments.

Micro poverty traps

Another class of models (such as those found in Galor and Zeira, 1993; and Banerjee and Newman, 1993) points to the potential for **micro poverty traps**, illuminating reasons why poor households might be unable to undertake profitable investment, and thus might remain mired in poverty, even while more prosperous households within the same economy undertake profitable investment and experience the benefits of growth. Again, increasing returns to scale at the micro level of individual investment projects are important to the theoretical arguments, which also point to imperfections in credit markets as an integral part of the story.

If investments that can raise productivity and income are profitable only when undertaken at a scale above some minimum threshold, then only investors with adequate financing for undertaking sufficiently large investments can hope to profit from investment. Potential investors for whom only smaller investments are feasible may rationally choose not to invest at all. Information problems in credit markets (relating to lenders' inability to fully assess borrowers' abilities and motivations or to fully monitor and supervise their use of credit, as discussed in Chapter 10) can cause lenders (such as banks) to offer credit only in proportion to the collateral that a borrower has to offer. The poor, who lack collateral (and lack savings, with which they could avoid the need to borrow for investment), are likely to find investments of adequate size infeasible and thus choose not to invest. Their incomes remain stagnant, even while the wealthy around them invest profitably and enjoy growing incomes.

In such models, redistributions of wealth or income from wealthy to poor households, and improved access to financial services for poor households, can speed rates of growth, by making it feasible for larger fractions of the population to undertake investments of adequate size. This raises the possibility that efforts to promote growth will be most successful when accompanied by efforts to reduce poverty and improve income distribution.

4.4F Deeper determinants of growth

Theoretical growth models of the last three decades point to many ways governments might encourage higher rates of investment, technical change, and economic growth. They might speed growth by investing in education, protecting intellectual property rights, coordinating investment decisions, and more generally creating **economic institutions**—economic policies, together with systems of contract law, property rights, and law enforcement—that allow investors and inventors to profit from their growth-enhancing activities. This raises a question about the determinants of economic growth at an even deeper level: Why haven't policymakers in poor countries put adequate growth-enhancing policies and economic institutions into place? For researchers such as Acemoglu and Robinson (2012), the answer has to do with history, politics, and political institutions. We take a closer look at this view and its implications in Chapter 13.

REFERENCES

Acemoglu, Daron, and James A. Robinson. *Why Nations Fail: The Origins of Power, Prosperity, and Poverty*. New York: Crown Publishers, 2012.

Banerjee, Abhijit V., and Andrew F. Newman. "Occupational Choice and the Process of Development." *Journal of Political Economy* 101(2): 274–298, 1993. http://www.jstor.org/stable/2138820

Chenery, Hollis B., and Alan M. Strout. "Foreign Assistance and Economic Development." *American Economic Review* 56(4): 679–733, 1966. http://www.jstor.org/stable/1813524

Domar, Evsey D. "Capital Expansion, Rate of Growth, and Employment." *Econometrica* 14(2): 137–147, 1946. http://www.jstor.org/stable/1905364

Durlauf, Steven N., Andros Kourtellos, and Chih Ming Tan. 2008. "Empirics of Growth and Development." In Amitava K. Dutt, and Jaime Ros (eds.). *International Handbook of Development Economics*, Volume 1. Northampton, Mass.: Edward Elgar Publishing, 2008, pp. 32–47.

Easterly, William. *The Elusive Quest for Growth: Economists' Adventures and Misadventures in the Tropics*. Cambridge, Mass.: MIT Press, 2001.

Galor, Oded, and Joseph Zeira. "Income Distribution and Macroeconomics." *The Review of Economic Studies* 60(1): 35–52, 1993. doi:10.2307/2297811

Harrod, R. F. "An Essay in Dynamic Theory." *The Economic Journal* 49 (193): 14–33, 1939. http://www.jstor.org/stable/2225181

Jones, Charles I. *Introduction to Economic Growth*. New York: W.W. Norton, 1997.

Knight, John. "China, South Africa and the Lewis Model." Centre for the Study of African Economies (CSAE) WPS/2007–12, 2007. http://www.csae.ox.ac.uk/workingpapers/pdfs/2007-12text.pdf

Lewis, W. Arthur. "Economic Development With Unlimited Supplies of Labour." *The Manchester School* 22(2): 139–191, 1954. doi:10.1111/j.1467-9957.1954.tb00021.x

Little, Ian M. *Economic Development: Theory, Policy, and International Relations*. New York: Basic Books, 1982.

Lucas, Robert E., Jr. "On the Mechanics of Economic Development." *Journal of Monetary Economics* 22(1): 3–42, 1988. doi:10.1016/0304–3932(88)90168–7

Mankiw, N. Gregory, David Romer, and David N. Weil. "A Contribution to the Empirics of Economic Growth." *The Quarterly Journal of Economics* 107(2): 407–437, 1992. doi:10.2307/2118477

Mincer, Jacob. "The Distribution of Labor Incomes: A Survey With Special Reference to the Human Capital Approach." *Journal of Economic Literature* 8(1): 1–26, 1970. http://www.jstor.org/stable/2720384

Murphy, Kevin M., Andrei Shleifer, and Robert W. Vishny. "Industrialization and the Big Push." *Journal of Political Economy* 97(5): 1003–1026, 1989. http://www.jstor.org/stable/1831884

Murphy, Kevin M., Andrei Shleifer, and Robert W. Vishny. "Why is Rent-Seeking So Costly to Growth?" *American Economic Review* 83(2): 409–414, 1993. http://www.jstor.org/stable/2117699

Romer, Paul M. "Endogenous Technological Change." *Journal of Political Economy* 98(5): S71–S102, 1990. http://www.jstor.org/stable/2937632

Romer, Paul M. "The Origins of Endogenous Growth." *Journal of Economic Perspectives* 8(1): 3–22, 1994. doi:10.1257/jep.8.1.3

Rosenstein-Rodan, P. N. "Problems of Industrialisation of Eastern and South-Eastern Europe." *The Economic Journal* 53(210/211): 202–211, 1943. http://www.jstor.org/stable/2226317

Solow, Robert M. "A Contribution to the Theory of Economic Growth." *The Quarterly Journal of Economics* 70(1): 65–94, 1956. doi:10.2307/1884513

QUESTIONS FOR REVIEW

1. Discuss the nature and purposes of theoretical growth-modeling exercises.

2. Discuss the implications of capital fundamentalism, structuralism, and dualism for growth policy.

3. For the Harrod–Domar growth model:
   a. Describe the technological assumptions.
   b. Describe the behavioral assumptions.
   c. Identify the key exogenous parameters that shape the economy's growth performance.
   d. Discuss what happens to the economy's growth performance when each parameter is increased.
   e. Discuss the implications the model was thought to yield for policy.
   f. Discuss the logical implications of the model that researchers ultimately found impossible to reconcile with empirical growth performance.

4. For the Lewis model:
   a. Describe the technological assumptions relevant to the subsistence sector and the capitalist sector.
   b. Describe the behavioral assumptions relevant to the subsistence sector and the capitalist sector.
   c. Define the notion of structural change that inevitably accompanies economic growth in this model.
   d. Employ Figure 4.1 to discuss what would happen to the initial rate of growth if the wage required to draw workers into the capitalist sector fell or if the value of the marginal product of labor in the capitalist sector were shifted up through policies that raise the capitalist sector output price.
   e. Discuss the implications the model was thought to yield for policy.

5. For the simple neoclassical growth model, and for the neoclassical growth model with technical change:
   a. Describe the technological assumptions.
   b. Describe the behavioral assumptions.
   c. Identify the key exogenous parameters that shape the economy's growth performance.
   d. Discuss what happens to the economy's growth performance when each parameter is increased.
   e. Discuss the implications the model was thought to yield for policy.

6. What does it mean to *endogenize* technical change in a formal growth model? Why was it difficult to endogenize technical change in growth models assuming constant returns to scale and perfect competition?

7. What is the significance of possible increasing returns to scale for our understanding of economic growth?

8. Describe the two approaches theorists took to endogenizing technical change, and describe some of the key implications of each approach.

9. Use Figure 4.4 to describe the conditions under which economies might have the potential to settle into two very different equilibria with regard to investment and prosperity. In such a model, in what sense is poverty the result of a *coordination problem*?

10. What is meant by the term *micro poverty trap*?

QUESTIONS FOR DISCUSSION

1. The Harrod–Domar model exhibits the knife-edge property that growth is consistent with continuously full employment only if $(s/k) - d$ just happens to equal n. This knife-edge property is eliminated in the simple neoclassical model, which is characterized by continuously full employment. Discuss the importance of assuming variable rather than fixed proportions production technology for working this change.

2. For each of the bodies of growth theory described in this chapter, state whether production technologies are characterized by constant or increasing returns to scale. Where production technologies are characterized by increasing returns to scale, state whether the increasing returns to scale are present only at the aggregate level (while individual producers continue to work under the assumption that their technology is characterized by constant returns to scale), or whether increasing returns to scale are also present and important at the level of the individual firm. What roles do these assumptions play in shaping the predictions of the models?

3. Discuss the role of empirical research (including simple empirical observations) in driving the evolution of growth theory.

PROBLEMS

1. As discussed in the text, the assumptions of the Harrod–Domar model may be summarized by the equations

$$Y = \left(\frac{1}{\nu}\right) K \qquad (4.A)$$

$$\dot{Y} = \left(\frac{1}{\nu}\right) \dot{K} \qquad (4.B)$$

and

$$\dot{K} = sY - dK \qquad (4.C)$$

where the notation is as defined in the text. (Equations 4.A and 4.B are two ways of stating the same assumption, but both expressions are useful to remember in the derivations you will be required to do below.)

a. Demonstrate that equations 4.B and 4.C together imply the following result regarding the growth rate of GDP. (Notice that the text offers guidance about how to derive this equation.)

$$\frac{\dot{Y}}{Y} = \frac{s}{\nu} - d$$

b. Show that equations 4.A and 4.C together imply the following result regarding the growth rate of K.

$$\frac{\dot{K}}{K} = \frac{s}{\nu} - d$$

2. Consider the neoclassical growth model with technical change, and its diagrammatic summary in Figure 4.3. Suppose the rate of population growth n increased. Which element of the graph (i.e., the $k^*(n+d+g)$ line or the $sf(k^*)$ curve) would change and in what way? Draw such a change into a graph like the one in Figure 4.3. When the rate of population growth increases like this, what happens to the steady-state level of income per capita? What happens to the steady-state rate of growth in income per effective worker? What is the immediate impact on the rate of growth in k^*? What is the immediate impact on the rate of growth of GDP per capita? Using intuitive, plain language, explain why the increase in the population growth rate has the short-run impact on growth that you just described and why that short-run impact eventually fades away.

3. Suppose the aggregate production function takes the form

$$Y = A(K)F(K, L)$$

where $A(K) = K^\beta$ describes an external, economy-wide effect of K on A, $F(K, L) = L^\alpha K^{1-\alpha}$ and $0 < \alpha < 1$.

a. Demonstrate that if you double both K and L while holding the initial value of A constant (i.e., ignoring the external effect of K on A), Y doubles.

b. Demonstrate that if you double both K and L, taking into account the external effect of K on A, Y more than doubles.

c. Derive an expression for the marginal product of capital while ignoring the external effect of K on A. That is, holding A constant (rather than treating it as a function of K), take the derivative of the aggregate production function with respect to K. Show that if K increases while L holds constant, this marginal product of capital falls.

d. Derive an expression for the marginal product of capital, taking into account the external effect of K on A. Show that if K increases while L holds constant, the marginal product of capital can fall or rise, depending on the values of α and β.

4. Critical to the construction of some models of macro poverty traps is the assumption that the profitability of setting up a modern, high-productivity establishment in any one sector depends positively on the size of the market the establishment will face (which in turn is taken to depend positively on the number of other sectors in which modern, high-productivity establishments have set up). In this problem you will examine a very simple technology for modern production, involving a *fixed cost* of setup, in which profitability of setting up indeed depends positively on the number of units of output the firm anticipates being able to sell. Suppose that modern production can take place only after incurring a fixed cost of F units of labor. Once that cost is incurred, each unit of additional labor produces $\alpha > 1$ units of output. The price of a unit of labor is 1. Suppose the price of a unit of output is 1 also. Let Q be the quantity of output the potential investor anticipates selling.

a. Derive an expression for the producer's profits (i.e., revenue minus labor costs) as a function of Q, F, and α.

b. Making use of this expression, show that if $F = 0$ (meaning that there are no fixed costs) then setting up is profitable regardless of the level of Q.

c. Now assume $F > 0$. Derive an expression for the minimum level of Q at which production is profitable. How does this minimum profitable scale change as F increases? As α increases?

5

Poverty, Inequality, and Vulnerability

Economic growth makes development possible, but rapid rates of economic growth alone are no guarantee of widespread improvements in well-being. A positive rate of economic growth in Bangladesh, for example, tells us that incomes there are rising *on average*, but it does not tell us what is happening in the lives of poor Bangladeshi households, like those we met in Chapter 2. Their incomes might be stagnant or falling. And even if their incomes are rising, their health may be deteriorating or they might face rising uncertainty about the future.

When evaluating development success at the macro level, therefore, most development analysts look not only to statistics on economic growth rates but also to an array of indicators describing how income gains are distributed across people and how lives are changing along nonincome dimensions. The indicators fall under three broad headings that are important in contemporary development discussions: poverty, inequality, and vulnerability.

This chapter first examines definitions and common measures of poverty, inequality, and vulnerability. It then takes a first look at the theoretical and empirical links between economic growth, on the one hand, and reductions in poverty, inequality, and vulnerability, on the other. In so doing, it reveals further motivation for Part III's more detailed study of the decisions, markets, and institutions through which development takes place.

5.1 Definitions and Measures

Poverty, inequality, and vulnerability are multidimensional problems that may be measured in diverse ways. In what follows, we define some of the most commonly employed measures, highlighting how each measure describes a different feature of the socioeconomic landscape and how development analysts' values and priorities might influence their choice of measures to use when evaluating development success.

5.1A Poverty

In general terms, people live in **poverty** when they experience well-being below some minimally acceptable level. Specific measures of poverty are defined by answers to three questions, which development analysts with differing values and priorities might answer in different ways. The first two pertain to the measurement of poverty at the individual or household level:

- What indicator of people's living standards should be considered when evaluating whether their well-being is above or below a minimally acceptable level?
- What constitutes the "minimally acceptable level" of this indicator?

The third question has to do with the aggregation of individual- or household-level poverty measures into a single summary measure for a group or region:

- What formula should be used to summarize information about the poverty levels of many people when constructing an aggregate poverty statistic, keeping in mind that each formula emphasizes distinct features of the distribution of poverty across people?

We address each of these questions in turn.

Choice of well-being indicator

The first choice reflected in the construction of a specific poverty measure is the choice of how to measure well-being for people in the population of interest. The most common choices are measures of per capita income or consumption expenditure within peoples' households. Examples of aggregate statistics employing such measures include the global income poverty statistics presented in Chapter 1 (Table 1.1). As we discussed in Chapter 2, however, income and consumption expenditure measures are only imperfect indicators of well-being and thus are only imperfect measures of deprivation. We might wish to supplement them with measures based on direct observation of peoples' food consumption, work hours, housing quality, health, asset holdings, or other dimensions of living conditions, and development analysts differ in which of these measures they consider most important in the assessment of well-being. Examples of nonincome poverty statistics were presented in Table 1.2.

Choices of whether to emphasize poverty statistics based on income or nonincome measures matter when defining policy goals, because the policies that are best for reducing income poverty and the policies that are best for reducing other kinds of deprivation need not be the same. In practice, countries that have achieved quite similar income poverty performance (by at least one of the measures defined below) have achieved quite different levels of performance along other dimensions. For example, the share of population living on less than $2 per day is nearly identical in Côte d'Ivoire and Indonesia (where the percentages are 46.1 and 46.3), even while their child health conditions are very different, with the number of child deaths before age five years per 1,000 live births at 35 in Indonesia and 123 in Côte d'Ivoire (World Bank, 2012).

Choice of poverty line

The second choice reflected in the construction of a specific poverty measure is the choice of poverty line. The **poverty line** is the value of the selected well-being indicator that marks the minimally acceptable level, below which people merit special policy attention.

Policymakers and development analysts take two broad approaches when defining poverty lines for income-based or consumption expenditure–based poverty measures, depending on whether they conceive of poverty as an absolute or relative phenomenon. People are identified as living in **absolute poverty** when they cannot afford to consume some minimally acceptable package of food, clothing, shelter, and other goods or services. To set absolute poverty lines, policymakers define a minimally acceptable package of goods and services and then estimate the minimum income required to obtain such a package. Policymakers might calculate quite different absolute poverty lines, depending on how generously or conservatively they define the minimally acceptable package, which might include only just enough food to maintain life or might also include some clothing, shelter, and other items required for full participation in society.

People are identified as living in **relative poverty** when their living standards are low relative to the typical level in their society. For example, policymakers might set a relative poverty line at 30 or 60 percent of the country's median income, reflecting their belief that special policy attention is always required for people who are relatively deprived, regardless of the absolute quantities of goods and services they are able to consume. Widespread improvements in income and living standards should eventually eradicate absolute poverty, but they need not diminish relative poverty.

When examining poverty statistics, development analysts must pay attention to the poverty lines employed, for two reasons. First, official poverty lines differ tremendously across countries. Most developing countries define their poverty lines in absolute terms, but they differ significantly in how generously they define the minimally acceptable package of goods and services, with higher-income countries tending to pick more generous packages. Some developed countries define poverty lines in relative terms. The net result is variation in official poverty lines around the world from the equivalent of $0.62 per day to $43.00 per day (Ravallion, 2010)! As a result, comparisons of official poverty rates across countries are seldom meaningful, and poverty statistics quoted without identifying the relevant poverty line are difficult to interpret.

Second, the poverty line employed when constructing a statistic reflects a judgment regarding how deprived someone must be to merit special policy attention. Development analysts should judge whether the poverty line employed in a specific set of poverty statistics is appropriate for answering a particular policy question, because statistics based on different poverty lines can yield different answers to the same question. Consider the question: How big is the challenge of eliminating global poverty? To facilitate the measurement of global poverty (and comparisons of poverty across countries), the World Bank constructs statistics based on the poverty lines of $1.25 and $2.00 per day. The $1.25 line is below the official poverty lines of most countries and is on par with official poverty lines in the world's 10 poorest countries. The $2 line is on par with official poverty lines in some middle-income countries. The use of these poverty lines has become so common that few people question how well the lines correspond to their notion of what it means to be poor. As Pritchett (2006) points out, however, even people living on $10 per day are very poor by developed country standards. If we counted as poor everyone living on less than $10 per day (rather than $2), the number of the global poor would double, and the challenge of eliminating global poverty would be much greater.

Choice of formulas for aggregating measures across households

The final choice reflected in the construction of an aggregate poverty statistic is the choice of how to aggregate poverty measures for many individuals into a single measure. Figure 5.1 offers one way of presenting all the information that must be summarized when the indicator of a person's

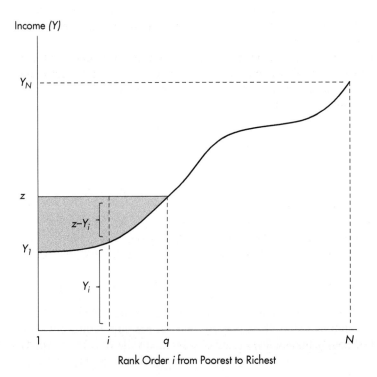

FIGURE 5.1
Incomes Ordered from Lowest to Highest

well-being is the per capita income in that person's household (Y). To construct the figure, we order the N individuals in a population from 1 to N, with individual 1 being the poorest and individual N the richest. We measure people's rank order (i) against the horizontal axis and their income (Y_i) against the vertical axis. As we move to the right in the diagram, we move to people with higher rank order and thus higher incomes. The resulting upward-sloping Y schedule tells us everything there is to know about incomes in the country. The average height indicates the average level of per capita household income, while the slope of the schedule indicates how rapidly incomes rise as we move from the poorest to the richest people and thus how unequally income is distributed in this population.

If we decide that the minimally acceptable level of per capita household income is z, then the horizontal line at height z in Figure 5.1 is a literal poverty line, and the figure completely describes the distribution of poverty (and prosperity) in the economy. The poverty line touches the Y schedule at person index q, indicating that q of the N people in this population are poor, and $N - q$ are nonpoor. For poor individuals, the vertical distance $z - Y_i$, is called person i's **income gap**, and is a measure of the depth of that person's poverty in units of income. If we divide this number by z, as in $(z - Y_i)/z$, we calculate person i's **proportional income gap**. If this number equals 0.30, the person's income falls 30 percent below the poverty line.

Any one aggregate poverty statistic summarizes only imperfectly the information in Figure 5.1, emphasizing some features of the poverty problem over others. The most commonly cited poverty statistics are headcount ratios. The **headcount ratio** (H) is the fraction (sometimes expressed as a percentage) of households in a population with incomes below the poverty line. In our notation,

$$\text{Headcount ratio} = H = q/N \tag{5.1}$$

The income poverty statistics in Table 1.1 are headcount ratios. The headcount ratio summarizes only a small fraction of the information contained in Figure 5.1. It measures the *prevalence* of poverty—that is, how widespread poverty is within the population—but it has nothing to say about the depth of poverty. In terms of Figure 5.1, H would remain the same even if the Y schedule turned down much more steeply to the left of q, indicating deeper poverty among the poor, as long as q and N remained unchanged.

The **total income gap** (TYG) is the total amount of money that would be required to bring every poor person's income up to the poverty line (if the money could be targeted perfectly and costlessly to the right people). Graphically, it is equal to the area of the shaded region below the z line and above the Y schedule, between 0 and q. We may write its formula as

$$\text{Total income gap} = TYG = \sum_{i=1}^{q} (z - Y_i) \tag{5.2}$$

where the final expression employs summation notation. (For a review of summation notation, see Problem 1 at the end of the chapter.) The TYG gives us a rough idea of how costly it would be to eliminate poverty, but it does not tell us about the number of people involved (q), the average depth of poverty, or the prevalence of very deep poverty among the poor. The total income gap may be large because many people are moderately poor or because a few people are extremely poor.

The **average proportional income gap** $(APYG)$ is just the simple average over all the poor of their proportional income gaps.

$$\text{Average proportional income gap among the poor} = APYG = \frac{1}{q} \sum_{i=1}^{q} \left(\frac{z - Y_i}{z} \right) \tag{5.3}$$

An *APYG* of 0.35 means that, on average, the incomes of the poor fall short of the poverty line by 35 percent. In terms of Figure 5.1, it measures the average extent to which the Y schedule falls below the z line to the left of q. While this measure picks up differences across countries in the typical depth of poverty, it would take the same value in countries with the same average poverty depth, even if the percentage of the population living in poverty was 10 percent in one country and 90 percent in the other.

The **poverty gap index** (PG) averages proportional income gaps across *everyone* in the population (poor and nonpoor), treating the nonpoor as having income gaps of zero (because they need nothing to bring their incomes up to the poverty line). That is,

$$\text{Poverty gap index} = PG = \frac{1}{N}\sum_{i=1}^{q}\left(\frac{z-Y_i}{z}\right) \tag{5.4}$$

The PG can be interpreted as the cost per person in the entire economy of eliminating poverty (if money could be targeted perfectly and costlessly), expressed as a share of the poverty line. A PG of 0.05, for example, indicates that bringing the incomes of the poor up to the poverty line would require a per capita expenditure of 5 percent of the poverty line.

Additional insight into the poverty gap index may be gained by re-expressing it this way:

$$PG = \frac{q}{N}\left(\frac{1}{q}\right)\sum_{i=1}^{q}\left(\frac{z-Y_i}{z}\right) = H*APYG \tag{5.5}$$

This says that the poverty gap index is equal to the product of the headcount ratio and the average proportional income gap, and it implies that the PG picks up variation across countries or over time in both the prevalence of poverty and its average severity. Like all the measures described thus far, however, it is unaffected by changes in the degree of income inequality among the poor and thus to the fraction of the poor who are in very deep poverty. That is, in a graph like Figure 5.1, as long as q and the average distance between the z line and the Y schedule (to the left of q) remain the same, the PG stays the same, even when the Y schedule becomes steeper to the left of q, implying a larger number of people living at very low levels of Y.

Poverty gap indices often pick up important variations in poverty conditions across countries or over time that are not reflected in headcount ratios. For example, looking only at headcount ratios, we might conclude that poverty is a similarly pressing problem in all four countries listed in Table 5.1, but poverty gap indices tell a different story. Given that its headcount ratio is similar to those for the other countries, the higher poverty gap for Haiti tells us that the average depth of poverty is greater there.

A measure that is sensitive not only to the overall prevalence and average depth of poverty but also to the prevalence of deep poverty among the poor is the **squared proportional income gap index** (sometimes called the P_2 measure). Like the poverty gap index, the P_2 measure averages an individual-level measure of poverty across all members of the population. Instead of

■ TABLE 5.1   **Poverty Measures for Four Countries**

Country	Headcount Ratio using $2 per Day Poverty Line	Poverty Gap Index using $2 Per Day Poverty Line
Bangladesh	76.5	30.4
Ethiopia	77.6	28.9
Haiti	77.5	46.7
Republic of Congo	74.4	38.8

Source: World Bank (2012).

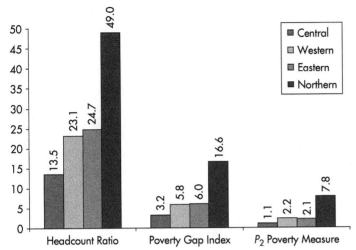

FIGURE 5.2
Poverty Index Values for Four Rural Regions in Uganda, 2009–2010
Source: Uganda Bureau of Statistics (2010).

using a person's proportional income gap as his contribution to the aggregate measure, however, it uses the square of his proportional income gap. That is,

$$\text{Squared proportional income gap index} = P_2 = \frac{1}{N} \sum_{i=1}^{q} \left(\frac{z - Y_i}{z} \right)^2 \tag{5.6}$$

The effect of the squaring is to magnify the contributions to the overall measure of the income deficits experienced by those in deepest poverty. Whereas someone whose income is 10 percent below the poverty line adds 0.01 to the overall measure, someone whose income is 50 percent below the poverty line adds 0.25 to the sum. The ratio of their poverty gaps is 5:1, but the ratio of their contributions to this aggregate measure is 25:1. The measure thus places greater weight on what is happening to the incomes that are farthest below the poverty line and is thus sensitive to changes in the fraction of the poor who are very poor, as well as to changes in the prevalence and average severity of poverty. Like H and PG, P_2 takes values between 0 and 1, with higher values indicating more serious poverty.[1]

Sometimes the headcount ratio, poverty gap index and P_2 measures yield different poverty rankings across countries or regions. Even when they yield similar rankings, study of all three is more revealing than study of any one alone. For example, Figure 5.2 presents poverty statistics for four regions in rural Uganda in 2009/10. They are based on a conservative poverty line, which includes only a little more income than is required to meet basic caloric needs. The headcount ratio statistics indicate that the prevalence of poverty is *twice* as great in Northern than Eastern Rural Uganda, but the poverty gap index shows that the average citizen would have to pay nearly *three* times as much to erase poverty in the Northern region as in the Eastern

---

[1]H, PG, and P_2 are three members of what is called the Foster–Greer–Thorbecke, or FGT, class of poverty indices, all of which rank poverty on scales from 0 to 1. (Sometimes they are multiplied by 100 and presented on a scale of 0 to 100.) The class is defined by the general formula

$$P_\alpha = \frac{1}{N} \sum_{i=1}^{q} \left(\frac{z - Y_i}{z} \right)^\alpha$$

and individual members of the class are defined by the value given to α. When α equals 0, each poor person's contribution to the aggregate poverty measure is 1 and the measure equals the headcount ratio (which is sometimes called P_0). When α equals 1, the formula yields the poverty gap index, or P_1, and when α equals 2, the formula yields the P_2 measure defined above. Higher values for α would yield statistics that place even greater emphasis on the incomes of the poorest among the poor (Foster, Greer and Thorbecke, 1984).

region, indicating that the average depth of poverty is also greater in the North. With the P_2 measure *four* times greater in the North than the East, *deep* poverty must be more significant in the North as well. Notice also that the Western region ranks better off than the Eastern region by the headcount measure (5.8 to 6.0), but worse off by the P_2 measure (2.2 to 2.1), though the differences are small.

Policymakers and policy analysts must sometimes select just one of the many possible poverty statistics for use in identifying policy priorities or evaluating poverty reduction success. For example, in the interest of replacing discretion and patronage by objective rules, the Mexican government tied its allocation of poverty reduction funding across regions to regional values of the P_2 poverty measure based on the official income-based poverty line. Similarly, in the interest of promoting accountability and comparability, a donor organization might require all its partner organizations to quantify their impacts using a common poverty measure.

As should be clear by now, the selection of a single aggregate poverty measure in such situations is a value-laden activity that should be undertaken with care. We've already seen that different poverty statistics can produce different conclusions regarding poverty-reduction priorities across countries, regions, or groups. For more on this, see Problem 2.

Different poverty measures can also yield different conclusions as to which of several competing policies is "the best" for reducing poverty. In fact, the use of headcount ratios for measuring success in poverty reduction implies somewhat disturbing priorities. According to headcount ratio measures, a program that raises the incomes of slightly poor people just enough to raise their incomes over the poverty line might look very successful, even while a program that raises the incomes of very poor people by much larger amounts—but not enough to raise their incomes over the poverty line—would look like a complete failure. Development analysts might judge that the PG or P_2 measure would produce a more desirable ranking of poverty reduction policies.

5.1B Inequality

In general terms, **inequality** exists when some people live at lower levels of well-being than others. Constructing a specific measure of inequality requires answering two questions:

> - What indicators of living standards should be considered when comparing well-being across members of the group?
> - What formula should be used for summarizing the relevant features of the distribution of living standards in the group?

By far the most commonly used inequality statistics are based on measures of per capita household income or consumption expenditure. Income-based inequality statistics are based on the same information we displayed in Figure 5.1: the level of per capita household income for every member of the population. For the purposes of constructing inequality measures, it is more useful to graph the same information in a different way, which emphasizes the comparison of incomes across income groups rather than the comparison of individual incomes to the poverty line. A diagram often used for this purpose is a **Lorenz curve** diagram, such as that presented in Figure 5.3.

To construct a Lorenz curve, we order everyone in the population from lowest income to highest income. We then ask: What percentage of total income is enjoyed by the bottom 1 percent of the population? What percentage of total income is enjoyed by the bottom 2 percent of the population? And so on, all the way up to: What percentage of total income is enjoyed by 100 percent of the population? To plot the answers we measure the cumulative percentage of the population (starting from the poorest) along the horizontal axis and the cumulative percentage of total income enjoyed by that group on the vertical axis. Both percentages range from zero to 100; thus the Lorenz curve always lies within a square box.

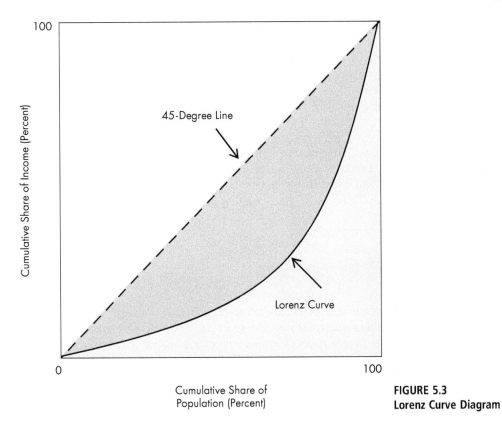

FIGURE 5.3
Lorenz Curve Diagram

If income in an economy were distributed perfectly equally, then everyone would have the same income, and we could line people up in any order for constructing the Lorenz curve. The first 10 percent of the population would enjoy 10 percent of total income, the first 50 percent would enjoy 50 percent of total income, and the Lorenz curve would be a straight line of slope 1, starting at the origin and ending at the northeast corner of the Lorenz curve square. It is useful to draw such a perfect equality reference line—called the **45-degree line**—into our Lorenz curve diagram, as is done in Figure 5.3.

What if one person enjoyed all the income in the economy? In such a case of extreme inequality, the share of income enjoyed by the first 20, 40, or 90 percent of the population would be zero. The Lorenz curve would be flat along the horizontal axis, until it shoots up to 100 percent at the very final point, indicating that 100 percent of the population—which includes the one rich person—does indeed enjoy 100 percent of the income. Thus, perfect inequality in this sense would be depicted by a backward L-shaped curve following the bottom and right sides of the Lorenz curve box.

For distributions between the extremes, we expect Lorenz curves to look something like that shown in Figure 5.3. It starts off with a slope lower than 1, indicating that the bottom percentiles of the population command less than 1 percent of total income each. But we know that ultimately 100 percent of the population must enjoy 100 percent of the income, so the curve must eventually reach the northeast corner. This requires that eventually the Lorenz curve become steeper, to a slope greater than 1, indicating that the top percentiles of the population command more than 1 percent of income each.

The shape of the Lorenz curve offers a thorough characterization of inequality in the distribution of income in the economy. It is silent, however, as to the mean level of income. Two economies can have vastly different mean levels of income but identical Lorenz curves.

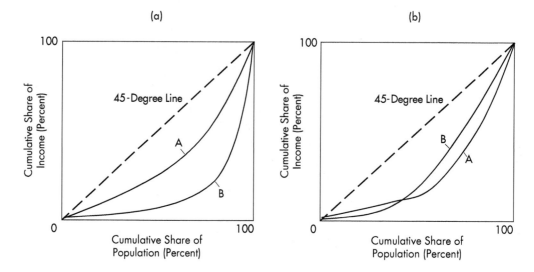

FIGURE 5.4
Comparing Lorenz Curves

In some cases the comparison of Lorenz curves across countries or time periods leads to an obvious conclusion about where inequality is worse. In Figure 5.4a, Lorenz curve B lies farther from the 45-degree line than Lorenz curve A at every population share. This indicates that no matter what x one picks, the income share of the lowest x percent of the population is smaller in country B than in country A; everyone would agree that inequality is worse in B than in A. The Lorenz curve for A is said to **dominate** that for B.

In other cases, however, Lorenz curves alone are not enough for drawing a conclusion about the relative significance of inequality. In Figure 5.4b, the Lorenz curves cross. If we look at the income share of the lowest 10 percent of the population, country A looks more unequal; but if we look at the income share of the lowest 50 percent of the population, country B looks more unequal. In cases like this, our conclusion regarding which distribution is more unequal depends upon our relative concern for those at the very bottom of the distribution.

Just as aggregate income poverty measures summarize key features of the information presented in Figure 5.1, so inequality measures summarize key features of the information presented in a Lorenz-curve diagram. When comparing the income distributions in two groups for which Lorenz curves do not cross, sensible income distribution statistics ought always to take a higher number for the Lorenz curve that lies farther from the 45-degree line. When Lorenz curves cross, different summary statistics can deliver different conclusions regarding where income is distributed more unequally, because they place differing emphasis on inequalities in the bottom, middle, and top of the distribution.

Several very simple summary statistics make use of only a small portion of the information contained in the Lorenz curve but are easy to interpret. It is common to describe income distributions by reporting the **shares of total income** enjoyed, for example, by the bottom 20 percent and top 10 or 5 percent of the population. We can also combine this information into a single statistic by taking the ratio of the income share of the top 10 percent to the income share of the bottom 40 percent.

A popular measure of inequality that makes use of much more Lorenz curve information is the **Gini coefficient**, which may be defined as the ratio of two areas in the Lorenz curve diagram. The numerator is equal to the area between the Lorenz curve and the 45-degree line (the darker shaded area in Figure 5.3). The denominator is equal to the area of the entire triangle lying below the 45-degree line (the sum of the darker and lighter shaded areas in Figure 5.3). If the distribution were perfectly equal, then the Lorenz curve would lie on the 45-degree line and the Gini coefficient would be zero. If one person enjoyed all the income, and the Lorenz curve took a backward

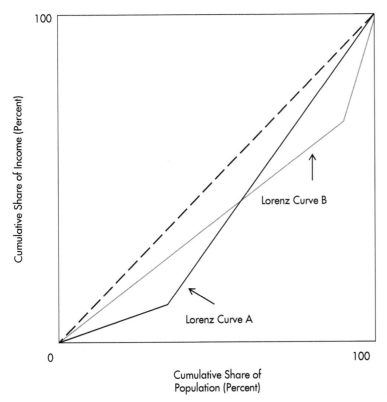

FIGURE 5.5
Lorenz Curves with Equal Gini Coefficients

L shape, the Gini coefficient would equal one. Thus, the Gini coefficient lies between 0 and 1, with higher values indicating higher inequality.

The Gini coefficient satisfies the logical requirement that it give a higher measure of inequality to the one of two distributions for which the Lorenz curve is dominated by the other. Even when Lorenz curves cross, the Gini coefficient calculation often provides a clear ranking of the distributions. Whichever Lorenz curve cuts off a larger area between the curve and the 45-degree line will earn a higher inequality ranking.

Would everyone agree with every ranking produced by the Gini coefficient? Probably not. Consider the case of the two Lorenz curves drawn in Figure 5.5. They have been drawn so that the areas between the 45-degree lines and the Lorenz curves are the same; thus their Gini coefficients are the same. Lorenz curve A describes a group in which the poorest one third equally share one ninth of total income, and the other two thirds equally share the remaining eight ninths. Lorenz curve B describes a group in which the poorest eight ninths equally share two thirds of total income, and the remaining one ninth of the population equally shares the other one third. Many (though not all) would consider inequality to be worse in population A than in population B, because many people instinctively place greater emphasis on the circumstances of the poorest when assessing inequality. The Gini coefficient formula does not build in that greater sensitivity.

Despite its imperfections, the Gini coefficient is a commonly used measure of inequality. Although in principal it can vary from 0 to 1, in practice, when describing income and wealth distributions, it tends to vary from about 0.2, reflecting very low inequality, to 0.7, reflecting great inequality. Table 5.2 provides Gini coefficient and income share reports drawn from diverse countries around the world.

The aims of reducing poverty and reducing inequality often provide similar guidance for policy, and the distinction between poverty and inequality is often blurred in popular discussions. Programs successful in raising the incomes of the poor also reduce inequality if they leave the

■ TABLE 5.2   Select Income Distribution Statistics

| Country | Gini Coefficient | Share of Income or Consumption Expenditure (Percent) | |
		Poorest 20 Percent of Population	Richest 20 Percent of Population
Ethiopia	0.30	9.3	39.4
Hungary	0.31	8.4	39.9
Turkey	0.39	5.7	45.1
United States	0.41	5.4	45.8
Costa Rica	0.51	3.9	55.9
Brazil	0.55	2.9	58.6
South Africa	0.63	2.7	68.2

Source: World Bank (2012).

incomes of the nonpoor unchanged. They reduce inequality even more if they are financed by taxes on the nonpoor.

Despite their overlaps, however, the objectives of reducing absolute poverty and reducing inequality are quite different and might lead to different conclusions about the best routes to development success. By identifying poverty reduction as a priority (when poverty is defined with respect to an absolute poverty line), policymakers indicate their judgment that it simply isn't right for human beings to live at less than some minimally acceptable standard of living. By identifying inequality reduction as the objective, they indicate the judgment that it is troubling or wrong for some people to have so much less than others in their society, or for some people to have so much more, regardless of the absolute living standards of the poorest. If all incomes in an economy were rising, but the incomes of the richest people were rising faster than the incomes of the poorest, then by the criterion of absolute poverty reduction, it would be a period of success but by the criterion of inequality reduction it would be a failure. Similarly, if the incomes of the richest were falling while the incomes of the middle class were rising and the incomes of the poor were holding constant, the period would be one of success in reducing at least some measures of inequality, though it would be one of failure in reducing absolute poverty.

5.1C Vulnerability

Vulnerability is a more complex concept than poverty or inequality. It arises out of the conjunction of two sets of circumstances: households' exposure to **fluctuations and shocks** (such as we described in Chapter 2) and households' lack of attractive mechanisms for ex ante and ex post responses to fluctuations, through which they can mitigate the effects of the fluctuations on their consumption and well-being. **Ex ante responses to fluctuations** include efforts to reduce susceptibility to risk, such as using insecticide-treated bed nets (to reduce exposure to malaria), undertaking precautionary saving, buying formal insurance, and participating in informal insurance arrangements. **Ex post responses to fluctuations** include the redirection of household labor from activities that have become unproductive as the result of shocks (such as labor on farms struck by drought) into other income-generating activities, and taking out loans to maintain consumption until times are better. A person's vulnerability may be reduced either by reducing the person's exposure to shocks (e.g., by eradicating malarial mosquitoes in the person's environment or building infrastructure that reduces the risk of local flooding) or by providing the person with better ways of coping with the shocks (e.g., by improving access to health care, crop insurance, or safety net programs).

In general terms, the vulnerability of concern to policymakers arises when people face "significant risk of significant future reductions in well-being." This vulnerability is a forward-looking concept: It pertains not to living standards today but to hopes and fears regarding future living standards. It is also a probabilistic concept, applying to entire groups of people facing some probability of loss, even though only a small fraction of the group might ultimately experience the loss. The inclusion of the "significant" qualifiers in the definition of vulnerability captures the idea that whereas every person in the world is at some risk of loss at all times, there are socially unacceptable levels of vulnerability that particularly merit policy concern.

The general definition of vulnerability raises many questions that we would have to answer when attempting to create more specific definitions and construct useful measures. These include:

- Is vulnerability a matter of objective probability or subjective fear?
- How high must a probability of loss be, and over what period of time, to be considered significant?
- To what kinds of loss must the hazards lead (e.g., in consumption expenditure, nutrition, disability, asset holdings)?
- Is the significance of the reduction in well-being a function of its size (relative, say, to the level of well-being before the reduction) or of the ultimate level to which it reduces well-being?
- Does it matter whether the feared reductions in well-being are likely to be temporary or longer lasting?

Different answers to these questions could easily generate hundreds of distinct notions of vulnerability. Among the most prevalent notions discussed by social scientists and policymakers are vulnerability of the nonpoor to falling into income poverty, vulnerability of the poor and near-poor to falling into malnutrition or "destitution" (defined by per capita consumption expenditure falling below a very low threshold), and vulnerability of anyone (including those with high incomes) to serious disruptions to their way of life or to disability or death (see Alwang et al., 2001; Dercon, 2006b).

To construct aggregate vulnerability measures comparable to aggregate poverty measures, we would need to answer all of the questions raised above, figure out how to quantify the resulting notion of vulnerability at the level of individuals or households, and then use formulas to turn all the micro measures into a single aggregate measure. Unfortunately, the forward-looking and probabilistic nature of vulnerability concepts renders such measurement extremely difficult.

Even without constructing direct measures of vulnerability itself, however, researchers can shed useful light on vulnerability by helping to quantify the probabilities with which households in various groups or geographic locations will be hit by bad weather, malaria, or other hazards; the availability and feasibility of various coping mechanisms for responding to shocks; and the fractions of groups that have suffered serious reductions in living standards in recent years.

An important source of information on vulnerability is **panel data sets**, which are constructed by administering the same questionnaires multiple times, over a series of seasons or years, to the same sample of households. Such data sets have revealed the widespread nature of vulnerability around the world. They demonstrate, for example, that the incomes of the poor and near-poor tend to vary a great deal from year to year. This suggests that many who are not poor today are vulnerable to becoming poor next year.

The figures in Table 5.3 are drawn from a paper by Baulch and Hoddinott (2000), which reviewed the studies of poverty dynamics available at the time of writing. The figures for different locations are drawn from studies performed by different researchers and employing different methods of measuring living standards and poverty and thus are not strictly comparable across locations. Even so, they are useful for demonstrating that the share of households that are "sometimes poor" is often much larger than the share of households who are "always poor." They suggest that in any one year there are many nonpoor households who *will* fall into poverty in the next year, and the number of nonpoor households who are *at risk* of falling into poverty is much larger.

■ TABLE 5.3   A Few Illustrative Results Regarding Poverty Dynamics

Location	Length of Study	Percent of Households:		
		Always Poor	Sometimes Poor	Never Poor
India	9 years	21.8	65.8	12.4
Zimbabwe	4 years	10.6	59.6	29.8
China	6 years	6.2	47.8	46.0
Pakistan	5 years	3.0	55.3	41.7

Source: Baulch and Hoddinott (2000), drawing on studies by other authors.

Transitory versus persistent poverty

The statistics in Table 5.3 suggest not only that some of today's nonpoor are vulnerable to falling into poverty, but also that some of today's poor are likely to exit poverty in the near future. This motivates interest in distinguishing among the poor those who are in **persistent** versus **transitory** poverty. Among those who are income-poor in any one year, some have moderate asset holdings but are experiencing an unusually bad year. Many of them are likely to exit poverty soon and are in transitory poverty. Others among the current income poor, however, have few assets and are likely to remain poor for a long time. They are in persistent or chronic poverty. Identifying whether a household's current poverty is persistent or transitory is a difficult task. One suggestion is to complement standard income-based or consumption expenditure–based measures of current poverty with asset-based measures that distinguish between those whose asset holdings are and are not great enough to provide them with income above the income-based poverty line in "average" years (Carter and Barrett, 2006).

5.2 Poverty, Inequality, Vulnerability, and Economic Growth

5.2A Values, beliefs, and development targets

Most development actors would agree that the aim in development is for some combination of economic growth and reductions in poverty, inequality, and vulnerability. Economic growth creates the potential for sustained and widespread improvements in well-being. Reductions in income poverty or income inequality demonstrate that the income gains associated with growth are distributed in a desirable manner, and reductions in nonincome-based measures of poverty or measures of vulnerability demonstrate that key nonincome dimensions of living standards are improving along with incomes.

Despite this common ground, development actors might argue for different kinds of policy for two quite different reasons. First, their *values* might differ. Some development advocates would be more willing than others to trade off reduced growth over the next five years in exchange for more rapid and widespread poverty reduction during the same period. Some would also be more willing than others to trade off reduced improvements in income-based poverty measures for more rapid reductions in nonincome measures of poverty or vulnerability. Development actors differ even more in the priority they place on reductions in inequality (relative to growth or poverty reduction). For some, reduced inequality is a critical feature of the better world they hope for. Many others, though, would consider development successful even when inequality is rising, as long as the economy is growing and poverty is falling.

A second reason development actors differ in the policies they prescribe is differences in their beliefs about how the world actually works. More specifically, they might disagree about the likely impacts on growth, poverty, inequality, and vulnerability of the various policies they might promote. These are differences in beliefs about *facts*. In principle, disagreements about facts can be resolved by appeal to empirical evidence, revealing which claims about the facts are true and which are false. Unfortunately, in practice, the available empirical evidence is not always clear-cut; on some questions evidence is lacking; and sometimes evidence is obscured by debaters who blur the distinction between facts and values. This text equips readers to identify important factual questions, understand what empirical research to date reveals about the answers to these questions, and become involved in research and experimentation that expands policy-relevant understanding of how the world works.

One broad disagreement about facts of enduring importance in development debates concerns the interrelationship between economic growth and poverty. If rapid economic growth almost always brings with it significant reductions in poverty, regardless of the policies employed to achieve the high growth, then the most effective way to pursue broad-based development might be simply to pursue policies that are good for growth. If, in addition, explicit policy efforts to reduce poverty tend to slow growth, then policy makers—even those for whom poverty reduction is a high priority—have even stronger reason to concentrate on speeding growth while letting poverty "take care of itself."

If, however, economic growth is a highly variegated phenomenon that does not always deliver poverty reduction, and especially if explicit efforts to reduce poverty and inequality have the potential to speed growth, then identifying the best development strategy is a more complicated task. Policymakers must then attempt to identify **pro-poor growth** policies from among the wider array of growth policy options, and they must also contemplate the use of explicit safety net policies focused on reducing poverty. The next section begins examining these interrelationships.

5.2B Mathematical relationships linking growth, inequality, and poverty

If we know that average income is rising (i.e., the "size of the pie" is increasing) and income inequality is holding constant or falling (i.e., the "share of the pie going to the poor" is staying constant or increasing), then mathematical relationships tell us that absolute income poverty is falling by at least some measure, because the absolute volume of income going to the poor is increasing. (To see that poverty need not fall by *all* measures, see problem 5.)

Ravallion (2001) offers a global summary of the historical relationships between growth and changes in inequality and poverty, drawing on data for 117 spells, or periods between pairs of comparable household surveys, pertaining to 47 developing countries in the 1980s and 1990s. He divides the spells into four groups, depending on whether average income is rising or falling, and whether inequality as measured by the Gini coefficient is rising or falling, and then observes what was happening to poverty as measured by the headcount ratio relative to the $1-per-day poverty line. His calculations are reported in Table 5.4. As we must expect, the largest reductions in poverty take place during spells in which growth is positive and inequality is falling.

The mathematical relationship tells us that *if* we could increase economic growth while holding the distribution of income constant, or *if* we could speed reductions in inequality

■ TABLE 5.4   **Median Annual Rates of Increase or Decrease in the $1-per-Day Headcount Ratio for Four Types of Spells**

	Spells in Which Average Income Growth Is:	
Spells in Which the Gini Coefficient Is:	**Negative**	**Positive**
Rising	+14.3%	−1.3%
Falling	+1.7%	−9.6%

Source: Ravallion (2001).

while holding economic growth constant, we would speed the rate of poverty reduction. But they tell us nothing about the likely effects on poverty of *actual* policy efforts to speed growth or reduce inequality. Not only might well-intentioned policy efforts to speed growth fail, but even successful policy efforts to increase growth might *also* increase inequality, leaving the net effect on poverty ambiguous. Similarly, efforts to redistribute income might slow growth, again leaving the net effect on poverty ambiguous. To understand these *policy-relevant* relationships among growth, inequality, and poverty, we must move beyond mere mathematical relationships to socioeconomic relationships.

5.2C Growth, inequality, and poverty as joint outcomes of the socioeconomic system

Our starting point for understanding deeper socioeconomic relationships is to recognize that growth and changes in inequality and poverty are joint outcomes of complex socioeconomic systems. A country's people, taking their current assets as given, and interacting with each other in markets and nonmarket settings, make many choices that together determine the levels and growth rates of each person's income, consumption expenditure, and well-being. The **exogenous factors** that shape these many decisions and outcomes—that is, the circumstances that are determined outside the system and taken as given by actors within the system—include the level, mix, and distribution of the country's initial assets, the external economic conditions the country faces, and the policies pursued by the government and other development actors. Measures of growth, inequality, and poverty reduction simply summarize different features of the multidimensional outcomes that emerge from the system. They are **endogenous** outcomes, jointly determined by initial conditions, policies, and external circumstances.

When formulating questions about the relationships among growth, inequality, and poverty reduction, then, we must be careful not to oversimplify. It does not make sense to think of growth or reductions in inequality as "causing" poverty reduction, as if we could somehow meaningfully impose a new growth rate or distribution outcome on the system and then observe what this does to poverty. It does, however, make sense to pose questions about changes in the exogenous factors that shape growth and distribution outcomes. For example, we might ask: Do the policies that are successful in speeding economic growth, regardless of their specifics, have a strong tendency to reduce poverty as well?

5.2D Theoretical connections from growth policies to poverty reduction

How *might* successful growth policies affect well-being and poverty? When policies succeed in speeding economic growth, they do so by speeding the economy's accumulation of assets (broadly defined, as in Chapters 2 and 3). Any *specific* set of growth policies encourages the creation of *specific* assets owned by specific members of society, and introduces specific kinds of change into the socioeconomic system. Some policies promote private investment in export manufacturing, for example, while others build roads that connect remote rural regions to markets. The new assets associated with growth tend to raise productivity and income for their owners or users. They also lead their owners to increase supplies to certain goods markets and their demands for certain types of labor. Their actions cause prices to rise in some markets and fall in others, and wages rise for some kinds of workers and fall for others. Policies, and price and wage changes, may furthermore place stress on traditional institutions and give birth to new institutions. The net result is a complex web of impacts that may raise well-being for some groups and reduce it for others, and the patterns of change may differ across growth policies of different sorts.

Policies promoting asset creation and growth have the potential to improve the well-being of the poor through four channels. First, they might increase the assets that the poor own or have direct access to, whether by giving the poor new assets or by encouraging the poor to undertake their own investments. Second, even if the new assets underlying growth are not owned by the poor, they might increase the incomes of the poor indirectly by driving up wages for low-skill labor or driving up the prices of goods produced by farms and household enterprises operated by the poor. Third, increases in assets owned by the nonpoor might lead to expansion of the supply of goods consumed by the poor, driving down their prices. Finally, with additional assets and income, the nonpoor might become more involved in public or private safety net institutions, which channel funds to the poor and vulnerable.

Unfortunately, none of these potential impacts of growth on the incomes of the poor is guaranteed to take place during all episodes of growth. Successful growth policies can fail to raise the asset holdings of the poor for a variety of reasons. Policies might, for example, encourage investment only by very large export manufacturing enterprises that are owned by the wealthy, and even when policies seek to encourage private investment more generally, they might fail to encourage investment by the poor, whose lack of collateral prevents them from obtaining investment financing (Chapter 10).

Growth might also fail to increase the income that poor workers earn from wage labor or household enterprises. Poor workers might live in remote areas not integrated into the larger markets in which growth is taking place (Chapters 8 and 9), and the new assets underlying growth might lead their owners to increase demand for skilled labor and specialized inputs produced by large suppliers rather than the unskilled labor and products that the poor have to offer. Remoteness from markets can also prevent the poor from enjoying consumer price reductions. Finally, growth can fail to stimulate greater transfers to the poor through safety net institutions. Such institutions might be absent, they may exist but exclude many poor people, and growth might even cause effective safety net institutions to break down (see Chapter 12).

Thus, while it is theoretically possible that the poor tend to share in growth under a wide range of policies, there are strong reasons to suspect that growth policies differ in the extent to which they are pro-poor. More specifically:

> Growth policies that explicitly create new assets owned or used by the poor, that address the financial constraints of the poor, that extend the reach of markets into more remote areas, and that emphasize accumulation of assets that stimulate the demand for unskilled labor or goods produced by the poor are more likely to bring poverty reduction than other policies that are equally successful at producing growth in average income.

5.2E Theoretical connections from poverty reduction policies to growth

How *might* poverty reduction policies affect growth? Explicit poverty reduction policies (such as those discussed in Chapters 15 and 16) tax the nonpoor (or draw on external funding) to finance the distribution of benefits to the poor. In the early days of development, most theorists and policy analysts assumed that such efforts would slow economic growth, for two reasons. First, if the poor save a smaller fraction of their income than do the nonpoor, then transferring income to the poor would reduce the rate of saving, tending to reduce the rate of investment and asset accumulation. (See the Lewis model described in Chapter 4.) Second, policies and programs that tax the incomes of the nonpoor and provide the poor with "handouts" might weaken the incentives of the nonpoor to work hard and innovate by reducing their share in the returns to such efforts, while also weakening the incentives of the poor to work by providing them with cash they do not have to work for (see Chapter 15).

In the 1990s new economic theories pointed to channels through which efforts to reduce poverty and inequality might instead *increase* economic growth (Aghion et al., 1999). One line of theoretical research highlights the tendency for financial market failures to deprive the poor of investment finance (which we examine closely in Chapter 10). If the poor lack financing at reasonable interest rates, then they may be prevented from undertaking investment projects with high returns. The projects that the poor must leave undone for lack of financing might have higher returns than the projects undertaken by the nonpoor. Policies that increase the income or assets of the poor might thus increase aggregate rates of saving and investment, and increase the average return on investment, by allowing the poor to undertake their high-return investment projects (Galor and Zeira, 1993).

Recent innovations in the design of poverty reduction programs create even greater potential for such programs to spur investment and growth by strengthening the incentives of participants to invest in the creation of human assets. For example, new "conditional cash transfer programs" direct benefits to poor households, conditional on the households' compliance with requirements that they send their children to school and make use of public clinics, and these programs appear to be successful in increasing investment in human assets (see Chapter 15).

5.2F Empirical relationships among growth, inequality, and poverty reduction

What do the data have to say about relationships between growth and poverty reduction? Empirical studies of aggregate cross-country data yield two key observations. First, on average over all countries for which adequate data can be mustered, economic growth has been associated with little change in income distribution (at least by some measures) and with significant reductions in absolute poverty. Second, the experience of individual countries has, however, been quite dispersed around that world average, with poverty sometimes falling significantly even when growth is very slow and sometimes falling only a little even when growth is rapid.

Figure 5.6 replicates a figure from a much-cited study by David Dollar and Aart Kraay (2002). The 285 data points plotted in the graph describe growth experiences for 92 countries over various time intervals (of at least five years in length) spanning a 40-year period. Each country-interval observation is represented by a point that indicates the rate of economic growth (measured along the horizontal axis) and the rate of growth of the income of the poorest 20 percent of the population (a measure of poverty reduction, measured along the vertical axis).

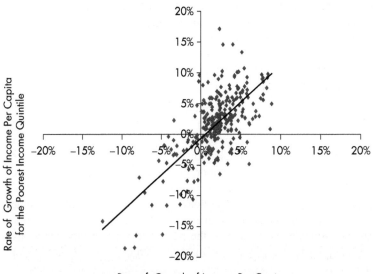

FIGURE 5.6
Cross-Country Correlation between Income Growth for the Bottom 20 Percent and the Rate of Economic Growth
Source: Dollar and Kraay (2002).

The slope of the regression line drawn through the middle of the scatter plot in Figure 5.6 is very close to one, indicating that on average, every 1 percentage point increase in the rate of economic growth is associated with a 1 percentage point increase in the rate of growth of average income for the poorest 20 percent. This implies that on average (over all the episodes included in the diagram) the income share of the poor (a measure of inequality) has tended to be unchanged by growth, and the incomes of the poorest 20 percent have risen at the same percentage rate as the incomes of the average members of the population. Authors like Dollar and Kraay (2002) emphasize this average relationship and conclude (as indicated by the title of their paper) that "growth is good for the poor."[2] Many policy advocates have interpreted this average relationship as reflecting a strong, worldwide structural tendency for growth to translate into significant poverty reduction, regardless of the policies used to promote growth.

We might question this interpretation for three reasons, however. Notice first that the data points representing particular places and time intervals are widely dispersed around the regression line. That is, among episodes with similar growth rates, the income shares of the poor have risen much in some cases, have risen little in other cases, and even have fallen in a few cases. In light of the theoretical discussion above, this is no surprise, given that the countries of the world are diverse in economic structure and have pursued quite different policies in recent decades.[3] It suggests that we cannot count on a strong structural tendency for growth to bring poverty reduction in any particular country or time period. It seems likely that the details of growth policies matter and that efforts to identify pro-poor growth policies will be required if policy-makers are to have simultaneous success in speeding growth and reducing poverty.

Notice, second, that even if there were a very high correlation between overall growth and the rate of income growth for the poorest 20 percent, that correlation need not indicate that growth-oriented policies *caused* the associated poverty reduction. It is possible that in some countries better-organized and better-motivated bureaucrats and politicians pursued policies that were good for both growth and poverty reduction, and that they would have succeeded in reducing poverty even if they had not pursued growth. The correlation might even arise out of reverse causation: It could be that government efforts to pursue poverty reduction improved their growth performance.

A third question we might raise about the results in Figure 5.6 is this: When the incomes of the poor grow at the same *percentage rate* as the incomes of the rich, do we necessarily conclude that the poor are sharing equally or adequately in the benefits of growth? Five percent of $100 is $5, while five percent of $10,000 is $500. The absolute benefits of growth are much greater for the nonpoor than for the poor when their incomes are growing at the same percentage rate.

More disaggregated case studies of economic growth episodes provide further reason to suspect that growth policy specifics—such as the extent to which they favor the regions and economic sectors where large fractions of the poor live and work and the extent to which they favor creation of infrastructure connecting remote regions to markets—must play an important role in shaping their poverty reduction impacts. For example, across states of India, rates of economic growth over the last 25 years ranged from 2.2 percent in Bihar to 7.2 percent in Karnataka. More rapid growth in nonagriculture than in agriculture contributed to a tendency for growth to be more rapid in states starting at higher levels of manufacturing development and per capita income. As a result, growth was associated with rising inequality in average income across regions (Chaudhuri and Ravallion, 2006).

---

[2]For a discussion of how measurement errors might cause a regression like this one to produce a slope estimate close to one, even when the true average coefficient is greater or less than one, see Deaton (2006).

[3]The authors attempt to study the role that policy differences might play in generating this dispersion, by looking for systematic tendencies for the income growth of the poorest 20 percent to rise more or less (while holding overall income growth constant) depending on the levels of several policy variables. They find no systematic relationship. Unfortunately, their policy variables include only a few broad macro outcome variables such as inflation rates and average years of primary education, which fall far short of measuring the detailed differences in policy that might determine the strength of the tendency for the poor to share in the benefits of growth.

In Ghana, export crop market liberalization and related infrastructure-building programs led to rapid growth in the rural forest zone, where most export crops are grown, but to stagnation and decline in other (poorer) rural areas, where food crops are grown (Aryeetey and McKay, 2007). Studies of Ethiopia (Dercon, 2006a) and Vietnam (Klump, 2007) highlight how incomes tend to grow more slowly in more remote regions than in places better connected to markets and for households living at greater distances from markets within regions. For other interesting case studies, see Ravallion and Chen (2007) on China and Thurlow and Wobst (2006) on Zambia.

Case studies also suggest that even when growth translates into reduction in income poverty, it need not translate into improvements in complementary nonincome measures of poverty. For example, growth in Ghana brought a large decline in income poverty rates, as well as improvements in school enrollment and the share of the population with access to potable water, but it was also accompanied by increases in malnutrition among children under five years old and reductions in health care use and life expectancy (Aryeety and McKay, 2007). This provides further reason to pay attention to policy details when seeking growth accompanied by multidimensional reductions in poverty.

On the basis of empirical evidence, we conclude that:

> While sustained development is impossible without economic growth, and growth often brings with it significant poverty reduction, single-minded pursuit of high growth through whatever means available need not always deliver success in broad-based development. Some kinds of growth deliver greater reductions in poverty than others, and safety net policies may be required to guarantee universal participation in the benefits of growth.

5.2G Growth and vulnerability

Just as the details of growth policies shape the extent to which growth brings poverty reduction, so the details are likely to shape the effects on vulnerability. For example, growth policies are more likely to reduce vulnerability to destitution if they raise the incomes of the poor (rendering it less likely that income reductions drive them all the way into destitution), if they create assets that reduce inherent risks of crop loss or ill health (such as floodwalls or immunization programs), or if they facilitate the development of market relationships through which the effects of some shocks can be spread out (see Chapter 8).

More than this, growth can even increase vulnerability unless explicit efforts are undertaken to prevent this. Effective growth policies often generate tremendous change at the microeconomic level, as some firms and sectors rise and others decline. Risk of unemployment can rise, and the geographic movement of people in response to new opportunities can cause traditional private safety net institutions to break down.

At the same time, policies explicitly targeted at reducing vulnerability might improve economic growth by insuring poor and near-poor households against the worst potential consequences of risky investments. If safety net programs provide households with the assurance that they may obtain program support if their risky investments work out badly, then households might become more willing to undertake investments, thereby contributing to economic growth (Chapter 10). Some workfare programs guaranteeing employment at low wages seem to provide such insurance (see Chapter 16).[4]

---

[4]Another related literature explores political economy channels through which higher initial levels of income or wealth inequality in a society cause lower subsequent growth rates. For example, Alesina and Rodrik's (1994) theoretical model suggests that in more equal societies, where the median voter derives a larger fraction of income from capital, governments tend to pursue policies that tax capital less and encourage growth more. Such models have more to say about which policies are likely to be pursued than about the likely growth-inducing impacts of redistributive policies, should they be pursued.

5.2H Further motivation for micro-level, context-specific study

At the end of Chapter 3 we argued that to understand growth and identify ways of raising growth rates, we must pursue disaggregated and context-specific study of the many decisions, markets, and institutions that influence growth outcomes. In this chapter, we have learned that if we are interested not only in raising the rate of growth but also in raising well-being for diverse groups throughout society, including the poorest groups, then we have even greater reason to pursue such detailed micro study. Growth improves a group's well-being only when it brings an array of changes in assets, prices, wages, and institutions that members of the group are well-positioned to enjoy. We must therefore study the ways diverse groups are affected by changes in assets, markets, and institutions of different types, and we must seek out sets of policies that together promote changes in assets, markets, and institutions that deliver benefits to many groups. With the next chapter we begin Part III, which presents an analytical framework and tools to facilitate such study.

REFERENCES

Aghion, Philippe, Eve Caroli, and Cecilia García-Peñalosa. "Inequality and Economic Growth: The Perspective of the New Growth Theories." *Journal of Economic Literature* 37(4): 1615–1660, 1999. doi:10.1257/jel.37.4.1615

Alwang, Jeffrey, Paul B. Siegel, and Steen L. Jørgensen. "*Vulnerability: A View From Different Disciplines.*" *Social Protection Discussion Paper No. 0115.* Washington, D.C.: World Bank, 2001. http://go.worldbank.org/45E0CHWNJ0

Aryeetey, Ernest, and Andrew McKay. "*Ghana: The Challenge of Translating Sustained Growth Into Poverty Reduction.*" In Tim Besley and Louise Cord (eds.). *Delivering on the Promise of Pro-Poor Growth: Insights and Lessons From Country Experiences.* Washington, D.C.: World Bank, 2007, pp 147–168. doi:10.1596/978-0-8213-6515-1

Baulch, Bob, and John Hoddinott. "Economic Mobility and Poverty Dynamics in Developing Countries." *Journal of Development Studies* 36(6): 1–24, 2000. doi:10.1080/00220380008422652

Carter, Michael R., and Christopher B. Barrett. "The Economics of Poverty Traps and Persistent Poverty: An Asset-Based Approach." *Journal of Development Studies* 42(2): 178–199, 2006. doi:10.1080/00220380500405261

Chaudhuri, Shubham, and Martin Ravallion. "*Partially Awakened Giants: Uneven Growth in China and India.*" *World Bank Policy Research Working Paper 4069.* Washington, D.C.: World Bank, 2006. http://go.worldbank.org/QMGRSSI1T0

Dercon, Stefan. "Economic Reform, Growth and the Poor: Evidence From Rural Ethiopia." *Journal of Development Economics* 81(1): 1–24, 2006a. doi:10.1016/j.jdeveco.2005.05.008

Dercon, Stefan. "Vulnerability: A Micro Perspective." In François Bourguignon, Boris Pleskovic, and Jacques van der Gaag (eds.). *Annual World Bank Conference on Development Economics— Europe 2006: Securing Development in an Unstable World.* Washington, D.C.: World Bank, 2006b, pp. 115–145. http://go.worldbank.org/GU6MX9DXN0

Dollar, David, and Aart Kraay. "Growth is Good for the Poor." *Journal of Economic Growth* 7(3): 195–225, 2002. doi:10.1023/A:1020139631000

Foster, James, Joel Greer, and Erik Thorbecke. "A Class of Decomposable Poverty Measures." *Econometrica* 52(3): 761–766, 1984. http://www.jstor.org/stable/1913475

Galor, Oded, and Joseph Zeira. "Income Distribution and Macroeconomics." *The Review of Economic Studies* 60(1): 35–52, 1993. doi:10.2307/2297811

Klugman, Jeni, Francisco Rodríguez, and Hyung-Jin Choi. "The HDI 2010: new controversies, old critiques." *The Journal of Economic Inequality* 9(2): 249–288, 2011. doi:10.1007/s10888-011-9178-z

Klump, Rainer. "Pro-Poor Growth in Vietnam: Miracle or Model?" In Tim Besley and Louise Cord (eds.). *Delivering on the Promise of Pro-Poor Growth: Insights and Lessons From Country Experiences.* Washington, D.C.: World Bank, 2007, 119–146. doi:10.1596/978-0-8213-6515-1

Pritchett, Lant. "Who is Not Poor? Dreaming of a World Truly Free of Poverty." *The World Bank Research Observer* 21(1): 1–23, 2006. doi:10.1093/wbro/lkj002

Ravallion, Martin. "Growth, Inequality and Poverty: Looking Beyond Averages." *World Development* 29(11): 1803–1815, 2001. http://ideas.repec.org/p/wbk/wbrwps/2558.html

Ravallion, Martin. "*Poverty Lines Across the World.*" *Policy Research Working Paper 5284.* Washington, D.C.: World Bank, 2010. http://go.worldbank.org/PLIZ7CWLL0

Ravallion, Martin, and Shaohua Chen. "China's (Uneven) Progress Against Poverty?" *Journal of Development Economics* 82(1): 1–42, 2007. doi:10.1016/j.jdeveco.2005.07.003

Thurlow, James, and Peter Wobst. "Not All Growth is Equally Good for the Poor: The Case of Zambia." *Journal of African Economies* 15(4): 603–625, 2006. doi:10.1093/jae/ejk012

Uganda Bureau of Statistics. *Uganda National Household Survey 2009/ 2010 Socio-Economic Module Abridged Report.* Kampala: Uganda Bureau of Statistics, 2010. http://www.ubos.org/UNHS0910

World Bank. *World Development Indicators 2012.* Washington, D.C.: World Bank, 2012. http://data.worldbank.org/data-catalog/world-development-indicators

QUESTIONS FOR REVIEW

1. What is a general definition of poverty, and what is involved in constructing a measure of poverty?

2. What is the distinction between absolute and relative approaches to constructing poverty lines?

3. Discuss the strengths and weaknesses of the following aggregate poverty measures:
   a. Headcount ratio
   b. Total income gap
   c. Average proportional income gap among the poor
   d. Poverty gap index (or P_1)
   e. Squared proportional income gap index (or P_2).

4. What is involved in constructing a measure of inequality?

5. Draw a Lorenz-curve diagram, label it carefully, and describe how it is constructed.

6. What does it mean for one Lorenz curve to dominate another?

7. Define the Gini coefficient and discuss the values embodied in its construction.

8. Compare and contrast the policy objectives of reducing poverty and reducing inequality.

9. Provide a general definition of vulnerability. What two sets of circumstances must combine to render a household vulnerable?

10. What are panel data sets, and what are their strengths and weaknesses for shedding light on vulnerability?

11. What is meant by the distinction between persistent and transitory poverty?

12. Why would many development analysts want to employ measures from all three of the following categories when measuring development success?
    a. A measure of economic growth
    b. Measures of income poverty or inequality
    c. Measures of nonincome poverty and vulnerability.

13. Discuss the roles of values and beliefs in explaining disagreements regarding the best policies to employ in pursuing development.

14. What mathematical relationship links growth rates, changes in inequality, and changes in poverty?

15. What are the four channels through which policies that promote asset accumulation (and thus economic growth) might lead to income increases for the poor?

16. Why might we worry that each of these channels might fail to be activated by particular growth policies?

17. Through what channels might poverty reduction efforts affect the rate of economic growth?

18. Discuss what we learn from Figure 5.6.

19. What are some channels through which growth policies might reduce or increase vulnerability, and what are some channels through which efforts to reduce vulnerability might affect growth?

QUESTIONS FOR DISCUSSION

1. Consider giving one dollar to a poor person, keeping in mind that among a country's poor people, some have much lower incomes than others. Consider each of the aggregate poverty measures defined in the text, and assume that per capita household income is the measure of individual-level well-being they summarize. For each measure, discuss how the impact on the measure would differ depending on whether the additional dollar were given to a person who is just barely poor (with income just below the poverty line) or to a person who is very poor.

2. Which of the aggregate poverty measures defined in this chapter appeals to you as the measure that best captures your concerns and priorities? Might your answer to this question depend on circumstances? Explain.

3. Do you think that your own concerns about people with low incomes and poor living standards are driven more by concerns regarding poverty or inequality? If you had to choose between two policies, one of which would reduce poverty while increasing inequality, and the other of which

would reduce inequality but increase poverty, which would you choose? Why?

4. Just as we can construct statistics to summarize poverty or inequality, so we can construct indices to summarize the state of "development." One such index is the Human Development Index, employed by the United Nations Development Program. It is intended to measure the country's achievements along three basic dimensions of human well-being: long and healthy lives (health), access to knowledge (education), and a decent standard of living (income). The life expectancy and GDP per capita indices are constructed by taking statistics on life expectancy at birth and GDP per capita and rescaling them so that they are expressed on a zero-to-one scale. The education index is constructed from data on mean years of schooling for adults aged 25 years and expected years of schooling for children of school-entering age, again on a zero-to-one scale. The education index is the geometric mean of the two education sub-indices. For a discussion of the issues involved in constructing such a measure, see Klugman et al. (2011). What do you think are the strengths of this index as a measure of development? What do you think are the weaknesses of this index? What might be the uses of such an index?

5. Pick a country you would like to learn more about. Access the most recent World Development Report, published by the World Bank and available online in the World Bank website. Find the "Selected Indicators" near the end of the text, and study the tables provided there on "Key development indicators" for countries around the world. What do you learn there about growth, poverty, and inequality in the country you picked? How does your country's performance in these areas compare to the performance of other countries with similar levels of GDP per capita? How does it compare to performance in the rest of the world?

PROBLEMS

1. This problem provides a brief review of summation notation, using an example related to the distribution of incomes in a population. Order the individuals in the population from 1 to N, with individual 1 being the poorest person and individual N being the richest. An individual's index is his rank number in this ordering. For example, the fifth-poorest person has person index 5. Let Y_i be the income of person i. In summation notation, the Greek letter Σ (capital sigma) denotes a sum. More specifically, the expression $\sum_{i=1}^{N} Y_i$, which is read as "the sum from $i = 1$ to N of Y-sub-i," can be defined as follows:

$$\sum_{i=1}^{N} Y_i = Y_1 + Y_2 + \cdots + Y_N$$

   a. Using summation notation, write down a formula for the mean (or simple average) of income in this population.
   b. Consider the expression

$$\frac{1}{q} \sum_{i=1}^{q} \frac{(z - y_i)}{z}$$

   where z is the income poverty line and q is the index of the individual with the highest income who remains under the poverty line. State in plain language the calculation this expression describes and offer an intuitive interpretation of the statistic that results from this calculation.

2. The following table lists the incomes for all individuals in each of three very small countries (just 10 people each). Incomes are listed in currency units (CUs) per week. The official poverty line is 10 CUs per week.

Incomes in Currency Units Per Week

Individual	Country 1	Country 2	Country 3
1	8	3	6
2	8	3	6
3	8	9	6
4	8	9	6
5	8	12	6
6	8	12	12
7	12	12	12
8	12	12	12
9	12	12	12
10	12	12	12

   a. Fill in the following table.

Poverty Measure	Country 1	Country 2	Country 3
P_0 (Headcount Ratio)			
P_1 (Poverty Gap Index)			
P_2			

   b. Fill in the following table. For each poverty measure, enter into the table the country rankings from most poor (1) to least poor (3) according to that measure.

	Country 1	Country 2	Country 3
Ranking according to P_0			
Ranking according to P_1			
Ranking according to P_2			

c. Write a brief essay on differences among the three poverty measures in the *values* underlying them and how these differences in values lead to differences in poverty *rankings* in the case of the three countries described in the tables.

3. Draw a diagram like that in Figure 5.1, including an initial income schedule. For each of the following cases, draw a new income schedule such that the shift from the initial schedule to the new one is associated with each of the following changes:

- Reduction in the headcount ratio but increase in average depth of poverty among the (remaining) poor
- Constant headcount ratio but reduction in poverty gap index
- Constant headcount ratio and poverty gap index but reduction in the P_2 measure.

4. The table below describes the distributions of income in two states (A and B) and in two subregions (rural and urban) of each state. Every individual in these states lives in a household of size one and has an income of exactly 100, 200, or 10,000 dollars per year (so it is easy to describe the distributions and calculate poverty statistics). The first two sections of the table present the numbers and percentages of individuals in each region at each income level.

a. Fill in the two rows of poverty statistics in each of the last two sections of the table. For the first of these sections, use a poverty line of $201. For the last use a poverty line of $101.

b. Suppose attention is restricted to headcount ratio statistics employing a poverty line of $201, and representatives of State A are attempting to argue that their state should be given priority in the allocation of poverty alleviation funds. Would they prefer to employ statistics calculated at the state level (columns 3 and 6) or subregion level (1,2,4, and 5)? Why?

c. Suppose attention is restricted to headcount ratio statistics calculated at the subregion level, and representatives of State A are still attempting to make the same argument. Would they prefer to employ a poverty line of $201 or $101? Why?

d. Suppose attention is restricted to poverty statistics calculated at the subregion level and employing a poverty line of $201, and representatives of State A are still at it. Would they prefer to use headcount ratio statistics or total income gap statistics?

e. Given that no single statistic captures everything that matters about poverty, what practical reasons might policymakers have for defining budget allocation rules based on a single simple statistic? In particular, why not just say: "Our civil servants know poverty when they see it; just give them *discretion* to allocate the funds as they see fit."?

	State A			State B		
	Urban	Rural	Total	Urban	Rural	Total
Population (Number of people)	10,000	10,000	20,000	10,000	90,000	100,000
Number of People with Income of:						
$100	0	0	0	0	45,000	45,000
$200	2,000	6,000	8,000	2,000	0	2,000
$10,000	8,000	4,000	12,000	8,000	45,000	53,000
Percentage of Population with Income of:						
$100	0	0	0	0	50	45
$200	20	60	40	20	0	2
$10,000	80	40	60	80	50	53
Poverty Statistics Using Poverty Line of $201:						
Headcount ratio (%)						
Total Income Gap ($)						
Poverty Statistics Using Poverty Line of $101:						
Headcount ratio (%)						
Total Income Gap ($)						

5. The first column in the following table describes the initial incomes of all 10 people in a very small country. The official poverty line in this country is 15.

a. Fill in the table in the following way. For the first 10 rows, in the second and third columns, fill in the income each person would have if each person's income exactly doubled or tripled, respectively. Then fill in the remaining rows, making use of the income information found in the first 10 rows.

b. Plot a Lorenz curve describing the distribution of income in the first column. How would the Lorenz curves for the distributions in the second and third column compare to this one? Explain.

c. Imagine that economic growth brings a change in incomes from the situation described by the first column to the situation described by the second column in just one year. What rate of economic growth would this imply? Describe in words what happens to the incomes of those who were officially poor at the beginning of the period. Is the improvement for the poor in this case picked up better by changes in the headcount ratio or changes in the average income among the officially poor?

d. Now imagine that economic growth brings a change in incomes from the situation described by the first column to the situation described by the third column in just one year. What rate of economic growth would this imply? Describe in words what happens to the incomes of those who were officially poor at the beginning of the period. Is the improvement for the poor in this case picked up better by changes in the headcount ratio or changes in the average income among the officially poor?

e. Study the absolute income increases enjoyed by various members of the economy over the course of growth from the first column to the second or third column. Comment on the statement: "If the distribution of income (as measured by the Gini coefficient) remains constant during growth, then everyone in the economy shares equally in the growth."

Person	Initial Income	Income after Distribution-Neutral Doubling	Income after Distribution-Neutral Tripling
1	1		
2	1		
3	1		
4	7		
5	7		
6	7		
7	19		
8	19		
9	19		
10	19		
Total Income	100		
Average Income			
Headcount Ratio			
Average Income among the Officially Poor			

chapter

6

Consumption, Time Allocation, and Production Choices

Development isn't something that just happens to people. People are active participants in development. Their choices help determine the speed of economic growth and how the benefits of growth are distributed. If we wish to understand the development process or design good development policies, we must study how people in developing countries make many important choices.

This chapter introduces readers to the role of choice in development and to how development economists study choices. It then begins building the analytical framework of Part III by examining three important sets of choices: consumption, time allocation, and production. The chapter reviews the basic theories that economists bring to the study of these choices and demonstrates their usefulness in empirical applications relating to nutrition policy, child labor, and the Green Revolution.

In later chapters, we argue the need to combine and modify these basic theories to better understand many development concerns. The basic theories nonetheless offer many insights of enduring value in development analysis.

6.1 Choices, Development, and Development Economics

Many choices influence the speed and character of development. Most obviously, when people choose to set up businesses, send their children to school, adopt new agricultural technologies, or cooperate with others in building roads, they create assets and contribute to economic growth. More subtly, when people choose how to interact with one another in market and nonmarket settings—choosing what to supply or demand in various markets and whether to comply with various institutional rules and norms—they help determine market prices and other critical socioeconomic outcomes (as we will see). In so doing, they help determine how the benefits of growth are distributed across households and what effects growth has on diverse dimensions of living conditions.

In this chapter, we examine peoples' choices regarding what to consume, how to spend their time, and what to produce (and with what inputs) on farms or in nonfarm enterprises. These choices are sometimes of direct interest, as when policymakers seek ways to increase the consumption of nutritious foods, reduce the time children spend working, or discourage the use of environmentally harmful farm inputs. These choices are also of more indirect and broader interest in development studies, because they help explain the quantities of goods, services, and labor that households demand or supply in various markets. We must understand these supplies and demands if we wish to understand how markets work, how the effects of policy may be transmitted to diverse households through markets, and how markets might contribute to development.

In the rest of Part III (Chapters 7–13), we will examine many other choices, including households' choices regarding whether or not to participate in markets at all, whether to participate in shorter- or longer-distance markets, where to work and live, how much to save and invest, what kinds of investment to undertake, and whether to comply with institutional rules and norms. In the policy analysis applications of Part IV, we will also examine people's choices regarding whether to participate in targeted transfer programs, use infrastructure services, enroll children in primary school, create or adopt new agricultural technologies, use microcredit, purchase insecticide-treated bed nets, and acquire health insurance.

Following common practice among development economists, we begin our study of each set of choices by applying **standard economic assumptions** about how people make choices. These are the assumptions to which readers have been exposed in introductory and intermediate microeconomics courses. The most fundamental of the standard assumptions is that people exhibit **neoclassical rationality**. This means that they make choices with the aim of maximizing their *utility* given the constraints they face. The utility they maximize is assumed to be a function only of the goods, services, and experiences they would possess after making choices. Additional assumptions regarding utility functions (which we will examine in Chapter 10) become relevant when defining neoclassical rationality for choices regarding saving and investment, which involve comparisons between present and future consumption and between safer and riskier outcomes.

In addition to assuming neoclassical rationality, standard economic models also assume that people have complete and accurate information about their options and constraints and that the only relevant constraints are inescapable resource constraints. These include the constraints that people cannot spend more money than they take in, cannot spend more time than they have available, and cannot obtain more output from production inputs than is technologically possible.

By invoking and applying the standard economic assumptions, we create simple theoretical models of how people make particular sets of choices. These models are useful because they help us work out lists of the many possible **determinants** of peoples' choices, or the features of their circumstances—such as how much land they own, how much education they have, or what prices they face—that they take as given in the present moment and that help to determine the choices they make. The models also remind us that any one choice a household makes (e.g., the choice of how much rice to consume) is inextricably linked to other choices (e.g., the choices of how much to consume of all other goods and services) and help us work out lists of the many possible choices that might be altered as the result of a change in a single determinant. These lists offer important guidance for empirical research, through which we seek to identify which of the theoretically *possible* cause–effect relationships (between determinants and outcomes) are indeed important in practice and to measure the sizes of these effects. Such research helps illuminate how socioeconomic systems work and what effects diverse policies are likely to have on peoples' choices and on development outcomes.

Research based on standard economic models has yielded many useful insights into development and policy, but we will often find it useful to question the standard assumptions and to carry out additional rounds of research guided by alternative assumptions.

The standard assumption that is most commonly questioned and rejected in development studies is the assumption that decision makers possess accurate and complete information. In reality, information is costly and difficult to obtain, especially in developing countries, and poor information flows inhibit development. People cannot take advantage of new investment opportunities—such as the opportunity to use a new and improved agricultural technology—unless they know about it (Chapter 20). Even when people are aware of certain opportunities, they may be discouraged from choosing them by inadequate, inaccurate, or untimely information. For example, people might fail to sell grain in a lucrative distant market because they lack up-to-date information about the price of grain in that market on any given day (Chapter 8). Similarly, they might fail to send a child to school because they lack accurate information about the benefits their children would derive from education (Chapter 19). We will also see that asymmetries of information—in which parties on one side of a market transaction know more about the quality of the good or service on offer than the parties on the other side—can cause markets to fail (Chapters 9, 10, and 13).

At times, development economists also question the assumption of neoclassical rationality. Taking their inspiration from the economics subdiscipline of **behavioral economics** or economic psychology (reviewed in DellaVigna, 2009), development economists sometimes define specific alternative models of how people make decisions and then undertake laboratory and field experiments to test whether peoples' choices are better explained by standard models of neo-classical rationality or models based on the alternative assumptions. The alternative assumptions explain some behaviors better and sometimes yield novel policy suggestions (Datta and Mullainathan, 2012).

In this textbook, we consider four kinds of departure from neoclassical rationality. We acknowledge, first, that the utility people derive from particular choices may be influenced by the behavior or beliefs of other people or by how their choices affect other people (Chapters 6 and 12), rather than depending only on the quantities of goods and services they themselves would possess after making the choices. Second, people's choices can depend not only on the utility they would experience after executing choices but also on their endowments, circum-stances, or emotions at the moment they must make a choice (see Chapter 22). Third, when people must weigh tradeoffs between present and future consumption (as they must when making choices regarding saving and investment), they might seek to maximize a utility function that exhibits *present bias*. This is a potential complication in how people evaluate utility as a function of consumption over time that is disallowed in standard economic models but can help explain why people procrastinate and why they sometimes lack the self-control to follow through on plans for saving and investment (see Chapter 10). Fourth, people's capacity to make the complex calculations required for maximizing utility may be diminished by attention limits or other deficits. Development and behavioral economists point out that while departures from neoclassical rationality appear equally relevant to human beings in all walks of life and in rich and poor countries alike, they can prove especially burdensome to people living in poverty (Mullainathan, 2006).

In addition to questioning the assumptions of perfect information and neoclassical ratio-nality, development economists also examine how people's choices are governed by constraints other than inescapable resource constraints. More specifically, taking their inspiration from another economics subdiscipline—the **economics of institutions**—development economists increasingly examine the impacts of institutional rules and norms, the humanly devised con-straints we introduced briefly in Chapter 2. Formal institutions include laws and regulations, which are enforced at least in part by the threat of codified penalties. Informal institutions can take the form of social norms. Many healthy institutional rules and norms encourage cooperation by prohibiting people from taking self-interested actions that detract from the common good (Chapter 12). Other norms seem to define systems of mental accounts, which limit the sets of uses to which people may legitimately devote income derived from specific sources (Chapters 7 and 22). Yet others, unfortunately, allow people with power to extract labor or wealth from powerless people. Development economists increasingly seek to understand not only how institutional rules affect peoples' choices but also how the rules come to exist and why people obey them (Chapter 12).

6.2 Consumption Choices, with Application to Nutrition Policy

6.2A A motivation

Nearly 1 million people in the developing world (16 percent of the population) are undernour-ished and hungry, consuming fewer calories per day than are required to maintain light activity and minimally acceptable weight (FAO, 2010). As many as 40 percent consume insufficient quantities of at least some micronutrients such as iron and vitamin A, and nearly 30 percent of children are seriously malnourished (World Bank, 2006). Malnourished children are more likely to die, and malnourished mothers give birth to more children with serious defects. Even among people who make it to adulthood without disability, inadequate nutrition increases susceptibility to illness and reduces productivity and earnings (Barrett, 2002). Thus malnutrition rightly demands policymakers' attention.

If we assumed narrowly that malnutrition is forced on people by poverty, we might jump to the conclusion that to improve people's nutritional status we must raise their incomes. Unfortunately, we'd become discouraged, because income has proved surprisingly weak as an instrument for improving nutrition (World Bank, 2006). Fortunately, economic theory allows us to identify a wider range of policy options, and empirical research guided by the theory allows us to identify effective interventions. In what follows, we review the basic economic theory of consumer choice and then demonstrate how to employ it in the study of nutrition policy.

6.2B Basic consumer theory: allocating budgets

Basic consumer theory examines how people allocate fixed budgets across the purchase of various goods and services, including food. It focuses on a consumer who seeks to maximize her utility subject to her budget constraint. Her **utility** is a measure of how attractive she would consider the results of any choice, and it is assumed to be a function only of the quantities of goods and services she consumes. Her **budget constraint** specifies that her total expenditure on all goods and services must not exceed her income.

A two-good case

Consider a consumer who must choose how to allocate income across expenditure on just two goods: food and nonfood. The **utility function**, $U(F, N)$, describes her utility as a function of the physical quantities of food (F) and nonfood (N) that she consumes. It describes her preferences, or her assessments of which combinations of F and N she prefers to others. $U(F, N)$ is assumed to exhibit positive but diminishing marginal utility of food consumption, where the **marginal utility** of food consumption (MU_F) is the amount by which utility rises when F rises by one unit while holding N constant.[1] By assuming that this is positive at any level of F, we assume that the consumer always prefers having more food to less (all else equal). By making the assumption of **diminishing marginal utility** of food consumption, we assume that the additional utility the consumer derives from an additional unit of food (MU_F) falls as the quantity of food she already has increases. We also assume that the marginal utility of nonfood consumption is positive and diminishing.

The consumer chooses F and N to maximize utility subject to her budget constraint, which is given by

$$p_f F + p_n N \leq Y, \tag{6.1}$$

where Y is the quantity of income with which she is endowed (measured in pesos), and p_f and p_n are the per-unit prices of food and nonfood (also measured in pesos).

Figure 6.1a summarizes this simple theoretical framework. The two axes measure the quantities F and N. All consumption pairs (F, N) that satisfy the budget constraint (equation 6.1) lie either along the diagonal **budget line** in the diagram or in the shaded region under that line. The budget line traces out the set of (F, N) combinations for which $p_f F + p_n N = Y$. It touches the horizontal axis at the point Y/p_f, indicating that if the consumer spent all of her income on food, she could purchase Y/p_f units of food. Similarly, it touches the vertical axis at Y/p_n. The slope of the budget line is $-p_f/p_n$, indicating that for each unit of food she gives up (moving one unit to the left in the diagram), she frees up p_f dollars, with which she can buy p_f/p_n units of nonfood (moving up by that amount in the diagram).

---

[1] When using calculus to describe and solve the consumer's utility-maximization problem, we define the MU_F to equal the partial derivative of $U(.)$ with respect to F.

To depict the consumer's preferences, we draw in **indifference curves**, such as the curves I_1, I_2, and I_3. Each indifference curve identifies all the combinations of F and N that would yield the consumer a particular level of utility. Every point in the graph lies on an indifference curve. The indifference curves describing a single consumer's preferences do not cross; and indifference curves that lie farther from the origin pertain to higher levels of utility. The assumptions we have made about the utility function imply that individual indifference curves are downward-sloping and convex (i.e., bowed toward the origin). That indifference curves are downward sloping follows from the assumption that utility is an increasing function of both goods; to maintain the consumer at a constant level of utility, a reduction in the consumption of one good must be accompanied by an increase in the consumption of the other good. That indifference curves are bowed toward the origin follows from the diminishing marginal utility of consumption. When a consumer consumes a high ratio of nonfood to food (closer to the vertical axis along an indifference curve), her marginal utility of nonfood is relatively low and the marginal utility of food is relatively high. The quantity of food she must receive to hold her utility constant when she gives up one unit of nonfood is therefore smaller than when she consumes a low ratio of nonfood to food (closer to the horizontal axis along the same indifference curve).

The quantities F and N that maximize the consumer's utility while satisfying the budget constraint are found by identifying the highest indifference curve that touches the budget line. This highest indifference curve is the one just tangent to the budget line at point a. The consumer depicted in Figure 6.1a chooses quantities F^* and N^*.

Effects of an increase in income

Recall that the endpoints of the budget constraint are given by Y/p_f and Y/p_n, and the slope of the budget line is $-p_f/p_n$. If Y increases while both prices remain constant, both endpoints of the budget line shift farther out from the origin while the slope remains the same. An increase in income from Y_1 to Y_2 thus causes the budget line to shift out from the origin in a *parallel* fashion, as in the shift from the solid budget line to the dashed one in Figure 6.1b.

An increase in Y has theoretically ambiguous effects on F and N. If the consumer's preferences are like those illustrated in Figure 6.1b, then the increase in income causes her consumption choice to change from point a to point b. The quantities she consume of both food and

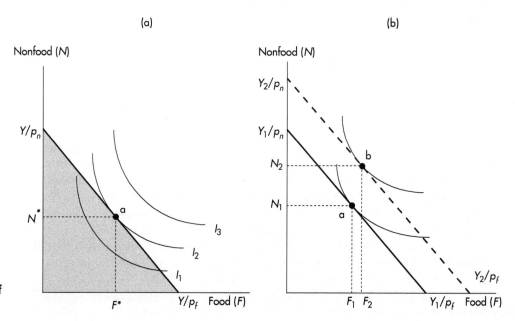

FIGURE 6.1
Basic Consumption Choices and the Effect of Increasing Income

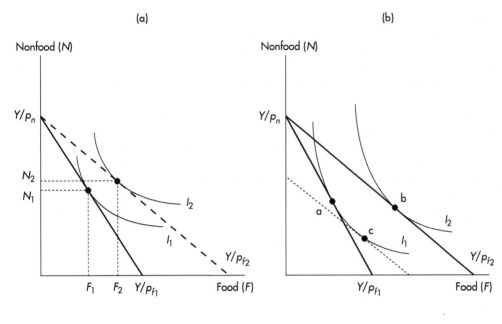

FIGURE 6.2
The Effect of a Food Price
Reduction on Basic
Consumption Choices

nonfood increase, with F rising more slowly than N. If her preferences were different, however, increases in income might cause F to rise more rapidly than N and could instead cause F to fall (see problem 2). A good whose consumption increases when income increases is called a **normal good**, and a good whose consumption decreases is called an **inferior good**. When Y rises, the consumption of at least one good must rise. We conclude that:

> An additional dollar of income is likely, but not guaranteed, to increase spending on food, and empirical research is required to determine the sign and size of this effect. If food and nonfood are both normal goods, then the additional dollar raises food consumption expenditure, but by less than one dollar, because some of the additional dollar is spent on nonfood.

Effects of a reduction in the price of food

Figure 6.2a examines the effect of reducing the price of food from p_{f_1} to p_{f_2}, while holding Y and p_n constant. This change pushes the budget constraint's endpoint on the horizontal axis out away from the origin (from Y/p_{f_1} to Y/p_{f_2}) but leaves the other endpoint fixed in place. Again, the impact on F is theoretically ambiguous. For the consumer whose preferences are illustrated in Figure 6.2a, both F and N rise, though F rises much more than N. A consumer with different preferences might have responded differently. All we know for sure is that the quantity consumed of at least one of the two goods must rise.

We gain further insight into the effect of a reduction in p_f, however, by decomposing it into two components: the income effect and the substitution effect. The decomposition is based on the observation that the reduction in p_f affects consumption through two channels. First, it increases purchasing power, in much the same way that an increase in *income* would. To see this, notice that if the consumer held her consumption choices constant at the initial levels F_1 and N_1 while experiencing the reduction in p_f, the total cost of her purchases would fall by $(p_{f1} - p_{f2})F_1$, a quantity of income that is now freed up and may be spent as she pleases. Second, the reduction in p_f reduces the price of food *relative to* the price of nonfood. This would induce the *substitution* of food for nonfood in the consumer's consumption basket, even if her purchasing power remained constant, because it means that food has become a better deal.

We decompose the effect of the food price reduction into substitution and income effects in Figure 6.2b, where the two solid budget lines starting at Y/p_n on the vertical axis describe the consumer's budget constraints before and after a food price reduction. The overall effect of the price reduction is to shift consumption from point a to point b. The dashed budget constraint represents a hypothetical situation in which the consumer is held at her initial level of utility but faces the new lower price of food. It has the same slope as the actual budget constraint she faces after the food price reduction, but it is tangent to the initial indifference curve I_1. The **substitution effect** of the food price reduction is defined to be the change in consumption from point a on the pre-price-reduction budget constraint to point c on the hypothetical budget constraint. This reflects the effect of making food cheaper relative to nonfood while holding the consumer's utility constant. The **income effect** is illustrated by the change from point c on the hypothetical budget constraint to point b on the post-price-change budget constraint. This reflects the effect of increasing real income or purchasing power while holding prices constant at the new levels. This decomposition attributes all the increase in utility arising out of the price reduction to the increase in purchasing power and thus to the income effect.

The income effect of the price reduction is identical to the effect of increasing income; both are represented by parallel shifts of a budget constraint. Thus the income effect of the reduction in p_f is to raise or lower F, depending on whether food is a normal or inferior good. The substitution effect of the food price reduction *must* be to raise F, because it is associated with a shift along an indifference curve from a point at which the slope is steeper to a point at which the slope is flatter. Given the convex shape of any indifference curve, this shift *must* be associated with a movement to the right (and down) along an indifference curve, and thus with an increase in F and reduction in N.

The overall effect of a food price reduction is the sum of the substitution effect, which must raise F, and the income effect which can raise or lower F depending on whether food is normal or inferior. We conclude that:

> If food is a normal good, then a reduction in the price of food raises the quantity of food consumed, and the impact on food consumption of the food price reduction is bigger than the impact of an increase in income that raises utility by the same amount. Empirical research is required to determine the size of this effect.

Allowing for multiple foods

In the real world, people allocate budgets across more than two items, including a variety of foods. Changes in income and prices can lead to changes not only in the overall levels of food and nonfood consumption but also in the relative importance of various foods in a consumer's diet.

Changes in the shares of food consumption expenditure devoted to different foods can weaken the effect of income on calorie intakes. Foods differ in taste, appearance, status, and convenience, as well as nutritional properties. If characteristics such as convenience or status are like normal goods, then increases in income might lead consumers to devote rising shares of their food expenditures to goods that offer more convenience and status. If such foods offer fewer calories per dollar spent, then income increases will have weaker effects on nutrient intakes than on total food expenditures.

Acknowledging the existence of multiple foods is especially important when examining the effects of a reduction in the price of a single food item, such as rice. Just as food price reductions induce substitution between food and nonfood in the consumer's overall consumption expenditure, so also do reductions in the price of rice induce substitution between rice and other foods within food expenditure. If rice is a normal good, then when the price of rice falls, the consumption of rice rises, and consumption of foods that people consider **complements** to rice also

Nonfood (N)

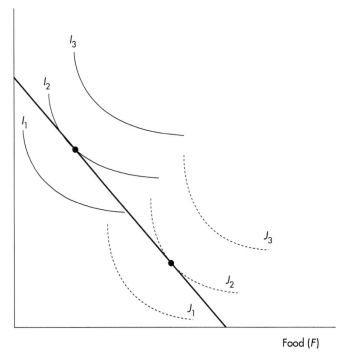

FIGURE 6.3
**Effects of Preference Differences or Preference Changes
on Consumption Choices**

Food (F)

rise, but consumption of foods that people consider **substitutes** for rice (such as wheat) fall. We conclude that:

A reduction in the price of a single food raises consumption of that food if it is a normal good. However, it will also reduce the consumption of substitute foods, weakening the overall effect of the food price reduction on calorie intakes.

Preference differences

When trying to understand differences across consumers in consumption choices, we must take into account not only differences in income and prices but also possible differences in preferences. Graphically, different preferences translate into different sets of indifference curves. For example, in Figure 6.3, indifference curves I_1, I_2, and I_3 might describe the preferences of Consumer i, while curves J_1, J_2, and J_3 describe the preferences of Consumer j, who apparently places greater priority on food consumption relative to nonfood consumption. Consumers' preferences regarding food and nonfood might differ because some have more dependent household members (increasing food consumption needs) or simply because their tastes differ.

Preference changes

In standard economic models assuming neoclassical rationality, the consumer's utility function is fixed and remains constant throughout any analysis. Her utility function might have been shaped by her early childhood experiences, as well as by her genes, but it is largely unchanging throughout her adult life. The details of her utility function help determine how she would respond to changes in income or prices, but the utility function itself does not change when socioeconomic conditions change.

It seems natural to question the standard assumption of fixed preferences regarding food consumption, however. If people value consumption of specific foods for their nutritional properties, taste, appearance, status, and convenience, then the relative value people place on the consumption of a specific food might change for at least three reasons. First, through schooling, public information campaigns, or their own experience, people might acquire new information about foods' nutritional properties or about the physical benefits of good nutrition. Second, they might perceive shifts in social norms regarding which foods are acceptable to eat or confer social status. Third, if their preferences are influenced by emotional associations, then persuasive advertising might alter the values they associate with consuming specific foods or other items.

We could represent a preference change graphically as a shift in a consumer's entire set of indifference curves. For example, the indifference curves I_1, I_2, and I_3 in Figure 6.3 could describe a consumer's preferences prior to a preference change, while J_1, J_2, and J_3 describe them after a change that raises the relative priority the consumer places on food consumption.

Once we admit that preferences might change for these reasons, we must conclude that:

> It may be possible to increase consumption of nutritious foods, even without raising income or altering prices, if nutrition education, general education, advertising, or social processes induce people to place increased priority on the consumption of nutrient-rich foods.

Empirical study of food demands

Efforts to estimate the size of income or price effects on food consumption choices often involve regression analysis using household survey data. A regression produces a good estimate of the causal effect of income on (say) rice consumption only if it controls adequately for *all* socioeconomic factors that differ across observations in the dataset and that cause differences in rice consumption. For a review of regression analysis and of the conditions under which it yields good estimates of causal effects, see Appendix A. Basic consumer theory helps us identify the list of "all socioeconomic factors" for which we must include controls in such regressions. We learn that:

> Regression analysis of household survey data delivers good estimates of the causal effect of income, prices, or other factors on the consumption of a particular food only when the regressions control adequately for *all* of the following variables that vary across households in the sample: household income; the price of the food in question; prices of goods that are significant substitutes or complements for the food in question; and demographic, cultural, and knowledge variables affecting preferences.

The theory also points to the importance of measuring income and prices in real or relative terms rather than nominal terms, because it implies that if Y, p_f, and p_n all rose by the same percentage, then Figure 6.1a, and the consumer's optimal choice of F and N, would remain unchanged. For more on econometric estimation of the impacts of income and prices on consumer choices, see Pollak and Wales (1992).

The magnitudes of demand relationships are often expressed as **elasticities**. If R is the quantity of rice consumed, then the elasticity of R with respect to Y measures the percentage change in R brought about by a 1 percent increase in Y (while holding prices constant). This **income elasticity** is positive for normal goods. Similarly, the elasticity of R with respect to p_r measures the percentage change in R brought about by a 1 percent increase in p_r (while holding Y and other prices constant). Except in unusual cases, we expect such an **own price elasticity** to be negative. For a refresher on how to interpret the magnitudes of elasticities, see problem 3.

6.2C **Nutrition policy**

It is natural to consider reducing malnutrition by increasing people's incomes, whether directly through a cash transfer program or indirectly through development policies aimed at raising incomes in wage and self-employment. Basic consumer theory reminds us, however, that households use additional income in the ways they consider best, and they do not necessarily spend it all on improving nutrition. Thus the theory leads us to ask the empirical question: How effective is additional income for improving the nutrition of the poor?

Empirical studies from around the world demonstrate that even very poor people spend at least 10 to 20 percent of their income on nonfood items. Banerjee and Duflo (2007) report much higher fractions. Some of the nonfood expenditure is used to meet urgent needs for home repairs, basic cooking utensils, children's clothing, fertilizer, or feed for goats or chickens, and some involves purchase of tobacco and alcohol (Alderman, 1986; Sadoulet et al., 2001; Barrett, 2002; Banerjee and Duflo, 2007; MCDSS/GTZ 2007).

Studies demonstrate further that calorie consumption rises much more slowly than total food consumption expenditure, because as incomes rise, people dedicate larger fractions of their food budget to foods that cost more per calorie but deliver more flavor, convenience, or status. For example, Bouis and Haddad (1992) estimate that the elasticity of calorie intake with respect to income among low-income households in the Philippines is very low, in the 0.08 to 0.14 range. Other estimates are somewhat higher than this, in the 0.3 to 0.5 range (e.g., Sub-ramanian and Deaton, 1996), but most researchers agree that the elasticity is significantly below 1. Box 6.1 discusses the estimation of the calorie–income elasticity. As a result, the World Bank (2006) and others conclude:

> Although general processes of broad-based economic growth, and more specific efforts to give cash to poor households, can and do improve nutrition, they tend to do so only slowly.

If giving cash to poor households has only modest impacts on nutrition, should policymakers consider giving these households food rather than cash? Basic consumer theory offers some surprising answers. Figure 6.4 examines the impact of distributing D units of free rice to a consumer under two alternative assumptions about the consumer's preferences. In both panels, the horizontal and vertical axes measure consumption of rice (R) and other items (O). The solid diagonal line segments extending from Y/p_o to Y/p_r indicate the budget lines before the distribution of rice.

The post-distribution budget lines are described by the dashed line segments in Figures 6.4a and b. If the consumer chose to spend all of her cash income Y on items other than rice, she would consume Y/p_o units of other items but would also consume D units of rice as a result of the distribution. Thus, instead of starting at Y/p_o on the vertical axis, the new budget line effectively starts D units to the right at the point a. (The consumer could also consume anywhere on the horizontal segment to the left of a, but would never choose to, because she would be letting some distributed food go to waste.) If she chose to spend all cash income on rice, she would consume $Y/p_r + D$ units of rice and no other items. Her budget line after the food distribution lies everywhere to the right of the original budget constraint by D units and is thus parallel to the original budget constraint. We may think of her post-distribution budget constraint in either diagram as described by two connected line segments: the horizontal segment from the vertical axis to point a and the dashed post-distribution budget line.[2]

---

[2]In drawing the food distribution budget line as in Figure 6.4, we are assuming that the consumer cannot resell the food she receives in the distribution. If she could sell any quantity she wishes of the distributed rice at the price p_r per unit and use the proceeds to purchase other items at the price p_o, then her budget constraint would continue up and to the left of point a, on a segment with the same slope as the rest of the budget constraint. The food would be as good as cash to her and would simply shift her budget constraint out in a parallel fashion, just as a cash transfer would. In Chapter 8 we will learn about transaction costs, which often deter people from trading away distributed foods in this way.

≡ Box 6.1 Estimating the Calorie–Income Elasticity

As in any econometric estimation, it is important to pay close attention to measurement when estimating the elasticity of calorie consumption with respect to income. Howarth Bouis and Lawrence Haddad (1992) point out that estimates of the calorie–income elasticity in early studies varied widely, from nearly 0.0 to 0.6. They argue that some of this variation arises out of differences in the measures of calorie consumption employed in the studies, and they argue further that studies employing what they consider the better measures produce estimates at the lower end of the range. Some early studies used measures of *calorie availability* within the household, which are constructed by taking households' reports of their food purchases and multiplying each food unit by its calorie content. Other studies used measures of *calorie intake by household members*, which are derived from observations of what household members actually consume. Calorie availability exceeds calorie intake when households use some of their food purchases to feed non-household members or when some food is wasted.

Bouis and Haddad point out two reasons why calorie–income elasticities might be overestimated when using calorie-availability measures rather than calorie-intake measures. First, as income rises, households tend to serve more meals to non-household members. Thus as income rises, calorie *availability* (which includes calories going to non-household members) rises more rapidly than calorie *intake* (which is the more relevant measure for nutrition policy purposes). Second, if people report the value of their food purchases inaccurately, this introduces errors into measures of calorie availability *and* total consumption expenditure, which is a commonly used proxy for income.

When peoples' food expenditure reports are too high or too low (relative to an accurate measure), measures of both their calorie availability and income are correspondingly too high or too low. As a result, this measurement error tends to make calorie consumption and income look more strongly positively correlated than they really are.

Bouis and Haddad assess the empirical importance of their arguments using data from the Philippines, which include measures of both calorie intake and calorie availability. They confirm that elasticity estimates employing calorie availability are much higher than estimates employing the preferred calorie intake measure. They also examine many variations in estimation methods. They conclude that the best estimates of the elasticity are quite low, in the 0.08 to 0.14 range, implying that a 10 percent increase in the incomes of the poor increases their calorie consumption by between just 0.8 and 1.4 percent.

Shankar Subramanian and Angus Deaton (1996) find such estimates implausibly low. In a careful study in which they measure food availability within the household net of meals provided to servants, they obtain calorie elasticity estimates in the 0.3 to 0.5 range. They argue that calorie intake measures such as those employed by Bouis and Haddad are probably measured with more error than food availability measures. If that measurement error is random (i.e., not correlated with the true calorie intake values or the regression error), then it is a source of attenuation bias, which causes the estimates to understate the true impact of income on calorie consumption (see Appendix A). Even if we accept their somewhat higher estimates, we must still conclude that calorie consumption rises substantially more slowly than income.

In each panel of Figure 6.4, the consumer's choice before the rice distribution is found at point b. In panel (a) the consumer's preferences are such that the highest utility she can attain after the rice distribution is at point c, where an indifference curve is tangent to the dashed budget line. At such a point, the consumer consumes all the rice distributed (*D*) *plus* some additional rice that she purchases out of her cash income *Y*. In panel b, depicting a consumer who places greater value on consumption of other items relative to rice, the post-distribution consumption choice is found at point a. This consumer consumes the entire rice distribution but purchases no additional rice, instead spending all of her cash income on other items.

Regardless of which diagram we use to analyze the consumption impact of the rice transfer, the basic theory forces us to recognize an important fact:

> When consumers receive distributions of free rice, the quantities of rice they consume are likely to rise by less than the quantity of rice received in the distribution.

We see this by noting that in both diagrams the horizontal distance between the pre- and post-distribution budget constraints is equal to the quantity of food distributed, and in both diagrams food consumption increases by *less* than this amount. The distribution allows consumers to cover some of their pre-distribution rice consumption with free rather than purchased rice, thereby freeing up cash that the consumers now choose to spend on whatever they wish. The increased purchasing power leads to increased purchases of *all* normal goods (and not just rice). Thus rice consumption rises by less than the quantity of rice distributed.

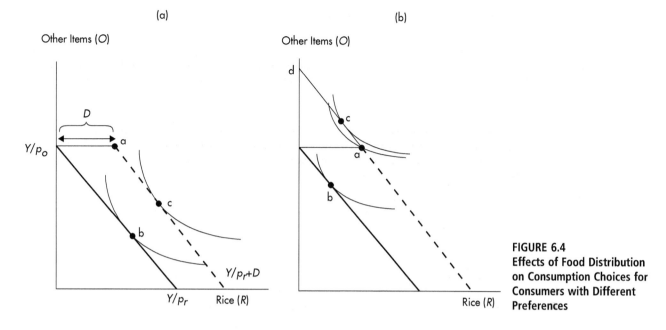

FIGURE 6.4
Effects of Food Distribution on Consumption Choices for Consumers with Different Preferences

In fact, the basic theory yields an even more striking implication:

> If, after they receive distributions of free rice, consumers choose to purchase additional rice out of their cash income, then (under the assumptions of the basic theory) the impact of the rice distribution on consumption choices is *exactly the same* as that of a cash distribution of equal value.

To see this, consider Figure 6.4a. When we cover the portion of the diagram to the left of point a, what does the uncovered portion of the diagram look like? It looks exactly like a diagram analyzing the impact of an increase in income, with a new budget constraint parallel to the original. The number of pesos of additional income that would be required to push the budget constraint to the right by D units is $p_r D$, which is the market value of the distributed rice. Thus the effect of the food distribution is the same as if the consumer had been given cash of comparable value. We can think of the consumer as using every unit of free rice to replace a unit of rice that the consumer would have purchased out of cash income in the absence of the distribution. This frees up $p_r D$ units of cash, which the consumer may now spend as she wishes.

Empirical studies confirm the theoretical prediction that food distributions to poor households increase food consumption by less than the quantities of food distributed. But they also often find that food distributions tend to increase consumption of the distributed foods by more than equivalent transfers of cash would, even when they spend some of their other income on the distributed food (Barrett, 2002), contradicting the basic theory. We consider possible reasons for this in Chapter 7. It remains the case, however, that food transfer impacts on food consumption are much more similar to cash transfer impacts than we might have guessed. (Their impacts can differ in other important ways, which we discuss in Chapters 8 and 15.)

Now consider the effect of the rice distribution for a consumer with preferences like those in Figure 6.4b. Here the rice distribution does increase rice consumption by more than if the consumer had been given a cash transfer of comparable value $p_r D$. After such a cash transfer, the budget line would pass through point a and would be parallel to the original budget constraint. It would thus be identical to the dashed budget line when looking to the right of point a, but it would continue up and to the left of point a along the solid line segment ending at point d. Facing this budget constraint, the consumer would have chosen to consume at point c and would thus have consumed *less* rice. We know this because the slope of the indifference curve touching point a must be less than the slope of the cash transfer budget line. (If it were higher, the consumer would maximize utility somewhere to the right along the dashed budget line rather than at the point a.) This means that the cash transfer budget line cuts through the indifference curve at point a, heading to the northwest, cutting from lower levels of utility to higher levels. The consumer thus achieves maximum utility under the cash transfer at a point to the northwest of a.

Notice, however, that had she been given cash instead of rice, the consumer depicted in Figure 6.4b would have enjoyed a *higher* level of utility. This leads to a stark and somewhat surprising conclusion of basic consumer theory:

> Under the assumptions of basic consumer theory, rice transfers have the potential to increase consumption of rice by *more* than would cash transfers of comparable value, but they do so only under conditions in which the rice transfers leave recipients *worse off* (i.e., at lower levels of utility) than comparable cash transfers.

Food distributions are most likely to have these consequences when the food distributions are large relative to household incomes (as would be the case in true emergency situations, in which households have little income with which to purchase additional food), or when the program distributes foods that are not commonly used and not much preferred locally (as when U.S. wheat received as food aid is distributed in regions of Africa where wheat is not commonly consumed). Anecdotal evidence suggests that food distributions sometimes do have these effects. Recipients of food transfers sometimes report wishing that they had received transfers in the form of cash rather than food and even engage in costly efforts to sell the unfamiliar grains in order to garner cash for purchasing more-familiar local grains and other urgently needed items.

For many years, explicit targeting of cash or food transfers to needy households was considered beyond the bureaucratic capacity of many developing countries. (See Chapter 15 on some of the difficulties involved.) Policymakers thus pursued an alternative approach to improving nutrition also suggested by the basic theory: reducing the economy-wide prices of key foods, thereby making the acquisition of adequate nutrition easier without the need for bureaucratic distributions of food or cash. For additional discussion of such **general consumer food subsidies**, see Chapter 17. Unfortunately:

> Basic consumer theory points to several weaknesses of using general food price reductions rather than targeted cash or food distributions to improve nutrition.

First, whereas a wheat price reduction increases a consumer's wheat consumption by more than a cash transfer of equivalent value, it increases the consumer's utility by less than the equivalent cash transfer would. Problem 4 establishes this, employing logic very similar to that employed in the comparison of cash and food distributions above. Second, general food subsidies channel costly benefits to *everyone* who purchases that food. Wealthy and well-nourished households often purchase larger absolute quantities of wheat than do the poor and malnourished. As a result, the cost per dollar of subsidy transferred to the poor tends to be very high for general food subsidies, because large fractions of the subsidy flow to the nonpoor. Finally, although a general consumer wheat subsidy increases consumption of wheat, it can also reduce consumption of foods that are substitutes for wheat. Results can sometimes be perverse. For example, a wheat subsidy in Brazil is widely thought to have *reduced* the nutritional status of the poor, because it caused them to shift consumption from rice toward bread, which offered fewer calories per dollar spent (Calegar and Schuh, 1988).

If consumers *choose* to spend only a fraction of a cash transfer on improved nutrition, the theory forces us to ask: On what grounds might policymakers claim it would be "better" for households to use cash transfers in more nutrition-enhancing ways? That is, on what grounds might a policymaker claim to be a better judge of what is best for a consumer than the consumer herself?

Such a claim is most defensible when policymakers have superior nutrition knowledge. We might wish to define "true" well-being as the utility households *would* derive from consumption *if* they had perfect information about the connections among food consumption, nutrient intakes, health, life expectancy, and well-being. Lacking such information, the utility they maximize differs from true well-being in a way that undervalues good nutrition. Under such circumstances, food subsidies that increase peoples' consumption of nutritious foods might indeed raise their true well-being by more than would a cash transfer, even though (as predicted by the basic theory) it reduces their perceived *utility* by less.

Empirical studies indeed suggest that exposure to nutrition information alters people's preferences in the direction of consuming more nutritious food. Block (2004), for example, shows that Indonesian mothers who have more schooling or who have acquired more nutrition knowledge through other sources use identical incomes to purchase more nutritious baskets of food relative to less knowledgeable mothers. Thus policymakers might indeed have reason to believe that they "know better" what poorly informed consumers would wish to consume if they had better nutrition knowledge.

But if the crux of the problem (of consumers spending what policymakers consider too small a fraction of cash transfers on nutritious food) is that consumers lack adequate nutrition knowledge, then policymakers should also consider attacking the problem directly by educating consumers about the nature and effects of good nutrition. Penny et al. (2005) offer an encouraging example of an intervention that improved nutrition in young children through nutrition education alone. The intervention informed new mothers in Peru about improved feeding practices for their children, including supplementary feeding with nutrient-dense chicken liver, eggs, and fish after six months of age. Randomized control trial results show that at 18 months of age, only five percent of children in intervention communities were significantly malnourished (with length at least two standard deviations shorter than the mean length for 18-month-old children in a well-nourished population), whereas 16 percent of children in the control group were significantly malnourished. It seems reasonable to conclude that:

> Nutrition education has the potential to improve nutrition outcomes significantly in some low-income settings.

A variety of programs now combine distributions of food or cash *and* nutrition education. Conditional cash transfer programs, such as Mexico's Progresa/Oportunidades program, combine cash transfers with requirements that beneficiaries attend nutrition education sessions (see Chapter 15). They have become popular in many parts of the developing world and appear to be successful in improving nutrition. In the United States the Women, Infants, and Children (WIC) program combines the distribution of food vouchers (for poor women) with nutrition education and is widely considered a great success (Barrett, 2002).

6.3 Labor Supply Choices, with Application to Child Labor

6.3A A motivation

The International Labour Organization (ILO) estimates that 152 million children aged 5 to 14 years and another 62 million aged 15 to 17 years are involved in child labor (ILO, 2010). Many observers see child labor as violating children's rights to proper childhoods, exposing them to harsh working conditions, and impoverishing their futures by preventing their education. Such concerns fuel efforts to condition international trade agreements on the enforcement of child labor prohibitions and to convince consumers in developed countries to buy only goods certified "child labor free" (Edmonds, 2008).

Economists instinctively respond to calls for child labor prohibitions by asking such questions as: Would child labor prohibitions leave children better off? Would they increase school enrollment rates? What other policy options are available for raising children's well-being and school attendance, and what are the relative merits of the various options? This section describes basic labor supply theory, which prompts economists to ask these questions and helps guide their efforts to answer them.

6.3B Basic labor supply theory: allocating time

Basic labor supply theory examines how people allocate time across competing uses. It emphasizes that work brings both benefits and costs. The primary benefit is the ability to buy goods and services with the income earned. The primary cost is the reduction of time available for other valuable activities.

The theory focuses on a decision-maker we will call a "labor supplier," who chooses how much time to allocate to wage labor and to other activities, seeking to maximize utility subject to time and cash constraints. His utility is assumed to be a function not only of his consumption of goods and services but also of the amount of time he is able to spend in nonlabor pursuits. His **time constraint** dictates that the total time he spends in wage labor and other pursuits cannot exceed the total waking hours he is free to allocate across these activities. His **cash constraint** dictates that his total expenditures on goods and services cannot exceed his total income, which includes both labor income he earns by working and any nonlabor income with which he is endowed. **Nonlabor income** includes transfer payments from the government or an NGO, gifts from other households, and receipts of rental payments on properties he owns and rents out.

A two-activity case

Consider a labor supplier endowed with T hours of time per week (not counting time required for sleep and meeting other basic needs) and M pesos of nonlabor income. He allocates time to just two activities: wage labor and home time. **Wage labor** (S) is time spent working for a wage of w per hour. **Home time** (H) is spent in recreation, education, child care, or other home activities, and it enters directly into his utility calculation as a good he values consuming. In developed-country discussions, nonwork time is sometimes labeled "leisure," but a broader label such as "home time" seems more appropriate in development studies.

His preferences are described by the utility function $U(C, H)$, which is a function only of the quantity of consumption items he consumes C and home time H, and exhibits positive but diminishing marginal utility in C and H. For convenience we set the price of consumption goods to 1 peso per unit, so that C represents both the physical quantity of consumption and the peso cost of consumption. This choice also implies that we will be holding the price of consumption goods constant throughout our entire analysis.

The labor supplier maximizes utility subject to the time constraint

$$S + H \leq T \tag{6.2}$$

and the cash constraint that

$$C \leq wS + M. \tag{6.3}$$

The requirements that $C \leq wS + M$ (from equation 6.3) and $S \leq T - H$ (from equation 6.2) together imply that $C \leq w(T - H) + M$. Rearranging, we learn that the labor supplier's choice of C and H must satisfy

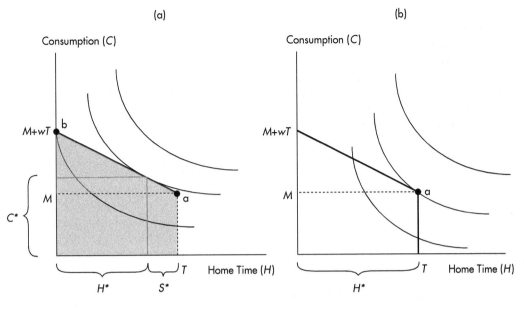

(a)   (b)

FIGURE 6.5
Basic Labor Supply Choices for Labor Suppliers with Different Preferences

$$C + wH \leq wT + M. \tag{6.4}$$

The right side of equation 6.4 is the total purchasing power the labor supplier would command *if* he allocated all available time to wage labor. This quantity, which economists call the labor supplier's **full income**, summarizes the market value of his time and nonlabor-income endowments and is entirely outside the labor supplier's current control. (Full income may be contrasted with the labor supplier's actual income, $wS + M$, which is determined in part by his choice of S.) The left side of equation 6.4 is a function of the choice variables C and H. Thus equation 6.4 tells us how the set of (C,H) options available to the labor supplier is limited by his endowments (T and M) and by the wage he faces in the labor market, as well as the price of consumption goods, which we are holding constant in the analysis.

Figure 6.5a summarizes this basic framework in a way that emphasizes its similarity to the consumer choice model described above. The two axes measure the two goods the labor supplier seeks to consume, C and H. Movements to the right in the diagram simultaneously indicate increases in home time (H) and reductions in labor supply ($S = T - H$).

The constraint described by equation 6.4 implies that the labor supplier may choose only combinations of C and H that lie on the solid sloped budget line connecting points a and b or in the shaded area below it. If he chose to spend all available time in home time, then he would enjoy T hours of home time but would earn no labor income and would be able to purchase only M pesos of consumption items, as indicated by point a in the diagram. If he devoted all time to wage labor, he would consume no home time but would earn the maximum possible labor income and would consume $M + wT$ in consumption items, as indicated by point b in the diagram. In between these extremes, each time he reduces H by one hour (moving to the left by one unit in the diagram) he increases his consumption expenditure by w pesos (rising by that amount in the diagram), and thus the slope of the constraint connecting point a and point b is $-w$.

We introduce the labor supplier's preferences into the diagram by drawing in indifference curves, and we identify the labor supplier's choice of C, H, and S by locating the point on the budget line where it just touches the highest possible indifference curve. The labor supplier in Figure 6.5a chooses to consume H^* home time, to supply $S^* = T - H^*$ hours of wage labor, and to enjoy $C^* = M + wS^*$ of consumption expenditure.

The similarities between Figure 6.5a and Figure 6.1a suggest that we can interpret equation 6.4 as a budget constraint in which full income, $wT + M$, plays a role similar to that of Y in the consumer choice model. The labor supplier may allocate this full income across the "purchase" of the two goods he cares about: consumption items and home time. The relevant cost of consumption goods is 1 peso per unit. The relevant per-hour cost of consuming home time, or the **opportunity cost of time**, is the full income given up by using an hour as home time rather than using it for work (w). The greater the wage, the greater the cost of home time relative to consumption goods and the steeper his budget constraint.

Corner solutions

As long as M is positive, the budget constraint has a *corner* at point a, rather than ending in an intercept along the horizontal axis. It is thus possible that the solution to the labor supplier's utility maximization problem is a **corner solution**, as depicted in Figure 6.5b. The labor supplier whose preferences are depicted in Figure 6.5b, as compared to the one in Figure 6.5a, places greater value on home time relative to consumption goods, perhaps because he has more young children requiring care. This labor supplier chooses to supply no labor, instead allocating all available time to home activities and consuming only what he can purchase with his nonlabor income.

Effects of an increase in nonlabor income

If we increase nonlabor income from M_1 to M_2 while holding w constant, then in graphs like those of Figure 6.6, the kink point a and the vertical axis intercept both rise by the same amount, and the budget constraint shifts up in a parallel fashion. For the decision maker depicted in Figure 6.6a, who supplies some labor prior to the increase, an increase in M (as the result, for example, of a program distribution of cash to poor households) shifts his budget constraint in much the same way that an increase in Y shifted the budget constraint for the consumer of Figure 6.1. If the labor supplier treats both consumption and home time as normal goods, then the increase in income leads to an increase in the consumption of both goods, as in the shift from b to c in Figure 6.6a. Under such circumstances, the receipt of additional nonlabor income leads to a reduction in labor supply and thus a reduction in labor income. This implies that the receipt of nonlabor income increases consumption expenditure by less than the amount of nonlabor income received.

For the decision maker of Figure 6.6b, who supplies no labor prior to the increase in M, labor supply and labor income do not change (remaining at zero), and consumption expenditure rises one full dollar for every dollar of additional nonlabor income received.

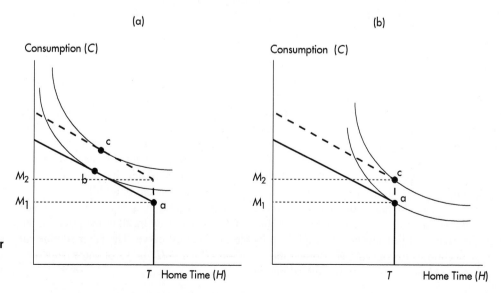

FIGURE 6.6
Effects of Nonlabor Income Increases on Labor Supply Choices for Labor Suppliers with Different Preferences

We conclude that:

> If a person initially supplies any labor, and if home time is a normal good, then an increase in nonlabor income causes the person to *reduce* labor supply, as he spends some of the additional full income on increasing home time. Empirical research is required to determine the size of this effect.

Effects of an increase in the wage

When we hold M constant and increase the wage from w_1 to w_2, the budget line's corner point a remains in the same place, while the intercept along the vertical axis rises, as in the shift from the solid to dashed budget constraint in Figure 6.7a. For the labor supplier depicted there, this leads to a shift in time allocation from point b to point c.

The wage change induces an income effect because it increases the cash value of the labor supplier's time endowment and thus his full income. It also induces a substitution effect, because it increases the cost of consuming home time in terms of foregone consumption expenditure. Formally, we may define the **substitution effect** of a wage increase as the effect on time allocation of an increase in w while holding the labor supplier's utility constant at the initial level. We define the **income effect** of a wage increase as the effect on time allocation of an increase in nonlabor income that raises the labor supplier's utility from the initial level to the level after the wage increase while holding the wage constant at the new higher level. The solid budget constraints in Figure 6.7b depict the labor supplier's full income constraints before and after an increase in the wage. The dashed budget constraint depicts the hypothetical situation in which the labor supplier faces the new higher wage but is held at his initial level of utility. The substitution effect is illustrated by the shift in consumption from point b to point d, and the income effect is given by the shift from point d to point c.

Notice that if home time is a normal good, then the income and substitution effects of the wage increase on labor supply work in opposite directions. The income effect of the wage increase is to increase home time (and reduce labor supply) if home time is a normal good. The substitution effect must reduce home time (and raise labor supply). We might surmise that the income effect on home time consumption would tend to be small at low wage and income levels, when increasing consumption of food and other basic necessities is more urgent, but that

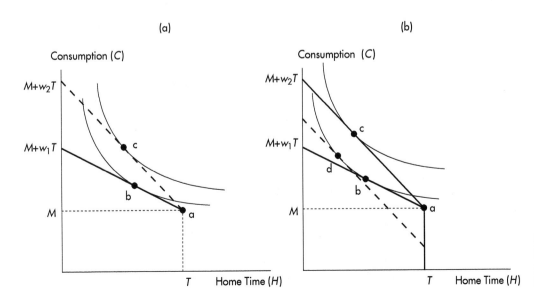

FIGURE 6.7
Effects of a Wage Increase on Basic Labor Supply Choices

the income effect might become larger at higher income levels. This suggests that the own price elasticity of wage labor might fall as the wage level rises, and it might even become negative.

Empirical estimates of wage elasticities of household labor supply in developing countries are few and far between, but they seem to suggest that labor supplies rise when wages rise, though the elasticities are low (Jayachandran, 2006). Thus:

> Theoretically, an increase in the wage can cause a person's labor supply to rise or fall. Empirical evidence suggests that it rises, though the elasticities may be low.

Multiple uses of time

In reality, people allocate time across more than two uses, including work, household chores, education, and recreation. Much of what we learned from the two-activity time allocation case extrapolates to the more complicated multiple-activity case. Increases in nonlabor income increase the time allocated to any uses that can be thought of as normal goods. An increase in an individual's wage brings an income effect that tends to increase all those same normal activities while reducing labor supply, and it also brings substitution effects that tend to increase labor supply relative to other time uses. Increases in the benefits of nonwork activities, or reductions in their explicit costs, tend to increase time devoted to those other activities and can reduce or increase work time, depending on whether those activities are substitutes for or complements to work time. Once we acknowledge the multiple uses of time, we recognize that:

> When a wage increase raises wage labor time, this time may be drawn out of various other uses, including household chores, recreation, and homework, as well as time in school, and empirical research is required to determine how these alternative time uses are interrelated.

Changes in the time endowment

We learned in Chapter 2 that households in developing countries often spend long hours carrying water from distant sources or searching for firewood. The time spent in such activities is unavailable either for income-generating work or for enjoying home time. Infrastructure projects that provide households with water or energy sources close to their homes, which reduce the hours per day required for collecting water and fuel, expand the total amount of time (T) that is available for wage work and home time. Expanding total available time from T to T^* would shift the budget constraint to the right and would increase the budget constraint's intercept on the vertical axis by $w(T^* - T)$. This suggests that:

> Interventions that reduce the time households must spend carrying water or collecting fuel free up time that households may allocate to home time (including time spent in school) or to work time (increasing labor income). Regardless of how they use the freed-up time, the intervention raises their well-being.

More generally, the basic theory highlights the important observation that *time is valuable*. Remembering this simple point will be of great importance later in the text, when we contemplate households' choices about whether or not to take advantage of new opportunities created by policies and programs.

Preference differences and preference changes

Social norms help shape preferences toward labor supply and other time uses. Cultural prohibitions can prevent households from allocating any time of its female members to wage labor outside the home, limiting the total time T that may be allocated to wage labor activities. Social norms might also shape the value parents place on sending their children to school rather than keeping them home to work in the fields.

Multimember households

Most potential workers live in multimember households. If we are willing to assume that a single decision maker within the household (or the entire household acting unanimously) makes a joint choice about the allocation of every member's time, then we can analyze such choices by treating home time for each member as a separate good that the household values consuming. (We will point out some inadequacies of this view of multimember households in Chapter 7.) This suggests that:

> If a household considers a particular member's nonwork time (including time in school) to be a normal good, then that member's nonwork time will rise when the household's nonlabor income or time endowment rises and when wages faced by other household members rise (increasing household full income). An increase in the person's own wage can reduce or increase his home time, depending on whether the substitution effect of this wage change outweighs the income effect.

6.3C Child labor

Familiarity with the basic labor supply model, and with economic logic more generally, helps us to identify and question three assumptions implicit in many calls for child labor prohibitions: that children are put to work by selfish decision makers who do not take the children's welfare fully into account, that children go to school if and only if they do not work, and that laws prohibiting child labor would be effective in eliminating all opportunities for children to work.

The basic labor supply model raises the possibility that parents put their children to work, even when they care deeply about their children's well-being, because the income from child labor provides children with food and other necessities, and the parents judge that these benefits outweigh the costs. If this is the case, eliminating child labor opportunities could leave children worse off.

Careful thought about time allocation choices furthermore raises the possibility that children might attend school even when they also work, and they might fail to attend school even when they do not work. Thus child labor prohibitions need not raise school attendance even if they successfully reduce child labor.

Economic logic more generally suggests that child labor prohibitions will be effective only if employers of children perceive a significant threat of detection and punishment for noncompliance. Child labor prohibitions may thus have little impact if it is costly and difficult to monitor and punish the employers of child labor.

The basic labor supply model also points to a wide array of alternative policies that might reduce child labor and that are more likely to raise child welfare and school enrollment rates than child labor prohibitions. These include efforts to raise family incomes, improve the rewards for schooling, reduce the cost of schooling, and reduce the time families must spend collecting water and fuel.

Motivated by these concerns, economists have generated a large body of empirical research on the causes and consequences of child labor. For an excellent review, see Edmonds (2008). Here we highlight just a few of the insights revealed by empirical study. We draw on Table 6.1, which presents a small subset of the household survey statistics assembled in Edmonds (2008). In the table, a child is recorded as engaged in a work activity if he or she devoted at least one hour to it in the last week. Children are identified as attending school if they have attended school in the

■ TABLE 6.1   Percentages of Children Aged 5 to 14 Years Undertaking Various Activities

Country	Any Work	Market Work Outside Home	Market Work Inside Home	Domestic Work	School	Any Work and No School	No Work and No School
Albania	62.7	3.5	29.5	56.1	54.7	32.6	12.7
Cameroon	85.2	30.8	42.7	81.1	94.5	5.0	0.4
Kenya	66.8	2.2	1.0	66.3	95.9	2.8	1.0
Mongolia	91.7	1.4	20.6	91.2	95.2	4.6	0.2
Venezuela	64.6	4.5	3.9	62.4	92.0	3.8	4.2
Vietnam	57.8	1.9	23.4	51.7	95.1	4.3	0.6

Source: Edmonds (2008).

last year. "Market work inside the home" involves production of goods and services on a family farm or in a family business. "Market work outside the home" involves work for pay for employers outside the home. "Domestic work" includes cooking, cleaning, carrying water, caring for siblings, and similar activities. Children are recorded as involved in "any work" if they are involved in any of these three work activities.

The definition of child work in Table 6.1 is somewhat broader than the ILO definition, which itself is very broad. The ILO counts as child laborers all children younger than 12 years who work at least one hour per week and children 12 to 14 years who work at least 14 hours per week in the production of goods and services. They also include children younger than 14 years involved in hazardous work and children younger than 18 years involved in "unconditional worst forms of child labor," which include forced labor, prostitution, armed conflict, and other illicit activities. The definition excludes children involved in domestic work, even when this absorbs many hours per day.

A first insight from empirical study is that most of the work that absorbs children's time in developing countries involves work on family farms, in family businesses, or in household chores, often working side by side with parents who are doing the same work. The first four columns of Table 6.1 indicate that market work inside the home and domestic work are much more common than market work outside the home. Other data sources document that large fractions of child market work are in agriculture, forestry, and fishing, but only a very small fraction is in manufacturing. This suggests that:

> Much child labor takes place in the children's homes or on farms and is thus likely to be outside the range of effective enforcement for child labor prohibitions.

The ILO estimates that 8.4 million children (a small fraction of all child laborers) are involved in the unconditional worst forms of child labor (ILO, 2002). Such activities demand attention, but they, too, are unlikely to be curtailed by standard approaches to enforcing child labor prohibitions.

A second insight from empirical study is that schooling is not generally incompatible with work. Table 6.1 reveals that the majority of working children attend school. This is possible because many working children are engaged in fewer than 10 hours of market work per week (see Figure 1 in Edmonds, 2008). Furthermore, in the countries in which larger fractions of working children do not attend school, large fractions of nonworking children also remain out of school (see Table 6.1), suggesting that obstacles other than child labor may be more important in preventing school attendance. Thus:

> Even if child labor prohibitions are effective in reducing child labor, they need not increase the schooling of child workers by as much as they reduce their labor.

In some cases, work by older siblings also appears to help cover the cost of sending younger siblings to school, and thus effective child labor prohibitions might even cause enrollment rates to decline by causing the siblings of child workers to drop out of school (Edmonds, 2008).

Third, child laborers tend to live in poor households and sometimes make a significant contribution to family income. Cross-country studies demonstrate that child labor is more prevalent in poorer countries, and studies that follow families over time often find that child participation in work rises significantly when the household is hit by an economic downturn, such as a crop failure or the loss of the household head's job (Beegle et al., 2006; Duryea et al., 2007). Studies estimate that labor by 13-year-olds contributed 13 percent of household income in Bolivia (Psacharopoulos, 1997) and that children in Nepal contribute 11 percent to the value of family agricultural production (Menon et al., 2005). Thus:

> Poverty can lead parents to put children to work, even when they take the children's welfare fully into account. Under such circumstances, eliminating children's contribution to family income can significantly reduce the households' ability to provide children and other family members with basic necessities.

Fourth, increases in family income (all else equal) tend to reduce child labor and increase schooling. Estimation of the effect of household income growth on child labor and schooling is complicated, because the forces that cause household incomes to rise often simultaneously raise the wages children could earn in child labor. The increase in household income tends to reduce child labor if child home time is a normal good (an income effect). The increase in child labor wages induces both an income effect that tends to reduce child labor *and* a substitution effect that tends to increase it, implying a net wage effect that may be positive or negative but that we might often guess would be positive, as described above. It is difficult to distinguish the income and wage effects, and the net effect may differ from place to place. In Brazil, a coffee boom that raised both income and wages brought an increase in child labor. As Kruger (2007) points out, the wage effect may have been especially strong in this case, because the coffee boom was expected to be temporary, and families expected children to return to school after the boom ended (thus the opportunity cost of temporary work was perceived to be quite low). Many parents of child laborers also owned no land and thus enjoyed no direct income gain from the increased coffee prices. In Vietnam, however, trade reform–driven increases in rice prices, in the presence of an unusually egalitarian distribution of rice farming land, led to widespread household income increases, including among many poor households. This gave rise to income responses that outweighed the wage responses and caused child labor to diminish (Edmonds and Pavcnik, 2006). See Box 6.2. Thus:

> In at least some contexts, rising household incomes appear to reduce child labor, but rising incomes are often associated with rising child wages, which can create countervailing pressure for child labor to increase. The net effect varies from context to context.

Fifth, empirical evidence also suggests that improvements in the benefits of schooling and reductions in the cost of schooling can raise school enrollment and, perhaps to a lesser extent, reduce child labor. For example, Foster and Rosenzweig (1996) argue that introduction of high-yielding rice varieties raised the returns to education in rural India and that where these returns rose the most, school enrollments rose the most. Kochar (2004) demonstrates that rural school enrollment is higher where returns to schooling are higher in nearby urban areas. Case and Yogo (1999) show that where pupil-to-teacher ratios are lower (and school quality is thus presumably higher) black children in South Africa are more likely to attend school, and Shafiq (2007) shows that boys are more likely to attend school and less likely to work where the costs of schooling are

≡ **Box 6.2** The Impacts of Rice Price Increases on Child Labor in Vietnam

During the 1990s Vietnam greatly reduced restrictions on both international and internal trade in rice. Across communities throughout Vietnam, the reform led to average rice price increases (relative to the consumer price index) of 30 percent. (For more on this policy reform, see Chapter 17.) These rice price increases might have affected the incidence of child labor through many channels. They raised farm profits and family income for the large fraction of rural Vietnamese households who produce and sell rice. If child home time is a normal good, such increases in income would tend to reduce child labor. On the other hand, the rice price increases reduced purchasing power for households that buy rice, inducing income effects that would raise child labor for those households. The rice price increases might also have increased the demand for labor by farmers who sell rice (see section 6.4 for qualifications), tending to raise the relative return to employing their own children in farm work and also tending to raise market demand and market wages for child labor. If the substitution effects associated with higher child wages outweigh their income effects, this would tend to raise child labor. Empirical work is required to determine the net effect of all these changes.

Eric Edmonds and Nina Pavcnik (2005) point out that the amount by which rice prices increased varied significantly from community to community in Vietnam (for reasons that will become clear in Chapter 8). The authors use this variation in rice price increases to study the effect of rice price changes on child labor. They employ household survey data on children between 6 and 16 years old in 115 rural communities in 1993 and 1998, including more than 4,000 children in each year. They treat children as child laborers if in the last seven days they worked at least seven hours in household production activities (including wood collection, household chores, and household repairs) or if they worked at all in agriculture, wage employment, or a family business. By this definition, the percentage of children laboring fell from 60 percent in 1993 to 48 percent in 1998. Through regressions examining the effect of the local rice price on a child's labor status, while controlling for community characteristics, child characteristics, and seasons, they find that larger local rice price increases led to larger reductions in child labor. They estimate that the 30 percent increase in rice price accounted for a 10-percentage-point reduction in child labor.

In an effort to confirm that the association they found between rice price increases and child labor reductions truly arose out of households' rational child labor supply responses to changing economic conditions (rather than to some spurious reason for correlation) and to understand better the strength of income effects on households' child labor choices, the authors engage in more detailed analysis guided by economic theory. They point out that (assuming child home time is a normal good) income effects should reduce child labor the most in households that sell the most rice and thus gain the most income from rice price increases, but they should tend to increase child labor in households that buy rice. They also point out that if rising market demand and wages for child labor induce substitution into child agricultural labor away from child home time, they should also induce substitution into child agricultural labor away from child time in household production. They limit attention to households in their sample that were observed in both 1993 and 1998, and they examine the effects of local rice price increases on child agricultural labor and child household production, allowing these effects to differ depending on the magnitude of household rice sales. They indeed find that child labor overall (whether in agriculture or home production) fell the most in the households experiencing the greatest income increases (consistent with a role for negative income effects on child labor) and that child labor time allocated to home production fell relative to time in agricultural labor (consistent with a role for positive substitution effects). For most households the income effects were large enough to outweigh substitution effects and reduce child labor.

This analysis of the income and substitution effects of rice price increases on child labor makes clear that even if all households around the world valued children's home time equally, rice price increases would have very different effects on child labor from place to place. Unusually equal land distribution, low levels of rural landlessness, and widespread involvement in rice production in Vietnam led most households to enjoy significant income effects, outweighing substitution effects and thus tending to reduce child labor. Where rice is an important staple for many households, but land is unequally distributed and few households sell rice, the income effects would be more muted relative to substitution effects, and child labor might rise.

---

lower in Bangladesh. School enrollment rates also tend to rise when road construction projects reduce the time cost and difficulty of walking to school.

Sixth, conditional cash transfer programs (CCTs), which simultaneously increase household income (inducing an income effect) and raise the net return to education relative to child labor (inducing a substitution effect in favor of schooling), seem to be particularly effective in raising enrollments for children in some circumstances. These programs raise household income by providing cash transfers, and they raise the net returns to education (relative to child labor) by allowing households to collect benefits only when their children are attending school regularly. Mexico's Progresa/Opportunidades CCT is considered very successful in raising school enrollment rates, especially among older children for whom school enrollment rates were not very high before the program. Schultz (2004) shows that for households eligible to participate in the program, children's wage and market work declined (though by less than school enrollment increased), and Skoufias and Parker (2001) show that domestic work for girls declined. de Janvry et al. (2006) show that Progresa transfers prevented families from withdrawing children from school when bad weather reduced family agricultural incomes, but it did not prevent children from entering the labor force at those times. CCTs in other Latin American countries show similar patterns of impact. We conclude that:

> A variety of school-related policies—including improvements in school quality, improvement in returns to education, reductions in money and time costs of schooling, and distribution of conditional cash transfers tied to schooling—have the potential to increase school enrollments and reduce child labor (though by less than they increase school enrollment). Because such policies expand household opportunities while child labor prohibitions reduce them, they are more likely to increase child and family well-being.

6.4 Basic Producer Theory, with Application to Green Revolution Labor Market Effects

6.4A A motivation

Over the second half of the 20th century, global incomes rose while the world population doubled, nearly tripling the world demand for food. World food supply kept pace as a result of technical change in agriculture, which allowed large increases in per-acre yields of basic food crops (Ruttan, 2002). Much of the increased food production took place in the developing world as a result of the Green Revolution, the adoption of high-yielding varieties of rice, corn, and wheat, which were developed by international crop research institutes funded by the Ford Foundation and Rockefeller Foundation (see Box 20.1).

The Green Revolution contributed to GDP growth and prevented real food prices from rising. Yet for many years, it remained controversial because of suspicions that it channeled disproportionate benefits to better-off farmers and even left some of the rural poor worse off. One suspicion was that it encouraged labor-displacing mechanization, which reduced the demand for agricultural labor, to the detriment of low-skilled and landless rural workers. Thus if we are to fully grasp the impacts of the Green Revolution, we must look closely at its impact on the demand for labor. The basic producer theory expounded in this section offers useful guidance for studying this and many other issues.

6.4B Basic producer theory: maximizing profits

Basic producer theory focuses on a producer who is endowed with a technology for producing goods or services and with **fixed factors of production**, such as capital and land, which she owns or has access to in quantities that are fixed, at least in the short run. She chooses how much labor to hire, how much to purchase of **variable inputs** such as fertilizer or cotton, and how much output to produce, seeking to maximize **profits**.[3] Her profits are the difference between the revenue she derives from selling her outputs and the costs she incurs when hiring labor and buying variable inputs. The technology she faces is summarized by a production function (as defined in Chapter 3). If she is a small participant in large, competitive markets for inputs and outputs, then she is a **price taker**, and market conditions dictate the prices she must charge for outputs and pay for inputs.

---

[3]The standard assumption of utility maximization reduces to profit maximization when the only choices open to the decision maker pertain to input use, production, and sales, and her utility is a function only of the goods and services she can consume by spending what remains of sales revenue after paying for inputs.

The case of one output and one variable input

Consider first a producer who manufactures a single output, cloth, according to the production function

$$Q = F(L; K, A) \tag{6.5}$$

where Q is yards of cloth, L is hours of low-skill labor, K is the quantity of capital equipment, A indexes the current state of technology, and the function $F(.)$ describes the maximum quantity of cloth that can be obtained from L hours of labor (given current levels of K and A). We focus on the **short run**, in which the producer may choose hours of labor (L) but takes the quantity of capital K and level of technology A as given. As in Chapter 3, we assume that the function $F(.)$ exhibits diminishing marginal returns to either input. If p is the price per yard of cloth and w is the hourly wage for low-skill labor, then the producers' profit is $pQ - wL$. (We ignore any fees she must pay for the use of capital when calculating costs and profits here, because she has no control over those costs in the short run; thus, whatever choice of L and Q maximizes profit while ignoring capital costs would also maximize profits while acknowledging them.) Not wishing to waste any hired labor, she chooses a combination of Q and L that is *on* the production function. Her choice reduces to one of picking the level of L (and implied Q) that maximizes profits.

The two panels of Figure 6.8 offer two useful ways to summarize basic producer theory for this simple case. In Figure 6.8a the horizontal axis measures hours of labor (L). The vertical axis measures pesos of revenue and cost. The downward-sloping schedule describes the contribution to total revenue of each successive unit of labor employed. It is equal to the value of the additional yards of cloth produced when each unit of labor is added to production (while holding K and A constant). That is, it is equal to the **value of the marginal product of labor** (*VMPL*), which in turn is equal to the (physical) marginal product of labor (*MPL*) multiplied by the price of a unit of output p. Its downward slope reflects the assumption of diminishing marginal returns.

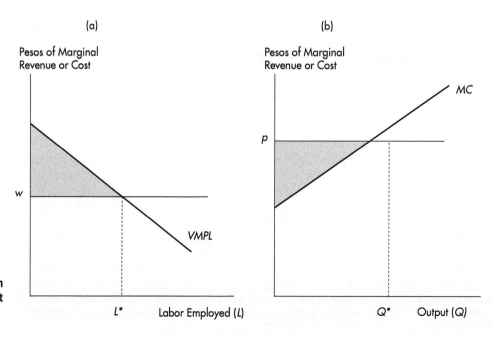

FIGURE 6.8
Labor Demand and Output Supply Choices in a Simple Model of Profit Maximization

The horizontal line is drawn at the height of the wage w. It represents the **marginal cost** of a unit of labor, or the amount by which total costs increase when a unit of labor is added to the payroll.

The profit-maximizing level of labor use L^* is found at the intersection of the $VMPL$ and w lines. If the producer chose to employ a quantity of labor less than L^*, and thus found herself using a quantity of labor to the left of L^* in the diagram, the $VMPL$ would be greater than the wage, and it would be possible to increase profits by increasing L. Similarly, if the producer started with more than L^* units of labor, she would be able to increase profits by reducing L. Only at L^* is there no potential to increase profits by increasing or decreasing L. The vertical distance between the $VMPL$ schedule and the wage line (to the left of L^*) indicates the addition to profits associated with each successive unit of production. The area of the shaded triangle is thus equal to total profits associated with employing L^* units of labor.

Figure 6.8b describes the very same profit-maximizing choice in another way. Here the vertical axis again measures revenue and cost in pesos, but the horizontal axis measures yards of cloth Q, rather than L. The line drawn at the height p indicates the addition to revenue associated with each additional yard of cloth produced. The marginal cost (MC) line indicates the addition to cost associated with each additional yard of cloth produced. The marginal cost equals the product of the wage w and the quantity of labor that would be required to produce the additional yard of cloth and thus equals w $(1/MPL)$. The marginal product of labor declines as L increases, and thus the marginal cost of producing an additional yard of cloth must increase as Q increases. As long as the marginal cost lies below the marginal revenue (p), producing one more yard of cloth would increase profits. Profits are maximized at the quantity Q^*, where the marginal cost just equals p. The vertical distance between the price line and the MC schedule to the left of Q^* indicates the addition to profit associated with each successive unit of output. In this diagram, too, the area of the shaded triangle equals profit. The two diagrams are two ways of illustrating the same production choice, and the two triangles have identical area.

Effects of changes in output price, wage, and technology

Using either of the diagrams in Figure 6.8, we can demonstrate the following:

- An increase in p, which shifts up the $VMPL$ schedule in Figure 6.8a and the price line in Figure 6.8b, while leaving the wage line and marginal cost schedule unchanged, leads to an increase in both the quantity of cloth supplied and the quantity of low-skill labor demanded.
- An increase in w, which shifts up the wage line in Figure 6.8a and the marginal cost schedule in Figure 6.8b, leads to reductions in both cloth supply and labor demand.
- Increases in K or A that increase the marginal productivity of labor, causing the $VMPL$ schedule to shift up in Figure 6.8a and the marginal cost schedule to shift down in Figure 6.8b, would lead to increases in labor demand and output supply.

Multiple variable inputs, single output

When low-skill labor is the only variable input (as in the model just described), the only way to expand production is to employ more low-skill labor. Thus any changes in prices, wages, capital, or technology that prompt the producer to expand production also increase her demand for low-skilled labor. When producers' variable inputs include skilled labor and other inputs as well as unskilled labor, and in the long run when capital inputs are variable as well, they may be able to increase production without increasing low-skilled labor. Producers with multiple variable inputs must choose both the **scale of production** (i.e., how many units of cloth to produce) and the **factor proportions** to use in producing each unit (e.g., whether to use lots of capital and little low-skill labor, or little capital and lots of low-skill labor).

For producers with multiple variable inputs, increases in output prices, reductions in input prices, capital accumulation and technical change all increase the value of a yard of cloth relative to the marginal cost of producing it and increase the desired scale of production (just as we saw in Figure 6.8b for the simpler case). Many of these changes, however, also cause some variable inputs to become cheaper or more productive relative to others, motivating the producer to substitute relatively cheaper inputs for relatively more expensive inputs. For example, when the wage for low-skill labor falls, the reduction in the cost of low-skill labor relative to the cost of other inputs can lead producers to employ more low-skill labor (and less of some other inputs) per unit of output produced.

We may decompose the overall effect of a change in a price, fixed factor, or technology on the demand for low-skilled labor (or any other input) into a scale effect and an input substitution effect. The **scale effect** refers to the increase in the demand for low-skill labor that would occur *if* the producer chose to increase the scale of production while continuing to use the same factor proportions. The **input substitution effect** refers to the increase or decrease in the demand for low-skill labor that would arise out of the producer's efforts to increase or decrease the relative importance of low-skilled labor in producing each unit of output (while holding the total quantity of output fixed). If high-skill and low-skill labor are **complements in production**, then the input substitution effect of the reduction in the high-skill wage encourages greater use of both high-skill and low-skill labor in producing a unit of output (while reducing the use of other factors). In such a case, both the scale and substitution effects of the reduction in the high-skill wage raise the demand for low-skill labor. If, however, high-skill and low-skill labor are **substitutes in production**, then the substitution effect of the reduction in the high-skill wage tends to reduce the demand for low-skill labor, and the net effect of the high-skill wage reduction on the demand for labor is theoretically ambiguous.

Labor-using and labor-saving technical change

By definition, a technological improvement makes it possible to produce a unit of the same output at lower cost or produce a higher value output at the same cost. It thus increases marginal revenue relative to marginal cost, encouraging an expansion of production, bringing a scale effect that tends to increase the demand for all inputs. Often technical change also induces input substitution effects, however, modifying the factor proportions used to produce a unit of output. The ultimate impact on the demand for low-skill labor (or any other input) thus depends on the exact nature of the technological improvement. We call a technological change **low-skill labor using** if it would tend to increase the demand for low-skill labor *while holding prices and fixed factors constant*, and we call it **low-skill labor saving** if it would tend to reduce the demand for low-skill labor under those conditions.

Agricultural production decisions

To understand agricultural production decisions, which affect the lives of many households in developing countries, it is useful to add two more dimensions to our discussion of production decisions. First, we must take into account the **seasonality** of input demands and output production. A calendar year may be broken down into one, two, or three agricultural crop cycles, and within each crop cycle land preparation activities (tilling, burning), are followed by planting activities (seeding fields, nurturing seedlings, and transplanting to fields), crop care activities (fertilizing, weeding, thinning, applying pesticides), and harvesting activities (cutting, picking, threshing). Labor requirements often differ greatly by season. A change in price, fixed factor, or technology might have diverse implications for labor use across the seasons. For example, a reduced price for chemical herbicides could reduce the demand for manual labor during the weeding phase of the agricultural cycle, but, by increasing the resulting yields of output per acre, it could increase the demand for harvest season labor. Construction of new irrigation equipment could increase yields and increase the demand for labor not only during traditional harvest times but also, by making it possible to complete a second or third crop cycle each year, greatly increase the demand for labor in months in which farm land was previously left idle.

Second, farmers often produce (or at least have the potential to produce) more than one crop. Farmers must choose how much of their land to allocate to the production of any one crop, and they allocate any one plot to the crop that yields the highest profit there. If a plot cannot be cultivated profitably under any crop (given current prices and technology) it is left **fallow** or idle. An increase in the price of corn can lead farmers to increase production of corn by increasing the intensity of production on land already devoted to corn cultivation (i.e., devoting more labor, fertilizer, and other inputs per acre), by expanding corn cultivation onto land previously left fallow, or by inducing **crop substitution**, in which land previously devoted to bean cultivation is now allocated to corn. The increase in the corn price can thus cause a reduction in the supply of beans. If bean cultivation tends to require more labor per acre than corn cultivation (when facing the same wages and other input prices), then shifting land from bean cultivation to corn culti-vation in response to the corn price increase can cause the demand for labor to fall!

Derived demands and linkages

Basic producer theory highlights that labor demand is a **derived demand**: producers' demand for labor is derived from consumers' demand for the goods and services that producers sell. When increases in the demand for goods and services raise the prices at which producers may sell their outputs, they also tend to increase producers' demands for labor (as well as other inputs). This is the source of important **linkages** among markets. When policies or circumstances increase the demand for agricultural goods, driving up prices in agricultural output markets, they also induce increases in the demand for labor, which can increase wages in labor markets.

Basic producer theory also raises the possibility of another less obvious but important linkage between markets for agricultural goods and markets for the goods and services produced by rural nonfarm businesses. Farmers facing higher output prices might demand more agricultural inputs produced by the rural nonfarm sector, and farmers and workers with rising incomes are likely to demand more nonagricultural consumer goods and services. Indeed, agricultural expansion tends to bring with it expansion of nonagricultural rural production as well (Reardon and Timmer, 2007). The nonagricultural expansion, in turn, can further increase the local demand for labor.

6.4C The green revolution's impact on rural labor

Mechanization and reductions in agricultural employment often followed closely after the adoption of Green Revolution seed varieties. This correlation in time led many observers to criticize the Green Revolution for displacing agricultural labor and worsening the plight of landless rural workers (Lipton and Longhurst, 1989; Hazell and Ramasamy, 1991). Does closer examination support the contention that the Green Revolution reduced the well-being of rural workers by reducing labor demand?

According to basic producer theory, when we want to understand what is happening to the quantity of labor demanded by a sector, it is useful to understand what is happening to techno-logical options. The main Green Revolution technological advance was the development of new varieties of rice, corn, and wheat that were more efficient at turning fertilizer and water into edible grain. They made higher yields per acre possible, but only when accompanied by greater fertilizer use, more carefully controlled watering, and more careful pest management.

Most analysts agree that if prices and wages had held constant, adoption of Green Revo-lution seed varieties would have *increased* the quantity of labor demanded in agriculture. The yields of the new varieties were much more responsive to increases in fertilizer use and weed control. By increasing yields, use of the new varieties increased the work that needed to be done at harvest time. The technology thus increased the marginal productivity of labor time devoted to production of rice and other Green Revolution crops, tending to raise *VMPL* schedules like that in Figure 6.8a, reduce *MC* schedules like that in Figure 6.8b, and increase the quantity of labor demanded at any wage. In most cases, Green Revolution seed use was adopted on land previously devoted to cultivation of traditional varieties of the same crops, tending to increase annual per-acre labor requirements by 20 or 30 percent (Lipton and Longhurst, 1989). In a few cases the greater profitability of Green Revolution seeds led to crop substitution, in which Green Revolution crops were planted on land previously devoted to crops employing more labor per acre, and they might thus have reduced the average per-acre demand for labor (see Bayri and Furtan, 1989, on Turkey), but such cases were rare.

Despite technological reasons to believe that the Green Revolution would have increased the quantity of labor demanded by 20 or 30 percent (had all else remained equal), agricultural employment tended to rise by much less than 20 percent over periods of Green Revolution expansion, and in some cases it even fell (Otsuka et al., 1994). This reduction in labor use, while farmers were adopting the Green Revolution technology and expanding output, was possible only because farmers simultaneously adopted other (labor-saving) technological advances. For example, among rice producers in the Philippines, tractors replaced oxen in land preparation, the practice of establishing seedlings in specialized seed beds and then transplanting them into flooded fields by hand (which required much labor per acre) were replaced by direct planting (in which rice was seeded directly into the field), and hand threshing was replaced by mechanical threshing.

There was nothing about the Green Revolution seed varieties that required these new labor-saving practices, so what motivated their adoption? Two observed changes stand out. First, in most cases wages were rising, encouraging farmers to adopt labor-saving technological changes on top of Green Revolution changes. Second, sometimes labor-saving technologies (which would have been profitable earlier, but were not available) were newly introduced during this period. For example, in the Philippines the development of chemical herbicides encouraged farmers to shift from transplanting seeds into flooded fields (where flooding prevented weed growth) to direct planting combined with herbicide use, and the development of smaller, more portable threshers encouraged small farmers to switch from manual to mechanical threshing. Regression analysis indicates that reductions in agricultural employment are better explained by rising wages and independent introduction of labor-saving technologies than by adoption of Green Revolution seed varieties (Otsuka et al., 1994).

The very fact that wages were rising must give us pause. If the only force for change during the period was the introduction of Green Revolution technologies, and if the Green Revolution technologies had reduced the demand for labor, then wages should have fallen rather than risen. Thus a simple story in which the Green Revolution forced labor displacement and impoverishment of rural labor cannot be right.

What caused wages to rise? The adoption of Green Revolution methods in agriculture itself tended to increase the agricultural demand for labor, as described above. On top of this, in many successful Green Revolution regions the rural nonfarm economy also expanded rapidly, raising that sector's demand for labor (e.g., Hazell and Ramaswamy, 1991). Many researchers believe that this expansion of the rural nonfarm sector was itself indirectly induced by the Green Revolution, as expanded agricultural production and incomes increased demand for agricultural inputs and consumer goods produced by the nonfarm sector. The resulting increase in prices of nonfarm goods and services led to increases in that sector's derived demand for labor. We thus conclude that:

> Contrary to suspicions that the Green Revolution hurt workers by reducing the agricultural demand for labor, the Green Revolution in most cases increased the demand for labor, not only in agriculture but also in the rural nonfarm sector. The resulting increase in rural wages encouraged the adoption of independent labor-saving agricultural technologies. In some cases, the net effect was a reduction in the quantity of labor employed in agriculture, even while wages were rising, as workers were pulled into the rural nonfarm sector.

REFERENCES

Alderman, Harold. *The Effect of Food Price and Income Changes on the Acquisition of Food By Low–Income Households*. Washington, D.C.: International Food Policy Research Institute (IFPRI), 1986. http://www.ifpri.org/sites/default/files/publications/oc5.pdf

Banerjee, Abhijit V., and Esther Duflo. "The Economic Lives of the Poor." *Journal of Economic Perspectives* 21(1): 141–167, 2007. doi:10.1257/jep.21.1.141

Barrett, Christopher B. "Food Security and Food Assistance Programs." In Bruce L. Gardner and Gordon C. Rausser (eds.). *Handbook of Agricultural Economics*, Volume 2, Part B. Amsterdam: Elsevier, 2002, pp. 2103–2190. doi:10.1016/S1574-0072(02)10027-2

Bayri, Tulay Y., and W. Hartley Furtan. "The Impact of New Wheat Technology on Income Distribution: A Green Revolution Case Study, Turkey, 1960–1983." *Economic Development and Cultural Change* 38 (1): 113–127, 1989. http://www.jstor.org/stable/1154163

Beegle, Kathleen, Rajeev H. Dehejia, and Roberta Gatti. "Child Labor and Agricultural Shocks." *Journal of Development Economics* 81(1): 80–96, 2006. doi:10.1016/j.jdeveco.2005.05.003

Block, Steven A. "Maternal Nutrition Knowledge and the Demand for Micronutrient-Rich Foods: Evidence From Indonesia." *Journal of Development Studies* 40(6): 82–105, 2004. doi:10.1080/0022038042000233812

Bouis, Howarth E., and Lawrence J. Haddad. "Are Estimates of Calorie–Income Elasticities Too High? A Recalibration of the Plausible Range." *Journal of Development Economics* 39(2): 333–364, 1992. doi:10.1016/0304-3878(92)90043-9

Calegar, Geraldo M., and G. Edward Schuh. "The Brazilian Wheat Policy: Its Costs, Benefits, and Effects on Food Consumption." Research Report 66. Washington, D.C.: International Food Policy Research Institute (IFPRI), 1988. http://www.ifpri.org/publication/brazilian-wheat-policy

Case, Anne, and Motohiro Yogo. "Does School Quality Matter? Returns to Education and the Characteristics of Schools in South Africa." NBER Working Paper No. 7399. Cambridge, Mass.: National Bureau of Economic Research, 1999. http://www.nber.org/papers/w7399

Datta, Saugato, and Sendhil Mullainathan. "Behavioral Design: A New Approach to Development Policy." CGD Policy Paper 016. Washington D.C.: Center for Global Development, 2012. http://www.cgdev.org/content/publications/detail/1426679

de Janvry, Alain, Frederico Finan, Elisabeth Sadoulet, and Renos Vakis. "Can Conditional Cash Transfer Programs Serve as Safety Nets in Keeping Children At School and From Working When Exposed to Shocks?" *Journal of Development Economics* 79(2): 349–373, 2006. doi:10.1016/j.jdeveco.2006.01.013

DellaVigna, Stefano. "Psychology and Economics: Evidence From the Field." *Journal of Economic Literature* 47(2): 315–372, 2009. doi:10.1257/jel.47.2.315

Duryea, Suzanne, David Lam, and Deborah Levison. "Effects of Economic Shocks on Children's Employment and Schooling in Brazil." *Journal of Development Economics* 84(1): 188–214, 2007. doi:10.1016/j.jdeveco.2006.11.004

Edmonds, Eric V. "*Child Labor*." In T. Paul Schultz and John A. Strauss (eds.). *Handbook of Development Economics*, Volume 4. Amsterdam: Elsevier, 2008, pp. 3607–3709. doi:10.1016/S1573-4471(07)04057-0

Edmonds, Eric V., and Nina Pavcnik. "The Effect of Trade Liberalization on Child Labor." *Journal of International Economics* 65(2): 401–419, 2005. doi:10.1016/j.jinteco.2004.04.001

Edmonds, Eric V., and Nina Pavcnik. "Trade Liberalization and the Allocation of Labor Between Households and Markets in a Poor Country." *Journal of International Economics* 69(2): 272–295, 2006. doi:10.1016/j.jinteco.2005.05.010

Food and Agriculture Organization (FAO). *The State of Food Insecurity in the World: Addressing Food Insecurity in Protracted Crises*. Rome: Food and Agriculture Organization, 2010. http://www.fao.org/docrep/013/i1683e/i1683e.pdf

Foster, Andrew, and Mark R. Rosenzweig. "Technical Change and Human-Capital Returns and Investments: Evidence From the Green Revolution." *The American Economic Review* 86(4): 931–953, 1996. http://www.jstor.org/stable/2118312

Hazell, Peter B. R., and C. Ramasamy. *The Green Revolution Reconsidered: The Impact of High–Yielding Rice Varieties in South India*. Baltimore: Johns Hopkins University Press, 1991. http://www.ifpri.org/sites/default/files/publications/hazell91.pdf

International Labour Organization (ILO). *Global Child Labour Developments: Measuring Trends From 2004 to 2008*. International Programme on the Elimination of Child Labour (IPEC). Geneva: International Labour Organization, 2010. http://www.ilo.org/ipecinfo/product/viewProduct.do?productId=13313

International Programme on the Elimination of Child Labour (IPEC). *Every Child Counts: New Global Estimates on Child Labour*. Geneva: International Labour Organization, 2002. http://www.ilo.org/ipecinfo/product/download.do?type=document&id=742

Jayachandran, Seema. "Selling Labor Low: Wage Responses to Productivity Shocks in Developing Countries." *Journal of Political Economy* 114(3): 538–575, 2006. doi:10.1086/503579

Kochar, Anjini. "Urban Influences on Rural Schooling in India." *Journal of Development Economics* 74(1): 113–136, 2004. doi:10.1016/j.jdeveco.2003.12.006

Kruger, Diana I. "Coffee Production Effects on Child Labor and Schooling in Rural Brazil." *Journal of Development Economics* 82(2): 448–463, 2007. doi:10.1016/j.jdeveco.2006.04.003

Lipton, Michael, and Richard Longhurst. *New Seeds and Poor People*. Baltimore: Johns Hopkins University Press, 1989.

Menon, Martina, Federico Perali, and Furio Rosati. "Estimation of the Contribution of Child Labour to the Formation of Rural Incomes: An Application to Nepal." CHILD Working Paper 10/2005. Rome: Centre for Household Income, Labour, and Demographic Economics, 2005. http://www.child-centre.unito.it/papers/child10_2005.pdf

Ministry of Community Development and Social Services, Government of Zambia/German Technical Cooperation (MCDSS/GTZ) "The Pilot Social Cash Transfer Scheme" *Zambia: Summary report*, 5th edition, Lusaka, 2007.

Mullainathan, Sendhil. "Development Economics Through the Lens of Psychology." Proceedings of the Annual Bank Conference on Development Economics, 2006. http://scholar.harvard.edu/mullainathan/publications/development-economics-through-lens-psychology

Otsuka, Keijiro, Fe Gascon, and Seki Asano. "Green Revolution and Labour Demand in Rice Farming: The Case of Central Luzon, 1966-90." *Journal of Development Studies* 31(1): 82–109, 1994. doi:10.1080/00220389408422349

Penny, Mary E., Hilary M. Creed-Kanashiro, Rebecca C. Robert, M. Rocio Narro, Laura E. Caulfield, and Robert E. Black. "Effectiveness of an Educational Intervention Delivered Through the Health Services to Improve Nutrition in Young Children: A Cluster-Randomised Controlled Trial." *The Lancet* 365(9474): 1863–1872, 2005. doi:10.1016/S0140-6736(05)66426-4

Pollak, Robert A., and Terence J. Wales. *Demand System Specification and Estimation.* New York: Oxford University Press, 1992.

Psacharopoulos, George. "Child Labor Versus Educational Attainment: Some Evidence From Latin America." *Journal of Population Economics* 10(4): 377–86, 1997. doi:10.1007/s001480050049

Reardon, Thomas, and C. Peter Timmer. "Transformation of Markets for Agricultural Output in Developing Countries Since 1950: How Has Thinking Changed?" In Robert Evenson and Prabhu Pingali (eds.). *Handbook of Agricultural Economics,* Volume 3. Amsterdam: Elsevier, 2007, pp. 2807–2855. doi:10.1016/S1574-0072(06)03055-6

Ruttan, Vernon W. "Productivity Growth in World Agriculture: Sources and Constraints." *Journal of Economic Perspectives* 16(4): 161–184, 2002. doi:10.1257/089533002320951028

Sadoulet, Elisabeth, Alain de Janvry, and Benjamin Davis. "Cash Transfer Programs With Income Multipliers: PROCAMPO in Mexico." *World Development* 29(6): 1043–1056, 2001. doi:10.1016/S0305-750X(01)00018-3

Schultz, T. Paul. "School Subsidies for the Poor: Evaluating the Mexican Progresa Poverty Program." *Journal of Development Economics* 74(1): 199–250, 2004. doi:10.1016/j.jdeveco.2003.12.009

Skoufias, Emmanuel, and Susan Wendy Parker. "Conditional Cash Transfers and Their Impact on Child Work and Schooling: Evidence From the Progresa Program in Mexico." *Economía* 2(1): 45–86, 2001. doi:10.1353/eco.2001.0016

Shafiq, M. Najeeb. "Household Schooling and Child Labor Decisions in Rural Bangladesh." *Journal of Asian Economics* 18(6): 946–966, 2007. doi:10.1016/j.asieco.2007.07.003

Subramanian, Shankar, and Angus Deaton. "The Demand for Food and Calories." *Journal of Political Economy* 104(1): 133–162, 1996. http://www.jstor.org/stable/2138962

World Bank. *Repositioning Nutrition as Central to Development: A Strategy for Large-Scale Action.* Washington, D.C.: World Bank, 2006. http://go.worldbank.org/SU9IR5JHY0

QUESTIONS FOR REVIEW

1. Describe some of the choices people make that help determine development outcomes.

2. Describe how development economists organize their study of how people make choices.

3. What assumptions define basic consumer theory? Be sure to define any terms you introduce.

4. Using a graph like the one in Figure 6.1a, demonstrate the effect on consumption choices of (a) an increase in Y, (b) a reduction in p_f, and (c) a change in culture or beliefs that causes the consumer to place greater value on providing adequate nutrition for her children.

5. Define the income effect and substitution effect associated with a reduction in the price of food. What does theory tell us about the signs of the income and substitution effects?

6. What does it mean for two goods to be complements in consumption? Substitutes?

7. What guidance does basic consumer theory offer for empirical research on the determinants of consumption choices?

8. What are some key empirical findings to date regarding the efficacy of income increases for improving nutrition among the poor?

9. Compare the impacts on a consumer's choices and well-being of the receipt of a bag of rice versus the receipt of a cash transfer equal to the value of a bag of rice (at the local market price), being careful to distinguish whether the consumer would or would not purchase any additional rice when given the rice distribution. Use diagrams like those in Figure 6.4 to explain your answer.

10. Discuss the weaknesses revealed by basic consumer theory of using economy-wide food price reductions to improve nutrition.

11. Under what conditions might nutrition education improve consumers' "true" well-being?

12. What assumptions define basic labor supply theory?

13. Using graphs like those in Figure 6.5, demonstrate the effects on the choices of potential labor suppliers who do and do not initially supply any labor of (a) an increase in M, (b) an increase in w, (c) an increase in T, and (d) a change in cultural norms that increases the relative value the labor supplier places on consumption expenditure relative to home time.

14. Define the income and substitution effects on labor supply associated with an increase in the wage. What does theory tell us about the signs of the income and substitution effects?

15. What questions does basic labor supply theory raise regarding the assumptions underlying many calls for prohibiting child labor?

16. Discuss some of the major lessons to be drawn from Table 6.1.

17. What assumptions define basic producer theory?

18. Using first a graph like that in Figure 6.8a and then a graph like that in Figure 6.8b, discuss the impacts on the production decision of (a) an increase in p, (b) an increase in w, (c) an increase in K (or A) that increases the marginal productivity of labor.

19. Discuss the seasonality of agricultural production and its implications for production decision analysis.

20. Define crop substitution and discuss how the possibility of crop substitution modifies our predictions regarding the effect of an increase in the price of corn on the demand for low-skill labor.

21. What is the significance of the statement that labor demand is a derived demand? What is a linkage between markets? What are some sources of linkage between agricultural markets and rural nonfarm markets?

22. Discuss the impacts of the Green Revolution on rural markets for low-skill labor.

QUESTIONS FOR DISCUSSION

1. Define marginal utility and offer an intuitive argument as to why it diminishes as the quantity of a good consumed increases. How do indifference curves relate to utility functions? Why do indifference curves slope downward? Why are indifference curves convex (i.e., bowed toward origin)? Offer a logical argument for why indifference curves cannot cross.

2. Describe how to determine the position and slope of the budget line in a diagram like the one in Figure 6.1. How do we know that the consumer will not choose to consume at a point inside the shaded region in Figure 6.1 rather than on the budget line? How do we know that the consumer will not consume in the unshaded region beyond the budget line? Explain why the combination of F and N that maximizes the consumer's utility subject to her budget constraint is found at a point on the budget line that is just tangent to an indifference curve.

3. Discuss the claim, "For a consumer with a utility function satisfying the assumptions of basic consumer choice theory, at least one good must be a normal good, but no good need be inferior."

4. Show that to determine the real quantities F and N consumed by the consumer whose preferences are shown in Figure 6.1a, it is enough to know the two ratios Y/P_n and p_f/p_n. We do not need to know all three quantities Y, P_f, and P_n independently.

5. Define a consumer's *true utility* to be the utility she would associate with consumption choices if she had complete understanding of the consequences of those choices for her health and nutrition. Define her *perceived utility* to be the utility she associates with consumption choices in her current state of imperfect knowledge regarding these consequences. Assume that because she lacks complete knowledge of health and nutrition consequences, she tends to undervalue the consumption of vitamin-rich vegetables relative to the consumption of other items. Using a diagram similar to that in Figure 6.1a, demonstrate that when she maximizes her perceived utility she fails to maximize her true utility.

6. Suppose a labor supplier allocates time to only two activities, work and home time, and has a total of 80 hours available per week to be allocated across these two activities. Show that under the assumptions of basic labor supply theory the following two circumstances would lead a labor supplier to make the same time allocation choice.
   a. The labor supplier receives 20 pesos in nonlabor income and is offered a wage of 5 pesos per hour of wage labor.
   b. The consumer is offered 420 pesos for a contracted work week of 80 hours but may buy time off (to allocate to home time) at a price of 5 pesos per hour.

7. Using diagrams like the one in Figure 6.5, describe the kinds of changes to a woman's labor supply choices that might be induced by her receipt of additional education. How might her budget constraint change? Why? How might her preferences change? Why?

8. What guidance does basic labor supply theory give us regarding the variables we should include in a regression examining the determinants of total household labor supply?

9. Consider a farmer who uses all of his available land to cultivate corn and beans, and assume that bean cultivation requires more labor per acre than corn production. Discuss the likely sign of the effect on corn production, bean production, and labor demand resulting from a reduction in the price of beans, an increase in the price of corn, an increase in the wage, and a reduction in the price of chemical herbicides. Explain your answers.

10. What guidance does basic producer theory give us regarding the variables we should include in a regression examining the determinants of a profit-maximizing farmer's supply of beans?

11. When studying any issue, economists instinctively identify the relevant *decisions* and *decision makers*, seek to understand the *constraints* and *preferences* that shape those decisions, work out the *logically possible implications*, and then undertake *empirical research* to determine which of the theoretical possibilities are important in practice. Suppose you are asked to study the likely effects on teacher and student performance of an effort to link teacher pay to how well their students perform on standardized tests. Which of the three basic models described in this chapter would serve as the best starting point for developing an appropriate analytical framework? Who is the most relevant decision maker? What is the most salient set of choices? What constrains those choices? What does the framework suggest regarding the possible impacts of the teacher performance-pay proposal?

PROBLEMS

1. Consider a consumer who chooses F and N to maximize $U(F,N) = F^{.75}N^{.25}$ subject to the budget constraint that $P_f F + P_n N = Y$. Making an appropriate substitution based on the budget constraint, this consumer may be construed as choosing F to maximize $F^{.75}[(Y - P_f F)/P_n]^{.25}$.

   a. Write down the first-order condition that must characterize the utility-maximizing choice F^*.

   b. Rearrange this condition to derive an equation for the utility-maximizing F^* as a function of Y, P_f, and P_n.

   c. According to this equation, how does the consumer's choice of F^* change as Y increases? As P_f increases? As P_n increases?

   d. Rearrange the condition one more time to derive an equation describing how the utility-maximizing food expenditure share, $(P_f F^*)/Y$, relates to the model's parameters. What do you learn from this expression?

2. Draw three identical graphs with axes labeled as in Figure 6.1a. Draw into the three graphs identical budget constraints, with a point a located in the same place on the budget constraint (like point a in Figure 6.1). In all three graphs draw in the new budget constraint that would become relevant after an increase in income (of the same amount in all diagrams). Now draw different sets of indifference curves into the three diagrams to indicate the preferences of three different consumers, in which their preferences lead to the following outcomes: All three consumers choose to consume at point a when facing the initial budget constraint. The first consumer spends the entire increase in income on food. The second consumer increases food and nonfood consumption in the same proportion. The third consumer reduces food consumption after the income increase. Draw at least two indifference curves in each diagram, making sure that they satisfy all the properties required by the basic theory.

3. Elasticities are useful measures, because we can roughly assess their size without reference to the units in which we measure goods consumption or price levels, simply by comparing their values to benchmarks of 1, 0, or −1.

   a. If the income elasticity of rice consumption equals 1, what happens to the ratio of rice consumption expenditure to total income when income rises (holding prices constant)? If the elasticity is greater (less) than 1?

   b. If the own price elasticity of rice consumption (R) is less than (greater than) −1, rice demand is said to be "price elastic"("price inelastic"). When rice demand is price elastic (inelastic), does total expenditure on rice ($p_R R$) rise or fall when the price of rice (p_R) rises?

4. Draw a diagram like Figure 6.2a. Suppose this diagram illustrates the impact on a consumer of a general food subsidy's reduction in the price of food (to the level associated with the dashed budget line).

   a. If the consumer still faced the initial prices, how much cash would she have to be given to be able to consume F_2 units of food and N_2 units of nonfood? Please answer using notation defined in the graph.

   b. Show that your answer to part a is equal to $F_2(p_{f1} - p_{f2})$.

   c. Now suppose the consumer had been given $F_2(p_{f1} - p_{f2})$ in cash while continuing to face the initial prices. Draw the budget constraint she would face into your diagram, and explain why you draw it as you do.

   d. Making reference to your graph and to any relevant assumptions of the model, demonstrate that if given the cash transfer described in part c, the consumer would consume less than F_2 units of food but would achieve a higher level of utility than that associated with consumption of F_2 and N_2.

5. Draw and label completely a diagram describing a consumer's choice regarding consumption of rice and other items when she has Y rupees of income and faces prices P_r and P_o in rupees per unit of rice and other items. Construct the new budget constraint she would face if she were offered the opportunity to purchase a limited quantity R of rice at a subsidized price P_s, which is lower than P_r. You may assume that R is less than Y/P_r.

6. Consider a manufacturer who produces cloth using low-skill labor, high-skill labor, and several other inputs. According to basic producer theory, what do we know (or not know) about the signs of the scale effect and input substitution effect on the demands for low-skill labor associated with each of the following changes:
    a. A reduction in the wage for low-skilled labor,
    b. A reduction in the cost of an input that is a complement to low-skill labor,
    c. A reduction in the cost of an input that is a substitute for low-skill labor,
    d. Low-skill labor-using technical change, and
    e. Low-skill labor-saving technical change.

7. Suppose every farmer in a region cultivates one acre of land, but their plots differ in quality. The quantity of output they produce, Y, as a function of the labor they devote to cultivation, L, is given by the production function $Y = e^{\alpha Q} L^{\beta}$, where Q measures land quality and $0 < \beta < 1$. The price of output is p, the wage is w, and farm profits are given by $pY - wL$. Take Q as given and treat L as a variable input. Derive an expression for the profit-maximizing value of labor input, L^*, as a function of Q. According to this expression, how does the value of labor input per acre vary across farmers with different land quality?

chapter

7

Households

People are diverse. In many developing countries, a few families own vast tracts of land, while most own little or none. Some live in densely packed cities, while others live in remote hamlets. Some breadwinners have college degrees, while others are illiterate. And even within households, some members are men in the prime of their lives, while others are women, children, or elderly. These differences matter, because socioeconomic changes tend to affect different people differently, raising well-being for some groups while reducing it for others. If we hope to identify the underpinnings of broad-based development success—which brings improvements in well-being for most groups—then we must take diversity seriously, and build it into our analytical framework from the very start.

After briefly expanding on the significance of diversity in development and policy analysis, this chapter introduces two sets of models used by development economists to organize study of how the impacts of change may differ, first *across households* of different types and then between women and men *within households*. We apply the first framework in studying the effects on world poverty of the global food price crisis that first peaked in 2008, and we derive lessons from the second about how to incorporate gender concerns into development policy analysis.

7.1 Diversity in Development and Policy Analysis

An important theme of this book is that people are diverse, and diverse people experience differentiated impacts of development policies. Working out a complete picture of a policy's differentiated impacts requires first examining the distribution of its **direct effects**, which are the effects on the people whose lives are touched most obviously and immediately. For example, the direct effects of policies that raise the price of corn are to raise incomes for farming households that sell corn and to reduce the purchasing power of households that buy corn. The direct effect of a policy that raises school quality is to raise the value of education for families who live near schools and can afford to send children to school, while bypassing many remote and poor families. Such policies might also benefit boys more than girls, who are less likely than their brothers to attend school.

As people experience the direct effects of policies, they respond in ways that generate **indirect or spillover effects**, which are also differentiated across diverse people. Many of these indirect effects are worked out through markets. For example, farmers who have been taught by agricultural extension agents to use improved seed varieties not only enjoy increased productivity and income but they might also increase their demand in rural labor markets and increase their supply to food markets. Through these channels the agricultural extension policy might raise wages and lower food prices, indirectly raising well-being for landless rural laborers and urban consumers and reducing it for farmers who have not adopted the new seed varieties.

Comprehensive analysis of policies' society-wide effects requires organized thought about the differentiation of direct and indirect effects. Development economists employ two sets of analytical tools for organizing such thought. The first organizes the study of impacts differentiated *across* households and is built up from the basic microeconomic building blocks reviewed in Chapter 6. The framework recognizes that while the abstract consumers, labor suppliers, and producers of Chapter 6 each engage in only one set of decisions at a time, real-world households engage simultaneously in consumption, time allocation, and (often) production decisions. This gives rise to tremendous differentiation across households in the nature and extent of their involvement in markets. The first half of the chapter builds up this framework and demonstrates its usefulness for studying the impact of the recent global food price crisis on global poverty.

The second set of analytical tools focuses on differentiation *within* households in developing countries, where women and girls often experience lower consumption, longer work hours, and fewer rights relative to men and boys, even within the same households. It recognizes that although the abstract decision makers of Chapter 6 and the households of the first half of this chapter are *unitary* decision makers, who seek simply and without conflict to maximize well-being as defined by a single utility function, real-world households are made up of multiple members whose interests and power can vary and who might engage in conflict as well as cooperation as they work out household decisions. The second half of this chapter introduces *non-unitary* models of household decision making and derives lessons from them regarding the incorporation of gender into development policy analysis.

All the models of household decision making examined in this chapter are **static** models. These are timeless models, in which households allocate their current time and income across uses with the aim of maximizing utility today, ignoring any possible connections between their present choices and future circumstances and thus ignoring any opportunities to save or invest. In Chapters 7 through 9 we will see that static models offer useful guidance for study of how households are affected by prices in markets for goods, services, and labor and also how households contribute to the determination of prices in those markets. Static models alone offer only incomplete guidance for the study of development, however, because households' saving and investment decisions play important roles in determining development success. In Chapter 10, therefore, we consider **dynamic** models of household decision making, which incorporate households' concern for the future as well as the present, and in which households make choices about borrowing, saving, and investing.

7.2 Unitary Household Theories: From Consumers, Labor Suppliers, and Producers to Households
7.2A A motivation

Advocates for the developing world have long argued that protection and subsidization of farmers in rich countries burdens developing countries by driving down world food prices and limits the ability of the poor in developing countries to profit from agricultural exports (Tokarick, 2008). Such advocates see higher global food prices as *good* for the world's poor.

Yet the dramatic increase in global food prices that reached a peak in 2008 ignited riots in many parts of the developing world and was deemed a global food price crisis, which undid the previous 10 years' work of global poverty reduction (World Bank, 2008). That is, suddenly it appeared that higher global food prices are *bad* for the world's poor.

How do we make sense of the apparent contradiction between these two views? What do we learn from the events of 2008 about the likely impacts on the world's poor of agricultural market liberalization in the developed countries? What empirical evidence should we gather to understand better the link between global food prices and global poverty? The household models discussed in the next four subsections provide a useful framework for analyzing such questions.

We differentiate our discussion across four broad archetypal categories of households, which we call wage labor households, farm households, nonfarm business households, and incapacitated households. We point out the importance of diversity both within and between these categories. The models we develop here are called **unitary household models**, because they treat the entire household as if it were a single or unitary decision maker, maximizing a single utility function. We may also call them *neoclassical* models of household decision making, because they are based on neoclassical assumptions, as described in section 6.1.

☰ Box 7.1 Notation Employed in Discussion of Wage Labor Households

M = endowment of nonlabor income(pesos)
T = total time endowment
w = wage in pesos per unit of time
S = labor supply time
H = home time

F = food consumption(bags)
N = nonfood consumption(bags)
p_f = per-bag price of food(pesos)
p_n = per-bag price of nonfood(pesos)

7.2B Wage labor households

In most developing countries, between one third and two thirds of workers earn their income as wage employees. We define **wage labor households** as households for whom wages are the main source of income, and we recognize that wage labor households are diverse. Some live in urban areas, while many others live in rural areas. A few of them earn high salaries in high-skill work, but many earn low wages in low-skill work, often in agriculture. What these diverse households have in common is that they function simultaneously as both labor suppliers and consumers. To begin studying their well-being and behavior, we combine the basic theories of consumption and time allocation presented in Chapter 6. Box 7.1 summarizes key notation used in this section.

As a *labor supplier*, a wage labor household is endowed with nonlabor income M and total time available (after accounting for sleep and other life-sustaining activities) T. It allocates time across wage labor S and home time H subject to the total time constraint that

$$S + H \leq T \tag{7.1}$$

As a *consumer*, the household chooses the quantities of various goods and services to consume, subject to a budget constraint. If the household faces a wage of w per hour of labor supplied, if the only two goods relevant to consumption decisions are food F and nonfood N, and if the household faces per-unit prices p_f and p_n, then the **budget constraint** may be written as

$$p_f F + p_n N \leq M + wS \tag{7.2}$$

The left side is the household's total **consumption expenditure** and the right side is the household's **income**, including both nonlabor and labor income. The household's utility is a function of the three quantities it values intrinsically: F, N, and H. The household maximizes its utility, $U(F, N, H)$, subject to the constraints described by equations 7.1 and 7.2.

As in the case of the basic labor supply model, we may re-express this problem in a way that emphasizes its similarity to the basic consumer choice model. Knowing that the household will not let any opportunities for consumption go to waste, we know that it will treat the constraints described by equations 7.1 and 7.2 as equalities rather than inequalities. Combining those two equalities and rearranging, we find that

$$p_f F + p_n N + wH = M + wT \tag{7.3}$$

The right side is the **wage labor household's full income**, or the market value of its time and nonlabor income endowments (identical to the labor supplier's full income in Chapter 6). Full income can vary greatly across households, which differ in the level of wages they face, numbers of able-bodied workers, hours available for work and home time (after hauling water and fuel), and nonlabor income. But any one wage labor household takes the value of its full income as given, much as the simple consumer of Chapter 6 takes actual income as given.

The left side of equation 7.3 indicates the three uses to which the wage labor household puts its full income: consumption of food, consumption of nonfood, and enjoyment of home time. We can think of these as the three goods the household buys with its full income. The household may purchase additional units of F and N at prices p_f and p_n, and may "purchase" an additional unit of H by devoting an additional hour to home time rather than wage labor, thereby causing actual income to fall by w relative to full income.

We may thus think of the wage labor household as solving a simple consumer choice problem, choosing quantities of three consumption goods (F, N, and H) to maximize utility, $U(F, N, H)$, subject to the budget constraint equation 7.3 in which full income, $M + wT$, takes the place of income. This gives us an easy way to think through the effects of change on the wage labor household's labor supply, because we know that labor supply falls by one unit whenever home time rises by one unit. To summarize the analysis thus far:

We can think of a wage labor household as choosing how much to consume of food, nonfood, and home time, seeking to maximize utility subject to a budget constraint that requires it to spend no more than its full income. Its full income is the sum of its nonlabor income endowment and the peso value of its time endowment when valued at the market wage, and the price it pays for consuming home time is equal to the wage it forgoes by not using that time for wage labor.

Impacts of endowment, price, and wage changes on behavior

If we think of wage labor households as maximizing $U(F, N, H)$, it is easy to describe the effects on household choices of changes in endowments, prices, and the wage. Increases in M, which increase full income without modifying the prices of the three goods, are like increases in total income (Y) in the basic consumer choice model. Thus if F, N, and H are all normal goods (as defined in Chapter 6), then increases in M lead the household to consume more of F, N, and H, and households choose to consume some of their increased full income in the form of increased home time, implying *reduced* labor supply. As always, whether this effect is large or small is an empirical question.

Increase in p_f or p_n reduce purchasing power and raise the relative prices of food or nonfood, as in the basic consumer choice model, although now they alter prices not only relative to other goods but also relative to home time. Again assuming that food is a normal good, an increase in p_f (holding w, M, and p_n constant) reduces F. The food price increase might cause H to rise, fall, or remain constant, depending on whether food and home time are substitutes, complements, or independent in consumption.

An increase in w raises the household's full income *and* increases the relative price of home time, as in the basic labor supply model. The income effect tends to increase H (and reduce S) if H is normal. The substitution effect tends to reduce H (and increase S). Thus the net effect of an increase in w is theoretically ambiguous, though empirical evidence tends to indicate that the net effect of an increase in wage is to increase labor supply (as we mentioned in Chapter 6).

Purchasing power impacts of food price increases

An increase in the price of food (holding income and other prices constant) reduces a wage labor household's well-being by reducing its **purchasing power** or **real income**. For poor wage labor households spending large fractions of their income on food, the effects may be large. When the price of food rises from p_f^1 to p_f^2, the total expenditure required to maintain the household's initial consumption levels rises by $(p_f^2 - p_f^1)F$, while income remains unchanged. This gap, which the household must close to satisfy its budget constraint, is like a tax to which the household must respond either by reducing F or N (reducing expenditures) or by reducing H (working longer hours and increasing cash income).

The tax implicit in a food price increase is larger for wage labor households that spend more on food, and it brings a larger *percentage* reduction in real purchasing power for households that spend larger fractions of their income on food. If ρ is the percentage increase in the price of food and f is the fraction of income the household typically spends on food, then the effect of the increase in food price is to reduce the household's purchasing power by approximately ρf percent. This expression only *approximates* the ultimate percentage impact on purchasing power (rather than measuring it exactly), because the consumer is likely to respond to the price increase by reducing the fraction of income spent on the relevant food and perhaps also by increasing labor supply. Both of these responses would tend to reduce the impact on purchasing power.

Purchasing power effects of simultaneous increases in food prices and wages

What if a wage labor household lives in a rural economy where increased food prices spur expansion of agricultural production and employment, causing wages to rise as well? To quantify the net change in a wage labor household's purchasing power when both the food price and the wage rise (relative to other prices in the economy), we again consider the gap that opens up between the total consumption expenditure required to maintain initial consumption levels and the household's income. When the price of food rises from p_f^1 to p_f^2, the cost of maintaining the household's initial consumption rises by $(p_f^2 - p_f^1)F$. This represents a reduction in the household's purchasing power. However, when the wage rises from w^1 to w^2, the income the household derives from its current labor supply rises by $(w^2 - w^1)S$, tending to raise its purchasing power. Whether the household's purchasing power rises or falls depends on the relative sizes of the two effects.

As before, if the price of food rises by ρ percent, and the household initially devotes a fraction f of consumption expenditure to food purchases, then the consumption expenditure required to maintain initial consumption rises by ρf percent. If each percentage point of increase in the price of food gives rise to an increase of ε percentage points in the wage (where ε may be called the **elasticity of the wage with respect to the price of food**), and if the household initially derives a fraction ω of its income from wage labor, then the income the household earns given its initial labor supply choice rises by $\rho\varepsilon\omega$ percent. We thus conclude that:

> If the price of food rises by ρ percent, and stimulates a wage increase of $\varepsilon\rho$ percent, while other prices in the economy and nonlabor income hold constant, then the approximate net percentage reduction in a wage labor household's purchasing power is $\rho(f - \varepsilon\omega)$, where f is the fraction of the household's consumption expenditure devoted to food and ω is the fraction of income it derives from wage labor. The household's purchasing power rises or falls depending on whether $\varepsilon\omega$ is greater or less than f.

This implies that the net effect on purchasing power of a food price and wage increase can differ greatly across wage labor households. Consider an increase in the price of wheat. For some wage labor households, wheat takes up a large fraction of the household's typical expenditure (so f is close to 1), and the wage rises very little in the wake of the wheat price increase (so ε is close to 0) or the household garners little of its income from wage labor (so ω is close to 0); the implicit tax on such households (associated with a wheat price increase) is large in percentage terms. For other wage labor households, however, wheat takes up only a small fraction of typical expenditures, the wage rises rapidly in response to the wheat price increase, and wages are an important source of household income (so that $\varepsilon\omega$ is greater than f). Such households ultimately *benefit* from the joint increase in the wheat price and wage.

Spending large fractions of their income on food, poor wage labor households tend to be particularly vulnerable to food price increases, especially in the short run before wages rise. However, even among poor wage labor households, the ultimate impacts of an increase in

≡ Box 7.2 Additional Notation Employed in Discussion of Farm Households

Q = quantity of food produced on farm
NMS = net marketed surplus of food
NLS = net market labor supply

I = quantity of purchased farm input
q = price of purchased input

the price of a particular food, such as wheat, can differ greatly across socioeconomic groups and places.

7.2C Farm households

Half the developing world's people, and three quarters of those living on less than $2 per day, live in rural areas. Of the developing world's rural households, half operate small farms (World Bank, 2007). In very poor countries like Malawi, 90 percent of the population lives in rural areas and nearly all of those households operate small family farms.

Farm households around the world are diverse. They might own vast plantations or rent tiny parcels of land, and they cultivate crops as diverse as rice (a food crop often raised in artificially flooded fields), cotton (an industrial input grown in dry areas, dependent on seasonal rainfall), and coffee (an export crop harvested from trees). For some the farm is their only source of income, but many also work for wages in agricultural or nonagricultural occupations or run small nonfarm businesses.

Farm households engage simultaneously in decisions regarding consumption, labor supply, *and* agricultural input use and production (Strauss, 1986). Unlike the consumers, labor suppliers and producers of Chapter 6 or the wage labor households of this chapter, farm households face choices about **market participation**. Because they both produce and consume food, they might sell none of a particular food crop that they produce and might buy none of a food they consume. In Mozambique, 94 percent of rural households operate farms, but only 29 percent sell any crops (Heltberg and Tarp, 2002). Similarly, farm households both supply and demand labor. They might hire little or none of the labor they employ on their farms, and they might hire out little or none of the labor they supply. Some households—often referred to as **subsistence** farm households—rarely engage in any market at all, instead simply devoting their labor time to cultivating their own farms and consuming what they produce.

In what follows we define terms for describing farm households' participation in markets, set up a simple model of farm household decision making when participating in markets is costless, use that model to analyze how the well-being of diverse farm households is affected by changes in market prices, and then use a simple modification of that model to demonstrate how a farm household's behavior can prove surprising when participation in markets is sufficiently costly that it chooses not to participate in one or more markets. Box 7.2 lists the new variables that become relevant in the discussion of farm households. (The variables of Box 7.1 are also relevant.)

Net marketed surplus and net market labor supply

Depending upon whether a farm household's production of a farm product exceeds or falls short of its consumption, the household may be either a net seller or net buyer of that item.[1] Letting Q represent the quantity of a crop called "food" that the farm produces, and letting F represent the household's consumption of food, we will define the household's **net marketed surplus** (*NMS*) of food as

$$NMS = Q - F \qquad (7.4)$$

---

[1] In reality, their relationships with markets may be more complicated. They might sell food in some seasons of the year and buy foods in other seasons. Given space limitations, we ignore such possibilities in this chapter.

If this takes a positive value, the household sells food in the market. If it takes a negative value, the household buys at least some food.

Similarly, letting L denote the total quantity of labor the household employs in cultivating its farm (including both family and hired labor), and letting S denote the total quantity of labor the household supplies to any kind of work, we define the household's **net market labor supply** (*NLS*) as

$$NLS = S - L \qquad (7.5)$$

Positive values indicate that some family labor is hired out through labor markets, and negative values indicate that some nonfamily labor is hired in through labor markets to help cultivate the family farm.

Endowments, constraints, and choices when participation in markets is costless

As a producer, the farm household is endowed with land, fixed factors of production, and a technology for agricultural production, which allow it to transform a quantity L of labor (whether family labor, hired labor, or a combination) and a quantity I of a purchased input (such as chemical fertilizer) into food according to the production function

$$Q = b(L, I) \qquad (7.6)$$

As a labor supplier, the farm household is also endowed with nonlabor income M and with total time T and must obey the total time constraint of equation 7.1. As a consumer, the household seeks to consume food and nonfood (in quantities F and N), and must satisfy a budget constraint, which restricts total spending on purchases of F and N to be no more than the net cash proceeds from all other activities.

Writing down the budget constraint is somewhat more complicated for farm households than for wage labor households. In this section, we keep the budget constraint as simple as possible by assuming that buying and selling prices for a single good or service are identical, and that there is no cost to participating in markets. (We later explain why participating in markets is costly and why purchase prices often exceed sales prices, and discuss the implications of these observations.) In particular, we assume that the price of food is p_f, whether the household is buying or selling food, and that p_n, q, and w are the prices of nonfood, purchased inputs, and labor, whether the household is buying or selling.

These assumptions simplify the task of writing down the budget constraint by allowing us to treat the household as if it buys everything it consumes and sells everything it produces, even when in fact it consumes some of what it produces and devotes some of the labor it supplies to the family farm. To see this, consider a household that produces Q units of food and consumes F units of food, with $Q > F$, so that it sells $Q - F$ units of food in the market and in so doing adds $p_f(Q - F)$ to the household budget. If the household had instead sold the entire quantity Q at the price p_f and then bought the entire quantity F at the same price, the net effect on the household budget would have been the same, because $p_f Q - p_f F = p_f(Q - F)$. We can, therefore, treat the household as selling everything it produces at the market price, selling some to the market and possibly some to itself. Similarly, we can treat the household as buying everything it consumes at the market price, buying some from the market and possibly some from itself. This simplifies the task of writing down the budget constraint, because it means that while we require notation for total consumption (F) and total production (Q), we do not require separate notation for net purchases and net sales, and we do not have to differentiate the prices that apply to purchases and sales. In a similar fashion, we can treat the household as selling all the labor it supplies S and buying all the labor it employs on the farm L at the market wage w, even though it might in fact use some family labor directly on the family farm.

Making use of this simplification, we may describe the **farm household's budget constraint** this way:

$$p_f F + p_n N \leq M + wS + (p_f Q - wL - qI) \tag{7.7}$$

The left side is a measure of the farm household's total consumption expenditure, in which we value everything it consumes at the market price, even if some of the food was produced on the family farm. The right side is a measure of total income, in which we value all farm produce and inputs at market prices, even if some of the produce was consumed at home rather than sold. The first two terms on the right side represent nonlabor income and wage labor income. The term in parentheses describes the contribution to total income from farm profits.

The farm household seeks to maximize utility as a function of food consumption, nonfood consumption, and home time, $U(F, N, H)$, subject to the constraints of equations 7.1, 7.6, and 7.7. As in the basic labor supply model and the wage labor household model, we may re-express this problem in a way that emphasizes its similarity to the basic consumer choice model. Recognizing that the utility-maximizing household will satisfy all constraints with equality, combining the three constraints and rearranging, we find that the farm household maximizes utility subject to the constraint

$$p_f F + p_n N + wH \leq M + wT + \left(p_f b(L, I) - wL - qI\right) \tag{7.8}$$

As in the wage labor household's full income constraint, the left side of equation 7.8 describes the total cost in terms of forgone full income of the household's consumption of three items (food, nonfood, and home time). The right side is a sum of three terms: nonlabor income, the market value of the time endowment, and farm profits.

The first step that this farm household would take toward maximizing utility is to choose L and I to maximize farm profits, $p_f b(L, I) - wL - qI$. In so doing the household maximizes the household income term on the right side of equation 7.8 without limiting the household's freedom to allocate that income across the three uses appearing on the left side (F, N, and H). Let's give the names L^* and I^* to the values of L and I that maximize farm profits. Having maximized farm profits, the farm household then maximizes utility subject to the constraint

$$p_f F + p_n N + wH \leq M + wT + \left(p_f b(L^*, I^*) - wL^* - qI^*\right) \tag{7.9}$$

where the right side is the **farm household's full income**.

This leads us to a conclusion that simplifies the analysis of how changes in prices, wages, and endowments affect the farm household's behavior:

> When market participation is costless (and buying prices are identical to selling prices), we may think of farm households as maximizing utility in two steps. First, they maximize farm profits (calculated valuing all inputs and outputs at market prices, even if they consume some of their produce and fulfill some of their labor demands with family labor). Second, they allocate their full incomes across the consumption of food, nonfood, and home time, seeking to maximize utility subject to a full-income budget constraint. Full income is equal to the sum of nonlabor income, the market value of the time endowment, and maximized farm profits. The prices households pay for food and nonfood are market prices, and the price they pay for home time is equal to the forgone wage.

Impacts of endowment, price, and wage changes on behavior when participation in markets is costless

In light of the above, we can work through the potential impacts on farm household behavior of changes in endowments, prices, and wages in two steps. First we think through the impacts on farm production decisions, and then we think through impacts on household consumption and time allocation decisions, taking into account that any changes affecting farm production decisions also affect farm profits and thus full income. For example, an increase in the price of purchased inputs q would reduce farm production and profits and reduce the use of purchased fertilizer I, and it can increase or decrease the profit-maximizing quantity of farm labor. The only channel through which the increase in q affects consumption and labor supply choices is through its impact on farm profits (and thus full income). The input price increase reduces farm profits and would thus be expected to reduce F, N, and H if all are normal goods.

Notice that the effect of an increase in q on net marketed surplus, NMS, is ambiguous. By increasing the cost of production, the increase in q reduces the profit-maximizing quantity of food produced Q, but by reducing profits and full income it also reduces food consumption F (if food is a normal good). The food consumption response tends to reduce the effect of the price increase on NMS, and it could even cause NMS to rise if the income reduction causes a very steep reduction in food consumption. Problem 2 asks you to think through several other comparative static implications.

More generally, to understand how changes in prices, wages, and other socioeconomic circumstances affect a farm household's involvement in markets, as indicated by its NMS and NLS, we must consider the impacts on both production *and* consumption and on both labor demand *and* labor supply. An increase in the price of corn motivates an increase in corn production, but the associated increase in farm profits and thus farm household income might stimulate a simultaneous increase in the household's corn consumption, rendering ambiguous the sign of the ultimate impact on corn *sales*. Thus, while a pure profit-maximizing agricultural producer would always increase corn sales in response to a corn price increase, a farm household that consumes some of what it produces might not.

Effects on farm household purchasing power of changes in prices and wages

Equation 7.7 allows us to analyze the approximate impact on the farm household's purchasing power of changes in agricultural prices and wages. If the price of food rose from p_f^1 to p_f^2, and if the household held its food production choices constant, farm revenue would increase by $(p_f^2 - p_f^1)Q$, tending to increase purchasing power. The expenditure required to maintain current consumption would also rise by $(p_f^2 - p_f^1)F$, however. Thus the net purchasing power increase of the food price increase is approximately

$$(p_f^2 - p_f^1)Q - (p_f^2 - p_f^1)F = (p_f^2 - p_f^1)NMS \qquad (7.10)$$

The expression on the right side emphasizes that the sign of the impact of a food price increase on a farm household's purchasing power depends on whether the household's NMS is positive or negative. If the NMS is positive, the household is a **net seller** of that crop and the price increase boosts household purchasing power. If the NMS is negative, the household is a **net buyer** and the price increase reduces its purchasing power.

Similarly, if the wage rose from w^1 to w^2, then the income the household derives from its current labor time would rise by $(w^2 - w^1)S$, but the profit it derives from its current farm production activities would fall by $(w^2 - w^1)L$. Thus, if the household did not alter its production and labor supply choices, the wage increase would bring a net purchasing power increase of

$$(w^2 - w^1)S - (w^2 - w^1)L = (w^2 - w^1)NLS \qquad (7.11)$$

If the household is a **net labor seller** (so that *NLS* is positive) a wage increase boosts purchasing power, but if the household is a **net labor buyer** (so that *NLS* is negative) the wage increase reduces purchasing power. If the price of chemical fertilizer rose at the same time, this would reduce the farm household's purchasing power even more.

We conclude that:

> If the price of a food rises by ρ percent, each percentage point of increase in that price ultimately gives rise to an increase of ε percentage points in the wage, and we let m indicate the ratio of the household's net marketed surplus of the food in question (valued at the market price of food) to its total consumption expenditure and n indicate the ratio of the household's net labor supply (valued at the market wage) to total income, then the approximate percentage change in the household's purchasing power is $\rho(m + \varepsilon n)$.

In problem 3 you will demonstrate that this formula is general enough to handle the special case of a wage labor household, which we may think of as "a farm household that sells no food and buys no labor." The formula tells us quite generally that:

> Goods price increases raise or lower a household's purchasing power depending on whether it is a net seller or net buyer of the goods in question. Wage increases similarly raise or lower its purchasing power depending on whether it is a net seller or net buyer of labor.

The net purchasing power effects of price and wage changes may be even more diverse among farm households than among wage labor households. Farmers who earn income primarily by producing corn for sale in the market tend to gain from a corn price increase, but other farmers might fail to benefit because they do not produce corn or because they produce corn only for their own consumption. Farmers who sell much of their family labor to the market tend to gain from wage increases, but farmers who hire market labor to cultivate their farms lose, and farmers who neither buy nor sell much labor are little affected by wage increases.

Transfer costs and nonparticipation in markets

Wage labor households have no choice but to participate in markets for food and labor, but farm households do have a choice, and in developing countries, many farm households choose not to participate in at least one relevant market. To understand why, we must explicitly recognize that participating in markets is costly. A household incurs **transfer costs** when it undertakes a market transaction. Transfer costs include transportation costs and transaction costs, where **transportation costs** include the costs of carrying goods or workers between the farm and the market center, and **transaction costs** include the costs of identifying buyers and sellers and reaching agreements regarding transactions. Transaction costs explain why the prices at which items may be purchased are higher than the prices at which they may be sold in the same location; retailers who purchase items from producers and then sell to consumers must earn enough on their sales to cover not only the price they paid producers for the goods but also the costs of locating producers, carrying out transactions with them, and setting out goods for sale in their market stall or shop. We dig more deeply into the nature of transfer costs in Chapter 8. Here we simply demonstrate how transfer costs might cause farm households to remain outside of markets and how households that are kept outside some markets by transfer costs might respond to change in surprising ways.

A simple farm household model focusing on labor demand, labor supply, and labor market participation in the presence of transfer costs

Consider a farm household that produces only a cash crop and consumes only food.[2] Such a household must participate in the cash crop market as a seller and must participate in the food market as a buyer. Focusing on such a household allows us to focus our analytical attention on the household's decision regarding participation in a single market: the labor market.

Critical to our discussion of labor market participation is the assumption that such participation is costly. Hiring labor out into the labor market is costly because a member of the family must travel to a hiring location or job site, find work, and submit to the authority of a nonfamily boss. Hiring labor in from the labor market is costly because hired workers must be located and brought to the farm, and they must be supervised. For convenience we assume that all the relevant transfer costs can be expressed in peso terms. Suppose w is the wage at the nearest hiring location in pesos per day, t_i is the per-day transfer cost of *hiring in* nonfamily labor from that market location, and t_o is the per-day transfer cost of *hiring out* family labor to that market. Under these conditions, for any day of labor the family hires in, they incur the total cost of $w + t_i$ pesos. For any day of labor the family hires out, the family brings home a net wage of $w - t_o$ pesos.

We assume that the household produces a quantity Q of the cash crop, which it sells at a price of p pesos per unit, with low-skilled labor L as the only variable input. It chooses to supply a total quantity of labor S to any work (whether on the family farm or in the labor market), knowing that total time available is T and thus as it increases S it reduces H. If $L > S$, the household wishes to employ more labor on its farm than it supplies itself, it hires labor in, and it spends $(w + t_i)(L - S)$ on hired labor. If $L < S$, the household wishes to supply more labor than it employs on the farm, so it hires labor out and earns $(w - t_o)(S - L)$ in wage labor earnings.

We assume, finally, that the household seeks to maximize its utility, $U(F,H)$, which is a function only of food consumption F and home time H. The cash it uses for purchasing food comes from cash crop sales, wage labor income, and nonlabor income M. To simplify the exposition, we set the price of food in the market to one peso per unit (so that F represents both total expenditure on food and the total real quantity of food consumed). Throughout all our analysis of changes in other prices and wages, we will be holding the price of food constant. The household's budget constraint may take two different forms depending on whether the household hires labor in or hires labor out. More specifically,

$$F = pQ + (w - t_o)(S - L) \quad \text{if} \ \ S > L$$
$$F = pQ - (w + t_i)(L - S) \quad \text{if} \ \ S \leq L \tag{7.12}$$

This says that total food consumption expenditure (the left side) is constrained to be equal to total receipts from cash crop sales plus labor income if the family is a net labor seller, and is equal to cash crop sales less the cost of hired labor if the household is a net labor buyer. If the household neither buys nor sells labor, its food purchases must just equal its receipts from cash crop sales.

The assumptions we have built into this simple model are convenient, because they imply that the household's entire set of decisions regarding consumption F, labor supply S, and production (Q and L) reduce to a simple pair of decisions regarding how much labor to use on its farm L and how much labor to supply S. Once we know L and S, we can figure out the values of all other choice variables through the use of simple identities. Once we know L, the production function tells us what Q must be. This also tells us the household's cash receipts from selling the cash crop, pQ. The choices of L and S together determine the costs associated with labor hired in

---

[2] The model developed in this section is a special case of a more general model examined by de Janvry, Fafchamps and Sadoulet (1991).

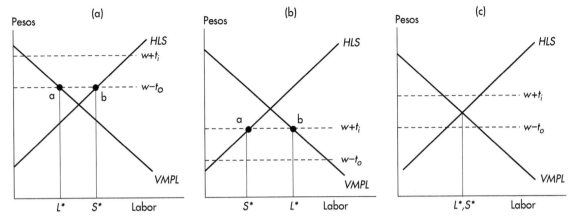

FIGURE 7.1
Labor Supply and Demand Decisions for Farm Households that Are Net Labor Sellers, Net Labor Buyers, and in Labor Autarky

or the receipts associated with labor hired out. Using equation 7.11 we can thus figure out the household's food purchases and consumption F.

We may describe the conditions influencing this household's choices using a single diagram that focuses on the choices of labor supply S and labor demand L. We wish to distinguish three configurations of this diagram as illustrated in Figure 7.1. The horizontal axis in each panel measures quantities of labor (whether L or S). The vertical axes are measured in pesos, which are useful for measuring the benefits and costs to the household of increasing labor supplies or labor demands.

We can think of the downward-sloping $VMPL$ (value of the marginal product of labor) schedule in each diagram as the farm household's demand for labor, just as the $VMPL$ schedule described the profit-maximizing farmer's demand for labor in Figure 6.6a. The $VMPL$ is the marginal benefit to the household—in terms of increased farm revenue and thus cash for food consumption—of employing another day of labor (whether family or hired labor) on its farm.

The upward-sloping household labor supply (HLS) schedule describes the cost to the household of giving up an additional day of its time to any kind of work (on the farm or in the market). Though the most natural way to think about the cost to the household of working is in units of utility lost as home time falls, we may translate this cost into the peso terms indicated by the HLS schedule by asking: "How many pesos must the household be given to just compensate for one less day of home time?" This cost rises as the household supplies more labor, because an additional day of home time becomes more precious as the quantity of home time enjoyed falls.

If the household had no access to labor markets, it would remain in **autarky**, neither buying nor selling labor. The quantity of labor it employs on its own farm L would then have to equal the quantity of family labor it supplies S. The household would maximize its utility by employing the quantity of labor associated with the intersection of its own farm labor demand ($VMPL$) and household labor supply (HLS) schedules. Let's call this quantity the **autarky labor quantity.**

To demonstrate that a household in autarky with respect to the labor market would maximize its utility at the intersection of its own labor demand and supply schedules, consider what would happen if the household devoted less than the autarky labor quantity to working its own farm. The household would be operating to the left of the intersection of the $VMPL$ and HLS schedules in any of the panels of Figure 7.1. With the $VMPL$ schedule above the HLS schedule, the increase in farm income associated with putting another day of labor to work in cultivating the farm ($VMPL$) would be greater than the income increase required to just compensate the household for losing a day of home time (the height of the HLS schedule). Adding another unit of family time to cultivating the farm would thus raise the household's utility. Similarly, if the household were operating to the right of the autarky labor quantity, it could increase household utility by reducing the use of family labor on the farm. Only when the heights of the *VMPL* and *HLS* schedules are equal is utility maximized (for a farm household in labor autarky). We'll call the height of the *VMPL* and *HLS* schedules at the autarky quantity the **autarky value of household labor**. It represents both the marginal cost to the household of working another day and the marginal benefit to the household of using another unit of labor on the farm, when starting from its autarky labor quantity.

In the presence of labor markets, households may be able to improve their utility beyond what they attain in autarky by hiring labor in or out. The line drawn at the height $w - t_o$ describes the marginal benefit to the family of selling a unit of family labor in the market. The horizontal line drawn at the height $w + t_i$ indicates the cost to the household of hiring in a unit of labor from the market. Notice that the more costly it is to participate in the market, the wider the gap between the $w + t_i$ and $w - t_o$ lines. Also, when t_o and t_i remain constant, an increase (decrease) in the market wage w causes the $w + t_i$ and $w - t_o$ lines to rise (fall) by the same amount, while the distance between them remains the same.

In Figure 7.1a the market wage w is sufficiently high (relative to the costs and benefits of labor use on the household's own farm) that both the $w + t_i$ and $w - t_o$ lines lie above the intersection of the *VMPL* and *HLS* schedules. This household can improve its utility relative to its autarky utility by selling some of its labor, because at the autarky labor quantity the benefit to the household of hiring labor out $(w - t_o)$ is greater than the cost to the household of working another hour (the autarky value of labor). We thus know that the household can increase its utility by selling some labor. (We can also tell that the household will not hire any labor in, because at the autarky labor quantity the cost of hiring labor in—$w + t_i$—is greater than the benefit of using that labor on the farm.)

The household described in Figure 7.1a devotes L^* units of family labor to cultivating the family farm while selling $S^* - L^*$ units of labor in the market. To see this, notice first that as long as the *VMPL* is greater than $w - t_o$, the family adds more to income by employing additional family time on the farm rather than in the market. Once the *VMPL* falls below $w - t_o$, however, the family would add more to income by selling additional labor in the market rather than using it on the farm. Thus we find the quantity of labor it devotes to own-farm cultivation (L^*) at point a, where the *VMPL* schedule and the $w - t_o$ line intersect. As long as the cost to the household of supplying more labor (the height of the *HLS* schedule) lies below $w - t_o$, the household increases its utility by supplying additional labor to the market. We find the household's utility-maximizing total supply of labor, S^*, at point b, where the *HLS* schedule intersects the $w - t_o$ line. Beyond this point the benefits of working fall short of the costs. The difference $S^* - L^*$ is the quantity of labor the household sells in the labor market.

In practical terms, when the $w - t_o$ line lies above the autarky price in a diagram like Figure 7.1a, we find the household's utility-maximizing choices of labor demand and labor supply by finding where the $w - t_o$ line crosses the *VMPL* and *HLS* schedules. Its labor supply exceeds its labor demand, and it chooses to participate in the labor market as a net labor seller.

In Figure 7.1b, the market wage w is sufficiently low that both the $w + t_i$ and $w - t_o$ lines lie below the intersection of the *VMPL* and *HLS* schedules. This household can improve its utility relative to the autarky level by hiring some labor from the market to help cultivate its farm, because at the autarky labor quantity, the benefit of employing another day of labor on the farm (*VMPL*) is greater than the cost of hiring in a day of labor from the market. This household uses family labor only on the family farm, and it supplements family labor by hiring in some market labor. Again we find the utility-maximizing level of total household labor supply (S^*) at the intersection of the *HLS* schedule with the relevant wage line, which is now the $w + t_i$ line; and we find the utility-maximizing level of total labor employed on the farm (L^*) at the intersection of the *VMPL* schedule and the same $w + t_i$ line. As long as the *HLS* schedule lies below $w + t_i$, the cheapest source of labor for cultivating the farm is family labor. Beyond point a, the cheapest source of labor for the farm is market labor, thus the household's utility-maximizing level of family labor supply S^* is found at point a. As long as the $VMPL$ remains above the cost of market labor $(w + t_i)$, hiring additional labor adds more to farm revenues than to costs. The household's utility-maximizing level of labor use on the farm L^* is found at point b. The difference $L^* - S^*$ is the quantity of labor the household hires from the market. The household chooses to participate in the labor market as a net labor buyer.

The story of Figure 7.1c is quite different. The intersection of the $VMPL$ and HLS schedules lies between the $w + t_i$ and $w - t_o$ lines. The cost of hiring labor $(w + t_i)$ is greater than the benefit of employing additional labor on the farm $(VMPL)$, and the return to hiring labor out $(w - t_o)$ is lower than the cost to the family of working more. Thus neither hiring in nor hiring out is attractive. The quantity of labor the household supplies (S^*) and the quantity of labor it demands (L^*) are identical. The household chooses to remain in autarky, not participating in the labor market.

If there were no transfer costs in this model, we would be unable to explain why some households remain outside of labor markets over long periods of time during which wages vary. If there were no transfer costs in labor markets, so that $t_i = t_o = 0$, then the $w + t_i$ and $w - t_o$ lines in graphs like those in Figure 7.1 would be identical and the household would almost always find itself in situations like those illustrated in panels a and b, in which it buys or sells labor. It would remain outside of labor markets only when the wage happens to be exactly equal to the autarky value of household labor.

We now have a framework for studying the forces that determine whether a farm household participates in the labor market, whether as buyer or seller. All else equal, increases in the costs and difficulty of participating in labor markets cause the gap between the $w + t_i$ and $w - t_o$ lines to expand, rendering it more likely that the household chooses not to participate in the labor market. Increases in the price of output or the marginal product of labor shift the $VMPL$ schedule up, rendering it more likely that the intersection of the $VMPL$ and HLS schedules lies above both wage lines, leading the farm household to buy labor. Increases in the household's willingness to supply labor at any level of compensation shift the HLS curve to the right, rendering it more likely that the intersection lies below the wage lines and the household sells labor. Thus:

> Farmers living in more remote areas or in areas connected to labor market centers by inferior infrastructure (for whom the cost of participating in the labor market is higher) are less likely to participate in labor markets than others. Improvements in infrastructure encourage participation in labor markets, and increases in fuel prices that raise the cost of transportation can reduce participation. Households with more or better land, or that experience labor-using technological improvements, are more likely than others to participate in labor markets as buyers, while households with many able-bodied workers and fewer household responsibilities that give value to home time are more likely to participate in labor markets as sellers.

More general models would yield similar predictions regarding participation in markets for agricultural outputs and inputs.

Implications of nonparticipation for behavior

The behavior of farm households that choose not to participate in labor markets may be quite different from that of profit-maximizing producers (such as those examined in Chapter 6), even when they make choices according to purely neoclassical assumptions. Most obviously, whereas a profit maximizer using labor as her only variable input would reduce labor demand and output supply in response to an increase in the wage, a farm household like the one in Figure 7.1c would make no behavioral changes in response to a small change in the wage. This does not mean,

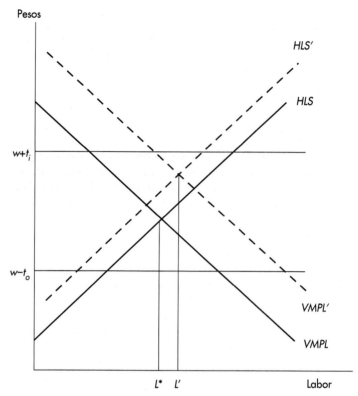

FIGURE 7.2
Effect of Cash Crop Price Increase on Farm Household in Labor Autarky

however, that farm households that remain outside of markets are entirely unresponsive to wage changes. A sufficiently large increase in the wage would cause a household initially in a situation like 7.1c to find itself in a situation like 7.1a, where it begins to hire labor out. Similarly, if the wage were to fall enough, the household might find begin to hire labor in.

Less obviously, a household not participating in labor markets for the reasons described in Figure 7.1c might respond very differently to a change in the price of the cash crop, p, than would a simple profit maximizer. For a price-taking profit-maximizing producer employing low-skill labor as the only variable input (as depicted in Figure 6.8a), an output price increase shifts the VMPL schedule up, inducing an increase in the quantity of labor demanded and in total production of the cash crop.

For a farm household in the situation described by Figure 7.1c, the direct impact of an increase in p is to shift the VMPL schedule up, as illustrated by the shift from the solid VMPL schedule in Figure 7.2 to the dashed VMPL' schedule. The new intersection of the HLS and VMPL' schedules lies to the right of the initial intersection, indicating a tendency for labor employed on the farm, and total farm output, to increase. But this is not the end of the story. The increase in p implies an increase in farm profitability and thus an increase in the household's full income. If home time is a normal good, then as profits and full income increase, the household's willingness to supply labor (at any level of compensation) falls, causing the HLS schedule to shift up and to the left, as indicated by the dashed HLS' schedule. This tends to attenuate the household's crop supply response to the price increase. If the shift in the HLS schedule is great enough, the increase in p might even cause the household to *reduce* its production of the cash crop! (As long as the percentage reduction in production is smaller than the percentage increase in price, the household still enjoys higher total crop income.) Thus:

When transfer costs prevent farm households from participating in labor markets, increases in crop prices can lead to much smaller increases in the supply of agricultural goods to markets than would be predicted by models of simple profit maximization, and they can even lead to reductions. If the same farmers had cheaper access to labor markets, and chose to participate in labor markets, the same output price increase might stimulate a significantly larger production response.

7.2D Nonfarm business households

Self-employment is much more common in developing than developed countries, not only in agriculture but also in rural nonfarm sectors and in urban areas. In urban Vietnam, more than 40 percent of men and more than 60 percent of women are self-employed (FAO/UNDP, 2002). The businesses of the self-employed are highly diverse and include selling umbrellas on city streets, performing freelance carpentry, operating small bakeries, and running larger family businesses. A very small number of the officially self-employed run large modern firms with many employees. Most work on their own, with family members, or with just one or two employees.

The farm household model of the previous section may easily be relabeled to accommodate analysis of nonfarm business households. The main difference is in the nature of the goods the households produce. Nonfarm households are less likely than food crop farmers to consume large quantities of the goods or services they produce, and thus they are more likely to be net sellers in output markets. As with wage labor and farm households, they benefit from goods price or wage increases depending on whether they are net sellers or net buyers of labor.

This implies that:

Increases in food prices tend to reduce the purchasing power of nonfarm business households, which are likely to be net buyers of foods. Associated wage increases boost their purchasing power if they are net labor sellers and reduce their purchasing power if they are net labor buyers. They may also benefit through increased prices for the nonfarm goods and services they produce, if the increased incomes of farmers and workers increase demand for the consumer goods they sell or if increased farm profitability raises demand for the agricultural inputs they sell.

7.2E Incapacitated households

Many of the poorest households in developing countries have little potential to generate income for themselves, either through wage labor or through the operation of farm or nonfarm enterprises. Their prime-age adult members may be disabled or absent, and the numbers of children, elderly, ill, injured, or disabled may be very high relative to the number of workers. Households headed by women and "skip generation" households in which grandparents care for grandchildren—because the middle generation has been taken away by violent conflict, HIV/AIDS, or other causes—are often among the most vulnerable and incapacitated. Governments of several countries in Africa estimate that at least 10 percent of their populations live in incapacitated and very poor households (Schubert, 2005).

We can think of such **incapacitated households** as special cases of wage labor households, whose total time endowments are very small or who face only very low wages. They might live almost entirely off nonlabor income in the form of gifts or loans from relatives, neighbors, or charitable organizations. Whereas the capacitated poor might hope to gain from workfare programs that offer low wages for manual labor, and might hope to share in growth that brings rising wages for low-skill labor, the incapacitated poor tend to be left behind by workfare programs and economic growth. Thus the incapacitated poor merit special attention in development policy analysis. As for food prices:

> Increases in food prices reduce the purchasing power of incapacitated households. Such households are largely unable to benefit from any associated increases in wages. Only if rising incomes inspire their capacitated neighbors to share more with the less fortunate through public or private safety nets might they derive any benefits from food price increases.

7.2F The poverty impacts of rising global food prices

After declining gradually for 30 years, world market prices of major staple food crops shot up in the first decade of the 21st century (relative to other prices). Rice prices rose most dramatically, rising more than 250 percent from 2004 to mid-2008. Maize and wheat prices rose more than 80 percent. Prices of meat, dairy, and cash crops also rose, but not as rapidly.[3] During the same period, world fuel prices doubled or tripled, and the prices of some fertilizers nearly quadrupled (Headey and Fan, 2008).

According to the unitary household theories just discussed, a first step in analyzing the short-run impact of such price increases on poverty is to gather data on the extent to which poor and near-poor households are net buyers or net sellers of the goods whose prices have increased. Maros Ivanic and Will Martin (2008) use household survey data to measure net purchases and sales of wheat, rice, dairy, maize, sugar, beef, and poultry for households in various income groups in Bolivia, Cambodia, Madagascar, Malawi, Nicaragua, Pakistan, Peru, Vietnam, and Zambia, and separately for rural and urban areas within each country. Using these data they ask questions of the form: If the world price of wheat rises 10 percent, and if we assume that wheat prices rise uniformly by 10 percent for all households throughout Bolivia, what happens to the purchasing power of poor and near-poor households, and what does this imply for poverty rates?

As we might expect, they find that rising food prices increase poverty rates in urban areas, where the poor produce little food and are predominantly food buyers. More surprising, however, they find that in many countries rising food prices also aggravate poverty in rural areas. Many of the rural poor live in landless or near-landless households, earning their living primarily by working for wages, and are net food buyers. An exception is Vietnam, where most rural households have some land and many of the rural poor are small commercial rice farmers.

They also find that the net poverty effects of food price increases differ across crops and countries. In Bolivia, rising wheat prices increase poverty and rising maize prices reduce it. Rising rice prices increase poverty in Cambodia and Madagascar, but they reduce it in Vietnam. In Uganda, locally grown staple foods such as matoke, tubers, and potatoes, which are not traded in international markets, are important in both consumption and production, muting the impacts of global food prices on the poor there (Wodon and Zaman, 2010).

Extrapolating from their basic calculations, Ivanic and Martin estimate that the short-run effect of the global food price increases observed between 2004 and 2008 was to increase the number of the world's people living on less than $1 per day (in real terms) by as many as 105 million people. If the authors had included the effects of rising prices for petroleum-based fertilizers and rising transportation costs in their calculations, they would have found fewer income improvements among poor net food sellers, and the estimated net increase in poverty would have been even greater. On the other hand, the true effect of global food price changes might have been somewhat smaller than they estimated, because they assumed that global food price increases are

---

[3] These figures pertain to dollar-denominated prices in major world markets (Heady and Fan, 2008).

fully transmitted to all households throughout each country and, as we will see in Chapter 8, global food price changes might have little effect on prices in rural areas that are poorly connected by infrastructure to larger markets. It nonetheless seems likely that global food price increases did indeed make poverty more pressing in many areas. Anecdotal evidence collected from around the world suggests that food price increases significantly reduced the purchasing power of many poor households, causing them to consume smaller quantities, choose less expensive foods, eat less frequently, and put their children to work (IFAD, 2008).

Given that large numbers of the world's poor are net food buyers, must we conclude that agricultural market liberalization in the developed countries, which would raise world food prices, would ultimately be bad for the world's poor? No, not necessarily. Higher global food prices might eventually increase production in agriculture and linked nonagricultural sectors, increasing the demand for labor and raising wages for rural workers. If we wish to predict the longer-run impacts of developed countries' agricultural liberalization, we must predict the extent to which increases in various crop prices will eventually translate into wage increases, both in the medium run as farmers adjust their variable inputs and in the longer run as farmers invest in capital improvements and technological innovation.

Unfortunately, surprisingly little research has been directed toward estimating the elasticity of low-skilled wages with respect to agricultural price increases. The few estimates to date are not very optimistic. For example, Boyce and Ravallion (1991) estimated impacts of rice price changes on agricultural wages in Bangladesh, allowing for the effects to grow over time as households adjust their production and employment decisions. They found a short-run elasticity of wage with respect to rice price of 0.22 and a long-run elasticity of 0.47, which is almost entirely realized within four years.

Ravallion (1990) uses these elasticity estimates to calculate the net impacts on poverty of rice price increases and induced wage increases in the short and long run. He finds that short-run wage effects are sufficiently small that rising rice prices increase poverty significantly even after taking related wage increases into account, and he finds long-run wage effects are only just strong enough to roughly balance price effects. Recall that the percentage reduction in a wage labor household's purchasing power associated with a one percent increase in food price is equal to $f - \varepsilon \omega$, using notation introduced earlier in the chapter. Because the typical wage labor household (in the population Ravallion studied) devoted less than half of its budget to rice purchases ($f < 0.5$), wage increases of less than half the rice price increases ($\varepsilon < 0.5$) were sufficient to set $f - \varepsilon \omega$ to zero, even in households that derived most income from wage labor (ω close to 1). Still, according to Ravallion's estimates, the wage effects only just balanced the price effects and did not bring net reductions in poverty.

Ravallion's conclusion may be overly pessimistic, because farmers may be more inclined to increase production and employment in response to the long-term price increases driven by liberalization than they are in the face of the temporary price fluctuations captured in the Bangladesh data. Many observers also suspect that farmers' longer-run responses to rising prices are currently constrained in many countries by lack of improved technologies, lack of market infrastructure, and lack of financing (Masters, 2008). This raises the possibility that rising food prices might lead to much greater expansion and poverty reduction if complemented by investments in agricultural research and extension, infrastructure, and improvements in financial markets. We return to these issues in later chapters.

Our household model framework reminds us, however, that even if agricultural liberalization in developed countries ultimately leads to agricultural expansion and rising wages in developing countries, many of the poor bear serious costs in the short run, and the incapacitated poor bear costs even in the long run, unless explicit efforts are made to increase transfers to them through public or private safety net institutions.

7.3 Non-unitary Household Theories: From Simple Utility Maximization to Cooperation and Conflict

7.3A A motivation

In many parts of the developing world, the lives of women and girls are much harder than the lives of men and boys (King and Mason, 2001; Kevane, 2004; World Bank, 2011). In South Asia and China girls receive lower quality food, are less likely to receive health care when sick, and die at higher rates. In many places girls receive less schooling than boys. Women often work longer hours than men, especially when hours spent cooking, fetching water, and performing other household chores are included in the calculations. They face more restrictions on their freedom and enjoy fewer rights to own property. Such differences suggest the importance of incorporating gender into development policy analysis. An important first step in this direction is to understand how gender enters into household decision making.

In what follows we describe three sets of theoretical models that together guide contemporary development economists' study of gender in household decision making and examine them in light of empirical evidence. We then summarize their implications for how we might incorporate gender concerns into policy analysis.

7.3B Gender in unitary household models

All the choice models considered in Chapters 6 and 7 thus far are models of *unitary* decision making. The defining characteristic of such models is that they treat the household as if it were a single actor, which seeks to maximize a single utility function.

We can easily incorporate concern for **intrahousehold distribution** (of food consumption, home time, and other goods) into unitary models of household decision making by assuming that the unitary decision maker maximizes a utility function in which food consumption, home time, and schooling enjoyed by female members, and food consumption, home time, and schooling enjoyed by male members, enter as distinct consumption items. After incorporating gender in this way:

> Unitary models of household decision making point to roles that income, time endowments, prices, and preferences might play in determining the extent to which households provide female members with less food, home time, or schooling than they provide for male members.

Unitary models suggest, for example, that rising incomes can reduce gender gaps in consumption if households treat female consumption as a more strongly normal good than male consumption. Some evidence suggests that this is the case. For example, women and girls in southern India receive less nourishment than men and boys in the dry season, when income is especially low, but their consumption rises enough to equal men's and boys' consumption in the harvest season when incomes are higher (Behrman, 1988). Thus, rising incomes may be expected to bring some reduction in gender gaps. More generally, in most of the 32 countries included in a study of infant mortality, the ratio of female infant mortality rates to male rates was higher among poor families than among wealthy families (King and Mason, 2001).

Unitary models also suggest that increases in household time endowments—arising, for example, out of infrastructure projects that build wells or power sources close to homes—may lower gender gaps in schooling if households treat female schooling time as a more strongly normal good than male schooling time. The observation that women and girls bear most of the large time burden associated with carrying water in the developing world suggests significant potential to reduce gender gaps in schooling rates by improving access to water, though direct estimates of the effects of such water projects on schooling are lacking (King and Mason, 2001).

Just as female consumption may be more sensitive to income and time endowment changes than male consumption in unitary models, so also it may be more sensitive to reductions in the cost of obtaining goods and services. Thus, general reductions in the prices of food, health services, and education can also decrease gender gaps. Several studies offer empirical evidence of such differences. Behrman and Deolalikar (1990), for example, find confirmation that some food price reductions would raise female nutrient intakes relative to male intakes, though the channels through which this happens are somewhat surprising. They find that reductions in the prices of foods that are relative luxury goods in rural south India (including rice and milk) *reduce* nutrient intakes for men (presumably by inducing a substitution from staple foods toward luxury foods that provide fewer nutrients per rupee spent), but they leave the nutrient intakes for women and girls largely unchanged or in some cases increase them.

Unitary models also suggest the potential to raise nutrition, schooling, and health care for girls relative to boys by reducing the costs of goods and services for girls while holding the costs for boys constant. Successful girls' scholarship programs bear out the significance of such efforts in education. For example, a secondary school scholarship program for girls in Bangladesh appears successful in raising girls' enrollment (King and Mason, 2001).

Finally, in the unitary household model, gender differences in consumption and time use are determined in part by the unitary decision makers' preferences.[4] This raises the possibility that advertising campaigns and education can alter gender gaps, even when income and prices remain constant.

Unitary models yield useful insights about gender and development, but:

Unitary theories suffer from three weaknesses as guides for research on gender in development.

One weakness is conceptual. Unitary theories assume that a household maximizes a single utility function. To apply this theory to a real-world household with multiple members, we must be willing to assume either that a single household head makes all the decisions for the household unilaterally or that all household members think alike and make unanimous decisions. A model that allows more nuanced possibilities, in which women may disagree with men (in the sense that their utility functions differ), and exercise at least some voice or autonomy, would be more compelling.

The other two weaknesses relate to unitary household model predictions that are contradicted by empirical evidence. First, to a unitary decision maker all income is equally useful for expanding the household budget and facilitating the purchase of goods and services, regardless of which family members bring the income into the household. Thus in unitary household models, household consumption decisions depend only on households' *total* income and not separately on the incomes of men and women (see problem 5). The unitary decision maker is said to **pool** income belonging to all household members before making choices about consumption.

Several empirical observations suggest, instead, that households do not treat men's and women's income as identical. For example, Thomas (1990) finds that nonlabor income in the hands of Brazilian women has bigger impacts on family health, and especially on child survival probabilities, than nonlabor income in the hands of Brazilian men, and Duflo (2003) finds that pension income received by women in South Africa improved the nutritional status of girls in their households, whereas pension income received by men did not. Such evidence suggests that channeling development program benefits to women rather than men can increase program

---

[4] For a more comprehensive review of what unitary models predict regarding intrahousehold allocations, see Strauss and Beegle (1996).

impacts on household nutrition and other investments in the human capital of children. Unitary models offer no guidance for deeper study of this possibility.

Unitary household models also predict that households will put resources to **efficient** use. This means that households allocate land, nonlabor income, and other resources across uses in such a way that it is impossible to raise one member's well-being without reducing the well-being of another. Unitary models predict efficiency as long as the unitary decision maker gives at least some positive weight to each member's individual well-being when assessing overall household utility. Under such circumstances, if household resource use were inefficient, household utility would not be maximized. Inefficiency (by definition) implies that one member's well-being could be raised without reducing other member's well-being and thus that household utility (which is a positive function of all members' well-being) could be increased. If household decisions are indeed efficient, then while gender biases can leave female members worse off than male members within households, they do not prevent households from making the most of their resources and exiting poverty.

Several studies suggest, however, that use of household resources may be inefficient in at least some contexts. For example, Udry (1996) offers provocative evidence of inefficient allocation of agricultural inputs across male and female plots of land among rural households in Burkina Faso (see Box 7.3 later). Dercon and Krishnan (2000) offer somewhat more subtle evidence of inefficiency within households in southern Ethiopia. They point out that intra-household efficiency requires that household members "insure" each other, in the sense that they share the burden of coping with income shocks, even when the shocks affect only one of them directly. That is, husbands and wives who have not been hit by shocks should provide transfers to spouses who have been hit by shocks. The authors demonstrate that in southern Ethiopia men do not provide their wives with much insurance against health shocks, instead leaving women to bear the burden on their own. This is inefficient, because the men could have made themselves better off without leaving women worse off if they had provided women with insurance (preventing women from having to bear the burden of health shocks alone) while requiring women to "pay" them for the insurance by allowing men to consume a larger average share of household resources.

7.3C Cooperative bargaining and other models of efficient collective decision making

A first set of **non-unitary household models** addresses the first two weaknesses of unitary models identified above: the unsatisfactory assumptions about how men and women with diverse interests interact within households and the inaccurate prediction regarding income pooling. In this set of models, husbands and wives are assumed to engage in **cooperative bargaining** over how to use household income, time, and other resources.

Cooperative bargaining theories recognize that husbands and wives might differ in their preferences and thus in their perceptions of how best to use household resources. Husbands and wives understand that **cooperation** in forming a household and coordinating work allows them to increase their joint productivity through specialization and economies of scale, and creates other benefits. They thus see the potential for cooperation to leave them both better off than if they were not married. The spouses also understand, however, that their interests are in **conflict**, because they would each like to enjoy as large a share as possible of the **surplus** (i.e., total potential improvement in well-being) created by cooperation. Cooperative bargaining theories thus assume that household decisions are reached through a bargaining process, in which each spouse seeks to get his or her way in allocating household resources and threatens to break up the household (causing the benefits of cooperation to disappear) if household allocations are not satisfactory.

Nash bargaining solutions

The bargaining processes in which wives and husbands engage may be complex and subtle and are difficult to model directly. Bargaining theorists argue that it is nonetheless possible to gain insight into the implications of bargaining by taking an approach proposed by John Nash (1950). Nash sets out axioms describing characteristics that we might reasonably expect to see in bargaining outcomes when the parties to the bargain are rational. He supposes these axioms are fulfilled and examines their implications.

More specifically, Nash suggests that a cooperative bargaining outcome should satisfy five axioms. First, it should be efficient, because rational parties to a bargain would not wish to overlook ways of improving the bargaining outcome for one party without worsening it for the other. Second, the solution should leave each party better off than he would be if they failed to cooperate, because each party must have a rational reason to participate in the bargain. This suggests that each party's **fallback position**, or the utility he would derive if household cooperation broke down, should play an important role in shaping the ultimate bargain. Third, interest in fairness suggests that if the parties to the bargain are identical in preferences and opportunities, then they should be treated equally by the ultimate bargain. The last two axioms proposed by Nash are more technical and subtle: that changing the scale in which utility is measured (without changing the way the parties rank order outcomes) should not change the real nature of the ultimate bargain, and that eliminating an un-chosen option (for how to allocate the household's joint resources) should not change the bargaining outcome.

Nash proved mathematically that if a bargaining outcome satisfies his five axioms, then it is identical to the outcome that would be achieved if the two parties simply agreed to choose household asset use, time allocation, and consumption allocations to maximize the product

$$(U_c - U_f)(V_c - V_f) \qquad (7.13)$$

where U_c and V_c are the utilities of husband and wife when they cooperate, and U_f and V_f are their utilities in their fallback positions. That is, the bargain maximizes the product of the gains to cooperation experienced by the two parties. (Problem 6 explores the intuitive appeal of this result for a simple case.) U_c and V_c are functions of the household's consumption, time allocation, and production choices. U_f and V_f are independent of household choices and are determined by a wide range of socioeconomic conditions that we discuss below. One implication is that:

> In Nash bargaining models, any change in circumstance that increases the wife's fallback utility (while leaving the husband's fallback utility unchanged) shifts the bargaining outcome in her favor. Having a stronger fallback position thus translates into greater **bargaining power**.

Some theorists interpret the parties' fallback utilities to be the utilities they would experience if the marriage failed and they divorced (McElroy and Horney, 1981). If this is the case, then the wife's fallback utility and bargaining power—and the household's ultimate decisions regarding consumption, labor supply, and production—should depend on the assets that would belong to her after divorce, the wage labor opportunities to which she would have access, her remarriage opportunities, and a wide range of legal institutions and social norms shaping her economic and social treatment as a single and divorced woman. The more vulnerable she would be in divorce, the less influence she will have in household decision making during marriage.

Other theorists interpret the fallback situation to be one of noncooperation while remaining married, in which husband and wife meet their individual needs as best they can, using only the resources over which they have individual control, rather than cooperating to achieve full economies of scale and specialization (Lundberg and Pollack, 1993). In this case, bargaining

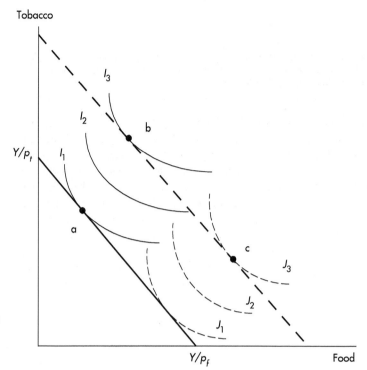

FIGURE 7.3
Household Consumption Choices in Unitary and Cooperative Bargaining Models

power can also depend on the wife's economic opportunities even while married, such as current opportunities for wage employment.

Bargaining power as a shifter of effective household preferences

Figure 7.3 is useful for illuminating differences between unitary and cooperative bargaining models of household decision making. Here we focus on a husband and wife endowed only with joint income Y, which they must allocate across the purchase of food and tobacco (at prices p_f and p_t). Whether the household is unitary or engages in a Nash bargain, it faces a budget constraint such as that depicted by the solid diagonal line. For a unitary household, the indifference curves I_1, I_2, and I_3 might represent the single unchanging set of preferences that shape the household's choices. Legal changes that assure the wife greater asset ownership in the event of divorce (and other variables affecting fallback positions as defined above) have no effect on this solution.

For a Nash bargaining household, by contrast, the indifference curves I_1, I_2, and I_3 represent what we could call the household's "effective preferences," which reflect a weighted average of the preferences of the husband and the wife, where the weights depend on their relative bargaining power.[5] If women place greater value on food relative to tobacco consumption, then changes to divorce law that increase the wife's bargaining power could cause the household's effective preferences to shift to the new configuration illustrated by the indifference curves J_1, J_2, and J_3, leading to greater food consumption out of any level of income. Bargaining models thus introduce the possibility that household choices are influenced by economic, legal, and social conditions that affect what life would be like for women in their fallback situations, even when they do not affect the household's current budget constraint.

---

[5] The use of the label "indifference curve" for this interpretation of the diagram is convenient but makes poor use of English. Along any one curve the weighted average of the husband's and wife's utilities holds constant, but neither husband nor wife need be indifferent between the consumption combinations along the curve.

We may use Figure 7.3 to demonstrate that:

> Cooperative bargaining models offer a possible explanation for the empirical evidence (cited earlier) that households do not pool income, and they admit the possibility that transfer program benefits can have stronger developmental impacts within households if targeted to wives rather than husbands.

Whether a household is unitary or engages in Nash bargaining, the receipt of a cash transfer by either spouse would shift out the budget constraint in the way illustrated by the shift from the solid to the dashed budget line in Figure 7.3. For a unitary household whose unchanging preferences are described by indifference curves I_1, I_2, and I_3, the cash transfer would lead the household's consumption to shift from point a to point b, regardless of whether the transfer is given to the husband or the wife. For a Nash bargaining household in which the wife places greater importance on the consumption of food relative to tobacco, however, the cash transfer might not only shift the budget constraint but also shift the household's effective preferences in the way illustrated by a shift in indifference curves to the positions of J_1, J_2, and J_3, leading consumption to shift from point a to point c. If the cash transfer had been given to the husband, the indifference curves might have stayed the same or shifted in the other direction. The transfer could thus have a bigger impact on food consumption if given to women rather than men, provided that the receipt of the transfer indeed increases the recipient's bargaining power and women value food consumption more highly relative to tobacco consumption than men do.

Perceived and true interests

In a thought-provoking essay, Amartya Sen (1990) extends the cooperative bargaining framework to a situation in which the objective that women seek to maximize through bargaining (which we have called *utility*) can differ from their true well-being, because their preferences are socially constructed. Women's **perceived interests** might differ from their true or **objective interests** because they have been raised to believe that men are more valuable than women, that men's contributions to the household (through income generation) are more valuable than women's contributions (through child care, water fetching, and other unpaid tasks), or that a woman's only legitimate objective is one that places little weight on her own needs and wants. These beliefs may be self-reinforcing if women living in male-dominated homes also believe they should not venture outside the home where their beliefs might be challenged. Sen points to the tendency for women in some cultures to acquiesce to their own ill treatment, and even to participate in punishing other female family members who deviate from cultural norms, as evidence of the important role that culture plays in reinforcing women's disadvantaged status.

When we allow for such a gap between women's perceived and objective interests, it becomes possible to improve women's well-being by changing their perceptions. Something as simple as creating new motivations for women to meet with other women (e.g., by creating opportunities for them to gather to learn about good nutrition) might ultimately improve their well-being if the opportunity for sharing about their needs and wants with each other legitimizes them, leading the women to revise their perceived interests to bear greater resemblance to their objective interests. Similarly, improved wage employment opportunities for women might increase women's well-being not only through improved household income, and not only by increasing their bargaining power, but also by bringing them into contact with new peer groups that reshape their perceived interests.

New insights

As was true in unitary models, changes in income, time endowments and prices, and advertising campaigns targeted at changing male household heads' preferences, all have the potential to alter gender gaps in resource allocations within cooperative bargaining models. Cooperative bargaining models also yield the new insight that women's treatment and influence within households might depend on institutional conditions, including legal and social rules defining property rights; rules relating to divorce, child custody, child support, and remarriage; and women's culturally determined perceptions of their own interests.

Continued weakness

One of the axioms defining a cooperative bargaining solution is that resource allocation is efficient. Thus empirical examples of inefficient allocation of resources across uses by men and women are as difficult to explain within cooperative bargaining models as they are in unitary models. This same difficulty applies to a more general class of theoretical models of household decision making introduced by Chiappori (1992), but it need not apply to the models in the next section.

7.3D Separated spheres and mental accounts

Anthropological studies of household decision making, especially in sub-Saharan Africa, provide two reasons for discomfort with all the household models described thus far. First, the models assume away any autonomous decision making by wives and husbands, who are assumed instead to reach joint decisions about all consumption, labor supply, and production choices. African men and women, by contrast, often seem to have clearly delineated spheres of activity in which they have autonomy (Kevane, 2004). In many parts of Africa, for example, farm households cultivate multiple plots of land, with some considered men's plots and others considered women's plots, and with cultivation decisions on separate plots being made autonomously.

Second, the models examined thus far assume that household members treat income as fully **fungible**, in the sense that any peso of income—regardless of where it comes from—may be channeled into any use within the household. This is hard to reconcile with anthropological descriptions of socially defined limits on the legitimate use of income from specific sources in some African cultures. For example, in Côte d'Ivoire, social norms dictate that income derived from yam cultivation be devoted to expenditure on staple foods and education of children, whereas only income from men's and women's cash crops may be used for the purchase of items of more individual interest to adults, such as tobacco, jewelry, or adult clothing (Duflo and Udry, 2004).

In light of these observations:

> We might wish to build models of household decision making in which cultural norms dictate husbands' and wives' **spheres of decision making** and the **mental accounts** that define lists of legitimate uses for income streams coming from specific sources.

In such models, husband–wife interactions are characterized more by self-interested trade than by cooperation. A wife may devote extra time to working her husband's plots in exchange for the husband's increased contribution toward the purchase of household food. More subtly, a husband may offer additional income support without requiring his wife to work on his land, if by so doing he relieves her need to earn income to meet her needs for clothing (by cultivating her own plots or working for wages), thus freeing her up to devote more time to child care and food preparation, which are of mutual interest. Hence the choices of wives and husbands remain interdependent.

Such models also raise the possibility that:

> Social norms defining decision-making spheres and mental accounts might prevent resources from flowing to their most efficient uses within households, and the problem may be compounded by lack of cooperation between semiautonomous husbands and wives.

☰ **Box 7.3** Inefficient Allocation of Inputs across Men's and Women's Plots in Burkina Faso

Many rural African households derive their meager livings from a number of very small plots of land and their own hard work. To maximize their income they must put their land and labor to efficient use. Efficiency requires that any labor the household uses be distributed across plots to maximize the total value of production. This in turn requires that the value of the marginal product of labor (*VMPL*) be set equal across plots (see Chapter 9). Any institutional constraint preventing households from equating the *VMPL* across plots would aggravate their poverty.

We might question whether labor is allocated efficiently across plots of land within African households, because many African cultures make distinctions between women's plots, men's plots, and communal plots. According to anthropological studies, women and men each control the income generated by their own plots, income from communal plots must be used to satisfy subsistence needs, and women and men also have some autonomy in making decisions regarding the uses of their plots. Lack of cooperation might prevent them from allocating labor, fertilizer, and other variable inputs efficiently across all plots.

Christopher Udry (1996) tests whether poor rural households in Burkina Faso allocate labor and other variable inputs efficiently across men's and women's plots, employing data on 150 households each observed in three agricultural years. Households and land arrangements in his sample are complicated: The median husband has 1.8 wives, and the median household cultivates 10 plots and produces six different crops.

To find evidence of inefficiency, Udry must find evidence that *VMPLs* differ across men's and women's plots within households. Simply demonstrating that average productivity (as measured by the value of production per hectare) tends to be higher for men's plots than

for women's plots is not enough. If production functions differ across crops, then average productivity can differ across plots devoted to different crops even when *VMPLs* are equated across plots (see problem 5 in Chapter 3), and average productivity can thus differ across men's and women's plots simply because men and women tend to cultivate different crops. Furthermore, where higher land quality raises *VMPL* schedules, more labor and fertilizer must be applied to drive down the *VMPL* to the same level. Thus average crop yields can differ across men's and women's plots, even when the *VMPLs* are equated, if average land quality differs between men's and women's plots.

Fortunately, Udry's data allow him to handle these complexities. In many of the households in his sample, one or more crops are cultivated on both men's and women's plots, and his data also contain excellent measures of topographical and soil characteristics for each plot. He can, therefore, compare yields on men's and women's plots within households, while controlling for crop choice and land quality. Such comparisons show average crop yields to be 30 percent lower on women's plots than on men's plots. The author speculates that this inefficiency arises because women are reluctant to encourage more use of their husbands' labor and fertilizer on their plots, fearing that this would lead to their loss of control over land and income.

Udry estimates how much household incomes could be increased by allocating labor more efficiently across men's and women's plots. He estimates that household incomes would rise by only about 6 percent. Thus, while he finds reason to reject the prediction that households allocate resources efficiently (and thus rejects unitary and cooperative bargaining models of household decision making), he finds that within-household inefficiency contributes only in a modest way to poverty in the study region.

For example, efficiency might dictate that the husband use some proceeds from cash crop production to purchase fertilizer for use on his wife's plots. He may be reluctant to do so, however, if the wife retains control over all income generated by her plots. Even though he could increase total household income by shifting some fertilizer from his own plots to his wife's, such a change might *reduce* the income over which he retains control.

The potential for such inefficiency in use of household resources implies that women's poor access to resources might not only reduce their shares in household consumption and leisure, it might also increase the average depth of the household's poverty. Changes in legal and social norms that redistribute resources like land from the husband's sphere to the wife's might thus be important not only for reducing gender-based inequality but also for reducing poverty more broadly. Box 7.3 describes Udry's (1996) assessment of the potential to raise household incomes in Burkina Faso by altering the allocation of resources across men's and women's plots within households.

New insights

Once we introduce separated spheres and mental accounts into models of household decision making, our list of potential determinants of intrahousehold distribution becomes longer and more complicated. Cultural institutions can influence intrahousehold distribution by helping to determine whether women are allocated control over any plots, how many plots they control, what crops they are allowed to cultivate, and the range of legitimate uses of income derived from plots of different sorts.

chapter

Domestic Markets for Goods and Services

People benefit from trading with each other in markets, and the benefits increase as markets expand in geographic scope, variety, and sophistication. Yet markets remain few, small, and unsophisticated in many developing countries. Understanding the barriers that might prevent market development, and the ways policymakers might help raise or lower those barriers, is important for understanding growth and development. Identifying the forces that cause market prices to rise and fall is also important in development studies, because price levels are important determinants of peoples' well-being (as we saw in Chapter 7).

This chapter argues that to understand the limited nature of many markets in developing countries we must acknowledge the existence of transportation and transaction costs, which tend to be high in developing countries but are ignored in introductory economic models of market equilibrium. The chapter then expounds a model of how market prices and quantities are determined in the presence of those costs and demonstrates the model's usefulness in two policy analysis applications. The chapter's final section examines the benefits of investment in infrastructure and institutions that reduce transportation and transaction costs, thereby promoting market development, and examines why governments and NGOs might have important roles to play in encouraging such investments.

8.1 Markets in Developing Countries

Developed-country markets offer consumers a tremendous variety of breakfast cereals, cars, appliances, and toys. Logistics companies deliver goods to customers' doorsteps, from halfway around the world, in a matter of days. Commodity price movements in one world capital lead almost instantaneously to price movements in distant capitals. Buyers pay by cash, check, credit card, or invoice and choose from a wide array of financing arrangements, and professional traders buy and sell futures and options.

Developing-country markets often appear sparse, small, and rudimentary when compared to markets in developed countries. Many farmers in developing countries have little to do with markets at all, mostly growing or building what their families consume and occasionally selling excess crops to buy fertilizer, clothing, or simple cookware. In nearby markets they have access to just a few goods produced in more distant locations, brought in by traders once a week. Shortages drive prices in some villages up sharply without encouraging an inflow of goods from neighboring villages where supplies are high and prices are lower. Buyers pay cash for goods in time-consuming face-to-face transactions only after they have personally inspected the quality of goods on offer. Not only are futures markets and financing options absent; many sellers do not even accept checks or invoices (Fafchamps and Minten, 2001).

These observations raise three sets of questions. First, why do markets in developing countries appear so small and unsophisticated relative to markets in developed countries? The answer we offer in section 8.2 is that market exchanges are costly to undertake and that many of the *transfer costs* associated with transporting goods and carrying out market transactions are especially high in developing countries.

Second, do the standard tools of market equilibrium analysis (as described in introductory economics courses) remain relevant for studying developing-country markets, despite their distinctive characteristics, or do we require new tools for analyzing market price determination in developing countries? We point out that the standard model of market equilibrium is based on the often-unstated assumption that transporting goods and carrying out transactions are costless activities. The standard model also makes no distinction between local and longer-distance transactions or between more- and less-sophisticated transactions. Section 8.3 modifies the standard model to account for transfer costs that vary with distance and across transactions of different types. The result is a more flexible model that builds on the insights of standard supply and demand analysis but is better suited for the study of development concerns. We illustrate the model's usefulness in applications involving transfer programs and agricultural pricing policies.

Third, what can and should be done to encourage market expansion in developing countries? The logic of comparative advantage (reviewed in Appendix 8A) suggests that new opportunities for exchange allow peoples to specialize in producing goods for which they are relatively well equipped, while trading for goods that are produced relatively well by others. Such specialization and exchange improves the economy's efficiency and productivity, expanding consumption possibilities for many people. Section 8.4 offers a more detailed examination of the potential benefits of expanding markets by reducing transfer costs. It then discusses the kinds of investment in infrastructure, institutions, and other assets that are required to reduce transfer costs, highlights the market and institutional failures that can prevent private actors from undertaking these investments, and discusses the roles that governments and NGOs might thus play in encouraging market development.

8.2 Transfer Costs

8.2A Market exchange and the costly transfer of goods

Goods market exchanges involve the transfer of goods from producers to consumers, or from upstream producers of raw materials and processed inputs to downstream producers of final goods, in exchange for the transfer of payments in the reverse direction. Sometimes producers sell directly to the consumers or downstream producers who will use the goods, and sometimes producers sell to intermediaries, who might sell to other intermediaries or to the ultimate users. Whether intermediaries are involved or not, the transfer of goods from producers to users is fundamental to market exchange.

The transfer of goods from producer to user can be quite costly. Goods must be transported from the producer's location to the user's, and they often must be stored along the way. Even when no storage is required, time is likely to elapse between production and payment, implying that producers or intermediaries require financing to cover the costs they incur before receiving payment. Buyers, sellers, and intermediaries also incur **transaction costs** when they undertake costly efforts to locate trading partners, reach agreements regarding transaction details, and monitor partners' compliance with agreements, and when they suffer losses to partners who fail to fulfill agreements. We use the term **transfer costs** to encompass all these transport, storage, financing, and transaction costs associated with the transfer of goods from their producers to their ultimate users.

8.2B Transfer costs in developing countries

Transfer costs tend to be high in developing countries as a result of limited infrastructure and weak institutions. Even where roads are wide and in good repair, transporting goods costs time and money, but transport costs are much higher where transport infrastructure is limited. For many communities in Africa, where less than half the population lives close to an all-weather road, transportation is very costly, time consuming, unpredictable, and physically risky (World Bank, 2007).

Poor communication infrastructure raises the cost of finding transaction partners and striking deals. Mobile phone networks have expanded rapidly in developing countries over the last few years, but major gaps in the network remain and very few buyers and sellers are connected to the Internet (Aker and Mbiti, 2010). In the absence of such technologies, sellers and buyers must seek partners in time-consuming and costly ways—such as traveling to distant marketplaces and waiting for suitable trading partners to walk by—and are capable of only very limited searches.

Poor storage infrastructure raises the cost of buying when supply is abundant in order to sell later when goods are scarce. Traders wishing to store goods must either pay high fees for the use of safe storage space or suffer high losses to spoilage and theft. Barrett (1997) reports on the dearth of improved storage facilities in Madagascar, and Fafchamps and Minten (2001) offer evidence that the high risk of theft raises the cost of storage to nearly prohibitive levels among Malagasy grain traders. In addition, financing is costly and difficult to obtain as a result of financial market failures we discuss in Chapter 10.

Transaction costs are high where legal and social institutions fail to support trust among potential trading partners (Greif, 2006; Platteau, 2000). Even when paying cash for a bag of vegetables in the market square, a buyer must either trust that the seller has not hidden rotten vegetables in the middle of the bag (risking loss to cheating) or spend time inspecting the entire bag. The value of trust is much greater when simple cash-and-carry transactions are unattractive. For example, a small factory wishing to can beans might prefer a more sophisticated transaction, in which it pays a farmer to deliver beans to the factory on a specified date. Both parties must trust that the other will fulfill promises. If the farmer fails to deliver on the contract date, the factory remains idle, and if the farmer delivers on the contract date, but the factory refuses to accept the beans or attempts to pay a lower price for the beans (taking advantage of the pressure the farmer faces once the beans are harvested and starting to spoil), the farmer might fare much worse than if he had taken the beans elsewhere. Lacking trust in their trading partners, farmers and potential factory owners might perceive that the sophisticated transactions required for effective factory operation are very costly, requiring them to monitor each other closely and exposing them to risk of large losses. These costs might be prohibitive, rendering the transactions unattractive and even preventing the factory's construction.

Unfortunately, surveys of firms in developing countries suggest that producers often lack trust that their suppliers and customers will fulfill contracts. As a result they undertake transactions only within small circles of trading partners with whom they have established long-term relationships (Bigsten et al., 2000). Such restrictions limit their potential to expand production and innovate. In section 8.4 we examine the ways healthier legal and social institutions might better support contract fulfillment and trust.

Taxes add yet another layer to transfer costs. International transactions are common targets of taxation because they must pass through seaports, airports, or customs stations on major highways or railways and thus are relatively easy to observe and regulate. For similar reasons, even within countries, transactions across longer distances are sometimes more heavily taxed. Some central governments give local governments the authority to tax agricultural goods passing through checkpoints along major roads within their jurisdictions. Other governments simply prohibit private transport of goods between communities in order to enforce the monopoly of a government marketing board on the buying and selling of specified agricultural products (see Chapter 17). In yet other cases, the local police (or other groups) decide for themselves to set up checkpoints along major routes at which they extract bribes from truckers.

In some developing regions the total transfer costs are very high indeed. Box 8.1 discusses the significance of transfer costs in Cameroon.

8.2C Market intermediaries and transfer costs

The activities that underlie transfer costs—transportation, marketing, storage, search, screening and financing—are very different from the activities of producing rice or clothing. Just as there are gains to specialization among producers of different goods, so there may be gains to specialization in the production of these **marketing services** as distinct from the production of

≡ Box 8.1 Transfer Costs in Cameroon

In late 2002, a reporter for the *Economist* magazine accompanied an 18-wheeler loaded with 30,000 bottles of beer and other beverages from the port city of Douala to the small town of Bertoua in Cameroon (The Economist, 2002). The 500-kilometer (313-mile) trip, which might have taken five or six hours in the United States, took four days. Given gridlock traffic, exacerbated by crumbling roads and car wrecks that could not be cleared until they had been examined by the police (who were in no rush), it took two hours simply to leave the city. Outside the city, progress was slowed by unpaved roads of rutted red dirt bordered with steep ditches, temporarily rendered impassable by rain three times during the trip. Once the rain delay lasted several hours longer than it might have because it was difficult to locate the person in charge of unlocking a gate used to prevent large vehicles from using the road when wet. Only after the gate was unlocked did the travelers discover that a bridge farther on had been washed out and they would have to find an alternative route. More dismaying than the condition of the road was the need to stop, often for hours at a time, at 47 road blocks operated by police, most of whom were seeking bribes in beer or cash.

Rough roads and dysfunctional law enforcement systems took their toll not only in time and in bribes but also high vehicle maintenance costs and high risks of injury and death from road traffic accidents.

The net result of transport difficulties for consumers in Cameroon is that a bottle of Coca-Cola that costs 300CFA (the local currency) in the capital city, where it is bottled, costs 315CFA in a small town 125 kilometers down the road and 350 CFA 100 kilometers farther. Consumers living off the main road fare even worse: a beer that costs 350 CFA in the port city of Douala on the western coast costs 450 CFA in villages that must be reached by foot in the country's eastern region.

In addition to increasing the average time and money costs of transport, and thus the prices paid by outlying consumers, transport difficulties like these make it nearly impossible to plan business operations with any accuracy. Uncertainties generated by poor infrastructure require Guinness Cameroon, the local subsidiary of the multinational beer producer, to retain 40 days of inputs in inventory, increasing production costs by perhaps 15 percent.

goods. Thus it is not surprising that many of the tasks that underlie transfer costs are often performed by specialized service providers or **market intermediaries** rather than by producers or consumers themselves.

In markets for agricultural produce, the intermediaries are highly diverse. On one end of the spectrum are the higglers of Jamaica, women who carry agricultural produce to town in baskets on their heads. On another end of the spectrum, and of growing importance throughout the developing world, are supermarket chains, which set up large regional warehouses, collect produce from farmers under contracts specifying quality standards and delivery dates, and package and distribute the produce to urban consumers. For more on supermarkets see Box 8.2. In between are diverse business people who engage in one or more of the activities involved in food marketing: crop collectors who gather produce from multiple farmers, truck drivers, grain millers,

≡ Box 8.2 Supermarketization of Food Markets in Developing Countries

In traditional domestic food markets, farmers sell to consumers in weekly open air markets or to traditional middlemen, who collect produce from multiple farmers and sell to wholesalers or to consumers in more distant towns. The food distributed through traditional marketing systems is often sold in unprocessed form and in bunches of mixed quality.

Over the last two decades food markets throughout much of the developing world have undergone *supermarketization*. Thomas Reardon and Peter Timmer (2007) describe how transactions between supermarkets and producers are more sophisticated than transactions in traditional markets. Supermarkets serve high-income urban consumers who value quality and consistent supply. To satisfy their customers' demands, supermarkets must enter into contractual relationships with farmers, who must promise to meet strict quality standards and delivery schedules. Working with farmers directly or through specialized brokers, supermarkets often also provide farmers with training, inputs, and equipment.

At the same time that supermarkets demand more sophisticated transactions, they introduce new technologies that can reduce the costs of sophisticated transfers. For example, they centralize collection and distribution of produce in large warehouses serving many retail stores

and sourcing from farmers over large areas. Taking advantage of economies of scale, they are able to reduce the costs of marketing high-quality foods. This allows them to offer urban consumers higher-quality produce at lower prices and to quickly gain market share over traditional retailers.

While delivering benefits to food consumers, the rise of supermarkets has more mixed implications for food producers. Creating the conditions for profitable trade in high-quality produce requires investment in warehouses, transport systems and the creation of productive relationships with producers. Supermarkets find that these investments are more profitable when dealing with larger farmers or with well-run associations of smaller farmers than when dealing with unorganized small farmers. They are also more profitable in regions with good infrastructure. Naturally, supermarkets only undertake investment where it is most profitable. Thus, the spread of supermarkets sometimes offers new opportunities to farmers who already enjoy larger farms, higher-quality land, and better infrastructure, while shutting out smaller, poorer, more remote, and more poorly-organized farmers.

Observing the disadvantages that smaller farmers face, some NGOs have begun efforts to organize and equip them for connecting to supermarket supply networks.

wholesalers who collect produce from multiple crop collectors, and more. In markets for fertilizer and other agricultural inputs, transactions are sometimes intermediated by the owners of general stores in small towns or by specialized input suppliers. In urban markets for nonagricultural goods, formal wholesalers and retailers purchase goods from producers and set out wares for sale in stores; and informal street vendors purchase goods in stores and carry the goods out to more dispersed and convenient locations around the city.

Sometimes the providers of transfer services charge explicit fees. For example, a trucker might charge a trucking fee for each ton of freight carried one kilometer. Often, however, marketers derive pay for their services by buying produce from upstream in the marketing channel and selling it downstream at a higher price. The difference between selling and buying prices is called the **marketing margin**.

It is sometimes thought that the mere existence of marketing margins implies exploitation of small farmers and businessmen, who are cheated out of receiving the full retail price for their produce by middlemen. It must be recalled, however, that middlemen perform services that are costly to produce. Even when marketers are perfectly competitive, and thus charge marketing margins equal to their costs of producing marketing services, marketing margins can remain high because the costs of transfer activities are high.[1]

In fact, the existence of specialized market intermediaries probably *reduces* marketing costs in many cases. If intermediaries benefit from specialization or larger scale, their costs of producing marketing services may be much lower than the costs producers would incur if they marketed produce on their own. If intermediaries charge competitive fees for their services, therefore, their existence might reduce marketing costs.

It remains possible, however, that some middlemen lack competition. Under such circumstances, they can command significant **marketing rents**, or excess profits derived by exploiting their privileged positions. Such rents raise transfer costs above the competitive market level. Sometimes rent-generating barriers to competition are created by policy. For example, when a government bestows the legal right to import chemical fertilizer on a single company, the lucky importer lacks competition and is able to raise price above cost without losing all customers to competitors.

Marketers might also lack competition in some remote regions. Many marketing tasks require the use of capital items such as trucks or storage silos, which require large investments by specialized investors. As a result of financial market failures (see Chapter 10), entrepreneurs might find it difficult to finance the purchase of such assets. In some rural regions, few entrepreneurs may have the local knowledge required to run profitable marketing businesses, and even fewer may have the necessary financing. The privileged few who set up marketing businesses may be able to reap rents. Using a year of detailed daily data on 10 wholesale grain traders in Ethiopia, Osborne (2005) finds evidence that traders in remote locations engage in noncompetitive behavior, depressing prices paid to farmers by an average of 3 percent, with price reductions higher in harvest seasons when supply is great. Such price reductions are especially deleterious for small farmers who do not have the means to store their produce at harvest and wait for better prices. Whether such market power is widespread is not known, because few empirical studies have addressed this concern.

8.2D Transfer costs and market limitations

As producers consider the array of buyers to whom they might sell their produce, they weigh the benefit they would derive from selling to a particular buyer (i.e., the price the buyer would pay) against the costs of producing the good *and* transferring it to the buyer. They choose to undertake the transactions for which the benefits most outweigh the costs. Producers might choose to trade only with neighbors, even when consumers in a distant city are willing to pay higher prices,

---

[1]For an explanation of why competition leads to a long-run equilibrium in which producers earn a normal return on their assets but zero "economic profits," and thus sell at a price equal to cost, see Pindyck and Rubinfeld (2008), Chapter 8.

because the transfer costs associated with shipping goods to the city outweigh the price advantage. High transportation costs can, therefore, help explain why many developing-country markets remain small in geographic scope.

High transfer costs of a different sort can explain why markets in developing countries remain limited in variety and sophistication. Where legal systems are costly to access and do not deliver fair judgments reliably, the risk associated with entering into contracts can render it very costly to carry out sophisticated transactions involving promises of future deliveries or payments. As a result, even though urban consumers may be willing to pay significantly higher prices for supermarket produce than they are willing to pay in traditional open-air markets, farmers might continue to supply only to traditional markets because the transfer costs when dealing with supermarkets are too high.

8.3 A Model of Market Equilibrium in the Presence of Transfer Costs

8.3A Motivation

Exercising good intuition about how markets respond to change is vital in development studies. Standard models of market equilibrium offer some useful predictions, but they are incomplete sources of intuition about markets in developing countries, because they have nothing to say about the geography or sophistication of markets or about the ways policies might encourage market development. This section expounds an otherwise standard model of market equilibrium that is more useful for development studies because it pays explicit attention to transfer costs.

8.3B Competitive equilibrium in a single market

Basic setup

As in introductory economics courses, we examine market equilibrium using diagrams that describe supply and demand relationships in a market of interest. Unlike in introductory courses, however, we acknowledge that transfer costs exist, that they differ between local and longer-distance trade, and that they differ between simpler and more-sophisticated trading arrangements. Thus, when defining the market of interest, we specify not only the good of interest but also the geographic contours of the market and any details regarding the nature of the good or its use that affect the sophistication and cost of related transfer activities.

We begin by identifying the geographic region of primary interest. When studying a small development project, this may be a rural village and the surrounding countryside. When studying a country's policies toward international trade, it is the entire country. We define the **local market** to encompass the supplies and demands of buyers and sellers who reside in that region. We identify the main center of trade within that region, as well as the primary **external market** that offers opportunities for longer-distance trade. For a single small village, the primary external market may be the market in the nearest larger town. For an entire country, the primary external market is the world market. We then describe local supply and demand relationships and opportunities for trade with the external market.

For example, Figure 8.1 describes the market for traditional green beans in Small Village, where the nearest and most attractive external market is found in Big City. Traditional beans are grown from traditional seed varieties, brought to weekly open-air markets in bulk, and sold in mixed quality by the kilogram through simple cash-and-carry transactions. (Later we will contrast such traditional produce with higher value-added crops requiring more costly and sophisticated transactions.) The horizontal axis measures quantities of beans supplied and demanded by households living in and around Small Village (in kilograms). The vertical axis measures the price of beans (in pesos per kilogram) in Small Village's open-air market in the

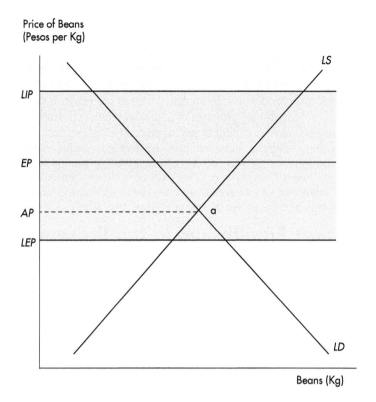

Price of Beans
(Pesos per Kg)

FIGURE 8.1
Market for Traditional
Beans in Small Village

Beans (Kg)

town square.[2] The local supply (*LS*) and demand *LD* schedules indicate the quantities of beans that households in and around Small Village would be willing to sell or buy in the town square at any price observed there. The horizontal lines, which we define below, describe the options that buyers and sellers within Small Village face for trade with partners in the Big City market.

The local supply and demand schedules reflect the behavior of households in Small Village or the surrounding area, which behave like the households studied in the first half of Chapter 7. They may choose to remain outside the market (consuming no beans or only beans they produce for themselves) or to participate in the market as competitive buyers or sellers. The **local supply schedule** is upward sloping, because as the price of beans in the town square rises (all else equal), some local farmers already producing and selling beans in the market find it profitable to produce and sell more, and because some farmers who had previously chosen to remain outside the market now find it profitable to produce beans for sale in the market. Similarly, the **local demand schedule** slopes downward because as the bean price in the town square rises, some buyers choose to purchase fewer beans, and some choose to leave the local bean market altogether.

In addition to buying and selling locally, Small Village residents may buy and sell in the Big City market. We give the name **external market price** (*EP*) to the price that people pay for traditional beans in the Big City market. We assume that the beans bought and sold in Big City are identical to those bought and sold in Small Village and that the Big City market is sufficiently large relative to Small Village that changes in Small Village's volume of trade with Big City have no impact on the *EP*.

---

[2]For simplicity we assume that the prices at which villagers may buy and sell within a single market location are the same. In reality, in the presence of transaction costs, the prices at which households are able to buy goods are likely to exceed the prices at which they can sell. As long as the transaction costs remain constant, the buying and selling prices rise and fall together. Including in our diagrams both buying and selling prices in the external market would introduce clutter without significantly changing the analytical results.

We define the **local import price** (*LIP*) to equal the *EP plus* the transfer costs associated with purchasing beans in Big City and transporting them back to Small Village. Local residents must choose between buying beans locally at the local price or buying them from Big City at a total cost per kilogram (including transfer costs) equal to the *LIP*. Buying Big City beans might involve traveling to obtain beans in Big City and paying the transfer costs explicitly, or buying Big City beans locally from market intermediaries and paying the transfer costs implicitly. The **local export price** (*LEP*) is equal to the *EP* minus the transfer costs associated with exporting beans from Small Village to Big City. Local residents must choose between selling locally at the local price or selling in Big City for total per-kilogram revenue net of transfer costs equal to the *LEP*. When goods require more sophisticated transactions, when local and external markets are farther apart, and when transport and communication connections between the local and external market are worse, transfer costs are higher and the gap between the *LIP* and *LEP* lines is wider.

Three types of equilibrium

Our goal in constructing a model of equilibrium in the Small Village bean market is to understand the forces that determine the local price of traditional beans and the quantities of beans exchanged in the local market and between the local and external market. In **market equilibrium** all potential traders succeed in buying or selling the quantities they wish to trade at the going local price, and no trader has an incentive to switch from buying or selling locally to buying or selling externally (or vice versa).

If trade with Big City were impossible, the Small Village bean market would remain in **autarky**, not engaging in trade with other markets, and we could ignore all the horizontal lines in Figure 8.1. The model would resemble the market equilibrium models expounded in introductory economics courses, and we would find the equilibrium price at the intersection of the local supply and demand schedules (point a in Figure 8.1). At this price the local quantity supplied just equals the local quantity demanded, and all buyers and sellers succeed in trading their desired quantities. We call the price associated with this intersection the **autarky price** (*AP*).

Once we acknowledge the possibility of trade with Big City, however, new types of equilibrium become possible, as illustrated in the three panels of Figure 8.2. For simplicity we leave out the *EP* lines, including only the more pertinent *LEP* and *LIP* lines.

When the *LEP* lies above the autarky price, as in Figure 8.2a, local producers would not remain content to sell beans locally at the autarky price, because they can sell as many beans as they like in Big City for a higher net return (*LEP*). Local consumers must pay prices at least equal

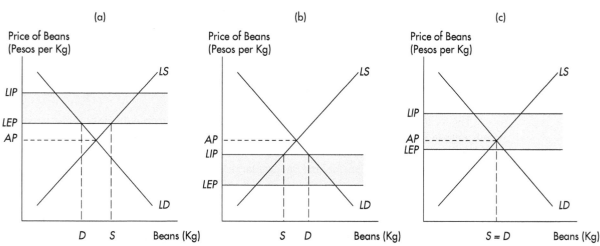

FIGURE 8.2
Exporting, Importing, and Autarky Equilibrium in the Small Village Bean Market

to the *LEP* if they wish to attract local producers to sell locally. At the same time, competition among local producers prevents the local price from rising any higher than the *LEP*. Thus when the *LEP* lies above the autarky price, the local price must equal the *LEP* in equilibrium, and the Small Village market finds itself in an **exporting equilibrium**. To find the equilibrium quantities supplied and demanded we observe where the *LEP* line intersects the local supply and demand schedules. With the *LEP* above the autarky price, the local quantity supplied S must exceed the local quantity demanded D, and the difference $X = S - D$ is the quantity local producers export to Big City. Because the *LIP* always exceeds the *LEP*, and because we are focusing on a case in which the *LEP* exceeds the autarky price, we know that local consumers have no interest in importing.

When the *LIP* lies below the autarky price, as in Figure 8.2b, the Small Village market finds itself in **importing equilibrium**. If local producers wish to sell any beans to local consumers they must charge prices no higher than the *LIP*. At the same time, competition among local consumers drives the local price up to the level of the *LIP*. Thus the local price must equal the *LIP* in equilibrium. The total quantity of beans demanded locally D is found where the *LIP* line crosses the local demand schedule, the total quantity supplied locally S is found where the *LIP* line crosses the local supply schedule, and local consumers import the difference $M = D - S$ from the Big City market. Local producers have no interest in exporting when the *LIP* lies below the autarky price, because the *LEP* always lies below the *LIP*.

In Figure 8.2c the *LIP* falls above the autarky price and the *LEP* falls below. At the autarky price, local producers have no interest in exporting, because the *LEP* is lower than the autarky price, and local consumers have no interest in importing, because the *LIP* is higher than the autarky price. With no importing or exporting, local equilibrium requires that the local price equal the autarky price, and the Small Village bean market finds itself in **autarky equilibrium**.

Sources of supply and demand shifts

Many kinds of socioeconomic change alter market equilibrium outcomes by inducing shifts in local supply or demand schedules. Socioeconomic changes shift local demand schedules to the right when they increase the quantity of beans local consumers would demand *while holding the local price constant at any given level*. The basic consumer choice model reviewed in Chapter 6 indicates several forces that might induce such shifts to the right, including an increase in local consumers' incomes (if beans are a normal good), reductions in the prices of goods that are complements to beans in consumption, and increases in the prices of substitutes.[3] Increases in the size of the local population would also shift demand to the right (assuming the newcomers bring the capacity to generate additional income or bring wealth that they can spend locally). More subtly, from Chapter 7 we know that reductions in the costs of transferring beans from the village market center to outlying homesteads might also shift the local demand schedule to the right by rendering the purchase of beans in town more attractive to outlying households, relative to consuming no beans or consuming beans they produce themselves.

The local supply schedule shifts to the right with good weather, reductions in the prices of inputs used in bean cultivation, increases in local stocks of fixed factors used in bean cultivation, improvements in bean production technologies, and reductions in the prices of goods that compete with traditional beans for land on local farms (see the review of basic producer theory in

---

[3]For net bean-selling farm households, the impacts of these demand-expanding changes may be to reduce net market sales (i.e. reduce their contribution to the local supply schedule) rather than to increase their net market purchases. For simplicity we treat them as shifting only the local demand schedule to the right. Despite this simplification, the graphical analysis yields correct predictions regarding the resulting changes in prices and quantities, because the rightward shift of the demand schedule and a leftward shift of the supply schedule of the same size lead to identical predictions regarding these changes.

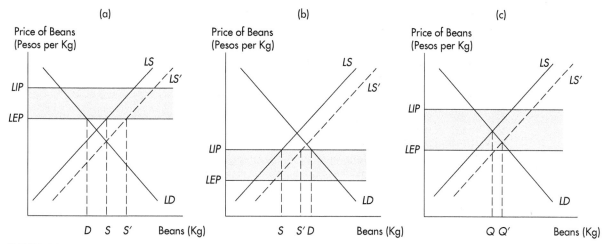

FIGURE 8.3
Effects of Local Supply Shifts on Markets in Exporting, Importing, and Autarky Equilibrium

Chapter 6).[4] Reductions in the costs of transferring beans between outlying homesteads and the village market can also shift the local supply schedule to the right.

Supply and demand shift effects differentiated by type of initial equilibrium

Unlike in standard models of market equilibrium, the effects of supply and demand shifts on equilibrium prices and quantities in the presence of transfer costs differ depending upon the nature of initial equilibrium. The three panels of Figure 8.3 examine the impacts of a rightward shift in the local supply schedule when starting from the three types of equilibrium. All three panels share the same initial local supply and demand schedules (LS and LD), as well as the same post-change local supply schedule (LS'). The three diagrams differ in the levels of the LIP and LEP, so that the market is initially in exporting equilibrium in the first panel, importing equilibrium in the second panel, and autarky equilibrium in the third panel. We consider a local supply schedule shift that is not large enough to shift the local market from one type of equilibrium to another.

Figure 8.3c, which describes a village bean market in autarky, produces predictions that are familiar from introductory microeconomics courses. Both before and after the supply shift, equilibrium is found at the intersection of the local supply and demand schedules. The shift from the solid to dashed supply schedule thus drives down the local price and increases the quantity purchased by local consumers (from Q to Q').

The impacts of the local supply expansion are quite different in the first and second panels, because trade with a large external market fixes the local price at a constant level. In Figure 8.3a, the local equilibrium price is equal to the LEP. The local supply shift leaves the LEP unchanged and thus leaves the equilibrium local price unchanged. With the local price and local demand schedule unchanged, the local quantity demanded by consumers D also remains unchanged. What changes is the volume of production by local producers (from S to S') and the quantity they export to the external market (now $X' = S' - D$), both of which increase. Similarly, in Figure 8.3b, the local supply expansion leaves the local price unchanged at the level of LIP. Local consumers continue to demand the same quantities at the same price, while local production increases and the quantity of imports from the external market falls.

Local demand shifts also induce effects that differ between cases of autarky equilibrium and trading equilibrium. Increases in local consumer incomes that shift the local demand schedule to

---

[4]Similar logic to that presented in footnote 3 allows us to treat these supply-expanding changes as only shifting the local supply schedule to the right, even though they might serve to reduce the quantities purchased from the market by net bean-purchasing households.

the right raise the equilibrium price only if the market is in autarky. If the local market imports or exports, an increase in local demand reduces exports or increases imports without inducing a change in local price or production.

More generally:

> Shifts in local supply and demand schedules bring changes in local prices only if the local market is in autarky equilibrium.

If the local market is in importing equilibrium (and if the local market is small relative to the external market) outward shifts in local demand raise local consumption and import quantities while leaving local price and production unchanged, and outward shifts in local supply raise local production and reduce imports while leaving local price and consumption unchanged. If the local market is in exporting equilibrium, outward shifts in demand only raise local consumption and reduce exports, and outward shifts in supply only raise local production and exports.

The effects of supply and demand shifts can differ across crops in the same location, because markets for some crops may be in autarky while markets for more easily traded goods are in importing or exporting equilibrium. For example, Alix-Garcia and Saah (2010) find that refugee inflows from Rwanda into western Tanzania (which shifted local food demands to the right) raised prices in markets near refugee camps for plantain, a food that is perishable and not much traded over long distances, while having little effect on the local prices of cereals, which are more easily transported and traded.

It is also useful to note the following. First, a policy's effects on prices or quantities are small unless the policy raises local quantities supplied or demanded at any price by a significant percentage. A policy that induces an increase of just 0.2 percent in the quantity supplied at any price causes a nearly imperceptible rightward shift in the local supply schedule and is unlikely to generate significant change in market conditions, but a policy that raises the quantity supplied at any price by 30 percent is much more likely to induce a significant price change. Second, in autarky equilibrium the sizes of price and quantity changes induced by a supply or demand shift depend on the elasticities of local supply and demand. Thus, while graphs like those in Figure 8.3 help us to predict the likely *direction* of changes in prices and quantities, empirical research is required to determine which effects are likely to be large and small in practice. Third, when a policy affects many local markets that together contribute a large fraction of the external market's supply or demand, the policy can induce a change in the external market price.

8.3C Relationships among markets at different geographic levels and in different geographic locations

In Figure 8.4 we use our model of market equilibrium in the presence of transfer costs to examine relationships among markets at different geographic levels (e.g., a small village market and the national market) and among markets in non-overlapping geographic areas (e.g., two small villages). The three panels depict the national market for rice in a rice-exporting country and the markets for rice in two villages within that country. Notice that the units on the horizontal axis are 10,000s of bags of rice for the larger national market and just individual bags of rice for the smaller village markets.

The local supply and demand schedules in the national market diagram represent the supplies of rice that producers within the country would be willing to ship into the capital city at any price, and the quantities of rice that consumers anywhere in the country would be willing to purchase in the capital city market at any price there. They include supplies and demands generated by people residing both in the capital city and in outlying locations that export to or import from the capital city. The *LEP* relevant to the national market is the *LEPN*, which is equal to the world market price of rice less the transfer costs associated with international export. Because we

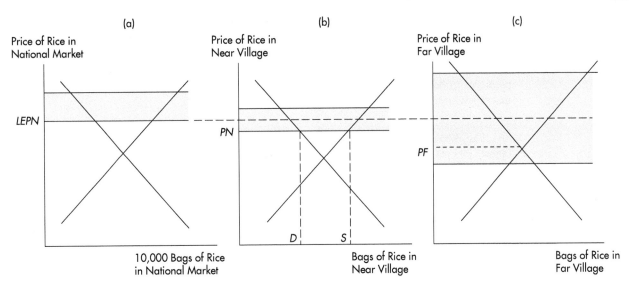

FIGURE 8.4
Equilibrium in the National Rice Market and the Local Rice Markets in Two Villages

wish to describe a national market in exporting equilibrium, we draw the *LEPN* line above the autarky price.

The second and third panels of Figure 8.4 depict the local markets in two villages. Local supply and demand conditions are identical in the two villages, but the transfer costs on trade between Near Village and the capital city are smaller than the transfer costs on trade between Far Village and the capital city.

We assume that the capital city is the external market most attractive to households in both Near Village and Far Village, so that the external market price relevant in both villages is *LEPN*. In Figures 8.4b and c the top edges of the shaded bands indicate the levels of the local *LIPs* and the bottom edges indicate the levels of the *LEPs*. Both bands are centered over the *LEPN*, but the band is wider in Far Village as a result of higher transfer costs. In the equilibrium depicted here, Near Village is in exporting equilibrium (with local price *PN*) and Far Village is in autarky equilibrium (with local price *PF*). Near Village's exports ($X = S - D$) constitute part of the total local quantity supplied to the national market at the price *LEPN*. In both Near Village and Far Village the local price is lower than the price of rice in the capital city, but Near Village is said to be **integrated** into the larger national market, because it engages in trade with the capital city, whereas Far Village remains un-integrated into the national market.

What happens if the world price of rice rises? In a diagram like Figure 8.4a, this raises the *LEPN* line. The equilibrium market price in the capital city rises. The quantity of rice demanded in the national market falls, and the quantities supplied to the national market and exported to the international market rise. The increase in *LEPN* also raises the *LIP* and *LEP* lines relevant to Near Village and Far Village. The price of rice in Near Village remains lower than the price in the capital city, but the two prices rise by the same amount. The international price increase is said to **pass through** to the Near Village market, which is integrated with the national market. The local quantity demanded in that village falls, the local quantity supplied rises, and Near Village's exports to the capital city market increase, helping to explain the increase in the local quantity supplied within the national market that is associated with the movement up and to the right along the national market supply schedule.

The external trade price band relevant to Far Village rises as well, but as long as Far Village remains in autarky equilibrium, prices there remain unaffected by changes in the world price. High transfer costs prevent the export price increase from being transmitted to Far Village. Only if the price increase in the national market is great enough will the lower edge of the external trade price band rise above the autarky price, causing Far Village to start exporting to the capital city. Far Village would then become integrated into the national market.

In models of competitive markets without transfer costs, prices for identical goods are predicted to be identical everywhere and to rise and fall together. In the model of competitive markets with transfer costs, by contrast:

> Prices for identical goods need not be identical everywhere and need not rise and fall in unison everywhere. Only the prices in markets that are integrated rise and fall together; even in markets that are integrated, price levels can differ as a result of transfer costs. National market price increases induce comparable local price increases in markets that are integrated into the national market and can induce some more remote markets to become integrated into the national market through exports, while leaving the most remote markets unaffected.

Often, price variation is only poorly correlated across markets within developing countries, suggesting that changes in world and national market prices might cause corresponding changes only over rather limited geographic regions within countries. For example, Ulimwengu et al. (2009) offer evidence that none of the 95 local Ethiopian maize markets they examine were integrated with the world market.

8.3D Policy analysis applications

When applying the market equilibrium framework to the analysis of specific policies, we begin by identifying the geographic region of primary interest and then asking whether the relevant market in that region is in importing, exporting, or autarky equilibrium. If the region is large, we also ask how much of the region is integrated into the central market and how much remains un-integrated. We then identify the ways the policy might cause the local supply schedule, the local demand schedule, or the *LIP* and *LEP* lines to shift. Observing the effects of these shifts in the graph, we identify the sorts of price and quantity impacts we would like to quantify. We illustrate this approach in the following discussion of two policy analysis applications.

Cash versus food transfers

Governments and humanitarian aid organizations have a long history of distributing free food to needy people. The distribution of food is motivated in part by a desire to meet obvious, basic needs in a direct way and in part by the need to make use of surplus grains sent to developing countries by rich country governments. Humanitarian organizations are increasingly experimenting, however, with distributing cash rather than food, even in emergency situations (Harvey, 2007).

One frequently voiced motivation for the shift from food to cash distributions is the belief that distributing food discourages development by driving down local food prices and discouraging local agricultural production, while distributing cash encourages development by raising local food prices and encouraging local agricultural production. Using the model of market equilibrium with transfer costs, we see that the comparison between the impacts of cash and food distributions on local markets is more complicated than this, and that whether cash or food transfers have more desirable market effects depends on context. (For a more complete comparison of cash and food transfer programs, see Chapter 15.)

To set up our analysis we recognize that food and cash distributions often take place in small rural communities where the incidence of poverty is high. We thus consider a rural village in which a transfer program targets a large enough fraction of the local population to

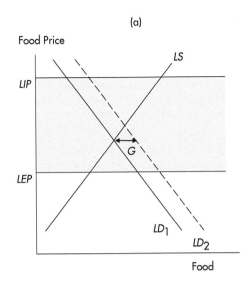

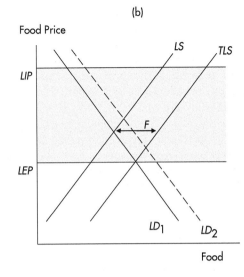

FIGURE 8.5
Effects on Autarky Food Market Equilibrium of Cash and Food Distributions of Equal Initial Value

induce significant shifts in local supply and demand schedules. Because we want to keep the analysis general, we recognize that the food market in this village may be in autarky equilibrium or importing equilibrium. (Humanitarian assistance programs are less likely to target communities in food exporting equilibrium.) In a complete analysis we would draw diagrams describing both autarky and importing equilibrium in a village food market and then identify the likely effects of cash and food transfers on the supply and demand schedules in each diagram.

In Figure 8.5 we illustrate the analysis of cash and food distributions in the case of autarky equilibrium. Panel a depicts a cash distribution and panel b depicts a food distribution. The primary direct effect of a cash distribution is to raise recipients' incomes, causing local food demand schedules to shift to the right. In Figure 8.5a we assume that at any price a cash distribution causes the quantity demanded to increase by G, and thus that the local supply schedule shifts to the right by G (from LD_1 to LD_2).

By contrast, food distributions can be thought of as shifting both demand and supply schedules to the right. Like cash transfers, they shift the food demand schedule to the right by increasing recipients' real incomes. In fact, under some conditions they shift the food demand schedule to the right by exactly the same amount as a cash distribution of the same value (see Chapter 6). We illustrate this in Figure 8.5b by a shift from LD_1 to LD_2. Assuming that the food distributed by the program is brought in from outside the village, the food distribution leaves the private local supply schedule LS unchanged, but it creates a new *total* local supply schedule TS (including food supplied by private local producers *and* food shipped in through the program) that lies to the right of the original local supply schedule by the amount of food distributed F. Because food distributions are likely to increase recipients' food consumption by less than the quantity of food distributed (see Chapter 6), we expect the local supply schedule to shift to the right by more than the local demand schedule shifts. We thus assume that the rightward shift of the total supply schedule (F) is greater than the rightward shift of the local demand schedule (G). Problem 2 asks readers to work out the implications of the supply and demand shifts under varying assumptions regarding the nature of initial equilibrium and the elasticity of local supply. Here we highlight several key conclusions.

First, the basic premise that cash and food transfers have differing effects on local food markets may be quite misleading when local food markets in program villages are integrated into larger food markets (through imports) and the programs are too small to induce food price changes in regional or national markets.[5] In such cases (not depicted here), both cash and food distributions leave the local food price and the local quantity produced unchanged, and they increase local consumption significantly. The main difference between cash and food distributions is that under cash distributions the additional food is brought into the region by the private sector (in response to the increased demands of cash transfer recipients) whereas under food distributions the additional food is brought into the region by government or NGO personnel. Thus, when the community is initially in a trading equilibrium, whether cash or food transfers are preferable hinges not on their impacts on local prices and production (which are identical) but on the relative speed and efficiency of public and private systems for bringing food into the target regions and the relative impacts on recipients' food consumption, nutrition, saving, investment, and well-being (as examined in Chapter 6).

Second, when the local food market is initially in autarky equilibrium (as in Figure 8.5), cash distributions do indeed tend to raise local food prices (by strengthening local demand) and food distributions tend to reduce them (by increasing local supply more than they increase local demand). However, these are not the only impacts on local food markets that are worth comparing. Both cash and food distributions bring costs as well as benefits, and whether cash or food distributions appear preferable will depend on local food supply elasticities.

Consider first the case of local markets in autarky equilibrium where local food supply is low and inelastic. We might have in mind, for example, a remote region hit by natural disaster that destroys crops and greatly limits agricultural production. With food supply highly inelastic in the short run, a food distribution would tend to reduce local food production only a little. Thus total food consumption in the area would rise by nearly the full amount F brought in by the program. Local food prices would fall steeply, tending to reduce the incomes farmers derive from what food they can supply to the market, but this effect may be small if local supplies are very low. By contrast, a cash distribution, which shifts local demand schedules to the right, raises local food prices a lot while encouraging very little increase in local production. The price increase reduces the real value of the cash distributed, and the program manages to increase total local food consumption only a little. Under these conditions food distributions are more attractive than cash distributions, because food distributions succeed in raising local consumption without much reducing local food production and farm incomes, whereas cash distributions fail to increase local food consumption much and stimulate local production only a little.

The picture is quite different if local food supply is elastic (while the local market is again in autarky equilibrium). Here we might picture a region in which labor markets work well and where farmers are able to expand acreage or intensify their production practices to increase production when higher prices make this attractive. The transfer programs of interest might serve refugees who have migrated into the area or chronically poor local households with very few assets and large numbers of dependents. If local food supply is highly elastic, cash distributions raise local food prices only a little while encouraging significant increases in local food production. They thus succeed in raising total local food consumption significantly. Food distributions, on the other hand, would significantly discourage local food production and would thus raise total local food consumption by much less than the quantity of program food distributed. Under such circumstances, cash transfers appear more attractive relative to food distributions. Cash transfers raise local consumption and stimulate local production significantly, whereas food distributions raise local consumption only a little and discourage local production. Thus:

---

[5]To analyze this case graphically, we would need to modify Figure 8.5 to reflect markets in trading equilibrium.

When local food markets are in autarky equilibrium, cash and food transfers differ in their impacts on the local food price, as well as the local quantities consumed and produced, and cash (food) distributions are more likely to be preferable when local food supply is elastic (inelastic). When local food markets are in importing (or exporting) equilibrium, cash and food distributions might have identical effects on local food consumption and probably have little effect on local food prices or the local quantities produced. Under such circumstances, cash (food) distributions are more likely to be preferable when the private (public) sector is more efficient at bringing food into the community.

Whether cash or food is more appropriate may vary from place to place even within small countries. For example, the World Food Programme (2007) finds that while markets in some rural Malawian communities are integrated with nearby urban markets, and even with markets in Mozambique, many of the more remote communities are not served by well-functioning markets. They find that whereas cash transfers may be appropriate in a few less-remote locations, food would be preferable in many locations.

World food prices and poverty

In Chapter 7 we learned that if the price of wheat rises by 10 percent and the ratio of a household's net marketed surplus in wheat to total income is m, then the household's real purchasing power rises by approximately $10m$ percent. Motivated by this observation, some researchers have estimated the effects on poverty rates of increases in global food prices by dividing the national population into income groups and using household survey data to estimate average values of m in each group. To estimate the effects of a 10 percent increase in wheat prices on poverty, they assume that all households within each income group experience purchasing power effects of $10m$ percent and observe for how many households these changes would lower or raise their real income enough to move them in or out of poverty. In Chapter 7 we cited such a study by Ivanic and Martin (2008).

Now we learn, however, that this approach can exaggerate the effects of international food prices or agricultural trade policies on poverty, because:

Many poor and near-poor households are located in remote regions with poor infrastructure that may be un-integrated into national and international food markets. Global food price increases might not raise the local prices faced by such households, and empirical research is required to describe the geographic distribution of price increases.

For example, Cudjoe et al. (2010) find that global food price changes drive comparable price changes in the markets of Ghana's largest cities but transmit only partially to more remote areas.

8.4 The Economics of Market Development
8.4A Market expansion and growth: the big picture

Markets expand in geographic scope and variety as people begin to trade goods over longer distances and for new products. Markets become more sophisticated when people undertake exchanges governed by more complex agreements regarding quality specifications or the timing of deliveries and payments. Economic logic suggests that:

> The creation and expansion of markets raises productivity by allowing producers to specialize, increase scale, and take advantage of agglomeration economies. Such market development also increases the variety of goods and services available and strengthens incentives toward investment.

Market exchange can raise productivity through many channels. At the most fundamental level, the logic of **comparative advantage**, which is reviewed in Appendix 8A, indicates that new opportunities for exchange between people with diverse production capabilities increase productivity and expand consumption opportunities by allowing people to specialize in the types of production they do relatively well.

Expanded market exchange can also raise productivity through three additional channels. Producers reap **intrinsic specialization advantages** when specialization in a single activity allows them to eliminate waste associated with their pursuit of multiple activities. For example, when farmers cultivate multiple crops, they might suffer waste associated with underproductive edges of individual fields or with the need to walk between plots spread out across locations suited to different crops, and they may be able to eliminate such waste when they specialize.[6]

If production is characterized by **economies of scale**, then expansion of trade that allows individual producers to serve consumers spread out over larger areas can also increase productivity. For example, producers might use low productivity handicraft methods when high transport costs limit them to producing processed food or clothing only for small village markets, but they might shift to higher-productivity factory-based methods when serving larger regional markets. (See problem 4 in Chapter 4.)

The development of rural–urban food markets makes possible the geographic separation of food production and consumption, allowing nonfarm producers to set up close to one another in cities. This can allow them to reap **agglomeration economies**, which render them more productive when located near one another than when separated from one another geographically. When firms operate near one another, their managers and workers more easily observe and learn from one another. Furthermore, with many firms in one location undertaking accounting, engineering, and other common business tasks, entrepreneurs might find it profitable to set up new firms that specialize in providing such business services. As a result of specialization and scale, they can produce these services at lower cost, thereby reducing the overall costs of production and raising aggregate productivity.

As households specialize and the scale of production increases, consumers enjoy a wider **variety** of goods and services. People seem to value variety itself, and increased variety also allows people with diverse needs and tastes to identify specific items that best suit their needs (Chamberlin, 1933; Lancaster, 1971).

The creation of markets can also raise incentives for investment in physical and human capital and in technological innovation. When people are restricted to producing only for small local markets, any investments they might make to increase production would drive down local prices; they might, as a result, perceive little scope for profitable investment. Once export to larger markets becomes possible, however, they can increase production without driving prices down, and investment becomes more attractive.

---

[6]When insurance markets work poorly (Chapter 10), individual producers may benefit from diversifying risks (e.g., remaining involved in the production of more than one good) and may thus perceive costs as well as benefits to specialization. Such costs (in addition to transportation and transactions costs) can inhibit specialization and market development.

8.4B Market expansion through transfer cost reduction: a closer look

The previous section offered general reasons to believe that the expansion of markets is good for growth and development but offered little detail regarding the likely nature and distribution of the benefits. Here we use the analytical framework of part 8.2 to uncover some of the more detailed consequences of improved market connections.

Connecting remote communities to larger markets

General improvements in transport and communication infrastructure have great potential to raise local growth rates and reduce poverty in remote communities. Such investments raise the *LEP* for local export crops in the remote communities (depicted by graphs like Figure 8.2a) and raise incomes for local farm households that are net sellers of the export crop. Higher selling prices and new access to a larger market also encourages these farmers to invest, contributing to economic growth. Dercon and Hoddinott (2005) find evidence for such impacts of transport infrastructure on growth rates in remote communities. Using data from 1,244 households in 14 rural Ethiopian communities during the period 1994 to 1999, they estimate that improving roads from being "accessible only to people, carts, and animals" to being "reasonably accessible by all vehicles" increased growth rates in average consumption by 3.5 percentage points, in a sample in which the mean growth rate was 2.5 percent.

Infrastructure improvements also reduce the *LIP* for imported consumer goods (in graphs like Figure 8.2b), tending to increase purchasing power not only for local exporting farmers but for other local households as well. By expanding local production and demand for labor (and perhaps by improving links to external labor markets), they can also raise wages, spreading benefits to landless laboring households in the community. Thus infrastructure improvements that reduce transfer costs on transactions with external markets have the potential to bring living standards improvements through many channels.

Our analytical framework reminds us, however, that the benefits of transfer cost reductions need not be shared equally throughout a community and that some households might even be made worse off. For example, when the local staple food and export crop is corn, when transfer cost reductions raise the local price of corn, and when there are few options to increase agricultural production in labor-using ways (so that wages rise little), landless households that spend large fractions of their budget on corn may be made worse off.

Fortunately, in many kinds of communities we would expect the benefits of improved market connections to be widely shared. For example, when a community exports unprocessed cotton and imports staple foods and clothing, reductions in transfer costs can raise the well-being of landless laborers as well as cotton producers, even if wages do not rise, by reducing the cost of importing most consumer items. Similarly, when a community exports rice and when most households own land and sell small quantities of rice, most households benefit from increased rice prices as well as reduced prices for imported consumer goods. The study described in Box 2.1 (Khandker et al., 2009) found that road improvements generated widely shared benefits in Bangladesh.

Connecting rural communities to one another

Reductions in basic transport and communication costs can also help increase food security by creating market connections between rural communities subject to localized agricultural supply shocks. In some developing countries, most rural communities face the risk of major crop loss to bad weather, crop disease, or insects every year, but only a few of the communities in fact

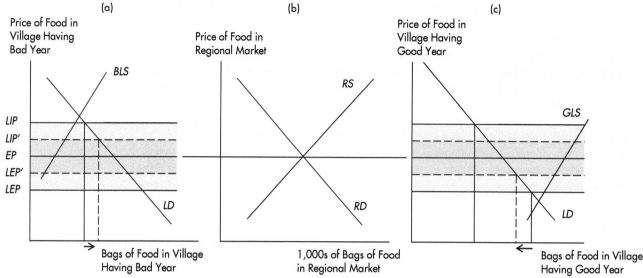

FIGURE 8.6
Regional Market Links between Communities Experiencing Good and Bad Agricultural Supply Conditions

experience the shocks in any one year. Aggregate food supply (across all communities) varies less than do food supplies within individual communities. Under such conditions, improved market connections among communities can help smooth out variation in food consumption over time and across communities by channeling food from communities having good years to communities having bad years.

To see how this works, consider Figure 8.6. Panel b represents a regional food market relevant to a large number of small communities. The *RD* and *RS* schedules indicate regional demand and regional supply. We assume that all communities within the region are identical in fundamental food supply and demand conditions, but half of them experience good weather in any one year, the other half experience bad weather, and the good weather is distributed across a different subset of communities each year. Thus, though supply conditions vary from year to year within individual communities, aggregate food supplies to the central market remain constant. Panel a describes the food market in a representative community experiencing a bad year (with local demand *LD* and bad local supply *BLS*), and panel c describes a community having a good year (with local demand *LD* and good local supply *GLS*).[7]

Both communities face the same high initial costs of trading with the regional market, and thus the same solid initial *LIP* and *LEP* lines. For communities experiencing poor supply years (panel a) the local price is driven up to the level of the initial *LIP*, and small quantities of food are imported from the regional market. For communities having good years (as in panel c), prices are driven down to the level of the initial *LEP*, and small quantities of food are exported. The local price in any one community fluctuates between the a low equal to the *LEP* in good years and a high equal to the *LIP* in bad years, and the quantity of food consumed locally also varies greatly between good and bad years.

---

[7]Reductions in income associated with supply contraction would tend to shift local food demand schedules to the left as well as shifting local supply schedules to the left. They would, however, tend to shift demand schedules to the left by less than they shift supply schedules to the left, and thus they tend to reduce local supply *relative* to local demand. Graphical analysis that shifts only the supply schedule should, therefore, provide an accurate qualitative picture of price and quantity fluctuations between good and bad years.

Now suppose that infrastructure improvements reduce the costs of trade with the regional market (and thus between communities having good years and bad years), making the dashed *LEP'* and *LIP'* lines relevant. The same fluctuations in local supply schedules now lead to much smaller fluctuations in local food prices and consumption quantities. Poor supply conditions (panel a) no longer drive local prices up as high, because consumers now face more attractive import opportunities and their demands are fulfilled to a greater extent through imports. Similarly, good supply conditions (panel c) no longer drive prices down as low, because export conditions have improved and farmers export larger fractions of their ample supplies. Transfer cost reductions allow the regional market to serve as a better shock absorber, channeling more food from communities with good weather to communities with bad weather. Indeed, Ahmed and Hossain (1990) find that better road infrastructure is associated with lower variation in crop prices.

Again, the benefits are spread unequally across households. Whereas households with little or no land, who are net food buyers, benefit from reduced fluctuation in food consumption, net food sellers can experience increased variation in their food sales revenue as reductions in their productivity are no longer counterbalanced to as great an extent by price increases.

Connecting markets through time

Just as intermediaries might wish to buy in villages having good production years and sell in villages having bad production years, so also might they wish to buy in months or years when crops are plentiful and sell later when they are scarce. To carry out such transactions, intermediaries must store crops. When storage facilities are in short supply and storage costs are high, few of these transactions are profitable. Reductions in storage costs encourage more purchases in good years (when prices are low), for the sake of storing and then selling in bad years (when prices are high). This increases demand when supply is high and adds to supply when supply is low, tending to reduce fluctuations in prices and in quantities consumed. Thus reductions in the transfer costs associated with buying, storing, and reselling can help stabilize food prices and food supplies through an additional channel.

Connecting small farmers to higher-value markets

Even in rural communities where exports of traditional crops are already profitable, the transfer costs associated with exporting higher-value crops—such as organic coffee or fresh vegetables for sale in urban supermarkets—can remain prohibitively high. Higher-value crops might require refrigerated transportation or other special handling and might require farmers to export under exacting contractual agreements with supermarket buyers or international exporters. They can also require quality sorting, certification, and delivery according to detailed schedules. The transfer costs associated with these more difficult exports may be very high for lack of appropriate infrastructure and the inability of farmers and buyers to commit credibly to fulfilling contractual promises. Thus even when farmers have access to technologies for producing the higher-value crops at low cost, they might refrain from adopting the technologies because the costs of marketing the crops would be too high. (Problem 3 asks you to draw graphs depicting this situation.)

Under such circumstances, reductions in the transfer costs associated with higher-value crops can lead farmers to upgrade their farms, shifting some land from production of lower- to higher-value crops. If the local market for the traditional crop is in autarky equilibrium, then local farmers' reduced supply of the traditional crop raises the local price for the traditional crop, tending to spread the benefits of upgrading even to farmers who do not upgrade, while tending to reduce the well-being of landless workers who are net buyers of traditional crops. If the new crops are more labor intensive than the traditional crops, however, then local demand for labor can increase, driving up wages and spreading benefits to landless workers as well.

8.4C Investments that encourage market expansion by reducing transfer costs

In light of the many benefits that market expansion can generate, it is worthwhile studying how to reduce transfer costs. In what follows, we point out that:

> Transfer costs are reduced through investment in the creation and improvement of infrastructure, institutions, and a variety of private business assets.

Investments in infrastructure

Investments in roads, bridges, and culverts help reduce transportation costs by allowing goods and people to travel along more direct routes, in greater safety, in larger and faster vehicles, and with less wear and tear. Railroads, river ports, and effective depots for moving trucked goods onto and off of trains and boats also help reduce transport costs.

Investment in telecommunications infrastructure reduces transfer costs by helping buyers and sellers identify transaction partners more quickly and easily. More subtly, improved communication can reduce the risks associated with trading in more distant markets. Farmers without access to telephones must transport themselves and their goods to a market before finding out the current price there. They might thus find long-distance transactions risky, because after transporting goods to a distant market they must sell there even if the current price is very low. Farmers with mobile phones can identify which of several external markets is paying the best price *before* taking their goods to market and thus face less risk of receiving disappointingly low prices.

Improvements in institutions

Over the last two decades, many economists have come to recognize the vital role of institutions in supporting market transactions. As defined in earlier chapters, institutions are formal rules and informal norms, together with related enforcement mechanisms, that constrain peoples' choices regarding particular sets of actions. Of specific interest are **contract enforcement institutions**. Even under fairly simple transaction agreements, buyers and sellers make promises to each other regarding future deliveries and payments. Undertaking such transactions is risky, and transfer costs are consequently high, when the partners to the transaction do not trust each other to fulfill promises. Either they must incur the costs of screening partners and monitoring and enforcing contract provisions, or they must bear large risks of loss to partners who cheat. Institutional rules, norms, and enforcement mechanisms that give people strong incentives to fulfill contractual promises, and thus give their trading partners reason to trust them, can reduce transfer costs significantly (especially for higher-value goods requiring more demanding contractual arrangements).

To facilitate discussion of trust, we use the term **agent** to describe a person who has made a promise to deliver goods or make payment, and we use the term **principal** to indicate the person to whom the promises have been made. We say that an agent **cheats** the principal if she intentionally fails to fulfill her contractual promises or if she reduces the principal's profits by exercising insufficient care in carrying out her contractual responsibilities.

The most visible trust-promoting institutions involve **formal contract law institutions**. When these institutions work well, they strengthen agents' incentives to fulfill their contractual promises by creating the expectation of punishments that outweigh the benefits of cheating. Unfortunately, legal systems often work poorly in poor countries, especially in rural areas and especially for urban firms that are small, new, or owned by non-elite outsiders (World Bank, 2001). We return to these issues below.

When formal legal systems fail to promote trust, **informal reputation-based institutions that promote fair dealing and trust** sometimes arise to facilitate market transactions. In small

☰ Box 8.3 The Maghribi Traders

In the 11th century, markets prospered in cities around the Mediterranean. Sea transport was costly and difficult compared to today, but it was well enough advanced to render trade between these cities potentially profitable. Merchants wishing to capitalize on trade opportunities faced high transfer costs, however, because transactions had to be worked out only after long sea voyages brought goods to their destination ports. Profits depended greatly on the care and skill exercised in finding buyers, striking deals, delivering goods, and obtaining payments in distant cities. Merchants either had to travel with their goods to carry out these activities themselves or trust agents to carry out these activities for them. Merchants who traveled with their goods had to curtail business in their home ports while traveling, and they were greatly restricted in their ability to diversify business across multiple ports. Merchants who entrusted trading to agents risked losses to agents' embezzlement or laziness. Formal courts offered little protection against such malfeasance, which took place in foreign territories, would come to light only months after the fact (when ships returned to home ports), and could be very difficult to prove, given the many other hazards that might affect the profitability of an expedition (e.g., shipwreck, piracy, spoilage).

According to Avner Greif (1993), informal rules and norms arose to support trust among the Maghribi traders. They were descendants of Jewish traders who had fled the area near Bagdad in the 10th century and settled initially in North Africa but eventually sent merchant colonists to many locations around the Mediterranean. By the mid-11th century, they had developed a network of trading relationships through which Maghribi traders in any one port served as merchants in their own dealings *and* as agents for Maghribi merchants in other ports. They operated according to rules and norms that dictated fair dealing,

employment only of other Maghribi traders as agents, the sharing of information about any Maghribi trader who cheated, and refusal to take as agent any Maghribi trader known to have cheated any other (until and unless he made restitution).

Greif argues that these rules and norms were *self-enforcing*, which means that they did not require enforcement by any government or outside authority. Because Maghribi traders dealt only with one another and had attained a valuable position in Mediterranean trade, individual traders knew that as long as they remained in good standing they would receive steady work and good profits. They perceived no incentive to cheat, because any short-run gains to cheating were outweighed by the loss of future profitable trading opportunities within the network. Members also had strong incentive to refuse to hire agents who had cheated. Such agents were best avoided, because they had already lost their hope of a lucrative future among the Maghribi, and thus they had little to lose from cheating on the current trade. The Maghribi successfully turned their cultural identity into a valuable asset, which reduced transfer costs and facilitated the expansion of long-distance trade, bringing benefits not only to the traders themselves but also to consumers and producers around the Mediterranean.

The Maghribi rules and norms facilitated some long-distance trade that otherwise might not have taken place, but they had their limitations. The rules were self-enforcing only so long as the Maghribi group remained limited in size and difficult to enter (except by inheritance). Greif argues that this prevented them from undertaking potentially lucrative trade with Italy, where it was unattractive to establish Maghribi communities and where trade would thus have required the use of outsiders as agents.

---

rural communities, where everyone knows everyone else and all are involved in multiple overlapping economic and social relationships, agents sometimes comply with norms of fair dealing to preserve their reputation and prevent social and economic ostracism (Platteau, 2000). We can think of such norms as supporting a form of cooperation in which all community members contribute to creating a more secure environment. Reputation-based institutions have also facilitated some longer-distance transactions. A much-cited example of such an institution is the set of rules and norms that constrained interactions among the Maghribi traders, a distinct cultural group important in long-distance trade around the Mediterranean in the 11th century (see Box 8.3). Similar reputation mechanisms operating within groups sharing common ethnicity and language may be at work today among Hausa traders in West Africa.

Transfer costs may also be reduced through the establishment of institutions that facilitate cooperation and coordination among producers. The rules and norms that shape behavior within agricultural producer cooperatives, for example, can help small farmers obtain fertilizer at lower prices by participating in collective bulk purchases or can help them obtain higher prices for their produce by participating in coordinated deliveries to supermarket chains or food-processing firms. Members of cooperatives can also obtain better access to agricultural extension system resources and to repairers of irrigation equipment, who would be more inclined to make a trip to meet many small farmers than to make the same trip to meet only a single small farmer.

Private business assets

Many of the investments required to reduce transfer costs involve infrastructure and institutions, but investment in many more mundane private business assets may also be important. For example, road construction yields its full transfer cost-reduction benefit only if simultaneous investments are made in deploying higher-capacity and faster vehicles, and reductions in storage and transfer costs require investments in warehouses, refrigeration equipment, and marketers' hard-won relationships with suppliers and buyers.

8.4D Barriers to private investment in transfer cost-reducing assets

Despite the wide-ranging benefits that might emerge from reducing transfer costs, transfer costs can remain high, because:

> Private actors might lack the incentive or the means to undertake critical transfer cost-reducing investments as a result of public goods problems, institutional failures, financial market failures, and other problems.

Many transport infrastructure assets are public goods, which provide benefits to large numbers of people and to which it is impractical to bar access. For example, many community members benefit from the construction of a road that connects the community to larger markets, but it may be impractical to set up toll booths to charge them for use of the road. Private entrepreneurs lack incentives to invest in such assets as a result of the **public goods problem**. Even though the total benefits (enjoyed by all users) far outweigh the costs, any single entrepreneur perceives no way to make a profit on the investment. Unable to charge tolls, the entrepreneur expects to enjoy only the private benefits from her own use of the public good, which in many cases is much smaller than the cost. Informal institutions sometimes arise through which community members cooperate in making joint investments in local public goods, but often they do not arise for reasons we discuss in Chapter 12.

Institutional failures can also prevent healthy private institutions from arising to promote contract fulfillment and trust or to encourage cooperation within producer groups. Again, such institutions often simply fail to arise even when they would generate significant value. They arise only through subtle forms of cooperation, which may be very difficult to catalyze. Moreover, as discussed in Chapter 12, even when they do arise they might exclude some groups and remain limited in scope. For example, reputation-based institutions that promote fair dealing and trust only promote trade within groups sharing a home community, language, or cultural identity (see Box 8.3). The institutions might exclude some groups with whom trade would be beneficial and who are in great need of the benefits that trade could bring. Thus, while informal institutions are helpful in early stages of development, it may be necessary to replace them with larger-scale formal legal institutions as development proceeds.

Financial market failures can prevent investments in private assets such as mobile phones, trucks, and storage facilities. In Chapter 10 we will see why financial market failures can prevent entrepreneurs with good investment projects from obtaining loans of adequate size or at reasonable interest rates. This is especially likely in poorer and more remote regions, where well-off entrepreneurs with the potential to self-finance are lacking and where information flows are inadequate to support outside finance. Lack of private sector entrepreneurship or experience can create additional barriers to transfer cost-reducing investments in such regions.

The problems mentioned thus far may be compounded by **coordination problems**. Investment in transfer cost-reducing assets may be privately profitable to some parties, but only when simultaneous investments are made by other parties. For example, a vegetable-canning company might find it profitable to improve a road connecting its cannery to a community of potential vegetable farmers, but only if it expects many farmers there to invest in the farm improvements required for producing high-quality vegetables. (Even though the road is a public good, the private benefits that the canning company would derive from the road may be sufficiently large that the investment is privately profitable.) At the same time, farmers may be willing to invest in farm improvements only if they expect the canning company to improve local roads and establish contracting relationships with them. If farmers do not expect the canning company to invest in roads, and the cannery does not expect the farmers to invest in upgrading their farms, then neither farmers nor the canning company will have incentive to invest, even though simultaneous investment would be profitable for all parties involved.

8.4E Government and NGO roles in encouraging market development

Most development analysts would agree that public goods problems and institutional failures create roles for governments to play in supporting market development through involvement in transport infrastructure investment, development of healthy legal institutions, and oversight of financial markets. Encouragement of infrastructure investment can take many forms, with governments building roads on their own account, paying communities or private contractors to build roads, or helping to catalyze local cooperation in community-based road maintenance. Chapter 18 examines the many challenges of infrastructure policy design and implementation. Government involvement in financial markets, too, can take many forms, as discussed in Chapters 10 and 21.

Formal legal institutions exist in all countries, but they are often ineffective in developing countries. Legal institutions prevent agents from cheating only if they lead agents to expect punishments for cheating that outweigh the benefits. Agents have such expectations only if they believe that principals will indeed take cheaters to court, that the court system is capable of detecting cheating, that the courts will render fair judgments (which find cheaters guilty, regardless of their economic or political power), and that the courts will impose fines or damage awards that are sufficiently high and quickly executed. Principals will take cheaters to court only if they can access the court system at low enough cost in time and money and if the courts can be expected to extract compensation of sufficient size and with sufficient probability and speed.

Agents' and principals' expectations, and thus the efficacy of formal contract law institutions, are shaped by many practical factors, including not only the details of the country's contract laws but also the details of court procedures and fees, court budgets, and the incentives of judges and other court personnel toward fulfilling their responsibilities quickly, well, and fairly (World Bank, 2001). Box 8.4 describes recent efforts to increase the efficacy of contract law institutions.

Some (but not all) development analysts also see potential to encourage the development of particular sectors through targeted efforts to reduce transfer costs along the sectors' value chains. A **value chain** is the sequence of activities that must be undertaken to facilitate production of a specific good and ultimately deliver it to consumers according to whatever process and product standards they demand. For example, the value chain linking a set of small farmers in Africa to European vegetable markets can involve actors who: market specialized inputs to vegetable farmers; provide financial, agricultural extension or quality certification services; sort, package or transport vegetables to the capital city; wholesale vegetables to exporters; oversee international transportation and customs clearance; and retail vegetables to European customers. In value chain development efforts, governments or NGOs identify specific products that a group of producers

≡ **Box 8.4** Legal System Reform

Formal contract law institutions are more effective when principals have access to the courts at low cost, courts deliver speedy and fair judgments, and systems enforce judgments (by collecting penalty payments) in a timely and consistent way. Performance along each of these dimensions is poor in many developing countries. Fortunately, there is enough variation in performance, even among developing countries, to suggest that improvements are possible. For example, the average duration of a commercial case is almost eight years in Ecuador, but it is less one year in the United States and Colombia. The average length of time between pronouncement of judgment and collection of penalties is 350 days in Senegal but 18 days in Ghana (World Bank, 2001).

In recent years, governments have implemented diverse legal system reforms, aiming to improve access, speed, and fairness. They have increased legal system budgets, hoping to improve speed and quality by reducing judges' case loads. They have attempted to increase efficiency in the use of budgets by eliminating duplication of records systems, simplifying procedures (e.g., shifting from written arguments to oral proceedings), and creating specialized courts that develop expertise in handling specific types of cases. Sometimes fees are reduced and procedures are simplified specifically for cases involving small sums through the creation of new small claims courts. By publishing facts regarding the number and nature of specific judges' rulings, they have sought to increase judges' accountability to local citizens, thereby improving their efficiency and fairness.

---

might profitably sell to exporters or supermarkets and that they do not yet produce or currently produce only for local markets. Government or NGO actors study the entire value chain, identifying the specific links along the chain at which private actors might lack the incentive or ability to undertake needed investments. They then introduce policies to undertake or promote those investments. They might also seek to overcome cooperation and coordination problems by coordinating the activities of diverse public and private sector actors. Their hope is that by strategically reducing specific transfer costs and coordinating investments, they will render private participation profitable throughout the entire value chain.

The partnerships forged for value chain development are highly diverse and tailor-made for specific markets. In Uganda, an NGO partnered with a farmer organization to link farmers with an urban fast-food restaurant to whom they could supply potatoes. The NGO helped the farmers gather the information necessary to create a successful collaboration. Through their organization, the farmers learned how to cultivate a new variety of potato, developed a system of staggered planting dates on plots of land at different altitudes, making year-round delivery possible, and made arrangements for storage and emergency purchase of potatoes from other farmers in order to fulfill their promised delivery schedule (Kaganzi et al., 2009). On a larger scale, the British nonprofit organization Infraco employs modest subsidies in helping to create collaborations between large outside private enterprises and farmer groups in remote areas of Africa with high-quality soils and climate, through which the private enterprises are given an incentive to undertake large mutually beneficial investments in transport and irrigation infrastructure (see www.infraco.com).

Case studies suggest that the creation of new value chains can indeed yield benefits for all parties involved. For example, the exporting firm Lecofruit, encouraged by government investments in infrastructure, undertook a variety of investments along the value chain linking small farmers in Madagascar to European markets for high-quality vegetables, apparently generating benefits for all parties involved (see Box 8.5).

Despite the success stories, government and NGO involvement in value chain development in specific industries remains controversial, because the risks of failure are high. Organizers must manage to pick winners, in the sense that they identify specific products that a group of producers will ultimately be able to sell profitably but that are not now produced. Their projects risk failure because predictions regarding production costs and the extent to which transfer costs will be reduced are difficult. Even if all project elements are implemented well, the resulting value chain might not deliver the profits anticipated. For example, Ashraf et al. (2009) describe an initially

≡ **Box 8.5** Contract Farming of High-Quality Vegetables for the European Market in Madagascar

High-quality vegetables command a substantial premium in European markets. For example, hand-picked green beans can earn two or three times the price of lower-quality beans. Given the intensive labor requirements of hand-picked beans and other high-quality vegetables, countries with low wages and long growing seasons are attractive locations for their production. Preferential trade agreements, such as the Everything But Arms Initiative, through which Madagascar and 47 other low-income countries gained duty-free and quota-free access to European Union markets, also encourage production in Madagascar.

Bart Minten, Lalaina Randrianarison, and Johan F. M. Swinnen (2005) describe how Lecofruit, a large multinational agricultural trading company, sought to take advantage of these conditions by contracting with local small-holder farmers. After initial experiments with gherkins, snow peas, asparagus, and mini-vegetables, the company now concentrates its Madagascar operations on hand-picked and hand-handled fine French beans, which it sells to seven European supermarket chains and other customers.

Production in Madagascar for export to Europe is profitable only if production meets exacting process and product standards, while production, processing, transport and other costs remain below the level of prices that the products command in European markets. Quality improvements and cost reductions required several kinds of investment that might be hindered by market failures. First, farmers must make long-term investments in learning how to cultivate new crops and using new methods (such as composting manure and vegetable matter, a practice they had not previously employed), as well as shorter-term investments in new seeds, fertilizer, and pesticides. Financial market failures that prevent small farmers from obtaining credit hinder these investments. Second, larger-scale investments are required in transport infrastructure and in institutions guaranteeing compliance with process and product standards. Production for export also requires farmers to exercise trustworthiness in fulfilling contractual promises.

The company developed an elaborate system of interaction with contracted small-holder farmers, aimed at encouraging many simultaneous investments. The company employs 300 extension agents, each of whom works with 30 contracted farmers, with the help of five or six assistants. Each contracted farmer devotes a specified small plot of land (usually involving only one third of his total small holding or less) to production for the company during a specified period, primarily in the off season of rice, which is the farmers' main staple crop. Through the extension agents the company trains the farmers in the methods required for production of high-quality beans. It provides seeds, fertilizer, and pesticides on credit, which the farmers pay back with the beans they produce in the first weeks of harvest. Extension agents visit them at least once a week, making sure they are following prescribed practices, sometimes applying the pesticides themselves, and also keeping a watchful eye to prevent farmers from selling to other buyers. The beans are transported to the capital city, where they are canned and sent to Europe. Exacting European buyers conduct chemical residue tests and send independent auditors to certify that standards regarding hygiene and work practices are maintained.

Use of this system with about 9,000 small farmers appears to be profitable for the company. Minten, Randrianarison and Swinnen's (2005) estimates suggest that participation has also been beneficial for the farmers. They receive a higher price for their produce than they would receive in local markets for traditional crops. Over the course of a year, a typical participating household earns about $45 in cash payments from contract farming (after loan repayments), about half the household's monetary income. Also important is the impact on timing of income. Contract income is received during what would otherwise be the hungry season between rice crops. The farmers report using some of the new practices (such as composting) on other off-season crops (on land not under contract), and econometric study suggests that their productivity in rice cultivation increases when the land used for rice cultivation is used for contract farming in the off season, because of the long-lasting effects of the composting and fertilizer application.

Lecofruit's experience suggests the potential for government and NGO investments in infrastructure, education, and agricultural cooperative development to encourage value chain development by the private sector. The company's dealings are restricted to farmers located near to the capital city, Antananarivo. In the wake of a government road-building project, they rapidly expanded operations to include 1,000 new contract farmers. The company also tends to work with farmers who are more educated than the average rural resident and expresses concern with the time and cost involved in training extension agents, given the low education levels in the local population. The large number of interactions between extension agents and farmers that Lecofruit must coordinate suggests that NGO efforts to identify good prospective contract farmers and organize them into cooperatives might significantly reduce contracting costs, encouraging companies like Lecofruit to expand their operations.

---

promising effort to encourage Kenyan farmers to produce French beans, baby corn, and passion fruit for export to European markets by providing farmers with information and input loans, facilitating negotiations between an exporter and the farmers, and coordinating crop collection at cooperatively run facilities where farmers grade and package their produce. The program succeeded in encouraging adoption of higher-value crops with only low levels of subsidization. But one year later the exporter dropped the farmers, who did not succeed in meeting high European process and quality standards.

REFERENCES

Ahmed, Raisuddin, and Mahabub Hossain. "Developmental Impact of Rural Infrastructure in Bangladesh." Research Report 83. Washington, D.C.: International Food Policy Research Institute (IFPRI), 1990. http://www.ifpri.org/sites/default/files/publications/rr83.pdf

Aker, Jenny C., and Isaac M. Mbiti. "Mobile Phones and Economic Development in Africa." *Journal of Economic Perspectives* 24(3): 207–232, 2010. doi:10.1257/jep.24.3.207

Alix-Garcia, Jennifer, and David Saah. "The effect of refugee inflows on host communities: Evidence from tanzania." *The World Bank Economic Review* 24(1): 148–170, 2010. doi: 10.1093/wber/lhp014

Ashraf, Nava, Xavier Giné, and Dean Karlan. "Finding missing markets (and a disturbing epilogue): Evidence from an export crop adoption and marketing intervention in Kenya." *American Journal of Agricultural Economics* 91(4): 973–990, 2009. doi:10.1111/j.1467-8276.2009.01319.x

Barrett, Christopher B. "Food Marketing Liberalization and Trader Entry: Evidence From Madagascar." *World Development* 25(5): 763–777, 1997. doi:10.1016/S0305-750X(96)00132-5

Bigsten, Arne, Paul Collier, Stefan Dercon, Marcel Fafchamps, Bernard Gauthier, Jan Willem Gunning, Abena Oduro, Remco Oostendorp, Cathy Pattillo, Måns Soderbom, Francis Teal, and Albert Zeufack. "Contract Flexibility and Dispute Resolution in African Manufacturing." *Journal of Development Studies* 36(4): 1–37, 2000. doi:10.1080/00220380008422635

Chamberlin, Edward H. *The Theory of Monopolistic Competition: A Re-Orientation of the Theory of Value*. Cambridge, Mass.: Harvard University Press, 1933.

Cudjoe, Godsway, Clemens Breisinger, and Xinshen Diao. "Local impacts of a global crisis: Food price transmission, consumer welfare and poverty in Ghana." *Food Policy* 35(4): 294–302, 2010. doi: 10.1016/j.foodpol.2010.01.004

Dercon, Stefan, and John Hoddinott. "Livelihoods, Growth, and Links to Market Towns in 15 Ethiopian Villages." FCND Discussion Paper 194. Washington, D.C.: International Food Policy Research Institute (IFPRI), 2005. http://www.ifpri.org/sites/default/files/publications/fcndp194.pdf

The Economist. "Trucking in Cameroon: The Road to Hell is Unpaved." December 19, 2002. http://www.economist.com/node/1487583

Fafchamps, Marcel, and Bart Minten. "Property Rights in a Flea Market Economy*." *Economic Development and Cultural Change* 49(1): 229–267, 2001. doi:10.1086/452501

Greif, Avner. "Contract Enforceability and Economic Institutions in Early Trade: The Maghribi Traders' Coalition." *American Economic Review* 83(3): 525–548, 1993. http://www.jstor.org/stable/2117532

Greif, Avner. *Institutions and the Path to the Modern Economy: Lessons From Medieval Trade*. New York: Cambridge University Press, 2006.

Harvey, Paul. *Cash-based responses in emergencies*. Overseas development institute (ODI). Humanitarian policy group (HPG), 2007.

Ivanic, Maros, and Will Martin. "Implications of Higher Global Food Prices for Poverty in Low-Income Countries." *Agricultural Economics* 39(S1): 405–416, 2008. doi:10.1111/agec.2008.39.issue-s1

Kaganzi, Elly, Shaun Ferris, James Barham, Annet Abenakyo, Pascal Sanginga, and Jemimah Njuki. "Sustaining Linkages to High Value Markets Through Collective Action in Uganda." *Food Policy* 34(1): 23–30, 2009. doi:10.1016/j.foodpol.2008.10.004

Khandker, Shahidur R., Zaid Bakht, and Gayatri B. Koolwal. "The Poverty Impact of Rural Roads: Evidence From Bangladesh." *Economic Development and Cultural Change* 57(4): 685–722, 2009. doi:10.1086/598605

Lancaster, Kelvin. *Consumer Demand: A New Approach*. New York: Columbia University Press, 1971.

Minten, Bart, Lalaina Randrianarison, and Johan F. M. Swinnen. "Supermarkets, International Trade and Farmers in Developing Countries: Evidence From Madagascar." Cornell Food and Nutrition Policy Program Working Paper 191. Ithaca: Cornell University, 2005. http://www.cfnpp.cornell.edu/images/wp191.pdf

Osborne, Theresa. "Imperfect Competition in Agricultural Markets: Evidence From Ethiopia." *Journal of Development Economics* 76(2): 405–428, 2005. doi:10.1016/j.jdeveco.2004.02.002

Pindyck, Robert S., and Daniel L. Rubinfeld. *Microeconomics,* 7th edition. Upper Saddle River, N.J.: Pearson Prentice Hall, 2008.

Platteau, Jean-Philippe. *Institutions, Social Norms and Economic Development*. Singapore: Harwood Academic Publishers, 2000.

Reardon, Thomas, and C. Peter Timmer. "Transformation of Markets for Agricultural Output in Developing Countries Since 1950: How Has Thinking Changed?" In Robert Evenson and Prabhu Pingali (eds.). *Handbook of Agricultural Economics, Volume 3*. Amsterdam: Elsevier, 2007, pp. 2807–2855. doi:10.1016/S1574-0072(06)03055-6

Ulimwengu, John M., Sindu Workneh, and Zelekawork Paulos. "Impact of Soaring Food Price in Ethiopia: Does Location Matter?" IFPRI Discussion Paper 00846. Washington, D.C.: International Food Policy Research Institute (IFPRI), 2009.

Williamson, John. "What Should the World Bank Think About the Washington Consensus?" *The World Bank Research Observer* 15(2): 251–264, 2000. doi:10.1093/wbro/15.2.251

World Bank. *World Development Report 2002: Building Institutions for Markets*. New York: Oxford University Press, 2001. http://go.worldbank.org/97WO9QUA50

World Bank. *World Development Report 2008: Agriculture for Development*. Washington, D.C.: World Bank, 2007. http://go.worldbank.org/ZJIAOSUFU0

World Food Programme (WFP). *Malawi: Assessment of Appropriateness and Feasibility of Cash Response Options*. Special Initiative for Cash and Voucher Programming (SICVP). Rome: World Food Programme, 2007. http://documents.wfp.org/stellent/groups/public/documents/ena/wfp142180.pdf

QUESTIONS FOR REVIEW

1. What are transfer costs and why do we suspect they are high in developing countries?

2. Discuss the roles that market intermediaries might play in determining the level of transfer costs associated with a particular set of market transactions.

3. Draw and discuss the significance of every element (local supply schedule, local demand schedule, external market price, local import price, local export price) in the market-equilibrium analysis diagrams developed in this chapter.

4. State the conditions under which a market will be found in importing equilibrium, exporting equilibrium, and autarky equilibrium.

5. What sorts of events might lead to a rightward shift of the local supply schedule? What sorts of events might lead to a rightward shift in the local demand schedule? Discuss how the impacts on the local market of a local supply or demand shift differ depending on whether the local market is in autarky, importing, or exporting equilibrium.

6. Discuss the relationship between the national market and the market in a small community that exports to the national market.

7. Through what mechanisms might the expansion of markets contribute to economic growth and development?

8. Discuss what the framework of section 8.3 implies about the likely benefits and costs of reductions in transfer costs that (a) connect remote communities to larger markets, (b) connect rural communities to each other, (c) connect markets through time, and (d) connect small farmers to higher value markets.

9. What kinds of investment might be required to reduce transfer costs? Why might the private sector fail to undertake some of these investments, even when the value to all affected parties exceeds the cost, and what roles might governments and NGOs play in reducing transfer costs and encouraging market expansion?

QUESTIONS FOR DISCUSSION

1. Use diagrams like those in Figure 8.2 to explain the statement: "If transfer costs were zero it would be difficult to explain why grain markets in some communities remain in autarky—neither importing nor exporting—over long periods, during which prices change at home and in external markets."

2. Suppose a development organization discovers that agroclimatic conditions in a poor rural community are ideal for producing a food that commands a high price in urban markets. The costs of producing a kilogram of the new crop are similar to the costs of producing a kilogram of traditional local crops, but the urban price of the new crop is double the price of the traditional crop. Will local production of the new crop necessarily increase local farm households' profits and income? Why might a shift from production of a traditional to a new crop fail to raise incomes? What does the transfer-cost discussion have to say about the kinds of investment that might be required before farmers and urban buyers both perceive the potential to profit from trade in the new crop?

3. Consider a rural community in which many households produce rice, and consider an agricultural extension program that causes some but not all local farmers to adopt new, more productive technologies.

a. In diagrams like those in Figure 8.2, what schedules or lines would shift, and in which directions, as a result of the agricultural extension program? If the rice market in this community is in autarky equilibrium (both before and after the introduction of the extension program), what happens to the price of rice?

b. Employing common sense, as well as the tools of the first half of Chapter 7, identify the diverse socioeconomic groups within the community that are likely to be affected by the extension program and related price changes in different ways. Which groups are likely to gain? Which groups are likely to lose?

4. Read Williamson (2000), which discusses different notions of what is meant by the "Washington consensus." Create a list of the various policy agenda items that are included as components of the Washington consensus within any school of thought. For each item, consider whether it has more to do with letting currently existing markets (shaped by current transfer costs) operate without direct government intervention (in the form of taxes on or regulation of transactions); reducing government involvement in production and marketing; or undertaking investment to reduce transfer costs and increase the geographic scope and sophistication of markets.

PROBLEMS

1. Using diagrams like those in Figure 8.2, discuss the potential impacts on the local price and local quantities of corn produced, consumed, imported, and exported of each of the following changes:
   a. An inflow into Small Village of refugees who bring wealth with them but do not have access to farm land
   b. A reduction in the price of fertilizer
   c. The construction of better paths connecting outlying homesteads to the Small Village center
   d. The construction of a better road connecting Small Village to Big City.

2. Elaborate on the discussion of cash and food transfers found in the text.
   a. Using diagrams like those in Figure 8.5 explain how and why cash and food transfers affect prices and quantities in local food markets that are in autarky equilibrium.
   b. Using diagrams similar to those in Figure 8.5, but modified to reflect importing equilibrium conditions, explain how and why cash and food transfers affect prices and quantities in local food markets that are in importing equilibrium.
   c. Discuss how the effects of cash and food transfers change as the local supply schedule becomes more inelastic, assuming that the local market is in autarky equilibrium.
   d. Discuss how the effects of cash and food transfers change as the local supply schedule becomes more inelastic, assuming that the local market is in importing equilibrium.
   e. How would you expect the elasticity of local food supply to differ in the short run and long run? What implications does this have for debates about the relative merits of cash and food distributions?

3. Draw a market diagram for a local rice market where buyers and sellers face an external market price that is higher than the local price, but in which high costs of importing and exporting cause the local market to remain in autarky. Suppose a road already exists between the local community and the external market, but costs of importing or exporting remain high because no external traders have set up routine business activities in the local market and no locals have set up routine business dealings in the external market.

   a. Draw what would happen to this diagram in the short run (during which costs of importing and exporting remain unchanged) if the external market price for rice rises, but the local market for rice remains in autarky.
   b. Explain why this change might stimulate private investment in the development of transport and marketing businesses that could reduce costs of exporting from the local community to the external market.
   c. Draw into the diagram and discuss what would happen if investments reduce transfer costs enough to make exporting attractive.
   d. In light of your answers to parts a through c, discuss possible differences between short-run and long-run responses of local prices in outlying areas to price changes in central markets.

4. Suppose that farmers in Small Village may use their land to cultivate either traditional green beans, for which transfer costs to the external market are moderate, or supermarket carrots, for which transfer costs to the external market are initially very high, and they fully cultivate all available land. The external market price for a kilogram of supermarket carrots is significantly higher than the external market price for a kilogram of traditional green beans.
   a. Draw two well-labeled diagrams depicting the Small Village markets for green beans and supermarket carrots, with the market for green beans in autarky equilibrium and the local market for carrots in an equilibrium in which local farmers supply *no* supermarket carrots and local consumers demand *no* carrots.
   b. Suppose that joint investments by supermarkets and NGOs reduce the transfer costs associated with exporting supermarket carrots to the external market (while leaving transfer costs on exports of traditional green beans unchanged). Depict in your diagram a reduction in transfer costs large enough to induce farmers in Small Village to begin producing and exporting supermarket carrots. What happens to the price (net of transfer costs) that farmers could expect to bring home from producing and exporting supermarket carrots?
   c. What might happen to the local supply schedule for traditional beans in response to this change in the local market for supermarket carrots? Explain.

Appendix 8A
Comparative Advantage and the Gains from Market Exchange

Through markets people sell the goods and services they produce and use the proceeds to buy the goods and services they wish to consume. A new opportunity for market exchange between two parties means a new opportunity for each to trade some of what she produces for some of what the other produces. One of the oldest and most profound results of economic theory is the **principle of comparative advantage**, which states that:

> New opportunities for market exchange between two parties leave both parties better off, even if one party is better at producing both goods, as long as they differ in their relative aptitudes for producing different goods.

Here we unpack this important claim and review the logic behind it.

Consider two farmers, Farzana and Hamid. Each farmer owns an acre of land and wishes to consume both rice and vegetables. They differ in their capabilities for producing the two goods. If Farzana used her entire acre for rice production, she would obtain 10 bags of rice, whereas if she used the entire acre for vegetables, she would obtain five bags of vegetables. More generally, if she grows rice on a fraction f of her acre while devoting the rest to vegetable production, she obtains $10f$ bags of rice and $5(1-f)$ bags of vegetables. Hamid's production capabilities are the reverse. He could obtain a maximum of five bags of rice or 10 bags of vegetables.

The two panels of Figure 8A.1 depict the two farmers' production capabilities. The shaded triangle in each panel identifies all the combinations of rice and vegetables that the farmer could feasibly produce. The line defining the diagonal edge of the triangle is the farmer's **production possibilities frontier** (*PPF*), or the set of all combinations of rice and vegetables that the farmer could produce while using his or her entire acre of land and cultivating each crop at maximum productivity.[a]

If exchange between the two farmers were impossible, each would remain in **autarky**, producing only for his or her own consumption and engaging in no trade. Each farmer would be restricted to consuming a combination of rice and vegetables that is feasible to produce on his or her farm. Not wanting to waste any resources, the farmer would produce and consume a combination of foods on his or her *PPF*. Using the language of Chapter 6, the *PPF* would constitute the farmer's budget constraint. Each farmer would choose to consume at the point along this budget constraint that maximizes utility. Let's suppose that Farzana chooses to consume at point a, and Hamid chooses point b.[b]

Our assumption about the farmers' differing production capabilities implies that their *PPFs* have different slopes, and this difference in slopes creates the potential for both farmers to benefit from trade. Farzana's *PPF* has a slope of -2, indicating that if she wishes to consume another bag of vegetables, while remaining in autarky, she must give up two bags of rice production. If offered the opportunity to trade for a bag of vegetables at a cost of less than two bags of rice, she would accept, because by trading she could increase her rice consumption without reducing her vegetable consumption: She could produce one bag less of vegetables, use

[a]The PPFs here are straight lines, because the farmers' per-acre productivities in the cultivation of each crop remain constant, no matter how much or little of their land they devote to cultivating each crop. In Chapter 11 we consider PPFs that are concave (i.e., bowed out from the origin) because productivity per unit of variable input in the production of either good falls as the quantity of variable input devoted to producing that good increases.
[b]We could introduce indifference curves (see Chapter 6) into the diagrams to illustrate each farmer's preferences and could then figure out where each farmer would consume by looking for a tangency between an indifference curve and the *PPF*. For our purposes here, however, it is more convenient to leave the indifference curves invisible.

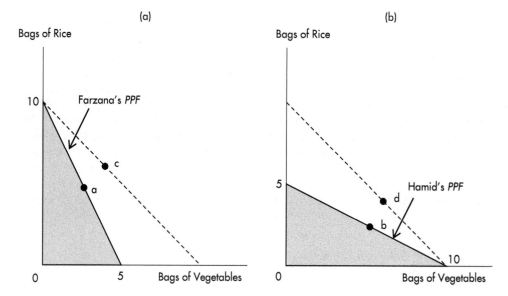

FIGURE 8A.1
Farzana's and Hamid's Production Possibilities and the Gains from Exchange

the freed-up land to produce two more bags of rice, and then give up only a fraction of that extra rice to obtain a bag of vegetables through trade. Hamid's *PPF* has a slope of $-1/2$. In autarky, Hamid would have to give up half a bag of rice to obtain an additional bag of vegetables. Turning this around, he would have to give up two bags of vegetables to obtain an additional bag of rice. If he could obtain a bag of rice through trade for a cost of less than two bags of vegetables, he would be able to consume more vegetables without reducing his rice consumption. At any rate of exchange, denominated in bags of rice per bag of vegetables, between two (the absolute value of the slope of Farzana's *PPF*) and $1/2$ (the absolute value of the slope of Hamid's *PPF*), both farmers are able to expand their consumption by trading.

When opportunity for trade arises, Farzana chooses to specialize in the production of rice and Hamid specializes in producing vegetables. To see this, suppose that the farmers agree to exchange rice for vegetables on a one-for-one basis. No matter how much of her land she devotes to rice cultivation, Farzana finds it cheaper (in terms of forgone rice consumption) to obtain vegetables through trade rather than through production on her own farm. It does not make sense for her to produce even a few vegetables, and thus she specializes in rice cultivation, producing at the point (0,10) at the upper left end of her PPF in Figure 8A.1a. The dashed line represents her consumption possibilities under exchange. This consumption possibilities schedule starts at the point (0,10), because she could choose to consume all 10 bags of rice she produces (and consume no vegetables). Its slope is -1, indicating that for each of the 10 bags of rice she chooses to trade she obtains one bag of vegetables in return. The new consumption possibilities schedule contains combinations of rice and vegetable consumption that lie to the northeast of point a; thus we know that she is better off under exchange than under autarky. (Indeed, no matter where she had chosen to consume along her autarky *PPF*, her consumption possibilities under exchange would include points to the northeast.) This means that through trades of appropriate sizes at the one-for-one rate of exchange, Farzana is able to consume more of both rice *and* vegetables than she would have consumed in autarky. We can think of exchange as offering Farzana a better technology for converting rice into vegetables than reallocating land from rice cultivation to vegetable cultivation on her own farm. A similar line of reasoning implies that Hamid, too, benefits from the opportunity to exchange vegetables for rice at the one-for-one rate of exchange; this leads him to specialize in vegetable cultivation.

As long as the two farmers have *PPFs* with different slopes, and they trade at a rate of exchange in between the absolute values of their *PPF* slopes, we can find particular trades that leave *both* farmers better off. In Figure 8A.1, an example of a trade that would leave both better off is a trade of four bags of Farzana's rice for four bags of Hamid's vegetables. This would cause Farzana to consume at point c and Hamid to consume at point d. Both are better off than if they had remained in autarky.

What's going on exactly? Farzana has higher **relative productivity** in rice cultivation, while Hamid has higher relative productivity in vegetable cultivation. This means that in autarky Farzana can produce an additional bag of rice at a lower cost in terms of forgone vegetable production than is true for Hamid, and Hamid can produce an additional bag of vegetables at lower cost in terms of forgone rice. When the farmers move from autarky to specialization and exchange, the joint resources of the entire two-person economy are put to better use. Land that is relatively well suited for rice cultivation is used for rice cultivation, and land that is relatively well suited for vegetable production is used for vegetable production. As a result, the economy's overall capacity to produce rice and vegetables is increased, and both parties to the voluntary exchange are able to benefit from expanded consumption.

Money-mediated exchange

The exchange just examined involved only two individuals and took the form of barter. In the real world, a household's integration into a local market is more likely to take the form of attending the village market day, where exchanges take place among many neighbors using money. Even so, the same intuition regarding the benefits of specialization and exchange applies. As long as the households have some differences in relative aptitudes for producing the various goods they all wish to consume, they benefit from specialization and exchange. Suppose many farmers like Farzana and Hamid, with *PPFs* having slopes between -2 and $-1/2$, come together for market exchange. We could find a market rate of exchange of rice for vegetables between 2 and 1/2 at which some of those who are relatively more productive in rice cultivation specialize in rice, while the others specialize in vegetables, and the total quantity that rice producers wish to sell just equals the total quantity of rice that vegetable producers wish to buy. All would be made better off by such exchange.

Relative and absolute productivity differences

What if one farmer had inferior capabilities for producing both crops? Would both farmers still find trade beneficial? The answer is yes, as long as their *relative* productivities still differ. Consider Figure 8A.2. Hamid's *PPF* is the same as in Figure 8A.1, but Farzana's production

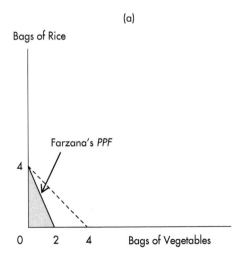

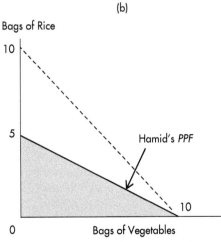

FIGURE 8A.2
Gains from Exchange when Farzana is Absolutely Less Productive than Hamid in Both Crops

possibilities have now shrunk (because, for example, her land is of lower quality). The most rice Farzana could produce is now four bags, and the most vegetables she could produce is two bags. We say that Farzana is **absolutely less productive** in both rice and vegetable cultivation relative to Hamid, who could produce five bags of rice or 10 bags of vegetables. Farzana's *PPF* is everywhere closer to the origin than Hamid's *PPF*. But Farzana's *PPF* remains steeper than Hamid's.

If offered an opportunity to trade rice for vegetables on a one-for-one basis, Farzana would again choose to specialize in rice cultivation. She would be able to consume anywhere along the dashed consumption possibilities schedule shown in Figure 8A.2a. When allowed to trade on a one-for-one basis, and assuming that there are enough farmers in the market like Farzana, who are willing to trade their rice for his vegetables at the one-for-one rate, Hamid would specialize in vegetable cultivation and consume along the dashed consumption possibilities schedule in Figure 8A.2b. Both farmers would be better off when trading than in autarky. What matters for trade to be beneficial is that farmers differ in their *relative* productivities and not their absolute productivities. When two parties exchange two goods, each party is by definition relatively more productive in one of the two goods. Farzana, despite her absolute disadvantages, is *relatively* more productive in rice cultivation. We say that Farzana has a **comparative advantage** in rice cultivation (and Hamid has a comparative advantage in vegetable production).

The gains from expanding and integrating markets

We have just seen the benefits that arise when individual farmers begin trading within their local markets. Further gains arise when exchange becomes possible between markets in different communities, turning the two smaller markets into a single larger one. Just as we can draw production possibility frontiers (*PPFs*) for individual farmers, so we can draw them for entire communities. We could re-label the graphs in Figure 8A.1 or Figure 8A.2, letting the *PPFs* represent the combinations of rice and vegetables (or food and textiles) that each of two communities could produce when putting all of their assets to good use. Again we could demonstrate that as long as their *PPFs* have different slopes, specialization and exchange allow both communities to consume more of both goods than under autarky. In fact, trade over longer distances is likely to allow greater gains from exchange than trade within local communities, because over longer distances relative productivities are likely to differ more.

Unfortunately:

> While the logic of comparative advantage implies that any new opportunity for exchange between two communities improves aggregate consumption opportunities in both communities, it does not guarantee that every individual within each community gains from the opening of trade. Indeed, the opening of trade between communities often leaves some individuals worse off even while aggregate consumption in their communities rises.

In our simple model, the opening of trade causes the rate at which rice is exchanged for vegetables to rise in one community and to fall in the other. In the community where rice becomes relatively more expensive, producers who specialize in rice gain while those who specialize in vegetables lose. (In Chapter 11 we take a more detailed look at the effect of expanded trade on the distribution of income within communities or countries using models that take account of markets for labor and other production inputs as well as markets for diverse goods.)

The logic of comparative advantage tells us that the consumption gains of the rice producers (in a community that begins to export rice and import vegetables) must be larger than the consumption losses of the vegetable producers (within the same community). Thus even if rice farmers gave gifts that just raised vegetable farmers' consumption back to the levels enjoyed before the opening of intercommunity trade, the rice farmers would still consume more

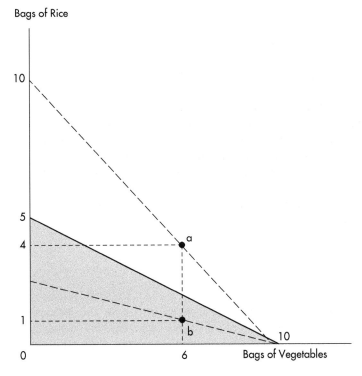

FIGURE 8A.3
Hamid's Options for Production and Exchange When Exchange Is Costly

than before the opening. This implies that everyone could be made better off if the opening of trade were accompanied by appropriate transfers from the "winners" (rice farmers) to the "losers" (vegetable farmers). Such transfers do not take place automatically, however, and creating tax and transfer programs to effect such transfers is a costly and difficult policy challenge (see Chapter 15).

It is important to recognize that even people who are made worse off by the opening of trade between communities continue to benefit from participating in the now-larger market. When the market's geographic expansion alters the local price at which rice trades for vegetables, it shrinks but does not eliminate individuals' gains from participating in the market.

How transfer costs inhibit trade

To see how transfer costs can inhibit trade, consider what happens to the analysis of Figure 8A.1 when exchange becomes costly. Figure 8A.3 reproduces the second panel of Figure 8A.1. When trade was costless, Hamid could bring four bags of vegetables to market and receive four bags of rice in exchange, allowing him to consume at point a.

Suppose now that trade is costly. For each bag of vegetables Hamid exchanges for a bag of rice, he must give up the equivalent of 3/4 of a bag of rice to cover the cost of getting the vegetables to market and finding a buyer. If Hamid gave up four bags of vegetables he would obtain four bags of rice in the market, but he would have to give up three bags of rice to cover trading costs. Bringing home only one bag of rice, he would end up consuming six bags of vegetables and just one bag of rice (at point b). This consumption pair lies inside his *PPF*. He effectively brings home only 1/4 bag of rice for every bag of vegetables he trades. His consumption possibilities schedule under exchange (the dashed diagonal line through point b) now lies *beneath* his *PPF*, and he chooses not to trade.

Labor Markets

Development requires change. Many necessary changes are worked out through labor markets, as people switch employers, migrate, acquire skills, perform new jobs, and produce new goods. We will see that well-functioning labor markets facilitate and guide these changes in ways that speed growth *and* help spread the benefits of growth more broadly throughout society. If we wish to understand development, therefore, we must study labor markets.

This chapter sets out a framework to guide study of developing country labor markets, highlighting the roles of labor mobility and skill acquisition in development, the barriers that might inhibit labor mobility and skill acquisition, and some of the ways policies might raise or lower those barriers.

9.1 Labor Markets and Development

Successful growth and development involve more than mere increase in the volume of economic activity. They involve important **structural changes**, or shifts in the nature and location of economic activity. They require workers to move from subsistence agriculture into commercial agriculture, from agriculture into manufacturing and services, from rural to urban areas, from self-employment and employment in tiny enterprises to wage employment in larger firms, and from firms where productivity is stagnant to more dynamic firms. Such movements are driven by investment and innovation that proceed more rapidly in some sectors, locations, and firms than others. For example, as incomes rise and households spend larger fractions of their income on nonfood items, entrepreneurs respond by investing more in nonfarm sectors. At the same time, the development of markets connecting rural and urban areas allows new nonagricultural producers to cluster near one another in rising urban locations, where their investments are made more productive by agglomeration economies (see Chapter 8). Even within sectors and locations, activity shifts from older, lower-productivity firms into the firms of the entrepreneurs who invest and innovate.

Structural change proceeds smoothly only when workers are willing and able to move out of familiar workplaces and into new ones. Their mobility enhances the productivity of investment in rising sectors and encourages new rounds of investment. Their movement also helps spread the benefits of investment to workers left behind in traditional sectors, because their movement into new markets reduces the supply of labor in traditional markets, creating pressure for wages there to rise.

For growth and structural change to proceed rapidly, many workers must also acquire new skills. Structural change requires workers to produce new goods, operate new equipment, comply with more-sophisticated management practices, and engage in work that is more technically demanding. Such changes are easier when workers acquire basic skills, such as literacy and numeracy. They may be impossible unless some workers also acquire the technical skills required in new occupations; the analytical, managerial, and communication skills required for work in more complex organizations; and the entrepreneurial skills required for innovating and starting new businesses. When workers acquire such skills, they encourage additional investment and expansion that may raise the demand for low-skill as well as high-skill labor, raising wages for many households.

Unfortunately, development economists suspect that diverse labor market frictions and imperfections slow development by inhibiting worker mobility and skill acquisition. After describing how labor markets would contribute to development if workers were perfectly mobile, section 9.3 defines and analyzes three types of friction that can misdirect or inhibit labor mobility in developing countries—migration frictions, search costs, and labor market segmentation—and explores ways governments and NGOs might improve or diminish labor market performance in these areas. Section 9.4 describes the developmental impacts of skill acquisition and how well-functioning labor markets might encourage it. It then describes how market imperfections can inhibit skill investments and suggests possible implications for education and job training policies. Chapter 19 takes a closer look at education policy challenges.

In the research on labor mobility and skill acquisition reviewed in this chapter, researchers often wish to assess how much better off workers would be in some jobs than others. If all work were the same, and if labor market transactions were always just simple exchanges of labor time for cash wages, then researchers could determine how much better off workers are in some jobs than others simply by comparing wages. In the real world, however, and especially in developing countries, working conditions vary across jobs, and workers receive compensation through diverse arrangements, many of them very different from simple exchanges of labor time for cash. Thus, before beginning our study of mobility and skill acquisition, we must describe the diversity of working conditions and employment arrangements in developing countries and consider how to incorporate it into empirical research. This is the task we begin with in section 9.2.

9.2 Multidimensional Work Arrangements and Worker Well-Being
9.2A Diversity in work and working conditions

Some workers labor in hot sugarcane fields or in underground mines, while others sit in air-conditioned offices. Some jobs offer autonomy, variety, and safety, while others are monotonous or dangerous. Variation in work and working conditions is especially striking in developing countries, where arduous work and undesirable working conditions are widespread. Thus it is useful to consider how differences in working conditions affect workers' choices regarding where to work, and how we should incorporate working condition diversity into empirical research on developing-country labor markets.

It is natural to assume that workers consider both wage levels and working conditions when choosing among job offers. Economists often assume, for example, that when offered a choice between jobs, workers evaluate the utility they would derive from each job—where utility is a function of the wage offered *and* working conditions—and choose the job offering the highest utility rather than the highest wage. Under such conditions:

> Competitive labor market equilibrium requires that all jobs for workers with the same skills provide workers with combinations of wages and working conditions that leave them equally well off.

In competitive labor markets, employers offering poor working conditions manage to attract workers away from those offering better working conditions only if they pay *higher* wages. In equilibrium they pay wage premiums just high enough to compensate workers for the extra discomfort or danger of their inferior working conditions, leaving workers indifferent about where they work. These wage premiums are referred to as **compensating differentials**. Many researchers would interpret the wage premiums that governments must pay to attract teachers to take rural posts as compensating differentials for the isolation and poor amenities in many rural locations (McEwan, 1999).[1]

---

[1] We only expect workers in inferior working conditions to receive compensating differentials when employers must compete for workers who are free to leave. Unfortunately, where law enforcement institutions are weak, some predatory employers shield themselves from competition through the use of deception, force, and coercion, thereby creating the power to drive their workers' working conditions and pay to tragically low levels. The International Labour Organization estimates that at least 12 million people are victims of practices labeled "forced labor," "bonded labor," "slavery," "sex trafficking," and "human trafficking," which are broadly condemned by the international community (U.S. Department of State, 2009).

Competition can provide employers with incentives to improve working conditions. Improvements are costly, but they also reduce the need to pay compensating differentials. More specifically, improvements in working conditions allow competitive employers to reduce wages by the amount in pesos that workers would be willing to pay for the better working conditions. Profit-maximizing employers in competitive labor markets therefore have an incentive to undertake all improvements in working conditions for which the peso value to workers exceeds the peso cost to employers. Moreover, if workers treat better working conditions as normal goods (as defined in Chapter 6), then the value they place on good working conditions rises as their income levels rise. This implies that the compensating differentials that employers must pay for poor working conditions rise as productivity and income levels rise, strengthening employers' incentives to invest in improved working conditions. For this reason, we might expect economic growth and rising labor demand to improve working conditions as well as wages.

For labor market competition to encourage employer investment in improved working conditions, however, workers must have accurate information about working conditions and must understand the implications of those conditions for their well-being. Unfortunately, workers might lack adequate information. They might not know, for example, that handling pesticides without protective clothing is harmful to their health and might, as a result, fail to demand compensating differentials for such work. Employers who do not have to pay compensating differentials for poor working conditions have little incentive to improve them. Employers might even be tempted to withhold information about working conditions and to fire workers who inform others about work hazards.

Governments often attempt to mandate better working conditions through labor regulation. The logic of compensating differentials implies that:

> When analyzing the potential impacts of working condition regulations, it is important to distinguish cases in which workers are and are not adequately informed about the conditions.

When workers are fully informed and labor markets are competitive, employers offering inferior working conditions must pay compensating differentials. When such employers improve working conditions in response to new regulations, they may be able to reduce wages at the same time, knowing that the need for compensating differentials has fallen. In such cases, even when the regulations are effective for improving working conditions, they fail to leave workers any better off. Moreover, if the regulations require employers to undertake improvements for which the costs to employers exceed the value to workers (and thus exceed the associated reductions in compensating differentials), then they raise total labor costs, potentially reducing labor demand and leaving some workers worse off.

When workers lack knowledge and receive no compensating differentials for poor working conditions, by contrast, competitive employers who improve working conditions in response to regulations cannot so easily reduce wages in compensation, and the regulations are more likely to raise well-being for the workers who remain employed in the improved workplaces. Promulgation of the regulations might also help inform workers elsewhere of the danger associated with certain working conditions, encouraging them to demand compensating differentials. Employers' increased costs can again reduce their labor demand, but policymakers may be willing to pay this price to protect workers from hazards of which they are unaware.

Implications for empirical comparisons of worker well-being

Later in the chapter we examine potential barriers to labor mobility in developing countries. When assessing the empirical importance of those barriers, we will look for evidence that some workers enjoy pay and working conditions that leave them substantially better off than they would be in other jobs requiring the same skills. Diversity in work and working conditions complicates this task. If work and working conditions were equally desirable in all jobs, then we could demonstrate that some jobs leave workers better off than others simply by demonstrating that they pay higher wages. To establish that some jobs leave workers better off than others when work and working conditions vary, empirical researchers must establish that wages are higher in some jobs than others *even when working conditions are held constant in the comparison* or must demonstrate that wages *and* working conditions are better in some jobs than others.

9.2B Diversity in employment contracts

In introductory models of labor market equilibrium, workers are hired under simple **fee-for-time transactions**, in which they are paid a fixed wage per hour, day, or month. In the real world, workers are often hired under more complicated arrangements, especially in rural areas in developing countries. For example, some workers in northeastern Brazil cultivate sugarcane under arrangements that give them the use of small homesteads, where they may live and grow food for their families, while also paying them cash wages for tending sugarcane. Their cash wages are calculated as a multiple of the acres they weed or the tons of cane they cut, rather than on the basis of the hours or days they work. Called *moradores* ("residers"), they tend to work for the same employers for many years. During the harvest season they work side by side with temporary workers who commute to the fields from nearby towns, and the *moradores* receive lower wages than the temporary workers for the same work (Schaffner, 1993).

The existence of unusual employment arrangements like this, especially when they involve low cash payments for poor workers in isolated locations and when workers appear to have long-term ties with their employers, has sometimes led policymakers to worry that employers have feudal power to tie workers to the land, thereby preventing competition from raising workers' pay. Such suspicions have led policymakers to outlaw troubling employment arrangements in the hope of modernizing agriculture and improving workers' well-being.

Economists point out, however, that:

> Complicated employment arrangements—including feudal-looking ones—can arise even when labor markets are fully competitive, and their use can generate mutual benefits for employers and workers.

We will see that employers might use the more complicated arrangements to reduce labor costs, even while leaving workers as well off as under simpler arrangements. Employers' ability to do so can increase their demand for labor, creating benefits for workers as well as employers. Under such circumstances, outlawing the use of the complicated employment arrangements may leave workers *worse* off and *reduce* productivity. In what follows we first describe employment contracts in more detail and then examine how employers can reduce labor costs through appropriate contract design.

Multidimensional employment contracts

We can think of employees and employers as exchanging work for compensation under **employment contracts** that can differ along many dimensions. In some cases the contracts are explicit and written, though often they are informal and unwritten. Employment contracts can differ in the **means of payment**, or the form in which compensation is transferred to workers. Payments may be made in cash or **in kind**, whether in the form of free or subsidized food, uniforms, transportation, or housing, or the use of land and other inputs. Employers may offer **nonwage benefits** such as paid weekly days off, paid holidays, paid sick leave, and pensions.

Employment contracts differ also in the **basis of payment**, which shapes the way remuneration is tied to the time and effort a worker puts in on the job. Rather than being paid an hourly rate, many workers earn **piece rates**, receiving specified pay per acre weeded, per kilogram harvested, or per package delivered. Other workers are paid fixed salaries per month or year, regardless of their hours, and some receive bonuses as rewards for high productivity.

In agriculture, labor is brought into production through even more diverse contractual arrangements. Often referred to as *agrarian institutions*, these arrangements include the use of **permanent** or **tied labor**, which may be contrasted with **temporary** or **casual labor**. Permanent workers are hired to work for the same employer year round. They usually receive lower daily wages than temporary workers and remain with the same employer for multiple years. Temporary workers are hired one day or season at a time, change employers frequently and often fail to find work in slack agricultural seasons.

Other agrarian arrangements look quite different from wage labor. Often landowners offer workers tenancy arrangements, in which workers cultivate plots of land in exchange for rental payments. Their "wage" is the difference between the total farm profits they generate from the rental plots and the rental payments they pay to their landlords. Under **fixed rent tenancies**, workers pay landowners a fixed amount of cash or produce at harvest time. Under **share tenancies**, workers pay landlords a specified fraction of what they harvest.

As suggested above, the use of more complicated employment contracts can help employers reduce labor costs while leaving workers just as well off. In what follows we discuss three of the most important ways they might do this: reducing the cost of effective labor by improving work incentives, reducing the total cost of compensation by making in-kind payments, and reducing average compensation costs by promising long-term and steady employment through which workers obtain implicit credit or insurance.

Improving work incentives

When they work harder, agricultural workers weed or harvest more acres per day or do a more thorough job. We say that they supply more **effective labor**—labor effort that completes valuable job tasks—when they work harder. When paid a simple wage per day and unsupervised, workers perceive little benefit to working hard (which does not improve their pay or employment prospects) while perceiving all the cost (of extra fatigue and discomfort). They might provide little effective labor, rendering the cost per unit of effective labor very high. They might work harder if paid on an hourly basis and supervised, but supervision is costly, so the cost per unit of effective labor (including supervision costs) can again be quite high.

Employers may be able to reduce the cost of effective labor by hiring workers under contracts providing **higher-powered work incentives** rather than under fee-for-time arrangements. Contracts provide higher-powered work incentives when they tie workers' pay to the quantity of effective labor they perform. They might do this by paying workers piece rates, offering bonuses for good performance, or hiring workers under tenancy arrangements. Under such arrangements, workers derive benefits from working hard, because working hard increases their piece-rate pay, increases their probability of receiving a bonus, or increases the profits they derive from cultivating rental plots. They are thus more likely to work hard under such contracts, even when they are subject to little direct supervision.

Foster and Rosenzweig (1994) employ a unique data set from a rural area in the Philippines to produce striking evidence that laborers do indeed work harder when working for piece rates than for hourly rates. Their data set follows workers over time as they move between jobs paying piece rates and time rates, and it simultaneously tracks workers' calorie intakes and changes in body mass. Holding calorie intake constant, harder physical labor should lead to smaller increases or greater reductions in body mass. They find that workers deplete body mass 10 percent more under piece rates than under time rates (holding calorie consumption constant). They also consume 23 percent more calories, consistent with their greater need for calories when working harder.

Reducing compensation costs through in-kind payment

Employers may be able to reduce labor costs by paying workers partly in kind. Suppose an employer initially pays workers entirely in cash at the competitive wage w per week and that workers use some of this cash to buy one or more bags of beans at a price of p per bag. If the employer began to pay each worker one bag of beans per week, together with a cash wage of $w - p$, the workers could still consume exactly what they consumed before. They would remain just as well off and would remain willing to work for this employer despite competition from other employers paying the cash wage w (and no in-kind payments). If the cost to the employer of providing a bag of beans c is less than what a worker pays for a bag of beans p, then by substituting a bag of beans for cash an employer reduces his total cost of obtaining one week of labor to $w - p + c$ which is less than w.

One reason agricultural employers may be able to provide workers with food at a cost c below the retail price p has to do with the transfer costs introduced in Chapter 8. In competitive markets, retail food prices must equal the cost of producing the food *plus* the cost of transporting the food to market and retailing it. When employers give food directly to workers who consume it nearby, many of these transfer costs may be avoided.

Throughout the 20th century, sugarcane plantation owners in northeastern Brazil were able to provide in-kind payments at low cost because they could allow workers to grow food for their own consumption on land that was of low quality for sugarcane cultivation. Food produced by the workers themselves needed no transportation and the labor required to produce it needed no supervision; thus the cost to employers of providing food this way was lower than the price workers would have had to pay for the food in markets. Heath (1981) offers historical evidence that economic incentives indeed motivated use of these contracts. The practice was especially prevalent when oscillating world sugar prices were low. When sugar prices were high, even low-quality land became valuable for producing sugarcane; in those periods plantation owners reduced the quantity of land allotted to workers for homesteads while increasing their cash wages.

Reducing labor costs through provision of implicit credit or insurance

A final way that employers may be able to reduce labor costs is by promising workers steady employment. As discussed in Chapter 2, human beings have an interest in smoothing consumption. This means that we prefer to avoid large swings in consumption over time, even if we must pay to avoid swings by accepting lower average consumption. People sometimes manage to smooth consumption by borrowing when income is low and then paying back (with interest) when income is high or by purchasing insurance. But poor rural workers—for whom wage-earning opportunities fluctuate profoundly with the seasons and the weather—often lack access to credit and insurance (for reasons discussed in Chapter 10).

When employers promise such workers steady year-round employment, they provide them with valuable opportunities to smooth consumption. Implicitly, they are providing workers with credit or insurance (in addition to wage payments). Just as workers sometimes accept lower wages in exchange for better working conditions, so also workers may accept lower average or annual wages in exchange for greater income stability. Permanent workers may, therefore, agree to work for lower wages than temporary workers in peak agricultural seasons, even when they are perfectly mobile and labor markets are competitive, because permanent employment shields them from unemployment in slack seasons (Bardhan, 1979). Wealthy employers with good access to financial instruments, for whom the cost of providing implicit credit and insurance is low, might therefore choose to reduce labor costs by offering permanent employment.

Explaining share tenancy

The agrarian institution examined in the largest number of journal articles by academic economists is share tenancy (see Otsuka and Hayami, 1988, for a review). Economists in the 1970s found the

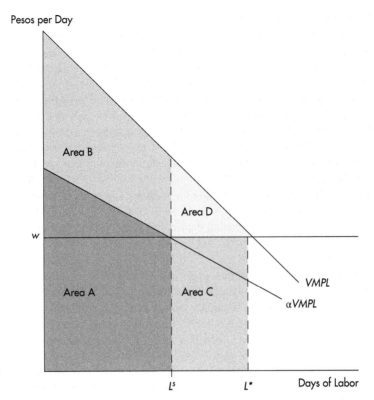

Pesos per Day

Area B

Area D

w

Area A   Area C

VMPL

αVMPL

L^s L^* Days of Labor

**FIGURE 9.1
Employer, Fixed-Rent
Tenant, and Share
Tenant Choices
Regarding the Quantity
of Labor to Employ on a
One-Acre Plot**

prevalence of share tenancy in South Asia and other parts of the world to be a puzzle that they could solve by drawing on recently developed theories related to incentive problems and risk.

At first glance, landlords' use of share tenancy was puzzling, because it appeared to foster inefficient land use. It should have been rejected by profit-maximizing landowners, who could have earned higher profits under more efficient fixed-rent tenancies. To see this, consider Figure 9.1, which examines choices regarding the quantity of labor to apply in cultivating one acre of land under various employment arrangements. The horizontal axis measures the days of labor devoted to cultivating the one-acre plot, and the vertical axis measures pesos of marginal revenue and cost.

For a landowner who cultivates the one-acre plot with wage labor paid w per day, and who is capable of supervising workers at no cost, each additional day of labor brings a benefit equal to the value of the marginal product of labor ($VMPL$), as defined in Chapter 6, and a cost equal to w. Devoting another day of labor to cultivating the plot thus increases profits as long as the $VMPL$ exceeds the wage, and the profit-maximizing level of labor L^* is found where the $VMPL$ equals the wage.

For a fixed-rent tenant who may also hire out his time to other employers at wage w, the choice is almost identical. Each additional unit of labor he devotes to the plot raises total plot revenue by the $VMPL$ and thus raises his tenancy income (i.e., total plot revenue minus the fixed rental payment) by the $VMPL$. Each additional unit of labor on the plot also reduces his earnings from wage employment by w, the opportunity cost of his time. Thus he maximizes his total income (from the plot and wage labor) by choosing the quantity of labor L^* at which the $VMPL$ equals the wage.

For the share tenant, work on the plot is less attractive relative to wage labor than for the fixed rent tenant. She expects to keep only the fraction α of any revenue from the plot; thus, while each additional unit of labor she devotes to the plot raises total plot revenue by the $VMPL$, it raises her *income* from the plot by only α times the $VMPL$. If she, too, may hire her labor out to other employers for the wage w, then each additional unit of labor she devotes to the plot costs her w in reduced wage income. Her total income from share tenancy and wage labor is maximized at the intersection of the $\alpha VMPL$ schedule and the wage line. Her income-maximizing choice of plot labor L^s is less than L^*, indicating that she cultivates the plot less intensively than would a fixed-rent tenant.

Under the conditions we have just described, it should be possible for the landlord to convert a share tenancy paying the tenant the share of α to a fixed-rent tenancy under which the tenant is left just as well off while *also* increasing the landlord's income. Under the share contract, the total revenue generated by the plot is equal to the area under the *VMPL* schedule to the left of L^s (area A plus area B in Figure 9.1).[2] Of this, the area under the $\alpha VMPL$ schedule (area A) goes to the tenant, leaving the landowner with income equal to area B. Under a fixed-rent tenancy, the tenant cultivates the plot more intensively, and the total revenue generated by the plot rises to equal the area under the *VMPL* schedule to the left of L^* (the total of areas A, B, C, and D). To keep the tenant just as well off as under the share tenancy, the landlord must allow the tenant to retain plot revenue equal to the revenue she would have retained under share tenancy (area A) plus enough additional revenue to compensate for the opportunity cost of the additional labor the tenant devotes to the plot under the fixed-rent tenancy (area C). The landlord may do this by charging a fixed rent equal to the sum of areas B plus D. In so doing, the landlord would keep the tenant just as well off as under the share tenancy, while increasing landlord income by an amount equal to area D.

So why might economically astute landlords choose to cultivate their land under this apparently inefficient and less profitable arrangement? Many development economists now see share tenancy as an employment arrangement that lies in the middle of a continuum between wage employment and fixed-rent tenancy and that just balances two mechanisms for reducing labor costs (Stiglitz, 1974b). Under (unsupervised and permanent) wage employment, workers have little incentive to work hard, but they enjoy income that does not fluctuate with variation in the weather (allowing employers to reduce average wages). At the other end of the spectrum, under fixed-rent tenancies, workers appropriate the entire *VMPL* and thus face strong work incentives, but they also bear all the risk associated with cultivation (and must be compensated for that with higher average annual earnings). Share tenancy might represent a good balance, providing workers with stronger work incentives than wage labor but without subjecting them to as much income fluctuation as under fixed-rent tenancy. It may thus be the type of employment contract that minimizes the cost per unit of effective labor. For an alternative view, see Otsuka and Hayami (1988).

Implications for labor market function and empirical research

What most of the theoretical papers on share tenancy, tied labor, and other agrarian institutions prove is that such contract choices *might* arise even when workers are perfectly mobile and employers are competitive. That is, they refute the claim that the mere existence of these contracts is evidence that workers are immobile and employers have feudal power. The theories do not, however, prove that workers *are* mobile and that labor markets *are* competitive. Employers might find these contractual forms useful even if workers are immobile or markets are not competitive.[3] This suggests that whether workers are paid under simple fee-for-time contracts or under more complicated contractual forms, deeper questions about worker mobility (to which we turn in the next section) continue to merit research.

A practical implication of the above discussion for empirical labor market studies is that researchers must take great care when using household survey questionnaires to measure workers' wages and working conditions. They must ask series of carefully designed questions that elicit adequate information about piece rates, shares, time rates, bonuses and in-kind payments, and they must recognize the need for compensating differentials when higher-powered

---

[2]Each unit of labor adds to revenue in an amount equal to the area of a narrow rectangle with width equal to one unit of labor and height equal to the *VMPL* associated with that unit of labor. Hence the area under the *VMPL* schedule to the left of the quantity of labor employed equals the total revenue generated by that quantity of labor.

[3]Schaffner (1995), for example, illustrates how employers might gain from offering permanent employment contracts while exercising a subtle form of exploitation, which allows them to hold workers' well-being below the level they would enjoy in fully competitive labor markets.

work incentives require workers to work harder and when less permanent employment arrangements provide workers with less implicit credit and insurance (Schaffner, 2000).

9.3 Mobility in Developing-Country Labor Markets
9.3A A simple model of labor mobility in development

In this section we illustrate how labor markets can facilitate growth and help spread the benefits of growth more broadly throughout society when labor is mobile. We examine a model of the national market for a single type of labor: low-skill labor. To keep the model simple, we assume that all jobs in this market involve equally attractive working conditions and that all workers are hired under simple fee-for-time contracts, so that the wage w fully characterizes how attractive a job is. We assume that workers supply more labor when the wage is higher,[4] and we assume that employers are perfectly competitive and maximize profits (as described in Chapter 6). This implies that the employers take the going wage as given and hire labor until the *VMPL* equals the wage.

Most important, we assume initially that workers are **perfectly mobile**. This means that they are always willing and able to leave one employer when another offers a higher wage. To highlight the significance of mobility while keeping the model small, we assume that the economy is composed of only two potential employers of low-skill labor, Producer 1 and Producer 2, who remain perfectly competitive despite their small number.

We describe the model graphically in Figure 9.2. In all three panels, the horizontal axes measure worker-days of labor, and the vertical axes measure wages in pesos per day. Panels a and b describe the demands for labor by Producers 1 and 2, which are given by their *VMPL* schedules (*VMPL₁* and *VMPL₂*). Panel c describes the entire national market for low-skill labor. The total labor demand schedule D is constructed by taking the *horizontal sum* of the two producers' labor demand schedules. That is, we identify the total quantity of labor demanded in the national market at any wage by adding together the quantities of labor demanded at that wage by each of the two producers. For example, at wage levels between those associated with the two horizontal solid

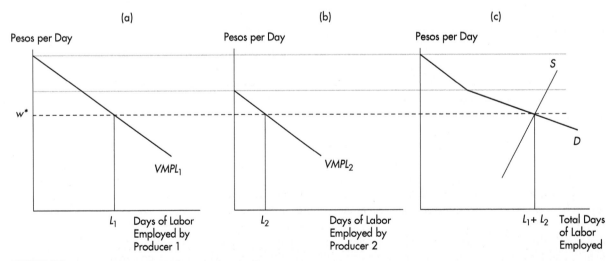

FIGURE 9.2
Labor Market Equilibrium When Workers Are Perfectly Mobile

---

[4]This is the standard assumption in labor market analysis, though we showed in Chapter 6 that it is theoretically possible for the quantity of labor supplied by utility-maximizing individuals to fall when the wage rises.

gray lines, Producer 2 demands no labor, and the total quantity demanded in the market is equal to the quantity demanded by Producer 1. At wages below the lower of the two solid gray lines, the total quantity demanded includes contributions from both producers.

The upward-sloping labor supply schedule (S) in Figure 9.2c indicates the total quantities of labor supplied by all low-skill workers in the economy at each wage. Because workers are perfectly mobile, it makes sense only to describe their total supply and not their supplies to Producer 1 and Producer 2 separately.

The labor market achieves **equilibrium** when no producer would prefer to hire or fire workers, every worker is content to remain in his current job, and every potential worker who is not working is content to remain out of the labor force. We ignore the possibility of international migration, so that we can focus more clearly on the developmental roles of domestic labor markets.

With employers perfectly competitive and workers perfectly mobile, the two employers must pay the same wage in labor market equilibrium. If Producer 1 paid a higher wage than Producer 2, Producer 1 would have an incentive to steal Producer 2's workers by offering them wages just above Producer 2's low wage. To avoid being replaced by such outsiders, Producer 1's workers would have to accept wage cuts. To avoid losing all his workers, Producer 2 would have to raise his wage. This process would continue until the two producers offered the same wage.

Labor market equilibrium also requires that the total quantity of labor demanded by both employers at the equilibrium wage equal the total quantity of labor supplied at that wage. Thus, the equilibrium wage w^* and equilibrium total employment ($L_1^* + L_2^*$) are found at the intersection of the total supply and demand schedules in Figure 9.2c. We find the equilibrium quantities of labor employed by individual producers by drawing a horizontal line at the height of the equilibrium wage and observing where it intersects the $VMPL$ schedules in the first two panels. In the equilibrium depicted in Figure 9.2, Producer 1 employs L_1^* units of labor and Producer 2 employs L_2^*.

Efficient allocation of labor across uses

Labor use is **efficient** when there is no way to make one person better off without making any other person worse off simply by reallocating labor across uses. Efficiency requires, first, that the $VMPL$ for low-skill labor be equated across all employers. To see why, notice that if Producer 1's $VMPL$ were higher than Producer 2's, then taking away one unit of labor from Producer 2 and moving it into Producer 1's firm would increase the value of Producer 1's production by more than it reduces the value of Producer 2's production. Such movement would raise the total value of production in the two-employer economy, creating the potential to leave everyone better off. Only when the $VMPL$s are equated across uses does it become impossible to raise the total value of production by reallocating labor. Efficiency requires, second, that the $VMPL$ for low-skill labor be equated to the value to workers (in pesos) of the last unit of home time they give up to supply labor (where home time is defined as in Chapter 6).

We may use the model illustrated in Figure 9.2 to demonstrate that:

> When workers maximize utility and are perfectly mobile, and when producers maximize profits and are perfectly competitive, their labor market interactions lead to an efficient allocation of labor.

The first requirement for efficiency is satisfied, because both employers pay the same wage, and both set their $VMPL$s equal to that wage, thereby setting their $VMPL$s equal to each other. Workers' mobility is vital to this result, because without their willingness to change jobs whenever one employer offers a higher wage than the other, wages and $VMPL$s would not be driven to equality across employers in equilibrium. The second requirement is satisfied because utility-maximizing workers supply labor until the value to them of an additional unit of home time is just equal to the wage (see Chapter 6), which is equal to the $VMPL$ as a result of employers' profit-maximizing behavior.

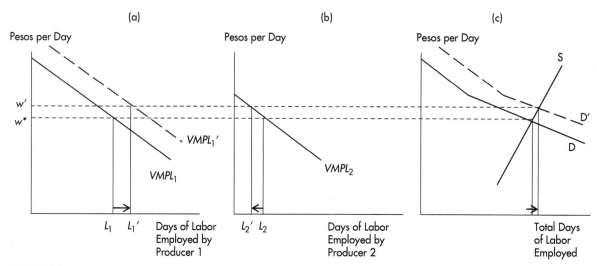

FIGURE 9.3
The Effects of an Employer-Specific Labor Demand Increase when Labor Is Perfectly Mobile

Labor mobility and economic growth

The model depicted in Figure 9.2 also illustrates how labor mobility facilitates growth when growth is driven by investment and innovation that are more rapid in some sectors than others. Suppose that Producer 1 invests in technological innovation that is low-skill **labor using**, in the sense that it causes the *VMPL* schedule to shift up, as illustrated by the dashed $VMPL_1'$ schedule in Figure 9.3a. At the initial level of employment, Producer 1's *VMPL* now exceeds the wage and Producer 1 sees the potential to increase profits by expanding employment and production. Producer 1 offers a higher wage (than the current market wage), seeking to draw new workers into its operations. Producer 1's higher wage provides the labor market signal that encourages workers to move into Producer 1's dynamic establishment.

When equilibrium is restored, both employers must again pay the same wage, and the total quantity of labor demanded must again equal the total quantity of labor supplied. Thus, we may identify the ultimate impact of Producer 1's investment on the equilibrium wage in Figure 9.3c. The shift in Producer 1's demand schedule implies a comparable shift in the total labor demand schedule in panel c (from *D* to *D'*), leading to a new equilibrium at the intersection of *D'* and the labor supply schedule. Drawing a line through all three panels at the height of the new equilibrium wage *w'*, we identify the new levels of employment by Producers 1 and 2 (L_1' and L_2').

The investment by Producer 1 induces two important labor flows: a movement of workers from Producer 2 (where employment has fallen) to Producer 1 (where employment has risen) and a movement of workers who were out of the labor force into employment (as seen by the movement up and to the right along the total labor supply schedule). It may also have induced some workers to supply more days of labor. These labor flows re-establish the equality of *VMPL*s across uses, adding to the impact of investment on the total value of production. Thus:

> Labor mobility into the labor force and from stagnant to dynamic sectors increases the rate of growth in GDP generated by sector-specific investment and innovation.

Labor market integration and the distribution of wage increases

As long as labor markets are perfectly competitive and workers are mobile, increases in the demand for low-skill labor in *any one* sector or location bring rising wages for *all* low-skill workers. To see this, look again at Figure 9.3. The investment that increased Producer 1's demand for labor raised wages for Producer 2's low-skill workers, even though Producer 2's business was shrinking while Producer 1's was expanding. Because Producer 2's workers were mobile, Producer 2 had to raise wages to retain some workers when Producer 1 began offering higher wages.

This indicates that:

> When labor is mobile, labor markets help spread the benefits of sector-specific labor demand growth to workers in other sectors and locations.

For example, workers in both agriculture *and* nonagriculture within rural communities benefit from labor demand increases in either agriculture *or* nonagriculture, as long as workers are freely mobile between sectors within rural communities. We saw an example of this in the discussion of Green Revolution impacts on wages in Chapter 6. Similarly, if workers were freely mobile between rural and urban areas, low-skill workers in both rural *and* urban areas would benefit from labor demand increases in rural *or* urban areas. (We examine reasons why this might not be the case later.) Under the assumptions of the basic model, labor markets in diverse sectors and locations are perfectly **integrated**, with wages in all low-skill labor markets rising and falling together.

Costly mobility

Now suppose that workers face a cost of moving from one producer's sector or location to the other producer's. We can think of workers as located nearer to one producer than the other at any time. Workers who are nearer to Producer 1 currently supply their labor to Producer 1's labor market, but they may also choose to incur a mobility cost and export their labor to Producer 2's market.

We describe such a situation in Figure 9.4. For the sake of comparison to the case of perfect labor mobility, the initial (solid) *VMPL* schedules for Producer 1 and Producer 2 in Figure 9.4 are identical to those in Figure 9.3, and the initial equilibrium involves the same wage (w^*) paid by both producers and the same employment levels (L_1^* and L_2^*). The main difference between Figures 9.3 and 9.4 is in the treatment of labor supply. In Figure 9.3, the two producers compete

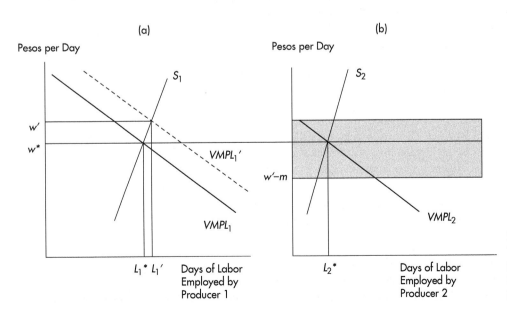

FIGURE 9.4
The Effects of an Employer-Specific Labor Demand Increase in the Presence of Mobility Costs

for labor in the same market, where supply is given by the total supply schedule S in panel c. In Figure 9.4 labor is supplied by the same total number of workers, but some of them are located near Producer 1 and supply labor according to the schedule S_1, while others are located near Producer 2 and supply according to the schedule S_2. The sector-specific supply schedules S_1 and S_2 are each steeper than the total supply schedule S, which is equal to the horizontal sum of the S_1 and S_2 schedules.

We assume that workers face mobility costs that are comparable to wage reductions of m pesos per labor-day. This means that in the initial equilibrium, workers in both markets compare the wage they earn in their home market, w^*, to the wage net of mobility costs that they would obtain if they exported labor to the other market, $w^* - m$, and decide to remain in their home market (because w^* is greater than $w^* - m$).

Again we consider the effect of investment or innovation that causes Producer 1's $VMPL$ to shift up to the level of the dashed VMP'_L schedule in Figure 9.4a. This shift raises the equilibrium wage in Producer 1's labor market to w'. (It now raises the equilibrium wage by more than in the case of perfect mobility, because the sector-specific supply schedule S_1 is steeper than the total supply schedule S.) The $VMPL$ shift also raises the net wage that Producer 2's workers would expect to enjoy if they moved into Producer 1's market to $w' - m$ (marked by the lower edge of the shaded region in panel b). Because Producer 1's wage rises by less than m, however, $w' - m$ remains below w^* (the wage still paid by Producer 2), and workers for Producer 2 have no incentive to move to take advantage of Producer 1's higher wage. As a result of mobility costs, the two labor markets are not integrated. In the new equilibrium, the $VMPL$s of labor are no longer equalized across uses, so the economy's labor is no longer allocated in a way that maximizes the value of production. Compared to the case of perfect labor mobility, the wage faced by Producer 1 rises more, and the innovation leads to lower increases in Producer 1's production and employment. Furthermore, the benefits of Producer 1's increased demand for labor are no longer shared with Producer 2's workers.

Within the simple model of this section, when workers are perfectly mobile, all workers with the same skills receive the same wage, no matter where they work, and any observed differences in wages for workers with the same skills constitute evidence of barriers to labor mobility. In a more realistic model that acknowledges the diversity in working conditions and employment arrangements discussed in section 9.2, wage differences would constitute certain evidence of labor mobility barriers only if working conditions were at least as good in the higher-wage jobs as in the lower-wage jobs.

Investment types, elasticities, and pro-poor growth

Before moving on from the basic model, it is useful to make two final observations. First, among the investments and innovations that lead to the same rate of economic growth, some are more likely to channel benefits to low-wage workers than others. Only if they are labor using—causing $VMPL$ schedules to rise—will they raise the demand for labor and drive up the wages earned by low-skill workers. Growth is thus more likely to raise the earnings of low-skill workers when based on the accumulation of physical and human capital that are complements in production with low-skill labor or on the adoption of new technologies that increase the productivity of low-skill labor. Such investments give rise to pro-poor growth.

Second, when investment increases the demand for low-skill labor, the size of the impact on low-skill wages—and on low-skill workers' well-being—depends critically on the wage elasticities of supply and demand (see problem 3). For example, when labor supply is inelastic, asset growth that increases the demand for low-skill labor raises wages and well-being significantly for the low-skill workers already in the market (and reduces profitability for employers of low-skill labor) while drawing few additional workers into employment. When the supply of labor is highly elastic, by contrast, the increased demand for labor generates few benefits for low-skill workers. The workers already in the market benefit little because their wages rise little. The workers drawn into the market are many, but the impact on their well-being is small; these worker chose not to work when the wage was only a little lower, suggesting that the opportunity cost of the time they give up to enter the labor market is only a little less than their new wage.

Estimation of labor demand and supply elasticities is subject to many econometric difficulties and is quite demanding of data and sophisticated estimation techniques, which unfortunately produce results that are not robust to small changes in their details (Fajnzylber and Maloney, 2001). Good estimates are rare, though a few studies mentioned in Chapter 6 suggest that rural labor supplies are rather inelastic.

Broad observations suggest that forces shifting up the demand for low-skill labor often raise low-skill wages significantly, implying that markets are characterized neither by extreme labor supply elasticity nor extreme labor demand inelasticity. For example, many episodes of expansion in agricultural production have been accompanied by rising rural wages (Hazell and Ramaswamy, 1991; Aryeetey and McKay, 2007). This suggests significant potential for investments that raise low-skill labor demand to reduce poverty.

9.3B Geographic mobility concerns

Over the course of development, the shares of manufacturing and service sectors in GDP tend to rise, while the agricultural sector declines, and the rise of nonagricultural production tends to shift jobs into urban areas. Within large countries, growth also tends to proceed more rapidly in some states and provinces than others (World Bank, 2008). Thus, workers' geographic mobility, or their willingness and ability to **migrate**, is important to development.

Migration flows are high within many developing countries, though their magnitudes vary greatly. The percentages of working-age populations who have ever migrated are 53 percent in Bosnia and Herzegovina (in data from 2001), 39 percent in Paraguay (2001), 19 percent in Sierra Leone (2003), 14 percent in Cambodia (2004) and 3 percent in Malawi (2005), according to the World Bank (2008). Rates of migration are increasing the world over; and many countries are witnessing especially large increases in **temporary migration**, in which migrants stay to work in destination regions only for a limited number of months or years before returning to their origin regions (Deshingkar and Grimm, 2005). Rural-to-urban migration flows are especially important in many countries, but they are by no means the only important type of migration flow. In Ethiopia, India, and Thailand the largest domestic migration flows are from stagnant rural areas to more dynamic rural areas, and in South Korea and Peru the largest flows are from cities to other cities (U.N. Population Division, as cited in Lucas, 1998).

Are observed migration flows too high or too low? Do they move people to the right destinations? What steps, if any, should policymakers take to improve migration flows or their consequences? Such questions are difficult to answer, because migration is more than just a labor market phenomenon. In addition to moving workers from one labor market to another, migration also requires individuals or families to change residence; it thus can bring many changes in migrant families' living conditions and in social institutions and policy challenges. We begin building toward answers by examining the way people make migration decisions and the societal impacts of their choices.

Migration decisions

Economists point out that workers move from one market to another only when households decide either to migrate as a unit or to send a member out as an individual migrant. Households decide not only whether to migrate but also whether to make a temporary or permanent move and where to go. It seems reasonable to assume that:

> Households weigh what they know about the benefits and costs of each migration option they face (relative to remaining where they are). Among migration options, they prefer the one for which the benefits are highest relative to the costs, and they exercise that option if its benefits outweigh the costs.

The benefits of migrating might include not only higher wages in more dynamic labor markets but also improvements along many other dimensions of household life. **Migration** costs include, at the very least, the initial costs of transporting people and belongings, the ongoing costs of transportation and communication required for staying in touch with family left behind, and the monetary and psychic costs of tearing up roots, finding work, crossing cultural and language barriers, and setting up new homes. They might also include the costs of risking unemployment or physical harm.

Many migration costs are incurred at the time of migration or shortly thereafter, whereas many of the income gains are enjoyed only in future years. Migration is thus an investment and is only feasible and attractive when potential migrants can easily finance the up-front costs, whether by borrowing, liquidating savings, or cutting back on current consumption. Migration may, therefore, be out of reach for the poorest households, who lack savings, lack access to credit, and have little scope to cut back consumption (see Chapter 10).

This overview of migration decisions suggests, first, that labor may be far from perfectly mobile across jobs in different locations if households perceive high costs to migrating, if they have difficulty financing the migration investment, or if they lack accurate information about conditions in distant labor markets. It suggests, furthermore, that migration flows can fail to move workers to where they are most productive if migrants choose destinations based more on non-wage features of life there (such as access to electricity) than on wage levels. Empirical research illuminating which types of benefits and costs strongly influence households' migration decisions is thus useful in development analysis.

Empirical research on the determinants of migration decisions has thus far yielded seven broad lessons (Lucas, 1997, 1998; Deshingkar and Grimm, 2005). First, working-age adults are more likely to migrate when the earnings gap between destination and origin is larger, suggesting that migration flows respond at least in part to labor market signals. Second, people are much more likely to migrate over very short distances (holding potential income gains constant) than over longer distances. The effect of distance on migration flows is so strong that it seems likely to represent much more than just the costs of transport and communication. It might represent high psychic or social costs of migrating away from home communities, as well as lack of information or high costs of bearing the uncertainty regarding life in unknown places.

Third, most migrants are young people. It thus seems likely that people indeed perceive migration as an investment, potentially yielding returns well into the future. Young people can expect to reap those returns for longer and, as a result, are more likely to find that the benefits of migration outweigh the costs. Fourth, often migration rates are higher among people with more education. This might indicate that the educated perceive higher returns to migrating into dynamic areas (where the returns to education may be higher), that they experience lower costs of migrating (being more adaptable) or that they have superior information regarding job opportunities. In some places, some of the least educated also migrate at high rates, though more commonly on a temporary basis.

A fifth lesson emerging from recent research is that migrants consider the amenities that a location has to offer, such as access to clean water, sanitation, education, and other social services, as well as labor market conditions. For example, Lall et al. (2009) find that even after controlling for earnings differentials, Brazilian migration rates are higher when differences (between sending and receiving locations) in access to clean water and sanitation services are greater. Governments' tendencies to provide more amenities in urban areas than in rural areas might create a non-labor-market stimulus for rural-to-urban migration.

Sixth, diverse social and economic institutions can slow or speed migration. On the one hand, social networks in sending locations can slow migration. Munshi and Rosenzweig (2009) argue, for example, that reluctance to lose the benefits of participating in private safety net institutions in potential sending locations slows migration flows in rural India. Weak land rights institutions (which we discuss in Chapter 12) can also prevent out-migration by households who cannot sell their land assets and thus stand to lose the value of their land rights if they move. On the other hand, migrants often choose destinations where relatives or acquaintances already reside, suggesting that social networks in destination locations can speed migration flows.

A final lesson is that when households contemplate sending only some members to migrate, they take into account potential impacts on the well-being of those left behind that are made possible when migrants send back **remittances**, or private money transfers. Remittances from members who have migrated elsewhere can allow sending households to purchase agricultural inputs or send children to school. By sending household members to live in different regions, where income fluctuations are not strongly correlated with income fluctuations at home, households can also improve their ability to cope with local shocks. For example, by sending daughters to different communities when they marry, households create the potential for family members in diverse locations to provide each other with mutual assistance, sending remittances when they are doing relatively well and receiving remittances when they are doing relatively poorly (Rosenzweig and Stark, 1989).

Migration impacts

Given that migrants often move to regions with higher wages:

> Migration probably reduces wage differentials between sending and receiving regions, at least for workers with the same skills as the migrants. In many cases, therefore, migration probably encourages efficiency, growth, and the spread of growth's benefits.

However:

> Migration flows fall far short of eliminating wage differentials, suggesting that workers are far from perfectly mobile across locations.

According to the World Bank (2008), wages for unskilled urban laborers exceed agricultural wages by more than 40 percent in a sample of 19 developing countries, and studies that attempt to control more carefully for possible differences between leading and lagging regions in average worker skills or in the nature of compensation arrangements also find large unexplained earnings gaps. For example, a study for Tanzania finds that consumption (as a proxy for earnings) grew an average of 36 percentage points more between 1992 and 2004 for people who migrated out of their initial communities in the remote Kagera region compared to other members *of the same households* who did not migrate (Beegle et al., 2011). If migrants and nonmigrants within the same households would have experienced similar consumption growth had they all remained in the sending location, this implies that migrants raised their earnings significantly by moving from lagging to leading regions.

Broader observations also suggest that geographic mobility is too low to fully integrate labor markets across regions within countries. Wages for similar workers tend not to rise and fall together across all regions within a country. For example, rising export crop prices in Ghana raised wages much more in regions producing those crops than in other regions (Aryeetey and McKay, 2007), and opening to greater international competition led to greater wage reductions in Indian regions where the most vulnerable industries were concentrated than in other regions (Topalova, 2007).

While migration brings labor market benefits, and might bring additional benefits to sending communities through remittance flows, it also imposes costs (Lucas, 1997, 1998; Deshingkar and Grimm, 2005). If migrants take with them important physical and human capital, and if this capital is complementary in production with low-skill labor, then their exodus might reduce the wages of low-skill workers who remain behind, aggravating poverty in lagging regions. Migration might also cause private safety net institutions in sending communities to break down, again reducing the well-being of those left behind (see Chapter 12). In addition, movements of people tend to raise transmission of infectious disease. Migrants themselves are also vulnerable to crime and harassment.

Of significant concern to policymakers is the migration-induced geographic shift in needs for sanitation, education, and other infrastructure and social services. If policymakers were committed to providing such services to all citizens regardless of their location, the population shift might constitute a benefit rather than a cost, because these services are often cheaper to provide in the more densely populated areas to which migrants move. In practice, however, governments often appear committed to providing services only in urban areas and thus see rural-to-urban migration as increasing the need to provide costly services.

Migration and policy

In the simple model of section 9.3A, frictions that prevent workers from moving to where wages are higher inhibit development, suggesting the developmental importance of investments that reduce migration frictions. These might include investments in transport and communication infrastructure, in the collection and dissemination of information about job openings, and in the creation of safety net programs (to compensate for migrants' loss of private safety net institutions in sending locations). Because these investments have some public goods qualities, private actors might not undertake them in the absence of intervention. Thus, governments and NGOs might have important roles to play in encouraging geographic mobility.

Migration is more than a mere labor market phenomenon, however, and can bring societal costs as well as benefits. Policymakers might therefore be reluctant to encourage migration despite its labor market benefits. They might also seek ways to reduce the societal costs and increase the societal benefits of migration. They might attempt to reduce the societal costs by reducing the spread of communicable diseases in and by migrant communities, protecting migrants' civil rights, and boosting the education of any low-skill workers in lagging regions left worse off by the exodus of skilled migrants. They might also attempt to boost the benefits of migration by providing improved means of sending remittances.

In practice, policymakers have often sought to stem the flow of migrants into cities and leading regions. China, Ethiopia, and South Africa long attempted to impose legal restrictions on movement, with only partial success. In many other countries migration is discouraged in subtler ways, involving urban zoning and land use laws that are unfriendly to the private supply of inexpensive housing, as well as infrastructure policies that deprive residentially segregated migrants of services or convenient transport between home and work. Given the potential economic benefits of migration, careful reevaluation of such policies would be valuable.

9.3C Interfirm mobility and related costs

Empirical studies that follow firms over five- or 10-year periods reveal that a process called **creative destruction**—involving the birth and expansion of innovative firms and the decline and death of other firms—can be responsible for a large fraction of productivity growth in developing as well as developed countries (see Aw et al., 2001, on Taiwan and Gebreeyesus, 2008, on Ethiopia). This implies that:

> Successful growth and development requires mobility of workers not only from region to region but also from firm to firm within regions.

Workers' mobility from firm to firm may be inhibited by **search costs**. Employers looking for workers with the right combinations of schooling, analytical ability, personality, strength, and other skills must advertise job openings, search for referrals, interview candidates, and administer tests. Workers must search for suitable jobs by reading advertisements, knocking on doors, standing on street corners, or completing applications and tests. These search activities are likely to be especially costly in developing countries, where infrastructure is weaker and the typical firm is much smaller than in developed countries (Tybout, 2000). With the same number of jobs spread out over a larger number of firms, workers must knock on more doors to find job openings and are less likely to know fellow workers who have information about a given employer.

Search costs can prevent labor markets from allocating labor efficiently across uses and can slow rates of economic growth. Because finding appropriate jobs is time-consuming, workers can experience periods of **unemployment** between jobs, when they are not working and are actively seeking employment at going wages. Because job search is an investment that may be difficult to finance, workers might also settle for **underemployment**—employment in jobs that make poor use of their skills or employ only a fraction of the labor time they are willing to offer— as they become desperate to find new sources of income.

Interfirm mobility costs and policy

In principle, governments could reduce unemployment, underemployment, and the duration of job vacancies by reducing search costs. They might attempt this by investing in better urban transport and communication infrastructure or by creating job centers that collect and disseminate information about job seekers and vacancies. They might try to improve the flow of information about worker skills by enforcing more uniform school curriculum standards or by accrediting training programs and certifying trained workers. Governments might also attempt to finance workers' job search efforts by creating **unemployment insurance** programs, which provide cash transfers to workers who have recently become unemployed. Such programs are considered difficult to administer, however (for reasons discussed in Chapter 15) and still cover few workers in developing countries.

Many developing-country governments attempt instead to reduce workers' vulnerability to unemployment through **job security regulations**, which require employers to give workers advance notice of firing, to make large lump-sum severance payments to workers they dismiss, or to obtain government approval before laying off workers. Unfortunately, whether or not such regulations improve security for employed workers, they introduce another mobility cost. By increasing the cost of replacing workers or downsizing, they reduce firms' ability to adjust to changing market conditions and reduce the expected profitability of hiring any given worker. This might reduce the demand for labor. A growing body of research suggests that stricter job security regulations indeed reduce worker mobility across jobs, reduce employment, and reduce productivity growth. Box 9.1 investigates the impacts of job security legislation (and other features of labor law) on manufacturing industries in India.

9.3D Sectoral mobility and labor market segmentation

The typical job in a developed country involves work for an employer with beautiful headquarters and hundreds or thousands of employees. Job responsibilities and compensation are spelled out in formal documents, and workers receive important nonwage benefits, as well as access to Social Security and other government-stipulated protections. Such jobs are the exception rather than the rule in developing countries, where large fractions of workers are self-employed or work for wages in very small enterprises, many jobs are performed on the streets or in rudimentary workplaces, written employment contracts are rare, and as few as 30 percent of workers are formally registered with government social security programs.

For decades, economists tried to organize the study of this striking difference between developing and developed countries by conceptually dividing developing countries' urban labor

☰ Box 9.1 Labor Regulations and Manufacturing Performance in India

Empirical study of labor regulation impacts is difficult, because most real-world variation in labor regulations is closely correlated with variation in other laws. In data that follow a single country over time, the periods in which labor regulations change are often reform periods in which many other policies change as well. In cross-country data, countries with more restrictive labor regulations tend also to impose heavier regulations in other areas. This makes it difficult to estimate the effects of labor regulations alone. Ahmad Ahsan and Carmen Pagés (2009), following the lead of Timothy Besley and Robin Burgess (2004), point out that state-level data from India are especially useful for studying impacts of labor regulations, because labor regulations vary across Indian states while most other laws and institutions are identical across the states, and because state-level labor regulations have changed over time, in different directions and with different timing in different states. Ahsan and Pagés use this variation to study the effects on manufacturing sector production, employment, and wages of two kinds of regulation: job security regulations and regulations governing the resolution of disputes between labor unions and employers.

The 1947 Industrial Disputes Act provides a national framework for Indian labor regulations, but during the 1980s many states exercised their constitutional authority to amend this legislation. Amendments in some states rendered the regulation less restrictive (or pro-employer) while others rendered it more restrictive (or pro-labor), generating significant variation across states. For example, some amendments reduced workers' ability to strike and are considered pro-employer amendments to dispute resolution laws. Other amendments increased the coverage of requirements that employers obtain government approval for dismissing workers and may be considered pro-labor amendments to job security regulations.

In their efforts to isolate labor regulation effects on production and employment, Ahsan and Pagés employ panel data for 16 Indian states over the period 1959 to 1997. They lag their regulation variables one year relative to their production and employment variables, recognizing that employers' responses to new legislation can take some time. They include in their regressions state fixed effects to account for all differences in laws and conditions across states that do not change over time. This implies that they derive their impact estimates from differences in the evolution of production and employment variables across states that modified their regulations in different ways and at different times. They include year fixed effects to account for nationwide changes in laws or circumstances that affect all states in the same way in any one year, and they add controls for some state-level variables that change over time.

They find that pro-labor changes in job security and dispute resolution regulations reduce nonagricultural output, especially in manufacturing, and their estimates suggest large effects. A pro-labor increase of one standard deviation in their measure of dispute resolution regulation reduces manufacturing output by 7.2 percent, and a pro-labor increase of one standard deviation in the job security measure reduces manufacturing output by 8.8 percent. The regulations also reduce employment. More pro-labor job security protection brings a small increase in wages and has little apparent effect on labor productivity, and more pro-labor dispute resolution laws reduce both productivity and wages.

---

markets into two sectors: the **formal sector** in which jobs conform to the developed country norm, and the **informal sector** in which jobs differ from that norm in at least one important way. They sought to understand why the informal sector is so much larger in developing countries and what the relationship is between the formal and informal sectors within developing countries. Many economists now see this dichotomous distinction between formal and informal as an unfortunate oversimplification of a multidimensional set of concerns. A more nuanced view of developing-country labor markets is emerging, in which distinctions within formal and informal sectors are at least as important as differences between the two (Perry et al., 2007). Before we can fully understand these debates regarding informality, we must define an important concept: labor market segmentation.

Segmented labor markets

In **competitive labor markets**, all workers with identical skills and preferences obtain jobs that leave them equally well off, and labor is allocated efficiently across uses. In **segmented labor markets**, by contrast, among workers with identical skills, some have "good jobs"—which offer packages of wages and working conditions that most workers would prefer—while others have "bad jobs" in which wages and working conditions are inferior. Though workers with bad jobs would gladly work for employers offering good jobs, even at lower wages than these employers pay to their incumbent employees, something prevents the good employers from lowering their wages and prevents the unlucky workers from moving into the better jobs. More specifically:

> Three sets of forces might prevent some employers (but not others) from lowering wages and taking on new workers, even when workers with the required skills are willing to work for less.

First, the government might set a legal minimum wage above the competitive equilibrium wage, and it might enforce this only for large, highly visible employers. Second, labor unions might achieve bargains with some employers that raise members' wages but succeed only in certain types of industries and firms.

Third, and more subtly, some firms might find it in their profit-maximizing interest to pay higher wages than many of their labor market competitors. For example, for some employers the costs of searching for and training new workers are large. This may be especially true for large employers with more capital-intensive production and more complex organizations, for whom downtime during job searches is more costly and for whom training is more important. Such employers would like to discourage workers from quitting when short-run commuting difficulties or family health problems render it tempting to drop out of the labor force temporarily or switch jobs. By paying higher wages than many other employers would pay for the same workers, these employers cause workers to weigh the short-run benefits of quitting against the long-run costs of losing premium wages, thereby providing workers with stronger incentives not to quit (Stiglitz, 1974a). The benefits of reduced search and training costs might outweigh the cost of paying higher wages. The higher wages that such employers offer are called **efficiency wages**, because they help these employers obtain a given quantity of labor at the lowest total cost. For an alternative rationale for paying efficiency wages, involving workers' incentives toward hard work, see Bulow and Summers (1986) and problem 4.

Figure 9.5 illustrates the effects of labor market segmentation within the simple framework of section 9.3A. If the two producers were perfectly competitive, the unique competitive equilibrium wage (w^c) would be found in panel c at the intersection of the total market labor supply schedule (S) and the total market demand schedule (D^c), which is just the horizontal sum of the two producers' $VMPL$ schedules. Under competition, Producers 1 and 2 employ L_1^c and L_2^c in labor.

We now let Producer 1 represent the high-wage sector in a segmented labor market and Producer 2 represent the low-wage sector. We suppose that minimum wage legislation, union power, or efficiency wage considerations prevent Producer 1 from reducing its wage below w^h. At this higher wage Producer 1 maximizes profits by hiring L_1^s units of labor. We determine the market wage, which is now relevant only to Producer 2's workers, by examining the effect of labor market segmentation on total labor demand in panel c. At any market wage below w^h the total market demand schedule (D^s) is now just equal to Producer 2's demand schedule plus the quantity L_1^s at

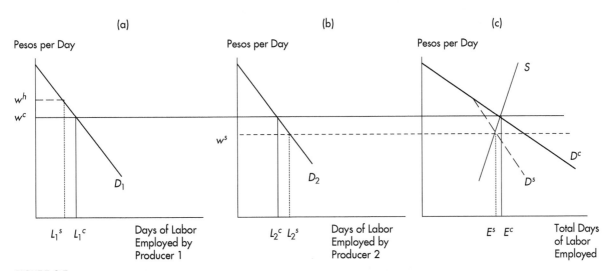

FIGURE 9.5
Labor Market Equilibrium when Markets Are Segmented

which Producer 1's employment is fixed. D^s lies to the left of D^c at wages below w^h, and thus the segmented labor market equilibrium wage w^s lies below w^c. The higher is w^h relative to w^c, the smaller is the high-wage sector, the larger is the low-wage sector, and the lower is w^s.

The graphical analysis points to three groups of workers hurt by segmentation. First, some workers who would have been employed by Producer 1 if labor markets were perfectly competitive work instead for Producer 2 at lower wages under segmentation. Second, workers who would have worked for Producer 2 even if markets were competitive receive lower wages under segmentation because workers forced out of the high-wage sector crowd into the low-wage sector, reducing their wages. Third, some workers leave the labor force because they are not lucky enough to obtain high-wage jobs and now find the wage in the other sector too low to outweigh the costs of working. The graphs also show that segmentation renders labor use inefficient, because it drives a gap between the *VMPL*s in the two sectors.

Informality: two views

For many years, development analysts tended to take one of two very different perspectives on informality. One view, predominant in the 1970s, held that the entire informal sector in developing countries should be understood as the low-wage sector in segmented labor markets. In this view, developing-country labor markets worked very poorly, being profoundly segmented, inefficient, and inequitable. Urban labor market segmentation was also thought to induce overly rapid migration into urban areas, as migrants entered urban labor markets on the chance that they could win a high-wage job, even while many of them ended up worse off in the informal sector (Harris and Todaro, 1970; Fields, 1975). The high rate of informality thus demanded policy attention, though how exactly policy might improve matters was a subject of debate.

According to the other view, predominant in the 1980s, developing countries' labor markets were perfectly competitive and not segmented at all. Employment arrangements differed between formal and informal sectors, but workers were perfectly mobile between sectors and workers with identical skills were equally well off in both sectors. In this view, labor markets could be counted upon to fulfill their developmental roles, and demanded little policy attention.[5]

Early empirical work

With the debate about developing-country labor markets formulated this way, empirical researchers felt called to divide labor markets into just two sectors, formal and informal, and to search for evidence of whether labor markets were segmented or competitive along this divide. They defined the dividing lines between formal and informal sectors in diverse ways and sometimes engaged in unproductive debates about which definitions were the best (as reviewed, for example, by Peattie, 1987). They then sought to assess whether wages were indeed higher in the formal sector, after controlling for workers' schooling, experience, and other productive characteristics. The results were mixed, depending to some extent on how researchers defined the informal and formal sectors. Wages tend to be higher (sometimes *much* higher) for larger employers relative to smaller employers (Velenchik, 1997; Schaffner, 1998) and for workers in jobs covered by labor regulations relative to workers in uncovered jobs. The results of comparing average hourly earnings between workers in wage employment and self-employment are more mixed (Perry et al., 2007).

---

[5]Even in this view it remains possible that high rates of informality are driven by distortions outside of labor markets that might demand attention. For example, complex and costly business regulation and taxation that is effectively enforced only for large and visible firms might give producers reason to remain small and avoid taxation, even while they hire workers from fully competitive labor markets.

The early approach to testing for segmentation suffered from a large inherent weakness. Even when data show large and robustly estimated wage differences between employers of different types, this need not constitute evidence of labor market segmentation. Large employers might pay higher wages than small employers (for workers with similar schooling and experience) for three reasons that are consistent with competition rather than segmentation. First, the higher wages might compensate for inferior working conditions (such as greater regimentation and monotony). Second, measured wages might appear higher for workers in larger establishments because wage data pertain to cash wage payments and larger employers might pay entirely in cash while smaller enterprises pay workers partly in the form of food, lodging, or training. Third, larger employers might employ workers with higher average skills along some dimensions other than schooling and experience. Researchers have tried to rule out these explanations for wage differences in various ways, but it is impossible to rule them out entirely using cross-section data alone.

More recent empirical work

More recent empirical work embodies two advances over earlier work. First, researchers have abandoned the practice of dividing the labor market into only two sectors and have begun to organize their research in less restrictive ways. For example, in a recent World Bank study, Perry et al. (2007) organize their research around a three-way division among self-employment, formal wage employment, and informal wage employment. Formal wage employment is employment under legally registered contracts. Informal wage employment is unregistered wage employment and takes place mostly in very small wage-employing establishments. Earlier work might have grouped self-employment and informal wage employment together, calling it the informal sector. Second, this newer empirical work moves beyond cross-section wage comparisons, adding studies of sector participation over the life cycle, panel data on the rates at which workers transition into and out of various sectors, and subjective questions about well-being and job satisfaction.

From the new empirical work a picture is emerging of profound differences between informal wage employment and self-employment. The informal wage sector often seems to relate to the formal wage sector in the ways suggested by models of labor market segmentation, whereas much self-employment does not. Informal wage jobs pay less than formal wage jobs, and many informal wage workers report wishing they had formal jobs. Transition rates out of informal wage jobs are quite high, while transition rates out of formal wage jobs are lower, consistent with the hypothesis that the payment of premiums to workers in better jobs renders them more reluctant to quit. Informal wage jobs are especially prevalent among young workers, suggesting that informal wage employment is an entry point (but not end goal) for young workers.

The self-employed, on the other hand, often report preferring self-employment over wage employment, and self-reported levels of well-being are similar for the self-employed and formal wage employees (after controlling for worker skills). More important, workers appear to move *into* self-employment as they age. Many self-employment activities appear difficult to enter. The evidence is consistent with the existence of financial constraints that require workers to save up, gradually accumulating the necessary capital (e.g., equipment, inventory, savings to provide a cushion during a start-up phase) before they can enter self-employment. See Perry et al. (2007) for a thorough look at the empirical patterns for several Latin American countries.

Government, informality, and segmentation

If labor markets are segmented as a result of imperfectly enforced minimum wage legislation, then governments might be able to reduce inefficiency and inequity by reducing the legislated minimum wage or expanding enforcement of the minimum wage more broadly throughout the economy. (Either reform would bring costs as well as these benefits. Additional analysis would be required before attempting to decide whether the benefits outweigh the costs.) Researchers studying diverse countries have, however, concluded that government regulations are unlikely to be the primary explanation for the existence of apparent high-wage sectors (Velenchik, 1997; Schaffner, 1998; Perry et al. 2007). If labor markets are segmented for reasons other than government regulation, it is unclear what actions the government might take to reduce or mitigate the consequences of the segmentation. Bulow and Summers (1986) argue that subsidizing the expansion of high-wage sectors might raise efficiency and improve earnings for many workers but that identifying the high-wage sectors and providing them with appropriate subsidies may be very difficult to do well. If labor markets are largely competitive, then policymakers might have no reason to intervene in labor markets, despite high rates of informality. Whether and why labor markets are segmented, and what the implications of segmentation might be for policy, remain matters of ongoing debate.

9.4 Skill Acquisition in Developing Country Labor Markets

Workers acquire skills through education and job training. **Education** refers to the acquisition of skills through primary and secondary schools, colleges, and universities, often by children and young adults before entering the labor market. **Job training** refers to the acquisition of skills after entering the labor market, usually through activities closely tied to specific lines of work or specific employers. Job training includes formal training, acquired through programs offered on employers' premises or off-site at training institutes, as well as informal training acquired on the job as mentors help newer workers learn the ropes or as new hires learn by doing.

Education and training are costly activities. They require workers to redirect time and energy from other valuable pursuits, and they are produced using the time of skilled teachers and trainers, as well as facilities, equipment, and materials. This means that a person acquires a new skill only if some interested party is willing and able to *invest* in making that happen, bearing the costs today in the hope of reaping future rewards. In what follows we examine the roles that labor markets might play in encouraging education and job training investments, the obstacles that prevent private actors from undertaking such investments, especially in developing countries, and the ways policymakers might intervene, hoping to improve education, training, and development outcomes.

9.4A A benchmark model of skills in labor markets

Consider first a simple benchmark model of how labor markets might encourage skill investments and help spread the benefits of such investments broadly throughout society. The model focuses on the interaction between the markets for two types of labor: low-skill and high-skill labor. High-skill workers are capable of performing some tasks that low-skill workers cannot perform; thus we treat low-skill and high-skill labor as distinct inputs into production. We assume initially that employers maximize profits and are competitive, and that workers are perfectly mobile across employers. At any moment, the numbers of low- and high-skill workers are fixed, but low-skill workers may invest in becoming high-skill workers through education or training.

We depict the simple model in Figure 9.6. In both panels the horizontal axes measure labor days and the vertical axes measure wages. The diagrams differ in two important respects. First, because high-skill workers are more productive than low-skill workers, the labor demand schedule is farther above the horizontal axis in panel b than in panel a, indicating that employers would be willing to pay more for any quantity of high-skill labor than for the same quantity of low-skill labor. Second, because high-skill workers are scarce relative to low-skill workers in developing countries, the labor supply schedule is closer to the vertical axis in panel b than in

(a)

Low-Skill Wage

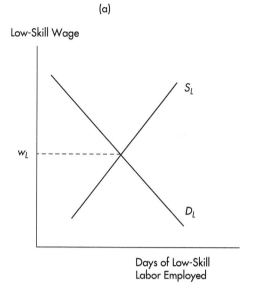

(b)

High-Skill Wage

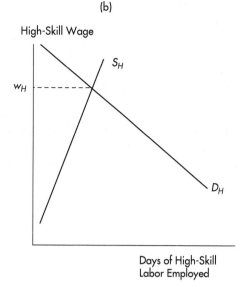

FIGURE 9.6
Equilibrium in Markets for Low- and High-Skill Labor

panel a, indicating that the quantity of high-skill labor supplied at any wage is smaller than the quantity of low-skill labor that would be supplied at that same wage.

In these well-functioning labor markets, the wage for high-skill workers (w_H) is higher than the wage for low-skill workers (w_L), both because high-skill workers are more productive and because they are more scarce. The markets thus offer to reward workers who acquire skills with wage premiums for the rest of their working lives (or at least until the skills become obsolete). In fact:

> Under the assumptions of the benchmark model, labor markets offer workers rewards for acquiring skills that are equal to the full value of the skills' impact on (marginal) labor productivity.

Competitive employers set the *VMPL* for each type of labor equal to its wage; thus the high-skill wage w_H exceeds the low-skill wage w_L by just as much as the *VMPL* of high-skill labor exceeds the *VMPL* of low-skill labor. The hope of such future wage premiums should provide workers with strong motivation to invest in acquiring skills that are valuable for growth and development.

Workers invest in skills when they bear the costs of acquiring skills. They might do this by paying explicit fees for programs offered by schools or formal job training institutes. In the case of training managed by employers, workers might instead bear the costs less obviously by accepting training period wages below what they could earn in jobs without training. (Job training is like a good working condition for which the wage reduction they accept is a compensating differential.) Under such circumstances, employers **provide** or **sponsor** the training—managing and seemingly paying for the curriculum, trainers, and materials—but they do not ultimately **bear the cost** of the training, because their training expenditures are offset by the discount they enjoy on the labor of low-wage trainees.

When workers acquire skills in this model, they transform themselves from low-skill to high-skill workers. This shifts the supply schedule for low-skill workers to the left (in Figure 9.6a) and shifts the supply schedule for high-skill workers to the right (in Figure 9.6b), tending to raise wages for low-skill workers and reduce wages for high-skill workers. If high-skill and low-skill labor are complements in production, then the productivity of low-skill labor also rises as the stock of complementary high-skill labor rises, and the productivity of high-skill labor falls as the stock of complementary low-skill labor falls. This would tend to raise the demand for low-skill labor and reduce the demand for high-skill labor, contributing to further increases in low-skill wages and reductions in high-skill wages.

This suggests, first, that:

> Workers' skill acquisition might contribute to economic growth both directly and indirectly.

We know from Chapter 3 that when workers acquire skills they add to the economy's stock of human capital, directly raising aggregate labor productivity. Here we see that their acquisition of skills also reduces the cost of high-skill labor. If the use of skilled labor is critical for the use of more capital-intensive methods of production or for the adoption of new technologies, then employers might find that investment in physical capital and technological innovation are unprofitable when high-skill labor is scarce and high-skill wages are high. When workers' investments in skills expand the supply and reduce the cost of high-skill labor, they might open up a bottleneck to growth and development, spurring additional growth through newly profitable physical capital investment and technical change.

The simple model also suggests that:

> Workers' acquisition of skills might contribute to reductions in poverty and inequality both directly and indirectly.

If low-skill workers are poor, then their acquisition of skills reduces poverty directly by increasing poor workers' productivity and earnings. Workers' transformation from low-skill to high-skill workers can also drive down high-skill wages and raise low-skill wages, as described above. In this way, labor markets help distribute some of the benefits of human capital investment to the low-skill workers who did not undertake skill investments themselves, further reducing poverty and inequality.

9.4B Skill types and the economics of skill investments

The skills imparted through education and job training are diverse, and the assumptions underlying the benchmark model make more sense for some skills than others. The nature of potential barriers to skill acquisition differs across skills of different types.

Skill types

The benchmark model is most applicable in the case of what economists call **general skills**, which raise workers' productivity in many jobs, are easily observed and, as a result, are valuable to many employers throughout the economy. They can include literacy, numeracy, and basic behavioral skills, which are useful in most jobs, as well as skills in computing and accounting, which are useful in a narrower range of jobs but nonetheless useful in many sectors and firms. They include most skills imparted through primary and secondary education and some imparted through job training. Because general skills are valuable to many employers, they inspire the competition among employers that bids wages for trained workers up to the level of their post-training productivity (as in the benchmark model). **Industry-specific skills**, an interesting subset of general skills, are valuable to multiple employers, but only to employers within a well-defined industry.

Labor markets are likely to treat **employer-specific skills** very differently from general skills. According to narrow definitions, a skill is employer-specific if it is valuable *only* to the single employer that sponsors the related training. Training that helps a worker gain competence in an employer's idiosyncratic manufacturing process might impart skills that are employer-specific in this extreme sense. According to broader definitions, skills are employer-specific, even if they have some value to outside employers, as long as they are significantly *more* valuable to the current employer (who provides the training) than to the outside employers. For example, when workers learn to do electrical or carpentry tasks associated with a particular production process, they might acquire some aptitude for electrical and carpentry work that is valuable in other jobs but that raises their productivity more in the current job than elsewhere.[6] We do not expect competition for such skills to raise trained workers' wages as much as in the case of general skills.

Barriers to investment in general skills

If employers compete for workers with general skills as suggested by the benchmark model, then their competition drives wages for generally trained workers up to the level of their post-training productivity. This implies that:

> Workers reap the full productivity benefit of general training in the form of increased wages.

In principle, therefore, labor markets provide workers with strong motivation to invest in general skills.

Unfortunately:

> Workers might fail to undertake investment in general skills training, despite high labor market rewards, for many reasons.

We discuss many of these reasons in Chapters 10 and 19. Here we mention just two. First, workers and their families might lack accurate information about the benefits of education. Second, they might lack adequate financing for the investment. That is, they might lack savings, be unable to borrow, and have no way to cover the training costs of acquiring skills without reducing their current consumption to unacceptably low levels.

If such barriers prevent workers and their families from paying for general skill acquisition, will employers step in to cover the costs? Unfortunately, if the skills are truly general, the answer is no, because competition among employers causes workers' wages to rise by just as much as general training raises their productivity. (If employers did not raise wages for generally trained workers this much, other employers would poach the workers away.) This means that an investment in a worker's general training raises a firm's costs by just as much as it raises firm revenues, generating no increase in profits. Unable to reap future increases in profits:

> Employers have no incentive to bear the costs of general skills training.

Barriers to households' investments in education and in general skills job training, therefore, represent significant obstacles to development in the absence of government or NGO intervention.

Barriers to investment in employer-specific skills

While we expect labor markets to reward workers with higher wages equal to the full productivity benefits of general training investments, and to offer employers no rewards for general training investments, we expect that:

> Workers and employers share the returns for investments in employer-specific skills.

---

[6]Acemoglu and Pischke (1998) and others argue that the theory of employer-specific skills applies even to many skills that appear quite general at first glance. The theory applies whenever bidding by outside employers bids wages up only to a level that is less than the value of the worker's productivity in work for the current employer. This is true if workers face costs of changing jobs, and if, for example, the particular combination of general skills that a worker acquires for the current employer is less valuable to outside employers, who require different combinations of general skills.

That is, we expect labor markets to raise the wages of workers with employer-specific skills to a level above what they would earn as untrained workers but below the level of their post-training productivity. We don't expect their wages to rise by as much as their post-training productivity (in work for the employers who trained them) because outside employers are not motivated to bid their wages up that high. We expect their wages to rise somewhat relative to untrained workers' wages, however, for one of two reasons. First, their new skills might have some value to outside employers, who bid their wages up. Second, even if their skills are not valuable to outside employers, their current employers might recognize that workers quit for many reasons (even when other employers are not attempting to poach them away) and might attempt to reduce trained workers' quit rates by paying them more than they could earn elsewhere.

With workers and employers each expecting to enjoy only a fraction of the productivity benefit from employer-specific training, both groups face only weak incentives toward unilateral investments in such training. They might nonetheless face strong incentives toward *joint* investments in employer-specific training if they are able to cooperate in sharing both the costs and the benefits. To share the cost, workers would have to accept training period wages that are below the wage for low-skill labor (implicitly transferring some of the training cost burden from their employers to themselves), but not so low that they bear the entire cost of training.

Unfortunately, many of the same obstacles that prevent workers in developing countries from bearing the costs of general training would also prevent them from bearing their share of employer-specific training costs. Achieving the necessary trust and cooperation between workers and employers may also be difficult, and financial constraints might further inhibit employers from contributing to such investments. Thus:

> Employers might perceive some incentive to invest in employer-specific training, especially if workers are capable of sharing the cost of training. Even so, we have reason to worry that they will underinvest in employer-specific skills training.

Barriers to investment in industry-specific skills

When employers within an industry compete with one another for workers with industry-specific skills, we expect competition to raise wages to the level of such workers' post-training productivity (as is the case with other general skills). Under these circumstances, individual employers have no motivation to invest in industry-specific skills. Cooperation among employers within an industry might, however, improve their motivation for investment in training. Acting together, as if they were a single employer, they might perceive the potential to profit from industry-specific training in much the same way that an individual employer might profit from employer-specific training. As is true with employer-specific training, however, we have reason to worry that employers will fail to undertake some valuable industry-specific training in the absence of intervention.

9.4C Education, job training, and policy
Education and policy

Most skills imparted through primary and secondary education are general skills. Empirical studies from around the world indicate, as expected, that labor markets offer workers rewards for acquiring such skills (see Box 9.2), and the rewards are often large.

Despite the high rewards to education in developing countries, and even though many governments subsidize education heavily, rates of investment in education remain low in many developing countries (see Chapters 3 and 19 for descriptive statistics). This suggests that

☰ Box 9.2 Schooling and Wages: Empirical Evidence

Empirical labor economists have long studied the effect of workers' schooling on their wages. Following the lead of Jacob Mincer (1974), they assume that worker i's wage (W_i) is related to his years of schooling (S_i), as well as his years of experience (E_i), according to an equation of the form:

$$\ln(W_i) = a + b S_i + c E_i + d(E_i)^2 + u_i$$

where $\ln(.)$ is the natural logarithm function, a, b, c, and d are unknown parameters, and u_i measures the effect on the wages of worker characteristics and circumstances (other than schooling and experience) that are randomly distributed across workers. (Often additional worker characteristics are included in the regressions as well.) Researchers then use regression analysis of household survey data to estimate the values of a, b, c, and d, paying special attention to the estimated value of b, which, when multiplied by 100, indicates the approximate percentage by which the wage increases for each one-year increase in years of schooling, while holding other characteristics constant. (See problem 5 for a derivation that justifies this interpretation.)

George Psacharopoulos and Harry Patrinos (2004) collected hundreds of studies of this type performed over many years using survey data from around the world. They report the following average estimates of b from studies pertaining to different regions of the world:

OECD	0.075
Asia	0.099
Latin America	0.120
Sub-Saharan Africa	0.117

This suggests that within the OECD an additional year of schooling tends to increase wages by about 7.5 percent, whereas in poorer regions of the world, where workers with more schooling are relatively scarce, an additional year of school tends to increase wages by 10 to 12 percent. Keeping in mind that a person spends just one year to acquire another year of schooling, but then reaps a 10 percent increase in wages for the rest of his working life, these numbers indicate that investments in education produce high returns.

Economists recognize one potentially important problem with all these estimates. If people with higher innate ability find schooling easier and more rewarding, and thus tend to obtain more schooling, then in a typical cross-section dataset, workers with more schooling are likely to have higher average ability. Most data sets contain no measure of ability, thus ability is omitted from the wage regressions, possibly introducing omitted variables bias into the estimation of the schooling impact on wages. The crux of the problem is that when we observe that workers who have obtained more years of schooling earn higher wages on average, we do not know the extent to which the higher wages reflect only the causal effect of their higher schooling (the effect we wish to estimate) rather than the effect of their higher average ability (an effect often referred to as *ability bias*). Fortunately, researchers have taken diverse approaches to eliminating ability bias and in most cases have found little evidence of bias in the standard estimation techniques. For an interesting example, see Duflo (2001).

---

barriers to household investment in education are serious, and that governments and NGOs might be able to improve development outcomes by devising ways to circumvent those barriers.

Many governments and other development actors have indeed placed education policies at the center of their development strategies. For decades they encouraged investments in primary education mainly by setting up government or NGO schools and offering their services at highly subsidized rates. Such policies succeeded in drawing many children into school but have failed to draw all children into school and often fail to provide school attenders with high-quality education.

The theory of general skill investments laid out above suggests a broader array of policies that development actors might use to expand primary education, including the distribution of education loans or scholarships for use in public or private schools, and efforts to inform parents about the benefits of education, among others. In Chapter 19, we dig deeply into the challenges that policymakers face when trying to draw more children into school and to ensure that schools provide high-quality education. We also examine the diverse reforms undertaken in recent years in attempts to improve the performance of education systems.

Job training investments and policy

Job training can impart skills that are general, industry-specific, or employer-specific. Good studies of job training, and of the labor market rewards for such training, are harder to find than studies of primary and secondary education impacts. The few studies available indicate that workers with training usually earn more than workers without training, but the studies often fail to differentiate between training of different types and intensities, and it is difficult to know whether the higher wages of trained workers represent rewards for training rather than rewards that these workers would have earned for their higher innate abilities, even if they had not received training.

We might expect training to be especially valuable in developing countries, where many workers reach the labor market without much education and where workers must adapt to so many changes. High reported rates of job training suggest that it is indeed quite valuable in developing countries. Drawing on the World Bank's World Business Environment Surveys for 28 countries, Batra and Stone (2004) find that 55 to 75 percent of firms train some workers. Employing the World Bank's Enterprise Surveys for 66 developing countries, Almeida and Aterido (2008) find that 45 percent of firms report having offered a formal training program to their employees. Schaffner (2006) finds that the incidence of job training among private sector male wage employees is higher in Colombia than in the United States, even after controlling for sector of employment and firm size. Batra and Stone (2004) also report that firms that train their workers are significantly more likely also to adopt innovations than firms that do not train.

The theory examined above gives us reason to worry that the private sector nonetheless invests too little in job training. Employers often complain that high turnover rates raise the costs of training in developing countries (McDermott, 1994; Perry et al., 1997), and producers claim that skills shortages prevent them from expanding production (Johanson and Adams, 2004).

Policymakers have historically devoted much less attention to job training than to education, though their interest seems to have grown in recent years. They might give lower priority to training than to education because the evidence regarding training's impact is less definitive or because they are more uncertain about how to design successful training policies. Looking only at the direct effects of training, they might also perceive investments in primary education as more valuable for reducing poverty and inequality than job training investments, because often the workers who obtain job training are nonpoor workers with secondary or even higher education. Growing recognition that job training might raise growth rates and reduce poverty indirectly, by opening up skill bottlenecks and encouraging investments that expand employment (even for low-skill workers), might help explain the recent rise in policy efforts to encourage job training.

Government efforts to encourage job training have often taken the form of setting up job-training institutes and offering their services at subsidized rates. Unfortunately, government-run programs have tended to provide skills that were not highly valued by the labor market, perhaps because they were insufficiently tailored to employers' immediate and specific needs (Johanson and Adams, 2004).

The theory reviewed above suggests that governments may be able to expand private sector training activities in many ways. They might offer workers loans or grants to use in purchasing job training from private providers. They might offer employers loans, grants, or tax breaks to provide job training to their workers. They might create partnerships with industry-specific employer groups that encourage cooperative training investments. Recent experiments also include efforts to partner with employers in creating apprenticeship programs. A fairly common practice is to tax employers from 0.5 to 3.0 percent of their payroll as a training levy and then allow employers to claim rebates up to the level of their tax payment for approved forms of training that they provide their own workers. For example, Malaysia's Human Resource Development Fund requires firms with more than 50 workers to contribute one percent of payroll to the fund, which is used to finance public training programs, but firms receive rebates of this tax for qualifying training expenditures that they make on their own. Evidence on the impacts of these schemes is mixed, but Tan (2001) concludes that Malaysia's rebate scheme significantly increased training and productivity.

Many questions about job training and related policies remain unanswered. Ongoing research may reveal new and better approaches for expanding job training investments in developing countries.

REFERENCES

Acemoglu, Daron, and Jörn-Steffen Pischke. "Why Do Firms Train? Theory and Evidence." *The Quarterly Journal of Economics* 113(1): 79–119, 1998. doi:10.1162/003355398555531

Ahsan, Ahmad, and Carmen Pagés. "Are All Labor Regulations Equal? Evidence from Indian Manufacturing." *Journal of Comparative Economics* 37(1): 62–75, 2009. doi:10.1016/j.jce.2008.09.001

Almeida, Rita K., and Reyes Aterido. "The Incentives to Invest in Job Training: Do Strict Labor Codes Influence This Decision?" Social Protection Discussion Paper No. 0832. Washington, D.C.: World Bank, 2008. http://siteresources.worldbank.org/SOCIALPROTECTION/Resources/SP-Discussion-papers/Labor-Market-DP/0832.pdf

Aryeetey, Ernest, and Andrew McKay. "Ghana: The Challenge of Translating Sustained Growth Into Poverty Reduction." In Tim Besley and Louise Cord (eds.). *Delivering on the Promise of Pro-Poor Growth: Insights and Lessons From Country Experiences*. Washington, D.C.: World Bank, 2007, pp. 147–168. doi:10.1596/978-0-8213-6515-1

Aw, Bee Yan, Xiaomin Chen, and Mark J. Roberts. "Firm-Level Evidence on Productivity Differentials and Turnover in Taiwanese Manufacturing." *Journal of Development Economics* 66(1): 51–86, 2001. doi:10.1016/S0304-3878(01)00155-9

Bardhan, Pranab K. "Wages and Unemployment in a Poor Agrarian Economy: A Theoretical and Empirical Analysis." *Journal of Political Economy* 87(3): 479–500, 1979. http://www.jstor.org/stable/1832019

Batra, Geeta, and Andrew H.W. Stone. "Investment Climate, Capabilities and Firm Performance: Evidence from the World Business Environment Survey." DFID-WB Collaboration on Knowledge and Skills in the New Economy working paper. Washington, D.C.: World Bank, 2004. http://siteresources.worldbank.org/EDUCATION/Resources/278200-1126210664195/1636971-1126210694253/Investment_Climate.pdf

Beegle, Kathleen, Joachim de Weerdt, and Stefan Dercon. "Migration and Economic Mobility in Tanzania: Evidence From a Tracking Survey." *The Review of Economics and Statistics* 93(3): 1010–1033, 2011. doi:10.1162/REST_a_00105

Besley, Timothy, and Robin Burgess. "Can Labor Regulation Hinder Economic Performance? Evidence from India." *The Quarterly Journal of Economics* 119(1): 91–134, 2004. doi:10.1162/003355304772839533

Bulow, Jeremy I., and Lawrence H. Summers. "A Theory of Dual Labor Markets with Application to Industrial Policy, Discrimination, and Keynesian Unemployment." *Journal of Labor Economics* 4(3, Part 1): 376–414, 1986. http://www.jstor.org/stable/2535059

Deshingkar, Priya, and Sven Grimm. *Internal Migration and Development: A Global Perspective*. IOM Migration Research Series No. 19. Geneva: International Organization for Migration (IOM), 2005. http://publications.iom.int/bookstore/index.php?main_page=product_info&products_id=178

Duflo, Esther. "Schooling and Labor Market Consequences of School Construction in Indonesia: Evidence from an Unusual Policy Experiment." *American Economic Review* 91(4): 795–813, 2001. doi:10.1257/aer.91.4.795

Fajnzylber, Pablo, and William Maloney. "How Comparable Are Labor Demand Elasticities Across Countries?" Policy Research Working Paper 2658. Latin America and the Caribbean Region. Washington, D.C.: World Bank, 2001. http://go.worldbank.org/41K2WDI8U0

Fields, Gary S. "Rural–Urban Migration, Urban Unemployment and Underemployment, and Job-Search Activity in LDCs." *Journal of Development Economics* 2(2): 165–187, 1975. doi:10.1016/0304-3878(75)90014-0

Foster, Andrew D., and Mark R. Rosenzweig. "A Test for Moral Hazard in the Labor Market: Contractual Arrangements, Effort, and Health." *The Review of Economics and Statistics* 76(2): 213–227, 1994. http://www.jstor.org/stable/2109876

Gebreeyesus, Mulu. "Firm Turnover and Productivity Differentials in Ethiopian Manufacturing." *Journal of Productivity Analysis* 29(2): 113–129, 2008. doi:10.1007/s11123-007-0076-0

Harris, John R., and Michael P. Todaro. "Migration, Unemployment and Development: A Two-Sector Analysis." *American Economic Review* 60(1): 126–142, 1970. http://www.jstor.org/stable/1807860

Hazell, Peter B. R., and C. Ramasamy. *The Green Revolution Reconsidered: The Impact of High-Yielding Rice Varieties in South India*. Baltimore: Johns Hopkins University Press, 1991. http://www.ifpri.org/sites/default/files/publications/hazell91.pdf

Heath, John R. "Peasants or Proletarians? Rural Labour in a Brazilian Plantation Economy." *Journal of Development Studies* 17(4): 268–281, 1981. doi:10.1080/00220388108421806

Johanson, Richard K., and Arvil V. Adams. *Skills Development in Sub-Saharan Africa*. Washington, D.C.: World Bank, 2004. http://go.worldbank.org/4GHBK9L0C0

Lall, Somik V., Christopher Timmins and Shouyue Yu. "Connecting Lagging and Leading Regions: The Role of Labor Mobility." Brookings-Wharton Papers on Urban Affairs: 151–74, 2009. doi:10.1353/urb.0.0024

Lucas, Robert E. "Internal Migration in Developing Countries." In Mark R. Rosenzweig and Oded Stark (eds.). *Handbook of Population and Family Economics Volume 1, Part B*. Amsterdam: Elsevier, 1997, pp. 721–798. doi:10.1016/S1574-003X(97)80005-0

Lucas, Robert E. "Internal Migration and Urbanization: Recent Contributions and New Evidence." IED Discussion Paper No. 91. Boston: Boston University, Institute for Economic Development, 1998. http://www.bu.edu/econ/files/2010/08/DP91.pdf

McDermott, Terry. "TQM: The Total Quality Maquiladora." *Business Mexico* 4(11): 42–45, 1994.

Mincer, Jacob. *Schooling, Experience, and Earnings*. Cambridge, Mass.: National Bureau of Economic Research, 1974.

Munshi, Kaivan, and Mark R. Rosenzweig. "Why is Mobility in India So Low? Social Insurance, Inequality, and Growth." NBER Working Paper No. 14850. Cambridge, Mass.: National Bureau of Economic Research, 2009. http://www.nber.org/papers/w14850

Otsuka, Keijiro, and Yujiro Hayami. "Theories of share tenancy: A critical survey." *Economic Development and Cultural Change* 37(1): 31–68, 1988. http://www.jstor.org/stable/1154179

Peattie, Lisa. "An Idea in Good Currency and How it Grew: The Informal Sector." *World Development* 15(7): 851–860, 1987. doi:10.1016/0305-750X(87)90038-6

Pencavel, John. "The Legal Framework for Collective Bargaining in Developing Economies." In Sebastian Edwards and Nora Lustig (eds.). *Labor Markets in Latin America: Combining Social Protection with Market Flexibility*. Washington, D.C.: Brookings Institution Press, 1997, pp. 27–61.

Perry, Guillermo E., William Maloney, Omar S. Arias, Pablo Fajnzylber, Andrew D. Mason, and Jaime Saavedra-Chanduvi. *Informality: Exit and Exclusion*. Washington, D.C.: World Bank, 2007. http://go.worldbank.org/SDJR6S3L20

Psacharopoulos, George, and Harry Anthony Patrinos. "Returns to Investment in Education: A Further Update." *Education Economics* 12 (2): 111–134, 2004. doi:10.1080/0964529042000239140

Rosenzweig, Mark R., and Oded Stark. "Consumption Smoothing, Migration, and Marriage: Evidence From Rural India." *Journal of Political Economy* 97(4): 905–926, 1989. http://www.jstor.org/stable/1832196

Schaffner, Julie. "Rural Labor Legislation and Permanent Agricultural Employment in Northeastern Brazil." *World Development* 21(5): 705–719, 1993. doi:10.1016/0305-750X(93)90028-8

Schaffner, Julie. "Attached Farm Labor, Limited Horizons and Servility." *Journal of Development Economics* 47(2): 241–70, 1995. doi:10.1016/0304-3878(95)00012-F

Schaffner, Julie. "Premiums to Employment in Larger Establishments: Evidence From Peru." *Journal of Development Economics* 55(1): 81–113, 1998. doi:10.1016/S0304-3878(98)00038-8

Schaffner, Julie. "*Employment*." In Margaret Grosh and Paul Glewwe (eds.). *Designing Household Survey Questionnaires for Developing Countries: Lessons From 15 Years of the Living Standards Measurement Study* (Volume 1 of 3). Washington, D.C.: World Bank, 2000, pp. 217–250. http://go.worldbank.org/3FI67NHLV0

Schaffner, Julie. "Job Training and Cross-Country Productivity Differences: New Hypotheses with Evidence from Colombia and the United States." Medford, Mass.: The Fletcher School, Tufts University, 2006.

Stiglitz, Joseph E. "Alternative Theories of Wage Determination and Unemployment in LDC's: The Labor Turnover Model." *The Quarterly Journal of Economics* 88(2): 194, 1974a. doi:10.2307/1883069

Stiglitz, Joseph E. "Incentives and Risk Sharing in Sharecropping." *The Review of Economic Studies* 41(2): 219–55, 1974b. doi:10.2307/2296714

Tan, Hong. "Malaysia's Human Resource Development Fund: An Evaluation of Its Effects on Training and Productivity." Washington, D.C.: World Bank, 2001.

Topalova, Petia. "Trade Liberalization, Poverty, and Inequality: Evidence From Indian Districts." In Ann Harrison (ed.). *Globalization and Poverty*. Chicago: University of Chicago Press, 2007, pp. 291–336.

Tybout, James R. "Manufacturing Firms in Developing Countries: How Well Do They Do, and Why?" *Journal of Economic Literature* 38(1): 11–44, 2000. doi:10.1257/jel.38.1.11

United States Department of State. *Trafficking in Persons Report: June 2009*. Washington, D.C.: U.S. Department of State, 2009. http://www.state.gov/g/tip/rls/tiprpt/2009/

Velenchik, Ann D. "Government Intervention, Efficiency Wages, and the Employer Size Wage Effect in Zimbabwe." *Journal of Development Economics* 53(2): 305–338, 1997. doi:10.1016/S0304-3878(97)00019-9

World Bank. *World Development Report 2009: Reshaping Economic Geography*. Washington, D.C.: World Bank, 2008. http://go.worldbank.org/O0F8YSCR41

QUESTIONS FOR REVIEW

1. What are compensating differentials and how do they arise in competitive labor markets? How might increasing competitive pressures during development give employers incentives to improve working conditions?

2. Why might we want to distinguish between working conditions about which workers do and do not have full information when analyzing the potential impacts of regulations to improve working conditions?

3. What do we mean by *employment contracts*? What are some of the key dimensions along which employment contracts differ?

4. What options do employers have for building higher-powered work incentives into the contracts they offer workers? Under what conditions might they be able to reduce labor costs by paying in kind? Why might they be interested in reducing the income fluctuations to which workers are exposed?

5. What is share tenancy? What puzzle did it initially present to economic researchers? What is one possible resolution to the puzzle?

6. What assumptions underlie the model depicted in Figure 9.2? Define all the elements of the graphs in Figure 9.2 and describe how to identify equilibrium wage and employment levels in this framework.

7. Define what it means for labor to be allocated efficiently across uses, and explain how labor mobility contributes to efficiency in the allocation of labor across uses.

8. How does labor mobility speed economic growth?

9. How do well-functioning labor markets help spread the benefits of growth broadly throughout the economy?

10. What roles do labor supply and demand elasticities play in determining the effects of investment or innovation on wages and employment?

11. Discuss the significance of migration in development.

12. What lessons does empirical research reveal about how households make migration decisions?

13. Discuss what is known or suspected about the impacts of migration.

14. What sorts of policies might be useful for improving the extent to which migration flows help move workers into their most productive uses?

15. Discuss the significance in development of workers' inter-firm mobility within urban areas.

16. How might governments or NGOs help or hinder interfirm mobility?

17. Define labor market segmentation and discuss its potential significance in development. What forces might cause labor market segmentation (by preventing some employers from reducing their wages to competitive market levels)?

18. How have labor market segmentation concerns entered into empirical research on formal and informal sectors in developing countries?

19. Discuss the potential significance of skill acquisition in development.

20. What are the main barriers to investment in education by workers or their families?

21. What are the main barriers to investment in job training by workers? By employers? How do the answers differ across training that provides general skills and training that provides employer-specific skills? How might governments or NGOs attempt to overcome those barriers?

QUESTIONS FOR DISCUSSION

1. Suppose a household survey asks all workers to report the pay they received last week. List as many reasons as possible for why reports of pay last week might vary across workers. Which of these reasons for reported wage differences imply that higher-wage workers are better off than lower-wage workers, and which are consistent with higher- and lower-wage workers being equally well off?

2. Suppose two firms produce clothing of identical value according to the same production function. Firm 1 provides workers with good working conditions and pays them $W per day, while Firm 2 provides workers with bad working conditions. Workers find employment in the two firms equally attractive only when Firm 2 pays a compensating differential of $D per worker per day. Firm 1's provision of nicer working conditions raises its costs by $C per worker per day relative to Firm 2's costs. Both firms maximize profits by setting the *VMPL* in clothing production equal to the marginal cost of labor (which includes the wage and any costs of providing good working conditions).
   a. If labor markets are perfectly competitive, what wage must Firm 2 pay?
   b. Assuming that the total supply of labor to the two firms is fixed, under what conditions would this labor be allocated across the two firms in the way that maximizes the value of production by the two firms?
   c. Now suppose that $D>C$. Compared to the allocation of labor across firms that maximizes the value of clothing production, is too much or too little labor allocated to Firm 1?
   d. If we think of the firms as producers of both clothing and workplace amenities to be enjoyed by their workers, might we nonetheless consider this equilibrium efficient?

3. Suppose a developing-country government is considering new legislation that would mandate the provision of sunscreen and eye-shielding hats to agricultural workers who work out of doors. You are asked to write a memo on whether or not this legislation is likely to generate more benefits than costs. What are some of the questions you would wish to research before offering your opinion?

4. Suppose the government sets up a workfare program that stands ready to hire anyone who comes forward to participate in the program. (The compensation rate is low because the aim is to attract participation only from the neediest households.) Although the main objective of the program is to provide jobs and income to needy households, program designers also hope to beautify roads and other public spaces by employing program participants in collecting trash. Initially the program offers to pay workers a fixed number of pesos for an 8-hour work day. What concerns might you have regarding the use of the fee-for-time contract structure? What alternative contract forms might you put forward for consideration?

5. Draw figures like those in the three panels of Figure 9.2, labeling them appropriately so that the first panel represents agricultural demand for low-skill labor, the second represents manufacturing demand for low-skill labor, and the third describes total national demand.
   a. Show what happens in this set of diagrams when investment in manufacturing equipment increases the demand for low-skill labor in that sector. Discuss how the analysis reflects the assumption of costless mobility of workers between agriculture and manufacturing.
   b. How do the impacts of the manufacturing investment change if the supply of low-skill labor becomes more inelastic? How does the change in elasticity affect the distribution of the benefits of growth in labor demand across those initially employed and those who are brought into the labor market as a result of growth?

c. How do the impacts of the manufacturing investment change if the manufacturing demand for labor becomes more inelastic?

d. How do the impacts of the manufacturing investment change if the agricultural demand for labor becomes more inelastic?

6. Consider a remote rural community where workers face very high costs of migrating out to obtain work elsewhere, and suppose that a single large landowner owns all the land and is the only source of employment. If the costs of commuting and migration are high enough, this employer might have *monopsony power*, lacking any effective competition for local workers. Such an employer can push wages down below the level that would obtain if the local labor market were competitive. What might prevent the employer from pushing wages down to zero? How might the employer's use of monopsony power in the local labor market (which allows him to push wages below the competitive level), combined with his power in local politics, affect the community's potential to grow through road construction or the setup of new local manufacturing enterprises?

7. Read Pencavel (1997). What potential benefits and potential costs of labor union activities does the author point out? What does the author argue to be the government' stance toward labor unions that best promotes development? Do you agree or disagree?

PROBLEMS

1. Re-read the discussion of Green Revolution impacts on rural labor markets in Chapter 6. That section presents a puzzle. The Green Revolution seemed to increase rural wages but *reduce* agricultural employment. This is difficult to explain as a result of a shift only in the agricultural demand for labor. The section argues that to understand these changes we must incorporate the rural nonfarm sector into our analysis. Draw figures like those in the three panels of Figure 9.2, labeling them appropriately so that the first panel represents agricultural demand for labor in a particular rural community, the second represents nonagricultural demand for labor in the same community, and the third represents the total demand for and supply of labor in the community. Draw in new agricultural and nonagricultural labor demand schedules (representing one shift of each schedule) that might follow from the adoption of Green Revolution technologies and that lead to a new equilibrium in which local wages have *risen* and agricultural employment has *fallen*. Please assume that the Green Revolution technologies are labor using. In what direction must the non-farm labor demand shift for the net result of the two demand schedule shifts to yield the indicated outcomes (i.e., higher wages and lower agricultural employment)? What are the impacts of such changes on nonagricultural employment and total employment? What impact must the adoption of Green Revolution technologies have on markets for goods produced by the nonagricultural sector to generate agricultural and nonagricultural demand shifts like this?

2. Consider four types of intervention that might be used to reduce the costs imposed on workers by unemployment and the threat of unemployment: (a) the creation of a job search assistance program that gathers information about vacancies and job seekers and helps workers and employers find good matches, (b) an unemployment insurance program that provides monetary assistance for several months to workers who are fired (funded out of general government revenue), (c) a regulation requiring employers who dismiss workers to pay the workers lump-sum severance payments, and (d) a regulation requiring employers to gain government approval for dismissing workers. Discuss the likely or possible impacts of each intervention on each of the following outcomes: (i) the rate at which employed workers are fired, (ii) the rate at which employed workers quit, (iii) the extent to which firing causes workers and their families to make drastic cuts in consumption, (iv) the length of time in unemployment among those who have lost jobs, (v) the length of time that first-time job seekers remain unemployed, (vi) the typical quality of match between worker and employer, and (vii) overall labor productivity. Explain.

3. Draw figures like the three panels of Figure 9.2, labeling them appropriately so that the first panel represents labor demand by large firms, the second represents labor demand by small firms, and the third represents the total supply and demand for labor by large and small firms combined.

a. Depict an initial equilibrium in which the market for low-skill labor is perfectly competitive. Analyze the impact of a minimum wage law that sets a legal minimum above the competitive equilibrium level and enforces it perfectly for all employers, both large and small. (*Analyze* here means "depict the change in your graphs and discuss the impacts on total employment, employment in each sector, and the earnings of any relevant classes of workers.")

b. Again depict an initial perfectly competitive equilibrium. Analyze the impact of a minimum wage law that sets a legal minimum above the competitive equilibrium level but is enforced only for large employers.

c. Draw a new set of figures depicting an initial equilibrium in which labor markets are segmented, with large employers paying wages above the competitive market level for efficiency wage reasons. (You may assume that the efficiency wage does not change throughout this problem.) Discuss the implications of this labor market imperfection for as many labor market outcomes as can be analyzed in these graphs.

d. Continuing in the graphs you drew for 3.c, analyze the impacts of a minimum wage law that sets the legal minimum wage to a level that is higher than the wage associated with perfect competition but lower than the efficiency wage paid by large firms and that is enforced only for large firms. Would large firms appear to be in compliance with the law? What impact would the law have on labor market outcomes?

e. Draw a set of figures identical to those you drew for part c. Analyze the impacts of a minimum wage law that sets the legal minimum wage to a level that is higher than the efficiency wage paid by large employers and is enforced only for large employers.

4. In this problem, we consider an employer who knows that he can get workers to work harder, and produce more effective labor per hour of work, if he pays them higher wages. More specifically, letting w be the wage in dollars per hour and letting $e(w)$ indicate the number of effective units of labor produced per hour of labor, the employer believes that the $e(w)$ function looks like the one illustrated in the diagram below, having a positive but diminishing slope. We could describe any ray from the origin in this diagram by an equation of the form $e = sw$, where s is the slope of the ray. This tells us that at any point along a ray, the ratio of w to e, w/e, must be equal to the same number, $1/s$.

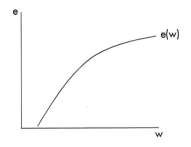

a. What are the units of the number w/e? Why might an employer wish to minimize this number?

b. To minimize w/e, while respecting the constraint that $e = e(w)$, the employer must find a point along the $e(w)$ schedule at which w/e reaches its lowest value and thus where $s = e/w$ reaches its highest value. Show how you might find this cost-minimizing level of w in the diagram. The wage associated with this point is this employer's efficiency wage.

5. Suppose $\ln(w) = a + bS + e$ where $\ln(w)$ is the natural logarithm function, w is a worker's wage in dollars per hour, S is the years of schooling the worker has completed, and e is a random error capturing the idea that even among workers with the same years of schooling, workers vary in ability and receive diverse wages.

a. Show that $b = [\partial w / \partial S] / w$, where $\partial w / \partial S$ is the partial derivative of w with respect to S.

b. Technically, the derivative $\partial w / \partial S$ tells us the rate of change in w per unit of S for infinitesimally small changes in S, but we might think of the value of $\partial w / \partial S$ as approximating the amount by which w would increase for every one-year increase in S. Making use of this approximation, what does the expression you derived in part a tell you about how to interpret values of b? (You may think of the w in the denominator as representing the pre-change level of w.) How should we interpret an estimate of b equal to 0.15?

c. Given that you spend one year in school to increase S by one, but might reap the resulting increase in w for many years in the labor market, would you think of an estimate of b equal to 0.15 as indicating a large or small effect of S on w? Explain.

chapter

10

Investment and Financial Markets

People make development possible when they choose to invest. The forces that determine who invests, how much they invest, and what kinds of investment they undertake determine the rate of economic growth and the character of development. Some of those forces operate through financial markets. Thus the study of investment decisions and financial markets is crucial in development economics.

After briefly describing the significance of investment decisions and financial markets in development, this chapter sets out a framework for studying private investment decisions and applies it in an exploratory study of the question "Why do African farmers use so much less fertilizer than farmers in other regions?" The chapter then examines the functions and malfunctions of markets for credit, savings-deposit services, and insurance in developing countries and considers the possible implications for development policy.

10.1 Investment, Financial Markets, and Development

Sustained and broad-based development is impossible without economic growth, and growth is impossible without investment. People **invest** when they undertake costly activities today with the aim of reaping returns in the future. Investment activities generate **returns**—streams of future improvements in income or well-being—by creating, upgrading, or maintaining assets or by moving assets into more productive uses. The assets involved are highly diverse, including many types of physical and human capital and technological knowledge (see Chapters 2 and 3).

Successful development requires not just a high total volume of investment, but also many kinds of investment undertaken by many kinds of investors. Economic growth is rapid when farmers and nonfarm entrepreneurs invest in equipment, structures, training, and new technologies and when workers invest in education and migration. Such investments are encouraged, and their growth impacts are enhanced, by collective investments in transport, communication, and power infrastructure (Chapter 3). Poverty reduction requires investments that raise the demand for low-skill labor, raise the skills of low-skill workers, expand the supply of consumption goods important to the poor, raise the profits of poor entrepreneurs, or connect remote communities to markets (Chapter 5). Reductions in nonincome poverty and vulnerability require investments in additional assets, such as clean drinking water and health care systems. To understand the full array of development outcomes, therefore, we must understand how people make decisions regarding many types of investment.

Investment decisions are more complicated than the decisions regarding consumption, time allocation, and production that we examined in Chapters 6 and 7, in two ways. First, they require **intertemporal comparisons**, or comparisons of costs and benefits that are spread out over multiple time periods. More specifically, they involve comparison of present costs to future benefits. Second, they involve **risk** or **uncertainty**. This means that the size of benefit that an investment will ultimately deliver depends on factors that are beyond the investor's control and are unknown at the time of the investment decision. Section 10.2 describes the models economists bring to the study of intertemporal and risky choices and then builds them into a more general model of private investment decisions. In later chapters, we will adapt this general model for more specific study of critical investments in infrastructure, education, agricultural technology, small business capital, and other assets and of the ways governments and NGOs might encourage such investments.

Because investments produce returns only after some delay and are risky, financial markets—markets for credit, savings-deposit services, and insurance—have important roles to play in facilitating investment, as we will see. Unfortunately, high transaction costs and deeper market failures appear to prevent financial markets in developing countries from fulfilling their developmental potential. Financial market weakness might impose *financial constraints* on some potential investors, which prevent them from undertaking valuable investments. Section 10.3 describes financial markets' developmental roles in more detail, examines reasons they might function poorly in developing countries, and discusses the possible implications of financial constraints for development policy.

10.2 Private Investment Decisions

10.2A A motivation

Farmers in sub-Saharan Africa use an average of 8 kilograms of fertilizer per hectare, while in most other regions of the world the average is more than 90 kilograms. Low fertilizer use contributes to African cereal grain yields that are one-third the size of yields in other regions (Morris et al., 2007).

Many analysts believe that increased fertilizer use is vital for poverty reduction, development, and prevention of environmental disaster in Africa. For Africa's many poor semi-subsistence farmers, increased productivity would mean larger harvests and shorter hungry seasons. Increased fertilizer use would slow the tremendous rate at which African soil quality is being depleted, as land scarcity rises, the practice of fallowing declines, and farmers increasingly harvest more nutrients than they return to the soil each year. Thus policymakers would benefit from insight into why so many African farmers use little or no fertilizer and how policy might make a difference.

Like other investment decisions, the decision to apply fertilizer involves intertemporal comparison and is risky. Farmers must devote money and time to applying fertilizer during planting and crop-care seasons, but they reap the benefits of increased crop yields only later, during harvest seasons, and the ultimate effects of fertilizer use on farm profits depend on weather conditions, market prices, and many other factors that farmers do not know when they make their fertilizer decisions. In what follows, we set out a general framework for studying private investment decisions in developing countries and then use it to guide an exploratory study of low fertilizer use by African farmers.

10.2B Investors and investment projects

A **potential investor** is any actor who might undertake investment, whether company president, self-employed carpenter, rice farmer, or community drinking water committee. We use the term **investment project** to signify the creation of a particular asset (or a particular costly shift in where or how an asset is used) by a particular investor. Examples include the construction of a crop storage shed by a poor farmer, the creation of a factory by a wealthy entrepreneur, and the migration of a rural family to a distant city in pursuit of higher earnings.

The primary benefits of investment are the **gross returns** the investment will generate over coming months or years. These are improvements in the investors' life circumstances, which flow from the creation or improved use of assets. For investments in capital equipment or the adoption of new technologies, they take the form of increases in farm or business profits. For investments in education, training, and migration, they include increases in wage earnings. Investments in wells for clean drinking water bring improved water quality and reductions in the time household members spend collecting water each day.

As an investor initiates a project, she incurs **up-front costs**, which include the money, time, and psychological costs of creating assets or putting them to new use. Some investments are

divisible, meaning that they can be undertaken at any size—even at sizes requiring only very small up-front costs—without altering the average profitability or desirability of the investment per peso of up-front cost. For example, small retail business owners may be able to purchase inventory in widely varying amounts, receiving similar per-peso returns regardless of whether they invest a little or a lot in inventory. Other investments seem to be **indivisible**, however, yielding no return unless the investor is capable of investing at least some minimum amount. For example, it may be impossible to invest profitably in setting up a tailoring business unless the investor is capable of buying at least an entire sewing machine. The minimum scale for profitable investment in a chemical manufacturing plant is much larger.

After the up-front costs have been paid and the project begins to produce returns, the investor may continue to incur **operation and maintenance costs**, which are the recurrent costs of any activities required to keep returns flowing from new or improved assets. In Chapter 18, we will take a closer look at operation and maintenance problems. In this chapter, we simply take the operation and maintenance requirements of a particular investment project as given. This allows us to define the **net return** an investment project will generate in each future month or year as the simple difference between the gross return and the operation and maintenance cost in that month or year.

As in standard consumer theory, the basic assumption underlying standard economic models of private investment decisions is that potential investors seek to maximize utility. In simple cases, they maximize utility by making the dichotomous choice of whether or not to undertake the investment, and they decide to undertake the investment if the benefits of doing so outweigh the costs. The decisions are complicated by the need to compare present costs to future returns and by the risky nature of the returns. In what follows, we first describe the analytical tools economists use to study choices involving intertemporal comparisons and risk and then set out a general model of private investment decisions.

10.2C Intertemporal comparisons and investment choices
Standard models of intertemporal choice

In standard economic models of intertemporal choice, people are assumed to evaluate the overall utility they would derive from any choice by first evaluating the **single-period utility** they would enjoy during each month or year affected by the choice, and then taking a weighted sum of the single-period utilities, with utilities enjoyed further in the future given smaller weights. More specifically, when considering choices involving the present (period 0) and T future time periods, a decision maker exercising neoclassical rationality maximizes a utility function of this form:

$$U(F_0, F_1, \ldots, F_T) = u(F_0) + \beta u(F_1) + \beta^2 u(F_2) + \beta^3 u(F_3) + \cdots + \beta^T y(F_T) \qquad (10.1)$$

where F_0 through F_T are quantities of consumption in periods 0 through T and $u(.)$ is a single-period utility function characterized by diminishing marginal utility. The parameter β is called the **discount factor** and takes a value between zero and one. The discount factor is included to capture human beings' inherent tendency to **discount** future consumption, or place less value on consuming a quantity F in the future than on consuming the same quantity in the present. Why do human beings discount the future? They may be impatient, or they might recognize that death or a major change in life circumstance could prevent them from enjoying future returns. They might also find it difficult to imagine their future circumstances or to identify with their future selves (Frederick et al., 2002).

Notice that while utility experienced one period into the future is multiplied by the fraction β to translate it into units comparable to current utility, the utility derived from consumption experienced two periods into the future is multiplied by the square of β (or β^2), and utility t

periods into the future is multiplied by β raised to the power t (or β^t). With β being a fraction between zero and 1, this implies that the decision maker discounts utility enjoyed further in the future at a higher rate. It implies, moreover, that when translating utility experienced in the future into equivalent units of utility in the present, she multiplies the future utility by *the same* discount factor once for each period it lies in the future. That is, she multiplies by the discount factor β once to utility experienced in period 1, twice to utility in period 2, and t times to utility experienced t periods into the future. She is said to employ **constant discounting** when assessing the value of future consumption and utility. (Later we examine the significance of this neoclassical assumption and consider an alternative to it.)

Investment decisions and financing concerns

Consider a potential investor deciding whether to undertake a project for which she must pay the (indivisible) up-front cost C in period 0 and from which she will reap the net return R in period 1. Applying the standard model of intertemporal choice, we can think of her as maximizing

$$U(F_0, F_1) = u(F_0) + \beta u(F_1) \tag{10.2}$$

Periods 2 and higher do not appear, because they are irrelevant to the decision. For simplicity we will call time period 0 "the present" and time period 1 "the future." The potential investor compares the utility she would enjoy if she undertakes the project to the utility she would enjoy if she does not, which we call her **status quo utility**.

   For the purposes of fixing her status quo utility, let's assume that she earns income Y in the present and again in the future, regardless of whether she invests, and that her consumption in each period is just equal to her income. Under these conditions, she achieves status quo utility

$$U^{SQ} = u(Y) + \beta u(Y) \tag{10.3}$$

The utility she would derive if she invests depends on how she chooses to **finance** the investment, or obtain the cash or other resources required to cover its up-front costs *before* the project produces returns. She may finance immediate investment in three ways. First, she may save out of current income to finance the up-front costs of investment. By definition, she **saves** when she chooses a level of consumption expenditure lower than her current income, freeing up some income for investment or other uses. Second, she may borrow money, inputs, or other resources to cover the up-front costs, promising to repay when the investment produces returns. Third, she may liquidate other assets to finance the investment. This means that she may sell off other assets and use the proceeds to cover the costs of the new investment. This option is available only to investors who own other assets that they accumulated through past saving or received as inheritance or gift.

   Investors taking a longer-term view may also choose to **save up**. This means that, instead of undertaking investments immediately, they save for several periods, until they have accumulated enough assets to finance the investment (by liquidating the assets they have accumulated).

   In general, we expect the investor to survey her financing options, identify the option that would yield the highest utility, and then undertake the investment project if the utility she would enjoy while using her best financing option exceeds her status quo utility. To understand her investment choice, therefore, we must examine the utility she would derive under each investment financing option.

Investment financed by current saving

If she undertakes the investment project and finances it by reducing current consumption, she consumes $(Y - C)$ in the present and $(Y + R)$ in the future and achieves utility

$$U^{IS} = u(Y - C) + \beta u(Y + R) \tag{10.4}$$

where the superscript IS indicates that this is the utility associated with investment financed by saving. This is only feasible for $C < Y$ and thus for investments that are small relative to current income. She chooses to undertake the investment if U^{IS} exceeds U^{SQ}, or (after rearranging) if

$$\beta[u(Y+R) - u(Y)] \geq [u(Y) - u(Y-C)] \tag{10.5}$$

The left side of equation 10.5 is the increase in overall utility associated with gaining the future return, and the right side is the reduction in overall utility associated with paying present costs.

Equation 10.5 indicates two reasons the investor might give smaller weight to a peso of future return than to a peso of present cost when evaluating the net benefit associated with investment. First, as indicated by the coefficient β, the investor discounts the future relative to the present. Second, for this investor who expects to earn regular income Y in both periods, the investment renders future consumption expenditure $(Y+R)$ higher than present consumption expenditure $(Y-C)$. Thus if $u(.)$ is characterized by diminishing marginal utility, the gain in utility from an additional peso of consumption in the future is smaller than the loss in utility from the last peso of consumption in the present.

For future reference, it is useful to express equation 10.5 in another way, which highlights the cost of having to delay consumption from the present to the future in order to carry out the investment. Let's let $a_1 = [u(Y+R) - u(Y)]/R$ denote the average increment to within-period utility per peso of future return R, and let $a_0 = [u(Y) - u(Y-C)]/C$ denote the average reduction in utility per peso of present cost C. Each peso of future return then increases total utility by approximately βa_1, and each peso of present cost reduces total utility by approximately a_0, and the investor makes the approximate comparison of $\beta a_1 R$ to $a_0 C$, where $a_1 < a_0$. Dividing both terms in the comparison by βa_1, this implies that the investor compares future return R to an adjusted up-front cost approximated by $C(a_0/a_1)(1/\beta)$, and invests if $R > C(a_0/a_1)(1/\beta)$ or if

$$R > C(1+r^a) \tag{10.6}$$

where $r^a = (a_0/a_1)(1/\beta) - 1$. r^a is a fraction between zero and 1 (similar to an interest rate) that describes the approximate premium the investor imputes to consumption in the present relative to the future and thus the cost of delaying consumption. For example, if $r^a = 0.20$, then each dollar of present consumption enters with approximately 20 percent more weight than each dollar of future benefit in the potential investor's comparison of benefits and costs. The lower the investor's β, and the more rapidly the investor's marginal utility declines with consumption, the greater is r^a, the greater the weight the investor places on present costs relative to future benefits, and the less likely the potential investor is to undertake any given investment project. We might guess that the cost of delaying consumption would be especially high for poor potential investors starting at very low consumption levels.

Investment financed by borrowing

Now suppose the investor is able to borrow at the interest rate r^b per period. This means that she can undertake the investment *without* having to reduce her present consumption, but she must pay back the loan with interest in the future. If she undertakes the investment, borrows at interest rate r^b to finance it, and plans to pay back the loan with interest, then her utility under investment financed by borrowing is

$$U^{IB} = u(Y) + \beta u\left(Y + R - C(1+r^b)\right) \tag{10.7}$$

This is feasible only if the investor has access to a loan large enough to cover C. U^{IB} is greater than U^{SQ}, and borrowing to invest is better than not investing, as long as

$$R > C(1 + r^b) \qquad (10.8)$$

U^{IB} is greater than U^{IS}, and financing the investment by borrowing is better than financing it by saving out of current income, as long as $r^b < r^a$. Thus, if interest rates on credit fall below r^a, investors with access to credit are more likely to invest than those without access, and among those with access to sufficient credit, those facing lower interest rates on borrowing are more likely to invest.

Investment financed by liquidating other assets

Now suppose the investor possesses a quantity of assets A that she may liquidate to finance the investment. The assets might be savings that she can withdraw from a savings account, or business inventory that she can sell to obtain cash. We assume that if she does not liquidate these assets in the present, then she will earn interest on them in the future at the rate r^s and will use the assets and interest to pay for $A(1 + r^s)$ of consumption in the future. If she liquidates enough assets to cover the up-front cost C, she may again undertake the investment in the present without reducing present consumption, but her asset balance falls to $(A - C)$ at the end of period 0, and her future consumption falls by $C(1 + r^s)$. Her overall utility under investment financed by liquidating assets is

$$U^{IA} = u(Y) + \beta \left(Y + R - C(1 + r^s) \right) \qquad (10.9)$$

This is greater than U^{SQ}, and liquidating other assets to finance investment is better than not investing, as long as

$$R > C(1 + r^s) \qquad (10.10)$$

If $r^s < r^a$, then U^{IA} is also greater than U^{IS}, and financing investment by drawing down other assets is better than financing it out of current saving. Thus, among investors with accumulated assets $A > C$, investors earning lower returns on those assets are more likely to undertake immediate investment. As long as the return on assets is less than r^a, investors with assets to draw down are also more likely to undertake investments than those without.

The cost of financing immediate investment

The preceding discussion suggests that we may think of an investor as incurring **financing costs**, no matter how she finances the investment. If she borrows a quantity C at the interest rate r^b, she explicitly pays borrowing costs of Cr^b in the future. If she draws assets on which she earns a return of r^s, she incurs the opportunity cost of forgone future interest earnings Cr^s. If she finances the investment by reducing current consumption, she incurs a cost of delaying consumption of Cr^a.[1] If she does invest today, she chooses—among feasible financing options—the one for which the financing cost is the lowest. Denoting the per-peso financing cost by r, she compares future returns R to the sum of up-front costs and financing costs, $C(1 + r)$, and invests if $R > C(1 + r)$. The existence of financing costs causes her to give greater weight to each peso of up-front cost than to each peso of future return when assessing whether the benefits of investment outweigh the costs. Investors for whom financing investments is more costly and difficult are more daunted by up-front costs, and they might fail to undertake certain investments, even while investors with better financing options would undertake them.

---

[1] If her accumulated savings A or the quantity of credit she may borrow B is less than C, she may also choose to finance the investment in part by drawing down savings or borrowing and in part by saving out of current income.

Saving up for investment

An investor taking a longer-term perspective might consider saving up over several periods to finance an investment. To see this, consider an investor who earns noninvestment income of Y in every period, who may invest C in period 0 to reap return R in period 1 *or* may invest C in the period 1 to reap return R in period 2. Under the assumptions of the standard model, and with periods 0, 1, and 2 relevant to this decision, she obtains status quo utility

$$U^{SQ} = u(Y) + \beta u(Y) + \beta^2 u(Y) \tag{10.11}$$

if she does not invest. Suppose her best option for financing investment immediately in period 0 is to finance by saving out of current income. If she undertakes the investment in period 0, she obtains utility

$$U^{I0} = u(Y - C) + \beta u(Y + R) + \beta^2 u(Y) \tag{10.12}$$

Drawing on results derived above, we know that if $R < C(1 + r^a)$, she will find this option unattractive. If, however, she saves $C/2$ in period 0, and if she can earn an interest rate of r^s on savings held from period 0 to period 1, then she need save only $C - (C/2)(1 + r^s)$ in period 1 to accumulate enough funds to undertake the investment in period 1. If she finances the investment this way she obtains utility

$$U^{I1} = u(Y - C/2) + \beta u \left(Y - C + (C/2)(1 + r^s) \right) + \beta^2 u(Y + R) \tag{10.13}$$

Because $u(.)$ exhibits diminishing marginal utility of consumption, saving the smaller amounts out of current income in two periods is less costly to her (in within-period utility loss) than saving the full amount C in one period. If r^s is positive, her ability to earn interest income on period 0 saving also helps her finance the period 1 investment. Delaying the investment's return from period 1 to period 2 diminishes its value to her in the present, but she might find that the utility associated with saving up and investing later (U^{I1}) exceeds her status quo utility (U^{SQ}), even when the utility associated with immediate investment (equation 10.12) does not, because saving up over two periods does not require her to cut consumption in any one period as acutely.

The possibility of saving up for investment over multiple periods complicates the relationship between investment choices and the rate of return (r^s) paid on other assets. When starting from a very low rate of r^s, an increase can render saving up more attractive, tending to encourage investment. Once the interest rate paid on saving reaches higher levels, however, increases might discourage the investor from investing, as it becomes more attractive to hold onto saved assets than to undertake a new investment project.

Saving for other reasons

People save up for purposes other than undertaking an investment project directly. Later we will see that people sometimes save in ways that channel financing to other people's investments, allowing savers to earn investment returns indirectly. As suggested in Chapter 2, they might also save to smooth consumption. Workers in their prime working years, for example, might save to finance consumption in their old age, and businessmen earning unusually high profits today might save to prop up consumption in future periods when they know income will be unusually low. When future income is uncertain, people might also engage in **precautionary saving**, through which they build up a buffer of assets that will allow them to sustain consumption if they are hit by shocks that reduce future income.

Implications of the standard model

Our discussion of investment financing under the assumptions of the standard model suggests that:

> Among investors facing comparable investment projects, investment is more likely by those who have access to more credit, can borrow at lower interest rates, have more assets to draw down, or are more willing to delay consumption. Those facing modest interest returns on saving may also be more likely to invest than those facing only very low returns on saving, because they find it easier to save up for investment over multiple periods.

Later in this chapter and in later chapters we will see a variety of empirical patterns consistent with these predictions. We will also see that poor households are especially likely to face higher financing costs because they earn low incomes, lack assets to liquidate, lack access to good savings instruments, and either lack access to credit or have access to credit only at high interest rates.

Present bias as a psychological barrier to saving and investment

Under the neoclassical assumption of constant discounting, potential investors assess investment opportunities in a way that is **time consistent**. This means that if, in period 0, they believe that their overall utility would be increased by undertaking an investment in period 1, and they therefore *plan* to undertake the investment in period 1, then after time elapses and they arrive in period 1, they indeed find the investment worthwhile and undertake it. Their future actions are consistent with their present plans.

To see this, consider an investor who is facing the opportunity to pay a cost C in period 1 to obtain a return R in period 2 and who otherwise earns income Y in every period. In period 0 she plans to undertake the investment in period 1 if doing so would raise her three-period utility. That is, she *plans to invest* if

$$[u(Y) + \beta u(Y - C) + \beta^2 u(Y + R)] > [u(Y) + \beta u(Y) + \beta^2 u(Y)] \qquad (10.14)$$

Simplifying, this requires that $\beta[u(Y + R) - u(Y)] > [u(Y) - u(Y - C)]$, indicating that the increase in single-period utility associated with the investment's return, multiplied by β, is greater than the reduction in single-period utility associated with the investment's cost. When she gets to period 1, she invests if her two-period utility under investment exceeds her two-period utility if she does not invest. That is, she *actually invests* if

$$[u(Y - C) + \beta u(Y + R)] > [u(Y) + \beta u(Y)] \qquad (10.15)$$

This, too, simplifies to $\beta[u(Y + R) - u(Y)] > [u(Y) - u(Y - C)]$. The two conditions are exactly the same. In both cases she compares the utility cost to the utility benefit multiplied by β. Thus, as long as Y, C, and R remain unchanged, she always makes the choice in period 1 that she planned in period 0 to make in period 1.

Behavioral economists and psychologists point to empirical evidence, however, that people might have **time-inconsistent preferences**, which sometimes lead them *not* to follow through on saving and investment plans (Frederick et al., 2002). To highlight the potential importance of time inconsistency in a simple fashion, let's examine the choices of a person whose utility function is characterized by **present bias**. A person subject to present bias finds it more difficult to delay consumption from the present to one period into the future than to delay consumption from any future period to one period further in the future. That is, when looking to a three-period horizon, she maximizes the utility function

$$U(F_0, F_1, F_2) = u(Y) + \delta[\beta u(Y) + \beta^2 u(Y)] \tag{10.16}$$

where δ is a parameter between 0 and 1 that measures present bias. When δ equals 1, there is no present bias, and the investor employs a constant discount factor β. Where δ is a fraction less than 1, the cost of delaying one unit of consumption is greater when the delay is from period 0 to period 1 than when it is from period 1 to period 2. She applies the discount factor $\delta\beta$ when comparing period 1 utility to period 0 utility, but she applies the discount factor β when comparing period 2 utility to period 1 utility.

A potential investor maximizing this utility function might in period 0 plan to undertake an investment in period 1 but then fail to undertake it when she gets to period 1. In period 0 she would plan to undertake an investment that costs C in period 1 and pays R in period 2 if $\delta\beta^2[u(Y+R) - u(Y)] > \delta\beta[u(Y) - u(Y-C)]$ or

$$\beta[u(Y+R) - u(Y)] > [u(Y) - u(Y-C)] \tag{10.17}$$

When the potential investor gets to period 1, however, period 1 becomes the "present" in which consumption is particularly valuable to her. At that point she undertakes the investment only if

$$\delta\beta[u(Y+R) - u(Y)] > [u(Y) - u(Y-C)] \tag{10.18}$$

With δ less than 1, this is a stricter criterion. She might thus fail to undertake the investment in period 1, even though she planned in period 0 to undertake it in period 1.

People characterized by present bias are said to have self-control problems. Looking forward from period 0 they believe they would be better off if they save and invest in period 1. Looking backward from period 2 or beyond, too, they might wish they had undertaken the investment. But in period 1, when the moment of decision is upon them, they find it too difficult to exercise the required denial of current consumption, and they do not invest. Similarly, present-biased individuals might plan to start saving up "tomorrow," whether to undertake an investment or to create a buffer against future shocks, but when tomorrow comes, they might have a hard time saving. Present bias might thus constitute a psychological barrier to saving and investment.

If people characterized by present bias are aware of their self-control problems, then they might benefit from opportunities to make commitments in the present that help them follow through on saving and investment plans in the future. Thus:

> Among investors who face comparable investment projects, those offered services that help them commit to saving and investing in the future might be more likely to undertake saving and investment.

Several recent experiments seem to confirm the potential for commitment devices to increase saving and investment by some people. Ashraf et al. (2006) partnered with the Green Bank of Caraga, in a rural area of the Philippines, to offer customers "commitment savings accounts." When customers open these accounts, they specify that they will save until a certain date or until they have reached a specified saving goal, and they agree to be penalized for making withdrawals before they have achieved their goal. Twenty-eight percent of the treatment group offered such accounts took up the offer, even though they already had access to savings accounts paying the same interest rate without the commitment device, and their use of the accounts increased their saving rates. Duflo et al. (2011) approached Kenyan farmers just after harvest and offered them a small encouragement (in the form of a time-limited offer of free delivery) to purchase fertilizer immediately. For farmers who were aware that present bias might lead them, during the next planting season, to use any money saved at harvest for consumption rather than fertilizer purchase, this offer encouraged them to commit in advance to making the fertilizer investment. Providing farmers with this nudge was more effective at increasing fertilizer use than a much more costly intervention that offered farmers fertilizer at half price during the planting season.

10.2D Risk and insurance

In this section we set aside discounting concerns to focus on risk, by assuming that an investment project's costs and returns both materialize at the same time in the near future. The investor thus cares only about the net return, R, which is equal to the gross return minus all up-front and operation and maintenance costs. We introduce risk by allowing the ultimate size and sign of R to depend on factors the investor does not know when she invests. More specifically, we acknowledge that the world can evolve in diverse ways after the investment has been made, achieving diverse possible **states of the world** at the time the return is realized, and that the return R differs across those possible states of the world. When contemplating the creation of a new tortilla-making business, for example, good states of the world are those in which the investor turns out to be an excellent tortilla maker and remains healthy, and the local demand for tortillas is strong. In bad states of the world, the cost of ingredients is high, the demand for tortillas is weak, or thieves abscond with equipment.

In standard economic models of investment choices in the presence of uncertainty, the investor does not know exactly what return an investment will produce, but she knows the **distribution of the investment's returns** across possible states of the world. To fully characterize an investment's distribution of returns, we identify all possible future states of the world, indicate the returns that would be realized in each state, and indicate how likely it is that each state occurs. In this text we will work with very simple distributions, in which we consider only two or three possible states of the world (and thus only two or three possible values of R). In reality, the possible returns can differ continuously over an infinite number of possible states of the world.[2]

Two features of the distribution of possible returns are especially important: the expected value and the variance. The **expected value** of the return is the weighted average of the returns across all possible states of the world, where the weights are equal to the probabilities with which the different states occur. The expected value of the return—or the **expected return**, for short— indicates how great the return is expected to be on average. The **variance** of an investment's return is a measure of how much the possible returns vary above and below the expected return across states of the world.[3] Among projects with the same expected return, those with higher variance are more **risky**.[4]

For example, suppose that only three states of the world—bad (b), normal (n), and good (g)—are possible, and suppose that the normal state occurs with probability 0.5, and the bad and good states each occur with probability 0.25. Consider two investment projects for which the returns in the three states are as follows:

---

[2] Such continuous distributions are characterized by functions called *probability density functions*, which describe the likelihood of occurrence as a function of possible return values. For a review of several common classes of such distributions—including the class of normal distributions—see Appendix B in Wooldridge (2012).

[3] More specifically, the variance of a random variable's distribution is defined as the weighted average, across all possible values the random variable might take, of the squared difference between the actual value and the expected value, where the weights are given by the probability of the random variable taking on the given value.

[4] Equating risk with variance is most intuitive when comparing investment projects with the same expected return. In such cases, higher variance implies higher probability of serious loss. When one investment project has higher expected return than another, it can carry lower probability of loss even if its variance is higher.

	R_b	R_n	R_g
Project 1	80	100	120
Project 2	50	100	150

The expected returns on these two projects are identical. Project 1's expected return is $0.25(80) + 0.5(100) + 0.25(120) = 100$, and Project 2's expected return is $0.25(50) + 0.5(100) + 0.25(150) = 100$. The equality of their expected returns indicates that neither project has a systematic tendency to produce a higher return than the other. Notice, however, that Project 1's actual return never lies farther than 20 away from the expected return in any state of the world, while Project 2's actual return is 50 away from the expected return half the time. Project 2's return has higher variance, and Project 2 exposes the investor to more risk than does Project 1.

Often it is useful to distinguish specific risks to which investors are exposed. Our tortilla maker faces risks related to fluctuations in ingredient prices, electricity costs, health, and other features of economic circumstance. In each of these areas she might be hit by **good shocks**, such as unusually high tortilla prices, or **bad shocks**, such as illness. Among projects with the same expected return, projects that are more likely to be hit by shocks, and projects for which shocks have larger impacts on returns, have higher variance and more risk.

Often we are interested in the extent to which project risks are correlated across projects. Some risks are highly **covariate** across investors within a community, tending to hit many in the community at the same time. For example, in low-lying villages, when flooding comes, many households are affected simultaneously. Other risks are **idiosyncratic**, associated with shocks that tend to hit only a few members of the at-risk group at once. For example, only a few community members might suffer road traffic accidents or fire in a given year, even though all members are at risk of such shocks. Risks of the same sort often appear more idiosyncratic when considered for a larger group. For example, while flood risk is highly covariate within a small community, it may be much less covariate when considering households throughout an entire country.

Expected utility and costs associated with risk

Risk matters because investors may be **risk averse**. This means that when comparing projects with the same expected return, they prefer lower-variance projects, which expose them to less risk of doing badly. Such investors might also prefer a project with lower expected return to a project with higher expected return *and* higher risk. We can thus think of risk as introducing a cost that makes an investment project less attractive to a risk-averse investor.

The standard economic model of decision making in the presence of risk assumes that decision makers maximize **expected utility**. Like an expected return, expected utility is calculated as a weighted average across all possible states of the world, with weights given by the probabilities of each state occurring. But while *expected return* is a weighted average of returns R, *expected utility* is a weighted average of the utility the investor derives from the returns, $u(R)$, where $u(.)$ is characterized by diminishing marginal utility of consumption. For example, when only two states of the world (g and b) are relevant, the decision maker seeks to maximize expected utility

$$EU(R_g, R_b) = pu(F_g) + (1-p)u(F_b) \qquad (10.19)$$

where F_g and F_b are the quantities of consumption in the good and bad states, p is the probability of the good state occurring, and $(1-p)$ is the probability of the bad state occurring.

Figure 10.1 is useful for teasing out the intuition about how the expected utility assumption builds risk aversion into the standard theory of investment decisions. The figure graphs an investor's real consumption expenditure F (in pesos) in any state of the world along the horizontal

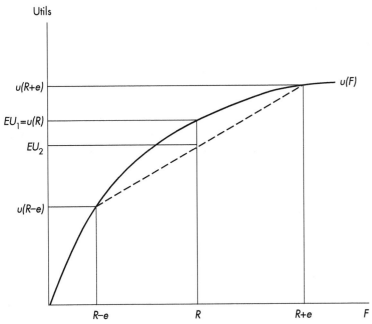

FIGURE 10.1
Expected Utility Comparison for Safe and Risky Projects with Same Expected Return R

axis and the utility $u(F)$ that the investor would derive from that consumption in that state of the world (in utils) along the vertical axis. The diminishing marginal utility of consumption is manifested in the concave shape of the $u(F)$ graph.

Let's suppose that only two future states of the world are relevant, each occurring with probability 0.5, and use Figure 10.1 to identify the expected utility associated with two projects whose returns in the good and bad states are as follows:

	R_g	R_b
Project 1	R	R
Project 2	$R + e$	$R - e$

Project 1 delivers the return R in either state of the world. That is, it delivers a *certain* return of R. The expected utility associated with Project 1 is

$$EU_1 = 0.5u(R) + 0.5u(R) = u(R) \qquad (10.20)$$

In Figure 10.1, this is given by the height of the $u(F)$ function when $F = R$.

Project 2 delivers the same expected return (R) but is risky. The expected utility the investor would associate with Project 2 is

$$EU_2 = 0.5u(R - e) + 0.5u(R + e) \qquad (10.21)$$

This is the simple average of $u(R + e)$ and $u(R - e)$. We can identify EU_2 in the graph by drawing the line segment of long dashes between the point $[R - e, u(R - e)]$ and $[R + e, u(R + e)]$ and identifying the height of this segment at its midpoint. Given the concave shape of the utility function, this *must* be less than the expected utility associated with Project 1.

If the $u(.)$ function were linear rather than concave, with $u(F) = F$, the decision maker would not be risk averse. Such a decision maker is said to be **risk neutral**, and she would undertake an investment project as long as the expected return on the investment is positive, regardless of the risk associated with it.

Why does the risky project yield lower expected utility than the safe project with the same expected return? As a result of the diminishing marginal utility of consumption, the reduction in bad state utility associated with moving from safe Project 1 to risky Project 2, $U(R) - U(R - e)$, is greater in absolute value than the increase in good state utility associated with the same move from the safe project to the risky project, $U(R + e) - U(R)$. Because the move from Project 1 to Project 2 reduces bad state utility by more than it increases good state utility, it reduces the weighted average of bad and good state utilities.

Insurance and the costs associated with risk

When investors can purchase appropriate insurance, they become capable of investing in risky projects without exposing themselves to severe reductions in consumption when hit by bad shocks, and they might thus become more willing to undertake risky investments. Under an **insurance contract**, an investor pays a fee, called a **premium**, to purchase a contract that promises payments, called **indemnities**, in specified bad states of the world. For example, weather-based crop insurance promises indemnities to make up for the value of farmers' lost crops when poor weather reduces yields. If an investor can simultaneously undertake a risky investment project *and* purchase insurance well-tailored to the project's risks, then the total of his investment returns *plus* indemnities (and thus his consumption) fluctuates little across states of the world.

For example, consider an investor with a certain income of 20 contemplating an investment project with a 50 percent chance of delivering a "good" return of 40, and a 50 percent chance of delivering a "bad" return of −20. The project's expected return is $0.5(40) + 0.5(−20) = 10$. The investor consumes the sum of her certain income and her investment return in any state. Thus she consumes 20 in either state if she does not invest, and she consumes 60 and 0 in the good and bad states if she does invest. Suppose further that her utility function is given by:

$$u(c) = \begin{bmatrix} c & if & c < 20 \\ 20 + 0.4(c - 20) & if & c \geq 20 \end{bmatrix} \qquad (10.22)$$

This utility function incorporates the diminishing marginal utility of consumption in a crude way, with each one-unit increase in consumption below 20 increasing utility by 1 full unit, and each one-unit increase in consumption above 20 increasing utility by only 0.4 units. If the potential investor does not invest, her expected utility is $0.5u(20) + 0.5u(20) = 20$. If she undertook the project without insurance, her expected utility would be $0.5u(0) + 0.5u(60) = 0.5(0) + 0.5(36) = 18$, which is less than 20. Thus, though the project's expected return is positive, she does not undertake the project, because this would reduce her expected utility. She is deterred by risk, because the utility cost associated with reduced consumption in the bad state more than outweighs the utility benefit of increased consumption in the good state.

Suppose now that the investor may pay a premium P for an insurance contract that pays 20 and waives the premium in the bad state of the world. If the investor undertakes the investment *and* purchases the insurance contract, she consumes $(60 - P)$ in the good state because she earns her certain income of 20 plus the investment return of 40 and must pay the premium P. She earns 20 in the bad state, because the insurance payout just compensates for her investment loss, allowing her to consume her certain income of 20. As long as $P < 40$, her consumption in the good state remains greater than 20, and her expected utility remains greater than $0.5u(20) + 0.5u(20) = 20$, which is the utility she would enjoy if she did not invest. Thus, as long as the premium charge is not too high, undertaking the investment *while also buying insurance* raises her consumption in the good state while leaving her consumption in the bad state unchanged, and she chooses to invest, even though she would not invest if she could not purchase insurance.

Whether or not insurance is available to the potential investor, the risky investment project carries with it **costs associated with risk**. Either the investor pays a premium to obtain insurance (thereby avoiding dramatic fluctuations in consumption) or she bears the consumption risk, which reduces her expected utility. Just as access to better borrowing and saving opportunities encourages investment by reducing the costs of financing, so access to better insurance opportunities encourages investment by reducing the costs associated with risk.

In our treatment of risk thus far we have assumed that potential investors know the distribution of returns for potential investments. This implies that they know a great deal: all the possible levels of net returns that might occur and the probability with which the investment produces returns at each of those levels. In practice, investors might face not just the known risk associated with returns that vary across states of the world but also deeper **uncertainty** regarding returns for which the expected value and variance across states of the world are simply unknown. If investors fear the unknown, then uncertainty can impose additional costs beyond the costs associated with known risks and can raise perceived investment costs even further.

We conclude that:

> Investors are more likely to undertake investment projects if they have better access to appropriate insurance policies or face lower insurance premiums.

Among investments paying the same expected return, investors are also more likely to undertake those associated with lower risk or associated with risks for which more appropriate insurance is available.

10.2E A model of private investment decisions

We incorporate the concerns of the previous two sections into a more general model of investment decisions by assuming that:

> A potential investor chooses to undertake an investment project only if she has adequate information about the project and if the highest expected utility she believes she can attain while undertaking the project (making best use of her financing and insurance options) exceeds the highest utility she can attain if she does not. In essence, she compares the expected stream of future net benefits to the costs, which include up-front costs and the costs associated with financing and risk.

In what follows, we lay out some of the most important implications.

Financial market conditions

Conditions in financial markets help determine which people invest and which investments they undertake. Holding investment projects' up-front costs and future returns constant, some potential investors might fail to undertake the projects because they lack adequate options for financing the investment or for insuring themselves against the projects' risks. Such financial constraints are especially likely to affect poor households, for reasons discussed later. Financially constrained investors might also forgo projects that deliver higher returns (per peso of up-front costs) while undertaking lower-return projects, because the higher return projects involve larger (indivisible) up-front costs and are more difficult to finance.

Potential investors' assets and investment projects' intrinsic returns

While holding financial market conditions and up-front costs constant, potential investors are more likely to undertake investments for which the future returns are higher, start sooner, last longer, or are less risky. Even when considering investment projects of the same type—for example, adoption of a new agricultural technology or sending a child to primary school—some households may be more likely to invest than others because differences in their assets or locations cause seemingly identical investments to produce intrinsic returns of different sizes. The effect of a new agricultural technology on crop production, for example, can depend on the quantity and quality of land a household possesses. Similarly, the impact of school attendance on later productivity and wages can depend on the quality of the local school.

Markets, institutions, and profitability

Even holding constant investment projects' intrinsic productivity, their profitability can differ across locations as a result of differing conditions in markets for goods, services, and labor. If technology investments increase farmers' production, for example, but also increase their demand for labor, then the investments are more profitable where output prices are higher relative to wages (see Chapter 20). Profitability may also vary across farmers and locations as a result of institutional differences. Cooperative institutions supporting bulk purchases and sales can improve output and input prices for members, and institutions supporting contract fulfillment and trust can reduce the transfer costs associated with participation in higher-value markets (as discussed in Chapter 8).

Institutions and risk coping

Holding expected returns constant, investment projects are more attractive where the returns are less risky or potential investors are better able to cope with risk. Sometimes where formal insurance markets are absent, informal insurance institutions arise to help people cope with shocks. For example, social norms requiring villagers to provide each other with mutual assistance offer some insurance against idiosyncratic shocks within communities (see Chapter 12). Formal public sector institutions, such as workfare programs, can also provide such implicit insurance (Chapter 16).

Institutions and the appropriation of returns

What matters to private investors' choices are not the overall returns their investments will generate but the fraction of the returns that they hope to **appropriate**, or make use of in ways that add to their own well-being. Fear that other people will appropriate the returns through fraud or theft, or that the government will appropriate the returns through taxation or expropriation, diminish the returns that investors expect to appropriate and increase the risk associated with investment. Investment is thus more attractive in the presence of healthy institutions protecting **property rights**. Such institutions protect investors' rights to use, claim the income generated by, and dispose of any assets they create or redeploy through investment. They include the formal and informal institutions that define investors' rights over land and other physical assets and that protect them from theft and fraud, as well as political institutions that shape their expectations regarding future taxation and expropriation. We take a closer look at land rights institutions in Chapter 12 and briefly consider political institutions in Chapter 13.

Unfortunately, investors' hopes of appropriating investment returns may also be diminished by some informal institutions. The same social norms of mutual assistance that can help investors cope with risk might also inhibit investment because they effectively require investors to pay neighbors some share of any returns their investments deliver. In addition, where husbands place higher value on consumption relative to saving than their wives, women might have difficulty protecting accumulated savings from appropriation by their husbands.

Institutions and commitment

The discussion of present bias suggested that where potential investors cannot borrow, the psychological difficulty of following through on plans to save might prevent them from undertaking valuable investments. The existence of institutions that allow potential investors to commit in advance to save and invest, such as the experimental offers of commitment savings accounts and nudges for fertilizer purchase described above, can encourage investment.

Knowledge and learning

Whether an investor undertakes an investment project depends on her beliefs and expectations regarding the project's returns. Potential investors might, therefore, fail to undertake investment projects with high and secure true returns simply because they lack accurate or complete knowledge regarding the returns. A farmer may be entirely unaware of a recently developed improved seed variety, for example. Parents might underestimate the extent to which schooling will increase their children's wages. Many investments involve **innovation**—doing something new or in a new place—and potential investors might view these innovations as risky, even if the investment projects are intrinsically safe, simply because they have not done such things before. The potential importance of knowledge and expectations raises interest in how information is transmitted and how people learn new practices or adjust their beliefs. We take a closer look at these issues in Chapters 20 and 22.

Tastes

Finally, some investors undertake investments that others do not because they place higher intrinsic value on the projects' nonmonetary returns. For example, some subsistence farmers in Africa are less inclined than others to adopt new higher-yielding varieties of sweet potato because they have stronger preferences for the taste and color of a traditional variety.

10.2F Application to the study of low fertilizer use in Africa

The preceding section suggests that when studying why farmers in Africa use less chemical fertilizer than farmers in Asia and Latin America, we should examine, at the very least, seven possible explanations. (1) Fertilizer investments may be intrinsically less productive on average in African agroclimatic conditions than in other places. (2) Even if fertilizer investments are just as *productive* on average, farmers may expect them to be less *profitable* in Africa, because fertilizer prices are higher relative to crop prices. Higher effective costs of labor and other complementary inputs may also reduce the profitability of fertilizer use. (3) African farmers might have weaker expectations of appropriating the returns because of weaker land rights institutions. (4) African farmers might also face greater financing difficulties. (5) Fertilizer investments may be more risky in Africa or (6) African farmers might have inferior opportunities for coping with risk. Finally, (7) African farmers may be less well informed about fertilizer investments.

Lower fertilizer use rates in Africa seem not to be the result of lower average intrinsic productivity. According to a survey of fertilizer profitability studies, the average physical response of crop yields to fertilizer use is just as high in Africa as elsewhere (Yanggen et al., 1998).

Fertilizer use is indeed often less profitable, however, because the ratio of fertilizer price to crop price is much higher in Africa. While ratios of fertilizer price per kilogram to crop price per kilogram range from 1 to 3 in Latin America, they range from 5 to 7 in East and Southern Africa. This suggests the importance of studying why farmers face such high fertilizer costs in Africa.

Fertilizer prices are higher in Africa relative to other places in part because African farmers face high costs of importing fertilizer. More than 90 percent of the chemical fertilizers used in Africa are imported (Morris et al., 2007). Importing costs are higher in Africa as a result of inferior port and international transport infrastructure (a problem to which we return in Chapter 11), and also because African countries import on such a small scale. Fertilizer imports in all of Africa constitute only 1 percent of global fertilizer consumption. Individual African countries import very small total quantities and often break their imports up into many smaller batches of diverse fertilizer types. As a result, they pay higher unit prices to shippers and fertilizer suppliers, who give discounts on larger-scale exports to other countries. On top of this, domestic transport costs are higher as a result of inferior domestic transport infrastructure, the scattering of farmers over greater distances, and the smaller quantities potentially demanded by farmers who have smaller farms. In the United States, transport costs are less than 5 percent of the final fertilizer price, but they are *one-third* of the final price in Zambia (Morris et al., 2007).

High mobility and transaction costs in rural labor markets, which might induce more farm households in Africa to remain outside of labor markets (Chapter 7), might also raise the effective cost of employing fertilizer by raising the effective cost of labor (especially in seasons of peak agricultural labor requirements) if fertilizer and labor are complements in production.

Higher costs of using fertilizer seem to be only part of the explanation for low fertilizer use in Africa, however, because fertilizer use often appears profitable in Africa, despite high costs, especially in maize and rice cultivation (Yaangen et al., 1998). Thus it is useful to consider additional potential barriers to fertilizer use.

At first glance, differences in land rights institutions might help explain differential investments in fertilizer use across continents, because formal land titling institutions cover a smaller fraction of farm land in Africa than in other places. As we will see in Chapter 12, however, customary land rights institutions often provide farmers with reasonably strong rights to harvest land they have cultivated and often allow them to continue cultivating the land as long as they wish. Even so, customary land rights institutions vary greatly within Africa, and their contribution to low fertilizer use in at least some places cannot be ruled out.

It seems likely that financing fertilizer use is also more costly and difficult in Africa relative to other places, though solid evidence is lacking. Broad measures constructed by Honohan (2008) suggest that access to financial services is less widespread in many African countries than in other parts of the world; thus it may be more difficult to finance investment by borrowing or saving up. Financing fertilizer use out of current income may also be more difficult in Africa, where farmers' income levels are especially low.

Risk and lack of insurance also seem likely to play important roles in explaining low fertilizer use in Africa. Weather-induced variability in crop yields appears to be much greater in Africa than in Asia (Morris et al., 2007). Crop price variation is also greater in Africa, adding further variability to the effect of fertilizer on profits. The price per metric ton of maize varied from US$50 to US$250 in Addis Ababa, Ethiopia, over a period (1996–2003) in which world prices were quite stable. Studies of the impact of risk on fertilizer use are rare, but Dercon and Christiaensen (2011) estimate for a sample of Ethiopian farmers that fertilizer use is profitable on average but increases risk, and that a reduction in risk would significantly increase fertilizer use.

The risk associated with chemical fertilizer use may be compounded by inadequate knowledge regarding how, exactly, to employ the fertilizers. Duflo et al. (2008) demonstrates that the profitability of fertilizer use can depend greatly on how exactly it is applied. Working with farmers in western Kenya, who each cultivated several experimental plots using different fertilizer quantities and seed varieties, they find that when cultivating traditional seed varieties, fertilizer use is highly profitable when one-half teaspoon is applied per planting hole, produces a much smaller profit when 1 teaspoon is applied, and produces a negative return when one-quarter teaspoon is applied. Troublingly, they also find that the use of 1 teaspoon per planting hole together with the use of high-yielding seed varieties, which is the recommendation that the Agriculture Ministry promotes to local farmers, produces a negative return. Broader experience suggests that returns also vary with the timing of application. Thus African farmers might perceive fertilizer use as risky if they do not have adequate knowledge regarding how to use it properly. Though no direct comparison is available, it is plausible that a longer history of fertilizer use in other regions of the world renders farmers better informed.

Agricultural extension agencies seek to inform farmers about the methods and benefits of fertilizer use, but they often work directly with only a small number of model farmers, hoping that knowledge will spread from farmer to farmer. Conley and Udry (2010) provide evidence raising serious questions about this approach, at least in Ghana. They examine four clusters of Ghanaian villages where farmers have recently started cultivating pineapples for export. Pineapple cultivation requires the use of chemical fertilizers, which had not been used much with crops previously cultivated. They found that farmers did not discuss farming practice with many other farmers in their communities, and they were often not even aware of how much fertilizer their neighbors used and what yields they obtained. This suggests that farmers might learn only little and slowly about appropriate fertilizer use from their neighbors' experiments, at least in the study region, and farmers in Africa might have inferior information regarding fertilizer use than farmers in other areas.

Following the guidance provided by economic models of investment decisions, we have uncovered many factors that probably contribute to low fertilizer use in Africa. Policymakers interested in increasing fertilizer use in a particular location may wish to consider investments in infrastructure (to bring down the local cost of fertilizer), agricultural research and extension (to improve profitability of and knowledge about fertilizer use and reduce its risk), education (to improve information acquisition about fertilizer use), formation of farmer cooperatives, international collaborations (to reduce fertilizer costs by coordinating larger-scale purchases), improvements in agricultural financing and insurance options, and creation of public safety net programs that improve farmers' ability to cope with risk.

10.3 Financial Markets, Financial Constraints, and Development

In section 10.2 we saw that peoples' opportunities for saving, borrowing, and obtaining insurance help determine their investment choices. In this section, we examine the markets in which such opportunities are determined: financial markets.

10.3A Basic financial market functions

When financial markets work well, they perform important developmental functions. We will see that:

Well-functioning financial markets contribute to development by channeling funds from savers to investors, helping investors and others cope with income fluctuations and risk, and reducing the cost of transactions in goods and labor markets.

Channeling funds from savers to investors (and other borrowers) through markets for loanable funds

Saving is defined as refraining from spending all of one's income on immediate consumption. Saving is important to investment, because all investments must be financed either by the investors' own current or past saving or by the saving of those from whom the investors borrow or inherit wealth. People save for diverse reasons, as indicated earlier.

When people save they accumulate wealth. They can hold their wealth in many forms, only some of which are useful for financing investment. When they use the savings to purchase equipment for farms or businesses, or to send their children to school, they employ savings directly in financing their own investments. When they lend their savings out to neighbors or relatives, they might help finance the borrowers' investments. When they deposit their savings in banks, the banks in turn lend the money out, again helping to finance investment by others. By contrast, when they save by stashing currency or gold jewelry under mattresses, or by paying a local money guard to hold their savings, the savings are not mobilized to finance investment.

The resources that savers make available for others to borrow may be called **loanable funds**, and it is through **loanable funds markets** that savings flow from savers to investors. When savers lend to investors, they transfer "money today" to investors in exchange for the investors' promises to return "money tomorrow." Investors return the savers' funds with interest, and the **interest rate** is the price they pay, per peso of borrowed funds, for the use of those funds.

Like exchanges in other markets, exchanges in the market for loanable funds leave both parties better off. Savers benefit when, by lending to investors, they increase the reward they derive from saving. If savers could not enter into exchange with investors, they would earn a return on their savings only by undertaking investments of their own. Lacking land, business acumen, or other prerequisites, some savers would be stuck investing in very low-return projects or even just storing cash under a mattress. Through markets for loanable funds, savers may instead finance other investors' higher-return projects, earning more through interest receipts on loans than they would have earned through returns on their own investment projects. Potential investors, too, benefit from exchanges in markets for loanable funds. Borrowing allows investors who have good investment projects to undertake profitable investments even when they lack enough savings to cover the up-front costs.

Potential investors are not the only ones who benefit from borrowing in markets for loanable funds. Households can smooth consumption in the face of income fluctuations by saving when income is high and drawing down savings when income is low, or by borrowing when income is low and repaying the debt when income is high. The market for loanable funds is a vehicle for mutually beneficial exchange between households experiencing unusually high income, who wish to save, and those experiencing unusually low income, who wish to borrow or draw down savings.

Just as goods market exchanges are sometimes carried out through intermediaries, so also transfers of loanable funds are sometimes carried out through **financial intermediaries**. Commercial banks, for example, borrow from savers who deposit their savings in bank accounts, and then lend to investors and other borrowers. They cover their costs and earn a return on their efforts by charging higher interest rates of their borrowers than they pay to depositors.

Well-functioning markets for loanable funds encourage economic growth and allow a larger set of investors to participate in growth. By offering savers better returns, they encourage saving and encourage savers to channel their savings into investment projects (rather than holding savings as cash under a mattress). By shifting financing away from savers' own lower-return investment projects toward higher-return projects managed by others, they raise the average return on investment. By increasing the volume and average quality of investments, they increase the rate of economic growth. In addition, by facilitating the flow of funds from wealthy savers with poor investment prospects to poor entrepreneurs with high-return investment projects, well-functioning markets for loanable funds can also render growth more inclusive. By helping households cope with fluctuations in income and needs, they reduce vulnerability.

Transferring and pooling risk through insurance markets

Insurance contracts transfer risk from buyers to sellers. The indemnity payments that insurance buyers receive when they are hit by shocks protect them from serious reductions in consumption, while imposing uncertain payout liabilities on insurance sellers. Buyers pay premiums to sellers for the service of bearing risk for them. Buyers and sellers of insurance enter into this mutually beneficial exchange when the cost of bearing risk is lower for the seller than for the buyer.

Insurance sellers may be able to bear risk at lower cost than insurance buyers because they are inherently less risk averse or have more wealth they can draw down to sustain consumption when hit by shocks, or because they can pool the risks faced by many insurance buyers. Insurers **pool risks** when they provide insurance contracts to many clients facing idiosyncratic risks. Under such circumstances, though each client faces significant risk each year (e.g., a 5 percent chance of needing major surgery), the insurer might face little risk, knowing that only a fairly stable fraction of clients (e.g., 5 percent) will be hit by shocks in any given year. If the fraction of the population hit by the shock each year is small, then by charging each client only a small premium the insurer may collect enough revenue to pay all indemnity claims (see problem 3).

Well-functioning insurance markets contribute to development through several channels. Most obviously, they reduce vulnerability to shocks. They may also speed growth by offering potential investors protection against the worst consequences of risky investments, thereby encouraging them to undertake more and higher-return investments. This may be especially important for poor potential investors who have no wealth they can draw down to sustain consumption when hit by shocks.

Facilitating the exchange of goods and services through markets for safe and convenient means of payment

If people exchanged goods and services only through barter transactions, they would incur high costs of carrying out transactions in goods markets. The use of paper currency and coins reduces transaction costs by allowing corn sellers to turn their corn into cash, which is easier and cheaper to carry with them as they seek out sellers of the goods they wish to purchase. Transaction costs associated with goods and labor market transactions often fall further when transactions are mediated by the banking system. When workers receive their pay in the form of checks or direct deposits into bank accounts, they do not have to expose themselves to risk by carrying cash on the street, and they can pay rent or pay for public utilities by sending checks in the mail or texting on a mobile phone rather than by traveling to pay the landlord in person. By reducing transaction costs, this encourages the expansion of markets, contributing to development through the channels examined in Chapter 8.

10.3B Financial markets in developing countries

In light of the important roles financial markets can play in encouraging growth and poverty reduction, it is troubling to observe that:

> Financial markets in developing countries, as compared to financial markets in developed countries, serve smaller fractions of the population, especially among the poor, and appear less capable of fulfilling their developmental functions.

Formal financial intermediaries serve much smaller fractions of the population in developing countries. Commercial and state-owned development banks are the primary providers of most formal financial services in developing countries, where stock and bond markets tend to be quite small, and even formal banking services reach much smaller fractions of the populations. According to Honohan (2008), the percentage of the adult population holding any kind of account (checking, savings, or loan) with a bank or other formal financial intermediary (such as a credit union or a registered microfinance institution), is more than 90 percent in most developed countries but lower than 50 percent and as low as 10 percent in developing countries.

Use of formal financial services is especially low among the poor in developing countries. Solo and Manroth's (2006) household survey of Bogota, Colombia, where financial services reach more households than in many developing areas, reveals that although 49 percent of all

☰ **Box 10.1** Rotating Savings and Credit Associations (ROSCAs)

In many places around the world, groups of neighbors and friends (often women) gather weekly to make small monetary contributions to a "pot," which is then given to a different member each week. In many cases, the order in which members receive the pot is determined by lottery. After every member has had a turn to use the pot, the group disbands or starts the process over. Called rotating savings and credit associations (ROSCAs) by social scientists, they are called *chit funds* in India, *susu* in Ghana, *hui* in China, and *tontines* in Senegal. ROSCAs are especially common in Africa and Asia, where often well over half of adults participate (Besley, 1995; Gugerty, 2007).

Participation in a ROSCA allows a member to turn a series of small saving installments into a larger lump sum through a combination of lending and borrowing. The contributions a member makes each week represent saving, or abstaining from consumption in order to free up income for other uses. The contributions she makes before receiving the pot are like small loans to the members who receive the pots. When she receives the pot, she is repaid by members who have already received the pot, while she also borrows from those who have not yet received it. Through the contributions she makes after receiving the pot, she repays those loans. This arrangement allows her to turn many small sums saved over time into a larger lump sum, with which she may undertake a small (indivisible) business investment, purchase a consumer durable, or obtain discounts on staple food items by buying in bulk. The arrangement has the added advantages of requiring no complicated accounting and of generating no stores of cash that must be protected from thieves.

Sometimes ROSCAs evolve into more complicated institutions, in which some funds are accumulated in a strong box or bank account. The group may use the accumulated funds to offer interest-bearing loans to members or nonmembers, thereby allowing members to earn a return on their savings. They may also use the fund to provide grants or interest-free loans to members struck by emergencies, thereby providing members with insurance.

---

adults use formal financial services, and 78 percent of adults in the top income decile use them, the rate of use is only 19 percent in the poorest income decile. Most households with formal financial accounts hold savings accounts or short-term consumer and business loans. Some kinds of formal financial services are nearly absent in developing countries, such as medium-term lending for home purchase or education and many forms of insurance.

Many households, even among the poor in developing countries, obtain financial services from informal sources. They obtain loans from moneylenders, friends and people with whom they have close business ties. They obtain savings services from neighborhood money guards and by participating in rotating savings and credit associations (see Box 10.1). They obtain some insurance through informal insurance arrangements, in which social norms lead neighbors who are doing relatively well to provide assistance to neighbors who are temporarily doing relatively poorly (see Chapter 12). Sometimes they obtain credit or insurance in ways that are tied to other transactions. For example, farmers might obtain credit from a food-processing company, which advances money to finance the purchase of planting season inputs and then deducts the cost of principal and interest when paying farmers for the crop at harvest. Tenants sometimes implicitly obtain credit from agricultural landlords, who collect rental payments only at harvest time. When they rent land under share tenancy agreements, tenants also implicitly obtain some insurance from landlords. Wage employees implicitly obtain credit and insurance from their employers, when they are hired under contracts that offer steady employment and pay in the face of fluctuating labor demand (as discussed in Chapter 9).

Informal financial services are often less attractive to clients or have more limited potential to promote development than formal financial services. Interest rates on loans from moneylenders are often very high and vary greatly across borrowers even within the same market (Banerjee and Duflo, 2010). When people hire money guards, they *pay* to save rather than collecting interest income on savings. While ROSCAs provide opportunities to save and borrow, they intermediate loanable funds only within small groups and thus facilitate only very limited flows of funds between savers and borrowers. Informal insurance arrangements protect people against only a limited class of risks and tend to fall apart when the need for insurance is greatest (again, see Chapter 12). The tendency to tie credit and insurance to tenancy, labor, or crop purchase agreements suggests that loanable funds might not flow freely toward the highest-return investments and that insurers might find it difficult to pool risks.

The multiplication and growth of **microfinance institutions** is changing the financial services landscape in some developing areas, especially among households that are moderately (but not very) poor (Helms, 2006). Many microfinance institutions offer small loans to poor or near-poor households, usually with the expectation that the loans will be used to expand or start small business endeavors, such as raising chickens, buying and selling used clothing, or purchasing equipment to expand a small furniture shop. Increasingly microfinance institutions also offer savings accounts or help catalyze the creation of savings groups similar to ROSCAs. The earliest microfinance providers were NGOs that provided their services on a not-for-profit basis with the aim of helping families move out of poverty. Many microfinance providers (including NGOs and for-profit financial institutions) now aim to earn profits, though only a fraction succeed in doing do, illustrating the difficulties that financial intermediaries seem to face when providing services to poor populations in developing countries. Furthermore, despite the rapid expansion of microfinance institutions over the last three decades, they still serve only a small fraction of the world's poor. We take a closer look at microfinance in Chapter 21.

We learned in section 10.3A that well-functioning financial markets have important roles to play in development. The evidence presented in this section suggests that financial markets might not, in fact, perform these roles very well in developing countries, especially among the poor. They deliver financial services to far fewer households, and the services they deliver are less attractive. The next several sections dig into potential explanations for poor financial market performance in developing countries.

10.3C Financial transaction costs

Just as high transfer costs can help explain the stunted nature of goods markets in developing countries (Chapter 8), so also high financial transaction costs can help explain the limited development of financial markets. In this section we point out that:

> In financial transactions, one party purchases a promise on which the other party may default. Parties to financial transactions (or their intermediaries) incur significant costs in their efforts to reduce the risk of default and, even so, experience costly defaults. These financial transaction costs are likely to be especially high in developing countries and for transactions involving poor clients.

Financial transactions are inherently risky because they involve the transfer of money today from a **principal** to an **agent** in exchange for the *promise* of a future payment by the agent to the principal. For example, savers (principals) lend money to borrowers (agents) in exchange for promises of future loan repayment with interest. Insurance clients pay premiums to insurers in exchange for the promise of future indemnity payments. Consumers place funds in checking accounts at banks against the promise that they may reclaim those funds whenever they wish.

These transactions are inherently risky for the principals because the agents might **default**, or fail to follow through on the promised payments. For example, investors could default on loans because their investments work out badly or because they simply refuse to repay. If all agents owned great wealth, and if legal and social institutions always allowed principals to claim full payment out of agents' wealth, default would be impossible. In practice, however, agents tend to have **limited liability** because their wealth is limited and because legal, social, or practical constraints prevent principals from extracting repayments that would force borrowers below minimally acceptable levels of consumption. Difficulties in forcing fulfillment of financial promises are especially great in developing countries, where formal legal institutions are weak, ownership rights to land and other assets are sometimes ill defined, and close-knit communities sometimes protect their own against outsiders attempting to claim repayment.

To reduce the inherent risk associated with financial transactions, principals and agents engage in costly information-gathering and trust-building activities. For example, lenders gather information about potential borrowers, seeking to identify trustworthy investors with solid investment plans. They might also monitor and supervise the borrower's investment activities. To guard against the borrower's fraudulent claims that repayment is impossible, the lender may gather information about the borrower's business performance and call on the courts or traditional institutions to enforce repayment. Lenders can also work at developing close relationships with borrowers, through which they may gather information more easily and motivate borrowers to repay. All these activities require time, expertise, and the collection of information. We'll give the name **supervision costs** to the costs of these information-gathering and trust-building activities.

Financial intermediaries probably reduce supervision costs significantly relative to the costs that borrowers and investors (or parties to other kinds of financial transaction) would have to bear if they carried out transactions without intermediation, because the intermediaries benefit from specialization and scale. Working with many savers but needing to screen each potential borrower only once, commercial banks can reduce the per-transaction cost of identifying good loan prospects. Their expertise and scale might allow them to reduce screening costs even further. By pooling risks, banks can offer savers low-risk returns without bearing much risk themselves. Insurance intermediaries are similarly advantaged relative to individuals for arranging insurance transactions.

Despite all their advantages, financial intermediaries nonetheless incur significant operating costs because they must devote time, energy, computers, buildings and vehicles to screening, monitoring, supervising, and enforcing repayments from borrowers, courting savers, and administering insurance. The costs are especially high in developing countries, where poor transport and communication infrastructure increases the cost of interacting with clients, and weak legal institutions increase the cost and difficulty of enforcing contracts.

The costs of carrying out financial transactions are even higher when providing financial services to poorer clients. The amounts the poor wish to borrow, save, or insure are small. Small transaction sizes increase supervision costs on a per-peso (of borrowed funds) basis, because screening, monitoring, and enforcement costs tend to be incurred on a per-client basis, regardless of how much they borrow, save, or insure. The smaller the loan each borrower takes out, the higher the ratio of fixed transaction costs to pesos of financial transaction. In addition, the poor tend to be located in difficult-to-reach places and to lack the education and connectivity required for streamlined written or electronic communication.

Cull et al. (2009) offer a useful window into the magnitude of these intermediation costs in developing countries. They examine financial data for a large number of for-profit and not-for-profit microfinance institutions, which specialize in making loans to low-income borrowers in developing countries. Some of these institutions are officially chartered as banks and tend to lend to borrowers who are only moderately poor or above the poverty line (though not very affluent). For them, the median ratio of operating cost to the value of their loan portfolio is 0.11. For those registered as nonbank financial institutions, who lend to somewhat poorer clients, the median ratio is 0.16, and for those registered as nongovernmental organizations, who lend to an even poorer population (though still not the very poorest), the median ratio is 0.21. These ratios imply operating costs of 11 to 21 cents per year per dollar of lending. For many institutions, operating costs are even higher than this and certainly much higher than the one to three cents per dollar for affluent clients in developed countries.

Lenders who wish to break even or earn profits must charge interest rates on loans that cover the cost of funds and costs associated with default as well as their supervision costs. For commercial banks the **cost of funds** is the interest rate they must pay to savers for the use of their funds plus any costs of seeking out savers and providing savings services. For other formal lenders the cost of funds is the interest rate at which they may borrow from private capital markets. For moneylenders making loans out of their own accumulated savings, the cost of funds is the rate of return on those savings that they forgo by not investing them in their next best use.

To see how defaults, the cost of funds, and supervision costs enter into the calculation of break-even interest rates on loans, consider bankers who must pay an interest rate of r^d per peso deposited by savers, who incur supervision costs of s per peso of funds borrowed from savers (payable at the end of the loan period), and who borrow from savers and lend to investors a total volume V in pesos. Suppose for simplicity that they expect a fraction d of borrowers to enter into complete default (paying back neither principal nor interest) and a fraction $(1-d)$ to repay in full with interest. To break even they must charge a borrowing rate r^b such that their receipts from borrowers who do repay, $V(1+r^b)(1-d)$, are at least as great as the sum they need to cover supervision costs and repayments to savers, $V(1+r^d+s)$. Rearranging this inequality, we find that breaking even requires that

$$r^b > (r^d + s + d)/(1 - d) \qquad (10.23)$$

The break-even level of r^b is greater than r^d, and the gap between the break-even lending rate and the deposit rate rises as s rises (holding d constant) and as d rises (holding s constant). The gap between the borrowing rate and deposit rate is called the **interest rate spread**. We use the term **financial transaction costs** to encompass both supervision costs and costs associated with default.

The high interest rates often charged by informal lenders, which in earlier decades were interpreted as evidence of monopoly power in small local credit markets, are now thought by many to reflect high financial transaction costs, and especially high supervision costs. Aleem (1990) studied informal money lending in a set of 16 villages near the market town of Chambar in Sind, Pakistan. According to data gathered from informal borrowers, interest rates charged by moneylenders were indeed high, averaging 79 percent per year, but average *costs* of lending were just as high. The costs included the costs of time and transportation devoted to screening potential borrowers, the administration of small trial loans, the costs of pursuing payments from delinquent borrowers, and the cost of funds. Though outright default was rare, the moneylenders also had to deal with high rates of late payments, often waiving some interest payments.

As financial transaction costs rise, financial markets become less successful in fulfilling their developmental functions. Higher financial transaction costs imply higher interest rate spreads. Higher spreads tend to raise the rates charged to borrowers and reduce the rates paid to savers, reducing the quantities deposited and borrowed, thereby reducing the rate of investment (see discussion question 4). Financial transaction costs probably reduce the average return on investment as well, by inducing savers to lend to relatives and close business associates (with whom financial transaction costs are lower), or to invest in their own low-return projects, rather than lending to the investors with the highest-return investment projects (see problem 2). Financial transaction costs prevent insurance markets from fulfilling their developmental functions in similar fashion.

10.3D Asymmetric information and financial market failures

Even after financial transaction costs have been paid, financial markets remain characterized by **asymmetric information**. Information is "asymmetric" in the sense that agents know more about their circumstances and character than their principals do. For example, borrowers know more about the risk and expected return of their investment projects, their work effort and honesty, and their actual investment returns than lenders know. Similarly, bankers know more about the risks they are taking with savers' funds than savers know.

We will see that:

Asymmetric information can cause financial markets to fail in ways that lead to credit rationing or missing credit and insurance markets.

Credit is rationed when some agents are unable to obtain as much credit as they would like at the going interest rate, or are unable to borrow at all, even in equilibrium. The extent of **credit**

rationing can differ across diverse credit markets distinguished by loan duration, type of borrower, and location. Insurance or credit markets are **missing** when credit or insurance tailored to specific loan uses or risks are simply unavailable for some types of clients and in some locations. In this section we concentrate primarily on how asymmetric information can lead to rationing in credit markets or to missing credit markets, but we mention its implications for insurance markets briefly at the end.

Asymmetric information problems can interfere with good credit market functioning by creating a tendency for default rates to rise when lenders raise the interest rates they charge on loans. When interest rates and default rates are linked in this way (for reasons we explain below), lenders might find it unprofitable to raise interest rates, even when the demand for loans exceeds the supply at current interest rates, because higher default rates would raise *costs* more than the higher interest rates would raise *revenue*. Unable to raise the interest rate they charge, they are also unable to raise the interest rate they pay to raise funds from savers, and the funds they are able to raise remain fewer than the funds demanded. The result is credit rationing: Some people who want credit at the current interest rate don't get it or get less than they wish. In extreme cases, lenders are unable to find *any* interest rate at which they may lend profitably, and the result is a missing credit market: no lending at all. In what follows we examine two mechanisms through which asymmetric information may create a tendency for default rates to increase as the interest rate charged for loans rises. They are known as *adverse selection* and *moral hazard*.

Adverse selection, missing credit markets, and credit rationing

Adverse selection arises when potential borrowers differ in their inherent default probabilities and when borrowers know their default probabilities but lenders do not. Unable to distinguish better risks (i.e., borrowers who are inherently more likely to repay their loans) from worse risks within a market, lenders must charge identical interest rates to all borrowers in that market. We will show that:

> In credit markets characterized by adverse selection, in which some borrowers are better risks than others, the better risks might drop out of the market more rapidly than the worse risks as interest rates rise. As a result, average default rates among the borrowers who remain in the market might rise as interest rates rise.

To see why rising interest rates can cause better risks to drop out of the market even while worse risks stay in, let's consider just two borrowers: a safe borrower with a riskless investment project, who repays in any state of the world, and a risky borrower with a risky investment project, who has a significant probability of defaulting. Only two states of the world—good and bad—are possible, and each occurs with probability 0.5. The returns the borrowers enjoy in good and bad states are distributed this way:

State of the World	Bad	Good
Safe borrower	R	R
Risky borrower	$R - e$	$R + e$

The risky borrower's project involves higher risk but the same expected return (R) as the safe borrower's project. Lenders cannot distinguish between safe and risky borrowers, so both are offered the same interest rate r^b. We assume that each borrower requires a loan of size L. We also assume that $R - e < L(1 + r^b) < R$, so that the safe borrower earns enough to repay the loan with interest in either state of the world, but the risky borrower can repay in full only in the good state. We assume that both borrowers are honest, in the sense that they repay in full whenever their investment returns are high enough to cover loan principal and interest. We capture limited liability in a simple way by assuming that in the bad state of the world the lender has no way of forcing the risky borrower to pay back more than some fixed amount P, which is less than the borrower's low return $(R - e)$. This implies that no matter what interest rate a lender charges, he can expect to extract only the fixed amount P from a risky borrower in the bad state of the world.

For simplicity we assume that the borrowers are risk neutral. This means that they undertake investment as long as the expected profit on investment is positive, where the expected profit is equal to the expected value of the return on the investment net of any loan payments. In either state of the world, the safe borrower earns R and must pay back $L(1 + r^b)$; thus her expected profit from taking out a loan and undertaking the investment project is

$$E^s = R - L(1 + r^b) \qquad (10.24)$$

The maximum interest rate at which it pays for the safe borrower to borrow and invest is the rate at which this expected profit falls to zero: $r^s = R/L - 1$. For the risky borrower the expected profit is

$$E^r = 0.5(R - e - P) + 0.5(R + e - L(1 + r^b)) = R - 0.5(P + L(1 + r^b)) \qquad (10.25)$$

The maximum interest rate at which this expected profit is positive is $r^r = (2R - P)/L - 1$. This is greater than the maximum interest rate at which the safe borrower would borrow, as long as $2R - P > R$, and we know this is true because $R > P$ by definition. Thus the risky borrower is willing to borrow at higher interest rates than the safe borrower, and an increase in interest rate from just below r^s to just above it would cause the safe borrower to drop out of the market while the risky borrower remains in.

We gain insight into this result by looking more closely at equations 10.24 and 10.25. We see that both borrowers compare their investment projects' identical expected returns (R) to the expected value of loan repayments, but that the risky borrower faces a lower expected loan repayment, $0.5(P + L(1 + r^b))$, than does the safe borrower (whose expected repayment is $L(1 + r^b)$), because he has a lower probability of repaying in full. Furthermore, as the interest rate rises, the expected cost of borrowing and investing rises faster for the safe borrower, who pays interest in both states of the world, than for the risky borrower, who expects to repay only half the time. Thus as the interest rate rises, the safe borrower's incentive to borrow and invest diminishes more rapidly than the risky borrower's. More generally, when the market is filled with a variety of borrowers facing different project risks, it is possible that first the safest borrowers and then riskier borrowers drop out of the market, and that the average default rate among those who remain in the market rises steadily, as the interest rate rises.

In the extreme:

> Adverse selection can cause a valuable credit market to disappear. Under less-extreme circumstances, adverse selection might lead to credit rationing.

A market may be developmentally valuable in the sense that lenders could break even or earn profits in the market if they could distinguish safe from risky borrowers and lend only to safe borrowers, and such lending would allow safe borrowers to undertake valuable investments. More specifically, if lenders charged some low interest rate r^l, safe borrowers would wish to borrow, and if lenders could limit their lending to safe borrowers the default rate would remain low enough that charging r^l would be sufficient to cover all the costs of lending. When lenders cannot distinguish safe from risky borrowers, however, both safe *and* risky borrowers would come forward to accept loans at the low rate r^l. As a result of this *adverse selection* of risky borrowers into the market, the market default rate would exceed the default rate among safe borrowers alone. Facing this higher default rate, lenders might be unable to cover costs by charging only r^l. Lenders might try raising the interest rate to cover the higher default costs, but in so doing they could drive safe borrowers out of the market, raising the average default rate even further. The interest rates required to cover the very high default rates of risky borrowers alone may be so high that even risky borrowers leave the market. In such cases lenders find it unprofitable to lend at any rate, and the market goes missing.

Under less extreme circumstances, lenders may be able to find a moderately low interest rate at which both safe and risky borrowers are willing to borrow and at which they can cover the costs of supervision and moderate default. They may nonetheless be unable to raise the interest rate profitably, despite an excess demand for loans, because the increase in the default risk (as safe borrowers drop out) would more than compensate for the increased interest revenue on loans that are repaid (see problem 5). Able to charge only low interest rates, lenders would also be able to pay only low interest rates to savers. At low interest rates, savers may be willing to save too little to meet all demand for loans at the low interest rates.[5] The result is credit rationing: Some profitable and safe investment projects lack financing and are not undertaken.

Moral hazard and credit market failures

Moral hazard arises when borrowers can improve their repayment probabilities by working harder (or being more honest) but lenders cannot force them to work hard. Lenders may be unable to enforce hard work either because they cannot observe the borrowers' work effort or because legal and social institutions do not allow them to punish borrowers for failing to work hard. Logic suggests that:

> In credit markets characterized by moral hazard, increases in interest rates can reduce borrowers' incentives to work hard, raising their default rates.

To see why, consider a borrower who can increase his investment project's expected return and reduce its risk by working hard. More specifically, this table indicates how his investment project would pay off if he works hard and if he shirks (i.e., fails to work hard), in two states of the world, which each occur with probability 0.5:

State of the World	Bad	Good
If he works hard	R	R
If he shirks	0	R

Working hard allows him to head off problems and prevent poor returns in the bad state of the world. Suppose this borrower is required to pay an interest rate of r^b and requires a loan of size L, which is less than $R/(1+r^b)$, so that the borrower is able to repay in full with interest when he reaps the return R. Suppose further that the reduction in utility he experiences from working hard is equivalent to a cost of C pesos in either state of the world. As a result of limited liability, he can be required to pay back no more than the return he earns on his investment. He thus repays in full with interest when his return is R, but he repays 0 when his return is 0. This

---

[5] The quantity of loans that banks are able to offer profitably may rise with the interest rate they charge on loans for two reasons. As indicated in the text, higher interest rates on loans allow them to pay higher interest rates on savings accounts, and higher interest rates on savings can attract more savings into the banks. Even if bankers have little capacity to raise the volume of savings by offering higher interest rates on saving, however, they may be able to raise the volume of saving by engaging in higher-cost activities—such as marketing campaigns or use of mobile banking facilities—that draw more funds into the banks without raising the rates offered to savers.

implies that he repays in both good and bad states of the world if he works hard, but he repays only in the good state if he shirks.

For simplicity we again assume that the borrower is risk neutral and invests as long as the expected profit from investing is positive. He chooses to work hard only if his expected profit when working hard exceeds his expected profit when he shirks. His expected profit when he borrows, invests, and works hard is

$$P^w = R - C - L(1 + r^b) \tag{10.26}$$

His expected profit if he borrows, invests, and shirks is

$$P^s = 0.5(R - L(1 + r^b)) \tag{10.27}$$

As long as $(R - C)/L - 1 > r^b$, both P^w and P^s are positive, and it pays to borrow and invest whether he plans to work hard or shirk. The net increase in expected profit associated with working hard is

$$P^w - P^s = 0.5(R - L(1 + r^b)) - C \tag{10.28}$$

where the first term on the right side is the increase in expected profits derived from working hard and the second term C is the cost of working hard. As the interest rate rises, the benefit to working hard, $0.5(R - L(1 + r^b))$, shrinks while the cost C remains constant, diminishing the incentive to work hard. When the interest rate rises high enough, $(r^b > ((R - 2C)/L) - 1)$, the borrower has no incentive to work hard, even though he still finds it profitable to borrow, invest, and shirk. Again, this generates a tendency for default rates to rise as interest rates rise, creating the potential for both credit rationing and missing credit markets.

Collateral and connections in credit markets

In some markets, lenders manage to mitigate asymmetric information problems by requiring borrowers to post **collateral**. When borrowers use assets such as vehicles, jewelry, or business equipment as collateral, they pledge to relinquish the assets to the lender in the event of default. When borrowers own such assets, and where legal and social institutions allow lenders to claim the assets in the case of default, the use of collateral reduces lenders' concerns about default in two ways. First, when borrowers post collateral, lenders are able to liquidate the assets and obtain some repayment even when borrowers default. Second, borrowers who have posted collateral have more to lose if they default; thus borrowers who post collateral have stronger incentives to make prudent choices and to work hard and repay. For collateral to serve these functions, the quantity of collateral must be large enough relative to the loan size to offer the lender significant security. Thus:

> In markets where lenders base lending on collateral, they tend to offer only small loans to borrowers with few assets to offer as collateral. Potential investors with no assets to offer as collateral are unable to borrow at all in such markets.

Another way lenders sometimes avoid the problems of asymmetric information is by lending only to relatives or close business associates. Lenders might direct their loans to close associates even when investment projects faced by other potential borrowers promise higher expected returns, because the transaction costs and information asymmetries that arise when working with more distant borrowers are too great.

Asymmetric information in insurance markets

Insurance markets might fail, too. As a result of adverse selection on the part of insurance buyers, insurance sellers may expect per-client indemnity payouts to increase as premiums rise. For example, consider the market for health insurance contracts, which promise to pay the buyers indemnities to cover health care costs if they are hit by illness or injury that requires hospitalization. Adverse selection arises when potential health insurance buyers differ in their inherent risks of illness or injury, and the buyers know their health risk status while insurers do not. The expected benefits of having an insurance contract are higher for those with greater health risks than for others. Thus as premiums rise, healthier individuals who are less likely to require indemnities leave the market while worse risks stay in, raising the expected level of indemnity payments per buyer. Unfortunately:

> This connection between premium rates and the average cost of providing insurance may cause insurance markets to go missing just as the connection between interest rates and default rates may cause credit markets to go missing.

Empirical evidence on asymmetric information

Direct evidence on the empirical importance of asymmetric information in financial markets is difficult to obtain. Box 10.2 describes a unique experiment designed specifically to study the effects of interest rates on loan default probabilities arising through adverse selection and moral hazard. Despite the limited direct evidence, many researchers suspect that asymmetric information problems help explain why some groups are unable to obtain formal credit and insurance.

10.3E Psychological and social barriers to saving

Financial markets in developing countries might fall short of fulfilling their developmental potential not only as a result of high financial transaction costs and asymmetric information problems but also because the social and psychological barriers to saving mentioned earlier can shrink the volume of funds flowing into the market for loanable funds at any interest rate. Social barriers include the difficulty of protecting savings from the demands of neighbors and spouses. Present bias might constitute a psychological barrier.

These social and psychological phenomena might help explain several empirical puzzles related to financial markets in developing countries. First, they might help explain why ROSCA participation is so widespread, even though ROSCAs offer savers no interest on their savings and expose them to significant risk of default by other group members. ROSCA participants might simply recognize that they "can't save alone" and value the discipline provided by group pressure (Gugerty, 2007). Similarly, social and psychological barriers might help explain the existence of money collectors, whom customers pay to collect deposits from them on a daily basis and then return the collected lump sum—less their fee—at the end of each month.

Finally, these social and psychological barriers might help explain why we do not see more saving up to make lucrative investments among people who lack access to credit. Even if a project requires a large initial investment, which is too large to undertake by saving out of current income alone, and for which credit is not available, potential investors could save up over several periods to accumulate large enough sums. Many investments, furthermore, can be undertaken in small increments and still generate high returns. For example, by saving up a little each day vegetable vendors could build up working capital of their own with which to purchase vegetables for sale each morning, reducing their dependence on the very costly loans they instead take out each day (Karlan and Morduch, 2010). The social and psychological phenomena discussed here might help explain why such saving is difficult. (For an experiment attempting to increase saving rates by helping participants counter the social and psychological barriers, see Box 22.2.)

☰ **Box 10.2** Searching for Evidence of Adverse Selection and Moral Hazard in Credit Markets

Dean Karlan and Jonathan Zinman (2009) collaborated on a study of asymmetric information and default rates with a South African lender that specializes in high-interest, short-term, noncollateralized lending of consumer credit to moderately poor workers. They identified 57,533 former clients with good repayment histories to which the lender sent letters offering preapproved loans at specified interest rates. These former clients were randomly divided into groups receiving higher and lower interest rate offers. Any clients coming forward were processed for loans. The clients responding to the higher interest rate offers were further divided into multiple groups, one receiving loans at the initial high offer and the others receiving loans at unexpected lower interest rates. All groups of borrowers were further divided randomly into two, with one group being promised future loans at attractive interest rates (provided they pay off the current loan) and the other receiving no such promise regarding future loans. To facilitate explanation of how the sample design allows the authors to draw inferences about adverse selection and moral hazard, a simplified version of it is shown in the following figure. (The figure includes only "high" and "low" interest rates, but the experiment in fact included many interest rates over a range.)

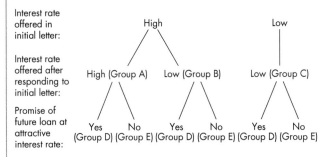

The study was designed to shed light on three ways alterations in credit contracts might lead to changes in default rates. First, default rates might rise when interest rates are increased because better risks drop out of the market, leaving a riskier set of clients in the borrowing pool (adverse selection). The study assesses this effect by comparing rates of

repayment problems between groups B and C. Both groups were ultimately given loans at the same (lower) interest rate, and thus they faced the same repayment challenges, but group B self-selected into participation in response to a higher interest rate offer than was made to group C. If adverse selection is significant, repayment problems should be more prevalent in the group that responded to the higher interest rate offer (Group B) than to the lower interest rate offer (Group C).

Second, default rates might rise when interest rates are increased because higher interest rates imply higher repayment burdens. Raising the repayment burden can increase default rates through two channels: reducing borrowers' diligence (moral hazard), and simply making it harder to cover the full repayment out of income (even if borrowers always work hard). The study assesses the overall repayment burden effect (not distinguishing the two channels) by comparing repayment performance for Groups A and B, which were selected in identical fashion but then allowed to borrow at different rates. If a higher repayment burden increases default rates, we should see higher repayment problems in Group A than in Group B.

Third, default rates might be reduced through the provision of a *dynamic incentive*, or a promise of access to future loans at attractive interest rates on the condition of good repayment performance on the current loan. The study assesses this effect by comparing Groups D to Groups E. Poorer performance in the absence of the dynamic incentive (Groups E) would indicate moral hazard.

The authors find strong evidence for moral hazard that is reduced through the use of dynamic incentives. Clients assigned dynamic incentives defaulted 13 to 21 percent less than the mean. The authors find weaker evidence of adverse selection and increased repayment burden problems.

The Karlan and Zinman study does not rule out the possibility that adverse selection and moral hazard effects might be larger in other contexts. The scope for adverse selection in their study was probably limited because initial loan offers went out only to the already-select group of former clients with good repayment histories. The scope for moral hazard might also have been smaller in this context, because the loans were made to people with steady wage jobs (for the purposes of financing consumption) rather than to small business owners for business investment.

10.3F **Financial constraints on investment**

When markets for loanable funds and insurance are imperfect in some of the ways just examined, some investors who would undertake investments if financial markets worked well might be prevented from investing by financial constraints of two sorts: liquidity constraints and insurance constraints. A potential investor is **liquidity constrained** when she would undertake a high-return investment if credit markets were free of problems, but she does not undertake the investment because credit market frictions and imperfections limit her access to credit, and she also lacks adequate income and savings to self-finance the investment. Such a person is eager to invest and would invest if given enough additional *liquidity*—whether in the form of credit, income, or wealth—to finance the investment. A potential investor is **insurance constrained** when she would undertake the investment if insurance markets were free of information problems, but she does not undertake the investment because she cannot obtain appropriate insurance or can obtain it only at a premium rate that is too high. Such a person would invest if given adequate access to appropriate insurance.

Financial constraints are of interest to development analysts because they raise the possibility that policymakers could encourage some high-return investments at relatively low cost simply by providing constrained potential investors with credit or insurance. Given that private lenders and insurers are unable to lend profitably to liquidity- or insurance-constrained investors as a result of financial market problems, governments and NGOs are also unlikely to cover all costs of providing these financial services. Even so, the cost of subsidizing loans or insurance may be much lower than the cost of other interventions with similar impacts on investment, such as government or NGO efforts to undertake the investments entirely on their own account.

Furthermore, because financial constraints are likely to be especially important for the poor, policies designed to overcome them might be especially useful for helping the poor escape poverty. Indeed, liquidity and insurance constraints might keep poor households stuck in **poverty traps**, with low incomes that remain unchanged even as nonpoor households around them invest and enjoy ongoing income growth. If high-return investments cannot be undertaken at very small scale, then the nonpoor who have plenty of collateral and financing may be able to undertake high-return investments while the liquidity-constrained poor find only low-return investments feasible. The poor might furthermore find that the low returns do not outweigh their financing costs and thus that it does not pay to invest at all. In light of these possibilities, researchers take great interest in searching for empirical evidence of liquidity and insurance constraints.

Empirical evidence on liquidity and insurance constraints remains fragmentary, but:

> A growing body of research is consistent with the existence of financial constraints that inhibit investment, especially among the poor.

A first arena in which researchers have searched for evidence of financial constraints on investment is among small- and medium-sized businesses. Many firms, especially small ones, complain that lack of access to credit prevents them from investing and growing. For example, Beck et al. (2005) survey more than 4,000 firms with at least five employees in 54 countries and find widespread reports that lack of adequate financing constrains their growth. Although this suggests liquidity constraints, it is not definitive evidence, because the firms may also be prevented from investing profitably by many other factors. It is thus not certain that injections of liquidity would expand their investment.

Recent experimental studies offer stronger evidence of liquidity constraints among small self-employment enterprises in Sri Lanka and Mexico. de Mel et al. (2008) provided grants worth $100 or $200 to randomly selected firms within a panel of 385 small self-employment enterprises in Sri Lanka. The median value of the enterprises' initial capital was less than $200. They found large average effects of the grants on profits, implying a rate of return on capital of at least 5 percent per month or more than 60 percent per year. This suggests that entrepreneurs should have found it profitable to borrow for investment even at interest rates well above local market rates. Liquidity constraints offer one potential explanation for their lack of investment before the study. When asked why they had not expanded their businesses before, most pointed to lack of financing as a significant constraint. The high variance in returns across firms suggests that the entrepreneurs might also perceive the investments as very risky; thus lack of insurance may have discouraged their investment. McKenzie and Woodruff (2008) performed a similar experiment among male-owned retail enterprises in Mexico, and they found even higher average rates of return. Again, the returns were heterogeneous, suggesting that financial constraints might have been binding for some entrepreneurs with high-return investment prospects, whereas they were irrelevant to other entrepreneurs facing only much lower returns on investments.

A second arena in which researchers have searched for evidence of liquidity constraints on investment is among families for whom the education of their children represents a significant investment. Even when school fees are low or zero, families must cover many costs of sending children to school, including the costs of textbooks and uniforms and the opportunity cost of any necessary reduction in the child's contribution to family income. In the face of such costs, the greater liquidity constraints faced by poorer families might explain why they are less likely to send their children to school. Edmonds (2004) finds evidence of liquidity constraints in an analysis of schooling decisions in South Africa. He finds that child labor falls and child schooling rises as soon as grandparents in their households start receiving payments from South Africa's old age pension program. Edmonds argues that because households knew in advance that they would receive the benefits, the only feature of household circumstances that changed upon receipt of the benefit was the household's liquidity.

Evidence on the roles of risk and missing insurance in constraining investment is still rather scarce, but it appears to confirm the potential usefulness of relaxing insurance constraints. Risk and vulnerability are certainly important features of life in developing countries, especially in rural areas, and evidence suggests that risk aversion is important among farmers, especially poor farmers (Dercon, 2005). Rosenzweig and Binswanger (1993) show that where Indian farmers face more variable rainfall, and thus where the risk attached to higher-productivity agricultural practices is greater, average incomes are lower, especially for poor farmers, suggesting that greater risk makes poor farmers more reluctant to invest in higher-productivity practices. In a similar vein, Morduch (1993) splits a sample of Indian farmers into two groups on the basis of their likely ability to smooth consumption if hit by crop failure, and he finds that the group for which such consumption smoothing would be more difficult is significantly less likely to adopt new higher-yielding seed varieties. In a field experiment, Karlan et al. (2012) find that grants of crop insurance (involving contracts that pay out indemnities when official measures of local rainfall are outside acceptable ranges) led Ghanaian farmers to undertake significantly more agricultural investment and to make riskier production choices.

10.3G Policy responses

We have seen that financial market weaknesses can inhibit growth and reinforce poverty in developing countries. In this section we point out how:

> Awareness of financial market imperfections, and of the potential for liquidity and insurance constraints to inhibit investment, now informs policy design and evaluation in many arenas.

In what follows we briefly discuss the relevance of financial market imperfections to policies of several types.

Prudential regulation of formal financial services providers

We have seen that financial market imperfections arise because the information required to support financial transactions is costly and difficult to obtain. This suggests that improvement in information flows might improve the performance of financial markets. This basic intuition underlies two classes of policies toward financial markets. The first involves efforts to enhance the performance of the commercial banking system through system-wide information-gathering and regulatory activities. For example, governments might assist bankers in assessing lending risks by encouraging the collection and dissemination of credit history information. They might also improve the flow of information between banks and savers who deposit their savings in banks. Savers might be reluctant to place their savings in banks, because they lack the expertise or scale to monitor banks' lending practices. Regulators are in a better position to audit banks' lending practices. They might use this capacity to impose regulations that prevent banks from taking on too much risk and then encourage savers to place deposits in regulated banks by providing them with deposit insurance. The hope is that by mitigating the effects of information problems regulators might expand commercial bank lending, thereby relaxing liquidity constraints for many potential investors.

Microfinance

The second class of financial market interventions involves the creation of microfinance institutions (MFIs). MFIs provide financial services to a poorer clientele than is typically served by commercial banks, using technologies for gathering information and relating to clients that are quite different from those employed by traditional commercial banks. MFIs require their loan officers to meet more frequently with their clients and to visit borrowers' homes and workplaces (rather than requiring borrowers to visit their offices). They require repayments that are more frequent and that begin sooner after the initiation of the loan. Sometimes they require borrowers to form groups that assume joint liability for the repayment of loans to any member. Many microfinance enthusiasts hope that these new technologies will (at least eventually) reduce supervision costs enough that they will be able to provide financial services to the poor while covering costs, even when commercial banks find this impossible. We take a close look at microfinance interventions in Chapter 21.

Broader policy implications

The potential significance of liquidity and insurance constraints expands the range of instruments that policymakers should consider in many policy areas. If poor households are prevented from sending their children to school by liquidity constraints, then policymakers seeking to increase school enrollment should consider reducing school fees and providing scholarships, in addition to building more schools. Because liquidity constraints are expected to be more serious among the poor, policymakers might wish to differentiate fees and scholarship offers depending on households' poverty status. Furthermore, liquidity constraints suggest that private sector schools might be absent not because private sector *supply* is lacking but because financing constraints prevent households from effectively *demanding* education. If this is the case, then it may be possible to expand school enrollment by providing households with loans or grants to use in purchasing education services from private providers.

Similarly, if families are prevented by insurance constraints from obtaining health care when ill, then private health care facilities may be absent in some populations not because supply is fundamentally lacking but because insurance constraints prevent households from effectively demanding health care. Households may be unable to pay the high costs of health care at time of need, but they may be willing to pay yearly premiums in exchange for the promise of help in paying health care bills when needed. If this is the case, then it may be possible to expand health care use not only by building government health care facilities and offering low-cost services but also by providing households with insurance arrangements that allow them to purchase health care from private providers (Chapter 22).

The potential importance of financial constraints also casts new light on safety net programs, such as targeted transfer and workfare programs (Chapters 15 and 16), which traditionally were considered useful "merely" for reducing poverty and vulnerability but not for promoting growth. By providing the poor with cash, such programs might relax liquidity constraints, allowing recipients to undertake investments that were previously infeasible. In addition, if safety net programs stand ready to prop up investors' incomes should their investments experience bad shocks, they might also stimulate investment by providing investors with implicit insurance. Thus safety net policies might not only reduce poverty and vulnerability but also contribute to investment and growth. We return to many of these issues in Chapters 15 through 22.

REFERENCES

Aleem, Irfan. "Imperfect Information, Screening, and the Costs of Informal Lending: A Study of a Rural Credit Market in Pakistan." *World Bank Economic Review* 4(3): 329–349, 1990. doi:10.1093/wber/4.3.329

Ashraf, Nava, Dean Karlan, and Wesley Yin. "Tying Odysseus to the Mast: Evidence from a Commitment Savings Product in the Philippines." *The Quarterly Journal of Economics* 121(2): 635–672, 2006. doi:10.1162/qjec.2006.121.2.635

Banerjee, Abhijit V., and Esther Duflo. "Giving Credit Where It Is Due." *Journal of Economic Perspectives* 24(3): 61–80, 2010. doi:10.1257/jep.24.3.61

Beck, Thorsten, Asli Demirgüç-Kunt, and Vojislav Maksimovic. "Financial and Legal Constraints to Growth: Does Firm Size Matter?" *The Journal of Finance* 60(1): 137–177, 2005. doi:10.1111/j.1540-6261.2005.00727.x

Besley, Timothy. "Savings, Credit and Insurance." In Jere Behrman and T.N. Srinivasan (eds.). *Handbook of Development Economics*, Volume III, Part A. Amsterdam: Elsevier, 1995, pp. 2123–2207. doi: 10.1016/S1573-4471(05)80008-7

Conley, Timothy G., and Christopher R. Udry. "Learning about a New Technology: Pineapple in Ghana." *American Economic Review* 100(1): 35–69, 2010. doi:10.1257/aer.100.1.35

Cull, Robert, Asli Demirgüç-Kunt, and Jonathan Morduch. "Microfinance Meets the Market." *Journal of Economic Perspectives* 23(1): 167–192, 2009. doi:10.1257/jep.23.1.167

de Mel, Suresh, David McKenzie, and Christopher Woodruff. "Returns to Capital in Microenterprises: Evidence from a Field Experiment." *Quarterly Journal of Economics* 123(4): 1329–1372, 2008. doi:10.1162/qjec.2008.123.issue-4

Dercon, Stefan. "Risk, Poverty and Vulnerability in Africa." *Journal of African Economies* 14(4): 483–488, 2005. doi:10.1093/jae/eji023

Dercon, Stefan, and Luc Christiaensen. "Consumption Risk, Technology Adoption and Poverty Traps: Evidence from Ethiopia." *Journal of Development Economics* 96(2): 159–173, 2011. doi:10.1016/j.jdeveco.2010.08.003

Duflo, Esther, Michael Kremer, and Jonathan Robinson. "How High Are Rates of Return to Fertilizer? Evidence from Field Experiments in Kenya." *American Economic Review* 98(2): 482–488, 2008. doi:10.1257/aer.98.2.482

Duflo, Esther, Michael Kremer, and Jonathan Robinson. "Nudging Farmers to Use Fertilizer: Theory and Experimental Evidence from Kenya." *American Economic Review* 101(6): 2350–2390, 2011. doi:10.1257/aer.101.6.2350

Edmonds, Eric V. "Does Illiquidity Alter Child Labor and Schooling Decisions? Evidence from Household Responses to Anticipated Cash Transfers in South Africa." NBER Working Paper No. 10265. Cambridge, Mass.: National Bureau of Economic Research, 2004. http://www.nber.org/papers/w10265

Frederick, Shane, George Loewenstein, and Ted O'Donoghue. "Time Discounting and Time Preference: A Critical Review." *Journal of Economic Literature* 40(2): 351–401, 2002. doi:10.1257/002205102320161311

Gugerty, Mary Kay. "You Can't Save Alone: Commitment in Rotating Savings and Credit Associations in Kenya." *Economic Development and Cultural Change* 55(2): 251–282, 2007. doi:10.1086/edcc.2007.55.issue-2

Helms, Brigit (ed.). *Access for All: Building Inclusive Financial Systems.* Washington, D.C.: World Bank, 2006. http://go.worldbank.org/AO9P9ZA220

Honohan, Patrick. "Household Financial Assets in the Process of Development." In James B. Davies (ed.). *Personal Wealth from a Global Perspective.* New York: Oxford University Press, 2008, pp. 271–292.

Karlan, Dean, and Jonathan Zinman. "Observing Unobservables: Identifying Information Asymmetries with a Consumer Credit Field Experiment." *Econometrica* 77(6): 1993–2008, 2009. doi: 10.3982/ecta5781

Karlan, Dean, and Jonathan Morduch. "Access to Finance." In Dani Rodrik and Mark Rosenzweig (eds.). *Handbook of Development Economics*, Volume 5. Amsterdam: Elsevier, 2010, pp. 4703–4784. doi: 10.1016/b978-0-444-52944-2.00009-4

Karlan, Dean, Robert Osei, Isaac Osei-Akoto, and Christopher Udry. "Agricultural Decisions after Relaxing Credit and Risk Constraints." CGD Working Paper 310. Washington, D.C.: Center for Global Development, 2012. http://www.cgdev.org/content/publications/detail/1426695

McKenzie, David, and Christopher Woodruff. "Experimental Evidence on Returns to Capital and Access to Finance in Mexico." *The World Bank Economic Review* 22(3): 457–482, 2008. doi:10.1093/wber/lhn017

Morduch, Jonathan. "Risk, Production and Saving: Theory and Evidence from Indian Households." Unpublished manuscript. Cambridge, Mass.: Harvard University, 1993.

Morris, Michael, Valerie A. Kelly, Ron J. Kopicki, and Derek Byerlee. *Fertilizer Use in African Agriculture: Lessons Learned and Good Practice Guidelines.* Washington, D.C.: World Bank, 2007. http://go.worldbank.org/DHJGCTE412

Rosenzweig, Mark R., and Hans P. Binswanger. "Wealth, Weather Risk and the Composition and Profitability of Agricultural Investments." *The Economic Journal* 103(416): 56–78, 1993. http://www.jstor.org/stable/2234337 http://www.jstor.org/stable/2234337

Solo, Tova Maria, and Astrid Manroth. "Access to Financial Services in Colombia: The 'Unbanked' in Bogota." *Policy Research Working Paper* 3834. Washington, D.C.: World Bank, 2006. http://go.worldbank.org/9XGFP84RT0

Wooldridge, Jeffrey M. *Introductory Econometrics: A Modern Approach,* 5th edition. Mason, Ohio: South-Western Cengage Learning, 2012.

Yanggen, David, Valerie A. Kelly, Thomas Reardon, and Anwar Naseem. "Incentives for Fertilizer Use in Sub-Saharan Africa: A Review of Empirical Evidence on Fertilizer Response and Profitability." MSU International Development Working Paper No. 70. East Lansing, Mich.: Michigan State University, 1998. http://purl.umn.edu/54677s

QUESTIONS FOR REVIEW

1. Making use of equation 10.1, describe the standard economic model of intertemporal choice.

2. What are the three ways investors may finance immediate investment? What cost is associated with each approach to financing?

3. Why might someone be willing to *save up* (starting immediately) for delayed investment, even when she is not willing to undertake the investment immediately?

4. What is present bias? In what sense do people characterized by present bias have a self-control problem?

5. Define in intuitive terms what it means for people to maximize expected utility. How is the assumption of risk aversion built into the assumption of expected utility maximization?

6. How might the opportunity to purchase insurance reduce the risk-related costs that a potential investor associates with a particular investment project?

7. Describe in general terms the conditions under which a potential investor undertakes a particular investment project and what the conditions imply about why some investors undertake investment projects even while other potential investors facing projects of the same type do not.

8. What guidance does the general model of private investment decisions offer as to possible explanations for low fertilizer use in Africa? What do we know about the empirical relevance of these explanations?

9. Discuss the roles that well-functioning financial markets can play in development.

10. Why are financial transactions costs especially high in developing countries? Why might they tend to be higher on transactions involving poorer clients?

11. What is adverse selection in the market for loans? Why might an increase in the interest rate charged on loans lead to an increase in the default rate in the presence of adverse selection?

12. What is moral hazard in the market for loans? Why might an increase in the interest rate charged on loans lead to an increase in the default rate in the presence of moral hazard?

13. How might a tendency for default rates to rise when interest rates rise lead to missing credit markets or credit rationing?

14. How might adverse selection in insurance markets lead to missing insurance markets?

15. What social and psychological barriers might prevent savings from flowing into loanable funds markets?

16. What kinds of empirical evidence suggest the existence of liquidity and insurance constraints on investment decisions?

17. Discuss the possible policy implications of liquidity constraints and insurance constraints that prevent private investors from undertaking valuable investments.

QUESTIONS FOR DISCUSSION

1. Suppose farmers may choose to invest in one or the other of two irrigation systems: a low-tech system or a high-tech system. The high-tech system costs more up front and requires more operation and maintenance expenditures, but it generates larger increases in crop yields and lasts longer. What differences across investors and locations might cause some farmers to choose the low-tech irrigation systems while others choose the high-tech systems?

2. Consider a potential investor who maximizes expected utility and consumes C in any state of the world if she does not invest. She faces a potential investment that pays net return $R + e$ in good states of the world and pays $R - e$ in bad states, where $R > 0$ and $0 < e < R$. Good states occur with probability 0.5.
   a. Use a diagram like the one in Figure 10.1 to show that if $u(F) = F$, so that utility in any state is just a linear function of consumption in that state, then she chooses to undertake the investment no matter what value e takes within its range.
   b. Draw a diagram in which $u(F)$ is concave as in Figure 10.1, rather than linear. Draw a case—defined by values

of R and e—in which the investor whose utility function you have drawn would choose *not* to undertake the investment. Using the diagram, explain why the investor chooses not to undertake this investment.

3. Use the simple model of private investment decisions expounded in this chapter to brainstorm a list of factors that might help explain why a particular family does not send their child to primary school.

4. Draw a diagram describing how the market for loanable funds would work if there were no transaction costs, no intermediaries, and no problems of asymmetric information. The horizontal axis should measure the quantity of loanable funds supplied by savers and/or the quantity of loanable funds demanded by investors and others. The vertical axis should measure the interest rate charged to borrowers and paid to savers, which is the price of loanable funds.
   a. Why might the supply schedule be upward sloping? Why might the demand schedule be downward sloping?

b. Imagine that all potential investment projects pay out their returns after one year but that potential investors face projects with differing levels of returns. If the market achieves equilibrium at the intersection of the supply and demand schedules, what can you say about the sets of potential investors who do and do not undertake investment in equilibrium? How are the potential returns on their investment projects likely to differ?

c. Imagine that the equilibrium you have drawn pertains to a population in which no one suffers from present bias. How would the diagram differ for a population that is in every way the same, except that some people exhibit present bias?

d. Suppose that lenders are prohibited from charging interest rates above a ceiling level r^c, which lies below the interest rate associated with the intersection of supply and demand. Use the diagram to explain how this gives rise to credit rationing. What can you say about the investment projects that are and are not undertaken under credit rationing?

e. Suppose that carrying out financial intermediation services costs a fixed rate c per dollar of loanable funds

transferred from lender to borrower and that intermediaries are competitive and always charge borrowers a rate r^b that is equal to $r^s + c$, where r^s is the interest rate they must pay to savers. How could you illustrate the introduction of such intermediation costs in your simple diagram describing equilibrium in the market for loanable funds? What happens to the quantity of loanable funds exchanged through the market? To the set of investment projects undertaken?

5. Many microfinance organizations offer poor borrowers loans under *joint liability* arrangements. This means that borrowers must form groups of five, 10, or more members in which each member bears responsibility not only for repaying his or her own loan but also for repaying the loan of any group member who defaults. Lending under joint liability is sometimes considered a substitute for requiring collateral. What is the purpose of requiring collateral, and how might lending under joint liability fulfill a similar purpose? How might joint liability lending mitigate the problem of adverse selection? How might it mitigate the problem of moral hazard?

PROBLEMS

1. Suppose that you save 10 pesos per month out of your noninterest income, you earn interest on savings of 5 percent per month, and you add all your interest income to your savings. How many months must you *save up* to accumulate 60 pesos? (You may assume that you deposit the 10 pesos saved during a month, plus the interest accumulated during the month, at the end of the month.) Holding all else the same, how many months must you save up to accumulate 60 pesos if you earn interest on savings of 10 percent per month?

2. The table describes a 10-person economy. Each person in this economy has 1 dollar that he might save or consume. He saves only if he can obtain a return on savings at least as high as the rate indicated in the first column. Each person also has access to an investment project paying the return listed in the second column. He is willing to undertake the investment using his own savings only if the return on his investment is at least as high as the return he requires to make saving attractive. He is willing to undertake the investment using a loan from a financial intermediary only if the investment pays a return greater than or equal to the interest rate he must pay on the loan. He prefers to finance the investment out of his own savings rather than a loan (if available) only if the return he requires to render saving attractive is lower than the interest rate he must pay on a loan.

Person	Saves If Return ≥ (Percent)	Available Investment Return (Percent)
1	5	5
2	5	8
3	5	9
4	8	5
5	8	5
6	8	5
7	10	9
8	10	10
9	20	9
10	20	15

a. Assume first that the costs of carrying out financial transactions are so high that no borrowing or lending takes place. As a result, the only way a person can earn a return on savings is by investing in his own investment project. Which people will invest in this case? What is the simple average of the returns on the investments undertaken?

b. Now assume that financial intermediation is costless, that all savings are deposited with financial intermediaries, and all investments are financed by loans from intermediaries. Because intermediation costs are zero and the market is competitive, the interest rate paid on savings is equal to the interest rate charged on loans. This interest rate adjusts to achieve equilibrium, in which the quantity of savings deposited with intermediaries just equals the quantity of loans extended by the intermediaries to finance investments. Describe the supply of savings deposits by listing possible interest rates and the quantities of deposits forthcoming at each interest rate. (That is, at each relevant interest rate, determine how many people would be willing to save.) Describe the demand for loans by listing possible interest rates and the quantities of loans demanded at each interest rate. (That is, at each relevant interest rate, determine how many people would be willing to undertake an investment if financed with a loan at that interest rate.) What is the equilibrium interest rate? At this rate, which people save? Which people invest? What is the simple average of the returns on investments undertaken?

c. Consider a change from having no financial intermediation (as in part a of this question) to having costless financial intermediation (as in part b). In what way does Person 1 gain from this change? Person 8? Person 10? What happens to economic growth? Why?

3. Consider an individual who faces two possible states of the world. With 20 percent probability he will face a bad state of the world, in which he must pay out $100 in health care expenses, and in the good state of the world he has no health care expenses. In either state of the world he earns income of $100 and consumes his income less his health care expenses. He is offered an opportunity to pay $20 up front (thereby reducing his consumption by $20 in either state of the world) for a health insurance contract that promises to pay him $100 to cover health care expenses in the bad state of the world. He seeks to maximize expected utility, where the utility he would derive in any state of the world is given by $C^{0.5}$, where C is his consumption in that state of the world.

   a. Calculate the *expected value* of his consumption, first assuming that he does not purchase insurance and then assuming that he does.

   b. Calculate his *expected utility*, first assuming that he does not purchase insurance and then assuming that he does. Would he choose to purchase the insurance?

   c. Now suppose that an insurer sells health insurance contracts to 10,000 individuals. Each individual faces a 20 percent chance of experiencing a health shock that requires payment of $100 in health care expenses. Their risks are idiosyncratic. This implies that in any one year approximately 20 percent of them will be hit by health shocks. Each insurance contract requires an up-front

payment of $20 and pays out $100 if the buyer experiences a health shock. Approximately how much will it cost the insurer to fulfill its promise of paying out $100 to every insurance contract buyer who experiences a health shock?

   d. If the cost of administering the insurance arrangement is $1 per contract holder, approximately how large a premium would the insurer have to charge to cover its total costs (including payouts for medical expenses and administrative costs)? Would the contract holders be willing to pay this premium?

   e. If the contract holders were risk neutral and sought to maximize the expected value of consumption rather than expected utility, would they be willing to pay this premium?

4. Consider a person who expects to earn Y in the present (period 0) and 0 in the future (period 1), and who seeks to maximizes utility as given by the function $U(C_0, C_1) = u(C_0) + \beta u(C_1)$; where $u(C)$ is a single-period utility function, C_0 and C_1 are quantities consumed in the present and future, and β is a parameter between 0 and 1.

   a. Suppose initially that $u(C) = C$ (so that the single-period utility function is characterized by constant rather than diminishing marginal utility) and $\beta = 1$ (so that this person does not discount the future). Would $U(Y, 0)$ be greater than, equal to, or less than $U(Y/2, Y/2)$?

   b. Now suppose that $u(C) = C$ and $\beta = 0.5$. Would $U(Y, 0)$ be greater than, equal to, or less than $U(Y/2, Y/2)$? Explain in intuitive terms why your answer here differs from your answer in a.

   c. Now suppose that $u(C)$ is the concave function described in the graph below, and $\beta = 1$. Making use of a ray that that extends from the origin through (and beyond) the point $[Y/2, u(Y/2)]$, identify the quantity $U(Y/2, Y/2)$ in the graph. Would $U(Y, 0)$ be greater than, equal to, or less than $U(Y/2, Y/2)$? Demonstrate this in the graph. Explain in intuitive terms why your answer here differs from your answer in a.

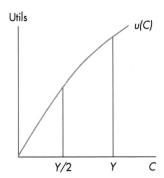

d. Continue to assume that $u(C)$ is the concave function described in the graph, and let $\beta = 0.3$. Would $U(Y, 0)$ be greater than, equal to, or less than $U(Y/2, Y/2)$?

5. A banker knows that when she offers loans at any interest rate less than 5 percent, the default rate is zero. For any interest rate I between 5 and 15 percent, the default rate is given by the function $D = 0.2 \times (I - 5) + 0.1 \times (I - 5)^2$. When the interest rate is I and the default rate is D, the banker expects to collect average returns on lending of $A = [(1 + I/100)(1 - D/100) - 1] \times 100$.

a. In a table, list integer values of I from 5 to 15. Calculate the default rate D and the average return on lending A associated with each interest rate. At which interest rate in your table is A maximized?

b. Now suppose that many competitive bankers face this same relationship between interest rates and default rates. Explain why equilibrium in this credit market might be characterized by rationing.

International Markets and General Equilibrium

Globalization is changing peoples' lives and reshaping the economic landscape. As international transactions become cheaper, people produce more for foreign markets, consume more foreign goods, and find new ways to invest and innovate. At the country level, export sectors expand, import-competing sectors decline, and economic activity shifts across geographic regions.

How policymakers in developing countries should respond to globalization remains a matter of debate. After years of insulating their economies from the influence of international markets, many developing-country governments reduced barriers to international trade in the 1980s and 1990s, expecting greater integration with the rest of the world to speed economic growth. They have achieved only mixed success, however, and some groups remain deeply critical of unfettered globalization, convinced that it brings costs borne mostly by the poor. Thus, careful study of the relationships between international trade and domestic development outcomes remains important in development studies.

After briefly describing the globalization of goods markets that has accelerated over the last two decades, this chapter presents three sets of analytical tools that economists bring to the study of international trade and development and employs them in searching for answers to three questions: What determines how successful a country is at exporting to world markets? What are the short- and medium-term effects of increased international trade on a developing country's production structure, income distribution, and poverty? And what are the longer-run impacts of increased international trade on economic growth?

11.1 Globalization and Development

Rising fractions of what people around the world produce and consume are bought and sold through international markets. In developing countries, the value of exports rose from 16 percent of GDP in 1980 to 32 percent in 2006, while the comparable percentage for developed countries rose from 20 to 27 (McMillan and Verduzco, 2010), and these percentages continue to rise (World Bank, 2012).

Falling costs of international transportation and communication are important driving forces behind globalization. The time and money costs of ocean transport have been falling for decades, and the speed of international transport has risen dramatically in recent years, as rapid reductions in air cargo rates have raised the fraction of world exports transported by air (Hummels, 2009). At the same time, the spread of mobile phones and Internet technologies have reduced the price and increased the speed of long-distance communication. In the terminology of Chapter 8, these changes have reduced the transfer costs associated with international market transactions.

Many governments have contributed to globalization through policy changes. In the 1930s and 1940s, most countries protected their economies from international trade through the imposition of **import tariffs** (i.e., taxes on imports) and other trade restrictions. Many countries have since **liberalized** their trade policies, reducing tariffs and lifting import restrictions. Average tariff rates in the industrial countries fell from roughly 40 percent of export value in the late 1940s to 4 percent in the late 1990s, although the agricultural and textile sectors within industrial countries continue to enjoy significant protection. Trade liberalization took place more recently and more rapidly in the developing countries, where high tariff rates were cut in half by a wave of unilateral reforms between the early 1980s and early 1990s (Bourguignon et al., 2002). Hummels (2009) argues that liberalization brought tariffs in many countries and for many goods down so low that transport costs became more important barriers to trade than tariffs in many markets.

Falling costs of international transactions and other forces have changed the composition of international trade as well as its volume. In the 1960s, developing countries largely exported **primary products** (i.e., agricultural goods and minerals) to the developed countries and imported manufactured goods in return. Now the share of manufactures in exports is greater than 80 percent in many developing countries, though it is still very small in some of the poorest countries (Martin, 2003; World Bank, 2012). The rising importance of manufactures among exports is matched by their rising share of GDP within many developing countries, especially in East Asia.

The nature of trade flows between developing and developed countries has also been reshaped by a profound **unbundling** of production and a related expansion of trade in partially processed goods (Baldwin, 2006). Rather than carrying out all stages of production locally, many firms in developed countries now complete only some production steps locally, having **outsourced** other production steps to subsidiaries or suppliers in other countries, often developing countries. Sometimes partially processed goods or components cross borders multiple times during production and distribution. For example, Japanese firms headquartered in Japan produce high-tech parts for electronic goods, ship them to producers elsewhere in East Asia for assembly, and then ship final goods back to Japan or to the United States for sale to consumers. Such relationships help explain why intermediate goods (i.e., parts, components, and partially processed goods) now make up 40 percent of world nonfuel merchandise trade flows (WTO, 2009).

A final global goods market trend worth noting is that developing countries are increasingly trading with each other. The share of developing country exports that is destined for other developing countries (rather than for developed countries) rose from 17 percent in the mid-1960s to 40 by the late 1990s (Martin, 2003), and that share continued to rise in all regions of the developing world between 2000 and 2010 (World Bank, 2012).

Most economists believe that greater integration into world goods markets—whether driven by falling transport costs or liberalizing policies toward international trade—ultimately raises average real income and consumption in all countries. At least after a period of **adjustment**, during which workers and other production factors must be shifted from declining import-competing sectors to rising export sectors, developing countries should enjoy aggregate gains from increased specialization and exchange. In Appendix 8A we illustrated the logic behind such gains in a model of trade between farmers with simple production technologies. In section 11.3, we illustrate the gains from exchange in models of trade between countries with more flexible production technologies. Greater integration into world markets might also bring longer-run gains through accelerated investment, productivity advance, and growth, for reasons discussed in section 11.4.

Most economists recognize, however, that the gains from increased international integration tend to be distributed unequally within countries and that integration can impose large costs on some groups, especially in the short and medium run. If policymakers hope to create safety net policies that protect vulnerable groups from having to bear those **adjustment costs** on their own, then they must understand how the benefits and costs of increased trade are distributed. Section 11.3 lays out the basic models that guide development economists' study of the distribution mechanisms.

The aggregate gains from improved international trade opportunities materialize as developing countries expand their production for export. Thus, developing countries can hope to gain significantly from globalization only if they succeed in growing their exports. Unfortunately, some developing countries have experienced much slower export growth than others in recent years. Average annual rates of growth in export volume between 2000 and 2010 varied from 25.9 percent in Sierra Leone to −4.9 percent in Zimbabwe (World Bank, 2012). Before examining the economy-wide impacts of increased international trade in sections 11.3 and 11.4, therefore, we first examine the challenges of expanding export volume.

The focus of this chapter is on the globalization of goods markets, but it is important to recognize that capital and labor markets are globalizing as well. International capital flows take three main forms. Through **foreign direct investment** (FDI), investors in one country directly undertake investment projects in other countries, establishing long-lasting ownership interest in, and management control over, firms in other countries. Through **portfolio investment**, savers purchase stocks or bonds in other countries, providing investors there with financing. Through **international bank lending**, savers in one country make deposits that are on-lent to investors in other countries. Capital flows into developing countries remain small relative to capital flows between developed countries, but they have risen over the last few decades (UNCTAD, 2012). The total volume of FDI flows into low- and middle-income countries, which have grown somewhat faster than other capital flows, is now more than four times the volume of official development assistance, but most of this FDI flows into a small number of relatively well-off developing countries.

International migration is on the rise as well, though labor markets remain much less globalized than goods and capital markets. The volume of remittance flows, to families back home in low- and middle-income countries from workers who have migrated, is now more than two and a half times as great as the volume of official development assistance (World Bank, 2012). Again, however, most of these remittances flow into a small number of developing countries.

11.2 A Partial Equilibrium Model of International Trade, with Application to Export Expansion

Why have some developing countries increased their exports so much more than others in recent years? And what might policymakers in developing countries do to encourage the expansion of exports? In what follows, we begin our study of international trade by examining the market for a developing country's export good, using the simple market equilibrium model of Chapter 8, and then take a closer look at three sets of potential determinants of developing country export volumes that are suggested by the model.

The model presented in this section examines **partial equilibrium** in the domestic and world markets for a single good. This means that it examines how changing circumstances affect equilibrium in these markets *while holding constant conditions in all other markets for goods and factors of production*. In later sections, we develop models of general equilibrium, which account for the effects of these same changing circumstances on markets for all goods and factors of production and which have more to say about the effects of international trade on the larger domestic economy.

11.2A Partial equilibrium model of international trade

Figure 11.1a depicts the national market for shoes in Indonesia, a shoe exporting country. The horizontal axis measures numbers of shoes in millions of pairs, and the vertical axis measures the local price of shoes in rupiahs, the Indonesian currency. The local supply and demand schedules indicate the total quantities supplied to and demanded from the main Indonesian market at any price by Indonesian firms and households. The gray horizontal line indicates the world market price for shoes, as measured in rupiahs, wp^{Rp}. The black horizontal lines at the heights of the local export price (*LEP*) and local import price (*LIP*) illustrate opportunities for exporting shoes to and importing shoes from the world market. Following the definitions of Chapter 8, the *LIP* equals the world price plus the transfer costs of importing shoes from the world market, and the *LEP* equals the world price less the costs of exporting from Indonesia to the world market. We draw the *LEP* above the autarky price because Indonesia is a shoe exporter. In exporting equilibrium, the local price of shoes in rupiahs, lp^{Rp}, is equal to the *LEP*.

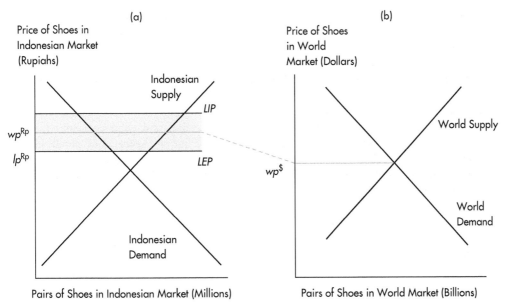

**FIGURE 11.1
Partial Equilibrium
Relationship between the
Indonesian and World
Markets for Shoes**

Figure 11.1b depicts the world market for shoes. The vertical axis measures the world market price for shoes in U.S. dollars. The horizontal axis measures the quantities of shoes exchanged in world markets, in billions of pairs. The world supply and demand schedules indicate the quantities of shoe exports forthcoming into world markets from all countries and the quantities of shoe imports demanded from world markets, at any price. The world market diagram contains no *LIP* or *LEP* lines, because no trade external to the world market is possible, and the world market equilibrium is always found at the intersection of the supply and demand schedules. The price associated with that intersection is the world price of shoes in dollars, $wp^\$$. It is useful to think of the world market as having a center in a major destination country for Indonesian shoe exports, such as the United States, but the graphical depiction of the world market reminds us that the price at which Indonesian exporters can sell to buyers in the United States is influenced by forces of supply and demand from around the world. For example, recovery from economic crisis in Europe shifts the global demand schedule for shoes to the right, and rising shoe supply in China shifts the global supply schedule to the right.

Figure 11.1 highlights a distinctive feature of many international transactions: buyers and sellers often live in countries with different currencies. The price of shoes is measured in rupiahs in the Indonesian market diagram (Figure 11.1a) but is measured in U.S. dollars in the world market diagram (Figure 11.1b). When Indonesian exporters sell shoes to buyers in the United States, they receive payment in U.S. dollars, but they pay their worker in rupiahs. They must, therefore, convert the dollars they receive into rupiahs through foreign exchange transactions, in which one currency is exchanged for another. The rate at which foreign currency may be converted into a country's domestic currency is called the country's **nominal exchange rate**, which economists measure in *units of domestic currency per unit of foreign currency*. We use e to denote the Indonesian exchange rate relative to the dollar, which is denominated in rupiahs per dollar. If the world price of shoes in dollars ($wp^\$$) is $40 and the Indonesian nominal exchange rate (e) is 9,500 rupiahs per dollar, then the world price of shoes as measured in rupiahs (wp^{Rp}) is $9,500 \times 40 = 380,000$.

When the Indonesian exchange rate measured in rupiahs per dollar rises, the rupiah is said to **depreciate** relative to the dollar, because more rupiahs are now required to purchase one dollar and each rupiah buys fewer dollars. If the world price of shoes in dollars remains constant, such a depreciation of the rupiah causes the world price line in Figure 11.1a (and the associated levels of the *LIP* and *LEP*) to rise. When the Indonesian exchange rate falls, fewer rupiahs are required to purchase each dollar, the rupiah is said to **appreciate**, and the world price line in Figure 11.1a falls. A depreciation of the Indonesian exchange rate tends to increase Indonesian exports, and an appreciation tends to reduce Indonesian exports.

The slanted light gray line connecting the world price in Figure 11.1b and the world price in Figure 11.1a reminds us that the two horizontal lines depict the same world price measured in different currencies. If the world price rises while the exchange rate remains constant, both price lines rise by the same proportion. If the world price in dollars remains constant while the Indonesian exchange rate fluctuates, the height of the price line in Figure 11.1b remains fixed while the height of the world price line in Figure 11.1a fluctuates.

When drawing Figures 11.1a and b, we are implicitly holding constant all prices and wages in the Indonesian and U.S. economies—other than the prices of shoes in Indonesia and the United States, which are determined in the diagrams.[1] This means that we are holding the Indonesian and U.S. price levels constant. The **price level** in Indonesia is the answer to the question: How many rupiahs would it currently cost to purchase a basket of goods and services that is representative of all goods and services produced or consumed in Indonesia? Indonesia experiences a positive rate of **inflation** over a given month when the Indonesian price level rises during that month. When price levels in Indonesia and the United States are both held constant, as they are in Figure 11.1, an increase in Indonesia's nominal exchange rate e, which raises the world price line, *also* represents an increase in Indonesia's **real exchange rate**, which economists define as $r = eP^*/P$, where P^* and P are measures of the U.S. price level in dollars and the Indonesian price level in rupiahs.

When seeking to understand the determinants of export sector performance in the real world (in which price levels change), it is the *real* exchange rate rather than the nominal exchange rate that matters for export sector performance. To see this, notice that P is the cost in rupiahs of purchasing a representative basket of goods and services in Indonesia, and eP^* is the cost in rupiahs of purchasing the same basket of goods and services in the United States (when using the nominal exchange rate to convert dollars into rupiahs). When the real exchange rate $r = eP^*/P$ rises, eP^* rises relative to P, and consumers in both Indonesia and the United States find it relatively more costly to purchase goods in the United States relative to Indonesia. As shoe consumers respond by demanding fewer shoes in the United States and more in Indonesia, they bid up the price of shoes in Indonesia, as illustrated by the increase in the world price line (and the related *LEP* and *LIP* lines) in Figure 11.1a. By contrast, if e doubled but P *also* doubled, so that the real exchange rate r held constant, the relative cost of buying shoes in the United States relative to Indonesia would not change, the world price in Figure 11.1a would remain unchanged, and Indonesian exports would remain unchanged.

When Indonesia's real exchange rate falls (representing a real appreciation of the rupiah relative to the dollar), the world price and *LEP* lines in Figure 11.1a fall, and Indonesian exports fall. The real exchange rate can fall because the nominal exchange rate e falls while the price levels P and P^* hold constant. But it can also fall because, for example, the Indonesian price level P rises at a faster rate than the U.S. price level P^*, while the nominal exchange rate holds constant.

Another distinctive feature of international transactions is that they may be taxed, subsidized or regulated by governments on both sending and receiving ends. Compared to many other transactions, imports and exports are relatively easy to tax, because they pass through a limited number of locations—major seaports, airports, or border crossings on road or rail lines—on their

---

[1]If all prices and wages in the Indonesian economy, including the price of shoes, were to double, the Indonesian market for shoes would experience no change in any real quantities. The profits that Indonesian shoemakers earn as measured in rupiahs would have doubled, for example, but with those profits they would be able to purchase just as many real goods and services as before the doubling. In market equilibrium diagrams like Figure 11.1a, we are studying the determination of the "real price of shoes," or the price of shoes *relative* to all other prices and wages in the economy, and thus relative to the Indonesian price level.

way in or out of a country. Taxes on exports and imports increase the transfer costs associated with those transactions. Thus, a country's tax on its exports lowers the *LEP* line in a diagram like Figure 11.1a, tending to discourage exports, and a tariff on imports raises the relevant *LIP* line.

11.2B Determinants of export volume

Simple though it is, the model of the previous section offers useful guidance for the study of export volume determinants, suggesting that:

> Export volumes can vary across countries and over time as the result of variation in three quite different sets of conditions, which are related to export transfer costs, real exchange rates, and domestic production costs. This suggests that policies of many sorts—some specific to export sectors and some more general—influence export sector performance.

Export transfer costs

In Figure 11.1a, Indonesia's shoe exports to world markets rise when the transfer costs associated with exporting fall, raising the *LEP*. Among the most important components of export transfer costs are the time and money costs of transporting goods to international destinations. Despite the reductions in transport costs that have encouraged globalization, transport costs remain significant, and producers in some countries face much higher costs of transporting to foreign markets than others. Box 11.1 documents tremendous variation across developing countries in the costs of transporting goods to the United States. Naturally, geography explains a large fraction of the variation. Countries that lie farther from the United States face higher costs of exporting to major markets there. **Landlocked countries**, which are countries without any direct access to the sea, are even more disadvantaged, lacking ready access to the cheapest mode of international transport: sea shipment.

Fortunately, transport costs may be reduced through investments in international transport infrastructure. High-quality seaport facilities significantly reduce costs. High-quality seaports are fully *containerized*, meaning that they are equipped for moving standardized shipping containers rapidly between trucks, railroad cars, and ships. They must also operate efficiently, processing ships without undue delays and charges. Londoño-Kent and Kent (2003) offer a detailed comparison of two ports in Central and South America, one of which is considered efficient and the other inefficient. They calculate that the cost of a typical visit is 30 percent higher in the inefficient port.

☰ Box 11.1 Geography, Infrastructure, Transport Costs, and Trade

Nuno Limão and Anthony Venables (2001) analyze rates charged by a Baltimore, Maryland, shipping company for shipping standard 40-foot containers to 64 destination cities around the world. (A standard shipping container has length of 40 feet, width of 8 feet, height of 8.5 feet, and volume of 2,720 cubic feet.) Using simple regression analysis, they relate shipping costs to kilometers of land and sea travel, an indicator of whether the receiving country is landlocked, and indices of infrastructure quality in destination and transit countries. The infrastructure index *inf* is the average of four indices measuring road, paved road, rail, and telephone network densities, and the authors include $1/inf$ in their regressions.

Their results show that the average rate among destination cities in nonlandlocked countries is $4,620. Costs rise by approximately $190 per 1,000 km of sea transport, $1,380 per 1,000 km of land transport, and—even after accounting for the distances involved—are $3,450

higher on average for destinations in landlocked countries. They find that among nonlandlocked destination cities, 40 percent of the variation in transport costs is explained by the quality of local infrastructure rather than by distance, that improving a country's infrastructure quality index ranking from the level of the 75th to the 50th percentile is the equivalent of reducing sea distance by 3,466 km, and that improvements in own and transit-country infrastructure greatly reduce the disadvantage of being landlocked.

The authors examine the effects of geography, infrastructure, and transport costs on the volume of trade flows between pairs of countries. They estimate that a 10 percent increase in transportation costs is associated with a 20 percent reduction in trade flows, and they argue that high transport costs explain much of Africa's lower volume of international trade.

Governments on sending and receiving ends raise export transfer costs in diverse ways. The costs of exporting rise when sending-country governments tax or regulate exports and when inefficiency and corruption raise the money and time costs of border-crossing procedures. Governments on the receiving end further raise developing countries' export transfer costs by taxing or regulating imports. As indicated earlier, tariff levels have come down to very low levels for many goods in many countries. Even so, developing country exporters often find it costly and difficult to enter foreign markets as a result of foreign government safety and sanitary regulations and their technical requirements for specific products. Such regulations can serve an important purpose in protecting receiving country consumers from hazards, but they remain contentious because they can also be used to protect domestic producers from international competition, and they may be administered in inefficient ways that raise transfer costs unnecessarily. For example, developing country producers often must work to satisfy multiple regulating agencies within a single destination country, and they often must comply with different technical specifications in each country to which they export.

Institutional innovations of diverse sorts could bring down these government-induced costs of sending goods across borders. Governments on both sending and receiving ends could improve the efficiency of border administration and improve coordination among their regulating agencies. International cooperation in the adoption of uniform technical standards would also reduce transfer costs (World Economic Forum et al., 2013).

Developing country producers face significant information costs when dealing with foreign buyers. To export successfully, they must understand not only the regulatory requirements in receiving countries but also the nature of foreign buyers' needs and preferences. Foreign buyers often require products that meet precise standards and are delivered in a timely fashion. Exporters might also have to invest in establishing good reputations among potential customers. Many of the necessary investments in collecting and disseminating information have public goods qualities. These investments may be prohibitively costly for individual exporters, especially small and medium-sized producers, but they may be profitable for groups of exporters that cooperate in sharing the costs. Coordination among exporters can also help reduce transport costs by increasing the scale of transactions. Such considerations have motivated the creation of many **export promotion agencies** around the world. These agencies undertake information gathering and dissemination activities, and they provide a forum for collaboration among small and medium-sized exporters. Effectiveness of export promotion agencies is a subject of debate, and it likely varies greatly depending on the nature and quality of operations (Lederman et al., 2010).

Even in today's globalized world, export transfer costs remain surprisingly large and remain significant inhibitors of international trade. Anderson and Wincoop (2004) estimate that even for goods traded between developed countries, the costs of border crossing and international transport add 74 percent to the cost of goods on average, and the costs of exporting are likely to be much higher for many developing countries.

Real exchange rates

When the Indonesian real exchange rate (relative to the dollar) rises, signifying a real depreciation of the Indonesian currency relative to the dollar, Indonesian exports tend to rise as consumers around the world find it more attractive to purchase goods in Indonesia relative to the United States. This suggests that any factors that help determine the real exchange rate help determine the volume of Indonesian exports. A complete discussion of the determinants of real exchange rates is beyond the scope of this chapter. Here we make just a few critical observations.

A variety of macroeconomic conditions and circumstances can cause the real exchange rate to appreciate, discouraging exports. For example, a government's efforts to hold the nominal exchange rate constant, while pursuing macroeconomic policies that cause the domestic price level to rise more rapidly than foreign price levels, lead to real exchange rate appreciation.

A country's imposition of tariffs or import restrictions can also cause real exchange rates to appreciate. Thus, the significance of the real exchange rate in Figure 11.1a reminds us that export performance may be influenced by broader macroeconomic policies and by policies toward imports, as well as policies toward the export sector.

Troublingly for natural resource–rich developing countries, a boom in a country's commodity exports can also cause its real exchange rate to appreciate, tending to discourage the development of its other export sectors. When the world price for one of the country's important commodity exports (such as oil or coffee) rises sharply, or when new oil fields are discovered in the country, the country's real exchange rate tends to appreciate.[2] Large inflows of foreign aid can have the same effect. The increase in the real exchange rate tends to discourage industries producing manufactured goods for export. This phenomenon is often called the "Dutch disease" in reference to the experience of the Netherlands after the discovery of natural gas deposits in 1959.

Domestic production costs and supply response

Two final alterations to Figure 11.1a that might raise export volume involve the supply schedule. Export volumes would rise if a reduction in domestic production costs caused the supply schedule to shift to the right, and movements along the supply schedule, in response to reductions in international transfer costs, would bring greater export expansion if the supply schedule were more elastic.

These observations remind us that the infrastructure and institutions relevant to export sector success are not only those specific to the export sector but also infrastructure and institutions that support market development and investment more generally. For example, improvements in *domestic* transport and communication infrastructure, which encourage domestic market development, also tend to raise export volumes, as they shift the local supply schedule to the right. The study described in Box 11.1 confirms that the quality of domestic transport infrastructure affects export success. Domestic regulations and the taxation of trucking, warehousing, and other trade logistics services can also raise the cost and difficulty of exporting and of market activity more generally.

Institutions that promote mobility in domestic labor markets and that encourage workers to acquire new skills can increase the elasticity of local export supply, even as they contribute to growth and development throughout the economy (Chapter 9). Similarly, institutions that protect property rights for domestic and foreign investors encourage investment throughout the economy (Chapter 10) and increase investors' responsiveness to improved export opportunities. All such improvements in the local business environment can encourage the expansion of production for the domestic market as well as for export, contributing to development more broadly.

The role of the local supply schedule in determining export volume suggests two additional channels through which a country's policies toward imports can affect its export performance. Policies taxing or inhibiting imports can discourage exports by raising the prices of imported inputs or by raising the demand for labor and other production factors in import-competing sectors, driving up production costs for exporters. (The models of the next section examine the latter mechanism further.)

The role of local supply also points to a way past policies toward imports or exports can influence current export success. If the productivity of firms in a particular export industry rises as the industry gains scale or experience, then temporary policies that subsidized or protected this

---

[2]Courses in international finance and open-economy macroeconomics equip students to understand the somewhat subtle logical connections between commodity booms and real exchange rates, and exchange rate determination more generally. One component of the explanation is that the commodity boom increases foreign buyers' need to exchange their currency for the local currency, thereby raising the supply of foreign currency and increasing the demand for local currency in foreign exchange markets.

industry in the past, when it was in its infancy, might have yielded long-lasting benefits of productivity growth that increase the industry's competitiveness today. We return to such issues in section 11.4.

11.3 General Equilibrium Models of Trade, Production Structure, and Income Distribution

In the 1970s and 1980s, many economists assumed that increased openness to international trade would reduce poverty and inequality within developing countries. In the 1990s, when newly available micro data revealed rising wage and income inequality in many prominent trade-liberalizing countries, including Mexico, Colombia, Argentina, Brazil, Chile, India, Hong Kong, and China (Goldberg and Pavcnik, 2007), economists were forced to rethink their understanding of the relationships between international trade and domestic development outcomes.

To understand why economists predicted that trade liberalization would reduce poverty and inequality in developing countries, and how the experiences of the 1990s altered their understanding of trade and development, we must lay out the logic embodied in two influential models of interaction between international markets and domestic economies: the specific factors model and the factor proportions model. Both are models of country-level **general equilibrium**. This means that they describe simultaneous equilibrium in the markets for all goods and all factors of production relevant to a country, and they emphasize the interconnections between these markets. For example, they emphasize the tendency for changes in goods markets to alter demands in labor markets and the tendency for expansion in some sectors to cause shrinkage in others, as fixed stocks of production factors are reallocated across uses.

We formally expound simple versions of these models, in which only two goods markets and two or three factor markets operate, and offer informal discussions of possible complications and extensions. We then describe how interactions between these theories and empirical research in the 1990s enriched economists' understanding of the relationships among international trade, income distribution, and poverty.

11.3A The specific factors model

Basic assumptions

Consider a developing country called Home that produces two goods, food and textiles, in quantities F and T. Its people derive income from owning three factors of production—land, capital, and labor—in quantities N, K, and L. The domestic prices for food (p_F) and textiles (p_T) are determined in Home's two goods markets, which are integrated with international goods markets. The per-unit returns earned by Home's factors of production—the rental rates on land (r_N) and capital (r_K) and the wage paid to labor (w)—are determined in the three factor markets. The economy is in general equilibrium when all five of its markets—the two goods markets and the three factor markets—are in equilibrium. Box 11.2 summarizes the model's notation and assumptions, which we elaborate in this section.

To analyze *equilibrium* in all markets, we must first describe our assumptions regarding local supply and demand in markets for each factor and good. Consider first the supply of factors of production. We assume that the total quantities supplied of land, capital, and labor are fixed. Labor is fully **mobile** across sectors, which means that workers can move between the food and textile sectors in pursuit of higher wages without incurring any costs. Thus, while the total labor stock L is fixed, the quantities of labor employed in the food and textile sectors, L_F and L_T, are determined through market interactions. Land and capital, by contrast, are **immobile** between sectors. Land is **specific** to (i.e., supplied only to) the food sector, and capital is specific to the

☰ Box 11.2 The Simple Specific Factors Model: Assumptions and Notation

Assumptions

- Two goods: food and textiles
- Three factors: labor, land, and capital
- Land is specific to food production
- Capital is specific to textile production
- Labor is mobile
- Producers maximize profits
- A representative consumer maximizes utility
- Markets are competitive
- The home country is small
- Transactions are costless

Notation

L, N, K = total quantities of labor, land, capital
L_F, L_T = labor employed in food, textiles
F, T = quantities produced of food, textiles

C_F, C_T = quantities consumed of food, textiles
X, M = quantities of exports, imports
p_F^w, p_T^w = world prices of food, textiles
p_F, p_T = domestic prices of food, textiles
w = wage
r_N, r_K = rental rates for land, capital
$f(L_F, N)$ = food production function
$t(L_T, K)$ = textile production function
$MPL_F(L_F, N)$, $MPL_T(L_T, K)$ = marginal products of labor in food production, textile production
$MPN_F(L_F, N)$ = marginal product of land in food production
$MPK_T(L_T, K)$ = marginal product of capital in textile production
$U(C_F, C_T)$ = representative consumer's utility function
$MU_F(C_F, C_T)$, $MU_T(C_F, C_T)$ = representative consumer's marginal utilities of food, textiles

textile sector. Land and capital are the *specific factors* that give the **specific factors model** its name. All units of labor, land, and capital are assumed sufficiently mobile *within* sectors that within-sector factor markets are competitive, all units of a factor in a given sector receive the same rental rate or wage, and all factors are fully employed in equilibrium.

The supplies of food and textiles and the demands for the factors of production are generated by competitive profit-maximizing producers. The food sector production function, $F = f(L_F, N)$, and the textile sector production function, $T = t(L_T, K)$, are characterized by diminishing marginal products and constant returns to scale (as defined in Chapter 3). Associated with these production functions are marginal product of labor functions, $MPL_F(L_F, N)$ and $MPL_T(L_T, K)$, which are decreasing in the labor arguments (indicating diminishing marginal returns to labor) and increasing in N or K (indicating that labor productivity rises when the land or capital employed per unit of labor rises). They are also associated with marginal product of land and capital functions, $MPN_F(L_F, N)$ and $MPK_T(L_T, K)$, which are increasing in the labor arguments and decreasing in the land and capital arguments. Producers are free to sell locally or in world markets.

The demands for food and textiles are derived from utility-maximizing consumers who earn their incomes as owners of Home's factors of production. For simplicity we assume that all Home consumers have the *same* preferences, and that as long as all consumers face the same prices for food and textiles, they all consume food and textiles in the same proportion, regardless of their income levels. Under these assumptions we can treat the country's many consumers as if they were a single big consumer whose preferences describe "national preferences." We describe national preferences with a standard utility function, $U(C_F, C_T)$, where C_F and C_T are the quantities of food and textiles consumed domestically. Associated with the utility function are the marginal utility functions $MU_F(C_F, C_T)$, which is decreasing in C_F, and $MU_T(C_F, C_T)$, which is decreasing in C_T. Consumers may buy locally or in world markets.

We assume that both goods are traded in international markets, where the prices of food and textiles are p_F^w and p_T^w when denominated in units of Home's currency. Home is a small country, in the sense that its export and import quantities (X and M) have no impact on world prices. We also assume initially that there are no transfer costs, but we will later discuss how the model's implications change when we acknowledge transfer costs.

We take $p_F{}^w$, $p_T{}^w$, N, K, and L, as well as the country's production functions and preferences, as **exogenous**, or determined outside the model. All other prices and quantities are **endogenous**, or determined within the model to satisfy general equilibrium conditions. In what follows we describe the equilibrium conditions (using both mathematical equations and graphs) and then use them in analyzing how changes in world prices affect the general equilibrium levels of endogenous domestic goods prices (p_F and p_T), production quantities (L_F, L_T, F, T), consumption quantities (C_F, C_T), and trade quantities (X and M). Asterisks (*) denote equilibrium values of the endogenous variables.

Equilibrium domestic prices

Because Home is a small country and because transactions are costless, competition drives domestic prices to equal world prices. Thus we know that $p_F{}^* = p_F{}^w$ and $p_T{}^* = p_T{}^w$ and that an increase in the world food price causes an identical increase in the domestic food price.

Equilibrium factor use and production

Labor is the only variable factor of production in either sector. Thus we completely describe the production side of Home's economy in general equilibrium by determining the equilibrium quantities of labor employed in the two sectors, $L_F{}^*$ and $L_T{}^*$. Two observations allow us to determine these quantities. First, the total quantity of labor is fixed and must be fully employed in equilibrium. Thus we know that

$$L_F{}^* + L_T{}^* = L \tag{11.1}$$

Second, because labor is mobile and labor markets are perfectly competitive, we know that the values of the marginal products of labor must be equated across food and textile production (see Chapter 9). Thus,

$$p_F{}^* MPL_F(L_F{}^*, N) = p_T{}^* MPL_T(L_T{}^*, K) \tag{11.2}$$

Equations 11.1 and 11.2 are two equations in two unknowns, and we may thus use them to solve for $L_F{}^*$ and $L_T{}^*$. Once we know these labor quantities, we may use the production functions to calculate the quantities of goods produced:

$$F^* = f(L_F{}^*, N) \tag{11.3}$$

and

$$T^* = t(L_T{}^*, K) \tag{11.4}$$

Figure 11.2 offers an insightful graphical depiction of Home's equilibrium production structure and factor use. The vertical and horizontal axes measure tons of food F and thousands of square yards of cloth T. We use equations 11.1, 11.3, and 11.4 to trace out Home's **production possibilities frontier** (*PPF*), which is the locus of all combinations of F and T that Home can produce when all its factors are fully employed. (See problem 2 for a numerical example.) In the figure, the *PPF* is the curved edge of the shaded region. At the upper left end of the *PPF* all labor is allocated to food production, at the lower right end all labor is allocated to textile production, and movements along the *PPF* from the northwest toward the southeast are brought about by reallocations of labor from the food sector to the textile sector.

The *PPF* is bowed out from the origin, becoming steeper as we move from left to right, as a result of the diminishing marginal product of labor in each sector. The slope of the *PPF* at any

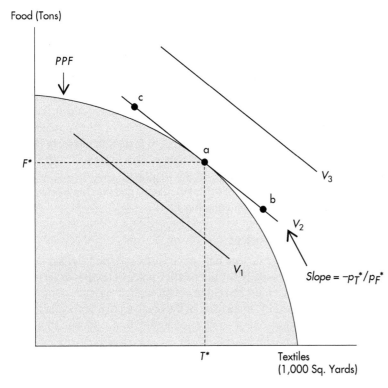

Food (Tons)

FIGURE 11.2
General Equilibrium Determination of Production Structure in a Simple Specific Factors Model

point is equal to the change in F associated with removing one unit of labor from food production, divided by the change in T associated with moving that unit of labor into textile production. It is thus equal to $-MPL_F/MPL_T$.[3] As we move to the right in the diagram, the quantity of labor in food production falls while the quantity in textile production rises (and the specific factors employed in each sector remain unchanged). With diminishing marginal returns to labor in both food and textile production, this implies that MPL_F rises and MPL_T falls as we move to the right, and the slope increases in absolute value.

The equilibrium combination of F^* and T^* must lie somewhere on the PPF, because all factors of production must be fully employed in equilibrium. To derive an expression that tells us *where* along the PPF production takes place, we rearrange equation 11.2 to get

$$MPL_F(L_F^*, N)/MPL_T(L_T^*, K) = p_T^*/p_F^* \qquad (11.5)$$

The left side (multiplied by -1) is equal to the slope of the PPF; thus this equation tells us that in equilibrium the economy must produce at a point on the PPF where the slope equals $-p_T^*/p_F^*$. To find this point in Figure 11.2, we find the point on the PPF that is just tangent to a line with slope $-p_T^*/p_F^*$. We may do this by drawing in a series of lines (V_1, V_2, and V_3) with this slope. These lines are called **isovalue lines**, because along any one of them the total value of production

---

[3]In Appendix 8A we introduced the notion of a production possibilities frontier (*PPF*) for a farm household and for a village. There the *PPF*s were straight lines rather than concave, because our assumptions about production technologies were simpler (and less realistic) than the assumptions in this chapter. In Appendix 8A, production of either crop required only a single input, land, and every unit of land on a farm or within a community was assumed to produce the same quantity of a given crop. The marginal product of labor in the production of either crop was thus constant, and moving one unit of land from rice production to vegetable production always yielded the same reduction in rice and same increase in vegetable production, regardless of how land was initially allocated across rice and vegetable production.

$p_F^*F + p_T^*T$ is constant (and the prefix *iso-* means "equal"). The *PPF* is just tangent to an isovalue line with slope $-p_T^*/p_F^*$ at point a, and in general equilibrium Home thus produces T^* units of textiles and F^* units of food.

Working out the effect of a change in world prices on the equilibrium structure of production is now easy! When p_F^* rises while p_T^* remains constant, for example, the isovalue lines in Figure 11.2 become flatter, and the tangency between the *PPF* and an isovalue line moves to the northwest. As we might expect, an increase in the price of food renders food production more profitable relative to textile production and increases the equilibrium level of food production. What we do not see in partial equilibrium models but we do see here is that the increase in the food price also leads to a *reduction* in textile production as labor is drawn out of textiles into the food sector, where the price increase raised the value of the marginal product of labor and intensified the demand for labor. Labor must flow out of the textile sector and into the food sector to reestablish the labor market equilibrium condition, equation 11.2.

The importance of relative, not absolute, prices

Notice that the equilibrium quantities F^* and T^* depend only on the ratio p_T^*/p_F^* and not on the absolute levels of p_T^* and p_F^*. We call the ratio p_T^*/p_F^* the **relative price of textiles in terms of food**, because it indicates the units of food that must be sold to obtain enough currency to buy one unit of textiles. Food production is encouraged by an increase in the relative price of food in terms of textiles, p_F^*/p_T^*, whether the change arises out of an increase in p_F^* or a reduction in p_T^*.

Equilibrium factor prices and the functional distribution of income

Food sector producers compete for the use of land, textile sector employers compete for the use of capital, and all producers compete for the use of labor. In equilibrium each factor of production must be paid the value of its marginal product. Thus we know that in equilibrium, these three relationships must hold:

$$w^* = p_F^*MPL_F(L_F^*, N) = p_T^*MPL_T(L_T^*, K) \tag{11.6}$$

$$r_N^* = p_F^*MPN_F(L_F^*, N) \tag{11.7}$$

$$r_K^* = p_T^*MPK_T(L_T^*, K) \tag{11.8}$$

Every variable appearing on the right side of these equations is either exogenously given (N, K) or an equilibrium outcome whose determination we have already discussed $(p_F^*, p_T^*, L_F^*, L_K^*)$. Thus these equations tell us directly the equilibrium levels of factor prices and the **functional distribution of income**, which is the distribution of income across the owners of different factors of production.

We may use these equilibrium conditions to work out what happens to factor payments in response to an increase in the world price of food. As we do so, we must pay attention not only to the nominal levels of w^*, r_N^*, and r_K^* but to the real purchasing power of the owners of the three factors of production. If, when the price of food rises, a factor's rate of pay (w^*, r_N^*, or r_K^*) rises faster than the price of food (and thus also rises relative to the price of textiles, which doesn't change), then its owners' real income rises. If a factor's rate of pay falls (and thus falls relative to the prices of both food and textiles), its owners' real income falls. If a factor's rate of pay rises relative to the price of textiles but rises less rapidly than the price of food, then its owners' real purchasing power can rise or fall, depending on the relative importance of textiles and food in their consumption baskets.

Working out what happens to the real returns to land and capital in response to an increase in the price of food is straightforward. From equation 11.7 we see that r_N^* rises both because p_F^*

rises and because the increased use of labor in the food sector raises the marginal product of land. Thus, r_N^* rises faster than p_F^*, and the real return to land increases. Similarly, from equation 11.8 we see that r_K^* falls as a result of the withdrawal of labor out of the textile sector. Because this represents a fall in r_K^* relative to both prices, the real return to capital falls. The increase in the relative price of food thus raises the real return to the food sector's specific factor and reduces the real return to the textile sector's specific factor.

The effect of an increase in the price of food on the real wage is ambiguous. Given the perfectly inelastic total supply of labor, the increase in the demand for labor in the food sector raises the nominal wage w^*. As labor is reallocated from textile production to food production, the marginal product of labor falls in the food sector and rises in the textile sector. Thus, from the first equality in equation 11.6 we infer that w^* rises less than p_F^* (in percentage terms) and from the equality of the first and third expressions in equation 11.6 we learn than w^* rises relative to p_T^*. Whether workers' real purchasing power rises or falls depends on the relative importance of food and textiles in workers' consumption expenditure. If they spend the majority of their earnings on food, their real purchasing power falls. If they spend the majority on textiles, their real purchasing power rises.

To summarize what we have learned thus far:

> An increase in the world price of food in terms of textiles leads to an increase in domestic food production and a decrease in domestic textile production. The real earnings of factors specific to the food sector rise and the earnings of factors specific to the textile sector fall. The earnings of mobile factors of production rise relative to the price of textiles but fall relative to the price of food, and thus the net effect on their real incomes is ambiguous.

Equilibrium consumption and trade

The total value in world or domestic markets of the equilibrium production quantities F^* and T^* is $Y = p_F^* F^* + p_T^* T^*$. This entire value is paid out to Home's citizens in the form of wages or rental payments. Home's consumers thus have access to aggregate income Y, which they may use to buy food and textiles at prices p_F^* and p_T^* (whether they buy locally or in world markets). In equilibrium they must consume a pair of total quantities C_F^* and C_T^* that satisfies the **aggregate budget constraint**:[4]

$$p_F^* C_F^* + p_T^* C_T^* = p_F^* F^* + p_T^* T^* \qquad (11.9)$$

In Figure 11.2 the aggregate budget constraint is depicted by the isovalue line (of slope $-p_T^*/p_F^*$) that is tangent to the *PPF* at the equilibrium production point a. If consumers choose to consume at a point like b, to the right of a, the economy must import textiles and export food, because F^* exceeds C_F^* and C_T^* exceeds T^*. To consume at a point like c, to the left of a, the economy would export textiles and import food.

Where along the aggregate budget constraint does the Home economy consume? Recall that under our assumptions we may treat Home's many consumers as if they were a single consumer characterized by a single utility function. We may thus determine Home's aggregate consumption choices by finding the point on the aggregate budget constraint at which the representative consumer's utility is maximized. Utility is maximized when the marginal utility

---

[4]If the economy borrows from abroad, the value of its consumption exceeds the value of its production. If the economy lends abroad, the value of production exceeds the value of consumption. For simplicity here, however, we assume that the country neither borrows nor lends abroad. The analysis would be much the same if we assumed the country could borrow a fixed amount.

associated with the last peso spent on food is just equal to the marginal utility associated with the last peso spent on textiles, as in[5]

$$(1/p_F*)MU_F(C_F*, C_T*) = (1/p_T*)MU_T(C_F*, C_T*) \tag{11.10}$$

We may solve equations 11.9 and 11.10 for the equilibrium quantities C_F* and C_T*. We can identify this solution graphically by introducing into our graph a series of indifference curves (I_1, I_2, and I_3), much like those we employed in Chapter 6, and locating the point on the aggregate budget constraint that is tangent to the highest indifference curve. The Home economy described in Figure 11.3 produces at point a and consumes at point b. Home produces more food than it consumes and exports the difference ($X* = F* - C_F*$). It consumes more textiles than it produces and imports the difference ($M* = C_T* - T*$). The shaded triangle connecting points a and b is called Home's **trade triangle**. The larger this triangle, the more important international trade is in Home's economy.

Terms of trade changes and their effects

A country's **terms of trade** is defined as the world relative price of its export product in terms of its import product. Home's terms of trade improve when the relative price of food rises. In Figure 11.3, an improvement in Home's terms of trade would cause the relevant isovalue lines to become flatter. Home would respond by shifting more labor into the production of its export, its trade triangle would expand, and it would manage to consume on a higher aggregate indifference

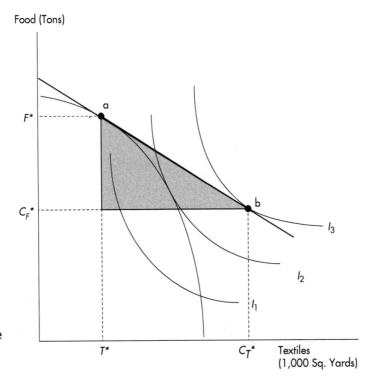

FIGURE 11.3
General Equilibrium Determination of Consumption and Trade in a Simple Specific Factors Economy

---

[5]The reader may verify that if this condition did not hold, it would be possible to increase utility by shifting a peso of expenditure from where the marginal utility is lower to where it is greater.

curve, indicating an improvement in aggregate consumption levels. Though aggregate consumption levels improve, we know from the preceding analysis that when the relative price of food rises, real incomes and consumption levels rise for owners of land and fall for owners of capital and that the effect on workers' real incomes is ambiguous. The observation that aggregate consumption levels improve indicates that the gains in real consumption by the "winners" must be greater than the loss in real consumption by the "losers."

Endowment differences, comparative advantage, the direction of trade, and gains from trade

World relative prices have important implications for Home's general equilibrium prices, production structure, and income distribution. But what determines world relative prices? And why does Home enter into international markets in the first place? Our answer here is very similar to the discussion in Appendix 8A regarding the gains from exchange between households or villages. If countries differ in their relative aptitudes for producing food and textiles, trade allows each country to exploit its comparative advantage, producing more of what the country is relatively well endowed to produce and then obtaining some of the other good through trade. To see how this works in the specific factors model, assume that the entire world contains just two countries, Home and Foreign, that they share the same production functions for food and textiles and the same representative consumer utility function, and that the ratio of land to capital is higher in Home than in Foreign. This causes Home's *PPF* to be steeper than Foreign's *PPF*, as illustrated in Figure 11.4.

If international trade were impossible, so that each country remained in autarky, each country would have to consume only what it produces. That is, it would have to produce *and* consume at a single point on its *PPF*. The *PPF* would essentially become the economy's aggregate budget constraint. To achieve maximum aggregate well-being, the economy would have to produce at the point along its *PPF* at which it is just tangent to an indifference curve.[6] Home's domestic relative price of textiles would adjust to the level associated with the dashed line in Figure 11.4a, which is just tangent to both the *PPF* and an indifference curve at point a.[7] Under our assumptions that render Home's *PPF* steeper and that render preferences identical in the two countries, we know that

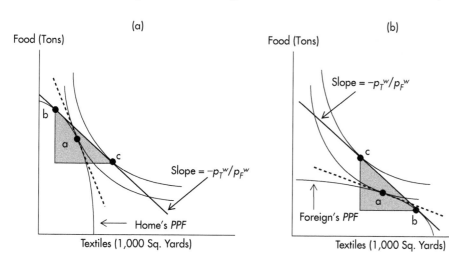

FIGURE 11.4
International General
Equilibrium and the Gains
from Trade

Foreign would achieve autarky equilibrium at point a in Figure 11.4b, with a *lower* domestic relative price of textiles (i.e., flatter domestic price isovalue line). We will see that this difference in autarky relative prices creates the potential for both countries to gain from trade.

What happens when (costless) international trade between Home and Foreign becomes possible? Home no longer has to consume only what it produces. The rate at which international exchanges of food for textiles take place is given by the world relative price (p_F^w/p_T^w), which would also become the domestic relative price in both countries. Knowing each country's *PPF* and preferences, we can determine how much each country would like to produce, consume, import, and export when facing any relative price. With only two countries in the world, equilibrium in international markets requires that what Home desires to export is just equal to what Foreign desires to import, and vice versa. The world relative price must therefore adjust until the two countries' trade triangles are identical but extend out in opposite directions from their production points. This equilibrium price will have to fall in between the relative prices that would obtain in each country in autarky. We see what this world market equilibrium looks like in Figure 11.4. Home produces at point b in Figure 11.4a and consumes at point c. It produces more food than it did in autarky and achieves a higher level of aggregate utility. Foreign exports textiles and imports food.

In world market equilibrium, each country exports the good for which its autarky relative price would be lower. With a higher ratio of land to capital, Home's *PPF* is steeper than Foreign's *PPF*, and with identical preferences, Home's *PPF* is tangent to an indifference curve at a point with steeper slope. This implies that the autarky relative price of food is lower in Home and that the autarky relative price of textiles is lower in Foreign. Home is said to have **comparative advantage** in food production, and Foreign has comparative advantage in textile production. When trade opens up between them, they exploit their comparative advantages by **specializing** in (i.e., shifting a greater fraction of their mobile factors into the production of) the good in which they have comparative advantage. As a result, both countries enjoy **gains from trade**, in the sense of expanding their aggregate consumption possibilities and reaching higher indifference curves. The theory does not tell us how large the gains from trade will be or how they will be shared between Home and Foreign.

Unfortunately, we know that the aggregate gains from trade do *not* translate into universal gains from trade at the level of individual citizens. When a country enters into trade, the relative price of the good that becomes its export rises. As we learned earlier, this raises the real rental rate on the fixed factor in its export sector, lowers the real rental rate on the fixed factor in its import-competing sector, and raises (or lowers) the real wage if workers devote small (or large) shares of consumption expenditure to the exported good.

11.3B Interpretation and extension of the specific factors model

The specific factors model as a model of the short run

For simplicity we have given the name "land" to the immobile factor in the food sector and the name "capital" to the immobile factor in the textile sector. We treated land and capital as permanently immobile, with no potential to find productive use outside their original sectors. We could instead have given the same name (e.g., "capital") to the fixed factors in both sectors, acknowledging some potential for these factors to be redeployed across sectors. We could then interpret the specific factors model as describing a **short run**, during which capital (whether physical or human) does not have time to shift across sectors, even while some more mobile factors (e.g., unskilled labor) do have time to move across sectors in response to wage changes. When interpreted this way, the model reminds us that when production in one sector becomes more profitable relative to the other, wages and rental rates paid to any factors that are not instantaneously mobile will rise in the favored sector and fall in the disfavored sector.

We would expect the emergence of premium pay in the favored sector to inspire eventual movement of specific factors out of the declining sector and into the rising sector, tending to erase the premium. To examine the resulting longer-run equilibrium we must leave behind the specific factors model and construct another model. One such longer-run model, the factor proportions model, is presented in the next section. First, however, we consider the implications of introducing goods market transfer costs and labor mobility costs into the specific factors model and examine the implications of the extended model for the effects of international market conditions and domestic trade policy on production structure, income distribution, and poverty.

Transfer and mobility costs, infrastructure, and institutions

We know from partial equilibrium analysis that when international transactions are costly, the domestic price of imports is higher than the world market price and the domestic price of exports is lower. International transfer costs thus worsen the effective terms of trade that any country faces in international markets. Improvements in infrastructure and institutions (along the lines suggested by section 11.2B) that reduce international transfer costs—important forces behind globalization—would improve a country's terms of trade, increase the relative importance of exports and trade in the economy, bring improvements in aggregate consumption levels, and increase real income for factors specific to its export sectors. They would also, however, bring reductions in real income for factors specific to import sectors and would result in ambiguous changes in workers' well-being.

From Chapter 8 we also know that if domestic trade between outlying areas and port cities is costly, some parts of the economy can remain unintegrated with national and international markets. Modest changes in world prices would leave the prices of goods and factors unchanged in those regions. We could think of a country's *PPF* as representing the production possibilities involving the factors only *in regions that are integrated into the national market*. Changing world prices would change goods and factor prices within the integrated regions, but they would leave goods and factor prices unchanged in more remote areas. Under such circumstances, improvements in the terms of trade have reduced potential to deliver aggregate consumption gains. Improvements in infrastructure and institutions that reduce domestic transfer costs thus increase the economy's capacity to gain from trade.

To exploit comparative advantage and gains from trade, an economy must shift labor into the export sector and out of other sectors. When production of different goods takes place in different parts of a country, this requires workers to migrate from regions specialized in the production of import-competing goods (or goods not traded in international markets) to regions specialized in export production. In the absence of migration costs, migration would immediately equalize wages in all regions of the country. When migration is costly, however, wages need not be equated everywhere. Workers might be mobile across sectors within a region but immobile across regions. In this case, real wages might rise more (or fall less) in regions where export production is concentrated than in other regions. Factors specific to import-competing sectors would also lose more in regions where export production is concentrated than in other regions. (We will see empirical evidence of this later.) Improvements in infrastructure and institutions that reduce migration costs (along the lines suggested in Chapter 9) might thus improve the economy's potential to gain from trade and would also alter the effects of trade on income distribution.

Import tariffs

When Home imposes a tariff on imports, the relative price of imported goods faced by local producers rises (even though the world relative price does not change). This raises general equilibrium production of import-competing goods (textiles) and reduces production of exports (food). Tariffs encourage domestic producers of the import-competing good by providing them with **protection** from international competition. By increasing the import-competing sector's demand for factors of production, the policy also implicitly taxes the export sector (by driving up the prices of factors of production), inducing its decline. Both imports and exports decline, reducing the extent to which the country participates in international markets. The policy thus prevents the country from enjoying some of the gains from trade, thereby reducing aggregate consumption levels. Not everyone in the country loses, however. According to the analysis above, only owners of factors specific to the export sector lose for sure. Owners of immobile factors in the import-competing sector gain, and workers might either gain or lose. The loss in aggregate consumption implies that the losses of the losers must be larger than the gains to the winners.

If foreign countries impose tariffs on their imports from Home and other countries, and if the foreign countries are large enough to affect world market prices, then their reduction in demand for Home's exports causes Home's terms of trade to deteriorate, again bringing aggregate losses for Home (and for the foreign countries themselves).

Trade and poverty

The specific factors model examines the impact of trade and world price changes on the real incomes of abstract laborers and of owners of land and capital, possibly differentiated by regions of the country in the presence of internal transfer and mobility costs. In the real world, as we saw in Chapter 7, households often derive income as owners of more than one factor of production. For example, farm households—even poor ones—derive income as owners of land as well as owners of labor. It is thus impossible to translate the model's predictions regarding the incomes of factors of production (and the functional distribution of income) into predictions regarding poverty (and the distribution of income across income classes) unless we bring in additional information regarding the way labor, skills, capital, and land are distributed across households living at different income levels.

Moreover, even among "the poor," some might earn income largely from labor, and others might earn income largely from land. Similarly, some might live in regions where the export sector is concentrated, while others live in regions where import-competing production is located and yet others live in locations largely outside the reach of international market influences. Thus, even among the poor, some might gain while others lose from changes in world market prices or domestic policies toward international trade. The distribution of the poor across categories is likely to vary greatly across countries. Thus, world prices and trade policy are likely to have different net impacts on aggregate poverty measures across countries.

General lessons

Despite its simplicity, the specific factors model yields some useful general lessons. First, it offers intuition as to why opportunities for international trade yield aggregate benefits for all countries, as each country better exploits its comparative advantage. Whether these aggregate gains are large or small is an empirical question. Second, the model suggests that in the short run increased trade (and the associated increase in export production) will benefit owners of relatively immobile factors at work in the export sector, including physical capital, sector-specific skills, and land on which export crop production is feasible. It will also harm factors that remain stuck in declining sectors producing import-competing and nontraded goods, again possibly including sector-specific skills and land specific to imported and nontraded crops, as well as capital. All of these effects may be stronger in regions where export producers are concentrated than in other regions, as a result of barriers to geographic mobility. Whether mobile and unskilled laborers gain, how large are the real income effects on specific factors, and how long this "short run" might last are all empirical questions meriting research in the study of international trade and its effects. We will see below how the experiences of the 1990s influenced researchers' answers to these questions.

11.3C **The factor proportions model**

In the short-run interpretation of the specific factors model, an increase in the terms of trade raises the rental rate on export sector capital (and other relatively immobile factors devoted to export production) and reduces the rental rate on import sector capital. Economic intuition suggests that this would stimulate additional rounds of change. Owners of import sector capital, seeing higher returns in the export sector, would have an incentive to move their capital. Such shifts in the supply of capital, out of the import-competing sector and into the export sector, would bring export sector rental rates down from their peak and raise the import-competing sector's rental rates up from their trough, eventually bringing rental rates into equality at some intermediate level. But would this new longer-run equilibrium rental rate lie above or below the rate capital owners enjoyed before the increase in the terms of trade? And how would the reallocation of capital affect the real wage? Such questions motivate interest in a second well-known model of general equilibrium and trade: the factor proportions model.

Basic assumptions

Consider a simple economy that produces two goods, textiles and chemicals, in quantities T and C, with just two factors of production, labor and capital, and assume that the capital stock K, labor stock L, and technology are constant. Critically, we also assume that both labor *and* capital are mobile across sectors.

We will see that in this model the distributional effects of trade hinge on the nature of technological differences between sectors. To focus attention on the critical dimension of technological difference, we assume that textile production is **labor intensive** relative to chemical production. This means that when both sectors face the same wage w and rental rate on capital r, the ratio of labor to capital chosen by profit-maximizing textile producers, L_T/K_T, is always higher than the comparable ratio in the chemical sector, L_C/K_C. By definition, if textile production is labor intensive, then chemical production is **capital intensive**. Intuitively, we are assuming that capital is inherently of greater relative importance in chemical production than in textile production. All other assumptions remain the same as in the specific factors model. We have just built a simple version of the **factor proportions model**.[8] Box 11.3 summarizes the basic assumptions and notation.

Capital mobility

We assume that capital is mobile across sectors, not because we believe that machines created for producing textiles can literally be moved and redeployed for producing chemicals, but because we want to acknowledge the potential for the owners of capital to gradually move their wealth out of declining sectors and into rising ones. Some machines may be redeployed after modest modification, and other machines that are no longer required may be sold for scrap, with the proceeds used for purchasing assets in rising sectors. Yet other assets may simply be allowed to depreciate, without being repaired or replaced and with the funds that might have been used to maintain their value instead used to create capital in other sectors. For simplicity, we examine the implications of capital mobility under the extreme assumption that all capital equipment is mobile across sectors and that producers therefore treat capital as a variable factor of production.

Because reallocation of capital across sectors takes time, the factor proportions model is often referred to as a model of trade and general equilibrium in the long run. Notice, however, that it is a rather artificial kind of long run, in which capital is capable of moving across sectors but the total quantity of capital and the nature of technology remain constant. We make these assumptions to focus our attention on the long-run effects of trade on production structure and income

---

[8]This model is often called the Heckscher–Ohlin model in honor of the two Swedish economists who developed it, Bertil Ohlin (1933) and his Ph.D. advisor, Eli Hechscher.

☰ Box 11.3 The Simple Factor Proportions Model: Assumptions and Notation

Assumptions

- Two goods: textiles and chemicals
- Two factors: labor and capital
- Labor and capital are both mobile
- Textile production is labor intensive relative to chemical production
- Producers maximize profits
- A representative consumer maximizes utility
- Markets are competitive
- The home country is small
- Transactions are costless

Notation

L, K = total quantities of labor, capital
L_T, L_C = labor employed in textiles, chemicals
K_T, K_C = capital employed in textiles, chemicals

T, C = quantities produced of textiles, chemicals
C_T, C_C = quantities consumed of textiles, chemicals
X, M = quantities of exports, imports
p_T^w, p_C^w = world prices of textiles, chemicals
p_T, p_C = domestic prices of textiles, chemicals
w = wage
r = rental rate
$t(L_T, K_T)$ = textile production function
$c(L_C, K_C)$ = chemical production function
$MPL_T(L_T, K_T), MPL_C(L_C, K_C)$ = marginal products of labor in textile production, chemical production
$MPK_T(L_T, K_T), MPK_C(L_C, K_C)$ = marginal products of capital in textile production, chemical production
$U(C_T, C_C)$ = representative consumer's utility function

distribution. In the next section we expand the discussion to include possible long-run impacts on investment (i.e., increases in the quantity of capital), innovation (i.e., technological improvements), and growth. To highlight this distinction, we refer to the factor proportions model as a model of the medium run.

Equilibrium domestic prices

Again, equilibrium domestic prices must equal world prices, and thus $p_T^* = p_T^w$ and $p_C^* = p_C^w$.

Equilibrium factor use and production

To determine equilibrium factor use and production in this economy, we must determine how both labor and capital are allocated across sectors. Knowing that labor and capital stocks must be fully employed in equilibrium, we know that

$$L_T^* + L_C^* = L \tag{11.11}$$

$$K_T^* + K_C^* = K \tag{11.12}$$

We also know that profit-maximizing producers in both sectors will set the value of the marginal product of labor equal to the same wage; thus in equilibrium labor will be allocated across sectors until the value of its marginal product is the same in both sectors. Similarly, the values of the marginal product of capital in the two sectors will be set equal to the rental rate and thus equal to each other. Hence we have

$$p_T^* MPL_T(L_T^*, K_T^*) = p_C^* MPL_C(L_C^*, K_C^*) \tag{11.13}$$

$$p_T^* MPK_T(L_T^*, K_T^*) = p_C^* MPK_C(L_C^*, K_C^*) \tag{11.14}$$

Given that we have already determined p_F^* and p_C^*, equations 11.11, 11.12, 11.13, and 11.14 constitute four equations in the four unknowns L_T^*, L_C^*, K_T^*, and K_C^*, allowing us to solve for equilibrium factor allocations. Having obtained the equilibrium levels of factor use, we may calculate the equilibrium levels of textile and chemical production by employing the production functions

$$T = t(L_T^*, K_T^*) \tag{11.15}$$

$$C = c(L_C^*, K_C^*) \tag{11.16}$$

Again we may examine the equilibrium factor use and production quantities implied by these equations using a *PPF* diagram. The *PPF* in Figure 11.5 traces out all combinations of textiles and chemicals that the economy could produce when all its production factors and technologies are put to most efficient use. With textiles T in thousands of square yards on the vertical axis and chemicals C in tons on the horizontal axis, we could trace out the *PPF* by determining the maximum quantity T that the economy could produce when already producing any given quantity of chemicals C. This maximization of T while holding C constant requires not only fully employing both factors as in equations 11.11 and 11.12 and making best use of the production functions equations 11.15 and 11.16 but also adjusting how the two factors are allocated across sectors until it is impossible to raise textile production without reducing chemical production. This requires that[9]

$$MPL_T(L_T^*, K_T^*)/MPK_T(L_T^*, K_T^*) = MPL_C(L_C^*, K_C^*)/MPK_C(L_C^*, K_C^*) \tag{11.17}$$

We know, by taking the ratio of the equalities in equations 11.13 and 11.14, that profit-maximization and competitive labor markets guarantee fulfillment of this condition.

In this model, as we move from the northwest to the southeast along the *PPF* (in a graph like Figure 11.5), we describe what happens as we move labor *and* capital out of textile production and into chemical production. Furthermore, as we increase the share of the economy's factors devoted to chemical production (the capital-intensive sector), we must also *increase* the ratio of labor to capital employed within each sector. To see why, recall that the labor—capital ratio in the capital-intensive chemical sector, L_C/K_C, is by definition always lower than the labor—capital ratio in the labor-intensive textile sector, L_T/K_T. If these ratios were to hold constant while we reduced textile production by one unit, each unit of capital released from textile production would bring with it more labor than would be absorbed with one unit of capital into chemical production, leaving some labor idle. Full employment of labor can be re-achieved only if the labor—capital ratios employed within sectors rise.

We may again demonstrate that equilibrium production is found at a point on the *PPF* that is just tangent to an isovalue line with slope equal to $-p_C^*/p_T^*$, such as V_1 in Figure 11.5.[10] As the world relative price of textiles rises, the relevant isovalue line in Figure 11.5 would become flatter, equilibrium textile production would rise, and chemical production would fall. Both labor and capital would shift from chemical production to textile production and the ratio of labor to capital employed in each sector would fall.

---

[9]When we withdraw one unit of labor from chemicals, we reduce chemical output by $MPL_C(L_C^*, K_C^*)$. We could restore C to its original level by moving in $MPL_C(L_C^*, K_C^*)/MPK_C(L_C^*/K_C^*)$ units of capital. Similarly, to maintain textile production when we add one unit of labor we would have to reduce capital by $MPL_T(L_T^*, K_T^*)/MPK_T(L_T^*, K_T^*)$. If $MPL_T(L_T^*, K_T^*)/MPK_T(L_T^*, K_T^*)$ is greater than $MPL_C(L_C^*, K_C^*)/MPK_C(L_C^*, K_C^*)$, then if we moved one unit of labor from chemicals to textiles but held textile production constant by removing capital, we could use some of the capital released to restore chemical production to its original level and still have some capital left over, with which we could increase production of either good. Only when equation 11.17 holds is it impossible to increase production in this way.

[10]Rearranging the second equality in equation 11.13, we find that in general equilibrium $MPL_T(L_T^*, K_T^*)/MPL_C(L_C^*, K_C^*) = p_C^*/p_T^*$. The ratio of marginal products on the left side of this equation is an expression for the slope of the *PPF*.

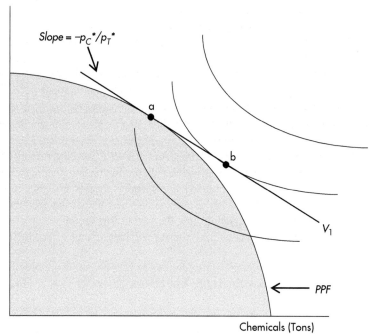

FIGURE 11.5
General Equilibrium in a
Simple Factor
Proportions Model

Equilibrium factor prices and the functional distribution of income

Each factor must be paid the value of its marginal product. Thus we know that

$$w^* = p_T^* MPL_T(L_T^*, K_T^*) = p_C^* MPL_C(L_C^*, K_C^*) \tag{11.18}$$

$$r^* = p_T^* MPK_T(L_T^*, K_T^*) = p_C^* MPK_C(L_C^*, K_C^*) \tag{11.19}$$

These equations describe w^* and r^* as functions of equilibrium quantities whose values we have already determined and allow us to examine how factor prices change in response to world price changes.

The implications for factor prices of an increase in the world price of textiles are somewhat simpler in this model than in the specific factors model. The equilibrium wage w^* must rise more than p_T^* (and thus relative to both goods prices) because the movement up and to the left along the PPF in Figure 11.5 requires a reduction in L_T^*/K_T^*, which raises $MPL_T(L_T^*, K_T^*)$. Similar reasoning indicates that r^* falls relative to both goods prices. Intuitively, as production falls in the chemical sector and rises in the textile sector, the ratio of labor to capital newly demanded in the textile sector is greater than the ratio of labor to capital released by the chemical sector. The incipient excess demand for labor (and excess supply of capital) drives the real wage up and the real rental rate down. It is this increase in the relative cost of labor that induces producers in both sectors to reduce their labor—capital ratios until both factors are again fully employed. Notice that workers in the chemical sector stand to gain from a reduction in the relative price of chemicals, even though it leads to a decline in the chemical sector, because the shift from chemical to textile production raises the relative demand for labor.

Comparative advantage and the direction of trade

As before, Home's aggregate budget constraint under trade is given by the isovalue line tangent to the PPF at the point of production (V_1 in Figure 11.5), and we may introduce aggregate indifference curves to identify the point along this aggregate budget constraint at which the Home economy consumes. As long as the production point is not the same as the consumption point, Home engages in the export of one good and the import of the other. If Home is a textile exporter (as in Figure 11.5), an increase in the relative price of textiles, p_T^*/p_C^*, causes it to produce and export more textiles and to reduce chemical production and increase chemical imports.

As in the specific factors model, trade improves aggregate consumption in both countries as long as one country has a steeper *PPF* than the other. Here the country with the steeper *PPF* exports textiles while the other country exports chemicals. (The country depicted in Figure 11.5 must have a steeper *PPF* than the rest of the world with which it trades.) In the specific factors model, differences in the slopes of *PPF*s arise out of differences in shares of immobile factors that are allocated to the two sectors. In the simple factor proportions model, differences in the slopes of *PPF*s arise solely out of differences in **relative factor abundance**, or differences in the ratios of total labor quantity (L) to total capital quantity (K). If the two countries have access to identical technologies for producing textiles and chemicals, then the country that is relatively abundant in labor (i.e., has a higher ratio of L to K) has a steeper *PPF* and has comparative advantage in the production of the labor-intensive good (textiles), whereas the other country has a flatter *PPF* and has comparative advantage in the capital-intensive good (chemicals).[11]

When trade is opened up between two countries in the factor proportions model, each produces more of the good that is intensive in its relatively abundant factor. For example, because labor is relatively abundant in the country depicted in Figure 11.5, the opening to trade leads to an increase in the country's production (and export) of the labor-intensive good, textiles. Again, both countries enjoy aggregate consumption gains from the opening of trade. However, as in the specific factors model, the gains are not shared equally by all people. According to the logic presented above, often referred to as the **Stolper–Samuelson theorem** (Stolper and Samuelson, 1941):

> In the medium run represented by the factor proportions model, the opening of trade increases the real return to the country's relatively abundant factor but reduces the real return to the country's relatively scarce factor.

Infrastructure and institutions

If Home is to gain from improved opportunities to trade with Foreign, it must be able to reallocate labor and capital out of its import-competing sector (chemicals) and into its export sector (textiles). In the model this involves only a simple movement along a smooth *PPF*, but in the real world it can require many kinds of investment: the creation of new firms by entrepreneurs, the acquisition of new skills by workers, cooperation among potential new exporters in acquiring information about foreign markets, the construction of roads to newly important regions, and the upgrading of port facilities. The labor market frictions examined in Chapter 9 and the obstacles to investment examined in Chapter 10 can slow or prevent the necessary reallocations. Thus:

> Involvement by governments and NGOs in such activities as creating public goods, coordinating marketing activities, overcoming financial constraints, and encouraging specific training may be required before a country can benefit fully from improved opportunities for international trade.

---

[11]Why does greater relative abundance of capital lead to a steeper *PPF*? Notice the following. We identify the leftmost end of the *PPF* by asking: "What quantity of textiles would we get if we devoted our entire factor stocks, K and L, to textile production?" Let's denote this quantity T_m. We identify the rightmost end by asking: "How much food would we get if we devoted all K and L to food production?" Let's call this quantity F_m. A country with a high ratio of K to L has factor endowments more suited to textiles production, and thus its ratio of T_m to L_m will be higher than in the other country. Its *PPF* will be steeper.

Will everyone favor such **complementary policies**? Probably not. In a country relatively abundant in low-skill labor, the owners of physical or human capital initially located in the export sector might prefer to retain barriers to the inflow of capital into their sector because such inflow would tend to drive down the real earnings they enjoy as owners of specific factors.

11.3D General lessons and questions

The specific factors and factor proportions models each yield quite stark implications for the effects of the opening of trade or changes in world prices on the functional distribution of income. The specific factors model predicts that an increase in the relative price of a country's export will raise real earnings for owners of factors specific to the export sector while reducing real earnings for owners of factors specific to the import competing sector. The factor proportions model predicts that in the medium run such a relative price increase would increase the real return to the country's relatively abundant factor and reduce the real return to the country's relatively scarce factor, regardless of the sectors in which the factors are employed.

Unfortunately, the simplicity of these theoretical models renders them difficult to map onto the real world. When attempting to use the factor proportions model for describing the real world, for example, does it make sense to focus on agriculture and manufacturing, which differ primarily in the intensity with which they use land, or to distinguish light manufacturing and agriculture from heavy manufacturing, emphasizing differences in capital intensity? And would some other mapping lead to even more accurate predictions regarding the effects of trade on economic structure and income distribution? In what follows we describe how empirical observations over the course of several decades have led to profound changes in economists' answers to these questions.

11.3E Trade liberalization and income distribution: surprises in the 1990s

In the 1970s and 1980s, the default model guiding economists' thoughts about trade, comparative advantage, and income distribution was a simple factor proportions model, in which developing countries had comparative advantage in low-skill, labor-intensive production and thus in which increased openness to trade was expected to reduce inequality and poverty in developing countries. Trade should raise the relative price of low-skill, labor-intensive goods in developing countries, shift productive resources into those sectors, raise the real wages of low-skilled labor, and reduce the real returns to human and physical capital. Thus, as indicated earlier, empirical evidence that trade liberalization was accompanied by *rising* inequality in many countries in the 1990s came as a surprise. A key feature of rising inequality in many of these countries was a rising *skill premium*, or rising wage differential between skilled and unskilled labor. In some countries, including China, interregional inequality was also rising, with incomes rising faster in regions where rising export industries were concentrated.

Upon closer inspection, the puzzle became more complicated. In a simple factor proportions world, rising trade should increase the real return of the country's abundant factor through a process that shifts production factors out of the import-competing sector into the export sector. But the data often showed very little change in the allocation of workers across sectors in response to liberalization. Instead, among workers with comparable skills and characteristics, average wages rose in sectors that were favored by trade reforms and fell in disfavored sectors. Within sectors, evidence suggested some reallocation of workers from smaller, less-productive firms to larger, more-productive firms with greater involvement in international markets (Bernard and Jensen, 1997).

If all these developments were the result of trade liberalization, then the simple factor proportions view of the world appeared inadequate. At the very least, significant frictions seemed to inhibit worker mobility across sectors, especially when different sectors were located in different geographic areas. The empirical observations thus increased interest in the specific factors model, suggesting that the "short run" represented by the model might last a long time empirically.

Empirical results also raised the question of whether the line dividing activities in which developing countries do and do not have comparative advantage might fall *within* sectors rather than between sectors. Trade can favor the larger and more productive firms within sectors that are capable of overcoming the hurdles to involvement in export markets. It can also favor firms specializing in specific segments of a sector's production process that are most likely to be outsourced from developed to developing countries. These activities, furthermore, might be low-skilled–labor intensive relative to other sectors in developed countries but nonetheless skill-intensive relative to other sectors within developing countries (Feenstra and Hanson, 1997). Exporting activities might also simply require more skill than producing for domestic markets. If this is the case, then skills development might be crucial for allowing developing countries to take better advantage of globalization and to spread the benefits of globalization more equitably throughout society.

Whether trade liberalization was, in fact, the prime determinant of the observed increases in inequality during the 1990s remains a matter of debate. In most countries trade liberalizations were accompanied by other reforms, including liberalizing changes in labor market regulations, privatization of state-owned enterprises, and an opening to international capital flows, which might also have driven the changes in inequality. Rising skill premiums might also have been driven by skill-biased technical change independent of trade liberalization.

In an effort to distinguish the effects of trade liberalization from the effects of other changes in policy or technology, several economists turned to data on households and enterprises within countries and considered whether income distribution changes were greater in sectors that experienced more dramatic trade liberalizations. They found that skill premiums increased more in sectors experiencing more dramatic liberalization, a correlation that is hard to attribute to changes in nontrade policies. These findings suggest that trade contributed to the increase in inequality *and* that production factors are not perfectly mobile across sectors (Goldberg et al., 2007). (In a simple factor proportions world with all factors perfectly mobile, factor returns should change in identical ways across *all* sectors.) Evidence that the ratio of skilled to unskilled labor in Colombia rose the most in sectors that liberalized the most also raises the possibility that increased trade encouraged more rapid skill-biased improvements in technology (Attanasio et al., 2004). Researchers continue to probe the role of increased trade in rising inequality (McMillan and Verduzco, 2010).

In light of the surprising evidence on income inequality, researchers also realized the need to take a more careful look at the potential connections between trade and poverty. They were forced to abandon the view (inspired by simple applications of the factor proportions model) that trade would unambiguously and uniformly reduce poverty in developing countries. They recognized that rising export prices (especially for food exports) would have differential effects on the real incomes of net buyers and net sellers of the export goods, that prices might not change to the same degree in all regions of the country, and that households might not benefit to the same degree from rising wages (because some are net sellers of labor and some are net buyers, and some incapacitated households neither buy nor sell labor). They thus recognized that trade was bound to generate both winners and losers among the poor in any country and that the net effect on poverty was likely to differ across countries. See the discussion of the poverty impacts of rising world food prices in Chapter 7 and the analysis of agricultural pricing policies (including policies toward agricultural imports and exports) in Chapter 17 for a more detailed look at these concerns.

One particularly compelling study of the causal effect of trade liberalization on poverty pertains to India (Topalova, 2007). The author argues that trade liberalization was differentially relevant across geographic regions, because sectors that had experienced greater tariff reductions employed greater fractions of the labor force in some regions of the country than others. She furthermore argues that the pattern of tariff changes across sectors was largely unrelated to the sectors' economic conditions or political influence because the pattern of changes was driven by the aim of rapidly rendering tariffs more uniform across sectors rather than by political maneuvering. She thus expects the correlation across regions between the intensity of liberalization and changes in poverty to represent the causal effect of differential liberalization on poverty changes.[12] She demonstrates that while poverty rates were declining throughout India during this period for many reasons, they declined *less* in districts more affected by trade liberalization, suggesting that the causal effect of greater trade opening was to *increase* poverty. Such research brings home the need for careful context-specific study of the likely poverty impacts of trade liberalization and for careful design of liberalization and safety net policy packages that protect the potential losers from severe losses.

11.4 Trade, Investment, Innovation, and Economic Growth

11.4A A motivation

Economists' opinions regarding the role that international trade should play in developing countries' growth strategies have undergone dramatic swings over the last 60 years. During the 1950s many economists encouraged policymakers to protect their economies from the effects of international trade by imposing tariffs and other import restrictions. By the 1980s, many economists urged developing country governments to open their economies to international trade and argued that such policies were of first importance in development strategies. Currently, most economists continue to believe that openness to international trade has potential to encourage economic growth, but many now consider trade policies just one set of institutions among many that are important for growth. The evolution of opinion regarding ideal trade policies reflects the influences of developing countries' experiences and academic empirical research. Before discussing this evolution in more detail, it is useful to lay out the theoretical channels through which greater involvement in international trade might affect economic growth rates.

In the models of section 11.3 we examined the impacts of international trade that occur even while holding constant an economy's technology and stocks of productive assets. To examine the potential impacts of trade on economic growth, we now turn to the longer run, in which investment can increase the stock of capital and technologies can improve.

11.4B Theoretical possibilities

We note first that:

> Opening to trade might increase or decrease the rate of growth by favoring or disfavoring sectors that are inherently more dynamic.

The specific factors and factor proportions models suggest that opening to international trade will encourage a shift of productive resources into sectors or activities in which a country has comparative advantage. If export activities are inherently more dynamic than other production activities—in the sense that they tend to experience more rapid productivity advance themselves or encourage more rapid productivity advance in other sectors—then opening to trade can raise overall growth by increasing the share of a country's resources that are allocated to dynamic sectors. If, however, import-competing sectors are more dynamic, then opening to trade can reduce overall growth.

---

[12]Topalova (2007) recognizes that liberalization may also have generated some base changes in poverty that were shared equally across all regions, which her study cannot illuminate. Her study speaks only to differences in poverty change driven by differences in the intensity of liberalization across regions.

Some sectors may be more dynamic than others for several reasons.[13] Producers in a nascent sector might exhibit low productivity while new and small, but they may be able to achieve rapid productivity advance if given the opportunity to grow or gain experience. Their productivity can grow rapidly through a process of **learning by doing**, in which they work out, through trial and error, how to operate most productively in the local environment. In addition, all producers in a sector can achieve rapid productivity growth when the sector is encouraged to grow if they benefit from **agglomeration economies**, or externalities that cause increases in any one firm's production to reduce production costs for other firms in the same sector and location (through mechanisms described in Chapter 8). In principle, temporary policies that encourage the expansion of such sectors today might allow these sectors to gain productivity-enhancing experience and scale, thereby encouraging more rapid expansion of the economy's *PPF*.

Some sectors might also be more dynamic than others in the sense that they generate externalities that increase productivity in the rest of the economy. For example, encouraging the expansion of the relatively high-tech semiconductor industry in a developing country might indirectly encourage local research and development activities, which have the potential to raise productivity in many sectors. Industries generating such **interindustry externalities** might, in principle, merit long-term support.

In addition to influencing the allocation of resources to more dynamic sectors:

> Opening to trade can speed growth, regardless of the sectors involved, if international competition, potential for international expansion, cheaper imports of intermediate goods, or involvement in export markets tends to speed investment or productivity advance.

Opening to trade can encourage greater efficiency by increasing competitive pressures on domestic import-competing producers and by expanding the export sector, in which international competition is inherently important. Trade opening may, furthermore, encourage more rapid investment by shifting firms' orientation away from small domestic markets toward larger external markets, where expansion is possible without driving prices down. Tariff reductions that reduce the cost of importing inputs and intermediate goods might encourage foreign multi-nationals to outsource production tasks to newly opened economies, further expanding investment. The opening to trade might also allow domestic firms better access to improved technologies by bringing them into business relationships with foreign buyers and suppliers and by allowing them to import new technologies embodied in intermediate inputs.

As always, we must ask which, if any, of these theoretically possible relationships between international trade and economic growth are in fact empirically important. We must also ask whether any long-run growth benefits of policies that encourage or discourage trade outweigh the short- and medium-run costs.

11.4C Trade policy and growth over the last 60 years

This section reviews the evolution of policies toward international trade in developing countries. For a related but broader discussion of evolving thought regarding the determinants of economic growth in developing countries, see Chapter 4.

Import-substituting industrialization

In the 1950s, development analysts found it natural to divide all goods in the world into the categories *primary commodities* and *manufactures* and to assume that developing countries had comparative advantage in primary commodities and comparative *dis*advantage in *all* manufactures.

---

[13]Harrison and Rodriguez-Clare (2010) examine the theoretical possibilities in more detail. They also review the logic of why, when some sectors are sufficiently more dynamic than others that they merit encouragement, domestic production subsidies are likely to deliver better results than taxes or subsidies on imports or exports.

As a result, they believed that openness to international trade would solidify developing countries' specialization in the production of primary commodities and prevent them from developing domestic manufacturing sectors.[14]

Specialization in primary production was widely believed to threaten long-run growth prospects for two reasons. First, the terms of trade for exporters of primary commodities (especially agricultural produce) were expected to decline continuously over time, as rising world incomes raised demands for manufactures more rapidly than demands for food, thereby causing the prices of agricultural goods to fall relative to the prices of manufactured goods.[15] Second, developing country producers were thought capable of rapid productivity advances in manufacturing production, but only if the sector and its workers were given the chance to learn by doing or experience agglomeration economies. If afforded temporary protection from international competition, these **infant industries** would eventually achieve productivity levels comparable to those in developed countries. The resulting increase in manufacturing productivity relative to primary sector productivity would render developing countries less dependent on manufactured imports from the developed countries and would allow them to gain comparative advantage in some manufacturing sectors. All this growth potential would be lost if developing countries instead remained specialized in primary production.

Economists at the time were well aware of the logic of the gains from trade and thus the short- and medium-term losses in aggregate consumption that such infant-industry protection would bring. Many assumed, however, that by temporarily sacrificing the gains from trade, developing countries would reap future gains in technological prowess that would more than outweigh the near-term cost.[16] Many paid little attention to policy impacts on income distribution or poverty, believing that poverty reduction would follow naturally from economic growth.

Motivated by these ideas, many developing countries pursued **import-substituting industrialization** (ISI) through at least the 1960s. They used high tariffs, together with quantitative restrictions on imports and foreign exchange purchases, to protect domestic manufacturing sectors from international competition. They allowed real exchange rates to appreciate significantly, encouraged investment in protected sectors by keeping the cost of imported capital goods low, and provided subsidized financing for investment in protected sectors. Many countries also taxed agricultural exports at high rates, raising revenue for use in industrialization efforts.

Problems with import-substituting industrialization

By 1970, empirical evidence had begun to cast doubt on many tenets underlying ISI policies and was bringing to light unanticipated problems with ISI. The terms of trade for primary commodity exporters were not declining, and the anticipated productivity increases in infant manufacturing sectors were not materializing. Agriculture was stagnating, preventing the rural poor from sharing in growth and curtailing the expansion of domestic markets for import-substituting manufactured goods. Even though many developing countries had enjoyed rapid growth in the 1960s, poverty rates were not falling. On top of this, tariff rates varied wildly across similar manufactured goods within countries, encouraging haphazard and wasteful patterns of investment. The potential to profit from tariff protection also led manufacturers to waste resources in costly efforts to lobby government officials for protection.

---

[14]The discussion of the rise and decline of import-substituting industrialization draws heavily on Bruton (1998) and Krueger (1997).

[15]In neither a specific factors world nor a factor proportions world does belief that the terms of trade will decline justify policies to prevent international trade. A fall in the terms of trade reduces what a country can gain from trade, but free trade remains better than the alternative. Thus, it was only in conjunction with infant industry arguments that these beliefs lent support to policies of protection.

[16]Some analysts believed the short-term costs associated with reduced exports would be small, because they rejected as irrelevant for developing countries the models of general equilibrium and international trade presented above. The Lewis model of labor surplus dualistic development (discussed in Chapter 4), for example, suggested that labor could be drawn out of agriculture into manufacturing *without* reducing agricultural production.

Trade liberalization and outer orientation

Even as empirical revelations cast doubt on ISI, the experiences of Korea and Taiwan suggested a new way to understand both comparative advantage and the relationship between trade and growth in developing countries. In the late 1950s and early 1960s these countries had begun to pull away from ISI policies. Though they did not remove tariffs on imports, they sought to neutralize their impact on the structure of production by providing subsidies to export activities and allowing their exchange rates to depreciate. By the late 1960s they were clearly out-performing other developing countries, with higher rates of growth in exports and per capita GDP, and they were exporting not traditional primary commodities but manufactured goods! Moreover, their manufacturing production was more labor intensive than in other developing countries, and their poverty reduction performance was better. This suggested that developing countries' comparative advantage might lie not only in primary commodity production but also in the production of labor-intensive goods, including some manufactured goods.

Conviction regarding the need to open developing economies to international trade strengthened in the 1980s. Encouraged by the emerging view of comparative advantage, and inspired by the success of Korea and Taiwan, a number of countries had begun to liberalize their trade policies in the late 1970s. They reduced tariffs, quantitative import restrictions, and export taxes, or they compensated for import protection by offering new encouragements to exports. They allowed their exchange rates to depreciate and opened their economies to foreign capital. When rates of growth dropped off in many developing countries in the 1980s, these more open economies appeared to fare better.

Economists began running regressions of country growth rates on a variety of country characteristics, including measures of their openness to international trade, often finding a systematic tendency for more open economies to grow faster (see Sachs and Warner, 1995, for a much-cited example). Eventually, economists started not only to reject earlier beliefs in the inherent dynamism of infant import-competing industries but also to believe that involvement in export markets was crucial for encouraging rapid productivity advance. The observation that exporting firms had higher average productivity than nonexporting firms within the same sectors appeared to support such belief. Soon many major international development organizations, and many developing-country governments themselves, began pushing for more trade liberalization.

Current perspectives on trade and growth

In recent years calls for trade liberalization as the route to rapid growth have become more qualified for several reasons. First, Rodríguez and Rodrik (2001), among others, called into question the results of earlier econometric studies relating country growth rates to trade openness. They pointed out problems with the measurement of trade openness, potential biases arising out of inadequate control for other policy reforms undertaken in conjunction with trade policy reforms, and inadequate control for the possibility that the correlation between growth and trade openness reflects the effect of growth on openness as well as the effect of openness on growth. They also demonstrated that the results were not robust to small changes in econometric specifications.

Second, closer study of panel data following individual firms over time raised doubts about earlier conclusions that increased involvement in export markets raises firms' productivity. Studies revealed that exporting firms were more productive than other firms even *before* they started exporting, suggesting that the correlation between exporting and firm productivity reflects, at least in part, the selection of more productive firms into export activities rather than a productivity-enhancing effect of involvement in export markets.[17] An early wave of studies

---

[17]Whether trade speeds growth and whether exporting enhances productivity remain subjects of debate. For an interesting recent contribution to the study of openness and growth, see Feyrer (2009).

demonstrated very little improvement in productivity after firms entered export markets. A later wave of studies, employing data from lower-income countries, found somewhat more evidence for learning by exporting; see Box 11.4.

Third, and perhaps more important, some countries that accomplished major liberalizing trade policy reforms in the 1990s failed to enjoy the anticipated growth success, or saw growth accelerate only many years after the reforms. Weak initial export expansion, especially in Africa, led many analysts to recognize the vital importance of investments in infrastructure and institutional development, both as complements to trade liberalization and as sources of growth in their own right (World Bank, 2005). More recently, exports and growth rates have risen precisely in the subset of African countries that have made significant progress in infrastructure construction, education expansion and democratization, and liberalizing trade policy (Radelet, 2010).

None of these recent qualifications suggest that trade is bad for growth. Indeed, successful growth almost always takes place in countries where participation in international markets is expanding, and most economists see integration into international markets as useful for growth. The qualifications merely point out that trade policy is only one component of a broader set of policies that have complementary importance for growth.

≡ **Box 11.4** Learning by Exporting?

One way trade liberalization might spur economic growth is by providing domestic firms with greater opportunity to *learn by exporting*, or experience productivity increases driven by involvement in export markets. By the mid-1990s many cross-section comparisons documented higher average productivity in exporting firms relative to non-exporting firms in the same industries, and many analysts interpreted this productivity difference as evidence of learning by exporting. The productivity differences might arise for a very different reason, however. If firms incur a fixed cost when they enter export markets, then only the firms whose higher productivity allows them to sell larger quantities profitably in foreign markets might find participation in export markets beneficial. The correlation between exporting and productivity might thus reflect the selection of higher-productivity firms into export activities.

Sofronis Clerides, Saul Lach, and James Tybout (1998) sought to distinguish the relative importance of learning by exporting and self-selection for explaining productivity differences by taking advantage of a new type of data set that was only just becoming available for developing countries: firm-level panel data sets that allow careful study of firms' productivity and exporting activity over five- or 10-year periods. They pointed out that if more productive firms select themselves into export market participation, then we ought to observe that exporting firms were more productive than others even *before* they started exporting. Similarly, if involvement in export markets raises firms' productivity, then we ought to observe that productivity levels or growth rates improve for firms *after* they start exporting.

Working with data on nearly all firms with at least 10 workers in Colombia (1981–1991) and Morocco (1984–1991), and with a sample of 2,800 larger firms in Mexico (1986–1990), the authors focus attention on firms in export-oriented industries that provided complete data for all years in their panels. They demonstrate that exporting firms indeed had lower average variable costs (implying higher productivity) than other firms in the two or three years before entering the export market. They found little evidence of cost reductions after entering export markets. In the interest of ruling out possible subtle omitted variables biases in these comparisons, they also fitted equations describing the determinants of export participation and average variable cost on an industry-by-industry basis, allowing export participation and cost in any period to depend on their own levels in previous periods, and acknowledging serial correlation over time for errors pertaining to individual firms. Estimation of these more elaborate relationships provided confirmation for their interpretation of the simpler relationships.

Over the subsequent decade many researchers sought to replicate, refute, or extend these results, using data from different countries or alternative estimation methods. Joachim Wagner (2007) reviewed many of these studies, concluding that while almost all studies find exporting firms to be more productive than nonexporting firms and find that exporting firms enjoyed higher productivity even before they began exporting (thereby providing evidence of self-selection), evidence of learning by exporting is weaker and more mixed. Ann Harrison and Andres Rodriguez-Clare (2010) point to a second wave of studies employing data from poorer countries, which suggest that while firms that export tend to be more productive than other firms even before they begin exporting, they also experience some productivity increase after entering export markets. This effect seems to be largest in the poorest countries, where potential exporters tend to be further from the technological frontier.

REFERENCES

Anderson, James E., and Eric van Wincoop. "Trade Costs." *Journal of Economic Literature* 42(3): 691–751, 2004. doi: 10.1257/0022051042177649

Attanasio, Orazio, Pinelopi K. Goldberg, and Nina Pavcnik. "Trade Reforms and Wage Inequality in Colombia." *Journal of Development Economics* 74(2): 331–366, 2004. doi:10.1016/j.jdeveco.2003.07.001

Baldwin, Richard. "Globalisation: The Great Unbundling(s)." Paper for the Finnish Prime Minister's Office. Helsinki, Finland: Economic Council of Finland, 2006. http://www.graduateinstitute.ch/webdav/site/ctei/shared/CTEI/Baldwin/Publications/Chapters/Globalization/Baldwin_06-09-20.pdf

Bernard, Andrew B., and J. Bradford Jensen. "Exporters, Skill Upgrading, and the Wage Gap." *Journal of International Economics* 42(1–2): 3–31, 1997. doi:10.1016/S0022-1996(96)01431-6

Bourguignon, François, Diane Coyle, Raquel Fernández, Francesco Giavazzi, Dalia Marin, Kevin H. O. Rourke, Richard Portes, Paul Seabright, Anthony J. Venables, Thierry Verdier, and L. Alan Winters. *Making Sense of Globalization: A Guide to the Economic Issues.* CEPR Policy Paper No. 8. London: Centre for Economic Policy Research, 2002. http://www.cepr.org/pubs/books/PP8.asp

Bruton, Henry J. "A Reconsideration of Import Substitution." *Journal of Economic Literature* 36(2): 903–936, 1998. http://www.jstor.org/stable/2565125

Clerides, Sofronis K., Saul Lach, and James R. Tybout. "Is Learning By Exporting Important? Micro-Dynamic Evidence From Colombia, Mexico, and Morocco." *The Quarterly Journal of Economics* 113(3): 903–947, 1998. doi:10.1162/003355398555784

Feyrer, James. "Trade and Income—Exploiting Time Series in Geography." NBER Working Paper No. 14910. Cambridge, Mass.: National Bureau of Economic Research, 2009. http://www.nber.org/papers/w14910.pdf

Goldberg, Pinelopi K., and Nina Pavcnik. "Distributional Effects of Globalization in Developing Countries." *Journal of Economic Literature* 45(1): 39–82, 2007. doi:10.1257/jel.45.1.39

Harrison, Ann, and Andres Rodriguez-Clare. "Trade, Foreign Investment and Industrial Policy." *Handbook of Development Economics* 5: 4039–4214, 2010. doi:10.1016/B978-0-444-52944-2.00001-X

Hummels, David. "Globalization and Freight Transport Costs in Maritime Shipping and Aviation." *International Transport Form Paper* 2009–3. Paris: OECD/ITF, 2009. www.internationaltransportforum.org/Pub/pdf/09FP03.pdf

Krueger, Anne O. "Trade Policy and Economic Development: How We Learn." *American Economic Review* 87(1): 1–22, 1997. http://www.jstor.org/stable/2950851

Lederman, Daniel, Marcelo Olarreaga, and Lucy Payton. "Export Promotion Agencies: Do They Work?" *Journal of Development Economics* 91(2): 257–265, 2010. doi:10.1016/j.jdeveco.2009.09.003

Limão, Nuno, and Anthony J. Venables. "Infrastructure, Geographical Disadvantage, Transport Costs, and Trade." *The World Bank Economic Review* 15(3): 451–479, 2001. doi:10.1093/wber/15.3.451

Londoño-Kent, María del Pilar, and Paul E. Kent. "A Tale of Two Ports: The Cost of Inefficiency." *Research Report 30140.* Washington, D.C.: World Bank, 2003. http://go.worldbank.org/H5J6NUAKE0

Martin, Will. "Developing Countries' Changing Participation in World Trade." *The World Bank Research Observer* 18(2): 187–203, 2003. doi:10.1093/wbro/lkg008

McMillan, Margaret, and I. Verduzco. "New Evidence on Trade and Investment." Washington, D.C.: Tufts University and International Food Policy Research Institute, 2010.

Ohlin, Bertil G. *Interregional and International Trade.* Cambridge, Mass.: Harvard University Press, 1933.

Radelet, Steven. *Emerging Africa: How 17 Countries Are Leading the Way.* Washington, D.C.: Center for Global Development, 2010.

Rodríguez, Francisco, and Dani Rodrik. "Trade Policy and Economic Growth: A Skeptic's Guide to the Cross-National Evidence." In Ben S. Bernanke and Kenneth Rogoff (eds.). *NBER Macroeconomics Annual 2000*, Volume 15. Cambridge, Mass.: MIT Press, pp. 261–338, 2001. http://www.nber.org/books/bern01-1

Sachs, Jeffrey D., and Andrew Warner. "Economic Reform and the Process of Global Integration." *Brookings Papers on Economic Activity* 1995(1): 1–95, 1995. http://www.earth.columbia.edu/sitefiles/file/about/director/pubs/brookings_q195.pdf

Stolper, Wolfgang F., and Paul A. Samuelson. "Protection and Real Wages." *The Review of Economic Studies* 9(1): 58–73, 1941. doi:10.2307/2967638

Topalova, Petia. "Trade Liberalization, Poverty, and Inequality: Evidence from Indian Districts." In Ann Harrison (ed.). *Globalization and Poverty.* Chicago: University of Chicago Press, 2007, pp. 291–336. http://www.nber.org/books/harr06-1

United Nations Conference on Trade and Development (UNCTAD), *Development and Globalization: Fact and Figures 2012.* United Nations, 2012. http://unctad.org/en/PublicationsLibrary/webgdsdsi2012d2_en.pdf

Wagner, Joachim, ed. "Exports and Productivity—Comparable Evidence for 14 Countries." The International Study Group on Exports and Productivity. *ESRI Working Paper 220.* Dublin: Economic and Social Research Institute, 2007. http://www.esri.ie/UserFiles/publications/20071211103332/WP220.pdf

World Bank. *Economic Growth in the 1990s: Learning from a Decade of Reform.* Washington, D.C.: World Bank, 2005. http://go.worldbank.org/6J3WXKCR50

World Bank. *World Development Indicators 2012.* Washington, D.C.: World Bank, 2012. http://data.worldbank.org/data-catalog/world-development-indicators

World Economic Forum, Bain and Company, and World Bank. *Enabling Trade: Valuing Growth Opportunities*. Geneva: World Economic Forum, 2013. http://www3.weforum.org/docs/WEF_SCT_Enabling Trade_Report_2013.pdf

World Trade Organization (WTO). *International Trade Statistics 2009*. Geneva: World Trade Organization, 2009. http://www.wto.org/english/res_e/statis_e/its2009_e/its09_toc_e.htm

QUESTIONS FOR REVIEW

1. How have the nature and volume of international trade changed in recent decades? What forces underlie these changes?

2. Define and discuss the significance of all the elements of Figure 11.1.

3. Describe and motivate the approach taken in section 11.2B to identifying the determinants of export volume. Discuss what we know about the empirical determinants of export volume.

4. What assumptions define the specific factors model? Which of the variables listed in Box 11.2 are exogenous and which are endogenous?

5. How are the general equilibrium levels of the domestic prices for food and textiles determined in the simple specific factors model?

6. What does Home's production possibilities frontier (*PPF*) represent, why is it bowed out from the origin in Figure 11.2, and how do we know that Home must produce somewhere on its *PPF* in general equilibrium?

7. Where along the *PPF* does Home produce in general equilibrium? Why?

8. How does the functional distribution of income change as the relative price of food rises and Home shifts resources out of textile production into food production? Why does the distribution change in this way?

9. Refer to Figure 11.3 and describe how to determine the quantities of food and textiles consumed in Home country in the specific factors model.

10. Using a diagram like Figure 11.3, illustrate the effects of an increase in Home's terms of trade on factor use, production, consumption, trade, and the functional distribution of income in the specific factors model.

11. Using a diagram like Figure 11.4, discuss the changes in aggregate production and consumption that take place in Home and Foreign when they move from autarky to trade with each other.

12. In what sense might we think of the specific factors model as a model of general equilibrium in the short run?

13. Discuss the possible effects of introducing international transfer costs, domestic transfer costs, and migration costs into the specific factors model.

14. What additional information would we require (beyond what we have assumed in setting up the model) to predict the effect of an increase in the terms of trade on poverty in a simple specific factors model?

15. What assumptions define the factor proportions model? In what sense does it examine general equilibrium responses over a longer run than the specific factors model?

16. Describe the nature of resource re-allocation that underlies a movement to the southeast along the *PPF* in the factor proportions model.

17. As the world relative price of textiles rises, what happens to production, factor allocation, and the functional distribution of income in the simple factor proportions model?

18. What is relative factor abundance, and how is it related to comparative advantage in the factor proportions model?

19. What complementary policies might be required to allow an economy to take advantage of the gains from trade?

20. Why was rising income inequality during the 1990s in developing countries that liberalized their trade policies a surprise? How did the inequality increases and related empirical research modify the way researchers think about the relationship among international trade, inequality, and poverty?

21. Describe one or more channels through which opening to international trade might slow growth, and describe one or more channels through which opening to trade might speed growth.

22. Discuss how and why beliefs regarding the nature of developing countries' comparative advantage and of the relationship between trade policy and economic growth have changed over the last 60 years.

QUESTIONS FOR DISCUSSION

1. Use Figure 11.1 to analyze the impacts of (a) a depreciation of the Indonesian exchange rate and (b) the introduction of a tax on shoe exports.

2. When residents of the United States take a safari vacation in Tanzania, Tanzania is said to "export tourism services" and the United States is said to "import tourism services." Draw

diagrams similar to those in Figure 11.1, modified to describe the Tanzanian safari tourism market and the world market for safari tourism services. Use the diagrams to brainstorm about the kinds of policy changes and programs that might be effective in increasing the volume of Tanzanian tourism service exports.

3. In the specific factors model, general equilibrium involves equilibrium in five markets. What are these five markets? Draw five market equilibrium diagrams (of the sort developed in Chapter 8) depicting equilibrium in all five markets, assuming that Home exports food and imports textiles. Suppose Home imposed a tariff on imports of textiles. Which of the five markets would be directly affected? Why and how would changes in this market (in response to the new tariff) bring change in the other markets? Why and how would changes in the other markets lead to new rounds of change in the first market? What do we learn from the specific factors model about what the new equilibrium will look like in each of the five markets after all rounds of change have worked themselves out and the system has attained the new general equilibrium?

4. Consider the PPF in Figure 11.2. Under the assumptions of the specific factors model, how would this PPF change as a result of investment that increases the stock of capital (while the stocks of land and labor remain fixed)? As a result of technical progress in the food sector only? Suppose the capital stock increases while world prices for the two goods hold constant. What would happen to the quantities of food and textiles produced and to the ratio of food to textile production?

5. Consider the country depicted in Figure 11.3. Suppose the rest of the world (from which this country imports textiles) experiences a technical advance in textile production, and the rest of the world is "large" relative to world markets. How would you depict the results of this change in Figure 11.3, and what would be the implications for the country's production, consumption, import, and export quantities?

6. Consider a factor proportions model in which the two goods are textiles and chemicals, the two factors are unskilled labor and skilled labor, and chemical production is relatively skilled-labor intensive. What impact would an increase in the world price of textiles have on the wage differential between skilled and unskilled labor in the textile-exporting country? Explain.

7. Drawing on the specific factors model, the factor proportions model, and extended versions of these models in which we allow for internal transfer and mobility costs, create a list of reasons why a particular poor household might fail to benefit from an increase in the price of the unskilled labor-intensive good.

PROBLEMS

1. Draw a pair of diagrams comparable to those in Figure 11.1 but modified to depict the market for bicycles in a bicycle-importing country and the world market for bicycles. Use this diagram to determine what would happen to this country's local price of bicycles, and to the quantities of bicycles the country produces, consumes, and imports, in response to each of the following changes:
   - An increase in the world demand for bicycles
   - An appreciation of the country's currency
   - An upgrading of the country's port facilities
   - A reduction in local wages
   - Technological advance in this country's bicycle-producing firms
   - The imposition of a tariff on bicycle imports

2. Consider a country endowed with $K = 100$ units of capital, $A = 100$ units of land and $L = 400$ units of labor and that produces two goods, food and textiles, in quantities F and T. The textile production function is $T = K^{0.5}L_T^{0.5}$ and the food production function is $F = A^{0.5}L_F^{0.5}$, where L_T

indicates the units of labor allocated to the textile sector and L_F indicates the units of labor allocated to the food sector. As in the specific factors model, land and capital are fixed while labor is mobile across sectors.

   a. Derive an equation for this country's PPF in a graph with units of food on the vertical axis and units of textiles on the horizontal axis.

   b. Derive an equation for the slope of this PPF.

   c. Under the assumptions of the specific factors model, if the world prices of textiles and food are both 1 and there are no transfer costs, what quantities of food and textiles would this country produce?

   d. Under these conditions, what would be the nominal wage? The per-unit return on land? On capital?

   e. If the world price of textiles rose to 2 while the price of food remained 1, what quantities of food and textiles would this country produce?

   f. Under these conditions, what would be the value of the wage, and what would be the per-unit returns to land and capital?

Institutions and Cooperation

People's interactions in market and nonmarket settings are governed by institutions, and we have seen that high-quality institutions enhance development in many ways. Unfortunately, institutional quality varies tremendously across countries. Many development economists argue that this variation is the primary reason some countries are so much richer than others (Rodrik, 2007; Acemoğlu and Robinson, 2012). In our search for the underpinnings of successful development, then, we must study how high-quality institutions arise and how they are sustained.

After briefly reviewing the diverse types of institutions relevant to development, this chapter focuses more narrowly on institutions that support cooperation at the community level. We prepare for such study by laying out key insights from two subdisciplines of economics that inform the study of cooperation and institutions: game theory and behavioral economics. We then propose a set of questions to guide policy-relevant empirical research on community-level institutions and apply them in studies of institutions governing common property resource use, informal insurance arrangements, and land rights.

In Chapter 13, we examine two additional sets of institutions: The institutions through which policymakers hope to provide good governance for policy implementation, and the political institutions that constrain policy choices.

12.1 Institutions, Cooperation, and Development

As indicated in Chapter 2, we label as an **institution** any set of formal rules, informal norms, and related enforcement mechanisms that constrain people's choices regarding a particular set of actions.[1] Some institutions are entirely informal, involving only unwritten and shared understandings among members of neighborhoods or communities or within larger cultures. Other institutions are more formal, involving codified rules as well as informal norms. Formal rules at the local level may be linked to local governments or to membership-based organizations such as agricultural cooperatives. Formal rules at the national level include laws, the rules defining government programs, and rules governing legal and law enforcement systems.

Healthy institutions contribute to development in diverse ways. In Chapter 8, we described the formal and informal institutions that encourage the development of goods markets by reducing transfer costs. Institutions that discourage fraud or prevent default on contracts increase people's confidence that others will fulfill contractual promises, thereby encouraging them to enter into long-distance and sophisticated market transactions. Informal norms supporting local cooperation, and the rules defining government infrastructure programs, encourage the road investments required to reduce transportation costs. Rules encouraging collective efforts within producer cooperatives allow members to obtain better prices on inputs and outputs. Some market-supporting institutions are particularly important for reducing the costs of exporting to world markets, as described in Chapter 11. In addition, as suggested in Chapter 9, healthy institutions can encourage labor mobility by facilitating flows of information between job seekers and employers or by providing new safety nets to replace traditional safety nets that migrants must leave behind.

---

[1]Many authors define institutions simply as "humanly devised constraints" on behavior, referencing North (1990). The definition provided here recognizes that institutions are humanly devised constraints, but it offers more detail that is analytically useful (which North, 1990, also highlights). For a thought-provoking and more complete discussion of how we might define institutions, see Greif (2006).

In Chapter 10, we learned how healthy institutions promote investment and growth. Customary rules and formal laws protecting agricultural land rights encourage farmers to invest in productivity-enhancing land improvements. Institutions that discourage vandalism and theft encourage investment in physical capital and in improved technologies that are embodied in physical capital. Political institutions that inhibit governments from expropriating assets and imposing punitive taxes give investors further confidence that they will be able to appropriate the returns to their investments.

Many of these healthy institutions encourage, and are sustained by, mutually beneficial cooperation and trust. Sometimes they encourage explicit cooperation among people who know one another well, as when village members agree to obey rules restricting the number of fish they each may harvest from the local pond, with the aim of preventing destructive overfishing and conflict. In other cases, the cooperation is more subtle and can involve larger groups. For example, when everyone agrees to respect one another's property rights and refrain from theft, everyone benefits, because greater security allows them to forgo costly efforts to protect their property, such as hiring guards, sleeping with shop inventory, or installing fences and locks. They enjoy additional benefits because greater security encourages people to participate in markets and to invest. Similarly, when most people agree to respect contractual promises, everyone benefits from the development of more sophisticated markets. By following such institutional rules and norms, each individual sacrifices some immediate gain, but when everyone submits to the rules' discipline, everyone benefits from a more prosperous economy and society.

Unfortunately, healthy institutions sometimes fail to arise, even when they would be highly valuable, and some institutions are far from healthy.[2] Some social norms that may have served beneficial purposes in the past now serve only to endanger or impoverish people. For example, traditional notions of beauty that encourage some young Ethiopian women to blacken their teeth, by breaking the enamel with needles, now expose them to risk of HIV infection, and social norms that require families to sacrifice livestock after the death of family members can deplete the assets of bereaved families to perilously low levels (Barrett, 2005).

Yet other institutions serve to enrich powerful groups at the expense of others. For example, rules that tied peasants to the land in medieval Europe enriched their feudal landlords. Rules that endowed a small number of Spaniards with rights to conscript labor from people living on vast tracts of land in the Americas in the 16th century served to enrich the colonial elite at the expense of indigenous populations. Rules giving executive power to greedy 20th-century autocrats allowed them to tax and control citizens without providing them effective government services. Acemoğlu and Robinson (2012) call such institutions "extractive" and argue that their depressing effects on the well-being of powerless groups can last for centuries.

Macro and development economists running cross-country growth regressions of the sort described in Chapter 3 have established important correlations between economic growth and diverse measures of institutional quality, including measures related to the nature and enforcement of contract law, law enforcement more generally, property rights, financial market governance, corruption, quality of government bureaucracy, and trust (Pande and Udry, 2006). Acemoğlu et al. (2001) argue, on the basis of instrumental variables estimation results, that the correlations indeed represent causal effects of institutional quality on growth.

All this leads us to ask: How do healthy institutions arise and what sustains them? If healthy rules and norms improve development outcomes by constraining people to behave in ways they otherwise might not, we must ask more specifically: What motivates people to obey institutional rules and norms? That is, how are the rules and norms *enforced*?

For development analysts trained in microeconomics, a natural way to begin studying such questions is to identify a specific institution of interest, carefully describe the rules and norms that

---

[2]Some institutions yield both developmental benefits and developmental costs, as we will see in section 12.3C.

☰ **Box 12.1** Three Sets of Community-Level Institutions

Institutions governing common property resources

Millions of families in the developing world derive their livelihoods from fishing grounds, forests, underground water reservoirs, and other resources held as common property within a community. Many other families supplement income or obtain cheap fuel by drawing on such common property resources (CPRs). When people harvest fish, wood, or water from sources held in common, they enjoy the full benefit of what they harvest but bear only a fraction of the cost, much of which falls on others as harvesting becomes more difficult or conflict breaks out. Economists thus anticipate that self-interested and rational people often overuse CPRs, ultimately degrading the environment and exhausting natural resources or igniting conflict. Many forests, fisheries, and other CPRs have indeed been degraded and even destroyed.

Yet many communities around the world manage to collectively restrain their use of local CPRs, often by agreeing to follow precisely defined formal use rules (Wade, 1987; Ostrom, 1990; Baland and Platteau, 1996). What is the anatomy of successful CPR governance institutions, and why do people comply with the rules? Under what conditions are good institutions most likely to arise; and what can we learn from them about how to catalyze cooperation in other community endeavors?

Informal insurance institutions

Self-interested and rational individuals would never give away something for nothing, would they? Yet in many communities around the world people comply with informal norms requiring them to give cash, food, or interest-free loans to neighbors who have fallen on hard times (Morduch, 1999). By complying with such norms, community members implicitly cooperate in providing one another with mutual insurance, making up for the failure of formal insurance markets (discussed in Chapter 10). Why do such norms arise, and why do people comply? Who participates? How might such institutions evolve in response to economic development or to the creation of public safety net programs?

Customary land rights institutions

Fertilizer use, irrigation system investments, and the adoption of advanced seed varieties have great potential to raise agricultural productivity and incomes. Farmers perceive incentives to invest in such practices only if they anticipate having the right to consume or sell the increased output derived from the plots of land on which they make the investments. Where farmers fear losing such rights, they may remain stuck with low levels of productivity and low incomes. Thus farmers benefit from living in communities in which all farmers cooperate in respecting one another's land rights.

Formal private property rights in land enforced by effective legal and law enforcement institutions could provide farmers with the necessary security, but many farmers in developing countries live beyond the reach of such formal institutions. Where formal institutions lack force, some farmers enjoy semiformal or informal land rights defined and administered by tribal authorities (Platteau, 2000). Others share in access to land held as common property, and yet others lack any confidence regarding their land rights. What explains variation in land rights institutions around the world, how important are land rights for investment, and what scope do governments have to strengthen these rights?

---

define the institution, identify the behaviors that the institution constrains and the contexts in which it constrains behavior, and then brainstorm about reasons why the relevant actors might obey the rules and norms.[3] To illustrate how such research might proceed, we narrow our focus to a set of institutions of great interest in contemporary development studies: institutions supporting cooperation at the community level. We begin by laying out key concepts in game theory and behavioral economics that support economists' brainstorming about why people might obey institutional rules and norms that support cooperation. Drawing on insights from these literatures, we then suggest a list of questions to guide policy-relevant research on community-level institutions and bring them to bear in the study of institutions governing the use of common property resources, informal insurance arrangements, and land rights. Box 12.1 introduces these institutions and raises some of the questions that motivate closer study.

12.2 Cooperation and Institutions: Key Concepts from Game Theory and Behavioral Economics

People's choices regarding whether or not to cooperate are strategic choices. Decisions are **strategic** when the objective benefits that any one person enjoys after making specified choices

---

[3]For an instructive discussion of why further econometric analysis of the relationships between institutional quality and growth rates at the aggregate level is unlikely to reveal useful insights into the underpinnings of healthy institutions, see Pande and Udry (2006).

depend on the choices made by other people. Decisions regarding cooperation and compliance with rules are strategic, because individuals benefit from choosing to cooperate only when others choose to cooperate, too. When searching for the underpinnings of healthy institutions, therefore, economists often draw insights from **game theory**, which is a branch of applied mathematics used by economists (and others) for studying choice in strategic settings.

Choices regarding cooperation, rule compliance, and rule enforcement are also choices in which decision makers may be keenly aware of how their choices affect other people or affect how other people perceive them. If they take these social impacts into account when comparing the well-being they would derive from various choices, then standard models of purely neoclassical decision making (as defined in Chapter 6) might offer inadequate guidance for the study of cooperation and institutions. Economists studying institutions therefore also draw insights from the field of **behavioral economics**, in which researchers construct and test specific hypotheses regarding departures from neoclassical rationality.

Sections 12.2A and 12.2B introduce readers to basic results regarding cooperation from the fields of game theory and behavioral economics.

12.2A Cooperation in standard game theory
Basic vocabulary and assumptions

A **game** is a strategic situation in which multiple decision makers make interdependent choices.[4] Each decision maker, called a **player**, must choose a **strategy**, which is a comprehensive plan of action. In a very simple game, each player chooses between just two actions, such as "help build the road" and "don't help build the road" or "play fairly" and "cheat," and all players must choose simultaneously, without knowing the actions others will take. In such cases a player's strategy is just her plan regarding which of the two actions she will take. In more complicated games players make choices at various stages, possibly knowing the actions others have taken at earlier stages. In such games, a player's strategy is a comprehensive statement of the actions she will take at all stages of the game, with actions at later stages contingent on choices made by any of the players in earlier stages. For example, if two players anticipate meeting each other for a simple game many times, a player's strategy is her plan regarding whether to play fairly or cheat at the first meeting, together with a plan for the way future choices regarding fair play will depend on what both players have chosen in previous meetings.

Each player is assumed to choose her strategy with the aim of maximizing her **payoff**, or the utility she will enjoy once all players have chosen and executed their strategies. In standard game theory, each player is assumed to evaluate the utility she would derive under various circumstances in a strictly **neoclassical** fashion. This means that her utility is a function only of her own present and future consumption (of goods, services, and leisure) and reflects no concern for the effects of her choices on others. The strategic nature of the game is reflected in how the payoffs that any one player receives after making a specific choice depend on what choices others have made.

Players are also assumed to have complete understanding of the choices available. Furthermore, the entire structure of the game—the set of actions that any player might take and the set of payoffs for all players resulting from any set of actions—is assumed to be **common knowledge** among all players. This means not only that each player knows all possible actions and payoffs for all players but also that each knows that the *other* players know the structure and can be expected to make rational use of all information.

In the games we examine here, players' rational behavior is assumed to lead them into **Nash equilibrium**, a situation in which each player has chosen a strategy that is the best possible

---

[4]For a broader look at the uses of game theory in development, see Wydick (2008).

response to the strategies chosen by other players.[5] That is, in Nash equilibrium no player can improve her payoff by changing strategy as long as others pursue their equilibrium strategies. Players thus behave as if they perfectly anticipate the choices of others. We use the term equilibrium **outcome** of a game to refer to the set of equilibrium strategies chosen by all players and the payoffs they ultimately receive. Games may have more than one Nash equilibrium, as we will see. To **solve a game** is to find all of the game's Nash equilibria.

Cooperation at its most difficult: the prisoner's dilemma game

A first simple game illustrates basic game theory concepts, while also highlighting the strong incentives that can discourage people from cooperating, even when cooperation would bring great mutual benefit. The well-known **prisoner's dilemma** (PD) game is often described by the following story: Two thieves are apprehended after carrying out a major robbery together. The police have enough evidence to send both thieves to jail for two years for a lesser crime, but they cannot convict either thief of robbery unless at least one of the thieves confesses. Interrogators cleverly offer the following deal to both thieves, who are interrogated in separate rooms: "If you confess and your accomplice does not, we will clear you of all charges and let you go free, while sending your accomplice to prison for 10 years. If he confesses and you do not, you will go to prison for 10 years and he will go free. If you both confess, you will both go to jail for seven years." The thieves also know that if neither confesses, they will both go to jail for only two years for the lesser crime.

Assuming for simplicity that each player's utility is equal to $10 - J$, where J is the number of years he spends in jail, we can summarize this game as in Table 12.1, where the first entry in each cell is the utility payoff to Thief 1 and the second entry is the utility payoff to Thief 2. For example, the entries in the upper right cell of payoffs tell us that if Thief 1 confesses and Thief 2 remains silent, then Thief 1 serves no jail time (and enjoys utility of 10), and Thief 2 serves 10 years (and experiences utility of 0).

The first step in solving a simple game of this sort is to consider each player's best response under every possible assumption regarding the behavior of the other player. For example, we identify which choice would yield Thief 1 the highest utility payoff if he knew Thief 2 would confess, and also identify which choice would yield Thief 1 the highest payoff if he knew Thief 2 would remain silent.

Comparison of the upper and lower cells in the first column of Table 12.1 tells us that if Thief 1 expects Thief 2 to confess, Thief 1's best response is to confess also, because he receives 10 years in prison (and utility of 0) if he remains silent but only seven years in prison (and utility of 3) if he confesses. The second column indicates that even if Thief 1 expects Thief 2 to remain

▥ TABLE 12.1 Utility Payoffs to Thief 1 and Thief 2 in a Classic Prisoner's Dilemma Game

If Thief 1:	If Thief 2:	
	Confesses	Remains Silent
Confesses	3, 3	10, 0
Remains Silent	0, 10	8, 8

[5]Games fall into two broad categories: cooperative and noncooperative games. In cooperative games, players are assumed capable of striking binding contracts at the beginning of the game, through which they can credibly promise to undertake specific actions at later stages of the game, regardless of the actions others take, and regardless of whether these choices will maximize the player's payoff once the game has reached that stage. This expands players' ability to promote cooperation through promises of rewards and threats of retribution. The Nash bargaining model of household decision making examined in Chapter 7 is an example of a cooperative game. In this chapter we focus on "noncooperative games," in which players cannot make such binding contracts. This means that each player must always assume that other players will at each stage of the game choose actions that maximize their payoffs, despite any (empty) promises or threats to the contrary that they made at earlier stages.

silent, Thief 1's best response is again to confess, as this wins him the reward of going free (utility of 10) rather than serving two years for a lesser crime (utility of 8). Thief 1 is said to have a **dominant strategy**, or a plan of action that yields the highest payoff no matter what he expects the other player to do. In this case, his dominant strategy is to confess. Comparable inspection of the two rows in Table 12.1 tells us that confessing is the dominant strategy for Thief 2 also.

We conclude that no matter what the thieves might expect of each other, they both choose to confess and both go to jail for seven years (utility of 3). This outcome is an equilibrium outcome for the game, because when both thieves confess, neither thief can improve his circumstances by doing otherwise.

Notice, however, that if both thieves had set aside purely self-interested instincts and chosen to remain silent, they would have achieved an outcome that is better for both of them: serving only two years for the lesser crime (achieving utility of 8). In game theory parlance, both thieves would have benefited from **cooperating** with each other, forgoing some personal gain in the interest of achieving a better outcome for all. Unfortunately, they both face strong incentives to **defect**, meaning that they choose not to cooperate. Individual rational choice leads both thieves to seven-year prison sentences, even though they could both have gotten off with just two-year sentences if they had cooperated in remaining silent.

What if the prisoners were given an opportunity to communicate before making their choices (but after the interrogators had laid out the offers)? Would they manage to achieve a better outcome by promising to remain silent? The answer is no, because such promises are not **credible**. A player's promise to make a specific choice is credible only if the promised action will indeed yield the player the highest utility at the time he is called upon to make the choice. In this PD game, even if both prisoners promised to remain silent, and even if each prisoner believed that the other would keep the promise, each would nonetheless break the promise and confess, because this leaves him better off. Thus an important lesson of the prisoner's dilemma game is that:

> Rational individuals may choose not to cooperate, even when all parties involved would benefit from cooperation. They might face such strong incentives to defect that they would fail to cooperate even if they expected others to cooperate.

Many choices affecting the well-being of households in poor communities are thought to have the PD structure, including choices regarding restrained use of common property resources (see Box 12.1 and section 12.3B) and choices regarding joint investment in local public goods. Here we examine choices regarding investment in a simple public good: a well-maintained road to market.

Consider a village populated by just two villagers, who must choose whether or not to participate in a road maintenance project intended to improve the connection between their village and a larger market town. (See Chapter 8 for a discussion of the roles such investments can play in development.) The project requires a total of L hours of labor and is set up so that the work will be divided evenly across any workers who choose to participate. If both villagers participate, each ultimately contributes $L/2$ hours and enjoys R units of improved road use benefit. If only one participates, she ends up contributing the full L hours by herself, but (because the road is a public good) both she and the nonparticipating villager enjoy R units of benefit. If neither villager participates, neither works, but neither enjoys the road benefits.

Assuming that each villager's utility is equal to the benefits she receives from road use less the hours she works, this road maintenance game may be summarized as in Table 12.2. To focus

■ TABLE 12.2 Payoffs to Villager 1 and Villager 2 in a Road Maintenance Prisoner's Dilemma

If Villager 1:	If Villager 2:	
	Shirks	Participates
Shirks	0, 0	R, $R - L$
Participates	$R - L$, R	$R - L/2$, $R - L/2$

on cases in which individuals would not wish to complete the road maintenance on their own but would benefit from cooperation in road maintenance, we assume that $R - L < 0$ but $R - L/2 > 0$.

The game described in Table 12.2 has the PD structure, because the dominant strategy for both villagers is to shirk (i.e., not participate). If Villager 2 shirks, Villager 1 would rather shirk (receiving payoff 0) than undertake the road project alone (receiving payoff $R - L < 0$). If Villager 2 participates, Villager 1 would prefer to enjoy the project's benefits while shirking (receiving payoff R) rather than to help Villager 2 (receiving payoff $R - L/2 < R$). This illustrates the players' desire to **free ride**, enjoying the benefits of the public good without contributing to its creation. Because they each have an incentive to free ride, neither can credibly promise to participate. In equilibrium, both villagers shirk and the road is not maintained, even though cooperation in road maintenance would leave them both better off. They are caught in a prisoner's dilemma.

A somewhat more tractable cooperation problem: the assurance game

Sometimes cooperation is not quite as difficult as in the PD game, because in some situations players find it in their best interest to cooperate if they expect others to cooperate as well. A second type of game, called the **assurance game** (AG, also called a ranked coordination game or stag hunt game) describes the value and difficulty of cooperation in such situations.

To highlight the subtle differences that distinguish AG from PD scenarios, let's examine a slightly modified version of the road maintenance game. Suppose again that the project requires a total of L hours of labor. Suppose, however, that the required work is divided up and each villager is given the responsibility for completing a designated portion of the road at her earliest convenience. The maintenance leads to new road use benefits of R for each villager, but only if the entire project is completed. If only zero or one villager participates, the project remains incomplete and fails to deliver any benefit.

This new situation is depicted in Table 12.3. If both of the villagers participate, they each enjoy the benefits of a maintained road (R) and each contributes half the cost of maintaining the road ($L/2$), thus enjoying net utility payoff $R - L/2 > 0$. If neither participates, then neither experiences any benefit or cost, and each receives utility payoff of 0. If only one participates, she loses $L/2$ in labor time, but neither villager gains any road use benefit. The most important difference relative to the game of Table 12.2 is that it is no longer possible for one player to benefit from free riding when the other player participates.

For the game described in Table 12.3, the outcome in which both villagers choose to shirk is again an equilibrium outcome. From the first column we see that if Villager 2 decides to shirk, Villager 1's best response is to shirk as well, because participating would cost her labor time ($L/2$) and would fail to generate any road maintenance benefits. Similarly, Villager 2 would choose to shirk if she expected Villager 1 to shirk.

The assurance game differs from the PD game, however, in having a *second* (better!) equilibrium in which the villagers cooperate in maintaining the road. When Villager 2 participates, Villager 1's best response is to participate as well, because the addition of her labor makes the project successful, and the successful project generates enough benefit (R) to warrant the labor involved ($L/2$). Villager 2 would similarly choose to participate if she expected Villager 1 to participate.

TABLE 12.3 Payoffs to Villager 1 and Villager 2 in a Road Maintenance Assurance Game

If Villager 1:	If Villager 2:	
	Shirks	Participates
Shirks	0, 0	0, $-L/2$
Participates	$-L/2$, 0	$R - L/2$, $R - L/2$

The assurance game is thus one of many games characterized by **multiple equilibria**, or multiple sets of mutually reinforcing choices. In the setting of Table 12.3, if each villager believes the other will shirk, she will shirk as well, confirming the other's belief. Yet if each villager believes the other will participate, she will participate as well, again confirming the other's belief. Mutual participation is better for the villagers than mutual shirking, but mathematical analysis of the game yields no prediction regarding which equilibrium will arise.

The assurance game suggests that:

> Sometimes rational decision making leads people to cooperate if (and only if) they believe that others will cooperate as well. Under such circumstances it may be possible to catalyze cooperation by coordinating expectations, giving each individual reason to believe that others will cooperate.

This suggests the valuable roles that communication, leadership, and a history of cooperation and trust might play in facilitating cooperation. If the villagers of Table 12.3 were to communicate before making their decisions, they might agree that participation is in their mutual interest and might promise to participate. Unlike in the PD game of Table 12.2, such promises to participate would be credible, because neither player would have an incentive to renege on the promise if she believed the other would indeed participate. One villager's exercise of leadership in initiating communication and coordinating expectations might also have a big payoff for both. Even if given no opportunity to communicate, having a history of cooperation might encourage individual players to expect continued cooperation by other players.

The role of expectations in determining which equilibrium arises in the AG setting suggests a possibility that is both troubling and hopeful: Groups of rational villagers might find themselves stuck in **poverty traps**, in which all make choices that lead to poor outcomes, because they expect others to do the same, even though they could all make choices that leave everyone better off. This is troubling, because it implies that some groups may be missing out on greater prosperity that could be theirs without any change in their objective opportunities. Nevertheless, it also offers hope for dramatic improvements in well-being within communities, without the need for large injections of external resources, because it may be possible for a leader to catalyze significant change simply by coordinating a collective change in expectations.

The comparison of the road maintenance games described in Tables 12.2 and 12.3 also suggests the importance of distinguishing between cooperation problems in which free riding is and is not a possibility, and seeking to organize collective challenges in ways that eliminate the potential for free riding. The only difference between the two games is in the organization of the road work. When villagers are asked to show up to help build the road and are told that the road will be completed no matter how many people show up, free riding is possible. When the road work is organized in a way that prevents benefits from emerging unless everyone does her part, on the other hand, free riding is not an option and a cooperative equilibrium becomes possible.

The significance of repeated interaction: the repeated prisoner's dilemma game

People living together in small rural communities face frequent opportunities to gain through cooperation. Roads and irrigation canals require frequent maintenance, for example. This raises the possibility that interest in retaining access to many *future* benefits of cooperation might encourage people to cooperate in the present. We examine this possibility with a third type of game, the (indefinitely) **repeated prisoner's dilemma (RPD) game**. Whereas the games described above are **one-shot games**, which players expect to play just once, the RPD is a **repeated game**, in which the same players face the same choices and payoffs multiple times.

Consider two villagers who know that their road will need maintenance every year into the indefinite future. More specifically, they anticipate playing the game of Table 12.2 many times.

Suppose further that when making their choices at any future date, the villagers will remember all the choices players have made at earlier dates. This allows them to pursue **contingent strategies**, in which they plan actions at future dates that depend on choices made earlier. For example, a villager might choose the strategy: "I will start out by participating. Then in the future I will continue to participate as long as everyone has always participated in the past. But if anyone has ever shirked, I will shirk." By adopting such a strategy, often called the **grim strategy**, a player can essentially threaten to punish a partner who shirks by closing off all potential for future cooperation and road maintenance benefits. If both players play this strategy, they will both participate in every period.

We would like to know whether, or under what conditions, the threats embodied in such contingent strategies might provide the discipline required for sustaining cooperation. In game-theory terms, we would like to know whether the choice of the grim strategy by both players satisfies the requirements for equilibrium. For this set of strategies to be an equilibrium, it must be the case that neither player has an incentive to depart from the grim strategy (by defecting rather than cooperating in any stage of the game), as long as the other player is expected to play the grim strategy, too.

For villagers in this repeated game, the payoffs relevant to today's choice of participation versus shirking are the payoffs they would enjoy both now *and* in the future. Following the discussion of intertemporal choice models in Chapter 10, let's assume that a unit of utility enjoyed one year from now is worth β units today, where $0 < \beta < 1$. Similarly, a unit of utility enjoyed t years from now is worth β^t units today.

If each player expects the other to play the grim strategy, then each expects his own choice of cooperation in the current year to be met with cooperation by the other player and to be followed by mutual cooperation in all future years. The choice of participation today is thus associated with long-term utility payoff of

$$U_p = (R - L/2) + \beta(R - L/2) + \beta^2(R - L/2) + \cdots \tag{12.1}$$

where the sum includes as many terms as there are years in the future. If the number of years is infinite, equation 12.1 becomes the sum of an infinite geometric series and simplifies conveniently to[6]

$$U_p = (R - L/2) + \frac{\beta}{1 - \beta}(R - L/2) \tag{12.2}$$

If a villager were to deviate from the grim strategy by shirking in the first year, however, he would avoid having to work while still enjoying the full road benefit (R) in the first year, but he would trigger shirking by both villagers in all future periods and would thus lose access to the stream of future road maintenance benefits. The long-term utility associated with shirking today is thus

$$U_s = R + 0 + 0 + \cdots = R \tag{12.3}$$

Participating is more attractive than shirking as long as U_p is greater than U_s. We may express this condition as

$$U_p = (R - L/2) + \frac{\beta}{1 - \beta}(R - L/2) > R = U_s \tag{12.4}$$

---

[6]In general, the infinite geometric series $A + \beta A + \beta^2 A + \cdots$ can be shown to equal $A/(1 - \beta)$. In equation 12.2, we separate out the first term because we wish to highlight the implications of cooperation and defection for utility today (the first term) and future discounted utility (the second term).

or

$$\frac{\beta}{1-\beta}(R - L/2) > L/2 \qquad (12.5)$$

Equation 12.5 says that if the players in this infinitely repeated game expect each other to play the grim strategy, they will prefer to participate in the road maintenance project today as long as the discounted sum of benefits arising from successful road maintenance in all future periods (i.e., the *benefit* of cooperating today, given by the left side of equation 12.5) is greater than the cost of working on the road project today (i.e., the *cost* of cooperating today, given by the right side of equation 12.5). The more weight the players place on the future (β), and the greater are the net benefits of road building ($R - L/2$) relative to the costs ($L/2$), the more likely this expression is to be true. If this is the case, then the outcome in which both players choose the grim strategy, and thus both choose to cooperate, is indeed an equilibrium outcome.

This result suggests that:

> If players foresee many opportunities for cooperation in the future, if cooperation is sufficiently valuable, and if players care enough about the future, then their concern for the future can help sustain their cooperation in the present.

Many development economists consider the potential for such cooperation to be especially great in small and stable communities in rural areas of developing countries. As modernization raises rates of movement into and out of such communities, the potential for cooperation might diminish.

Readers might find the assumption that players expect to play a game an *infinite* number of times unrealistic. They might also (rightly) suspect that if players know a PD game will be repeated only a finite number of times, then cooperation is not an equilibrium. In a game that is repeated only a finite number of times, there is a *last* period, in which no future interactions are expected, and in which there is, therefore, no reason to cooperate. Working backward, this implies that there is no reason to cooperate in the second-to-last period, because there is no potential for future cooperation. The same can be said for the period before that, and the period before that, back to the first period (see problem 3).

Fortunately, what matters for sustaining cooperation in the RPD game is not that the number of future interactions is literally infinite but that it is **indefinite**. This means that the game has some positive probability of continuing on from any stage of the game that is played. For example, suppose that in any stage of the game that takes place, there is a probability δ that the game will be repeated in the next period, but a probability $1 - \delta$ that the current period is the last, because one or both players could move away, die, or otherwise become uninterested in future cooperation. The players then have the realistic expectation that the game will eventually end, but they still perceive a chance for future play during any stage of the game that is played. As long as the probability of the game continuing is not too small, and players do not discount the future too much, the future retains the potential to discipline the present and support cooperation as described earlier.[7]

Although indefinite repetition of the PD game can allow players to achieve cooperation, it does not *guarantee* cooperation. We have shown that *if* both players choose the grim strategy,

---

[7]Readers might wish to raise one further shortcoming of our analysis of the infinitely repeated prisoner's dilemma game: The threat contained within the choice of grim strategy does not appear credible. The strategy requires a player to respond to a single episode of the other's shirking by retaliatory shirking for all future periods. This would be very costly for the punisher as well as the punished, and the punisher might not wish to impose such severe punishment when the need arises. This suspicion is indeed correct. It can be shown, however, that mutual cooperation may nonetheless be supported by the use of strategies somewhat more complicated than the grim strategy, in which all threats of punishment are credible. In groups larger than two, such strategies could involve not only punishing shirkers but also punishing those who fail to punish shirkers.

their choices are mutually reinforcing and allow them to sustain cooperation. We have not shown that both players *will* choose the grim strategy. In fact, the RPD has an *infinite* number of equilibrium strategy combinations, only some of which involve cooperation. For example, another equilibrium is one in which both players decide to shirk in every single period! (This is an equilibrium, because when both players play this strategy, neither can improve his payoff by participating today.) Repetition turns the PD game with a single (bad) equilibrium into a game with multiple equilibria (some good and some bad). As in the assurance game, mathematical analysis of the model does not tell us which kind of equilibrium will arise. Thus:

> Even when players' concern for the future makes present cooperation possible, players are not guaranteed to cooperate. Communication and leadership again have roles to play in catalyzing cooperation.

The significance of rules, rewards, and punishments: overview

Standard game theory, as illustrated by the PD, AG, and RPD games, hints at the potential value of institutional rules and norms while also raising difficult questions about how such rules and norms would come to be respected. Effective rules prohibiting defection would be of great value in a simple PD game. Unfortunately, merely stating a rule that prohibits defection would not induce cooperation in a PD setting, because players face strong incentives to disobey such rules. This suggests the importance of examining how rules are **enforced**, or made effective at changing players' behavior. We expand on this point below.

Rules prohibiting defection are of less obvious value in AG settings. In an AG, when each player believes others will cooperate, she cooperates as well. In such circumstances, players have no incentive to defect when they expect others to cooperate, in which case rules prohibiting defection are not necessary. If institutional rules and norms play any role in AG settings, it is one of coordinating expectations, or helping each player form the expectation that other players will cooperate. The model provides no explanation, however, for why the coordinating mechanism should take the form of a specific set of rules and norms.

The role that institutional rules might play in RPD settings is similarly subtle. Institutional rules and norms might simply be ways of articulating equilibrium contingent strategies of the form: "I'll cooperate as long as you cooperate, but if you defect I will punish you by defecting in the future." But institutions observed in many real-world settings call for immediate punishment of defectors using fines, physical punishments, or public rebukes, rather than mere threats of future noncooperation. Thus the interpretation of institutional rules and norms as equilibrium RPD strategies is not fully satisfying, and a complete theory of cooperation-supporting institutions requires more detailed study of when and how threats of explicit, immediate punishment might support cooperation.

Rules and third-party enforcement in one-shot prisoner's dilemma games

We may easily demonstrate that rules accompanied by explicit punishments for cheating can improve well-being in a simple PD game. Return to the game of Table 12.2, but suppose now that a **third party** external to the village (such as a representative of the central government) enforces a rule that prohibits shirking. Assume that this external party is able to observe both players' choices and extract a utility penalty P from any player who breaks the rule by shirking. The transformed game is described in Table 12.4, which is the same as Table 12.2 except that the punishment P is subtracted from the relevant payoffs in cases of shirking.

Examination of the second column in Table 12.4 tells us that as long as the punishment for shirking (P) is greater than the cost to each player of contributing her "fair share" to the project ($L/2$), then when Villager 2 participates, Villager 1 finds participation more attractive than free

TABLE 12.4   Payoffs to Villager 1 and Villager 2 in a Road Maintenance Game with Third Party Enforcement

If Villager 1:	If Villager 2:	
	Shirks	**Participates**
Shirks	$0 - P, 0 - P$	$R - P, R - L$
Participates	$R - L, R - P$	$R - L/2, R - L/2$

riding (and being punished), because $R - L/2 > R - P$. Thus if the punishment is large enough ($P > L/2$), then if one villager expects the other to participate, she chooses to participate, too. Examination of the first column tells us that in this two-person game, when $P > L/2$, Villager 1 would choose to participate even if she expected Villager 2 to shirk, because with $P > L/2$ and $R > L/2$, it must also be the case that $R - L > - P$. It may be shown, however, that in a similar game with more than two players, noncooperation in equilibrium is also possible.[8] We learn here that:

> Rules against defection, when enforced by third parties who observe and punish defection, can support cooperation and raise players' well-being if the threat of punishment eliminates the incentive to free ride.

The game of Table 12.4 demonstrates the potential benefit of well-enforced rules, but it says nothing about the cost. It assumes that some external authority, such as a central government, enacts a rule requiring villagers to cooperate in road maintenance projects, has access to an enforcement technology, and is willing to pay the cost of employing this technology. An **enforcement technology** is a mechanism for monitoring compliance and for exacting penalties or bestowing rewards. Such technologies are costly to employ, involving the time, effort, or social sacrifice of monitors, guards, judges, or fine collectors, as well as the use of vehicles, hardware, software, or other inputs.

Rules and shared enforcement costs in one-shot prisoner's dilemma games

Unfortunately, willing and capable external enforcers are lacking in many developing-country communities, where the formal institutions of central and state governments often have little effective reach, especially in rural areas. In the absence of third-party enforcers, might the parties who stand to gain from cooperation create and enforce rules for themselves? We will find that:

> When potential cooperators must pay for rule enforcement themselves through a shared expenditure, the existence of a cheap enforcement technology can help make cooperation possible. It does not guarantee cooperation, however, because the enforcement technology is a public good. Potential cooperators might, therefore, face a secondary cooperation problem and fail to undertake the joint investment in the enforcement technology.

To establish this, suppose that community members are able to hire a third party to catch and fine villagers who do not participate in community projects. For example, suppose that the two villagers contemplating road maintenance choices as in Table 12.2 may now pay a total cost

---

[8]With N players, when all participate, each contributes labor L/N and enjoys payoff $R - L/N$. Punishments that are large enough to render cooperation possible ($P > L/N$) may nonetheless be small enough that participants choose not to participate if they believe no one else will participate, because the loss from carrying out the project on one's own ($L - R$) is greater than the punishment for shirking (P). In such cases, third-party enforcement transforms the PD game into an AG, rather than transforming it into a game in which the dominant strategy of both parties is to cooperate.

■ **TABLE 12.5   Payoffs to Villager 1 and Villager 2 in the First Stage of a Road Maintenance Game with Collective Payment for Enforcement**

| If Villager 1: | If Villager 2: | |
	Doesn't contribute	Contributes
Doesn't contribute	0, 0	$0, -C/2$
Contributes	$-C/2, 0$	$R - L/2 - C/2, R - L/2 - C/2$

C to hire a punishment agent (PA) to monitor both villagers' behavior and impose a penalty of $P > L - R$ on any villager who shirks. If each villager contributes $C/2$, the village hires a PA and gains an effective mechanism for punishing shirking. If only one villager contributes, or if neither contributes, then the village fails to hire the PA and shirking goes unpunished.

The villagers now face a **two-stage game**. In the first stage, they must decide whether or not to contribute $C/2$ toward hiring a PA, and in the second stage they must decide whether to participate in the road-maintenance project or shirk, already knowing whether or not a PA has been hired. To solve a two-stage game like this, we must work backward, first considering all possible configurations of the second-stage game and identifying the equilibrium for each of them. We may then analyze the first-stage game, assuming that all players are aware of the equilibria in the second stage to which their first-stage choices might lead them.

In the present example, the second stage can take two forms depending on whether or not the village succeeds in hiring a PA in the first stage. If the villagers fail to hire a PA, then in the second stage they face the PD game of Table 12.2, they both choose to shirk, and each receives a utility payoff of zero. If, instead, they succeed in hiring a PA, then in the second stage they face the game of Table 12.4, and with $P > L - R$, they both choose to participate, each deriving utility $R - L/2$.

Having drawn these conclusions about the second stage, we may now describe the first-stage game as in Table 12.5. Each villager must decide whether or not to contribute $C/2$ toward hiring a PA. If neither pays, then they hire no PA, they each face the second-stage PD, and they each derive zero utility. If both pay, then they hire a PA, they each face the second-stage game of Table 12.4, and they each derive total utility of $R - L/2 - C/2$ (their second-stage payoff less the cost of their first-stage contribution). We assume that C is small enough for this payoff to be positive. If one pays and the other does not, then no PA is hired. We also assume that if one pays and the other does not, the one who pays suffers some loss that cannot be recovered, while the other derives utility of zero. For simplicity we assume that the one who pays loses her full payment and derives utility of $-C/2$.

This game has the AG structure. If each villager expects the other to help cover the cost, they both choose to contribute, and the community successfully creates an institution to support collective participation in road maintenance projects. If, however, each expects the other not to contribute, then neither will choose to contribute, no cooperation-supporting enforcement mechanism is created, and they remain in the PD with regard to road maintenance. Thus the existence of a costly technology for third-party enforcement of cooperation does not guarantee cooperation, because the villagers might find themselves facing a **secondary cooperation problem**. That is, they might fail to create a mechanism for enforcing participation in road maintenance because the enforcement mechanism is itself a public good. By transforming the PD into an AG, the existence of an enforcement technology can nonetheless expand the role for leadership in catalyzing cooperation.

Rules and decentralized enforcement in one-shot and indefinitely repeated prisoner's dilemma games

Rather than hiring a third-party enforcer, the villagers might instead contemplate monitoring each other and administering punishments in a more decentralized way. That is, each might monitor the other and threaten immediate punishment upon detection of shirking. However:

When potential cooperators must punish each other for shirking in a decentralized fashion, the existence of a cheap punishment technology can allow them to make credible threats of punishment that support cooperation, but only if they expect to interact indefinitely. Again, although the existence of the punishment technology creates the potential for cooperation, it does not guarantee cooperation.

Return yet again to the two villagers facing the road maintenance game of Table 12.2. Suppose now that each villager is able to extract a punishment of P from the other player, but that the punisher must bear a personal cost of c. For example, one villager may punish the other for shirking by bringing the shirker before the village council and demanding that he be fined. This would impose a significant cost on the shirker, but it would also impose some cost on the punisher, who must expend time and energy in monitoring the shirker and bringing the complaint to the council, and she could suffer social and psychological costs from serving as the accuser. Could mutual threats of such punishment have the force required to sustain participation in the road maintenance project?

In a one-shot game under the assumptions we have made thus far, the answer is no. Punishment, by definition, must take place *after* shirking has already occurred, and thus the villagers would find themselves in a two-stage game. In the first stage of this road maintenance game with decentralized punishment for shirking, they decide whether to participate in the road maintenance project, and in the second stage they decide whether to exact any punishments on shirkers. Unfortunately, once they get to the second stage, neither villager has an incentive to punish the other, because so doing would cost her c but would produce no subsequent benefit. Villagers might threaten at the start of the game to punish each other for shirking, but such threats would not be credible, because each villager knows that the other will ultimately have no incentive to follow through on the threat.

As with the simple PD game without explicit enforcement, indefinite repetition might improve the chances for cooperation in this two-stage game. Villagers might have an incentive to punish defection in the present if by so doing they can support cooperation in the future. Furthermore, the existence of the low-cost technology for immediate punishment could improve the potential for cooperation, because the hope of future cooperation benefits may be enough to outweigh the cost of punishing defectors today (c), even if they are not enough to outweigh the full cost of participating today ($L/2$). In such circumstances, the combination of indefinite repetition and the existence of a low-cost technology for decentralized punishment might make cooperation possible. We must conclude, however, that:

The existence of inexpensive technologies for monitoring compliance and immediately punishing noncompliance could expand the potential for cooperation supported by institutional rules and norms, but cooperation is far from guaranteed. Healthy institutions might simply fail to arise even when they would generate great mutual benefits.

Summary

From standard game theory we learn that cooperation is particularly difficult when people are able to free ride, enjoying the benefits of collective undertakings while letting others bear the costs. When all attempt to free ride, no benefits materialize. We learn also that even purely self-interested individuals might nonetheless choose to cooperate when they care about the future and expect to face repeated opportunities for cooperation with each other into the indefinite future. Threats of punishment by third-party enforcers also have the potential to raise well-being by encouraging self-interested individuals to cooperate. In the absence of third-party enforcement, the existence of low-cost enforcement technologies that potential cooperators themselves can purchase or impose could facilitate cooperation, especially when the parties involved expect to interact indefinitely, but they do not guarantee cooperation.

In the next section we learn that people often cooperate even when they do not expect to interact again, and even in the absence of third-party enforcement. This behavior is difficult to explain using standard game theory. For possible explanations of such behavior, we turn to a discussion of behavioral economics.

12.2B Behavioral economics, reciprocity, and cooperation

As mentioned in Chapter 6, researchers in the field of behavioral economics test for specified departures from the assumptions of standard neoclassical models of decision making using carefully designed laboratory and field experiments. They examine departures of many sorts, including the existence of present bias, which we discussed in Chapter 10. Here we discuss one additional departure from neoclassical rationality that is particularly pertinent to the study of cooperation, and to the role of institutional rules and decentralized enforcement mechanisms in supporting cooperation: the observed tendency for people to make choices exhibiting "reciprocity" (Fehr and Gächter, 2000b).

Reciprocity

People exhibit **positive reciprocity** when they choose actions that are more beneficial to other people (and more costly to themselves) after they witness the others acting in a manner they perceive as fair or generous. They exhibit **negative reciprocity** when they choose actions that are more costly to other people (even if extracting these penalties is costly to themselves) after they witness the others acting in a manner they perceive as unfair or selfish.

Laboratory experiments seeking to measure and understand reciprocity often engage volunteer participants in simple **ultimatum bargaining games**, in which two players are asked to divide a fixed sum of money. A first person is given the role of Proposer. She must make a proposal to a second player, called the Responder, regarding how to split the sum between them. If the Responder accepts, the players receive the agreed amounts, but if the Responder rejects the proposal, neither player gets anything.

If both players in an ultimatum game had strictly neoclassical utility functions, the Responder would accept any positive amount offered, because he would always consider obtaining something better than nothing. Anticipating this, the Proposer would offer only the smallest possible amount, so as to keep as much as possible for herself. In many experimental studies with this game, in which real people are placed in the roles of Proposer and Responder, however, Proposers offer sums significantly larger than the minimum possible, and when they offer the Responders less than 30 percent of the total sum, the Responders often reject the proposals. Such results have been demonstrated in many countries, even when the sums of money involved are substantial. In post-experiment interviews, participants report choosing to reject low offers (despite the personal loss) because they consider them "unfair" (Fehr and Gächter, 2000b). Studies suggest that between 40 and 66 percent of subjects behave in this reciprocal manner, though at least 20 percent behave in the purely self-interested manner suggested by neoclassical game theory. (Frank et al., 1993) find that students who have taken economics courses are more likely to behave in the neoclassical fashion than other students.)

Reciprocity and cooperation

We might initially question whether reciprocal behavior truly violates neoclassical assumptions. We know from section 12.2A that when neoclassical decision makers play indefinitely repeated games, they might in equilibrium employ contingent strategies in which they respond in kind to cooperative and uncooperative behavior in their opponents (as in the grim strategy). The evidence shows, however, that experimental subjects treat each other in reciprocal fashion even when they have no relationship with each other and have no expectation of interacting again in the future (Fehr and Gächter, 2000b). This suggests that people engage in reciprocal behavior because they derive utility directly from engaging in acts that reward cooperative people and punish uncooperative people, and not only out of the hope of encouraging future cooperation.

Reciprocal preferences are of interest in the study of cooperation and institutional rules because:

> Reciprocal preferences (and especially negative reciprocity) might provide the cement that holds cooperative arrangements together by providing people with motivation to follow through on threats of punishing defectors.

Players with negative reciprocal preferences experience a utility boost when they punish players who have defected. If this utility boost is big enough to outweigh the direct cost to a punisher of inflicting a punishment, then threats of decentralized punishment become credible (even in one-shot games), and credible threats of punishment can make cooperation possible by eliminating the reward for free riding. Positive reciprocity can furthermore cause people to derive a utility bonus from the very act of cooperating when others cooperate (regardless of the material rewards), thereby reducing their incentive to free ride and reducing the size of the explicit penalty required to induce their cooperation.

To see this, return to the road maintenance game of Table 12.2, but suppose now that each player is able to exact a punishment of size P on the other player at a direct utility cost of c. Suppose further that each player enjoys a negative reciprocity utility payoff of N when he punishes a shirker, as long as he has not himself shirked. (It seems reasonable to assume that players enjoy punishing a lack of community spirit only when they themselves have exhibited such spirit.) Finally, suppose that each player enjoys a utility bonus of G for being good by cooperating (when the other player cooperates).

As long as $N > c$, each player would choose to punish the other player for shirking, even at the end of a one-shot game, and the threat of decentralized punishment is credible. The first-stage game thus takes on the form of that in Table 12.6.

If both shirk, both receive utility payoffs of zero. If both cooperate, they both enjoy the second-stage returns to cooperation in road maintenance $(R - L/2)$ plus the internal utility bonus for being good (G). If one participates and the other shirks, both receive the road-maintenance benefit R, the one who participates completes the project and punishes the shirker, for a net reward of $R - L - c + N$, and the one who participates is punished, for a net reward of $R - P$.

Reciprocal preferences make cooperation possible in this one-shot game. As long as $P + G > L/2$, then $R - L/2 + G > R - P$, and when one villager participates, the best response of the other is to participate as well (see column 2 of Table 12.6). The greater the positive reciprocity reward (G), the smaller the penalty (P) required to render free riding unattractive. If $R - L - c + N > 0$, then the losses from maintaining the road alone $(L - R)$ and exacting punishment (c) are greater than the gain from negative reciprocity (N), and when one player shirks the other shirks as well. In such cases, the game has an uncooperative equilibrium as well as a cooperative equilibrium. If the gain from negative reciprocity were great enough $(N > L - R + c)$, participation would be the dominant strategy for both players.

■ TABLE 12.6 **Payoffs to Villager 1 and Villager 2 in the First Stage of a Road Maintenance Game with Decentralized Enforcement when Players Experience Internal Rewards for Reciprocal Behavior**

	If Villager 2:	
If Villager 1:	**Shirks**	**Participates**
Shirks	0, 0	$R - P$, $R - L - c + N$
Participates	$R - L - c + N$, $R - P$	$R - L/2 + G$, $R - L/2 + G$

It is useful to highlight two points regarding the game of Table 12.6. First, negative reciprocity supports cooperation by encouraging each player to monitor the other's actions and to mete out immediate, explicit punishments. Reciprocity would have little scope to improve cooperation if players were unable to observe each other's actions or had no technology for delivering punishments.

Second, negative reciprocity may be a more potent force for supporting cooperation than positive reciprocity. In the absence of negative reciprocity, threats of punishment are not credible, and one villager who expects the other to participate would participate as well only if the *reward for positive reciprocity* (G) were great enough to outweigh the cost of participating in the project ($L/2$). By contrast, as long as the *punishment* (P) is large enough to outweigh the cost of participating in the project ($L/2$), the reward for negative reciprocity (N) need only be large enough to outweigh the cost of meting out punishment (c), and with a sufficiently cheap enforcement technology, the necessary negative reciprocity reward may be quite small.

Laboratory experiments designed to replicate public goods investment decisions confirm that people often cooperate even in one-shot games and that cooperation is stronger when players have access to decentralized punishment technologies. In experiments performed by Fehr and Gächter (2000a), players were told they would play a game six times. In each round they were given the opportunity to contribute varying amounts to the creation of a public good (i.e., a fund that delivers mutual benefits to all players). Players were divided into four groups. For two groups, the games allowed players to exact punishments at some cost to themselves, and for the other two no such punishment technology was available. Within each of those pairs, in one group the same sets of players continued with each other through all rounds of play, and in the other group the players were placed in new groups of strangers in each round. Players knew in advance whether or not they would be playing all rounds with the same partners.

Participants given the ability to punish did indeed inflict punishment on uncooperative partners, despite the cost to themselves and even when they did not expect to meet the offending parties again. The punishments tended to be larger the further the offender's contribution was below the average contribution to the public good. Furthermore, groups with access to a punishment technology exhibited much higher levels of cooperation than the groups without the technology. High levels of cooperation were maintained even when players did not expect to play with the same partners in all rounds and even in the last round of the game.

The underpinnings of reciprocity

If reciprocity (or some other effect of social interactions on preferences) is important for enforcing institutional rules and norms and sustaining cooperation, then more detailed knowledge of the forces that determine how people evaluate which behaviors merit reciprocal treatment, and of what determines the strength of these feelings, might shed valuable light on institution-building efforts. Two additional experimental results suggest that:

> Efforts to facilitate communication among potential cooperators might strengthen their reciprocal tendencies, thereby rendering cooperation more likely. Third-party efforts to impose rules and incentive schemes on potential cooperators, however, might weaken reciprocal tendencies, thereby rendering internally motivated cooperation less likely in the future.

The potential significance of communication is highlighted by experimental results showing that contributions to public goods games increase when players are allowed to communicate. In fact, they are higher not only when players are allowed to talk but even when they are allowed only to see each other, relative to the case in which they interact only remotely from computer terminals (Bohnet and Frey, 1999). This suggests that efforts by outsiders to bring potential cooperators into face-to-face conversation might improve chances for cooperation, even when the potential cooperators seem to be facing a PD.

The potential detrimental effect on cooperation of externally imposed rules is demonstrated by Frohlich and Oppenheimer (1996). In the first stage of a two-stage experiment, they engaged two groups of participants in PD games. One group played a simple PD game, and the other played a PD-like game to which an externally enforced system of rewards and punishments had been added (similar to that in Table 12.5). In the second stage, both groups played simple PD games without the externally imposed rules. In the first round, the group facing the externally imposed incentive scheme exhibited higher cooperation than the other, but in the second round, after the external reward system had been removed, they cooperated less than the other group.

Other varieties of social preferences

People who exhibit positive and negative reciprocity are said to exhibit preferences that are "social," in the sense that the utility they enjoy depends not only on their own consumption and circumstances but also on how their actions affect other people. Preferences may be social in other ways that also shape and support institutional rules and norms. For example, people seem to derive higher utility from undertaking particular actions when larger fractions of the people around them also undertake those actions, giving them a tendency to conform to behavioral norms, and perhaps creating a tendency for cooperative and uncooperative behavior to propagate over time. Thus broader research into *social economics* might yield valuable insights into institutions and development (Barrett, 2005).

12.3 Economic Analysis of Community-Level Institutions

12.3A An agenda for research on community-level institutions in developing countries

Institutions supporting cooperation at the community level are of great interest in current development discussions. They merit close study for three reasons. The first relates to practical policy analysis: Community-level institutional rules and norms constrain people's choices and could, therefore, alter the way they respond to policy. If we want to understand and predict the direct and indirect impacts of policy, therefore, we must understand the nature of the institutional rules that govern people's choices.

The second reason for studying community-level institutions relates to current debates about program governance: Policymakers increasingly wish to harness or replicate successful community-level institutions for improving the implementation of development programs. Study of indigenous local-level institutions could yield insights about how to design policy reforms aimed at increasing community participation. We offer an overview of such reforms in Chapter 13 and consider many specific cases of such reforms in Chapters 15 through 22.

The final reason relates to the development community's larger interest in the institutions introduced in section 12.1. The study of specific healthy institutions at the local level might yield lessons about how to create the broader array of large-scale healthy institutions required for successful development.

In this part we suggest that:

> Policy-relevant empirical study of community-level institutions first identifies where specific institutions seem to be at work and then asks a series of probing questions regarding their nature, impacts, and evolution.

Researchers identify that an institution is at work when they observe people exhibiting a regularity of behavior, in circumstances that arise repeatedly, especially when the behavior conforms to articulated rules or norms and especially when actors who comply appear to bear an associated cost. For example, as we saw in Box 12.1, researchers have observed people cooperating in the restrained use of local CPRs, even when free riding seems feasible and even though unrestrained use would yield them greater profit.

Once we identify an institution that merits study, the most obvious first question is *What exactly are the institutional rules and norms constraining peoples' choices in this context?* The details are important for understanding how institutions affect peoples' behavior and could yield insight into the kinds of rules—rigid or flexible, general or differentiated—that institution builders should seek to construct.

The second and much more difficult question is *Why do people comply with these rules and norms?* That is, how are they enforced? When an individual believes that others will comply, does he have an incentive to comply as well, as in the assurance game? If so, then coordination of expectations might have been the route to the institution's success, and we should examine the roles of communication, leadership, and history in bringing such coordination about. If instead individuals have incentives to free ride, as in a prisoner's dilemma, then how important are explicit rewards and punishments for enforcing compliance? How important are expectations of repeated interaction and threats of future retaliatory noncompliance? How important are socially conditioned preferences through which people experience internal rewards for cooperative behavior, internal punishments for uncooperative behavior, or internal rewards for punishing uncooperative behavior in others?

The next several questions probe any positive function that an institution serves and how well it fulfills this function. *What benefits do community members enjoy as a result of mutual respect for the institutional rules? Under what conditions are effective institutions of this sort most likely to arise? How well does the institution perform its apparent function for those who enjoy its benefits? Who is included in or excluded from its benefits?* Answers to such questions shed light on where government and NGO policies that fulfill similar functions are most needed and on the potential benefit of complementing or replacing private institutions with public institutions.

Next, knowing that people's many important choices are interconnected, we ask: *What collateral effects might the institution have on other dimensions of peoples' choices?* For example, might institutional rules and norms that promote beneficial cooperation *also* have deleterious side effects in some circumstances? And do the rules alter our expectations regarding the way people will respond to policy changes?

The final set of questions examines the dynamics of institutional change: *How did the institution come into existence and how has it evolved over time? How might the institution change in response to the introduction of related policies?*

The empirical literature on private and customary community-level institutions in developing countries is still quite young and offers only partial answers to this body of questions. Furthermore, much of the research on specific institutions involves case studies offering answers that are more suggestive than definitive. The research is nonetheless thought-provoking. In the rest of this section, we introduce readers to three sets of institutions that have caught the attention of development economists and review some of the key findings of research to date.

12.3B Institutions governing local common property resources

The livelihoods of many developing-country households are tied to local common property resources (CPRs) such as fishing grounds, canal-based irrigation systems, common grazing land, and forests. Like public goods, CPRs are effectively **nonexcludable**, meaning that members of groups holding joint use rights cannot be prohibited from using them. Unlike public goods, however, CPRs are **rival**. This means that as one person increases use, the value available to all others falls. For example, as one farmer puts more animals out to graze on common land, it becomes more difficult for the animals of all other commons users to obtain grass. Similarly, the more water one farmer pumps out of an aquifer, the less water is left for other farmers, the more difficult it becomes to pump water out, and the more likely conflict becomes.

We focus here on CPRs that are renewable and local. **Renewable** CPRs are replenished each year, as grass grows and fish reproduce. Excessive use can degrade or destroy such CPRs, but as long as use is not too intense, users retain access to the resource indefinitely. **Local** CPRs belong to groups of small or medium size, such as members of small rural communities. Unlike global common property resources, such as Earth's ozone layer, local CPRs are often managed by sets of people who communicate and interact on a frequent basis.

The tragedy of the commons

Each of a CPR's users must decide how much to harvest or extract from a CPR each season. Users' decisions are often interdependent in a way that is thought to resemble a prisoner's dilemma. To see this, suppose that two people, Fisher 1 and Fisher 2, have access to a fishing ground and that each may choose to harvest fish in either a restrained or unrestrained fashion. If they both exercise restraint (e.g., fishing for only six hours per day with one boat and crew each), they both earn profits of 10. If they fish in unrestrained fashion (e.g., fishing for longer hours or with more boats), they each catch more fish, but their per-fish costs rise as it becomes more difficult to find fish, and they earn profits of only 5 apiece. Total profits derived from the pond are thus 20 when both fishers exercise restraint, but profits fall to 10 when neither exercises restraint. If one fisher exercises restraint while the other does not, they jointly derive total profits of 16, with the restrained fisher earning 4 and the unrestrained fisher earning 12. This game is shown in Table 12.7.

This game has the prisoner's dilemma structure, leading to predictions of a **tragedy of the commons**, in which the CPR is overused (Hardin, 1968). Community members would be better off if they cooperated in restraining their use of the resource, but self-interest inevitably leads to unrestrained use.

Case studies demonstrate, however, that overuse of local CPRs is not inevitable in the real world. Often harvesting is governed by indigenous institutions, which involve locally devised and locally enforced rules and norms. In what follows we review some of the key insights from research on successful local CPR management institutions and on the conditions under which successful institutions are most likely to arise. Ostrom (1990, 2005) and Wade (1987) are particularly useful references. We will see that:

> Local CPR governance institutions are often surprisingly sophisticated, involving explicit rules tailored to local circumstances. Explicit punishments, repeated interaction, and socially conditioned preferences all appear to play roles in enforcing them. Central governments sometimes contribute more to the protection of local CPRs by supporting local management institutions than by imposing regulations from outside or privatizing the resources.

Rules

Successful community cooperation in local CPR management often involves much more than friendly feelings and vague commitments to conserve local resources. Often, successful cooperation in CPR management involves detailed and clearly articulated rules. The rules tend to be

■ TABLE 12.7 **Payoffs to Fisher 1 and Fisher 2 in a CPR Prisoner's Dilemma**

	If Fisher 2:	
If Fisher 1:	Does Not Use Restraint	Uses Restraint
Does Not Use restraint	5, 5	12, 4
Uses Restraint	4, 12	10, 10

☰ **Box 12.2** Two Successful Local Common Property Resources Management Institutions

Canal-based irrigation system governance in a southern Indian village

Robert Wade (1987) describes the management of a canal-based irrigation system in "K village." Located near the downstream end of a large government irrigation system, the community faces a limited water supply. If too much of the flow is directed onto upstream fields within the community, fields downstream get too little, leading to loss of rice crops downstream and to conflict. To ensure restrained use and sharing, the village council employs 12 common irrigators for the two months during which the rice crops require irrigation. The common irrigators are instructed to "adequately wet" each field in rotation, not returning to a field until all others have been adequately wetted. If common irrigators catch farmers trying to steal water out of turn, the offenders are required to pay small fines and are reprimanded in front of the village council. Farmers contribute to the irrigators' pay in proportion to the amount of land they irrigate. These fees are collected in kind at harvest. This arrangement imposes discipline on day-to-day water use, encourages farmers to restrain their irrigated acreage, and pays for itself through the collection of fees in a manner farmers find very difficult to evade. The village council is dominated by the village elite and therefore commands necessary respect among the elite. Fortunately, the interests of the elite are aligned with those of the wider community, because large landowners own multiple plots of land distributed across upstream and downstream locations.

Fishery in Alana, Turkey

Elinor Ostrom (1990), drawing on a study by Fikret Berkes (1986), describes a fishery where competition for the best fishing spots among 100 or so fishers threatened the fishery and led to wasted time and violence. Over 10 years of experimentation, the local fishing cooperative developed a workable solution. They listed all the fishing sites in the area, delineating sites large enough to make efficient use of fishing boats and far enough apart to prevent conflict. At the beginning of each fishing season they make a list of all licensed fishers in the area, whether members of the cooperative or not, and allocate them to fishing sites by drawing lots. A few unlucky ones might fail to obtain access to the fishery in a given year. The fishers endorse the list of assignments and deposit it with the local sheriff. Each day from September to January each fisher moves one site to the east, and each day from January to May they move one site to the west. This gives each fisher equal access to the fish stocks, which migrate east and then west during the fishing season. Fishers can easily monitor each other's compliance with the scheme because any attempt to usurp a good fishing site would be detected and rebuffed by the fisher allotted that site for the day. Occasional disputes are resolved through conversations in local cafes. Ostrom points out that detailed local knowledge of the fishery was crucial in working out a system that seems fair to everyone involved and that is easy to monitor and enforce.

remarkably sophisticated, in the sense that they are cleverly tailored to local circumstances, but they are also simple to follow, involving no complex calculations. They often incorporate some flexibility and can be modified through a process in which users believe they have some voice. The rules are devised in ways that people consider fair and that facilitate monitoring of compliance, either by the users themselves or by people they hire. The arrangements are highly diverse. Box 12.2 describes two examples.

Enforcement mechanisms

Formally defined and immediate punishments often play prominent roles in the enforcement of successful local CPR management institutions. Sometimes the monitoring and enforcement mechanisms are centralized, as in the first example of Box 12.2, and sometimes they are decentralized, as in the second example. Often violators are required to pay codified fines, and sometimes violators are publicly reprimanded, creating the potential for social sanctions as well. The penalties are often graduated, with small fines for first-time offenders but larger fines for repeat offenders.

Successful institutions are more likely to arise in small, close-knit communities. This might reflect the importance to enforcement of repeated future interaction or of past interaction through which community members developed socially conditioned preferences supporting cooperation. Researchers' frequent observation that the creation of fair rules is important for success hints more specifically at a role for reciprocal preferences in supporting compliance. Thus, explicit punishment, repeated interaction, and socially conditioned preferences might all contribute to the enforcement of successful CPR management rules.

Contextual factors

Successful CPR institutions appear more likely to arise where the benefits of cooperation are higher relative to the costs. For example, Wade (1987) reports that the users of canal-based irrigation systems in India are more likely to create successful institutions if the canal is located in the bottom third of a larger government irrigation system. In such locations, water is more likely to be in limited supply and cooperation is thus more important for preventing conflict. Successful institutions are also more likely to exist where people live closer together, perhaps because the costs of monitoring each other are lower.

Exclusion

Successful management of CPRs requires cooperation by all potential users with physical access to the designated resource. Thus, where successful CPR management institutions arise, they tend to incorporate most interested parties living in a designated geographic area, regardless of their socioeconomic status. Disadvantaged groups might nonetheless have inferior access to CPRs if advantaged groups are capable of excluding them from residence in the relevant geographic areas, and conflict over CPRs can contribute to poverty. Indeed, conflicting desires to control water and other natural resources have contributed to many violent conflicts in the developing world. Successful CPR management institutions might also be less likely to arise where inequality is greater and where the interests of the elite are not well aligned with the interests of the poor (as suggested by Wade, 1987).

Interactions with policy

The logic of the tragedy of the commons initially convinced many policymakers and analysts that central governments must protect local CPRs from overuse, either by regulating their use or (where feasible) by dividing the resources and privatizing them. Privatization gives individual owners exclusive rights to use a pond or a section of land or forest and was expected to prevent overuse of resources by putting them into the hands of private owners who would bear all the costs (as well as all the benefits) of harvesting them. Case study evidence on effective community-level institutions suggests, however, that neither central government regulation nor privatization may be necessary. Furthermore, privatization is often infeasible and regulations can make matters worse when they displace healthy local cooperative management institutions.

Ostrom (1990) argues that local groups have a great advantage over external government authorities when it comes to designing feasible and inexpensive systems of rules, monitoring, and punishment. They have much better access to detailed information regarding the nature of the resources involved (e.g., the location of local fishing sites), the interests of people involved, and the nature of potential conflicts. They are thus better able to create rules and enforcement technologies that are perceived as fair and are effective at low cost. External authorities would find it much more costly, and perhaps impossible, to gather the information necessary to design such rules. Furthermore, external authorities often lack the personnel and budget to monitor compliance and follow through on punishment. As a result, a takeover by central government sometimes replaces effective local management with *no* real management, leading to CPR degradation.

External authorities might nonetheless have valuable roles to play in encouraging effective local management. They might, for example, back up the rights of local rule-enforcement agents (such as the local sheriff in the second example of Box 12.2) to monitor rule compliance and administer punishments. Over the last two decades many governments and international organizations have experimented with methods of supporting rather than displacing community-level natural resource management institutions (World Bank, 1998). Few rigorous studies have yet been undertaken assessing the impacts of these efforts on CPR use or on well-being among CPR users.

12.3C Informal insurance institutions

In many communities around the world, people who are doing relatively well provide assistance to neighbors in urgent need, expecting that neighbors will reciprocate when circumstances are reversed in the future (Morduch, 1999). Aware of the tremendous fluctuations in income and needs to which developing-country households are exposed (see Chapter 2), and equipped with the analytical tools of section 12.2, development economists have come to see the rules and norms that govern such mutual assistance as examples of **informal insurance institutions**. These institutions encourage a subtle form of cooperation among people subject to idiosyncratic shocks: When everyone in the group agrees to contribute by giving gifts when they are doing better than their neighbors, they all enjoy reduced vulnerability, because they know that when they are hit by bad times they will receive gifts that allow them to sustain consumption and avoid selling off productive assets. We will see that:

> Informal insurance institutions are highly diverse in form and offer people valuable protection against fluctuations and shocks of moderate size. Unfortunately, they tend to fall apart when they are most needed, often exclude many of the neediest people, even when they are functioning well, and might inhibit development by weakening peoples' incentives to invest. Their existence might also alter the impacts of public safety net programs in diverse ways.

Norms and rules

Often mutual assistance is governed by informal norms that call on families who are doing relatively well (within the communities or networks in which the norms apply) to provide cash, food, or interest-free loans to families that have been hit by crop failure, unemployment, illness, death in the family, or other sudden needs. Some indigenous insurance institutions are more formal. In rural Ethiopia, for example, most households belong to burial societies, called *iddir*, to which households make specified payments in good months and from which their families receive payments to help cover the daunting cost of funerals when family members die (Dercon et al., 2006). These groups meet once or twice per month, have written rules, and keep written records of contributions and payments.

Enforcement mechanisms

The cooperation problem underlying the need for informal insurance institutions is more complicated than the simple prisoner's dilemma, because the costs and benefits are uncertain and are spread out over time. The expectation of repeated future interaction must play some role in sustaining such institutions. As was the case with CPR governance institutions, however, immediate punishments for defection also appear to play some role. Contributions are sometimes encouraged by threats of malicious gossip or exclusion from community activities, for example. Sometimes the punishments are even more troubling. Platteau (2000) describes how in some African cultures, people who are prosperous and stingy are accused of witchcraft and become the victims of poisoning.

Limitations

Informal mutual insurance institutions reduce people's vulnerability to some shocks, but they have many shortcomings as social safety nets. First, informal insurance institutions do not arise and thrive equally in all places. Case studies reveal differences in the size and coverage of such institutions. In addition, according to survey data, private transfers of cash or food from household to household—which might signal the existence of informal insurance institutions—are much less prevalent in some countries and communities than others. Second, even where informal mutual insurance institutions arise, they are unlikely to channel many resources to the permanently destitute, who have little chance of reciprocating assistance in the future.

Third, informal insurance institutions often provide insurance in segmented and exclusionary ways. For example, Munshi and Rosenzweig (2005) show that although some mutual insurance takes place among Indian households, it takes place largely within subcaste networks. Members of poorer castes have opportunities to share risk only with other poor households, suggesting that the protection they derive from participation is lower. Goldstein (2004) argues that mutual assistance is more prevalent within groups of male or female friends than between husbands and wives within Ghanaian households. Wealthier Ethiopian households belong to larger numbers of funeral societies than poorer households and are better protected against shocks (Dercon et al., 2008).

Fourth, because informal insurance institutions tend to operate only within small, close-knit groups, they tend to provide protection against only a small range of shocks, and not the most devastating. Norms of mutual assistance offer reasonable protection against shocks only when the typical number and magnitude of shocks within the group in a given year is small enough that the contributions by those who are not hit by shocks are adequate to cover the needs of those who are hit by shocks. This implies that informal insurance institutions have little scope to help groups cope with shocks that are covariate within the groups or that generate very large needs. Informal insurance institutions thus cannot help groups cope with covariate shocks such as floods and droughts. Gertler and Gruber (2002) documents that while informal insurance arrangements appear to provide Indonesian households with protection against common but idiosyncratic health shocks of moderate size, they offer much less protection against health shocks that are less frequent but very costly, such as those associated with serious illness requiring hospitalization.

Effects on behavior

Researchers point out two ways informal insurance institutions might slow growth and poverty reduction. First, norms dictating that any community member earning unusually high income give transfers to members with lower incomes reduce individuals' incentives to invest and innovate, because individuals must bear the full cost of innovation while expecting to enjoy only a fraction of the returns. Sharing institutions might thus create a drag on growth and development, helping to trap communities in poverty. Anecdotes describe, for example, how potential entrepreneurs find it difficult to succeed in setting up new general stores in their closely knit home communities, because family and friends demand that they share their inventory. Second, informal insurance institutions might also inhibit labor mobility. Workers may be reluctant to migrate out of home communities in which they benefit from mutual assistance norms, even when wages elsewhere are higher. Munshi and Rosenzweig (2009) offer evidence of this for India.

Interactions with policy

When a household receives a transfer from a public safety net program, other households who would have felt obligated by mutual assistance norms to provide that household with private transfers might no longer feel so obligated. Thus receipt of a public transfer may cause a household to lose private transfers. In such cases the net effect of the public transfer on the recipient household's income may be far smaller than the size of transfer distributed to the household, and the true beneficiaries of public poverty reduction transfers may be the (possibly nonpoor) households who withdraw their private support from public transfer recipients. Several recent randomized control trials of cash transfer programs in Latin America, however, find evidence that this crowding out of private transfers by public transfers is at most quite small (Fiszbein and Schady, 2009).

12.3D Customary and informal land rights institutions

Formal institutions protecting private property rights in land, which are documented in land titles and enforced by courts and law enforcement systems, can be understood as solving a public goods problem. If everyone respects everyone else's rights to use and claim the produce of the land they cultivate, everyone benefits. Community members respect one another's rights by refraining from encroaching on land or stealing produce. If everyone respects rights in this way, each land user can forgo costly fences and guards, and each can invest in land improvements without great fear of loss to theft, vandalism, or expropriation. By clarifying ownership and offering peaceful means of resolving disputes, formal private land rights institutions also help prevent conflict.

Many people in the developing world lack formal title to land and live outside the reach of formal legal and law enforcement systems. This is especially true in less commercialized rural areas and in the squatter settlements around large cities. Concerned that lack of strong property rights inhibits efficiency and investment, many governments have mounted programs aimed at providing titles to farmers and slum dwellers. Such land titling initiatives are costly and difficult to administer, however. Land must be surveyed and mapped. Program personnel must attempt to identify current possessors of specific plots and resolve disputes over who should own the land, and they must create systems for recording both initial rights and the changes in rights associated with sales, gifts, inheritance, and foreclosure.

Knowing that community-level institutions sometimes arise to facilitate cooperation, analysts must consider the possibility that communities manage to protect land rights even in the absence of central government involvement. If community-level institutions provide nearly as much security as formal private property institutions, then costly government titling efforts might not merit the expense. Thus it is useful to take a close look at land rights institutions where formal private property institutions are absent. We will find that:

> Customary land rights institutions often provide rural land users with enough security to encourage investment, even when they do not guarantee the full range of rights associated with formal private property regimes. They are diverse, however, and offer varying degrees of security.

The introduction of formal private property rights through titling programs thus improves land use efficiency and investment in some rural contexts but not others. Formal land rights are more likely to improve efficiency and investment in urban slums, where effective customary land rights institutions are less likely to exist.

Unfortunately, we will also learn that:

> Even where customary land rights institutions support efficiency and investment, they are often highly exclusionary, offering few rights to women and pastoralist groups.

Customary and informal land rights

In rural areas, and especially in close-knit communities with long-shared histories, land rights are often governed by customary institutions, which are enforced by tribal or lineage authorities. Sometimes land is held as common property and governed by CPR governance institutions like those discussed earlier. Often, however, plots of land are allocated to individual users, who enjoy individualized rights of some sort. In fact, individualized land rights are becoming increasingly common within customary institutions, especially where lucrative market opportunities are becoming available.

Customary land rights institutions provide users with diverse packages of rights that often look quite different from the package of rights conferred under formal private property regimes. Under formal regimes, title holders are entitled to use land and claim its produce for as long as they like. Title holders may be required to obey legal regulations, but they otherwise enjoy autonomy in decisions regarding land use. They may leave the land idle or rent it out without losing ownership. In addition to full **use rights**, they have full **transfer rights**, meaning that they may give their land away, sell it, or bequeath it to whomever they wish. When land is sold, the new owner acquires all these rights and the previous owner retains no right to reclaim the land.

Under customary land rights institutions, land users typically have the right to claim the produce of their current crops, but they might lack full land use rights and often lack full transfer rights. They may be prohibited from planting trees or may be required to obtain approval for their plans from elders, chiefs, or spiritual leaders. In some cases users must allow pastoralist groups to graze their animals on the stubble after crops are harvested. Sometimes current users expect to retain use of land for as long as they wish, but sometimes they perceive a high probability of losing land use, knowing that tribal or family leaders have the right to reclaim land. Users can also find it difficult to retain rights to land if they leave it idle or rent it out. They might have no right to give away or sell the land or may be able to sell only to other group members, though in some cases they are allowed to sell even to outsiders. Sometimes they retain the right to reclaim the land by refunding the purchase price. Who receives the land when a land user dies may be governed by strict rules, decided by elders, or left up to the land user's discretion.

Residents of urban squatter settlements are often recent in-migrants from other places. With weaker ties to their neighbors than residents of close-knit rural communities, they are less likely to enjoy property rights governed by customary authorities. They might thus need to protect their claims to land through their own vigilance and resistance or by paying local strongmen for protection.

Rural land rights, productivity, and investment

Policymakers worry that customary and informal institutions provide only weak protection for property rights in land. Weak land rights might inhibit investment and productivity growth through several channels. First, land users may be discouraged from making investments tied to land—such as investments in irrigation ditches, tree crops, and houses—because they fear losing control over the land. Second, even if they believe they can retain use of the land for as long as they wish, they may be put off from investment if a lack of land sales rights renders them unable to realize or liquidate the value of their investments should they wish to move. Third, weak land rights institutions might prevent land users from obtaining credit to finance investment by preventing the use of land as collateral. Land lacks value as collateral if lenders from outside a community do not expect customary institutions to allow them to claim use of the land. Fourth, customary land rights regimes that prohibit sales or discourage rentals can prevent land from being cultivated by the highest-productivity farmers.

Most empirical studies of the effectiveness of customary land rights institutions for encouraging investment and raising productivity involve comparisons of productivity and investment outcomes across titled and untitled land or across lands held under different sets of customary rights (e.g., land over which users have temporary versus longer-term control, or land that users are allowed to bequeath versus other land). Drawing inferences about the causal effect of land rights status on investment and productivity is difficult, because correlations between land rights and investment might reflect not only the effect of land rights on investment but also causation in the reverse direction. Farms with better investment outcomes may be more likely to have strong property rights for several reasons. Farmers might have made investments in trees and structures in order to obtain stronger land rights under customary regimes that reward investments with stronger rights. When obtaining title is costly, farmers who face better investment opportunities and thus have more to gain from titling may also be more likely to purchase titles, and titling programs might tend to focus on regions with better investment opportunities. Most studies of land rights and investment are thus subject to important caveats, though some do a more compelling job than others at controlling for variation in land quality and investment opportunities.

Platteau (2000) and Deininger (2003) offer reviews of the large empirical literature on rural land rights, productivity, and investment. Here we highlight only a few critical lessons that emerge from that literature. First, stronger land rights certainly can increase investment significantly, but formal titling is neither necessary nor sufficient for guaranteeing strong land rights.

Within Africa, for example, some customary systems seem to provide more security and better investment incentives than others, but most studies find little effect of formal titling on productivity or investment. Second, formal titles are more likely to strengthen land rights and investment in regions of resettlement or rapid migration, where strong traditional land rights institutions are less likely to be present.

Third, the strengthening of individualized *use* rights appears to be more important for encouraging investment than is the strengthening of *transfer* rights. The 1988 decollectivization of agricultural production in Vietnam, which gave farm families the right to reap and control the harvest of their own plots, but did not give them strong transfer rights, is credited with kicking off a tremendous boom in agricultural productivity. A further reform in 1993 that issued titles increased transfer rights but, in contrast, had only a small effect on productivity (Do and Iyer, 2008).

Finally, the issuing of formal titles, which bestow transfer as well as use rights, appears useful for helping farmers acquire credit. Thus, the effects of titles on productivity and investment are greater where credit markets are active. Unfortunately, this also implies that the impacts of titles on productivity and investment tend to be larger for wealthier farmers, because small farmers have difficulty accessing credit even with land titles (Carter and Olinto, 2003).

Rural land rights and exclusion

The empirical literature on land rights and investment highlights the potential for customary systems to confer strong rights, as well as the difficulties of rendering formal titling systems effective. It thus suggests that policymakers interested in strengthening land rights at low cost should consider ways of strengthening customary institutions, rather than replacing them with formal private property institutions. For example, policymakers might give formal titles to tribal or lineage authorities, thereby reducing conflict between groups, while letting local authorities govern individualized land rights through customary means. Unfortunately, even when this is a cost-effective way of strengthening investment incentives and reducing intercommunity conflict, it might reinforce and exacerbate intracommunity inequities.

One of the most striking features of many customary land rights systems in Africa is the disparity in treatment of women relative to men (Kevane, 2004). Men may be able to obtain use of land by asking their fathers, other relatives, or tribal elders, as well as by inheritance or the clearing of previously uncultivated land. After a young man cultivates land for some time, it comes to be accepted as "his." In these same cultures, all of these routes to acquiring land may be closed to women, who gain only temporary rights to cultivate small quantities and lower qualities of land through agreements with their husbands or fathers. In some places, women lose all access to land when widowed or divorced. Thus, even when customary land rights regimes provide land rights security for men, they might maintain profound insecurity for women.

Policymakers face daunting challenges in strengthening land rights while also improving gender equity in access to land. If policymakers attempt to impose new property rights regimes that give greater rights to women, they might find these regimes very difficult to enforce, because the rules might have little legitimacy among tribal and lineage enforcers. If policymakers attempt to impose inheritance rights for wives, they might succeed only in encouraging men to choose informal over formal marriage (Kevane, 2004). Thus great care must be taken in efforts to expand women's land rights.

Another dimension of land rights exclusion that merits attention is the exclusion of pastoralist groups. Historically, many customary land rights systems among settled groups protected pastoralists' rights to graze animals on crop residue after harvest. Agreements between settled and pastoralist communities were mutually beneficial, providing pastoralists with animal feed and cultivators with manure. As customary land rights regimes are replaced by formal systems of private property, pastoralists tend to lose grazing rights.

☰ Box 12.3 Effects of Land Titling in Urban Peru

Prior to 1996, residents in urban Peru could obtain a formal title to their land only by paying high fees and dealing with large bureaucratic difficulties. As a consequence, many residents lacked formal titles. In 1996, the government initiated a program in eight cities that allowed residents to obtain titles quickly and at very little cost. Project teams started work in several neighborhoods within each participating city, digitally mapped all lots in those neighborhoods, and required residents only to verify that they had resided there before the program began. After completing registration of titles in one community each team moved on to a nearby community. Between 1996 and 2003 more than 1.2 million households obtained titles through this program.

Erica Field (2007) analyzes data on 2,750 households collected in the year 2000, at which point the program had reached some communities but not others. This allows comparison of household labor supply and other outcomes for households in communities that had and had not already received titles. This simple comparison would yield a biased estimate of the impact of titling if the communities that had already received titles were systematically different from the communities that had not. Field offers a way of accounting for this possibility.

She observes that in all communities, some residents possessed titles even before the program was introduced. The introduction of the program should have had no direct effect on such households. Any differences across the treated and untreated communities for households that possessed a title before the program should thus reflect differences in neighborhood characteristics. If differences in neighborhood characteristics induce differences in household labor supply that are the same for households that did and did not have a title prior to the program, then an unbiased estimate of titling impact may be obtained by calculating the difference across treated and untreated communities in household labor supply among households that *did not* have a title prior to the program and subtracting off the difference across treated and untreated communities among households that *did* have a title prior to the program. Using this difference-in-differences approach, she estimates that providing the opportunity for easy and cheap acquisition of title increased household labor supply by 13.4 hours per week on average. Receipt of a title was also associated with a higher incidence of adults working outside the home rather than at home and a lower incidence of child labor.

Urban land rights, efficiency, and investment

We might expect formal titling efforts to have greater impacts on investment and efficiency in urban squatter settlements than in rural areas, because urban residents are less likely to benefit from strong customary land rights institutions, and because it may be easier to create effective formal institutions in urban areas. Stronger urban land rights might boost investment in housing improvements and might free households from spending time and money on protecting their property. Again, empirical estimation of titling effects is complicated by multiple reasons for correlation between title holding and investment. Qualitative evidence links title holding to substantial investments in housing improvements (de Soto, 1993). A particularly compelling quantitative study by Field (2007) establishes that receipt of a formal title in urban Peru increased average family labor supply by 13.4 hours per week and reduced child labor (see Box 12.3), presumably because adult family members no longer needed to remain at home to resist expropriation by other households.

Di Tella et al. (2007) offer one last somewhat surprising observation about the possible impacts of titling. They compare slum dwellers in Buenos Aires who live and work in very similar conditions, except that some have had legal title to their land for more than 10 years while others have no legal title. They find that the homeowners with legal title have substantially different *beliefs* relative to the others. For instance, they are more likely to believe that one can succeed on one's own (not needing the support of a strong group), that one can get ahead by working hard, and that money is necessary for happiness.

REFERENCES

Acemoğlu, Daron, and James A. Robinson. *Why Nations Fail: The Origins of Power, Prosperity and Poverty*. New York: Crown Publishers, 2012.

Acemoğlu, Daron, Simon Johnson, and James A. Robinson. "The Colonial Origins of Comparative Development: An Empirical Investigation." *American Economic Review* 91(5): 1369–1401, 2001.

Baland, Jean-Marie, and Jean-Philippe Platteau. *Halting Degradation of Natural Resources: Is There a Role for Rural Communities?* Rome:

Food and Agriculture Organization of the United Nations, 1996. http://www.fao.org/docrep/x5316x/x5326e00.htm

Barrett, Christopher. *The Social Economics of Poverty on Identities, Communities, Groups and Networks*. London: Routledge, 2005.

Berkes, Fikret. "Marine Inshore Fishery Management in Turkey." In Proceedings of the Conference on Common Property Resource Management, 63–84. Washington, DC: National Academy Press, 1986.

Bohnet, Iris, and Bruno S. Frey. "The Sound of Silence in Prisoner's Dilemma and Dictator Games." *Journal of Economic Behavior & Organization* 38(1): 43–57, 1999. doi:10.1016/S0167-2681(98)00121-8

Carter, Michael R., and Pedro Olinto. "Getting Institutions "Right" for Whom? Credit Constraints and the Impact of Property Rights on the Quantity and Composition of Investment." *American Journal of Agricultural Economics* 85(1): 173–186, 2003. doi:10.1111/ajae.2003.85.issue-1

De Soto, Hernando. "The Missing Ingredient: What Poor Countries Need to Make Their Markets Work." *The Economist,* September 11, 8–12, 1993.

Deininger, Klaus. *Land Policies for Growth and Poverty Reduction.* Policy Research Report 26384. Washington, D.C.: World Bank, 2003. http://go.worldbank.org/7MMU0ACIB1

Dercon, Stefan, Joachim De Weerdt, Tessa Bold, and Alula Pankhurst. "Group-Based Funeral Insurance in Ethiopia and Tanzania." *World Development* 34(4): 685–703, 2006. doi:10.1016/j.worlddev.2005.09.009

Dercon, Stefan, John Hoddinott, Pramila Krishnan, and Tassew Woldehannnam. "Collective Action and Vulnerability: Burial Societies in Rural Ethiopia." *CAPRi Working Paper No. 83.* Washington, D.C.: International Food Policy Research Institute, 2008. http://dx.doi.org/10.2499/CAPRiWP83

Di Tella, Rafael, Sebastian Galiani, and Ernesto Schargrodsky. "The Formation of Beliefs: Evidence from the Allocation of Land Titles to Squatters." *The Quarterly Journal of Economics* 122(1): 209–241, 2007. doi:10.1162/qjec.122.1.209

Do, Quy-Toan, and Lakshmi Iyer. "Land Titling and Rural Transition in Vietnam." *Economic Development and Cultural Change* 56(3): 531–579, 2008. doi:10.1086/533577

Fehr, Ernst, and Simon Gächter. "Cooperation and Punishment in Public Goods Experiments." *American Economic Review* 90(4): 980–994, 2000a. doi:10.1257/aer.90.4.980

Fehr, Ernst, and Simon Gächter. "Fairness and Retaliation: The Economics of Reciprocity." *Journal of Economic Perspectives* 14(3): 159–182, 2000b. doi:10.1257/jep.14.3.159

Field, Erica. "Entitled to Work: Urban Property Rights and Labor Supply in Peru." *The Quarterly Journal of Economics* 122(4): 1561–1602, 2007. doi:10.1162/qjec.2007.122.4.1561

Fiszbein, Ariel, and Norbert Schady. *Conditional Cash Transfers: Reducing Present and Future Poverty. A World Bank Policy Research Report.* Washington, D.C: World Bank, 2009. http://go.worldbank.org/H9PAWAIX70

Frank, Robert H., Thomas Gilovich, and Dennis T. Regan. "Does Studying Economics Inhibit Cooperation?" *Journal of Economic Perspectives* 7(2): 159–71, 1993. http://www.jstor.org/stable/2138205

Frohlich, Norman, and Joe A. Oppenheimer. "Experiencing Impartiality to Invoke Fairness in the N-PD: Some Experimental Results." *Public Choice* 86(1–2): 117–135, 1996 doi:10.1007/BF00114878

Gertler, Paul, and Jonathan Gruber. "Insuring Consumption Against Illness." *American Economic Review* 92(1): 51–70, 2002. doi:10.1257/000282802760015603

Goldstein, Markus. "Intrahousehold Efficiency and Individual Insurance in Ghana." Development Economics Discussion Paper Series No. 38. London: London School of Economics and Political Science, 2004. http://sticerd.lse.ac.uk/dps/DE/DEDPS38.pdf

Greif, Avner. *Institutions and the Path to the Modern Economy: Lessons from Medieval Trade.* New York: Cambridge University Press, 2006.

Hardin, Garrett. "The Tragedy of the Commons." *Science* 162(3859): 1243–1248, 1968. doi:10.1126/science.162.3859.1243

Kevane, Michael. *Women and Development in Africa: How Gender Works.* Boulder, Colo.: Lynne Rienner Publishers, 2004.

Morduch, Jonathan. "Between the State and the Market: Can Informal Insurance Patch the Safety Net?" *The World Bank Research Observer* 14(2): 187–207, 1999. doi:10.1093/wbro/14.2.187

Munshi, Kaivan, and Mark Rosenzweig. "Economic Development and the Decline of Rural and Urban Community-Based Networks." *Economics of Transition* 13(3): 427–443, 2005. doi:10.1111/ecot.2005.13.issue-3

Munshi, Kaivan, and Mark Rosenzweig. *Why is Mobility in India so Low? Social Insurance, Inequality, and Growth.* No. w14850. Cambridge, Mass.: National Bureau of Economic Research, 2009.

North, Douglass C. *Institutions, Institutional Change and Economic Performance.* New York: Cambridge University Press, 1990.

Ostrom, Elinor. *Governing the Commons: The Evolution of Institutions for Collective Action.* New York: Cambridge University Press, 1990.

Ostrom, Elinor. *Understanding Institutional Diversity.* Princeton, N.J.: Princeton University Press, 2005.

Pande, Rohini, and Christopher Udry. "Institutions and Development: A View From Below." In Richard Blundell, Whitney K. Newey, and Torsten Persson (eds.). *Advances in Economics and Econometrics.* New York: Cambridge University Press, 2006.

Platteau, Jean-Philippe. *Institutions, Social Norms and Economic Development.* Vol. 1. London: Routledge, 2000.

Rodrik, Dani. *One Economics, Many Recipes: Globalization, Institutions, and Economic Growth.* Princeton, N.J.: Princeton University Press, 2007.

Wade, Robert. "The Management of Common Property Resources: Finding a Cooperative Solution." *World Bank Research Observer* 2(2): 219–234, 1987. doi:10.1093/wbro/2.2.219

World Bank. "The International Workshop on Community-Based Natural Resource Management (CBNRM)—Workshop Report." Washington, D.C.: World Bank, 1998. http://info.worldbank.org/etools/docs/library/97605/conatrem/conatrem/documents/May98Workshop_Report.pdf

Wydick, Bruce. *Games in Economic Development.* New York: Cambridge University Press, 2008.

QUESTIONS FOR REVIEW

1. Give examples of healthy and unhealthy institutions.

2. Why might the study of game theory and behavioral economics be useful in the study of institutions?

3. Explain the significance of every element of Table 12.1, making use of the terms "player," "strategy," "payoff," "cooperate," and "defect." What is the solution to this game? Why?

4. Define the prisoner's dilemma, assurance game and indefinitely repeated prisoner's dilemma classes of game, and discuss what we learn from each about cooperation.

5. Discuss the potential value of rules and related enforcement mechanisms that punish uncooperative behavior in prisoner's dilemma, assurance game and repeated prisoner's dilemma situations.

6. Discuss how researchers in behavioral economics use ultimatum games played by research subjects in laboratories to learn about reciprocity.

7. Discuss the significance of reciprocity for cooperation.

8. Suppose we discover evidence that members of a community are obeying a particular set of institutional rules or norms, and we wish to set up research to illuminate this institution. What questions would we wish to address in our research and why?

9. In the cases of the three sets of institutions examined in sections 12.3B, 12.3C and 12.3D, what tentative answers are offered to each of the questions raised in section 12.3A (and which remain unanswered)?

QUESTIONS FOR DISCUSSION

1. Contrast the way the word *institution* is used here with the ways it is used in common parlance.

2. Describe the institutional rules or norms that might constrain peoples' behavior in the following circumstances. What roles do you think communication, leadership, explicit punishment, repeated interaction, and socially conditioned preferences play in catalyzing or sustaining compliance?
   a. Two people approach each other on a narrow path. How do they avoid collision or conflict?
   b. Two drivers in the United States reach an intersection with four-way stop signs, one from the south and one from the east, and stop at the same time. Who proceeds first?
   c. Residents of a remote rural community in a developing country could try to steal grain from each other's fields. Why don't they?
   d. Residents of a U.S. suburb could try to steal each other's belongings. Why don't they?

3. Under what conditions may one individual or group successfully impose institutional rules on another group? What examples of this come to mind? Do you think the rules imposed are likely to create benefit or harm for the group on which they are imposed?

4. Suppose you knew that the utility rewards that punishers derive from punishing "unfair" behavior play an important role in supporting community-level cooperation. Suppose further that you are asked to design an experimental institution-building program that would support community-level cooperation in some activity that is new to the community. Describe your design for this program.

5. What general lessons do you take away from the discussion of CPR governance, informal insurance, and land rights institutions regarding the importance of local institutions in shaping a policy's impacts?

PROBLEMS

1. Consider a small rural area inhabited by just two small farmers, Farmer A and Farmer B. The farmers must each choose whether or not to make investments that would allow them to produce a higher-value crop. If either farmer continues cultivating traditional crops, he earns a profit of 0. To switch to cultivating a higher-value crop, he must incur an investment cost of 10. Having made the investment he will obtain revenue of 20 if an urban-based food processing company decides to set up a trucking route to collect produce in his area, but he earns no revenue if the food processing company does not do this. Both farmers know that the food processor will set up local crop collection if and only if both farmers invest in producing the high-value crop. If only one farmer invests or if neither farmer invests, neither farmer will have an opportunity to sell his higher-value product to the processor. If both farmers invest, the processor will certainly collect their produce and pay them each 20.
   a. Fill in the following table of payoffs to describe the game these two farmers are faced with, assuming their payoffs are equal to any revenue they receive from the food processor less any investment costs they undertake.

	If Farmer B:	
If Farmer A:	Does Not Invest	Invests
Does Not Invest		
Invests		

b. Does Farmer A have a dominant strategy? Explain.
c. Is this game a prisoner's dilemma, an assurance game, or some other sort of game? Explain.
d. What does the structure of this game imply about the kinds of activities an NGO might experiment with to encourage a shift to high-value crop production in this area?

2. A village's two villagers hold as common property a local forest from which they harvest nuts. If a villager exercises restraint, he exerts a quantity of labor equivalent to 5 in cost. If he does not exercise restraint, he exerts a quantity of labor equivalent to 10 in cost. If both exercise restraint, they each obtain a harvest worth 15. If neither exercises restraint they each obtain a harvest worth 18. If one exercises restraint and the other does not, the one who exercises restraint obtains revenue of 9, and the one who does not obtains revenue of 22.
a. Fill in the following table to describe the payoffs in this game.

	If Villager B is:	
If Villager A is:	Unrestrained	Restrained
Unrestrained		
Restrained		

b. Suppose an external authority imposes a rule requiring each villager to exercise restraint. Any villager caught harvesting in an unrestrained fashion must pay a fine F. F must be an integer. At least how high must F be to create the potential for a good equilibrium in which both exercise restraint (but not necessarily guarantee a good equilibrium)? At least how high must F be to make restrained use the dominant strategy for both players?
c. Now suppose that the external authority is able to detect unrestrained use with probability of only 0.5. Suppose further that each villager maximizes expected profits. This means that the payoff he obtains when facing a probability p of paying a fine F is equal to $R - L - pF$, where R is his revenue and L is his labor cost. At least how high must F be to create the potential for a good equilibrium in which both exercise restraint?

3. Suppose two villagers know that they are going to play the game of Table 12.2 two times (in two years). Consider the grim strategy "I will participate in the first year. In the second year I will participate if both of us participated in the first period, but I will shirk if either of us shirked."

a. Is the outcome in which both players choose the grim strategy a possible equilibrium of the game? Why or why not?
b. More generally, is any outcome in which either player participates in the first year a possible equilibrium in this game? Why or why not?

4. Suppose that each year two villagers play a two-stage game. In the first stage they play the game of Table 12.2. In the second stage each villager faces the opportunity to impose a punishment of P on the other, at a cost of c to himself, with $P > L/2$.
a. If each villager believed that the other player would punish him in the second period if he shirked in the first period and the other player cooperated, what first-stage game would they face and what strategy would they choose?
b. Now suppose that the villagers expect to play this two-stage game once a year for an infinite number of years. If one villager knew that by punishing the other villager for shirking in the first year he could ensure that the other player would participate in road maintenance in all future years, and he knew that by failing to punish shirking in the first year he would lose all opportunity for future cooperation, what benefits and costs would he perceive to punishing the other for shirking? Under what conditions (on the values of the game's parameters) would he choose to punish in the first year?
c. Suppose the conditions you just described are met. Consider the strategy: "I will participate in the first stage of the first year. In the second stage of the first year I will punish the other villager if he shirked in the first period. In subsequent years I will participate in the first stage if both of us have always participated in the past, but I will shirk if either of us has shirked in the past, and I will punish in the second period if the other has shirked while I participated." If one player credibly commits to play this strategy, would the other player have any reason to deviate from the same strategy? Why or why not?
d. Compare the condition you derived in 4.b to the condition in equation 12.5 of the text. Discuss how the availability of the decentralized punishment technology employed here might expand the range of conditions under which cooperation is possible in the infinitely repeated road maintenance prisoner's dilemma.

5. Consider a restricted version of an ultimatum game in which the Proposer is given $10. In the first stage of the game the Proposer may choose to offer either $1 or $5 to the Responder. In the second stage the Responder may choose to accept or reject the Proposer's offer from the first stage. If she accepts, the Proposer gives the offered amount and keeps the rest of the $10. If the Responder rejects the offer, neither receives anything.
a. Describe the second stage of the game by recording payoffs to the Responder in the following table. What is

the Responder's best response to the Proposer's offer of $5? Of $1? Explain.

	If the Proposer Offered:	
If the Responder:	$1	$5
Rejects		
Accepts		

b. Taking into account the Responder's best responses in the second stage of the game, describe the first-stage game faced by the Proposer using the following table to record payoffs to the Proposer. What strategy does the Proposer choose? Explain.

If the Proposer offers:	
$1	
$5	

c. Now suppose that the Responder has access to a punishment technology that would allow her to impose a fine of 6 on the Proposer at a cost of 1 to herself. She now faces three options in the second period: accept, reject and not punish, and reject and punish. Use a table similar to the one found in 5.a (but allowing for all three Responder choices) to describe the second stage of this game. What is the Responder's best response to the Proposer's offer of $5? $1? What does this imply about the first-stage game faced by the Proposer and the solution to the game? Explain.

d. Now suppose that the Responder continues to have access to the punishment technology but also has preferences that exhibit negative reciprocity in the following way. If (and only if) the Proposer offers anything other than a fair even split, the Responder enjoys a utility boost from punishing the Proposer that increases her payoff by 3. Use a table similar to the one in 5.a (but again allow for all three Responder choices) to describe the second stage of this game. What is the Responder's best response to the Proposer's offer of $5? Of $1? Taking into account the Responder's best responses in the second stage, use a table similar to the one found in 5.b to describe the first-stage game faced by the Proposer. What strategy does the Proposer choose? Explain.

chapter

13

Policy, Governance, and Political Economy

People guided only by markets and private institutions encounter obstacles to development. Policies introduced by governments and NGOs have the potential to improve development outcomes by helping people overcome these obstacles. Unfortunately, many policies fail to realize their developmental potential. Even where policymakers are well intentioned, policies sometimes fail because they are poorly designed or poorly implemented. Where policymakers pursue selfish interest rather than development, policies' impacts are often far worse, serving to enrich the powerful at the expense of the powerless and trapping many people in poverty.

This chapter examines the conditions under which policies indeed enhance development outcomes. It first describes briefly how policies interact with the households, markets, and private institutions analyzed thus far in Part III. It then examines the underpinnings of good policy design, the ingredients of good governance for policy implementation, and the political conditions under which policymakers choose policies that foster development.

13.1 Policy, Governance, Politics, and Development

Development outcomes are determined in great part by the households we have studied throughout Part III, as they make important choices related to production, consumption, labor supply, saving, and diverse household and community investments. Development is most successful when peoples' many choices—and the resulting impacts on assets, markets, and institutions—bring rapid economic growth and widespread reductions in poverty and vulnerability.

Even in the absence of intervention by governments and NGOs, people make many choices that contribute to development. Their interest in building better futures for themselves and their families gives them reason to save and invest, thereby spurring economic growth. Markets encourage them to specialize and to engage in mutually beneficial exchange. Prices in goods and factor markets help them identify which goods are most valuable to produce and where their labor and other assets will be put to best use. Financial markets help direct savings toward high-value investment projects and help people cope with risk. Private institutions sometimes encourage cooperation for the protection of local natural resources and the creation of local public goods.

When guided only by markets and private institutions, however, people make some choices that slow development. For example, in Chapter 8 we described how private actors might choose not to undertake critical market-enhancing investments in transport infrastructure, as a result of the public goods problem. This is just one of a longer list of **market and institutional failures** that can prevent ideal development performance in the absence of intervention.

Development-oriented governments and NGOs intervene in socioeconomic systems seeking, at least in part, to improve development outcomes. Their policies connect with the socioeconomic system by altering the opportunities and constraints that define people's choices. This means that policies ultimately alter macro-level development outcomes by altering specific people's opportunities, incentives, and choices at the micro level. Policies are most likely to enhance development success when policymakers identify activities that private actors choose to do too little or too much when guided only by imperfect markets and private institutions, and then design policies to counterbalance those imperfections. Section 13.2 pulls together a comprehensive list of the market and institutional failures that can raise barriers to development, identifies the types of policy design that might help people overcome the barriers, and offers a cautionary discussion of why well-intentioned policy designs sometimes prove inadequate.

Even when well designed, policies can fail if they are implemented poorly. Policymakers must entrust the execution of policies to agents, who have discretion over critical implementation choices. When the public sector institutions that constrain agents' choices provide *good governance*—a concept we will define carefully—policies are implemented effectively and without generating unnecessary cost. Poorly governed agents, at best, deliver low-quality services. At worst, they create new obstacles to development through bureaucratic rigidity and corruption. Section 13.3 documents the many symptoms of governance failure in developing-country government institutions, identifies the ingredients of good governance, describes the governance structure design choices available to policymakers, and introduces readers to four varieties of governance reform that have become popular in recent decades: decentralization, increased community participation, increased use of performance contracting, and introduction of private sector competition.

Principles of good policy design and implementation contribute little to development when policymakers choose to ignore them. Many countries have failed to develop, not because policymakers lacked understanding but because they pursued selfish objectives rather than development. At a deep level, therefore, politics and political institutions play important roles in determining development success. A full treatment of the political economy of development is beyond the scope of this text, but section 13.4 offers a brief discussion of the political pre-conditions for development success.

13.2 Intervention Rationales and Policy Design

A **rationale for intervention** is a reason why private actors, guided only by markets and private institutions, might make **socially suboptimal** choices. This means that compared to some societal ideal, they choose to do either *too little* or *too much* of some activity. Such circumstances open up the possibility that **public actors** such as governments or NGOs could improve development outcomes through appropriate intervention in the socioeconomic system. Our first step toward defining and analyzing specific rationales for intervention is to make more precise our comparison between private and socially optimal decisions.

13.2A Private versus social decisions

Private decision makers

When choosing *whether or not* to undertake a particular activity, such as adopting a new technology or vaccinating a child, a private decision maker chooses to undertake the activity if he is aware of the opportunity and if he judges that the private benefits outweigh the private costs. The **private benefits** include any resulting improvements in his living conditions, and the **private costs** include any deteriorating changes. If the activity involves investment, the private costs also include those associated with financing and risk (as defined in Chapter 10).

When choosing *how much* of an activity to undertake, such as how much corn to produce, a private decision maker assesses the **marginal private benefit (MPB)** and the **marginal private cost (MPC)** of each additional unit, and chooses the quantity of activity at which the *MPB* just equals the *MPC*, as depicted in the three panels of Figure 13.1. In each panel, we measure the quantity of activity undertaken Q along the horizontal axis, and we measure the *MPB* and *MPC* along the vertical axis. For meaningful comparison we must measure the *MPB* and *MPC* in the same units, and it is convenient to measure these benefits and costs in pesos. Thus we define the *MPB* as the maximum number of pesos the private actor would pay to obtain the benefits he derives from the last unit of Q and define the *MPC* as the minimum number of pesos the decision maker must be paid to compensate for the cost of undertaking the last unit of Q.

Sometimes we have reason to believe that the *MPB* holds constant as Q increases while the *MPC* rises (as in Figure 13.1a). For example, for a farm household that faces perfectly

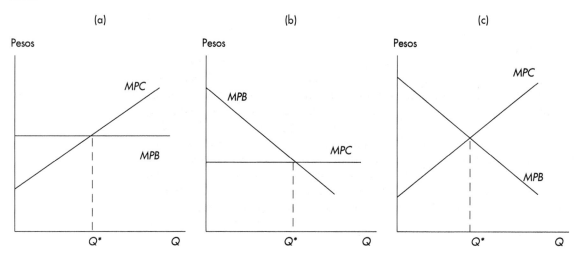

FIGURE 13.1
Private Choices Regarding How Much of an Activity to Undertake

competitive markets and that maximizes household well-being by maximizing farm profits, the *MPB* of increasing corn production by one unit is just the price obtained by selling the unit, which remains the same no matter how many units are sold. The *MPC*, meanwhile, is the market cost of the labor and other inputs required to produce one unit, which rises as Q rises as a result of diminishing marginal returns in production (see section 6.4).

In other cases, we expect the *MPB* to fall as Q rises, while the *MPC* holds constant (as in Figure 13.1b). For example, when a producer contemplates his demand for an input in a perfectly competitive input market (section 6.4), or when a consumer contemplates her demand for a consumer item in a perfectly competitive goods market (section 6.2), the *MPC* is just the price of the input or consumer item, which remains constant as Q rises. The *MPB* falls as Q rises, as a result of diminishing marginal returns in production or diminishing marginal utility in consumption.

More generally, the *MPB* schedule might fall with Q while the *MPC* schedule rises, as in Figure 13.1c. For a farm household isolated from labor markets by high transportation and transaction costs, the family labor supply decision takes this form (section 7.2C).

Regardless of whether Figure 13.1a, b, or c offers a more accurate depiction of a private decision, the private decision maker chooses to undertake at least some of the activity (setting $Q>0$) if the *MPB* associated with the first unit of Q (i.e., the height of the *MPB* schedule at the vertical axis) exceeds the *MPC* of that first unit (i.e., the height of the *MPC* schedule at the vertical axis). The decision maker maximizes the activity's net contribution to his well-being by choosing the quantity Q^* at which the *MPB* just equals the *MPC*.

The social decision maker

For the study of development policy, we define socially ideal decisions by imagining a hypothetical ideal **social decision maker** who wishes to maximize achievement of the development objective (defined along the lines of Chapter 1). She observes all the options available to each private decision maker throughout the socioeconomic system and calculates the decisions each must make to maximize achievement of the development objective given the system's current assets and its technological and international opportunities.

This social decision maker does *not* represent a real-world policymaker, who might pursue personal and political gain rather than development alone. Rather, the social decision maker is a theoretical construct we use to facilitate clear discussion of the rationales for intervention. In principle, development analysts with different values (e.g., differences in the relative priority they place on growth versus immediate poverty reduction) must hypothesize somewhat different ideal social decision makers pursuing their somewhat different development objectives, but for our purposes these differences will not matter.

Like the private decision maker, the social decision maker compares benefits and costs when making choices about the activities a particular private decision maker should undertake. Rather than comparing *private* benefits and costs, however, she compares *social* benefits to social costs. **Social benefits** include any improvements in living standards that would be enjoyed by any individual in the socioeconomic system when everyone makes socially ideal decisions (improvements we will call the **society-wide consumption benefits** of the activity), as well as any additional value the social decision maker imputes when activities transfer well-being across individuals in ways that improve attainment of societal equity ideals (which we will call the **distributional benefit** of the activity). Similarly, the **social costs** of an individual decision maker's activity include the reductions in living standards that would be experienced by anyone in the socioeconomic system, when everyone makes socially ideal decisions. When determining the optimal quantity of an activity, the social decision maker compares the **marginal social benefit (*MSB*)** and **marginal social cost (*MSC*)**.[1]

When the private benefits or costs of an activity differ from the social benefits or costs, private decision makers undertake too little or too much of the activity. For example, when the social decision maker perceives benefits to each unit of an activity that the private decision maker does not (in addition to the benefits the private decision maker perceives), the *MSB* lies above the *MPB* schedule, as in Figure 13.2. The quantity of activity chosen by the private decision maker Q^P lies below the quantity desired by the social decision maker Q^S, and the private decision maker chooses too little of the activity. When the *MPC* lies below the *MSC*, the private decision maker chooses too much of the activity.

Broad differences between private and social decisions

We may now observe that:

> The social benefits and costs of an activity can differ from the private benefits and costs for five broad sets of reasons.

First, while the social decision maker evaluates the total value of benefits and costs that accrue to *anyone* in society, a private decision maker values only benefits that he can appropriate and considers only the costs that he must bear. The benefits he can **appropriate** are the benefits he can claim for himself and dispose of as he wishes. Below we will consider how public goods problems, externalities, common property resource problems, market power, and weak institutions for securing property rights and enforcing contracts might cause private decision makers to appropriate only a fraction of the society-wide marginal consumption benefits or to bear only a fraction of the society-wide marginal costs.

Second, financial constraints (arising out of asymmetric information problems) of the sort described in Chapter 10 can cause the private costs associated with investment financing and risk to exceed the social costs.

Third, while a private decision maker evaluates an action's benefits and costs given his current expectations about the behavior of others, the social decision maker evaluates the benefits

---

[1] In standard economics discussions of the rationales for intervention, the social benefits are defined to include only what we have called the society-wide consumption benefits. Equity considerations are not incorporated into the comparison of social benefits and costs. Implicitly, the social decision maker is assumed capable of costlessly using taxes and transfers to redistribute income to achieve equity objectives *after* making sure—through equating marginal social benefits and costs—that resources are being used efficiently throughout the economy. The standard analysis also limits attention to market failures, largely ignoring institutional concerns, and therefore ignores the possibility that private institutions might, for example, induce some redistribution in the absence of public sector intervention. For studying the pursuit of development in a world where institutions matter, and in which costless policy mechanisms for taxes and transfers do not exist, it seems preferable to treat the pursuit of equity and efficiency as interrelated problems.

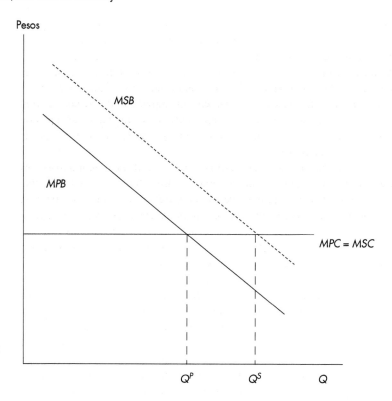

FIGURE 13.2
Private and Socially
Ideal Choices when
Marginal Social Benefit
Exceeds Marginal
Private Benefit

and costs that would materialize *when all other actors make ideal choices*. If an action's private benefits are higher (or private costs lower) when other actors make complementary choices, then a failure of markets and private institutions to orchestrate coordinated action (i.e., a coordination problem as defined in Chapter 8) can cause private benefits to fall short of social benefits.

Fourth, even when true private benefits and costs are equal to social benefits and costs, private actors might have incorrect *perceptions* of the benefits and costs. They may be entirely unaware of a valuable opportunity, may be aware of an opportunity but possess inaccurate information about its benefits and costs, or might impute excessively high costs to an activity about which they feel fear of the unknown for lack of adequate information or experience. Some departures from neoclassical rationality (such as present bias, as defined in Chapter 10) can also generate differences between private and social assessments of how choices affect well-being.

Finally, whereas private decision makers care only about changes in living conditions that enter directly into assessments of individual or household well-being, the social decision maker cares also about broader societal outcomes related to poverty and inequality. She might thus attribute additional social benefit (beyond the society-wide consumption benefits) to actions that reduce poverty or improve equity.

The next section offers a more detailed list of possible rationales for intervention and briefly describes the policy designs that development actors might use to counteract each imperfection. Most of these rationales are discussed at greater length elsewhere in the text.

13.2B Rationales for intervention and their implications for policy design

The public goods problem

Public goods are nonrival and nonexcludable. A good is **nonrival** when consumption by one person does not reduce the potential for consumption by others. A good is **nonexcludable** when it is impossible (or at least uneconomical) to preclude people who live within its reach from consuming its services. The nonrivalry of public goods means that the society-wide consumption benefits of creating them include improvements in well-being for everyone living near them.

Nonexcludability implies that a private producer of a public good cannot demand payments from its many consumers, because the producer cannot withhold the good from consumers who don't pay. This means that public goods producers cannot appropriate any of the society-wide benefits that accrue to other people. The only private benefit an individual would derive from creating a public good is his own enjoyment of it, which may be a small fraction of the society-wide benefit and may be far less than the cost. This **public goods problem** can prevent private investment in socially desirable public goods.

For many years the logic of the public goods problem convinced most economists that private actors would always fail to provide public goods in the absence of intervention. Increasingly development economists recognize that even when *markets* fail to provide adequate incentives for creating public goods, *private institutions* might succeed (see Chapter 12). If investment in a public good would truly be socially beneficial, then the society-wide benefits it would produce must exceed the total cost. This means that if the cost of production were shared by all consumers in proportion to the benefits they enjoy, each consumer's private benefit would exceed his share of the cost. An institution that encourages cooperation among a public good's consumers, then, might facilitate collective investment in creating the public good. Unfortunately, such institutions tend to arise only in small, close-knit communities, and they often fail to arise even in such contexts, for reasons discussed in Chapter 12. Markets *and* private institutions thus often fail to support investment even in community-level public goods, and they almost always fail to support socially optimal investment in larger-scale public goods.

Many investments vital to development have public goods qualities. These include critical infrastructure assets, such as rural roads and many community water-treatment systems. Less-tangible public goods include national defense, some technological ideas, and the shared sense of nationhood arising out of a national education curriculum. On a smaller scale, efforts to eradicate local malarial mosquitoes, organize collective bulk purchases of inputs by neighboring farmers, collect information regarding foreign markets (of relevance to multiple small export manufacturers), and apply for community grants from national governments also have public goods qualities.

For large-scale public goods, government actors might hope to counteract the public goods problem by creating the public goods directly or by paying private contractors to create them. With smaller-scale public goods, governments or NGOs might also be able to catalyze investment by local groups, without having to provide most of the necessary resources, by helping communities create institutions that support local collective action. Guided by such institutions, private individuals might become willing to contribute private resources for investment in local public goods. Many recent efforts to involve communities in the design, implementation, and financing of infrastructure investments reflect this new perspective on local public goods provision (see Chapter 18).

Externalities

Private actions carry **externalities** when they generate benefits or costs that are experienced by anyone other than the individual undertaking the action (and that this same actor does not come to appropriate or bear through market transactions).[2] **Positive externalities** are *benefits* enjoyed by

---

[2] When someone produces a good for sale, his action ultimately generates a benefit for the consumer who buys and consumes the good. Though the benefit is experienced directly by someone other than the producer, this is not an externality, because the consumer pays the producer. In competitive markets, consumers purchase the quantity of a good at which the marginal private benefit equals the market price. Thus, when the producer receives the market price for producing the good, he appropriates the entire *marginal* benefit accruing to the buyer. Similarly, when producers pay for inputs in competitive markets, they bear the marginal private cost experienced by the owners of the inputs.

others that private actors cannot appropriate and they create a tendency for private actors to undertake *too little* of the activity. For example, consider an employer's investment in general job training for his workers (as defined in Chapter 9). Such investments produce social benefit by raising the value of goods and services the workers will produce over the rest of their working lives. An individual employer may be able to appropriate some of that social benefit through increased profits, if he is able to retain some trained workers without having to raise their wages too much. The private benefit may nonetheless be smaller than the social benefit, if the employer knows that workers might quit and take their increased productivity to work for other employers. Thus employers tend to invest too little in general training.[3]

Many broad development strategies have been motivated by a belief that production in certain economic sectors carries positive externalities. For example, some international trade policy reforms in the 1980s and 1990s were guided in part by the belief that some production activities—such as semiconductor production or production for export more generally—would yield positive externalities that raise productivity for other local producers (Chapter 11).

More recently, Hausmann and Rodrik (2003) have argued the importance for development of a positive externality–generating activity they call **self-discovery**. Development often requires production of new products or adoption of new production processes that have been developed in other parts of the world. Adapting methods to local contexts requires costly experimentation and tinkering, and it is also risky, because producers do not know beforehand whether the tinkering will succeed in rendering the new industry competitive. For example, only through investment in self-discovery by a few bold entrepreneurs did the world learn that Colombia could develop a successful flower industry or that India could excel in the production of computer software. Unfortunately, although producers bear all the costs of self-discovery, including the entire cost of failed experiments, they bear only a fraction of the social benefits. Many of the benefits of successful experimentation are enjoyed by other entrepreneurs who observe and imitate the innovators' successes.

To counteract the market failure associated with a positive externality, governments or NGOs must either undertake more of the desirable activity on their own account or boost the private rewards attached to the relevant activity, seeking to close the gap between the *MPB* and *MSB*. They could do this most directly by offering private actors specified subsidy payments per unit of Q (over and above the payments the private actors obtain through market transactions).

Negative externalities are *costs* experienced by others that private actors do not bear and are associated with a tendency for private actors to undertake *too much* of an activity. Negative externalities are of increasing concern in developing countries. As manufacturing sectors expand and auto use increases, problems of air and water pollution become more acute, and rising income increases the priority societies place on reducing such problems. Policymakers might discourage activities associated with these negative externalities by extracting a tax per unit of output or unit of pollution, by imposing regulations (and related enforcement mechanisms) that limit production or pollution, or through more sophisticated efforts to assign pollution rights and create markets in which producers come to bear a marginal cost for their pollution.

The common property resource problem

Common property resources (CPRs) are nonexcludable (like public goods) but rival (unlike public goods). A local fishing ground is nonexcludable when locals cannot be precluded from fishing there, and it is rival because as one fisher harvests more fish he renders it more difficult for

---

[3] Employers' tendency to invest too little in general training might not matter if workers faced no barriers to investment, because workers face strong incentives to bear the cost of general training (see Chapter 9). Unfortunately, workers may be prevented from undertaking the investment by financial constraints, inadequate information or other problems discussed later in this section.

others to find fish, raises everyone's vulnerability to conflict, and increases the chance of destroying the fishery. A fisher appropriates the entire social benefit of harvesting another fish by selling it in the market, but he perceives only a fraction of the social cost, which is shared by all and thus largely falls on other fishers. Markets thus fail to motivate socially optimal restraint in CPR harvesting. As in the case of local public goods, community institutions can arise to encourage cooperation in local CPR management, but they do not always arise, even when they would generate great benefits (see Chapter 12).

For large-scale CPRs, such as large watershed regions or Earth's ozone layer, governments may be able to restrain use only by imposing regulatory rules backed up by monitoring and punishment. For smaller-scale CPRs, governments or NGOs may also be able to encourage restraint by building or supporting local institutions. That is, at least in principle, they may be able to encourage the development of locally devised and locally enforced rules that support cooperation.

Market power

When producers face perfect competition in goods markets, they cannot raise their prices above the price charged by competitors without losing all customers to the competition. A producer has **market power** in a goods market when he is able to raise his price (through some range) without losing all customers. In the extreme case of **monopoly**, a single producer lacks any competition at all. In the case of **oligopoly**, only a few producers participate in a market and they collude in raising prices together. In the more subtle case of **monopolistic competition**, many producers manage to differentiate their products enough that each has scope to alter her price (relative to prices charged by competitors) without losing all customers, but competition nonetheless prevents producers from earning monopoly profits.

Under perfect competition, a producer takes the market price as given. His marginal private benefit from producing another unit of the good equals the market price, regardless of how many units he produces. This is significant, because the competitive market price reflects the marginal benefit derived by the good's consumers.[4] Thus, under competition, and in the absence of externalities and other complications discussed below, the producer's *MPB*, which equals the market price, also equals the *MSB*.

When a producer has market power, she takes the market demand schedule for her product as given, rather than taking the market price as given. The demand schedule tells her how the quantity she will sell falls as she increases the price she charges, and thus the maximum price she can charge while selling a given quantity Q. To increase Q she must reduce her price. This implies that the marginal revenue she associates with producing and selling an additional unit is *less* than the price at which she sells the unit; selling the unit adds directly to revenue in the amount of the price at which it is sold but also reduces revenue indirectly by reducing the price received from all units previously sold at the higher price. As a result, the *MPB* lies below the price charged and thus below the *MSB*. With the *MPB* below the *MSB*, producers with market power tend to produce too little of the good in question (relative to the socially optimal quantity). They also sell at a price above the competitive equilibrium level.

Similarly, producers have market power in input markets when they can reduce the price they pay for an input without losing all suppliers. In the extreme case of **monopsony** in the labor market, a single employer constitutes the sole source of employment for all workers of a given skill level in a particular region. The local labor supply schedule tells such producers the minimum wage they can pay to obtain any given quantity of labor. To increase the quantity of labor employed, they must raise the wage to induce greater labor supply. For such producers, the marginal cost of increasing production by one unit is *greater* than the market price for labor and

---

[4] See footnote 2.

other inputs required for producing that unit, because when they increase labor by one unit, they incur not only the direct cost of hiring that unit (the wage) but also the indirect cost of having to increase the wages paid to all units of labor previously employed. Producers with monopsony power would thus hire fewer workers than is socially optimal and would pay workers less than they would get in a competitive market.

Producers might have market power in goods markets for several reasons. First, economies of scale in their technology of production can render their production sector a **natural monopoly**. If per-unit production costs fall over a very long range as a firm's level of production increases, then a single firm serving the whole market can enjoy lower unit costs than any competitors who might try to enter the market at smaller scale. The single large producer can thus prevent competitors from entering the market profitably. For example, the networks of pipes or cables required to deliver water, power, or landline telecommunication services to households can create conditions of natural monopoly in some infrastructure sectors. We will see in Chapter 18, however, that technical change is expanding the potential for competition even in these sectors.

It is often suspected that the small size of local markets in developing countries can support market power even in industries that would not be considered natural monopolies in larger markets. In remote areas within developing countries, high transportation and communication costs can effectively isolate local markets from external competition, and a single producer or small number of producers might enjoy market power simply because they are the only entrepreneurs in the relevant geographic areas with the capital and know-how to supply a given good. Similarly, a farmer owning most of the land within a small geographic region may be the only source of employment for local laborers, especially if his political power allows him to prevent the inflow of nonagricultural employers into the region.

Even national markets centered in urban areas may be quite small relative to the minimum scale at which firms in an industry can operate efficiently. If transfer costs or tariffs effectively seal a small number of local firms off from international competition, then they may be able to exercise market power.

In some cases, governments or other actors may be able to reduce market power by intervening to reduce transfer cost barriers that prevent competition. For example, they might build good roads that reduce transfer costs and increase the competitive pressure from producers in other regions. (Such roads tend not to be produced in the absence of intervention, because they are public goods.) Similarly, by reducing barriers to international trade they may increase competition in urban markets. Governments can also use antitrust regulation to prohibit a single firm or small number of firms from taking over an entire local industry.

In the case of natural monopolies, governments might respond by leaving the industry in the hands of a single firm (for whom unit costs are low), and attempt to counteract the firm's market power by regulating the price it may charge to consumers. With the price fixed at the regulated level, the marginal revenue associated with increasing production by one unit is set equal to the regulated price, and it no longer lies below the price charged for the last unit. If regulators set the regulated price equal to the price that would obtain in a perfectly competitive market, consumers would demand the competitive equilibrium quantity and producers would maximize profit by fulfilling that demand. The consequences of market power would be eliminated and the *MPB* would equal the *MSB*.

Weak property rights and contract enforcement institutions

Private investors expect to appropriate the full social returns from investing in agricultural land improvements only if they expect to retain ownership (or at least some control) over the land for as long as their investments increase yields. Similarly, investors reap the full social returns on investments in nonagricultural production equipment only if they expect to retain control over their firms for the life of the equipment. That is, private actors perceive strong incentives to invest only if they believe that they will retain **property rights** to the assets they create (Chapter 10). Investors' property rights are insecure when they fear the loss of assets to theft, vandalism, fraud, or expropriation by powerful neighbors or the government. Property rights to physical capital such as buildings, machines, irrigation canals, and tree crops are secure only when investors' **land rights** are secure. Unfortunately, while customary **land rights institutions** sometimes arise to offer investors reasonable security, at other times they do not, and even when they do encourage investment, they may do so only for a select group, while denying rights to others (see Chapter 12). The most obvious policy response to the lack of secure property rights is an effort to create formal **property rights institutions** backed up by legal and law enforcement systems. Policymakers might also attempt to strengthen customary property rights institutions.

Lack of strong **contract enforcement institutions**, too, may cause private actors to perceive private marginal benefits of production and investment that are lower than social marginal benefits. Investments that increase production of goods and services generate private returns only when investors expect to sell the additional output and obtain required inputs at attractive prices net of transfer costs. As discussed in Chapter 8, some higher-value goods and services must be supplied in a continuous and timely fashion and in consistent quality. Participation in such markets requires buyers and sellers to give and receive promises regarding future payments and deliveries. The transfer costs associated with these sophisticated transactions may be prohibitively high in the absence of strong contract enforcement institutions, which facilitate trust between buyers and sellers. While private institutions sometimes arise to support fulfillment of contractual promises within small groups of people with some common bond, they often fail to arise and seldom arise on a large scale. The most obvious policy response is to try to create effective contract law institutions (a challenge discussed in Chapter 8).

Financial constraints

Chapter 10 offered theory and evidence suggesting that some potential investors are prevented from investing in high-return projects by liquidity or insurance constraints. A potential investor is **liquidity constrained** when she would undertake a high-return investment if credit markets worked well, but she does not undertake the investment because she cannot finance the investment on the terms a well-functioning credit market would provide. This is the case when, in addition to lacking access to credit on well-functioning market terms, she also lacks adequate savings to cover the cost of the investment and would find it very difficult to cover the cost by reducing current consumption expenditure. A potential investor is **insurance constrained** when she would undertake the investment if insurance markets worked well, but does not undertake the investment because she cannot obtain appropriate insurance or can obtain it only at a premium rate that is too high. Lacking adequate insurance, she is put off from investing by the risks involved. Liquidity and insurance constraints can also prevent households from smoothing consumption in the face of fluctuations and shocks.

In the social decision maker's ideal plan, potential investors who are liquidity- or insurance-constrained in the real world would undertake their investments. Whereas liquidity-constrained investors effectively discount the future at very high rates (with present costs weighing heavily in their decisions relative to future benefits, as described in Chapter 10), the social decision maker discounts future returns using the **social discount rate**. This rate reflects the willingness of the country's savers to give up resources today in exchange for resources in the future. If financial markets were free of information problems, the social discount rate would be revealed by the interest rate that equilibrates the market for loanable funds.[5] Investors who are liquidity

---

[5] Exactly what interest rate the social decision maker should use when accounting for the costs to society of financing an investment is a matter of academic debate, but in practice governments tend to evaluate the social desirability of investment projects using social discount rates on the order of 3 to 7 percent in developed countries and on the order of 8 to 15 percent in developing countries (Zhuang et al., 2007).

constrained in the real world discount the future at a rate higher than this ideal and thus fail to undertake some investments that the social decision maker would prefer them to undertake.

The social decision maker would also prefer that insurance-constrained investors undertake their investments. From her perspective, many risks that investors face are idiosyncratic at the societal level. Ideally, investors would join together for mutual insurance, as they would if insurance markets were free of information problems. They would thus face low costs associated with risk. Insurance-constrained investors face significantly higher costs associated with risk and thus fail to undertake socially desirable investments.

As argued in Chapter 10, liquidity and insurance constraints can affect investments in almost any sort of asset, including physical capital, human capital, and improved technologies, but they are more likely to affect poor households than nonpoor households and smaller firms than larger firms. Poorer households and smaller firms are less capable of self-financing or self-insuring and the costs of providing financial services to poorer clients are higher than the cost of providing such services to wealthier clients interested in larger transactions.

In principle, policymakers might counteract liquidity constraints by providing constrained investors with additional liquidity. For example, they could provide constrained investors with loans at the social discount rate. (Given that policymakers are likely to face the same difficulties that prevent private lenders from breaking even on such loans, this is likely to require some subsidy.) Policymakers might instead encourage the liquidity-constrained to invest by providing them with transfers rather than loans. To encourage insurance-constrained investors, policymakers could provide them with insurance at low premiums or could create flexible safety net programs that provide them with the assurance of alternative sources of income in the case of bad investment outcomes.

Policymakers might also respond to liquidity and insurance constraints at a deeper level, attempting to counteract the underlying information asymmetries that cause financial markets to malfunction. In Chapter 10, we discussed ways government regulations might relax some financial constraints. For example, regulations might improve financial market operation by improving the sharing of credit history information or by increasing savers' confidence in financial institutions.

Coordination failures

A set of private investments is inhibited by a **coordination failure** when the investments would all prove profitable if undertaken *simultaneously* but would each prove unprofitable if undertaken on its own. We saw examples of this in Chapter 8's discussion of value chains. Farmers might be happy to make the on-farm investments required for high-value crop production if a supermarket stands ready to buy their crops. Similarly, a supermarket may be happy to invest in the physical and organizational infrastructure required to purchase produce in a given region if that region's farmers stand ready to supply the produce. Nonetheless, farmers and supermarkets might each be reluctant to invest unilaterally. We saw possible examples of coordination failure on a larger scale in the discussion of macro poverty trap models in Chapter 4. Governments or NGOs may be able to catalyze private investment in all the required assets by undertaking them on their own account, by subsidizing them, or simply by coordinating expectations. (See also the discussion of the assurance game in Chapter 12.)

Coordination problems arising out of informal insurance institutions might hold back investment in small communities. As we saw in Chapter 12, when community norms require households whose incomes are relatively high to share with households whose incomes are relatively low, individuals might fail to undertake profitable investments because they must share the proceeds of successful investments with their neighbors while bearing the full cost themselves. If all community members were to invest simultaneously, however, all their incomes would rise and social norms would demand no transfers. Thus governments or NGOs might be able to help a community out of a poverty trap by coordinating simultaneous investments by all community members. Public actors might also be able to stimulate investment by creating public safety nets that supplant private safety net institutions, thereby freeing group members to invest without having to share out the proceeds.

Problems of inadequate information

Private actors might fail to undertake a socially valuable activity, such as the adoption of a new agricultural technology or a valuable hygiene practice, simply because they are not aware of the opportunity. Private actors have little incentive to engage in costly dissemination of such information unless the activity requires purchase of some input (e.g., seeds embodying a new agricultural technology), in which case private input sellers might have some incentive to provide the information (Chapter 20). Furthermore, even when private actors are aware of an opportunity—for example, to use fertilizer or to send a child to school—they might possess *inaccurate* information regarding the benefits and costs. They might thus perceive benefits lower than the true (private and social) benefits or costs higher than the true costs. The most obvious policy response to inadequate or incorrect information is to supply such information (or pay a private actor to provide it). In some cases, people may be able to acquire the necessary knowledge only through experience that dissipates fear of the unknown. In such cases, temporary financial incentives that encourage people to experiment with the activity might be useful for counteracting the information failure.

Sometimes market participants lack the expertise or scale required to acquire, at low cost, accurate information about the qualities of goods or services they might purchase (such as chemical fertilizers, medicines, or doctors' diagnostic services) or about the health and safety implications of jobs they might accept. In such cases, governments, which benefit from economies of scale and expertise in quality inspection activities, might have roles to play in regulating product quality and safety standards.

Present bias and other departures from neoclassical decision making

Research in behavioral economics reveals reasons why individuals might make choices that, in some sense, are not in their own best interest (DellaVigna, 2009). In Chapter 10, for example, we described how people whose preferences are characterized by present bias can find it difficult to undertake activities in the present that they planned to do at earlier times and that they will wish they had undertaken when looking back at a later date. Policies that provide such individuals with small nudges to encourage them in the desired direction might lead to significant improvements in well-being. Policymakers might similarly have the potential to improve well-being by designing policies that encourage restraint in the consumption of addictive goods.

Equity considerations

The social decision maker might impute additional social benefit (that private actors do not appropriate) to some activities that reduce poverty or improve the distribution of well-being. The social decision maker might, for example, value household-to-household transfers that redistribute income toward the poor. The transfers may be explicit and untied to any other transactions, or they may be implicit, taking the form of transactions in which poor buyers obtain goods at prices below cost, poor producers sell at prices above competitive levels, poor workers obtain wages above competitive levels, or poor investors obtain credit at interest rates below the cost of supplying the credit. Private institutions, such as informal insurance institutions, might support some of these transfers even in the absence of intervention, but they probably fail to support many of them. The most obvious policy response to inequity in the distribution of income is to undertake explicit or implicit transfers on the public actor's own account. In response to perceived inequity in access to services that are considered necessary for achieving a minimally acceptable standard of living—such as safe drinking water services or basic education—policymakers might also subsidize service provision for households who would not otherwise have effective access to them.

To conclude:

> Market and institutional failures related to public goods, externalities, common property resources, market power, weak property rights and contract enforcement institutions, financial constraints, coordination failures, inadequate information, non-neoclassical decision making, and equity considerations might constitute rationales for intervention.

Policymakers might respond to these failures by designing policies that provide transfers, loans, or information to private actors; tax or regulate private activities; or create legal systems to govern interactions among private actors. They might also respond to failures (as they have historically) by involving the public sector directly in the activities handled imperfectly by the private sector, including the provision of infrastructure, education, financial, and health services; and the creation and dissemination of new technological ideas. Any of these interventions *might* generate social benefits greater than social costs, though only if they are well designed and well implemented.

13.2C Incorrect diagnosis and policy design failure

When a policy's design reflects incorrect assumptions about underlying market and institutional failures, it can fail in diverse ways, even when implemented by well-intentioned policymakers. Consider a policy that seeks to catalyze investment in community latrines by providing information about the benefits of using latrines and by encouraging the creation of community sanitation committees as forums for collective action (but offers the committees no outside resources). The policy design reflects the implicit assumption that just two market and institutional failures prevent investment in community latrines: inadequate information about their benefits and the lack of institutions to solve the public goods problem. If instead, or in addition, the communities are liquidity-constrained, then, even if the program successfully informs community members and motivates them for collective action, the community might fail to undertake the investment for lack of finance.

Other errors in the diagnosis of underlying market and institutional failures might lead to policies that succeed in catalyzing targeted activities but do so at a greater cost to the government or NGO budget than is necessary. Policymakers might, for example, encourage the creation of an asset they consider socially valuable—such as a small grain mill with its own power generator—by offering an individual a grant to cover the purchase of the required assets. Policymakers might implicitly believe that the social returns on the investment are high as a result of positive externalities, but that the private returns would be too low to inspire private investment, even if financing were available at a moderate interest rate. If, in fact, a private investor *is* capable of appropriating ample returns but is prevented from investing only by liquidity constraints, then policymakers might have been able to catalyze the same investment at lower cost by offering a loan rather than a grant.

Finally, policymakers' assumptions may be mistaken in a more fundamental way. The private sector might decline to undertake activities that policymakers perceive as valuable, not as a result of market or institutional failures but because private actors rightly expect that the activities produce too few benefits (social and private) relative to the costs. That is, the policymakers might be mistaken in their belief that the activities are socially desirable. The private sector might understand better than government bureaucrats, for example, that certain electrical generators are doomed to irresolvable maintenance problems or that certain households cannot operate microenterprises profitably.

13.2D An important caveat

In the **theory of the second best**, economists point out that a choice that is socially desirable when all other actors in the system are making socially ideal choices might *not* be socially ideal when other choices in the system are flawed. This implies that designing a policy to correct one market and institutional failure can do more harm than good when other failures remain uncorrected. For example, suppose a firm has market power *and* pollutes. A well-executed policy to regulate the firm's price might succeed in expanding production and reducing price, counteracting the effects of market power. In the absence of appropriate policy responses to the pollution externality, however, the policy that counteracts market power would aggravate pollution, and the costs of such unintended consequences could outweigh the benefits.

We saw earlier that policies can fail because their designs are based on incorrect assumptions regarding underlying market and institutional failures. The logic of the second best suggests that even when a policy is created in response to a true market and institutional failure, and even when it is well designed to compensate for that failure, it might nonetheless bring unintended costs and fail to generate a net improvement in development outcomes. Thus, while the list of intervention rationales identified earlier offers useful guidance in the search for beneficial policy designs, it offers no guarantee that policymaker's well-intentioned efforts to correct market and institutional failures will deliver benefits that outweigh the costs. Policymakers' interest in correcting market and institutional failures leads to good policymaking only when accompanied by keen interest in the empirical study of context and in comprehensive evaluation of policy impacts.

13.3 Good Governance of Policy Implementation

Implementing policies well is difficult, because policymakers cannot implement policies by themselves. They must instead work through agents, who have at least some **discretion** (i.e., decision-making power) over how to do their jobs. Development-oriented policymakers welcome agents' use of discretion when the agents have greater expertise or local knowledge than the policymakers and when the agents use these advantages to improve policy impact. Unfortunately, agents might instead—and all too often do—use their discretion to divert funds, take bribes, show favoritism, exert little effort, or make well-intentioned but poor choices. Policymakers would like to guide agents into productive exercise of their discretion. That is, they would like to create institutions—rules, norms, and related enforcement mechanisms—that provide **good governance** for their agents' many policy implementation choices.

After briefly documenting governance failures that detract from policies' impacts in developing countries, this section examines the underpinnings of good governance and the ways policymakers might attempt to improve governance.

13.3A Governance failures

A growing empirical literature documents that:

> Poor governance of policy implementation in developing countries often leads to corruption, poor service quality, inappropriate service design, and imbalance in resource allocations across regions and facilities.

Corruption

Corruption, which we may define as "the misuse of public office for private gain (Svensson, 2005)," is the governance failure that inspires the most outrage. Corruption at the highest levels of government can divert vast sums away from effective policy implementation. Mobutu Sese Seko, then president of Zaire (now Democratic Republic of Congo), for example, diverted an estimated $5 billion of government funds into his own coffers before he was overthrown in 1997. We return to the discussion of corruption at this level in section 13.4.

Sadly, the smaller sums of public money diverted into private uses at lower levels of government often add up to large sums as well. Reinnika and Svensson (2004) tracked Ugandan central government funds intended for primary schools and discovered that schools received on average only 13 percent of the funds sent their way, the rest having been diverted by local government officials and politicians. Olken (2006, 2007) estimates that 29 percent of road project funds and 18 percent of subsidized rice are diverted in Indonesia.

Much of the corruption that touches everyday life involves government officials' demands for bribes rather than their diversion of government resources. Many firms must pay bribes to obtain necessary government service and permits, and demands for bribes affect myriad trans-actions on a daily basis. Svensson (2003) estimates that 80 percent of the firms in a Ugandan sample paid bribes in a typical year. Enumerators hired to travel with truck drivers on trips into and out of Aceh province in Indonesia observed 6,000 illegal payments to police, soldiers, and weigh station attendants in just 304 trips (Olken and Barron, 2009)!

When government officials charge bribes for fulfilling their responsibilities, they raise the cost of doing business and discourage investment. For the 80 percent of Ugandan firms who reported any typical annual bribe payments, their estimated payments averaged about 8 percent of total cost (Svensson, 2003), and Fisman and Svensson (2007) estimate that corruption is a greater inhibitor to Ugandan firms' growth than taxation. The truckers driving into and out of Aceh, Indonesia, spent on average about $40, or 13 percent of their total costs, on bribes (Olken and Barron, 2009).

In addition to *demanding* bribes for fulfilling their responsibilities, government officials sometimes *accept* bribes for disregarding the rules and procedures they were hired to implement. This form of corruption, too, appears widespread. According to a 2006 survey of 11,000 firms in 125 countries, 14 percent of developed country firms report that "firms like theirs" pay bribes to obtain government contracts, while 50 percent of firms in low-income countries make such reports (D'Souza and Kaufmann, 2011). When officials award contracts to the firms offering the best bribes rather than the firms putting forward the best proposals, they decrease the efficacy of public spending. When judges accept bribes for delivering favorable verdicts, they prevent the justice system from providing either justice or support for contractual exchange. When regulators accept bribes for issuing permits without properly scrutinizing compliance with regulations, they put citizens at risk. For example, when they issue building permits without assessing compliance with safety codes, they increase the risk of catastrophic building collapses. Inadequate inspections by government officials also expose citizens to substandard medicines and ineffective fertilizers (World Bank, 2003).

Poor service quality

The quality of government services is often very low in developing countries. Many primary schools fail to equip students even with basic literacy and numeracy skills. Many piped drinking water systems deliver contaminated water. Many roads are impassable, and electricity grids are often so unreliable that firms cannot stay in business without running their own generators. Some of the most alarming evidence of poor service quality comes from the health sector. A study in Zambia found that only 30 percent of diarrhea cases in children were correctly assessed by health care providers, and only 19 percent of children with diarrhea were correctly rehydrated (World Health Organization, 1998). In Benin, one in four sick children was given unnecessary or dan-gerous drugs (Rowe et al., 2001). In surprise visits to health clinics in six developing countries, Chaudhury et al. (2006) found that on average 35 percent of health workers were absent, and many of those present were not working. Spending scarce resources on the delivery of low-value services obviously diminishes the government's potential to enhance development.

Poor service design

Services are often poorly tailored to local needs, further diminishing the efficacy of government spending. Many schools operate according to standardized schedules that conflict with local parent's needs for their children's assistance in harvesting crops or hauling water, creating unnecessary barriers to enrollment. Similarly, health facilities' schedules are often inconvenient and erratic, and roads sometimes create connections for which there is little demand.

Imbalance across regions, communities, and facilities

Supply of government services is almost always more ample in urban areas than in rural areas and in well-off communities relative to poor communities. In addition, per capita rates of financing for education and health care often vary widely across schools and health facilities. This diminishes the distributional effect of policy implementation and probably diminishes efficacy as well, given that the marginal returns to additional spending are likely higher in communities where funds are scarce.

13.3B The underpinnings of good governance

Policy implementation is successful when the agents who implement policy make good *choices*. Their choices are *good* when they help realize the intentions of development-oriented policy-makers while putting available resources to best possible use. Thus we begin study of good governance by identifying the kinds of choices that policy implementers must make and the conditions under which they make good choices.

Implementation choices

Some **policy implementation choices** help to define policies' fundamental designs. In primary education policy, for example, decision makers at some level must define curriculum content, school schedules, and school fees. More generally, for policies that offer cash, loans, goods, or services to beneficiaries, implementing agents must define the nature of the good or service offered and the criteria people must satisfy to become beneficiaries. For policies that impose taxes or regulations, implementing agents must define the exact nature of the policies' restrictions and related details pertaining to monitoring and punishment for noncompliance.

The quality of some these *policy design choices* is enhanced when they are made by central-level decision makers and applied in a uniform fashion throughout a country. For example, primary education curricula contribute the most to a shared culture among a nation's many youth if the same curriculum is employed in all regions, communities, and ethnic groups. Many detailed policy design choices generate better results when tailored to local circumstances, however. Decisions regarding school schedules, for example, might lead to higher enrollment rates (on the same budget) if tailored to avoid conflict with local children's work responsibilities. Similarly, decisions regarding the design and construction of a community's water system might yield better outcomes when shaped by local information on income levels, preferences, and conditions in markets for labor and construction materials.

Policy implementation choices of another sort define in greater detail how policies affect their target populations. Teachers, nurses, agricultural extension agents, loan officers, water fee collectors, and other **frontline service providers** make many *daily implementation choices* about how to interact with their clients, which shape the quality of the education, health care, technological information, or financial services provided. Judges, customs officials, and building inspectors must decide how to interact with citizens seeking verdicts and what verdicts to reach, thereby affecting the quality of justice supplied and the difficulty of bureaucratic procedures. In general, high-quality services are tailored to the needs of individual clients. The managers of frontline service providers, too, affect service quality through their decisions about how to assign employees to diverse tasks, discipline workers, and equip service providers with facilities, supplies, and information.

A final important set of implementation choices determines the *level of central-level spending* that is devoted to a policy and the *allocation of that spending across locations*. Overall spending in the many locations must be coordinated in some way so that it does not generate large total budget deficits. Ideally, the resources are also allocated across locations and uses in ways that balance policymakers' interests in efficiency and equity.

Inputs to high-quality implementation choices

Common sense and the study of implementation failures suggest that:

> Good policy implementation choices require varying combinations of five key inputs: motivation, local information, resources, capacity, and coordinating oversight.

The most obvious input that agents must bring to good decision making is appropriate **motivation**. Agents must seek to maximize objectives similar to policymakers' objectives. Problems of corruption and absenteeism suggest important deficiencies in motivation.

A second input that receives much attention in current governance discussions is **local information**. Policy designs can be tailored to local circumstances, and services can be delivered in ways that meet individual needs, only when agents have access to local information and are given the discretion to use it. Often frontline service providers and their immediate managers have easier access to local information than administrators at higher levels.

In addition to good intentions and local information, implementing agents also require **resources** and **capacity**. The resources they require can include textbooks, chalk, thermometers, medicines, computers, vehicles, and fuel. The capacity they exhibit may be a function of their innate skills; the education, training, and experience they have acquired; and the access they have been given to external or expert information, such as information regarding best practices in disease treatment or information on crop prices in markets around the country. Decision-making committees also require the capacity to cooperate, debate, and reach agreements.

Finally, implementation choices benefit from some level of **coordinating oversight**. To avoid large budget deficits, expenditure decisions made in many localities must be rendered consistent with central-level budget constraints. They must also be coordinated to yield distributions across locations that are consistent with policymakers' equity and efficiency goals. Some decisions benefit from uniform application across all locations or from coordination that allows implementers to reap economies of scale.

13.3C   Governance structure design choices

In this section we describe how:

> Policymakers influence the inputs brought into implementation choices through their **governance structure design choices**, which are choices regarding: the allocation of decision-making authority across agents of different types; the allocation of expenditures and revenue collection responsibilities across locations; the criteria for selecting employees, contractors and partners; the provision of capacity-building services; and the design of accountability mechanisms.

In this section we describe each of these design choices. In the next section we see how these choices interact with one another and with context to determine the quality of implementation outcomes.

Allocation of decision-making authority across agents

Policymakers must decide which agents have responsibility for any particular set of implementation choices. When policymakers implement policies through **centralized civil-service bureaucracies**, they allocate authority over most choices to central government employees in central-level offices.[6] They might instead **deconcentrate** decision making by transferring responsibility for some choices to agents at lower levels of the central government bureaucracy or **delegate** decision-making authority to officials in regional or local governments. When they hire an NGO or for-profit firm to complete a specific task—such as the distribution of emergency food packages or the construction of rural roads—policymakers transfer frontline service-provision choices to the NGO or firm while retaining control over higher-level decisions within the government. Sometimes policymakers delegate authority for some choices to civil society organizations, community committees, or other partnering organizations. In special cases, they allow private sector producers to take over provision of critical services—such as the distribution of domestic water or electricity—on a for-profit basis, while retaining a more limited role for government decision makers who regulate or subsidize the firms.

We will see that when policymakers transfer decision-making authority from one set of agents to another, they are likely to alter the nature and magnitude of several of the inputs—motivation, local information, resources, capacity, and coordinating oversight—that affect the quality of implementation choices. For example, when they transfer decision-making authority from central-level administrators to local-level bureaucrats or community committees, they transfer decision-making responsibilities to agents who might have better access to local information and stronger motivation to please local citizens but who might also have inferior decision-making capacity; they also relinquish some coordinating oversight.

Rules for allocating expenditure and collecting revenue

Policymakers sometimes allow central-level administrators to allocate central government funds across locations and uses as they see fit. For example, decision makers in the central offices of the education and infrastructure ministries often have control over central government spending throughout the country within their sectors. Policymakers might instead impose rules that allocate funds to localities in proportion to the numbers of households living below the poverty line, the number of school-aged children, or some other measure, thereby reducing central administrators' discretion over the allocation of central budgets. Policymakers may also impose rules that require, encourage, restrict, or prohibit efforts by local agents to raise local revenue by charging user fees or taxes or by soliciting voluntary contributions.

Changes in rules regarding the allocation of expenditures and the collection of revenue might influence not only the quantities of budgetary resources available to local decision makers but also their motivation. For example, rules that award community schools with central government funding on a *per-student* basis provide local agents with stronger incentives to expand school enrollment than rules that award funding on a *per-school* basis.

Criteria for selecting employees, contractors, and partners

Policymakers set the criteria or procedures used to determine who may hold positions as employees, contractors, or community representatives. For example, they might set minimum

---

[6] For simplicity in exposition, we examine implementation options from the perspective of central government policymakers. Policymakers in local governments and NGOs face many of the same options and concerns.

qualifications for public secondary school teachers or define the process for electing or appointing members of community drinking water committees.

Alterations in these criteria may alter the typical agent's capacity and motivation. For example, reductions in the minimum level of education required for obtaining employment as a community health worker might reduce the typical level of capacity among health workers, but might also increase the potential to fill a community's health care positions with people born and raised locally, thereby increasing the typical health worker's motivation to please local clients and to remain in her post (rather than quitting and opening up a vacancy that is difficult to fill). Similarly, requiring democratic elections for members of community drinking water committees might reduce their typical education level but might increase their motivation to serve the interests of many in the community rather than the interests of the elite.

Capacity-building services

Policymakers provide capacity-building services when they allocate resources for training local-level bureaucrats in technical skills, management, or decentralized policy design and when they assist community committees with needs assessment or institution-building activities.

Accountability mechanisms

Agents are held **accountable** for their choices when, with at least some probability, they are rewarded for high-quality choices or punished for low-quality choices. Policymakers might encourage increased accountability of agents to their superiors by requiring the use of **performance contracts**, through which agents' pay, promotion, or continued employment is tied to their high-quality and honest performance. This is possible only when the superiors are capable of monitoring their agents' performance.

An agent might instead be held accountable by his clients. This is possible only when the clients are able to monitor and evaluate his performance and to administer rewards and punishments based on their evaluations. Policymakers might improve clients' capacity to monitor agents by providing clients with information about agents' budgets or about the performance of comparable agents in other places. If clients have social relationships with the agent, they may be able to administer social rewards (e.g., praise and respect) for effective service and to administer social punishments (e.g., complaints or disapproval) for poor performance. Policymakers might strengthen clients' ability to punish agents by tying agents' pay or promotion to measures of client satisfaction. If the agent is a local democratically elected official, then clients can punish his poor performance by voting him out of office.

A final mechanism through which agents may be held accountable involves **competition**. When clients are free to choose among competing agents, and when agents are rewarded in some way for attracting more clients, then clients can hold agents accountable for providing good service by threatening to take their business elsewhere. Policymakers can strengthen competition among public sector service providers by assigning them to serve overlapping geographic areas and allowing citizens to choose among them. They can introduce private sector competition by allowing private sector firms to compete for government contracts or by shifting from government provision of services to government provision of **demand-side financing**. Under demand-side financing arrangements, the government distributes to citizens the financial means for purchasing services or goods (such as education services or food) from competitive private providers, rather than providing the services or goods directly.

When policymakers strengthen accountability mechanisms, they increase agents' motivation to improve performance along the dimensions that the mechanisms reward. For example, when their pay is tied to the number of clients they serve, agents face stronger incentives to attract new clients, and when their pay is tied to client satisfaction, they face stronger incentives to improve service quality along the dimensions valued by clients. We will see, however, that strengthening incentives to perform along the dimensions rewarded by employers or clients can also *reduce* performance along other important dimensions.

Thus, as is true of every governance structure design choice described in this section, modifications in accountability mechanisms have the potential to yield both beneficial and detrimental effects on implementation choices and outcomes. The exact nature and magnitude of the benefits and costs depend on the details of the governance reform and on context. In searching for ways to improve governance, as in searching for appropriate policy designs, empirical research is of great importance.

13.3D Governance reforms

For many years, developing-country governments implemented many policies through centralized civil service bureaucracies, sometimes concentrating decision-making authority at the central level to a remarkable degree. For example, education ministry central offices sometimes not only set curriculum content, school schedules, and school fees for entire countries, but also took charge of hiring and training all teachers and of allocating all teachers, textbooks, and chalk to individual schools. This left school principals with almost no discretion over spending and with little scope to manage and discipline personnel. Often the scope for local decision making was reduced further by public sector employment rules that restrict firing or that link pay to tenure rather than to performance. Clients often had no choice of frontline service provider and no way to voice complaints about corruption or poor service quality.

Motivated by accumulating evidence of governance failures, policymakers around the world have initiated diverse governance reforms in recent decades. In this section we introduce four classes of reform: decentralization, increased community participation, increased use of performance contracting, and the introduction of private sector competition. We will see that:

> Usually the primary aim of a governance reform is to improve the quality of a targeted set of implementation decisions by increasing one or two of the five critical inputs to high-quality decision making: motivation, local information, resources, capacity, and coordinating oversight. Unfortunately, success in raising the intended inputs is not guaranteed and reductions in other inputs are possible. A reform's ultimate impacts on the five inputs and on implementation quality depend greatly on the details of the reform's design and on context.

Decentralization

Decentralization reforms shift responsibility for specified implementation choices from a small number of agents in central offices to a larger number of agents closer to the local level. Often the primary aim is to increase the local information and motivation brought to the specified decisions, by transferring decision-making responsibility to agents who have better access to local information and who are more easily held accountable by clients.

Despite their similarities, decentralization reforms differ in many important ways. Some shift the locus of decision making to the state or provincial level, while others shift it even lower, to municipalities, communities, or individual facilities (such as schools or clinics). Some reforms deconcentrate decision making within central government bureaucracies, while others delegate decisions to local governments. Some maintain central government funding at pre-reform levels, or even improve funding for many localities, while others reduce central government financing and increase local agents' responsibilities for collecting revenues. Reforms also differ in the breadth of decision-making authority given to local decision makers and in the efforts made to build the capacity of local decision makers.

Unfortunately, decentralizing reforms need not always succeed in improving use of local information and enhancing accountability. Details of the reform design and of context can stand in the way. Reforms that transfer decision-making authority only to the state or provincial level, for example, are less likely to increase the input of local information and motivation than are reforms that transfer decision-making authority to the local or facility level.

Even decentralizing reforms that shift the locus of decision making to the community or facility level fail to raise agents' motivation unless local citizens are truly able to hold local agents accountable. This means that citizens must have the capacity to monitor and evaluate the local agents' performance, and they must be able to provide agents with rewards or punishments. Citizens might, however, lack the expertise or equipment to judge the quality of government services such as teaching, health care, road construction, or domestic water supply. Often parents feel unable to judge the quality of teaching in their children's schools, and Banerjee et al. (2004) suggest that citizens sometimes have such low expectations that they consider services acceptable, and issue no complaints, even when the objective quality of these services is very low (from the perspective of an outside observer).

Furthermore, even when citizens have the capacity to evaluate performance, they might lack the means or desire to administer significant punishments or rewards. When decentralized decision makers are local elected officials, citizens can punish poor performers by voting them out of office. In other cases, however, the only rewards and punishments that citizens may be able to administer are the social rewards of praise and respect and the social punishment of disapproval. Such enforcement mechanisms might not be enough to hold agents accountable. Citizens might also prefer not to criticize government professionals to whom they feel socially inferior.

A growing number of NGO experiments demonstrate, however, that interventions can raise local clients' capacity for holding decentralized decision makers accountable. A widely cited effort by the Public Affairs Center in India (an NGO) collected users' ratings of municipal government services in Bangalore. The resulting "citizen report cards," which revealed high rates of corruption and low quality of service, were used to open up dialogue between service providers and users and eventually led to the creation of task forces and then to significant improvements in delivery of services (World Bank, 2003).

In a more narrowly focused effort in 2004, a Ugandan NGO sought to improve community oversight over public health care dispensaries. NGO personnel used a baseline household survey to create health facility report cards and then brought community members and facility staff into organized conversation about how to improve services. They encouraged community members to monitor the health workers' follow-up on action plans, but community members had no formal power to sanction poor performance. A follow-up survey six months later revealed large improvements in effort, use of facilities, and community health outcomes, even though community members were unable to judge the quality of health care at a technical level. Community members were able to monitor waiting time, absenteeism, cleanliness, and the use of equipment (such as thermometers) during exams. Performance in all of these areas improved (Björkman and Svensson, 2009).

Even when decentralization does allow community members to exert pressure on agents, it can fail to motivate in the intended fashion, particularly when the pressure on agents comes mostly from the local elite and when the elite pursue self-serving objectives. **Elite capture** can lead local decision makers to place infrastructure improvements in locations beneficial only to the elite or to direct cash transfers to people favored by the elite rather than to the poorest households.

Whether or not decentralized decision makers are better motivated and better informed than centralized decision makers, they might still deliver inferior implementation choices if they have lower capacity for making good decisions. Early decentralization experiments often revealed that decision makers at lower levels of government bureaucracies lacked adequate decision-making capacity. Having worked for many years in centralized command-and-control bureaucracies, these agents often lacked basic management and bookkeeping skills, lacked expertise in the sectors they administer, and even lacked an interest in making real decisions. Many governments and NGOs are currently working to enhance decentralization outcomes by providing capacity-building services of many types. Rigorous evaluation of such efforts is unfortunately rare, and little is known about which kinds of capacity-building efforts indeed have significant impacts.

The effects of decentralization on the resources available for providing local-level services vary greatly, depending on the expenditure- and revenue-sharing rule changes that accompany the reform. Many decentralizing reforms have taken place during periods of budgetary stress and have thus been accompanied by significant reductions in central-level financing for local activities, together with significant increases in expectations of local revenue collection. Under such circumstances, decentralization often leads to the introduction or increase of user fees (whether official fees or informal voluntary contributions), rendering services less accessible for the poor, and to sharp reductions in the resources brought to local decisions and in service quality. In fact, budget shortages can be so severe that newly authorized local decision makers have no real scope to render decisions. Per-household expenditure levels can also become more uneven across communities, as agents in higher-income communities find it easier to raise local revenue.

In other cases policymakers have made little effort to set firm budget limits for new decentralized decision makers. Under such circumstances, local decision makers have little incentive to contain costs and the result may be large budget deficits and macroeconomic instability.

Bolivia's (unusually positive) experience with decentralization demonstrates the potential for success in increasing equity in the geographic distribution of expenditures, improving the availability of resources to local decision makers and allowing local decision makers to improve the allocation of resources across uses. In 1994, the Bolivian government increased to 20 percent the fraction of central government funds transferred to the municipal level, began distributing the funds across municipalities in proportion to population levels, and transferred the titles to (and responsibility for) all infrastructure assets to the municipalities. By allocating funds across locations according to rule rather than allowing high-level ministry officials to exercise discretion, the reform greatly reduced imbalances in spending across communities and led to a significant redirection of spending across uses. Infrastructure spending, which was concentrated in the transport, hydrocarbons, and energy sectors before the reform, shifted significantly toward investments in urban development, water, and sanitation. Faguet (2004) demonstrates that individual municipalities increased spending most on the sectors in which they had the greatest deficits, suggesting that local decision makers took advantage of the opportunity to tailor spending better to local needs.

Increased community participation

One of the most frequent calls in current development discussions is to increase **community participation** in the design and implementation of development policies. In principle, participatory reforms transfer the authority over specified implementation choices to communities. The relevant communities might be villages, neighborhoods, or sets of households that use particular schools, clinics, or irrigation systems. Community representatives may be asked to assess local households' eligibility for cash transfer programs, to select blueprints for new water systems, to contribute time and money toward the construction, operation, and maintenance of electrical generators, or to manage local schools.

The primary aim in participatory reforms, as in decentralizing reforms, is to increase the local information and the motivation brought to targeted decisions. Participatory reforms sometimes inspire greater hope for such improvements than do decentralizing reforms, because, in comparison to local bureaucrats, community members are likely to have better knowledge of their own needs, better knowledge of their neighbors' circumstances, more opportunities to observe frontline service providers, and greater personal interest in local service quality.

When evaluating whether participatory reforms are likely to deliver on these hopes, however, we must recognize that in practice participatory development programs do not work directly with entire communities. They work directly only with particular community members who belong to community committees or who attend community gatherings. Participatory reforms improve motivation as intended only if community committees are indeed responsive to the needs of the entire community. They can fail because committees, like local government officials, are susceptible to elite capture. Policymakers may be able to avoid some of the worst forms of elite capture through care in designing the procedures through which community committees are formed. Fritzen (2007) finds that requiring communities to elect committee members through democratic processes (rather than allowing them to form committees without much oversight) changed the composition of the committees involved in an Indonesian infrastructure program in a subtle but beneficial way. Both before and after the change, most committee members belonged to elite groups. After the change, however, committee members came more often from new elite groups of younger, better educated individuals, who exhibited stronger interest than the old elite in furthering the interests of the poor.

Even when not captured by self-serving elite, community groups can pursue objectives that are somewhat different from those of policymakers. For example, while policymakers probably prefer that workfare program benefits go to the poorest households within communities, community committees running workfare programs in South Africa preferred to use beneficiary selection methods that appeared transparent and fair, such as drawing names out of a hat (Adato and Haddad, 2001).

Participatory reforms might increase the motivation and local information brought to decisions, but they also often transfer decision making authority to agents with lower capacity. To compensate for community committees' capacity deficits, governments and large NGOs often contract with smaller NGOs to provide communities with facilitators, who provide some training and help the communities to organize. Motivating the facilitators to encourage true community decision making, rather than imposing their own preferences on communities' decisions, is an additional challenge.

The evidence on community capacity for direct involvement in the management of service delivery is mixed (see Chapters 18 and 19). School-based management reforms in El Salvador, Honduras, and Nicaragua provided funding for schools run by committees of parents and teachers. The committees were given the power to hire and fire teachers, set salaries, maintain school buildings, and manage school operations. Econometric comparisons of community-based and traditional schools suggest that community management raised student test scores in El Salvador and Honduras but not Nicaragua. More detailed data suggest that performance improved along dimensions that parents without expertise in teaching could monitor (such as teacher attendance), whereas the technical quality of classroom methods, which parents were less capable of evaluating, may have deteriorated (Umansky and Vegas, 2007).

As with decentralization, the impact of participatory reforms on the resources brought to local decisions depends on the accompanying changes in central-level funding. Often an important motivation in participatory reforms is to shift some of the financing burden for service provision from the central government or NGO budget onto communities. As we saw in Chapter 12, community institutions might encourage community-level cooperation in the financing of local public goods investments. Designers of participatory reforms often hope to harness or catalyze such cooperation, thereby drawing new funds into the financing of central government policy. Most participatory programs require, at the very least, that community committee members work for free or for token payments, thereby performing at low cost what NGO or government employees would otherwise undertake at professional salaries. Especially in the case of infrastructure programs, communities are often required to contribute 20 percent of the cost of construction (whether paid in cash, materials, or labor time) and *all* of the ongoing costs of operation and maintenance. Community committees must raise these funds locally by collecting user fees, dues, taxes, or voluntary contributions.

Requiring significant local contributions can benefit central governments by reducing their budgetary responsibilities, but it may also alter implementation outcomes in undesirable ways.

Some of the poorest communities may be unable to muster the resources required to cover 20 percent of construction costs, and they may thus be excluded from participation. In addition, the need to charge user fees can exclude some of the poorest households within participating communities. Communities also often fail in effectively financing and executing operation and maintenance activities.

Introduction of performance contracting

Some more narrowly focused reforms introduce performance contracting for frontline service providers within government bureaucracies. The primary aim in such reforms is, of course, to improve the motivation that agents bring to their implementation choices. To succeed in improving performance, the contracting reforms must tie pay to measures of performance that agents have sufficient scope to improve, and they must link measured performance to sufficiently large rewards or punishments. Some reforms tie agents' pay more closely to performance information already available. For example, reforms might link teachers' pay to their students' performance on national academic achievement exams (see Box 13.1) or give health center administrators the authority to fire low-performing health professionals. Other reforms intensify the use of already-existing monitoring technologies. For example, in the interest of reducing the corrupt diversion of government funds, policymakers might increase the probability with which road construction managers' books are audited (as in the experiment evaluated by Olken, 2007). Increasingly, performance contracting reforms take advantage of emerging surveillance technologies. See Box 13.1 for a discussion of how cameras with tamperproof date-and-time stamps were used to remotely monitor teachers' attendance at rural schools, making possible a new link between attendance and pay. Cameras with GPS are also being used to track progress on the construction and repair of irrigation systems in conflict-ridden Afghanistan.

≡ Box 13.1 Two Experiments with Performance Contracting in Education

Tying pay to test scores

Paul Glewwe, Nauman Ilias and Michael Kremer examine an NGO initiative in Kenya, which offered teachers prizes tied to the performance of students in grades 4 through 8 on standardized end-of-year exams administered by district governments (Glewwe et al., 2010). In schools achieving top average scores, and in schools registering the greatest improvement over their baseline, all teachers in grades 4 through 8 would receive a prize worth 20 to 40 percent of their monthly pay. To encourage cooperation within the schools, the prizes were awarded on the basis of school-wide performance rather than individual class performance. To discourage teachers from preventing weak students taking the exam, the program announced that students not taking the exam would be assigned a very low score. To study the impact of this prize scheme, 100 low performing schools were randomly divided into two groups, only one of which was offered the prize scheme. The results offer a discouragingly stark picture of "teaching to the test" in this case. The program had no impact on teacher attendance or pedagogy, other than an increase in the number of special test prep sessions offered to their students in advance of the exam. Students' scores on the district exam increased in the year of the prize scheme, but their scores on other exams did not rise, and even their scores on the same exams in subsequent years showed no persistent improvement.

Remote monitoring of teachers' attendance

Esther Duflo and Rema Hanna (2005) examined a successful experiment focused on a more basic dimension of teacher choice. The experiment offered financial incentives for good attendance to teachers operating one-room nonformal education centers in rural India. The scheme made use of a clever technological innovation aimed at increasing the potential to observe and monitor attendance in remote schools at low cost. The teachers were issued cameras with tamper-proof date-and-time stamps and were instructed to verify their attendance at school each day by having a student take a photo of the teacher and other students at the beginning and ending of each school day. Each day in which the beginning and ending photos contained a minimum number of students and were at least 5 hours apart was counted as a valid work day. Depending on the number of days they attended, they could earn anywhere from 500 to 1,300 rupees per month. Teachers in comparison schools earned a fixed 1,000 rupees per month.

The program immediately reduced teacher absence rates from 42 percent to 22 percent, and it increased teaching time over the course of the school year by about one third. Teachers in program schools were just as likely to be teaching while in school as teachers in comparison schools, suggesting that teachers did not compensate for greater attendance by reducing their effort while in school. Students' test scores increased significantly, and the authors calculate that the ratio of student test score improvement to program cost was high relative to other interventions aimed at increasing students' performance.

A variety of performance contracting reforms have proved successful. Increased auditing of road construction managers in Indonesia saved more than enough money, through reduction in the corrupt diversion of funds, to pay for itself (Olken, 2007). Remote sensing of teacher attendance also proved cost-effective (see Box 13.1). In Rwanda a "pay for performance" scheme tying pay for primary health care center workers to a variety of indicators related to outreach, quality of service, and health outcomes significantly increased the quantity and quality of prenatal care (Basinga et al., 2010).

Even when performance contracting improves performance along the contracted dimensions, however, it need not improve performance overall, for two reasons. First, as Holmstrom and Milgrom (1991) point out, when workers are responsible for multiple tasks, tying their pay to performance of one task can *reduce* their motivation toward other tasks. For example, if teachers' pay is tied to their students' test scores, teachers might teach to the test, spending more time running drills of facts important to performance on the exam and less time helping students become more creative problem solvers. The first example in Box 13.1 finds some evidence of this for a test score–based teacher incentive scheme in Kenya.

Second, sometimes superiors must introduce rules that define agents' responsibilities more rigidly before they can tie pay or continued employment to any measure of performance. In such cases, as rules take on greater roles in defining how agents do their jobs, agents' discretion to respond to local information can diminish, possibly decreasing the overall effectiveness of their work. Such concerns were borne out in experiences around the world with the Training and Visit approach to agricultural extension (see Chapter 20). The Training and Visit approach sought to hold agents more responsible by requiring agents to visit client farmers on more-rigid schedules, requiring them to provide more rigidly defined sets of messages during those visits, and requiring their superiors to monitor their compliance with these rules. The new approach probably improved agents' discipline, but it also reduced agents' ability to respond to farmers' idiosyncratic, changing, and time-sensitive needs. For this and other reasons the approach ultimately fell into disfavor (Feder and Slade, 1986).

Introduction of private sector competition

Policymakers can introduce private sector competition into frontline service provision in two ways. First, they can require administrators to hire private sector contractors to complete specified tasks (that would otherwise be done by public sector employees) through a process of competitive bidding. The primary aim would be to increase service providers' motivation to find low-cost ways of providing the specified services. Such reforms successfully increase motivation only if three conditions hold: the government officials charged with awarding contracts have the capacity to monitor the quality of providers' proposals and promises, multiple providers truly compete for the government's business, and government officials indeed award contracts to the firms offering the best proposals. Sometimes the number of private sector firms available to participate in bidding is very small, however. Furthermore, as indicated by the evidence of bribe-taking by officials who award contracts, creating effective approaches to competitive bidding is a difficult governance challenge in itself.

Policymakers might instead harness private sector competition by shifting to demand-side financing. They can take funds that would otherwise have been used to finance a government food distribution program and use them to instead distribute food stamps, which recipients may use in payment for food provided by private vendors. Similarly, they can take funds that would otherwise have been used to provide primary education through government schools and use them to distribute vouchers, which recipients may use to purchase education services from any qualifying provider, including private sector providers. Often the main aims in demand-side financing reforms are to increase providers' motivation to reduce cost and to design services that better satisfy clients. Sometimes the main aims of the reforms are somewhat different, however. When private sector firms are subject to fewer regulations and bureaucratic difficulties than government providers, the main aim may be to expand the supply of services more quickly and cheaply than is possible within the government.

The potential for demand-side financing to improve performance probably differs across policies involving goods and services of different types. A shift from government food distributions to the distribution of food stamps, for example, seems likely to generate true accountability-enhancing competition. Food stamp recipients have no incentive to take bribes in exchange for poor food delivery, and they are probably capable of judging and comparing the quality of food provided by different vendors; thus they may do a better job than government bureaucrats of choosing private food providers. Furthermore, at least in urban areas, and when the government stands ready to redeem food stamps collected by many food retailers, competition among retailers is likely. Whether the conditions required for effective competition hold in education is more difficult to guess. On the demand side, clients find it more difficult to judge education quality than food quality. This may be particularly true among poor parents, suggesting that better-off families might get more out of voucher reforms than poor families. Government monitoring and certification of school quality, alongside efforts to inform and train parents in assessing the quality and fit of education services, might help. On the supply side, economies of scale in the supply of education services might prevent the creation of multiple schools in small rural communities, thereby precluding real competition.

Even when it is effective at increasing motivation for efficient service provision, demand-side financing can reduce other critical inputs to implementation choices. For example, as education supply decisions are taken up by diverse private-sector providers, policymakers lose the scope to build a widely shared culture through the use of uniform school curricula. Such reforms can also give rise to greater social differentiation, if well-off families club together in sending their children to exclusive schools. Distributing vouchers only to poor families, requiring schools that receive voucher payments to accept applicants of all sorts, and enforcing other provisions can help contain such problems. In practice, school voucher efforts have been reasonably successful, though more so in urban than rural areas and when limited to poor beneficiaries. For a closer look, see Chapter 19.

13.4 The Political Economy of Development

Many real-world policymakers bear little resemblance to the social decision makers of section 13.2, who single-mindedly pursue the development objective. Even policymakers who care deeply about development face pressure to sacrifice the pursuit of some development goals in order to maintain political support, and many policymakers throughout history have pursued selfish and partisan interests rather than development. In some countries, the authority of would-be policymakers to enforce policies is also severely limited by ongoing disputes over who has the right to set policy. It is therefore natural to ask: Under what conditions do policymakers have the capacity and motivation for effective pursuit of the development objective?

Answers to this question must be found in the study of politics and political institutions. Following Acemoğlu and Robinson (2012), we may define **politics** as "the process by which a society chooses the rules that will govern it" and define **political institutions** as the rules—formal and informal—that "determine who has power in society and to what ends that power can be used," together with the political mechanisms that enforce compliance with these rules. In what follows we suggest the importance of two key political preconditions for successful development and acknowledge some of the serious questions they raise regarding contemporary development work. The first precondition is the consolidation of power in a sufficiently strong state. The second is the existence of political institutions that constrain policymakers to use that consolidated power in ways that foster development.

Consolidated power

Some of the market and institutional failures highlighted in section 13.2 can be overcome only by governments capable of protecting property rights, establishing security, and financing investment in public goods on a national scale (Acemoğlu and Robinson, 2012). To fulfill such functions, a government must have the power to enforce rules, levy taxes, and provide services throughout its territory, and investors must expect the government to retain this power well into the future. Where power is fragmented across competing groups, and where the threat of civil war or coups creates uncertainty over who will wield power in the future, investors lack such confidence and resources are wasted in conflict. One political prerequisite for successful development, therefore, is the consolidation of power in a sufficiently strong state.

If this is the case, then what are the prospects for development in some of the world's poorest countries, which are plagued by civil wars and coups? NGOs might succeed in providing valuable humanitarian assistance to poor and vulnerable populations in such countries, but widespread and sustained improvements in well-being are unlikely without the establishment of security, order, and peaceable institutions for resolving conflict. Collier (2007) argues that military intervention by external forces may, in fact, be required to help such countries escape the conflict trap and achieve development success.

Institutional constraints on the use of power

Policymakers with consolidated power face strong temptation to use that power to enrich themselves and their fellow elite rather than to pursue widespread improvements in well-being. Policymakers of impressive character might ignore such temptation, but many leaders who succeed in consolidating power do not. This suggests that development is most likely where healthy political institutions constrain policymakers' use of consolidated power.

What are the essential characteristics of political institutions that foster development in this way? In their search for answers to this question, many researchers have considered the possible importance of formal political rules, as defined by constitutions and formal government structures. For example, they have examined whether democracy or authoritarianism is better for growth and whether development performance differs systematically across presidential and parliamentary democracies.

Drawing on both theoretical and empirical studies, many researchers have concluded, however, that there is no clear ordering of formal political institutions. For example, theory offers no clear prediction as to whether democratic or authoritarian institutions are superior for growth and development (Przeworski and Limongi, 1993). By holding policymakers accountable to a broad constituency, democratic institutions might have an advantage in allowing policymakers to promise more credibly not to expropriate investors' assets, but democratic governments might also face greater pressure to redistribute income and to spend on consumption rather than investment. Formal democratic institutions may also be subverted by patronage, vote-buying, and other abuses. Authoritarian regimes might experience less pressure for spending on consumption, and authoritarian rulers might benefit from greater policymaking autonomy, but authoritarian rulers might use their power for personal gain rather than development. Empirical studies of the relationship between economic performance and formal political institutions also produce equivocal results (Williams et al., 2011).

To understand the political preconditions for development success, therefore, we must look beyond formal political rules to broader notions of political institutions (including their informal components) and to the mechanisms that enforce them. This leads us to ask: Under what fundamental *political conditions* do the individuals involved in policymaking find themselves accountable for using consolidated power in ways that foster development?

Acemoğlu and Robinson (2012) offer one possible answer to this complex question. They argue that to understand the political underpinnings of development, we must study how political power is distributed between the elite and other groups in society. In their view, in most societies throughout history, elite groups have used consolidated power to create *extractive* policies and economic institutions, which enrich the elite by extracting labor and wealth from powerless groups. Such institutions stifle growth and development by depriving most of the population of secure property rights and investment opportunities. They argue, furthermore, that development has become possible only in countries where, at some critical moment in history, diverse non-elite interest groups—each with sufficient political power—cooperated in overthrowing the extractive elite and establishing political institutions that prevent any one group from acquiring extractive power.

Under these new and better political institutions, each of the cooperating interest groups accepts checks on its own accumulation of political power and helps enforce checks on other groups. In this way, each group helps hold policymakers accountable to all collaborating groups. Acemoğlu and Robinson label such political institutions *inclusive*, because they hold policymakers accountable for securing the property rights and education opportunities of a diverse set of groups rather than for a narrower elite group alone.

Even though such inclusive institutions must be enforced by a balance of political power among diverse interest groups, they might not require the involvement of groups representing *all* of society, and they might therefore arise even in the absence of fully fledged democracy. Indeed, Acemoğlu and Robinson argue that the Industrial Revolution—the fundamental source of modern economic growth and development in their view—was made possible by the Glorious Revolution of 1688 in England, which rendered monarchic political institutions somewhat more inclusive than before the revolution but endowed only a small, well-off fraction of the population with the right to vote.

If the key to successful development is such sharing of political power by diverse interest groups (and the inclusive political institutions that they hold in place), then we must ask: What is the nature of political power, and how might diverse groups with sufficient power come to collaborate in holding policymakers accountable? Acemoğlu and Robinson suggest that interest groups derive their **political power** from their economic power (which gives them the capacity to offer rewards or threaten punishments to other groups) and from the effectiveness of their organization (which gives their members the capacity to cooperate in the use of pooled economic power). If this is the case, then to encourage the creation of more development-friendly political institutions in countries currently governed by extractive institutions, development actors might wish to enhance the economic power, and improve the organization, of the interest groups with greatest potential to participate in sustaining inclusive institutions, and to work at creating alliances among these interest groups. Development actors' efforts to expand education opportunities and to guarantee the freedom of the press might also improve the interest groups' collective capacity to hold policymakers accountable.

This way of understanding the political economy of development raises some difficult questions for development actors. For example, if, in some countries, the key to long-run development success is political change, then might it make sense to redirect some energy and resources away from focused poverty-reduction activities and toward activities that empower less-poor but more politically important interest groups for putting better political institutions into place? If middle class and college educated groups are more likely than the poor and less educated to organize relevant interest groups, for example, then development actors might increase their long-run success by directing a larger fraction of resources toward the promotion of business associations and investments in college education.

A final set of questions suggested by this brief political economy discussion pertains to foreign aid. Might foreign aid sometimes do more harm than good, by weakening civil society's capacity to hold policymakers accountable? And how might we reform foreign aid institutions to enhance their contribution to development? Foreign aid helps finance much-needed investment in the sorts of development-enhancing interventions identified in section 13.2. But by providing an external source of finance to the elite groups that control extractive governments, foreign aid might weaken the elite's accountability to the rest of society; it might weaken their need to extract tax revenue, thereby weakening their incentives to protect property rights and provide effective services for potential tax-paying groups. External financing may also provide the elite with resources to use in subverting formal democratic processes. Thus, although foreign aid can bring direct developmental benefits, it might also contribute indirectly to a deterioration of political institutions. Which of these effects outweighs the other, and how the political costs of foreign aid might best be avoided, remain important questions for empirical research (Collier, 2007).

REFERENCES

Adato, Michelle, and Lawrence J. Haddad. "Targeting Poverty Through Community-Based Public Works Programs." FCND Discussion Paper No. 121. Washington, D.C.: International Food Policy Research Institute, 2001. http://www.ifpri.org/sites/default/files/publications/fcndp121.pdf

Acemoğlu, Daron, and James Robinson. *Why Nations Fail: The Origins of Power, Prosperity, and Poverty.* New York: Crown Business, 2012.

Banerjee, Abhijit V., Angus Deaton, and Esther Duflo. "Health Care Delivery in Rural Rajasthan." *Economic and Political Weekly* 39(9): 944–949, 2004. http://economics.mit.edu/files/771

Basinga, Paulin, Paul Gertler, Agnes Binagwaho, Agnes L. B. Soucat, Jennifer R. Sturdy, and Christel M. J. Vermeersch. "Paying Primary Health Care Centers for Performance in Rwanda." Policy Research Working Paper 5190. Washington, D.C.: World Bank, 2010. http://go.worldbank.org/EMLMIYCE40

Björkman, Martina, and Jakob Svensson. "Power to the People: Evidence From a Randomized Field Experiment on Community-Based Monitoring in Uganda." *The Quarterly Journal of Economics* 124(2): 735–769, 2009. doi:10.1162/qjec.2009.124.2.735

Chaudhury, N., J. Hammer, M. Kremer, K. Muralidharan, and F. H. Rogers. "Missing in Action: Teacher and Health Worker Absence in Developing Countries." *The Journal of Economic Perspectives* 20(1): 91–116, 2006. doi:10.1257/089533006776526058

Collier, Paul. *The Bottom Billion: Why the Poorest Countries are Failing and What Can Be Done about It.* Oxford: Oxford University Press, 2007.

D'Souza, Anna, and Daniel Kaufmann. "Who Bribes in Public Contracting and Why: Worldwide Evidence from Firms." Washington, D.C.: The Economic Research Service and Brookings Institution, 2011. http://dx.doi.org/10.2139/ssrn.1563538

DellaVigna, Stefano. "Psychology and Economics: Evidence from the Field." *Journal of Economic Literature* 47(2): 315–372, 2009. doi:10.1257/jel.47.2.315

Duflo, Esther, and Rema Hanna. "Monitoring Works: Getting Teachers to Come to School." Working Paper No. 11880. Cambridge, MA: National Bureau of Economic Research, 2005. http://www.nber.org/papers/w11880

Faguet, Jean-Paul. "Does Decentralization Increase Government Responsiveness to Local Needs? Evidence From Bolivia." *Journal of Public Economics* 88(3–4): 867–893, 2004. doi:10.1016/S0047-2727(02)00185-8

Feder, Gershon, and Roger Slade. "The Impact of Agricultural Extension: The Training and Visit System in India." *The World Bank Research Observer* 1(2): 139–161, 1986. doi:10.1093/wbro/1.2.139

Fisman, R., and J. Svensson. "Are Corruption and Taxation Really Harmful to Growth? Firm Level Evidence." *Journal of Development Economics* 83(1): 63–75, 2007. http://dx.doi.org/10.1016/j.jdeveco.2005.09.009

Fritzen, Scott A. "Can the Design of Community-Driven Development Reduce the Risk of Elite Capture? Evidence From Indonesia." *World Development* 35(8): 1359–1375, 2007. doi:10.1016/j.worlddev.2007.05.001

Glewwe, Paul, Nauman Ilias, and Michael Kremer. "Teacher Incentives." *American Economic Journal: Applied Economics* 2(3): 205–227, 2010. doi:10.1257/app.2.3.205

Hausmann, R., and D. Rodrik. "Economic Development as Self-Discovery." *Journal of Development Economics* 72(2): 603–633, 2003. http://dx.doi.org/10.1016/S0304-3878(03)00124-X

Holmstrom, Bengt, and Paul Milgrom. "Multi-Task Principal-Agent Analysis: Incentive Contracts, Asset Ownership, and Job Design." *Journal of Law, Economics and Organization* 7(special issue): 24–52, 1991. doi:10.1093/jleo/7.special_issue.24

Olken, Benjamin A. "Corruption and the costs of redistribution: Micro evidence from Indonesia." *Journal of Public Economics* 90(4): 853–870, 2006. doi:10.1016/j.jpubeco.2005.05.004

Olken, Benjamin A. "Monitoring Corruption: Evidence From a Field Experiment in Indonesia." *Journal of Political Economy* 115(2): 200–249, 2007. doi:10.1086/509548

Olken, Benjamin A., and Patrick Barron. "The Simple Economics of Extortion: Evidence from Trucking in Aceh." *Journal of Political Economy* 117(3): 417–452, 2009. doi: 10.1086/599707, http://www.jstor.org/stable/10.1086/599707

Przeworski, Adam, and Fernando Limongi. "Political Regimes and Economic Growth." *The Journal of Economic Perspectives* 7(3): 51–69, 1993. doi: 10.1257/jep.7.3.51

Reinikka, R., and J. Svensson. "Local Capture: Evidence from a Central Government Transfer Program in Uganda." *The Quarterly Journal of Economics* 119(2): 679–705, 2004. doi: 10.1162/0033553041382120.

Rowe, Alexander K., Faustin Onikpo, Marcel Lama, Francois. Cokou, and Michael S. Deming. "Management of Childhood Illness at Health Facilities in Benin: Problems and Their Causes." *American Journal of Public Health* 91(10):1625–1635, 2001. doi:10.2105/AJPH.91.10.1625

Svensson, Jakob. "Who must pay bribes and how much? Evidence from a cross section of firms." *Quarterly Journal of Economics* 118(1): 207–230, 2003.

Svensson, J. "Eight Questions about Corruption." *The Journal of Economic Perspectives* 19(3): 19–42, 2005. doi: 10.1257/089533005774357860

Umansky, Ilana, and Emiliana Vegas. "Inside Decentralization: How Three Central American School-Based Management Reforms Affect Student Learning Through Teacher Incentives." *The World Bank Research Observer* 22(2): 197–215, 2007. doi:10.1093/wbro/lkm006

Williams, Gareth, Alex Duncan, Pierre Landell-Mills, and Sue Unsworth. "Politics and Growth." *Development Policy Review* 27(1): 5–31, 2009. Available at SSRN: http://dx.doi.org/10.1111/j.1467-7679.2009.00433.x

World Bank. *World Development Report 2004: Making Services Work for Poor People.* Washington, D.C.: World Bank, 2003. http://go.worldbank.org/PLF4W7YI81

World Health Organization, Division of Child Health and Development. *CHD 1996–97 Report.* Geneva: World Health Organization, 1998. http://www.who.int/

Zhuang, Juzhong, Zhihong Liang, Tun Lin, and Frnaklin De Guzman. "Theory and Practice in the Choice of Social Discount Rate." ERD Working Paper No. 94 Manila: Asian Development Bank, 2007.

QUESTIONS FOR REVIEW

1. Define every element in the graphs of Figure 13.1. What is the significance of the intersection between the *MPB* and *MPC* schedules?

2. What is the significance of the social decision maker defined in this chapter?

3. Why might the *MSB* schedule lie above the *MPB* schedule, as in Figure 13.2?

4. For each of the rationales for intervention discussed in section 13.2C, describe the relevant market and institutional failure, state some economic sectors or activities for which it is most likely to be relevant, and state the kind(s) of policy that might be useful for counteracting the failure.

5. Describe the diverse varieties of governance failure in developing countries.

6. What kinds of choices are made by policy-implementing agents?

7. Discuss the significance of the five critical "inputs" to high quality implementation decisions.

8. Describe the governance structure design choices available to policymakers.

9. For each of the four classes of governance reform discussed in the text, describe (a) the one or two critical inputs to good decision making that the reforms often aim to increase, (b) the conditions that must hold for the reforms to succeed in increasing these inputs, (c) reasons the reforms might fail to increase these inputs, and (d) ways the reforms might also affect other critical inputs (often in deleterious directions).

10. Discuss the significance of consolidated power and of political institutions in providing policymakers with the capacity and motivation to pursue the development objective.

11. Describe Acemoğlu and Robinson's perspective on the political underpinnings of development success, and discuss some of the questions this view raises regarding contemporary development practice.

QUESTIONS FOR DISCUSSION

1. For each of the rationales for intervention in the text, discuss (a) whether and how we might expect it to inhibit economic growth and (b) whether and why it may be a problem of particular relevance to the poor.

2. What are some of the reasons a government bureaucrat responsible for issuing business registration papers might perform her responsibilities very slowly? What sorts of governance reform might be effective in increasing the speed at which she processes licenses? Describe the logic of how the reforms might increase her speed. What other benefits or costs might follow from such reforms?

3. What are some of the reasons a primary school teacher might have little impact on his students' human capital? What sorts of governance reform might be effective in increasing the quality of education he provides? Describe the logic of how the reforms might increase his impact. What other benefits and costs might follow from such reforms?

PROBLEMS

1. A small NGO sets up a project in a remote community in Cameroon, intending to provide local women with a sustainable source of cash income: the processing and sale of shea butter (which is used in cosmetics and chocolate production). The shea tree grows in this community, and local families consume its fruit, but they have never before dried, ground, and processed the nuts inside the fruits to make shea butter. The project provides the women (free of charge) with a single motorized crusher that they may all take turns using to process the nuts, and it trains them in processing techniques. The project plans, for the first two years, to send trucks to help the women with transporting their shea butter to a regional capital city, where they may sell it to an exporter. After two years, the NGO plans to exit the community and expects to leave behind a self-sustaining shea-processing business.

   a. What diagnoses as to why local women would not enter the shea butter processing business in the absence of intervention seem to underlie this project? (You might want to differentiate the diagnosis of underlying problems—or lack thereof—between the introductory two-year period and the subsequent period.)

   b. Describe one or more alternative diagnoses under which this project design would be ineffective in stimulating sustainable new income generation.

   c. Describe another alternative diagnosis under which this program would succeed in stimulating sustainable income generation but might cost more to the NGO initiating the project than absolutely required to make the investment happen.

2. A city's domestic water market is a natural monopoly. The city's government initially owns and operates the city's water utility, which supplies the whole market with water services. The utility charges a low base per-gallon fee for the first gallons of water consumed by any household each month and then charges a higher per-gallon fee for water consumed over the base level. This allows poor households to pay low rates for small quantities and allows nonpoor households to pay higher average rates for larger quantities. The utility is inefficiently run and provides poor service. It also operates at a loss, receiving subsidies to cover its losses out of general government revenue. In a major reform, the government auctions off the right to run the water utility to a private firm. At the same time, the government ceases to provide any subsidy to the firm out of general government revenue.

   a. Which of the "governance structure design choices" discussed in the chapter are altered by this reform? (Base your answer only on what you have been told about the reform.)

   b. How would you expect each of these changes in a governance structure design choice to alter the motivation, local information, resources, capacity, or coordinating oversight brought to bear on the decision regarding the *level of the base fee* charged by the utility? Which of these changes in input would tend to raise the level of the base fee and which would tend to lower it?

Policy Analysis

Policymakers contribute the most to development when their policies are well designed and well implemented and when they choose sets of policies that together achieve the best array of development outcomes possible given any practical constraints. Policy analysts encourage and support good policy choices by illuminating the benefits and costs that are likely to emerge from any policy and by analyzing how those benefits and costs would change with modifications in the policy's design or implementation or with the introduction of complementary policies.

After defining core policy analysis concepts and objectives, this chapter introduces a systematic approach to policy analysis. The approach is organized around seven questions, which together guide their users through comprehensive study of a policy's benefits and costs. The remaining chapters of the text then demonstrate how to apply the approach (which draws on the analytical tools of Part III) in analyzing diverse questions related to targeted transfer and workfare programs, agricultural pricing policies, and policies toward infrastructure, education, agricultural technology, microfinance, and health.

14.1 Policy Analysis Concepts and Objectives

We use the term **policy** as a shorthand reference to any policy, project, or program implemented in pursuit of development objectives. A policy may be established by a government, intergovernmental agency, NGO, community group, or corporation. The policies may be large scale or small scale, one-time or ongoing. They include taxes on imports, projects to build wells for drinking water, the creation of microfinance institutions, programs to provide cash transfers to needy households, and interventions of many other sorts.

A policy connects with the socioeconomic system, and ultimately affects development outcomes, by connecting with people. Most policies can be understood as offering new opportunities to, or imposing new constraints on, certain groups. For example, targeted transfer programs offer people who meet eligibility criteria the opportunity to collect transfers of cash or food. Education policies offer families the opportunity to send their children to schools of certain types in certain locations, provided they pay specified fees. Agricultural extension policies offer farmers information, training, and advice regarding crop cultivation, while minimum wage policies constrain specified employers to pay wages at least as high as some legislated minimum to all of their workers (or face specified penalties).

Only some of the people who are offered new opportunities accept them, and only some who are legally subject to regulations change their behavior to comply. Those who accept a policy's opportunities or change their behavior to comply with a policy's regulations are the policy's **directly affected groups**. Members of the directly affected groups, like everyone else, are people who make interrelated choices as they seek to achieve as much well-being as possible for themselves and their families (as described in Chapter 2). When they respond to new opportunities and constraints, they and their families might alter their behavior in many ways, revising their choices regarding what to do with their time, how to run their farms or businesses, what to consume, what health precautions to practice, what to save, and which investments to

☰ Box 14.1 Example Policies: Introduction

Mexico's Progresa program

In 1997, the Mexican government introduced a program called Progresa, which continues today under the new name Oportunidades. We may classify Progresa as a cash transfer program, which seeks to distribute cash benefits to a carefully defined set of eligible poor households. More specifically, it is a *conditional* cash transfer program, which conditions households' continued receipt of program cash on their compliance with requirements that they send their children to school and make use of public clinics. The program employs a multistage process for identifying eligible households, calculates transfer sizes using formulas that depend on the sex and grade level of children in the household (as well as other household characteristics), and enforces school and clinic use conditions through a careful set of administrative procedures. It also requires that beneficiary households send female members to attend the meetings at which the cash transfers are distributed. For a more detailed description of the program, see Box 15.1

World Learning's CAGE program in Benin

With funding from USAID, the Washington, D.C.–based NGO World Learning implemented the Community Action for Girls' Education (CAGE) project in rural Benin. The program hired several local NGOs to send project facilitators to selected communities, where they helped form the local committees that would become the program's local partners. The committees were given responsibility for developing a collective vision for girls' education, assessing local barriers to girls' education, and developing proposals for small projects aimed at reducing those barriers. The program offered "community mini grants" that provided funding for up to half the cost of these projects, while the communities were responsible for the remainder of the funding. Projects included local campaigns to increase awareness of the importance of education, construction of blackboards or study spaces, and creation of monetary prizes for academic performance, skilled teaching, or school attendance. For a more detailed description of the program, see Carter (2005).

understanding their logic, and explaining why they are large or small is a daunting task! How should the policy analyst begin?

This section introduces a systematic approach to policy analysis, which guides the policy analyst through comprehensive study of a policy's benefits and costs. It takes the form of seven questions, which encourage the user to break the analysis down into tractable pieces and to examine all the potential pathways linking policy to impacts. The analyst must use the theoretical tools of Part III, together with detailed knowledge of policy design and governance structure, to work out logically possible answers to each question and must then seek out empirical evidence regarding the likely sizes of the benefits and costs.

Box 14.1 introduces the reader to two example policies. Subsequent boxes discuss the application of the seven questions to the analysis of these example policies.

Question 1: What are the policy's objectives?

A policy's **objectives** are the intended social benefits that motivate policymakers to expend resources on the policy and that shape the policy's design. Fully successful development requires welfare-enhancing change along many dimensions for many people, as we discussed in Part II. Individual development policies, however, typically aim at achieving improvement along only a subset of these dimensions and for subsets of people. Defining a policy's objectives requires identifying the **target groups** for whom the policy aims to improve living standards (e.g., pastoralists or poor urban women) and the dimensions of living conditions that the policy seeks to improve (e.g., current food consumption, future business income, or access to health care). Box 14.2 describes the objectives of the example policies.

When defining a policy's objectives it is also useful to describe the logical chain linking the policy to its objectives, when this is not obvious. For example, a program of credit for small and medium enterprises may aim to reduce poverty indirectly by increasing the demands of participating enterprises for low-skill labor, thereby raising incomes for low-skill wage laborers and their families.

Identifying a policy's objectives at the start of the analysis is useful for both policy analysts and policymakers. Question 1 alerts the analyst to some of the most important benefits and logical links that will require empirical study. It reminds policymakers that articulating objectives is an important first step in skillful policy design. It also reminds them that the ultimate objective of a policy must be to improve *well-being*, and not merely to achieve program implementation targets

☰ Box 14.2 Example Policies: Objectives

Mexico's Progresa program

Progresa's innovative design reflects creative thought about policy objectives. Traditional cash transfer programs aim solely to achieve the short-run objective of reducing current poverty by increasing the consumption expenditure of today's poor, but Progresa's design reflects dual objectives. In addition to reducing short-term poverty, the program seeks to reduce long-term poverty and contribute to economic growth by encouraging families to invest more in the education and health of their children. Adding this second objective is not costless. If households must send children to school to remain eligible, they might have to reduce their children's income-generating work. Household income from regular economic activities might thus fall, offsetting the cash injection provided by the program. As a result, Progresa might reduce current poverty by less than would be the case for more traditional, unconditional cash transfer programs offering transfers of the same size. However, policymakers may be willing to accept this sacrifice if the additional impact on future poverty is large enough. (Chapter 15 offers a more comprehensive analysis of the tradeoffs associated with conditioning cash transfers on school attendance.)

World Learning's CAGE program in Benin

Thorough evaluation of the CAGE program, too, requires appreciation of its dual objectives. CAGE shares one objective with Progresa: effecting long-run improvements in well-being through increased investment in education, especially for girls. Its other objective is very different, however. Whereas Progresa aims to increase households' current consumption expenditure, CAGE does not. In fact, households must *sacrifice* current consumption as they contribute to the local co-financing of CAGE projects. CAGE's second objective is to create additional long-run improvements in community well-being through institution building. Program facilitators hope to improve the community's capacity to cooperate in solving problems of mutual concern by bringing community members together and by training leaders to assess needs, design projects, seek funding, and execute projects. The hope is that communities will be better able to take advantage of other programs offered by governments and NGOs and that they will also be better equipped for undertaking investments on their own, without the involvement of governments or NGOs. When compared to other programs seeking to increase school enrollments, CAGE might therefore produce smaller enrollment increases per dollar, but the smaller enrollment impact must be weighed against the program's stronger impacts on community institutions.

by distributing many loans, visiting many farmers, or enrolling many children in school. Meeting such targets may be a necessary condition for improving well-being, but it is not a sufficient condition.

Question 2: What design details define the policy on paper?

Policies introduce change into the socioeconomic system by offering people new opportunities or imposing new constraints on them. We will see that seemingly small changes in the details of these opportunities and constraints can lead to large changes in the numbers and types of directly affected groups, the effects of the policy on directly affected peoples' well-being and behavior, the spillover and feedback effects that result from their changed behavior, and budgetary costs. Thus it is important to describe policies in detail before beginning to analyze their impacts.

For policies that offer benefits (such as cash transfers or community infrastructure grants) or services (such as education or health care), the nature of the new opportunities they offer are ultimately shaped by choices regarding

- Program eligibility requirements;

- The nature, size, and quality of benefits or services provided;

- Any fees charged for services;

- Any conditions or requirements placed on recipients; and

- The procedures for disseminating information about the program, assessing eligibility, and distributing benefits or services.

For policies that regulate activities, the new constraints are shaped by choices regarding

- The nature of the regulations;
- The rules determining who is liable for compliance with the regulations;
- The provisions for monitoring compliance; and
- The penalties for noncompliance.

With some of these design details, policymakers may choose either to determine the details themselves or to delegate this responsibility to lower-level administrators, community committees, other development organizations, or the private sector. For example, they might ask community committees to select which type of water system will be built in each community (rather than directly selecting which type of system will be built in all communities). With other design details, such as the exact nature and quality of services provided by teachers and other front-line service providers, policymakers have no choice but to leave them in the hands of **policy-implementing agents**. Thus a complete answer to Question 2 must state any of the above design details that are set directly by policymakers in a centralized fashion *and* the design of the governance structure through which policymakers hope to shape the decisions of decentralized decision makers and other policy implementers.

To describe a policy's **governance structure** (as defined in Chapter 13), a policy analyst must identify the decentralized decision makers (e.g., lower-level bureaucrats within central government ministries, local government officials, community committees) to whom various decisions have been delegated, as well as the managers and service providers (e.g., school principals, teachers, customs officials) who shape the use of funds and the quality of service provision or rule enforcement. Having done this, the analyst then seeks to identify the details of

- Any guidelines, rules, resources, or capacity-building services provided to any decentralized decision makers;
- Any rules or procedures determining who may occupy these decision-making positions;
- Any contributions of goods, cash, or labor required of the decentralized decision makers; and
- The mechanisms through which they are held accountable for making choices consistent with policymakers' intentions.

Students new to policy analysis find it unexpectedly difficult to describe a policy's design in the necessary detail. Often policy documents devote more space to what policymakers hope and believe they will accomplish (i.e., the policy's objectives) than to the actual details of how the policy is set up. In addition, students who are used to analyzing economic problems only in general terms, using scale-free diagrams, may initially lack instinctive interest in important numerical details, such as the sizes of transfer payments, the levels of workfare program wages, or the magnitude of school enrollment fees. Furthermore, the nature and significance of **policy design details** may be difficult to grasp without first becoming familiar with the populations, technologies, and institutions involved. Making the effort to describe design details in an organized, specific and comprehensive way is, however, vital preparation for the analysis of a policy's impacts. Chapters 15 through 22 describe the nature of critical design choices for policies of diverse types. For brief descriptions of the example policies' designs, the reader may review Box 14.1. (Box 15.1 provides a more detailed description of the Progresa program.)

Question 3: What design details define the policy's impact in practice?

Question 3 acknowledges that policies often look different on the ground than they look on paper. For policies that have already been implemented, a first task in policy analysis is to examine the policy's de facto design details, which we will call the policy's **implementation outcomes**.[2] For policies in which decentralized decision makers have been given authority to make some of the detailed design decisions, the analyst examines

- The choices decentralized decision makers have made and the extent to which they reflect skilled and well-motivated tailoring of design to local circumstances.

When the policy offers any education, health, agricultural extension, credit, infrastructure, or other services, the analyst examines

- The nature and quality of the services actually provided and the efficiency with which they are provided.

When the policy imposes regulations, the analyst considers

- The rigor with which compliance is monitored and penalties are carried out.

The analyst also considers

- The extent to which program funds are wasted or stolen,
- The extent to which local funds are drawn into policy efforts, and
- The nature of any bureaucratic difficulties created by the policy.

In an effort to understand implementation outcomes, the analyst must first identify the individuals within a policy's implementing hierarchy or partnership who have *de facto* authority to make decentralized policy design and implementation choices. The analyst then seeks to understand why the implementing agents make the choices they do and brainstorms about how policy design and governance structure changes might improve the quality of their choices. Following the discussion of good governance in Chapter 13, this involves examining the local information, capacity, resources, and coordinating oversight these individuals would require to make good decisions; the local information, capacity, resources, and coordinating oversight brought to bear on their choices in practice; and the effectiveness of the mechanisms through which they are held accountable for making high-quality decisions. Box 14.3 highlights what would be involved in applying Question 3 to the study of the example policies.

Question 4: What sorts of individuals, households, or firms are directly affected by the policy, how large are these groups, and how might the identity and sizes of the groups change over time?

Having worked out a careful description of the opportunities and constraints created by the policy in practice, and of the groups to whom these opportunities and constraints are presented, the

---

[2] In some discussions of program evaluation, what we call implementation outcomes (emphasizing the role that policy implementers play in determining them) are called program *outputs*, and the term *outcomes* is reserved for the program's ultimate impacts on well-being, which we call *development outcomes*.

≡ **Box 14.3** Example Policies: Implementation

Mexico's Progresa program

The Progresa program's multistage approach to identifying eligible households calls on local program staff to administer questionnaires to all households in the community and to use the information collected to identify households they believe are poor enough to satisfy the program's eligibility criteria. These lists are then discussed and adjusted by community members in community meetings. The program also calls on schoolteachers and health care workers to fill out forms verifying school attendance and use of health care facilities by program families, and it calls on women designated as *promoters* to gather participating women for meetings, encourage them to comply with program requirements, and collect program payments. To describe the eligibility requirements as they are worked out in practice, the analyst must examine how thoroughly the program staff seeks out households to be interviewed, what rules they use for determining which households are placed on the tentative beneficiary lists, and what kinds of corrections community members make to these lists. To determine whether the behavioral conditions are implemented according to the program design, the analyst must question whether teachers and health care workers provide accurate and complete information regarding program compliance and whether they take advantage of their role by extracting favors from

beneficiaries. To understand how the program intersects with women's lives and how benefits are distributed in practice, the analyst must study how the promoters go about their assigned tasks.

World Learning's CAGE program in Benin

The CAGE program is explicitly designed to involve communities in determining the details of community projects. The program hires NGO facilitators to help form community committees and guide them through the needs assessment, project selection, and proposal process. Whether the program indeed leads to the selection of projects well suited to local needs and interests, and what local benefits and costs are generated by the projects, depends on the composition of the community committees that the facilitators help form and the nature of the guidance and capacity-building services that the facilitators provide to the committees (e.g., whether the facilitators indeed encourage true local decision making or whether they instead pressure committees to make choices that the facilitators deem best). In answering Question 3 for this program, the analyst takes interest both in the local decision-making process and in the set of projects ultimately chosen and implemented.

policy analyst turns in Question 4 to the first points of contact between the policy and the socioeconomic system: the people who are directly affected by the policy. Policy analysts adapt and apply economic models of household and firm decision making from Part III (especially Chapters 6, 7, 10, and 12) in identifying the community, household, or firm characteristics that are most likely to play important roles in determining whether individuals become directly affected. They then seek out empirical evidence on the sizes and identities of the groups that are directly affected by the policy in diverse ways. For example, they identify which groups among the poor and nonpoor in a region do and do not ultimately participate in a cash transfer program. For large-scale policies and programs, the analyst often starts by identifying which communities within a region participate in the program and then identifies the groups within program communities that do and do not participate.

When policies seek to achieve their objectives by channeling benefits directly to their target groups, the analyst's primary concern is to compare the policy's target groups (i.e., the groups the policy *aims* to reach) with the groups who in practice are directly affected by the policy (i.e., the groups the policy *actually* reaches). Such policies are susceptible to two sorts of **targeting failure**: the leakage of benefits to nontarget groups and noncoverage by the program of some target group members. For example, lax administrative procedures, or eligibility criteria poorly correlated with true poverty, might allow many nonpoor households to collect a transfer program's benefits. At the same time, the program might fail to deliver benefits to some households in deep poverty who live far from roads and find it too difficult to collect benefits (Chapter 15).

When policies seek to regulate behavior, a primary aim in answering Question 4 is to identify how many in the target group indeed modify their behavior in response to the policy. Many target individuals might fail to change their behavior because poor monitoring or small penalties give them little reason to fear being caught in noncompliance. Others might fail to change their behavior because they would have made choices that meet regulatory requirements even in the absence of regulation.

Measuring the *sizes* of the directly affected groups is important. A program will not achieve great success in reducing poverty if it reaches only a tiny fraction of the poor. Likewise, a regulation will have little impact on society if only a few people change their behavior in response.

Often it is useful to distinguish and measure the sizes of multiple groups that will be affected by the policy in different ways and to different degrees. For example, flexibly designed safety net policies might provide immediate cash benefits to households in current severe need while also providing a greater sense of security to households that are not currently in need (and are thus not current program participants) but are vulnerable to shocks that could send them into destitution in the future. It is useful to identify and measure the size of both these groups. Similarly, girls' secondary school scholarship programs might help some households that would not otherwise do so to send their girls to secondary school while also increasing the disposable income of other households that would have sent their girls to school even in the absence of the program. A tariff policy that raises the price of rice has varied effects across groups, depending on whether they are net buyers, net sellers, or nonparticipants in rice markets (see Chapter 7).

The first step toward answering Question 4 is to rephrase it in a more specific way, tailoring it to the type of policy under consideration. The rephrasing often points to a behavioral choice made by households or firms that brings them into contact with the policy. For example, when studying agricultural pricing policies (Chapter 17), this question becomes: Who will *buy or sell* the relevant crops in markets affected by the policy? When studying programs of investment in irrigation systems (Chapter 18), the question becomes: Who will *use* the new irrigation systems? When studying targeted transfer programs (Chapter 15), it becomes: Who will *participate* in the program?

The next step toward answering Question 4 is to identify and apply analytical tools that help structure thought about which households will and will not engage in the behaviors required for direct contact. Often microeconomic models of basic decisions regarding whether or not to participate in a program, how much rice to consume, or whether or not to send a child to school is of great use in the analysis. In subsequent chapters, we identify the analytical tools from Part III (or adaptations and extensions of those tools) that are most useful for answering Question 4 in each policy area. Box 14.4 discusses the application of Question 4 to the example policies.

Question 5: What effect does the policy have on the well-being and behavior of the directly affected groups in the short, medium, and long run?

We care about impacts on the *well-being* of everyone directly affected by a policy because these impacts usually constitute important components of the policy's overall social benefits and costs.

☰ Box 14.4 Example Policies: Directly Affected Groups

Mexico's Progresa program

For a cash transfer program like Progresa, Question 4 may be restated as a question about which households do and do not ultimately become recipients of program cash. Given the program's poverty reduction aim, it is especially important to ask: How well does Progresa do at reaching the poor? Who among the poor is left out, and why? To what extent are Progresa benefits delivered to nonpoor households and why? It will also be useful to consider how flexibly the program will drop households who rise out of poverty and incorporate households who fall into poverty in future years. In Chapter 15, we develop a simple model of program participation that offers useful guidance for systematic study of such questions.

World Learning's CAGE program in Benin

For a community grant program with dual objectives like CAGE, a complete answer to Question 4 overlaps somewhat with the answer to

Question 3, but it pushes further. To fully identify who is directly affected either by participation in community committees or as beneficiaries of the local projects, we must ask: Which communities (i.e., at which income and schooling levels) will choose to write proposals and succeed in obtaining grants from CAGE? Which individuals join CAGE committees within participating communities, what kinds of projects do they choose, and which households make use of any infrastructure or services provided by the projects? The program might fail to reach the poorest households because the poorest communities do not have the capacity to form committees and write proposals, because only self-interested members of the elite join the committees, because well-meaning committee members misjudge local needs, or because the interventions that would help the poorest households require far more funds than are forthcoming through the program's mini grants.

To obtain a complete picture of how a household's well-being is affected by a policy, the analyst must consider possible impacts on many dimensions of living standards—including food consumption, working hours, health, and security—and for diverse household members. Some of the effects may be unintended and unfortunate. For example, even when a microfinance program directed toward women increases women's income and influence within their families, it might also trigger domestic violence toward women in some participating households.

Without careful attention to the many dimensions of living conditions that may be affected by a policy, a policy analyst might fail to detect important improvements in well-being. For example, participation in a cash transfer program might fail to increase a woman's total income and consumption expenditure, but it might nonetheless raise her well-being if it allows her to reduce her working hours or send her child to school. It might also raise her current income but not her current consumption if she chooses to save and invest out of the increased income (thereby raising future income and consumption). In such cases, studies that look only at impacts on current consumption expenditure might incorrectly conclude that women obtained little benefit from participation. Chapter 2's discussion of the many interrelated choices that households make in their pursuit of well-being helps the analyst brainstorm broadly about possible impacts.

We care about a policy's effects on the *behavior*, or choices, of directly affected groups for at least three reasons. First, in some cases policies aim specifically to encourage socially desirable behaviors, such as consumption of micronutrient-rich foods or use of insecticide-treated bed nets, or to reduce costly behaviors, such as smoking or use of air-polluting cook stoves. Second, some behavioral responses to programs can partially un-do intended program impacts. For example, when an NGO sets up a school or offers small loans, households might simply switch from obtaining comparable services from the private sector to obtaining program services. In such cases, the new publicly provided services are said to **crowd out** the use of private services by directly affected households. Third, changes in the behavior of the directly affected groups can give rise to important spillover and feedback effects, which we examine in Question 6.

In searching for possible impacts on the directly affected, it is useful to ask a series of more specific questions for each of the groups affected by the policy: In what specific ways does this policy change the opportunities or constraints of the directly affected? What behaviors might be altered as a result of these changes in opportunities and constraints, whether now or in the future? After the directly affected have done their best to take advantage of new opportunities and to mitigate the effects of new constraints, what will have happened to their living standards (along multiple dimensions)? What, if anything, can we say about the net effect of all these changes on their well-being? Chapters 15 through 22 familiarize readers with the features of behavior and living standards that are most important to consider when analyzing policies of particular types. Again, the tools of Chapters 6, 7, 10, and 12 are especially useful. After identifying the theoretically possible impacts on well-being and behavior, the policy analyst then seeks empirical evidence on how large or small the impacts are in practice (Box 14.5).

Question 6: When changes in the behavior of the directly affected induce changes in markets, institutions, and the physical environment, what spillover and feedback effects result, and how do these effects vary over time?

Analysis of spillover effects may be important in several ways. Some policies achieve their primary objectives only indirectly through spillover effects.[3] For example, a program that

---

[3] Notice that the distinction between direct and spillover effects is quite different from the distinction between intended and unintended effects. Some spillover effects are very much intended, and some direct effects are unintended.

≡ **Box 14.5** Example Policies: Direct Effects

Mexico's Progresa program

As a cash transfer program, Progresa provides households with additional cash, which they may use in many ways. As a conditional cash transfer program, which requires parents and children to devote time to school and health center visits, Progresa also imposes a constraint on household time allocation. Applying Question 5 in a comprehensive study of Progresa impacts requires careful study of what happens in participating households to school attendance, health center use, work by children (which can fall if their time in school rises), work by adults (who could take advantage of extra cash to reduce labor supply, but who might instead compensate for reduced child labor by working more), current income, and consumption expenditure (which might not rise by the full amount of the program transfer if their labor supply falls). Given the possible existence of liquidity constraints (Chapter 10), households might even use extra cash to undertake investment in financial or physical assets, adding another boost to future well-being (while reducing the impact on current consumption). A complete evaluation would consider all of these possible impacts.

World Learning's CAGE program in Benin

The CAGE program requires community participation in the financing and execution of projects to expand girls' schooling, and it provides community committees with institution- and capacity-building assistance and grants. It can affect local committee members by providing them with skills and information and by placing demands on their time. It may thus be important to consider how their new skills and time constraints affect their involvement in other community activities. The projects ultimately completed might affect households with school-aged children whose values and beliefs are affected by community-awareness campaigns, who take advantage of new school facilities, or who are motivated to work harder by the offer of prizes. To the extent the program increases the time their children spend in school, it might alter household's allocation of time to work or other activities. The need to gather community contributions to help finance local projects implies that the program might also reduce the disposable income of some families, thereby potentially reducing their consumption and saving.

provides loans to the nonpoor owners of medium-sized businesses might aim to reduce poverty indirectly by expanding small business employment and driving up wages for low-wage workers. For other policies, the primary objective is to improve the well-being of the directly affected, but spillovers effects help spread the benefits to additional groups. For example, agricultural research and extension programs might aim primarily to increase the incomes of the farmers who adopt new technologies, but they might also benefit consumers and landless laborers as increased food supplies drive food prices down and increased labor demand raises wages. Unfortunately, policies' spillover effects can also represent unintended social costs. The same food price reductions and wage increases that benefit landless laborers in the wake of agricultural research and extension programs can also hurt other farmers who were unable to adopt the new technologies.

As in the examples just given, many spillover effects are worked out through markets—whether goods markets, labor markets, or financial markets. Such spillover effects are likely to be significant only when policies' direct effects are large relative to the markets in which the directly affected participate. A small targeted transfer program in a large urban area where many markets are well integrated across neighborhoods would induce such small shifts in the relevant demand and supply schedules as to leave market conditions virtually unchanged. A targeted transfer program of the same size can have much more important effects on local markets if implemented in small rural communities where local markets are poorly integrated into larger markets (see Chapter 8).

Other spillover effects are worked out through private institutions. Sometimes institutional rules currently in force induce social responses to policies that alter opportunities or constraints for groups other than the directly affected. For example, in communities where informal insurance institutions require households who are doing relatively well to provide gifts or interest-free loans to households who are doing relatively poorly, a poor household's receipt of cash from a public transfer program might lead other community members to refrain from giving institution-mandated gifts to that household (Chapter 12). Program participants might also feel compelled by social norms to share their good fortune with neighbors. In either case, the program increases the income of households not directly affected by the program (i.e., those who would have given gifts in the absence of the program or those who receive gifts from program participants).

In other cases, the introduction of a new public policy can cause traditional institutions to break down, thereby altering the opportunities and constraints for everyone originally governed by the institutions. The introduction of public safety-net programs might, for example, cause informal insurance arrangements and other private safety-net institutions to fall apart. Any community members who would have received assistance through the private safety nets, and who are not reached by the new public safety net program, are left worse off.

Yet other spillovers are worked out within public institutions. Some policies place additional strain on the limited time or limited budgets of local schools, clinics, and bureaucracies. When a community infrastructure program increases the responsibilities of busy local bureaucrats, they have less time for other responsibilities. This can generate costs elsewhere in the community. When a scholarship program increases the number of children attending school, the resulting rise in student-to-teacher ratios might cause a decline in school quality for other children attending those schools. On the other hand, many current programs seek to generate positive spillovers by providing local decision makers with skills in needs assessment, proposal writing, and financial management that will improve their effectiveness in other areas.

Finally, some spillovers are the result of physical externalities. When directly affected farmers increase their use of chemical fertilizers, for example, the quality of drinking water in downstream communities can decline.

The same forces that generate spillover effects can generate feedback effects that modify the impacts on the directly affected groups. For example, the receipt of a cash transfer allows a household to buy and consume more food. But if many households in a small, remote community receive cash transfers, their increased food demands might drive up the local price for food, reducing the quantity of additional food they enjoy as a result of the cash transfer (in addition to increasing profits for local net food sellers and reducing real incomes for local net food-buying households that do not participate in the program).

In Chapters 15 through 22 we point out the types of spillover and feedback effects most likely to be at issue in various policy discussions. We draw on the analytical tools of Chapters 8, 9, 10, 12, and 13 in working out the possibilities. Box 14.6 discusses spillover and feedback effects for our example policies.

≡ Box 14.6 Example Policies: Spillover and Feedback Effects

Mexico's Progresa program

Cash transfer programs tend to increase beneficiary household spending on food and other basic consumption items. If the effects on individual households are large and if a large fraction of the relevant population receives transfers, then the program can drive up prices for basic goods. Cash transfer programs can also reduce labor supply, tending to drive up wages for comparable low-skilled workers, if the program effects are large relative to the relevant labor markets. Effects in both food and labor markets might tend to create a multiplier effect of the program on local incomes, as incomes rise for wage laborers and small farmers outside the program. Rising prices also induce a feedback effect on those directly affected, however, reducing the transfers' impacts on participants' real consumption.

A program like Progresa might also generate spillovers through various social channels. As indicated in the text, private safety net institutions might induce nonprogram households to reduce their gifts to program households, and program households might give new gifts to neighbors, raising the consumption expenditure of nonprogram households indirectly. By design, Progresa program benefits are distributed only to women within participating households, and the women must gather periodically at pay points to receive the cash. The hope is that the program enhances women's decision-making role within their households and generates more solidarity among women in the community. It is possible that such changes could spill over into changed roles of women within nonparticipating households as well. It is also sometimes feared that programs like Progresa, which provide benefits to some but not all members of a community, might create social divisions and bitterness that reduce the community's ability to live in harmony and cooperate for mutual benefit. Looking further into the future, the program might be expected to drive down the differential between workers with more and less human capital if by raising schooling rates it significantly raises the supply of skilled relative to unskilled labor. It might thus help to reduce income inequality.

World Learning's CAGE program in Benin

The small projects undertaken by CAGE communities are unlikely to have large effects on local markets for goods, services, or labor. If the program sets any important spillover effects into motion, they are likely to be associated with role model effects (in which households directly touched by CAGE projects send more girls to school, perhaps tending to improve the attitudes of their neighbors toward sending girls to school), future increases in the supply of educated labor, and future impacts of the program's institution- and capacity-building efforts on nonprogram community activities.

Question 7: What are the budgetary costs of the policy, and how do they vary over time?

A policy's budgetary costs include the total cost of any subsidies implicit in the provision of transfers or services, as well as any administrative costs of assessing eligibility, monitoring compliance with program requirements or with regulations, distributing benefits, and exacting punishments. The **subsidy** implicit in service provision is the difference between the total cost to the government or NGO of providing the service less any costs recovered by requiring service users to pay fees or requiring beneficiaries or their communities to make contributions or repay loans with interest. The true budgetary costs of a program can differ from the costs appearing in official budgets when the program draws on resources of other programs. Sometimes, for example, a program is run by personnel from a pre-existing program or department, and the full cost of their time is charged to the pre-existing budget rather than to the new program budget. Leaving these costs out might yield an accurate depiction of the costs to this organization, assuming the employees can handle the increased work load by using their time more efficiently. But it might lead to an inaccurate reflection of what it would cost to replicate or expand the program in situations where implementation would require the creation of new bureaucracies.

Program expenses and receipts tend to evolve over time. With time, program staff might improve their capacity to collect fees locally or learn how to divert program resources into private ventures. Beneficiaries might learn ways of evading user fees. Rising awareness can also expand program participation.

Often it is useful to distinguish between one-time and recurrent budgetary costs. Many policies require one-time expenditures for creating assets (such as roads and irrigation systems) or institutions (such as a new microfinance institution). For such programs, it is useful to distinguish between the subsidy required to create the asset (a one-time subsidy) and the subsidy required for ongoing operation and maintenance. Many contemporary development organizations aim for their programs to achieve operational **sustainability**, in the sense that after they have subsidized the creation of an asset or institution, they can leave the financing and execution of operation and maintenance to recipient households or communities. If and when programs achieve sustainability in this sense, lead organizations have no need to stay involved with recipient communities and may **exit**, having handed off all responsibilities to local actors.

It makes most sense to ask Question 7 last (rather than earlier) when policymakers are prepared to cover whatever costs a policy generates, or when policymakers wish to predict the approximate cost of a proposed policy. In such cases the analyst will wish to draw on answers to Questions 2, 3, 4, and 5 in working out the costs (Box 14.7). For example, when predicting the likely budgetary cost of a cash transfer program, it will be important to know or estimate not only the size of benefits to be distributed to households (Question 2), but also the efficiency and integrity with which the bureaucracy will administer the program (Question 3) and the number of households that will participate in the program (Question 4). When predicting the likely

☰ Box 14.7 Example Policies: Budgetary Costs

Mexico's Progresa program

In a cash transfer program like Progresa, the cost of the transfers themselves can make up 70 to 90 percent of total budgetary costs. For the purposes of comparing with other cash transfer programs, it is often useful to express total budgetary costs on a *per–participating household* basis and to break the total down into the cost of the transfers themselves and the administrative costs. Even better, the analyst might recognize that part of the cost of reaching targeted households is the cost of transfers that inadvertently go to nontarget households. It may thus be useful to calculate and compare total program cost *per targeted individual correctly reached by the program*.

World Learning's CAGE program in Benin

While the CAGE program offers some financing for small projects to participating communities, the cost of the grants themselves is small relative to the cost of the personnel and travel involved in the people-intensive work of building community institutions.

budgetary cost of a consumer food subsidy, analysts must consider how many households will consume some of the subsidized food (Question 4) and how much of this food they will choose to consume (Question 5).

Sometimes, however, it makes more sense to address the question of total budgetary costs earlier in the analysis. In some policy analyses the total budget is firmly fixed at the outset. In such cases, total budgetary costs are easily determined, and the challenge for the policy analyst is to figure out how many people can be reached, what value of goods and services can be provided, and what assets can be built and operated from that fixed budget. That is, one must take the fixed total budget into account when answering Questions 2 through 6.

In Chapters 15 through 22, we identify the most important contributions to budgetary costs in each policy area and identify ways of expressing the costs (e.g., on a per-beneficiary or per-kilogram basis) that are most useful in policy comparisons.

14.3 Putting the Seven Questions to Work

The most obvious use of the seven questions is in analyzing the impacts of a policy already in place. The policy analyst may use the seven questions to work out a comprehensive list of the policy's potential benefits and costs and then seek out empirical evidence to illuminate the actual or likely sizes of these benefits and costs in practice. For a discussion of empirical methods, see Appendix A.

Having used the seven questions to sketch out a complete assessment of direct and indirect impacts, the analyst almost always needs to *reorganize* research results for creating clear and useful policy analysis documents. Often it is most useful to divide documents into sections that: describe in detailed fashion the policy under consideration and the context in which it is being implemented; discuss the nature and size of the benefits the policy produces (both directly and indirectly); and describe the nature and size of the costs it produces (both directly and indirectly). (See Chapter 15 for an example.)

Though some rephrasing might be required, the seven questions are also useful for guiding research on other kinds of policy analytic questions, including: What benefits and costs are likely to emerge from a proposed policy? What were the benefits and costs of a recent policy reform? What might be the benefits and costs of modifying a program's design in a specific way? What would be the relative merits of two alternative approaches for trying to achieve the same objective?

When using the seven questions to study policy design changes or policy reforms, or when comparing alternative policy approaches, analysts can answer the seven questions carefully for each of the two policies or designs to be compared (e.g., the "before reform" policy and the "after reform" policy, or alternative policy A and alternative policy B) and then carefully compare the answers, looking for all the dimensions along which the impacts of one policy might look better or worse than the impacts of the other policy. Chapters 15 through 22 provide many examples of such comparisons.

REFERENCES

Carter, C. J. "Rethinking Evaluations in International NGOs: A Study of the CAGE Evaluation in Benin." Master's Thesis, The Fletcher School, Tufts University, 2005.

Kirkpatrick, Colin H., and John Weiss, eds. *Cost–Benefit Analysis and Project Appraisal in Developing Countries*. Northampton, MA: Edward Elgar Publishing, 1996.

QUESTIONS FOR REVIEW

1. Describe in general terms how policies introduce change into socioeconomic systems and how they give rise to both direct and indirect effects.

2. State the "seven questions to guide policy analysis" and for each discuss why we ask it and how we go about answering it.

Targeted Transfer Programs

chapter

Targeted transfer programs distribute cash or food to people in need. Forty years ago such programs were considered relevant to short-term poverty reduction but irrelevant to long-term development, and they were therefore given little attention in development discussions. Today targeted transfer programs are considered essential components of many development strategies. Governments and NGOs use them to raise consumption for destitute households, to encourage investments in children's education, to help ex-combatants reintegrate into post-conflict society, and for many other purposes.

This chapter equips readers to apply Chapter 14's policy analysis approach in the study of targeted transfer programs. Sections 15.1 and 15.2 set out the necessary analytical tools. Sections 15.3 and 15.4 then apply the seven questions in evaluating the benefits and costs of Mexico's Progresa program and in analyzing several important targeted transfer program design choices.

15.1 Targeted Transfer Programs in Developing Countries

15.1A Targeted transfers and development

At first glance, targeted transfer programs do not look very "developmental." They aim merely to distribute supplemental cash or food, rather than to catalyze sustained improvements in people's earnings from regular economic activities; and they have little obvious connection to the asset creation required for economic growth. Even so, transfer programs have gained popularity within development strategies for four reasons.

First, the international development community has come to recognize that some socioeconomic groups have little potential to share directly in the benefits of economic growth. This is true even in rich countries, where disability or old age limit some people's participation in dynamic labor markets. In developing countries, additional groups—such as orphans or those with little education—are likely to remain in great need in the short and medium run. If development is to raise well-being for all groups in society, therefore, policymakers must create **social assistance** institutions, which transfer resources from those whose living standards are high and rising to those whose living standards are low and unlikely to grow soon in the absence of direct intervention.

Second, the development community now recognizes how greatly well-being falls when people are *vulnerable* to fluctuations and shocks, as defined in Chapter 5. The magnitude and frequency of shocks are especially great for the poor and near-poor in developing countries, but shocks—whether to wealth, earnings, or health—remain a part of life even in rich countries. Broad-based development thus also requires the creation of institutions that provide **social insurance**, or the transfer of resources from those whose living standards are normal or unusually good to those hit by sudden loss, so as to prevent living standards from falling too far, and to increase security.

Third, accumulating evidence suggests that liquidity and insurance constraints (as defined in Chapter 10) prevent the poor from investing and thus that transfers directed to the poor can speed economic growth. If the chronically poor are liquidity constrained, then simple transfers might free them to make high-return investments in livestock, equipment, or their children's education. If the poor are insurance constrained, then the availability of safety-net programs might free them to make investments in their farms or businesses without having to fear destitution in the event of investment failure.

Fourth, recent innovations in the design of transfer programs have expanded their potential to produce sustained benefits. For example, **conditional cash transfer programs**—which condition poor families' receipt of benefits on their sending children to school—simultaneously raise beneficiaries' current income levels *and* encourage them to invest in human capital (Rawlings, 2005).

15.1B Targeted transfer program objectives

Most targeted transfer programs share the general objective of reducing current poverty. They differ, however, in their more specific objectives, and these differences have important implications for their design and evaluation. For example, they differ in **target groups**, or the specific groups among the poor and vulnerable that they aim to assist. They might focus on the incapacitated poor, the unemployed, poor families with school-aged children, pregnant and nursing mothers, infants, or drought-stricken farm families. They might seek to provide social assistance to the chronically poor or social insurance to the vulnerable.

Targeted transfer programs differ also in the **target level of income or well-being** to which they hope to raise participating households. Some programs seek to raise incomes above the relatively generous poverty lines of middle-income countries, but the **social cash transfer programs** recently introduced in sub-Saharan Africa seek merely to help destitute households obtain the calories required for survival (Schubert and Slater, 2006). Increasingly, targeted transfer programs also aim to encourage **targeted behaviors**, such as consumption of micronutrients, investments in education and health, or resettlement and reintegration of ex-combatants into civilian society.

15.1C Targeted transfer program design and implementation

Design elements

A targeted transfer program's character and impacts are defined by six sets of design elements: eligibility requirements, behavioral conditions, benefits specifications, recruitment procedures, procedures for distributing benefits, and choice of governance structure. For a description of a targeted transfer program that highlights these design elements, see Box 15.1 on Mexico's Progresa program.

Eligibility rules define which types of individuals or households are officially entitled to receive benefits and typically incorporate some combination of means tests, categorical restrictions, and geographic targeting. **Means testing** requires measurement of potential beneficiaries' incomes or asset levels and awards eligibility only to households with income or assets below specified levels. **Categorical restrictions** limit participation to households with certain easy-to-observe characteristics, such as whether they have at least one child (as in the family allowance policies of Eastern Europe), own land that has historically produced certain crops (as in Mexico's PROCAMPO program), or include members who are older than 60 years (as in some Latin American social security programs). Use of categorical restrictions is also known as **indicator targeting**. In the special case of **geographic targeting**, benefits are distributed only to people residing in certain neighborhoods or villages.

Some programs employ **proxy means tests**, which lie somewhere between formal means tests and simple categorical restrictions. They employ short questionnaires (sometimes called "poverty score cards") containing 10 to 20 simple questions regarding household characteristics that program designers consider good predictors of consumption expenditure or asset levels, and they limit eligibility to people for whom a simple function of these indicators falls within a certain range. For example, program designers might limit eligibility to people for whom at least 5 of 10 indicators of low living standards—such as living in a dwelling with dirt floors—are present. See Schreiner (2009) for an example.

≡ **Box 15.1** The Design of Mexico's Progresa Program

In 1997, Mexico launched an innovative program called Progresa, which was designed to reduce future as well as current poverty. Its most innovative design feature was its use of behavioral conditions, which condition beneficiaries' receipt of transfers on their investment in children's education and health, but every detail of the program's design reflects careful regard for its potential impact on the program's performance.

Eligibility for Progresa transfers is determined through a two-stage process intended to institutionalize objectivity in the distribution of benefits. First, program officials select communities that meet two criteria: They must be among the most marginal localities in Mexico according to an index derived from statistics on illiteracy and access to clean water, and they must have access to public schools and clinics. Second, within program communities, program personnel select households based on a proxy means test. After administering socio-economic questionnaires to all residents of program communities, the program staff identifies households with living-standard measures that meet the proxy means test criteria. They then convene community assemblies at which community members are asked to identify errors in the initial screening and to correct the list of eligible households.

The maximum cash benefit that a household may receive depends on its family structure. Initially, households received education grants for each child younger than 18 years who attended grade 3 through 9. Later, households also received such grants for children in higher grades. Education grants are larger for children attending higher grades and are larger for girls than for boys at the secondary school level. Households also receive grants intended to boost consumption and nutrition. In 2003, the education grants ranged from $10.50 per month for boys and girls in third grade to $66 per month for girls in the third year of upper secondary school; households also received nutrition grants of roughly $15.50 per month. Pregnant and nursing mothers, children four months to two years old, and any children between two and five years who show signs of malnutrition receive nutritional supplements in addition to cash.

The program's innovative use of behavioral conditions attracted worldwide attention. Households' receipt of education grants is conditioned on their children maintaining school attendance records of at least 85 percent. Attendance is verified through documents filled out by school staff. Similarly, receipt of nutrition grants is conditioned on participation in a variety of health-related activities, including preventive-care visits to clinics and attendance at health lectures. Nutritional supplement distribution is conditioned on children's monthly visits to clinics for growth monitoring. The program contains no explicit provisions to facilitate compliance with the behavioral conditions, such as building, staffing, or equipping schools and clinics, but policymakers remain aware of the need for complementary measures, and over time they have made some additional investments in such facilities.

Even the program's logistical details were designed with an eye to their potential impacts on beneficiaries' behavior. Benefits are given directly to the mothers in beneficiary families, with the aim of involving women as much as possible in the disposition of program benefits. The women come to posts near their communities to receive wire transfers, in the form of checks, which they cash immediately. One woman in each community is selected to be the community *promotora*, who channels complaints and problems from the communities to the program and provides beneficiaries with reminders about such things as the need to make clinic visits.

Despite program designers' attempts to involve communities in eligibility assessment, the program's governance structure is, in fact, highly centralized, being executed by a new federal government bureaucracy. In principle, local program implementers are provided with sufficient funding to fulfill program promises to all qualifying families. In practice, while the main cash transfer components appear to have been funded adequately, the nutritional supplements have been available in only limited supply within some communities and were rationed, with priority given to the neediest cases among the eligible.

One final innovative feature built into Progresa's design was the use of the program's roll-out phase for rigorous evaluation of the program's impact using a randomized control trial. The 506 communities to which the program would ultimately be extended during that period were randomly divided into two groups, with the first group of 320 communities receiving treatment by the program in 1998 and the remaining 186 communities receiving treatment only in 1999. Household survey data collected in 1998 (before the program was introduced anywhere) and follow-up data collected in 1999 (when the first set of communities had been treated but the second set had not) thus allow estimation of program impacts using simple and difference-in-differences comparisons of outcomes for sets of treated and untreated communities rendered virtually identical by randomization.

Despite changes in government administration, the Progresa program continues with great popularity, though now under the new name Oportunidades.

Sources: Adato et al. (2000), Behrman et al. (2009), Skoufias and Parker (2001).

At least as important as the eligibility rules themselves are the procedures regarding when, how, and by whom eligibility is assessed. The simplest means tests are based on potential beneficiaries' own answers to the question "What is your income?" while more rigorous tests are based on program officials' administration of questionnaires during visits to applicants' homes or on community elders' identification of needy families within their communities.

Behavioral conditions describe actions that participants must take to remain eligible for transfers. For example, beneficiaries of Mexico's Progresa program continue to receive benefits only if their children attend school and obtain routine physical examinations (Box 15.1). To fully describe such a program, analysts must describe not only the conditions themselves but also the procedures through which compliance with the conditions is monitored and enforced and any efforts made to facilitate poor households' compliance with the conditions (e.g., construction of additional classroom space to facilitate compliance with school attendance conditions).

In some cases, behavioral conditions help render a program self-targeting. A program is **self-targeting** when its behavioral conditions or logistical requirements discourage participation by the eligible nonpoor. For example, program designers might condition the receipt of benefits on the use of government health care facilities, hoping to discourage participation by nonpoor households, who prefer to use higher-quality private clinics. Similarly, by tying the receipt of benefits to the performance of manual labor in a workfare program (a possibility to which we return in Chapter 16), program designers might discourage participation by nonpoor households, for whom the opportunity cost of time is greater than for poor households.

Targeted transfer programs differ most obviously in the nature of benefits they deliver. **Cash transfer programs** distribute cash, whether in the form of currency, debit cards, or electronic transfers to bank or cell phone accounts. **Food-based transfer programs** distribute free or low-cost food or food-stamp documents that may be used to purchase food from the private sector. Food-based transfer programs are defined also by choices regarding which food(s) are distributed and whether they are distributed as cooked meals, nutritional supplements, or unprocessed staple foods.

Critical to the description of transfer programs are the **transfer size specifications**. Transfer sizes may be defined in units of currency or units of food. In the case of **rationed food subsidies**, which allow households to buy limited quantities of staple foods at lower-than-market prices, the size of the implicit transfer depends on the quantity of food households may purchase at the low price (the ration limit) and the difference between the subsidized and market price (the subsidy per unit of food).

Often transfer sizes are calculated according to formulas relating them to individual or household characteristics. Public pension programs, for example, often link the size of a beneficiary's transfer to her pre-retirement earnings, her current age, and the number of years over which she contributed social security tax payments. Food distribution programs might link the quantity of food a household receives to the number and ages of the household's dependents. Policy analysts are especially interested in two features of the formulas that determine transfer sizes. First, what do they imply about the typical generosity of the program? Second, what characteristics and behaviors are rewarded (whether intentionally or unintentionally) with higher benefits payments?

Transfer programs differ also in how people are recruited for participation and in the processes through which people apply for and collect benefits. Some programs send staff door to door to identify the eligible and offer them benefits directly. Others disseminate information about the benefits they offer—through mass media advertisements, dramatic performances on market days, or word of mouth—and require potential beneficiaries to apply.

The time and energy required for participants to collect benefits depends on the number and geographic spread of benefits distribution sites, the staffing of those sites, and the frequency of benefits distributions. Beneficiaries may be required to show special documents or to undergo fingerprint scans to prove their eligibility. Some programs **target individuals** within households by requiring that benefits be delivered only into the hands of particular family members, such as women or school children.

Targeted transfer programs often cover large geographic areas including many communities, and policymakers often determine the program's character and impacts within a given community only indirectly, through their **governance structure design choices**. In fully centralized programs, policymakers make all fundamental design decisions—such as decisions regarding eligibility requirements and transfer sizes—at the highest administrative level, rendering these details uniform across communities. In decentralized programs, policymakers delegate these decisions to local governmental or nongovernmental groups, thereby allowing diversity in program design details across communities. Complete descriptions of transfer programs highlight which actors—central government bureaucrats, local government officials, or community committees—have responsibility for these design decisions.

Even when design decisions are centralized, policymakers might delegate eligibility assessment to local government officials or community committees rather than to central government bureaucrats. They might also delegate some benefits-distribution activities to local officials, community committees, or even private sector agents under contract. For example, some programs employ private banks or mobile phone companies in the distribution of cash benefits, and some hire private procurement companies or caterers to distribute food packages or school lunches.

Given the importance of bureaucrats, committees, private firms, and other agents in implementation, a transfer program's impacts can depend on the budgetary resources, rules, guidelines, and capacity-building services provided by central policymakers to community-level agents; the selection criteria or processes for employees, committees or contractors; and the mechanisms through which implementing agents are held accountable for pursuing program objectives and completing their tasks efficiently (as described in Chapter 13). Officials at the central level might have discretion to allocate program funds across regions or communities as they see fit or may be required to distribute funds according to a rule, such as a rule requiring communities to be given a fixed quantity of funding per capita.

Implementation concerns

What ultimately determines a program's impact is not how it is designed on paper but how it is implemented in practice. When beginning to analyze a transfer program's impact, therefore, it is important to study its implementation outcomes: the funding ultimately provided to diverse communities; the capacity and motivation local implementers bring to their activities; what choices they ultimately make about local program design; and their efficacy, efficiency, and integrity in disseminating information, assessing eligibility, enforcing behavioral conditions, and distributing benefits. Even when local implementers are skilled and well-motivated, they may be prevented from fulfilling all official rules simply because they receive too little funding from the central level. In such cases, they must either introduce de facto eligibility rules that reduce the number of transfers distributed or reduce transfer sizes below official levels.

15.2 The Economics of Targeted Transfer Program Participation and Impacts

We prepare for practical analysis of targeted transfer programs by working through the economics of how targeted transfer programs can affect people, markets, and institutions. More specifically, we prepare to apply Chapter 14's policy analysis approach by developing tools that help us identify: who is likely to be directly affected, what impacts a program might have on the directly affected, the spillover and feedback effects that might arise as the behavioral responses of the directly affected introduce change into markets and institutions, and the program's budgetary cost. Our starting point is the observation that households are directly affected by a targeted transfer program when they **participate** in the program. This means that they receive program benefits.

15.2A Participation decisions and targeting concerns

An important goal of most targeted transfer programs is to reduce current poverty and to do this in a very direct way: by giving cash or food to poor households. To achieve significant poverty reduction without unnecessary cost, a transfer program must attract many poor households to participate while preventing the participation of most nonpoor households. Policy analysts thus concern themselves with two types of transfer program **targeting failure**: **noncoverage of the poor** (or exclusion errors) and **leakage** to the nonpoor (or inclusion errors).

Common sense, together with the economic logic of household decision making discussed in Chapters 6 and 7, tells us that:

> A household will participate in a transfer program only if the household is aware of the program, believes that the private benefits of participation will outweigh the private costs, and is deemed eligible by program implementers.

The **private benefits of participation** might include not only cash or food transfers but also subsidiary benefits such as job counseling services, nutrition lectures, and opportunities to meet with other participants. A transfer's value to beneficiaries might depend on the form in which it is distributed, as well as the program's generosity. The **private costs of participation** include the time, money, and psychological costs of traveling to application and distribution sites, waiting in line, complying with behavioral conditions, dealing with program personnel, and experiencing any stigma associated with participation.

This view of participation decisions suggests that poor households might fail to participate in a transfer program for three sets of reasons. First, some poor households might fail to apply for benefits because they are unaware of the program or their eligibility for it.

Second, some of the targeted poor might fail to pass eligibility tests. Indicator targeting tends to exclude many poor households because poverty is poorly correlated with simple category indicators (see problem 1). For example, programs that limit eligibility to households with elderly members exclude the many poor who live in households without elderly members. Similarly, geographic targeting excludes the poor who live in untargeted communities. Even when programs employ means tests, they can exclude some of the poor, if program implementers apply means tests in a biased fashion or fail to obtain accurate and complete information about households' living standards.

Finally, even among the poor who are aware of a program and are eligible for it, some might fail to participate because they perceive that the costs of participation exceed the benefits. This is more likely to be true when the program is less generous, when the household lives far from application or distribution sites, when application procedures are daunting, and when participants are treated poorly by program staff. Behavioral conditions can also create barriers to participation by the poor. For example, requirements that households send children to school might prevent participation by households that live far from schools.

This simple model of program participation also indicates how difficult it may be to prevent leakage of funds to the nonpoor. Some nonpoor households might participate legally because of inaccurate means testing, because they satisfy categorical or geographic restrictions, or because they are not daunted by behavioral conditions that were meant to deter them. Some leakage to nonpoor households might also arise through fraudulent participation, possibly involving collusion with program implementers.

Unfortunately, policymakers often face a tradeoff between success in preventing leakage and success in covering the poor, because program design changes that discourage the nonpoor from participating tend also to discourage participation by the poor. For example, when means tests based on self-reported income are replaced by means tests based on more demanding procedures for assessing eligibility, implementing agents gain greater ability to identify and reject nonpoor applicants, but the procedures can also prove more daunting for poor, illiterate households. Similarly, when geographic targeting is used to concentrate benefits in a small number of very poor communities, the many poor who live in untargeted communities are excluded. Behavioral conditions tying benefits to use of public clinics might discourage participation by the poor as well as the nonpoor.

In practice, targeting failures are common and can be surprisingly large. Coady et al. (2004) studied 122 targeted transfer programs from around the world, in which poverty reduction was a primary objective. They found that one quarter of these programs were **regressive**, in the sense that a larger share of program benefits went to nonpoor recipients than to poor ones.

15.2B Effects of participation on household well-being and behavior

Effects on well-being

Targeted transfer programs affect participating households' well-being by increasing their non-labor income and by requiring them to undertake any behaviors necessary for collecting benefits or satisfying program conditions. As long as participation is voluntary and participants have accurate information about what a program entails, we expect participation to increase well-being. We also expect that:

> The increase in a household's well-being resulting from participation in a targeted transfer program becomes larger (all else equal) when the program raises the household's nonlabor income by more or requires households to undertake fewer costly behaviors that they would not otherwise have undertaken.

Whether a transfer program is capable of significantly raising well-being depends in great part on the program's generosity, as measured by **official transfer sizes**. If transfers are very small (when considered on a per-household-member basis), the program is unlikely to reduce participants' poverty much. In cash transfer and food stamp programs, official transfer sizes are directly defined by program rules. For food transfers and subsidies, the cash value of the transfer (T) may be calculated as

$$T = (p_u - p_s)F$$

where F is the quantity of food to which households are entitled (in units of, say, bags or kilograms of specific foods), p_s is the subsidized price the household must pay to receive the food (often zero), p_u is the unsubsidized price that the household would have paid for the food in the absence of the program, and $(p_u - p_s)$ is the subsidy per unit of food received through the program. In assessing whether transfers are likely to have a significant impact on poverty, it is useful to compare transfer sizes to the typical levels of income in the target group and to the typical gaps for that group between income and the poverty line. A program makes a greater difference for well-being when it raises income by 50 percent rather than 5 percent, but even so it will have little impact on the headcount ratio if the 50 percent increase leaves most households below the poverty line.

Unfortunately, participants' nonlabor income might rise by less than the full official transfer because participants must pay for transport to collect benefits, local officials demand kickbacks, or budget constraints lead local program implementers to distribute transfers smaller than the official size.

Because net increases in nonlabor income are difficult to measure directly, researchers often seek to quantify a program's impact on well-being by estimating its impact on current consumption expenditure. Care is required when drawing inferences about well-being impacts from impacts on current consumption expenditure, however, because households can use increased nonlabor income to raise well-being in two ways that do not increase current consumption expenditure: reducing labor supply and increasing saving. Thus to get a complete picture of program impacts on well-being, it is useful to estimate impacts on time use, savings, and asset holdings, as well as consumption expenditure (Chapter 2).

Effects on behavior

When analyzing the impacts of transfer programs on participants' behavior, we must recognize that:

> Participation in a transfer program can alter a household's behavior for four reasons: It (1) raises the household's nonlabor income and (2) increases the reward to any behaviors necessary for satisfying behavioral conditions, eligibility requirements, or benefits collection. It can also (3) alter the way women's or children's interests enter into household decision making or (4) relax liquidity constraints.

First, and most obviously, participation increases nonlabor income, thereby relaxing budget constraints and inducing **income effects**. The simple models of consumption and time allocation decisions in Chapter 6, which we combined into a simple model of unitary decision making by wage labor households in Chapter 7, remind us that when households receive more nonlabor income, they use the additional income to increase consumption of all normal goods, while possibly reducing their spending on some inferior goods. From Chapter 10 we know that they might also choose to allocate some additional income to saving and investment. Empirical evidence reviewed in Chapter 6 leads us to expect that an income transfer will raise a poor household's food consumption expenditure by a smaller percentage than it increases the household's income (because as income rises households devote increasing shares to nonfood purchases) and to increase the household's calorie consumption by a smaller percentage than it increases their food consumption expenditure (as the household substitutes toward tastier and more convenient foods that cost more per calorie).

One normal good on which households might spend additional income is home time, or time spent in activities other than income generation, such as rest, child care, schooling, or leisure. When households consume more home time they reduce their labor supply and labor income. In such cases, the transfer raises the household's total income (i.e., the sum of labor and nonlabor income) by less than it increases nonlabor income, and the transfer is said to **crowd out labor income**. Empirical evidence reviewed in Chapter 6 suggests, however, that transfer programs' effects on labor supply tend not to be large.

Second, transfer programs strengthen incentives toward behaviors that are rewarded by eligibility requirements, behavioral conditions, and transfer size calculations, thereby inducing **incentive effects**. Some incentive effects are fully intended. Designers of conditional cash transfer programs, for example, design behavioral conditions with the aim of increasing school enrollment rates. Some incentive effects are unintended, however, and are sometimes undesirable. For example, when geographic targeting limits eligibility to households residing in certain villages, they might encourage families to migrate into the relatively poor target villages or to send their children to live with relatives there. Similarly, when programs tie the size of family allowances to the number of children in a family, they might encourage parents to have more children.

Third, the nonunitary household models examined in Chapter 7 raise the possibility that transfer programs can alter household behavior by altering women's or children's control over household resources. Indeed, program designs often target individuals within households, with the aim of inducing such **intrahousehold effects**. By targeting women within households, program designers hope to increase women's say over how transfers are spent or more generally to improve the treatment of women. By targeting food to schoolchildren at school they hope to increase the share of transfers enjoyed by the children rather than other members of their families and also to improve children's ability to learn while in school.

Unitary models of household decision making, such as those studied in Chapter 6 and the first half of Chapter 7, suggest that attempts to target transfer program benefits to individuals within households might not succeed. If households approach decision making by first taking stock of all household resources, regardless of who brings them into the household, and then

≡ **Box 15.2** Empirical Study of the Flypaper Effect

Seeking to measure the empirical strength of the flypaper effect, Hanan Jacoby (2002) analyzed data on 3,189 children in 159 schools in metropolitan Cebu, the Philippines. Approximately 15 percent of the children participated in a school feeding program, which provided them with snacks containing 20 percent of recommended daily calorie consumption. If the flypaper effect is strong, then participation in the program should raise students' total calorie consumption (including consumption at home and at school) by nearly the full number of calories contained in the snacks. If instead households divide the additional resources among multiple members in the way predicted by unitary household models, then families should reduce the calories consumed by students at home and students' total calorie consumption should rise by much less than the amount contained in the snacks.

Simple comparisons of mean total daily calorie consumption for children who did and did not participate in the program are likely to yield biased estimates of program impact, because the families of children who participate are likely to differ in important ways from nonparticipating families. For example, program officials might have introduced the program only into schools of particularly needy communities. As a result, incomes might be lower in participating households, and this might imply that calorie consumption would have been lower for participating children than for nonparticipating children even in the absence of the program. Under such circumstances, even if the program increased participants' consumption by the full number of calories contained in the snacks, participating children's average total consumption levels might look little better than those of nonparticipants.

To circumvent this problem, Jacoby makes clever use of the difference-in-differences strategy for estimating impact. He argues that if a household shares a child's school snack calories with other household members by reducing the child's food consumption at home, then it is likely to do this on school days, when the children receive snacks, but not on other days. If this is true, then children's consumption on nonschool days should reflect the way children were fed *before* their households were treated by the program, whereas school days reflect their consumption *after* treatment. The difference in average consumption from nonschool days to school days among participating children should thus contain information about program impact.

Unfortunately, this before-to-after change for participants might also include another effect: Nonschool days are holidays and weekends, when families might traditionally eat special meals or otherwise alter their eating patterns. Thus the change in participants' consumption from nonschool days to school days might include the effect of such eating habits as well as program impact and offer a biased impact estimate. Jacoby points out that if such eating habits are the same for participating and nonparticipating families, then he may use the difference-in-differences strategy to obtain an unbiased impact estimate. This involves calculating the increase in consumption from nonschool to school days for participating children (which includes program impact plus habitual consumption differences between school and nonschool days) minus the comparable increase for nonparticipating children (which includes only the habitual consumption differences).

Jacoby finds evidence of a strong flypaper effect. He estimates that the total school-day consumption of participating children increases by 90 to 100 percent of the size of the supplement they receive through the program. This indicates very little sharing of benefits with other household members.

---

deciding how to allocate the resources across uses, then efforts to target individuals should have no impact on household choices. For example, a household might treat food received by a child at school in the same way it would treat a transfer received by an adult at home, using it to raise consumption of all household members. The household might succeed in doing this, even when the child eats all the food provided at school, by reducing the food the child receives at home and using the food freed up to raise the consumption of other household members.

The nonunitary household models discussed in the second half of Chapter 7 create more theoretical space for individual targeting to work. Transfers distributed to specific household members might raise their bargaining power, allowing them to enjoy a disproportionate share of the transfer's benefits. Culturally defined mental accounts might also prevent untargeted household members from appropriating benefits received by targeted members outside the home.

Only a few empirical studies have attempted to estimate the strength of the **flypaper effect**, or the extent to which benefits targeted to specific household members stick to those members (rather than being shared with other members). Somewhat surprisingly to economists schooled in unitary models of household decision making, the evidence gathered thus far seems to indicate that food distributed to children in school feeding programs does indeed stick to the children. See Box 15.2 for an example.

The final mechanism through which transfer program participation might alter behavior involves **liquidity effects**. As discussed in Chapter 10, poor households may be liquidity constrained as a result of financial market imperfections. This means that they face high-return investment opportunities that they would undertake if credit markets worked well but that they do not undertake because they do not have access to adequate financing. If poor households are liquidity constrained, then cash or food transfers might allow them to undertake investments, such as sending children to school, purchasing modern inputs for farm production, or improving the roofs on their homes. This creates the possibility that a transfer program will encourage families to send more children to school even when it places no behavioral conditions on recipients. The logic of liquidity effects also suggests that programs aimed at immediate poverty reduction might yield long-lasting benefits. For households running farms or firms, relaxation of liquidity constraints can also increase production and the demand for labor and other inputs.

15.2C **Targeted transfers and vulnerability**

Some targeted transfer programs seek not only to raise the well-being of the currently poor by increasing their nonlabor income but also to raise the well-being of the vulnerable by promising them income transfers in the future should they fall into need. It stands to reason, though, that:

> Targeted transfer programs are capable of reducing households' perceived vulnerability to shocks only when the programs are characterized by flexibility in targeting, are capable of delivering benefits quickly, and are backed by credible promises of long-term funding.

Few targeted transfer programs achieve the necessary **flexibility in targeting**. Targeting is flexible when program implementers frequently and quickly detect and enroll households who fall into poverty and when they detect and remove from distribution rolls participant households whose circumstances have improved. Means-tested programs in developing countries tend to assess eligibility infrequently and thus lack such flexibility, because means testing is costly and time consuming. In principle, geographically targeted programs could be rendered flexible by redefining the set of program communities each season or year in response to information on where needs are greatest. In practice, however, this may be difficult. For discouraging evidence on the responsiveness to changes in need of geographically targeted emergency food distribution programs in Ethiopia, see Jayne et al. (2002). The workfare programs examined in Chapter 16 have somewhat greater potential to achieve targeting flexibility and reduce vulnerability.

15.2D **Targeted transfers and markets**

Many of the behaviors that change as a direct result of participation in transfer programs relate to participants' supplies and demands in various markets. Such behavioral changes generate spillover effects for other households and feedback effects for the participants themselves. It is thus useful to identify the markets most likely to be affected and the conditions under which the resulting effects might be large enough to matter.

We learned in Chapter 8 that:

> Cash and food transfer programs can have important effects on local markets for food and other basic consumer goods, but only when the programs are large relative to local markets and the local markets are poorly integrated into larger external markets.

In such cases, cash transfers and food stamp programs tend to raise local food prices by increasing local demands for food. This raises well-being for local food sellers and reduces well-being for nonparticipating households that buy food. It also reduces the program's net impact on participant's real income and consumption. Food transfer programs that truck food into remote communities from outside, by contrast, tend to raise local food supply more than local demand, tending to reduce local food prices, thereby benefiting local food buyers and hurting local food sellers.

According to the time-allocation model of Chapter 6, if home time is a normal good, then the receipt of transfer income reduces participating households' labor supply. At the same time, if the program stimulates demand for locally produced goods and services (for which markets are in autarky equilibrium) then increased prices for those goods and services can increase the derived demand for labor by their producers. Liquidity effects can also generate increases in production and labor demand among participating households with farms and nonfarm businesses. Thus,

> When local labor markets are not well integrated into larger labor markets, targeted transfer programs can raise wages through several channels, thereby creating spillover benefits for nonparticipant workers.

Especially when evaluating large transfer programs in remote areas, therefore, it is useful to examine impacts on local prices, local wages, and the real labor incomes of nonparticipants.

15.2E Targeted transfers and institutions

People interact not only in markets but also in nonmarket forums such as neighborhoods, community committees, and public schools, and their interactions are governed by institutions, as defined in Chapter 12. Transfer programs can alter interactions within these forums, and can also alter the institutions that govern them. Here we emphasize that:

> The introduction of targeted transfer programs might induce spillover and feedback effects through impacts within and upon private safety-net institutions, community institutions supporting local cooperation, and public institutions providing education, health care, and other services.

Private safety-net institutions

Consider first the informal insurance institutions described in Chapter 12. Such institutions sometimes guide extended family, neighbors, and co-members of ethnic or religious groups to provide mutual assistance. This means that when any member household is doing relatively well, it must provide assistance to others who are doing relatively poorly. If transfer program participants would have been on the receiving end of such transfers in the absence of the program, then their receipt of public transfers might cause them to lose private assistance from other households, who no longer feel compelled by social norms to help out. In such cases, public transfers are said to **crowd out private transfers** (i.e., replace some or all of the private transfers that program beneficiaries would have received).

Mutual assistance norms can also cause community members to regard public transfer benefits as income that should be shared with other community members (who were not so fortunate as to receive any public transfers directly). Participants in public transfer programs might thus share the benefits with others.

The crowding out of private transfers and the sharing of benefits with others diminish a transfer program's direct impact on participants by reducing the net impact on their nonlabor income (a feedback effect). At the same time, though, these changes bring positive spillover effects for other households as they increase the income retained by the households that would have given gifts in the absence of the program or increase the gifts households receive from beneficiaries.

At least in principle, public transfer programs might so alter socioeconomic conditions within a community as to cause informal insurance institutions to fall apart altogether. When this happens, even some nonparticipating households who would have benefited from neighbors' gifts might lose out on private assistance when the public program is introduced. Community members might also become less likely to provide mutual assistance in the future. Although such displacement of private safety-net activities may be costly for some households, it might also enhance investment and growth by reducing community members' need to share the benefits of their investments with neighbors.

Households might give private transfers to other households even when they have no expectation of receiving return transfers in the future. Such transfers may be governed by altruism and local egalitarian norms rather than by informal insurance motivations. These broader private safety-net transfers, too, may be crowded out by public transfers. Of the handful of recent studies seeking to quantify the crowding out of private transfers by specific transfer programs, however, most find that they crowd out only small quantities of private transfers (Fiszbein et al., 2009). Crowding out might nonetheless be significant for the few households affected, and crowding out may be greater in some contexts.

Institutions supporting community cooperation

Community members benefit from cooperation in creating public goods and protecting local common property resources. Institutions sometimes arise to encourage cooperation at the community level, as we saw in Chapter 12, but such cooperation does not always arise and may be fragile. The forces that determine whether or not communities manage to cooperate are not fully understood, but we might suspect that feelings of solidarity and perceptions of mutual fair treatment help support such cooperation. We might thus worry that the introduction of targeted transfer programs into close-knit rural communities might disrupt cooperation when they privilege some community members over others or create a divide between program insiders and outsiders. On the other hand, transfer programs might strengthen community cooperation when they help create community committees, involve them in program administration, and provide them with training.

Social service institutions

Participants' receipt of benefits from a new targeted transfer program might alter their use of other public programs and services. A first possibility is that they must give up participation in other public programs. This reduces the net impact of the new program on their nonlabor income and well-being, but it can generate a spillover benefit for the government of reduced spending on other programs. A second possibility is that receipt of benefits from transfer programs leads participating households to make greater use of public schools and clinics. This is likely to generate deleterious spillover effects, either for the government, if it spends more on schools and clinics to expand supply in tandem with demand, or for other users of public schools and clinics, who experience increased crowding and reduced quality of education and health services. A third spillover effect mediated by public institutions arises when the implementation of a new targeted transfer program absorbs the time of local officials or bureaucrats, reducing the time they devote to other valuable public-service activities.

15.2F Targeted transfers and the environment

Policy analysts are increasingly sensitive to the environmental implications of policies and programs, and targeted transfer programs can affect the environment through diverse channels. Some school feeding programs degrade the environments around schools, through use of fuel for cooking and disposal of waste. Transfer programs that encourage an expansion of agricultural production, whether by relaxing participants' liquidity constraints or by stimulating demand in local food markets, might also encourage the clearing of valuable forests. On the other hand, income increases might lead households to substitute purchased fuels for collected firewood, reducing pressure on local natural resources and reducing air pollution caused by cooking fires.

15.2G Budgetary costs of targeted transfer programs

A targeted transfer program's total budgetary cost includes both the **total value of transfers distributed** by the program and the **administrative costs**. Administrative costs cover the personnel, vehicles, computers, offices, security services, and other inputs required for disseminating information, assessing eligibility, monitoring and enforcing behavioral conditions, and distributing benefits. They often represent between 10 and 30 percent of total program budgets, but they can rise even higher.

Analysts often compare targeted transfer programs' efficiency by comparing the shares of administrative costs in total program costs. Unfortunately, even when this fraction is very low, leakage rates may be very high, implying that only a small fraction of total program expenditures is reaching the targeted poor. It would, therefore, make more sense to compare total program cost *per dollar correctly delivered to the targeted poor*, which is low only when both per-beneficiary administrative costs and leakage rates are low.

15.3 Evaluating Targeted Transfer Programs

Rigorous evaluation of policies' benefits and costs is vital to good stewardship of scarce development resources. The seven questions introduced in Chapter 14 offered a general guide to identifying all the potential benefits and costs that merit empirical study. Parts 15.1 and 15.2 described what might be involved in applying those questions in the study of targeted transfer programs. Box 15.3 summarizes the practical implications by suggesting how we might customize the seven questions for the case of targeted transfer programs.

After working through the questions in Box 15.3 to identify a program's potential benefits and costs, and studying any available evidence regarding their empirical magnitudes, the policy analyst must synthesize her findings and write them up effectively. It seldom makes sense to organize the presentation of research findings around the "seven questions." Rather, the analyst *re-organizes* her findings in a way that renders them the most coherent and memorable for her readers. For example, the discussion of the Progresa program's benefits and costs in Box 15.4 first offers a comprehensive examination of the program's impact on current poverty, pulling together

---

≡ Box 15.3 Questions to Guide Analysis of Targeted Transfer Programs

Question 1: Objectives

Is the program intended primarily to reduce current poverty, reduce vulnerability, or encourage targeted behaviors? What is the program's target population? What is the target level of income? What are the targeted behaviors?

Question 2: Design

What eligibility requirements, behavioral conditions, benefits specifications, procedures for recruitment and benefits distribution, and governance structure choices define the program on paper?

Question 3: Implementation

Which communities are included in the program, and how are program funds distributed across them? What design choices are made by decentralized decision makers? In practice, what eligibility requirements and behavioral conditions are enforced, what benefits are distributed, and how are participants recruited and benefits distributed?

Question 4: Directly affected groups

Who participates in the program? Which groups among the poor does the program reach (and fail to reach)? How well does the program limit leakage to the nonpoor?

Question 5: Direct effects

How much does participation in the program raise participant households' nonlabor income (taking into account the size of transfers distributed in practice and the costs of collecting benefits), and what costs does it impose? How does participation affect consumption expenditure, nutrition, saving, investment, household labor supply, intrahousehold distribution, and any behaviors rewarded or penalized by behavioral conditions, eligibility requirements, or other program design features?

Question 6: Spillover and feedback effects

What effect does the program have in or on goods and labor markets, informal insurance and other private safety-net institutions, institutions that support community cooperation, public institutions, or the environment, and what spillover and feedback effects result?

Question 7: Budgetary costs

What is the program's total budgetary cost? How do total costs break down into benefits correctly distributed to the target poor, benefits leaked to the nonpoor, and administrative costs?

≡ **Box 15.4** The Benefits and Costs of the Progresa Program

The creators of the Progresa program incorporated plans for rigorous and comprehensive evaluation into the program's design. As a result, much more is known about Progresa's benefits and costs in its early years (1998–2000) than about most other targeted transfer programs in developing countries. The evaluation yielded strong evidence of program success, contributing to its political popularity.

Analysis of benefits

The program's primary objectives were to reduce current poverty through the distribution of cash transfers to poor families and to reduce future poverty by increasing poor households' investments in nutrition, health, and education. The program's design also reflects the subsidiary objective of increasing women's say over how their households spend income.

The program succeeded in reducing current poverty significantly, reaching many of Mexico's rural poor and raising their current income and consumption expenditure substantially. The program distributed benefits to 40 percent of the rural population as a whole and 80 percent of households within the especially poor communities selected for participation (Coady, 2003). Average program benefits equaled roughly 20 percent of average income, and many participants also received nutritional supplements containing 20 percent of daily calorie requirements and 100 percent of micronutrient requirements. Qualitative evidence suggests that Progresa raised some recipient households' nonlabor income by less than the official transfer size, because their *promotoras* charged admittance to meetings, they incurred costs travelling to transfer distribution sites, or they shared benefits with neighbors out of fairness considerations (Adato et al., 2000). The average diversion of official transfers away from recipients cannot have been very great, however, because the program raised participants' average total consumption expenditure by 14 percent, even while some of the additional income was used to increase saving and even though income from child labor fell (Skoufias et al., 2001; Gertler et al., 2012).

Despite the program's broad outreach, it failed to reach some groups among the poor. Geographic targeting naturally excluded the poor who lived in nonprogram communities. Some excluded communities were very poor, having been excluded because they lacked adequate access to schools and clinics. Even within program communities, an estimated 20 percent of the very poor were bypassed (Coady and Parker, 2009). A process evaluation report suggests that some of the very poor may have been missed because they were not home when interviewers came to administer the household census or because they refused to participate in the census (Adato et al., 2000). Community meetings provided little opportunity to identify and incorporate these households, because, in practice, only families already awarded eligibility attended the mandated meetings. Difficulties in obtaining forms for registration at schools and clinics prevented some eligible households from collecting benefits, and some families (especially very poor ones) may have perceived that the cost of sending children to school (and losing their help at home) exceeded program benefits.

The Progresa program seems to have spread some indirect benefits to nonparticipants within program communities. Barrientos and Sabatés-Wheeler (2009) estimate that the program raised food consumption among nonparticipants in program communities by 5 to 12 percent (depending on the year). The authors do not identify the channels through which the program generated such spillover effects,

but several possibilities suggest themselves. Local farmers might have benefitted from increased local demand for food, at least in more remote communities where we would expect such demand increases to drive prices up. They might have responded by increasing the demand for labor, tending to raise wages. Participants might have added further to the increase in labor demand, if the transfers relaxed liquidity constraints, allowing them to invest in expanding their farms or nonfarm businesses. Some nonparticipants also received gifts from participants.

The Progresa program succeeded in improving nutrition, health, and school enrollment, thereby presumably reducing future poverty. Participants increased food consumption expenditure by 11 percent and calorie consumption by 7.1 percent (Coady, 2003). Participation also raised consumption of micronutrient-rich meat and vegetables.

The program's impact on health appears especially impressive. Participation reduced infant mortality rates by an estimated 17 percent (Barham, 2011), reduced newborn illness by 25 percent, increased child height by 1 to 4 percent, and increased child weight-for-height ratios by up to 3.5 percent, while also increasing clinic use, prenatal care, and the frequency of weight checks (Coady, 2003).

Impacts on school enrollment were concentrated among middle-school–aged children. As expected, primary school enrollment rates rose only a little, because primary enrollment rates were already more than 90 percent before the introduction of the program. Middle school enrollment rates, which were much lower prior to the program, rose 7 to 9 percentage points for girls and 3 to 6 percentage points for boys (Skoufias and Parker, 2001).

Focus group discussions suggest that the program had some success in female empowerment, though it is difficult to judge the size and significance of this effect. Women reported that attendance at monthly meetings allowed them to enjoy new kinds of relationships with other women, that they acquired more self-confidence, and that they obtained more control over household resources (Adato, 2000; Coady, 2003).

Analysis of costs

A large program like Progresa naturally carries with it a large budgetary cost. By 1999 the program reached 2.6 million families, with a total budget of $777 million. This is about 0.2 percent of GDP and about $300 per year in total cost per family (Coady, 2003).

Compared to many targeted transfer programs, Progresa's administrative costs were low. Coady et al. (2005) estimate that average administrative costs amounted to 10.6 pesos for every 100 pesos of Progresa benefits delivered in 2000. Recurrent costs were even lower, because this figure includes some costs of a one-time external evaluation and the entire value of some capital expenditures. In 2000, 34 percent of costs related to identifying beneficiaries, 22 percent of costs related to delivering cash transfers, and 18 percent related to certifying compliance with behavioral conditions.

Although significant fractions of Progresa benefits are estimated to have leaked to the nonpoor, the program's targeting approach is considered quite effective at limiting leakage when compared to other social programs in Latin America. According to Coady (2003), 58 percent of program benefits were delivered to households in the bottom 20 percent of the national income distribution, and 80 percent were delivered to households in the bottom 40 percent. Much of the program's success in limiting leakage derived from its use of geographic targeting, which limited participation to residents of very poor communities. Means testing within program communities played a somewhat smaller role. The flow of greater benefits to households with larger numbers of school children helped increase the share of benefits going to the poorest households, because larger families are more likely to be poor in this region. Widespread advertisement of the program, presenting it as intended for the poor, may have helped prevent leakage by discouraging nonpoor households from seeking benefits (Coady and Parker, 2009). Even so, participants, school directors, and others complain that some recipients were not needy (Adato et al., 2000).

The program's outreach among the poor and its impact on school enrollment and clinic use were facilitated by policymakers' efforts to expand supply of education and health services. The costs of this expansion do not appear in the program's budget and are difficult to quantify but are worth acknowledging.

Imperfect means testing within program communities seems to have generated some social cost. According to Adato et al. (2000), many community members felt that *all* community members were poor and in need of assistance, and that the distribution of benefits only to those deemed eligible was unfair. The program thus engendered feelings of resentment and some division between participants and non-participants. Qualitative evidence indicates that in some communities non-beneficiaries reduced their participation in communal work days and stopped paying school fees.

The economic stimulus generated by the Progresa program may have brought with it deleterious environmental effects. As transfers increased households' demand for food and fuel, it might have placed pressure on local natural resources. Alix-Garcia et al. (2010) present evidence that the introduction of Progresa benefits increased rates of local deforestation, but only in communities served by poor roads, where residents presumably had fewer opportunities to meet new demands for resource-intensive goods through imports.

evidence on how many of the poor were reached directly and who among the poor was left out (from research on Question 4) and how large a net effect the program had on the nonlabor income, consumption, labor income, and saving of poor participants, after taking into account both direct and feedback effects (from research on Questions 5 and 6), as well as how many of the poor might benefit indirectly and how much and through what channels they benefit (from Question 6). It then goes on to discuss all additional potential benefits before turning to a comprehensive discussion of the costs.

15.4 Analyzing Transfer Program Design Questions

When policy analysts identify a transfer program's benefits and costs, they provide policymakers with the facts to be weighed when deciding whether or not to continue funding the program in its current form. When analysts identify the benefits and costs of a particular *change* in program design—for example, a change in eligibility requirements, the addition of a school enrollment condition, an increase in transfer size, or a switch from food to cash benefits—they provide policymakers with the facts to be weighed when deciding whether to alter a current program in a particular way or whether to include a particular design feature in a new program. In this section, we describe how policy analysts might use the approach summarized in Box 15.3 to guide research on such **policy design questions**, and we apply the approach in discussing several transfer program design questions of current interest.

15.4A Comparing impacts for two program designs

Policymakers suggest changes to transfer programs in the hope of achieving specific improvements in program performance, such as expanded outreach among the poor, reduced leakage, or improved behavioral impacts. We call such performance enhancements the **design change benefits**. Unfortunately, even when the logic motivating a design change is impeccable, the actual benefits that emerge in a specific empirical context may be small, and the changes almost always bring **design change costs** as well as benefits. Changes that improve impacts on school enrollments can also reduce the program's outreach among the poor, for example, and changes that enhance the program's impact on beneficiaries' well-being often increase budgetary costs.

Thus policymakers ought to weigh the likely empirical benefits and costs carefully when contemplating design changes.

We introduce here the general principle that:

> To identify the potential benefits and costs of altering a program's design in a specific way, the policy analyst compares the potential impacts of two programs: the actual program and a hypothetical program that differs in one or several well-specified design details but is otherwise identical to the actual program.

For example, to identify the benefits and costs of adding school attendance conditions to a social cash transfer program, the analyst would compare the program's actual impacts to the potential impacts of a hypothetical program that is identical except for the addition of the condition that children attend school.

We argue, furthermore, that:

> The seven questions of Chapter 14, applied in careful parallel fashion to two such comparison programs, help policy analysts to specify a design question precisely and to identify potential design change benefits and costs.

In the case of targeted transfer programs, the seven questions of Chapter 14 become the more specific seven questions of Box 15.3. Comparing answers to Question 1 (about program objectives) helps the analyst articulate the primary motivation for the change. Does the design change primarily reflect a change in program objectives or a desire to achieve the same objectives in greater measure or at lower cost?

Working out parallel and detailed answers to Question 2 (on program design) helps the analyst think out in practical terms what would be involved in making the design change and in identifying the features of program design that must be held constant to make the comparison most meaningful. For example, in a Progresa-like program without school enrollment conditions, would transfer sizes still depend on the age and gender of children in the same way, and would the program still bypass communities without adequate access to schools and clinics? When comparing an actual food-based transfer program to a hypothetical cash transfer program, what size of cash transfer would render the two programs comparable, thereby rendering the comparison fair and meaningful?

When applying Question 3 (on implementation) to each of the two programs, the analyst questions whether the design change on paper would indeed translate into an effective design change in practice and looks for implementation problems that might be aggravated or reduced by the design change. When considering the addition of a school enrollment condition, for example, the analyst assesses whether the condition is likely to be enforced and effective. When contemplating a change in governance structure, such as a shift toward greater community participation in assessing eligibility, she considers the potential impacts on the inputs to good decision making—motivation, local information, resources, capacity, and coordinating oversight—brought to bear on decisions regarding eligibility (as discussed in Chapter 13).

Parallel application of Question 4 (on who is directly affected) encourages the analyst to identify groups among the *poor* who would gain or lose coverage as a result of the design change, groups among the *nonpoor* who would gain or lose coverage, and the likely net effects on coverage of the poor, leakage, and total program size. Question 5 (on direct effects) reminds the policy analyst to examine whether the design change might increase or decrease the program's impact on the well-being of households that participate under both designs and whether it might lead to greater or smaller impacts on behaviors of interest (e.g., school enrollment). Question 6 (on spillover and feedback effects) raises similar questions about how spillover and feedback effects might be increased or decreased.

Finally, applying Question 7 (on budgetary costs) reminds the analyst to examine the effect of the design change on administrative cost per beneficiary, leakage rates, total program cost per peso of benefit correctly delivered to the poor, and total program cost.

In what follows we discuss several example questions about transfer program design. The discussions incorporate the results of comprehensive research guided by the seven questions, but they are organized and articulated with the aim of highlighting the tradeoffs policymakers face when making design choices, and thus they make little explicit reference to the seven questions.

15.4B To condition or not?

The tremendous popularity of conditional cash transfer programs (CCTs) is easy to understand.[1] School attendance requirements turn programs of mere income redistribution into programs that promote investment in human capital and growth, and they seem to guarantee that beneficiaries put program benefits to good use. But is this popularity justified? Does the inclusion of school attendance conditions truly increase program impacts on school attendance significantly, and in what ways might it cause program performance to deteriorate? That is, might cash transfer programs without school enrollment conditions—which are called **unconditional cash transfer programs** (UCTs)—perform just as well and in some ways even better than CCTs, at least in some contexts?

The addition of a school attendance condition might have little effect on school enrollments for several reasons. The conditions may be poorly enforced, and even if they are well enforced, the conditions might have little scope to improve enrollment rates, because enrollment rates might already be high even in the absence of the program. More subtly, even when enrollment rates are low in the absence of a transfer program, liquidity constraints may be the primary barrier to school enrollment, and UCTs may be just as effective as CCTs at increasing liquidity and raising enrollments. Thus policy analysts must question how large an improvement in school attendance will result from the inclusion of school attendance conditions.

The most obvious cost of including a school attendance condition is the increase in administrative cost associated with the need to enforce it. Three subtler costs may be more important. First, if the addition of a school attendance condition leads households to undertake schooling investments that they would not otherwise have undertaken, then it probably reduces the program's impact on beneficiaries' current consumption expenditure (as it requires them to redirect some income from consumption expenditure to financing investment in education) and probably reduces the program's impact on their well-being overall.[2]

Second, some of the poorest households may be forced out of the program by school attendance conditions, either because they live in communities without schools or because the private costs of sending children to school (and losing their contributions to household income and child care) are greater than the private benefits of program participation. Imposing school attendance conditions may also exclude households without children, though this cost may be avoided through care in the design of the program change (i.e., inclusion in program design of unconditional transfers for households without children).

A final cost arises if the design change is successful in increasing school attendance. As school attendance rises, policymakers must either incur costs of expanding supply to meet the

---

[1] The text focuses here on conditional *cash* transfer programs, which have come to be known by the popular acronym CCTs, but the issues discussed here relate equally well to conditional food-based transfer programs, such as Bangladesh's Food-for-Education program, which distributed food transfers conditioned on recipients' use of schools.

[2] In a unitary household model, the imposition of a new constraint leaves the single household decision maker worse off. In bargaining models of household decision making, it is possible that the constraint improves the impact on less powerful household members, but it must leave more powerful members worse off. In mental accounts models of household bargaining, it is possible (though by no means necessary) that the imposition of a constraint could leave all members better off, if it increases efficiency in allocation of household resources.

new demand, or they must bear with reductions in school quality as ratios of students to teachers, textbooks, and school facilities rise.

Several recent studies examine impacts of including school attendance conditions in targeted transfer programs. de Brauw and Hoddinott (2008) examine the schooling impacts of Mexico's Progresa program. They identify two groups of participating households for whom (the authors argue) the school attendance conditions were and were not enforced. The first group received the documents required for verifying school attendance and (according to self-report) believed that school attendance was required for receipt of benefits. The second group failed to receive the documents (implying that program officials could not monitor their school attendance) and did not believe that benefits were conditioned on school attendance. The authors conclude that the inclusion of school enrollment conditions added little to the program's impact on enrollment rates for primary school-aged children, for whom enrollment rates were very high even in the absence of the program (and program impacts were very small overall). They find, however, that the enforcement of school attendance conditions increased the rate of older children's entry into secondary school by as much as 18 percentage points. Unfortunately, the study had little to say about the costs of including the behavioral conditions. In particular, it sheds no light on the extent to which the inclusion of behavioral conditions excluded poor families for whom the private cost of compliance with the condition was too high.

Baird et al. (2011) employed a randomized control trial to examine the benefits and costs of adding school attendance conditions to a cash transfer program in a very poor country. They compare the impacts of a conditional cash transfer program and an unconditional version of the same program on girls aged 13 to 22 years in Zomba District, Malawi. They focused on girls who were initially in school and never married and followed the girls for two years. They found that the inclusion of the school attendance condition indeed increased the program's impact on school enrollment, with the CCT program raising the enrollment rate by 11.3 percentage points after two years, whereas the UCT raised it only by 3.3 percentage points (relative to a control group enrollment rate of 70.4 percent). The CCT raised enrollments substantially even when the transfers were as little as $5 per month!

The authors also found, however, that the addition of the school attendance condition prevented some families from participating in the program and that this exclusion prevented the program from generating long-run benefits of a very different sort: reduction in risky sexual behavior and early marriage. Two years after its introduction, the UCT reduced marriage and pregnancy rates among the targeted girls by 8.6 and 7.7 percentage points, but the CCT had little discernible impact on these rates. The results suggest that among adolescent girls who are unlikely to remain in school (even if offered monetary incentives), and who are thus likely to be excluded from CCT programs, the receipt of *un*conditional transfers reduces pressure for marriage and unprotected sex. The inclusion of school enrollment conditions thus prevented participation by families in which additional cash would have significantly reduced risky sexual behavior and early marriage.

15.4C Cash versus food?

Many targeted transfer programs distribute food packages or meals rather than cash. School feeding programs, supplementary feeding programs for women and infants, emergency food distributions, and other food-based transfer programs are often more popular politically than cash transfer programs because they seem to ensure that recipients put all transfer resources to proper use addressing basic nutrition needs. Such programs also seem to be the most natural uses for foreign aid sent to developing countries in the form of food, a significant mode of international development assistance since the enactment of U.S. Public Law 480 in 1954.

The basic model of consumer choice calls into question the assumption that food transfers yield bigger impacts on food consumption, nutrition, and health than cash transfers of comparable size. As we saw in Chapter 6, a food transfer is unlikely to increase the consumption of program foods by the full quantity transferred, because some of the free food substitutes for food the recipient would have purchased out of nonprogram income in the absence of the program. This effectively frees up cash that participants may use to increase spending on all normal goods, including nonfood items, and on saving. In fact, under the assumptions of the basic theory, if the quantity of rice that a program distributes is sufficiently small relative to a household's rice demand, then the rice distribution would have the *same* impact on the household's food consumption and nutrition as would a transfer of cash of comparable value. Food transfers *might* have somewhat greater impacts on food consumption than comparable cash transfers if the food transfers are large relative to nonprogram income, are distributed in the form of foods households prefer not to consume, or if (as in the nonunitary household models of Chapter 7) women have greater say in how to use food transfers than cash transfers, but the differences need not be large. Empirical research is somewhat mixed. Often food transfers have larger impacts on food consumption than comparable cash transfers do, but food transfer impacts nonetheless appear more similar to cash transfer impacts than proponents might have guessed.

Even when food transfers raise food consumption by more than comparable cash transfers, they need not have better impacts on health. When the distribution of food rather than cash leads households to spend larger fractions of their income on food, it might also lead them to spend smaller fractions of their income on shoes, purified water, health care, or other nonfood items also important to health (Barrett, 2002).

Whether or not the use of food rather than cash raises a transfer program's nutrition impact, it can have several other benefits worthy of consideration. First, and most important, when transfers must be distributed in the immediate aftermath of a disaster, and when local food supply is thus low and inelastic (and assuming communities are cut off from larger markets by high transfer costs), the distribution of food transported in from outside the communities may be far more effective at increasing local food consumption than a cash distribution. Under those conditions, cash transfers tend to drive up local food prices, reducing the real value of the cash transfers and failing to raise local consumption (see Chapter 8). Even if the private sector eventually responded with increased supply to the higher local food prices caused by cash transfers, it might do so only with a long lag, as private actors set up new distribution channels. Thus public sector food distributions may be more effective, or simply quicker, than cash transfers at raising recipients' real consumption under such circumstances.

Second, the distribution of food rather than cash might help to reduce leakage. If a transfer program distributes foods that are not highly desired by local populations, especially by nonpoor households, or if the distribution of food is more bothersome and stigma-inducing than cash distributions, then the use of food rather than cash might reduce leakage to nonpoor households. (Unfortunately, it might also cause some poor households to drop out.)

A final potential advantage of food transfer programs relative to cash programs is that transfer sizes specified in units of food maintain their real value over time during inflation, without the need for adjustment by administrators or legislators, while the real value of cash transfers diminishes. Similarly, a uniform transfer size specified in units of food provides uniform real benefits to households in different communities, whereas a uniform transfer size specified in cash would provide different real benefits to households in communities with differing price levels. We expect, for example, that among community markets in food-importing equilibrium, local food prices tend to be higher in more-remote communities (see Chapter 8). Uniform cash transfers would provide smaller real benefits to more remote beneficiaries under those circumstances.

Although the distribution of food rather than cash can bring design change benefits, it also brings design change costs. First, under the assumptions of basic consumer theory (Chapter 6), when food-based transfers increase food consumption by more than comparable cash transfers, the use of food rather than cash also *reduces* the program's impact on recipients' well-being. Thus food transfers might generate less satisfaction among recipients than comparable cash transfers. Second, when transfers are distributed in remote communities, the food brought in from outside can discourage local food production and depress the local economy (by driving prices down in the presence of elastic supply), whereas the distribution of cash would push local prices up and encourage local production (Chapter 8). We expect the stimulation of the local economy to be important primarily for long-term transfer programs in remote communities, where food markets are cut off from larger markets by high transfer costs but local producers have the scope to increase production in response to price increases. Third, food may be easier to pilfer en route to distribution than some forms of cash transfer, such as checks or electronic transfers.

Many practitioners (and even many well-trained economists!) assume that the budgetary cost of distributing a food transfer is higher than the budgetary cost of distributing a comparable cash transfer because food transfers require the government or NGO administering the program to bear the cost of transporting and distributing food (which is bulky and perishable). This reflects imprecise thinking, however, which implicitly assumes that the cost of transporting food into food-short communities somehow disappears when policymakers switch from distributing food to distributing cash. These costs do not disappear, because recipients of cash transfers must purchase food from private vendors, who must transport food into the food-short communities. If the local market is in competitive importing equilibrium, the local price of food includes the cost of purchasing the food in the external market *plus* the cost of transporting the food into the community and distributing it (see Chapter 8). The shift from food to cash transfers thus brings a shift of food transport and distribution activities (for the food ultimately consumed by transfer recipients) from the public to the private sector.

A precise comparison of the budgetary costs of distributing food and cash transfers becomes possible when we carefully define what we mean by food and cash transfers "of comparable size." In a fair comparison, we compare the cost of distributing a bag of food in a given community to the cost of delivering enough cash that a recipient could buy a comparable bag of food from the private sector *in the same community*. The total budgetary cost of delivering the bag of food is equal to the price of the food in, say, the capital city (where the government procures it) plus the public sector's cost of transporting and distributing it. If the private sector, too, must truck the food in from the capital city, then the total cost to the government of delivering the comparable cash transfer equals the local price of the bag of food (which includes the cost of procuring the food in the capital city plus the private sector's transport and distribution costs) *plus* the costs of distributing the cash itself. After working through this precise comparison, we see that the total budgetary cost of delivering a food transfer is greater than the total cost of delivering a cash transfer of the same real value to the recipient only if the public sector's cost of transporting and distributing a given quantity of food is greater than the private sector's cost of transporting and distributing that quantity of food *plus* the public sector's costs of transporting and distributing the relevant cash.

Whether food distributions bring higher budgetary cost than distributions of comparable cash transfers therefore depends on context. Where an efficient public sector bureaucracy benefits from scale and experience in food distribution, especially where cash distributions are made costly by the need to carry currency from the capital city into remote areas in heavily guarded trucks, the total cost of providing food transfers may be smaller than the cost of providing recipients with enough cash to purchase the same quantities of food from the private sector. Cash transfers may be significantly cheaper than comparable food transfers, however, when competitive pressures lead to better governance and greater efficiency in private sector distribution. The private sector might do a better job of preventing loss to food decay and might procure food for sale to beneficiaries from nearby communities, while the public sector ships food in from farther away. The cost advantage of cash transfers also tends to be greater where more-developed financial systems allow program staff to obtain currency from local bank branches (rather than transporting it from the capital) or to avoid the use of currency altogether by distributing cash transfers electronically.

In summary, context matters when deciding whether a transfer program should distribute benefits in food or cash. Food transfers are the most attractive compared to cash transfers in the immediate aftermath of supply shocks that limit local food supply, especially when local food markets are poorly integrated into larger markets. The potential advantages of food distributions also tend to be higher when the foods distributed discourage participation by the nonpoor (but not the poor), when public sector food distribution systems are well governed, and when financial institutions are poorly developed and security is poor.

15.4D Involve the community?

In the governance of transfer programs, as in the governance of many other interventions, policymakers increasingly hope to improve performance by increasing "community participation" (Conning and Kevane, 2002). To increase **community participation**, policymakers give community representatives authority over specified design or implementation choices, which would otherwise have been made by government bureaucrats. In several recently introduced social cash transfer programs in sub-Saharan Africa, community responsibilities are borne by small, newly formed community welfare committees, and the committees are charged with assessing eligibility according to criteria set by central-level policymakers (Schubert and Slater, 2006). The Uzbek government took a somewhat different approach, involving preexisting quasi-religious community organizations called *mahallas* in program implementation. The *mahallas* were called upon not only to assess eligibility but also to determine local eligibility rules and transfer sizes, subject to a budget constraint (Micklewright and Marnie, 2005).

Policymakers hope that by moving eligibility assessments and benefits distribution from bureaucrats into the hands of local decision makers, they will improve targeting outcomes and program performance more generally. Targeting might improve because local decision makers have better information about local households' living standards and activities, which allows them to assess eligibility more accurately. They might also have greater capacity to use moral suasion to keep nonpoor neighbors from seeking benefits, and they might have stronger motivation to please their neighbors by disseminating information about the program, recruiting applicants, and distributing benefits efficiently. Policymakers might also hope to improve the population's satisfaction with transfer programs by shifting the definition of eligibility requirements and transfer sizes into the hands of decision makers with better knowledge of what local households consider fair and important. In addition, policymakers often hope that community-oriented reforms will reduce administrative costs by shifting administrative tasks from paid bureaucrats to local committee members who work as volunteers or for token payments.

Unfortunately, as emphasized in Chapter 13, reforms that increase community participation can fail to produce the desired benefits. Community committees might divert funds to personal uses or put little effort into assessing eligibility. Elite capture might lead them to assess eligibility in a biased fashion, and they might simply lack capacity for reaching collective agreements and administering programs effectively. In communities where households are spread out geographically or segmented into social groups that interact very little, the assumption that they have better information about community members' living standards than government bureaucrats may also be incorrect.

Even when community participation increases the quality of targeting *within* each community, it can worsen the targeting of benefits *across* communities. Communities must be given firm limits on the total volume of benefits they may distribute. Without such limits they would be tempted to exaggerate the extent of poverty in their communities in order to bring in more central government funding. Unfortunately, the fixed budget limits must be determined before communities assess eligibility, and thus before they gather accurate information on local living standards. This means that the government must determine how large a budget to allocate to a community on the basis only of external and imperfect data. At best, the government might have access to recent census or survey data, which indicate roughly how poverty counts vary across communities. More often, all they know about communities are the approximate sizes of their total populations, and the best they can do is to allocate funds to communities according to a per capita funding rule. The social cash transfer programs mentioned earlier, for example, provide community committees with budgets just large enough to fund transfers for 10 percent of their populations, regardless of how many local families are poor by an absolute standard. Such a budget allocation rule can lead to the exclusion of many poor households in communities with high poverty rates.

Few empirical studies offer rigorous impact estimates for participatory reforms. Case studies suggest that some community committees are captured by the elite, whereas others perform their tasks fairly and well (Conning and Kevane, 2002). The *mahallas* of Uzbekistan, for example, appear to do a good job of targeting benefits to the poor, although they exhibit a small bias in favor of Muslim households. The *mahalla*-based transfer program also suffers from targeting errors induced by poor allocations of funds across regions (Micklewright and Marnie, 2005). Box 15.5 describes a thought-provoking randomized control trial designed to illuminate the relative merits of involving communities rather than bureaucrats in eligibility assessment in Indonesia.

☰ Box 15.5 Proxy Means Testing versus Community Eligibility Assessment in Indonesia

In 2008, Vivi Alatas, Abhijit Banerjee, Rema Hanna, Benjamin Olken, and Julia Tobias collaborated with the Indonesian government in fielding a randomized comparison of three approaches to assessing eligibility for a transfer program: proxy means testing, community-based eligibility assessment, and a hybrid of the two (Alatas et al., 2012). They randomly assigned 640 communities into three treatment groups. In each of the three treatments, households within each community were ranked by a measure of well-being, and transfers were distributed to an externally determined number of households from the bottom of the ranking. The three treatments differed in the methods used for ranking households. In the proxy means test (PMT) treatment, the households were ranked by estimates of household per-capita consumption expenditure based on 49 relatively easy-to-observe indicators related to household assets and demographics. The formulas used to predict consumption expenditure based on these indicators were derived through econometric study of preexisting household survey data, and program staff obtained the indicator data by administering questionnaires to all households. In the community assessment treatment, program staff invited community members to meetings at which they ranked the communities' households from richest to poorest. On average, meeting attendees had to rank 54 households and the process took 1.7 hours. In the hybrid treatment, the community ranking exercise was performed first and then eligibility was determined by performing the PMT only on households that ranked below or near the eligibility threshold in the community-ranking exercise.

To create an objective standard against which to measure the targeting performance of the three approaches, the researchers used baseline data to rank households by a direct measure of per capita consumption expenditure and identified households as poor when this measure fell below $2 per day. The PMT is meant to approximate such a means test based on per capita consumption expenditure but might yield targeting errors because the PMT index constructed from 49 indicators estimates per capita consumption expenditure only imperfectly. Community ranking might produce fewer targeting errors, because communities might have more accurate and complete information about households' consumption expenditure than is included in PMT indices, but community ranking might instead produce more targeting errors for two reasons. Community meetings might produce poor rankings because the elite take over and bias the assessments or because weak effort prevents accuracy. Alternatively, community meetings might produce accurate assessments of well-being but draw on community members' broad knowledge of households'

circumstances to award eligibility based on a better, more-holistic welfare standard than per capita consumption expenditure. They might, for example, base their assessments on households' vulnerability and hope for the future, in addition to their current per capita consumption expenditure.

The results indicate that all three approaches to eligibility assessment produce significant errors relative to the per capita consumption expenditure standard, with 32 percent of all households mistargeted, 20 percent of nonpoor households incorrectly receiving benefits and 53 percent of poor households incorrectly excluded. Somewhat reassuringly, most of the errors involved households either just below or just above the poverty line. Overall, the community and hybrid approaches produced more targeting errors than the PMT, though only by a few percentage points. Among the very poor (with consumption expenditure per capita below $1 per day), however, the community method performed at least as well as the PMT.

The authors argue that some of the apparent errors in community-based targeting reflect communities' use of more holistic measures of well-being rather than elite capture. In a randomly selected subset of community treatment locations, all community members were invited to participate in the ranking meetings, while in others only the "elite" (i.e., seven people invited by the village head) participated, and this made no difference for targeting outcomes. This does not rule out elite capture, because the elite may be capable of imposing their will even on larger meetings, but neither does it give cause to worry that elite capture is a serious problem. Furthermore, researchers found that households related to the community elite were no more likely to receive transfers than others. The community assessment method left more community members satisfied with the program than they were with the PMT, and rankings provided by randomly selected community members correlated more strongly with community-based rankings than with consumption expenditure rankings. Regressions revealed that after controlling for households' per capita consumption expenditure, communities were more likely to award benefits to households headed by widows and less likely to award benefits to households related to the community's elite or with relatives living outside the village.

Fatigue may be a greater barrier to targeting accuracy in community ranking exercises in Indonesia than elite capture. Researchers found that targeting errors were significantly worse for households considered later in the ranking meetings. We might also suspect that the quality of such rankings depends greatly on the skill and effort of the program staff who lead the ranking exercises.

REFERENCES

Adato, Michelle. "The Impact of Progresa on Community Social Relationships." Washington, D.C.: International Food Policy Research Institute, 2000. http://www.ifpri.org/sites/default/files/publications/adato_community.pdf

Adato, Michelle, David Coady, and Marie T. Ruel. "An Operations Evaluation of Progresa From the Perspective of Beneficiaries, *Promotoras*, School Directors, and Health Staff." Washington, D.C.: International Food Policy Research Institute, 2000. http://www.ifpri.org/sites/default/files/publications/adato_operations.pdf

Alatas, Vivi, Abhijit Banerjee, Rema Hanna, Benjamin A. Olken, and Julia Tobias. "Targeting the Poor: Evidence from a Field Experiment in Indonesia." *The American Economic Review* 102(4): 1206–1240, 2012. doi: 10.1257/aer.102.4.1206

Alix-Garcia, Jennifer, Craig McIntosh, Jarrod R. Welch, Jarrod and Katharine R. E. Sims. "The Ecological Footprint of Poverty Alleviation: Evidence From Mexico's Oportunidades Program," 2010. http://ssrn.com/abstract=1568245 or http://dx.doi.org/10.2139/ssrn.1568245

Baird, Sarah, Craig McIntosh, and Berk Özler. "Cash or Condition? Evidence From a Cash Transfer Experiment." *The Quarterly Journal of Economics* 126(4): 1709–1753, 2011. doi:10.1093/qje/qjr032

Barham, Tania. "A Healthier Start: The Effect of Conditional Cash Transfers on Neonatal and Infant Mortality in Rural Mexico." *Journal of Development Economics* 94(1): 74–85, 2011. doi:10.1016/j.deveco.2010.01.003

Barrett, Christopher B. "Food Security and Food Assistance Programs." In Bruce L. Gardner and Gordon C. Rausser (eds.). *Handbook of Agricultural Economics*, Volume 2, Part B. Amsterdam: Elsevier, 2002, pp. 2103–2190. doi:10.1016/S1574-0072(02)10027-2

Barrientos, Armando, and Rachel Sabatés-Wheeler. "Do Transfers Generate Local Economy Effects?" Brooks World Poverty Institute (BWPI) Working Paper 106. Manchester, UK: University of Manchester, 2009. http://www.bwpi.manchester.ac.uk/resources/Working-Papers/bwpi-wp-10609.pdf

Behrman, Jere, Susan W. Parker, and Petra E. Todd. "Schooling Impacts of Conditional Cash Transfers on Young Children: Evidence from Mexico." *Economic Development and Cultural Change* 57(3): 439–477, 2009. doi: 10.1086/596614

Coady, David P. "Alleviating Structural Poverty in Developing Countries: The Approach of Progresa in Mexico." Washington, D.C.: International Food Policy Research Institute, 2003. http://go.worldbank.org/IA5P54CRT1

Coady, David P., Margaret E. Grosh, and John Hoddinott. "Targeting Outcomes Redux." *The World Bank Research Observer* 19(1): 61–85, 2004. doi:10.1093/wbro/lkh016

Coady, David P., and Susan W. Parker. "Targeting Performance Under Self-Selection and Administrative Targeting Methods." *Economic Development and Cultural Change* 57(3): 559–587, 2009. doi:10.1086/596778

Coady, David P., Raul Perez, and Hadid Vera-Llamas. "Evaluating the Cost of Poverty Alleviation Transfer Programs: An Illustration Based on Progresa in Mexico." FCND Discussion Paper 199. Washington, D.C.: International Food Policy Research Institute, 2005. http://www.ifpri.org/sites/default/files/publications/fcndp199.pdf

Conning, Jonathan, and Michael Kevane. "Community-Based Targeting Mechanisms for Social Safety Nets: A Critical Review." *World Development* 30(3): 375–394, 2002. doi:10.1016/S0305-750X(01)00119-X

de Brauw, Alan, and John Hoddinott. "Must Conditional Cash Transfer Programs be Conditioned to be Effective?: The Impact of Conditioning Transfers on School Enrollment in Mexico." IFPRI Discussion Paper 00757. Washington, D.C.: International Food Policy Research Institute, 2008. http://www.ifpri.org/sites/default/files/publications/ifpridp00757.pdf

Fiszbein, Ariel, Norbert Schady, Francisco H.G. Ferreira, Margaret Grosh, Niall Keleher, Pedro Olinto, and Emmanual Skoufias. *Conditional Cash Transfers: Reducing Present and Future Poverty*. A World Bank policy research report. Washington D.C.: World Bank, 2009. http://documents.worldbank.org/curated/en/2009/01/10298306/conditional-cash-transfers-reducing-present-futurepoverty

Gertler, Paul, Sebastian Martinez, and Marta Rubio-Codina. "Investing Cash Transfers to Raise Long-Term Living Standards." *American Economic Journal: Applied Economics* 4(1): 164–192, 2012. doi: 10.1257/app.4.1.164

Jacoby, Hanan G. "Is There an Intrahousehold 'Flypaper Effect'? Evidence From a School Feeding Programme." *The Economic Journal* 112(476): 196–221, 2002. doi:10.1111/ecoj.2002.112.issue-476

Jayne, Thomas S., John Strauss, Takashi Yamano, and Daniel Molla. "Targeting of Food Aid in Rural Ethiopia: Chronic Need or Inertia?" *Journal of Development Economics* 68(2): 247–288, 2002. doi:10.1016/S0304-3878(02)00013-5

Micklewright, John, and Sheila Marnie. "Targeting Social Assistance in a Transition Economy: The Mahallas in Uzbekistan." *Social Policy & Administration* 39(4): 431–447, 2005. doi:10.1111/spol.2005.39.issue-4

Rawlings, Laura B. "A New Approach to Social Assistance: Latin America's Experience With Conditional Cash Transfer Programmes." *International Social Security Review* 58(2–3): 133–161, 2005. doi:10.1111/j.1468-246X.2005.00220.x

Schreiner, Mark. "A Simple Poverty Scorecard for Cambodia," 2009. http://www.microfinance.com/#Cambodia

Schubert, Bernd, and Rachel Slater. "Social Cash Transfers in Low-Income African Countries: Conditional or Unconditional?" *Development Policy Review* 24(5): 571–578, 2006. doi:10.1111/j.1467-7679.2006.00348.x

Skoufias, Emmanuel, and Susan Wendy Parker. "Conditional Cash Transfers and Their Impact on Child Work and Schooling: Evidence From the Progresa Program in Mexico." *Economía* 2(1): 45–86, 2001. doi:10.1353/eco.2001.0016

QUESTIONS FOR REVIEW

1. For what reasons are targeted transfer programs considered important in development strategies?

2. What are some ways policy objectives can vary across targeted transfer programs?

3. What policy design features distinguish one targeted transfer program from another?

4. What policy design and implementation outcomes merit consideration when examining how a targeted transfer program functions in practice?

5. Why are households' program participation decisions of interest in the study of targeted transfer programs' impacts?

6. Describe the simple model of program participation examined in the text and discuss the guidance it offers for studying the impacts of targeted transfer programs.

7. Why might a program's impact on a household's nonlabor income be overstated by the official size of the transfer program? Why might it be understated by estimates of the program's impact on household consumption expenditure?

8. Why and how might participation in a targeted transfer program cause a participating household to change its behavior?

9. Under what conditions might a targeted transfer program reduce vulnerability for households who do not currently participate?

10. Discuss the possible impacts of targeted transfer programs on goods and labor markets, private and public institutions, and the environment, and discuss the spillover and feedback effects that might result.

11. What are the key categories of targeted transfer budgetary costs, and what might policymakers want to know about them?

12. How, in general, can we employ the questions in Box 15.3 for studying the benefits and costs of possible *changes* in the design of a targeted transfer program?

13. Discuss the benefits and costs of adding school attendance conditions to a targeted transfer program.

14. Discuss the benefits and costs of transforming a food transfer program into a cash transfer program with comparable eligibility requirements, behavioral conditions, and generosity.

15. What are some ways policymakers have tried involving communities in the design or implementation of cash transfer programs? Discuss the potential benefits and costs of shifting from a centralized governance structure to greater community participation.

QUESTIONS FOR DISCUSSION

1. Consider the questions listed in Box 15.3.
   a. Discuss why each question is of interest in policy analysis.
   b. For each sub-question listed under questions 3 through 6, describe the analytical frameworks that policy analysts might use when brainstorming about possible answers, and discuss how the details of a program's design and context might influence the answers.
   c. Answer each question for Mexico's Progresa program, drawing on the information presented in Boxes 15.1 and 15.4.

2. Outline the points made in Box 15.4. Identify which of the questions in Box 15.3 might have prompted you to uncover each of the points you just outlined.

3. Read Micklewright et al. (2005) on the *mahalla*-based cash transfer program in Uzbekistan. Think through the questions in Box 15.3 and for each one consider: "What more specific questions should I ask when applying this question to this program?" and "What (if anything) do I learn about the answers to these questions from this paper?"

4. Consider the question: "What are the potential benefits and costs of transforming an unconditional cash transfer (UCT)

program into a conditional cash transfer (CCT) program, by adding a school attendance condition?"
   a. How would you use the questions in Box 15.3 to help you work out a comprehensive answer? More specifically, describe the two programs for which you would examine potential impacts in parallel fashion.
   b. Discuss the potential benefits and costs that are brought to light by comparing answers to each of questions 4 through 7.
   c. Compare your list of potential benefits and costs with the potential benefits and costs discussed in section 15.3B.

5. In some countries affected by HIV/AIDS, as many as 20 percent of children younger than 15 years are orphans. They may be maternal orphans (who have lost their mother), paternal orphans (who have lost their father) or double orphans (who have lost both parents). Some orphans live with a surviving parent, some live in child-headed households, and some are cared for by adults under informal fostering arrangements. Foster parents may be grandparents, other relatives, or unrelated adults in the children's communities. Many orphans and other members of the households in which they live are poor, and many orphans are vulnerable to exploitation or ill treatment, having no adults to look out for

their interests. Most foster families care as best they can for foster children, but some foster children are taken in by foster parents who treat them more like unpaid servants than like children.

a. Suppose you are asked to design a targeted transfer program that will help orphans or foster families in some way. What are some possible *objectives* that might guide your program design? Please state each possible objective as specifically as possible, identifying the target group and the primary dimensions of well-being or behavior the program might aim to improve.

b. Suppose you are asked to create a program that pays foster parents of orphans to help defray the costs of fostering and to encourage more fostering. What practical questions would you have to answer when defining *eligibility rules* and *eligibility assessment procedures*?

c. Discuss the potential benefits and costs of a program that provides monthly transfers of a fixed per-orphan amount to any adult household head who provides foster care for one or more child orphans in his or her home. To answer this question, first use the questions in Box 15.3 to brainstorm about the program's potential direct and indirect impacts. When brainstorming answers to the questions listed under questions 4 and 5 in the box, notice that different groups of households might be affected in different ways. For example, households that were already fostering orphans are affected differently than households that take in foster children in response

to the program. Notice also that different groups of households (e.g., those headed by well-intentioned parents and those headed by exploitative parents) enter into policy analysis in different ways.

d. Now discuss the potential benefits and costs of replacing the program described in part c by a program that is in every way identical except for the addition of the behavioral conditions that (1) the orphans attend school at least 85 percent of the time and (2) the orphans are receiving adequate care, as evidenced by the results of unannounced home visits by program staff. To answer this question, take the approach described in section 15.4A.

6. Suppose a sample survey reveals that 30 percent of the truly poor fail to participate in a cash transfer program. You are hired to prepare a report in which you list potential program changes that might reduce this nonparticipation rate, discussing the costs and benefits of each potential change. Which program design features would you consider changing? What potential costs and benefits would be associated with each?

7. Suppose a sample survey reveals that 50 percent of participants in a cash transfer program are, in fact, not poor. You are hired to prepare a report in which you list potential program changes that would reduce this leakage rate, discussing the costs and benefits of each potential change. Which program design features would you consider changing? What costs and benefits would be associated with each change?

PROBLEMS

1. You are asked to evaluate two very simple alternative transfer programs that provide transfers of $100 to all eligible households in a particular region. In both programs, targeting is based solely on a single categorical restriction. Policy A limits eligibility to households with illiterate household heads. Policy B limits eligibility to households with disabled household heads. The following table describes the population in the program region.

	Poor Households	Nonpoor Households	All Households
Total number of households	1,000	2,000	3,000
Percentage of household heads who are illiterate	80	1	27.3
Percent of household heads who are disabled	20	5	10

a. Assume for this part that program staff are able to accurately identify whether a household head is illiterate or disabled (or both), and that they indeed provide transfers to all eligible households and withhold transfers from all ineligible households. Fill in the following table.

	Policy A	Policy B
Percentage of poor households covered by the program		
Total dollars transferred to poor households		
Total dollars transferred to nonpoor households		
Total dollars transferred to all households		

b. Now abandon the assumption that program staff can identify illiterate and disabled household heads perfectly and think practically about the challenges of implementing categorical restrictions tied to illiteracy and disability in a real-world program. First for Policy A and then for Policy B discuss:

- What practical rules and procedures might be involved in testing for eligibility?
- For what reasons might the actual coverage of the poor be lower or higher than the coverage rate you calculated in part a?
- For what reasons might the volume of funds leaked to the nonpoor be lower or higher than you calculated in part a?

c. For which of the two programs do you expect the practical difficulties of part b to lead to larger increases in leakage rates relative to the (unrealistic) calculations of part a?

d. How might the two programs differ in their ability to target funds to the poorest and most vulnerable among the poor?

e. How might the two programs differ in the way they modify the incentives of potential program participants?

f. Write up a succinct, clear paragraph summarizing your analysis of the relative merits of Policies A and B, drawing on everything you learned in parts a through e. That is, write up a summary discussion of the likely benefits and costs of choosing Policy A *relative to* Policy B (or vice versa).

2. Mexico's PROCAMPO program was introduced to compensate farmers for crop price reductions associated with the North American Free Trade Agreement (NAFTA) and to support farmers as they transitioned away from producing the affected crops into new economic activities. Farmers were eligible if they cultivated one of nine qualifying crops in the three years just before NAFTA went into effect. Farmers received payments equal to about $70 per hectare of qualifying land (i.e., land on which qualifying crops had been grown in 1991–1993). The program was implemented by program staff located in government offices in major market towns and was publicized on radio and TV. At the beginning of each planting season, eligible farmers could claim payments at program offices, as long as they continued to cultivate any crops (not just the crops affected by NAFTA) on their qualifying land. To put this another way, farmers could not continue to collect benefits if their qualifying land was idle, and no one could collect benefits if the land had been sold or given to new owners. The program was originally designed to make these payments at the initial levels for 10 years, and then to reduce the per-hectare payments down to zero over a five year phase-out period.

a. What are PROCAMPO's eligibility requirements? What are PROCAMPO's behavioral conditions? Why do you think eligibility is tied to historical cultivation of NAFTA crops rather than to current cultivation of those crops?

b. Given what you know about the program's design, what concerns do you have about potential poverty targeting failures?

3. Discuss the potential benefits and costs of replacing a means-tested cash transfer program implemented in every one of a country's communities by a program that first employs geographic targeting to identify program communities and then implements the same means test to assess eligibility within communities. Use the approach described in section 15.4A to develop a list as comprehensive and specific as possible of the potential benefits and costs. Be sure to identify the groups most likely to experience the various benefits and costs.

4. Consider two quite different food-based transfer programs that might be used to encourage school attendance. A *food-for-education* program offers monthly distributions of uncooked bulk food for households whose children attend school on the days food is distributed. A *school feeding program* provides a prepared meal to children daily at school. Discuss the potential benefits and costs of shifting from the food-for-education bulk distribution program to the school feeding program, while leaving the total caloric content of the benefits roughly the same per month per household.

Workfare

Workfare programs provide opportunities for poor households to earn income by performing low-skill labor in public works projects. They can be thought of as targeted transfer programs in which the distribution of benefits is conditioned on the recipients' fulfillment of work requirements. They have greater potential than other transfer programs to reduce poverty in a "self-targeting" fashion while also reducing vulnerability and speeding economic growth. Success in all of these areas is far from guaranteed, however. Economic analysis offers useful insights into workfare programs' potential and limitations.

16.1 Workfare in Developing Countries
16.1A The multidimensional appeal of workfare programs

Workfare programs—also known as programs of direct employment, labor-intensive public works, cash for work, or food for work—are highly appealing to many development analysts and policymakers (Ravallion, 1991; Subbarao, 2003). When they offer low wages for hard work, they attract participation by the poor without attracting the nonpoor, thereby reducing current poverty in a **self-targeting** fashion. This means that they discourage leakage to the nonpoor without requiring program personnel to administer costly eligibility tests. When they stand ready to employ workers hit by crop failure or job loss, they provide households with a secure mechanism for coping with shocks, thereby reducing vulnerability. When they put the poor to work building roads, irrigation networks, or other infrastructure, they add to asset creation, speeding economic growth and long-run poverty reduction. We will see, however, that they cannot fulfill their promise in any of these areas without careful attention to detail in program design and governance.

16.1B Workfare program objectives

Most workfare programs aim to achieve some combination of three objectives: reducing current poverty for participants, reducing vulnerability for households at risk of falling into poverty in the future, and creating infrastructure assets that speed economic growth and contribute to long-term poverty reduction. Some programs also pursue subsidiary objectives, such as improving community decision-making capacity or investing in the human capital of young workers. The relative importance of these objectives differs significantly across programs, as may be seen in Boxes 16.1 and 16.2, which describe well-regarded workfare programs in India and Argentina. When making specific program design choices, policymakers often face difficult tradeoffs, because design choices that enhance achievement of one objective often cause performance to deteriorate along other dimensions. It is useful, therefore, to identify the relative priority of a program's multiple objectives before embarking on design or evaluation.

Workfare programs aim to achieve their objectives through two broad channels: distributing wages to needy participants and creating infrastructure. In this chapter we focus primarily on their impacts as employment programs. We examine the challenges of infrastructure creation in more detail in Chapter 18.

Implementation concerns

A first step in analyzing the impact of workfare programs is to study in detail the array of employment opportunities ultimately created by the program and how they are allocated, asking: In which communities does the program initiate work projects? How much funding is allocated to each participating community? How much of this funding is used to cover legitimate program costs, rather than being siphoned off by corrupt officials or contractors? What policy design choices—regarding wage specifications, eligibility assessment, and project type—are made at the local level? How well do local implementers succeed at recruiting workers, assessing eligibility, enforcing work requirements and supervising work? If the program claims to guarantee employment, is this guarantee truly honored? If not, what de facto eligibility rules apply?

16.2 The Economics of Workfare Program Participation

We prepare for analyzing the design and impact of workfare programs by studying the determinants of who participates in workfare programs, the direct effects of participation on participating households, the effects on vulnerable households, the nature of possible spillover and feedback effects, and the budgetary costs of providing workfare jobs. Many of the concerns are similar to those raised for targeted transfer programs in Chapter 15. Here we highlight the *additional* concerns raised by the inclusion of work requirements in a transfer program's design.

16.2A Workfare program participation and targeting

In general terms, the conditions under which households participate in workfare programs are the same as the conditions for participating in targeted transfer programs (Chapter 15). That is,

> Households participate in a workfare program only if they are aware of the program, believe that the benefits of participation outweigh the costs, and are deemed eligible by program implementers.

Because workfare program benefits are conditioned on involvement in work projects, however, households' workfare participation decisions are tied closely to their labor supply and time-allocation choices. In what follows, we develop a simple model of workfare participation that emphasizes these connections.

Basic model

As in the basic labor supply model of Chapter 6, we examine the time-allocation choices of utility-maximizing individuals who derive utility from home time H and consumption expenditure C, allocate total time T across home time and work activities, and receive nonlabor income M. In the absence of a workfare program, they may work as many days as they wish for a wage w_a in other income-generating activities, which we will refer to as their **alternative activities**. By allowing w_a to vary across individuals, we recognize that some people face better opportunities to earn income outside the program than others, because they are healthier, have more education, own more farm or nonfarm business assets, or live in communities where labor market conditions are better. If labor markets are segmented, some individuals might also face higher alternative wages than others because they have better luck or better connections (Chapter 9). Wages in alternative activities can, furthermore, vary across seasons and years as labor demand fluctuates with the weather or macroeconomic conditions.

Figure 16.1 illustrates the time-allocation choices of two individuals, who are identical in every respect except that they face different wages in alternative activities. In each panel, the horizontal axis measures home time H in days per month and the vertical axis measures consumption

(a)

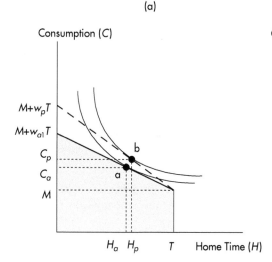

(b)

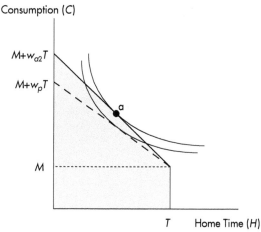

**FIGURE 16.1
Decisions to
Participate in a
Workfare Program
for Workers with
Different Alternative
Wages**

expenditure C in pesos per month. The solid budget constraint in each diagram indicates all the combinations of H and C that the individual may consume when she faces only the choice of how many days to work in her alternative activity. If she chooses not to work, she enjoys T days of home time and M pesos of consumption expenditure. For each day she allocates to work in her alternative activity, she loses one day of home time but increases her consumption expenditure by w_a. The individuals in panels a and b face alternative wages of w_{a1} and w_{a2}, with $w_{a2}>w_{a1}$, and the slopes of their (solid) alternative activity budget constraints are $-w_{a1}$ and $-w_{a2}$.

We introduce the opportunity for workfare participation simply, by assuming that an individual may work as many days as she wishes in a workfare program at the program wage w_p, but that if she chooses to work at all, she must work either in the program or in her alternative activity (but not in both). We also assume initially that workers know about the program, that anyone who wishes to participate may do so, that there are no fixed costs of participation (a concept we define below), and that working conditions are comparable in program and alternative work. Figure 16.1 illustrates a case in which $w_{a2}>w_p>w_{a1}$. The dashed schedules there indicate all the combinations of H and C that the individuals could consume by allocating their time in different ways across work in the workfare program and home time.

Under the assumptions made thus far, an individual may choose to consume anywhere along *either* her (solid) alternative activity budget constraint or her (dashed) workfare program budget constraint. As a utility maximizer, she chooses to participate in the workfare program if the highest utility she can attain is found on the workfare budget constraint rather than the alternative activity budget constraint. As in Chapter 6, we identify where her utility is maximized along the budget constraints in Figure 16.1 by introducing indifference curves. We can think of the potential participant as first identifying the highest levels of utility she could achieve while allocating time to her alternative activity and while allocating time to the workfare program (by identifying points on her two budget constraints that are just tangent to indifference curves) and then choosing to participate if the indifference curve just tangent to the workfare program budget constraint is farther from the origin than the indifference curve just tangent to her alternative activity budget constraint.

The logic of self-targeting

The individual whose choice is depicted in Figure 16.1a chooses to participate in the workfare program because the highest utility she can attain is found along her workfare program budget constraint, while the individual in Figure 16.1b chooses not to participate because the highest utility he can attain is found along his alternative activity budget constraint. More generally, under the assumptions we have made thus far, individuals facing alternative wages less than the workfare program wage participate, while those facing higher alternative wages do not.[1] This suggests that:

> If people from nonpoor households face higher wages in their alternative activities than people from poor households, and if a workfare program's wage is set at an appropriate level, then the program may be self-targeting, in the sense that individuals from nonpoor households choose not to participate, even while many poor households choose to participate.

To achieve self-targeting under these conditions, the program wage must be set at a level below the alternative wages faced by the nonpoor and above the alternative wages faced by the poor.

The self-targeting potential of workfare programs may be even greater when we acknowledge possible differences in working conditions between workfare jobs and alternative activities. If program work is more physically demanding or monotonous, for example, then the logic of compensating differentials (Chapter 9) suggests that people choose to participate in workfare only if the program wage equals at least the workers' alternative wage *plus* a wage premium to compensate for less-pleasant work. Moreover, if good working conditions are like normal goods, then individuals from better-off households might value them more highly and may be willing to accept inferior working conditions only if paid larger wage premiums. A workfare program wage that attracts workers from poor households into program work might, therefore, fail to attract nonpoor people out of their alternative activities, even when the program wage is somewhat greater than the wage in those alternative activities.

Potential for leakage

In practice:

> Workfare program benefits might leak to nonpoor households either because programs are designed poorly for discouraging participation by the nonpoor or because some members of nonpoor households have little opportunity to earn income in alternative activities.

Programs are poorly designed to discourage participation by the nonpoor when program wages are set to high levels and when program work requirements are light or poorly enforced. Even when programs are designed as well as possible for self-targeting, however, some members of nonpoor households might participate because they face few opportunities for alternative work. Some members of nonpoor households, especially female and younger members, might face poor earnings in alternative activities because they possess little human capital or face social restrictions on the types of private sector work they may perform. If their participation in program work is deemed socially acceptable and safe, they might find participation attractive, even while other members of their households do not. Some members of nonpoor households may also possess significant human capital but may be unable to find alternative work because macroeconomic crisis or other shocks have left local labor markets in disequilibrium, with some skilled workers unemployed (i.e., desiring to work for the current market wage but unable to find work).

---

[1] We could generalize this statement further to account for the possibility that some workers cannot obtain as many hours or days of work as they wish at the market wage. In this case, workfare programs can offer better income-generating opportunities by allowing workers to work more hours (at similar wages), as well as by allowing them to work for higher wages (see problem 3).

Potential for exclusion of the poor

Whether or not they are self-targeting (in the usual, limited sense that they discourage most nonpoor households from participating):

> Workfare programs can fail to provide benefits to many poor households because the excluded households lack able-bodied workers, lack workers who can be freed from child care responsibilities, live far from workfare project sites, suffer more serious social costs of participation, do not know about program opportunities, or are not deemed eligible by program staff.

Workfare programs often exclude some of the poorest and most vulnerable households, such as skip-generation households (in which elderly grandparents are rearing young grandchildren) and households in which the adults are seriously ill or disabled, for whom program work is infeasible. The more strenuous the program work, the more a program is likely to exclude such households. Programs that do not provide child care or otherwise accommodate children at project sites might also exclude some particularly vulnerable female-headed households, in which the lone adult is capable of program work but cannot participate without leaving children alone.

Even poor households capable of supplying labor may be excluded from workfare participation if they face fixed participation costs. **Fixed costs** of participation are costs that workers must bear to derive any benefits from the program and that do not increase as the hours or days they work in the program increase. For example, a worker might have to pay to travel to a program work site or for accommodations or tools. These costs are likely to vary, even among workers facing identical wages in alternative activities, because workers live at different distances from work sites and because the social costs of participation are higher for some workers than for others.

Figure 16.2 illustrates workfare participation choices in the presence of fixed participation costs. The two panels describe individuals facing the same alternative work opportunities (associated with the solid budget constraints) and the same program wage. The first graph pertains to a worker who faces a **fixed monetary cost** of participation, such as the cost of buying a bus ticket or a required tool. No matter how many hours or days she chooses to work in the program, her income is reduced by this amount. The effect is like that of a reduction in nonlabor income. Hence the dashed budget constraint relevant if she chooses to participate is given by the vertical

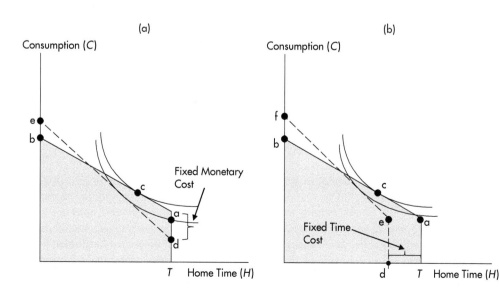

FIGURE 16.2
Workfare Program Participation Decisions for Workers Facing Fixed Monetary and Time Costs of Participation

line segment below point d and the diagonal line connecting point d and point e. This budget constraint reflects a reduction in nonlabor income (in the amount of the fixed cost) as well as an increase in the wage, relative to the solid pre-program budget constraint.

The second panel of Figure 16.2 pertains to a worker who faces a **fixed time cost** of participating. For example, he might need to walk several kilometers to reach the project site, and this reduces the total amount of time he has available for work or other activities. Once he chooses to participate in the program, it is as if the maximum number of hours or days available to him per month T falls, shifting the vertical section of his budget constraint to the left by the amount of the fixed time cost. The (dashed) budget constraint relevant if he chooses to participate in the program (connecting points d, e, and f) reflects a shift to the left in the vertical segment, as well as an increase in the wage, relative to the (solid)) alternative activity budget constraint.

People with preferences like those depicted in both panels of Figure 16.2 achieve higher utility by remaining in their alternative activities (at point c) than by joining the program, even though the program wage exceeds the wages in their alternative activities. The fixed costs of participation outweigh the potential benefits of receiving higher wages.

One implication of Figure 16.2 is that geography is important in defining a workfare program's coverage of the poor. Workfare participants must be put to work in specific projects in specific geographic locations. When workfare programs do not provide adequate assistance with transportation and lodging, poor households may be excluded from workfare benefits because they do not live in communities where workfare projects are set up or because they live in more remote locations within project communities. Their communities might be excluded because central-level administrators do not expect infrastructure investments in those communities to yield high returns, because their communities lack the capacity to create successful grant proposals, or because liquidity constraints prevent their communities from making necessary local contributions to program financing.

Some poor households can also face fixed social or psychological costs of participating if, for example, the gender or caste of their household heads renders them vulnerable to ill treatment at project sites. We might think of such costs as imposing the equivalent of a monetary fixed cost (equal to the price they would pay to avoid the social or psychological discomfort). Figure 16.2a suggests that such costs, too, might prevent some poor households from participating, even when program wages are higher than their alternative wages.

Notice that:

> In the presence of fixed costs, raising the program wage can raise participation by the poor.

In either panel of Figure 16.2, an increase in the program wage would cause the diagonal portion of the (dashed) program budget constraint to rotate up around the pivot point a, cutting through the alternative activity budget constraint farther to the right. If the program wage were to rise high enough, the program budget line would cut through the alternative budget line to the right of point c. The workers depicted there would then achieve higher utility by entering the program than by remaining in their alternative activities.

In practice, workfare programs can exclude the poor, even when the poor wish to participate, for additional reasons discussed in Chapter 15. Some poor households may be unaware of workfare program opportunities or fail to satisfy program eligibility requirements. Even when programs contain no formal eligibility requirements, some poor households might fail to obtain program jobs because local administrators are given insufficient funding. Even if jobs are allocated in a reasonably fair manner—by lottery or on a first come, first served basis—some poor workers may be left without jobs. When elite groups capture control of the local allocation of jobs, and thus gain power to exercise favoritism and discrimination, the poorest households fare even worse.

Empirical targeting outcomes

Empirical examples reveal that targeting is far from perfect even in top-performing workfare programs and that budgetary constraints can worsen targeting outcomes. Survey evidence showed that 60 to 70 percent of workers in Maharashtra's EGS belonged to households qualifying as officially poor in its early days (Ravallion et al., 1991). Often those belonging to nonpoor households were women with few other income-generating opportunities. Households with disabled workers failed to participate. According to Gaiha (1996), the share of benefits going to nonpoor households rose over a period in which the program wage rose and budgetary constraints caused the program to begin rationing jobs.

Leakage rates were similar in the Trabajar program, with 60 to 70 percent of participants coming from officially poor households, and 80 percent from the poorest 20 percent of households in Argentina (Jalan and Ravallion, 1999). Because the program was small, however, many more of the poor (even in households with able-bodied workers) failed to receive coverage (Jalan and Ravallion, 1999). Of particular concern was the failure to cover the poor in some of the poorest communities, which may have eschewed participation because they lacked the resources and capacity to make required copayments and develop project proposals.

Leakage rates were somewhat higher for the Jefes program, with only half of participants coming from the poorest 20 percent of households. Evidence suggests that eligibility requirements (which required that participants be unemployed household heads with dependents) were not well enforced. The work requirement was also weak and inconsistently enforced, though Galasso and Ravallion (2004) conclude that it nonetheless played some role in preventing participation by the nonpoor.

16.2B Direct impacts of workfare participation on well-being and behavior

Impacts on well-being

Figures 16.1 and 16.2 suggest that:

> Workfare program participation raises a participant's well-being more, all else equal, the more the program wage exceeds the wage in the participant's alternative activity and the smaller are the participant's fixed costs of participation. It also raises well-being more when program working conditions are more attractive relative to working conditions in the alternative activity.

For the worker whose time-allocation choices are depicted in Figure 16.1a, the introduction of a workfare program effectively rotates her budget constraint up around the pivot point a, from the solid position associated with work in her alternative activity to the dashed position associated with participation in the workfare program. The effect on her well-being is the same as that of a simple wage increase from w_{a1} to w_p. From the analysis of Figure 16.2, we know that this benefit of obtaining a higher effective wage must be weighed against any fixed costs of participation. From the logic of compensating differentials (Chapter 9), we know that if working conditions in the program are better (or worse) than in her alternative activity, then her well-being rises more (or less).

As with targeted transfers, a workfare program raises well-being primarily by raising household income. As compared to other targeted transfer programs, however, workfare programs have greater potential to **crowd out** (i.e., cause a reduction in) participating households' income from other sources. Transfer programs without work requirements reduce labor income largely as a result of income effects that raise the consumption of home time (and reduce total labor supply). A workfare program can crowd out other labor income, even while participating households' total labor time holds constant or rises, by inducing participants to switch out of alternative income-generating activities into program work.

One practical implication is that the total wage payment a household receives from a workfare program may be a poor estimate of the program's *impact* on the household's income from all sources. In Figure 16.1a, for example, the participant receives a total wage payment from the program of $w_p(T - H_p)$, but the program raises her total income only from $C_a = M + w_{a1}(T - H_a)$ to $C_p = M + w_p(T - H_p)$. Wage payments are good estimates of income impacts only when participants would have been unemployed or out of the labor force in the absence of the program. Although this may be the case for many workers in periods of macroeconomic crisis, when labor markets are in disequilibrium (as described below), this is unlikely to be the case in other settings.

Empirical estimates confirm that workfare programs sometimes crowd out significant quantities of nonprogram labor income, and they demonstrate that the extent of this crowding out rises as program wages rise (drawing in more participants who would have worked in the absence of the program) and as local economic conditions improve (strengthening alternative income-generating opportunities). Datt and Ravallion (1994) studied the labor supply and income effects of Maharashtra's Employment Guarantee Scheme in two villages. They estimated that in Shirapur, a relatively poor village, only one fifth of the time devoted to program work came out of other work. The rest came out of leisure, domestic work, and self-reported unemployment. On average, the crowding out of income from other work amounted to 21 percent of gross program wages. The estimated magnitude of crowding out was somewhat larger in Kanzara, a better-off village with higher agricultural productivity and better opportunities for alternative employment. In this village, one third of program time was drawn out of paid employment and another one quarter was drawn out of work on participants' own farms. Crowding out of alternative income amounted to 32 percent of the gross program wage.

Crowding out was significant in the Trabajar program, too, even though the program was created as a response to high unemployment. Jalan and Ravallion (1999) estimate that the program raised participants' income, on average, by only half of what participants received in program payments. Perhaps because the crisis precipitating the Jefes program was more severe, estimates suggest that crowding out was somewhat smaller under that program, with net income gains equal to about 70 percent of gross program payments (Galasso and Ravallion, 2004).

Impacts on behavior

As with targeted transfer programs:

> Participation in workfare programs can alter participants' behavior through four channels. Participation (1) increases income and (2) alters incentives, especially by raising the value of participants' work time. It can also (3) alter the way women's interests enter into household decision making or (4) relax liquidity constraints.

The main potential differences between the behavioral effects of workfare programs and the behavioral effects of other transfer programs have to do with the effective wage increase, which can encourage households to devote more time to work and less time to other activities. If children are eligible to participate, a workfare program may encourage children to work, at the expense of school attendance and other activities, though the income effects of increased wages for adults in their households might counterbalance this incentive change. To avoid encouraging child labor, some workfare programs limit eligibility to workers at least 18 years of age. Even when children are not allowed to participate, workfare programs might create incentives for families to remove children from school by raising the value of children's time in housework and caring for siblings, as the children's parents are drawn into workfare participation outside the home. If programs improve employment opportunities for women, and especially if they improve women's opportunities more than they improve men's opportunities, then they might encourage households to allow women to work outside the home. This might induce increases in women's influence in household decision making through various channels discussed in Chapter 7.

16.2C Impacts on vulnerability

Transfer programs reduce vulnerability (to severe reductions in consumption), when households are confident that the programs will enroll them and quickly provide them with benefits, in the event of crop failure, job loss, or other shocks that reduce income. Reductions in vulnerability increase well-being directly and can also encourage investment by insurance-constrained households (as defined in Chapter 10).

Transfer programs reduce vulnerability in this way only when they are characterized by flexibility in targeting, are capable of delivering benefits quickly, and are backed by credible promises of continued funding into the future. Targeting is flexible when programs admit households soon after they fall into poverty and graduate households as soon as their economic circumstances improve. In means-tested targeted transfer programs, this would require program implementers to perform frequent means tests and would require administrative procedures that quickly add people to and remove people from distribution lists. In practice, means tests are often performed only infrequently.

Our discussion of workfare program participation decisions implies that:

> Workfare programs are capable of reducing vulnerability for workers whose income in regular economic activities is subject to shocks, but only when the programs' wage levels are well chosen, the programs truly guarantee employment, and the programs are expected to remain in place for the foreseeable future.

If program wages are set at levels that attract many poor workers but few nonpoor workers, then programs can achieve good targeting outcomes without having to employ means tests. If employment is also truly guaranteed, then targeting is flexible, because workers simply select themselves into the programs when their potential earnings in regular economic activities fall below program earnings, and they select themselves out again when their alternative income-generating opportunities improve.

Unfortunately, achieving such flexibility is a great governance challenge for two reasons. First, if participants' labor time is to be put to valuable use, it must be deployed on well-designed projects, and implementers must be ready to initiate such projects at any time and in any location. Second, the program must have access to funding that is adequate for hiring everyone who wishes to work at the program wage. When weather or unemployment shocks hit many workers at once, even low wages can attract many workers, and budget constraints can prevent implementers from satisfying all requests for employment. In such cases, households cannot count on obtaining program work in the event they need it.

Even when workfare programs offer well-chosen wages and guarantee employment, they cannot address all types of vulnerability. They are helpful when households suffer shocks that reduce what they are able to earn in their regular economic activities, but they are little help when households are hit by shocks that render their breadwinners incapable of working. For example, they may offer households little protection against health shocks, which drive many households into deep poverty.

16.2D Workfare and labor markets

Workfare programs are more likely than other targeted transfer programs to generate spillover effects through labor markets because they can significantly increase the local demand for labor. The spillover effects take different forms, depending on which of two models offers the better

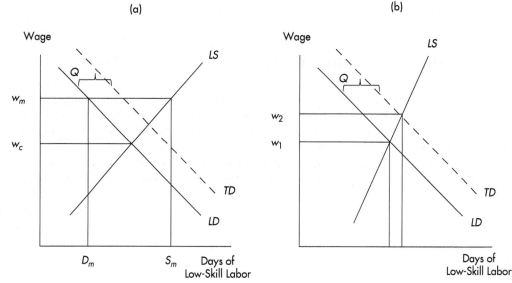

FIGURE 16.3
Labor Market Impacts of Workfare-Induced Demand Shifts under Two Sets of Labor Market Conditions

description of how local labor markets work: a model of labor markets characterized by unemployment or a model of labor markets in competitive equilibrium.

Labor market effects in the presence of unemployment

Implicit in many discussions of workfare programs is the assumption that participants would have been unemployed or underemployed in the absence of the program. This means that they would have wished to work for the current market wage but could not find work or could not find as much work as they wanted. Such assumptions are plausible when we have reason to suspect that the market wage for low-skill labor is stuck above the competitive equilibrium level, as in Figure 16.3a. In competitive equilibrium, the wage would adjust to level w_c, where the (solid) local supply (LS) and local demand (LD) schedules intersect and where all workers who wish to work at the market wage are in fact working as much as they wish. If the market wage remains stuck at w_m, above w_c, by contrast, workers wish to supply S_m days of labor, employers demand D_m days of labor, and $U_m = S_m - D_m$ days of labor remain unemployed.

The assumption that labor markets are in disequilibrium like this is most plausible in the immediate aftermath of a macroeconomic shock that reduces labor demand. In such cases, we would expect the unemployment to disappear with time, as the wage adjusts downward, inducing local employers to increase the quantity of labor they demand, and as workers reduce their labor supply or migrate out to stronger labor markets.

It is also theoretically possible for unemployment to arise as an equilibrium phenomenon, having no such tendency to disappear with time. According to the "nutrition-based efficiency wage hypothesis," for example, rural employers may be reluctant to reduce wages for agricultural labor below some low threshold, even when the unemployed offer to work for less, because employers believe that workers receiving lower wages would eat so little as to be unproductive in agricultural tasks (Bliss and Stern, 1978a and 1978b). Profit maximization would require these employers to hire labor only to the point at which the value of the marginal product of labor equals the threshold wage they are willing to pay, and this could leave some poor workers unemployed. The empirical importance of such conditions is a matter of debate.

Careful examination of Figure 16.3a indicates that:

> When labor markets are characterized by unemployment, a workfare program induces no change in low-skill wages and crowds out no private sector employment. Even so, it can induce significant spillover effects for some non-participating workers, especially when the program wage is higher than the market wage for low-skill labor.

Consider what happens in Figure 16.3a when a workfare program demands a fixed quantity of labor Q at a wage just below w_m. The program would attract workers who would have been unemployed or underemployed in the absence of the program, but it would not attract fully employed workers (who were already working as many hours as they wish at the higher market wage). The program effectively creates a new total labor demand schedule (TD) that lies to the right of LD by the quantity Q, because no matter what the market wage (and quantity of labor demanded by the private sector), the program demands the additional quantity Q. More specifically, at the market wage w_m, the private sector continues to demand D_m in labor, while the program employs the additional Q. If Q is less than $U_m = S_m - D_m$ (as in Figure 16.3a), it reduces but does not eliminate unemployment and underemployment. The increase in demand creates no pressure for wages to rise, because the total quantity demanded continues to fall short of the total quantity supplied.

Under these conditions, the workfare program increases employment by the full quantity of labor it demands and increases the total income of low-skill workers by the full quantity of wages it pays out. If all participants would have been fully unemployed in the absence of the program, then these increases in employment and earnings are enjoyed fully by participants. If, however, some participants would have been underemployed (rather than fully unemployed) in the absence of the program, then as they move into the program, they might give up work hours in the private sector. Under such circumstances, the program's direct effect on their total incomes is smaller than the pay they receive from the program, and the program also generates spillover effects for other workers drawn into private sector employment. Other workers must be drawn into the private sector to replace any workers who leave to participate in the workfare program, as long as the private sector continues to demand a total of D_m days of labor.

If a workfare program demanding Q in labor days were to offer a somewhat higher wage, greater than or equal to w_m, then it might attract fully employed low-skill workers as well as unemployed and underemployed workers. Under such conditions, crowding out of nonprogram income among participants is even more likely. Again, however, as long as Q is less than $U_m = S_m - D_m$, the program raises incomes for participants *and* for any workers who are drawn into private-sector employment to replace them, but it does not alter the market wage.

When unemployment is a disequilibrium phenomenon, we expect it to disappear over time. This suggests that workfare program impacts on employment and earnings can diminish over time, even while program employment holds constant. In the absence of the program, workfare participants who were unemployed when the program was introduced might have obtained employment in subsequent months, as the labor market adjusted toward equilibrium. The program's impact on their earnings, defined as the difference between their program earnings and what they would have earned in the absence of the program, can thus diminish over time. Furthermore:

> When introduced into markets in disequilibrium, workfare programs may initially improve participants' immediate consumption and well-being a great deal, but they can also prevent participants from making transitions into new private sector work.

For this reason, program designers sometimes introduce time limits on participation, or they condition participation on completion of job training or job search activities, with the aim of encouraging transitions into new private sector employment. Box 16.3 reports on experiments

≡ Box 16.3 Encouraging Transitions from Workfare to Private Employment in Argentina

In 1993, many residents of the Argentine town Confluencia lost their jobs when an oil refinery was privatized. Even five years later, participation in the local Trabajar workfare program remained very high in this company town, leading policymakers to worry that the program was encouraging workfare dependency. In October 1998 they undertook a randomized trial of two programmatic efforts to discourage dependency by encouraging workfare participants to transition into private employment. Under the first program, randomly selected workfare participants were presented with voucher documents to bring to potential private sector employers. With the vouchers, the employers who hired them could claim a wage subsidy of $150 per month for workers over 45 years of age ($100 per month for younger workers) for 18 months. With the legal minimum wage at $200 per month, this represented a substantial wage subsidy. The second program provided the same vouchers plus opportunities to obtain training and small training-period stipends. Emanuela Galasso and coauthors (2004) report the results of following 953 workers (distributed across the two treatments and control) over 18 months.

Neither treatment proved to be dramatically effective, but the results nonetheless shed interesting light on how labor markets work. Receipt of wage subsidy vouchers modestly increased workers' probability of transitioning into private employment from 9 percent in the control group to 14 percent. It is striking that the receipt of a voucher increased employment probabilities even though almost none of the employers redeemed the vouchers, and that workers chose to transition into private employment even though most of them reported their new jobs as temporary and the transition did not increase their earnings.

Labor regulations probably help explain why employers did not redeem the vouchers for substantial wage subsidies. Most operated in the informal sector. To redeem the vouchers they would have had to register the subsidized workers, thereby becoming liable for payment of social security taxes equal to 30 percent of their gross wages. Having registered the subsidized workers, they might have had to register their other workers as well, and severance pay regulations would have rendered it difficult to fire them after the subsidies ran out.

If employers did not take advantage of the wage subsidies, then why did receipt of vouchers help workers obtain private employment? The authors speculate that for poor workers accustomed to finding jobs through informal networks, the voucher may have served as a letter of introduction that encouraged them to apply for more jobs. Employers may have (mistakenly) believed the vouchers were distributed to workfare participants who had shown special merit. Workers may have taken the private sector jobs, even when they paid no more than workfare, because they appeared more likely to last.

The addition of the training opportunity did not much increase the program's impact on employment. Thirty percent of workers offered training did not even take up the offer, raising questions about the relevance and quality of the training offered.

with using wage subsidies and training to encourage transitions of workfare participants into private sector employment.

Labor market effects when labor markets are in equilibrium

If labor markets were in the sort of disequilibrium described by Figure 16.3a, then modest fluctuations in supply and demand would leave the market wage for low-skill labor unchanged. Even in low-wage rural areas, however, wages seem to fluctuate with supply and demand, and they tend to rise in response to development interventions that raise the demand for labor. Under such conditions, it is more appealing to assume that labor markets are in competitive equilibrium rather than exhibiting the conditions depicted in Figure 16.3a. We will see that:

> When introduced into labor markets in competitive equilibrium, workfare programs raise wages for low-skill workers and crowd out some private sector employment at the aggregate level. By raising wages, they increase well-being for all participating and nonparticipating low-skill workers alike, and reduce well-being for employers of low-skill labor.

(We are assuming here that the workfare programs are large relative to local labor markets and that local labor markets are poorly integrated into larger markets.) Figure 16.3b illustrates such a case. Before a workfare program is introduced, this market is in equilibrium at wage w_1. If the workfare program were to offer a wage below w_1, it would attract no participants, because everyone willing to work at a lower wage is already employed at the higher wage w_1.

If a workfare program offers to match the market wage and demands the labor quantity Q, it again effectively creates a (dashed) total market demand schedule (TD) that lies to the right of LD by Q. The program competes with the private sector for workers, driving the local wage up to w_2.

As the wage rises, some new workers are drawn into the labor force (as the intersection of the supply and demand schedules moves up along the labor supply schedule). Because total employment rises by less than Q, however, we know that some of the labor drawn into the program has been drawn out of private employment. That is, program employment has crowded out private employment at the aggregate level.

When labor markets are competitive, a workfare program might reduce poverty and inequality a lot, even when it raises low-skill employment only a little. In fact, the more inelastic is the local supply of labor, the less the program increases total employment and the more it increases wages. Following the logic of Chapter 7, larger increases in low-skill wages mean larger increases in well-being for low-skill workers, who are likely to be poor, and larger reductions in well-being for employers of low-skill labor, who are likely to be nonpoor. This potential for workfare programs to raise low-skill wages explains why farmers in India sometimes lobby against the introduction of EGS workfare projects in their communities, especially in agricultural peak seasons (Imbert and Papp, 2012).

The poverty-reducing impacts of workfare programs in competitive labor markets may be small, if labor supply is highly elastic. Under such conditions, workfare programs raise low-skill wages little. They might draw many workers into employment, but these new workers would not have been unemployed in the absence of the program. They would have been *out of the labor force*, having *chosen* not to work at the market wage, which would have been only a little lower than the wage in the presence of the workfare program. This implies that the opportunity cost of their time in nonwork activities is high, and that the net impact of participation on their well-being is low. Empirical research is required, therefore, to assess the potential for workfare programs to raise well-being for low-skill labor.

Empirical estimates of workfare program labor market impacts are rare. One recent study of a national workfare program in India (which was modeled after Maharashtra's EGS) found that the spillover effects arising through increases in wages for low-skill labor were in fact large, constituting at least half of all program effects on the well-being of poor workers (Imbert and Papp, 2012). Estimates also indicate that the program might have crowded out nearly as much employment in the private sector as was created by the program.

16.2E Other short-run spillover effects

When food-for-work or cash-for-work programs are introduced in remote rural communities, where local food markets are not integrated into larger regional markets, they can induce changes in local food prices. The analysis of these effects is much the same as in the case of cash and food transfers as discussed in Chapters 8 and 15. Chapter 15's discussion of possible impacts within and on local institutions—including private safety-net institutions, community institutions supporting cooperation, and the public institutions that govern schools and clinics—also applies to workfare programs.

16.2F Longer-run infrastructure impacts

Like the conditional cash transfer programs described in Chapter 15, workfare programs have the potential to reduce future poverty as well as current poverty. They reduce future poverty if they use participants' labor to invest in the creation of valuable infrastructure that delivers benefits to the poor. We reserve a detailed examination of the challenges and impacts of infrastructure policies for Chapter 18. Here it suffices to point out that:

> Workfare programs have greater impact on future poverty when they provide participants with stronger work incentives, when they employ participants in infrastructure projects that are better located and better designed, and when any infrastructure assets they create are adequately operated and maintained.

16.2G Budgetary costs

Workfare program budgetary costs fall into three main categories: wage payments, nonwage construction costs, and administrative costs. Some programs also incur costs of providing on-site child care, lodging, or transportation. When projects are labor intensive, wage payments are a large fraction of the cost of constructing any infrastructure created by program workers. If administrative costs associated with assessing eligibility and distributing pay are also low, then wage payments take up a large fraction of total program expenditures. In a group of projects reviewed by the World Bank in the mid-1990s, the share of wages in total costs varied between 30 and 60 percent, with most in the 50 to 60 percent range (Subbarao, 2003). The average has probably increased somewhat in recent years, as emphasis in new programs has shifted toward achievement of short-run poverty-reduction objectives rather than infrastructure creation.

If a program truly guarantees employment at the program wage to anyone who wants it, then the government or organization funding the program must stand ready to finance as many projects as are required to provide all the jobs demanded. Estimating costs for any period then involves estimating the number of workers who will find participation attractive relative to their alternative activities. Costs tend to rise when general economic conditions deteriorate and the demand for program jobs increases.

If instead, as is often the case, a program faces a fixed budget limit, B, then total program costs are largely fixed in advance, and policy analysts may wish to ask: How many workers are likely to obtain employment through the program? If program administrators have set the program wage w and the target ratio n of nonwage to wage costs (a measure that falls as the target level of labor intensity rises), then the budget will finance the creation of roughly $B/[w(1+n)]$ worker-days of employment. Estimating how many workers will be reached by the program then requires educated guesses—based on both program rules and the nature of the local economy—of how many days the typical worker will participate. If the program expects to retain the same group of workers for the entire duration of the project, then the number of workers is just the number of worker-days divided by the project's expected duration in days.

Public works projects are notorious for corruption. Officials might siphon program funds away by claiming payments for ghost workers or by overbilling for construction materials. As more funds are siphoned away, a program with fixed total funding reaches fewer workers or produces infrastructure of lower quality. Thus governance reforms that reduce the diversion of funds can lead to significant improvements in a program's short- or long-run impacts. As mentioned in Chapter 13, Olken (2007) describes several experimental efforts to reduce corruption in road construction projects. The most effective experimental reform was relatively simple, because it required only an increase in the probability with which the contractors in charge of construction at the local level had their books audited.

In summary:

> For a workfare program with a fixed budget, the number of workers reached by the program tends to fall as the program wage rises, as the labor intensity of work projects falls, and as deteriorations in governance increase the volume of program resources diverted away from program activities.

16.3 Workfare Program Evaluation and Design

Box 16.4 adapts the seven questions of Chapter 14 for use in evaluating workfare programs. When applied in parallel fashion to programs with different designs, they illuminate the tradeoffs involved when making program design choices. We examine several difficult tradeoffs below.

≡ **Box 16.4** Questions to Guide Analysis of Workfare Programs

Question 1: Objectives

Is the program intended primarily to reduce current poverty, reduce vulnerability, or speed growth and reduce future poverty by creating infrastructure? What is the target population? What subsidiary objectives do policymakers hope to achieve with this program?

Question 2: Design

What wage and benefits specifications, eligibility requirements, employment guarantees, work project specifications, and governance structure choices define the program on paper?

Question 3: Implementation

In which communities are work projects undertaken? What design choices are made by decentralized decision makers? In practice, is employment truly guaranteed, what wages and benefits are distributed, what eligibility requirements are enforced, and what kinds of work projects are undertaken? How effective is the supervision of program work?

Question 4: Directly affected groups

Who participates in the program? Which groups among the poor does the program reach (and fail to reach)? What fraction of the target poor population does it reach? How well does the program limit leakage?

Question 5: Direct effects

What is the program's impact on participating households' incomes and home time? How much income from alternative activities is crowded out? How does participation affect nutrition, saving, investment, labor supply of adults and children, and intrahousehold distribution? What impact does the program have on vulnerability?

Question 6: Spillover and feedback effects

What is the program's total effect on low-skill employment and wages, and what spillover and feedback effects does this imply? What effect does the program have on goods markets, informal insurance and other private safety-net institutions, institutions that support community cooperation, and public institutions, and what spillover and feedback effects result? What longer-run effects are generated by any infrastructure constructed?

Question 7: Budgetary costs

What is the program's total budgetary cost? How do total costs break down into wage and benefits payments, nonwage construction costs, and program administrative costs?

16.3A **Wage setting**

When setting a workfare program's wage, program designers must grapple with ethical concerns as well as empirical evidence on local labor market conditions. To clarify the tradeoffs involved, it is useful to consider the potential benefits and costs of raising the program wage, starting from a low level.

The most important benefit of increasing the program wage is improvement in the program's impact on participants' well-being; with a higher wage, the program is more effective at raising a participant's family out of poverty. Raising the wage can bring at least four additional benefits. The wage increase can improve coverage among poor households as program benefits begin to outweigh the high fixed participation costs faced by some poor households. Higher wages can increase pressure on private employers to raise wages, generating greater spillover benefits for poor workers who do not participate, especially if the program seeks to guarantee employment at the program wage. Larger wage payments (holding the number of participants constant) imply greater increases in participants' consumer demands, increasing the program's stimulus to the local economy. Finally, paying higher wages can raise productivity in infrastructure construction by improving morale and reducing the potential for strikes and labor conflicts, as seems to have been the case with some South African workfare programs (Adato and Haddad, 2001).

Raising the program wage naturally brings costs as well as benefits. The most obvious cost is the increased per-participant budgetary cost. Total program costs are likely to rise even more, as the program attracts additional participants. The additional workers are likely to be better off than incumbent workers, and thus leakage of benefits to the nonpoor may rise as well. Furthermore, as total budgetary costs tend to increase, budget limits become more likely to bind, causing deterioration in program coverage and in the program's potential to reduce vulnerability by guaranteeing employment. Once budget constraints bind, increases in the wage (and thus in per-worker cost) necessitate reductions in the number of participants. Unless an effective (and costly) means test is in place to direct jobs to the neediest workers, the fraction of jobs going to the neediest workers is likely to fall. With the total number of jobs *and* the fraction of jobs going to the truly poor both falling, coverage of the target poor population deteriorates. With employment no longer guaranteed, the program also provides workers with less confidence that they can prop up their consumption by participating in the program if they are hit by shocks.

Starting with the program wage at a very low level (i.e., well below the market wage for low-skill labor), many analysts and policymakers would conclude that the benefits of increasing the wage outweigh the costs. If the labor market is in competitive equilibrium, and if program work is comparable to local low-wage work, then the program will not even begin to attract workers until the wage reaches the market level. If some workers are unemployed, then the program might attract workers even at below-market wages, but many policymakers would still judge the benefits of increasing the wage toward the market level greater than the cost, because the increase would render the program more capable of raising participants and their families out of destitution, without beginning to attract fully employed workers, and thus without encouraging much crowding out or leakage.

When the wage rises to the level of the local market wage for low-skill workers, however, the benefits of increasing the wage fall farther and the costs rise, and the debate regarding further increases becomes more contentious. Raising the program wage above the market level would continue to enhance the program's direct impact on the poverty of participants, but now the costs of raising the wage are higher. At wages above the market level a workfare program ceases to be self-targeting. The program begins to attract fully employed workers and workers at higher skill levels. If the program's total budget is fixed, coverage of poorer workers is likely to fall as well.

Organizations funding workfare programs differ in beliefs regarding the most appropriate way to set wages. Many policy analysts conclude that workfare programs perform best when the program wage is near the level of the local market wage for comparable unskilled work. They judge that the benefit of raising participants' incomes further, to a more-desirable level, is outweighed by the increase in leakage and the reduction in the number of the truly poor served by the program. For some, including the International Labour Organization, the need to pay fair or decent wages trumps concerns about program outreach among the poor. For them it is unethical to pay market wages when market wages are too low to provide workers' families with adequate nutrition, clothing, and lodging. Recognizing that workfare programs fail to self-target at above-market wages, they encourage the use of eligibility testing to improve targeting.

Even when policymakers agree that a workfare program's wage should be set to the market level, they may be prohibited from doing so by minimum wage legislation. One of the rules defining Maharashtra's EGS ties its wage to India's official agricultural minimum wage. In the program's early days, when the minimum wage was held at low levels (near the market wage), the EGS succeeded in self-targeting and guaranteeing employment to the poor. After the official minimum wage doubled in 1988, however, leakage rates increased, the program ran into budget constraints, and the program no longer truly guaranteed jobs for all interested workers (Ravallion et al., 1991). The Trabajar and Jefes programs in Argentina managed to pay wages below the legal minimum by calling the program payments "social assistance" rather than wages, thereby legally side-stepping minimum wage requirements.

The program wage that best balances the benefits and costs of wage increases is likely to differ across communities where labor market conditions differ. Program wage setting should also take into account the nature of the work participants are asked to do, with more unpleasant or dangerous tasks paying higher wages. Centralized wage setting can thus lead to poor program performance, with projects failing to attract workers where the program wage is too low for local labor market conditions and can lead to benefits that are poorly targeted where the program wage is too high, as was true with a Food for Work program in India (Deshingkar et al., 2005).

The experience of the Community-Based Public Works Programme (CBPWP) in South Africa highlights some of the difficulties of wage setting and a possible advantage to community involvement in selecting the program wage (Adato and Haddad, 2001). Program wages were initially set at below-market levels in the hope of achieving good targeting outcomes. Objection to the low wages catalyzed labor strikes, leading many communities to increase wages to higher levels, comparable to formal sector wages. Because the local programs faced budget constraints, the higher wages meant fewer jobs. Projects run by participatory community-based organizations tended to pay lower wages than projects run by larger NGOs or government agencies, perhaps because the community organizations were more successful at helping local workers understand the link between lower wages and larger numbers of jobs to share within the community.

16.3B Supervision and piece rates

Work requirements mobilize labor for creating infrastructure only if the requirements truly motivate participants to exert significant effort. When workers are paid a fixed sum per day, regardless of what they accomplish while at the work site, and if supervision is minimal (beyond the monitoring of attendance), then workers may be poorly motivated for work. If workers need not work hard to obtain pay, the work requirement might fail to render the program self-targeting.

Work requirements have more bite—proving more effective at discouraging leakage and encouraging work—when they are specified in **piece rate** terms, which tie pay to the quantity of tasks a worker completes, rather than **time rate** terms, which tie pay to days or hours of presence on the job. An anecdote from northeastern Brazil illustrates the potential impact of choosing piece rates over time rates. An emergency employment program initiated in the late 1980s began hiring workers to pick up trash around public buildings and along roadways, paying a fixed wage for an eight-hour work day. The program attracted poor workers and succeeded in increasing their incomes, but public places and roadsides showed few signs of trash collection. Eventually, program managers switched from time rates to piece rates. They estimated the meters of road that a typical worker could police in an eight-hour day and set the piece rate for roadside cleanup so that a worker who completed that "full day's work" would receive the same daily payment as before. To contain cost and spread benefits, they also limited the meters of road a worker could clean per day. The results were striking. The workers continued to participate and take home the same daily income as before, but now they completed their full days' work in just four hours per day, and the roadsides were clean!

Paying piece rates is not without difficulty or cost, however. In some places, labor regulations prohibit payment of piece rates. In Mexico, for example, the constitution itself prohibits piece rate payments. Even where piece rates are lawful, their use can increase the physical burden associated with participation, making the program less accessible to workers weakened by malnutrition or illness. In Chapter 22 we will see how malnutrition and anemia can be endemic in poor communities. In such contexts, requiring participants to engage in rock breaking, which can raise daily food requirements by as much as 1,000 calories, can serve to exclude some needy families who would participate if work requirements were not as demanding. Paying workers for the quantity of tasks they complete can also reduce their attention to the quality of their work. Thus, when choosing whether to specify program wages in piece rates rather than time rates, program designers must weigh the benefits of increased participant work effort against the potential costs of greater exclusion of poor workers with lower physical capacity and participants' reduced attention to quality in their work.

16.3C Priorities and governance structures

In principle, workfare programs can simultaneously reduce current poverty, reduce vulnerability, and create infrastructure that contributes to economic growth and long-term poverty reduction. In practice, however, program designers appear to face a tradeoff between excellence in reducing poverty and vulnerability, on the one hand, and in creating valuable infrastructure, on the other, because the workfare program governance structures that yield greatest success in reducing poverty and vulnerability differ from the governance structures that yield greatest success in creating infrastructure.

Some tradeoff is inevitable, because the public works projects that would best reduce poverty and vulnerability on a given budget are likely to differ in location, timing, and nature from the projects that would add most value to the infrastructure stock. To maximize impacts on poverty and vulnerability, programs must implement projects wherever and whenever they are needed, must implement them in many dispersed locations, and must use methods that are as labor-intensive as possible. This might mean implementing projects that are small and easy to complete during agricultural slack seasons, when employment needs are greatest. Program designers seeking to produce high-value infrastructure at low cost, by contrast, might prefer to work at larger scale and on a continuous rather than seasonal basis so as to economize on the fixed costs of setting up work sites and of employing professionals year round. They would choose to build infrastructure where its value is greatest rather than where needs for employment are greatest, and they might be willing to use less-labor-intensive methods if use of heavy equipment would improve construction quality. Yet the tradeoff need not be dramatic, because most poor communities could benefit from infrastructure projects of modest size.

Historically, however, governments have found it very difficult to create public works programs that deliver strong performance in both poverty reduction and infrastructure construction. They have typically employed people in public works projects through two quite different kinds of program. **Emergency employment programs** are temporary programs designed to provide safety net assistance in the wake of drought, conflict, or macroeconomic downturn. Created and implemented very rapidly, these programs often succeed in providing significant assistance to poor workers' families, but they also draw criticism for creating infrastructure of low quality and little enduring value. In many cases, they do not even attempt to create infrastructure, employing workers instead in tasks like trash collection. **Infrastructure construction programs** are ongoing developmental efforts focused on building infrastructure to speed growth and encourage long-run reduction in poverty. Such programs are relatively good at producing valuable infrastructure (though far from perfect, as we see in Chapter 18) but have generated relatively little employment for unskilled workers. In fact, they often use equipment-based construction methods (e.g., using heavy machinery to even out roadbeds) even when labor-based methods (e.g., using workers with hand tools to perform the same tasks) are also feasible.

Over the last four decades, the International Labour Organization, the World Bank, and other development organizations have promoted reforms of emergency employment programs and infrastructure construction programs, aiming to improve their performance in their areas of traditional weakness, but these efforts have proved costly and difficult. A brief review of their experiences sheds additional light on challenges to workfare program governance.

One of the primary reasons for the poor infrastructure performance of emergency employment programs is the need to implement projects quickly. As we will see in Chapter 18, creating infrastructure that delivers large and long-lasting benefits requires not only technical excellence in the design of the physical assets but also the creation of effective institutions for operating and maintaining the assets, and all of this takes time. It may be possible to improve the infrastructure performance of emergency employment programs by replacing one-off, temporary programs (implemented in the wake of crisis) by permanent programs that stand ready to provide employment when needed. The permanent staff of such programs would have time to develop high-quality infrastructure projects. Replacing temporary emergency employment programs by permanent ones might yield the additional benefit of improving safety net performance, because programs that stand ready to implement projects when needed might deliver benefits to distressed families more quickly and might offer greater reassurance to the vulnerable. Such programs are difficult to create, however, because they require political support and funding for emergency employment even in the absence of emergency. They also require a staff with expertise in the technical and institution-building aspects of infrastructure creation but that also remains sensitive to poverty and employment needs. Maharashtra's EGS is considered a successful example, but few governments have come even close to creating such a program.

One of the primary reasons why infrastructure construction programs tend to have only modest impacts on poverty is that they use equipment-based methods. Reforms that would improve their poverty-reduction impacts would replace equipment-based construction methods by labor-based methods in at least some important construction tasks. In addition to increasing the number of jobs created during the construction of any given asset, such a reform might deliver many additional benefits. Making larger total payments to local workers and demanding tools created by the local nonfarm sector, labor-based projects might provide greater stimulus to local economies. Avoiding the use of fuels and heavy machines, they might be better for the environment. Allowing local workers to learn relatively simple construction techniques, they might equip communities better for later maintenance. In economies that have abundant unskilled labor and where wages are low and equipment is scarce, labor-based construction techniques might even reduce total construction costs.

Believing all of these benefits to be significant, the World Bank and other organizations sought ways to encourage the use of more labor-based methods in infrastructure construction. Suspecting that the resistance to labor-based methods came from staff engineers trained in developed countries, whose training led them to assume incorrectly that labor-based methods yield lower-quality results, these development organizations undertook studies of infrastructure construction tasks and identified many for which labor-based methods produced results of equal or higher quality than equipment-based methods. Examples include the construction and maintenance of low-traffic gravel feeder roads, irrigation canals, small dams, erosion-control projects, forestry projects, and buildings such as community centers and teachers' houses. In the late 1970s, they ran small pilot programs in many countries in which labor-based methods not only yielded results of comparable quality to equipment-based methods but also did so at lower total cost. The results convinced a few countries to pursue more labor-based methods, but in most countries infrastructure programs reverted to equipment-based methods as soon as the pilot programs ended.

Stock and de Veen (1996) offer several reasons why infrastructure program officials tend to resist the use of labor-based methods. First, even though labor-based methods may be cheaper than equipment-based methods when evaluated using market wages and prices, they might appear more costly to officials in infrastructure ministries because minimum wage and other labor legislation raises the cost of labor above the market level, and donor grants for equipment imports render equipment artificially cheap. Given their mandate to construct infrastructure, the officials might simply be unwilling to accept higher costs for the sake of improved poverty reduction.

Second, labor-based projects place much greater demands on supervisory capacity. When performing construction in house, government agencies must train many more staff to supervise teams of low-skill labor. For example, it can take 200 to 300 workers, in groups of 20 to 30, each with a supervisor, to accomplish the work of one bulldozer operated by one or two skilled workers (Stock and de Veen, 1996). When governments undertake construction through private-sector contractors, the use of labor-based methods requires them to shift from working with a small number of large contractors (who specialize in equipment-based methods) to working with a large number of smaller contractors (who have ready access to local labor in many locations). Such contractors require supervision by government staff and can require significant training when they are new to government contracting.

Third, labor-based projects also require much better administration of payments than equipment-based projects do, and infrastructure programs often lack adequate capacity. Equipment vendors and equipment-service contractors accept lump-sum payments and are somewhat flexible regarding the timing of payments. Low-wage workers, in contrast, must be paid weekly and suffer significant distress when payments are late. Public works programs around the world have experienced difficulties in making regular, timely wage payments, and late payments lead to work stoppages and even riots, slowing project completion and raising costs. Even India's highly regarded Employment Guarantee Scheme runs into wage-payment problems, though computerized registration, the issuing of worker cards, and payment through savings accounts in banks and post offices appear to have reduced such problems in the state of Andra Pradesh (Lal et al., 2010).

A final source of resistance to labor-based methods may be the professional culture and incentives shaping the decisions of individual program engineers. They might see labor-based projects as second class and perceive that career advancement follows only from pursuing equipment-based projects.

REFERENCES

Adato, Michelle, and Lawrence J. Haddad. "Targeting Poverty Through Community-Based Public Works Programs: A Cross-Disciplinary Assessment of Recent Experience in South Africa." FCND Discussion Paper No. 121. Washington, D.C.: International Food Policy Research Institute, 2001. http://www.ifpri.org/sites/default/files/publications/fcndp121.pdf

Bliss, Christopher, and Nicholas Stern. "Productivity, Wages and Nutrition: Part I: The Theory." *Journal of Development Economics* 5(4): 331–362, 1978a. doi:10.1016/0304-3878(78)90016-0

Bliss, Christopher, and Nicholas Stern. "Productivity, Wages and Nutrition: Part II: Some Observations." *Journal of Development Economics* 5(4): 363–398, 1978b. doi:10.1016/0304-3878(78)90017-2

Datt, Gaurav, and Martin Ravallion. "Income Gains for the Poor from Public Works Employment: Evidence From Two Indian Villages." LSMS Working Paper No. 100. Washington, D.C.: World Bank, 1994. http://go.worldbank.org/EWMQ8YMJ80

Deshingkar, Priya, Craig Johnson, and John Farrington. "State Transfers to the Poor and Back: The Case of the Food-for-Work Program in India." *World Development* 33(4): 575–591, 2005. doi:10.1016/j.worlddev.2005.01.003

Gaiha, Raghav. "Wages, Participation and Targeting—The Case of the Employment Guarantee Scheme in India." *Journal of International Development* 8(6): 785–803, 1996. doi:10.1002/(ISSN)1099-1328

Galasso, Emanuela, and Martin Ravallion. "Social Protection in a Crisis: Argentina's Plan Jefes y Jefas." *The World Bank Economic Review* 18 (3): 367–399, 2004. doi:10.1093/wber/lhh044

Galasso, Emanuela, Martin Ravallion and Agustin Salvia. "Assisting the Transition from Workfare to Work: A Randomized Experiment." *Industrial and Labor Relations Review* 58(1): 128–142, 2004. http://www.jstor.org/stable/4126640

Government of Maharashtra State. *Tenth Five Year Plan 2002–2007 and Annual Plan 2002–2003*, 2002

Imbert, Clement, and John Papp. "Equilibrium Distributional Impacts of Government Employment Programs: Evidence of India's Employment

Guarantee." Paris: Paris School of Economics, 2012. http://www.parisschoolofeconomics.eu/docs/imbert-clement/2012-03-19-pse-working-paper-equilibrium-distributional-impacts-of-government-programs–imbert-papp.pdf.

Jalan, Jyotsna, and Martin Ravallion. "Income Gains to the Poor From Workfare—Estimates for Argentina's Trabajar Program." Policy Research Working Paper No. 2149. Washington, D.C.: World Bank, 1999. http://go.worldbank.org/B2Q6WI87J0

Lal, Radhika, Steve Miller, Maikel Lieuw-Kie-Song, and Daniel Kostzer. *Public Works and Employment Programmes: Towards a Long-Term Development Approach*. Working Paper No. 66. Brasilia: International Policy Centre for Inclusive Growth, 2010. http://www.ipc-undp.org/pub/IPCWorkingPaper66.pdf

Olken, Benjamin A. "Monitoring Corruption: Evidence From a Field Experiment in Indonesia." *Journal of Political Economy* 115(2): 200–249, 2007. doi:10.1086/509548

Ravallion, Martin. "Reaching the Poor through Public Employment: Arguments, Evidence, and Lessons from South Asia." *World Bank Research Observer* 6(2):153–175, 1991. doi:10.1093/wbro/6.2.153

Ravallion, Martin, Gaurav Datt, and Shubham Chaudhuri. "Higher Wages for Relief Work Can Make Many of the Poor Worse Off: Recent Evidence From Maharashtra's "Employment Guarantee Scheme"." Policy, Research, and External Affairs Working Paper No. 568. Washington, D.C.: World Bank, 1991. http://go.worldbank.org/G5TJIWY2C1

Stock, Elisabeth A., and Jan de Veen. "Expanding Labor-Based Methods for Road Works in Africa." World Bank Technical Paper No. 347. Washington, D.C.: World Bank, 1996. http://go.worldbank.org/N263XHODZ0

Subbarao, Kalanidhi. "Systemic Shocks and Social Protection: Role and Effectiveness of Public Works Programs." Social Protection Discussion Paper No. 0302. Washington, D.C.: World Bank, 2003. http://go.worldbank.org/4V42BZLET0

QUESTIONS FOR REVIEW

1. What objectives might policymakers hope to achieve by implementing workfare programs?

2. What design details distinguish one workfare program from another on paper? In practice?

3. Define all the elements of the graph in Figure 16.1a. How do we know that the person whose opportunities and preferences are depicted in this graph would choose to work in the absence of the program? How do we know she would choose to participate in the workfare program?

4. Define *self-targeting* and use graphs like those in Figure 16.1 to explain how a workfare program can be self-targeting.

5. Under what conditions might workfare program benefits leak to the nonpoor?

6. Under what conditions might a workfare program fail to provide benefits to a poor household?

7. Explain why the dashed program budget constraints in Figures 16.2a and b take the shapes given in the graphs.

8. How and why might changes in the nature of a workfare program's work and working conditions alter targeting outcomes?

9. Under what conditions might participation in a workfare program have little impact on a worker's well-being, even when the worker works full time in a workfare program and receives pay for full-time participation?

10. Why do workfare programs have greater potential to crowd out labor income at the level of the individual participant than other targeted transfer programs?

11. Through what channels might a workfare program alter participants' behavior? What kinds of behavior might be altered?

12. Under what conditions might a workfare program reduce vulnerability?

13. For each of the two graphs in Figure 16.3, discuss (a) the initial labor market conditions described by the solid *LD* and *LS* schedules and (in panel a) the w_m line; (b) whether a workfare program offering a wage lower than the initial market level would attract workers; (c) the effect on the market wage for low-skill workers, and on total low-skill employment, of introducing a workfare program that matches the market wage and hires Q in labor; (d) the direct and indirect effects of such a program on low-skill workers; and (e) how these effects might change if the program paid a wage significantly higher than the market wage for low-skill labor.

14. What short-run spillover effects and long-term impacts might change when a workfare program's design is altered?

15. What broad categories of cost must be covered by workfare program budgets?

16. Discuss the benefits and costs of raising a workfare program's wage from the level of the market wage for low-skill workers to a significantly higher level.

17. Discuss the benefits and costs of switching from time rates to piece rates.

18. Discuss some of the reasons policymakers appear to face a tradeoff, when designing or funding public works programs, between greater success in poverty and vulnerability reduction, on the one hand, and creation of more valuable infrastructure, on the other.

QUESTIONS FOR DISCUSSION

1. Draw a graph like Figure 16.1a.
   a. Define all the elements of the graph.
   b. Explain how we know that this person chooses to participate in the workfare program.
   c. Let *Y* be the quantity of income this participant receives from the workfare program. Which vertical distance in your graph is equal to *Y*?
   d. Which vertical distance in your graph is equal to the impact of the program on this worker's income?
   e. Draw the budget constraint this person would have faced had she been given *Y* as an unconditional transfer rather than earning it through a workfare program. Would she have been better or worse off?

2. Why might some analysts conclude that public employment schemes are unlikely to reach the "poorest of the poor"?

3. Draw a graph with budget constraints similar to those in Figure 16.1a but that depicts a worker who (a) chooses not to work in the absence of the program, (b) chooses to participate when the workfare program is introduced, but (c) is not made much better off by the program (despite earning the full program wage).

4. Discuss the possible channels through which workfare program participation might affect children's school attendance, even when the program does not allow children younger than 18 years to participate and this restriction is well enforced.

5. Drawing on the discussion of workfare program impacts on labor markets, discuss the conditions under which major employers in a small rural community would be most likely to oppose the creation of a workfare project in or near their community.

6. Discuss the significance of each of the questions listed in Box 16.4.

7. Discuss the potential benefits and costs of replacing a means-tested cash transfer program by a workfare program.

8. Discuss the possible rationale for *combining* a large workfare program with a small, explicitly targeted cash transfer

program when designing a strategy for poverty reduction in some regions. What approach to targeting of the cash transfers would render the cash transfer program most *complementary* to the workfare program?

PROBLEMS

1. Consider a workfare program that employs no means testing or categorical restrictions. That is, it is a program that provides jobs to any workers who come forward to accept program jobs at the program wage.
   a. *List* some details of program design that could be modified to reduce leakage to the nonpoor. (Please do not consider the introduction of means testing or categorical restrictions.)
   b. State the *direction* in which those design details should be modified to reduce leakage, and *explain* how such a change might reduce leakage.
   c. *Discuss the potential costs* associated with modifying the program in the indicated directions.

2. The following table describes some features of income distribution and workfare program participation in Village X. The program provides employment to anyone who wishes it at the program wage. "Quintile 1" refers to the poorest 20 percent of the population. In this village there are 1,000 households; thus "Quintile 1" refers to the poorest 200 households, "Quintile 2" refers to the 200 households with the next lowest incomes, and so forth. The *poverty line* is such that only households in Quintile 1 are considered poor. Total income for each household is the sum of program income (the wages received for work in the program) and nonprogram income (income from any other source, including labor income and receipt of private transfers).

Quintiles Based on Nonprogram Income	Average Nonprogram Income per Household*	Average Total Income per Household (Including Program and Nonprogram Income)*	Percentage of Households Participating in the Program
1	100	200	70
2	200	210	10
3	300	302	2
4	500	500	0
5	1,000	1,000	0

*These figures average over both participants and nonparticipants within quintiles.

   a. Do leakages to the nonpoor appear to be large or small relative to total transfers to the poor? Explain.
   b. What do you learn about noncoverage of the poor from this table? What more might you guess about the groups among the poor that are excluded from benefits?

   c. Explain how the numbers in the table can be used to derive the conclusion that among *poor program participants*, total income (including program income) is *more than* double their nonprogram incomes.
   d. Do the figures in the table justify the conclusion that the program *impact* on the income of participating poor households is to more than double it? Why or why not?

3. Draw three graphs in which the horizontal axis measures home time H and the vertical axis measures consumption expenditure C, as in Figure 16.1a.
   a. In the first graph, draw in and label the alternative activity budget constraint and the workfare program budget constraint for a situation in which the market wage for low-skill labor is greater than the program wage, but the individual in question is unemployed and unable to find any private sector work at the market wage. You may treat this as a situation in which the individual effectively faces a wage of zero; for each additional day she attempts to work, she reduces home time by one day and increases consumption expenditure by zero.
   b. In the second graph, draw in and label the alternative activity budget constraint and the workfare program budget constraint for a situation in which the market wage for low-skill labor is greater than the program wage and in which the individual in question is underemployed, in the sense that she can find only a small, fixed number of days of work per month at the market wage. (After exhausting those days, any additional days of work she might devote to alternative activities would generate no increases in labor earnings.) Draw in indifference curves to demonstrate that a worker might choose to participate in the workfare program under these conditions.
   c. In the third graph, first replicate what you have drawn for part b. Now add in a third budget constraint that depicts the possibility of first working the limited number of hours at the market wage and then allocating additional work hours to the workfare program.

4. Draw a diagram depicting the local market for low-skill labor in competitive equilibrium. Describe (in the graph and in words) the impact on the market wage of introducing a workfare program that offers a wage higher than the initial equilibrium wage and that truly guarantees employment for anyone who wishes it at the program wage. You may assume that there are no fixed costs of participation and that work in the program and work in alternative activities are

9. Read Deshingkar et al. (2005) on the Food-for-Work program in India. On the basis of this reading, what do you think are the key design flaws that led to the disastrous performance of this program?

equally attractive. What happens to the competitive wage paid by private sector employers?

5. By some estimates, over 3,000 farmers in the Indian state of Karnataka committed suicide between 2000 and 2006. (Though large enough to be troubling, 3,000 is a small number relative to the total number of farmers in the state.) In many cases the farmers had been hit by shocks—such as poor rainfall, irrigation system failures or pest attacks—which rendered it difficult for them to feed their families and repay debts. The state government implemented a cash transfer program which can be thought of as a *suicide compensation program*, in which the families of farmers who commit suicide are compensated for the loss of their main breadwinner with a sum of money equivalent to about U.S. $2,000 (a very large sum of money relative to local incomes and debt burdens). Consider replacing this suicide compensation program by a *workfare program* that truly guarantees employment and that puts participants to work building infrastructure. The program would pay a daily wage below the wage typically paid to low-skill manual labor in this region, and below the typical daily returns to farmers cultivating farms that have not been hit by shocks, but high enough to provide workers and their families with at least enough food to subsist. List the main potential benefits and costs associated with replacing the suicide compensation program by the workfare program, and provide a brief explanation as to why each benefit or cost might emerge.

chapter
17

Agricultural Market Interventions and Reforms

Governments intervene in markets when they tax, subsidize, or regulate market transactions. By raising or lowering important prices, such policies raise or lower real incomes for net sellers of the relevant goods and push real incomes in the opposite direction for net buyers (Chapter 7). They also initiate chains of impact that can ultimately alter many important development outcomes, including poverty, inequality, production structure, international trade flows, and economic growth.

In this chapter we develop tools for analyzing market interventions and reforms. We focus on **agricultural market interventions**, which have especially important connections to poverty and growth in developing countries, where poor and middle-income households spend large fractions of their incomes on food, and where many households earn their livelihoods in agriculture (see Chapter 2).

17.1 Developing-Country Government Intervention in Agricultural Markets
17.1A Background and focus

In the 1930s, 1940s, and 1950s many developing-country governments intervened in agricultural markets—using diverse policy instruments described below—with the aim of reducing urban food prices. Finding theoretical support in the Lewis model of labor-surplus dualistic development and related research (Chapter 4), policymakers considered growth of the manufacturing sector essential for development, and they hoped that by holding down urban food prices—thereby holding down the wages that urban employers had to pay to draw workers out of agriculture—they would speed the expansion of manufacturing. Seeking to hold down the budgetary cost of subsidizing urban food consumption, many governments also held down the prices paid to food crop farmers, implicitly taxing them to pay for the consumer food subsidies. Governments furthermore taxed exports of coffee, cocoa, cotton, and other cash crops and used the tax revenue to help finance investment in manufacturing infrastructure.[1]

By the 1960s and 1970s, researchers and policymakers began to realize that the rural poor were not benefitting from economic growth, and they began to suspect that high taxation of agriculture was slowing growth by choking off the production of food and exports. Their initial efforts to encourage agriculture left farm prices artificially low for many farmers, but they attempted to compensate for this by providing farmers with subsidized inputs and credit. To protect small farmers from what they believed to be exploitative market middlemen, many governments, especially in Africa, also provided public sector agricultural marketing services and prohibited most private sector involvement in marketing.

In the 1980s and 1990s, changing thought about how developing economies work and about what roles governments should play in development, together with budgetary crises and pressure from foreign aid donors, led many developing-country governments to undertake

---

[1] Governments also taxed agriculture indirectly with policies that protected manufacturing sectors from international trade and that maintained overvalued exchange rates (see Chapter 11).

liberalizing reforms of policies toward agricultural markets. More specifically, greater confidence in markets (Chapter 4) and greater conviction about the importance of integration into international markets for economic growth (Chapter 11) motivated efforts to reduce taxes, subsidies, and regulations on agricultural market transactions and to reduce government involvement in markets more generally. Policymakers hoped such reforms would speed growth, shrink government budget deficits, and reduce poverty. The results differed greatly across countries and sometimes proved disappointing, as we will see. Despite extensive reforms, taxation of agriculture remains significant in some developing countries, and especially in low-income countries.

This chapter equips readers to understand the differentiated impacts of past agricultural market interventions and reforms and to brainstorm about the design and evaluation of future policies toward agricultural markets.

Agricultural market reforms are often undertaken together with reforms of other policies important for agricultural performance, such as policies toward rural infrastructure and agricultural research and extension. While we make reference to these important policies in this chapter, we reserve thorough analysis of them for later chapters, because they are best understood using additional analytical tools.

Agricultural performance in any one developing country is influenced by agricultural market interventions in the developed countries and in other developing countries. Developed countries tend to subsidize agriculture rather than tax it, and such policies tend to drive down world prices for agricultural commodities, thereby reducing developing countries' potential to profit from agricultural exports (World Bank, 2007). In Chapter 7 we briefly examined the potential impact on developing economies of rising global food prices, such as might follow from the removal of agricultural subsidies in the developed countries. In this chapter we focus on the impacts of developing countries' policies toward their own agricultural markets, noting their implications for other countries.

17.1B Design and implementation of agricultural market interventions and reforms

Policy design choices

A first step toward understanding agricultural market reforms is to become familiar with the many ways governments intervene in agricultural markets. At the broadest level, an agricultural market intervention is defined by the choice of which commodity is involved, whether the policy increases or reduces the prices paid by consumers and paid to producers for that commodity, and the size of the resulting price increases or reductions. Policies that lower consumer prices relative to free-market levels are said to impart **general consumer subsidies**. The adjective *general* means that the subsidies are available to all households and contrasts with the *targeted* food subsidies distributed through the food-based targeted transfer programs described in Chapter 15. Policies that raise producer prices impart **producer subsidies**, whereas policies that reduce producer prices below free-market levels imply **taxation of producers**. Because these policies begin to alter socioeconomic outcomes by altering agricultural prices, we sometimes refer to them as **agricultural pricing policies**.

At a more detailed level, agricultural pricing policies are defined by the types of taxes, subsidies, and regulations involved. Among explicit taxes on agricultural transactions, the most widely used are **import tariffs** (i.e., taxes on import transactions) and **export taxes** (i.e., taxes on export transactions), which have long served as important sources of revenue for developing country governments. Taxing imports and exports is easier than taxing domestic agricultural commodity transactions, many of which are small and informal, and take place among neighbors in dispersed geographic locations. Tax rates usually vary across precisely defined categories and qualities of goods, and taxes may be specified as **ad valorem taxes** (i.e., percentages of total sales value) or **unit taxes** (i.e., specified currency values per physical unit).

Governments sometimes discourage imports or exports with **quantitative restrictions** rather than taxes, prohibiting such transactions or limiting their quantities. When they impose **import quotas**, for example, they require traders to obtain licenses for importing, and they grant only a limited number of licenses. They might give away the valuable licenses free of charge or auction them off to the highest bidders. We will see that quantitative restrictions on imports have impacts very similar to import tariffs.

In principle, governments can also set the prices at which specified goods must be sold or can impose legal minimums or maximums for these prices. Their scope for employing such **price regulations** is limited by their capacity to enforce them. Often, legal minimum prices (above free-market levels) are enforceable only when governments stand ready to buy any produce farmers wish to sell to the government at the minimum price. The Brazilian agricultural price-support scheme described in Helfand and Castro de Rezende (2001) is an example of such a policy.

In addition to regulating private transactions, policymakers can mandate government purchases and sales of agricultural produce at market prices. A government might, for example, purchase grain in years of ample supply, building up **buffer stocks**, and sell them during times of shortage, with the aim of stabilizing prices. It might also purchase quantities of staple foods to distribute through a targeted transfer program.

Many developing-country governments have intervened in a more comprehensive way by setting up state-owned **agricultural marketing boards** with exclusive rights to buy and sell specific crops. Marketing boards for export crops like coffee and cocoa buy the crops from domestic producers at prices set by policymakers, sell them in international markets at world prices, and undertake all the marketing activities required to transfer the commodities from farms to foreign buyers. Farmers are required by law to sell their produce only to the marketing boards or to licensed traders who deliver their produce to the marketing boards.

When governments set purchase prices above what farmers could get by exporting directly, then farmers gladly sell to the marketing boards. More often, however, export-crop marketing boards set purchase prices below the levels that farmers would receive if they were allowed to export directly. The difference between the low price paid to farmers and the higher price (net of transfer costs) that the farmers would receive if they exported directly represents an implicit tax on exports. Sometimes the taxes have been very large indeed; for example, during the 1970s and 1980s, cocoa farmers in Africa implicitly paid a tax of approximately 51 percent of the world price (McMillan, 2001). In such cases governments must enforce marketing boards' exclusive purchase rights by detecting and punishing illicit sales. Often enforcement efforts focus on preventing the private transport of commodities along major roads or through major border crossings.

Marketing boards for domestic staple food crops like wheat or maize sell mostly to domestic food processors or consumers rather than to international markets, either buying the food from domestic farmers or importing it. They must pay world market prices for imported goods, but policymakers have discretion over the prices paid to domestic farmers and the prices charged to domestic buyers. Often they subsidize domestic consumers. Policies are said to provide consumers with **explicit subsidy** when the costs of the consumer subsidy are borne by the marketing board, which operates at a deficit financed by the government. Consumer subsidies on imported food must be financed explicitly, because foreign suppliers cannot be forced to accept below-market prices. Policies are said to provide consumers with an **implicit subsidy** when governments push some or all of the cost of the consumer subsidy onto domestic producers by paying farmers at below-market prices.

Direct government involvement in agricultural markets through marketing boards usually requires the establishment of government **buying stations** at which the marketing boards collect produce from farmers and government **distribution systems** through which they sell the produce to international markets or to domestic food processors, retailers, or consumers. Often marketing boards have engaged in **pan-territorial** and **pan-seasonal pricing**, in which they set prices that are the same in all locations (despite the greater transportation costs associated with buying in more remote regions) and in all seasons of the year (despite the natural tendency for market prices to fall during harvest seasons and to rise after harvests are exhausted). We will see that impacts of marketing boards' policies are shaped by the geographic distribution of buying stations and shops.

Many marketing boards have engaged not only in buying and selling crops but also in providing subsidized fertilizer, agricultural extension services, and short-term credit. Even when governments do not establish marketing boards, they sometimes subsidize, tax, or regulate fertilizer sales.

Many current agricultural pricing policy questions have to do with the wave of liberalizing reforms in developing countries that began in the mid-1980s and gathered momentum in the 1990s. These reforms involved changes of two broad types: (1) reductions in taxes, subsidies, and quantitative restrictions on transactions and (2) reduced government involvement in the provision of marketing services for agricultural outputs and inputs, agricultural extension services, and agricultural credit. The exact nature of the reforms differed greatly across countries, as did their impacts. Liberalizing reforms in Vietnam's agricultural markets in the 1990s, described in Box 17.1, primarily involved relaxation of quantitative restrictions on rice exports and fertilizer imports. Reforms in many African countries, which we discuss later in the chapter, involved the partial or complete dismantling of agricultural marketing boards.

Disappointed with the results of direct government involvement in agricultural marketing activities, and also with liberalizing reforms, some policymakers are now attempting to craft more focused government interventions in agricultural markets; these reforms are aimed at encouraging and expanding markets rather than altering prices or replacing private market institutions

≡ Box 17.1 Reforms of Rice and Fertilizer Market Policies in Vietnam in the 1990s

For Vietnam in the 1990s, "agricultural market liberalization" meant liberalization of markets for rice and chemical fertilizer. As of the early 1990s, 85 percent of rural households in Vietnam produced rice and 42 percent sold rice (Benjamin and Brandt, 2004). The largest quantities of rice produced for sale were produced in the Mekong Delta region in the south and (to a lesser extent) the Red River Delta region in the north, with smaller quantities of rice produced primarily for local consumption in the mountainous areas in between and farther inland. Of the two major rice-producing regions, the Mekong Delta region in the south was the more natural breadbasket for the country, with greater total acreage, lower population density, and larger farm sizes (Minot and Goletti, 2000).

Three major policies defined government involvement in agricultural markets prior to reform in the mid-1990s: quantitative restrictions on international rice exports, quantitative restrictions on sales of rice from the south to the north within the country, and quantitative restrictions on chemical fertilizer imports. Though the private sector was active in producing, transporting, milling, and selling rice to wholesalers or retailers in the 1990s, only a small number of state-owned enterprises had the legal right to export rice. By restricting the quantity of licenses granted for exporting, the government restricted the quantity of rice that could be exported to international markets. Perhaps to protect the older rice culture of the Red River Delta region, the government also used licensing requirements to restrict the sale of rice from the breadbasket area in the south to the north. No chemical fertilizers were produced domestically, and the limits on chemical fertilizer imports effectively fixed chemical fertilizer availability at a low level.

Liberalizing reforms over the 1990s relaxed all three sets of restrictions. Quantitative restrictions on exports were virtually eliminated,

as the value of export licenses issued expanded from 1 million metric tons in 1992 to 4.5 million metric tons in 1998, a limit that was no longer binding. Barriers to transport and sale of rice from south to north were reduced. The government also tripled the quantity of chemical fertilizer imports allowed into the country.

As is almost always the case with agricultural market reforms, the reforms just described were components of a larger wave of reforms affecting every sector of the Vietnamese economy (Glewwe, 2004). Vietnam embarked on the *Doi Moi* or "renovation" reforms in the late 1980s, transforming a previously socialist economy into a regulated market economy. The basic institutions of agricultural production were radically changed in 1988, when agricultural land was decollectivized, individual farmers were given long-term leases to pieces of the land they had farmed collectively, and sale of crops to private-sector marketers was legalized. These reforms brought rapid expansion of agricultural production. In fact, over the next few years Vietnam was transformed from a rice importer to the third largest rice exporter in the world. Land rights were further strengthened in the late 1990s, when farmers gained longer-term leases and the rights to transfer, inherit, and mortgage their land. Legal land rights changed little during the period of the rice and fertilizer market reforms in the early and mid-1990s, though the effects of the earlier land rights reforms might have continued to accumulate during the period. Privatization and improved macroeconomic policies were fueling rapid urban growth during the 1990s, increasing demand for agricultural goods, but the direct effects of this growth on rural markets and livelihoods were limited by restrictions on migration into the major cities.

with government marketing boards. In Chapter 8 we examined such policies, which seek to correct market and institutional failures and reduce transfer costs. **Transfer costs** include all the transport, storage, financing, and transaction costs associated with the transfer of goods from their producers to their ultimate users through markets. Policies to reduce transfer costs include efforts to improve enforcement of contracts between buyers and sellers, establish systems for grading agricultural produce qualities, help farmers organize cooperatives, and invest in transport and communication infrastructure.

Implementation concerns

The impacts of agricultural pricing policies depend on the quality of governance within the public sector institutions assigned to enforce them. Governance is an especially great concern in the case of marketing board policies, because marketing boards take over many marketing activities that would otherwise be performed by the private sector, and poorly governed marketing boards might perform these activities less efficiently than private traders. Thus, when analyzing the implementation of agricultural market interventions, it is important to examine how and how well taxes, regulations, and quantitative restrictions are enforced, how effectively marketing boards control crop transactions, how efficiently they perform their marketing functions, and the nature and quality of the agricultural extension and credit services they provide.

17.2 The Economics of Agricultural Market Intervention and Reform

Agricultural pricing policies directly affect people's lives by altering the prices at which they may buy or sell agricultural outputs and inputs. In the first two sections below we describe how to use Chapter 8's graphical models of market equilibrium for studying the impacts of agricultural pricing policies on agricultural prices. In later sections, we discuss how to analyze the direct and indirect effects of those price changes on households of diverse types.

17.2A Market-level analysis: taxes and subsidies

We may think of agricultural pricing policies as altering agricultural prices through two types of activity: (1) taxing, subsidizing, and regulating agricultural transactions and (2) altering the (nontax) transfer costs on agricultural market transactions by altering the institutions that govern marketing activities. In this section we use the market equilibrium models of Chapter 8 to examine the impacts on prices of the first set of activities. We discuss the impacts of the second set in the next section.

Explicit export taxes

Consider first the impacts of introducing an explicit tax on exports. We will see that:

> In addition to raising government revenue, an explicit export tax reduces the export crop's domestic price. This effectively taxes domestic producers and subsidizes domestic consumers. The sizes of impacts depend critically on local supply and demand elasticities.

The solid local demand (*LD*), local supply (*LS*), and local export price (*LEP*) schedules in Figure 17.1 depict a national market in exporting equilibrium before the introduction of an export tax. The local supply and demand schedules indicate the tons of export crop that would be sold or purchased by the country's residents in the country's central market at any price charged there. The local export price (*LEP*), which equals the world price less all per-ton transfer costs incurred

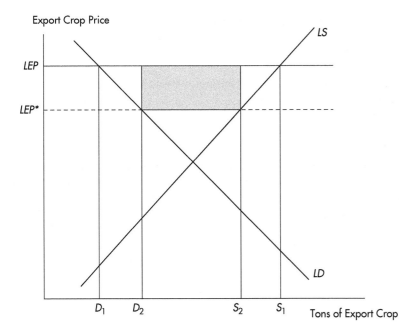

FIGURE 17.1
Introduction of an Export Tax

by exporters, lies above the autarky price.[2] In equilibrium, the domestic price equals *LEP*, domestic consumers purchase D_1 tons of the crop, domestic producers sell S_1 tons, and $X_1 = S_1 - D_1$ tons are exported.

The introduction of an export tax adds a new component to the transfer costs associated with selling in world markets and reduces the revenue that farmers bring home from international sales. If the country is a small supplier to international markets, the tax leaves the world price unchanged but reduces the *LEP*. If it falls to the level of *LEP** in the diagram, the market remains in exporting equilibrium and the domestic price also falls to *LEP**. In addition to explicitly taxing farmers who export, the policy implicitly taxes farmers who sell in any domestic markets affected by the policy and implicitly subsidizes households who purchase in those markets. Buyers and sellers in more remote communities, which remain un-integrated into national markets, are not directly affected. Domestic purchases in the national market rise to D_2, sales by domestic farmers (whether to domestic or international buyers) fall to S_2, and the quantity exported falls to $X_2 = S_2 - D_2$. The difference between *LEP* and *LEP** is the per-unit export tax. Thus the total revenue collected by the government through this export tax is represented by the area of the shaded rectangle.

Further thought about Figure 17.1 reminds us that the sizes of an export tax's impacts on the quantities supplied, demanded, and exported and on the government budget depend on the elasticities of the local supply and demand schedules (as well as the size of the tax). If local supply and demand schedules are both highly elastic, then the tax reduces exports a great deal, as the tax leads to a large contraction in the quantity supplied and a large increase in the quantity purchased domestically. If this shrinkage in the tax base is strong enough, then imposing the new tax might generate little revenue, and increasing the tax rate could even cause tax revenue to fall. Empirical studies of producer and consumer behavior, such as those guided by the models of Chapter 6, are thus of great importance for predicting the aggregate impacts of agricultural market interventions on sales, purchases, trade flows, and government budgets.

---

[2] We know that the world price lies above the *LEP*, and the local import price (*LIP*) lies above that. They do not figure into our analysis here, so we leave them out of the diagram to reduce clutter.

In the 1940s and 1950s, many prominent development thinkers took a **structuralist view** of the developing world, thinking of most elasticities—and especially agricultural supply elasticities—as very low (see Chapter 4). If agricultural supply were highly inelastic, then export taxes would bring large increases in tax revenue while causing little contraction in agricultural production. Thus the structuralist view of the world helped to motivate high rates of taxation of agricultural exports.

With the benefit of hindsight, and of a much larger body of empirical research on agricultural producers around the world, most economists now reject the strict structuralist view of the world. When farmers have access to inputs, credit, technological ideas, and markets, agricultural supplies have often proved to be quite elastic. For example, reforms that raised producer prices for coffee and cocoa in the 1990s led to large increases in production in many reforming countries, though sometimes only after a delay of several years (Akiyama et al., 2001). At the same time, however, supply responses to higher prices were much smaller in regions where farmers lacked good infrastructure connections to markets and lacked access to agricultural research, extension, and credit services.

Some countries are sufficiently large suppliers to world markets that reductions in their exports would cause world prices to rise, contrary to the assumption we have made thus far. For example, Warr (2001) reviews estimates suggesting that the world rice price rises by 1 to 2 percent for every 1 percent reduction in Thailand's rice exports. Such world price increases partially compensate domestic farmers for increased tax rates, reducing the net impact on their incomes.

Quantitative restrictions on exports

Figure 17.2 illustrates how to analyze a quantitative export restriction using a domestic market equilibrium diagram. The solid *LD*, *LS*, and *LEP* schedules again describe equilibrium in the absence of intervention. Under such conditions, $X_1 = S_1 - D_1$ units of the crop would be exported. Now suppose that the government limits what may be exported to the smaller quantity Q. In

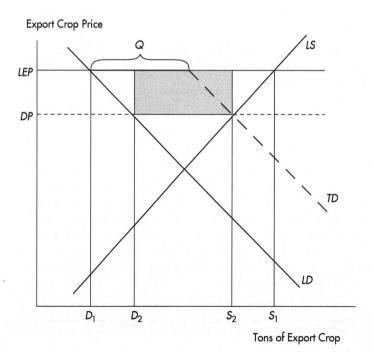

FIGURE 17.2
Introduction of a
Quantitative Export
Restriction

practical terms, this policy limits international demand for local produce to the quantity Q. At any domestic price below *LEP*, the total demand for local produce is now just equal to the quantity demanded by local consumers (as indicated by the *LD* schedule) plus the quantity Q. We may thus trace out a new (dashed) **total demand schedule** *TD*, which lies parallel to *LD* and to the right of it by the quantity Q, and which indicates the total quantity of local produce effectively demanded by local and world buyers at any domestic price. The new equilibrium domestic price *DP* is found at the intersection between the new total demand schedule *TD* and the unchanged local supply schedule, and this new price lies below *LEP*.

Figure 17.2 demonstrates that:

> A quantitative restriction on exports has many of the same effects as an export tax.

By limiting the impact of international demand on the domestic market, it reduces domestic prices, as well as local quantities supplied and exported, while increasing the local quantity demanded. In fact, it is possible to identify an export tax rate that is **equivalent** to this quantitative export restriction, in the sense that it has the same impacts on the domestic price and on the quantities produced, consumed, and exported. For the case illustrated in Figure 17.2, the equivalent tax rate is given by the vertical distance between the *LEP* and *DP* lines.

The quantitative export restriction and the equivalent export tax differ in one important respect, however. Under an export tax, the value represented by the shaded rectangle in Figure 17.2 is channeled directly to the government as tax revenue. Under a quantitative export restriction, this value represents a windfall gain to the privileged exporters who are granted export rights. Such rights allow them to buy Q (which is equal to $X_2 = S_2 - D_2$) of the export crop in the domestic market at the lower domestic price *DP* and sell it in the world market, bringing home *LEP* per unit. If the government simply gives these valuable rights to favored individuals or firms, the quantitative restriction generates no government revenue and encourages firms to waste resources competing for the favor of the government officials in charge of distributing the rights. The government may instead extract much of the value attached to the shaded rectangle by auctioning off the export rights.

Input market taxes and subsidies

Governments often intervene in agricultural input markets as well as output markets. Box 17.1 described the example of Vietnam's quantitative restriction on the import of chemical fertilizer. We can work out the potential effects of such input market policies on producer and consumer crop prices in two steps. First, we use diagrams describing equilibrium in the relevant input markets to work out the likely impacts on domestic input prices. Second, we use diagrams describing markets for the agricultural crops that are produced using the relevant inputs to examine the effects of the input price changes on producer and consumer crop prices.

The reader could demonstrate, for example, that a quantitative restriction on fertilizer imports increases the domestic price of fertilizer. The model of profit-maximizing production decisions in Chapter 6 suggests that if fertilizer is an important input to rice production, then the increase in the fertilizer price reduces the quantity of rice that farmers supply at any price, shifting the local rice supply schedule to the left. The reader could further demonstrate that if the market for rice is in exporting equilibrium (with or without an explicit export tax or subsidy), a leftward shift in the supply schedule reduces the quantities of rice produced and exported but leaves local producer and consumer prices unchanged. If the market for rice is instead in autarky equilibrium or is governed by a quantitative restriction on exports, then the leftward shift of the local supply schedule tends to increase consumer and producer rice prices. The rice price increase then constitutes an implicit tax on consumers and attenuates to some extent the net taxation of farmers (see problem 1).

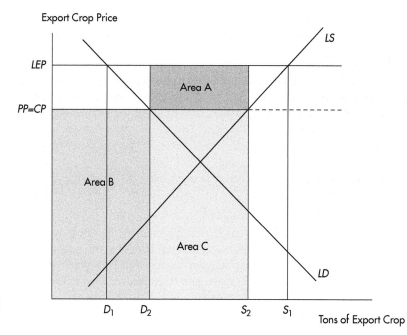

FIGURE 17.3
Introduction of an
Export Crop Marketing
Board That Taxes
Farmers and Subsidizes
Consumers

Marketing boards

Introducing a marketing board for an export crop is a much larger and more complicated intervention than imposing an export tax, yet we may begin our analysis of such interventions with market diagrams very similar to those we employed above. For simplicity, we assume initially that all of the country's producers and consumers live near the central market and face similar, very low transport costs. This simplifies our discussion of Figure 17.3. We relax this assumption below.

Figure 17.3 illustrates the effects on market-level outcomes of introducing an export crop marketing board that implicitly taxes farmers. The government sets up a marketing board and gives it the sole legal right to buy, sell, and export the relevant crop. The *LD* and *LS* schedules remain relevant, because they describe the quantities that local producers and consumers would supply and demand in the central market at any prices the marketing board sets. The *LEP* schedule remains relevant, too, because the marketing board must sell to world markets at the world price and "take home" (after paying the cost of transferring exports to the world market) *LEP* on any quantities exported. (Here we assume that the marketing board faces the same export transfer costs as the private sector. We relax this assumption in the next section.)

The marketing board implicitly taxes farmers when it pays them an **administered producer price** *PP* less than the *LEP*. To determine how much produce farmers would deliver to the marketing board at such a price, we introduce a horizontal line at the height *PP* into Figure 17.3 and observe where it crosses the local supply schedule. At this price, farmers supply the quantity S_2.

In principle, the marketing board may set the price charged to domestic consumers at any level. In practice, the government might find it difficult to charge consumers a price higher than *PP*, because this would give consumers and producers an incentive to engage in parallel market transactions at an intermediate price. For export crops that are not staple foods, the government may also perceive little pressure to reduce consumer prices below *PP*. Thus, in the interest of simplicity, we assume that the **administered consumer price** *CP*, at which the marketing board sells the export crop to domestic consumers, is equal to the administered producer price. This implies that domestic consumers are subsidized while producers are taxed, as was the case with an explicit export tax and a quantitative export restriction. To determine the local quantity deman-ded, we observe where the line at the height CP (which equals PP) crosses the local demand schedule.

The impact of this marketing board intervention is to reduce the quantity supplied locally (from S_1 to S_2), increase quantity demanded (from D_1 to D_2) and decrease exports (from $X_1 = S_1 - D_1$ to $X_2 = S_2 - D_2$). The government receives the world price for all exports and takes home export revenue equal to the sum of area A and area C in the diagram (the area of the rectangle with base X_2 and height LEP). It receives payments from domestic consumers equal to area B (the rectangle with base D_2 and height CP). It must pay domestic farmers a total amount equal to area B plus area C (the rectangle with base S_2 and height PP). The difference between its receipts and expenditures, given by area A (the darker shaded rectangle) is the budget surplus derived from its marketing operations. This is the implicit tax revenue collected on exports. From the similarities between Figures 17.3 and 17.1, we observe another type of equivalence, this time between an explicit export tax policy and the creation of a marketing board that implicitly taxes exports.

Marketing boards for staple food crops often aim to subsidize domestic consumers and often function in markets characterized by importing equilibrium. Under such circumstances, they purchase food from both domestic farmers and world markets. Schedules LD, LS, and LIP in Figure 17.4 illustrate a national food crop market in importing equilibrium in the absence of intervention. We again ignore geography and transport costs by assuming that all domestic producers and consumers live near the central market. In the absence of intervention, local consumers or processors would purchase D_1, local farmers would produce S_1, and $M_1 = D_1 - S_1$ imports would fill the gap between local demand and local supply. Because the marketing board seeks to subsidize consumers, we know that the administered consumer price CP lies below the LIP. If, as is often the case, the marketing board finances the consumer subsidy in part explicitly (i.e., through marketing board budget deficits) and in part implicitly (i.e., by paying farmers lower prices than they would receive in the absence of intervention), then the administered producer price PP lies between the LIP and CP. (In some cases governments seek to subsidize producers as well as consumers. To accomplish this they must pay administered producer prices above LIP.)

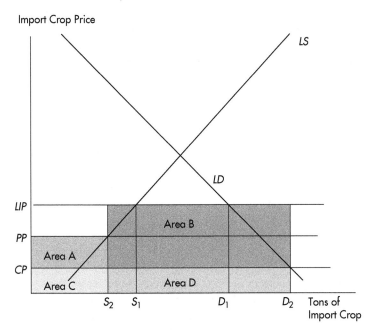

FIGURE 17.4
Introduction of an Imported Food Crop Marketing Board That Subsidizes Consumers

To find the local quantity purchased D_2, we find where the CP line cuts the local demand schedule. To find the local quantity sold S_2, we find where the PP line cuts the local supply schedule. The difference $M_2 = D_2 - S_2$ is the quantity that the marketing board must import, assuming that it supplies consumers with as much of this food as they desire at the low administered consumer price. The revenue received from selling the total amount D_2 to consumers at the price CP is given by the sum of area C and area D in the diagram. The marketing board's cost of purchasing from domestic farmers is given by the sum of area A and area C, while its expenditure on purchases from international markets (including transfer costs associated with international transactions) is given by the sum of area B and area D. The budget deficit, which is the difference between its receipts and expenditures, is given by the sum of area A and area B.[3]

Our analysis indicates that:

> Governments can use marketing boards to tax or subsidize domestic producers or consumers. Unlike in the cases of explicit export taxes and quantitative export restrictions, their effects on producer prices can differ from their effects on consumer prices. Again, the impacts on total quantities supplied, demanded, imported, and exported, and on the government budget, depend critically on the elasticities of local demand and supply.

Geographic variation in policy impacts

Agricultural marketing board policies sometimes induce complex patterns of price changes across geographic locations, with important implications for poverty and income distribution. We use Figure 17.5 for illustrating this point. The figure depicts local markets for an export crop in two rural communities, Near Village and Far Village. Near Village lies closer to the central market

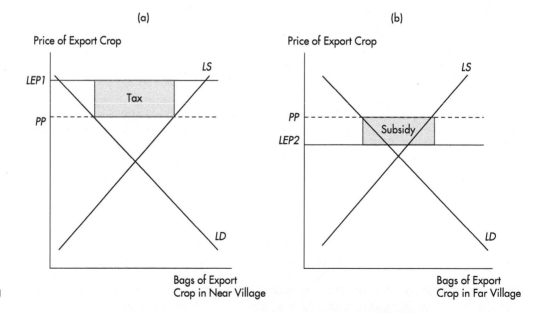

FIGURE 17.5
Introduction of
Pan-Territorial Pricing

---

[3] Often budget limits force marketing boards of this sort to limit, or ration, the quantities of imported food supplied at the subsidized consumer price. In this case, total domestic demand would be held to an administered level, lower than the quantity D_2 in Figure 17.4, and the costs of administering the ration scheme would be added to the government's budget deficit. Some consumers who cannot obtain the goods they want at the administered price would be willing to offer farmers more than the administered price to obtain some of the good. Unless the government takes costly steps to prevent it, parallel markets will emerge through which farmers supply directly (and illegally) to consumers (at a price between CP and PP).

than Far Village, and the transfer costs associated with exporting goods to the central market are higher for Far Village than Near Village. Local supply and demand conditions (given by *LS* and *LD* schedules) are the same in the two markets, and we assume initially that the markets operate freely without government intervention. Thus the only difference between the two markets is that the relevant local export price is higher in panel a than in panel b. In the absence of intervention, the local price in Near Village would be *LEP1*, while the price in Far Village would be *LEP2*. The difference between *LEP1* and *LEP2* is equal to the difference in the transfer costs (associated with exporting to the central market) relevant to the two villages.

We now introduce a marketing board that sets up buying stations in both villages, requires all producers to sell only to buying stations, and engages in pan-territorial pricing. This means that it buys (and sells) the export crop at the same administered price *PP* at both buying stations. Such a policy eliminates the price differential between these two markets.

If the administered pan-territorial price lies at a level like *PP* in Figure 17.5, which is less than *LEP1* but greater than *LEP2*, then the policy effectively taxes producers in the near market while simultaneously subsidizing farmers in the far market! The marketing board implicitly collects tax revenue in Near Village equal to the area of the shaded rectangle in the first diagram, while it distributes a subsidy in Far Village equal to the area of the shaded rectangle in the second diagram. The government could have achieved the same effect if it had imposed an explicit tax on all crops arriving in the central market while also paying out subsidies to farmers equal to their costs of bringing goods to the central market. For the case illustrated in the diagram, the net effect of the export tax and transport subsidy in Near Village is to tax farmers. The net effect in Far Village, where farmers have more to gain from the transfer cost subsidy, is to subsidize farmers there. If the administered price *PP* had been set lower, the implicit tax on crops arriving in the central market would have been larger relative to the transport cost subsidy, and the net effect might have been to tax farmers in both communities.

The analysis suggests that:

> Even when a marketing board implicitly taxes the average farmer, it might nonetheless subsidize farmers living near the most remote buying stations if it engages in pan-territorial pricing.

Pan-territorial pricing encourages a shift in the geographic distribution of export crop production from less- to more-remote locations and a redistribution of income from less- to more-remote producers.

Once we acknowledge the significance of geography, transport costs, and pan-territorial pricing, the aggregate-level analysis of marketing board policies becomes somewhat more complicated than illustrated in Figure 17.3. If the marketing board pays the administered price *PP* not only in the central market but also in outlying markets, then the quantity supplied to the national market by net exporting communities at any administered price *PP* would be greater than illustrated by the standard local demand schedule, because the price in more distant communities would be *PP* rather than *PP* less all relevant transfer costs. Thus the introduction of pan-territorial pricing (while holding the price paid in the central market constant), would effectively shift the local supply schedule to the right. The total quantity of exports would rise, tending to increase government revenue. At the same time, however, the shift to pan-territorial pricing requires the marketing board to subsidize all the transfer costs associated with exporting the crop from out-lying areas into the central market. This tends to reduce net government revenue collection. Though not adjusted for these effects, Figure 17.3 nonetheless generates the right predictions regarding the signs of marketing board policy impacts on aggregate quantities, even when the marketing boards employ pan-territorial pricing, as long as the increase in export tax collections exceeds the additional expenditure on transport.

To fully understand the geographic distribution of taxes and subsidies under marketing board policies, analysts must consider not only whether the marketing board engages in pan-territorial pricing but also the geographic distribution of buying stations. Notice that if no buying station had been set up in Far Village, farmers would have had to cover the costs of transporting their product from Far Village to the nearest buying station, and they would not have enjoyed the entire subsidy indicated in Figure 17.5. Government efforts to restrict private crop movements might even have prevented them from transporting their produce to any buying station, thereby preventing them from participating in national and international markets.

The full impacts of marketing board policies are influenced also by the geographic distribution of the government shops at which the government sells crops at subsidized prices to consumers or processors. Often the shops are located only in urban areas, preventing rural consumers from benefiting directly. Sometimes they are located in poor neighborhoods, in an attempt to better target the benefits to the poor.

Policy impacts on price variation

In the absence of agricultural market intervention, crop prices tend to fall in harvest seasons, when supplies are plentiful, and to rise in the hungry season in between harvests, when supplies are less plentiful. The potential to sell at higher hungry-season prices can provide private traders with the incentive to store up crops during the harvest season for later sale. Such efforts tend to increase demand when supplies are plentiful and increase supplies when they would otherwise be low. Such activities tend to reduce price fluctuations. They tend not to eliminate price fluctuations entirely, however, because traders only store crops if the price premiums they can obtain by selling at a later date are at least as great as the costs of storage. Fluctuations from year to year in local agricultural supply conditions or in world market prices also lead to fluctuations in agricultural prices and to private storage activities that tend to reduce the fluctuations.

Policies of intervention in agricultural markets often reduce the degree of fluctuation in agricultural prices as well as altering their average levels. This is most obvious in the case of marketing boards that engage in pan-seasonal pricing. It is also true when marketing boards set administered prices that fluctuate less than world market prices from year to year. If they hold administered producer prices for export crops constant while world prices fluctuate, they implicitly levy larger taxes on farmers when world prices are high than when world prices are low. They might even subsidize farmers when world prices fall very low.

17.2B Market-level analysis: institutional concerns

In section 17.2A we saw how agricultural market interventions can extract taxes from, and distribute subsidies to, agricultural producers and consumers. In this section we examine how agricultural market interventions alter the rules and norms that govern **agricultural marketing services**, which include the transport of crops from farms to central markets, between national markets and international trading partners, and between surplus and deficit communities within rural areas. They also include the aggregation of crops from small farmers into larger lots (often performed by small local traders, who sell to transporters or wholesalers), as well as wholesaling, retailing, and storing crops, transporting and selling agricultural inputs, and providing agricultural credit.

Creating and abolishing marketing boards

When governments establish marketing boards, they shift these marketing activities from the private sector to the public sector. Marketing board bureaucrats become responsible for collecting crops from farmers, transporting them to central markets, and selling them to international or domestic buyers. Often they also become responsible for providing farmers with inputs and credit. Responsibility for marketing activities is thereby transferred to public sector employees governed by public sector institutions from private traders governed by a combination of private institutions and government regulations.

Over their history, marketing boards developed a reputation for poor governance and inefficient execution of transport, wholesale, and retail activities. Facing weaker incentives to work hard and avoid waste than competitive private traders, marketing board bureaucrats diverted funds to corrupt uses and performed these marketing activities at costs well above the efficient level. In effect, this inefficiency caused public sector transfer costs (i.e., the costs of public sector collection, transport, grading, and distribution of crops to buyers) to exceed private sector transfer costs. Holding constant the prices marketing boards pay to producers (and the prices they receive from international buyers), higher transfer costs imply lower net tax revenue collection or higher marketing board budget deficits. Holding constant target revenue collection (and the prices received from international buyers), higher transfer costs imply lower prices paid to farmers. Pan-territorial pricing increases average transport costs and budget deficits even further by encouraging a redistribution of crop production from locations near central markets toward markets farther away.

Marketing boards also tended to displace private sector storage activities. By erasing inter-seasonal and inter-year price differences, they eliminated private sector incentives to store crops. By committing to buy and sell at steady prices in the face of supply shocks, they ended up absorbing and storing surpluses in good supply years and selling them off in bad supply years, taking over the storage activities from the private sector. Again, weaker incentives led to inefficiency in the performance of these functions.

At the same time, marketing boards might have *increased* variability in food availability and prices in some rural communities hit by idiosyncratic supply shocks. Private traders might have transported goods directly from surplus rural communities to deficit rural communities, thereby helping to smooth out price and quantity fluctuations in all communities (see Chapter 8). Marketing boards, by contrast, sometimes established rigid channels for transporting food only from outlying surplus areas into central markets, and from central markets to outlying areas, and might have had little capacity to shift food directly from surplus to deficit rural regions.

All this suggests that:

> If liberalizing reforms replace marketing boards by fully competitive and efficient private marketing sectors, then these reforms could significantly reduce the transfer costs attached to crop and input transactions.

To understand the significance of such changes for the overall impact of marketing board liberalization on agricultural prices, imagine eliminating a marketing board in two steps. The first hypothetical step leaves the marketing board in charge of all marketing activities but eliminates its collection of tax revenue and distribution of subsidies by adjusting the prices it pays to farmers and charges to consumers. More specifically, this step sets the price that an export crop farmer receives from the marketing board equal to the world market price less all the board's costs of transporting and marketing the farmer's produce. For farmers who had been taxed by the marketing board, this implies a price increase, and for farmers who had been subsidized (usually the more remote farmers under pan-territorial pricing), it implies a price reduction. Similarly, this step sets the price that a consumer must pay for imported food equal to the world market price plus all the board's costs of obtaining and distributing the food.

After eliminating all tax collection and subsidy distribution by the marketing board, the second hypothetical step in liberalization is an institutional change: the shift of all marketing activities from marketing board bureaucrats (governed by public sector institutions) to private sector traders (governed by private sector institutions and any relevant regulations). If private traders are competitive and more efficient than the bureaucrats, this reduces the transfer costs associated with crop and input transactions. Such a reduction in the transfer cost on crop exports would tend to raise both the *LEP* and prices received by farmers. This augments the price increase enjoyed by farmers who had been taxed by the marketing board, and it counteracts the price reduction experienced by any remote farmers who had been subsidized by the board. If the transfer cost reduction is large enough, even farmers who had been subsidized by the board might benefit from liberalization. The transfer cost reduction also tends to reduce prices paid by consumers. Again, if the transfer cost reduction is large enough, consumers might gain from liberalization even if they had been subsidized by the board. Such logic provided liberalization proponents in the 1980s and 1990s with reason to hope that the benefits of liberalization would be widespread, even among groups that had been subsidized by the boards.

We must, however, recognize two reasons why the liberalization of marketing boards might *reduce* efficiency in marketing activities, at least in the short run. First, liquidity constraints (as defined in Chapter 10) might prevent investments that are necessary for the emergence of a competitive and efficient private marketing sector. Private agents must undertake investments to enter the newly opened market for marketing services. Some small-scale and low-tech marketing services—such as the collection of crops from neighboring farmers for delivery to a trucker or wholesaler—can be done at small scale and require only small start-up investments. We might thus expect rapid entry into these activities and rapid emergence of competition.

Other marketing activities, however, require much larger investments and may be held up by liquidity constraints. To provide long-distance transport services, for example, an entrepreneur must purchase a truck, which is a large investment. Similarly, the investments required to provide storage and wholesaling services are large (Barrett, 1997). Such investments are also risky, especially when potential investors fear that governments will soon re-nationalize marketing activities. Thus liquidity constraints and institutional failures can prevent entrepreneurs from undertaking the large investments required for competition and efficiency. Farmers in some locations might face only small-scale and high-cost marketing options. In other locations, lone entrepreneurs might undertake the large investments required for low-cost production of marketing services but take advantage of market power to charge farmers prices well above cost. Consequently, at least in the short run, liberalization might fail to reduce transfer costs and might even raise transfer costs for some farmers.

The second reason why the elimination of a marketing board need not uniformly increase efficiency in marketing activities is that financial market failures might prevent the replacement of public sector agricultural credit by private sector credit on comparable terms. The fundamental source of friction and failure in private credit markets is the potential for borrowers to default (as discussed in Chapter 10). The possibility of default raises costs for lenders, who must either bear high default losses or spend a lot on reducing default rates through screening, monitoring, and enforcement activities. Asymmetric information about borrowers' default risks can furthermore induce rationing or cause some private credit markets to disappear altogether. Marketing boards might have an advantage relative to private lenders in extending credit to farmers that reduces these frictions and failures. As the only buyer to whom farmers may legally sell their crops, a marketing board can simply deduct loan principal and interest before paying farmers for their produce at harvest time and may thus be able to preclude default at low cost. As a result:

> Marketing boards may be able to provide farmers with better access to credit than they would get in the absence of intervention, even if policymakers choose not to subsidize the credit transactions. Liberalization may thus bring a reduction in credit availability, resulting in leftward shifts of crop supply schedules.

The reduction in credit supply associated with liberalization need not be uniform across all sectors. For some commodities and in some locations, large private sector crop buyers might enjoy advantages similar to the market boards for supplying credit to the farmers from whom they purchase crops. Supermarket chains or exporters, for example, sometimes offer to provide farmers with inputs—or with credit to purchase inputs—in exchange for farmers' contractual promise to sell their produce to the buyers (and pay off their debts) at harvest time. Such arrangements appear to be profitable in some contexts, as suggested by the example of Lecofruit in Box 8.5. Unfortunately, where contract law institutions are weak and contractual promises are poorly understood by farmers, default risks can remain prohibitively high and private buyers might find such contracts unattractive. Thus even where marketing boards are replaced by large private sector crop buyers, credit availability can deteriorate when marketing boards are eliminated.

Enforcing contracts and quality standards

Especially in recent years:

> Governments sometimes seek to improve the institutions that govern private sector marketing activities rather than replacing them by public sector marketing board institutions. Such efforts have the potential to reduce transfer costs and encourage market development.

As discussed in Chapter 8, policymakers might seek to reduce private sector transfer costs by establishing institutions that promote trust and that facilitate the use of more sophisticated contracts. Contract law institutions, which punish buyers or sellers for failure to fulfill contractual promises, reduce the probability of cheating by contractual partners and increase trust. Regulations defining product grades and standards, together with certification procedures that promote respect for the grades, reduce transfer costs by eliminating the need for repeated visual inspections of goods as agricultural produce makes its way from seller to buyer. When such regulations of agricultural market transactions reduce transfer costs, they tend to raise prices received by farmers and reduce prices paid by consumers (while holding constant any government tax collection or subsidy distribution).

17.2C The distribution of direct impacts on real income and well-being

Agricultural market interventions directly affect many peoples' lives by altering the prices of agricultural outputs and inputs. The previous two sections demonstrated how to use market equilibrium diagrams to identify the likely directions of change in agricultural consumer and producer prices and how the sizes and signs of these changes might differ across geographic locations and time periods.

In this section and the next two we illustrate the kinds of direct and indirect impacts that might result from policy-induced price changes, while focusing on the relatively simple example of a maize price increase that is uniform across producers and consumers in all locations.[4] We consider a country where maize is important in both production and consumption.

Impacts of a uniform maize price increase on real income and well-being

From studying unitary household models in Chapter 7 we know that:

> A uniform increase in the price of maize raises the real income (and well-being) of households that are net sellers of maize and reduces the real income of households that are net buyers.

---

[4] Two of the behavioral responses to price changes that we examine in what follows were already introduced in the analysis of market equilibrium diagrams: changes in the quantities of crop demanded and supplied in response to price changes. It is the strength of these behavioral responses that dictate the slopes of the local supply and demand schedules.

We know, furthermore, that the price increase has larger proportional effects on real income in households where the ratios of net maize sales or purchases to total income are higher. The price increase has no direct effect on households who neither buy nor sell maize.

All this implies that a uniform price change can generate a complicated pattern of direct real income impacts across groups and locations. Nonfarm households (i.e., wage labor, nonfarm business, and incapacitated households, in the terminology of Chapter 7), whether in rural or urban areas, suffer reductions in real income and well-being when the maize price rises while their nominal incomes hold constant, because their real purchasing power falls. Households with higher incomes tend to consume larger absolute quantities of maize per capita but spend lower fractions of their total consumption expenditure on staples like maize. Hence, better-off nonfarm households experience a larger *absolute* reduction in real purchasing power from a staple food price increase, but poorer nonfarm households tend to experience a greater *proportional* reduction in their purchasing power.

The pattern of a maize price increase's direct impacts across farm households at different income levels is harder to predict, because farm households may be net maize buyers, net sellers, or uninvolved in maize markets, and the relative importance of these different kinds of households can vary in diverse ways across income groups. Thus it is impossible to predict how a maize price increase will affect the distribution of real income without gathering empirical evidence on net maize purchases and sales.

We may describe the approximate distribution of an agricultural market intervention's real purchasing power effects across groups and locations using household sample survey data collected before the price increase (following Deaton, 1989). Using data on income or consumption expenditure levels, other household characteristics and location, we may group households into sets that are of distinct interest to policymakers and that we suspect will be affected differently by the maize price increase. For example, we might divide households into groups defined by income level and whether they live in rural or urban locations. Using data on the values of household maize production and consumption, we then estimate the average value of net maize purchases or sales per capita within groups. Often we divide the net per capita purchase or sales measures by total income or consumption expenditure per capita (and multiply by 100), to obtain indicators of the average percentage by which real purchasing power tends to rise or fall in each group. Studies cited in Chapter 7 applied this approach in estimating the impact of global food price increases on global poverty. In section 17.3 below, we apply this approach in the study of agricultural market reforms in Vietnam in the 1990s.

Nonuniform price changes and well-being

The analysis of pricing policies' real income effects is more complicated than the analysis of the uniform maize price increase just considered, because policy-induced price changes tend to differ across locations. In some cases this differentiation is socially and politically significant. In eastern and southern Africa during colonial times, for example, pricing policies raised prices for farmers in less remote areas, where European settlers cultivated large farms, while reducing prices for farmers in more remote areas, which were populated by African smallholders (Jayne and Jones, 1997).

Impacts of changes in price variability

Often policies of market intervention reduce the variability of agricultural prices as well as raising or lowering their mean levels. When the main reason for variation in domestic prices is variation in world market prices, policies that mute price fluctuations reduce real income variability for domestic net buyers and net sellers alike. When the main reason for local price variation is variation in local agricultural supply conditions, however, policy efforts to mute price variation again reduce variability in real income for consumers but can increase real income variation for farmers whose productivity fluctuates. In the absence of intervention, prices tend to rise when farmers' productivity is low and tend to fall when farmers' productivity is high, thereby tending to moderate variability in their revenue and income. A policy that eliminates price variation would eliminate this moderating influence.

17.2D Behavioral responses of the directly affected

Models of household decision making in Chapters 6, 7, and 10 suggest that a maize price increase might alter a household's behavior for four reasons, which we can associate with effects of four types. First, the maize price increase raises or lowers the household's real income (as described in the previous section), inducing **income effects**. Second, the maize price increase represents an increase in the price of maize relative to other goods the farm might consume or produce and relative to agricultural inputs, inducing **substitution effects**. Third, if the burdens of maize purchases or the profits of maize sales are differentially attached to women in households' mental accounts (Chapter 7), then the maize price increase could introduce **intrahousehold effects** as it alters women's influence in household decision making. Finally, if households are liquidity constrained (as defined in Chapter 10), then as a price increase raises or lowers real income it can also relax or tighten liquidity constraints on investment, inducing **liquidity effects**.

The unitary household models presented in Chapter 7 help us organize our study of the income and substitution effects. Wage labor households, nonfarm business households, and incapacitated households, as well as farm households that do not produce maize, might consume maize but do not produce it. As a result, they respond to a maize price increase as consumers and as suppliers of labor but not as producers. As their real purchasing power falls, the income effect of the maize price increase leads them to reduce consumption of all normal goods. If home time is a normal good, the income effect increases their total labor supply and might even increase their supply of child labor. The substitution effect encourages them to substitute away from the consumption of maize (and goods complementary to maize in consumption), thus reducing the quantity of maize they demand even further, while possibly increasing their consumption of substitute grains. They mitigate the impact of the price increase on their purchasing power by shifting consumption expenditure toward goods that have become relatively cheap. We conclude that:

> Non-maize-producing households for whom maize and home time are normal goods are likely to respond to a maize price increase by reducing the consumption of maize and other complementary goods. They might increase consumption of substitute grains and might increase their supply of labor, including child labor.

Maize-farming households (assuming they also consume maize) respond to a maize price increase as producers, consumers, and suppliers of labor. As producers, they experience substitution effects, as the price of maize rises relative to other agricultural inputs and outputs. According to the analysis of Chapter 7, if they are active in goods and labor markets, they respond to the maize price increase in the same way a profit-maximizing firm would. They are likely to increase production, whether by bringing new land into cultivation, cultivating land already devoted to maize more intensively, or reallocating land from the cultivation of other crops to the cultivation of maize. All of these changes tend to increase the quantity of labor and other inputs demanded for maize cultivation. In many cases their *total* demands for labor and other inputs (for use in producing all crops) also rise, though labor demand might fall if the price increase causes them to expand maize production onto land previously devoted to crops that use more labor per acre than maize.[5]

---

[5] When maize farmers are active in the maize market but not the labor market (a set of circumstances also discussed in Chapter 7 and thought relevant to many African communities), their production response is attenuated by the need to fill additional labor requirements by sacrificing home time. As family labor supply increases, the cost to the household of giving up increasingly scarce home time rises, tending to reduce the benefit of additional expansion of family farm production. Under unusual circumstances, the increase in maize price could even *reduce* maize production, as farm households take advantage of the increased per-unit maize price to reduce family labor supply without experiencing much reduction in maize revenue.

As consumers and labor suppliers, maize-farming households experience both substitution and income effects. As with non-maize-farming households, the substitution effect (arising as maize becomes relatively more expensive) tends to reduce their demand for maize and increase demands for substitute grains. The sign of the income effect for maize-farming households depends on whether they are net sellers or net buyers of maize. If they are net buyers, their real incomes fall, tending to reduce their demands for normal goods, as was the case for all nonfarm households. If they are net sellers, however, their real income rises (as their farm profits rise by more than the cost of what they consume), tending to increase their demands for normal goods.

To determine the ultimate effects of a maize price increase on maize farmers' market purchases and sales of goods and labor, we must consider the net effect of their **production side responses** (i.e., their crop production and input demand responses) and their **consumption side responses** (i.e., their consumption demand and time use responses). We expect that:

> Maize-farming households that are involved in markets, whether as buyers or sellers, tend to respond to a maize price increase by increasing the quantity of maize they produce, and in many cases by raising their demand for labor. If maize and home time are normal goods, then net maize-selling households, whose real income rises, increase maize consumption and reduce labor supply, while net maize-buying households, whose real income falls, reduce maize consumption and increase labor supply.

In light of the "separated spheres and mental accounts" models of household decision making presented in Chapter 7, an increase in the price of maize might also alter women's scope for decision making within their households. It is impossible to predict the nature of these effects without careful study of the local institutions that define men's and women's decision-making spheres and mental accounts.

If households are liquidity constrained, then, as an increase in the maize price increases net sellers' real purchasing power, it can free them to undertake profitable investments in education, farms, or nonfarm businesses. The price increase may, therefore, contribute to growth in agricultural production not only in the short run, as households find it profitable to produce more maize with the assets they already own, but also in the medium and long run, as they undertake investments to expand production further. At the same time, the maize price increase might restrict investment by net maize buyers, for whom real purchasing power falls.

As always:

> The nature and size of households' behavioral responses to price changes depend on context and on the nature of complementary policies.

For example, maize supply will expand in a more price-elastic way, and perhaps raise labor demand more, where some land of reasonable quality is currently left fallow, where agricultural research and extension services are active, and where farmers have access to short-term financing and good transport and communication infrastructure.

17.2E Spillover and feedback effects

The behavioral responses of directly affected households can give rise to spillover and feedback effects that radically alter policies' ultimate impacts on poverty, inequality, and production. In this section we sketch the potential spillover and feedback effects, again focusing on the example of a uniform maize price increase.

Aggregate change in real income

Earlier we saw that net maize-selling and net maize-buying households tend to respond to a maize price increase by altering their supplies and demands in goods or labor markets in opposite directions, as real incomes rise for one group and fall for the other. More specifically, net maize-buying households are likely to reduce their demands for many normal goods and to increase their household labor supply, while net maize-selling households are likely to increase their demands for many normal goods and to reduce their labor supply. Assessing which group's behavioral changes are likely to dominate is, therefore, a useful step to take before attempting to predict the impact of a maize price increase on prices and wages in other markets.

If the demands and supplies of maize-selling and maize-buying households are similarly sensitive to changes in income, then the changes for the group experiencing the larger real income change dominates. For example, if the increase in real income for net maize sellers is greater than the reduction in real income for net maize buyers, then it is likely that the overall effect of a maize price increase will be to increase the total quantities of normal goods demanded at any price. Thus to predict whether aggregate demands for normal goods will rise or fall, and whether aggregate labor supply is likely to fall or rise, we must determine whether the real income gains of net sellers exceed the real income losses of net buyers, and thus whether aggregate real income rises or falls.

Because changes in real income at the household level are approximately proportional to net maize purchases and sales, we can compare approximate sizes of the aggregate real income gains for net sellers and the aggregate real income losses for net buyers by comparing the total volume of net sales to the total volume of net purchases. Mathematically, this is the same as comparing the total volume of production to the total volume of consumption.[6] We conclude, therefore, that:

> The net effect of a maize price increase on total real income in a region (taking into account the real income gains of the net sellers and real income losses of the net buyers) is to raise total real income if the region is a net maize exporter, implying that total maize production in the region exceeds total maize consumption. If the region is a net maize importer, the maize price increase tends to reduce the region's total real income.

In rural areas, which are likely to be net maize exporters, a maize price increase tends to raise regional real income, raising market-level demand for normal goods and reducing market-level labor supply. In urban areas, which are net maize-buying regions, a maize price increase reduces aggregate real income, tending to reduce demand for normal goods and increase the supply of labor. If a country is a net exporter, we expect the real income gains in rural areas to exceed the real income losses in urban areas.

Rural labor markets

An increase in the maize price is likely to raise rural wages. Maize farmers (whether net sellers or net buyers) are likely to increase the demand for labor. Net maize-selling households might increase the supply of labor while net maize-buying households reduce their labor supply, but as long as the rural area is a net maize exporter, we expect the real income gains of the net sellers to exceed the real income losses of the net buyers and expect that the net effect of the change is to reduce labor supply. If rural labor markets are not well integrated with larger labor markets, we expect the wage to rise as demand rises and supply falls. If labor is mobile between farm and

---

[6] Let P_i and C_i be the quantities of a crop that household i produces and consumes. The quantity $P_i - C_i$ is household i's net marketed surplus. It is positive if the household is a net seller and negative if the household is a net buyer. Let households 1 through n be net sellers and households $n+1$ through N be net buyers. Then total net sales are $TNS = \sum_{i=1}^{n}(P_i - C_i)$ and total net purchases are $TNP = \sum_{i=n+1}^{N}(C_i - P_i)$. The difference between total net sales and total net purchases is $TNS - TNP = \sum_{i=1}^{N}(P_i - C_i)$. This, in turn, is equal to $\sum_{i=1}^{N}P_i - \sum_{i=1}^{N}C_i$, which is the difference between total production and total consumption.

nonfarm sectors within rural areas, wages rise not only for maize farm workers but also for low-skill workers in all farm *and* nonfarm rural activities (see Chapter 9). The size of the wage increase depends on the elasticities of local labor supplies and demands.

Notice that an increase in the rural wage for low-skill labor spreads some of the real income benefit of the maize price increase to rural landless laborers, who are often poor. Wage increases also tend to reduce the profits and well-being of net labor-buying households, including large farmers and owners of medium and large nonfarm businesses, who are not poor (some of whom benefited directly from the maize price increase).

The rural nonfarm sector

Nonagricultural activities contribute significant fractions of production and employment in the rural areas of most countries, and rural nonfarm sectors are closely linked to agricultural sectors in important ways (Haggblade, Hazell, and Reardon, 2007). An increase in the price of maize may, therefore, generate important spillover effects worked out through changes in the nonfarm sector. Here we emphasize three channels of indirect impact. First, if the rural area is a net maize exporter, then aggregate rural real income rises, increasing demands for all normal goods and services, some of which are produced in the rural nonfarm sector. Second, an increase in the price of maize also tends to increase the demand for nonlabor maize cultivation inputs, some of which may be supplied by the rural nonfarm sector. If rural markets for any of these consumer goods or agricultural inputs are not well integrated into larger markets, the increased demand raises local prices and stimulates local production. A third effect works in the opposite direction: Increased wages (driven by rising agricultural labor demand) tend to reduce profits in nonfarm business and discourage nonfarm production. Many empirical studies suggest, however, that the first two effects often swamp the third, so that policy changes that expand agricultural production also expand the rural nonfarm sector (Haggblade, Hazell, and Dorosh, 2007).

Urban labor markets

An increase in the price of maize tends to reduce aggregate urban real income and increase urban labor supply, because urban areas are net maize importers. If urban labor markets are not well integrated with rural labor markets, this tends to reduce urban wages, though the effect need not be large. If urban and rural labor markets are integrated through rural-to-urban migration, however, then as wage increases in rural areas reduce the flow of rural workers into urban areas, urban labor supply falls and urban wages rise, transmitting some of the benefits of agricultural expansion to urban areas. Such effects might take time to fully materialize.

Markets for non-maize goods

If a country is a net maize exporter, an increase in the maize price generates a net increase in aggregate real purchasing power. This tends to increase spending on normal goods, some more strongly than others. The shares of consumption expenditure devoted to luxury foods such as meat, vegetables, and more convenient processed foods, as well as clothing, furniture, and home construction services, tend to rise and can even cause prices for such goods to rise more rapidly than the maize price. Such price increases tend to encourage an increase in production of non-staple food crops, livestock, and nonfarm consumer items. At the same time, as increased demand for labor in maize production raises wages and draws labor into maize production, labor costs in other sectors rise. The net effect may be to encourage expansion of sectors producing goods for which demands are rising most rapidly, while causing other sectors to shrink.

Revisiting household-level real income effects

In section 17.2C, we described how analysts can use household survey data on net maize purchases and sales to approximate the distribution of a maize price increase's direct real income effects across groups at different income levels and in different locations. We have since described how a maize price increase can induce an important second round of change in wages and prices of other goods and services. Policy analysts can incorporate these changes into their estimates of real income effects across groups and locations, if they have data on households' net purchases or sales in all the affected markets. An increase in rural wages, for example, would tend to increase the real purchasing power of rural net labor suppliers while reducing the real purchasing power of rural net employers of low-skill labor.

Environmental spillovers

Agricultural pricing policies can also generate spillover and feedback effects through increases or decreases in agricultural production practices that generate environmental externalities. See Chapter 9 in Norton et al. (2006) for an introduction to environmental concerns in agriculture.

In general,

> Many important effects of a maize price increase may be indirect rather than direct. It is especially important to examine indirect effects on rural labor markets, the rural nonfarm sector, urban labor markets, non-maize goods markets, and the environment.

17.2F Impacts on economic growth

Notice that the primary direct effects of an agricultural pricing policy change are one-time changes in the real incomes of households that are net sellers or net buyers of the relevant items and one-time changes in the government budget. These direct effects can lead to one-time changes in wages, other prices, and the structure of production. These effects might imply profound changes in the distribution of real income and possible one-time changes in total real income.

Often, proponents argue that major liberalizing reforms in agricultural markets will speed economic growth. Yet the most obvious effects of these policy changes are one-time changes in the level and distribution of income, rather than changes in long-term rates of economic growth. What connections might we find between pricing policies and economic growth? Several possibilities suggest themselves.

First, if the pricing policy changes allow countries to take better advantage of their comparative advantage in international trade (see Chapter 11), if they lead to significant efficiency improvements in the operation of agricultural markets, or if they reduce the scope for rent-seeking behavior (Chapter 3), then the policy change might give rise to a significant (one-time) increase in the total value of production per capita, which takes time to work itself out. A large and slowly-emerging one-time increase in real income per capita may add to the rate of economic growth for five or ten years.

Second, increases in real income among liquidity-constrained farmers might allow them to exit poverty traps and begin investing, adding to rates of economic growth (Chapter 10). Third, a pricing policy change might raise growth rates through the theoretical channels described in section 11.4. For example, if a policy change leads to an increase in the size of a production sector that is inherently more dynamic or that gives rise to externalities that raise productivity in other sectors, then the change might speed the rate of productivity advance. Whether these effects are large in practice is an empirical question with answers that depend on context.

17.3 Analyzing the Benefits and Costs of Agricultural Market Reforms

17.3A General observations

Many of the most pressing questions regarding agricultural market interventions pertain to the liberalizing reforms begun in the 1980s and 1990s. Analyzing a reform is more complicated than analyzing the kinds of policy design changes we examined in Chapters 15 and 16. The analysis of a policy design change involves comparison of an actual policy to a hypothetical policy that differs from the actual policy in just one way or a very small number of ways. The analysis of a reform, by contrast, involves the comparison of two sets of actual policies—before and after the reform—that can differ in many important ways. Empirical analysis of agricultural market reforms is further complicated by their tendency to take place at the same time as reforms in other policy arenas.

A useful starting point in the study of policy reforms is to carefully describe the full array of relevant pre-reform policies and then to identify all the detailed changes in those policies wrought by the reform. Box 17.2, which adapts the seven questions of Chapter 14 for the study of agricultural market reforms, takes this approach. The analytical tools presented in section 17.2 guide policy analysts in their efforts to answer these questions, though the correspondence between the tools and the questions is not as straightforward as in Chapters 15 and 16.

≡ **Box 17.2** Questions to Guide Analysis of Agricultural Market Reforms

Question 1: Objectives

To what extent was the reform motivated by the desire to speed growth, raise tax revenue, reduce spending, redistribute real purchasing power, or encourage agricultural or industrial expansion?

Question 2: Design

Before the reform, what taxes, subsidies, quantitative restrictions, and regulations did the government impose on transactions involving agricultural crops and inputs? Were marketing boards in place? If so, what restrictions were placed on private agricultural marketing activities? Where did the marketing board place its buying stations? What prices did the marketing board pay to farmers located near the central market and to those farther out? What agricultural inputs, credit, or services did the marketing board provide to farmers? What prices did it charge to urban consumers, processors, or wholesalers? How much did its prices vary across seasons and years? What changes did the reform bring in each of these areas?

Question 3: Implementation

How effectively were any relevant taxes, quantitative restrictions, or regulations enforced, and for which sellers and buyers, before and after the reform? What explicit and implicit taxes (on crop sales or on purchases of crops or inputs) were increased or reduced by the reform? If the reform altered the institutions governing agricultural marketing, what effects did this have on the efficiency of agricultural crop marketing and short-term agricultural credit supply? What average price changes did the reform bring for farmers and consumers of different types or in different locations? What changes did it bring in the variability of prices over seasons and years?

Question 4: Directly affected groups

Who purchased or sold the affected crops and inputs in markets affected by the reform?

Question 5: Direct effects

How large were net purchases and sales of the affected commodities (prior to the reform) in groups distinguished by income level, location, ethnicity, and any other characteristic of interest to policymakers? Taking into account the distribution of average net purchases and sales across groups, together with information on the actual reform-induced price changes experienced by each group, what direct effect did the reform have on the distribution of real income? What impacts did the reform have on production, consumption, time allocation, and investment choices within the various groups and regions? What were the aggregate impacts on production, consumption, imports, and exports of the crops in question and on agricultural investment?

Question 6: Spillover and feedback effects

What effects did the reform have on rural labor markets, the rural nonfarm sector, urban labor markets, and other goods markets? What impacts did reform-induced changes in agricultural production have on the environment? When all these changes are taken into account, which groups throughout society benefited a little or a lot and which were hurt a little or a lot?

Question 7: Budgetary costs

What was the effect of the reform on the government budget (including marketing board budgets)?

In an interesting twist, white maize market reforms in eastern and southern Africa left consumers better off, even though the reforms reduced consumer maize subsidies (Jayne and Jones, 1997). Prior to the reforms, marketing boards had sold white maize to millers at subsidized prices. They sold to only a few large-scale millers, who produced highly refined maize flour. To maintain marketing board control over crop collection, they prohibited the private transport of maize into urban areas, thereby preventing the emergence of any competition for the government-supplied millers. Reforms brought increases in the prices that marketing boards charged to the large-scale millers, but reforms also legalized private transport of grain and private milling. This facilitated the emergence of a small-scale milling sector producing more coarsely ground maize meal, which is cheaper and more nutritious than the highly refined meal produced by large-scale millers. By switching to coarse meal, consumers avoided major increases in maize consumption costs and probably enjoyed improved nutrition as well. Consumers in deficit rural areas also benefited from liberalized grain transport because it became possible for them to purchase grain directly from neighboring surplus areas rather than obtaining grain only after it had been transported into central markets for milling and then transported back out to deficit rural areas.

REFERENCES

Akiyama, Takamasa, John Baffes, Donald F. Larson, and Panos Varangis (eds.). *Commodity Market Reforms: Lessons of Two Decades.* Washington, D.C.: World Bank, 2001. http://go.worldbank.org/WNBAVJZNC0

Alderman, Harold, and Kathy Lindert. "The Potential and Limitations of Self-Targeted Food Subsidies." *The World Bank Research Observer* 13 (2): 213–229, 1998. doi:10.1093/wbro/13.2.213

Barrett, Christopher B. "Food Marketing Liberalization and Trader Entry: Evidence From Madagascar." *World Development* 25(5): 763–777, 1997. doi:10.1016/S0305-750X(96)00132-5

Benjamin, Dwayne, and Loren Brandt. "Agriculture and Income Distribution in Rural Vietnam Under Economic Reforms: A Tale of Two Regions." In Paul Glewwe, Nisha Agrawal, and David Dollar (eds.). *Economic Growth, Poverty, and Household Welfare in Vietnam.* Washington, D.C.: World Bank, 2004, pp. 133–186. http://go.worldbank.org/JTIPQV8AX0

Deaton, Angus. "Rice Prices and Income Distribution in Thailand: A Non-Parametric Analysis." *The Economic Journal* 99(395): 1–37, 1989. http://www.jstor.org/stable/2234068

Edmonds, Eric V., and Nina Pavcnik. "The Effect of Trade Liberalization on Child Labor." *Journal of International Economics* 65(2): 401–419, 2005. doi:10.1016/j.jinteco.2004.04.001

Edmonds, Eric V., and Nina Pavcnik. "Trade Liberalization and the Allocation of Labor Between Households and Markets in a Poor Country." *Journal of International Economics* 69(2): 272–295, 2006. doi:10.1016/j.jinteco.2005.05.010

Glewwe, Paul. "An Overview of Economic Growth and Household Welfare in Vietnam in the 1990s." In Paul Glewwe, Nisha Agrawal, and David Dollar (eds.). *Economic Growth, Poverty, and Household Welfare in Vietnam.* Washington, D.C.: World Bank, 2004, pp. 1–26. http://go.worldbank.org/JTIPQV8AX0

Haggblade, Steven, Peter B. R. Hazell, and Paul A. Dorosh. "Sectoral Growth Linkages Between Agriculture and the Rural Nonfarm Economy." In Steven Haggblade, Peter B. R. Hazell, and Thomas Reardon (eds.). *Transforming the Rural Nonfarm Economy: Opportunities and Threats in the Developing World.* Baltimore: Johns Hopkins University Press, 2007, pp. 141–182.

Haggblade, Steven, Peter B. R. Hazell, and Thomas Reardon (eds.). *Transforming the Rural Nonfarm Economy: Opportunities and Threats in the Developing World.* Baltimore: Johns Hopkins University Press, 2007.

Helfand, Steven M., and Gervásio Castro de Rezende. *Brazilian Agriculture in the 1990s: Impact of the Policy Reforms.* Texto Para Discussão No. 785. Rio de Janeiro: Instituto de Pesquisa Economica Aplicada, 2001. http://www.ipea.gov.br/portal/images/stories/PDFs/TDs/td_0785.pdf

Jayne, T. S., and Stephen Jones. "Food Marketing and Pricing Policy in Eastern and Southern Africa: A Survey." *World Development* 25(9): 1505–1527, 1997. doi:10.1016/S0305-750X(97)00049-1

Kherallah, Mylène, Christopher L. Delgado, Eleni Z. Gabre-Madhin, Nicholas Minot, and Michael Johnson. *Reforming Agricultural Markets in Africa.* Baltimore: Johns Hopkins University Press, 2002.

McMillan, Margaret. "Why Kill the Golden Goose? A Political-Economy Model of Export Taxation." *The Review of Economics and Statistics* 83(1): 170–184, 2001. doi:10.1162/003465301750160135

Minot, Nicholas, and Francesco Goletti. "Rice Market Liberalization and Poverty in Viet Nam." *Research Report* 114. Washington, D.C.: International Food Policy Research Institute, 2000. http://www.ifpri.org/sites/default/files/publications/rr114.pdf

Norton, George, Jeffery Alwang, and William A. Masters. *The Economics of Agricultural Development: World Food Systems and Resource Use.* New York: Routledge, 2006.

Swinnen, Johan F. M., Anneleen Vandeplas, and Miet Maertens. "Liberalization, Endogenous Institutions, and Growth: A Comparative Analysis of Agricultural Reforms in Africa, Asia, and Europe." *The World Bank Economic Review* 24(3): 412–445, 2010. doi:10.1093/wber/lhq017

Warr, Peter G. "Welfare Effects of an Export Tax: Thailand's Rice Premium." *American Journal of Agricultural Economics* 83(4): 903–920, 2001. doi:10.1111/ajae.2001.83.issue-4

World Bank. "World Development Report 2008: Agriculture for Development." Washington, D.C.: World Bank, 2007. http://go.worldbank.org/ZJIAOSUFU0

QUESTIONS FOR REVIEW

1. Describe policy design options for agricultural market intervention.

2. Define all the elements of Figure 17.1 (after reviewing Chapter 8, if necessary). Describe and explain what the graph indicates about the effects of introducing an export tax on the *LEP*, domestic sales, domestic purchases, exports, and export tax revenue.

3. Discuss the significance of agricultural supply elasticities to export tax policies.

4. What does it mean for a particular quantitative export restriction and a particular export tax to be *equivalent*?

5. Describe and explain what Figure 17.3 indicates about how the introduction of an export crop marketing board that taxes farmers affects domestic sales, domestic purchases, exports, and the government budget.

6. Describe and explain what Figure 17.4 indicates about the impacts of a food crop marketing board that subsidizes consumers and that finances the subsidy partly implicitly and partly explicitly.

7. Use Figure 17.5 to explain the impact on the geographic distribution of agricultural production of introducing a marketing board that engages in pan-territorial pricing.

8. Why might the creation of a marketing board increase transfer costs in agricultural output markets? Why

might the creation of a marketing board reduce transfer costs?

9. Why might a marketing board be able to lend to farmers at a lower interest rate than is offered by private and competitive lenders, without having to subsidize the lending activity?

10. Which groups in society benefit directly from a maize price increase? Which groups are hurt directly? Explain.

11. Describe the kind of data we might use to study the real income effects generated by agricultural price changes. What calculations might we undertake?

12. Discuss the likely direct impacts of a maize price increase on the consumer demands, labor supplies, maize sales, and demands for labor and other farm inputs, for households of different types?

13. Describe the possible spillover effects of a maize price increase that involve rural labor markets, the rural nonfarm sector, and urban labor markets.

14. Describe some of the differences in pre-liberalization agricultural pricing policies around the world. How might these differences help explain differences across countries and crops in the impacts of agricultural market reform on agricultural growth?

QUESTIONS FOR DISCUSSION

1. Draw two figures similar to Figure 17.1, except that in one of the figures the local supply of the export crop is highly inelastic and in the other the supply is highly elastic. Draw the *LEP* and *LEP** lines at the same height in the two graphs, so that in both you examine the impact of imposing an export tax of the same size.
   a. In which case is the new tax more effective at raising tax revenue?
   b. Demonstrate in each figure what happens to tax revenue collection when the tax rate increases (by the same amount in each figure). Discuss the conditions under which an increase in the export tax rate might *reduce* tax revenue.

2. Draw a market diagram describing a national crop market in importing equilibrium. How would you illustrate the

imposition of an import tariff in this diagram? What does the diagram have to say about the potential impacts of imposing an import tariff?

3. Use Figure 17.2 to describe and explain what happens when a government imposes a quantitative restriction on a crop's export. If the market price remained at the pre-restriction level, the market would be in disequilibrium. Which kinds of actors would find it impossible to achieve the purchases or sales they wish to make at the going price? How might their reaction to this situation help move the market toward the new equilibrium?

4. Use a graph like Figure 17.3 to describe an export crop market in which a marketing board taxes farmers and subsidizes local consumers. How would you illustrate the

effects of a policy reform that raises the price paid to farmers while holding the price charged of domestic consumers unchanged? What would happen to domestic sales, domestic purchases, exports, and total export tax revenue?

5. Use a pair of graphs like those in Figure 17.4 to describe the impact of a marketing board that engages in pan-territorial pricing. Suppose that Near Village is very close to the central market and that the transfer cost of exporting produce from Near Village to the country's central market is zero. Suppose further than the transfer cost of shipping produce from Far Village to the central market (or Near Village) is equal to the vertical distance between the *LEP1* and *LEP2* lines.

   a. At what level of the administered pan-territorial price would the marketing board neither collect tax revenue from Near Village nor distribute subsidy to Near Village?

   b. Illustrate the impacts in both villages of a policy change that sets the pan-territorial administered producer price to the level you just identified.

   c. Assume that in addition to making the policy change of part b, policymakers wish to eliminate subsidies for farmers in Far Village. What per-unit fee could they charge Far Village farmers that would just compensate for the subsidy implicit in the high pan-territorial price? How would this fee compare to the cost of transporting goods from Far Village to the central market?

   d. Suppose policy makers always set administered prices in Near Village and Far Village to the local export prices relevant to those villages. (This means that when the local export price in a village rises, the administered price also rises.) Illustrate the effect of an institutional change that reduces transfer costs (both the costs of exporting from the central market to world markets and the cost of exporting from Far Village to the central market).

6. Read Alderman and Lindert (1998). What does it mean for a general consumer food subsidy to be *self-targeting*? What

empirical evidence suggests that when choosing the foods to use as vehicles for general consumer subsides, policymakers might have to trade off greater effectiveness at directing a large fraction of subsidies to the poor against reduced absolute improvements in well-being for the poor?

7. Suppose you are asked to make predictions regarding the distribution of the direct real income effects associated with an increase in the price of rice in a particular rural region.

   a. What information would you like to collect and why? Think first about how you might break down the entire population of interest into groups that might be affected by the price increase in different ways and to different degrees. Then indicate what you would like to know about each group, as well as about the policy and the nature of the region's economy.

   b. Describe some conditions under which a large fraction of the direct benefits accrue to the households with the highest incomes, but a large fraction of the ultimate benefits (including both direct and indirect benefits) accrue to low-income households.

8. Read Deaton (1989). How do the relationships shown in Figures 2 and 7 help explain Deaton's two main conclusions that (1) a higher price of rice would bring benefits to rural households at all levels of living and (2) it is households in the middle of the income distribution who stand to enjoy the largest percentage income gains. How might the story change if his analysis took labor market spillovers into account?

9. Through what logical channels, and under what conditions, might an increase in the world price of coffee lead to an increase in school enrollment rates among girls in a rural area of a developing country?

10. Discuss the significance of each of the questions listed in Box 17.2. To which of these questions is the analysis of market equilibrium diagrams relevant? To which of these questions is the analysis of data on net purchases and sales relevant?

PROBLEMS

1. This question examines the effects of a quantitative restriction on fertilizer imports.

   a. Draw a diagram illustrating a fertilizer market in initial importing equilibrium. Introduce into the graph any additional features necessary for examining the effects of a quantitative import restriction. What are the effects of this restriction on price, purchases, sales, imports, and import tax revenue?

   b. Now draw a graph like Figure 17.1 to describe an export crop market in equilibrium after the introduction of an export tax. Use the graph to analyze the impact on this market of the imposition of a quantitative restriction on

imports of the fertilizer that is used in export crop production.

   c. Now draw a graph like Figure 17.2 to describe an export crop market in equilibrium after the introduction of a quantitative export restriction. Use the graph to analyze the impact on this market of the imposition of the quantitative restriction on imports of the fertilizer that is used in export crop production.

2. Here are some statistics for two countries. In which country does an export tax on rice seem likely to be the most progressive, in the sense that on average it taxes higher-income

groups at a higher rate (or subsidizes them at a lower rate) than lower-income groups. Explain, making explicit reference to the information provided in the table.

	Country 1		Country 2	
	Poor	Nonpoor	Poor	Nonpoor
Number of people	100,000	200,000	100,000	200,000
Average expenditure on rice as share of average total consumption expenditure	60%	20%	50%	40%
Average value of production of rice as a share of average total consumption expenditure	70%	10%	40%	50%

3. Consider a country that exports corn, and assume that:
   - Corn is cultivated using highly labor-intensive methods.
   - The primary way corn production can be expanded here is by expanding cultivation onto previously fallow land.
   - There is no migration or commuting between rural and urban areas.
   - Markets for the output of the rural nonfarm sector are in autarky.
   a. Describe the likely effects of an increase in the price of corn on the well-being of each of the following groups, being careful to describe all relevant channels through which the price increase might affect the group's well-being and the likely direction of the effect.

   - Small commercial corn farmers who sell corn but do not buy or sell labor
   - Rural poor households who run small nonfarm businesses using only family labor
   - Rural poor wage laborers
   - Urban poor wage laborers
   b. The table below shows some statistics describing the corn-exporting country's population. If this country *reduced its import tariff* on corn, would you expect the number of *poor who benefit* from the change to be *greater or smaller* than the number of *poor who are hurt* by the change? *Explain*. Please assume that this country is a small importer in world corn markets.

Among All Households:	
Percentage urban	20
Percentage rural	80
Among All Urban Households:	
Percentage poor	20
Percentage nonpoor	80
Among All Rural Households:	
Percentage poor	60
Percentage nonpoor	40
Among Poor Rural Households:	
Percentage small commercial corn farmers	70
Percentage nonfarm self-employed	15
Percentage wage laborers	15

Infrastructure Policies and Programs

Infrastructure assets are physical assets that generate drinking-water, sanitation, irrigation, power, transportation, and communication services, which are essential for healthy living, modern production, and well-functioning markets. Through infrastructure policies, governments and NGOs undertake or encourage the creation, operation, and maintenance of these assets.

For many years, policymakers measured their infrastructure investment success in physical units, such as kilometers of road paved or numbers of wells dug. They now appreciate that infrastructure investment contributes significantly to development only when new infrastructure assets generate high-quality services and remain productive for many years, and when many households or businesses put those services to good use. This requires not only the construction of high-quality wells, power plants, roads, and other physical assets but also the creation of effective institutions to finance and govern their operation and maintenance.

18.1 Infrastructure in Developing Countries

18.1A Infrastructure stocks in developing and developed countries

Infrastructure stocks (i.e., current volumes of infrastructure assets accumulated through past infrastructure investments) are much smaller in developing countries than in developed countries. Table 18.1 offers a sketch of the differences. Poorer countries have fewer roads per square kilometer than richer countries, and very few roads in low-income countries—just 21 percent—are even paved (rows 1 and 2). In many poor countries, large fractions of the rural population live several kilometers or more from the nearest all-weather road. Cross-country differences in electricity stocks are even greater, with power-generating capacity per capita 40 times greater in high-income countries than in low-income countries (row 3).

Despite significant investments by the international development community over the last decade, drinking water and sanitation infrastructure stocks also remain scarce in many poor regions (rows 4 and 5). More than one third of the population in low-income countries lacks access to improved drinking water sources (such as household or public taps or protected wells or springs). This understates the cross-country difference in accessibility, because a household is counted as having access as long as the improved water source lies within 1 kilometer of its residence, and many households with access in low-income countries must walk 20 minutes round trip to fetch each bucket of water, whereas most households in high-income countries have water piped directly into their homes. The differential between low- and high-income countries in access to improved sanitation facilities (including pit latrines and flush toilets) is even greater.

Communications infrastructure has historically been much scarcer in poor countries than rich countries, but mobile telephones are rapidly changing things. The sixth row of Table 18.1 reports numbers of fixed telephone lines plus mobile phone subscriptions per 100 people. These numbers might overstate differences across country groups in the share of people with effective telephone access, because households in poorer countries are more likely to share phones. The differences are also declining rapidly, because mobile phone use has been expanding rapidly in recent years, even in very poor countries. Another way of measuring access to telephone services is to calculate the share of the population living in geographic locations covered by mobile phone

■ TABLE 18.1 **Average of Infrastructure Access Indicators in Low-, Middle-, and High-Income Countries**

Infrastructure Indicator	Low-Income Countries	Middle-Income Countries	High-Income Countries
Road density, 2009 (km of road per 100 sq km of land area)	Not available	23	46
Roads paved, 2000–2009 (percentage of total road length)	21	54	81
Electricity consumption per capita, 2009 (kilowatt-hours per person)	229	1,675	9,064
Access to improved water source, 2010 (percentage of population)	65	90	100
Access to improved sanitation facilities, 2010 (percentage of population)	37	59	100
Access to telecommunications infrastructure, 2010 (fixed lines plus mobile phone subscriptions per 100 people)	34	92	155
Access to Internet, 2010 (Internet users per 100 people)	6	24	73

Source: World Bank (2012).

towers. Aker and Mbiti (2010) report that even in sub-Saharan Africa, 60 percent of the population has access in this sense. Internet use is spreading more slowly, as illustrated by the last row of the table (row 7).

The aggregate figures in Table 18.1 hide great variation in access to infrastructure among low-income countries. For example, Africa's paved road network is just one fourth as dense as in other low-income countries, and its electrical-generation capacity is just one eighth as great (Foster and Briceño-Garmendia, 2010). Irrigation statistics, which are available for too few countries to include in Table 18.1, also indicate large differences in coverage across regions of the world, even among lower-income countries. For example, the percentage of agricultural land that is irrigated is 74 percent in Pakistan but only 0.5 percent in Ethiopia (World Bank, 2012).

More detailed statistics demonstrate great variation in access to infrastructure within low-income countries. Whereas 86 percent of the urban population in low-income countries had access to improved water sources in 2010, only 57 percent of the rural population had such access (World Bank, 2012). In urban Mysore, India, 32 percent of all households have water connections, but only 8 percent have connections in slums (Briceño-Garamendia et al., 2004). More generally, access to infrastructure is lowest for the poorest populations. Estache and Fay (2010) report that among the poorest 20 percent of households in low-income countries, only 10 percent have access to modern electricity services, 41 percent have access to improved drinking water, and 27 percent have access to improved sanitation.

The absolute magnitude of need is great. More than 1 billion people around the world lack access to roads, 1.2 billion lack access to improved water, and 2.4 billion lack access to improved sanitation (OECD, 2007).

18.1B Infrastructure services in developing and developed countries

Infrastructure assets contribute to development not merely by existing but by generating **infrastructure services**, such as transportation of people and goods, provision of clean drinking water, and the flow of electricity to light homes or refrigerate medicines. Low-income countries' deficits (relative to richer countries) in the value of infrastructure *services* are even greater than their deficits in infrastructure *stocks*, because infrastructure assets in developing countries often generate only low-quality services and quickly fall into serious disrepair. Electricity outages and voltage fluctuations capable of damaging equipment are common. Rural roads are filled with potholes. Water from "improved" sources is often unsafe to drink and available only intermittently, and many wells become unusable within a few years. Telephone connections are often lost. Commercial users give especially low ratings to electricity, railroad, and port services in low-income countries (Briceño-Garamendia et al., 2004).

18.1C Infrastructure policy objectives

The ultimate objective guiding infrastructure policies, as with all development policies, is to improve well-being. With the provision of some infrastructure services, such as domestic power and drinking water services, the primary objective is to raise well-being directly for households using the new services, whether by improving their health, raising incomes, freeing up time, increasing comfort, or reducing vulnerability. With the provision of other services, such as industrial power and port services, the primary aim is to encourage investment and employment expansion by the entrepreneurs who use the services, with the aim of raising wages for workers and contributing to growth.

Articulating an infrastructure policy's ultimate objectives carefully, and identifying all the choices various actors must make if the program is to achieve these objectives, is a useful first step toward effective policy design. We will see, for example, that domestic water infrastructure programs improve health only if water system operators choose to exercise consistent care in daily water treatment and pipe maintenance and if households choose to use the improved water consistently and for important hygienic practices. This suggests the need for care in designing institutions to govern water system operation, maintenance, and use.

18.1D Infrastructure policy design and implementation

A first step in analyzing an infrastructure policy's impacts is to identify how it changes households' and firms' physical access to infrastructure services, alters the cost and quality of those services, or alters the information available to potential users about the value of proper use. Although policymakers at the central level determine some of these implementation outcomes directly, they influence many of them only indirectly through their governance structure choices. In what follows we first describe the implementation outcomes in more detail and then describe the policy design choices through which policymakers hope to influence them. We concentrate here on the implementation outcomes that determine impacts after the infrastructure is in place. For a treatment of the shorter-run impacts associated with hiring workers to construct the infrastructure, see Chapter 16.

Implementation outcomes

Opportunities for using infrastructure services tend to be shared by households or firms within a community even while they differ across communities. For example, some communities have water-treatment systems or connections to electricity grids and others do not, but households within a particular village or neighborhood often experience the same water quality and face the same electricity fees.

A policy's impacts within a community are influenced most obviously by the nature of any new infrastructure assets constructed there as a result of the policy. What matters is not only whether the new assets are sanitation systems or roads but also where the assets are located within the community; whether households obtain services through household connections or at communal sites; the nature of inputs and skills required to construct, operate, and maintain the assets; and the assets' environmental implications.

Impacts are determined also by the fees that households and firms must pay for services. Households may be charged one-time **connection fees** to obtain access to a domestic water or electricity network, or they may be charged ongoing **use fees** per unit of service they consume. Use fees can differ depending on the volume of services a household or firm consumes or the time of day when the services are consumed. Sometimes households are asked to make voluntary contributions of labor or money. When the volume of services supplied is too small to meet demand at the specified fees, impact is determined also by the way operators ration services.

Policymakers sometimes combine efforts to expand the availability of infrastructure with education and promotion programs, which encourage households to make effective use of the infrastructure services or educate them about use fees. For example, they might encourage households to use new, safer drinking water sources (rather than pre-existing sources that deliver unsafe water), to protect safe water from contamination, to use water for frequent hand washing, or to obtain electricity at lower cost by using it during off-peak hours.

Finally, an infrastructure policy's impacts within a community depend on the quality and longevity of the infrastructure services provided. New drinking water systems contribute most to local development when they deliver safe water over a long time. This in turn might require that operators add appropriate quantities of chlorine each day and consistently maintain the pipes.

Holding a policy's impacts within a community constant, implementation outcomes are better when the services are provided **efficiently**. This means that the actors in charge of generating infrastructure services deliver as much quality in operation and maintenance as possible on a given budget and (to put it another way) generate any given quantity and quality of infrastructure services and maintenance at the lowest possible cost. Efficiency is diminished when the firms, community committees, or government bureaucrats in charge of operation and maintenance lack adequate expertise and information, lack adequate operation and maintenance budgets, or are not adequately held accountable for avoiding waste and working hard. Resources are wasted when infrastructure capacity remains idle, and service quality suffers when operators seek to supply services to too many users given physical capacity constraints. For example, when power-generating capacity is too low relative to demand, some users experience blackouts, and when domestic water provision capacity is too low, some households obtain only intermittent water supply.

Policy design choices

To begin describing and analyzing an infrastructure policy's governance structure, it is useful to identify the way authority over seven sets of policy design and implementation choices is allocated across central-level administrators, local-level bureaucrats, community committees, private firms, and NGOs. *Project selection decisions* determine the general type, quality, and location of the infrastructure assets to be constructed. *Project design decisions* define the more detailed technical specifications and create blueprints. Day-to-day *construction management decisions* guide the procurement of labor and materials for construction and the supervision of construction activities. Day-to-day *operation decisions* guide procurement of the labor and materials required for generating infrastructure services on a daily basis, and they determine, when necessary, how the services are allocated across users. *Fee-setting decisions* determine the fees charged for connection to networks or use of services. *Maintenance decisions* guide ongoing efforts to maintain and repair the assets. *Decisions regarding education and promotion activities* determine the content of any education provided to potential users and the methods employed for education and promotion.

In centralized governance structures, central-level administrators select and design projects, set fees, bear responsibility for maintenance, and determine the content and methods of education and promotion activities while relying on local employees to manage construction and operation. Governments might deconcentrate some decision making by giving local employees more say over the nature of projects to be constructed. They might also involve the private sector in design, construction, operation, and maintenance activities through competitive contracting, while retaining control over what gets built and what fees are charged.

Increasingly, policymakers seek **community participation** in infrastructure programs, giving community committees authority over some of the design and implementation decisions outlined above. In the Swajal Water and Sanitation Project, for example, community committees are asked to select (from a menu) the type of water infrastructure to be constructed and to oversee construction, fee-setting, operation, and maintenance, with the assistance of local NGOs and private-sector suppliers and contractors, while central government employees make technical

☰ Box 18.1 The Swajal Water and Sanitation Project

World Bank documents showcase the Swajal Project as an example of best practice in "community-based and demand-responsive" water and sanitation infrastructure programs. Piloted in 1,200 villages by the government of India, the program offered villages assistance in forming water and sanitation committees, provided partial funding for water and sanitation infrastructure construction, and offered the committees menus of technical designs from which to choose. The menu of technical options included water systems that differ greatly in convenience, complexity, and cost, from hand-powered pumps delivering water through communal taps to water systems that pipe water directly to households. Eligible sanitation projects included construction of latrines, drainage systems, or compost pits.

To receive program grants, communities had to commit to pay 10 percent of capital costs for water projects (with 1 to 5 percent of costs paid up front), 60 percent of capital costs for sanitation infrastructure, and *all* operation and maintenance costs. They were also required to take responsibility for overseeing construction by private-sector contractors and overseeing operation and maintenance by hired technicians.

Several program design features were intended to improve the quality of decision making by community committees. The program required that committees have 7 to 12 democratically elected members, at least 20 percent of whom were from socially and economically backward groups and at least 30 percent of whom were women. It provided the committees with simple accounting systems. The government identified local NGOs to partner with the community committees in making decisions and to provide training and help manage project bank accounts. The government specified rules and guidelines in a 100-page contract that was to be signed by community committees, their assisting NGOs, and the government's Project Management Unit. The government provided community committees with lists of contractors with good reputations and other information to help them locate high-quality inputs or services at good prices. The government supported cross-community visits through which committee members in one community could learn from the experience of committee members elsewhere. The program also provided the communities with education regarding health and environmental sanitation and women's development.

The World Bank (2001) presents the Swajal Project as a success because it attracted participation by many communities, despite requiring them to make financial contributions, and because— compared to the more centralized infrastructure program it replaced—it yielded more rapid project completion while holding construction quality and costs at acceptable levels. We will learn, however, that such assessments are far from complete.

design decisions and support community decision making in various ways (see Box 18.1). Under Social Investment Fund programs, communities develop and propose project designs with the help of NGOs or private-sector contractors, and a central-level committee selects which community projects get funding.

In some privatized governance structures, governments select, design, and construct infrastructure assets and then award contracts over operation, maintenance, fee-setting, and promotion efforts to private sector firms. In more fully privatized structures, private sector firms take charge of selecting, designing, and constructing assets, as well as all the other decisions, subject to regulation by the government and perhaps with the assistance of government subsidies. The government might allow multiple private firms to compete in these activities, or it might allocate authority over these decisions to a single firm under a concession contract.

As suggested in Chapter 13, additional governance structure choices are likely to play critical roles in infrastructure policy performance. Policymakers at the central level determine the volume of funding to provide for the program, how those funds are allocated across projects or communities, and how the transmission of funds to the local level is governed. They might also set rules regarding what steps local decision makers may, may not, or must take to raise local funds. In addition, they set the criteria and processes for selection of employees, contractors, and community committee members; provide decentralized decision makers with rules, guidelines, and institution- and capacity-building services; and determine how local decision makers are held accountable for making good choices.

18.2 The Economics of Infrastructure Service Use and Supply

Households and firms are directly affected by an infrastructure policy if they *use* infrastructure services affected by the policy, either before or after the policy is introduced. In what follows, we first survey the ways households and firms might use and derive benefits from new infrastructure services. We then develop simple frameworks for studying who uses the services supplied by a particular infrastructure asset and the direct and indirect impacts of that use on the well-being of diverse groups. Next, we examine private sector infrastructure service supply and potential rationales for public sector intervention. We conclude this preparation for policy analysis by highlighting critical questions regarding infrastructure program costs.

18.2A New infrastructure service uses and benefits

New infrastructure services allow people to fulfill important needs or wants in new ways. In the absence of new infrastructure, people fulfill those needs and wants by employing **substitute services or goods**. For example, in the absence of protected wells, people might obtain drinking water from rivers. In the absence of electricity, they might light their homes with kerosene, cook with collected firewood, and mill grain by hand or using animal power. In this section we highlight that:

> When evaluating the potential benefits people might derive from new infrastructure services, it is important to identify the uses to which people might put the new services and the substitute services or goods they would employ in the absence of the new infrastructure.

In what follows, we offer an overview of the uses of infrastructure services and how the switch from using substitute services to using new infrastructure services can improve well-being.

Domestic water infrastructure projects can take many forms: piping water from distant sources into community centers, piping water to homes from nearby wells, or installing treatment systems to improve water quality. Households may use the new domestic water services for drinking, cooking, cleaning, and bathing. In the absence of new water infrastructure, many people around the world, mostly women and girls, walk hours each day to obtain water, carrying every ounce they use over long distances. Ray (2007) cites an estimate that 40 billion woman-hours per year are spent fetching water in sub-Saharan Africa alone. Many people also consume water that is contaminated by bacteria, parasites, and toxic chemicals.

When new infrastructure brings water closer to home, it frees up valuable time. When it purifies water, it protects households against many waterborne illnesses, including diarrheal diseases, which kill 1.5 million children under five each year, and guinea worm infestation, which leaves victims painfully incapacitated. When new drinking water infrastructure improves health or frees time, it can also increase labor supply and income or encourage greater school attendance, especially by girls. In urban slums where the only alternative way to obtain water is to purchase it from vendors at high prices, the new infrastructure can reduce the monetary cost of obtaining water.

Sanitation infrastructure assets include latrines or toilets for communal use, sewer systems that transport waste water from homes and businesses to disposal or treatment points, wastewater treatment systems, and solid-waste disposal systems. Such assets allow people to dispose of waste in ways that do not contaminate their local environment. In the absence of such assets, people would dispose of waste in other ways. As we saw in Chapter 1, many people around the world use open fields and forests as their toilets. In some places, women are permitted to relieve themselves only when nighttime darkness allows them some privacy. Trash accumulates in ditches, causing stench and providing breeding grounds for flies and other pests. New sanitation infrastructure can therefore increase convenience, comfort, and privacy, as well as improving health by reducing disease transmission. Freed-up time and improved health, again, can also increase income.

Investments in **irrigation infrastructure** include construction of wells, pumps, dams, reservoirs, canals, and pipes that help collect and distribute water for use in agricultural production. In the absence of such infrastructure, farmers must either carry water or rely on rainfall to water their crops. New irrigation infrastructure can raise farmers' yields and reduce the variability of their yields by reducing losses to inadequate rainfall. It can allow farmers to shift into the cultivation of higher-value crops or higher-yielding varieties of traditional crops, to cultivate a second or third crop per year, or to expand onto land previously not suited to cultivation. As they expand cultivation, farmers might increase food supply, tending to reduce food prices, and might increase their demand for labor, creating pressure for wages to rise. The new supply of irrigation services can thus directly improve the well-being of users' households by raising their average income or reducing the variability of their incomes over seasons and years, and it can indirectly raise well-being for many more households by reducing food prices, expanding employment opportunities and raising wages.

Electricity infrastructure assets include the large networks of cables that connect communities and households to national grids and the power plants that supply electricity to those networks, and they also include smaller solar-, wind-, biomass-, or hydroelectric-power generators that provide electricity only to small communities. Electricity users include households, farms, firms, and communities.

Households can use electricity for lighting, cooking, running appliances that speed or ease household chores, and obtaining the information and entertainment services offered by radios and televisions. In the absence of electricity, households might use kerosene for lighting, firewood for cooking, and travel, word of mouth, or community gatherings for information and entertainment. Often electricity is a cheaper source of power than substitute sources, and thus switching to new electricity services can reduce the unit cost of lighting and cooking. It can also free up time if it eliminates the need to collect firewood. The switch to electricity can increase the quality and reduce the cost of lighting, encouraging households to use more lighting in the evenings. This can facilitate study or allow housework to be performed at later hours, freeing daytime hours for additional income-generating activities. Electric lighting and cooking can improve health by eliminating kerosene- and fire-based indoor air pollution. Radio and television can provide households with more and more-timely information and with new entertainment options. The creation of new electricity infrastructure can thus free up money and time, improve health, and increase educational attainment, income, and consumption of entertainment.

Farms can use electricity to run irrigation systems, and businesses can use it for running computers and manufacturing equipment and for lighting shops. Without access to larger-scale electrical infrastructure, farms and businesses might run their own small-scale generators at higher average cost, or they might irrigate and manufacture using only human and animal power. A switch from private generators to grid-based electricity can reduce production costs. New access to electricity can render it possible for farms and firms to adopt much more productive technologies and can allow offices and shops to remain open for longer hours. As they innovate and expand, they can create more and better jobs. Thus, through various channels, new electricity infrastructure can increase farm or firm productivity, raising profits, increasing the demand for labor, and contributing to economic growth.

Finally, communities can use new electricity infrastructure for lighting streets and community centers or running health center refrigerators. In so doing they can improve safety, encourage social gatherings, facilitate community business meetings, encourage adult literacy education, or improve local health care.

Transport infrastructure includes roads, bridges, culverts, railroads, depots, seaports, and airports, all of which contribute to the movement of goods and people. In the absence of any such infrastructure, people must transport themselves and their goods on foot or perhaps with the help of pack animals. As transport infrastructure improves, it becomes possible first to ride animals or walk more quickly and safely and to use carts to transport somewhat larger quantities. With continued improvement, the use of motorized vehicles and more-direct routes becomes possible. Further improvements allow the use of larger-capacity and faster trucks, buses, trains, and ships and faster trans-shipment between the various forms of transport.

As vehicle capacity increases and the wear and tear on vehicles falls, transport costs fall. In rural communities, this reduction in transfer costs increases the effective prices of local exports, reduces the prices of local imports, and eases travel, encouraging households and communities to engage in more exporting, importing, use of services, commuting, migrating, and visiting, as we saw in Chapters 8 and 9. Better export prices increase incomes and encourage labor demand and investment, better import prices increase real purchasing power and reduce production costs, and improved access to services can improve education and health and speed the adoption of new technologies.

Improved market connections between regions subject to different agricultural shocks reduce variability in food prices and consumption. Improved seaports and airports raise the profitability of international exporting and reduce the cost of international imports. Increased transport speed can make feasible the export and import of higher-value, more-perishable items. Investment in transport infrastructure, therefore, has the potential to spread benefits to many groups by expanding farm and nonfarm business opportunities, raising wages, reducing consumer prices, stabilizing prices and supplies, and improving access to services.

Communications infrastructure includes mobile phone towers, landline phone or Internet networks, and call exchanges. Households, farms, and businesses use communication technologies to obtain information, coordinate activities, and maintain relationships. Without access to phones, households obtain these services only through travel and face-to-face communication. New communication infrastructure might allow farmers to obtain timely information about prices in several markets without having to travel. By allowing them to obtain price information before transporting crops, telecommunication services might increase the average price they receive, reduce the risk of taking their crops to market, and improve supply to markets that might otherwise have experienced shortages. With improved communication, manufacturers can reduce work stoppages and reduce costs by better coordinating the activities of their suppliers, and they can increase the value of their production by better tailoring their goods and services to customers' needs. As farms and firms become more productive and expand, they might expand employment opportunities and raise wages. AIDS and tuberculosis patients can receive reminders to take their medicines, improving the efficacy of treatment. Family members can stay in touch over longer distances. Increasingly, improved communication technologies also allow people to send money, make payments, and save at lower cost and with greater security.

18.2B Who uses infrastructure services?
Decisions regarding whether to use infrastructure services

Infrastructure assets contribute to development only when people use their services. Basic theories of consumption, time allocation, production, and investment suggest that:

> A household (which might operate a farm or firm) uses an infrastructure service if it perceives that the private benefits of using the new infrastructure service (rather than substitute services or goods) outweigh the private costs.

At the very least, the household must perceive that the benefits of current use outweigh the costs of current use, but:

> If the household must bear significant one-time costs to gain access to the service, then the decision to use it becomes an investment decision, and the household uses the service only if the stream of future net benefits outweighs the one-time costs, including the costs associated with financing and risk.

The **private benefits** are the benefits a household associates with switching from the use of substitute services to the use of new infrastructure services. As suggested in the previous section, switching from substitute services to the new services can reduce the money or time cost of performing basic functions, such as obtaining drinking water, lighting homes, or watering crops, thereby relaxing money or time constraints. Using new infrastructure services can also generate direct consumption benefits, such as opportunities to drink better-tasting or safer water or to consume television entertainment. The new services may instead (or in addition) allow households operating farms or firms to adopt new technologies, thereby improving productivity and incomes. By improving health or reducing the variability of productivity or profits, the switch to new services can also reduce households' vulnerability.

The **private costs** of current infrastructure service use can also take diverse forms. The switch from substitute to new services can raise the monetary cost of performing basic functions if households are charged use fees for the new services (e.g., water from a new treated drinking water system) while substitute services are available free of charge (e.g., water collected from a river). Switching to new infrastructure services can also require households to expend more time and effort in performing basic functions, to bear new risks, or to give up traditional ways of cooking or carrying out other daily activities.

Households face **one-time costs** of obtaining effective access to infrastructure services when they must pay connection fees and when they must purchase or construct sinks, toilets, electrical appliances, irrigation canals, machinery, computers, carts, bikes, trucks, or phones before they can make use of new services.

Households' choices regarding infrastructure service use depend not only on the objective benefits and costs of use but also on their preferences. Their preferences, and thus the relative weight they place on the benefits and costs of use, might depend on their understanding of the benefits (e.g., the health benefits of using clean drinking water) and on social norms (e.g., regarding the importance of cooking food the traditional way, over wood fire). If women and children would benefit more than other members of their families from new infrastructure use, then whether a household uses the new infrastructure might also depend on the distribution of decision-making authority within households.

Infrastructure and the poor

This simple framework suggests several reasons why the poor are less likely to use new infrastructure services than the nonpoor. First, if the use of new infrastructure services costs time and money, and if households treat the consumption or time-saving benefits of new service use as if they were strongly normal consumption goods, then poor households may be less likely to use new infrastructure services simply because, at their low income levels, they place greater value than richer households on consumption of staple foods relative to consumption of higher-quality water or home time. Second, when connection fees or other up-front costs are significant, liquidity constraints can cause poor households to weigh up-front costs more heavily relative to future benefits (than do less-poor households that are not liquidity constrained), rendering them less likely to take up the opportunity to connect to new services. Third, having smaller farms, fewer appliances, and fewer complementary assets of other sorts, they might have less to gain from use. Fourth, they tend to live in more remote locations and to have less education, and they may thus be more likely to lack physical access or to lack knowledge of use benefits. Finally, the institutions that govern the rationing of infrastructure services might discriminate against them, whether because they are of lower economic status or because they belong to disadvantaged ethnic groups.

All this suggests that policy designers must consider how every detail of infrastructure policy design might affect the number of households that will use new services, and especially how they might affect use of the new services among the poor. Use rates among the poor might drop off, all else equal, as fees rise, service quality falls, physical access to the services by the poor becomes more difficult, the methods for rationing scarce services become more discriminatory, and efforts to educate households about the benefits of use diminish. Even the structure of fees can matter, because liquidity-constrained poor households are more likely to be put off by high up-front connection fees than by ongoing use fees (even when comparing fees that ultimately collect the same revenue over several years).

A review of World Bank–financed rural electrification projects offers two examples of how program design details have served to exclude the poor (World Bank, 2008). First, poorer households are less likely to use electricity because poorer communities are less likely to obtain connections to electricity grids. Program planners tend to give higher priority to connecting communities where the cost of connecting to the grid is lower, and these tend to be less-remote, less-poor communities. Second, the utilities created to operate the electricity networks often charge connection fees on the order of $100, which liquidity-constrained poor households find difficult to pay. As a result, even in communities where electricity has been available for 15 to 20 years, it is common for 20 to 25 percent of households to remain unconnected, even though estimates suggest that households are willing to pay significantly more per month than the average cost of providing the electricity service.

The Swajal Project introduced in Box 18.1 offers additional examples of ways the poor are excluded. Case studies suggest that the poorest households are sometimes excluded by their inability to make large one-time monetary contributions. The program requires village water and sanitation committees to finance 10 percent of their projects' capital costs. To fulfill this requirement, they sometimes demand one-time contributions from village members. To enforce payment of such contributions, they choose to construct systems that pipe water directly to houses and do not include any public standpipes in their proposals. This allows them to enforce payment of contributions by denying access to households that do not pay. Sometimes powerful individuals hijack program resources, paying the community contribution out of their own pockets, and then using program funds to build private tanks or wells (Sampat, 2007).

18.2C Effects of infrastructure service use on users' well-being

From preceding sections we know that the switch from substitute services to new infrastructure services can reduce the time or money costs of performing basic functions, improve the quality of services used in consumption or production, or facilitate adoption of new technologies, thereby improving health, increasing consumption of goods, services, or home time, increasing saving and investment, or reducing vulnerability. It can also bring costs of many kinds. Careful observation suggests that:

> The nature and magnitude of the net benefits a user derives from using new infrastructure services can depend on the user's choices regarding how to use the new service and how much of it to use, as well as the price and quality of the service, the physical ease of access to the service, and the length of time the asset remains operational.

A key observation here is that even when households choose to use new infrastructure services, they might fail to derive all the benefits policymakers might hope for, because they do not use the services in the ways intended by policymakers. For example, households might fail to derive the full health benefits of new water infrastructure if they fail to protect water from contamination during transportation and storage, if they fail to use the treated water consistently (even when at school or in the marketplace), if they use too little water or if they fail to develop good hand washing habits. Similarly, electricity use fails to deliver its full potential health benefits if households use the electricity for lighting but continue to cook over wood fires. Improved roads also deliver fewer benefits to users who opt to walk along them rather than to purchase transport from new bus and truck services. Users' benefits from new infrastructure also depend on how much they use the new services. For example, some farmers gain larger benefits from irrigation systems because they use them to irrigate more acreage.

Given the importance of users' decisions regarding *how* and *how much* to use new infrastructure services, it is useful to examine those decisions more closely. When we do we find that:

> Whether a household puts a new infrastructure service to a particular use and how much a household uses the service in that way depend on the household's appreciation of the benefits of that use, the strength of the household's preferences favoring traditional practices, the quantities of complementary assets the household owns, and the nature of complementary policies, as well as the price charged for the service (relative to the cost of substitute services) and the quality and convenience of the new service.

These relationships among household circumstances, infrastructure service uses, and infrastructure policy benefits have five practical implications for policy analysis.

First, an increase in use fees can reduce the net benefits that users derive from new infrastructure in two ways: by reducing their purchasing power and by motivating them to cut back on use—using less water per day or using fewer electrical appliances, perhaps to the point at which some of the desired benefits disappear.

Second, reductions in an infrastructure service's quality, convenience, or reliability can similarly reduce use benefits in two ways: by reducing the efficacy of the service in any given use and by discouraging some beneficial uses. For example, unreliability in rural electricity supply can prevent its use for powering rural manufacturing enterprises, thereby limiting its impact on rural nonfarm employment. Unreliability can also prevent the use of electricity for refrigeration. For more on household choices regarding use of electricity, see Box 18.2. Unreliability of irrigation water supply (which sometimes derives from unreliability of the electricity that powers the pumps) similarly reduces the benefit of irrigating water-sensitive crops, and unreliability in domestic water supply prevents consistent use of safe water.

Third, effective education and promotion campaigns have the potential to increase infrastructure program benefits. A review of water and sanitation program evaluations found

≡ Box 18.2 Uses and Benefits of Rural Electricity

A review of World Bank rural electrification programs underscores the importance of household choices in determining the nature of program benefits (World Bank, 2008). The review reveals that the benefits of rural electrification programs often differed from the benefits policymakers expected, because people made unexpected choices regarding how to use the new electricity services. Policymakers had hoped that improving access to electricity in rural areas would reduce the money or time costs of lighting and cooking, increase school participation and learning by facilitating night-time studying, improve access to information transmitted by television, reduce indoor air pollution associated with the use of wood-burning stoves, expand employment by catalyzing the creation of nonfarm businesses, and improve vaccination and health care by improving capacity to refrigerate vaccines and medicines.

New users did indeed put new electricity services to some of the anticipated uses. Of electricity used in rural areas, by far the largest fraction is used for lighting, for both residences and streets. The second largest fraction is used for television. This suggests that electrification delivered at least some benefits related to extended hours for homework or chores and increased flows of information and entertainment.

Several desired impacts have not materialized, however, because households have not put electricity to other anticipated uses. For example, very few households have adopted electricity for cooking, except in Asia, where some households use rice cookers. Strong preference for food cooked in traditional ways appears to be an important

barrier. Even so, electrification has brought some reduction in indoor air pollution by encouraging a switch from kerosene to electrical lighting.

At least as disappointing, in the cases reviewed, rural electrification catalyzed the creation of almost no rural factories and very few nonfarm household enterprises. Even where rural manufacturing enterprises already existed, they often preferred to use their own high-cost generators rather than new grid-based electricity, because the grid-based service was too unreliable.

Rural electrification of health centers seems to have had little impact on vaccination rates, perhaps because the service is too unreliable to guarantee effective refrigeration. Electrification might nonetheless have improved health outcomes through a very different channel: Electrification of health care workers' residences might have helped rural health centers attract and retain staff.

Despite rural electrification programs' failure to generate some desired benefits, estimates of households' willingness to pay for electricity—even when used only for lighting and television—suggest that program benefits far outweigh the costs. Cheaper and better lighting, in particular, transforms lives in quite fundamental ways that households apparently value a great deal.

Unfortunately, the poorest households sometimes benefit less than they might, because they do not fully understand the fee schedules. Often the utilities offer a single low, fixed lifeline fee for households that use up to 25 kilowatt-hours per month. Poor households that do not understand this sometimes use significantly less electricity than they have paid for.

multiple examples of water system investments that failed to reduce diarrheal disease, in part because households chose not to use the new infrastructure or failed to use it effectively (World Bank, 2010). A review of rural electrification projects found that many poor households failed to use as much electricity as they had paid for because they did not understand the rate schedule (see Box 18.2).

Fourth, governance reforms that prolong or expand use of infrastructure services by improving maintenance might multiply the benefits of creating new infrastructure. The longer new infrastructure continues to deliver services, the greater the benefits generated by a single investment. One way to quantify the value of maintenance is to compare the cost of maintenance to the cost of new investment to replace assets that decay through lack of maintenance. The World Bank reports that an additional $12 billion spent on road maintenance in Africa over a decade could have prevented enough deterioration to save $45 billion on road reconstruction, and that $1 million spent on maintenance of cable networks could have extended the number of households served enough to save $12 million in construction of additional electricity-generating capacity (World Bank, 1994). Yet governments and donors consistently take inadequate care with maintenance. As a result, roads crumble, wells cease to supply water, and irrigation systems fail.

Fifth, better-off households often derive greater direct benefits from the construction of new infrastructure assets because they use infrastructure services in larger quantities. Households with more agricultural land can benefit more from new access to irrigation. Households that own more appliances, or have greater ability to finance their purchase, benefit more from new access to electricity. A corollary to this observation is that **general subsidies for using infrastructure services**—which reduce the price of infrastructure service use below the cost of production—tend not to be well targeted. Lower fees might encourage use by the poor, but they might also direct a large fraction of costly subsidies to nonpoor households that use larger quantities.

Paying attention to how users actually use new infrastructure services, and to how effective their uses are in delivering desired improvements in health or other outcomes, is important for comprehensive and meaningful evaluation of infrastructure programs. Again the Swajal Project is a case in point. Despite its excellent performance in completing projects and raising funds, its impact on health might have been weak. Systematic evidence on health impacts is unavailable, but Asthana (2003) report that interviewees in many of their case-study villages complained about implementation problems that could reduce health impacts, such as rusting pipes (which can admit contamination from surrounding soil), lack of daily chlorination, lack of motivation by committees to oversee operation and maintenance, and failure of committees to collect fees for covering the cost of operation and maintenance. They also report that a number of water systems were already defunct less than five years after construction. Comprehensive evaluation of the Swajal Project would include systematic study of such problems on a larger scale, as well as study of impacts on health outcomes.

18.2D Other direct and indirect effects of infrastructure service use

The use of new infrastructure services can also alter users' behavior in ways that give rise to important spillover and feedback effects. More specifically,

As use of new infrastructure services alters users' money and time costs of performing basic functions, improves the quality of the services they use, or allows them to adopt new technologies, it can generate indirect effects through the impacts of users' behavioral responses on goods and labor markets, the physical environment, and the efficacy or cost of other policies and programs.

Spillovers through goods and labor markets

When policymakers invest in infrastructure that encourages production and marketing—including irrigation, electricity, transport, and communication infrastructure—indirect effects worked out through goods and labor markets may be crucial for fulfilling their objectives. Policymakers might hope that expansion of irrigation, transport, and communication infrastructure in rural areas will induce an expansion of agricultural production that improves rural employment opportunities and raises rural wages while also driving down food prices and reducing variation in food supply. Similarly, they might hope that investments in urban electricity, transport, and communication will induce expansion of nonagricultural production and employment, and that improved ports will further expand labor demand by encouraging exports of labor-intensive goods.

As with policies that increase crop prices, infrastructure programs that raise agricultural productivity or improve rural communities' links to markets can lead to direct or indirect impacts for all members of rural communities, with some groups benefitting greatly, some benefitting only a little, and others losing. For example, irrigation systems can raise productivity and incomes for irrigation system users and can raise wages and reduce food prices for landless workers, but they may also reduce profits for farmers unconnected to the new irrigation systems as crop prices fall and labor costs rise. See Box 2.2 for a discussion of the community-wide impacts of rural road projects in Bangladesh on the well-being of diverse groups.

Physical externalities

Many infrastructure projects have the potential to generate important externalities, many of them negative. One community's domestic water and sanitation infrastructure might pollute the drinking water of downstream communities. Overuse of irrigation and poor drainage can reduce productivity in surrounding areas by raising water tables and salinity and can provide malarial mosquitoes with stagnant water in which to breed. Dam projects used to generate electricity or irrigation water sometimes destroy habitats and displace people. Road improvements can reduce safety for pedestrians and increase urban air pollution. Off-grid rural electricity projects that use solar or wind power have better environmental implications than many grid-based projects.

Spillover effects on the performance of other policies and programs

Investments in infrastructure can increase the efficacy and reduce the cost of many other policies. If they reduce diarrheal disease, new water and sanitation systems can increase the effectiveness of school building programs (by improving children's attendance and attention), nutrition interventions (by improving beneficiaries' retention of nutrients) and even agricultural market liberalization (by increasing farmers' physical capacity to work harder when crop prices rise). New irrigation infrastructure can open up more promising avenues for productivity advance through agricultural research and extension. Improved telecommunication, and expanded tele-vision use, can speed and reduce the cost of transmitting information and recruiting program participants. Better transportation infrastructure encourages children to attend school, encourages mothers to seek health care, increases the potential for microfinance clients to set up profitable businesses, reduces the cost of agricultural extension activities, and raises the profitability of adopting higher-yielding crop varieties.

18.2E Private sector supply of infrastructure services and rationales for intervention

In this section we examine private actors' decisions regarding the supply of infrastructure ser-vices, seeking to identify circumstances under which they might fail to provide services that policymakers judge socially beneficial. In so doing, we identify rationales for intervention, in the terminology of Chapter 13. More specifically, we first consider private actors' decisions regarding *investment* in the creation of community-level infrastructure assets. We then examine private actors' choices regarding *operation and maintenance* activities, which determine the price, quantity, quality, and longevity of the services provided after the assets have been created. We will see that:

> The diverse assets that fall under the label "infrastructure" have very different properties and thus suggest quite different potential rationales for intervention. Rationales for intervention might relate to public goods problems, liquidity constraints, externalities, knowledge deficits, market power, or equity concerns. Different rationales, in turn, have different implications for policy design.

Rationales for intervention in community-level infrastructure investment

A first step toward delivering infrastructure services to a new community is investment in the creation of a community-level asset, such as a drinking water or sanitation system. We concentrate here on infrastructure investments that policymakers judge to be socially beneficial, in the sense that they would generate more social benefits than social costs if well-constructed, operated, and maintained.

Some community-level infrastructure assets are unlikely to be provided by the private sector because they are public goods. A classic example (discussed in Chapters 8 and 13) is a rural road connecting a remote community to a larger road or market town. Many of the lower-cost options for providing other sorts of infrastructure service also involve public goods. Examples include neighborhood standpipes (where hiring an attendant to collect fees is infeasible), communal latrines, investments that protect communal wells from contamination, and installation of street-lights or electricity for a community center. By definition, infrastructure assets that are public goods generate services from which residents cannot be excluded and thus for which private actors cannot charge fees. Able to capture only their small private benefits, private actors are unwilling to pay the full cost of creating the assets. Where local institutions support cooperation, communities might, but often do not, manage to undertake collective investment in such public goods (Chapter 12).

If the public goods problem is the only barrier to investment, and if governments or NGOs are able to catalyze local cooperation, then they may be able to encourage local investment in public goods without having to subsidize much of the up-front cost. If they cannot catalyze such cooperation, then they might have to subsidize most or all of such costs. They might put their subsidies to work directly, through public-sector construction efforts, or indirectly, by providing subsidies to private contractors or community actors.

Sometimes broad-brush discussions of infrastructure investment treat all infrastructure services as if they were public goods, but in fact many—perhaps most—are not. Where it is feasible and inexpensive to charge and collect fees, the services are not public goods. Infrastructure investment might nonetheless be prevented in such circumstances by four other market and institutional failures.

First, infrastructure investment may be prevented by liquidity and insurance constraints, whether on individual potential investors or on communities contemplating collective investments. Such constraints are most likely for large investments (e.g., hydroelectric dam projects) and for poor communities contemplating collective investments that are large relative to local means. Governments and NGOs might succeed in catalyzing these investments, without having to subsidize a substantial portion of the asset-creation cost, by providing subsidized financing or insurance for the investment.

Second, private investors might fail to invest in socially beneficial infrastructure, because many of the benefits arise through positive externalities, which they cannot appropriate. For example, much of the social benefit of an individual's latrine use is in the prevention of disease transmission to others. If private investors charged fees equal to the cost of providing latrine services, they might attract no users, even though the social benefit of use far outweighs the cost. In such cases, investment might not take place without substantial subsidization by governments or NGOs.

Third, demand may be insufficient to motivate investment because users lack knowledge regarding the benefits of use. Users who would be willing to pay fees in excess of cost if they fully appreciated the benefits of drinking clean water, for example, may be unwilling to pay such fees simply because they do not have full knowledge of the benefits. Even under such conditions, private actors might undertake the investments if they could combine such investments with an effective and sufficiently low-cost method for educating users about the benefits. If they do not, governments or NGOs may be able to catalyze private-sector investment by subsidizing user education or by subsidizing the investment costs.

A final reason a community-level infrastructure investment might be socially desirable but privately unprofitable is that the high prevalence of poverty in the community renders its residents unwilling to pay fees that cover the costs of provision. Even in the absence of public goods problems, externalities, and information problems, low-income households may be unwilling to purchase infrastructure services that are provided at fees that cover costs because they place greater priority on consumption of staple foods or other necessities. With too few households willing to pay prices at or above cost, it may be unprofitable for a private infrastructure service provider to enter the community. Policymakers might nonetheless consider service use in the community to be socially beneficial, because such use helps satisfy equity objectives.

Low incomes are most likely to present problems for profitability where the costs of providing infrastructure are especially high, as is the case for communities located in more-remote and difficult locations. In such cases, governments or NGOs might be able to encourage private investment by subsidizing the difference between what local users are willing to pay and the revenue private investors must receive for the investment to be profitable. Subsidizing efforts to develop lower-cost technologies for serving such communities might also help.

For some infrastructure investments, private actors may be quite willing to undertake investment as long as they are legally permitted to do so and do not face too many costly regulations or a too-high risk of expropriation. Relaxation of restrictive regulations or credible promises not to expropriate, rather than new intervention by governments and NGOs, may be useful for encouraging private-sector investments in such assets. Mobile-phone towers may be an example.

Rationales for intervention in operation and maintenance

Investments in infrastructure assets yield their full social benefits only when they are well operated and maintained and when they are used by all of the nearby households for which policymakers believe the social benefits of use exceed the costs. Unfortunately, even after an infrastructure asset has been created, market and institutional failures can prevent private actors from undertaking ideal operation and maintenance activities in the absence of continued intervention. Operation and maintenance activities are costly, and thus they are only performed by private or community actors who can expect to recoup those costs in some way.

Many of the same market and institutional failures that motivate intervention in infrastructure investment can also motivate intervention in operation and maintenance. Just as roads or wells are public goods, so also the operation and maintenance of roads and wells are public goods; and just as positive externalities and lack of knowledge can imply insufficient willingness to pay for construction of latrines or water treatment systems, so also might they imply insufficient willingness to pay for the services of latrines or water-treatment equipment after they have been created.

Because operation and maintenance costs are lower than the costs of operating, maintaining, *and* amortizing investment costs, it is *possible* but not inevitable that private actors or communities could operate and maintain an infrastructure asset profitably without subsidization, even after having required subsidization for the initial investment costs. Thus it is possible that governments and NGOs can exit from involvement in some infrastructure projects after having subsidized or participated in the creation of infrastructure assets, without jeopardizing effective operation and maintenance. Such hopes underlie many contemporary infrastructure programs.

Successful operation and maintenance after public actors exit is not guaranteed, however. Where private actors would find it impossible to charge fees that cover the full costs of adequate operation and maintenance, government or NGO subsidies may be important for sustaining infrastructure benefits. If, as a result of economies of scale or other advantages, governments or NGOs are able to provide training or technical assistance to communities at costs below what communities would have to pay for comparable services in the market, the public actors might wish to deliver some of their ongoing subsidies in the form of training and technical assistance rather than cash.

With yet other types of infrastructure, private actors may be more than willing to cover costs of investment, operation, and maintenance, but they would exploit market power to charge fees well above costs. Such high fees would price some users out of the market (or constrain their use), even though their use would be socially beneficial. Market power may be a problem for infrastructure services delivered via networks of pipes or cables or for power-generation projects that are efficient only at large scale. The market might sustain only a single network or project and might allow the owner of that asset to exercise market power. Such concerns motivate governments to regulate fee-setting by private service providers or to become directly involved in providing the service through a state-owned enterprise.

Some infrastructure services are likely to be *over* used rather than *under* used because they are common property resources. As discussed in Chapter 12, common property resources are nonexcludable, like public goods, but are rival. This means that it is infeasible to charge fees for their use, but each individual's use depletes the benefits available to others. Many irrigation systems have this property, because it is difficult to charge farmers for their use of ground or canal water, but the more one farmer draws from the resource, the less is left for other farmers. Paying inadequate attention to the social costs of their actions, farmers can deplete the resource through overuse or can incite conflict. Some communities create effective institutions to prevent overuse of, or conflict over, common property resources, but many do not. Government efforts to establish and enforce use rules may be helpful, but this is a daunting task.

Technical change has diminished the rationales for intervention in some infrastructure areas over time. For example, the minimum scale at which fossil fuel–based electrical power generation plants can operate has fallen over time, rendering private-sector competition more likely. Satellite, microwave, and mobile telephone technologies have reduced the importance of cable networks in the delivery of telecommunications services, and the development of electronic monitoring devices has increased the feasibility of charging for road use in some contexts.

Finally, we must acknowledge that equity concerns can motivate government intervention during operation and maintenance, as well as during investment. Public actors might believe that equity requires universal effective access to critical infrastructure services. Where low incomes and/or high costs imply that users are unwilling to pay fees high enough to cover operation and maintenance costs, policymakers might have to subsidize operation and maintenance, if they are to achieve such equity objectives. In the absence of government institutions capable of distributing targeted transfers, policymakers might also wish to make implicit income transfers to poor households by providing infrastructure services to them at fees below cost (though such transfers tend not to be well targeted).

18.2F Budgetary costs

The costs that ultimately matter to governments and NGOs are the subsidies they inject into infrastructure activities. Subsidies are equal to expenditures less any revenue gathered by charging fees or requiring contributions. Total subsidies are also equal to the total costs of investment, operation, and maintenance, plus the costs of any capacity- or institution-building services that public actors provide to local agents and the cost of any education or promotion campaigns, less all the resources contributed or paid by community groups, private firms, and users.

It is often useful to distinguish between **one-time subsidies** provided to encourage an asset's construction or installation, or to help partners create institutions for governing operation and maintenance, and **recurrent subsidies** incurred on a repeated basis while supporting or undertaking operation and maintenance. Many current development actors hope to catalyze the provision of high-quality, widely used, and long-lasting infrastructure services by providing only one-time subsidies. They assume that private or community actors are willing and able to perform operation and maintenance activities adequately without ongoing subsidy. Whether this assumption is true in any given case is an empirical question.

18.3 Evaluating Infrastructure Programs and Design Changes

18.3A Evaluating infrastructure programs

Box 18.3 adapts the seven questions of Chapter 14 for use in evaluating infrastructure programs. (The questions ignore the short-run impacts associated with hiring workers to construct the infrastructure assets, which were examined in Chapter 16's discussion of workfare programs.) In general, they point to the importance of asking questions about who *accesses* new infrastructure services, the *uses* to which users put the services, the *quality* of infrastructure services they

---

≡ **Box 18.3** Questions to Guide Analysis of Infrastructure Programs

Question 1: Objectives

Do policymakers intend the creation of infrastructure under this program primarily to improve the well-being of infrastructure users themselves? If so, do policymakers aim to improve users' health, income, school enrollment, security, comfort, or free time? Do policymakers instead, or in addition, aim to encourage users to invest and expand production and employment, thereby indirectly raising incomes and improving well-being for other groups?

Question 2: Design

What policy design choices regarding physical infrastructure assets, fees and contributions, education and promotion campaigns, and governance structure define the program or policy on paper?

Question 3: Implementation

In which communities are infrastructure assets created? Who makes local policy design and implementation decisions within communities? What local information, capacity, motivation, and coordinating oversight (as defined in Chapter 13) are brought to these decisions? In practice, what kinds of assets are built, what fees are charged, what contributions are demanded, how well do education and promotion campaigns convey their messages, what quality of services are provided, how efficiently are the services provided, how well are the assets maintained, and how long are they likely to remain operational?

Question 4: Directly affected groups

Who uses the infrastructure services? Are poor communities less likely to obtain service? Are poor households less likely to use the services within communities?

Question 5: Direct effects

What quantities of the new infrastructure service are used by households at different income levels? Do they use the new services in the ways required to deliver the intended impacts? What impacts does the switch from alternative services to the new infrastructure services have on their health, income, school enrollment, security, comfort, or free time? What additional impacts does use have on their consumption, time allocation, production, saving, and investment choices? How long are these impacts likely to last (before the infrastructure breaks down or wears out)?

Question 6: Spillover and feedback effects

What effects does the program have on rural labor markets, the rural nonfarm sector, urban labor markets, and goods markets? What effects does modified infrastructure use have on the environment? How does the availability of the new infrastructure increase the effectiveness or decrease the cost of other policies and programs? When all these changes are taken into account, which groups throughout society benefit a little or a lot and which are hurt a little or a lot?

Question 7: Budgetary costs

How much subsidy does the lead government or NGO provide on a one-time basis for initial infrastructure construction, institution building, capacity building, and education and promotion activities? How much subsidy does it provide on an ongoing basis for operation and maintenance activities?

receive, the *direct impacts* of use on users' well-being and behavior, the *longevity* of the services and impacts, *spillover* effects, and *budgetary costs*. With some rephrasing, these questions can also be used to guide study of reforms in policies toward privately owned utilities.

When applied in parallel fashion to programs with different designs, or to policies before and after reform, the questions in Box 18.3 help policy analysts identify the potential benefits and costs of proposed program design changes or policy reforms. In what follows we examine several design changes.

18.3B Raising fees

Many infrastructure policy reforms over the last two decades—including efforts to privatize, decentralize, and increase community participation—have included provisions that raise user fees to levels that cover at least the costs of operation and maintenance. Even so, subsidies remain common. For example, most national water utilities and one third of electricity utilities charge subsidized rates to all customers, and most offer subsidized rates to at least some customers (Komives et al., 2007).

The primary potential design change benefit of raising fees to cost-covering levels is an increase in revenue. The additional revenue can be used to reduce the infrastructure sector's net drain on the government budget or to increase the quantity or quality of services provided while holding the total budget constant. Fee increases are most effective in raising revenue when many members of the target populations are willing to pay cost-covering fees for the infrastructure services (and, as a result, continue to use the service despite the fee increase). In some cases, a secondary motivation for fee increases is to deter over-use of infrastructure services (such as irrigation water) that can generate negative externalities.

Raising fees to cover-covering levels may bring design change costs of three types, however. First, raising fees might cause some households—especially poorer households—to stop using the service. This reduction in coverage can be large when many households in the target population are unwilling to pay fees that cover cost, and it may be a cost of significant concern to policymakers if they believe that the social benefits of using the affected service outweigh the social costs. The social benefits of use may outweigh the social costs, even for people unwilling to pay cost-covering fees (who must perceive private benefits of use that fall short of costs) if potential users do not fully appreciate the benefits of use, if their use generates positive externalities, or if their use is important for fulfilling equity objectives. Second, among those who continue to use the service, raising fees might reduce the quantity of the service they use. Again, this may be an important cost if the benefits of using larger quantities are poorly appreciated by potential users or if greater use generates positive externalities. Third, a fee increase reduces the size of the implicit income transfers that users receive through the use of services at subsidized prices. The social costs of eliminating these subsidies may be important if the transfers implicit in low fees are well targeted to the poor and if policymakers lack better policy tools for distributing transfers to the poor.

The sizes of the design change benefits and costs may differ greatly from context to context. Ahuja et al. (2010) argue that, even among domestic water infrastructure projects, the benefits of raising fees are likely to outweigh the costs for some types of infrastructure projects but not others. They argue that raising fees is least likely to make sense for projects that provide poor rural communities with access to higher-quality, treated water. They point out first that many poor households appear unwilling to pay cost-covering fees for higher-quality water. Case studies of projects that make treated water available for a fee in poor rural communities show that many households fail to use the new water systems, preferring instead to use untreated water from rivers or ponds that is available for free. Similarly, many households are unwilling to pay for chlorine to treat their water at home, and in a study of Kenyan household choices regarding use of treated and untreated wells at different distances from their homes, Kremer et al. (2011) found that households were willing to pay very little—in valuable travel time—to obtain higher-quality water. Policymakers are likely to consider reduced use of new treated water systems an important cost of raising fees, because people may not fully appreciate the health benefits of using treated water, because use of treated water probably generates positive health externalities, and because policymakers are likely to consider use of clean water by the poor important for fulfilling equity objectives.

Other water projects, by contrast, primarily improve the convenience of water use rather than improving water quality. For example, some urban water projects construct pipe networks that deliver water directly to houses, in neighborhoods where people already had access to water from the same treated source through public standpipes. Ahuja and coauthors (2010) argue that households in the target populations for such projects appear willing to pay for the additional convenience of in-home water taps. In a study in urban Morocco, randomly selected households were offered loans to help them pay one-time connection fees for a new water service that piped water directly to houses. In the absence of this service, they obtained water of the same quality from public standpipes. When offered the financing scheme, nearly 70 percent of households accepted, suggesting significant willingness to pay for greater convenience, as well as the presence of significant liquidity constraints (Devoto et al., 2012). Furthermore, even if higher fees prevent some households from using piped water services that increase convenience, policymakers may not consider this an important design change cost, because people are likely to understand and appropriate the full social benefit of increased convenience, and it seems unlikely that policymakers consider mere convenience in water use essential for attaining equity objectives. In principle, higher fees could reduce the health benefits of piped water projects, by reducing the *quantities* of water used by households, but in the Morocco study health outcomes were no better among Moroccan households who were offered the financing plan than among other households. Thus charging cost-covering fees appears much more attractive for some urban piped water projects than for many projects that improve water quality in poor rural areas.

Fee schedules and differentiated subsidies

Many of the costs of raising fees would be reduced if fees could be raised to cost-covering levels in a selective manner, requiring higher payments from households that are less poor and more willing to pay, while targeting continued subsidies to households that are poor and unwilling to pay. Policymakers around the world have taken three main approaches to the design of fee schedules that target subsidies to the poor: quantity targeting, administrative targeting, and service-level targeting (Komives et al., 2007).

By far the most common approach for targeting subsidies to the poor involves **volume targeting**, in which average fees (per unit of service) rise with the volume of the service a household uses. Volume targeting can take the form of **increasing block tariffs**, in which all customers pay low fees for the initial quantities of service they use each month and then pay larger fees for additional quantities used above some threshold. For example, when electricity providers meter households' electricity use, they often charge a very low "life-line price" below the cost of production for the first 25 kilowatt-hours consumed per month, while billing additional kilowatt-hours at a higher rate. Volume targeting may also be attempted through the use of **volume-differentiated tariffs**, in which customers using quantities below some threshold pay a low rate on all units used, while customers using quantities above the threshold pay a high rate on all units used. If the correlation between poverty and service-use volumes is strong, then such fee structures are likely to result in the poor paying significantly lower average unit prices than the nonpoor.

Administrative targeting of infrastructure service subsidies employs means tests or categorical restrictions (of the sorts introduced in Chapter 15) to target subsidies to the poor. Sometimes policymakers charge low fees to people who have passed means tests for other social programs. Sometimes they set rates at lower levels for pensioners or war veterans, and sometimes they target the subsidies geographically, charging lower rates for households that live in low-income neighborhoods.

Infrastructure service providers engage in **service-level targeting** when they offer services at two levels of convenience or quality and charge subsidized rates only for the lower-quality service. They might, for example, charge cost-covering fees for water piped directly into homes, while providing water from public standpipes for free. In a few cases, subsidized rates are provided for lower-voltage electricity or for electricity used at night.

Whether the benefits of delivering subsidies through any of these mechanisms (relative to charging fees that cover costs for all users) outweigh the costs depends on how well they target benefits to the poor. Komives et al. (2007) survey studies of targeting performance for 45 electricity-subsidy schemes and 32 water-subsidy schemes (some actual and some hypothetical). They find that most schemes do a poor job of covering the poor, because the poor do not use the services. Often the poor lack physical access to services in their neighborhoods or are prevented from acquiring connections to services by high connection fees and liquidity constraints.

They find that even among users, subsidies are poorly targeted to the poor under volume-targeting schemes, because service-use volume is much more weakly correlated with poverty than we might have guessed. While the richest households do indeed use infrastructure services in significantly higher volumes than other households, usage patterns are quite similar for the poor and middle class. Thus, subsidies directed to low-volume users are not much more likely to go to the poor than to the middle class. Volume-pricing schemes deliver a smaller fraction of subsidies to poor households than is the case for most targeted-transfer programs. In fact, they deliver a smaller fraction of benefits to the poor than would be the case if subsidies were distributed randomly throughout the population!

Komives and coauthors find that administrative targeting approaches tend to deliver somewhat larger fractions of benefits to poor households than do volume-pricing approaches. As we would expect after our study of targeted-transfer programs in Chapter 15, however, administrative targeting is nonetheless far from perfect.

The authors suggest that service-level targeting merits more experimentation. In the few cases they observed, service-level targeting appears more effective at limiting leakage to the nonpoor than other approaches. The provision of free public taps in Bangalore and Katmandu, combined with delivery of water piped to homes at cost-covering fees, channeled large fractions of subsidy to poor households. Even so, many of the poor lacked access to the subsidies because they did not live in the poorer neighborhoods where the public taps were provided.

18.3C Governance of operation and maintenance

Poor maintenance of infrastructure is a widespread problem in developing countries. According to the World Bank (2003), one third of South Asia's rural water infrastructure is not functional, and such maintenance deficits are not unusual. For many years, policymakers assigned to central government ministries the responsibility for constructing roads, wells, and other infrastructure assets, but they left responsibility for maintaining the assets ill defined. Recent years have brought governance reforms intended to improve maintenance.

One class of governance reforms on which many policymakers have pinned their hopes involves increased community participation. These reforms often include five essential elements: government assistance in creating committees charged with overseeing relevant infrastructure activities at the community level, participation by the committees in selecting the assets to be constructed, the requirement that communities (through their committees) contribute resources to construction, the designation of communities as the legal owners of the infrastructure created, and the delegation of full responsibility for operation and maintenance to the committees.

In principle, such reforms could solve maintenance problems by improving accountability for maintenance and guaranteeing a source of maintenance funding. As members of the local community of users, committee members might have stronger personal interest (relative to government bureaucrats) in preserving local assets and might also be more susceptible to pressure from other community members, especially if they are democratically elected. Giving committees legal ownership of assets and requiring community contributions to capital costs could further increase communities' commitment to maintenance by increasing their psychological sense of ownership; research in psychology and behavioral economics reveals that people tend to exhibit "loss aversion," tending to be more concerned about losing something they believe they already own than they are about obtaining something of equal value that they do not own (Kahneman et al., 1990). Community members might also be willing to pay for effective operation and maintenance, especially if the creation of new community institutions solves any public goods problems and if they believe they can hold committees accountable for putting the fees to good use.

At least in principle, such reforms could deliver benefits in addition to improvements in infrastructure maintenance. Community committees with better access to local information than central government bureaucrats would be capable of selecting and designing infrastructure assets better suited to local needs. For example, some committees might recognize that local needs would be better served by simple water systems that deliver water to community taps than by more expensive systems that pipe water to homes. Community members would also be better able to identify the least costly ways of carrying out construction, and they might be more motivated to complain about corruption among bureaucrats charged with delivering funds for community projects. Development of community institutions for governing infrastructure operation and maintenance might generate spillover benefits by rendering communities more capable of cooperating in other ventures.

Unfortunately, reforms that increase community participation are not guaranteed to solve the maintenance problem. Community committees might lack adequate access to the technical expertise required for good maintenance. In principle, they might hire experts, but such expertise can come at very high cost to communities requiring expertise only on a small scale; professionals' time is put to more efficient use (and thus acquired at lower unit cost) in larger-scale organizations overseeing maintenance for multiple communities. Committees might also prove ineffective at raising the necessary funds, if they fail to catalyze local cooperation or if poverty renders too few community members willing to pay fees that cover the costs of operation and maintenance.

Even when communities are capable of high-quality maintenance, they might lack adequate motivation. The committees might be captured by the elite and choose not to focus energy on maintenance activities of community-wide value. Even if operating in a more democratic way, community committees might perceive little pressure to undertake maintenance. Donnges et al. (2007) indicate, for example, that community members seldom complain about lack of routine road maintenance. Rather, they complain only when roads become impassable, at which point the opportunity to save on reconstruction costs through routine maintenance is already past.

Increasing community participation in infrastructure programs can also bring important costs. Budgetary costs may be increased as the small scale of construction prevents cost savings through bulk purchase of construction materials. Demands for community participation in project selection, design, and financing might render the program inaccessible to some of the poorest communities, and even within communities, the need to charge fees and demand community contributions might prevent poorer households from participating in the benefits of infrastructure use (as discussed in the previous section). Participation in committee work can divert members' time away from other valuable community activities.

Many attempts to improve maintenance outcomes through increased community participation have proved disappointing. Earlier we saw anecdotal evidence of poor maintenance performance in the Swajal Project. Similar experiences have been observed around the world, especially in water, sanitation, and road projects. Some of the failures of participatory reforms have also plagued decentralizing reforms, which devolve responsibility for infrastructure to local governments rather than to new, single-purpose community committees. For example, decentralization of infrastructure investment to the local level in the Philippines led to a complete breakdown in rural road maintenance. On average, individual communities were responsible for maintaining just 4 kilometers of road. At such scale they could not afford to hire the required expertise and were unable to raise even small quantities of local funding (World Bank, 1994).

Two new options for the governance of infrastructure maintenance are now attracting attention, and experiments are yielding some promising results. One option is to leave communities in charge of maintenance but to provide them with ongoing funding and technical assistance. For example, various NGOs are experimenting with circuit-rider programs that provide rural village water committees with periodic visits from water system technicians, who can help local committees to solve problems and obtain chlorine and spare parts. They also increase committees' accountability for good performance. Such efforts appear successful at improving the quality of water consumed by local households in Honduras (Kayser, 2011).

Another option is for central governments to claim responsibility for maintenance and to contract competitive private firms to execute the maintenance. This approach takes better advantage of scale economies and expertise than community participation, and it employs competition to hold firms accountable for high quality and low-cost maintenance. It is also susceptible, however, to the same governance failures that lead to rampant corruption in centralized infrastructure construction. The results of a Kenyan experiment cited in Ahuja et al. (2010) are encouraging. In a randomized control trial, researchers compared the maintenance performance of three governance structures: user committees with no outside financing, user committees provided with outside financing, and government contracting of private-sector firms. The maintenance activities required were relatively simple: cleaning storm drains and trenches associated with protected springs. Providing grants to committees raised their overall performance measure by 30 percent of one standard deviation on average, and replacing user committees (who lacked outside financing) by paid contractors improved outcomes by 50 percent of one standard deviation.

Regardless of the governance structure employed, maintenance will be inadequate if too little funding is forthcoming to finance it. For politicians, construction of new infrastructure is much more appealing than providing routine maintenance for assets created by political predecessors. They may also be loath to spend funds on the maintenance of assets that benefit people who already have infrastructure at the expense of spending on new infrastructure for people who have none. Policymakers must therefore search for ways to institutionalize maintenance funding and render it politically acceptable. Some countries have created road funds, which levy taxes on road users of 7 or 8 cents per liter of gasoline and dedicate the revenue generated to road maintenance.

REFERENCES

Ahuja, Amrita, Michael Kremer, and Alix Peterson Zwane. "Providing Safe Water: Evidence From Randomized Evaluations." *Annual Review of Resource Economics* 2(1): 237–256, 2010. doi:10.1146/annurev.resource.012809.103919

Aker, Jenny C., and Isaac M. Mbiti. "Mobile Phones and Economic Development in Africa." *Journal of Economic Perspectives* 24(3): 207–232, 2010. doi:10.1257/jep.24.3.207

Asthana, Rohit. "Evaluation of Varied Approaches for Enabling Sustainable and Equitable Access to Drinking Water in Uttaranchal." New Delhi: Development Centre for Alternative Policies, 2003. http://planningcommission.nic.in/reports/sereport/ser/stdy_uttrnl.pdf

Briceño-Garmendia, Cecilia, Antonio Estache, and Nemat Shafik. 2004 "Infrastructure Services in Developing Countries: Access, Quality, Costs and Policy Reform." Policy Research Working Paper 3468. Washington, D.C.: World Bank, 2004. http://go.worldbank.org/9NHV6JAL20

Chattopadhyay, Raghabendra, and Esther Duflo. "Women as Policy Makers: Evidence From a Randomized Policy Experiment in India." *Econometrica* 72(5): 1409–1443, 2004. doi:10.1111/ecta.2004.72.issue-5

Devoto, Florencia, Esther Duflo, Pascaline Dupas, William Pariente, and Vincent Pons. "Happiness on Tap: Piped Water Adoption in Urban

Morocco." *American Economic Journal: Economic Policy* 4(4): 68–99, 2012. doi: 10.1257/pol.4.4.68

Donnges, Chris, Geoff Edmonds, and Bjorn Johannessen. "Rural Road Maintenance: Sustaining the Benefits of Improved Access." Socio-Economic Technical Papers (SETP) No. 19. Geneva: International Labour Organization, 2007. http://www.ilo.org/emppolicy/pubs/WCMS_ASIST_8001

Estache, Antonio, and Marianne Fay. "Current Debates on Infrastructure Policy." In Michael Spence and Danny Leipziger (eds.). *Globalization and Growth: Implications for a Post-Crisis World*. Washington, D.C.: World Bank, 2010, pp. 151–193. http://www.growthcommission.org/storage/cgdev/documents/globalization/globalizationebook.pdf

Foster, Vivien, and Cecilia Briceño-Garmendia (eds.). *Africa's Infrastructure: A Time for Transformation*. Washington, D.C.: World Bank, 2010. http://go.worldbank.org/YTCI6ZOPW0

Kahneman, Daniel, Jack L. Knetsch, and Richard H. Thaler. "Experimental Tests of the Endowment Effect and the Coase Theorem." *Journal of Political Economy* 98(6): 1325–1348, 1990. http://www.jstor.org/stable/2937761

Kayser, Georgia. "Moving Beyond the Millennium Development Goal for Water: Testing Safe and Sustainable Drinking Water Solutions in Honduras and El Salvador." PhD Dissertation. The Fletcher School, Tufts University, 2011.

Komives, Kristin, Jon Halpern, Vivien Foster, Quentin Wodon, and Roohi Abdullah. "Utility Subsidies as Social Transfers: An Empirical Evaluation of Targeting Performance." *Development Policy Review* 25(6): 659–679, 2007. doi:10.1111/dpr.2007.25.issue-6

Kremer, Michael, Jessica Leino, Edward Miguel, and Alix Peterson Zwane. "Spring Cleaning: Rural Water Impacts, Valuation, and Property Rights Institutions." *The Quarterly Journal of Economics* 126(1): 145–205, 2011. doi:10.1093/qje/qjq010

Monari, Lucio. "Power Subsidies: A Reality Check on Subsidizing Power for Irrigation in India." Viewpoint Report 24277, 2002. http://go.worldbank.org/YKBI74MTC0

Olken, Benjamin A. "Monitoring Corruption: Evidence From a Field Experiment in Indonesia." *Journal of Political Economy* 115(2): 200–249, 2007. doi:10.1086/509548

Organisation for Economic Co-operation and Development. *Promoting Pro-Poor Growth: Policy Guidance for Donors*. DAC Guidelines and Reference Series. Paris: OECD Publishing, 2007. doi: 10.1787/9789264024786-en

Ray, Isha. "Women, Water, and Development." *Annual Review of Environment and Resources* 32(1): 421–449, 2007. doi:10.1146/annurev.energy.32.041806.143704

Sampat, Preeti. "'Swa'-jal-dhara or 'Pay'-jal-dhara-Sector Reform and the Right to Drinking Water in Rajasthan and Maharashtra." *Law, Environment and Development Journal* 3(2): 101–125, 2007. http://www.lead-journal.org/2007-2.htm

World Bank. *World Development Report 1994: Infrastructure for Development*. New York: Oxford University Press, 1994. http://go.worldbank.org/CA3VU9YGR0

World Bank. "Community Contracting in Rural Water and Sanitation: The Swajal Project, Uttar Pradesh, India." Field Note 22798. Washington, D.C.: World Bank, 2001. http://go.worldbank.org/U8KYIX45Y0

World Bank. *World Development Report 2004: Making Services Work for Poor People*. Washington, D.C.: World Bank, 2003. http://go.worldbank.org/PLF4W7YI81

World Bank. *The Welfare Impact of Rural Electrification: A Reassessment of the Costs and Benefits*. An Independent Evaluation Group (IEG) Impact Evaluation. Washington, D.C.: World Bank, 2008. http://go.worldbank.org/S6C9P8B6A0

World Bank. *Water and Development: An Evaluation of World Bank Support, 1997–2007* (Volume 1). Independent Evaluation Group (IEG) Study Series. Washington, D.C.: World Bank, 2010. http://go.worldbank.org/8CF0ZVJ0E0

World Bank. *World Development Indicators 2012*. Washington, D.C.: World Bank, 2012. http://data.worldbank.org/data-catalog/world-development-indicators

QUESTIONS FOR REVIEW

1. Describe differences in the per capita quantities of infrastructure assets and services across countries at different income levels, among countries at similar income levels, and within countries.

2. Describe the objectives that might motivate infrastructure programs and policies, the infrastructure policy design options, and the implementation outcomes that ultimately shape infrastructure policy impacts.

3. For each category of infrastructure assets, discuss the ways their creation might improve well-being. How might the nature of these benefits depend on the nature of substitute services and goods available in a community?

4. Discuss the conditions under which a household uses a new infrastructure service. According to this economic model of infrastructure service use decisions, what are some reasons the poor are less likely to use a new infrastructure service than the nonpoor?

5. Why might households' choices about *how* or *how much* to use new infrastructure services affect the nature and size of an infrastructure project's benefits? What policy features might affect users' choices regarding how and how much to use the service? Why might better-off households tend to experience greater direct benefits from infrastructure investments?

6. Through what channels might infrastructure investments generate spillover and feedback effects?

7. Describe the market and institutional failures that might justify government or NGO intervention in infrastructure investment or infrastructure service provision. For each rationale, give examples of particular types of infrastructure for which the rationale might be relevant and describe the sorts of intervention it might motivate.

8. Discuss the potential benefits and costs of raising the fees charged for using infrastructure services.

9. Discuss the potential benefits and costs of reforms to centralized infrastructure investment programs that increase community participation.

QUESTIONS FOR DISCUSSION

1. Suppose you work for an NGO that has built wells for drinking water in several villages. Reports indicate that the wells are not used much. You are asked to brainstorm about the kinds of program design change that might improve use.
  a. What basic questions about the program and context would you want to ask as you begin your investigation?
  b. What kinds of design change might merit consideration?

2. Suppose you are asked to design assessments of the impacts of community infrastructure construction projects on the well-being and behavior of households that use their services. For each of the following assets, what would you include in a reasonably complete list of the impacts you would like to study?
  - A well providing safe drinking water
  - A new network of household electricity connections
  - A new irrigation system
  - A new landline providing a community with a pay telephone

3. How might choices made during the selection, design, and construction of an infrastructure asset affect its likely longevity?

4. For which kinds of infrastructure would you expect the study of spillover effects to be the most important for understanding the size and distribution of overall impacts?

5. What complementary policies might increase the extent to which a rural electrification program increases rural non-farm employment?

6. Why and how might the rationales for government intervention differ between road investments and railroad investments?

7. Why might private investors fail to invest in the provision of socially beneficial latrine services? Would you guess that for-profit provision of latrine services is more likely to arise (in the absence of intervention) in urban or rural areas? Explain.

8. Discuss the significance of each of the questions in Box 18.3.

9. Read Monari (2002).
  a. What do you learn about the objectives, design, implementation, direct beneficiaries, direct impacts, spillover effects, and budgetary costs of the Indian government's policy toward electricity for agriculture?
  b. Discuss the potential benefits and costs of raising fees for agricultural electricity (without any governance reform).
  c. Discuss the potential benefits and costs of installing water meters and charging for electricity on the basis of metered use rather than on the basis of pump size.
  d. What might be involved in a governance reform that could increase quality and reduce cost in providing electricity for agriculture by increasing community participation in local electricity distribution?
  e. Describe the logic of how a governance reform involving increased community participation might bring improved electricity service quality *and* widespread improvements in well-being throughout a rural community *without* increasing the central government's expenditure on electricity for that community.
  f. What details of the reform design would you wish to know before offering an opinion regarding whether the reform is likely to succeed in doing this?

10. Read Chattopadhyay and Duflo (2004). Why might we be interested in the question of whether female and male leaders make different decisions regarding infrastructure investments? Why is it difficult to tell from simple cross-section correlations (between gender of leader and policy choices) whether the gender of the leader truly makes a difference for policy outcomes? What unusual feature of the Indian data and context make it possible to get a better answer to this question? What do they find?

11. Read Olken (2007). Describe the nature of the corruption that is the subject of this study. Describe the approaches to reducing such corruption examined in the paper, the study design, and the result.

PROBLEMS

1. An NGO brings electricity to remote communities by setting up small diesel-powered generators, together with electric grain mills large enough to meet the grain-milling needs of the community. Before the intervention, women spent hours each day grinding grain into meal using mortar and pestle. The NGO organizes the communities' women into groups and then sells the generators and mills to the groups at a price that covers cost, while also providing them with loans so that they may pay off the purchase in installments. Except for collecting loan repayments, the NGO has no further interaction with the communities after installing the machines and training designated operators in operation and maintenance. In addition to running the grain mill, the generator may be used for charging batteries or running equipment directly connected to the generator. The women are free to give or sell the electricity or mill services as they see fit.

   a. Are the services of these diesel-powered generators public goods? Why or why not?

   b. What market and institutional failures might have prevented local investment in such generators?

   c. What features of program design give you reason to worry that some poor households might fail to benefit from this program? Explain.

   d. What direct and indirect impacts would you want to measure within participating communities?

   e. Why might some communities fail to take advantage of the NGO's offer?

2. A government program has just constructed a new road connecting a set of small villages to a larger market town. For residents too poor to own their own motorized vehicles, the new road provides them with cheaper and faster transport services only if it leads a private entrepreneur to set up a business that sells minibus services between the villages and the market town. Only one local resident has sufficient access to capital to start up a minibus service, and nonresident entrepreneurs choose not to start up such a business because they will not be able to keep close enough watch on the employees they hire to drive their buses. The following table describes local demand for minibus round trips (in average trips demanded per day) within three income groups and for three fare levels.

	Poor		Near Poor		Nonpoor	
Fare	Percent Who Ever Ride	Avg. Daily No. of Round Trips	Percent Who Ever Ride	Avg. Daily No. of Round Trips	Percent Who Ever Ride	Avg. Daily No. of Round trips
$3	40	3	50	3	30	8
$4	0	0	40	2	30	8
$6	0	0	0	0	30	8

a. Suppose the cost of running a minibus for a day is $28 (a fixed cost) plus $2 per rider (a marginal cost). The minibus can seat up to 16 passengers. Fill in the first five columns of the following table, using the minibus service demand information presented in the table above, as well as the cost information.

Fare	Round Trips (Average Daily Number)	Average Daily Revenue (Fare × Number of Round Trips)	Daily Fixed Cost	Average Daily Variable Cost (2 × Number of Round Trips)	Average Daily Profit[a]	Average Daily Profit after Subsidy
$3						
$4						
$6						

[a]Average daily profit = Average daily revenue – daily fixed cost – average daily variable cost. (Negative indicates loss.)

b. The potential minibus entrepreneur seeks to maximize profits and sets up the new minibus service only if he can derive a positive profit on an average daily basis. The entrepreneur faces no competition and expects to supply all the services demanded at any fare he charges. Will he choose to set up business? If so, which of the three prices in the table would he prefer to charge? Why?

c. The government creates a minibus service subsidy policy that would pay the entrepreneur $20 per day, but only if he charges a fare of $3 or less. Use the final column in the table to indicate the average daily profits associated with charging each fare after accounting for the subsidy (which provides revenue of $20 if the fare is $3 or less).

d. In the presence of the subsidy, will the entrepreneur set up business? If so, which of the three prices in the table would he prefer to charge? Why? (Please assume that the fare limit is well enforced.)

e. Discuss the benefits and costs of introducing the minibus service subsidy, including both benefits and costs that you learn about in the table *and* any other benefits and costs that you would like to measure.

3. Consider the Swajal Project as described in Box 18.1. Discuss the potential benefits and costs of imposing the restriction that communities can receive funding for piped domestic water systems only if they *also* include in their system design a community tap at which people may collect water without charge. You may assume that the program operates in villages where community members have easy access to untreated river water.

chapter 19

Education

The ultimate aim of education policies is to speed development by strengthening investment in human capital. Toward that end, governments and NGOs create and operate schools or offer scholarships, information, uniforms, textbooks, and other assistance to students and their families. Governments can also regulate or subsidize schools run by NGOs and private for-profit providers. In their pursuit of greater success, policymakers search for ways to draw more children into school, encourage children to remain in school longer and increase the value of what children learn while in school.

19.1 Education in Developing Countries
19.1A Education investment in developing and developed countries

Primary school enrollment rates have risen dramatically over the last half-century, and many countries have achieved nearly universal primary enrollment. The first three rows of Table 19.1 present **gross enrollment rates** (GERs) in primary, secondary, and tertiary education in low-, middle-, and high-income countries. The primary GER is calculated by taking the number of children enrolled in primary school (usually from school administrative records) and dividing by the number of children of primary school age (from a census or survey). The number can exceed 100 percent, because some children in primary school may be older than primary school age. Average gross primary enrollment rates now exceed 100 percent within all country groups shown in the table. This represents tremendous expansion in primary education since 1960, when average primary GERs were 65 and 83 percent in low- and middle-income countries. In sub-Saharan Africa, the average primary GER was still only 77 percent in 2000, but even that average rate reached 100 percent by 2009, reflecting the international development community's tremendous push to expand primary education in recent years (Glewwe and Kremer, 2006; World Development Indicators, 2012).

GERs greater than 100 percent indicate primary school systems with the capacity to serve all children of primary school age, but they can significantly overstate the fraction of children ever enrolling in school, because many primary school students in developing countries are older than official primary school age (having started school late or repeated grades). This motivates interest in complementary statistics on **net enrollment rates** (NERs), as shown in the fourth row of Table 19.1. The primary NER is calculated by identifying the number of children who are enrolled in primary school *and* are of official primary school age and then dividing by the number of children of primary school age in the population. Here we see that despite high growth in enrollment rates, 20 percent of primary school–aged children in low-income countries yet remain out of school. This group includes some children of early school ages who will eventually start school when they are older, but it also includes children who will never attend school. Most out-of-school children of primary school age live in sub-Saharan Africa and South Asia.

Enrollment rates at the secondary and tertiary levels have also risen significantly in the last half-century, but they remain much lower in low- and middle-income countries than in high-income countries (rows 2 and 3 of Table 19.1). More detailed figures (not shown) demonstrate that enrollment rates remain lower for girls than for boys in sub-Saharan Africa, South Asia, and the Middle East/North Africa, and enrollment rates remain lower in rural and poorer regions relative to urban and richer regions in many countries.

■ TABLE 19.1   Education Statistics for Low-, Middle-, and High-Income Countries

	Low-Income Countries	Middle-Income Countries	High-Income Countries
Gross Enrollment Rates, 2010			
Primary	104	109	101
Secondary	39	69	100
Tertiary	7	24	70
Net Primary Enrollment Rates, 2010	80	89	95
Primary School Pupil–Teacher Ratios, 2010	46	23	15
Literacy Rates, 2010 (Percentage of Population)			
Males Aged 15–24	75	94	99
Females Aged 15–24	68	88	99
Adults 15+	61	83	98

Source: World Bank (2012).

The disparity between poorer and richer countries in what children ultimately learn before leaving school is even greater than suggested by the differences in school enrollment rates, because the quality of teaching and learning also tends to be lower in poorer countries. Often schools lack basic equipment such as desks, blackboards, and school buildings. Many primary school teachers have less than a secondary education themselves, and teachers may be poorly motivated for their work. When researchers made unannounced visits to primary schools in six developing countries, they found that teachers were absent nearly 20 percent of the time, and in many cases teachers were not teaching even when they were present in the school (Chaudhury et al., 2006). Class sizes tend to be much larger than in developed countries, as suggested by the pupil-to-teacher ratios presented in Table 19.1. Textbooks are often in such short supply that 10 or more students must share a single copy, and many schools lack budgets for basic teaching supplies such as chalk and paper.

Under such conditions, it comes as no surprise that in comparative studies of academic achievement, the cognitive skills demonstrated by average fourth- or eighth-grade students are much lower in some developing countries than in developed countries (Glewwe and Kremer, 2006). Indeed, many students in developing countries complete primary school without learning how to read. Thirty percent of Malian youth aged 15 to 19 who had completed six years of schooling, and 50 percent of comparable Kenyan youth, could not read a simple sentence (World Bank, 2011).

One result of low enrollment rates and the low quality of teaching and learning is low rates of basic literacy and numeracy in the adult workforce. The literacy rates presented in the last row of Table 19.1 indicate important differences across countries in **education stocks** (i.e., levels of education among workers accumulated through past education investments), and probably understate the size of the deficits in developing countries. Most literacy statistics are based on subjective measures obtained by asking people whether they can read and write. In developing countries, such rates are often much higher than objective measures obtained by administering tests. For example, Kenny (2010) cites a study for five states in India in which 68 percent of respondents reported themselves as literate, while only 38 percent could write their names correctly and only 12 percent could read easily from a textbook at the second- to third-grade level.

19.1B Ultimate and proximate objectives in education policy

The ultimate objectives in education policy are to generate widespread improvements in well-being and to spur economic growth, especially in the medium to long run. Policymakers expect education to generate such benefits by increasing workers' productivity and income and by improving households' capacity to obtain information, access social services, make informed choices, participate in democratic processes, resolve conflicts, and adapt to change. Belief in the developmental value of education is supported by empirical studies at the micro and macro levels.

Micro-level studies examine how earnings and other indicators of household living standards are related to education levels within samples of households drawn from the same country. Hundreds of such studies from around the world show that earnings tend to rise by 10 percent or more with each additional year of schooling completed (see Box 9.2). Micro studies also demonstrate that people with more education are more likely to adopt new technologies, make use of social services, participate in civic functions, and have healthier children and smaller families (Foster and Rosenzweig, 1996; Glewwe, 2002; Grossman, 2006).

Macro-level studies examine how the levels and growth rates of GDP per capita relate to the levels or rates of change in education stocks across countries. The results of growth and development accounting exercises (as described in Chapter 3) are consistent with the hypothesis that increases in education per worker contribute significantly to increases in average labor productivity and income. Studies of growth rate determinants (also described in Chapter 3) also find that growth rates are higher where countries begin a period with higher typical levels of schooling, suggesting that higher levels of education can facilitate improvements in technology and organization (Hanushek and Woessman, 2007). In more recent data, relationships between the rate of economic growth and the quantity of schooling have become less robust (Pritchett, 2001). This might reflect that recent school enrollment expansions have drawn children into schools of lower average quality. Attempts to control for cross-country differences in the quality as well as quantity of education seem to support this conjecture (Hanushek and Woessman, 2007).

Most of the potential benefits of current education efforts are realized only in the future, when today's schoolchildren have become workers, citizens, and parents. This makes it difficult to measure the impact of current policies on their ultimate objectives. Often policy analysts are willing to assume, however, that policies make progress toward achieving the ultimate objectives when they make progress toward achieving three shorter-term or proximate objectives: increasing the number of children who start school, increasing the number of years children complete before leaving school, and increasing the value of what children learn while in school.

19.1C Primary and secondary education policy design and implementation

Policymakers pursue the proximate objectives just described by altering households' education opportunities. Here we first describe the dimensions of primary and secondary education opportunities that policies might alter and that shape policy impacts. We then describe the policy design choices through which policymakers influence these implementation outcomes.

Implementation outcomes

Households' schooling opportunities are defined by "supply-side" and "demand-side" policy implementation outcomes. **Supply-side** elements include the number and geographic distribution of schools, and—for each school—the numbers of classrooms at different levels and grades, the quality and content of education services, the primary language of instruction, the comfort and security of the facilities, and any limits on the number or types of students the school accepts. **Demand-side** elements influence households' desire or capacity to send their children to school, without directly altering the nature of education services offered. They include the fees charged directly (e.g., for tuition) or indirectly (e.g., by requiring households to purchase books or uniforms), as well as the details of any programs offering scholarships, conditional cash transfers, school meals, or other support for school attendance.

Policymakers care not only about how their policy choices alter households' schooling opportunities but also about how much it costs to provide any given set of opportunities. Thus a final implementation outcome of interest is the efficiency with which education policies are implemented. Education policy implementation is more **efficient** when a given set of education opportunities is provided at lower cost.

Policy design options

With some implementation outcomes, policymakers may either choose the outcomes directly or delegate such choices to agents closer to the local level. These include the number and distribution of schools, school building designs, language of instruction, curriculum, advancement and graduation requirements, school schedules, fees, scholarship and meal programs, and education promotion campaigns. Policymakers may delegate some or all of these **school policy choices** to district or school-level administrators, parent–teacher associations (PTAs), community committees, NGOs, or for-profit education providers.

Policymakers have only indirect influence over other critical school-level implementation outcomes, including the quality of instruction, informal local efforts to encourage enrollment, and the efficiency of school management. They influence these outcomes indirectly through their governance of what we will call **school management choices**, which they sometimes charge to central-level administrators and sometimes delegate to agents closer to the local level. These include school-specific choices regarding numbers of teachers and textbooks; quantities of other supplies; teacher hiring, pay, mentoring, promotion, and firing; and daily management of teachers, students, and resources.

Education policy designs are defined by the way responsibilities for the various school policy and management choices are allocated across central-level administrators and other agents closer to the local level, by the specific school policy choices set by policymakers at the central level, and by the design of the governance structure through which policymakers influence agents' choices. Many developing-country school systems have long histories of highly centralized governance, in which most schools are owned and operated by national or regional governments, and most school policy and management choices are made at high levels of government bureaucracies. In the most centralized systems, policymakers and national or regional administrators determine where to build schools; design buildings and curricula; choose the language of instruction and fees; train, hire, and allocate teachers to schools throughout the country; design, publish, and distribute textbooks; procure and distribute chalk and other supplies; and even pay, discipline, and fire teachers.

Education policy reforms and programs

In recent decades, governments have undertaken a variety of education policy reforms. Some reforms have retained centralized control, while changing specific school policy or management choices made at the central level. Through such reforms, governments have eliminated school fees throughout the country, increased the rate of school construction, altered teacher hiring standards, or introduced new mandatory curricula and textbooks.

Other reforms have sought to decentralize some school policy and management choices within government school systems or create new openings for communities and NGOs to participate in providing education. Yet other reforms have subsidized private sector participation in providing education. One approach to subsidizing private sector education is to distribute vouchers, which parents may use to purchase education services from qualifying private providers.

The details of education policy reforms differ greatly from case to case. The local agents given new authority over school policy and management choices by decentralizing or privatizing reforms are sometimes given very limited control over day-to-day school management decisions, while in other cases they are given much broader scope to hire and fire teachers, choose curricula,

≡ Box 19.1 Universal Primary Education Reforms in Uganda

Uganda's Universal Primary Education reforms of 1997 combined five elements: eliminating tuition fees, increasing per-student transfers from the central government to schools, expanding teacher training, constructing new schools and classrooms, and introducing governance reforms aimed at preventing diversion of education funds to other uses.

In principle, both before and after the reform, the central government paid teacher salaries, constructed schools, and disbursed **capitation grants** (i.e., grants to schools calculated on a per-student basis) to cover nonwage expenditures. School district administrators hired civil service teachers and allocated them to schools, and school management committees (or parent–teacher associations—PTAs) oversaw daily school operations.

Before the reform, official policy called for central government capitation grants to schools of 2,500 Ugandan shillings (USh) per child enrolled in lower primary and USh4,000 per child in upper primary (approximately US$2.50 and $4.00). In practice, schools received few funds from this source. Rampant corruption and diversion of funds resulted in schools receiving on average only 28 percent of the funds disbursed by the central government for their capitation grants. Official policy also mandated that parents pay tuition fees of USh2,500 and USh4,000 per child in lower and upper primary school, matching the official capitation grants. In practice, only small fractions of the official fees were collected, and schools were required to transfer all but a small fraction of the fees they collected to school district administrators. Thus schools received very little discretionary funding through government sources.

School management committees generated funding for schools by charging PTA fees, which averaged USh7,400 per student but varied greatly across regions and schools. They used these funds—a large fraction of all funds invested in primary education—to pay for materials, pay supplementary salaries for teachers receiving low government

salaries, and hire additional teachers. When trained teachers were unavailable they hired untrained teachers; just before the reform, 40 percent of all teachers had no training. In addition to tuition and PTA fees, households were also responsible for buying uniforms, supplies, and textbooks.

On paper, the 1997 reform eliminated tuition fees and outlawed PTA fees. It also doubled official capitation grants from the central government to schools. Governance reforms, including the publication of the capitation grants disbursed to schools, aimed to increase the share of disbursed funds reaching schools by increasing community members' capacity to hold the school system accountable. The reform also increased the rate of teacher training by creating a distance education program, and it committed the government to providing more textbooks and constructing more facilities (while requiring communities to provide the labor). Finally, the reform included a new campaign to promote girls' education.

In practice, the reform significantly reduced, but did not eliminate, fee payments by households. Average total reported fee payments fell 87 percent between 1995 and 2000, but in 2000, 13 percent of households continued to report paying tuition fees, and 15 and 56 percent reported paying PTA and "school development fund" fees. Governance reforms succeeded in increasing the fraction of grants reaching schools to 90 percent, though the delivery of grant money remained slow and unpredictable. The number of teachers rose by 25 percent between 1996 and 2001, and the share of teachers lacking training fell from 40 to 25 percent and the numbers of textbooks increased. Later in the chapter we examine the impacts of this reform.

Sources: Aguti (2002); Dauda (2004); Deininger (2003); Penny et al. (2008); Ablo and Reinikka (1998).

and set fees. Policymakers influence the behavior and accomplishments of the local agents through their choices regarding what buildings, teachers, textbooks, or monetary grants for discretionary spending they provide to schools; the rules that determine the distribution of such resources across schools; the capacity-building services they provide; and the mechanisms through which local agents are held accountable for pursuing policy objectives.

In recent years, governments and NGOs have also introduced programs to complement preexisting government school systems. Such programs provide additional teachers, textbooks, or facilities to schools, or they offer scholarships, conditional cash transfers, meals, uniforms, and other encouragements to families whose children attend government schools. Other programs build the capacity of PTAs or train communities to monitor the use of local school budgets.

Often education policy reforms contain multiple components, as in the case of Uganda's Universal Primary Education reforms of 1997, which are described in Box 19.1.

19.2 The Economics of Primary and Secondary Education in Developing Countries

We begin preparing for the analysis of education policy reforms by studying the determinants of which children enroll in school, the direct and indirect effects of schooling, and education policy costs. We then take a closer look at how policymakers might influence the quality of teaching and learning. Finally, we examine the rationales for intervention by governments and NGOs in the education arena and their possible implications for policy design.

19.2A School enrollment decisions

A general model

Understanding households' decisions regarding whether or not to send children to school each year is important for understanding which children ever start school and how many years they ultimately attain.[1] We begin study of their decisions by observing that:

> A household sends a particular child to school in a given year if the household's decision makers expect the private benefits of doing so to outweigh the private costs. This is an investment decision, because most of the costs must be borne immediately, while many of the benefits accrue only in the future.[2]

In many economics discussions, the main benefit of enrolling a child in school for a year is the impact of the additional education on her future income. Additional schooling can improve workers' incomes by increasing their productivity in any given type of work (whether on a farm, in a nonfarm family enterprise or in wage employment) or by helping them move into more productive occupations. Such labor market rewards are greater when students learn more valuable skills while in school and when strong employer demands for skilled workers raise the wage premium paid to educated workers.

Parents might value their children's future income gains out of altruistic concern for the children's well-being or because they expect to share in those gains, believing that better-off children will provide them with greater income support later in life. Parents might also value non-income benefits their children can derive from education, such as improved access to social services or more effective voice in local politics. They might value education for its own sake or for the prestige it brings, and they also value the more immediate benefits of scholarships, conditional cash transfers, and school meals.

The most obvious private costs of sending a child to school are the explicit costs: tuition and fees; the costs of books, uniforms, and supplies; and the costs of any transportation, lodging, and board required for attending school. As suggested by the analysis of time allocation decisions in Chapter 6, the full cost of attending school also includes the **opportunity cost of the child's time**, or the value given up when the child's time is withdrawn from other activities. The opportunity cost may be high because some of the time the child spends in school (or traveling to and from school) comes out of time the child would have spent working for wages or working on a farm. It might also be high if spending more time at school requires children to spend less time caring for siblings or doing housework; this might require their mothers or older siblings to reallocate time from income generation to child care. Beyond this, sending a child to school can entail discomfort, whether because sending a young or female child to school is considered socially inappropriate or because spending time outside the home raises the child's risk of physical harm.

We know from Chapter 10 that financing education investments is costly and that liquidity constraints can elevate financing costs, especially for poor households. Liquidity-constrained households must place greater weight on the up-front costs of schooling, when comparing them to future benefits, than other households. As a result, poorer households might send fewer children

---

[1] Households also make important choices regarding how often, or under what circumstances, students attend school during the years in which they are enrolled. When children do not attend consistently, they often fall behind in school and repeat grades.
[2] If a household has more than one option regarding where to send a child to school—for example, the household may send a child to a public school or a private school—it sends the child to the school for which the expected benefits most outweigh the costs.

to school, even when their children face the same education benefits, fees, and opportunity costs as other children.

Households can differ in their school enrollment choices not only because they anticipate different objective benefits and costs but also because differences in preferences, norms, or the intrahousehold distribution of decision-making authority cause them to value the benefits and costs differently. Some might consider education intrinsically more valuable than others do. Some might place greater value on the future income impacts of schooling, because their children are bound by stronger cultural obligations to support their parents in old age. If educating girls is a higher priority for mothers than for fathers, then households in which women play a greater role in decision making are more likely to send their girls to school (Chapter 7).

Households' school enrollment choices differ across children at different ages and different levels of schooling already attained. These differences define the age at which children begin school and the number of years they attain before leaving school. In some countries, many children do not begin school until they are eight or nine years old. They may be kept home at earlier ages because parents believe that children are too young to gain from schooling, because the risks of long walks to school are especially great at young ages, or because social norms render it socially costly to send young children to school. Children enter school when parents perceive that the benefits of schooling begin to exceed the costs.

Children who enter school eventually cease attending, because the perceived benefits of additional schooling fall far enough, or the perceived costs rise high enough, that the benefits of additional schooling no longer outweigh the costs. The perceived benefits of additional schooling might fall as the level of learning already achieved rises, because, for example, parents believe that their children will benefit from becoming literate but will not benefit from learning beyond that level. The direct cost of additional schooling can rise with years of schooling already attained if schools at higher grade levels are more distant or charge higher fees. The opportunity cost of children's time is also likely to rise as they age, because their potential earnings in wage labor markets or in family businesses rise or because societal demands create increasing pressure for them to marry and start families. If the opportunity costs of their time rise abruptly to high levels in their mid-teens, regardless of how many years of schooling they have attained, then the forces that cause children to start school only at older ages also reduce the years of schooling they ultimately attain.

A household's enrollment choices can differ across children of different gender, status, or ability. Many parents enroll girls at lower rates than boys. The simple model of enrollment choices suggests many possible reasons for this. Parents might value girls' future well-being less than boys', or they might accurately perceive that the benefits of schooling are lower for girls, who will face discrimination in labor markets later in life, or that the costs are higher for girls, who are more vulnerable to harm outside the home.

Empirical evidence on the determinants of enrollment

The preceding discussion suggests that households' enrollment choices can depend on many characteristics of the education opportunities they face, as well as local socioeconomic conditions, their own household characteristics, and the gender, status, and abilities of their children. Empirical study of these relationships is useful for policymakers who hope to alter education opportunities in ways that will draw many children into school at low cost. Here we highlight a few critical findings from empirical research to date. For more detailed reviews, see Glewwe and Kremer (2006) and Kremer and Holla (2009).

Physical access to school

Children who live farther from the nearest school must spend more time and energy in getting to school, might also face higher monetary costs for transportation or boarding, and may be exposed to greater risks. If these effects on cost are significant, then efforts to reduce distances to school, by building schools in new locations, can raise enrollment rates significantly. Many household surveys confirm that school enrollment rates drop off quickly as the distance from a child's home to the nearest school rises above one or two kilometers, even after controlling for household income and other factors. This suggests that construction of additional schools might raise enrollment rates significantly in regions where many children live more than two or three kilometers from the nearest school. Duflo's (2001) study of rapid school construction efforts in Indonesia generates evidence consistent with this hypothesis.

Household surveys also make clear, however, that school construction efforts alone are unlikely to bring all remaining children into school, because enrollment rates often remain low even among children who live within one kilometer of the nearest school (see Box 19.2).

Actual and expected income gains

If parents value the long-run impacts of schooling on their children's earning power or well-being, then education policy reforms that raise school quality, and broader economic policies that raise the labor market rewards for education, can raise school enrollment rates. Where the labor market rewards are already high, policy efforts to raise parental understanding of those labor market returns might also raise enrollment rates.

Several studies suggest that parents' schooling decisions indeed depend on the likely impacts of schooling on their children's earning power. Foster and Rosenzweig (1996) show that the income gains associated with education in rural India in the 1960s and 1970s were higher in regions where adoption of high-yielding crop varieties was more profitable, and that farmers invested in more schooling for their children where the income benefits of education were higher. Kochar (2004) demonstrates that rural Indian families also invest more in educating their children where the returns to schooling in nearby towns—to which their children might migrate for better jobs—are greater.

Two recent studies demonstrate that improved information regarding the labor market rewards for schooling can raise enrollment rates. In the Dominican Republic (Jensen, 2010) and Madagascar (Nguyen, 2008), providing families with information about earnings differentials by education level reduced dropout rates by 3 to 4 percentage points.

Even so, the evidence is somewhat mixed regarding the likely impact of school quality improvements on school enrollments. An effort to increase teachers' attendance in remote schools by linking teachers' pay to teachers' attendance (described in Box 13.1) improved school quality, and parents and children responded with higher attendance rates. Several Kenyan programs that raised school quality by increasing schooling inputs or providing teachers with stronger incentives, however, did not raise enrollment (Kremer and Holla, 2009). This suggests that parents might find it easier to observe and evaluate changes to obvious school quality indicators, such as teachers' attendance rates, than to observe and evaluate subtler changes in teaching methods and teachers' effort.

Liquidity constraints, fees, and demand-side programs

If a significant fraction of households are liquidity constrained, then modest increases in household income, and modest reductions in the up-front monetary costs of sending children to school, might raise school enrollment rates significantly. The enrollment rate increases would be especially large among poorer households, which are more likely to be liquidity constrained. As mentioned in Chapter 10, Edmonds (2006) presents evidence of liquidity constraints on school enrollment decisions in South Africa, where children's enrollment rates rose when grandparents living in their homes started receiving anticipated old age pension benefits.

In an earlier study, Jacoby (1994) presented very different evidence of liquidity constraints. He demonstrated that children from lower-income families in Peru are more likely to miss school and repeat grades than other children. He points out that while weaker preferences for education among lower-income families might explain correlations between income and the years of schooling that children ultimately complete, they cannot explain a correlation between income and school repetition rates, because families should always (i.e., regardless of their preferences toward education) wish their children to complete schooling as quickly as possible so as not to delay the higher incomes they will earn once they leave school. Liquidity constraints, which increase the urgency of pulling children out of school periodically to help generate family income, offer a more plausible explanation for why poorer children are more likely to fall behind.

More recent studies offer direct evidence that reducing out-of-pocket costs and increasing conditional transfers attached to school enrollment can raise enrollment rates, especially among the poor. As noted in Chapter 15, the Progresa conditional cash transfer program in Mexico, which provided monthly transfers of up to $27 per month per child attending school, increased enrollment rates among middle-school girls by 7 to 9 percentage points. Conditional monthly transfers as low as $5 per month raised enrollments for secondary school–aged girls in Malawi (Baird et al., 2011). We will see later that simply eliminating modest school fees raised enrollment rates dramatically in several countries. Two randomized control trials from Kenya also found that giving families free uniforms worth just $6 raised enrollments significantly (Kremer and Holla, 2009).

Preferences

If household preferences toward educating children are malleable, then efforts to persuade families or communities of the importance of sending children to school may be useful, and if women value education more than men, then efforts to raise women's say over the use of household resources might also raise enrollment rates, perhaps especially for girls. Emerging evidence encourages further exploration of these mechanisms. Jensen and Oster (2007) found, for example, that the introduction of cable television raised female school enrollment rates in India. They suggest that access to television might have altered households' attitudes toward girls' education by broadening the range of role models and opinions to which parents were exposed. Studies reviewed in Chapter 7 also offered evidence that increases in household income were more likely to raise girls' enrollment rates when the income entered households through the mother than when it entered through the father.

Other features of local school supply

School policy and management choices can affect enrollment rates not only by affecting school location, fees, and quality but also by altering more detailed features of the services schools provide. Changes in schools' hours of operation and vacation schedules might increase school attendance by reducing the conflict between children's school attendance and their home responsibilities, thereby reducing the opportunity cost of their time in school. Small improvements in local footpaths and bridges, or arrangements for parents to escort groups of children to school, can reduce the difficulties or risks of school attendance. Modifying the curriculum to include elements that parents value highly, and developing relationships of trust between parents and school staff, can also encourage enrollment. Systematic evidence on the impacts of such changes is lacking, though anecdotal evidence offers some support (see Box 19.2 for examples).

Identifying critical barriers to enrollment

The policies that are likely to draw the most children into school on a fixed budget differ from context to context. Where there are no schools nearby, only very large scholarships would convince households to send their children to school (presumably in distant towns), and building schools is likely to be a more cost-effective approach to raising enrollment rates than creating scholarship programs. Similarly, where all households already are located close to schools, building additional schools is unlikely to raise enrollment rates in a cost-effective manner; and

Box 19.2 Policies for Achieving Universal Primary School Enrollment in Ethiopia: Lessons from Household Survey Data

According to Ethiopia's Welfare Monitoring Survey of 2004, only 39 percent of rural children of primary school age (7 to 14 years old) were enrolled in school in that year. This represented a huge improvement over a decade earlier, but it also signified that getting all primary school–aged children into school remained a great challenge for Ethiopian policymakers. Even simple descriptive statistics from household surveys shed important light on the mix of policies that would be required to achieve universal primary enrollment in rural areas. As of 2000, one third of rural children lived at least 5 kilometers from the nearest school. It was unlikely that many such children would be brought into school without building more schools. At the same time, even among rural children living less than 1 kilometer from the nearest school, more than half remained out of school. Building schools in more locations would do little for such children. Thus it appeared likely that policymakers would have to combine both supply- and demand-side efforts to bring all children into school.

Econometric estimates relating enrollment rates to community, household, and child characteristics shed additional light on the likely importance of various policies. They indicated, for example, that even after controlling for differences across households in income, parents' education, remoteness from roads and markets, and community characteristics, households located farther from the nearest school are significantly less likely to send their children to school. In fact, the estimates imply that building schools in communities that were previously 10 kilometers from the nearest school would increase school enrollment rates by 20 to 30 percentage points. The effects would be even larger for girls, tending to reduce gender differences in enrollment rates, and for younger children, tending to reduce the age at which children begin school. The effects of distance on schooling rates were especially profound for the first one or two kilometers of distance between the child's school and home, suggesting that the Ethiopian government's aim to build large schools intended to enroll all students within a five-kilometer radius might require revision. Building a larger number of smaller, more-dispersed schools might have a much larger impact on enrollment.

According to the estimates, increases in income, while holding distance from school and the other factors constant, led to only small increases in enrollment rates. This was true even among children living close to the nearest schools, for whom we would expect income to make a greater difference than for children without any feasible

schooling opportunities. This does not rule out the possibility that in some local contexts, income transfers could have a large impact on enrollment rates, especially if the transfers are made conditional on sending children to school, though it casts doubt on the desirability of a widespread and costly income transfer policy as the means for getting children into school.

Many children were reported to be both working and attending school, suggesting that many child work activities were compatible with attending school, especially in rural areas. The tendency for boys' enrollment rates to be lower and their work rates to be higher in communities with tighter labor markets suggests, however, that some work activities did compete with schooling for boy's time. At the time of the survey, almost all children who were enrolled in school were enrolled in government schools following strict, Western-influenced school schedules, which did not coordinate well with rural child labor requirements. It remains possible that changes in school schedules would reduce the opportunity cost of schooling by rendering school and work more compatible. NGOs experimenting with more flexible school schedules in Ethiopia indeed report that when given the chance, parents choose school schedules that are quite different from government school schedules, either starting and ending earlier in the day or being offered in two shifts, so that some of their children can go to school in the morning and others go in the afternoon, leaving some to help out at home all day long.

A variety of indirect evidence suggests a strong role for parents' exposure to, and beliefs about, the benefits of education. Only 21 percent of rural household heads were literate, and many children lived in remote communities where none of the adults had ever been to school. Even after controlling for household income and distance to the nearest school, the literacy of a child's parent or household head and the rate of literacy among other household heads in the child's neighborhood both had large estimated effects on primary school enrollment rates. Enrollment rates were also higher among households that engaged in "modern" practices such as listening to the radio. Taken together, these patterns raise the possibility that primary school promotion and adult literacy campaigns, which offer adults an enhanced appreciation of what education can offer their children, might help raise enrollment rates.

Sources: Schaffner (2004), and calculations based on the Ethiopian Welfare Monitoring Survey 2004.

where households are already convinced that education is highly valuable, education promotion campaigns would do little good. Context-specific empirical work is thus useful for identifying the array of policies that might be required to draw all children into school (see Box 19.2 for an example).

19.2B The direct and indirect effects of schooling
Long-run direct and indirect effects

The most important effects of education policies arise in the long run, as students put their learning to use in adulthood. A brief review of empirical evidence on such effects was presented in section 19.1B. Many of these long-run benefits are direct effects enjoyed by the students and their families.

Some of the anticipated long-run benefits of education are indirect, however, arising as externalities. Policymakers hope, for example, that when schooling provides children with a common language and history, it imbues them with a shared national identity and sense of social responsibility. If this is the case, then any one child's participation in schooling could benefit other members of society by encouraging peace and cooperation. Similarly, when schooling improves workers' ability to communicate about, experiment with and adopt improved technologies, one child's schooling could benefit others by speeding the rate of productivity growth, as suggested by some endogenous growth theories reviewed in Chapter 4. When acquisition of basic literacy and numeracy skills renders it easier for others to communicate with her, a student's schooling reduces the costs of carrying out transactions with her or providing her with social services; and when education reduces students' propensity to engage in crime, one child's schooling reduces risks faced by other households. Finally, if schooling renders people capable of greater discernment in exercising rights to voice and vote, then one child's schooling can benefit others in society by improving the quality of democratic processes.

Children's acquisition of education can also induce indirect effects worked out through labor markets. As discussed in Chapter 9, as education investments reduce the supply of less-educated labor and increase the supply of more-educated labor, they can drive down the wage premiums earned by more-educated labor while driving up wages for less-educated labor, thereby reducing poverty and inequality indirectly.

When analyzing policy reforms, it will be important to recognize that:

> The nature and magnitude of education's direct and indirect long-run impacts depend on the quality and content of what children learn while in school and differ across levels and grades of schooling.

Where schools offer low-quality instruction, even investments that draw many children into school at low cost can generate few long-run benefits. If decentralized or segregated education systems fail to provide children with a common language and culture, they do little to promote peace and cooperation. Schools that emphasize rote learning might encourage productivity growth much less than schools that emphasize problem-solving skills.

Differences in the long-run benefits of schooling by level and grade can complicate policymakers' choices over whether to use scarce funds to expand primary or higher levels of schooling. If primary education investments yield higher long-run benefits than investments in secondary or tertiary schooling, then scarce budgetary resources might yield greater impacts on growth and equity when they are used to expand primary education rather than higher levels of education. If secondary or tertiary education generates larger impacts on the rate of productivity growth than primary education, however, then shifting more resources into secondary or tertiary education might raise the growth impacts of education policy, and policymakers might face a tradeoff between improving equity with additional primary school investments and raising growth rates with additional investments in higher levels of education. Furthermore, if highly educated labor is complementary in production with low-skill labor, then expanding investment in higher education might even help speed increases in wages for un-educated workers by increasing the demand for low-skill labor (Bloom et al., 2006). Such possibilities merit empirical investigation.

Short-run effects

The impacts discussed thus far are all "long-run" impacts of school enrollment, in the sense that they accrue after students have left school and throughout their adult lives. In comprehensive policy analysis, it is useful to remember that when improved education opportunities induce a household to send a child to school, they might also alter the household's current consumption level and its other investments. Consumption might fall, as households pay explicit or opportunity costs, or it might instead rise, if scholarship, transfer, or meal programs are sufficiently generous. For families who would send their children to school regardless of fee levels, reductions in fees increase real income without affecting their schooling investments.

19.2C Governance and the quality of teaching and learning

Policymakers influence the quality of teaching and learning through their choices regarding the governance of school policy and management choices. These choices, whether made by central-level administrators, local-level bureaucrats, community committees, or others, affect the quality of learning through multiple channels. Most obviously, they help determine the quality of the services provided by teachers.

Teachers influence education service quality when they make choices regarding how frequently to report to work, what time and energy to spend in teaching while at school, what effort to expend in preparing lessons, how to allocate their teaching time across subjects, what methods to employ for teaching and motivating students, and how, exactly, to respond to the needs of individual students. Using the language of Chapter 13, they make high-quality teaching choices, and supply high-quality teaching services, when they bring a healthy combination of capacity, motivation, resources, and coordinating oversight to these choices. School managers can influence teaching quality, therefore, through their choices regarding hiring standards for teachers, the training and mentoring that teachers receive on the job, the curriculum teachers are asked to teach, how they are held accountable for effective teaching of this curriculum, the scope they are given to tailor their methods to the needs at hand, and the quantities and types of textbooks, wall charts, blackboards, chalk, pencils, pens, library resources, lab equipment, and computers available for use by them and their students.

While holding constant the motivation, capacity, and resources a teacher brings to her teaching, the quality of learning achieved by her students is likely to fall as the number of her students rises. It is also likely to fall as the level and diversity of needs among her students rise and as her students' preparation and motivation fall. Students' capacity to pay attention and digest information can depend on how well rested and well fed they are while in school, as well as on the nutrition, health care, and cognitive stimulation they received as young children. If competition or cooperation among students is important in learning, then any one child's learning can depend on the capacity and motivation of other students in the class. Students might also learn better where electric lighting, tutoring opportunities, or educational television programming reinforce lessons outside of school.

This suggests that:

> School managers can influence learning directly through their supply-side choices regarding the numbers of teachers to hire and the governance of teaching choices, and also indirectly through their demand-side efforts to draw more children into school. Learning outcomes depend also on many factors beyond school managers' immediate control.

Empirical evidence on the determinants of learning

Policymakers seeking to provide good governance for school management choices would benefit from empirical evidence on the production function relating learning outcomes to school management choices and other circumstances. For many years empirical evidence on the determinants of learning was drawn largely from *retrospective studies*, in which researchers ran regressions of learning outcome measures—usually average student scores on standardized language and math achievement tests—on various measures of "education inputs" or "policies," such as dollars available per student in school budgets, student-to-teacher ratios, and student-to-textbook ratios, using data on random samples of schools.

Unfortunately, retrospective studies can yield biased estimates of the causal impacts of education inputs on learning, because they might suffer from important omitted variables biases (Glewwe and Kremer, 2006). Retrospective studies are likely to overestimate the causal effect of some inputs, such as textbooks. The social and political processes that lead some schools to acquire larger numbers of textbooks per student probably allow the same schools to acquire more of other inputs as well, and they can also reflect greater interest among local parents in investing in their children's education outside of school. When some of these other inputs and parental investments are unmeasured, the regression coefficients on measures of textbook availability are likely to pick up some of their effects (as well as any causal effect of textbook availability) in retrospective studies.

In recent years, researchers have begun to study the determinants of learning using estimation methods more convincing than simple retrospective studies. Some use randomized control trials. Others identify natural experiments in which critical policy elements vary across schools or students for reasons that are arguably unrelated to all other determinants of learning outcomes. Empirical evidence to date regarding what matters for learning is far from complete, but a few interesting lessons are emerging.

Textbooks and other physical inputs

Retrospective studies typically attribute large learning impacts to increases in the numbers of textbooks and other supplies available per student, but randomized control trials produce more nuanced conclusions. Glewwe et al. (2009) found that providing additional textbooks to schools in Kenya produced no improvements in test scores on average, though it improved test scores among the best students. The authors point out that the textbooks were written in English (the third language for many students) and at a high level. Additional textbooks might have had greater impact on learning if their content were tailored better to the needs of the typical student.

Several studies suggest the usefulness of well-designed technological assistance. Radio-based enhancements to primary education in Nicaragua (Jamison et al., 1981) and computer-assisted teaching in India have shown good results (Banerjee et al., 2007).

Teacher incentives

Two randomized control trials reviewed in Box 13.1 examined the effects on school quality of two quite different efforts to improve teachers' performance by tying teachers' pay to performance measures. An initiative that tied the pay of teachers in small remote schools to their attendance as measured using cameras with date-and-time stamps proved successful at reducing teachers' absenteeism and raising student test scores (Duflo et al., 2008). A more complicated effort to improve pedagogy, effort, and attendance, by tying teachers' rewards to students' performance on standardized tests, encouraged teachers to "teach to the test" without bringing about more fundamental improvements in teachers' performance (Glewwe et al., 2010). In a more recent randomized control trial in India, the results of tying teacher pay to student test performance were more promising and had greater impacts on student test scores than interventions of similar cost that provided schools with additional teachers or block grants for purchasing supplies (Muralidharan and Sundararaman, 2011).

Early childhood nutrition and care

Studies by psychologists and neurologists highlight the tremendous importance for cognitive development of good nutrition, health care, and stimulation among young children from conception to age three years (Alderman, 2011). Children from poorer backgrounds, who are less likely to be well-nourished, enroll in school at lower rates, remain in school for fewer years, and tend to learn less. Provision of preschool programs at ages four and five years can compensate to some extent for earlier deprivation, but interventions to improve nutrition between conception and age three appear more cost-effective at improving cognitive attainment than remedial interventions at later ages.

19.2D Budgetary costs

The total budgetary costs borne by central governments or NGOs naturally tend to grow with the numbers of children they draw into school. They also rise with efforts to improve students' learning by increasing the per-student quantity and quality of teaching inputs in the system. Holding constant the quantity of students served and the quality of education provided, budgetary costs fall with improvements in the efficiency of education service provision and with increases in the share of costs borne by parents and communities. The efficiency with which schools produce a given number of students with complete, high-quality primary school education may be increased by reducing repetition and dropout rates, as well as by reducing waste and the corrupt diversion of resources.

19.2E Rationales for intervention

High social returns to education investments, on their own, need not justify government or NGO intervention in education. If parents perceive high private returns to education, they might invest in it, even in the absence of intervention, by purchasing education services from private for-profit schools. To identify possible rationales for intervention, it is useful to ask why too few private sector education services might be bought and sold in the absence of intervention. In what follows, we point out that:

> Diverse rationales might justify government or NGO intervention in education. Education might generate positive externalities and other social benefits that parents cannot appropriate, households' schooling choices might be liquidity constrained, households might have inadequate information (about the benefits, costs, or quality of education), and policymakers might consider education vital for achieving poverty reduction and equity objectives. These potential justifications for intervention differ in their implications for education policy design.

Externalities

A first possible rationale for intervention arises if education generates positive externalities of the sorts described in section 19.2B. Parents might also give less weight than policymakers might wish to the interests of their children (relative to their own interests) when deciding how to use scarce household resources. Parents might, therefore, demand too little education, even if they faced no liquidity constraints and even if private sector schools sold high-quality education services at competitive fees. Under such circumstances, governments or NGOs might be able to improve education outcomes by subsidizing the purchase or sale of education services. As long as parents perceive at least some private benefit to educating their children, partial subsidies (which reduce fees below the cost of providing education services but do not eliminate fees) may be enough to raise education investments to the socially optimal level. If externalities are equally relevant to all children, then subsidies of similar magnitude for all students may be desirable.

Liquidity constraints

If liquidity constraints prevent some households from effectively demanding education services, then the pattern of subsidy required to achieve ideal outcomes may be quite different. Because the poor are more likely to be liquidity constrained than the nonpoor, it may be desirable to target larger subsidies to the poor. The partial subsidies suggested by externalities may also be too small to counter liquidity constraints, because the up-front costs that liquidity-constrained parents find difficult to bear often include the opportunity costs of their children's time and the costs of purchasing school clothes and transportation, as well as the fees charged to cover the costs of providing the education services. The subsidies required to overcome liquidity constraints can thus equal or even exceed the cost of providing education services. That is, policymakers might need to *pay* severely liquidity-constrained households to send their children to school. In principle, policymakers could try to relax liquidity constraints by providing education loans rather than by reducing fees or providing grants, but practical difficulties with enforcing loan repayment often seem to rule out that option.

Notice that while externalities and liquidity constraints can provide rationales for government or NGO *subsidization* of schooling services, they do not necessarily justify government or NGO *provision* of the subsidized services. Governments and NGOs might be able to counter these imperfections by subsidizing households' purchase of education services from private, for-profit providers. A possible exception arises if coordinated provision of a uniform curriculum to all students is required to achieve nation-building externalities, in which case centralized government provision may be important.

A combination of liquidity constraints and collective action problems might justify intervention of a different sort in some poor communities. Even when all parents in a community are willing and able to pay fees that would cover the cost of schooling their own children, liquidity constraints might prevent any one of them from undertaking the investment required to set up a school. Under such circumstances, the community's children attend school only if parents succeed in creating a school through a cooperative investment. As we know from the discussion of public goods in Chapter 12, however, institutions to support such cooperation are not always present. Such constraints might justify government or NGO efforts to catalyze local cooperation in the creation of new schools.

Misperceptions of schooling benefits

If inadequate knowledge or incorrect information regarding the benefits and costs of schooling lead some parents to underinvest in schooling for their children, governments and NGOs might also have a role to play in disseminating information. Such a rationale for intervention is most likely relevant in more remote communities and in communities where few parents have attended school.

Parents might also find it difficult to evaluate the quality of services that schools provide. This asymmetry of information between parents and schools might allow private providers to charge fees well above cost for low-quality services, and parents' fears of being cheated in this way might prevent them from investing. Governments might respond to this information asymmetry by setting school quality standards and seeking to monitor and enforce compliance with the standards.

Poverty reduction and equity objectives

A final set of possible rationales for public sector intervention in education relates to poverty reduction and equity objectives. Even in the absence of externalities, liquidity constraints, and information problems, and thus even when parents could be expected to make efficient education decisions in the absence of intervention, policymakers might wish to encourage education investments by poorer households out of concern for poverty reduction and improved equity. As with concerns about externalities and liquidity constraints, poverty reduction and equity concerns might motivate subsidization of education, especially for poorer households, but need not motivate public sector provision of education.

19.3 Evaluating Education Policy Reforms
19.3A Education reform objectives

In the 1960s and 1970s, developing-country governments and other development actors invested in education primarily by increasing the number of government-run schools, each built, staffed, and operated according to pre-existing models. The models they followed often employed curricula, schedules, and building designs reflecting schooling norms of developed countries. They also required all students to pay identical fees, which were lower than the cost of supplying education services but were not trivial. In so doing, they provided all students with partial subsidies, as would be appropriate if education generates positive externalities and other social benefits that parents do not appreciate.

Such policies drew many children into school, but they left many children out of school and provided many children with only low-quality education. The policies also placed major demands on government budgets, often amounting to several percent of GDP. In recent years, policymakers have therefore searched for reforms that would improve education systems' outreach and quality while containing cost. Constraints on per-child spending in developing countries are particularly tight, because children represent much larger fractions of the population in developing as compared to developed countries. This implies that although developing and developed countries spent similar fractions of GDP on education in the late 1990s, average education spending amounted to more than $3,000 per student in high-income countries but just $600 per student in middle-income countries and less than $50 per student in low-income countries (Glewwe and Kremer, 2006).

Recent decades have witnessed diverse education policy reforms, many motivated in part by a re-thinking of the rationales for intervention. Recognizing that larger subsidies may be required to draw the children of liquidity-constrained parents into school, policymakers have experimented with eliminating school fees and with providing targeted scholarships. Concerned about inadequate information and the possible need for collective action, NGOs have worked at engaging communities in building and governing their own schools, especially in more remote locations. Recognizing that liquidity constraints and externalities might call for central governments to subsidize education but not to provide education services, policymakers have experimented with decentralization, increased community participation, and privatization, hoping to improve schools' efficiency and quality by improving school governance. Sometimes these reforms also aim to reduce the share of total education costs borne by the government, by requiring or encouraging greater contributions from parents or communities.

19.3B Evaluating education reforms

Box 19.3 adapts Chapter 14's seven questions for analysis of education policy reforms. The questions highlight that education policy reforms tend to affect at least two groups directly: the families of children who are drawn into school by the reforms, and the families of children who experience changes in the costs or quality of schooling but who would have attended with or without the reform. These groups tend to differ in socioeconomic status and location, and they tend to be affected in very different ways. In some cases comprehensive evaluations also require consideration of additional groups, such as families of children who remain out of school but would have attended in the absence of reform, and families induced by the reform to move from public to private schools or vice versa.

In what follows, we study the benefits and costs of three very different types of government education policy reform. The first involves a change in a centralized school policy choice (the elimination of school fees), without major changes in the allocation of decision-making authority across actors of different types. The second and third reforms reallocate authority over some school policy and management decisions from the central government to community committees and to private sector education providers.

≡ Box 19.3 Questions to Guide Analysis of Education Policy Reforms

Question 1: Objectives

To what extent do policymakers intend the reform to draw more children into school, keep children in school longer, improve the value of what children learn while in school, improve efficiency in the provision of education services, or shift responsibility for school finance from the central government to parents or communities?

Question 2: Design

Prior to the reform, what school policy and governance structure choices characterized education policy? What changes did the reform bring in school policy choices made in a centralized fashion? What changes, if any, did the reform bring in the governance of school policy and management choices?

Question 3: Implementation

How effectively were any changes in centralized policy choices enforced and executed? What happened to the number and distribution of schools? What happened to the volume of central government resources disbursed to schools, the fraction of those funds reaching schools, and the distribution of those resources across schools? Who took on new school policy and management decision-making authority? What happened to the local information, capacity, motivation, and coordinating oversight (as defined in Chapter 13) brought to school policy and management choices? How did school policy choices change in practice? What effect did the reform have on the quality and content of instruction, and on the efficiency of school management?

Question 4: Directly affected groups

As a result of the reform, in which groups of households did children enter school, exit school, or experience change in school cost or learning quality as incumbents? Among children who would have attended school with or without the reform, which groups shifted from government to nongovernment schools or from nongovernment to government schools?

Question 5: Direct effects

Among households in each of the groups directly affected by the reform, what effect did the reform have on what children learned (and thus on the future benefits they derive from learning) and on current household consumption?

Question 6: Spillover and feedback effects

What indirect effects were generated by entry into schooling, exit from schooling, or changes in learning, whether through externalities or labor market impacts?

Question 7: Budgetary costs

What was the effect of the reform on the government's budget, taking into account the effects on numbers of students, total cost per student, and the share of total costs borne by the government?

19.3C Eliminating school fees

Of the 79 countries surveyed by Kattan and Burnett (2004), 40 percent charged official tuition fees for primary schooling and almost all charged at least one fee of some sort (e.g., for PTA dues, textbooks, exams, uniforms, or community contributions to district school boards). In searching for ways to draw more children into school, it is natural to consider reducing or eliminating school fees. In what follows, we lay out the potential benefits and costs of education policy reforms that eliminate school fees, and we examine their empirical magnitudes in four cases of such reform: Malawi in 1994, Uganda in 1996, Tanzania in 2001, and Kenya in 2003.

The primary potential benefit of eliminating school fees is an increase in enrollment, especially among children from poorer households. By reducing the private costs of schooling relative to the private benefits, the elimination of fees might encourage additional schooling investments by households at any income level, but it is most likely to encourage enrollment among poorer children, for whom liquidity constraints are more pressing.

The elimination of school fees can fail to raise enrollment rates significantly, however, for two quite different reasons. First, policies that eliminate school fees may be difficult to enforce in practice. When policymakers abolish official school fees, local school managers might respond to the loss of fee revenue (which is sometimes their main source of discretionary funding) by demanding "voluntary contributions" from parents. In most reforms that abolish official fees, policymakers compensate schools for the loss of fee revenue, at least to some extent, by increasing central government transfers to schools financed out of general revenue. More generous compensatory financing can reduce pressure to charge unofficial fees.

Second, policies that eliminate school fees can reduce schooling costs by *too little* to convince many more parents to send their children to school. Even when parents pay no school fees, they might incur costs for transportation, clothing, and books, as well as the opportunity cost of their children's time and nonmonetary costs. Even in the absence of tuition fees, therefore, the costs can continue to outweigh the benefits, especially among the liquidity-constrained poor, and especially if parents have low expectations regarding the benefits of education or serious concerns regarding the risks of sending children to school.

In the four cases reviewed here, the elimination of school fees indeed increased school enrollment rates dramatically, despite some evidence of increased demands for "voluntary contributions" (Kattan and Burnett, 2004).[3] In Malawi and Uganda, total enrollments rose 50 and 70 percent, respectively, and their primary gross enrollment rates reached 134 and 124 percent. Enrollments increased more for poor children than for nonpoor children and more for girls than for boys. The elimination of fees nonetheless failed to bring all children into school. The primary net enrollment rates in Uganda and Tanzania remained at only 83 and 85 percent after reform.

The elimination of fees can bring important policy design change costs as well as benefits. Unless the central government greatly expands its funding of schools out of general revenue, learning outcomes are likely to deteriorate for several reasons. First, even if enrollments were to hold constant, the elimination of school fees without compensating increases in other funding would significantly reduce per-student expenditures. It is not uncommon for school fees to constitute 30 percent of total public plus private spending on government primary education, and in extreme cases (as in Cambodia) school fees can constitute as much as 80 percent of financing. Second, even if the government maintained total funding for primary schools, per-student funding would fall as enrollment rates rise. Third, because the new students drawn in by the elimination of school fees are likely to be poorer than the average incumbent student, their entry might reduce the average student's preparation for learning. This would raise the burden on teachers and might diminish the potential for incumbent students to learn from their peers. Fourth, some analysts worry that when parents are freed from paying fees, they might become less diligent in monitoring teachers and demanding high-quality education. The elimination of school fees is thus likely to bring some combination of increased burden on central government budgets and reduced school quality and learning outcomes.

All four reforming governments examined here attempted to compensate for reduced fee revenue by instituting or increasing the size of capitation grants disbursed to schools by the central government. The budgetary implications were nearly as dramatic as the enrollment increases. In Uganda, government spending on primary education rose from 0.6 percent of GDP to 2.5 percent. In Malawi, spending tripled, reaching 7.5 percent of GDP! Even so, spending failed to keep pace with enrollment, and spending per student declined in these two countries. Per-student spending declined less in Tanzania and Kenya, where strong government commitment and international support allowed even more rapid spending increases.

Despite the spending increases, learning outcomes appear to have declined in all four countries (Kattan and Burnett, 2004). The case of Malawi is particularly disturbing. After the reform, the school system served an average of 119 pupils per class, 21 pupils per textbook, and 38 pupils per desk. Government funding for nonsalary expenditures at the school level dried up. To accommodate the huge increase in student population, policymakers increased the number of teachers by 75 percent. To achieve such a rapid expansion of the teaching staff, they had to recruit untrained teachers and deploy them to schools after only three-week induction periods. Despite these efforts, many schools remained understaffed, and some teachers lost interest in teaching when faced with overwhelming numbers of students. It is impossible to quantify the impact of these changes on student learning and test scores because pre-reform test scores are unavailable. Post-reform test scores confirm, however, the very low levels of post-reform learning. According to the 1998 Southern African Consortium for Monitoring Education Quality exam, for example,

---

[3] An important caveat must be applied to the discussion of reform impacts in this section. The data permit study only of before—after changes in enrollment rates and other outcomes, rather than more rigorous estimates of causal impact. Observed changes may be driven not only by the elimination of school fees but also by other changes over time in policy and economic conditions.

less than 25 percent of Malawian students in Standard 6 had reached the minimum level of reading mastery, and less than 1 percent had attained the desired level of mastery. Perhaps as a result of low quality, rates of repetition and dropout were also very high. After the reform it took the average student 13 years to complete 8 grades of primary school, and only 18 percent of school starters completed primary school. Many dropped out too early to have achieved functional literacy and numeracy.

In Uganda, the increases in pupil-to-classroom and pupil-to-teacher ratios were somewhat smaller; but even there the fraction of school children who could read a simple sentence declined after the reform, and average scores on national assessment exams fell significantly. Per-student spending fell little in Kenya, but Bold et al. (2011) argue that school quality fell even there. They base this conclusion on the observation that many better-off families moved their children from government to private schools, despite rising private school costs. They argue that school quality and peer effects on learning (at least as perceived by better-off parents) diminished in government schools with the influx of poorer students, motivating an exodus of better-off students.

In light of the budgetary difficulties caused by eliminating school fees, it is useful to consider whether enrollments might be increased through other, less-expensive means. Many NGOs involved in **nonformal education** or **alternative basic education** believe such means exist. Often working in communities lacking government schools, these organizations operate on the assumption that parents are willing to contribute money, materials, and labor to building and running schools for their children, as long as the schools are well designed to suit their interests. They assume further that requiring parents and communities to contribute money and time has the beneficial effect of encouraging parents' interest and oversight, thereby improving the quality of the education ultimately provided.

The key to increasing enrollments, in their view, is not to reduce the financial cost but to design curricula that are more tailored to parents' perceived needs than are state school curricula, to develop a school schedule that conflicts less with local needs for children's help on family farms, and to promote the importance of education among families for whom formal school systems are alien and off-putting. They also work to improve school safety, to seek out female teachers for female students, and to build separate latrines for boys and girls, in an effort to find investments of modest cost that reduce important barriers to school attendance. In an effort to keep costs more manageable, they often build school buildings to much cheaper specifications (and sometimes dispense with buildings entirely, holding classes under big trees) and use curricula that can be covered in fewer hours per grade level. Whether these measures, too, lead to reduced school quality is an important question. Little systematic evidence is available on the quality and outreach of the education achieved by these programs.

Another alternative to universally eliminating fees is introducing means-tested fee waivers, scholarships, or stipend programs, which reduce schooling costs only for households with income or assets below specified levels. If such programs could be designed to target fee waivers largely to liquidity-constrained households, then they might increase enrollments by nearly as much as universal fee waivers while placing much less pressure on central government budgets and school quality. To gain insights into the feasibility, design, and impacts of such programs, see the discussion of conditional cash transfers in Chapter 15.

19.3D School-based management reforms

School-based management reforms shift responsibility for some school policy and management decisions from government administrators in national or regional offices to local school management committees composed of parents or community leaders. The committees sign contracts with their Ministries of Education, accepting responsibility over specified school policy and management decisions and agreeing to meet specified conditions in exchange for central government provision of funds or teaching inputs.

The primary motivation behind some school-based management reforms is much-needed improvement in school quality. More specifically, policymakers hope to improve school quality by improving the way teachers and other school resources are managed. They expect to improve management quality by shifting management decisions from remote bureaucrats in central government offices to local actors, who are better able to observe what is happening in schools and whose greater personal stake in schooling outcomes gives them stronger motivation to manage well.

The motivation behind other school-based management reforms is to expand school access into previously un-served locations more cheaply and quickly than would be possible under more traditional, centralized governance. Local school management committees may be able to operate with greater speed and efficiency than central government administrators, not only because they have better local information and motivation but also because they are less encumbered by civil service rules regarding hiring, firing, pay scales, and procurement. Often policymakers also hope to reduce per-student central government spending by requiring school management committees to finance larger fractions of local costs out of local resources through the collection of fees or voluntary contributions.

Policy analysts recognize that although school-based management reforms might succeed in increasing the local information and motivation brought to school management decisions, they might also fail to do so for several reasons. Even if local committees are well motivated for involvement in the schools, the reforms might give them too little decision-making authority to put their local information and motivation to productive use. For example, even well-motivated school committees might find it difficult to strengthen teachers' incentives and improve teachers' performance if they are not given authority to hire and fire teachers.

The motivations of school committee members might also be less than ideal. A committee might be captured by the self-interested elite, who divert resources to their own uses. More subtly, committee members might be well-intentioned parents of children already attending school, who work hard at improving the quality of their children's education but are unaware of the barriers to enrollment they create for other families when they decide to raise school fees. They might thus fail to balance enrollment and quality objectives in the way policymakers would like them to.

The rules determining how government resources are allocated to schools can also skew committees' incentives in inefficient directions. For example, rather than providing school committees with simple capitation grants, the Kenyan government offers to provide them with one teacher for any number of students per grade up to 30, as long the committees provide school buildings and cover any non-salary expenditures out of local resources. Kremer et al. (2003) argue that this policy causes communities to construct too many schools, use too many teachers, use too few complementary teaching supplies, undertake too little school maintenance, and charge fees that prevent poorer children from attending school.

School-based management reforms might also reduce the quality of school management by reducing the capacity or resources brought to school management decisions. If school committees are to improve teaching quality, they must provide good governance for teachers. This means that they must create conditions under which teachers are well motivated and are equipped with the necessary skills and resources. School committee members—who often have little education themselves—might have little capacity to evaluate the quality of teaching or identify managerial changes that would improve quality. School-based management reforms furthermore reduce the resources brought to school management when locally managed schools are given less central-level funding per student than is allocated to traditional, central-government-run schools, especially when schools are prohibited from charging fees or are located in poor communities.

The discussion thus far suggests that careful attention to design details might increase the potential for success with school-based management reforms. Reform designers may be able to improve committees' scope for good management, for example, by increasing the range of management decisions over which they are given authority. Policymakers may be able to improve school committee motivation by requiring democratic elections of committee members or requiring that committees include representatives of under-served groups within the community. Reforms might generate better results when committees are provided with more central government funding, more sensible funding rules, and more training. Committees might also achieve more where they are subject to more frequent monitoring by Education Ministry officials or where standardized testing allows some assessment of their performance.

Examination of three school-based management reforms—the EDUCO program in El Salvador, the PROHECO program in Honduras and the School Autonomy program in Nicaragua—offers insight into the potential and limitations of such reforms, though it leaves many questions unanswered. For descriptions of these reforms and studies of their impacts, see Di Gropello (2006) and Umansky and Vegas (2007).

The primary goal of the reforms in El Salvador and Honduras was to facilitate the rapid creation of schools in remote, previously un-served communities. They allowed communities that did not have schools and that had a minimum number of school-aged children to establish community-managed schools. NGOs and other liaisons were hired to help organize and train committees. The committees were composed of community members, most of them parents of school children. They received a fixed quantity of government funding per teacher plus a fixed amount for facilities maintenance and materials, and they were not allowed to charge fees. They were given control over the hiring and firing of teachers and school directors, but they were somewhat restricted by regulations regarding how to spend their funds.

Statistical comparisons of community-managed and traditional schools reveal similar patterns in El Salvador and Honduras. Survey results seem to confirm that the reform represented a real change in the locus of management; parents in community-managed schools were more likely than parents in traditional schools to report that they have influence over what happens in school. The results also suggest that community committees chose a different approach to school management, as compared to traditional school administrators. Community-managed schools hired teachers who were younger and less experienced, paid them less, and provided them with fewer benefits. They also hired the teachers under one-year renewable contracts. At the same time, they hired more teachers on a per-student basis, thereby maintaining smaller class sizes.

Community committees devoted effort to managing the schools but seemed more capable of disciplining attendance than of improving classroom activities. Teachers in community-managed schools attended school more frequently, worked longer hours, and assigned more homework, suggesting improvements in the most visible dimensions of their performance. At the same time, teachers in community-managed schools were more likely to use traditional teaching methods (i.e., dictation and teaching from the blackboard) rather than newer methods involving more student participation. Teachers also felt they had less influence over school decisions, had lower morale, and felt more distant from parents. School directors, too, reported having less influence in community-managed schools than in traditional schools. Thus, while smaller class sizes and higher teacher effort might have improved teaching quality, lower teacher experience, deterioration in teacher morale, and reduced influence of trained teachers and directors over school activities might have caused it to deteriorate.

Despite the mixed effects on teaching inputs and pedagogy, the net effects of reform were more than satisfactory in El Salvador and Honduras. The reforms allowed rapid expansion of schools in previously un-served areas. The new schools seem to have done just as well at enrolling children within their communities as traditional schools. Thus the reform was an effective vehicle for achieving its primary objective: expanding access to school.

Though school quality was of secondary concern, policymakers hoped that the new schools would at least maintain the same quality as traditional schools. Here, too, the reforms appear successful. In both countries, students in locally managed schools performed better on standardized Spanish language tests than students in traditional schools, and in Honduras they also performed better in math and science. The test score differences were statistically significant but modest in size. Given that the community-managed schools were located in poorer and more-remote communities, where parents were less educated, the test score differences seem likely to understate the performance gains caused by reform. Dropout rates were also lower in community-managed schools.

The Nicaraguan reform was quite different. There the primary aim of the reform was to increase efficiency in pre-existing well-resourced schools and to shift some of the financing burden from the central government to communities, rather than to create new schools in un-served areas. Again, school quality was only a secondary concern. No eligibility criteria limited which schools or communities could participate, but schools participated only if teachers and school directors voted to do so. The school committees, which included school directors as well as parents, received less government funding than traditional schools. They received funds calculated on a per-student basis, which might have given them more interest in increasing enrollment and less reason to reduce class size, as compared to the financing rules relevant for school committees in El Salvador and Honduras. They were allowed and encouraged to raise local voluntary contributions. Initially they could also charge tuition fees, and although fees were later officially prohibited, some community-managed schools continued to charge fees illegally. The committees were given control over hiring and firing of teachers but not of school directors, and the committees had great flexibility regarding how they spent their funds.

The results of the Nicaraguan reform also differed from the El Salvador and Honduras cases. Nicaraguan schools participating in the reforms tended to be located in better-off communities and to have more resources than traditional schools. The reform appears to have transferred management authority to local school directors rather than parents. Parents in community-managed schools did not report more influence over school affairs than parents in traditional schools. Parents became more involved in financial concerns, but not in the classroom. As in the other countries, the community-managed schools hired teachers with lesser qualifications on one-year contracts and paid them less. In Nicaragua they also used larger class sizes.

The results of the Nicaraguan reform were less satisfactory. Estimates of the reform's impact on enrollments are unavailable, but it seems likely that barriers to enrollment rose as schools attempted to raise more local funding through fees and voluntary contributions. The reforms also led to greater inequality in resources across schools, as community-managed schools in well-off communities pulled in more local revenue. Statistical comparisons provide no evidence of increased teacher attendance, and student test scores were no higher in community-managed schools than in control schools, despite the resource advantage of the community-managed schools. Dropout rates were no lower. Thus the Nicaraguan reforms appear not to have raised the quality of teaching and learning.

19.3E Voucher-based privatization

Education voucher programs provide eligible families with government funds to use in purchasing education services from eligible schools—often including private and public schools. The effect is to introduce a new range of government-subsidized schooling opportunities outside the government school system. As a reform to the governance of government-subsidized education, voucher reforms shift some school policy and management decisions from public to private sector providers, and they increase the accountability of public sector providers to students and families by requiring them to compete for students.

In developed countries, and sometimes in urban regions of developing countries, the primary aim in introducing voucher programs is to encourage competition among schools, thereby ultimately raising the quality of teaching and learning or increasing the efficiency of education provision. By encouraging the creation of new schools, voucher programs can also increase the diversity of subsidized education options, giving parents greater opportunity to find education services well suited to their idiosyncratic needs.

In developing countries, however, vouchers might be used to expand the reach of subsidized education systems in poor or remote places where government schooling opportunities are in short supply. Policymakers might hope that the private sector will expand the supply of schooling opportunities more rapidly and more cheaply than would be possible through the government system, because private education providers (like the school management committees discussed in the previous section) are unencumbered by civil service hiring, pay, and procurement rules. Voucher programs are unlikely to encourage much competition in poor and remote locations, where the numbers of students per community are too small to be served by more than one school at a minimally efficient scale.

Naturally, voucher reforms can bring costs as well as benefits. Governments introducing voucher programs must give up some control over the content of subsidized education. As the number and diversity of schools rises, the difficulties of monitoring and regulating schools also increase. Unless governments increase expenditures on accreditation activities, parents can fall prey to profit-seeking schools providing low-quality education.

Voucher programs can also increase inequality in education outcomes across socioeconomic classes. If voucher schools are allowed to charge tuition fees greater than voucher values (or accept "voluntary contributions" in addition to vouchers), then better-off parents might use the vouchers at more expensive and higher-quality schools than poorer households. Even if all voucher schools are required to charge only the voucher amount, the poor might experience fewer benefits if voucher schools are allowed to employ selective admissions criteria, or if poor parents are less aware of what is at stake in their school choices and are less likely to exercise their right to switch schools. The quality of the schools attended by poorer students may even decline, as better-off students transfer to better schools. Schooling options can also decline in less densely populated or poorer areas, where the per-student costs of providing education services are higher, if the voucher amount is too low to attract private participation and pre-existing government schools are unable to cover costs and must be shut down.

Voucher reform impacts are likely to vary depending on many detailed policy design choices, including, most obviously, the size of the voucher payment and the rules determining eligibility for receiving vouchers. The impacts also depend on whether voucher-receiving schools may charge parents fees in addition to the voucher amount, the range of schools considered eligible for voucher use, the regulations placed on voucher schools, and efforts made to inform and educate parents about the program. In practice, the impacts of voucher programs also vary depending on whether they are financed by add-on funding (which leaves all previous funding for the government school system in place) or by shifting an unchanged total quantity of funding from traditional funding of government schools to funding by voucher programs. In some cases they may even be accompanied by a reduction in total government funding.

Chile and Colombia have undertaken the largest voucher programs in developing countries to date. Carnoy and McEwan (2001) provide a succinct review of their designs and impacts. In Chile, voucher funds are available for all primary and secondary school students, and they may be used to pay any education provider (public or private) that agrees not to charge any tuition in addition to the voucher amount. The introduction of this program transformed the Chilean school system into one in which the private sector plays a large role. The impacts of the reform differed significantly between rural and urban areas, however. In urban areas, where enrollment was already nearly universal before the reform, the introduction of vouchers had little impact on enrollment. The reform seems to have increased competition in urban areas, where it encouraged the entry of many new private for-profit schools, but Hsieh and Urquiola (2006) find little effect of private entry on average student test scores. The program's more significant effect in urban areas was to increased socioeconomic segregation, as parents of higher socioeconomic status clubbed together in sending their children to private schools with selective admissions. In rural areas, by contrast, the reform encouraged the entry of few private schools and many rural families continued to face only one school option.

The Colombian voucher experiment was much smaller and very different. Policymakers intended the program to expand secondary school capacity in an inexpensive way, especially for the poor in selected urban areas. Vouchers were offered only to households who lived in especially poor urban neighborhoods and included children who had completed public primary school. Recipient households could use the vouchers to send their children only to private schools, and the schools were allowed to charge additional tuition. The program was introduced at a time of substantial excess capacity in the private school system and substantial overcrowding in the public system. The vouchers were intended to provide new schooling opportunities for some poor families who previously were kept out of government-subsidized education by capacity constraints in government schools, as well as to shift some students out of overcrowded public schools into less-crowded private schools.

Careful empirical studies (including Angrist et al., 2002) indicate that the program increased secondary school enrollment and completion rates for voucher recipients. It also increased their performance on academic achievement tests, either because private schools offered better education or because the voucher program, which cut off payments to students who failed to pass exams, gave students an incentive to work harder. Even though the program did not allow or require government schools to compete with private schools for voucher students, it might have increased the quality of public-sector education by reducing overcrowding problems.

REFERENCES

Ablo, Emmanuel, and Ritva Reinikka. "Do Budgets Really Matter? Evidence from Public Spending on Education and Health in Uganda." Policy Research Working Paper 1926. Washington, D.C.: World Bank, 1998. http://go.worldbank.org/5609IJ89I0

Aguti, Jessica N. "Facing Up to the Challenge of Universal Primary Education, (UPE) in Uganda through Distance Teacher Education Programmes." Department of Distance Education, Makerere University, 2002. www.col.org/pcf2/papers/aguti.pdf

Alderman, Harold (ed.). *No Small Matter: The Impact of Poverty, Shocks, and Human Capital Investments in Early Childhood Development.* Washington, D.C.: World Bank, 2011. doi:10.1596/978-0-8213-8677-4

Angrist, Joshua, Eric Bettinger, Erik Bloom, and Elizabeth King. "Vouchers for Private Schooling in Colombia: Evidence from a Randomized Natural Experiment." *The American Economic Review* 92(5): 1535–1558, 2002. doi:10.1257/000282802762024629

Baird, Sarah, Craig McIntosh, and Berk Özler. "Cash or Condition? Evidence from a Cash Transfer Experiment." *The Quarterly Journal of Economics* 126(4): 1709–1753, 2011. doi:10.1093/qje/qjr032

Banerjee, Abhijit V., Shawn Cole, Esther Duflo, and Leigh Linden. "Remedying Education: Evidence from Two Randomized Experiments in India." *The Quarterly Journal of Economics* 122(3): 1235–1264, 2007. doi:10.1162/qjec.122.3.1235

Bloom, David, David Canning, and Kevin Chan. "Higher Education and Economic Development in Africa." Washington, D.C.: World Bank, 2006. http://siteresources.worldbank.org/INTAFRREGTOPTEIA/Resources/Higher_Education_Econ_Dev.pdf

Bold, Tessa, Mwangi Kimenyi, Germano Mwabu, and Justin Sandefur. "Why Did Abolishing Fees Not Increase Public School Enrollment in Kenya?" CGD Working Paper 271. Washington, D.C.: Center for Global Development, 2011. http://www.cgdev.org/content/publications/detail/1425590

Carnoy, Martin, and Patrick McEwan. "Privatization through Vouchers in Developing Countries: The Cases of Chile and Colombia." In Henry Levin (ed.). *Privatizing Education: Can the Marketplace Deliver Choice, Efficiency, Equity, and Social Cohesion?* Boulder, Co: Westview Press, 151–177, 2001.

Chaudhury, Nazmul, Jeffrey Hammer, Michael Kremer, Karthik Muralidharan, and F. Halsey Rogers. "Missing in Action: Teacher and Health Worker Absence in Developing Countries." *Journal of Economic Perspectives* 20(1): 91–116, 2006. doi:10.1257/089533006776526058

Dauda, Carol L. "The Importance of De Facto Decentralization in Primary Education in Sub-Saharan Africa PTAs and Local Accountability in Uganda." *Journal of Planning Education and Research* 24 (1): 28–40, 2004. doi:10.1177/0739456X04266602

Deininger, Klaus. "Does Cost of Schooling Affect Enrollment by the Poor? Universal Primary Education in Uganda." *Economics of Education Review* 22(3): 291–305, 2003. doi:10.1016/S0272-7757(02)00053-5

Di Gropello, Emanuela. "A Comparative Analysis of School-Based Management in Central America." World Bank Working Paper No. 72. Washington, D.C.: World Bank, 2006. http://go.worldbank.org/R1XU9Z71Z0

Duflo, Esther. "Schooling and Labor Market Consequences of School Construction in Indonesia: Evidence from an Unusual Policy Experiment." *American Economic Review* 91(4): 795–813, 2001. doi:10.1257/aer.91.4.795

Duflo, Esther, Rema Hanna, and Stephen Ryan. "Monitoring Works: Getting Teachers to Come to School." CEPR Discussion Paper No.

DP6682. London: Centre for Economic Policy Research, 2008. http://www.cepr.org/pubs/dps/DP6682.asp

Edmonds, Eric V. "Child Labor and Schooling Responses to Anticipated Income in South Africa." *Journal of Development Economics* 81: 386–414, 2006. doi:10.1016/j.jdeveco.2005.05.001

Foster, Andrew, and Mark R. Rosenzweig. "Technical Change and Human-Capital Returns and Investments: Evidence from the Green Revolution." *American Economic Review* 86(4): 931–953, 1996. http://www.jstor.org/stable/2118312

Glewwe, Paul. "Schools and Skills in Developing Countries: Education Policies and Socioeconomic Outcomes." *Journal of Economic Literature* 40(2): 436–482, 2002. doi:10.1257/002205102320161258

Glewwe, Paul, Nauman Ilias, and Michael Kremer. "Teacher Incentives." *American Economic Journal: Applied Economics* 2(3): 205–227, 2010. doi:10.1257/app.2.3.205

Glewwe, Paul, and Michael Kremer. "Schools, Teachers, and Education Outcomes in Developing Countries." In Eric Hanushek and Finis Welch (eds.). *Handbook of the Economics of Education*. Amsterdam: Elsevier, 2006, pp. 945–1017. doi:10.1016/S1574-0692(06)02016-2

Glewwe, Paul, Michael Kremer, and Sylvie Moulin. "Many Children Left Behind? Textbooks and Test Scores in Kenya." *American Economic Journal: Applied Economics* 1(1): 112–135, 2009. doi:10.1257/app.1.1.112

Grossman, Michael. "Education and Nonmarket Outcomes." In Eric Hanushek and Finis Welch (eds.). *Handbook of the Economics of Education*. Amsterdam: Elsevier, 2006, pp. 577–633. doi:10.1016/S1574-0692(06)01010-5

Hanushek, Eric, and Ludger Woessmann. "The Role of School Improvement in Economic Development." CESifo Working Paper No. 1911. Munich: CESifo (Institute for Economic Research), 2007. http://www.cesifo-group.de/portal/pls/portal/docs/1/1187806.PDF

Hsieh, Chang-Tai, and Miguel Urquiola. "The effects of generalized school choice on achievement and stratification: Evidence from Chile's voucher program." *Journal of Public Economics* 90: 1477–1503, 2006. http://dx.doi.org/10.1016/j.jpubeco.2005.11.002

Jacoby, Hanan G. "Borrowing Constraints and Progress through School: Evidence from Peru." *The Review of Economics and Statistics* 76(1): 151–160, 1994. doi:10.2307/2109833

Jamison, Dean T., Barbara Searle, Klaus Galda, and Stephen P. Heyneman. "Improving Elementary Mathematics Education in Nicaragua: An Experimental Study of the Impact of Textbooks and Radio on Achievement." *Journal of Educational Psychology* 73(4): 556–567, 1981. doi:10.1037/0022-0663.73.4.556

Jensen, Robert. "The (Perceived) Returns to Education and the Demand for Schooling." *The Quarterly Journal of Economics* 125(2): 515–548, 2010. doi:10.1162/qjec.2010.125.2.515

Jensen, Robert, and Emily Oster. "The Power of TV: Cable Television and Women's Status in India." NBER Working Paper No. 13305.

Cambridge, MA: National Bureau of Economic Research, 2007. http://www.nber.org/papers/w13305

Kattan, Raja Bentaouet, and Nicholas Burnett. "User Fees in Primary Education." Departmental Working Paper 30108. Washington, D.C.: World Bank, 2004. http://go.worldbank.org/R7JOFRITA0

Kenny, Charles. "Learning about Schools in Development." CGD Working Paper 236. Washington, D.C.: Center for Global Development, 2010. http://www.cgdev.org/content/publications/detail/1424678

Kochar, Anjini. "Urban Influences on Rural Schooling in India." *Journal of Development Economics* 74(1): 113–136, 2004. doi:10.1016/j.jdeveco.2003.12.006

Kremer, Michael, and Alaka Holla. "Improving Education in the Developing World: What Have We Learned from Randomized Evaluations?" *The Annual Review of Economics* 1: 513–542, 2009. doi:10.1146/annurev.economics.050708.143323

Kremer, Michael, Sylvie Moulin, and Robert Namunyu. "Decentralization: A Cautionary Tale." Poverty Action Lab Paper No. 10. Cambridge, MA: Poverty Action Lab, 2003. http://www.povertyactionlab.org/sites/default/files/publications/23_Kremer_Decentralization.pdf

Muralidharan, Karthik, and Venkatesh Sundararaman. "Teacher Performance Pay: Experimental Evidence from India." *The Journal of Political Economy* 119(1): 39–77, 2011. doi:10.1086/659655

Nguyen, Trang. "Information, Role Models and Perceived Returns to Education: Experimental Evidence from Madagascar." 2008. http://www.povertyactionlab.org/sites/default/files/documents/Nguyen%202008.pdf

Penny, Alan, Michael Ward, Tony Read, and Hazel Bines. "Education Sector Reform: The Ugandan Experience." *International Journal of Educational Development* 28(3): 268–285, 2008. doi:10.1016/j.ijedudev.2007.04.004

Pritchett, Lant. "Where Has All the Education Gone?" *The World Bank Economic Review* 15(3): 367–391, 2001. doi:10.1093/wber/15.3.367

Schaffner, Julie A. "The Determinants of Primary School Enrollment in Ethiopia: Evidence from Three Household Surveys." Africa Region Human Development Working Paper Series. Washington, D.C.: World Bank, 2004. http://siteresources.worldbank.org/AFRICAEXT/Resources/no_85.pdf

Umansky, Ilana, and Emiliana Vegas. "Inside Decentralization: How Three Central American School-Based Management Reforms Affect Student Learning through Teacher Incentives." *The World Bank Research Observer* 22(2): 197–215, 2007. doi:10.1093/wbro/lkm006

World Bank. "Learning for All: Investing in People's Knowledge and Skills to Promote Development." World Bank Group Education Strategy 2020. Washington, D.C.: World Bank, 2011. http://siteresources.worldbank.org/EDUCATION/Resources/ESSU/Education_Strategy_4_12_2011.pdf

World Bank. *World Development Indicators 2012*. Washington, D.C.: World Bank, 2012. http://data.worldbank.org/data-catalog/world-development-indicators.

QUESTIONS FOR REVIEW

1. Describe what we know about differences in the rate of human capital investment, and in education stocks, across countries at different income levels.

2. Discuss the meaning and significance of *proximate objectives* in education policy.

3. Describe the education policy implementation outcomes that determine households' education opportunities. Describe the policy design options through which policy-makers seek to determine the implementation outcomes.

4. Describe briefly the economic model of school enrollment decisions presented in the text.

5. What are some of the lessons learned from empirical evidence to date regarding the determinants of school enrollment choices?

6. How might household survey data be used to shed light on the set of policies required to get all remaining out-of-school children into school?

7. Describe the possible long-run effects of education. How might they differ depending on the nature and quality of school governance?

8. Describe how education policies might affect the families of school children in the short run.

9. Describe the determination of the quality and content of learning by a school's students.

10. What are some of the lessons learned from empirical evidence to date regarding the determinants of learning?

11. Discuss the factors that tend (all else equal) to raise the average central government budgetary cost of providing a child with a complete primary education.

12. What market and institutional failures might motivate government or NGO intervention in primary and secondary education, and what possibilities do they raise regarding policy design?

13. What are the potential benefits and costs of eliminating school fees? What do we know about these benefits and costs in practice?

14. Contrast the potential impacts of a universal elimination of primary school fees and a more restricted elimination of school fees only for households passing a means test.

15. Discuss the potential benefits and costs of reforms that transfer authority over school management decisions from central government bureaucrats to school management committees. Discuss how changes in the details of reform design can alter their impacts.

16. What are education voucher programs? Describe the parameters that define a voucher program, and discuss the potential benefits and costs of such programs.

QUESTIONS FOR DISCUSSION

1. Many children complete primary school but do not complete secondary school. Within the simple model of school enrollment decisions presented in section 19.2A, what might explain why their parents choose to send them to school for all primary school years but not for all secondary school years? What kinds of policies might be useful for increasing secondary school completion rates among children who complete primary school?

2. Consider the impacts of an education policy reform that increases the years of schooling an individual must have to obtain a position as a primary school teacher. Through what channels might this reform affect school quality and learning outcomes? How might the impact on learning differ depending on whether teachers are hired by schools receiving capitation grants from the central government (which do not change) or are allocated to schools by the central government (which pays their salaries)?

3. Discuss the significance of each question in Box 19.3.

4. Consider a country where policymakers have long dictated that a single language be employed for instruction in all schools throughout the country, and where this single language is the second or third language for many children. Discuss the potential benefits and costs of a reform that allows individual schools to select their own primary language of instruction.

5. Consider an education reform that is financed by additional international funding and that increases the ratio of textbooks to students throughout the school system. Discuss as comprehensively as possible the potential benefits and costs of this reform.

6. Consider an education policy reform that shifts authority over many school management decisions from central-level government bureaucrats to school principals, while holding constant the level of per-student funding. What hopes and worries would you have regarding the effect of the reform on the five ingredients—local information, motivation, resources, capacity and coordinating oversight—brought to the affected school management decisions? What effects might the reform have on school policy and management choices, and thereby on implementation outcomes?

7. In the Education for All movement, international development actors rallied around the goal of getting all children into primary school by 2015. In so doing, they prioritized the spending of development funds on expanding primary school enrollment rates over spending on expansion of secondary enrollment rates or improvements in the quality of learning at the primary school level. Describe how the benefits and costs of these three types of spending might differ. Do you think the emphasis on expanding primary school enrollments would be appropriate even if expansion of secondary enrollments has a greater impact on labor productivity and growth?

8. Education programs are often used by governments or NGOs to instill beliefs and values, as well as to teach basic skills. What development outcomes might they hope to improve by altering values? How would you draw the line between acceptable and unacceptable efforts by policymakers to reshape values and beliefs?

PROBLEMS

1. In some regions girls receive less education on average than boys.
   a. State at least two reasons parents might perceive the benefits of educating their daughters to be lower than the benefits of educating their sons, and state at least two reasons they might perceive that the costs of educating girls are higher than the costs of educating boys.
   b. What sorts of policies might be useful for raising girls' enrollment rates relative to boys'?

2. Consider a region in which there are two villages, Village A and Village B. In each village there are 100 poor families and 50 nonpoor families. Each family has one school-aged child and decides to send the child to the nearest school if the following inequality is satisfied:

   Tuition cost + Transport Cost + Opportunity Cost
   ≤ Household's Valuation of Future Education Benefits
   + Scholarship

   Initially *Tuition costs* and *Scholarships* are zero for all households, and Village A has a school but Village B does not, implying that *Transport Costs* for all households in Village A are zero and *Transport Costs* are 20 for households in Village B. The *Opportunity Cost* of a child's time is 10 in a poor household (where children are expected to work and help with chores) and 0 in nonpoor households. Poor households value *Future Education Benefits* at 5, and nonpoor households value them at 15; this difference reflects the higher rate at which liquidity-constrained poor households discount future benefits.
   a. Which of the four groups of households (nonpoor in A, poor in A, nonpoor in B, poor in B) would send their children to school under the initial conditions?
   b. After each of the following policy initiatives, which of the four groups would send their children to school?
      - The government builds a school in Village B (but makes no other policy changes).
      - The government institutes a means-tested scholarship program under which a payment of 5 is made to any poor household, in either village, that sends a child to school (but builds no schools and makes no other policy changes).
      - The government builds a school in Village B and charges tuition of 10 to anyone who attends that school (while continuing to charge no tuition in Village A and offering no scholarships).
      - The government builds a school in Village B, charges tuition of 15 for all nonpoor households in either village that send their children to school, and pays scholarships of 5 to all poor households in either village that send their children to school.
   c. Suppose that it costs 500 to build a school, and that there are no costs to administering tuition collection or scholarship programs, so that tuition fee policies add to the budget the full amount of fees collected from enrolled students, and scholarship programs cost only the full value of scholarships distributed to students who take them up. What is the net impact on the government budget of each of the four policies described in part b?
   d. Under the circumstances described in this problem, which of the following equity objectives is/are achievable on a fixed budget of 500:
      - equality (across all four groups) in the *offer of education services and subsidy*,
      - equality in the *receipt of education subsidy*, or
      - equality in the *receipt of education services*?
   Explain.

3. Consider a highly decentralized government school system in which the central government provides annual grants to school administrators. The administrators may use the grants for hiring teachers; buying textbooks, desks, and other supplies; and running any other school-level programs that they wish, including demand-side programs. The grants are capitation grants, which means that the size of the grant that a school receives is equal to the number of students enrolled multiplied by a per-student grant level. School administrators are also given the authority to charge modest tuition fees if they wish. What would be the main potential benefit(s) and cost(s) of introducing into this school system an incentive scheme for principals, in which principals receive pay bonuses tied to the average scores of their students on standardized academic achievement exams? Explain.

Agricultural Research and Extension

Technical change in agriculture has great potential to speed growth and reduce poverty in developing countries. Governments and NGOs promote such technical change through their policies toward agricultural research and extension. **Agricultural research** activities are purposeful efforts to develop new and better agricultural technologies, and **agricultural extension services** help farmers acquire the skills and information necessary for using new agricultural technologies profitably. Government and NGO policies include both direct investments in public sector agricultural research and extension programs and efforts to encourage investment in agricultural research and extension by private actors.

20.1 Technical Change in Developing Country Agriculture

20.1A Agricultural technical change and development

Technical change is change in the way goods or services are produced, which enables producers to generate given quantities of goods at lower cost or to produce higher-value goods at comparable cost. Technical change in agriculture merits the concern of development economists for three reasons. First, technical change can be an important source of economic growth, as we saw in Chapter 3's review of growth-accounting studies. Technical change in agriculture, more specifically, has significant potential to raise aggregate growth rates in many of the world's poorest countries, where large fractions of the population are engaged in agriculture (see Chapter 2).

Second, technical change in agriculture has the potential to reduce poverty for many groups within a developing country. It can help commercial farmers produce and sell more crops, raising their profits and income. For small farmers who produce food only for their families, it can increase the quantity or nutritional value of what they eat and can reduce their vulnerability to hunger. For the landless rural poor, it can bring rising wages if it increases the demand for labor. In areas not fully integrated into global markets, local agricultural technical change can drive down local food prices, increasing the real incomes of poor households that own little land and are net food buyers.

Third, agricultural technical change on a global scale will be required to hold down average world food prices in coming years (Ruttan, 2002), thereby preventing recurrences of recent global food price crises. Over the second half of the 20th century, world food demand tripled. Technical change allowed world food supply to grow even faster, encouraging a slow decline in world food prices. In recent years, this price trend seems to have reversed, as the pace of agricultural technical change has slowed and growth in food demand has accelerated. Global food demand is likely to double again over the next half century. If food production is to keep pace without expanding onto ecologically important and fragile land and while adapting to global warming, additional technical change will be required.[1]

Despite tremendous increases in agricultural productivity over the last 50 years, per-hectare and per-person productivity levels remain much lower in many developing countries than in developed countries, suggesting significant potential for productivity advance in the developing

---

[1] By increasing temperatures, making rainy seasons less predictable, increasing the incidence of extreme weather events, and in other ways, global warming is expected to reduce agricultural productivity in poor countries significantly, unless new technologies that are more resilient in the face of these stresses are developed (Keane et al., 2009).

world. According to the FAO Statistical Yearbook 2010, the average per-hectare cereal yield was 7.5 tons in France in 2009, but just 3.9 tons in Bangladesh and 1.6 tons in Malawi. Agricultural GDP in dollars per person in the agricultural population was $25,000 in France but just $210 and $70 in Bangladesh and Malawi, respectively. Unfortunately, although technical change and productivity increases in developing countries are possible, they are by no means guaranteed, as we will see.

20.1B The Nature and diversity of technical change in agriculture

Technical change in agriculture takes many forms. The most famous improvements in agricultural technology in recent history involved the creation and adoption of new seed varieties for traditional staple food crops. The **Green Revolution** that began in the 1960s was founded on the development of new varieties of wheat, rice, and maize that increased per-acre yields by improving plants' ability to convert fertilizer and water into grain (see Box 20.1). Other new seed varieties produce crops with shorter growing seasons, which reduce farmers' exposure to late-season droughts and increase their ability to produce multiple crops per year. Others produce crops more resistant to disease, insects, or soil deficiencies. Yet other new seed varieties yield crops with superior qualities, such as higher nutrient content, better appearance or taste, or greater ease of harvest, transport, storage, and packaging.

The range of potential technical change extends beyond the development of new seed varieties. Some researchers seek to enhance soil fertility by devising new compositions of chemical fertilizer, new methods for the use of manure and compost, new methods to prevent soil erosion, or new ways of alternating crops over time that improve nutrient availability without the application of fertilizers. New technologies for well- or river-based irrigation, rain-water harvesting, and prevention of run-off enhance water resources. New methods based on labor tasks, chemicals, cropping practices, or biological interventions (such as the introduction of predator wasps, as in Box 20.1) help control pests. The development of new machines or tools can reduce labor requirements in critical months when labor markets are tight or can increase the speed of

≡ Box 20.1 Examples of Technical Change in Agriculture

Green Revolution technologies

The new agricultural technologies at the heart of the Green Revolution were new semi-dwarf varieties of the world's most widely consumed staple food crops: wheat, rice, and maize. Developed by scientists using traditional plant-breeding methods in international and national agricultural research centers, the new varieties were more efficient than traditional varieties at turning fertilizer and water into grain. This meant that farmers could increase per-acre yields by shifting from traditional to new varieties, but only if they combined the new seeds with additional fertilizer and an ample and steady water supply. To develop successful varieties, researchers had to select not only for higher-yielding plants but also for dwarf plants with shorter, sturdier stems, so that the heavier heads of grain would not lodge in the soil. The yields of early Green Revolution varieties were more sensitive to departures from ideal water conditions and to pests than traditional varieties and thus increased the risk farmers faced. Soon, scientists began breeding for resilience as well as yield, and later Green Revolution varieties increased yields without increasing risk. The ongoing stream of new varieties, together with investments in irrigation and increased use of fertilizer, contributed to tremendous yield increases in many parts of Asia and Latin America. Indian rice yields, for example, rose from two tons per hectare in the 1960s to six tons per hectare by the mid-1990s.

Technological responses to cassava threats in africa

Two new agricultural technologies reversed devastating losses in the cultivation of cassava (also called manioc or yuca), a staple food crop native to South America but now important in the diets of many African populations. The first new technology was a response to the accidental spread to Africa of South American cassava mealy bugs and green mites, which caused African farmers to lose up to 80 percent of their crops in the early 1980s. Collaborative work between national and international research centers led to the distribution of predator wasps that controlled the cassava pests biologically, virtually eliminating the threat by 1988. The second innovation was a response to a particularly devastating strain of cassava mosaic virus, which reduced Ugandan cassava production by 90 percent within five years of its first appearance in the 1990s. Four years of collaboration between Ugandan and international research centers produced a new variety of cassava resistant to the disease and restored production to its pre-crisis level.

Sources: IFPRI (2002), Gabre-Madhin et al. (2004).

planting, weeding, harvesting, or crop-grading activities. Improvements in on-farm storage technologies reduce losses to decay or rodents, allowing farmers to store their own food and seed, rather than selling when prices are low at harvest only to buy later when prices are high. Through improvements in farm management, farmers can reduce waste and obtain better prices for their produce.

As we begin to brainstorm about the potential impacts of technical change, three observations stand out. First, new technologies can change the nature and results of agricultural production and farm life along many dimensions. When studying a new technology, we will be interested in its implications not only for the crop's average **yield** (i.e., the average quantity a farmer can produce per hectare), but also for the crop's quality; the variability of output in the face of insects, disease, and weather hazards; the seasonality of output and sales; labor requirements in various seasons of the year; requirements for use of purchased inputs; necessary investments in machines, tools, and structures; and health and environmental quality.

Second, technical changes almost always bring costs for farmers as well as benefits. The Green Revolution technologies raised output per hectare, but they simultaneously required farmers to use more fertilizer, labor, and irrigation water. In the early years, they also increased farmers' risks of crop failure. Similarly, new fertilizers increase yields and new pesticides reduce risk of crop loss, but they can also expose farmers to new health and environmental hazards. Zero tillage cropping systems, in which farmers leave crop residue where it stands at the end of harvest (rather than plowing it under) and plant the next crop while the residue still retains moisture, reduce farmers' needs for labor, water, and fertilizer, but they increase the difficulty of pest management (World Bank, 2007). Recognizing the tradeoffs is important for understanding why new technologies might not be attractive to all farmers and for analyzing the broader benefits and costs of technology policies.

Third, the managers of agricultural research institutions have significant scope to influence the **direction of technical change**. They choose which crops to work on and whether to set up and staff facilities for developing new seeds, new machines, or new cultivation methods. When using traditional plant-breeding methods, scientists choose the plant characteristics (e.g., higher yields or resistance to a particular disease) for which they will select. Because different kinds of technical change yield very different benefits and costs for individual farmers and for society, policymakers must examine the impacts of their policies on the direction as well as the speed of technical change.

20.1C The process of technical change in agriculture

Agricultural technology changes when farmers put new technologies to effective use on their farms. They can do this only if new technologies have been developed and if they have acquired adequate knowledge of them. Thus, we are interested in three sets of actors: researchers, who invest in the development of new technologies; extension agents, who inform and teach farmers about the use of new technologies; and farmers, who adopt new technologies.

In the most general sense, **agricultural researchers** include any actors who identify new and improved ways of cultivating crops or raising livestock. Farmers themselves are researchers when they identify better methods through trial and error. In this chapter, however, we focus on professional researchers who intentionally invest time, skill, land, and equipment in their pursuit of better technologies. Researchers or their managers influence the rate and nature of technical change through their choices regarding how much research to undertake, the methods they employ, and thus the kinds of new technology they create.

Rapid agricultural technical change in developing countries is possible only if they develop at least some local agricultural research capacity, because agricultural technology is **circumstantially sensitive** (Evenson and Westphal, 1995). This means that agricultural technologies deliver results that vary with agroclimatic conditions. For example, high-yielding rice varieties that double rice yields in the Indian state of Punjab might raise yields by only 20 percent in the state of Bihar. It also means that technologies that deliver excellent results in one location must often be altered—through local adaptive research—to deliver top results in new locations. For example, high-yielding rice varieties developed at the International Rice Research Institute in the Philippines must be crossbred with local varieties, so that they become more resilient in the face of local stresses, before becoming successful in India or Madagascar. Thus, developing countries cannot experience rapid technical change in agriculture solely by importing new technologies from developed countries.

Agricultural extension agents include any actors who inform or teach farmers about the use of new technologies. We will use the term **messages** to refer to the specific kinds of information and training they might bring to farmers. Some messages inform farmers about the existence of recently developed technologies or teach them how to employ the new technologies most successfully. Other messages teach farmers about old technologies or management practices that farmers elsewhere have employed for many years, but that are new to client farmers. Yet other messages train farmers in problem-solving or decision-making skills, encourage them to create organizations for collective action, or transmit information about input and output prices or evolving process and product standards that farmers must meet to sell in specialized markets (such as markets for certified organic produce). Extension agents can also facilitate rapid technical change by transmitting information about farmers' needs and preferences back to agricultural researchers.

Farmers might informally provide extension services when they share knowledge about technologies or markets with their neighbors. In this chapter we focus primarily on agents with professional interest in spreading such knowledge. They include government or private-sector employees hired to serve as extension agents. They might also include private-sector input retailers, who provide farmers with information in the hope of increasing farmers' input demands, and employees of supermarket chains or exporting companies, who guide farmers' efforts to cultivate new, higher-value crops under contract. Extension agents or their managers influence the rate and nature of technical change through their choices regarding how much to invest in extension activities, what information and training to carry to farmers, to which sets of farmers they carry these messages, and the methods they employ for transferring knowledge.

Extension agents' work is challenging and costly, especially in developing countries. Agents must contact many small farmers, who are geographically dispersed and who may be illiterate and lack access to electronic media, and their job involves more than merely repeating information. The circumstantial sensitivity of agricultural technology and the changing nature of threats to agricultural productivity mean that agents must employ diagnostic and problem-solving skills if they wish to convey information that is well tailored to farmers' circumstances and needs. The tacit nature of technological knowledge further complicates their job (Evenson and Westphal, 1995). Knowledge is **tacit** when it cannot be imparted from one person to another simply by handing over a written list of instructions or a physical input in which the technology is embodied (e.g., a seed). To convey adequate working knowledge of how to use a new variety of soybean, for example, agents might need to train farmers through hands-on demonstrations, guided practice, and other teaching methods.

Research and extension activities produce no fruit unless farmers choose to adopt the new technologies. Farmers influence the rate and nature of technical change through their choices of which technologies to adopt and how much of their land to devote to them.

20.2 The Economics of Technical Change in Agriculture

Agricultural research and extension policies introduce change into socioeconomic systems when they induce farmers to *adopt* new technologies. We define the term *new technology* very broadly to include any farming practices that are new to the farmers involved. In this section, we first examine how farmers decide whether to adopt a new technology, as well as the direct and indirect impacts of their adoption. We highlight how these decisions and impacts depend on the nature of the new technologies created by agricultural researchers, the content and quality of the messages offered to them by extension agents, the state of local markets and institutions, and the presence of complementary policies. We then examine the types of research and extension activities that the private sector is most likely to supply and the types for which government or NGO intervention may be required.

20.2A Agricultural technology adoption decisions

Drawing on the general discussion of investment decisions in Chapter 10, we organize study of technology adoption decisions by observing that:

> A farmer adopts a particular new technology if she possesses adequate knowledge of it and judges that the benefits of adoption outweigh the costs. More specifically, she adopts if she judges that the ongoing increases in utility she will enjoy each year once she has learned how to put the technology to best use will more than outweigh any up-front costs, including any costs of acquiring agricultural extension services and costs associated with financing and risk.

Farmers might require several types of **knowledge** before adopting a technology. In addition to knowing of the technology's existence, they must acquire working knowledge of how to use it, and must learn about its likely benefits and costs when employed on their farms. They might also require information about where to obtain the best prices on fertilizer and produce or about the certification standards they must satisfy to sell at premium prices in markets for organic or Fair Trade products.

Adoption can bring **up-front costs** that farmers must bear either before they begin using the new technology or in early seasons of use, before they have learned how to put the technology to best use. These include the costs of capital equipment and structures, such as tractors and greenhouses. They also include any costs of learning, including explicit fees for extension services, opportunity costs of time devoted to training, and implicit losses during an early learning-by-doing phase, in which the new technology performs worse than the old technology. For tree crops, they include several years of forgone production before the trees begin to produce fruit.

Even after farmers have learned how to put a new technology to best use, adoption brings **ongoing costs** as well as **ongoing benefits** relative to continued use of an old technology. Adopting a new technology can alter work and life in many ways, as indicated above. Switching from the old technology is likely to improve farmers' lives along some of dimensions while causing deterioration along others. A necessary condition for adoption to be attractive is that farmers expect the ongoing benefits to exceed the ongoing costs and thus expect adoption to raise their ongoing expected utility. Farmers adopt a new technology only if they judge that the streams of future increases in utility more than compensate for the up-front costs of capital investment and learning, together with the costs of long-term financing and one-time adoption risks.

This simple economic model of adoption decisions implies that whether a farmer adopts a particular technology can depend on the nature of her opportunities to learn about it and the relevance of the technology to her circumstances, as well as local market and institutional conditions affecting the profitability of adoption, her access to insurance and financing, and her preferences.

Learning

Empirical studies confirm that farmers must learn how to use new technologies well, that this takes time, effort, and thoughtful observation, and that lack of adequate learning opportunities can inhibit adoption. Foster and Rosenzweig (1995) demonstrate that the profits Indian farmers derived from the cultivation of new high-yielding seed varieties grew over the farmers' first several years of experience with them in the early years of the Green Revolution. Duflo et al.

(2008) find that Kenyan farmers randomly selected to participate in fertilizer-use experiments on their own farms were more likely than others to use fertilizer in later years, suggesting that the experiment gave them a valuable opportunity to learn. Thus, careful study of how farmers learn may offer important insights for policy.

Farmers sometimes appear to gain valuable knowledge by observing their neighbors. Foster and Rosenzweig (1995) find evidence for this in the observation that Indian farmers' profits from using Green Revolution technologies were higher where the collective experience with the new technologies among other farmers in their villages was greater. While this suggests potential for knowledge to spread from farmer to farmer, it also suggests that farmers may be reluctant to pay extension agents for knowledge they might hope to acquire from neighbors. The extent to which farmers learn from their neighbors probably differs from place to place. Conley and Udry (2010) found that farmers in Ghana knew little about their neighbor's fertilizer use and yields and thus seemed not to learn much about the cultivation of a new crop (pineapples) from their neighbors.

Farmers also appear to learn by experimenting with new technologies, but may tend to underinvest in such experimentation, hoping to free ride on experimentation by others. Foster and Rosenzweig (1995) observe that Indian farmers with more land, who had more to gain from learning about a good new technology, were more likely to begin cultivating the Green Revolution varieties soon after they became available. The authors then demonstrate that small farmers whose neighbors had large farms were *less* likely to experiment with the new varieties in early years than small farmers surrounded only by other small farmers. They argue that small farmers with large-farm neighbors expected to benefit from their neighbor's costly experimentation and thus waited to adopt until their neighbors had undertaken most of the work required to determine how best to apply the new seeds locally.

Survey data from many locations indicate that farmers with more education are more likely to adopt new technologies, or adopt them more quickly, than farmers with less education, even at quite low levels of education. For example, farmers who have completed primary school adopt new technologies more rapidly than farmers with no education.

The exact nature of the link between education and technology adoption has important implications for policy. If more-educated farmers adopt new technologies more quickly only because they have better access to information, then it might be possible to speed technology adoption by improving the flow of information to uneducated farmers. If instead education is of intrinsic value in helping farmers to experiment with and learn about new technologies, then education may be crucial for speeding agricultural technical change. Foster and Rosenzweig (1996) argue that education is indeed intrinsically valuable, improving farmers' ability to *learn* about new technologies. They demonstrate that the profits from cultivation of Green Revolution crops rose more quickly over the first few years of use for Indian farmers with primary education than for farmers with no education. Farmers who have experienced the benefits of technical change seem to recognize the valuable role that education played in allowing them to do so. Indian farm households in geographic areas where the Green Revolution technologies raised yields by larger percentages (because the technologies were better suited to local growing conditions) invested more in the schooling of their children (Foster and Rosenzweig, 1996).

While empirical research to date highlights the importance of learning and of education for agricultural technology adoption, it leaves open many practical questions about how best to facilitate and encourage learning about new technologies.

Geography

The crop-specific nature of most agricultural technologies and their circumstantial sensitivity imply that agricultural technologies developed for any one crop and in any one location deliver top physical performance only in very similar locations. Some farmers, therefore, might have little interest in adopting a particular new technology simply because it is not relevant or does not work very well on their farms. For example, early Green Revolution research efforts focused on wheat, rice, and maize and targeted areas with high agricultural potential because researchers' primary aim at the time was to increase world food supplies. As a result, while early Green Revolution technologies greatly increased average yields in South Asia, they largely bypassed some of the poorest rural areas within the region, which lacked irrigation, dependable rainfall, level terrain, and rich soils. The early Green Revolution technologies also largely bypassed Africa because wheat, rice, and maize were not the most important staple food crops there and because growing conditions were very different from those in the high-potential South Asian region. Only later, in the 1980s and 1990s, did researchers adapt improved varieties to a wider range of conditions, facilitating their spread into un-irrigated areas within South Asia. Increased attention to additional staple food crops and to African conditions also encouraged some productivity advance in Africa, though the Green Revolution continues to lag behind there for many reasons (World Bank, 2007).

Output and input markets

The rate at which farmers adopt a new technology can vary dramatically, even among farmers with very similar physical production conditions, if the farmers face different conditions in markets for crops and inputs. To see this, consider a new technology that raises a crop's expected per-hectare yield by ΔY, raises the per-hectare fertilizer requirement by ΔF, raises the harvest season per-hectare labor requirement by ΔL, and does not require any one-time investment in capital equipment or learning.[2] We ignore for simplicity the need to finance the fertilizer purchase with short-term credit. Let p, q, and w represent the crop price, fertilizer price, and harvest-season wage. A necessary condition for adoption is that the farmer expects the switch to the new technology to increase her expected profits (i.e., the expected value of her profits, as defined in Chapter 10) enough to outweigh any cost of increased risk. We can see that market prices influence her adoption decision, because the change in her per-hectare expected profits $\Delta \pi$ is

$$\Delta \pi = p \Delta Y - q \Delta F - w \Delta L \tag{20.1}$$

and is thus a function of p, q, and w. This impact of adoption on average profits is smaller, all else equal, in countries where q is higher relative to p in national markets. It is also smaller in remote locations within countries where high transfer costs raise input prices and reduce export crop prices relative to national market levels. The technology is also less attractive to farmers for whom the effective cost of labor is higher relative to the crop price, whether because local labor markets are tighter or because high mobility costs prevent labor-constrained farmers from hiring labor in local labor markets. Higher ratios of fertilizer prices to output prices and greater isolation from labor markets probably help explain why farmers in Africa have been less likely to adopt fertilizer and Green Revolution technologies than farmers in Asia and Latin America (see Chapter 10).

Poorly developed markets are less likely to prevent adoption of technologies that require no purchased inputs. Examples include disease-resistant varieties of crops that can be grown without purchased inputs, new patterns of intercropping (i.e., planting two or more crops in alternating rows within the same field) that increase yields or reduce fertilizer requirements, or new ways of managing farm resources that reduce waste.

Insurance and liquidity constraints

Risk and insurance enter farmers' adoption decisions in two ways. First, when a farmer looks ahead to what life would be like after learning how to use a new technology, she might expect the switch from the old technology to the new one to increase or decrease the risks she faces on an annual basis. A new technology might increase risk by increasing how sensitive her crop yields

---

[2] The delta symbol, Δ, may be read as "change in." Thus ΔY represents the change in per-acre yield associated with the switch from the old technology to the new.

are to variation in growing conditions or by requiring her to purchase new inputs of uncertain quality from retailers she does not trust. The better her access to annual crop insurance, the less likely any increases in risk are to deter her from adopting. Second, regardless of whether the new technology is expected to increase or decrease the risk she faces each year after she has learned how to implement the technology, the initial period of experimentation may be risky if she is uncertain about her abilities or about the suitability of her farm for the new technology.

Indirect evidence is consistent with risk playing an important role in farmers' crop choice decisions. Morduch (1993) finds, for example, that smaller farmers, for whom insurance constraints are likely to be more important (see Chapter 10), are more likely than wealthier farmers to cultivate less-risky crops and tend to diversify their crops more. He also finds that this effort to diminish risk is costly to them because it reduces their average profits.

If risk is important in farmers' adoption decisions, then the introduction of new crop insurance opportunities might increase adoption rates (see Chapter 10). Testing this hypothesis can be difficult, because farmers' take-up rates of insurance offers tend to be low (Cole et al., 2013). Understanding why insurance take-up rates are low is an area of active research. (We return to such issues when we discuss health insurance in Chapter 22.) Emerging experimental studies (e.g., Karlan et al., 2012) suggest that insurance protection can indeed encourage farmers to use more purchased inputs and to undertake riskier production choices, at least in some contexts.

Access to financing, too, might affect adoption decisions in two ways. When a farmer looks ahead to annual production needs, she might expect the technology to increase or decrease her need to purchase fertilizer, labor, or other inputs during each year's planting season and thus to increase or decrease her annual need for short-term financing. A farmer who anticipates chronic short-term liquidity constraints would be less likely to adopt a technology that increases her annual need for purchased inputs. Farmers might also require longer-term financing to cover any up-front costs of capital equipment or of income foregone while learning.

In practice, farmers who adopt new technologies often make use of credit, and many analysts believe that liquidity constraints prevent the adoption of new technologies by many farmers. Definitive evidence that improved access to credit catalyzes adoption is difficult to find, however, because in cross-section datasets, the farmers who manage to obtain credit probably enjoy superior farm or farmer traits, or have better access to other programs and services, than farmers who do not use credit. It is, therefore, difficult to tell whether their adoption rates are higher because they have access to credit or because they have other advantages. Experimental studies involving small nonfarm businesses cited in Chapter 10 find evidence of significant liquidity constraints, but few such studies have been conducted for agriculture. A recent experimental study by Karlan et al. (2012) finds little evidence of liquidity constraints on farm input use in Ghana. Further research in this area is warranted.

Poor access to credit and insurance among potential *suppliers* of agricultural inputs might also constrain adoption. In some regions only a few entrepreneurs have the local knowledge and land required to successfully produce high-yielding seeds for sale or to retail fertilizer to local farmers. Where credit or insurance constraints prevent entrepreneurs from setting up input-supply businesses, local farmers might find it infeasible, or at least very costly, to obtain the inputs required for adopting new technologies.

Institutions

Even among farmers facing identical agroclimatic and market conditions, adoption rates might vary depending on the nature of local institutions. For example, farmers belonging to well-functioning agricultural cooperatives might face several advantages: Through coordinated action they can reduce the per-farmer cost of agricultural extension visits or can obtain better prices for inputs and outputs through bulk arrangements for purchase and sale. Weak land rights institutions might discourage farmers from adopting technologies that require investments in land improvements, such as terracing of sloped fields, construction of irrigation systems, or planting of trees. Access to workfare programs and other public safety-net institutions might encourage farmers to adopt, by providing them with implicit insurance against crop loss. Strong local norms of mutual assistance might help or hinder adoption. On the one hand, they might provide a substitute for formal insurance; on the other hand, they might reduce the gains from adoption that farmers expect to appropriate if the norms require them to share increased profits with their neighbors (see Chapter 12). As suggested in Chapter 10, the availability of institutions that help present-biased investors commit in advance to saving and investment might also facilitate farmers' investment in technology adoption.

Preference differences

Differences in farmers' preferences might render some more likely than others to adopt new technologies. Most obviously, farmers who are less averse to risk and who are more willing to delay consumption are more likely to undertake such investments. Other dimensions of preferences might also matter. When a new technology alters the nutritional properties, taste, and appearance of a crop that a farmer produces for her family's own consumption, her adoption choice can depend on the relative importance she attaches to various food properties. NGOs trying to encourage the use of more nutritious varieties of sweet potato in Africa, for example, have run into resistance because the more nutritious varieties have orange flesh and farmers and their families are more comfortable with traditional varieties that have yellow flesh.

Gender

According to the Food and Agriculture Organization (FAO, 2011), women make up 43 percent of the agricultural labor force in the developing world, though the fraction varies across regions. In Africa, women's share of the agricultural labor force is 50 percent. Women often cultivate plots of land with some autonomy, and they often bear much of the responsibility for their households' subsistence food production. Thus many of the farmers whose technology-adoption decisions influence agricultural productivity are women.

Often the conditions under which women make technology-adoption decisions are very different from those of men, even when compared to men in the same communities and households. Often women cultivate subsistence crops while men cultivate cash crops. Women might cultivate smaller and lower-quality plots of land, and their property rights over land are often much more tenuous (Chapter 12). Often they have less education and face greater barriers to participation in agricultural cooperatives or financial markets. Culturally defined gender roles can render it more difficult for women to produce crops for sale rather than consumption and can also place greater demands on their time by allocating to them the responsibilities for water carrying, fuel gathering, and child care. Women and men sometimes obtain information and help through segregated networks, and poorer endowments mean women's networks are likely to be less effective. Sadly, development programs sometimes widen gender gaps by developing better technologies only for men's crops or designing extension programs with only men in mind. Thus for many reasons female farmers tend to use fewer modern inputs than men.

Implications for agricultural research and extension

This economic perspective on adoption decisions has important implications for policy and policy analysis. First, if agricultural research is to yield direct benefits for specific target groups, researchers must seek to understand the target farmers' preferences and the agroclimatic, market, and institutional conditions they face and then create technologies well suited to those conditions. If the farmers they wish to reach are poor and remote and face only poorly developed markets for crops, inputs, labor, and financial services, for example, researchers should focus on developing new technologies that maintain or reduce per-hectare requirements for purchased inputs and harvest-season labor and that maintain or reduce farmers' exposure to risk. Such technologies would be quite different from the early Green Revolution technologies. If the farmers they wish to reach are women as well as men, they must seek to understand the distinct constraints that women face.

A second implication is that, while agricultural extension agents have the potential to catalyze adoption by conveying messages to farmers, they will succeed only if their messages are well suited to local circumstances, if local farmers have not received the messages through informal channels, and if agents are effective in helping farmers learn and experiment. This means that extension agents' potential to improve agricultural practices depends on their access to high-quality and locally relevant new technologies (and thus on the quality and reach of the agricultural research system) and on the timeliness, skill, and effort with which they carry messages to farmers. Again, if extension programs are to be successful among farmers who are women, they must consider women's distinct needs.

A final implication is that agricultural research and extension policies may be strongly complementary with policy efforts in other areas. Investments in infrastructure and institutions that reduce transfer costs in agricultural markets, for example, might greatly increase rates of adoption for new technologies that require the use of new purchased inputs. Policies that encourage investment in education and that improve farmers' access to finance and insurance may also be important. In addition, adoption of new technologies might be enhanced by regulatory oversight of quality standards in agricultural input markets or by efforts to provide potential input retailers with training or credit.

20.2B Direct and indirect effects of technology adoption
Direct effects

Farmers who adopt new technologies pay the up-front cost of adoption and then reap the ongoing net benefits as described in the previous section. They enjoy greater rewards to adoption when the new technology is better suited to their circumstances, when local market and institutional conditions are more conducive to adoption, and when they possess more land and other complementary assets. They continue to reap returns on their adoption investments until they cease using the new technologies. They might cease because the adopted technology is displaced by an even better one, because the technology deteriorates over time, or because changing market conditions render the adopted technology unprofitable.[3]

Drawing on the discussions of household decision making in Chapters 6, 7, 10, and 17, we recognize that technical change can alter adopting households' lives and behavior in many ways. As agricultural producers, they might respond to a new technology by increasing production of the affected crops, reducing production of other crops, and altering their demands for labor and other inputs. If adoption increases their profit and income, then as consumers they are likely to increase their consumption of normal goods and reduce their labor supply (if home time is a normal good). For households that are liquidity constrained, increases in income can facilitate additional investment, leading to impacts that grow over time. If the technical change has differential effects on the income streams of men and women, then it might influence the intra-household distribution of decision-making authority and well-being.

---

[3] Some agricultural technologies deteriorate over time for biological reasons. For example, high-yielding seed varieties become more vulnerable to insect and disease attacks over time unless maintenance research prevents such deterioration.

Spillover effects

As with agricultural market reforms that increase crop prices, technology improvements that raise agricultural productivity have the potential to induce spillover effects for many groups throughout society. Most obviously, when technical change increases local food supplies, it can drive down food prices, improving the well-being of net food-buying households, including rural households with little or no land as well as urban households. When technical change is labor-using (see Chapter 9), it raises the agricultural demand for labor, further improving the circumstances of landless rural households. Adoption can also lead farmers and workers to demand more inputs and consumer goods from the rural nonfarm sector.

Unfortunately, productivity-enhancing technical change can also hurt some groups through two main channels. First, by driving down output prices and driving up wages, adoption of new technologies can squeeze the profits of non-adopting farmers producing the same crops (or crops that are close substitutes in consumption). If better-off farmers adopt a new productivity-enhancing technology while poorer farmers do not, then the new technology can increase income inequality among farmers.

Second, technical change can generate environmental externalities. New technologies can encourage increased use of irrigation water, which leaches nutrients from the soil and raises salinity levels. They can also encourage erosion, or the expansion of cultivation onto land previously covered in rainforest, which is important for carbon sequestration and biodiversity. The availability of new seed varieties often encourages a shift toward monoculture, in which most agricultural land within a region becomes devoted to the same breed of the same crop. Diverse crops and breeds are vulnerable to different insects and diseases; thus the spread of monoculture eliminates natural diversification of risks and renders a region vulnerable to catastrophic crop failure. Increasingly, however, researchers are attempting to develop crops with characteristics that mitigate environmental harms and that can even improve environmental conditions.

We conclude that:

> To fully appreciate the impact of technology adoption in agriculture, we must examine the impacts on average income, the variability of income, nutrition, health, and environmental conditions not only for adopting farmers but also for rural workers, entrepreneurs in the rural nonfarm sector, urban consumers, and non-adopting farmers.

We see the importance of such comprehensive analysis in the case of the Green Revolution (Box 20.2).

≡ Box 20.2 Green Revolution Impacts

After synthesizing the results of hundreds of studies of Green Revolution impacts, Peter Hazell (2002) argues that the adoption of Green Revolution technologies often spread benefits broadly throughout the regions well suited to them. Large farmers tended to adopt first, but eventually small farmers adopted as well, and they all enjoyed rising average incomes. Though early Green Revolution varieties increased risk of crop failure, later Green Revolution technologies brought little increase in risk. Adopters increased their demands for goods and services produced by the rural nonfarm sector, and rising labor demands in agriculture and nonagriculture raised rural wages for low-skill workers (as discussed in Chapter 6). Where income growth lagged was in geographic regions unsuited to use of the new technologies. Net food buyers in such areas benefitted from lower food prices, but net sellers of unimproved varieties of Green Revolution crops suffered from lower prices and higher input costs.

Unfortunately, rapid expansion of Green Revolution technologies, supported by policies that subsidized the use of irrigation water and chemical fertilizers, also brought environmental costs: water pollution, health problems among agricultural workers, groundwater depletion, and long-run productivity-reducing buildup of soil salinity levels. More careful attention to the details of later Green Revolution technologies and to accompanying policies has helped to reduce these environmental effects. Hazell (2002) observes that in the absence of the Green Revolution technologies, expansion of agricultural production would have required greater spread of cultivation onto lands valuable for their forests, biodiversity, watershed protection, or other benefits.

20.2C Investment in agricultural research and rationales for intervention

Research investment

Agricultural research is a costly, long-lived, and risky investment. To develop a technology satisfying specified criteria, research organizations might have to employ scientists, land, and equipment for five to 10 years or more, and sometimes research programs fail.

The directors and managers of research organizations make many decisions that shape the nature and speed of technical change. At the broadest level, they decide how much to invest, what crops to work on, and what directions of technical change to pursue. At a more detailed level, they choose how many agricultural research stations and fields to set up, how to distribute the research stations geographically, which researchers to hire, and what training, resources, and discretionary budgets to give them. Managers also define the goals they wish researchers to pursue and design mechanisms to hold them accountable.

These research management decisions help determine four important dimensions of research system performance: the number, type, and quality of the technologies generated, and the efficiency with which they are generated. New technologies are of higher quality when they are better tailored to the circumstances of target farmers or bring larger gains along any particular dimension (e.g., yield increase). New technologies are produced more efficiently when researchers produce technologies of given type and quality at lower cost.

Rationales for intervention in agricultural research

Private actors undertake costly research activities only if they expect to reap sufficient profits once their research succeeds. Unfortunately, such profits might not be forthcoming for some socially beneficial research. Some new technologies can be thought of as disembodied ideas about how to turn traditional agricultural inputs into output, and can be adopted without having to purchase new specialized inputs. For example, farmers might adopt improved methods of managing farm resources—such as planting nitrogen-fixing trees or weed-resistant ground-cover crops between rows of grain—that increase yields or reduce vulnerability to pests without purchasing new inputs. Such technological ideas are *nonrival*, because one farmer's use of the idea does not preclude other farmers from using it. Such ideas are also *nonexcludable* if farmers can easily acquire them by observing other farmers. They are therefore public goods (see Chapter 13). Unable to exclude farmers from using such ideas, private researchers are unable to charge for their use and have little motivation to invest in developing them.

In principle, government creation of patent law systems—and other institutions for defining and protecting intellectual property rights—could improve private researchers' incentives to invent technologies with public goods qualities. Such systems can help transform technological ideas into excludable goods by protecting their inventors' exclusive rights to use them. If governments effectively identify and punish farmers who use protected ideas without license, then they allow researchers to profit from the ideas they invent, either by employing them exclusively in their own production or by charging licensing fees for their use by others.

In practice, enforcing patent protection for disembodied technological ideas in developing-country agriculture would be very difficult. Where crops are produced by large numbers of small and geographically dispersed farmers, it is very costly to monitor production methods and penalize farmers for using technologies without license.

Many new agricultural technologies are better characterized as toll goods rather than pure public goods, however. **Toll goods** are nonrival but excludable. Many new agricultural technologies take this form, because they are embodied in specialized inputs. For example, farmers can use Green Revolution technologies only if they obtain improved seeds. Similarly, they can use new ideas about mechanical technologies only by purchasing the related farm equipment.

Enforcement of intellectual property rights for such technologies may be feasible, because monitoring just a few input producers is easier than monitoring many small farmers. Indeed, patent protection institutions, and similar institutions to protect plant breeder rights, are under development in many developing countries (World Bank, 2006). Researchers may be able to retain control over the use of some technologies, even without patent protection, by keeping secret some of the details regarding how the related inputs are produced. In the case of new seed varieties, inventors might even retain control of seed distribution by using genetic modification techniques to introduce "terminator genes," which render second-generation seeds sterile, thereby requiring farmers to purchase seeds every year only from licensed distributors.

The scope for private-sector development of toll-good technologies is likely to be limited, however, even for technologies that have high social value, when the technologies are intended for poor farmers in developing countries. Such farmers may be prevented from purchasing specialized inputs by liquidity constraints or by failures in agricultural extension or input markets. In such cases, private sector researchers anticipate little potential to profit by licensing new technologies, and they therefore refrain from investing in the relevant research.

Even if patent and breeder rights protection of technologies for small farmers in developing countries were feasible, and even if it would encourage additional private sector research, it might not be socially desirable. Although patent protection strengthens research incentives, it also reduces the value that societies derive from the new technologies created. Patent protection works only by allowing researchers to charge more for their specialized inputs than it costs to produce them; this generates the profits that motivate research. The resulting high input prices cause farmers to use fewer of these inputs than is socially desirable. High input prices also reduce the profits of the small farmers who use them and may prevent other small farmers from using them at all, limiting their usefulness for poverty reduction. Governments attempt to balance the research-increasing benefits of intellectual property rights systems against the use-inhibiting costs by limiting the duration of patent rights and designing systems of exemptions. For a discussion of these design choices, see World Bank (2006).

All this leads to a somewhat nuanced view of the rationales for intervention in agricultural research:

> For technologies embodied in inputs, and tailored for use in regions where farmers are nonpoor and unhindered by liquidity constraints, the private sector might face robust incentives for investment in research, even in the absence of intervention. In some cases, creation and enforcement of patent laws and plant breeder rights systems can enhance these incentives. The private sector is unlikely, however, to develop technologies that are not embodied in inputs, or technologies that are embodied in inputs but intended for use by poor and liquidity-constrained farmers. Policymakers may be able to improve research system outcomes by subsidizing the development of such technologies.

This view of private sector research incentives has two important implications. First, the types of new technologies that are likely to be of most benefit to poor farmers facing poorly developed markets (as discussed in section 20.2A) are precisely the kinds of technologies that the private sector is *least likely* to invent in the absence of intervention. This suggests that public sector promotion of such research may be warranted. Second, although the public sector may be justified in subsidizing such research, it may not be justified in employing those subsidies within public sector agricultural research institutions. It may be possible to improve research outcomes by instead, or in addition, subsidizing private sector research activities. This opens the door to experimentation with diverse institutional approaches to the governance of subsidized agricultural research.

Intervention in international and national agricultural research

Many levels of research are required to produce new technologies, from **basic research**, which illuminates general scientific principles or creates general methods for technological development (e.g., genetic modification techniques), to **applied research**, which adapts the results of basic research to the specific needs of farmers in particular regions. The technologies that farmers adopt are ultimately the result of applied research carried out near them and are of relevance within somewhat limited geographic areas. Their development would be impossible, however, in the absence of basic research, which produces results that are relevant over much larger geographic areas. Often the results of basic research are public goods on an international scale. National governments are likely to underinvest in such basic research because they face strong incentives to free ride on other countries' basic research investments. Free riding slows down technological progress throughout the world. Rapid agricultural technical change in the developing world is thought, therefore, to require international cooperation in basic agricultural research.

Such concerns led the Rockefeller and Ford Foundations to establish international agricultural research centers in Mexico, the Philippines, Colombia, and Nigeria over the course of the 1940s, 1950s, and 1960s. These centers developed genetic material that, through adaptive local research, became the basis of the Green Revolution varieties of maize, rice, and wheat. In 1971 these four centers were brought together under the newly created Consultative Group on International Agricultural Research (CGIAR), funded by 16 donors, including the governments of the United States and other developed countries. By 2004, the CGIAR system had grown to include 15 centers worldwide.

The need for internationally funded agricultural research relevant to developing countries is probably greater today than 40 years ago (Alston et al., 2006). In the 1970s and earlier, the majority of agricultural research in developed countries was carried out by public sector research centers producing publicly available technologies. Over time, the share of the public sector in developed-country agricultural research has fallen as private sector agricultural research has expanded, and private sector research is protected to a much greater extent by patents and trade secrets. Thus, fewer and fewer technological advances in developed country agriculture are available to scientists or farmers in developing countries. The research performed in the developed countries has also become less useful to the developing countries, as it has shifted away from efforts to increase productivity of basic food crops toward efforts to improve food quality or facilitate processing, and it has shifted toward the development of more capital-intensive high-tech methods.

Despite an arguable increase in the need for international collaborative research on developing countries' staple food crops, funding for such efforts declined significantly in the late twentieth century (Alston et al., 2006). The 1990s witnessed a decline in the total volume of developed country aid to developing countries and a decline in the share of aid directed to agriculture. Developed countries' support for the CGIAR system suffered a somewhat less severe contraction than agricultural aid overall, but it stagnated nonetheless. At the same time, the breadth of the CGIAR mission increased, as it devoted increasing shares of resources to non-research activities and to research on environmental issues, non-staple crops, forestry, and fishing. This further squeezed the resources available for pursuing productivity advance in staple food crops. The funding for international agricultural research has picked up again more recently out of growing interest in catalyzing a new Green Revolution for Africa and increasing concern about global food price crises.

20.2D Agricultural extension service supply and rationales for intervention

Agricultural extension service supply

Agricultural extension services are diverse. Agricultural extension agents can inform farmers about technologies of many types, train them to use new technologies, provide them with opportunities to observe the performance of new technologies, or inform them about market prices and standards. They might simply transmit messages given to them by extension managers in a top-down fashion or instead create messages more tailored to farmers' needs after observation and discussion. Sometimes extension agents also help farmers with the logistics and paperwork of obtaining credit or inputs or with organizing cooperative undertakings.

Many of these extension activities must be done face to face. Even transmitting simple information can require personal contact when target farmers are not literate and have little contact with broadcast media. In-person communication is even more important when attempting to pass on tacit knowledge.

Extension managers often hope to transmit information through two types of person-to-person interaction. Extension agents contact some farmers directly. We'll call these their **contact farmers**. Managers might also hope to contact additional farmers indirectly by encouraging or requiring the contact farmers to spread what they have learned to other farmers.

The managers of an extension organization shape its performance through their choices regarding how many resources to invest in extension activities, which types of services to provide, the allocation of services across regions and farmer types, and what fees to charge for the services they provide. They also make more detailed choices regarding the numbers and qualifications of extension agents; their training, pay levels, and pay structure; the conditions under which they are promoted or fired; and the curricula, budgets, and equipment with which they are provided. Managers might also define protocols for how agents should identify contact farmers, how often they should interact with them, and what requests or demands they should make regarding contact farmers' interactions with other farmers.

These agricultural extension management choices help determine several critical dimensions of extension service performance: how many and which types of farmers are offered direct contact, the nature and quality of the messages and other services offered to contact farmers, how many and which types of farmers are offered services indirectly by contact farmers, the nature and quality of those services, and the efficiency with which services are provided. Agricultural extension services are of higher quality when they are better tailored to farmers' circumstances and when they are provided in a more timely and effective manner. Efficiency increases when it becomes possible to provide any given set of services to a given number of farmers at lower cost.

Rationales for intervention in agricultural extension

Private firms provide extension services only when they can charge farmers fees that are high enough to cover costs. Farmers may be unwilling to pay fees greater than costs, even for services that would generate large private and social benefits, for two reasons tied to the nature of extension services. First, they might simply be unaware of the existence and potential value of technological knowledge and thus fail to demand it. This is especially likely in regions where farmers have no history of useful contact with extension agents.

Second, even when farmers believe extension agents possess valuable information, they might hope to acquire the information, at least imperfectly, by observing their neighbors. That is, some extension information has public goods qualities, inclining farmers to free ride on their neighbors' acquisition of extension services, as we saw earlier.

These market failures do not apply to all extension services, however. Some extension messages, such as the results of soil-testing services, must be customized to individual farms and are therefore excludable. Extension services may also be excludable when they transmit knowledge that is highly tacit, which can be disseminated only by agents with skill and motivation beyond what neighboring farmers can provide, and when they transmit market price information, which is valuable only when received in a timely fashion. Other technologies are embodied in purchased inputs, suggesting that agricultural input retailers might profit from combining extension activities with their efforts to retail seeds or fertilizer.

In special cases, private actors might even perceive incentives to disseminate information with strong public goods qualities. Large buyers of produce—such as exporting firms or supermarket chains—may be able to profit from providing extension services that help farmers produce the crops they wish to buy. Such buyers might be willing to provide extension services to many local farmers within a small geographic region in exchange for the farmers' contractual promises to sell their crops to the buyers. When working with many neighboring farmers, any sharing of information between farmers reduces the per-farmer cost of providing extension services, and exclusive purchase arrangements allow buyers to charge farmers for the extension services by deducting extension fees before paying farmers for their crops. This is attractive to buyers only when farmers can be expected to fulfill their promises to sell to the contracting buyers, and it might thus be most relevant for export crops or high-end supermarket produce, for which farmers have few alternative local sales opportunities.

Farmers themselves might also overcome local public goods problems by creating farmer cooperative organizations, through which they purchase extension services for the group. By coordinating extension visits with multiple farmers, they may also reduce the cost of providing extension services.

Even when farmers are aware of the value of extension information and have little opportunity to free ride, they may be prevented from purchasing extension services by liquidity constraints. The poor are especially likely to be shut out, not only because they face inferior access to financial services but also because the fees extension agents would have to charge to cover costs are probably higher for poor farmers who live in more remote locations and often have less education. Again, coordinating with other farmers in ways that reduce the cost of extension services might help, but farmer organizations sometimes exclude the poor; and they do not always arise spontaneously, even when they would be valuable.

We conclude that:

> Private actors might perceive incentives to supply particular kinds of extension services to farmers who are not liquidity constrained. This is most likely for providing knowledge that must be customized to individual farms, is not easily passed on from farmer to farmer, or is relevant to crops of interest to large buyers. Public actors may be able to improve development outcomes by subsidizing the purchase or sale of extension services that have strong public goods qualities, pertain to crops with many buyers, and are intended for use by poor farmers. In some cases, the creation of farmer cooperatives might help by circumventing free-riding problems and reducing the per-farmer cost of extension services.

This suggests that some public sector agricultural extension efforts might crowd out private sector extension services. Policymakers might wish to focus public sector programs on the farmers and the messages of least interest to the private sector.

20.3 Agricultural Research and Extension Policy Design and Evaluation

20.3A Agricultural research and extension policy objectives

Agricultural technical change, and the research and extension policies that promote it, have the potential to raise well-being for many groups throughout society: subsistence farmers, commercial farmers of all sizes, rural laborers, rural nonfarm households, and urban consumers. They also have the potential to improve well-being along many dimensions: increasing average income, reducing vulnerability, improving nutrition, preserving the environment, or freeing up time. If agricultural technology policies are to raise the well-being of any *specific* group, however, they must be well tailored to that purpose. Thus identifying target groups and understanding their preferences and constraints is an important first step in designing and evaluating agricultural research and extension policies.

20.3B Agricultural research policy design, implementation, and evaluation

At the broadest level of agricultural research policy design, policymakers decide how much to invest in subsidizing agricultural research at national and international levels. They also choose how to allocate funds across crops and across broad directions of technical change, and they choose the institutional structures that govern subsidized agricultural research.

Historically, most developing countries' agricultural research has been carried out in centralized civil-service systems. Policymakers might consider reforms of two broad types. The first type alters research priorities or the volume of spending without significantly altering the governance structure. For example, a reform might shift research spending from export crops to domestic food crops while retaining a centralized civil-service governance structure. The second type alters governance structures, with the aim of improving efficiency or effectiveness. Such reforms might introduce higher-powered work incentives, shift decision-making authority from national to regional personnel, or encourage more interaction between researchers and farmers within civil-service systems. They might instead seek to privatize some research management decisions by, for example, contracting private firms to carry out specified research programs. Kremer and Zwane (2005) suggest an alternative approach to privatization: offering awards for the first private researchers to create technologies that satisfy specified technical criteria and are adopted by specified numbers of farmers. We take a closer look at this proposal later.

Box 20.3 adapts Chapter 14's seven questions for the case of agricultural research policies. Because agricultural research is a long-lived investment, the ideal evaluation would take a long-run perspective. It would study the (actual or hypothetical) results of pursing a set of research policies for 10 years or more, and it would examine the speed with which research generates new

≡ Box 20.3 Questions to Guide Analysis of Agricultural Research Policies

Question 1: Objectives

To what extent do policymakers aim to improve the well-being of small-farm households, rural landless laborers, poor food consumers, or other groups? To what extent do they aim to raise well-being by raising average farm incomes or wages, reducing variability in rural incomes, reducing the average level or variability of food prices, or improving nutrition?

Question 2: Design

What choices regarding total funding, research priorities, and governance structure define the policy on paper?

Question 3: Implementation

What local information, capacity, motivation, and coordinating oversight (as defined in Chapter 13) do researchers and their managers bring to their work? How many and what types of new agricultural technologies are generated by subsidized research? How quickly and efficiently are they generated?

Question 4: Directly affected groups

How many farmer and which farmers adopt new technologies generated by the subsidized research system? How do adoption rates differ across poor and nonpoor households and between women and men?

Question 5: Direct effects

What effect does adoption of these new technologies have on the average level and variability of adopting farmers' profits and total incomes and their choices regarding crop production, labor and input demands, consumption, time allocation, saving, and investment? How are these impacts likely to evolve over time?

Question 6: Spillover and feedback effects

What effects do adopters' behavioral changes have on rural labor markets, the rural nonfarm sector, urban labor markets, and urban goods markets? What changes in wages and prices result? What effects does adoption have on the environment? Which groups are affected indirectly and in which ways through these channels?

Question 7: Budgetary costs

What is the total budgetary cost of the subsidized agricultural research over the period in question?

technologies, the speed and spread of the technologies' adoption, and the wide-ranging impacts of adoption, as well as the budgetary cost.[4]

20.3C Agricultural extension policy design, implementation, and evaluation

Policymakers must choose how many funds to invest in subsidizing agricultural extension services, the types of extension services to subsidize, the criteria used to determine which farmers are offered services, what fees are charged, and the institutional structures through which extension managers and agents are governed.

Historically, many governments have provided subsidized agricultural extension services through centralized civil service systems providing their services for free. Over the last half century, governments have undertaken many reforms within public sector extension systems, often simultaneously reforming total spending, extension priorities, and governance. We consider examples of such reforms below. Policymakers might instead seek to privatize agricultural extension services, either by contracting directly with private agricultural extension providers or by distributing vouchers that farmers may use to purchase extension services from qualifying private sector agents.

Increasingly, development actors also encourage private provision of extension services in more subtle ways. Working on the assumption that agricultural input retailers would provide valuable extension services if they weren't held back by credit constraints or lack of knowledge, they subsidize retailers' investments in training and new inventory, thereby encouraging them to expand their retail and extension activities.

Box 20.4 presents questions to guide research on agricultural extension policies. Subsidization of agricultural extension services can have long-lasting effects if it leads farmers to adopt technologies that they never would have adopted in the absence of intervention. The true impact of subsidized extension services might be shorter lived, however, if the services simply help farmers adopt new technologies *sooner* than they would have in the absence of intervention. In the extreme, subsidized extension services might have little impact at all if they merely crowd out private extension services that would have reached farmers just as quickly.

20.3D How valuable are public sector investments in agricultural research and extension?

How high are the returns on investments in agricultural research and extension? That is, if we were to value all the effects of a research or extension program in monetary terms, how would the stream of benefits compare to the costs?

Comprehensive answers to such questions are lacking, because to construct them, researchers would have to estimate all the society-wide impacts of a research or extension program and then translate all those impacts into comparable monetary terms—a value-laden activity. Many researchers have, however, estimated rates of return to research or extension program spending based more narrowly on the programs' impacts on agricultural productivity, farm profits, or farm household incomes. Such estimates might understate the society-wide returns if they miss important positive spillover effects, though they might also fail to account for societal losses arising out of environmental externalities.

Even when maintaining the narrower focus on yield or income impacts, analysts face difficult estimation challenges, as discussed in Evenson (2001). No single study is flawless, but

---

[4] For simplicity, Box 20.3 ignores the potential for subsidized agricultural research to crowd out unsubsidized private-sector research.

☰ Box 20.4 Questions to Guide Analysis of Agricultural Extension Policies

Question 1: Objectives

To what extent do policymakers aim to improve the well-being of small farm households, rural landless laborers, poor food consumers, or other groups? To what extent do they aim to raise well-being by raising average farm incomes or wages, reducing variability in rural incomes, reducing the average level or variability of food prices, or improving nutrition?

Question 2: Design

What choices regarding total funding, types of services offered, criteria used to determine which farmers are offered services, fees, and governance structure define extension policies on paper?

Question 3: Implementation

What local information, capacity, motivation, and coordinating oversight (as defined in Chapter 13) do extension agents and their managers bring to their work? What types of messages and other services are offered by extension agents? To whom do they offer these services? What quality of service do they offer? What fees do they charge? What extension messages do contact farmers pass on, and to which other farmers do they pass them on?

Question 4: Directly affected groups

How many farmers and which farmers ultimately purchase or accept subsidized extension services, whether from agents or contact farmers?

Question 5: Direct effects

What new technologies do the directly affected farmers adopt, and how quickly do they adopt them? When, if at all, would they have adopted these technologies in the absence of subsidized extension services (after learning about them from private extension agents or other farmers)? What effect does adoption, or the change in the timing of adoption, have on the average level and variance of farm profits and income and on their households' choices regarding crop production, labor and input demand, consumption, time allocation, saving, and investment over the short, medium, and long run?

Question 6: Spillover and feedback effects

What effects do behavioral changes among those directly affected have on rural labor markets, the rural nonfarm sector, urban labor markets, and urban goods markets? What changes in wages and prices result? What effects does adoption have on the environment? Which groups are affected indirectly and in which ways by these changes?

Question 7: Budgetary costs

What is the total budgetary cost (net of fees collected) of the subsidized agricultural extension policies over the period in question?

---

the large body of research—including hundreds of studies for research and extension programs around the world, using many datasets and estimation approaches with diverse strengths and weaknesses—suggests that the returns to investment in research and extension are very high. For comparison purposes, most studies calculate the **internal rate of return (IRR)** on investments in research or extension that are implied by estimates of costs and impacts. The IRR indicates the interest rate at which the discounted stream of benefits would just equal the discounted costs; thus higher internal rates of return indicate better investments. Among the many studies reviewed in Evenson (2001), 82 percent of the estimated IRRs for research programs, and 74 percent of the estimated extension program IRRs, were over 20 percent per year, and mean and median estimated IRRs were much higher. Some estimated returns are negligible, and publication biases might mean that low return estimates are under-represented in the sample of published studies, but Evenson (2001) concludes that the evidence of high returns to investment in agricultural research and extension is more conclusive and extensive than for any other type of development intervention.

Though most economists agree that historical investments in agricultural research and extension have produced high average returns, most also agree that many agricultural research and extension systems exhibit signs of weak governance. Poorly developed markets for inputs, outputs, and financial services have also inhibited farmers' responses to research and extension spending. Institutional reforms that improve the governance of subsidized research and extension services and that encourage market development might therefore raise the returns on agricultural research and extension investments to even higher levels (World Bank, 2007).

20.3E Redirecting research subsidies from push toward pull mechanisms

Policymakers would like agricultural researchers to perform subsidized research efficiently and to pursue only research programs with the greatest social value. Guaranteeing efficient use of subsidies is difficult, however, because policymakers lack researchers' expertise and therefore have only limited capacity to monitor researchers' performance and hold them accountable. Researchers' desire for academic success or intellectual satisfaction might lead them into research that is technically challenging but unlikely to generate great social benefit. Similarly, lacking social science expertise and preferring the familiar, they might devote too little effort to understanding farmers' preferences or to studying the state of market development in target regions. They might also waste resources by continuing to pursue research agendas after they have proved unpromising.

Two sets of observations seem to confirm the weakness of the link between researchers' objectives and farmers' needs (Kremer and Zwane, 2005). First, many technologies that have fulfilled researchers' expectations and been released to the public with great hopes have failed to inspire adoption by many farmers. Second, several crop varieties rejected by researchers have been widely adopted after escaping from agricultural research stations. For example, Indian researchers rejected a rice variety called *mashuri*, which eventually spread throughout Asia after a local farmer started cultivating it. Similarly, a potato variety rejected by researchers in China became popular after a field worker planted it outside the research station.

In response to perceived governance weaknesses, Kremer and Zwane (2005) propose a new institutional vehicle for subsidizing agricultural research, which simultaneously privatizes subsidized research and offers stronger incentives for researchers to tailor research to farmers' needs. They propose that the public sector offer awards for development (by private sector researchers) of technologies that meet specified technical criteria *and are adopted* by specified numbers of farmers in target regions. They characterize such an award system as an effort to *pull* agricultural research by paying for research outputs (i.e., adopted new technologies), in contrast with traditional efforts to *push* research by paying for civil-service research inputs (e.g., salaries and equipment).

Pull financing has the potential to improve the direction, speed, and efficacy of agricultural research. By offering awards for specified new technologies, policymakers guide researchers into broadly defined research areas they deem socially valuable, while allowing competitive firms with technical expertise to identify the most efficient ways of achieving research success in those areas. By tying awards to adoption, moreover, policymakers provide researchers with incentives to study target farmers' preferences and constraints and to tailor their research accordingly.

In addition to improving the impact of subsidized agricultural research, a shift to pull financing might encourage the private sector to invest its own resources in research, extension, and agricultural input retail. When award-worthy new technologies are embodied in specialized inputs (e.g., new seeds) and may be of interest to well-off farmers, private-sector firms might see a potential to recoup some of their research costs by selling the specialized inputs. In such cases they might invest some of their own resources into the research, in the sense that they invest more than they expect to recoup by winning awards. More generally, with awards tied to adoption, research firms might invest in the development of agricultural extension systems to encourage greater adoption of their technologies. For example, they might invest in training agricultural input retailers or providing them with credit.

The logic behind the pull financing proposal is compelling, but no attempt has been made to implement it. Careful thought about the details of design and implementation might help explain why. Successful implementation would require policymakers to identify socially valuable types of new agricultural technology and to convince private sector researchers that the private benefits of developing those technologies will outweigh the private costs. This implies three sets of practical challenges. First, policymakers must carefully define the technical specifications that new technologies must meet to qualify for awards. Significant investments in social science research might be required to identify types of new technology that would generate large social benefit. Researchers in the physical and social sciences would also have to brainstorm about the potential social and environmental costs of adopting certain types of new technology, and they would have to specify additional technical requirements to safeguard against such costs.

Second, policymakers must specify award sizes. The awards must be large enough to motivate private sector investment, but not so high that the costs ultimately exceed the social benefits. Policymakers would probably have to specify award sizes as complicated formulas rather than specific dollar values. To encourage researchers to achieve the highest levels of technological quality and adoption possible (rather than encouraging them to just barely meet minimum technical criteria), they might tie award sizes to adoption rates and technology quality measures, such as average yields under specified conditions. They might also tie award sizes to adoption rates over multiple years so that researchers have long-term interest in maintaining the quality and use of their technologies.

Third, policymakers must create trustworthy mechanisms for identifying winners and paying out awards. They must specify the details of the experiments and survey methods that will be used to determine whether a given technology has met technical and adoption rate standards, and researchers must believe that these procedures will deliver unbiased and accurate judgments. Policymakers must also create institutions through which they can make credible promises of paying out awards five or 10 years hence, despite changes in government administration. Significant international cooperation and commitment might be required to provide researchers with adequate confidence in the system.

Kremer and Zwane (2005) point out that even if all these challenges could be overcome, pull financing should be employed only as a complement to, rather than a replacement for, push financing. Although pull mechanisms offer strong incentives for applied research leading to the development of adoptable technologies, they offer little incentive for the basic research that makes applied research possible. They also discourage researchers from undertaking exploratory research in areas that have not yet come to policymakers' attention, and they discourage researchers from pursuing ideas generated as serendipitous byproducts of other research.

20.3F Agricultural extension governance reforms

Governance problems may be greater in agricultural extension than in agricultural research, because monitoring extension agents' job performance is especially difficult. To deliver high-quality services, agents must diagnose farmers' needs and respond appropriately. It is difficult to assess the quality of such work without redoing it, and when extension agents are assigned to large territories, it is difficult even to monitor their work hours.

Often problems of low-powered incentives have been compounded by other barriers to agents' productive contact with farmers: inadequate funding for transport and frequent requests for extension agents to perform other tasks, such as administering census questionnaires. Having only limited resources and large numbers of potential clients, agents also tend to select relatively well-off contact farmers, which whom visits are easier to arrange and more likely to be productive.

With the hope of improving service coverage and quality, policymakers have undertaken numerous extension system governance reforms over the last 35 years. Experience with one wave of reforms illuminates some of the difficult tradeoffs inherent in governance choices. Between 1975 and 1995 more than 70 countries, with World Bank support, introduced the Training and Visit approach to agricultural extension (Anderson and Feder, 2004, 2007). The reforms sought to raise service quality and increase the number of farmers ultimately contacted (either directly or indirectly), by holding agents more accountable to their superiors, increasing the number of agents, and increasing the role that contact farmers play in passing extension messages on to other farmers.

To increase agents' accountability, policymakers redefined agents' responsibilities in a way that would permit measurement of their performance, and they created hierarchies of supervisors to monitor that performance. Under the new system, agents were required to follow a strict schedule in two-week cycles. Each cycle began with a mandatory training session, at which specialists trained agents for delivering particular sets of messages to their contact farmers over the next two weeks. Agents then met with contact farmers according to a predetermined schedule, rendering it possible for their supervisors to check up on whether they were fulfilling their job responsibilities. Requiring biweekly meetings reduced the number of contact farmers that any one agent could feasibly serve, but policymakers hoped to increase the total number of farmers receiving extension messages by increasing the number of agents and encouraging contact farmers to spread messages to other farmers more frequently and effectively.

In many cases, the benefits of Training and Visit reforms proved elusive. While the new system succeeded in creating strong incentives for agents to follow biweekly schedules, this seems not to have translated into an increase in the value of the services agents provided to farmers. In fact, farmers soon complained that agents brought too few new messages to warrant biweekly meetings. Furthermore, agents given strict orders to communicate the specialists' messages were less motivated, and had less opportunity, to elicit and respond to farmers' information needs, and they were less willing to provide farmers with other services, such as assistance with obtaining inputs. The total numbers of farmers reached by extension systems also tended to fall, even while the numbers of agents rose, because the number of contact farmers per agent fell and contact farmers did not increase their transmission of extension messages to other farmers as intended. In practical terms, one of the biggest drawbacks to the Training and Visit reforms was their tendency to increase total budgetary costs by 25 to 40 percent. Eventually, most Training and Visit systems were significantly revised or abandoned entirely.

The Training and Visit reforms strengthened agents' incentives to transmit messages handed down to them by specialists and supervisors, but they weakened their incentives to diagnose farmers' needs and respond accordingly. Many current reforms, by contrast, seek precisely to increase extension systems' responsiveness to farmers' needs. These efforts to render extension services more **demand driven** or **farmer driven** sometimes introduce competition among agents for client farmers. The assumption underlying such reform is that farmers are in a better position than supervisors to judge the quality of services an agent provides. If farmers are allowed to choose among competing extension agents, and if agents' pay or employment is linked in some way to the number of clients they attract, then farmers may hold agents responsible for meeting their needs by threatening to take their business elsewhere.

Competition among agents may be introduced, even within public sector extension systems, by assigning agents to overlapping territories and allowing farmers to choose among agents. Competition may be extended further to include private for-profit and NGO agents, even while the government continues to subsidize extension services by distributing vouchers to finance farmers' purchase of extension services.

Competition-enhancing reforms may incorporate two additional elements: charging fees and organizing farmers into cooperative groups. Policymakers hope that charging fees will motivate farmers to exercise greater care in choosing among agents, while also shifting some of the extension system cost burden onto farmers. By organizing farmers into groups that meet jointly with agents, they hope to reduce per-farmer extension costs. Unfortunately, connecting with farmers through cooperative organizations and charging fees can significantly reduce the use of extension services by the poorest farmers. For a review of experience with such reforms, see Anderson and Feder (2007).

REFERENCES

Alston, Julian M., Steven Dehmer, and Philip G. Pardey. "International Initiatives in Agricultural R&D: The Changing Fortunes of the CGIAR." In Philip G. Pardey, Julian M. Alston, and Roley R. Piggott (eds.). *Agricultural R&D in the Developing World: Too Little, Too Late?* Washington, D.C.: International Food Policy Research Institute, 2006. doi:10.2499/089629756XAGRD

Anderson, Jock R., and Gershon Feder. "Agricultural Extension: Good Intentions and Hard Realities." *The World Bank Research Observer* 19(1): 41–60, 2004. doi:10.1093/wbro/lkh013

Anderson, Jock R., and Gershon Feder. "Agricultural Extension." In Robert Evenson and Prabhu Pingali (eds.). *Handbook of Agricultural Economics, Volume 3.* Amsterdam: Elsevier, 2007, pp. 573–628. doi:10.1016/S1574-0072(06)03044-1

Cole, Shawn, Xavier Giné, Jeremy Tobacman, Petia Topalova, Robert Townsend, and James Vickery. "Barriers to Household Risk Management: Evidence from India." *American Economic Journal: Applied Economics* 5(1): 104–135, 2013. doi: 10.1257/app.5.1.104

Conley, Timothy G., and Christopher R. Udry. "Learning About a New Technology: Pineapple in Ghana." *American Economic Review* 100(1): 35–69, 2010. doi:10.1257/aer.100.1.35

Duflo, Esther, Michael Kremer, and Jonathan Robinson. "How High Are Rates of Return to Fertilizer? Evidence From Field Experiments in Kenya." *American Economic Review* 98(2): 482–488, 2008. doi:10.1257/aer.98.2.482

Evenson, Robert E. "Economic Impacts of Agricultural Research and Extension." In Bruce L. Gardner and Gordon C. Rausser (eds.). *Handbook of Agricultural Economics, Volume 1, Part A.* Amsterdam: Elsevier, 2001, pp. 573–628. doi:10.1016/S1574-0072(01)10014-9

Evenson, Robert E., and Larry E. Westphal. "Technological Change and Technology Strategy." In Jere Behrman and T. N. Srinivasan (eds.). *Handbook of Development Economics Volume 3, Part A.* Amsterdam: Elsevier, 1995, pp. 2209–2299. doi:10.1016/S1573-4471(05)80009-9

Food and Agriculture Organization. *The State of Food and Agriculture 2010–2011: Women in Agriculture: Closing the Gender Gap for Development.* Rome: Food and Agriculture Organization, 2011. http://www.fao.org/docrep/013/i2050e/i2050e00.htm

Foster, Andrew D., and Mark R. Rosenzweig. "Learning By Doing and Learning From Others: Human Capital and Technical Change in Agriculture." *Journal of Political Economy* 103(6): 1176–209, 1995. http://www.jstor.org/stable/2138708

Foster, Andrew, and Mark R. Rosenzweig. "Technical Change and Human-Capital Returns and Investments: Evidence From the Green Revolution." *American Economic Review* 86(4): 931–953, 1996. http://www.jstor.org/stable/2118312

Gabre-Madhin, Eleni Z., and Steven Haggblade. "Successes in African Agriculture: Results of an Expert Survey." *World Development* 32(5): 745–766, 2004. doi:10.1016/j.worlddev.2003.11.004

Hazell, Peter B. R. *Green Revolution: Curse Or Blessing?* Washington, D. C.: International Food Policy Research Institute, 2002. http://www.ifpri.org/publication/green-revolution

Karlan, Dean, Robert Darko Osei, Isaac Osei-Akoto, and Christopher Udry, "Agricultural Decisions after Relaxing Credit and Risk Constraints." *National Bureau of Economic Research Working Paper* 18463. Cambridge, MA: National Bureau of Economic Research, 2012.

Keane, J., S. Page, A. Kergna, and J. Kennan. *Climate Change and Developing Country Agriculture: An Overview of Expected Impacts, Adaptation and Mitigation Challenges, and Funding Requirements,* ICTSD–IPC Platform on Climate Change, Agriculture and Trade, Issue Brief No.2. Geneva: International Centre for Trade and Sustainable Development, and Washington, D.C.: International Food & Agricultural Trade Policy Council, 2009.

Kremer, Michael, and Alix Peterson Zwane. "Encouraging Private Sector Research for Tropical Agriculture." *World Development* 33(1): 87–105, 2005. doi:10.1016/j.worlddev.2004.07.006

Morduch, Jonathan. "Risk, Production and Saving: Theory and Evidence From Indian Households." Unpublished Manuscript. Cambridge, MA: Harvard University, 1993.

Ruttan, Vernon W. "Productivity Growth in World Agriculture: Sources and Constraints." *Journal of Economic Perspectives* 16(4): 161–184, 2002. doi:10.1257/089533002320951028

World Bank. *Intellectual Property Rights: Designing Regimes to Support Plant Breeding in Developing Countries.* Agriculture and Rural Development Department. Washington, D.C.: World Bank, 2006. http://siteresources.worldbank.org/INTARD/Resources/IPR_ESW.pdf

World Bank. *World Development Report 2008: Agriculture for Development.* Washington, D.C.: World Bank, 2007. http://go.worldbank.org/ZJIAOSUFU0

QUESTIONS FOR REVIEW

1. Discuss the significance of agricultural technical change for developing countries.

2. Describe the range of possible "directions of technical change" in agriculture.

3. Discuss the roles played by agricultural researchers, agricultural extension agents, and farmers in determining the rate and nature of agricultural technical change.

4. Discuss the roles of learning, education, geography, goods and labor markets, financial markets, institutions, preferences, gender, and the specific nature of a new agricultural technology in determining which farmers adopt the technology.

5. How might researchers need to tailor the direction of technical change they pursue if they wish poor farmers to adopt their new technologies?

6. What role might policies toward infrastructure, education, agricultural markets, and financial markets play in determining which farmers adopt a new technology?

7. What factors help determine how much adopting farmers benefit from adopting a new technology?

8. What spillover effects might be important to consider in a thorough evaluation of the effects of agricultural technology adoption?

9. What rationales might justify intervention by governments or NGOs in agricultural research and extension activities?

What implications do these rationales have for policy design?

10. What objectives might motivate policies toward agricultural research and extension?

11. Describe the array of design choices that define government or NGO policies toward agricultural research.

12. Describe the array of design choices that define government or NGO policies toward agricultural extension.

13. Describe Kremer and Zwane's proposal for an award program to "pull" agricultural research, and contrast it with traditional "push" approaches to subsidizing agricultural research. Discuss the relative merits of push and pull mechanisms for subsidizing agricultural research.

14. Describe the Training and Visit approach to agricultural extension, and discuss the benefits and costs of introducing Training and Visit reforms into pre-existing centralized civil service extension agencies.

QUESTIONS FOR DISCUSSION

1. Describe the early Green Revolution technologies. How would you describe the direction of technical change associated with the switch from the technologies farmers were using before to these technologies? Discuss how the details of this technical change affected: (a) which farmers around the world were likely to benefit and (b) the nature of the direct and indirect effects of adoption.

2. What direct and indirect effects would you want to measure for a thorough study of each of the following types of technical change? What potential barriers to adoption would you want to study?
   - Adoption by food crop farmers of chemical fertilizer
   - Adoption by soybean farmers of tractor-pulled plows and harvesting equipment
   - Adoption by subsistence farmers of a new technology capable of storing grains and legumes safely for many months

3. Discuss the significance of each question in Boxes 20.3 and 20.4.

4. Suppose you are asked to write a report on the likely benefits and costs of shifting some government agricultural research spending away from export crops toward domestic

food crops. What information would you wish to gather before writing your report? What sorts of potential benefits and costs would you consider?

5. Consider an NGO working in rural development in a particular poor region of a developing country. What kinds of advocacy and liaison activities involving the national agricultural research system might it find useful?

6. Read Anderson and Feder (2007). Discuss the benefits and costs of redirecting agricultural extension funding away from traditional extension approaches toward the Farmer Field School approach?

7. If private agents (e.g., input retailers) are quite active in extension even without subsidy, how might policymakers want to tailor public sector and NGO extension policies to complement, rather than substitute for, this private extension activity?

8. If an NGO were to train or hire people to provide extension services in a poor community, how might they define "quality" services, and how might they design a system that provides agents with strong capacity and motivation for providing high-quality services?

PROBLEMS

1. You are hired by the new government of a developing country to write a report on the extent to which the current government agricultural research program is targeted

toward poverty reduction and to generate a list of potential changes in the research program that would improve its poverty reduction impact (without increasing total spending). What features of the agricultural research program would you study, and what changes would you consider? Explain.

2. Consider a national agricultural extension service in which the agents have three sets of responsibilities:
   - Informing and teaching farmers about new technologies produced by the agricultural research system
   - Helping farmers cope with frequent and diverse problems with insects, crop diseases, and weather variations that hit their crops
   - Spreading public health messages to the farming population

   The agency currently offers its services free of charge, and the agents provide services of moderate quality. Each agent is paid a fixed salary and is assigned as the sole agent in a region. The agents allocate their time across farmers within their regions as they see fit.

   Discuss the potential benefits and costs of a reform with two key elements:

   - Charging fees: Agents must start charging farmers a modest fee per scheduled extension visit. Farmers may organize themselves into groups through which they can share the costs of extension visits. Agents may make unscheduled visits to inform farmers of the services they offer and to encourage farmers to form groups, but they may not charge for such visits. Farmers pay fees only for official, scheduled extension visits.
   - Competition among agents: Agents are assigned to overlapping areas. Farmers may request official visits from any of the agents available in their region, and agents' pay is tied to the number of official farm visits they make. The pay scale is set so that agents attracting enough requests to require full-time work would continue to receive the same level of pay as before, but agents who are not much requested receive less than before.

Microfinance

Government, NGO and for-profit **microfinance programs** offer credit, savings, and other financial services to clients poorer than those typically served by commercial banks. Thousands of microfinance institutions have sprung up over the last 30 years, supported by many governments and intergovernmental development organizations, as well as by NGOs of all sizes and by citizens of rich countries who lend to microentrepreneurs online. Much goodwill, talent, and money that could be employed in other development endeavors is devoted to microfinance. Thus microfinance activities, like other development interventions, merit close study by policy analysts.

21.1 Microfinance in Developing Countries
21.1A The microfinance idea

Microfinance was born in the mid-1970s, when Nobel Prize–winning economist Mohammad Yunus and his graduate students at Chittagong University in Bangladesh began making small loans to poor villagers. They demonstrated that their clients—often women—not only were eager to borrow small amounts but also were able to pay off their loans with interest. Yunus's efforts soon attracted worldwide attention and inspired replication and experimentation around the world. According to the 2012 report of the Microcredit Summit Campaign, more than 3,600 institutions now provide microfinance services and serve close to 205 million clients in 147 countries (Maes and Reed, 2012).

Supporters are often drawn to microfinance by an appealing idea: Rather than give the poor handouts, which provide them only temporary help, we can offer them small loans for financing business investments. As they create or expand **microenterprises** (i.e., very small businesses), their incomes rise in a sustained fashion, allowing them to grow their families out of poverty. We may, furthermore, target the loans to women, empowering them for greater influence in their homes and communities. And we can do all this at little per-household cost because recipients will repay their loans with interest, allowing the funds to be recycled for raising many families out of poverty.

To some supporters, this idea seems a matter of simple logic, but policy analysts recognize it as a set of assertions about empirical relationships that may or may not be true in all circumstances and that therefore require careful, context-specific study. This chapter helps readers identify the assumptions underlying the microfinance idea and reviews the empirical evidence gathered to date regarding the achievements and limitations of microcredit, the oldest and most prevalent type of microfinance.

21.1B Microfinance program objectives

Most microfinance institutions (MFIs) aim to improve the lives of poor clients and their families, though they differ in how, exactly, they define their target groups. Some explicitly target the "very poor" or "poor," and carefully articulate the poverty lines that define these groups. Many others target the "poor" or "near poor," without defining precisely the poverty lines they have in mind. Many target women, aiming to empower them for larger roles in their families and communities, and some pursue additional social objectives, such as improving borrowers' nutrition knowledge or conflict-resolution skills.

MFIs differ also in the way they expect to reduce poverty. Many expect to raise clients' incomes in a sustained way by helping them create or expand microenterprises. Others take a broader view of how access to financial services might improve clients' well-being. Financial services can help clients cope with income fluctuations, pay off loans to moneylenders, or aggregate the small sums they can save each week into the larger lump sums required to purchase durable consumer goods (such as mattresses) or to pay infrequent and significant fees (such as school fees). MFIs and donors might also aim to reduce poverty indirectly by increasing their clients' demands for workers to help in their microenterprises.

Many of the MFIs that pursue poverty-reduction objectives simultaneously pursue financial sustainability. An MFI is **financially sustainable** when its revenue (from interest and fees on loans) exceeds its operating cost, allowing it to continue operation at its current scale or even expand (through reinvestment of profits) without the need for new injections of donor subsidy.[1] Some seek to **commercialize**. This means that they seek to achieve a higher level of profitability, at which they can attract capital from purely profit-seeking investors.

Some microfinance sector leaders argue that all MFIs should pursue financial sustainability. Whether financial sustainability is a valid objective of all microfinance programs, however, is not immediately obvious. Well-articulated objectives in poverty reduction and development work (as defined in Chapter 14) identify the dimensions of well-being that policy designers hope to improve and the target populations for whom they hope to bring about these improvements. Financial sustainability, which describes MFI profitability rather than household well-being, is not an objective of this sort. In fact, we will see that microcredit program design changes that increase financial sustainability have mixed implications for a program's outreach and impact among the poor. It is therefore important to explore the potential benefits of financial sustainability, the empirical magnitude of any tradeoffs between sustainability and poverty reduction, and the implications of such tradeoffs for development policy.

21.1C Microfinance program design and implementation

Current microfinance programs are incredibly diverse. They differ in the nature of the financial products they offer, the training and other subsidiary services they provide to clients, the recruitment practices and eligibility criteria they use to identify clients, their formal institutional structures, and the personnel practices and informal institutional norms that govern their daily operations.

Loan product designs

The microfinance products of primary concern in this chapter are loans. Most microcredit programs offer any potential client not just a single loan but a sequence of loans of increasing size, in which the receipt of later loans is conditioned on successful repayment of earlier loans. Each loan must be repaid over the course of a **loan cycle** of three, four, six, or 12 months, at the end of which a borrower in good standing may either start a new loan cycle or leave the program. Typically, borrowers are required to begin repaying a loan only a week or two after receiving it and must make weekly or biweekly payments at mandatory meetings throughout the loan cycle.

Although most microloans are smaller than the loans typically offered by traditional commercial banks, the label *microcredit* is applied to loans of widely varying sizes. The Grameen Bank offers loans of as little as $10 in its program of interest-free loans for beggars

---

[1] By this definition, an MFI may be considered financially sustainable even while continuing to benefit from the use of donor capital or social investor capital on which it pays below-market returns. We expand on this definition below. Exact definitions of financial sustainability (and related terms) differ across MFIs. For an overview of income statement and balance sheet definitions important in analyzing MFIs' financial sustainability and repayment performance, see CGAP (2003).

(MicroFinance Transparency, 2011), while Banco Compartamos, a Mexican MFI, offers loans as large as $7,000.[2] Average microloan sizes range from around $100 in India to $1,500 in Bolivia.[3]

Microcredit interest rates vary widely across countries, institutions, and loan types, though most are higher than the rates typically charged by commercial banks. For example, the interest rates on most Grameen Bank loans are near 20% per annum, while for-profit MFIs like Banco Compartamos can charge 100% or more per annum (Cull et al., 2009).

In the early days of microfinance, most MFIs followed the Grameen Bank example of requiring borrowers to form small groups in which members are held jointly liable for loan repayment. Under such **group liability**, if any member of the group fails to make a payment, the other members of the group must make the payment for her or lose access to further microcredit. Some MFIs offering group liability loans work with solidarity groups of five members, while others work with village banks, with 20, 30, or 50 members.

Group liability lending remains popular, but the share of MFIs offering loans under **individual liability** has grown over the years. Even the Grameen Bank shifted to individual lending in 2002. Under individual liability, borrowers are obligated to make only their own loan payments, though often they are still required to form groups and make loan payments at group meetings. Under both individual and group liability, borrowers who fail to fulfill their repayment obligations are denied access to future credit.

Often MFIs require borrowers to use loans for investment in microenterprise, and they might attempt to enforce such restrictions by distributing the loan in the form of business assets rather than cash. Other MFIs place no restrictions on loan use.

Savings product designs

A growing number of organizations offer microsavings services. A few MFIs offer formal savings accounts, such as might be offered by commercial banks, in addition to microcredit. The savings accounts they offer differ in the rates of interest they pay savers (if any), the fees charged (if any), and the minimum deposits required to open or maintain accounts. Two innovations in savings accounts that have drawn attention in recent years are the offer of deposit collection services (Ashraf et al., 2006a) and the offer of commitment savings accounts. The latter allow savers to specify savings goals and then penalize them for withdrawing savings before they have met their goals, except in documented cases of emergency (Ashraf et al., 2006b).

A variety of organizations, including MFIs and NGOs with broader social missions, have become involved in the creation of informal savings groups, through which members accumulate savings outside of formal financial institutions. The catalyzing organizations provide groups with the organizational help and training required to carry out their own financial activities, but they do not become directly involved in financial transactions with group members. Some informal savings groups are **savings clubs**, which require members to attend weekly meetings and to make weekly deposits of small sums, which are stored away in locked boxes that members take turns guarding. The savings clubs meet for specified numbers of weeks, at the end of which the boxes are opened and members are free to use their accumulated savings.

Other informal savings groups promoted by NGOs are rotating savings and credit associations (ROSCAs), similar to the indigenous ROSCAs described in Chapter 10 (see Box 10.1). Like savings clubs, ROSCAs require members to make weekly contributions for a specified number of weeks, but the pot of deposits collected at any meeting is distributed to a different member each week, rather than being placed in a locked box. For most members, the ROSCA is part savings instrument (allowing them to accumulate savings over the weeks before obtaining the pot) and part loan (which they repay through deposits after they take the pot). Like savings clubs,

---

[2] http://www.compartamos.com.
[3] http://www.forbes.com/forbes/2008/0107/050.html.

ROSCAs provide members with an opportunity to aggregate a sequence of small deposits into a larger lump sum, but ROSCAs do this without the need to guard money in a locked box and allow most members to make use of the lump sums sooner.

An **accumulating savings and credit association** (ASCA) is a somewhat more flexible savings group. Like savings clubs, most ASCAs require members to make savings deposits each week and share out the accumulated savings at the end of a fixed cycle of 6 or 12 months. As in ROSCAs, members have the opportunity to borrow from the group as well as save. ASCAs are more flexible, however, because members have more choice regarding when and how much to borrow. They pay back the loans with interest, and the interest proceeds are distributed to all members with the accumulated savings at the end of the fixed term. Sometimes members also contribute to an insurance fund that may be used to help members in emergency.

A distinctive informal savings group structure indigenous to India is the **self-help group**. As with other savings groups, self-help group members are required to make weekly or monthly deposits at group meetings. Groups accumulate these deposits over early weeks or months, and they eventually begin making loans to group members out of the accumulated savings. After establishing records of good account keeping and loan repayment over several years, many groups become capable of borrowing as a unit from commercial banks, a practice that is encouraged by Indian government policy. Special regulatory provisions allow Indian banks to lend to unregistered self-help groups, and a special line of credit from a national development bank provides the banks with a small subsidy for such activities (Wilson, 2002).

Insurance products

Many MFIs have begun to experiment with insurance products as well. We postpone discussion of insurance product design until Chapter 22, where we discuss health insurance programs.

Training and other nonfinancial services

Although some MFIs specialize in providing financial services and focus narrowly on providing those services as efficiently as possible, others pursue broader microenterprise development objectives, helping borrowers with market research or providing them with training in record keeping, management practices, or specific skills (e.g., furniture construction). Others pursue even broader social missions and use mandatory group meetings as platforms for promoting health practices, gender equality, or literacy.

Recruitment, eligibility, and creditworthiness assessment

Most microlenders expect their loans to be self-targeted toward poorer households, at least to some extent, because they expect well-off households to have access to more attractive financing opportunities. Even so, some also impose simple eligibility requirements intended to target services to the poor. They might, for example, lend only to women with asset holdings below some threshold.

Even microlenders that explicitly target the poor also limit eligibility to clients who are **creditworthy**, or likely to fulfill all their loan repayment obligations. They might lend only to women who have already run small businesses for at least one year or who enjoy a steady source of wage income out of which they can make weekly payments in the near term while getting a business off the ground.

Legal and regulatory status

Many MFIs are NGOs with legal status as nonprofit institutions. Nonprofits face lower taxes and less burdensome reporting requirements than for-profit institutions. They might earn profits but are legally prohibited from distributing profits to investors. This means that any profits they earn must be plowed back into their work. A growing number of MFIs have taken on for-profit status. Other microfinance programs are run by governments.

☰ Box 21.1 Two Microfinance Institutions

The Grameen Bank

According to Mohammad Yunus, the inspiration for the Grameen Bank presented itself in the mid-1970s, when he met a woman named Sufiya, who made beautiful bamboo stools in the village of Jobra, Bangladesh. Despite working long hours, she could not get ahead. She relied on a local moneylender for cash to purchase bamboo, and he charged high interest rates and demanded that she sell her stools only to him. After researching the matter further, Yunus loaned a total of $27 to Sufiya and 41 other villagers who were similarly indebted, generating great excitement in the village. These women and many additional borrowers repaid their loans in full. After failing to convince commercial banks to take on such clients, Yunus founded the Grameen Bank ("Village" Bank in Bengali).

The Grameen Bank introduced a novel methodology for lending to borrowers without collateral. Bank staff invited villagers to form groups of five and offered them one-year loans, for which they would be jointly liable and which they would pay back in 52 weekly installments. The bank restricted participation to households with less than one-half acre of medium-quality land. Each week borrowers were expected to attend a meeting of their center, which is a set of 8 to 10 borrowing groups. At these meetings, bank staff collected loan payments and sometimes provided nonfinancial services, such as low-cost inputs or advice on health, hygiene, or family planning. Borrowers made mandatory weekly savings deposits and recited the bank's 16 Decisions, in which they committed to maintaining their homes in good repair, growing vegetables, keeping their families small, educating their children, building pit-latrines, rejecting the payment of dowries, making investments to raise income, and helping each other out.

Bank loan officers are selected carefully and undergo one year of training, during which they are schooled in poverty as well as finance. Loan officers each oversee eight to 10 centers, and their pay is tied in part to annual surveys of well-being among their borrowers.

The bank has evolved over the years, adding housing loans (of about $125) in 1984, offering emergency loans after the flood in 1998, and undergoing a broader reform in 2001, when it switched to individual lending, made loan products more flexible, and increased emphasis on collecting deposits from nonborrowers.

Regulated under special legislation, the Grameen Bank is a nonprofit institution, but it is also a regulated financial institution that may legally collect deposits. Yunus conceives of the bank as a "social business," which primarily pursues social goals rather than personal gain.

According to Yunus, social businesses should work to break even or make profits, so that they are not reliant on donor funding, but they should plow any profits back into the pursuit of their social objectives, and they must be willing to forgo some profits in the interest of enhancing their social impacts.

Compartamos

In 1990, a Mexican NGO called Gente Nueva used a USAID grant to finance training for its staff in the village banking microcredit methodology. Over the next 10 years, supported by grants and concessional loans from the World Bank, the Inter-American Development Bank, and other development organizations, the NGO expanded its village banking operations. Through its primary loan product, Woman Credit, it provided joint liability loans, in sizes varying from roughly $100 to $1,000, to women organized into groups of 10 to 50, in four-month loan cycles with weekly or biweekly payments.

In 2000, the NGO launched a for-profit, regulated finance company, Financiera Compartamos, in which it shared ownership with a combination of development organizations, the company's managers and directors, and other private investors. In 2006, the finance company became a full bank (but did not begin to collect deposits). Banco Compartamos continued to serve rural women, even while successfully pursuing high profits and using many of those profits to expand operations. The bank's directors considered high profits crucial for achieving their goal of reaching one million clients. Their pursuit of profits and expansion is reflected in the compensation of their loan officers, who can earn bonuses of up to 120 percent of their base salary on the basis of monthly evaluations tied to number of clients and repayment rates.

In 2007, Banco Compartamos undertook a public offering of 30 percent of its shares, in which investors received 12 times the book value of those shares. About $150 million of the proceeds went to private investors. The public offering initiated heated debate throughout the microfinance community as to whether, by charging interest rates of 100 percent per year, Banco Compartamos was inappropriately enriching private investors (and shareowning development organizations) at the expense of poor borrowers.

Sources: Ashta and Hudon (2009); Dowla and Barua (2006); Dugan and Goodwin-Growen (2005); Partida and de Mariz (2008); Yunus (2007).

Some MFIs (among both nonprofit and for-profit) are also formal, regulated financial institutions—either commercial banks or nonbank financial institutions. Becoming a regulated financial institution opens up greater legal capacity to collect savings deposits, but it requires MFIs to meet capital requirements, more stringent reporting requirements, and other prudential regulations designed to protect depositors.

Box 21.1 describes two high-profile MFIs with quite different designs.

Implementation and governance

Microfinance programs alter development outcomes by offering new financial service opportunities to potential clients. The front-line service providers in microlending are the **loan officers**, who recruit borrowers, oversee formation of groups, distribute loans, meet with borrowers weekly to collect loan payments, and in some cases help groups develop constitutions. They might also provide training in financial literacy, business management, disease prevention, or conflict resolution. The governance structures through which MFI designers seek to constrain loan officers' implementation choices differ in hiring standards and compensation schemes and in the training and mentoring provided to loan officers. Differences in such governance structure choices can lead to important differences in the motivation and capacity brought to bear on loan officers' decisions, and thus in the quality, content, and efficiency of the services provided to clients.

The microfinance landscape

A database assembled by Gonzalez and Rosenberg (2006) offers a useful snapshot of the microfinance sector. The database includes information on 2,600 MFIs serving 94 million borrowers—representing the great majority of the world's MFIs and microloan borrowers in that year. According to the data, the geographic spread of microfinance is uneven, with seven-eighths of microfinance clients living in Asia. Asia's share is large both because several Asian countries are very large and because the shares of households involved with microfinance are much higher in some Asian countries than in other parts of the world. The data also indicate that most microfinance clients are served by a few very large MFIs, while the vast majority of MFIs are very small. Three quarters of clients are served by the largest 10 percent of MFIs, and the remaining 90 percent of MFIs serve just one quarter of all clients.[4] MFI clients are served by a diverse array of institutional types: 24 percent are served by NGOs, 30 percent by government institutions, 29 percent by self-help groups, and 17 percent by regulated financial institutions (including banks and nonbank financial institutions, some of which are for-profit and some nonprofit).

21.2 The Economics of Microcredit

We prepare for empirical study of microcredit by examining the conditions under which households participate in microcredit programs, the potential direct and indirect effects of participation, the costs of microlending, and the potential rationales for intervention in microcredit. In this section we highlight how the details of program design and context might influence program impacts. Section 21.3 reviews empirical evidence on some of the questions raised here.

21.2A Participation in microcredit programs

A microcredit program has greater **outreach** when it engages a larger fraction of the poor households in its target population and when it reaches households farther down in the distribution of well-being among the poor. To gain insight into the determinants of outreach, we examine the conditions under which any one potential borrower joins a microcredit program. We first examine the conditions under which an individual would wish to borrow—for business investment or for other reasons—on a microcredit program's terms, and what this implies about possible outreach patterns. We then consider how behavioral conditions, nonfinancial services, and eligibility and creditworthiness criteria might alter those outreach patterns.

Borrowing for business investment

The activity at the heart of many microcredit success stories is borrowing for business investment. Many of the businesses that microcredit clients operate involve the sale of goods, meals, or services door to door, in open air markets, or in small shops, or to owners of somewhat larger enterprises. Some borrowers purchase staple foods or used clothing in large district markets for

---

[4] The statistics cited here are derived from the Gonzalez and Rosenberg (2006) database, but they are found in Cull et al. (2009).

☰ Box 21.2 Microcredit Clients' Businesses in Sri Lanka

Judith Shaw (2004) offers a rich description of the microenterprises run by microcredit clients of two MFIs in a poor region of Sri Lanka. Her study was motivated by earlier researchers' observation that upper-poor and near-poor microcredit clients tend to benefit the most from microcredit, while clients who start out poor or very poor tend to gain less. Seeking to illuminate the reasons this might be, she administered structured questionnaires to 253 current MFI clients and conducted focus group discussions and in-depth interviews with staff and clients. Using retrospective questions, she measured respondents' incomes just before they joined the program (or five years prior to the survey, if they had been participating for longer than five years). She also collected information on the microenterprise occupations they pursued and their current income, as well as various demographic characteristics and where they lived.

She noticed a tendency for borrowers who started out poorer to pursue very different occupations from those who started out above the poverty line. To quantify this, she classified occupations into two groups. Any occupation for which within-sample median income on the survey date was above 80 percent of the poverty line she labeled an "entrepreneurial activity," and those with lower median incomes she labeled "survival activities." Entrepreneurial activities included carpentry, motor mechanics, electrical repairs, hair dressing, tractor hire, rice milling, ocean fishing with motorized vehicles, cattle herding, wholesaling, retailing from a permanent shop or a licensed weekly market stall, or irrigated multi-season agriculture. The survival activities were quite different, tending to require less capital, less skill, and less-sophisticated technologies, and they were more subject to seasonal or periodic scarcity of inputs. They included brick making, rock breaking,

sea-shell crushing, lagoon fishing from a canoe, vending from a small kiosk or cart, free-range poultry raising, production of coir (a fiber extracted from coconut husks), and single-season rainfed agriculture.

She observed that most clients who started out poor or very poor chose survival activities, and then tended to experience only small increases in income during participation, while those who started out at higher income levels tended to choose entrepreneurial occupations and fared better. (She is careful to point out that the income changes she observes are not estimates of program impact, because there is no control for how participants' incomes would have changed had they not participated.) This led her to probe more deeply into the reasons why poorer clients did not choose entrepreneurial activities.

Drawing on qualitative and quantitative information, she suggests that the poorer clients were inhibited from choosing higher-return occupations by a wide variety of barriers. Some live in stagnant rural areas, where they lack market opportunities and access to roads and electricity. Even in areas with more vibrant markets, many are put off by the large capital investments required to set up entrepreneurial micro-enterprises, which are larger than they can finance with small micro-loans and which they might perceive as too risky. They also lack necessary technical skills and have little capacity to sustain loan payments and consumption during the long gestation periods that many of those investments require. In some cases, their opportunities are restricted because they are of low caste or are female household heads. Some also appear to be held back by lack of entrepreneurial experience and aspirations. They report making occupational choices that "copy others," having no skills or propensity for assessing potential business opportunities themselves.

---

resale in smaller local markets. Some produce and sell beverages, meals, bricks, or handicrafts, and some work as self-employed carpenters or mechanics. Box 21.2 describes the businesses run by microcredit clients in a poor region of Sri Lanka.

The theories of financial market failure examined in Chapter 10, and the emerging evidence that some poor households are liquidity constrained, encourage the hope that poor households will eagerly accept offers of microcredit and that their participation in microcredit programs will allow them to undertake high-return business investments. The theories also suggest reasons why better-off households are much less likely to be liquidity constrained and thus unlikely to find microcredit's high interest rates and inconvenient payment schedules attractive. All this suggests that microcredit might be an effective and self-targeted tool for reducing poverty.

A simple economic model of borrowing for business investment reminds us, however, that even if some poor households are liquidity constrained, microcredit programs might find it difficult to achieve broad and deep outreach among the poor and that the breadth and depth of their outreach may depend critically on the loan terms they offer. We begin articulating a simple model of borrowing for business investment by assuming (along lines suggested in Chapter 10) that:

> If a potential borrower were offered microcredit without any behavioral conditions or nonfinancial services, she would accept the loan and use it to finance business investment if she perceived that the benefits of using the loan to finance her best feasible investment project outweighed the costs and if she had no better way to finance the investment.

The primary benefits of borrowing for business investment are the increases in future business profits made possible by creating or expanding a microenterprise. The costs include the up-front fixed costs of purchasing inventory or equipment, the increase in time the borrower must devote to running the business, the microcredit interest payments, the expected cost of any penalties associated with repayment difficulties, the costs of cutting back consumption in order to make early loan payments, and any costs associated with bearing more risk. If the potential borrower is offered not just a single loan but a series of loans of increasing size, then she might take up the offer even if the benefits of the first loan fall short of the costs, so long as she believes that the benefits of a sequence of microcredit-financed investments will eventually outweigh the costs.

Borrowing for business investment is attractive only for borrowers who expect their best feasible investment projects to increase their business profits in coming months or years by more than they must repay in principal and interest. Holding loan terms constant, households with worse business investment prospects are less likely to find microcredit attractive. Unfortunately, we have reasons to suspect that even among liquidity-constrained households, poorer households on average face worse business investment prospects. Borrowers who are healthy or who have carts, plots of land, well-located homes, specialized skills, or useful connections, and those who have already established successful businesses, might have the capacity to turn small sums of working capital into ample profits. Potential borrowers who have few skills, no business experience, and no complementary assets might find it much more difficult to set up a sufficiently profitable business with just a small loan. The prospects of paying back loans with interest rates of 20 percent or more per year are even slimmer for those who are unhealthy or disabled or who are caring for ill family members.

Holding loan terms constant, households living in more remote and poorer locations are also less likely to find microcredit attractive. A microenterprise's profits rise with increases in the local prices of the goods and services it sells, and fall with increases in the prices of inputs and inventory. Where transfer costs are low and markets are well integrated into larger markets, microentrepreneurs can expand supply without driving down local output prices and can obtain inputs dependably and cheaply.[5] In remote locations, where transfer costs are high, nonfarm microenterprises are less likely to be profitable. Households whose main investment prospects lie in agriculture are also less likely to find microcredit attractive, because the lag between planting season investments and harvest season returns makes it difficult to comply with strict weekly repayment schedules.

Even among households with modest assets and facing robust markets, some poor households simply do not have strong enough entrepreneurial traits to set up a microenterprise. They may be unwilling or unable to bear the risks involved or be unprepared for self-employment. The descriptive evidence offered in Box 21.2 is consistent with significant variation among the poor in the propensity to profit from microcredit, with poorer households often facing poorer business investment prospects than less-poor households.

Our model of borrowing for business investment also suggests that households' participation choices are likely to depend on the program's loan terms. For example, as interest rates rise, the costs of borrowing rise relative to the benefits, and borrowers with the least-lucrative investment prospects might drop out. As the minimum loan size rises, again the borrowers with weaker investment projects might drop out because they are unwilling to bear more risk, though some better-off households might also enter the program if the larger loans allow them to undertake investments with large fixed setup costs. As loan-repayment schedules become more stringent, potential borrowers whose investments would deliver unstable or delayed returns might drop out. Shifting from individual to group liability lending can also reduce demand, all else equal, because group liability brings the additional risk of having to cover other group members' loan payments and the additional pressure of ongoing scrutiny by peers.

---

[5] See Chapter 8 for a definition of transfer costs and for the behavior of markets that are and are not integrated into larger markets.

Borrowing for other purposes

Whether or not they wish to borrow for business investment, households might wish to borrow for other reasons, such as paying for unusual medical expenses (without having to cut consumption drastically or sell off assets), making home improvements, or paying off higher-interest-rate debt. The use of credit for these purposes may be attractive to nonentrepreneurial as well as entrepreneurial households among the poor.

Behavioral conditions and nonfinancial services

Behavioral conditions (such as requirements to attend weekly meetings) increase the costs of participation, possibly preventing some households from participating. Time-consuming behavioral conditions may be more off-putting for the nonpoor than the poor, but they may be daunting also to poor businesswomen, whose incomes depend heavily on their presence in the marketplace.

On the other hand, strict requirements for attending weekly meetings and for repaying installments made in public among peers can raise the value of participation for some clients, who face social or psychological barriers to saving, of the sorts discussed in Chapter 10. By committing to a loan contract that threatens penalties if she fails to make weekly loan installments, a present-biased borrower (who is aware of her tendency toward indiscipline) obtains a valuable device for imposing discipline on her future self. Unable to save up to purchase a desired durable good, she might be willing to pay interest in exchange for a microcredit arrangement that helps her commit to exercising thrift. Field experiment evidence in Bauer et al. (2012) seems to support this conjecture. A borrower might also value the way a microcredit arrangement provides her with a legitimate use of weekly savings, helping her protect any money she sets aside each week from claims by spouses or neighbors.

Offers of training and other nonfinancial services can expand program outreach in two ways. First, occupational and business training, and other business development services, can improve the menu of investment options available to potential borrowers. This might encourage participation by clients who would not otherwise have expected to profit from borrowing and investing. Second, potential participants might also value training, nutrition information, and gatherings with other women for reasons unrelated to business investment, and these added benefits might tip the scale in favor of participation for some potential borrowers.

Recruitment, eligibility requirements, and creditworthiness assessments

Even households for whom the likely benefits of participation outweigh the costs will not participate if they are unaware of the program or are not accepted into the program. Some microlenders set eligibility requirements, or design recruitment procedures, to target the poor, and such program design features can inadvertently exclude some of the poor as well as preventing participation by nonpoor households (see Chapter 15). In addition, most microcredit programs limit participation to applicants satisfying creditworthiness requirements, and these requirements often exclude some of the poorest potential clients. For example, when program personnel recruit only among women who are selling wares in market places and who can prove that they have operated businesses in those markets for at least one year, they restrict participation to households that already have enough assets to run successful businesses. Even when programs accept women who are starting businesses for the first time, they sometimes reject women with the lowest incomes who cannot demonstrate the capacity to make weekly loan payments dependably. When participation requires acceptance into joint liability groups or the posting of collateral, the poorest women might find it even more difficult to enter microcredit programs.

Many microcredit programs lend only to women. This restriction may be irrelevant for many households, because often the majority of participants are women, even when programs are open to men. Microenterprise development may be more attractive to women than to men, if it is more compatible with child care than wage employment or farm work is, or if they face fewer wage-employment opportunities than men do. Restricting participation to women can, however, prevent participation by some households in which women and men would benefit from microloans offered to men.

Outreach concerns

The discussion thus far suggests that:

> Whether a microcredit program is capable of reaching many households among the poor and very poor is an empirical question. Poor and very poor households might lack sufficiently attractive investment prospects, may be put off by burdensome behavioral conditions or investment risks, and can fail creditworthiness tests or eligibility conditions.

It also suggests that:

> Microcredit programs' outreach performance can differ significantly across programs with different designs and in different contexts.

More specifically, outreach may be diminished by higher interest rates, larger minimum loan sizes, more-demanding lending terms and behavioral conditions, more stringent creditworthiness tests, and the offer of fewer nonfinancial services. Outreach may also be inhibited by remoteness, caste- or gender-based restrictions on potential clients' business activities, and levels of education, health, and business experience in the local population. This implies the importance of case-by-case empirical assessment of microcredit program outreach.

21.2B Direct effects on well-being

Possible impacts

The aim of many microcredit programs is to raise participants' income and well-being sustainably by helping them to start or expand small businesses. Economic models of household choices in Chapters 6, 7, and 10 suggest that the improvements in well-being might manifest themselves in different ways, because participants might use increased income to increase food consumption and nutrition, to purchase durable consumer goods, to pay for home improvements, or to undertake additional saving and investment. If the businesses generating the income are operated by women, it is possible—though not guaranteed—that the new income will increase their voice over how their households spend resources. Increases in income may be counterbalanced to some extent by longer work hours.

If clients borrow for reasons other than business investment, the impacts can take different forms. Participants might use microloans to replace borrowing from moneylenders at higher interest rates, in which case participation increases their disposable income simply by reducing their interest payments. They might use microloans to obtain otherwise unattainable health care, in which case they might avoid disability, illness-induced job loss, or even the death of a household member. If they use a loan to finance payment of a daughter's dowry, they might avoid having to sell off livestock.

Regardless of how borrowers use the credit, the impacts on their well-being may be of any size. Participation can even leave borrowers worse off, because business investments are risky. Even when borrowers make well-informed investment choices, they might reap little return because they fall ill or because local demand for what they produce falls. To repay their loans under such circumstances they might have to cut back consumption, sell off assets, or obtain loans from other sources. If they default, they could suffer social ostracism and even retaliation by the group members who were forced to pay off their loans. If borrowers make poorly informed investment decisions, the potential for harm is even greater.

The size and nature of direct impacts are likely to vary with program design. As interest rates rise, borrowers undertaking the same business investments enjoy smaller net increases in income. Longer grace periods between taking out the loan and making the first installment might allow business investments with longer gestation periods and higher returns. If offered fewer nonfinancial services, borrowers might reap lower business profits or lose out on other developmental benefits.

Empirical study of impacts

Obtaining comprehensive and reliable empirical assessments of microcredit program impacts is difficult for many reasons. Here we mention three.

First, as indicated earlier, the direct impacts on participants' well-being can manifest themselves as improvements in diverse living condition indicators. This implies that caution must be exercised when evaluations measure impacts on only a few indicators. For example, an evaluator measuring only impacts on consumption expenditure might incorrectly infer that a program has no impact on well-being, even when households benefited significantly by avoiding a sell-off of assets. Narrow assessments focusing only on business outcomes may be particularly misleading. For example, even if the program helps borrowers start successful businesses, it might have little net impact on income and well-being if borrowers succeed in operating new businesses only by giving up other income-generating activities.

A second complication that affects assessment arises because impacts can evolve over time in diverse ways. If borrowers use credit to finance business investments with very short gestation periods, then participation can raise business income and consumption expenditure almost immediately upon joining the program. If borrowers finance longer-term investments, participation can bring *reduced* consumption during a gestation period lasting from several weeks to several loan cycles, as borrowers make early loan payments out of other income, even when participation will ultimately produce large benefits. Consumption in early months can fall even more if borrowers seek to augment microloans with additional savings so that they can undertake larger investments than are feasible with microcredit alone. (See problem 2.)

After a participant leaves a microcredit program, impacts can continue to evolve over time in diverse ways that matter to evaluators. Participation might allow a borrower to build up long-lived business assets (e.g., by acquiring a sewing machine), raising her income to a new level that she sustains after leaving the program. It might even allow her to graduate to continued business growth financed by borrowing from commercial banks or by reinvestment of profits. On the other hand, she might use loans only for working capital—using each loan to purchase rocks that she breaks and sells over the course of the loan cycle, starting over at the same income and asset level with each loan—and experience only temporary income effects, which soon disappear after she exits the program.

This diversity in possible time paths of impact suggests the need for cautious interpretation when impacts are measured at only one or two time intervals after participants join a program. The end of the first loan cycle or the first year of participation may be too soon to observe much of the program's ultimate impact. And even if evaluators happen to observe peak impact, they might draw incorrect conclusions about the value of the program because they do not know whether that impact will be sustained.

A third complication arises because impacts are likely to differ across households that use loans for different purposes, that begin with different initial income or asset levels, or that have differing degrees of luck with risky investments. This implies that estimating only a program's *average* impact can obscure important features of the program's consequences. For example, average income might rise significantly because a few participants achieve great business success, even while *most* participants gain little. Indeed, average impacts may be positive and substantial, even while some households are seriously hurt—an outcome of importance to social actors seeking to "do no harm." Thorough evaluations would examine not only overall average impacts but also the percentages of participants who gain much, gain little, or are harmed, and the way average impacts vary across borrowers of different types.

In summary,

> Ideal assessments of a microcredit program's direct impact would illuminate how participation affects multiple dimensions of living conditions, how these impacts evolve over time, and how the nature, size, and evolution of impacts differ across borrowers.

In practice, even high-quality assessments illuminate impacts on only some household-level indicators and at only one or two points in the evolution of impact, and they can fail to provide precise estimates of how impacts vary across borrowers. Caution must therefore be exercised when interpreting results.

21.2C Spillover and feedback effects

Spillovers through markets for goods, services, and labor

Microcredit programs can reduce poverty indirectly as participants alter their supplies or demands in markets for goods, services, and labor. Microentrepreneurs can improve poor villagers' access to telecommunication services by selling time on cell phones, or they can improve job opportunities by hiring additional workers to help them in production of handicrafts or meals. Evidence to date has revealed few cases of significant employment creation by microcredit clients, however.

Spillover effects on other potential lenders

New microcredit programs may also induce spillover effects through their impacts on other lenders. If, before a new microcredit program was created, moneylenders or other MFIs lacked competition and were charging interest rates above the competitive level, then the new program might benefit clients of all local lenders by introducing competition that drives down interest rates. (Under those circumstances, the program's net effect on the total volume of borrowing in the community may be smaller than the volume of loans distributed by the program, because some of the program's loans might merely crowd out loans from other local lenders.) Unfortunately, a new microcredit program might instead increase other lenders' costs by increasing the difficulty of assessing whether potential borrowers are already deeply indebted and by making it easier for borrowers to default without losing access to future credit.

Other spillovers

Many MFIs hope to generate broader economic and social benefits by introducing new role models for women and girls, encouraging better hygiene and nutrition, or encouraging cooperation in overcoming local barriers to development.

21.2D Microlending costs and financial sustainability

Microcredit program costs

Lending is a costly activity. From Chapter 10 we know that the costs of lending include the cost of funds, supervision costs, and costs associated with default. The cost of funds is the return lenders must pay to deposit holders or investors for the use of their funds. Supervision costs include the costs of all the people, buildings, vehicles, and equipment used in recruiting clients, assessing creditworthiness, helping clients understand loan terms, and collecting payments. Default costs include the principal and interest unpaid when borrowers run into payment difficulties. In addition to all these costs of lending, microcredit programs incur the costs of providing any nonfinancial services and of performing means tests. We will use the term **operating costs** to refer to the total of all these costs.

We have reason to suspect that:

> Operating costs, per peso of loans provided, tend to be greater for poorer borrowers than for less poor borrowers, for MFIs offering nonfinancial services (as well as credit) relative to those that do not, for MFIs with for-profit rather than nonprofit status, and for formal, regulated MFIs than for other MFIs. Operating costs might also depend in important ways on contextual factors such as population density, borrowers' access to communication technologies, and local levels of financial literacy.

The costs of administering the smaller loans that poorer borrowers typically demand are greater on a per-peso (of lending) basis, because many supervision costs are largely fixed on a per-borrower basis. Populations' remoteness, illiteracy, innumeracy, geographic dispersion, and lack of familiarity with loan concepts tend to increase supervision costs. While holding constant all of these conditions, operating costs rise when MFIs offer more services because service provision is costly. Operating costs may be higher for for-profit MFIs than nonprofits as the result of higher tax liabilities, and they may be higher for formal regulated institutions than for other MFIs as the result of more stringent regulations on operation and reporting standards.

Sustainability

For financial sustainability, an MFI's revenue from interest and fee payments must be at least as great as its operating costs.[6] MFIs with higher ratios of revenue to operating costs are said to be more sustainable, and any excess of revenue over operating costs is referred to as **profit**. This is a liberal definition of profit, because MFIs often enjoy a cost of funds well below the market rate for borrowed funds: They might continue to use donated capital, on which they pay little or no interest, or they might borrow from social investors, who accept below-market interest rates. They might also benefit from the tax breaks associated with nonprofit status.

To achieve commercialization, MFIs must pursue a more rigorous standard of profitability. Their revenue must be high enough that it would exceed their operating cost, even if they had to provide investors with competitive returns for all capital and even if they had to pay taxes at for-profit rates. An MFI that is profitable at this level could continue operating without the involvement of socially minded donors or investors, and it could expand by obtaining capital in commercial capital markets (Cull et al., 2009). MFIs that do not meet this more rigorous standard of profitability are **subsidized**, and the total volume of **subsidy** they employ is the difference between their total adjusted operating costs (calculated using the market cost of funds and for-profit tax rates) and their revenue. Many enjoy only the small subsidies implicitly provided by social investors who accept below-market rates for the use of their funds. More heavily subsidized MFIs require ongoing donor grants even to cover the basic costs of supervising loans and providing nonfinancial services.

Because the costs of lending to poorer borrowers tend to be higher:

> The interest rates that lenders must charge to achieve profitability tend to be higher for poorer borrowers. Unfortunately, there is no guarantee that borrowers at a particular level of poverty are willing to pay interest rates high enough to cover the cost of lending to them. It might, therefore, be impossible to lend profitably to the poorest potential borrowers.

---

[6] Often MFIs exclude the costs of providing nonfinancial services from their cost calculations when assessing financial sustainability. We include them here because we are aiming to identify the total subsidy that underlies the impact of entire microcredit programs (including financial and nonfinancial elements).

Costs and lending technologies

Prior to the advent of microcredit programs, commercial banks tended not to lend to poor or near-poor households. This suggests that they could not profitably lend to such borrowers, being unable to charge interest rates high enough to cover the costs. If this is true, then MFIs' hope of lending profitably to those same poor populations must rest on the use of new technologies that are superior to those of commercial banks. Just as new agricultural technologies allow farmers to produce given quantities of wheat at lower cost, so new lending technologies might allow MFIs to provide given quantities of credit services to given populations at lower cost. While new agricultural technologies might involve new packages of seeds, fertilizers, and cultivation practices, new **lending technologies** might involve new loan product designs, new ways of training and motivating loan officers, and new ways of organizing interactions between loan officers and clients. New lending technologies reduce lending costs when they reduce default rates without raising supervision costs or reduce supervision costs without increasing default rates.

Several features of MFI lending technologies are considered especially important for allowing them to serve poor borrowers at lower cost than traditional commercial banks. The first innovative feature of microlending technologies to attract the attention of academic economists and development practitioners was the use of group liability lending. Beginning in the early 1980s, academic economists argued that by holding groups jointly liable, MFIs shifted some of the burden of screening and supervising clients from loan officers onto group members, thereby economizing on loan officers' time while achieving very high repayment rates (see Ghatak and Guinnane, 1999). When a group member knows that she is liable for other group members' repayments, she should be motivated to accept only good credit risks into her group and to provide any assistance and pressure necessary to guarantee that other members make their payments. Group members' social and economic ties can also give them greater scope (than loan officers have) to punish one another for making poor choices. More positively, if one group member runs into a temporary cash shortage, jointly liable group members might have an incentive to provide her with short-term loans, allowing the group to remain in good standing.

Although joint liability can help reduce lending costs in some circumstances, many academics and practitioners no longer view it as the essential and complete explanation for MFI successes. A growing number of MFIs (including now the Grameen Bank) offer individual liability loans with comparably high repayment rates.

A second innovative practice that can reduce screening and monitoring costs is the practice of starting borrowers with very small loans and offering them a sequence of loans of increasing size, each conditional on timely repayment of previous loans. This practice is thought to provide borrowers with **dynamic incentives** for repayment. Borrowers expecting to reap larger benefits from larger loans in the future have reason to repay their current loans, even when this is difficult, because they do not wish to lose access to future benefits. An experiment reviewed in Box 10.2 offered support for the hypothesis that dynamic incentives improve repayment rates.

A third practice that can reduce default rates on lending to poor borrowers is requiring borrowers to begin repaying their loans only one or two weeks after loans are disbursed. This practice can help reduce lending costs if investment projects that are larger and have longer gestation periods also tend to be more risky. Knowing that payments will be required very soon, some potential borrowers facing only risky investments with large setup costs might choose not to borrow, and borrowers facing multiple investment options might choose projects that have shorter gestation periods and are also safer. This could reduce the time loan officers must spend evaluating borrowers' investment plans, though it also increases the frequency with which they must meet with clients. Requiring borrowers to begin weekly payments soon after loan disbursement can also help borrowers develop habits of thrift and money management that improve their payment performance. On the other hand, it can also reduce the benefits they derive from microcredit by restricting their investment options.

Two more mundane features of microlending technologies can help reduce lending costs. First, even when borrowers are not jointly liable, they often make loan payments at weekly group meetings. This allows loan officers to meet with many borrowers at one time in a single location. Second, the use of loan payment sizes that are constant over the life of a loan, and the requirement that the leaders of borrowing groups collect members' loan payments and deliver a single group payment to the loan officer, reduce the time and skill required for bookkeeping by loan officers.

All these innovations probably reduce the cost of lending to poor borrowers, but they do not reduce the costs to levels that are low in absolute terms. Recruiting clients in dispersed locations and meeting with them weekly are personnel-intensive activities; thus microlending costs are high, despite low default rates. As reported in Chapter 10, MFIs' lending costs are often on the order of 20 percent per year.

Debate continues over which features of microcredit lending technologies are most essential for guaranteeing high repayment rates. In MFIs' pursuit of further cost-reducing technical change, they continue to experiment with program design changes. We examine some of these in section 21.3B.

Sustainability and poverty reduction

Many MFIs charge interest rates higher than those typically charged by commercial banks, and use innovative lending technologies, but nonetheless fail to cover costs or earn only profits that are too low to attract and retain commercial investors (Cull et al., 2009). For reasons we discuss below:

> Many MFIs feel pressure to increase their financial sustainability. They can attempt to do this in two ways, with very different implications for outreach and impact.

A first route to increasing sustainability is through modifications to lending technologies that leave the credit services at least as attractive to borrowers as before but somehow economize on loan officers' time or strengthen borrowers' repayment incentives. For example, requiring biweekly rather than weekly meetings might reduce per-borrower and per-peso supervision costs by expanding the number of clients that a single loan officer can serve. If MFIs could make this change without raising default rates, then they could offer loans that are at least as attractive as before the change, while reducing lending costs. Other approaches to efficiency gains might involve alterations in loan officer hiring standards, training, or supervision.

A second route to increasing sustainability is through changes in loan product and program designs that render program services less attractive. In their efforts to increase sustainability, MFIs can (and often do) raise interest rates, increase minimum loan sizes, offer harsher responses to payment difficulties, or eliminate nonfinancial services. Such attempts to improve sustainability are not foolproof. For example, while an increase in interest rate certainly increases the revenue collected on any loans fully repaid, it can also increase the default rate enough to reduce total revenue (see the discussions of adverse selection and moral hazard in Chapter 10). Similarly, eliminating nonfinancial business-development services certainly reduces nonfinancial program costs but can also increase default rates by reducing the profitability of borrowers' businesses.

Even when innovations of this second type increase financial sustainability, they can have the unfortunate consequence of reducing program outreach and impact among the poor. We return to a discussion of this potential tradeoff below.

Microfinance institutions' setup costs

Microcredit program costs have a natural tendency to fall over the first few years of an MFI's existence. When they first open, MFIs must recruit borrowers for every new loan they issue and provide only loans of smallest size. Over time, as they retain incumbent borrowers, per-loan recruitment costs fall and loan sizes rise, tending to reduce supervision costs on a per-peso (of lending) basis. Early experimentation may also be useful for adapting a lending technology to local context. These processes help explain a tendency for MFIs to require more subsidy in their first several years of existence than in later years. We might think of the excess costs in the early years as a kind of fixed cost of setting up a new MFI.

21.2E Rationales for intervention in microcredit

If an MFI uses no subsidy at any stage of operation, then its activities are similar to those of any other private-sector, for-profit producer of goods or services. It uses up none of the scarce resources that governments, NGOs, or other social actors might devote to improving development outcomes. It embodies no policy intervention and requires no rationale for intervention to justify its existence.

This does not guarantee that fully profitable MFIs supply credit services in socially ideal fashion. If an MFI lacks competition, it might charge interest rates greater than the social ideal. In addition, if potential borrowers lack the capacity for accurate assessment of borrowing opportunities, and especially if loan officers have incentives to encourage too much borrowing, then policymakers might wish to impose transparency requirements or other customer protections.

Microcredit programs that are subsidized, by contrast, do constitute policy interventions, and the subsidies they require have greatest potential to improve development outcomes if the programs are well-designed responses to market or institutional failures (from the list discussed in Chapter 13). The most obvious possible rationale for subsidizing microcredit has to do with poverty reduction. Social actors might wish to raise the well-being of poor clients by a significant amount, even if this requires them to charge interest rates well below cost. They might consider microcredit a particularly attractive vehicle for channeling transfers to the poor because it requires beneficiaries to participate in their own advancement. This suggests that subsidies for microcredit may be well justified if they allow MFIs to reach poorer clients, or provide larger benefits to poor borrowers, than would be possible without subsidy.

A more subtle possible rationale for subsidizing microcredit relates to liquidity constraints. Some households may be prevented by liquidity constraints from undertaking high-return investments, even while the economy's loanable funds are used to finance lower-return projects. If this is true, then subsidization of lending to liquidity-constrained investors might redirect loanable funds from investments with lower to higher returns, increasing the efficiency of investment and the rate of economic growth. Subsidization of microcredit might also relax liquidity constraints on other highly valuable household activities, such as meeting critical needs for health care or smoothing consumption in the face of income fluctuations. Liquidity constraints might therefore help justify subsidization of microcredit, but only if the subsidies help channel financing to especially high-return uses.[7]

Even MFIs that ultimately achieve sustainability often enjoy significant subsidization by donors in early years. Donors probably provide such subsidies to "infant" MFIs in the expectation of establishing sustainable institutions for reducing poverty, pursuing other social objectives, or relaxing liquidity constraints. Such subsidies are well motivated only if the infant MFIs go on to generate significant social benefits after achieving sustainability. Thus, policymakers might have

---

[7] If the new technology developed through an MFI's costly experimentation is a public good, then policymakers may be able to improve development outcomes by subsidizing such experimentation. (See Chapter 20's discussion of rationales for intervention in agricultural research.) This might take the form of providing temporary subsidies to pioneering MFIs entering new geographic regions or attempting to reach new borrower types. Such subsidies are well motivated, however, only if the technologies developed by pioneers are easily replicated and quickly put to profitable use (without subsidies) by competitors.

reasons for interest in estimating the social impact of mature MFIs, even after they have become fully profitable.

All this suggests that:

> Policymakers may be able to improve development outcomes by regulating microcredit activities, if microcredit markets lack competition or potential borrowers are unable to accurately assess the benefits and costs of borrowing. Policymakers may also be able to improve development outcomes by providing either one-time subsidies for microcredit program setup costs or ongoing subsidies to microcredit operations, if subsidies allow microcredit programs to reach poorer clients, achieve greater improvement in well-being among poor borrowers, or help liquidity-constrained borrowers to undertake investments with particularly high social returns.

21.3 Evaluation and Design of Microcredit Programs

21.3A Evaluation of microcredit programs

Box 21.3 summarizes many of the empirical questions raised earlier, by adapting Chapter 14's seven questions for study of microcredit programs. The questions emphasize that comprehensive microcredit program evaluations must examine outreach and impact as well as financial sustainability and must pay careful attention to the multidimensional nature of impacts, the evolution of impacts over time, and the heterogeneity of impacts across borrowers of different types.

≡ **Box 21.3** Questions to Guide Analysis of Microcredit Programs

Question 1: Objectives

Is the program intended primarily to reduce poverty, achieve other social objectives, or generate profits for investors? If the aim is poverty reduction, does the program target primarily the moderately poor, the very poor, or households above official poverty lines?

Question 2: Design

What loan terms, behavioral conditions, nonfinancial services, recruitment practices, eligibility and creditworthiness criteria, formal institutional structures, personnel practices, and other governance structure choices define the program on paper?

Question 3: Implementation

What capacity, motivation, and oversight (as defined in Chapter 13) do loan officers bring to their work? What loan terms, recruitment, eligibility assessment, and creditworthiness testing practices define the program in practice? What behavioral conditions are enforced? How efficiently are the credit services provided? What type and quality of nonfinancial services are provided?

Question 4: Directly affected groups

Who joins the program in a given year? How many participants continue from previous years? Among those who join and those who continue, how many are near poor, poor, and very poor? What is the average depth of poverty represented among borrowers and how poor are the poorest participants? What fraction of the target poor population is covered by the program?

Question 5: Direct effects

What are the average effects of participation on households' consumption expenditure, time allocation, asset holdings, and intrahousehold distribution, evaluated one loan cycle, one year, and several years after joining? How likely are these impacts to persist? How do these patterns of impact differ across households with different initial asset and income levels? How many participants experience large or modest improvements in well-being, and how many are made worse off? What are the program's impacts on behaviors targeted by the program's nonfinancial services? What are the effects on microenterprise output supplies and demands for labor and inputs?

Question 6: Spillover and feedback effects

What effects do the behavioral responses of participants have on markets for goods, services, and labor? To what extent does this program crowd out, or alter the costs of, credit services provided by moneylenders or other MFIs? To what extent does the program provide nonparticipants with new role models, new information, or new propensity for cooperation or conflict?

Question 7: Budgetary costs

How much subsidy is required annually to sustain the array of impacts revealed by the previous questions? How much subsidy was required in earlier years to bring the MFI to its current level of efficiency and efficacy?

The handful of rigorous impact assessments undertaken to date do not permit broad generalizations regarding microcredit outreach, impact, and profitability. The programs they examine are diverse, but they are far from representative of the entire microcredit sector. Most of the assessments also focus on estimating direct impacts on participants, having less to say about outreach, spillover effects, and profitability. The studies have nonetheless produced some intriguing results. In what follows we briefly review the results of several seminal studies.

Coleman (2006) studied the impacts of two MFIs in Thailand that provide group liability loans starting at $60 to women in village banks of 20 to 60 members. In principle, the MFIs targeted the poorest of the poor, but in practice they largely left formation of village banks up to community leaders. Coleman constructed credible impact estimates by comparing participating households to a set of households that should have been very similar in every way, except that they had not yet received program services. The comparison households were located in communities that were soon to receive program intervention (suggesting that the NGOs considered them very similar to the communities already participating), and the comparison households had already declared their intention to participate in the program (suggesting that they were very similar in personality and circumstances to the households that were already participating).

The results were rather dismaying. Better-off village women were more likely to participate than poorer women, who sometimes were excluded against their will and who sometimes thought that the village bank was "for rich people." Wealthier members obtained more credit than poorer members by fraudulently obtaining credit under multiple names. Participation had no discernable impact on the well-being of rank and file village bank members, though it raised business income and assets for the village banks' officers. The concentration of benefits among better-off households is disappointing, but the impacts nonetheless support the hypothesis that some households are liquidity constrained and that microcredit programs have the potential to encourage business investment by relaxing liquidity constraints.

Karlan and Zinman (2010) studied a South African MFI offering four-month consumer loans at an annual interest rate of 200 percent to urban wage employees. Marginal potential borrowers, whose scores on the MFI's creditworthiness rating scale were just below the usual cutoff for lending, were randomly assigned to treatment and control groups. Six to twelve months after loan disbursement, treated households exhibited higher food consumption and somewhat higher subjective measures of well-being, suggesting that even high-priced short-term loans to wage-earning households have the potential to improve the well-being of some borrowers. But the impact results are incomplete and mixed. Borrowers reported more stress and more symptoms of depression. The authors rule out negative *average* impacts on food consumption, but they do not examine whether food consumption might have declined for some borrowers at the lower end of the impact distribution, and they did not assess impacts on total consumption expenditure or assets.

Box 21.4 describes a final randomized control trial, Banerjee et al. (2010), in more detail. The studies reviewed here offer some compelling (though partial) assessments of direct impacts, but they have little to say about the potential outreach of microcredit programs among the poor or whether microcredit harms some clients.

21.3B Financial sustainability, commercialization, and poverty impact

According to the Consultative Group to Assist the Poor (CGAP), "best practice" in microcredit is to use subsidies as little as possible and only during the start-up years, and to push for sustainability, if not commercialization. They encourage MFIs to take any measures necessary to achieve profitability. In fact, one document on the consortium's website teaches MFIs to calculate how much they must raise their interest rates to achieve sustainability (Rosenberg, 2002).

≡ **Box 21.4** The Impact of Opening of New Branches by the MFI Spandana in Hyderabad, India

Spandana is an Indian NGO that provides joint liability loans to groups of 6 to 10 women at annual interest rates of approximately 20 percent. Borrowers must be women between 18 and 59 years of age who have resided in the same area for one year and have valid ID and proof of residence. At least 80 percent of borrowers in any group must own their own homes. Borrowers form their own groups, must repay loans in 50 weekly installments, and are not required to undertake business investments. Spandana loan officers do not evaluate women's loan-use plans. The minimum loan size is Rs10,000, which is equivalent to $200 using market exchange rates and $1,000 using purchasing power parity exchange rates.

In 2005, when Spandana was about to expand operations within the large city of Hyderabad, Abijit Banerjee and coauthors (2010) worked with the organization to rigorously evaluate the impact of opening new Spandana branches. Spandana identified 104 neighborhoods of interest, where households are "poor but not the poorest." Residents live in concrete houses with some public services. Many of their incomes are well above the $2 per day poverty line, and school enrollment rates are high. Spandana and the research team sorted the 104 neighborhoods into pairs with similar characteristics and randomly selected one neighborhood from each pair for treatment. A baseline survey collected in 2005 confirmed that the distributions of household characteristics were very similar in treatment and control groups and that very few households were borrowing from MFIs at that time. Spandana then proceeded to open branches in the treatment communities.

The researchers returned in 2007 to undertake a follow-up survey in two steps. First, they conducted a census of all households in the study neighborhoods. Second, using the census as their sample frame, they drew random samples of households that had been in the area for at least three years and contained women 18 to 55 years old. They then conducted interviews for over 6,800 households between August of 2007 and April of 2008.

Because randomization was performed at the level of entire neighborhoods, the study is most obviously suited for delivering unbiased estimates of the impact of Spandana branch opening on entire neighborhoods (rather than on Spandana borrowers alone). Other MFIs entered both treatment and control communities over the study period, but the fraction of households borrowing from MFIs rose to 27 percent in treatment communities while rising to only 18.7 percent in control communities. The neighborhood-level impacts must be understood as arising out of the extension of credit to the extra 8.3 percent of households.

The opening of a Spandana branch raised the share of a neighborhood's households starting businesses during the previous year by 1.7 percentage points, implying that about one in five Spandana loans led to the creation of a new business. Other Spandana loans were used for investment in existing businesses and for other purposes.

Recognizing that impacts may be heterogeneous, the authors examined impacts for three groups. Households in the first group already owned businesses one year before the final household survey and were assumed to have owned businesses before borrowing from Spandana. The second and third groups of households did not own

businesses one year earlier and were classified as either likely or unlikely to open a business during the intervening year. To measure households' likelihood of opening a business, the authors first used control sample data to estimate the relationship between households' characteristics and their probabilities of opening businesses during the year. Using the estimated coefficients from this relationship, together with data on household characteristics, they then calculated predicted business-opening probabilities for all households in treatment and control samples. Households with predicted probabilities above the 75th percentile were classified as likely to open businesses. Before treatment, the incomes of households who already owned businesses and of those who were likely to open them were higher by about 10 percent relative to the incomes of those unlikely to open businesses.

The impact estimates suggest that participants use Spandana credit for diverse purposes and that potential entrepreneurs face large fixed costs of setting up new businesses. Households in all three groups were equally likely to borrow from Spandana (with uptake rates of just 8 to 10 percent) but exhibited quite different impacts 15 to 18 months after branch opening. The borrowers who already owned businesses increased spending on durable goods (including durable goods for use in business) and maintained nondurable consumer spending. The borrowers who did not have businesses and were likely to start them increased spending on durables even more, and they *reduced* nondurable consumer spending, with especially large reductions in their consumption of temptation goods such as tobacco and alcohol. The borrowers who did not have businesses and were unlikely to start them, by contrast, increased nondurable consumer spending while exhibiting no increase in durables spending.

These patterns are consistent with the hypothesis that owners of pre-existing businesses find Spandana loans useful for carrying out small expansions of their businesses, which are feasible without additional saving on their part, while potential entrepreneurs who wish to start new businesses must supplement Spandana loans with additional saving during a significant gestation period. Both of these groups might enjoy consumption gains in the future as their investments mature, though such gains can only be conjectured on the basis of the study data. The results are also consistent with little program impact on business investment among the households that did not own businesses and were unlikely to start them. They might have used loans to increase consumption without undertaking measures to increase income; thus their consumption gains might be short-lived. Alternatively, they might have used Spandana loans to pay off debt at higher interest rates; this would have increased their incomes net of loan payments during their Spandana participation and might have generated longer-term impacts if it allowed them to work their way out of perpetual debt.

The results thus suggest significant but modest microcredit impacts on business investment in this context, but they leave open the question of whether and how much these investments will raise well-being in the future. They also suggest that many microloans are not used for business investment. The authors failed to find short-term impacts on measures of school enrollment or women's empowerment.

Many development organizations participating in CGAP see sustainability and commercialization as worthy goals, because they hope to bring financial services to the world's many unbanked poor households and they see commercialization as the only route to achieving this. They argue that the poor are willing to pay cost-covering interest rates, whatever those rates might be, and that the real constraint on outreach is the limited quantity of donor funding for micro-credit. Only by freeing themselves from the need for donor funds, and financing expansion by borrowing from commercial banks, attracting equity investments in commercial markets, or collecting deposits, can MFIs reach the several billion people they assume would wish to borrow on their terms.

The theoretical discussion in section 21.2 offered reasons to question many of the assumptions underlying this view. (For more on these assumptions, see Morduch, 2000.) For example, we must question whether all the world's poor would indeed demand credit at interest rates that cover the cost of lending to them. We might worry especially that raising interest rates and taking other measures to increase profitability would cause MFIs' poorest potential borrowers to refrain from participating.

Empirical study of the tradeoff between outreach and profitability is difficult, because few MFIs make sufficient financial information publicly available, and even fewer collect high-quality data on outreach. Comparisons of outreach and profitability across MFIs are also complicated by the great diversity in program design and context.

Evidence available to date suggests five tentative conclusions, though additional research is warranted. Many of these conclusions are supported by evidence reported in Cull et al. (2009). The authors employ data gathered by the nonprofit Microfinance Information Exchange on 346 MFIs. Their sample of MFIs is not randomly drawn from the entire population of MFIs, but it is useful for studying sustainability concerns, because it contains MFIs for whom sustainability objectives are particularly important. The sample includes MFIs that are nonprofit NGOs, non-bank financial institutions (which may be nonprofit or for-profit), and full commercial banks (most of which are for-profit).

A first tentative conclusion is that microcredit programs can reach at least moderately poor households while achieving financial sustainability. Most MFIs began with subsidy, but many MFIs in the sample—even nonprofit NGOs—have achieved financial sustainability. In the Cull et al. data, 57 percent of all MFIs and 54 percent of NGOs are financially sustainable. Where data are available (not reported specifically in Cull et al., 2009), they suggest that microcredit clients are poor by developed country standards, though they are not all officially poor by developing country standards.

Second, sustainable MFIs probably do not reach many households among the poorest of the poor, and many of their borrowers probably have incomes significantly above the $2.00 per day poverty line. Sustainable microfinance seems to reach farther below the poverty line in Asia than in other regions, however.

Third, a unique study for Indonesia provides strong reason to doubt that sustainable microcredit would reach most poor households, even if it could expand without limit using commercial capital. Johnston and Morduch (2008) studied a random sample of 1,438 households that are representative of the Indonesian population. Their enumerators were loan officers of an MFI well known for reaching many poor households while earning profits. They were therefore able to assess the creditworthiness of each household in the sample, whether borrower or not, according to the standards of an efficient, sustainable MFI. Using carefully worded questions, they also measured the sizes of loans that households would request if they were to borrow. The study found that among poor households, only 38 percent met the creditworthiness test. Of the creditworthy poor, moreover, 48 percent would want loans of less than $210, which is the breakeven loan size, below which the MFI believes it cannot lend profitably. Thus, only 22 percent of poor households were deemed creditworthy *and* likely to demand loans large enough to be provided profitably. Even among these 22 percent, it is unclear how many would indeed choose to take on debt if offered a loan of the desired size. In practice, only 7.5 percent of poor households borrow from any MFI or bank.

Fourth, it appears difficult for MFIs to increase financial sustainability without moving up market to households that are less poor. Although the Cull et al. (2009) dataset offers no direct measures of borrowers' incomes, it includes several indicators that are thought closely correlated with outreach among poorer households and strength of social missions: average loan size, percentage of loans made to women, percentage of loans made in rural areas, and percentage of loans offered under group rather than individual liability. In their sample, commercial banks are more likely than NGOs to be profitable (87 percent versus 57 percent), enjoy larger typical profits, and appear to lend to a significantly better-off clientele. Their average loans sizes are four times as large as NGOs' average loan sizes, when measured as percentages of income at the 20th percentile of the country's income distribution (224 percent versus 48 percent). Fewer of their loans are to women or in rural areas, and more require individual rather than group liability.

Frequent expressions of concern by MFI practitioners about *mission drift* also suggest that in practice donor pressure to achieve sustainability leads them to increase interest rates, increase minimum loan sizes, increase the share of lending in more prosperous and urban locations, and make other changes that tend to increase the average income of borrowing households. One such anecdote is found in the conclusion to the Shaw (2004) study discussed in Box 21.2. Dehejia et al. (2012) offer more rigorous analysis of a natural experiment in which an MFI raised its interest rates in some neighborhoods but not others. The increase indeed caused some of the poorest borrowers to drop out.

Fifth, although subsidies probably allow MFIs to achieve greater impacts on poverty and other social objectives, too little is known about the magnitudes of these effects. Allocating subsidies to microcredit programs is a wise use of scarce donor funds only if the array of impacts generated by each dollar of subsidy is more desirable when used to subsidize microcredit than when used to subsidize other poverty-reducing interventions. For the incapacitated poor, targeted transfer programs might generate better impacts per dollar of subsidy than subsidized microcredit programs. For the remote poor, subsidization of road construction, road maintenance, or electrification might put subsidies to better use than subsidized microcredit programs. In more urban contexts, subsidizing credit for medium-scale enterprises might prove more useful for poverty reduction (via employment creation) than subsidizing credit for microenterprises. Further research is warranted.

21.3C Microcredit program design changes

MFIs would like to increase sustainability, outreach, or impact without sacrificing performance in any of these areas. Several recent randomized control trials examine design changes that might yield such improvements. For broader reviews of design change studies, see Karlan and Morduch (2010) and Bauchet et al. (2011). Here we describe three.

Individual versus group liability

Gine and Karlan (2011) worked with the Green Bank of Caraga in the rural Philippines to examine the effects of shifting from group to individual liability. The bank forms centers of 15 to 30 borrowers, divided into groups of five, and allows them to grow over time without limit. Borrowers are jointly liable at two levels: They must pay off the loans of any group members who do not make full payment, and they must pay off the loans of any other groups in their center who do not make full payment. In a first experiment, the researchers eliminated group liability for members of pre-existing groups that were formed under group liability. In a second, they compared the performance of new groups formed under individual and group liability. Borrowers appear to prefer individual liability. In pre-existing groups, the elimination of group liability brought more new members and higher retention rates. Centers opened under individual liability were also larger. Default rates, furthermore, were no higher under individual liability than under group liability. Even so, the shift to individual liability probably reduced profitability by increasing the time loan officers spent on repayment activities. It might also have reduced program outreach for an unanticipated reason: Loan officers were more reluctant to open new centers under individual liability.

Grace period

Typical microcredit arrangements offer only small loans and require borrowers to begin repaying one or two weeks after loan disbursement. If many of the high-return investment opportunities available to poor households are characterized by significant setup costs and gestation periods, then such arrangements can limit outreach and impact by rendering it infeasible to undertake high-return investments with microloans. Introducing a grace period, which increases the number of weeks between loan disbursement and first payment, could, therefore, improve both outreach and impact. Investments with larger fixed costs and longer gestation periods may also be more risky, however, in which case the introduction of a grace period could raise lending costs by raising default rates or increasing the time loan officers must devote to screening borrowers' investment projects.

An experiment reported in Field et al. (2011) appears to confirm that when an MFI introduces a grace period it trades off expanded investment options for borrowers against higher default rates. The authors examined the effect of delaying the first payment—from two weeks after disbursement to two months after disbursement—on individual liability, low-interest one-year loans of $90 to $225, for women with microenterprises in Kolkata, India. Introduction of the grace period allowed borrowers to save less out of their loans to cover first loan payments, and to invest 6 percent more in inventory and raw materials for their businesses. When allowed grace periods, borrowers also extended more credit to customers and provided a wider variety of goods—impacts the authors interpret as increasing business risks. Three years after disbursement, average business profits in the treatment group were 30 percent higher, and household incomes were 17 percent higher, but the variance of profits also increased, and default rates rose from 2 percent in the control to 9 percent in the treatment group.

Weekly versus biweekly payments

Many MFIs insist on weekly meetings because they are thought to reduce default rates by encouraging self-discipline, increasing peer pressure, or helping group members develop the trust required to provide each other with reciprocal assistance in meeting loan payments. Group members often complain about the burden of meeting attendance, however, and loan officers' involvement in such frequent meetings increases lending costs. If MFIs could reduce the frequency of meetings without raising default rates too much, they would be able to improve profitability while also rendering participation more attractive to borrowers.

Feigenberg et al. (2010) randomly assigned borrowing groups in West Bengal, India, to weekly or monthly meetings. Group members received individual liability loans of $100 to be repaid over 46 weeks. Members of groups that met weekly were significantly more likely to have contact with each other outside meetings and to trust that group members would help them out in an emergency. They were also more likely to make transfers to each other. No differences in default rates appeared during the first loan cycle. The authors observed, however, that default rates on first loans are extremely low, and that this might reflect the power of dynamic incentives; borrowers considered the initial loans small and often accepted them with the hope of obtaining larger loans in subsequent cycles. The authors followed study households through a second loan cycle, during which both treatment and control groups met at the same frequency, and found that those who met weekly during the first loan cycle were 8 percentage points less likely to default on their second loans! Rough calculations suggest that the savings on loan officer time associated with the shift from weekly to monthly meetings very nearly equaled the losses from increased default. Whether weekly meetings are preferable to monthly meetings therefore seems to depend on whether the benefits to borrowers of increased ties of friendship and mutual assistance are valuable enough to outweigh the increased time burden of attending more frequent meetings.

21.3D The Shift from credit-led to savings-led microfinance

In recent years, many development practitioners who wish to improve poor households' access to financial services have shifted their focus from microcredit toward microsavings. Many now devote their time and energy to **savings-led microfinance** programs, which encourage the creation of savings groups much like the self-help groups indigenous to India (Ashe, 2009). Such programs help villagers form savings groups, which tend to progress through several stages. At first, group members make mandatory weekly contributions at group meetings, which the group accumulates. After establishing basic discipline and accumulating enough funds, many groups begin to use accumulated funds to offer short-term interest-bearing loans to members. Often the interest rates charged on loans are quite high, allowing the group to pay high rates of interest on members' accumulating deposits. After establishing good records of loan repayment and book-keeping, these savings groups sometimes begin borrowing jointly from commercial banks or MFIs. NGOs often help the groups organize, and train them in basic bookkeeping and thrift practices, and later help them make contact with commercial banks.

Promoters of savings-led microfinance point to several ways microcredit programs have proved disappointing and suggest how savings-led approaches might perform better. First, many poor households—especially among the poorest—either do not wish to join microcredit programs or would not pass creditworthiness tests. The poorest households seem not to face investment opportunities with returns that would allow them to pay credit back at high interest rates, and even many less-poor households prefer not to go into debt, regardless of whether they could undertake sufficiently profitable investments. Access to safe, interest-paying savings instruments may be of broader interest among the poor, and by choosing very small mandatory weekly savings contributions, savings groups can be tailored to use by very poor households.

Second, because they require borrowers to take on significant risks, microcredit programs have the potential to increase households' apprehensions about the future and to do harm when risky investments do not work out. Savings groups, by contrast, are likely to reduce vulnerability by encouraging households to accumulate savings, which they can use for buying health care when hit by illness or for sustaining consumption when faced with temporary income loss.

Third, in some cases microcredit programs absorb significant subsidies in their early years, even when they eventually became financially sustainable, and achieving financial sustainability is a struggle. Writing about the experience of Catholic Relief Services (CRS), Wilson (2002) estimated that the subsidies required by some MFI partners before they achieved financial sustainability amounted to as much as $150 to $300 per client. The costs of promoting formation of savings groups are more naturally limited because they include only the costs of encouraging group formation and training groups. Groups handle financial transactions entirely on their own, requiring no ongoing subsidization. Wilson estimates that the cost of assisting a savings group until it becomes self-sustaining works out to about $6 to $12 per member.

Wilson (2002) articulates a fourth difference between NGO involvement in microcredit programs and savings-led microfinance programs, which illuminates a governance dilemma inherent to the pursuit of social objectives through the provision of microcredit. As she puts it, microcredit programs ask "bankers to become social workers or social workers to become bankers." Again writing about the experiences of Catholic Relief Services (an NGO that decided to divest itself of its many microcredit activities in 2005), she describes how their grassroots partners and local staff often found that excellence in fulfilling their duties as loan officers diminished their effectiveness in their other relief and development roles. For example, as loan officers working for profit-seeking MFIs, they were required to concentrate attention on locations with access to markets rather than on more remote locations, where the neediest households lived. Local staff also regretted how their role as loan collectors reduced clients' willingness to discuss needs with them and caused them to be seen as enemies rather than allies.

Savings-led microfinance programs, by contrast, require diverse actors to carry out more natural tasks. NGO staff and partners undertake promotion and training activities rather than loan officer duties. If groups grow to the point at which they wish to obtain credit from outside, the credit services they obtain are provided by commercial banks or other specialized financial institutions.

The discussion thus far suggests that when an NGO shifts funds from supporting micro-credit programs to supporting savings-led microfinance programs, it may enjoy the benefits of reaching poorer households, reducing vulnerability rather than increasing it, reaching a larger number of households per budget dollar, and creating a better institutional platform for delivering social and development services. But what is the cost? The typical impact per household might be much smaller and might develop much more slowly with savings-led microfinance than with microcredit. When groups of very poor women save pennies per week, their capacity to provide loans of helpful size may remain very limited for a long time. While microcredit programs bring loanable funds into poor communities from outside, savings groups merely encourage the flow of loanable funds from savers to borrowers within communities. In poor communities, the volumes of funding involved can remain far too small to finance high-return investments, or even to help households weather significant health shocks, for a long time. Before we can fully appreciate the relative merits of the savings-led approach, therefore, we will require rigorous assessments of savings groups' impacts over periods of at least several years.

REFERENCES

Ashe, Jeffrey. "Savings-Led Microfinance and Saving for Change: Low Cost, Mass-Scale, Self-Replicating and Profitable Microfinance for the Rural Poor." Boston: Oxfam America, 2009. http://www.microfinancegateway.org/p/site/m/template.rc/1.9.34515/

Ashraf, Nava, Dean Karlan, and Wesley Yin. "Deposit Collectors." *Advances in Economic Analysis & Policy* 6(2): Article 5, 2006a. http://www.bepress.com/bejeap/advances/vol6/iss2/art5

Ashraf, Nava, Dean Karlan, and Wesley Yin. "Tying Odysseus to the Mast: Evidence From a Commitment Savings Product in the Philippines." *The Quarterly Journal of Economics* 121(2): 635–72, 2006b. doi:10.1162/qjec.2006.121.2.635

Ashta, Arvind, and Marek Hudon. "To Whom Should We be Fair? Ethical Issues in Balancing Stakeholder Interests from Banco Compartamos Case Study." Centre Emile Bernheim (CEB) Working Paper No. 09/036. Brussels: Université Libre de Bruxelles, 2009. http://www.microfinancegateway.org/p/site/m/template.rc/1.9.39319/

Banerjee, Abhijit V., Esther Duflo, Rachel Glennerster, and Cynthia Kinnan. "The Miracle of Microfinance? Evidence From a Randomized Evaluation." Working Paper, 2010. http://econ-www.mit.edu/files/6093

Bauchet, Jonathan, Cristobal Marshall, Laura Starita, Jeanette Thomas, and Anna Yalouris. "Latest Findings From Randomized Evaluations of Microfinance." Access to Finance Form: Reports by CGAP and Its Partners. Washington, D.C.: Consultative Group to Assist the Poor (CGAP)/World Bank, 2011. http://www.cgap.org/gm/document-1.9.55766/FORUM2.pdf

Bauer, Michal, Julie Chytilová, and Jonathan Morduch. "Behavioral Foundations of Microcredit: Experimental and Survey Evidence From Rural India." *American Economic Review* 101(2): 1118–1139, 2012. doi 10.1257/aer.102.2.1118

Coleman, Brett E. "Microfinance in Northeast Thailand: Who Benefits and How Much?" *World Development* 34(9): 1612–1638, 2006. doi:10.1016/j.worlddev.2006.01.006

Consultative Group to Assist the Poor (CGAP). "Microfinance Consensus Guidelines: Definitions of Selected Financial Terms, Ratios, and Adjustments for Microfinance." Washington, D.C.: Consultative Group to Assist the Poor (CGAP)/World Bank, 2003. http://www.cgap.org/gm/document-1.9.2784/Guideline_definitions.pdf

Cull, Robert, Asli Demirgüç-Kunt, and Jonathan Morduch. "Microfinance Meets the Market." *Journal of Economic Perspectives* 23(1): 167–192, 2009. doi:10.1257/jep.23.1.167

Dehejia, Rajeev, Heather Montgomery, and Jonathan Morduch. "Do Interest Rates Matter? Credit Demand in the Dhaka Slums." *Journal of Development Economics* 97(2): 437–449, 2012. doi:10.1016/j.jdeveco.2011.06.001

Dowla, Asif and Dipal Barua. *The Poor Always Pay Back: The Grameen II Story.* Bloomfield, CT: Kumarian Press, 2006.

Dugan, Maggie, and Ruth Goodwin-Groen. "Donors Succeed By Making Themselves Obsolete: Compartamos Taps Financial Markets in Mexico." Case Studies in Donor Good Practices No. 19. Washington, D.C.: Consultative Group to Assist the Poor (CGAP), 2005. www.cgap.org/gm/document-1.9.2295/cs_19.pdf

Feigenberg, Benjamin, Erica M. Field, and Rohini Pande. "Building Social Capital Through Microfinance." NBER Working Paper No. 16018. Cambridge, MA': National Bureau of Economic Research, 2010. http://www.nber.org/papers/w16018

Field, Erica, Rohini Pande, John Papp, and Natalia Rigol. "Term Structure of Debt and Entrepreneurship: Experimental Evidence From Micro-finance," Harvard University, Princeton University and MIT, 2011. http://www.centrobaffi.unibocconi.it/wps/allegatiCTP/repayment_default_may_11_1.pdf

Ghatak, Maitreesh, and Timothy W. Guinnane. "The Economics of Lending With Joint Liability: Theory and Practice." *Journal of Development Economics* 60(1): 195–228, 1999. doi:10.1016/S0304-3878(99)00041-3

Giné, Xavier, and Dean Karlan. "Group Versus Individual Liability: Short and Long Term Evidence From Philippine Microcredit Lending Groups." Working Paper, 2011. http://karlan.yale.edu/p/Group versusIndividualLending.pdf

Gonzalez, Adrian, and Richard Rosenberg. "The State of Microcredit: Outreach, Profitability, and Poverty: Findings From a Database of 2600 Microfinance Institutions." Washington, D.C.: Consultative Group to Assist the Poor (CGAP), 2006. http://www.microfinancegateway.org/gm/document-1.9.26787/25.pdf

Johnston, Don, Jr., and Jonathan Morduch. "The Unbanked: Evidence From Indonesia." *The World Bank Economic Review* 22(3): 517–537, 2008. doi:10.1093/wber/lhn016

Karlan, Dean, and Jonathan Morduch. "Access to Finance." In Dani Rodrik and Mark R. Rosenzweig (eds.). *Handbook of Development Economics*, Volume 5. Amsterdam: Elsevier, 2010, pp. 4703–4784. doi:10.1016/B978-0-444-52944-2.00009-4

Karlan, Dean, and Jonathan Zinman. "Expanding Credit Access: Using Randomized Supply Decisions to Estimate the Impacts." *The Review of Financial Studies* 23(1): 433–464, 2010. doi:10.1093/rfs/hhp092

Maes, Jan P., and Larry R. Reed. *State of the Microcredit Summit Campaign Report 2011.* Washington, D.C.: Microcredit Summit Campaign

(MCS), 2012. http://www.microcreditsummit.org/pubs/reports/socr/2012/WEB_SOCR-2012_English.pdf

MicroFinance Transparency. *Pricing Certification Report: Grameen Bank.* Lancaster, PA: Microfinance Transparency, 2011.

Morduch, Jonathan. "The Microfinance Schism." *World Development* 28 (4): 617–629, 2000. doi:10.1016/S0305-750X(99)00151-5

Partida, Juan M, and Frederic de Mariz. *Banco Compartamos: Market Leadership Sustained by Superior Efficiency.* JP Morgan Chase and Co. 2008. http://www.spanish.microfinancegateway.org/content/article/detail/50430

Rosenberg, Richard. "Microcredit Interest Rates." CGAP Occasional Paper No. 1. Washington, D.C.: Consultative Group to Assist the Poor (CGAP), 2002. http://www.cgap.org/gm/document-1.9.2696/OP1.pdf

Shaw, Judith. "Microenterprise Occupation and Poverty Reduction in Microfinance Programs: Evidence From Sri Lanka." *World Development* 32(7): 1247–1264, 2004. doi:10.1016/j.worlddev.2004.01.009

Wilson, Kim. "The New Microfinance: An Essay on the Self-Help Group Movement in India." *Journal of Microfinance / ESR Review* 4(2): 217–246, 2002. https://ojs.lib.byu.edu/spc/index.php/ESR/issue/view/162

Yunus, Muhammad. *Creating a World Without Poverty: Social Business and the Future of Capitalism.* New York: Public Affairs, 2007.

QUESTIONS FOR REVIEW

1. Describe the range of objectives pursued by microfinance programs.

2. Microfinance programs are highly diverse. Along what design dimensions do they differ?

3. Describe the simple model of borrowing for business investment examined in the text, and discuss its implications for how and why microcredit program participation can vary across households of different types.

4. How might microcredit programs' loan terms, behavioral conditions, nonfinancial services, recruitment procedures, eligibility requirements, and creditworthiness assessment procedures affect program outreach?

5. What dimensions of households' living standards and behavior might be affected by microcredit program participation? How might these impacts come about?

6. How and why might a microcredit program's impacts evolve over time? How might they differ across participants?

7. Discuss the possible spillover effects that a microcredit program might generate through markets for goods, services, and labor; interactions with other potential lenders; and through other channels.

8. Describe the components of microcredit programs' operating costs, and discuss how they might vary across contexts and borrower types.

9. Describe some of the innovations incorporated into microcredit lending technologies that might allow them to lend to poor populations at lower cost than commercial banks, and explain how these innovations might reduce costs.

10. Discuss the ways a microlender might try to increase its financial sustainability.

11. Discuss the rationales for intervention in microcredit operations.

12. Describe the results of recent evaluations of microcredit programs.

13. What tentative lessons can be drawn from empirical research to date regarding the potential to reach the world's many unbanked poor with profitable microcredit programs and the tradeoff MFIs face between profitability and outreach?

14. Through what channels might each of the following microcredit program design changes alter a microcredit program's outreach, impact, and profitability: a shift from joint to individual liability, the introduction of a grace period into repayment arrangements, and a shift from weekly to monthly meetings?

15. Discuss the relative merits of savings-led microfinance programs as compared to microcredit programs.

QUESTIONS FOR DISCUSSION

1. What assumptions about empirical reality underlie the microfinance idea articulated in section 21.1A?

2. Suppose you wanted to modify a microcredit program with the aim of reaching a poorer set of households than the program currently reaches, and within the same communities. What design changes would you contemplate?

3. Suppose you are asked to participate in an evaluation of microcredit program impact, and suppose a methodology has been worked out for estimating impacts on any outcomes of interest one year after borrowers join the program. What outcomes would you wish to measure and why?

4. Discuss the significance of each of the questions in Box 21.3.

5. Discuss the relative strengths and weaknesses of the three microcredit program impact studies profiled in section 21.3A.

6. Discuss the potential benefits and costs of each of the following modifications to a microcredit program:
    - Increasing the interest rate charged on loans
    - Doubling the initial loan size and increasing the loan cycle from 6 months to 12 months
    - Limiting participation to women
    - Shifting from unregulated for-profit status to status as a regulated, for-profit commercial bank

7. When a microcredit borrower or a member of her family becomes seriously ill or injured, it becomes very difficult for her to continue making loan payments. Microcredit program designers might wish to build in provisions that waive or delay some payments for borrowers hit by serious illness or injury. How exactly might such provisions be specified? What benefits and costs might be associated with building in such provisions?

8. Discuss the potential benefits and costs of replacing a targeted transfer program that pays households $50 every six months by a microcredit program that offers households loans with starting size of $50 to be paid back in weekly installments over six-month loan cycles?

9. Discuss the potential benefits and costs of replacing a microcredit program that provides each of 20 women in a joint liability group with loans of $100, which they use to run individual small businesses, by a program that provides a group of 20 women with a single loan of $2,000 that they are to use in undertaking a cooperative investment in setting up a mill for grinding grain into flour (or some other small- or medium-sized food-processing or manufacturing operation).

10. Consider a community lacking a good road connection to market. Why might construction of a high-quality road to market increase the potential poverty reduction impact of a microcredit program located in the community, and why might the presence of a microcredit program increase the impact of road construction on the community?

PROBLEMS

1. A single microcredit organization (MCI One) currently operates in a certain region. It provides loans of up to $400 and lends at an interest rate of 20 percent. It has been in operation for seven years and has only just barely managed to achieve financial sustainability. A new microcredit organization (MCI Two) is considering entering the same region, offering loans of up to $50 and charging an interest rate of 15 percent. Other details regarding the specifics of the program it would set up remain to be determined.
    a. Given what we know about MCI One's experience, explain carefully why it seems unlikely that MCI Two will be able to operate without subsidy, even after an initial startup phase.
    b. What objective might MCI Two hope to achieve through its offer of subsidized loans at lower interest rates (than those charged by MCI One) that is not already being met by MCI One? Explain the logic behind why MCI Two might be able to achieve this objective even though MCI One has not.
    c. What concerns might MCI One have regarding the consequences for its own operations of entry by MCI Two?
    d. What choices could MCI Two make regarding its program design that would reduce its potential to create the adverse consequences for MCI One that you just described?

2. The population of Community A includes three kinds of households. The following table describes numbers of households in each group, the income they obtain each period from sources other than business investment, and their business skill level.

Group	Number of Households	Income from Other Sources in Each Period	Business Skill Level
Group 1	40	30	Low
Group 2	40	30	High
Group 3	20	80	High

Two types of business investment opportunities are available in Community A: small retail businesses and small sewing businesses. The returns to investments in setting up these businesses do not depend on how many people choose to undertake them. The following table describes the structure of their setup costs and the profits they generate in each of three periods, for potential entrepreneurs who have low and high business skill.

Project Description	Skill Level	Setup Cost	Profits Delivered by Business in Each of Three Periods		
			Period 1	Period 2	Period 3
Purchase inventory for small retail operation	Low skill	50	25	25	0
	High skill	50	40	40	0
Purchase sewing machine for tailoring business	Low skill	70	0	0	0
	High skill	70	0	60	60

Households have two sources of financing to cover the setup cost of an investment: a loan from the local microcredit program (taken out at time zero, before the beginning of period) and saving out of Period 1 income from other sources. Initially, the local microcredit program offers loans of 50, which borrowers must pay back in two installments of 30 each in Periods 1 and 2. This means that borrowers can finance immediate investment in a small retail business, but they can finance investment in a sewing business only by adding 20 saved out of other income in period 1 to the loan of 50. Borrowers consider an investment feasible only if it does not require them to push consumption below 30 in any period. As long as consumption remains above 30 in all periods, the utility a household derives over the three-period horizon is given by the simple sum of consumption in periods 1, 2, and 3. Consumption in any period is equal to income from other sources *minus* any saving out of income used to help finance investment *plus* any business profits derived from an investment *minus* any loan repayments. Households seek to maximize utility as they decide whether to borrow and invest, and which investment project to undertake.

a. For each group (1, 2, and 3) state which business investment, if any, they will undertake at time zero, given the conditions described thus far, and indicate what level of consumption they will enjoy in each period.

b. State what percentage of Community A households participates in the microcredit program and fill in the following table describing the microcredit program's impacts. The impact on consumption in any period is consumption in the presence of any microcredit-financed investment minus consumption in the absence of any such investment. If they do not participate, then the impact in each period is zero.

	Participate (Yes or No)	Period 1	Period 2	Period 3
Average Impact on Consumption for:				
• Group 1				
• Group 2				
• Group 3				
• All microcredit program participants				
Percentage of microcredit program participants whose consumption is raised by at least 15				

c. Suppose evaluators are able to perfectly estimate the impact of the program on consumption in any period and for any group. Discuss how their conclusions regarding the program's success in raising consumption might differ depending on the period in which they observe consumption.

d. Focus only on period 2. If evaluators consider a program successful if it raises average consumption among participants by at least 15, would they judge this program successful? If they consider a program successful if it raises the consumption of at least half the participants by 15 and reduces consumption for no participants, would they judge this program successful?

e. Suppose the interest rate rises so that microcredit program participants must make payments of 35 rather than 30 in periods 1 and 2. Now who participates and which projects do they undertake?

f. Suppose the microcredit program is restructured to give borrowers a grace period before beginning to repay their loan. They still obtain loans of size 50, and now must pay off the loan in two installments of 40 each in periods 2 and 3. No payment is required in period 1. How does this change affect the investment choices of Group 2 households?

Public Health, Health Care, and Health Insurance

Public health policies seek to prevent illness and injury by encouraging health-protecting investments and practices. **Health care interventions** provide medical services at subsidized prices to people struck by illness or injury. **Health insurance programs** allow healthy people to pay premiums in exchange for the promise of reduced health care costs in the event of illness or injury. All such policies have the potential to improve health and protect households from the financial catastrophe that often accompanies ill health. Successful policies, therefore, contribute to economic growth by increasing the stock of human capital, while also reducing poverty and reducing vulnerability to some of the world's most devastating shocks.

22.1 Health and Health Policy in Developing Countries

22.1A Health, health care, and health spending in developing and developed countries

Health conditions in many developing countries have improved rapidly over the last 50 years. Life expectancy at birth in low- and middle-income countries rose from just 47 years in 1960 to 68 years in 2010.[1] The number of deaths before age five years per 1,000 live births—the **under-five mortality rate**—fell from 157 in 1970 to 63 in 2010 (World Bank, 2011, 2012). Although rising incomes and education levels help to explain some of this improvement, successful health policy interventions, such as campaigns to vaccinate against measles and promote the use of oral rehydration therapy for children with diarrheal disease, have also played important roles (Jamison, 2006).

Despite the improvements, illness and early death remain much greater threats in poorer countries than in richer countries, as documented in Table 22.1. Life-expectancy statistics (row 1) indicate that the average newborn in a high-income country can expect to live 21 years longer than the average newborn in a low-income country. Infants in low-income countries are 14 times more likely to die during their first year than infants in high-income countries (row 2), and more than 1 in 10 children in low-income countries still die before age five years (row 3). Maternal mortality rates show that expectant mothers in low-income countries are 39 times more likely to die before or during delivery than expectant mothers in high-income countries (row 4), and according to statistics on lifetime risk of maternal death, 15-year-old girls in low-income countries are 100 times more likely than their high-income counterparts to die during childbirth eventually (row 5).

People living in poorer countries face a different mix of health threats than people living in richer countries. To quantify these differences we turn to calculations of the **disability-adjusted life years** (DALYs) lost to particular health threats in countries at different income levels. The DALYs lost to a particular health threat is a commonly used measure of the **burden of disease** or the death and disability (broadly defined) associated with an illness or injury. To calculate the number of DALYs lost to a disease in a given year, statisticians gather data on the age and gender of everyone struck by the disease in that year. For victims who die, they use mortality rate tables to estimate how many more years each victim would have lived had she not succumbed to the

---

[1] Life expectancy at birth is calculated from current age-specific mortality rates and indicates the number of years the average person born today would live if current mortality rates remain relevant throughout her life.

■ TABLE 22.1   Health Indicator Averages in Low-, Middle-, and High-Income Countries

	Low-Income Countries	Middle-Income Countries	High-Income Countries
Life expectancy at birth, 2010 (years)	59	69	80
Infant mortality, 2010 (deaths before age 1 per 1,000 live births)	70	38	5
Under-five mortality, 2010 (deaths before age 5 years per 1,000 live births)	108	51	6
Maternal mortality ratio, 2008 (deaths of mothers per 100,000 live births)	590	210	15
Lifetime risk of maternal death, 2008 (fraction)	1/39	1/190	1/3900

Source: World Bank (2012).

disease during that year, and they count those years as lost. For victims who survive, they calculate the average duration (until the end of the episode or end of life) of any disability and count those years as partially lost, with the fraction of each year lost to a given disability determined by a panel of experts. For example, the disability weights for blindness, moderate depressive episodes, and severe iron deficiency anemia are 0.594, 0.350, and 0.090, respectively (World Health Organization, 2008b). After applying a 3-percent discount rate (which causes years of life lost farther in the future to count less) and nonuniform age weights (which reduce the weight placed on the earliest and latest years of life relative to the straight 3-percent discount rate), the statistician adds together the losses due to death and disability to produce the final statistic.

The DALY statistic has many weaknesses as a measure of the harm wrought by a disease: The severity of a disability is measured in a somewhat arbitrary way and the overall calculation largely ignores the broader implications of an illness for victims' families. To its credit, however, the DALY statistic does incorporate both death and the loss of function among victims who do not die, and it gives greater weight to diseases that end lives sooner.

Table 22.2 uses DALY statistics to describe the distribution of the burden of disease across country groups and health threats. It shows that more than half the world's burden of disease

■ TABLE 22.2   Disability-Adjusted Life Year (DALY) Statistics in Low-, Middle-, and High-Income Countries, 2004

	Low-Income Countries	Middle-Income Countries	High-Income Countries
Population (millions)	2,413	3,045	977
Total DALYs lost (thousands)	827,669	572,859	122,092
Average DALYs lost per 1,000 persons	343	188	124
DALYs lost to various diseases as percentage shares of total DALYs lost:			
All infectious and parasitic diseases	29.1	10.1	2.3
Tuberculosis	2.7	2.0	0.2
HIV/AIDS	5.2	2.6	0.5
Diarrheal disease	7.2	2.3	0.4
Malaria	4.0	0.2	0.0
Respiratory infections	9.5	3.1	1.1
Maternal conditions	3.5	1.6	0.5
Perinatal conditions	11.3	5.5	1.4
Nutritional deficiencies	3.2	2.0	0.6
Cancers	2.3	7.2	14.6
Diabetes mellitus	0.7	1.8	3.0
Unipolar depression	3.2	5.1	8.2
Cardiovascular disease	6.9	13.3	14.6
Unintentional injuries	7.9	11.5	6.2

Source: World Health Organization (2008a).

■ TABLE 22.3   Health Care Supply Indicators in Low-, Middle-, and High-Income Countries, 2005–2010

	Low-Income Countries	Middle-Income Countries	High-Income Countries
Physicians per 1,000 people	0.2	1.2	2.8
Nurses and midwives per 1,000 people	0.5	2.0	7.1
Hospital beds per 1,000 people	n.a.	2.4	5.7

Source: World Bank (2012).

strikes in low-income countries, where only one third of the world's population resides. According to the third row of Table 22.2, for every 1,000 people living in high-income countries, the diseases that strike in a year cause people to lose the equivalanet of 124 years of life, whereas for every 1,000 people living in low income countries, people to lose 343 years of life to the diseases that strike in a year. Much of the differential in DALYs lost per person between low- and high-income countries is attributable to the higher burdens of infectious and parasitic diseases and to problems related to childbirth in the low-income countries. At the same time, non-communicable diseases such as heart disease and cancer now cause more than half of the burden of disease in low- and middle-income countries and are rising in importance.

The burden of disease is greater in low-income countries, not only because people living there are more likely to contract diseases but also because they find it more difficult to obtain health care when they become ill and the quality of care is lower. As indicated in Table 22.3, the numbers of doctors, nurses, and hospital beds per 1,000 people are much lower in poorer countries. Rates of absenteeism among health professionals are also very high, especially in rural areas (Chaudhury et al., 2006). Some facilities lack basic equipment and medicines, and even where equipment and medicines are available, medical professionals sometimes put them to poor use. Das et al. (2008) studied health care providers' knowledge and practices in four developing countries and documented low levels of both competence and effort. They report, for example, that when diagnosing illness in patients with diarrhea or cough, the average provider in an Indian public sector health care facility asks just one question ("and that one was often asked rudely"). When presented with vignettes, the average doctor knew to complete only 30 percent of tasks deemed essential by experts and actually completed only 8 percent of those tasks when observed in consultation with patients.

The burdens of ill health are financial as well as physical. Health care expenditure absorbs more than 5 percent of GDP in low- and middle-income countries, as indicated in Table 22.4, and a much higher fraction of health expenditure in poorer countries is paid **out of pocket**, by households paying fees to health care providers, rather than by the public sector. Health care spending is particularly burdensome, because it is spread unevenly across families and over time; a few families experience major health problems in a given year and incur very large health care costs, while many others require little or no care that year. Facing high out-of-pocket costs, many families that are struck by serious illness or injury forgo care or are turned away by health care providers, and many others are impoverished. Despite significant out-of-pocket expenditure, total spending per capita remains much lower in low-income countries.

■ TABLE 22.4   Health Financing Indicators in Low-, Middle-, and High-Income Countries, 2010

	Low-Income Countries	Middle-Income Countries	High-Income Countries
Health expenditure as percent of GDP	5.4	5.7	12.7
Out-of-pocket expenditure as percent of total health expenditure	48	36	14
Per capita health expenditure in PPP$	61	369	4,660

Source: World Bank (2012).

≡ **Box 22.1** Poor Health and Health Care in Udaipur, India

In an exploratory study designed to identify the nature and prevalence of health and health care problems in a poor Indian district, Abhijit Banerjee, Angus Deaton, and Esther Duflo conducted surveys of households, health care facilities, and health care workers in 100 hamlets in Udaipur district in the state of Rajasthan (Banerjee et al., 2004). In these very poor communities, 40 percent of residents live below the official poverty line, few are literate, and very few have electricity.

The statistics reveal a shocking picture of pervasive ill health. More than half the population is anemic. Ninety-three percent of men and 88 percent of women have body mass index below 21, which is the official cutoff for low nutrition in the United States. Average lung capacity measures suggest significant respiratory difficulty. According to self-reports, 30 percent of adults would have difficulty working unaided in the fields or walking five kilometers, and 18 to 20 percent have difficulty squatting or standing up from a sitting position. Such difficulties must present significant barriers to generating income for workers with little education in small rural communities.

The problem with health care in these communities seems not to be that households cannot access it but that its quality is very low and the costs are a significant burden. On average people had to walk 1.4 kilometers to reach a health facility. Even in the bottom third of the income distribution within this poor population, the average person visits a health facility nearly once every two months. Less than a quarter of the visits are to public facilities. Most of the rest are to private facilities, though some are to traditional healers.

That residents visit public health care facilities as often as they do is somewhat surprising, given how difficult it can be to find a health facility open and staffed. Official policy dictates that public health centers should be open six hours per day for six days per week and should provide virtually free care. The researchers hired assistants to conduct random visits to health facilities over many weeks and found that on average almost half the medical personnel were absent and facilities were closed half the time. Moreover, whether a facility would be open or closed on any given day was unpredictable. Attendance was worst in facilities farthest from the road and where the facilities included no living quarters for personnel.

In private sector health care, the most striking problem is the low level of training among its providers. Forty-one percent of doctors at private facilities had no medical college degree, 18 percent had no training at all, and 17 percent didn't even have a high school degree. Diagnostic tests of any sort were performed in only 3 percent of visits, but injections were administered in 68 percent of visits.

Though public sector health care was supposed to be virtually free, households reported spending nearly as much per visit to a public facility (71 rupees) as to a private facility (84 rupees). Even visits to traditional healers cost only a little less (61 rupees). On average, households spent about 7 percent of their budgets on health care. In summary, households in these very poor communities spend a lot on health care and seem to get little for their money. They face high risks of death and serious disability, and even when they escape these direst results, they suffer diminished capacity for work and other physical activities.

Within developing countries, ill health is a greater burden for the poor than for the nonpoor, for many reasons. Poor households are more likely to live in locations that lack water and sanitation infrastructure, where they are more exposed to infectious disease and pollution, and they tend to undertake more dangerous work. When they become ill or injured, they are less likely to obtain care, because they live farther from health care facilities, are more daunted by fees, and are more likely to consider illness "normal." When they get care, the quality is often lower than for wealthier patients. Box 22.1 illustrates the pervasive effects of ill health and the inadequacy of health care systems in some poor communities.

22.1B **Causes and consequences of health outcomes in developing countries**

A person's **health** is her multidimensional state of physical and psychological well-being (or ill-being). A healthy person enjoys strength, vitality, comfort, and capacities for many physical and mental activities. The health a person can expect to experience in any year is a function of the health stock she brings into the year, the probabilities with which she is hit by various health shocks during the year, and the nature and quality of any health care she would receive. People are hit by **health shocks** when they experience episodes of illness or injury. Health shocks include infectious and noninfectious diseases, nutritional deficiencies, and injuries resulting from accidents, childbirth traumas, and other physical stresses. A person's **health stock** is the potential for health with which she begins the year. It is determined in part by genetics and in part by her history of past health shocks, heath care, and other health-related choices. It indicates the health she will enjoy throughout the year if she experiences no health shock, and it also helps determine her susceptibility to health shocks.[2]

The probabilities with which a person is hit by various health shocks depend on her health environment, the health inputs she uses, and the health behaviors she undertakes, as well as her health stock. The quality of her **health environment** is determined by local climate, pollution levels, prevalence of communicable disease, and any other factors outside her control that influence the likelihood of illness or injury. **Health inputs** are items she may use to shield herself against health risks in her environment, such as insecticide-treated bed nets, condoms, and vitamin-rich foods. **Health behaviors** include activities such as hand washing, exercise, abstaining from unprotected sex, delaying age at first pregnancy, increasing spacing between pregnancies, and breastfeeding infants, which reduce health risks without requiring the use of health inputs, as well as activities such as smoking or use of pesticides without protective clothing, which people might undertake for reasons unrelated to health and which increase their exposure to health risks.

Health shocks have consequences for physical and mental health and also for many other dimensions of household well-being and behavior. Without any health care, an individual experiences the full physical impact of the shock: temporary or permanent pain, discomfort, or disability. These physical effects can, in turn, reduce her capacity to work and earn income and to attend school (Strauss and Thomas, 1998; Kremer and Miguel, 2007). With reduced physical capacity, she might also have to purchase equipment that others do not require, such as eyeglasses or leg braces, simply to maintain normal daily activities. A health shock affects not only the victim but also other members of her family as they reduce consumption, increase time spent caring for her, or increase time earning income in her place. Severe health shocks can cause death, in which case the victim loses years of life and her family loses all her contributions to household well-being. When men die, the losses for widows and young orphans are often especially profound.

A person struck by a health shock obtains **health care** when a health professional—a doctor, nurse, medical technician, community health worker, midwife, medicine vendor, or traditional healer—provides her with diagnostic, curative, or palliative services. Health care providers supply diagnostic services when they deliver advice about appropriate treatments, usually based on the results of interviews, physical exams, or testing. Curative care seeks to eliminate the underlying causes of health problems, and palliative care seeks to reduce pain or other symptoms. The prescribed course of action might involve health care procedures (such as bone setting or surgery), medication, and follow-up activities by patients (such as rest or reha-bilitation exercises). If the patient agrees, the health professional might provide the prescribed medication and health procedures. Often the patient's family must purchase medications and supplies (such as surgical dressings) from outside vendors.

Effective health care can help recipients avoid many of the worst consequences of health shocks, reducing the intensity or duration of pain, improving the patient's capacity to generate income or attend school, or preventing death. The nature and magnitude of these health care impacts depend on the quality of diagnostic services, medical procedures, and medicines that patients obtain, as well as their choices regarding how closely to follow prescribed courses of action.

Even when the ill and injured receive effective health care, thereby avoiding many of the worst physical impacts of the shocks, they can experience financial trauma, as they are called

---

[2] The World Health Organization (WHO) defines health as a "state of complete physical and mental well-being, and not merely the absence of disease or infirmity." This definition seems to discourage an emphasis on merely combating illnesses and injuries when defining health policy goals. For policy analysis purposes, however, it is useful to emphasize illness and injury in the way we model health, because, in practice, health policies achieve their goals only when they reduce the incidence of health shocks or reduce the deleterious consequences of health shocks, and because the diversity of these shocks and their probabilistic character play important roles in defining practical health policy challenges.

upon to pay for the care. For minor illnesses, the treatment costs are relatively low, but for many health shocks, the fees for required care far exceed the quantities of cash that households keep on hand. Treatment for major health shocks, such as heart failure, can cost the equivalent of several years of income. To cover the costs of health care, households might have to sell off livestock or business assets, thereby reducing their capacity to generate income for many months or years into the future. They might instead go into debt and then work at repaying the debt for months or years, by cutting back on consumption or increasing the time their children spend working. Health shocks are among the most common reasons households fall into poverty (Dercon et al., 2005; Krishna, 2006).

The risk of health shocks is a significant source of vulnerability for *all* households in developing countries, whether they anticipate obtaining appropriate health care or not. Without care they must suffer the full physical consequences of health shocks, while with care they must bear the financial burden of **user fees**, or fees charged at the time of service. Such vulnerability diminishes well-being directly, and it can also alter household choices in ways of concern to policymakers. Households might attempt to create financial cushions for coping with health shocks by holding savings in the form of cash or jewelry, rather than in the form of productive assets. In so doing they diminish their productivity and income. High probabilities of death or disability can also increase the rates at which households discount the future, tending to reduce their interest in productive investments. High risks of losing children to health shocks can diminish parental incentives to invest in children's early nutrition and schooling and can encourage them to have many children (to increase the chance of rearing children to adulthood), rendering it more difficult for them to raise their households' per-capita income.

Households might attempt to protect themselves against the burden of future health shocks by purchasing health insurance. When a household purchases a **health insurance contract**, the household agrees to pay a fee or **premium** in exchange for the promise of **indemnities**, or financial assistance with paying health care bills, should a family member experience a covered health shock. Owning such a contract reduces the effective cost of obtaining care at time of need. Reduced immediate costs render it more likely that the insured will obtain care when hit by health shocks and reduce the financial impact of obtaining care. Unfortunately, households in developing countries often lack opportunities to purchase health insurance.

22.1C Health policy objectives and broad policy options

Health policies aim to reduce the physical, mental, and financial burdens that households experience when health shocks strike and to reduce households' vulnerability to the burdens that future health shocks might bring. Success in these endeavors increases well-being directly and can contribute to growth by increasing the stock of human capital and encouraging other investment. In practice, health policymakers work toward their ultimate objectives by pursuing one or more of four proximate objectives: reducing the risk of health shocks, increasing the share of households that obtain health care when hit by health shocks, improving the quality of health care, and reducing the financial trauma inflicted on households by health care costs. Specific health policies emphasize different combinations of these proximate objectives, and they might concentrate more narrowly on reducing the burdens associated with particular diseases. Some reflect deep concern with equity in access to healthy environments and health care, concentrating especially on improvements for the poor and other disadvantaged groups.

Policymakers may pursue these objectives through at least five types of intervention. First, *public health policies* seek to reduce risks of illness or injury. They include immunization programs, campaigns to promote use of health inputs (e.g., bed nets) and good health behaviors (e.g., hand washing), the construction of health-improving infrastructure (e.g., treated drinking water systems), and the enforcement of regulations to reduce environmental risks (e.g., regulations on industrial pollution). Second, *health care programs* create and operate health centers, clinics, and hospitals or deploy community health care workers. Third, *health insurance programs* offer participants the promise of help with paying health care costs in the event of illness or injury, often in exchange for the payment of fixed monthly or yearly premiums.[3] Fourth, *regulations* that require providers of health care services or pharmaceuticals to meet minimum quality standards seek to protect consumers from for-profit suppliers selling low-quality health care or ineffective medications. Finally, *medical technology policies* encourage research and development of cheaper or more effective methods of preventing, diagnosing, or treating health problems.

Comprehensive analysis of policies in all these areas is beyond the scope of this chapter. In what follows, we focus on two important fields of health policy discussion in which the tools of economic analysis are particularly useful: public health efforts to encourage use of health inputs and the introduction or reform of health insurance programs.

22.2 Economic Analysis of Programs Promoting Health Input Use

Insecticide-treated bed nets, water filters, condoms, and vaccinations against childhood illnesses have great potential to reduce the burden of infectious disease. Researchers estimate that the social benefits of using such health inputs far outweigh the costs (Laxminarayan et al., 2006), yet the shares of developing country households using them remain low (Dupas, 2011). In what follows, we set out the theory that informs current research on decisions to acquire and use health inputs, and we discuss private health-input supply and the rationales for intervention in this area. We then summarize the implications for designing and evaluating programs that promote use of health inputs, and we apply the framework in studying the benefits and costs of charging fees for insecticide-treated bed nets.

22.2A Households' acquisition of health inputs

Households are directly affected by programs promoting use of health inputs when they **acquire** health inputs, whether by purchasing them or accepting them free of charge. In general, we expect households to acquire health inputs when they judge that the benefits of acquisition outweigh the costs. Current economic models of how households evaluate the benefits and costs incorporate insights from basic consumer choice models, but they also acknowledge potential complications related to learning, decision framing, and barriers to borrowing and saving.

Basic economic models of decisions to acquire health inputs

In basic economic models of household decision making, such as those examined in Chapter 6, households allocate fixed time endowments across work, schooling, leisure, and time spent acquiring goods and services. They simultaneously allocate their total incomes across the consumption of various goods and services, including health inputs. In the simplest models, households are assumed to have complete information about the consequences of their choices and to maximize standard, fixed utility functions. Such models offer a useful starting point for analyzing health-input programs, because they remind analysts that rates of health input acquisition can fall as the money or time costs of acquisition rise and as income falls (if households treat the benefit associated with health input use as a normal good). Dupas's (2011) assessment of the empirical evidence to date is that households' acquisition of health inputs indeed tends to drop

---

[3] The distinction between health care programs and health insurance programs is not sharp. When health care programs charge fees below cost for the health care they provide, they are implicitly providing households with zero-premium health insurance, and many health insurance programs distribute their benefits in the form of low-cost health care rather than cash.

sharply as prices rise, especially among poor households. Acquisition rates also fall as households' distances from sale or distribution sites rises.

Basic models of household decision making emphasize that households compare the *private* benefits of health input use to the private costs. The private benefits may be small relative to the social benefits when a household's health input use generates positive externalities. Use of health inputs that prevent households from contracting disease also reduces the rate at which diseases are transmitted to others. Such externalities are especially strong when rates of health-input use surpass critical levels. For example, entire communities enjoy reduced malaria transmission rates when at least 50 percent of households use bed nets (Hawley et al., 2003).

Information and learning

As long as households face even small time or money costs of acquiring health inputs, they will choose to acquire them only if they believe that owning and using the inputs confers some benefit. Unfortunately, although the costs of acquiring a health input are immediate and fairly obvious, the benefits take the intangible form of a reduction in the probability of contracting disease. Compelling models of decisions to acquire health inputs must, therefore, pay close attention to how households acquire knowledge and understanding of the benefits.

To understand the benefits of health input use at the deepest level, households would have to understand the complex biological processes that determine health risks and the role that using health inputs plays in altering those processes. People with little science education might find it difficult to understand, for example, how vaccinations reduce the risk of illness, especially when the scientific explanations clash with their long-standing beliefs, or mental models, about the cause of illness. Banerjee and Duflo (2011) cite a case in which parents were reluctant to bring their children for vaccinations because they believed that the "evil eye" was the primary cause of childhood illness and death and that allowing children to be seen in public during the first year of life rendered them vulnerable to the evil eye. In a similar vein, Datta and Mullainathan (2012) conjecture that Indian parents fail to use inexpensive, readily available, life-saving oral rehydration therapy for their young children with diarrhea because in their mental models of illness, diarrhea is a problem of too many fluids flowing through the body, which would only be aggravated by using oral rehydration therapy (which requires ill children to drink a mixture of water, sugar, and salt).

Households might come to appreciate the benefits of using health inputs, even without fully understanding the underlying processes, if they learn through experience that use tends to improve health. For example, even without understanding the role of bacteria in transmission of waterborne disease, they might learn that adding chlorine to water reduces illness by observing their own experience and that of their relatives and neighbors. If such learning is possible, then temporary interventions that encourage households to gain experience might increase the rate at which those households and their neighbors purchase the inputs in the future.

Experience need not always increase acquisition rates, however. Drawing good inferences about the effects of using health inputs may be very difficult when households observe only small samples of family and friends. Experience might also reveal information about the costs as well as the benefits of use. If households had underestimated the costs, then experience can *reduce* future acquisition. Kremer and Miguel (2007) find that households with larger numbers of social connections to people who had obtained free deworming drugs in the past were *less* likely than others to purchase deworming drugs themselves, perhaps because they learned through their contacts' experience about the unpleasant physical side effects of taking the drugs.

When households do not understand the underlying processes and cannot easily infer the benefits of use through observation, they might nonetheless acquire the necessary appreciation of benefits through efforts by others to inform them. Transmitting information about benefits of health inputs requires more than mere repetition of facts, however. If hearing or reading information is to change a household's behavior, household decision makers must *believe* the information and must, therefore, trust that the people or organizations providing the information are well informed and well motivated to communicate truthfully.

Several studies reviewed in Dupas (2011) suggest that some households lack information about the benefits of using health inputs and that providing information can change health behavior. Often the impacts are only modest, however, and emerge only when households judge the source of the information to be trustworthy. Madajewicz et al. (2007) found a large effect on households' water use choices of informing them that water from their primary source had an unsafe level of arsenic: 60 percent of households randomly chosen to receive information about arsenic contamination switched to safer water sources, whereas only 8 percent of comparable households in the control made this switch over the same period. Jalan and Somanathan (2008) found a smaller effect of information on household water purification activities: Households informed of fecal contamination in their drinking water were 11 percent more likely to adopt new techniques than the control. An aggressive campaign in Egypt to distribute oral rehydration therapy kits and to inform parents about their effectiveness in preventing children's death from diarrheal disease brought dramatic reductions in infant mortality in the 1980s, but 10 years of oral rehydration therapy campaigns in India brought little change, perhaps because people distrusted a government that had engaged in forced sterilization in the 1970s.

Contextual factors and decision framing

Psychologists and behavioral economists point out that when people must choose between two options, their choices might depend not only on their expectations regarding the utility they would experience after choosing each option (as in standard economic models) but also on **contextual factors**, or details of the circumstances under which they are called upon to make the choice (Bertrand et al., 2006). Current research on decisions to acquire health inputs acknowledges the potential importance of many such factors. Here we highlight just two.

First, when households must choose between two options, their choices can depend on which of the two options they perceive to be the status quo. In many experimental contexts, households exhibit **loss aversion**, or a tendency to value goods and services more highly when asked to give them up (e.g., when asked to sell them) than when offered an opportunity to acquire them (e.g., through purchase). This suggests that the way choices are **framed**, or portrayed, can influence households' responses. For example, households may be more likely to purchase and use bed nets if the choice is framed as one of losing their children's good health through refusal to purchase a net than if it is framed as one of gaining their children's good health by opting to buy a net.

Second, people can behave as if they have different **identities** that differ in values and ideals, and their choices at any given moment can depend upon which identity is most salient to them at the time. For example, women in Trenton, New Jersey, who had been asked questions to bring out their "social selves" were less likely to express interest in opening a savings account than otherwise identical women who had been asked questions to bring out their "family selves" (Bertrand et al., 2006). It may, therefore, be possible to increase uptake of health input offers by framing choices in ways that bring out identities especially interested in family health.

Unfortunately, identifying effective ways of framing decisions is not easy. Dupas (2009) experimented with several framing approaches to encourage purchases of bed nets: marketing messages emphasizing the losses of morbidity and mortality that follow from malaria, messages emphasizing the financial gains from avoiding malaria, and efforts to elicit a verbal commitment to purchase a bed net in the future. None of these approaches generated a statistically significant impact on purchases.

Dynamic considerations

When households purchase bed nets, water filters, or other durable health inputs, they are making investments. From Chapter 10 we know that poor households may be prevented from undertaking socially valuable investments—even when they fully appreciate the benefits—by the difficulty of financing the one-time expenditures required. The expenditures may be too large to pay out of current cash income without severely reducing consumption, and credit market failures can leave them without access to credit. Saving up to make the investments, by setting aside small sums of money each week, can also be difficult if needy neighbors expect excess cash to be shared with them or if spouses demand that such cash be spent on current consumption goods. If individuals are present biased (as defined in Chapter 10), then the disproportionate weight they place on immediate costs relative to future benefits can also prevent them from exercising the discipline of saving and investing, even when they know that they would consider health-related investments worthwhile after the fact.

In the presence of such barriers to saving and investment, choices to acquire health inputs can depend on households' options for financing health investments. Tarozzi et al. (2011) found that when Indian households were offered one-year loans at 20 percent interest rates for purchasing bed nets, 52 percent purchased at least one net, whereas only 2 percent of control households (who were offered nets for the same price without financing) did so. Box 22.2 describes an experimental study of the impact on acquiring health inputs (and household financing of emergency health care needs) of introducing several simple new opportunities for saving.

Present bias might represent a barrier to acquiring health inputs even when the up-front costs take the form of discomfort or inconvenience rather than cash fees. If present bias is significant, then even small inconveniences—such as having to walk a kilometer to obtain free immunizations—can represent significant barriers to acquisition. Efforts to reduce the immediate inconvenience or to compensate for it with small and immediate rewards might then have large impacts on uptake. According to Banerjee et al. (2010), present bias might help explain the success of an experiment in which they offered households two pounds of dried beans for each immunization obtained at an NGO immunization camp. The immunization rate in treatment villages rose from 17 to 38 percent.

To summarize:

> Whether a household acquires a health input might depend not only on the time and money costs of acquiring the input and the household's income and preferences but also on the nature of the household's opportunities to learn about the input and on how the acquisition choice is framed. For a durable health input, the decision to acquire is an investment decision, which may also be influenced by the household's opportunities to borrow and save and by the offer of small immediate incentives that offset the immediate inconvenience of acquisition.

22.2B Health input supply, rationales for intervention, and program design options

The social cost of equipping a household with a health input includes the cost of manufacturing the input and then transporting and distributing it to the household. Public health experts believe that the social benefit of using a bed net, water filter, or other proven health input far exceeds this social cost for households living in locations where malaria and waterborne diseases are endemic. Private profit-seeking retailers might fail to distribute socially beneficial health inputs, however, because the retailers must pay the full social cost of purchasing, transporting, and distributing the inputs but may be able to appropriate only a fraction of the social benefit as a result of households' low willingness to pay. A household's **willingness to pay** for a health input is the highest price at which the household would choose to purchase the item. We will see that:

> Externalities, lack of knowledge, and liquidity constraints can reduce households' willingness to pay for socially desirable health inputs to a level below retailers' costs and can therefore constitute rationales for intervention. The diversity of rationales suggests a menu of possible policy responses worthy of more careful study.

Where households lack information about benefits of health inputs, dissemination of information might increase their willingness to pay. In some cases, private retailers might invest in disseminating information with the aim of increasing sales and profits, but they are likely to underinvest because such efforts tend to raise demand for their competitors' goods as well as their own. In the presence of such information externalities, governments and NGOs might have a role to play in informing households about the benefits of using health inputs. They might also have some advantages over for-profit retailers in disseminating information, because households might expect retailers to exaggerate the benefits of their wares and might, therefore, consider public actors more trustworthy in some cases.

If lack of information is the only barrier to using health inputs, then policymakers might have the capacity to catalyze widespread use through education activities alone, without directly subsidizing the manufacture or distribution of health inputs. To achieve success at lowest cost,

≡ Box 22.2 Encouraging People to Save for Health Input Purchases and Health Emergencies

Searching for cheap and effective ways to increase household saving for purchases of health inputs or emergency health care, Pascaline Dupas and Jonathan Robinson identified 113 rotating savings and credit associations (ROSCAs) in a Kenyan district and randomly divided them into four treatment groups and one control group (Dupas and Robinson, 2011). In all five groups they made presentations to promote savings for health-related expenditures. In the four treatment groups they also offered new opportunities for saving.

In the *safe box treatment* group, researchers offered each participant a metal box, with padlock and key, and a passbook. Box owners could deposit money through slits in the boxes' lids without having to unlock them, and they were encouraged to use the passbooks to keep track of their deposits and withdrawals. They were also asked to record in the passbooks their health saving goal, or the health input (e.g., bed net or water filter) for which they were saving up. For the *lock box treatment* group, researchers again offered metal boxes and passbooks, but they arranged for a local NGO's program officer to hold the keys, under instructions to relinquish a key only when a box owner reached her savings goal.

In the *health pot treatment* group, researchers encouraged each ROSCA's members to organize a small special-purpose ROSCA activity, in which any interested members would agree to make weekly contributions just large enough that the pot would allow one participant to purchase a designated health input each week. In the *personal health account treatment*, the researchers arranged for ROSCA treasurers to hold members' savings in individual accounts, under instructions to allow members to make withdrawals only in the case of health emergencies.

Six and 12 months after introducing the treatments, researchers interviewed a total of 771 individuals across the four treatment groups and one control group, seeking to measure and understand the impacts of the treatments on savings, purchases of health inputs, and participants' ability to cope with health shocks. High rates of uptake for all treatments suggest the existence of unmet demand for good modes of saving. The shares of participants who made at least some use of the savings tools offered were 74, 69, 65, and 93 percent in the groups offered safe boxes, lock boxes, health pots arrangements, and individual health accounts, respectively.

Estimated treatment impacts indicate that even providing rather weak protection for savings can significantly increase saving and spending on health inputs. Even the safe box treatment, which provided the weakest encouragement to saving, raised expenditure on health inputs by 68 percent relative to mean control group expenditure. It also raised the probability of achieving the owner's health input saving goal from 34 to 47 percent. Post-experiment qualitative interviews suggest that the most valuable service provided by the safe box was the opportunity to leave savings at home rather than carrying them when outside the home, perhaps protecting them against demands for immediate assistance for neighbors and against temptations for unnecessary expenditures. The safe box treatment was also somewhat more effective among married relative to single participants, suggesting some value in providing a legitimate way to prevent spouses from redirecting savings to other purposes.

Differences in impact across treatment groups suggest, however, that requiring participants to commit to use savings *only* for purchase of health inputs *reduces* saving. Compared to the safe box treatment, the lock box treatment embodied a stronger commitment to use savings only for health input purchase and was less effective at raising spending on health inputs; in fact, the researchers detected no significant impact of the treatment on health input expenditure. The individual health account treatment, by contrast, embodied stronger commitment than the safe box treatment to use savings only for health emergencies and appeared effective for increasing savings; it reduced the probability of being unable to afford needed care by 12 percentage points. This suggests that participants highly value the availability of savings for use in emergency.

Despite the strong commitment implicit in the health pot treatment to use savings only for purchasing health inputs, participants who were encouraged to form health pot groups increased saving (and expenditure on health inputs) more than those offered safe boxes (129 percent relative to the control mean), suggesting great value to the social pressure and credit provided by ROSCA arrangements.

In a follow-up study three years after introducing the treatments, the researchers found evidence that simply conveying ideas about new modes of saving sometimes can have long-lasting impact on saving rates. They found that rates of using savings tools in all treatment groups were still quite high and that the treatment practices had even spread to some of the control-group ROSCAs. When asked why they had not made use of such practices before the experiment, most respondents indicated that they simply had never thought of it. The follow-up study also raises the possibility that traditional ROSCA arrangements exert more pressure than some participants find ideal: when groups were offered safe boxes or lock boxes (modes of saving that do not require ROSCA participation), ROSCAs were more likely to disband over the three years than were the ROSCAs in other groups.

policymakers would have to address detailed questions about the design of activities to disseminate information, such as: What messages should the program deliver and to whom? Through what media should the messages be delivered? Who should deliver the messages in person? How should the choices regarding acquisition and use of health inputs be framed?

Provision of information alone may, however, be insufficient for catalyzing widespread use. Willingness to pay for health inputs might fall short for several reasons, implying a role for subsidization. In the presence of important health externalities, *general and permanent* subsidies may be required to achieve high levels of use. *Temporary* subsidies might be useful if households' own experiences and the experiences of neighbors provide them with opportunities to learn, raising their subsequent willingness to pay. *Targeted* subsidies or financing might be most appropriate if the liquidity-constrained poor cannot finance purchases of health inputs. Among present-biased households, policymakers may be required not only to fully subsidize the manufacture, transport, and distribution of health inputs but also to provide additional small incentives just large enough to outweigh the immediate inconvenience and time cost of collecting the inputs.

Even when externalities, learning through experience, or liquidity constraints provide a rationale for governments or NGOs to subsidize the purchase or sale of health inputs, they need not justify direct public sector involvement in the retailing of health inputs. Policymakers might therefore wish to consider distributing subsidies in the form of vouchers, which households may use to purchase inputs from private sector providers, rather than through direct distribution of low-cost inputs.

22.2C Direct and indirect effects of acquiring and using health inputs

Decisions to use health inputs

When designing programs to promote use of health inputs, policymakers must consider not only how design choices affect households' acquisition of health inputs but also how they affect households' daily decisions regarding use, because:

> Many health inputs deliver health benefits only if people use them effectively on a daily basis.

After acquiring durable health inputs such as bed nets or water filters, households face daily choices regarding whether and how to use them. Barriers to use may be significant, because proper use can be costly in time or comfort. In a one-room hut, using a bed net can entail hanging the net each night and taking it down each morning, and sleeping under a net can be uncomfortable. Using water filters and water storage units properly requires knowledge and care, and filtered water cannot be obtained in large quantities as quickly as unfiltered.

Contextual factors and dynamic considerations can impinge on daily use decisions, even after inputs have been acquired. Some marketers of health inputs believe that the price the household paid for a health input is an important contextual factor influencing their subsequent use decisions. More specifically, they believe that decisions to use health inputs are subject to a **sunk-cost effect**, which renders households more likely to use a health input if they have paid more to acquire it. (Whether this is the case is an empirical question, to which we return below.)

Present bias can also turn small inconveniences into significant barriers to daily use. On any given evening, households compare the inconvenience of setting up a bed net to the future benefits of a reduced probability of contracting malaria, and in the presence of present bias, the immediate inconvenience can loom large. If this is the case, then efforts to redesign health inputs in ways that render them more convenient and comfortable could increase use rates significantly.

Direct and indirect effects

Among households that use health inputs effectively, some fraction avoid illness, ultimately enjoying better health, improved income-generating capacity, and reduced health care expenditures. Similar benefits can extend to the users' neighbors through positive externalities.

Some analysts argue that increased demand for health inputs by some households may also improve the supply of health inputs to other households by encouraging market development. At least in principle, such an indirect effect might arise if potential retailers of health inputs must cover fixed costs of setting up operations in particular communities. In the face of fixed costs, they may be unwilling to set up operations unless they anticipate sufficient demand; some remote communities with weak demand might attract no retailers at all, and others might attract only lone, monopolistic retailers. Policies that succeed in raising demands above critical levels in such locations might encourage new private retailers to enter, thereby providing lower-cost sources of health inputs even to households with no direct connection to the policies. Whether such effects on market development are important in practice is an empirical question.

22.2D Evaluating health input policies

Box 22.3 adapts Chapter 14's seven questions for use in evaluating health input programs. It emphasizes the need to study impacts on the numbers of households that acquire health inputs, the extent to which households that own health inputs also *use* them consistently and correctly, the direct impacts of use on health and economic well-being, the spill over effects of use on neighbors' health and economic well-being through externalities, the impacts of current use on users' future demands and demands by neighbors, and the impacts on private health input markets, as well as costs. As always, answering these questions in parallel for two different program designs is useful when studying the benefits and costs of program design changes.

22.2E Free distribution or sale of insecticide-treated bed nets?

Thanks to a concerted effort by the international development community, the number of malaria deaths per year has fallen 13 percent over the last decade, but malaria still claimed 655,000 lives in 2010, mostly among pregnant women and children and mostly in Africa (WHO, 2011). The disease also debilitates workers and creates financial stress for households and health systems. The spread of three practices has helped reduce malaria transmission and mortality rates: spraying long-lasting insecticide inside homes (to kill malaria-carrying mosquitoes), appropriately treating malaria cases (to increase survival rates and reduce the rate at which mosquitoes pick up and transmit the malaria parasite), and sleeping under insecticide-treated bed nets (to reduce the rate at which people are bitten by malarial mosquitoes).

Although bed nets alone cannot eradicate malaria, they have been shown to reduce overall mortality rates by as much as 20 percent in areas where malaria is still endemic (Lengeler, 2004). Bed nets, which retail at unsubsidized prices of $5 to $12, save lives at low cost. Many governments and NGOs therefore promote increased use of bed nets.

Some of these programs distribute bed nets for free. Others undertake aggressive **social marketing campaigns** to inform and persuade households of the benefits of using bed nets, while also selling bed nets at subsidized prices. They argue that asking households to pay fees for bed nets is critical for good program performance, for several reasons. First, by charging fees they recover some costs, allowing them to distribute more bed nets on the same budget. Second, charging fees should prevent the waste associated with distributing bed nets to people who will not use them. Third, if households are subject to sunk cost effects, or if they infer the value of new items like bed nets from the prices charged for them, then charging fees might also increase rates

☰ Box 22.3 Questions to Guide Analysis of Programs That Promote Use of Health Inputs

Question 1: Objectives

For what health input does the program promote acquisition and use? What dimensions of household well-being do policymakers most hope to improve, for which households, and for which household members?

Question 2: Design

What policy design choices regarding information dissemination and promotion activities, prices charged or incentives offered, targeting of discounts or incentives, and governance of health input distribution activities define the program on paper?

Question 3: Implementation

In which communities and to which households does the program attempt to deliver information and promotion activities? How effectively are information dissemination and promotion activities executed? In which communities are program-subsidized inputs distributed? What price is charged for them? How efficiently are input promotion and distribution activities carried out?

Question 4: Directly affected groups

Who acquires health inputs as a result of program activities? Which households fail to acquire health inputs? Among households that acquire health inputs, which households would have purchased them even in the absence of the program?

Question 5: Direct effects

How consistently and correctly do the directly affected households use the health inputs? Which household members benefit from using the health inputs? What impact does this use have on household members' survival, health, income, school enrollment, security, and comfort? What effect does current use have on their future willingness to pay for health inputs?

Question 6: Spillover and feedback effects

What are the effects of health input use by directly affected households on the rates at which other households in their communities acquire health inputs or contract the relevant infectious diseases? What effects does the program have on private health input markets, and how do market changes affect nonparticipating households?

Question 7: Budgetary costs

What is the total budgetary cost of the program? To what extent are the costs of purchasing and distributing the health inputs subsidized?

---

of use among the households who acquire them. Fourth, when households pay for bed nets, program designers may use these payments to provide high-powered work incentives to the program personnel distributing the nets.

Charging fees for bed nets may, in principle, improve program performance in these ways, but the effects need not be large in practice, and charging fees can also bring an important cost: a reduction in the share of target households that acquire bed nets. Empirical evidence on the relative magnitudes of the benefits and costs is therefore required before deciding whether to charge fees or not.

Using a randomized control trial, Cohen and Dupas (2010) estimate the sizes of these benefits and costs in one Kenyan district. They randomly assigned the district's prenatal clinics to multiple treatments. Patients in the diverse treatment groups were offered opportunities to acquire bed nets at varying prices, starting at zero. The highest price charged in any treatment group was only 10 percent of the unsubsidized price, just below the (highly subsidized) price at which bed nets are typically sold by social marketers.

The experimental results demonstrate that, at least in this Kenyan context, the costs of charging fees are large, and the benefits are small. Charging even the low price typically charged by social marketing groups caused the share of households acquiring nets to drop by 60 percent, and households that paid for bed nets were no more likely to use them than households that received them for free. Follow-up research demonstrated, furthermore, that those who received bed nets for free, and their neighbors, were more likely to purchase bed nets in the future. Taking into account these longer-run and spillover effects, the authors conclude that in the Kenyan district they studied, programs that distribute bed nets for free are more cost effective in saving lives than programs that sell them at low prices!

Hoffmann (2009) points out an additional potential cost to charging fees for bed nets. Bed nets reduce infant mortality rates only if children sleep under them. Results from a randomized control trial in rural Uganda suggest that when households must pay fees for bed nets, they acquire fewer nets and are more likely to have too few nets to cover all household members at night than when they obtain nets for free. Moreover, in households that own too few nets to cover the whole family at night, it is the adults rather than the children who sleep under them. Thus, charging fees for bed nets reduces program impact on child mortality even among households that continue to purchase at least one net. Among households offered nets for free, 79 percent of children slept under nets, whereas among households offered bed nets at a low price, only 56 percent of children slept under nets.

22.3 The Economics of Health Insurance Programs

When people experience illness or injury, the ultimate impact on their physical and financial well-being depends on whether and how quickly they obtain health care, the quality of care they receive, and the user fees they must pay for care. In the absence of government and NGO intervention, and often even in its presence, many ill and injured people go without care, and many of those who obtain care are impoverished by the fees. Much of the care they receive is also poor in quality.

In decades past, many governments and NGOs responded to these apparent symptoms of health care system failure in a **supply-side** fashion, setting up government or NGO hospitals and clinics to supply health care. In the interest of equity, governments set official user fees at low levels for all patients. This meant that the services had to be financed largely out of general tax revenue, supplemented by foreign aid.

Experience revealed that this supply-side response to health care system failure was itself prone to policy failure. The limited capacity of developing country governments to raise general tax revenue meant that funding always fell short of what would be required to provide even basic health care at low cost to entire populations. Political pressures directed scarce system resources into the creation of urban and high-level hospital facilities, rather than more dispersed clinics and rural health posts, limiting the number of households with physical access to service, especially for poorer households. Low salaries—and even lower budgets for medicines and supplies—encouraged government health care professionals to charge unofficial fees or require patients' families to purchase medications and supplies from outside vendors. This created additional barriers to use of government services by the poor. Government health care systems also failed to deliver high-quality care.

Encouraged by the World Bank, many countries sought to improve the performance of government health care systems in the 1990s by introducing or raising user fees. They hoped that by recovering larger fractions of cost per person served, they could stretch limited budgets further, reaching more people or providing higher-quality care. In practice, however, few benefits emerged, while health care utilization rates fell, the financial burden of health shocks on households increased, and health care policy impacts became even less equitable. Since 2000, some countries have abolished the user fees introduced in the 1990s, improving health care utilization rates, especially among the poor (Yates, 2009). Unfortunately, government budget constraints and governance problems continue to restrict the outreach and quality of government health care systems.

Many current efforts to increase health care utilization rates, improve the quality of care, and reduce the financial burden of care involve creating health *insurance* programs. These programs offer participants the promise of transfer payments to help cover the cost of health care in the event of specified health shocks, usually in exchange for the payment of premiums. In the next two subsections we examine the rationales for creating health insurance programs. We then set out the detailed design choices that define particular health insurance programs and raise questions about the determinants of their costs, outreach, and impacts. Finally, we take a closer look at a particular class of health insurance programs of current interest: community-based health insurance programs.

22.3A Health insurance, health care utilization, and out-of-pocket spending

In the absence of intervention by governments or NGOs, and in the absence of health insurance, people who become ill or injured would have to purchase health care from private providers, who charge user fees that cover costs. Serious health shocks might require care for which user fees equal months' or years' worth of household income. Under such circumstances, health shocks are a troubling source of risk for all households, rich and poor alike, because households hit by shocks must either obtain care and pay high out-of-pocket fees or must forgo care and suffer the worst physical and economic consequences of ill health.

Facing such costly risks, households should be willing to pay at least some fee to purchase health insurance contracts, which promise to pay for any necessary care in the event of health shocks. For households with the financial means to pay for care when hit by shocks, such contracts reduce vulnerability to financial shocks and poverty. For those who would have forgone care when hit by health shocks, such contracts would improve their health by allowing them to obtain health care.

If insurance markets were free of information problems, and if insurance transactions were costless to carry out, insurers would come forward to supply health insurance to many households while charging premiums that households are willing to pay. They could supply insurance at such premiums while covering costs, because they would benefit from **risk pooling**. They engage in risk pooling when they take on liability for the cost of any necessary health care for many people, only some of whom will in fact be struck by health shocks in a given year. They can take on these liabilities without having to bear much risk themselves because, although the cost of care that any one person will require in a year is highly uncertain, the cost of care required by a large population of clients in a year is much easier to predict. They can therefore estimate with reasonable accuracy the cost of fulfilling their insurance promises and can charge small premiums of all clients that together provide sufficient revenue to cover that cost.

For example, suppose each of 10,000 individuals faces a 2 percent chance of requiring a surgery that costs C pesos. If their risks are uncorrelated (or idiosyncratic, in the terminology of Chapter 10), then an insurer would know that close to 2 percent of them (200) will require surgery in any year. The number of surgeries required would fluctuate somewhat from year to year, but would average out to 200 over time. If the insurer charged each of the 10,000 individuals a premium equal to two percent of the cost of surgery ($0.02C$), the insurer would raise $10,000 \times 0.02C = 200C$ in revenue, which is enough to cover the cost of the promised surgeries (on average over time). Risk-averse clients would be willing to pay premiums even higher than this, because they would prefer to pay $0.02C$ for certain, than to face a 2 percent chance of paying the full cost C. This is the case because whether they pay this premium for insurance or go without insurance, the expected value of what they must pay (either in premiums or in user fees for surgery) is $0.02C$, but paying the certain premium is less risky. (For a review of expected value and risk-aversion concepts, see Chapter 10.) Liquidity-constrained clients who would be unable to pay C if hit by health shocks (but who are able to pay the smaller premiums) might be willing to pay even more for insurance, because without it they would have to forgo surgery and suffer the full health consequences of health shocks, possibly including pain, suffering, disability, or death. If insurance markets were free of frictions and imperfections, therefore, competitive for-profit insurers might often be able to charge premiums high enough to compensate them for their time (and for bearing the small risk they face), as well as for the necessary surgery costs.

The existence of a well-functioning health insurance market would reduce people's vulnerability to health shocks. The benefits of insurance would be especially great for poorer households, who would have to forgo health care in the absence of insurance, but insurance would also reduce the vulnerability of richer households to financial trauma. The insurance arrangements would achieve these benefits by spreading the cost of health care (for contract holders who fall ill) across all contract holders (including the many who remain healthy). It thus allows a redistribution of income from those who remain healthy to those who become sick, while leaving everyone better off, because even those who ultimately remain healthy benefit from reduced risk.

Unfortunately, formal health insurance markets are largely absent in developing countries. Chapter 10 described the transaction costs and asymmetric information problems that are thought to prevent their emergence. Informal insurance institutions (as described in Chapter 13) can help people bear the smaller costs of care for common health shocks, but they appear incapable of shielding people from the major financial burdens associated with less-frequent but more-serious illness and injury (Gertler and Gruber, 2002). Failure of insurance markets may therefore be understood as contributing to two critical symptoms of the failure of the health care system in the absence of intervention: low rates of health care utilization and high rates of impoverishment among those who obtain care.

The logic of health insurance market failures suggests that where households must pay significant user fees for health care, NGOs and governments may be able to increase health care utilization and reduce the financial burden associated with care by introducing new health insurance programs. Where private firms are unable to supply health insurance services profitably, public sector health insurance programs are likely to require subsidy, but the necessary subsidy might not be large. That is:

> It may be possible to provide insurance benefits to many households, increasing the rate of health care utilization and reducing the rate of health-shock-induced impoverishment, while charging premiums that cover large fractions of cost, because households' willingness and capacity to pay low and steady premiums when healthy may be greater than their capacity to pay sudden and large user fees when ill.

As always, while logic suggests the potential for health insurance programs to generate significant benefits at low cost, it does not guarantee that in practice the benefits will be large and the costs small. The nature and magnitude of impacts are likely to depend on the details of program design and context and to require careful empirical study.

22.3B Health insurance, health care quality, and efficiency

Health care improves people's lives by preventing death and disability, reducing pain and discomfort, and speeding recovery from health shocks. It is of high quality when its providers ask good questions, perform appropriate tests, draw sound conclusions from the information they gather, and perform procedures skillfully. Its value is also enhanced when it can be obtained speedily, in clean facilities, and from providers who treat patients with respect.

Health care is provided efficiently when a given array of services (defined by type and quality) is provided at lowest cost, and when providers expend any effort or resources on a patient's care for which the likely social benefits outweigh the social costs. The efficiency of health care provision suffers when health care equipment, supplies, and medicines are wasted or diverted to other uses, when health care professionals divert their work hours to other uses, and when health care professionals fail to administer high-value tests and procedures. In the presence of profound budget constraints, health care is also inefficient when providers administer costly tests and procedures that have very low expected benefit. Because some tests and procedures require specialized and costly equipment and staff, efficiency can require that many services be provided by widely dispersed and less-costly clinics and health posts, while a few are treated at a smaller number of higher-cost hospital facilities.

Doctors, nurses, and other frontline health care providers contribute to quality and efficiency by making good choices about how many hours to work, how quickly to work, what tests and procedures to perform, and how to perform them. To make good choices, they require appropriate knowledge and skills, timely availability of appropriate equipment, supplies and medications, and appropriate motivation.

Health care managers—whether policymakers or private health care providers—help determine the quality and efficiency of care when they decide on the geographic distribution of facilities of different types and the institutional structure through which they govern the activities of health care professionals. They set hiring standards and determine what training, mentoring, equipment, supplies, medicines, and discretionary budgets to provide to staff. They set guidelines and protocols for diagnosis and treatment, design mechanisms for monitoring performance, and design pay and promotion schemes. To make good management choices, they, too, require appropriate knowledge, skills, resources, and motivation.

Patients influence the efficiency of health care when they decide when and where to seek care and how much care to demand. They can contribute to inefficiency by waiting too long before seeking care, seeking treatment for simple health conditions at high-cost facilities, or demanding high-cost tests and procedures that deliver little benefit.

Markets are unlikely to yield high-quality and efficient health care in the absence of intervention, for several reasons. Most households lack expert medical knowledge, and thus they have much less information than providers about the quality and necessity of the care provided. Providers might take advantage of this asymmetry of information by charging high fees for low-quality care. Paid on a fee-for-service basis, providers might also seek to raise profits by prescribing unnecessary tests, procedures, and medications. Households' lack of knowledge regarding when and where to seek care might further diminish efficiency. In addition, financial market limitations can render it difficult for health care providers to manage stocks of medicines and supplies in the face of randomly fluctuating demands for care and inflows of user fee revenue.

Health insurance programs and health care governance

Health insurance programs have the potential to improve health care quality and efficiency by creating a new institutional interface between health care consumers and health care suppliers, which improves the governance of health care management and health care use decisions. Rather than paying health care providers directly, participants in some health insurance programs empower program staff to strike contracts with and pay health care providers on their behalf. Some insurance programs contract directly with health care professionals and provide covered health care in house, while others contract with third-party health care organizations run by independent managers.

The new institutional arrangements can help health care consumers coordinate their demands and negotiate better contractual arrangements, which improve the governance of health care management decisions. Working together through an insurer, health care users can hire expert staff to monitor and hold providers accountable, an investment no one user would undertake on her own. Working through a health insurance program, they can also hire providers under new contractual forms. For example, rather than paying providers on a fee-for-service basis, they may pay them fixed fees per patient (under **capitation** pay schemes) or per health shock episode (with fees differing across episodes involving health shocks in different diagnostic groups). Such pay schemes motivate providers to avoid unnecessary tests or procedures. (They might also discourage them from spending time and supplies on patients, and they thus make most sense when accompanied by well-enforced health care quality standards.) Health insurance programs may also offer providers a steadier stream of payments, possibly facilitating improvements in health care quality and cost by improving management of medicine stocks. By negotiating with providers collectively, health insurance program participants can also raise their bargaining power relative to health care providers.

Further efficiency gains may be possible when health insurance programs encourage households to make more efficient use of the health care system. By requiring consumers to see primary care providers first (except in cases of emergency) and obtain referrals before seeking care at hospitals, insurance programs can encourage consumers to obtain effective care from the least-cost providers. Coverage of primary care visits can encourage households to enter the health care system at earlier stages of illness, when treatment is more effective and less costly. Efforts to promote good hygiene, use of bed nets, and other preventive measures can also improve health at low cost.

In summary:

> Health insurance programs have the potential to improve health care quality and efficiency by providing health care managers and professionals with higher-powered incentives or more predictable financing, by increasing health care users' bargaining power, or by improving their use of the health care system through rules or education.

When a health insurance program is created as part of a larger government health sector reform, which simultaneously raises the user fees charged for government health care at time of need, it represents a shift from supply-side to **demand-side financing** of government-subsidized health care. When governments supply low-cost health care in public sector facilities, policymakers and administrators suffer all the usual challenges to good governance within civil service bureaucracies. When they instead supply insurance, empowering households to demand health care from private providers, they put health care management decisions into the hands of private sector agents, who are free from bureaucratic rigidities, and who may be motivated to improve quality and efficiency by the need to compete for contracts or patients. When policymakers go one step further, and provide households with financing to purchase health insurance from competing private providers, they might hope to improve the efficiency of health insurance service provision as well as health care provision.

22.3C Design and implementation of health insurance programs

Health insurance programs are among the most complicated programs examined in this text. They distribute transfers (i.e., indemnities) that are triggered by random events (i.e., health shocks) and are tied to the use of health care. Basic policy design choices define the conditions under which indemnities will be paid and the sizes of indemnity payments; premium levels; procedures for recruitment, enrollment and distribution of indemnities; and eligibility requirements. In addition, policymakers face many critical governance structure choices.

Basic policy design choices

Health insurance programs differ greatly in the details of the **insurance coverage** they offer. Some programs offer coverage for the care of **catastrophic health shocks**, which are life-threatening and require surgery, hospitalization, or costly medication. Other programs offer coverage for the smaller and more frequent costs of **primary health care** services, which include the diagnosis and treatment of common illnesses, usually in clinics or health posts. Whether covering catastrophic care or primary care (or both), programs might specify lists of conditions and types of care that they will or will not cover. Some exclude coverage for particularly costly conditions such as HIV/AIDS, and many exclude coverage for medications. A few programs cover the cost of transport from participants' home communities to health care facilities. Some cover only the costs of care provided in house (i.e., by employees of the insuring organization), while others cover care provided by a list of qualifying third-party providers.

Within any class of covered health shocks and treatments, the generosity of coverage is defined by deductibles, coinsurance rates, and caps on out-of-pocket spending or indemnity payments. In some programs, participants must pay out of pocket for health care costs up to specified **deductible** levels (per health shock episode or per year), before additional costs are covered by indemnities, while others offer **first dollar coverage** (i.e., zero deductibles). Very generous programs might cover 100 percent of health care costs beyond the deductible level, while others might cover only 60 percent, thereby imposing 40 percent **coinsurance rates** on participants. Some programs impose per-episode **out-of-pocket payment caps**, promising to cover any costs in excess of that cap, and others impose **insurer payment caps**, requiring participants to cover any costs over the cap.

In addition to determining program coverage, designers must set the premiums or registration fees that participants pay. Programs differ in the levels of the fees and how they vary across income levels or demographic characteristics.

Additional design choices set the procedures for enrolling participants, collecting their premiums and verifying their eligibility when they attempt to claim benefits. Because health insurance is a complicated concept and new in many developing areas, enrollment drives sometimes include efforts to educate households about the potential value of insurance, as well as about the existence of the program and their eligibility for it.

Once enrolled, participants who become ill or injured must claim the indemnities promised by the program. Sometimes they must first pay for health care out of pocket and then fill out applications for reimbursement. Some recent programs allow participants to claim benefits in a **cashless and paperless** fashion, simply by presenting identification and asking for care from a participating provider.

Definition of eligibility requirements is critical to the design of poverty-targeted health insurance programs like India's National Health Insurance Scheme, described in Box 22.4 below. The targeting options are the same as those for targeted transfer programs (as analyzed in Chapter 15), including assessments based on means tests or proxy means tests, community discussions, geographic location, or demographic characteristics. In some cases, participation is limited to members of specific communities, agricultural cooperatives, microcredit programs or other local organizations, or to employees of specific employers.

A final distinguishing design feature is whether participation is mandatory or voluntary. Many of the oldest health insurance programs in developing countries are **mandatory** for all formal sector workers. Formal sector workers are wage employees, usually in urban establishments with at least 10 employees, whose employers are legally registered and comply with payroll tax law. The mandate is enforced by using payroll taxes to deduct premiums before workers receive their pay. Mandatory programs are limited to formal sector workers (and their families), because this is the only group for which enforcement of the mandate is feasible in developing countries. In Latin America, mandatory programs were introduced as far back as the 1930s, and the programs now cover over half the population. In today's poorer countries, however, very few people work in the formal sector, and mandatory programs might cover as little as 10 percent of the population.

In programs targeting the many developing-country households outside the formal sector, participation is voluntary. Our primary focus in the remainder of the chapter is on voluntary programs.

≡ Box 22.4 India's Poverty-Targeted National Health Insurance Scheme

In February 2008, the Indian government introduced an ambitious and innovative National Health Insurance Scheme, which seeks to cover the costs of hospital care for all households identified as living below the poverty line. The program subsidizes the purchase of health insurance, which participating households can use to pay for care from competitive health care providers. To enroll, households must be officially recognized as below the poverty line (BPL), through proxy means tests that are conducted by their state governments. The program provides eligible households with first dollar coverage for in-patient hospital care for more than 725 procedures and up to five members per family. Total health care benefits per household per annum are capped at 30,000 rupees. The program also covers up to 100 rupees of transport cost per visit, up to a total of 1,000 rupees per household per year. Households may begin to claim these benefits one month after enrolling and paying an annual per-household registration fee of 30 rupees.

The program's administrative structure is designed with careful attention to ease of use by beneficiaries and to the incentives of all program-implementing parties. Essential to the design is the use of smart card technology. Upon enrollment, households are provided with smart cards, which store photo and fingerprint information for all enrolled family members. Participating health care providers must acquire smart card readers, which allow them to check eligibility, transmit the identity of health care recipients and the nature of the health care they receive to insurers and program officials, and charge the cost of care against the coverage cap recorded on the participants' cards. This allows health care providers to bill health insurers for payment, and it allows enrollees to claim health insurance benefits in a cashless and paperless fashion.

The central government sets participant registration fees and minimum standards for insurance coverage. It also sets technological standards so that smart cards issued in any state and by any insurer may be read in any participating health care facility throughout the country. It offers to cover 75 percent of program costs for state governments that agree to cover the other 25 percent of costs and comply with program standards. To obtain funds, state governments enter into contract with the central government, provide staff to monitor insurers in the field, and provide insurers with electronic lists of eligible BPL households. The sharing of cost between states and central government should encourage states to comply with standards and contribute funding, while also encouraging them to contain costs.

Insurance services are provided by public and private sector organizations that compete to win contracts with state governments, under which they become the sole providers of program insurance within districts (which are geographic units smaller than states). They are assigned to enroll eligible households during a four-month enrollment period each year. Their enrollment efforts are overseen by state government field officers, who must verify household heads' identities. A smart card may be issued only when a field officer indicates approval by inserting his smart card into the smart card printer. Insurers must also identify health care providers that meet program standards and make state-specified payments to health care providers for covered services

provided. Insurers compete for contracts by bidding a level of premium that the state government must pay them per enrolled household. Competition should provide them with motivation to hold down costs, while payment tied to the number of enrolled households should motivate them to spread awareness and make enrollment easy for households. They are prohibited from denying enrollment to eligible households on the grounds of pre-existing health conditions. The least-healthy households, who have the most to gain from an insurance contract, are likely to enroll first; thus interest in reducing per-participant costs by broadening outreach might provide insurers with additional motivation to pursue high enrollments. Insurers are required to engage NGOs to assist with educating participants about how to claim benefits.

Health care services are provided by public and private sector hospitals selected by insurers. They must provide covered procedures in exchange for fees that are set by the state government and paid by the insurers, and they must set up 24-hour desks equipped with smart card readers. Rules prohibit them from charging fees to participants and require them to pay transportation benefits to participants upon admission. When a patient is discharged, use of the smart card triggers payment by the insurer to the provider.

According to the papers in Palacios et al. (2011), early implementation outcomes are encouraging though imperfect. Most states have signed on, and insurers have come forward to offer bids. The winning bids have come in below ceilings set by the central government, and they were lower in the second year than in the first, averaging 560 rupees per household per year. In 2011, insurers enrolled 23 million households. Although this is a large number, it represents less than half of the target population in program regions.

Implementation shortcomings have arisen where implementers' incentives are not well aligned with policymakers' goals, however. Insurers, who are paid on a per-enrolled-household basis, sometimes enrolled only one member per household, rather than the five members they are required to cover. Paid a uniform fee for enrollment of households in any location, they also failed to run enrollment drives in some more costly and remote locations. Initially, enrollments were often delayed by the failure of state government field officers to appear at enrollment sites. Some states improved the enrollment process by offering the field officers small bonuses per enrollment. Insurers are slow to hire NGOs to educate clients about making claims. Health care providers seldom pay transportation benefits to patients, and they often charge fees. One fifth to one third of patients report paying at least some health care costs out of pocket. State governments are sometimes slow to pay insurers, who in turn are slow to pay providers.

The most common criticism of the program is that its targeting is highly flawed, for reasons beyond the direct control of program implementers. The state-provided lists of BPL households are out of date, suffer from data entry errors, and are based on proxy means tests that are thought to be highly imperfect.

Source: Palacios et al. (2011).

Implementation and governance

Health insurance programs offer households the opportunity to pay a premium in exchange for help paying the cost of specified types of health care. The implementation outcomes that ultimately shape program impacts include, most obviously, the geographic distribution of communities that become involved in the program, the basic program design choices made by any decentralized or private sector decision makers, and the way recruitment, education, eligibility assessment, and indemnity distributions are carried out in practice. Because indemnity payments are tied to the use of health care, program impacts are also shaped by the quality and accessibility of health care for diverse health conditions.

Program impacts thus depend on the quality of three sets of implementation decisions: any **decentralized choices regarding basic program design** (as described above), **insurance program implementation choices** (which help determine how enrollment efforts and eligibility assessments are carried out in practice, how rapidly and reliably claims are processed, and the efficiency with which these services are provided), and **health care management choices** (which determine the quality, locations, and efficiency of covered health care). Policymakers influence these implementation outcomes through their governance structure choices.

Health insurance program governance structures differ in the extent to which the management of insurance services and covered health care services are integrated into program institutions. In **fully integrated programs**, program employees manage and provide both health insurance and health care services. Such programs provide subsidies for health insurance and health care in a supply-side fashion, by directly providing low-cost health care. Within such integrated programs, governance structures can differ in the extent to which insurance service and health care management choices are made in a centralized fashion and in the resources, capacity-building services, and accountability mechanisms provided to any decentralized decision makers.

Rather than managing health care provision directly within integrated organizations, health insurance programs might allow participants to purchase health care from **third-party health care providers**. The list of eligible third-party providers can include public or private providers in hospitals, clinics, health care institution networks, or private practice. When they allow use of third-party health care providers, policymakers must determine eligibility criteria for participation by providers, the scope participants are given to choose among providers, the standards and protocols the providers must comply with to retain eligibility, and the arrangements through which they are paid for their services.

Yet other programs, including the program described in Box 22.4, make use of **third-party health insurance providers** as well as third-party health care providers. By distributing vouchers or arranging for participants to enroll at low premiums, such health insurance programs subsidize participants' purchase of program insurance from qualifying public or private sector insurers. Program designers specify the standards that third-party insurers must meet to qualify for participation and the nature of any competition through which they are selected. They must also determine how much latitude to give the third parties in designing insurance products and promotion programs, enrollment and claims procedures, and the extent to which program participants may exercise choice among insurers. Typically third-party insurers are given responsibility for designing and implementing the governance of health care providers. Some private insurers choose to provide health care as well as health insurance through integrated for-profit organizations, while other insurers allow their clients to work with third-party care providers.

Large programs differ in the extent to which decision making is allocated across central, state, district, and community levels. Many current programs fall under the label of **community-based health insurance** (CBHI) programs, in which members of communities or local organizations are asked to collaborate in designing and administering health insurance programs for members. The governments or NGOs that seek to initiate and nurture such programs must choose the rules and guidelines by which the local decision-making bodies are formed, and what resources, capacity-building services, and accountability mechanisms to provide for them. We take a closer look at these programs in the next section.

22.3D **Health insurance program costs and subsidies**

Insurance programs take in revenue from any premiums or fees charged to participants, and they incur costs of three broad types: the costs of covered health care (i.e., the cost of fulfilling indemnity promises), the financial transaction costs associated with providing insurance services, and the costs of fulfilling any other program functions, such as eligibility assessment or participant education. The costs of covered health care can take the form of reimbursements to participants or direct payments to health care providers.

The per-person subsidy required to sustain an insurance program is equal to the difference between the average per-person cost and any per-person premiums or registration fees collected. The two most obvious ways to reduce the per-person subsidy also reduce the value of the program to participants: increasing the premium and reducing program generosity. But these are not the only ways to reduce cost.

> Program designers might hope to reduce the per-person subsidy required to sustain a health insurance program, without reducing the value of the program to participants, in four ways: mitigating adverse selection, mitigating moral hazard, improving the governance of health care, and improving the governance of health insurance and program implementation activities.

Per-person costs are elevated by the **adverse selection** into the program of only the least healthy people, who expect to make more claims for health care coverage. Program designers might induce more participation by healthier individuals in several ways. By requiring participants to pay premiums for at least one month before claiming benefits, they discourage people from waiting until they become ill to join the program. By requiring families to join as a unit, they prevent households from signing up only their least-healthy members. By requiring members of an agricultural cooperative to make joint decisions regarding participation, they can draw in some healthier members who would not have chosen to participate on their own, and by promoting participation as a way that neighbors can help each other they can encourage some healthier community-minded people to contribute.

Per-person costs are elevated also by the **moral hazard** of excessive health care use generated by insurance. When households obtain insurance, the effective user fees they must pay when hit by health shocks drop to low levels. This might encourage them to demand costly tests and procedures with little potential benefit. Health care providers compensated on a fee-for-service basis may be happy to provide such services. Health insurance programs might attempt to mitigate moral hazard by shifting from fee-for-service payment of health care providers to other contractual arrangements, by requiring providers to follow specified protocols for care, and by covering only a list of essential health care services.

Improved governance of health care implementation choices can also reduce per-client costs by improving the efficiency of providing health care services. They might improve health care governance by improving the design or enforcement of contractual arrangements with health care providers or by providing clients with rules or education that improve their health care choices.

Finally, program designers might hope to reduce per-person costs by improving the governance of health insurance and program activities. The transaction costs involved in enrolling participants, collecting premiums, verifying claims, reimbursing clients, paying health care providers, assessing eligibility, and implementing education and promotion activities can be large. Designers might try to improve governance of these activities by improving accountability mechanisms or information technologies, altering hiring requirements and training programs, finding lower-cost delivery mechanisms within public sector bureaucracies, or by privatizing insurance functions.

22.3E Impacts and enrollment

Direct impacts

Households may anticipate three types of benefit during a year of insurance coverage. When hit by covered health shocks for which they *would* have obtained health care even without insurance, households may enjoy reductions in out-of-pocket spending on health care or improvements in the quality of care they receive (with associated improvements in health). When participants are hit by covered shocks for which they *would not* have obtained care without insurance, the receipt of indemnities may also increase their use of health care (again improving health). When health insurance leads them to get health care they otherwise would have gone without, participation may *increase* out-of-pocket spending if the program requires participants to pay deductible or coinsurance rates, but care might save their lives, prevent long-term disability, or improve their health in other ways. The private and social returns to this care may be high, because the insurance might relax a liquidity constraint that had prevented them from obtaining highly valuable care. Any of these impacts can raise well-being in the long run as well as the short run by improving health, preventing households from selling off assets, or preventing households from falling into debt.

The magnitude, duration, and distribution of benefits can differ significantly across program designs and context. Simple models of expected utility maximization under perfect information, as introduced in Chapter 10, highlight how the value of benefits can depend on details of program design. Most obviously, households derive greater benefit when programs cover a larger subset of the health shocks they face, cover costlier health shocks, or offer more generous coverage for given health shocks. Increases in the generosity of coverage might raise the benefits more for the poor than the nonpoor, because reductions in out-of-pocket costs might allow some poor households to take advantage of health insurance and obtain care in cases of large health shocks that they would have left untreated under less generous programs.

More subtly, we might expect insurance covering catastrophic illness to raise well-being by more than insurance covering primary care (while holding the per-participant expected value of indemnity payments and health care quality constant in the comparison). Intuitively, health insurance that provides no coverage for devastating health shocks reduces vulnerability only a little. More technically, for a risk-averse household, anticipated receipt of an indemnity payment when hit by a catastrophic health care shock would tend to raise well-being by more than the receipt of an indemnity payment of the same size when only primary care is required because for risk-averse individuals, marginal improvements in finances or health tend to increase utility more when the initial state of finances or health is lower. (See problem 3.) Catastrophic coverage may, furthermore, be less likely to crowd out coverage by informal insurance institutions, which help households cope with small health shocks but not large ones, as mentioned above.

Simple models of decision making under uncertainty also suggest that less-healthy households would place greater value on given health insurance coverage than healthier households, because they are more likely to require care and receive indemnities.

To derive any health insurance benefits at all, households must anticipate *using* indemnities to obtain high-quality health care and successfully claiming the indemnities when hit by covered health shocks. Households might therefore perceive few benefits to participating in a health insurance program if they live far from health care facilities or if they live near facilities providing only low-quality care. They may be put off from claiming benefits by the cost or difficulty of transportation to health care facilities, capacity constraints that induce rationing of care, bureaucratic difficulties with establishing eligibility or making claims, or the financial difficulty of making payments up front (when programs distribute indemnities as reimbursements after the fact). Health care providers may be unwilling to provide covered care if the payments they receive from clients and insurers do not cover their costs.

The benefits of participation rise with programs' success in improving health care quality, both by improving health in the wake of shocks for which households would have obtained care even in the absence of insurance and by increasing the rate at which households make use of health care and claim benefits. Programs involving strategic purchasing of health care by program managers or private health insurers are more likely to improve quality than programs reimbursing health care on a fee-for-service basis (Carrin et al., 2005). Unfortunately, the creation of health insurance programs might instead reduce health care quality by increasing the number of people seeking treatment. Boosting demand can increase congestion unless suppliers respond elastically. The nature and magnitude of program benefits therefore depend also on the elasticities of supply for diverse sorts of health care.

In summary:

> The value participants derive from health insurance programs increases with the breadth and generosity of insurance coverage, the initial accessibility and quality of available health care, the policy attention given to improving health care quality, the ease and speed of obtaining care and claiming benefits, and the elasticity of health care supply. The value is also greater for people who anticipate greater health care needs. It may be lower for poorer households if liquidity constraints and coinsurance requirements render them less able to take advantage of insurance benefits.

Health insurance programs can generate spillover effects as well. Health care quality might rise or fall for nonparticipant users of participating health care facilities. If insurance speeds participants' recovery from infectious diseases, nonparticipants might benefit from reduced disease transmission. Any impacts of health improvements on participants' consumption, time allocation, production, and investment choices might also alter prices and wages important to nonparticipants' real incomes.

Enrollment

Health insurance programs increase health and financial security for many people only if they succeed in enrolling many households. In practice, achieving high enrollments appears to be one of the greatest challenges faced by developing-country health insurance programs, many of which enroll only small fractions of their target populations. We begin exploring this challenge by observing that a household head enrolls in a health insurance program only if he is aware of the program, is deemed eligible, and judges that the benefits of participation outweigh the costs. The costs of participation include premium payments and any other time or money costs associated with participation, including the financing costs associated with paying premiums at the beginning of the coverage period. Households compare these costs not to the actual benefits, as described earlier, but to what they understand and value about the benefits.

To fully understand the benefits of health insurance, a household would have to know its chances of being hit by various health shocks, the potential benefits of obtaining health care, the user fees it would have to pay for care without insurance, and the indemnities it would receive with insurance. Household members would have to understand the notion of paying for conditional promises of assistance, for which there is no rebate if assistance is not required. Given the evidence we examined earlier regarding the limited effects of education on use of health inputs, we might guess that well-designed education programs have the potential to increase enrollment but that designing effective education programs may be a significant challenge. Temporary subsidies that encourage households and their neighbors to gain experience with health insurance and health care might raise subsequent willingness to pay if households tend to underestimate the benefits or overestimate the costs.

Enrollment may be diminished by households' lack of trust in those who offer insurance. Lack of trust may be an even greater inhibitor to purchases of health insurance than health inputs. Households must pay premiums in exchange for a promise of future and uncertain indemnity payments, and such a promise has little value unless they trust the insurer to be honest and prudent. A legal and institutional structure that regulates insurers' activities and stands ready to finance their temporary budgetary shortfalls might encourage enrollment.

Local institutional rules and norms that promote mutual assistance and cooperation may encourage participation in community-level insurance programs. Households may value the opportunity to assist neighbors by paying premiums and participating. They might also cooperate in the hope of achieving improvements in the quality of local health care that are possible only through collective action.

Liquidity constraints can prevent some households from making premium payments, just as they prevent some households from purchasing health inputs. Program design changes that reduce the difficulty of mustering the necessary liquidity—such as moving premium payment deadlines to harvest seasons, when many households have cash, or collecting small payments frequently throughout the year—might increase enrollment rates.

In summary:

> Enrollments can fall as premiums rise, and there is no guarantee that voluntary health insurance programs can enroll large fractions of their target groups while charging premiums that cover large fractions of cost. Holding objective benefits constant, it may be possible to increase households' willingness to pay for insurance through education, by temporarily subsidizing (more heavily) their acquisition of experience, through institutional changes that enhance confidence in the program's integrity and solvency, through efforts to harness local institutions' encouragement for mutual assistance and cooperation, and by helping households overcome liquidity constraints on premium payments.

Naturally, enrollment rates might rise as objective program benefits rise (holding premiums constant). Enrollments may also be lower among poorer households, who are more likely to be liquidity constrained, and for whom remote location and lack of education can constitute barriers to participation.

Several forces that can reduce willingness to pay for socially valuable insurance may be stronger for catastrophic insurance coverage than for primary care coverage. First, concerns that insolvency will prevent insurers from fulfilling promises may be greater for insurers offering catastrophic coverage, especially when programs cover only small populations. Small fluctuations from year to year in the number of participants requiring expensive treatments such as heart surgery can cause large shortfalls of premium receipts relative to indemnity costs in high-claim years, and in the absence of adequate reserves or credit, insurers might find themselves unable to cover all claims. Second, households can gain confidence-boosting experience with insurance more easily and quickly in the case of primary care coverage, because they and their neighbors are more likely to experience the relevant health shocks and receive indemnities during a first year of coverage. Third, program participants might perceive greater potential for programs to improve the quality of primary care in local facilities than of catastrophic care in more distant facilities. Fourth, behavioral economists point out that people often under-appreciate the significance of low-probability events and underinsure themselves against such events (Camerer and Kunreuther, 1989; Laury et al., 2009). For all these reasons, difficulties in achieving high enrollment rates may be especially great for programs offering catastrophic coverage.

22.3F Evaluation of voluntary health insurance programs

Sections 22.3A and 22.3B provided reasons to hope that health insurance programs will improve health care utilization and quality, and reduce impoverishment by health shocks, at low cost. Subsequent sections explained why it may be difficult for health insurance programs to fulfill these hopes. Box 22.5, which adapts Chapter 14's seven questions for use in the study of voluntary health insurance programs, therefore emphasizes the need for careful empirical study of insurance programs' outreach; their impacts on health care utilization, health care quality,

≡ **Box 22.5** Questions to Guide Analysis of Voluntary Health Insurance Programs

Question 1: Objectives

To what extent do policymakers intend the program to increase health care utilization, reduce out-of-pocket expenditures on health care, or improve the quality or cost of health care? What is the program's target group?

Question 2: Design

What policy design choices regarding insurance coverage and premiums; eligibility requirements; procedures for enrollment, recruitment, claims, and education; and governance structure define the policy on paper?

Question 3: Implementation

In which communities does the program enroll participants? Who makes any local-level policy design and implementation choices and what choices do they make? In practice, who is deemed eligible, how costly and difficult is it to enroll, what efforts are made to recruit and educate participants, what premiums and other fees are charged, what insurance coverage is provided, how costly and difficult is it to access health care, what quality of health care is available, and how efficiently are health care and health insurance program services performed?

Question 4: Directly affected groups

Who enrolls in the program? What fraction of the target group enrolls? To what extent does the program reach the poorest households within its target group?

Question 5: Direct effects

What effect does participation have on participants' use of health care services and out-of-pocket spending? What effect does the program have on the quality of care participants receive? What is the program's impact on their health, time use, income, consumption, saving, and investment? How do these impacts differ across poor and nonpoor households and across households in different locations?

Question 6: Spillover and feedback effects

What spillover effects does the program generate for nonparticipants through changes in health care quality and efficiency or through changes in participants' involvement in markets for goods, services, and labor?

Question 7: Budgetary costs

How much subsidy is required on average to sustain the program at its current levels of participation and insurance coverage? How much does the level of subsidy required vary from year to year?

out-of-pocket spending, health, and household asset holdings; and the subsidies required to sustain the programs.

22.3G Community-based health insurance

People are protected against the worst consequences of health shocks when they have effective access to quality health care at costs that do not impoverish them. Many countries provide such protection to formal sector workers through mandatory health insurance programs that charge cost-covering premiums. A few middle-income countries offer highly subsidized protection to the poorest households. The great majority of developing-country households, however, lack access to mandatory and poverty-targeted programs because their members work outside the formal sector and either fail poverty-targeting eligibility tests or live in countries without poverty-targeted programs. Some governments, microfinance institutions, and NGOs hope to provide health insurance protection to this large and diverse group, even on very limited budgets, through the creation of **community-based health insurance** (CBHI) programs.

Also known as mutual health organizations or micro health insurance programs, CBHI programs are voluntary, nonprofit health insurance schemes, usually organized at a subnational level, through which members of communities, agricultural cooperatives, microcredit programs, or other local organizations cooperate in program design, administration, and financing. Most have simple structures, charge flat-rate premiums, and encourage an ethic of mutual assistance and solidarity. Some are homegrown collaborations among members of single communities, seeking to improve their access to health care. Others are the creations of nonprofit hospitals, seeking to improve their outreach by allowing households to prepay for health care. Yet others are catalyzed and supported by large NGO or government programs that work in many communities.

The hope that CBHI programs can protect many poor and near-poor households against health risks while covering most costs—even while for-profit insurers and large government programs have been unable to do so—rests on the belief that community groups have important cost advantages in providing insurance over private insurers and government bureaucracies. Community organizations can hold down costs by using volunteers (or local leaders paid token fees) as administrators and by keeping programs simple. They may be able to mitigate adverse selection problems by requiring all members of an agricultural cooperative or microcredit group to make collective enrollment decisions or by encouraging many community members to participate in a spirit of mutual assistance. They might also have greater capacity than nonlocal actors to reduce health care costs (and increase quality) through bargaining with local health care providers.

CBHI programs might also inspire higher willingness to pay for similar benefits, allowing them to reach comparable groups while charging higher premiums and covering more costs. Local organizations might inspire more trust, if they provide households with opportunity for close involvement. Participatory organizations might also have greater capacity to design coverage and logistical details well suited to local needs.

Although the logic of these potential advantages inspires hope, careful empirical study of CBHI performance is required, because community organizations might also suffer disadvantages relative to other insurers, and even if the advantages outweigh the disadvantages, they may not be great enough to ensure success. As we know from Chapter 12, local-level cooperation is difficult, and healthy local institutions often fail to develop, even when they would be valuable. From Chapter 13 we know that when local institutions do arise, they are often captured by the local elite. Community members might also lack the knowledge and skills required for excellence in designing benefits packages, setting premiums, negotiating with health care providers, or managing money.

Furthermore, CBHI programs might suffer disadvantages related to their small scale. When pooling risks, insurers covering only small populations face greater fluctuations from year to year in the percentage of clients requiring costly care and thus face greater risks of insolvency. When they cover clients only within small geographic areas, they also become susceptible to covariate health shocks, such as local epidemics, that strike many of the insured simultaneously. Small scale might also elevate per-member administration costs and reduce the organizations' ability to exercise influence over quality or fees at large hospitals.

Few studies of CBHI performance combine details on program design, enrollment performance, and subsidy levels with rigorous estimation of program impacts on health care utilization, financial protection, and other household outcomes. Even so, we may draw a few cautious conclusions from experience to date.

CBHI programs appear capable of enrolling households in poor communities while charging nontrivial premiums. For example, many CBHI programs have arisen in the Thiès region of Senegal, where the average per-capita income of the richest quintile is about $28 per month (Jütting, 2004). The premiums are low, but they are nontrivial for this population: a typical scheme charges a one-time entrance fee of approximately $1.50 and then monthly per-capita fees of $0.15 to $0.30.

CBHI programs also appear capable of increasing health care utilization and financial security for participants. Aggarwal (2010) finds that participants in the Yeshavini program in India increased the number of visits to medical facilities by 6 to 7 percent, reduced borrowing to pay for care by 30 percent, and reduced payment for care out of savings and other sources by even more. Anecdotal evidence suggests that some CBHI programs also succeed in improving the availability of essential drugs, setting up simple primary care facilities within their communities, or improving cleanliness and attendance by medical professionals at local health care facilities.

Despite the evidence that CBHI programs *can* significantly improve households' protection against health shocks, the performance of the CBHI sector as a whole has proved disappointing. CBHI programs seldom attract enrollment by large fractions of their target populations. A few unusual schemes enroll more than half of eligible households, but few schemes cover more than 25 percent and many cover less than 15 percent (Carrin et al., 2005). Even in Senegal, where CBHI programs have multiplied and grown over two decades, they still reach only 5 percent of the population (Bonan et al., 2011). CBHI outreach is especially limited among poorer members of their target groups, unless governments, religious organizations, or other outside actors subsidize premium payments for the poorest (Preker and Carrin, 2004). The poor are sometimes put off by the difficulty of paying fees, and they are sometimes shut out by institutional restrictions, such as the limiting of enrollment to members of agricultural cooperatives.

Even among CBHI participants, few obtain comprehensive protection against health shocks. Many programs cover only primary health care costs. Among programs offering coverage for hospital care and other catastrophic costs, many charge 40 or 50 percent coinsurance rates, which can prevent poor households from obtaining care for serious illnesses even if insured, and which leave them exposed to large financial shocks. In addition, very few CBHI programs attempt to improve the quality, accessibility, or cost of local health care. In an International Labor Organization (ILO) review (Baeza et al., 2002), only 10 of the 62 programs for which information was available engaged in any sort of strategic purchasing of medicine or health care.

A final limitation in CBHI performance to date is the programs' inability to cover large fractions of cost, despite offering only weak benefits and charging premiums that are off-putting to at least some households (Preker et al., 2004). We might guess that programs achieving higher enrollment rates probably require greater per-person subsidy, but systematic evidence is unavailable.

What limits CBHI performance? And what scope is there to improve performance through better program design or through the provision of additional NGO or government support? Comprehensive answers to these questions will require much additional research. Two recent sets of research results, however, suggest the complexity of the health insurance challenge.

First, as we might expect, people have a hard time understanding the insurance concept and appreciating the benefits of paying for a service they might not need. Nonparticipants indicate lack of understanding as a reason for nonparticipation, and participants complain when premiums are not returned after years in which they make no claims. Even so, recent randomized control trials in Senegal and Kenya find no impact on CBHI enrollment rates of financial literacy programs emphasizing risk and insurance concepts, which were provided by experienced and well-respected NGOs (Bonan et al., 2011; Dercon et al., 2011).

Second, a growing body of research suggests that lack of trust in insurers' promises of indemnities might seriously limit households' willingness to pay for health insurance. Enrollment rates rise with measures of households' trust in CBHI providers and are more sensitive to premium rates among those who lack trust (Dercon et al., 2011). Enrollment rates also *fall* as measures of risk aversion rise in some populations. If households trusted insurers to pay promised indemnities, then we would expect more risk-averse households to value insurance more highly. When insurers cannot be trusted to pay indemnities, however, purchasing insurance creates a new possible state of the world that is worse than any other, in which households are hit by serious health shocks and receive no indemnities after paying out premiums, and the most risk-averse households might find this unacceptable (Dercon et al., 2011). Unfortunately, research has not yet provided a clear guide to boosting trust. Policymakers might wish to experiment with efforts to increase transparency, provide local CBHI programs with reinsurance (to reduce risks of insolvency), create and enforce prudential regulations for nonprofit insurers, or alter the institutions that govern CBHIs in other ways.

REFERENCES

Aggarwal, Aradhna. "Impact Evaluation of India's 'Yeshasvini' Community-Based Health Insurance Programme." *Health Economics* 19(S1): 5–35, 2010. doi:10.1002/hec.1605

Baeza, Cristian, Fernando Montenegro, and Marco Núñez. "Extending Social Protection in Health Through Community Based Health Organizations: Evidence and Challenges." Discussion Paper. Geneva: International Labour Organization, 2002.

Banerjee, Abhijit V., Angus Deaton, and Esther Duflo. "Health Care Delivery in Rural Rajasthan." *Economic and Political Weekly* 39(9): 944–949, 2004. http://epw.in/epw/user/viewAbstract.jsp

Banerjee, Abhijit V., and Esther Duflo. *Poor Economics: A Radical Rethinking of the Way to Fight Global Poverty.* New York: PublicAffairs, 2011.

Banerjee, Abhijit V., Esther Duflo, Rachel Glennerster, and Dhruva Kothari. "Improving Immunisation Coverage in Rural India: Clustered Randomised Controlled Evaluation of Immunisation Campaigns With and Without Incentives." *British Medical Journal* 340 (1): c2220, 2010. doi:10.1136/bmj.c2220

Bertrand, Marianne, Sendhil Mullainathan, and Eldar Shafir. "Behavioral Economics and Marketing in Aid of Decision Making Among the Poor." *Journal of Public Policy & Marketing* 25(1): 8–23, 2006. doi:10.1509/jppm.25.1.8

Bonan, Jacopo, Olivier Dagnelie, Philippe LeMay-Boucher, and Michel Tenikue. "Is it All About Money? A Randomized Evaluation of the Impact of Insurance Literacy and Marketing Treatments on the Demand for Health Microinsurance in Senegal." CISEPS Working Paper No 1/2012. University of Milano Bicocca, 2011. http://ssrn.com/abstract=1990203

Camerer, Colin F., and Howard Kunreuther. "Decision Processes for Low Probability Events: Policy Implications." *Journal of Policy Analysis and Management* 8(4): 565–592, 1989. http://www.jstor.org/stable/3325045

Canning, David. "The Economics of HIV/AIDS in Low-Income Countries: The Case for Prevention." *Journal of Economic Perspectives* 20(3): 121–142, 2006. doi:10.1257/jep.20.3.121

Carrin, Guy, Maria-Pia Waelkens, and Bart Criel. "Community-Based Health Insurance in Developing Countries: A Study of Its Contribution to the Performance of Health Financing Systems." *Tropical Medicine and International Health* 10(8): 799–811, 2005. doi:10.1111/j.1365-3156.2005.01455.x

Chaudhury, Nazmul, Jeffrey Hammer, Michael Kremer, Karthik Muralidharan, and F. Halsey Rogers. "Missing in Action: Teacher and Health Worker Absence in Developing Countries." *Journal of Economic Perspectives* 20(1): 91–116, 2006. doi:10.1257/089533006776526058

Cohen, Jessica, and Pascaline Dupas. "Free Distribution or Cost-Sharing? Evidence From a Randomized Malaria Prevention Experiment." *Quarterly Journal of Economics* 125(1): 1–45, 2010. doi:10.1162/qjec.2010.125.1.1

Das, Jishnu, Jeffrey Hammer, and Kenneth Leonard. "The Quality of Medical Advice in Low-Income Countries." *Journal of Economic Perspectives* 22(2): 93–114, 2008. doi:10.1257/jep.22.2.93

Datta, Saugato, and Sendhil Mullainathan. "Behavioral Design: A New Approach to Development Policy." CGD Policy Paper 016. Washington, DC: Center for Global Development, 2012. http://www.cgdev.org/content/publications/detail/1426679

Dercon, Stefan, Jan Willem Gunning, and Andrew Zeitlin. "The Demand for Insurance Under Limited Credibility: Evidence From Kenya." Working Paper, 2011.

Dercon, Stefan, John Hoddinott, and Tassew Woldehanna. 2005. "Shocks and Consumption in 15 Ethiopian Villages, 1999–2004." *Journal of African Economies* 14(4): 559–585, 2005. doi:10.1093/jae/eji022

Dupas, Pascaline. 2009. "What Matters (and What Does Not) in Households' Decision to Invest in Malaria Prevention?" *American Economic Review* 99(2): 224–230, 2009. doi:10.1257/aer.99.2.224

Dupas, Pascaline. "Health Behavior in Developing Countries." *Annual Review of Economics* 3(1): 425–449, 2011. doi:10.1146/annurev-economics-111809-125029

Dupas, Pascaline, and Jonathan Robinson. "Why Don't the Poor Save More? Evidence From Health Savings Experiments." NBER Working Paper 17255. Cambridge, MA: National Bureau of Economic Research, 2011. http://www.nber.org/papers/w17255

Gertler, Paul, and Jonathan Gruber. "Insuring Consumption Against Illness." *American Economic Review* 92(1): 51–70, 2002. doi:10.1257/000282802760015603

Hawley, William A., Penelope A. Phillips-Howard, Feiko O. Ter Kuile, Dianne J. Terlouw, John M. Vuvule, Maurice Ombok, Bernard L. Nahlen, John E. Gimnig, Simon K. Kariuki, Margarette S. Kolczak, and Allen W. Hightower. "Community-Wide Effects of Permethrin-Treated Bed Nets on Child Mortality and Malaria Morbidity in Western Kenya." *American Journal of Tropical Medicine and Hygiene* 68: 121–127, 2003. http://www.ajtmh.org/content/68/4_suppl

Hoffmann, Vivian. "Intrahousehold Allocation of Free and Purchased Mosquito Nets." *American Economic Review* 99(2): 236–241, 2009. doi:10.1257/aer.99.2.236

Jalan, Jyotsna, and E. Somanathan. "The Importance of Being Informed: Experimental Evidence on Demand for Environmental Quality." *Journal of Development Economics* 87(1): 14–28, 2008. doi:10.1016/j.jdeveco.2007.10.002

Jamison, Dean T. "*Investing in Health.*" In Dean T. Jamison, Joel G. Breman, Anthony R. Measham, George Alleyne, Mariam Claeson, David Evans, Prabhat Jha, Anne Mills, and Philip Musgrove (eds.). *Disease Control Priorities in Developing Countries.* Washington, D.C.: Disease Control Priorities Project (DCPP), 2006, pp. 1–34. http://www.dcp2.org/pubs/DCP

Jütting, Johannes P. "Do Community-Based Health Insurance Schemes Improve Poor People's Access to Health Care? Evidence From Rural Senegal." *World Development* 32(2): 273–288, 2004. doi:10.1016/j.worlddev.2003.10.001

Kremer, Michael, and Edward Miguel. "The Illusion of Sustainability." *The Quarterly Journal of Economics* 122(3): 1007–1065, 2007. doi:10.1162/qjec.122.3.1007

Krishna, Anirudh. "Pathways Out of and Into Poverty in 36 Villages of Andhra Pradesh, India." *World Development* 34(2): 271–288, 2006. doi:10.1016/j.worlddev.2005.08.003

Laury, Susan K., Melayne Morgan McInnes, and J. Todd Swarthout. "Insurance Decisions for Low-Probability Losses." *Journal of Risk and Uncertainty* 39(1): 17–44, 2009. doi:10.1007/s11166-009-9072-2

Laxminarayan, Ramanan, Jeffrey Chow, and Sonbol A. Shahid-Salles. "Intervention Cost-Effectiveness: Overview of Main Messages." In Dean T. Jamison, Joel G. Breman, Anthony R. Measham, George Alleyne, Mariam Claeson, David Evans, Prabhat Jha, Anne Mills, and Philip Musgrove (eds.). *Disease Control Priorities in Developing Countries*. Washington, D.C.: Disease Control Priorities Project (DCPP), 2006, pp. 35–86. http://www.dcp2.org/pubs/DCP

Lengeler, Cristian. "Insecticide-Treated Bed Nets and Curtains for Preventing Malaria." *Cochrane Database of Systematic Reviews* (2): CD000363, 2004. doi:10.1002/14651858.CD000363.pub2

Madajewicz, Malgosia, Alexander Pfaff, Alexander van Geen, Joseph Graziano, Iftikhar Hussein, Hasina Momotaj, Roksana Sylvi, and Habibul Ahsan. "Can Information Alone Change Behavior? Response to Arsenic Contamination of Groundwater in Bangladesh." *Journal of Development Economics* 84(2): 731–754, 2007. doi:10.1016/j.jdeveco.2006.12.002

Palacios, Robert, Jishnu Das, and Changqing Sun (eds.). *India's Health Insurance Scheme for the Poor: Evidence From the Early Experience of the Rashtriya Swasthya Bima Yojana*. New Delhi: Centre for Policy Research, 2011.

Preker, Alexander S., and Guy Carrin (eds.). *Health Financing for Poor People: Resource Mobilization and Risk Sharing*. Washington, D.C.: World Bank, 2004. http://documents.worldbank.org/curated/en/2004/

05/3522037/health-financing-poor-people-resource-mobilization-risk-sharing

Strauss, John, and Duncan Thomas. "Health, Nutrition, and Economic Development." *Journal of Economic Literature* 36(2): 766–817, 1998. http://www.jstor.org/stable/2565122

Tarozzi, Alessandro, Aprajit Mahajan, Brian Blackburn, Dan Kopf, Lakshmi Krishnan, and Joanne Yoong. "Micro-Loans, Insecticide-Treated Bednets and Malaria: Evidence From a Randomized Controlled Trial in Orissa (India)." ERID Working Paper Number 104. Durham, N.C.: Economic Research Initiatives at Duke, 2011. http://ssrn.com/abstract=1881075

World Bank. *World Development Indicators 2011*. Washington, D.C.: World Bank, 2011. http://documents.worldbank.org/curated/en/2011/01/14407866/world-development-indicators-2011

World Bank. *World Development Indicators 2012*. Washington, D.C.: World Bank, 2012. http://data.worldbank.org/data-catalog/world-development-indicators

World Health Organization (WHO). *The Global Burden of Disease: 2004 Update*. Geneva: World Health Organization, 2008a.

World Health Organization (WHO). *The Global Burden of Disease: 2004 Update: Disability Weights for Diseases and Conditions*. Geneva: World Health Organization, 2008b.

World Health Organization (WHO). *World Malaria Report 2011*. Geneva: World Health Organization, 2011. http://www.who.int/malaria/world_malaria_report_2011/en/

Yates, Rob. "Universal Health Care and the Removal of User Fees." *Lancet* 373(9680): 2078–2081, 2009. doi: 10.1016/S0140-6736(09)60258-0

QUESTIONS FOR REVIEW

1. How do health, health care, and health care financing differ between low- and high-income countries?

2. What factors help determine the level of health a person enjoys?

3. Describe the array of potential consequences of a health shock.

4. What ultimate and proximate objectives guide health care policy, and what broad types of policies might be used in pursuit of these objectives?

5. Describe the economic theory that guides study of health input acquisition decisions, and describe some of the empirical evidence gathered to date about the determinants of those choices.

6. What market or institutional failures might constitute rationales for intervention in health input markets, and what are their implications for the design of health input promotion programs?

7. Discuss the significance of the design and evaluation of health input programs in people's daily decisions to use health inputs.

8. What direct and indirect impacts might follow from effective efforts to encourage use of health inputs?

9. Discuss the benefits and costs of charging fees for insecticide-treated bed nets (rather than distributing them for free).

10. Explain how the existence of well-functioning health insurance markets could increase health care utilization, reduce impoverishment caused by health shocks, and leave all parties better off.

11. For what reasons might health insurance markets fail to function well for most households in developing countries?

12. Why might it be possible for governments or NGOs to increase health care utilization and reduce health-shock-related impoverishment, at low cost, through the creation of health insurance programs?

13. Why might health care markets fail to deliver quality and efficiency in the absence of intervention?

14. How might the creation of insurance programs improve quality or efficiency?

15. What are the three main components of the costs of health insurance programs?

16. Discuss the ways program designers might attempt to reduce the per-person subsidy required for operating a health insurance program.

17. Describe the potential direct and indirect impacts of participation in a health insurance program.

18. Discuss the determinants of household decisions to enroll in health insurance programs.

19. Why might CBHI programs be more successful at providing health insurance to poor and near-poor households in the informal sector than governments or for-profit insurers? Why might they be less successful?

20. Discuss what we have learned from experience to date about the potential for CBHI programs to provide satisfactory health insurance coverage to the many developing country households that are covered neither by formal-sector mandatory health insurance programs nor by highly subsidized health insurance programs targeted to the poorest households.

QUESTIONS FOR DISCUSSION

1. Discuss the significance of each question in Box 22.3.

2. Compare and contrast the challenges of two approaches to increasing effective use of clean drinking water in rural communities: distributing water filters for use in homes versus helping communities build clean drinking water systems that deliver water to household taps.

3. Consider the experiment described in Box 22.2, which offered participants new ways of saving to buy health inputs or to buy health care in emergencies. The researchers might have chosen instead to design treatments that facilitated saving up for a goal unrelated to health or for no specified goal at all. Discuss the relative merits of policies that provide improved modes of saving *for health* relative to

policies that provide improved modes of saving untied to any specific saving goal. Under what conditions are the benefits of tying saving in new modes to health-related goals most likely to outweigh the costs?

4. Discuss the significance of each question in Box 22.4.

5. Discuss the potential benefits and costs of increasing the premium charged by a CBHI program.

6. Read Canning (2006). Discuss the potential benefits and costs of shifting a fixed quantity of funding away from the treatment of HIV/AIDS toward the prevention of HIV/AIDS.

PROBLEMS

1. When programs distribute free bed nets, they are distributing in-kind transfers. In Chapter 15, we examined the relative merits of distributing cash transfers versus food transfers (a particular type of in-kind transfer). Drawing on the analytical tools presented there, as well as the concepts presented in this chapter, articulate as carefully and completely as possible the potential benefits and costs of replacing a program that spreads information about the importance of using bed nets and distributes free bed nets to targeted households by a program that spreads the identical information and that follows the same targeting criteria but that distributes cash transfers equal in value to the local cost of buying a bed net (rather than distributing the bed nets themselves). Under what conditions are the benefits most likely to outweigh the costs?

2. Consider two potential buyers of health insurance. Each maximizes expected utility, and each experiences utility in any state of the world that depends on his consumption expenditure (in pesos) C and his level of health H. Each knows that he will be hit by a health shock with probability

0.5. If not hit by a health shock, he will enjoy $C = 100$ and $H = 100$. When hit by a health shock, his health will fall to zero if he does not obtain care, but his health can be maintained at 100 if he purchases health care for 100 pesos (causing his consumption expenditure to fall to zero). Potential Buyer A's utility function is

$$u_A(C, H) = C + 2H,$$

and Potential Buyer B's utility function is

$$u_B(C, H) = C^{0.5} + 2H^{0.5}.$$

An insurer charges a premium p for a health insurance contract that pays the buyer 100 pesos in the event the buyer is hit by the health shock. The premium must be paid before the state of the world is revealed.

a. Which potential buyer is risk neutral? Which is risk averse? How can you tell? (You might wish to review the discussion of risk and expected utility in Chapter 10.)

b. Show that in the absence of insurance, both potential buyers would choose to obtain health care if hit by the health shock (rather than suffer the health loss associated with the shock).

c. What is the expected value of the insurer's indemnity payout to a buyer?

d. What is the highest premium Potential Buyer A would just be willing to pay for the health insurance contract? What is the highest premium Potential Buyer B would pay? Why is one willing to pay more than the other?

e. Extrapolating from what you have seen here, discuss in intuitive (i.e., nonquantitative) terms the conditions under which an insurer could break even when supplying health insurance contracts, even when the insurer incurs transaction costs in addition to the costs of expected indemnity payouts.

3. Consider two potential buyers of health insurance who purchase health care (preventing any impact on their health) whenever hit by a health shock (much like the potential buyers in question 2). We may therefore think of health shocks as affecting only the potential buyers' consumption expenditure, and we may describe their utility in any period as a function only of their consumption expenditure. Potential Buyer A's utility in any state of the world is given by

$$u_A(C) = C,$$

and Potential Buyer B's utility is given by

$$u_B(C) = C^{0.5},$$

where C equals consumption expenditure in pesos. Each faces three possible states of the world, each of which occurs with probability of 1/3. In the best state, the potential buyer is hit by no health shock and enjoys $C = 200$. In both the intermediate and worst states of the world, he is hit by a primary health shock that reduces his consumption by 30 pesos. In the worst state of the world, he is *also* hit by a catastrophic health shock that diminishes his consumption by 60 pesos. In the absence of insurance, then, his consumption falls to 170 in the intermediate state of the world and to 110 in the worst state of the world. An insurer offers two insurance contracts. Contract 1 pays 30 pesos in the event of a primary health shock. Contract 2 pays 60 in the event of a catastrophic health shock.

a. What is the expected value of the insurer's indemnity payout to a buyer under each contract?

b. If offered the opportunity to purchase only Contract 1 for a premium of 20, paid before the state is revealed, would Person A accept? Would Person B? Explain.

c. If offered the opportunity to purchase only Contract 2 for a premium of 20, paid before the state is revealed, would Person A accept? Would Person B? Explain.

d. If offered the opportunity to purchase only one of the two contracts for a premium of 20, would Person A prefer Contract 1, prefer Contract 2, or be indifferent between the two? What about Person B? Explain.

e. Explain as intuitively as possible why, for at least one of the two potential buyers, Contract 2 (which offers catastrophic care insurance) is more valuable than Contract 1 (which offers the same expected value of indemnity payments but covers primary care shocks).

Appendix A

Interpreting and Evaluating Empirical Evidence

When studying the development process or evaluating policies, development analysts raise many **empirical questions**, which can be answered only through observation or experiment. Some of the empirical evidence they examine is clear-cut and easy to interpret, but other evidence is partial, weak, or susceptible to multiple interpretations. To avoid drawing incorrect conclusions—and making costly policy mistakes—they must examine the evidence knowledgeably and critically. This appendix offers an overview of key concepts and concerns that should inform the interpretation of empirical evidence and the evaluation of its quality.

The focus here is on **quantitative empirical research methods**, which involve statistical and econometric analysis of information that is recorded in numerical form and has been collected in comparable fashion from a large sample of households, firms, countries, or other units of observation. Quantitative methods may be contrasted with **qualitative methods**, which include focus-group discussions, structured interviews of key informants (such as NGO program officers or village leaders), casual conversations and other methods of gathering information that involve smaller numbers of informants, and more open-ended and flexible methods of eliciting information. Most good research projects make careful use of both quantitative and qualitative methods. We focus on quantitative methods, because greater technical knowledge is required to interpret their results and because we can discuss and evaluate their potential weaknesses in greater detail.

A.1 Empirical Research Questions

We use the term **variable** as a shorthand reference to a quantity or characteristic that can be defined in comparable fashion for all units in a sample. A variable describes a circumstance, attribute, belief, behavioral choice, or systemic outcome that takes different values for different sample members. For example, a *per capita GDP* variable in a sample of countries might describe each country's per capita GDP in U.S. dollar equivalents. The characteristics described by variables must be recorded in numerical form, but they may include characteristics that are inherently qualitative or non-numerical. A *traditional gender beliefs* variable, for example, may take the value 1 for people who report believing that it is "acceptable for men to beat wives who burn the cooking" and 0 for those who do not.

We are interested in two main categories of empirical question. Each question in the first category seeks to describe a feature of a single variable's distribution in a population of interest. Examples include:

What is the average level of per capita household income in urban Peru?

What share of Thai households are net rice consumers?

Each question in the second category examines the causal effect of one variable on another, as in:

What is the average effect of a year of schooling on a person's hourly wage?

By how much do rice prices in a local market rise when local farmers are hit by bad weather?

What is the average effect of a particular microcredit program on participating households' per capita consumption expenditure?

Before we can answer either type of question, we must measure the variables involved. In what follows, therefore, we examine three quantitative research tasks: measuring variables, estimating features of a single variable's population distribution, and estimating the causal effect of one variable on another.

A.2 Measuring Variables

Researchers take many approaches to measuring variables. They might use scales to measure children's weights, use customs records to measure firms' export quantities, or use global positioning systems and records from weather stations to measure the quantities of rain to which farms have been exposed during a growing season. Often they measure variables simply by asking people about them, using identical questionnaires to elicit the relevant information in comparable fashion from representatives of all sampled households, firms, or communities.

High-quality empirical research begins with measurement methods that are valid and reliable. A method is **valid** if it indeed measures the concept or quantity that the researcher aims to measure. To construct a valid measure, a researcher must first carefully define what she is trying to measure and then devise an accurate way of gathering any relevant information. For example, when measuring *income*, an economist might seek to quantify "the total value of resources a household earns in some period of time through the employment or rental of its human, physical, and financial assets." This concept of income represents the total value of resources available for consumption expenditure or saving during the period, and it includes not only cash wages but also in-kind payments, bonuses, profits derived from the sale of goods or services produced by family enterprises, and the value of any food that the family consumes out of its own farm production. A measure of income derived simply by asking a household representative, "How much income did your household earn over the last 12 months?" might fail to produce a valid measure for many reasons. Household representatives might not think of food received from employers, or food grown on their own farms, as "income," and, if they worry that the interviewer has connections to tax authorities, they might have an incentive to under-report their income.

A measure is **reliable** to the extent that it produces the same result every time the fundamental circumstances of interest are the same. For example, fully reliable measures of income (as defined above) would produce identical measures for every household earning the same total income, regardless of how households earn their income and despite any differences in their education levels or attitudes. The most valid and reliable measures of income are derived from series of questions that cover all the ways that households might acquire income, that leave no ambiguity to be resolved by respondents, and that refer to periods of time for which respondents are capable of remembering quantities accurately. For a discussion of how to design questionnaires to obtain good measures of many household-level and individual-level variables, see Grosh and Glewwe (2000).

Some quantities that we would like to measure—such as a household's overall well-being—are impossible to measure directly. Often we hope to draw inferences about how such un-measurable variables change over time or differ across people, however, by observing measurable variables that contribute to or are correlated with them. For example, Chapter 2 discusses the strengths and weaknesses of using income, consumption expenditure, labor time, asset levels, and other measures as indicators of household well-being.

Practical implications

All this suggests that when evaluating the quality of empirical evidence, it is useful to ask the following:

- How, and how carefully, did the researcher define the variables that require measurement?

- How, exactly, were the variables measured? How closely do those measures correspond to what the researcher wanted to measure?

- For variables measured by administering questionnaires, would the respondents have accurate information about the variables? Would they remember the information accurately? Would they have adequate motivation to calculate or assemble the relevant information and report it honestly and accurately?

A.3 Estimating Means, Proportions, and Other Population Distribution Parameters
Population distribution parameters

The term **population** refers to all the individuals, households, firms, communities, or other observational units that are of interest when asking an empirical question. For example, when asking "What is the average level of education among adults in urban Peru?" the population of interest is all adults residing in urban Peru. When asking "At what rate did average total factor productivity increase in the Indian manufacturing sector?" the population of interest is all Indian manufacturing firms. A variable's **population distribution** is a statement of all the values it takes on throughout the population, together with a statement of the fractions of the population for which the variable takes on values in specific ranges. The population distribution of a variable measuring per capita income for households in Peru, for example, indicates the percentages of Peruvian households with per capita incomes in various ranges.

In policy analysis we are often interested in quantifying key **parameters**, or summary features, of population distributions. When investigating whether incomes in a population are typically high or low, we might wish to know the mean or median of the population distribution. The **population mean** of a household-level per capita income variable is the simple average of per capita income across all households in the population. The **population median** is the income of the household that falls in the middle when all households in the population are arranged from lowest to highest per capita income. The median tends to be more useful than the mean for describing a variable's typical level in a population when the variable's distribution is positively skewed, in the sense that a small fraction of the population has values much higher than most members of the population; population distributions of income, consumption expenditure, and wages tend to be skewed in this way. We may also be interested in a **population proportion**, such as the fraction of the population for which income per capita falls below \$2 per day.

When seeking to understand a variable's degree of dispersion in a population, we might wish to know the population variance, the population standard deviation, or one of the inequality measures examined in Chapter 5. The **population variance** of a variable Y is defined by

$$Var(Y) = \frac{1}{N} \sum_{i=1}^{N} (Y_i - \mu)^2 \qquad (A.1)$$

where N is the number of units in the population, Y_i is the value of the variable for the ith unit in the population, and μ is the population mean, which may be calculated as[1]

$$\mu = \frac{1}{N} \sum_{i=1}^{N} Y_i \qquad (A.2)$$

This says that to calculate the population variance of Y, we measure how far each Y_i is above or below the population mean, square these differences (so that whether Y_i is above or below the mean, an increase in the distance between it and the mean increases the overall measure), and then take the average of the squared differences across all units in the population. The **population standard deviation**, which is defined as the square root of the variance, expresses the variance information in units that are easier to interpret than the variance itself. For example, if Y is income in pesos per capita, then the variance of Y is measured in *pesos per capita squared*, and the standard deviation is measured in *pesos per capita*. The population standard deviation of an income variable, therefore, describes the average extent to which the incomes of population members lie above or below the mean (in pesos per capita).

Samples

Quantitative researchers learn about population distributions by analyzing **samples**, which are subsets of populations. Ideally, the samples are constructed in disciplined ways that render them representative of the relevant populations. Researchers may use **simple random samples**, in which each sample unit is identified by drawing a member at random from a complete list of the population (called the **sample frame**). Values for the variable that are common in the population are likely to appear on any one random draw and thus are likely to appear in many simple random sample observations, whereas values that are uncommon in the population are unlikely to appear in many sample observations. Thus, in a simple random sample, a variable's **sample distribution**—a statement of all the values the variable takes on in the sample, together with a statement of the fractions of the sample for which the variable takes values in specific ranges—should resemble the variable's population distribution. The larger the sample, the more closely the sample distribution resembles the population distribution. Another approach to creating a representative sample is to create a **systematic sample**, by obtaining an ordered list of all population members and choosing every third, tenth, or one hundredth member on the list.

Researchers sometimes draw **stratified random samples** rather than simple random samples, first dividing the total population up into subpopulations of interest, and then drawing random samples from each subpopulation. Sometimes they draw samples of similar size from each subpopulation, even when some make up much larger fractions of the total population than others, because they require large enough subsamples to draw good inferences about subpopulation distribution parameters, even for smaller subpopulations. For example, researchers attempting to quantify not only the average of household income in an entire country, but also the income averages in rural and urban areas of the country, might decide to draw random samples of equal size from urban and rural areas, even when the urban population is one third the size of the rural population. A variable's distribution in a stratified sample of this sort becomes representative of its distribution in the population only if researchers employ sample **weights** or **expansion factors**, which indicate that each sample unit taken from the under-represented subpopulation represents a larger number of population units than those taken from over-represented

---

[1] For a review of the summation notation employed here, see problem 1 in Chapter 1.

subpopulations. In the case just described, each rural observation in the sample represents three times as many population households as does each urban sample observation.[2]

Simple random samples, systematic samples, and stratified random samples are called **probability samples**, because it is possible to determine the probability with which any member of the population would be selected into such a sample. In simple random samples and systematic samples, each population unit has the same probability of selection into the sample. In stratified random samples, the probabilities of selection can differ across subpopulations, and researchers can use information about these probabilities to construct sample weights and estimate population parameters. Variables' distributions in nonprobability samples—including **convenience samples**, which are created by obtaining information only for the members of the population that happen to be easy to contact—cannot be expected to offer good reflections of population distributions because the distribution of the variable of interest can differ across groups that are easier and harder to contact, the groups that are harder to contact will be under-represented, and researchers are unable to construct weights that allow them to adjust for the under-representation.

Sample statistics as estimates of population parameters

Researchers use the process of drawing a sample and calculating a sample **statistic**—a numerical measure calculated using sample data—to estimate a population parameter. To **estimate** a population parameter is to make an educated guess regarding its value. Sample statistics include the **sample mean**, **sample median**, and **sample proportion**, which are defined in the same ways as their population counterparts, except that they are calculated over all members of the sample rather than all members of the population.

Researchers would like their estimates of population parameters to be close to the true parameter values. An estimate is *close* to the true value if it *tells the same story* as the true value. This means that it would not lead policymakers into costly mistakes or lead social scientists to draw incorrect conclusions about economic or political conditions. Evaluating whether two values are close requires a context-specific judgment call. For example, if the true proportion of the population intending to vote for the opposition candidate is 56 percent, then for most purposes we would consider an estimate of 55 percent to be close to the true value because it tells the same story of the opposition commanding a small majority, while we would consider an estimate of 30 or 75 percent to be far from the true value because those numbers suggest very different political conditions.

Unfortunately, the process of drawing a sample and calculating a sample statistic is not guaranteed to yield an estimate close to the true value of the analogous population parameter. To appreciate the nature of the problem, imagine trying to estimate the population mean of a variable Y by drawing a sample of size n and calculating the sample mean. If sample size n is significantly smaller than the population size N, then there are many possible samples of size n that we might draw from the population, and the value of the sample mean would be different in each of those samples. In most samples the sample mean would differ from the population mean, at least a little, and we give the name **sampling error** to the difference between a sample statistic calculated from a particular sample and the population parameter it is meant to estimate. The sample mean may be close to the population mean in many samples, but at least some of the samples would be unusual ones, in which the sample mean is far above or below the population mean. We give the name **sampling distribution** (in this case, for the sample mean statistic) to the list of values the sample mean takes across all possible samples of size n that we could draw from the population, together

---

[2] Some stratified random samples are self-weighting. This means that the probability of selection into the sample is the same in all subpopulations (i.e., smaller samples are drawn from smaller subpopulations), so that no weights are required to render the sample distribution representative of the population distribution.

with the shares of all those possible samples in which the sample mean takes values in various ranges.[3] If, across all the possible samples of size n, the sample mean is close to the population mean in a large fraction of the samples, then the probability of drawing a *single* sample in which the sample mean is close to the population mean is also high. We judge that an estimate is "high quality" when this probability is high, because it means that the one statistic we calculate (using data from the one sample we draw) has a high probability of being close to the true value.

A statistic has a high probability of being close to the true value of the population parameter that it estimates if it satisfies two conditions: it is an unbiased estimate of the true parameter value, and it is a precise estimate. Technically, a statistic provides an **unbiased** estimate of a population parameter if the mean of its sampling distribution (i.e., the average of the statistic's value across all possible samples of size n that we might draw from the population) is equal to the true value. More intuitively, the estimate is unbiased if we have no particular reason to suspect that the statistic will be either too high or too low when we draw a single sample. An estimate is **precise** if it has a high probability of taking a value close to the mean of its sampling distribution (which is equal to the true population value if the estimate is unbiased). That is, a statistic is precise if we believe the statistic's value does not vary much across the many samples of size n that we might draw from the population. This requires that the variance and standard deviation of the statistic's sampling distribution are small, in a context-specific, practical sense (defined below).

We cannot observe directly whether an estimate is unbiased and precise, because we cannot observe directly the true parameter value or the sampling distribution. (We don't observe all possible samples of size n.) We can, however, use careful study of the sampling and estimation process to make educated guesses about unbiasedness; and we can evaluate the precision of an estimate by calculating the estimate's 95 percent confidence interval (defined later).

Evaluating whether an estimate is unbiased is largely a matter of evaluating the validity of the measure employed, how carefully and successfully the sample was constructed, and whether appropriate weights were employed when calculating sample statistics. It may be shown, for example, that the sample mean provides an unbiased estimate of the population mean as long as the variable is measured well and the sample is a simple random sample or systematic sample drawn from a comprehensive and accurate sample frame. To obtain an unbiased estimate of a population mean using a stratified random sample, we must calculate sample means using appropriate weights.[4]

Unfortunately, problems with measurement, sample selection, or data collection can introduce **bias**. Use of an invalid measure—such as a measure of income collected in a way that gives respondents incentive to under-report—can create a tendency for the sample mean to understate or overstate the population mean. Logistical difficulties that prevent interviewers from locating certain types of sampled units, or a tendency for sampled individuals of certain groups to refuse to participate in a survey, can cause simple random samples to become unrepresentative. For example, if smaller manufacturing enterprises are more difficult to interview than larger enterprises, and if larger enterprises tend to be more productive than smaller ones, then the average of a productivity variable in the sample (in which smaller enterprises are under-represented) will tend to overstate the true population productivity average.

---

[3] When we discuss the sample mean's sampling distribution, we are treating the sample mean as an **estimator**. This means that it is a rule or formula describing how to use any sample drawn from a population to obtain an estimate of a population parameter. The estimator has a sampling distribution because there are many possible random samples of size n that we could draw from the population, and in each sample the application of the rule would yield a different result. Estimators are examples of **random variables**, which are functions or processes that assign numerical values to the outcomes of random or chance activities, such as drawing random samples. After drawing a particular sample, and plugging the sample data into the sample mean formula, the result we obtain is an **estimate**, which is a constant (i.e., a single number) rather than a random variable. Note that the true population mean, which we hope to estimate, is a constant, not a random variable.

[4] For example, if a sample included one out of every 1,000 urban households, but only one out of every 3,000 rural households, then if we employ weights indicating that each urban sample household counts for 1,000 population households, and each rural sample household counts for 3,000, the weighted sample mean constitutes an unbiased estimate of the population mean.

Just as we can show that the sample mean provides an unbiased estimate of the population mean in well-executed simple random samples and systematic samples, so we can show that the sample proportion provides an unbiased estimate of the population proportion under those circumstances. We can also show that the following statistic, which we call the **sample variance**, provides an unbiased estimate of the population variance of Y

$$S^2 = \frac{1}{n-1} \sum_{i=1}^{n} (Y_i - \overline{Y})^2 \tag{A.3}$$

where $\overline{Y}$ is the sample mean of Y. But again, data collection difficulties can introduce bias. For example, if interviewers fail to interview many of the most geographically remote households, who also tend to be among the poorest households, and if many of the richest households refuse to participate, then a simple calculation of the variance of income in the sample of households successfully interviewed will tend to understate the variance of income in the population.

Evaluating an estimate's precision is a matter of calculating the estimate's standard error and using the estimate and its standard error to calculate its 95 percent confidence interval. A statistic's **standard error** is an estimate of the standard deviation of its sampling distribution. It is a measure of how much the sample statistic would tend to vary across all possible samples of size n that could be drawn from the population. More practically, it may be thought of as a summary measure of how much confidence we should place in the accuracy of our estimate, given the characteristics of the particular sample we have to work with (with larger standard errors corresponding to lower levels of confidence).

Remarkably, we may estimate the standard deviation of the sample mean's sampling distribution, even though we observe only a single sample, rather than the many possible samples of size n relevant to its sampling distribution. For example, we may show that the following statistic is an unbiased estimate of the variance of the sample mean's sampling distribution[5]:

$$\widehat{Var}(\overline{Y}) = S^2/n \tag{A.4}$$

where S^2 is the sample variance of Y as defined above and n is sample size. The square root of this estimate is the **standard error of the sample mean**. Introductory statistics textbooks provide comparable formulas for calculating standard errors for sample proportions and other sample statistics.

The expression in equation A.4 ties our educated guess about the standard deviation of the sample mean's sampling distribution to two important features of our sample. First, the appearance of n in the denominator implies that the sampling distribution's variance falls—and the sample mean becomes a more precise estimate of the population mean—as sample size rises. This makes sense, because when drawing only small samples, the chance of drawing an unusual sample (in which the sample mean is very different from the population mean) is high, and as the sample size rises relative to the population size, the scope for drawing samples with unusual means falls. This result also conforms to the intuition that the larger quantity of information contained in a larger sample improves our ability to estimate accurately. Second, the appearance of S^2 in the numerator implies that the sample mean becomes a less precise estimate of the population mean as the within-sample variation in Y around the sample mean increases (holding n

---

[5] The estimated variance of the sampling distribution of the sample mean ($\widehat{Var}(\overline{Y})$) should not be confused with the population variance of the variable in question ($Var(Y)$). The latter concept is a constant (rather than a random variable, as defined in footnote 3) that has socioeconomic implications, describing how Y varies across members of the population. The former has statistical implications, describing how the value taken by the sample mean varies across all possible samples of size n that might be drawn from the population.

constant). This, too, makes sense, because when Y varies greatly within the sample, then the variance of Y in the population is also likely to be large. As the values of Y in the population become more dispersed, the probability that a sample of size n will contain unusual values (that pull the sample mean significantly above or below the population mean) also rises.

We may use our calculation of an estimate's standard error (together with the estimate itself) to calculate a **95 percent confidence interval** for the estimate. This is an interval calculated in such a way that it has a 95 percent chance of containing the true value of the population parameter. For the sample mean, we use the following formula to calculate a 95 percent confidence interval:

$$[\overline{Y} - 1.96 \times s.e.(\overline{Y}),\ \overline{Y} + 1.96 \times s.e.(\overline{Y})] \tag{A.5}$$

where $s.e.(\overline{Y})$ is the standard error of the sample mean $\overline{Y}$ (as defined above). We may show that an interval calculated this way has a 95 percent chance of containing the true value of the population mean.[6] That is, if we used this formula to calculate an interval (around the sample mean) in each of the many possible samples of size n that we could draw from the population, the intervals would contain the true value in 95 percent of the samples.

To assess whether the sample mean is a precise estimate of the population mean in a given application, we calculate this confidence interval and evaluate whether it is *narrow* (and our estimate is precise) or *wide* (and our estimate is imprecise). The interval is narrow if the two end values tell very similar stories about the population mean, and it is wide if they tell very different stories. Evaluating whether the interval is wide or narrow requires a context-specific judgment call on whether the values at the two ends of the interval are *close* or not. For example, when estimating the mean years of schooling in the adult population, we might consider a confidence interval of [10.9, 11.2] to be narrow, because the values at both ends of the interval (and all values in between) suggest that the average adult has completed primary school but not completed secondary school. We would consider an interval of [5.1,13.3] to be wide, because one end of the interval suggests that the average worker has not even completed primary school, while the other end suggests that the average worker has completed more than secondary school. When the two ends of the confidence interval tell very different stories like this, the data are telling us that they do not contain sufficient information to justify confident conclusions about the average level of schooling in the population of interest. This is most likely to happen when our sample size is small (i.e., with n less than 50) and when the values of the variable of interest vary widely in the population.[7]

Practical implications

When evaluating the quality of estimates of population means, proportions, and other population distribution parameters, development analysts should ask the following questions:

- What is the population of interest? What population distribution parameter is the researcher trying to estimate?

- What type of sample (e.g., simple random sample, systematic sample, stratified random sample, convenience sample) is employed?

---

[6] Technically, this statement holds only if the sample size n is sufficiently large.

[7] When researchers design samples and surveys to use for estimating a population mean, they use formulas like equations A.4 and A.5, together with a guess about the magnitude of S^2, to calculate the minimum sample size n required to estimate the population mean with a target degree of precision (e.g., a target width for the 95 percent confidence interval).

- What sample statistic is calculated to estimate the population parameter? If the sample is a stratified random sample, are appropriate weights employed when calculating the sample statistic?

- Did data collectors have difficulty obtaining data from some subpopulations, whether because of refusal to participate or logistical difficulties? If so, how would we expect the variable's distribution to differ between members of the undersampled subpopulation and the rest of the population? How would this under-representation tend to bias estimation of the population parameter?

- Is the 95 percent confidence interval for the sample statistic narrow, indicating that the statistic provides a precise estimate of the population parameter, or is it wide, implying that we cannot draw strong conclusions about the population parameter from the current sample? If 95 percent confidence intervals and standard errors are not presented, is the sample small (i.e., less than 50 observations), in which case we should be particularly worried about imprecision?

A.4 Estimating Causal Effects[8]
Causal effects

Rather than estimating a parameter of a single variable's population distribution, development analysts often wish to estimate a population *relationship* among variables. More specifically, they wish to estimate the **causal effect** of a determining variable or **determinant** on an **outcome variable**. The causal effect of a determinant X on an outcome Y can be measured as the change in Y that *results from* a one-unit increase in X. We might also call it the **ceteris paribus effect** of X on Y, because it answers the question: "If we increased X by one unit, *while holding all other determinants of Y constant*, what would happen to Y?" (If no other determinant of Y changes, then any change in Y that follows from a change in X must be the *result* of the change in X.) For example, the causal effect of years of schooling on a Peruvian person's wage is the answer to the question: "If we could increase by one the years of schooling a Peruvian resident received earlier in life, while allowing nothing else about the person's innate characteristics or his circumstances to change, what would happen to his wage?"

The causal effect of X on Y must be distinguished from the **correlation** between X and Y in the population of interest. The correlation between X and Y measures the extent to which Y tends to rise or fall as we shift attention from subpopulations with lower to higher levels of X, *not holding constant the other possible determinants of Y*. In the real world, the many potential determinants of any Y tend to be correlated with one another (as well as with Y). As we shift attention from subpopulations with lower to higher levels of X, the typical levels of other potential determinants are changing as well. Thus the change in typical level of Y observed as we shift attention from lower to higher levels of X might result not only from the changes in X but also from change in the other determinants. For example, people with higher innate ability might find school easier and tend to obtain more schooling. If so, then people with more years of schooling will have higher average levels of innate ability. If innate ability has a positive causal effect on wages, then when we shift attention from people with lower to higher levels of schooling, wages might rise not only as a result of schooling's causal effect but also as a result of an associated change in the average level of innate ability. We would be picking up a *correlation* between schooling and wages, but not the *causal effect* of schooling on wages.

---

[8] This section offers a brief overview of critical econometric concepts and methods typically presented in introductory econometrics courses. For a more complete treatment see Wooldridge (2012).

Samples

A causal effect is a **population relationship**. Just as we use statistics describing sample distributions to estimate population distribution parameters (such as the population mean), so we use statistics describing sample relationships to estimate causal effects. We will see that in most cases the samples must include not only data on the outcome Y and the determinant of interest, which we will call X or X_1, but also on other potential determinants of Y, which we will call $X_2, ..., X_k$.

The most common type of sample is a simple **cross-section** sample, which is a probability sample in which all units are observed only once, all at roughly the same time. Most cross-section samples are **observational** samples, meaning that after researchers select units into the sample, they simply observe the values of Y, and X_1 through X_k, without attempting to manipulate the values of any variables. Observational samples may be contrasted with samples tied to randomized control trials (discussed in more detail later), in which researchers collaborate with policymakers to *set* the values of one or more possible determinants of Y for randomly selected subsamples. **Repeated cross-section** datasets include subsamples drawn from the same population in two or more time periods. Subsamples for each time period are drawn to be representative of the same population, but the particular units selected into the samples are different in each period. **Panel** or **longitudinal** datasets follow a sample of households, firms, or other units over time. Like repeated cross-section datasets, they allow study of change over time for sampled populations. Unlike repeated cross-section datasets, however, panel samples include the *same* individuals in each time period, allowing examination of individual-level changes over time. A simple **time series** dataset contains information for only a single unit of observation, often an entire country, but it contains observations from many consecutive time periods.

In what follows, we examine what is required to obtain good estimates of causal effects under several sets of circumstances, defined by the way Y is determined and by the nature of the sample available. Initially we assume possession of the most common type of sample, a random cross section.

Simple linear regression models and ordinary least squares estimation

Consider first the challenge of estimating the causal effect of X on Y when the true model of how Y is determined (in the population) takes a very simple form, described by three assumptions. The first assumption is that

$$Y_i = a + bX_i + u_i \quad \text{for all } i \tag{A.6}$$

where i indexes members of the population (n of which are drawn into our sample), Y_i and X_i are values for observation i of variables measured in our dataset, and u_i is the value for observation i of a variable for which we do not have a measure and which we will call an **error term**. a and b are parameters of the population relationship that we would like to estimate. This first assumption states that Y varies only as a result of variation in X and u and that the relationship of Y to X and u is a simple linear one, described by just two parameters, a and b.

The second and third assumptions are that the average value of u in the population is zero, and that u and X are uncorrelated in the population. Together these assumptions indicate that when we limit our attention to a subpopulation in which all members have the same value of X, the average of u within that subpopulation is zero (no matter what value of X we focus on).[9] This means that the average value of Y within a subpopulation defined by $X=X^*$ is equal to $a+bX^*$, and the values of u are mere *noise* that causes some people to be above average (for people with their levels of X) and others to be below average, and that has no tendency to rise or fall as X rises.

---

[9] We are thinking of a population that is so large that even when we focus on individuals with $X = X^*$, the number of individuals over which we must average is large.

By including u in the equation, we acknowledge that X is not the only determinant of Y. By imposing the second and third assumptions, however, we are making the strong assumption that the net effect of all determinants of Y other than X is to induce variation in Y that is uncorrelated with X. This means that as we shift attention from subpopulations with lower to higher levels of X, there is no tendency for other determinants of Y to change, and we are essentially observing a ceteris paribus change in X. Later we must relax this unrealistic assumption.

Within this simplest model, the coefficient b quantifies the causal effect of X on Y because it answers the question: "If we increased X by one unit, while holding u (the only other determinant of Y) constant, what would happen to Y?" To interpret the magnitude of b, we would need to know the units in which X and Y are measured. To make good judgments about whether a magnitude indicates a large or small effect, we would need additional knowledge about the context. For example, if X measures the years of schooling that individuals have completed, and Y measures their hourly wages in U.S. dollar equivalents per hour, then a value for b of 1.45 implies that a one-year increase in schooling increases a worker's hourly wage, on average, by \$1.45. If the mean wage in the population (an important descriptor of context) is \$10, this would constitute a 14.5 percent increase in wages for the average worker. Given that a person spends just one year to obtain an additional year of schooling but could reap this 14.5 percent wage increase for many years throughout his working life, this would constitute a large causal effect of schooling on wages. We would consider an effect of this magnitude **economically important**, or big enough (in absolute value) to have important implications for our understanding of the world or our evaluation of policy.

We may describe this model using a simple graph, as in Figure A.1a, where X is measured against the horizontal axis and Y is measured against the vertical axis. The line with intercept a and slope b describes how *average Y* is related to the level of X in the population. This is known as the **population regression line**. Each of the points scattered around the line plots the values of X and Y for an individual member of the population. The 30 points in the graph describe a random sample of just 30 individuals from this population. The error term u causes the actual levels of Y for these individuals to fall above and below the line. Because (by assumptions 2 and 3) the average level of u is zero and has no tendency to rise or fall as X rises, the points are scattered fairly evenly above and below the line at all levels of X.

The graph suggests how we might use a cross-section sample to estimate the parameters a and b. If we draw a random sample of size 30 from the population and observe the values of X and Y for each unit in the sample, we could create a **scatter plot** of the resulting data, or a graph in which we plot one point (indicating the values of X and Y) for each observation in the sample. The scatter plot would look like the scatter of points in Figure A.1a, except that we would not see

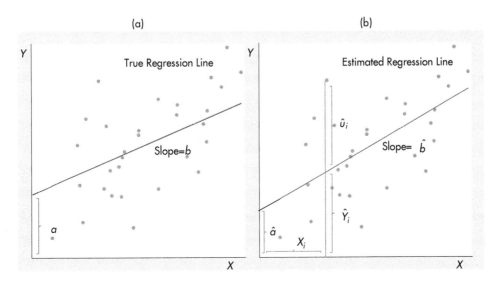

FIGURE A.1
Scatter Plots of Data with True and Estimated Regression Lines

the population regression line. If we know that the true model generating our data conforms to the assumptions above, however, then we would guess that the population regression line goes through the middle of the scatter plot, in the sense that the points from our dataset should be (roughly) evenly scattered above and below it. This suggests that we could estimate the population parameters a and b by putting a line through the middle of the scatter plot and using the intercept and slope of that line as our estimates of a and b. The method of **ordinary least squares (OLS) regression** does just this.[10]

When we use OLS to estimate this simple model, we say that we are running a regression of Y on X. Many computer programs designed for data analysis are capable of performing the required calculations. Running such a regression yields estimates of a and b that we will call $\widehat{a}$ and $\widehat{b}$ (read as "a hat" and "b hat"). The line defined by $\widehat{a} + \widehat{b}X$ is called the **estimated regression line**. Figure A.1b takes the same scatter plot of data as appears in Figure A.1a and plots the estimated regression line obtained by running an OLS regression of Y on X (using the data analysis program STATA). The estimated regression line is not exactly the same as the population regression line, for the same reason that a sample mean is not exactly equal to the population mean it estimates (i.e., *sampling error* causes $\widehat{a}$ and $\widehat{b}$ to differ from the true a and b). When we plug the value X_i into the equation for the estimated regression line, we obtain the OLS **predicted value** for observation $i, \widehat{Y}_i = \widehat{a} + \widehat{b}X_i$, which is the height of the estimated regression line at $X=X_i$. The difference between the actual and predicted values of Y for observation $i, \widehat{u}_i = Y_i - \widehat{Y}_i$, is called the OLS **residual** for observation i, and it is equal to the vertical distance between the scatter plot point for observation i and the estimated regression line in Figure A.1b.

We consider an estimate $\widehat{b}$ to be of high quality when we judge that it has a high probability of being close to the true value b. Again, determining whether the true value of b and an estimated value are close requires a context-specific judgment call. If two values tell the same story about a causal effect, and they would not lead policymakers into costly mistakes (or lead researchers into faulty conclusions about how the world works), then they are close. For example, if X is years of schooling, Y is hourly wages in U.S. dollar equivalents per hour, and the true value of b is 1.45, then we would probably judge the value 1.39 to be close to the true value, because both values indicate an economically important (but not huge) effect of schooling on earnings (as argued above). We would not, however, judge the values of 0.09 and 4.67 to be close to the true value, because they imply very small and very large effects of schooling on earnings.

As was true with the sample mean statistic discussed above, the OLS regression statistic $\widehat{b}$ has a sampling distribution describing the distribution of values it would take across all possible samples of size n that we might draw from the population. The sampling distribution indicates the probability of $\widehat{b}$ taking a value in any particular range when we draw a single sample and run an OLS regression of Y on X. Our estimate is of high quality, having high probability of taking a value near the true value in a single sample, when $\widehat{b}$ is unbiased and precise, where the terms unbiased and precise are again defined as in section A.2.

We can show that the OLS estimate $\widehat{b}$ is unbiased if the population relationship between Y and X truly takes the very simple form described by the three assumptions above, if we employ a well-executed random sample from the population, and if we obtain good measures of Y and X.[11] If the assumptions of the simple model are true, the primary sources of potential bias are problems with measuring Y and X and sample-collection problems that prevent us from obtaining fully

---

[10] More specifically, OLS regression identifies the line that *best fits* the scatter plot of data by choosing the values of $\widehat{a}$ and $\widehat{b}$ that minimize the sum (across all observations in the data set) of the squares of the vertical distances between each point in the scatter plot and the line defined by $\widehat{a}$ and $\widehat{b}$. It can be shown that the estimated regression line that results from this procedure puts the line through the middle of the scatter plot, in the sense that the sum of the vertical distances between the scatter points and the regression line (not squared) equals zero, indicating an even scatter of points above and below the estimated regression line.

[11] If, as assumed here, the value of b is the same for all subpopulations, then we do not need to employ sample weights to obtain unbiased estimates in stratified random samples.

representative samples among people with X in every relevant range.[12] Below, when we consider more realistic models of how Y is determined (in which we allow for other determinants of Y that are correlated with X), we will consider a much more common and more important reason why an OLS slope coefficient estimate might be biased (omitted variables bias).

In general, the use of inaccurate measures of Y and X can introduce biases of diverse sorts. A useful benchmark result pertains to cases in which X is measured with a seemingly benign sort of error called **classical measurement error**, which randomly causes some values to be too high and others to be too low but has no systematic tendency to rise or fall as X rises. We may show that in such cases the OLS estimate of the causal effect of X on Y is biased in a way that understates the importance of the effect of X on Y. This tendency for OLS to understate effects in the presence of classical measurement error on a regressor is called **attenuation bias**.

We evaluate the precision of an OLS estimate by calculating its 95 percent confidence interval. We may show that if the variance of the error term u (describing the degree of u's variation across members of the population) is equal to the same value (which we call σ^2) within any subpopulation (defined by level of X), then the following statistic is an unbiased estimate of the variance of $\widehat{b}$'s sampling distribution:

$$\widehat{Var}(b) = \frac{\widehat{\sigma}^2}{\sum_{i=1}^{n} (X_i - \overline{X})^2} \tag{A.7}$$

Here

$$\widehat{\sigma}^2 = \frac{1}{n-1} \sum_{i=1}^{n} \widehat{u}_i^2 \tag{A.8}$$

and is an unbiased estimate of σ^2.[13]

The expression in equation A.7 has three sensible implications about the conditions under which the sampling variance tends to be smallest and our estimate of b most precise. First, holding the average distance of the X values from their sample mean constant, an increase in sample size n increases the denominator; this implies that the OLS estimator becomes more precise as sample size rises. Second, holding n constant, the estimate becomes more precise as the average distance of the X values around their sample mean rises (increasing the size of the denominator). This conforms to the intuition that samples with greater variation in X offer us greater opportunity to learn about the effect of X on Y. Third, the variance tends to fall as the average size of the squared OLS residuals falls, reducing the numerator; in populations in which actual observations are more dispersed around the population regression line, the probability of drawing unusual samples in which the OLS estimated regression line is very different from the true population regression line

---

[12] For example, suppose that X is years of schooling and Y is the hourly wage, and we expect b to be positive, indicating that the causal effect of schooling on wages is positive. Suppose further that if people with income (Y) above a certain level (that is usually attained only by people with high levels of schooling, X) often refuse to participate in the survey, and people with income below that level mostly choose to participate. Under these circumstances, among people with low levels of schooling, the sample may be reasonably representative, even while among people with high levels of schooling the highest incomes are seriously under-represented. As a result, the sample average of income among people with low levels of schooling may be nearly unbiased, while the sample average of income among people with high levels of schooling seriously underestimates the true population average. This implies that the sample average of Y rises more slowly than the true average of Y as X increases, and the OLS regression coefficient $\widehat{b}$ will tend to understate the causal effect of X on Y.

[13] The right-hand side of equation A.8 is the sample variance of the OLS residuals. It indicates, therefore, that we use the sample variance of the OLS residuals to obtain an unbiased estimate of the true variance of the error terms.

is higher. In summary, the probability that we have drawn an unusual sample, in which the OLS estimate $\widehat{b}$ is far from the true b, shrinks as sample size rises, as the variation in X rises, and as the degree of noise around the regression line falls.

We may calculate the 95 percent confidence interval for an OLS regression coefficient $\widehat{b}$ using the formula

$$[\widehat{b} - 1.96 \times s.e.(\widehat{b}), \ \widehat{b} + 1.96 \times s.e.(\widehat{b})] \tag{A.9}$$

where $s.e.(\widehat{b})$ is the standard error of $\widehat{b}$ and is equal to the square root of the variance described in equation A.7.[14] To evaluate whether this confidence interval is wide or narrow, we must use knowledge of units and context to assess whether the values at the lower and upper ends of this interval tell the same story (in which case the confidence interval is narrow and our estimate is precise) or tell different stories (in which case the confidence interval is wide and our estimate is imprecise). If the interval is wide, then we must conclude that our data are not strong enough to allow confident conclusions about the size of the causal effect of X on Y. For example, if X is years of schooling and Y is average hourly earnings in dollar equivalents per hour as above, and if the lower end of the confidence interval is 0.12 and upper end is 10.3, then the lower end of the confidence interval implies virtually no effect of schooling on the wage, while the upper end implies a large effect. In such a case, the data do not allow us to distinguish with high confidence whether or not schooling has an economically important effect on the wage.

Statistical significance versus economic importance

Researchers often report whether OLS estimates of slope coefficients are *statistically significant* or not. A coefficient estimate is **statistically significant at the 95 percent confidence level** if 0 is not included within its 95 percent confidence interval.[15] That is, an estimate is statistically significant if the entire 95 percent confidence interval lies either above or below zero. Under such circumstances we can conclude with confidence that the coefficient is "not zero," but this is not a very strong statement. All too often, researchers mistakenly treat an estimate that is statistically significant as if it must also be economically important (as defined earlier). Astute readers realize that this need not be the case. Even if the entire 95 percent confidence interval lies to the right of zero, rendering the estimate statistically significant, the values at both ends of the interval might be so small as to imply economically unimportant effects; in such cases we have strong evidence *against* an important effect. If the value at the low end is small while the value at the upper end is large, then the data do not allow us to draw a confident conclusion about whether the effect is important. Only if both ends of the confidence interval indicate large effects can we conclude with confidence that the effect is economically important.

Similarly, researchers often mistakenly treat an estimate that is not statistically significant (or that is **statistically insignificant**) as if it provides evidence of X having *no* causal effect on Y. Again, this might not be the case. A coefficient estimate is statistically insignificant when the 95 percent confidence interval includes zero; its lower limit is negative while its upper limit is positive. If the estimates at both ends of the confidence interval are economically small in absolute

---

[14] Technically, the interval described by equation A.9 may be interpreted as a 95 percent confidence interval only if sample size n is sufficiently large or if the distribution of u in the population of interest is a normal distribution.

[15] The theoretical underpinnings of statistical significance assessments lie in the theory of hypothesis testing, which we do not review in this appendix. The reader is referred to textbooks on statistics and econometrics. A coefficient is statistically significantly different from zero if we reject the null hypothesis that the coefficient is equal to zero, in favor of the alternative hypothesis that it is either greater or less than zero. We can show that we reject such a null hypothesis at the 95 percent confidence level if the 95 percent confidence interval for the coefficient does not contain zero.

value, then we have a precise estimate that is near zero and we indeed have strong evidence of virtually no effect. One or both of the ends of the confidence interval may, however, be large in absolute value, consistent with an economically important effect, while the confidence interval *also* contains zero. In such cases we cannot draw a confident conclusion about whether X has an important effect on Y or not.

Development analysts must, therefore, demand that researchers report standard errors for OLS estimates. Knowing the estimate and its standard error, analysts can eyeball a 95 percent confidence interval, knowing that such an interval stretches from approximately two times the standard error below the OLS estimate to two times the standard error above the estimate.[16] They should draw inferences about economic importance based on confidence intervals and not merely on statements of statistical significance or insignificance (or OLS coefficient estimates alone).

Multiple regression models and ordinary least squares regression

Now consider the challenge of estimating the causal effect of X (which we'll now call X_1) on Y under the somewhat more realistic assumptions that

$$Y_i = a + b_1 X_{1i} + b_2 X_{2i} + \cdots + b_k X_{ki} + u_i \tag{A.10}$$

and that u_i has mean zero in the population and is uncorrelated with X_{1i} (after holding all other Xs constant at any levels). We will refer to X_1 through X_k collectively as the **right-hand side variables** or **regressors**. The key difference between this set of assumptions and the previous set is that Y might now depend not only on X_1 and an error term that is uncorrelated with it but also on variables X_2 through X_k, which *might* be correlated with X_1. Again we assume that the relationship between Y and its determinants is linear, and our primary interest is in the coefficient b_1, which answers the question: "If we increased X_1 by one unit, while holding constant all other determinants of Y (which now include X_2 through X_k and u), what would happen to Y?"

Now the second and third assumptions together indicate that when we limit our attention to a subpopulation defined by each regressor taking a specific value, the average of u within that subpopulation is zero (no matter what levels of the right hand side variables we focus on). This means that the average value of Y within any subpopulation defined by $X_1 = X_1^*, X_2 = X_2^*, \ldots$ $X_k = X_k^*$ is equal to $a + b_1 X_1^* + b_2 X_2^* + \cdots + b_k X_k^*$, and u again represents the noise that causes some people to be above average while others are below average, and it has no tendency to rise or fall as X_1 rises (while holding the other regressors constant). X_2 though X_k represent all other determinants of Y that might be *correlated* with X_1, while u captures the net effect of all other determinants of Y that are *not correlated* with X. Significantly, we assume that we have measures of all the determinants X_1 through X_k in our dataset. Later we relax this assumption.

Now that Y depends on k measured determinants, it is no longer possible to describe the model in a simple two-dimensional graph. Even so, the intuition we derived from Figure A.1 remains relevant. If we draw a random sample and observe Y and X_1 through X_k for each sample unit, we may use OLS regression to put a line through the middle of the resulting (k+1-dimensional) scatter plot of data and use the intercept and slopes of that line as our estimates of a and b_1 through b_k. We can show that if the population relationship between Y and X_1 through X_k truly

---

[16] Researchers sometimes report t ratios instead of standard errors. A coefficient's t ratio is the coefficient estimate divided by its standard error. If this ratio is greater than 2 (or, more precisely, greater than 1.96) in absolute value, then the coefficient estimate is statistically significant at the 95 percent confidence level. Many researchers would argue that it is preferable to report standard errors rather than t ratios, because t ratios allow easy assessment only of statistical significance, while standard errors also allow easy assessment of what the data do or do not say regarding economic importance.

conforms to the three assumptions above, and if we employ a well-executed probability sample with good measures of Y and X_1 through X_k, then our OLS estimates are unbiased. Most important, our OLS estimate of the causal effect of X_1 on Y, $\widehat{b}_1$, is unbiased.

Notice how remarkable this result is! By assuming the true model conforms to equation A.10, we are acknowledging that the determinant of interest, X_1, may be correlated with other determinants of Y. This means that if we simply observed how Y rises or falls as we shift attention from subpopulations with lower to higher levels of X_1, we would observe a correlation between X_1 and Y but would not observe the ceteris paribus effect of X_1 on Y. Even so, we can tease out an estimate of the ceteris paribus effect of X_1 on Y by running an OLS regression of Y on X_1 *and all the other determinants of Y that may be correlated with X_1*. By including X_2 through X_k in the regression, we control for their variation in our sample. The OLS procedure estimates the causal effect of X_1 on Y by examining only the variation in X_1 and Y that remains *after eliminating any variation in Y that can be explained on the basis of variation in the other RHS variables*. This ability to estimate the effect on Y of a single regressor while holding other RHS variables constant is what makes OLS regression such a powerful and important analytical tool.

As always, even when we believe an estimate is unbiased, sampling error (i.e., the possibility that we have drawn an unusual sample) might render the estimate misleading; thus we must evaluate its precision by examining its 95 percent confidence interval. We may show that if the variance of the error term u is equal to σ^2 within any subpopulation (defined by levels of X_1 through X_k), then the following statistic is an unbiased estimate of the variance of $\widehat{b}_1$'s sampling distribution, in this model with multiple regressors:

$$\widehat{Var}(\widehat{b}) = \frac{\widehat{\sigma}^2}{\sum_{i=1}^{n} (X_{1i} - \overline{X}_1)^2 (V_1^2)} \tag{A.11}$$

where V_1^2 is a measure of the variation in X_1 that remains *after holding X_2 through X_k constant* and $\widehat{\sigma}^2$ is again an estimate of the variance of u_i.[17] As in the case of the simpler model, the expression for $\widehat{b}_1$'s sampling variance tells us that the variance becomes smaller, and our estimate becomes more precise, as sample size n rises, as the average degree of variation in X_1 around it sample mean rises, and as the estimated variance of the error term (the numerator) falls. In addition, the inclusion of V_1^2 in the denominator tells us that our estimates become more precise when X_1 has more variation *that is independent of the other RHS variables*. If X_1 is closely correlated with another RHS variable (or, more generally, is near to being a perfect linear function of the other regressors) then, after holding the other Xs constant, there is very little variation in X_1 left from which we can learn about X_1's ceteris paribus effect on Y. Thus our estimate also becomes more precise as the variation in X_1 that remains after holding the other regressors constant rises.

Again, we may calculate the 95 percent confidence interval for the OLS estimate $\widehat{b}_1$ according to the formula:

$$[\widehat{b}_1 - 1.96 \times s.e.(\widehat{b}_1),\ \widehat{b}_1 + 1.96 \times s.e.(\widehat{b}_1)] \tag{A.12}$$

where $s.e.(\widehat{b}_1)$ is the standard error of $\widehat{b}_1$ and is equal to the square root of the variance described in equation A.11. Computer programs capable of estimating OLS regressions typically report

---

[17] More specifically, V_1^2 is equal to $(1-R^2)$, where R^2 is the R-squared measure from a regression of X_1 on $X_2, \ldots, X_k$. The R-squared statistic measures a regression's goodness of fit. It takes values between 0 and 1, with higher values indicating better fit. A regression's fit is better when the sum of squared differences between the actual and predicted values is smaller. When the R-squared measure from a regression of X_1 on $X_2, \ldots, X_k$ is high (and V_1^2 is low), variation in X_1 is closely tied to variation in $X_2, \ldots, X_k$, and very little variation in X_1 remains after holding $X_2, \ldots, X_k$ constant.

both the coefficient estimates and the related standard errors, allowing calculation of these confidence intervals. (Often they report the confidence intervals as well.) Again, we may use the same approach described earlier to evaluate whether this confidence interval is wide or narrow.

A more general view of multiple regression models

The model described in equation A.10 is more realistic and general than the model in equation A.6 because it allows that Y might be determined by any number of variables and that those variables might be correlated with one another. At first glance, equation A.10 still seems relevant only to a narrow class of circumstances, however, because it requires that the population relationship between Y and its determinants be *linear*. This is restrictive, because linearity implies that the size of the effect on Y of a one-unit increase in X_1 is the same, no matter how much or little X_1 we start with and no matter how much or little we have of the other determinants. For many real-world relationships that we might like to estimate, this assumption is not reasonable. For example, if Y measures firms' outputs, X_1 measures their labor inputs, and X_2 measures their capital inputs, then we would expect that the effect of X_1 should diminish as the initial level of X_1 rises (while holding X_2 constant), because we expect diminishing marginal returns when we increase individual production inputs while holding other inputs constant (see the discussion of production functions in Chapter 3). We would also expect that the effect of X_1 on Y would rise as X_2 increases, because increasing the number of workers from, say, 10 to 11 would add more to output in a firm with more capital than in a firm with less capital.

Fortunately, the model in equation A.10 is less restrictive than it might seem, because the variables we place on the left- and right-hand sides of the linear relationship may themselves be *non*linear functions of other, more fundamental, variables. For example, our left-hand side variable might be $\ln(Y)$ rather than Y, where $\ln(.)$ is the natural logarithm function, and our regressors might include $\ln(X_1)$, X_2^2, $1/X_3$, or $X_1 \times X_3$. When we employ functional transformations of these sorts on the left- and right-hand sides, we can use OLS estimates of linear regression models to estimate nonlinear relationships between the more fundamental Y and Xs. For example, the equation

$$\ln(Y_i) = a + bX_i + cZ_i + u_i \tag{A.13}$$

which describes a linear relationship between $\ln(Y_i)$, X_i, Z_i, and u_i, implies the nonlinear relationship between Y_i and the other variables:

$$Y_i = e^a e^{bX_i} e^{cZ_i} e^{u_i} \tag{A.14}$$

(We derive equation A.14 by exponentiating both sides of equation A.13.) In this model, the effect on Y of a one-unit increase in X rises as the initial level of X or the level of Z increases (assuming b and c are positive). We may estimate this model by constructing a new variable (call it *lnY*) that is equal to the natural logarithm of the variable Y we find in our data set and then running a regression of *lnY* on X and Z.

A complete treatment of OLS regressions employing functional transformations is beyond the scope of this appendix. It is important, however, for readers to know how to interpret the magnitudes of coefficients in such models, which are often employed in applied papers, such as those cited in this text. Table A.1 therefore presents key facts required for interpreting coefficient estimates in models involving functional transformation. The first column lists common functional form choices. The reader may employ the information in the second column to interpret individual coefficient estimates for regressions of those sorts. The symbol Δ is read "change in." For example, the entry in the second column for the log-lin model (second row) states "$b \times 100 =$ percentage ΔY for one-unit ΔX." This indicates that if the coefficient on X (years of schooling) in

■ TABLE A.1   Basic Facts Regarding OLS Regression Models Employing Functional Transformations

Model Name	Equation	Interpretation of b	Comments
Lin-lin model	$Y = a + bX + cZ + u$	b = units ΔY for one-unit ΔX	
Log-lin model	$\ln(Y) = a + bX + cZ + u$	$b \times 100$ = percentage ΔY for one-unit ΔX	Implies $Y = e^a e^{bX} e^{cZ} e^u$
Log-log model	$\ln(Y) = a + b \ln(X) + c \ln(Z) + u$	b = percentage ΔY for 1 percent ΔX	Implies $Y = e^a X^b Z^c e^u$
Quadratic model	$Y = a + bX + cX^2 + dZ + u$	b = units ΔY for *first* one-unit ΔX	$b+2cX^*$ = units ΔY for one-unit ΔX when starting from $X = X^*$ (It is useful to calculate this for X^* equal to the sample mean or to some other salient value of X.)
Model with interaction effect	$Y = a + bX + cZ + dXZ + u$	b = units ΔY for one-unit ΔX when $Z = 0$	$b+dZ^*$ = units ΔY for one-unit ΔX when starting from $Z = Z^*$ (It is useful to calculate this for Z^* equal to the sample mean or to some other salient value of Z.)

a regression with left-hand side variable $\ln(Y)$ (where Y is the wage in pesos per hour) is 0.05, then the estimate implies that a one-unit increase in X (i.e., a one-year increase in schooling) increases Y (the wage) by $0.05 \times 100 = 5$ percent. For more on the log-lin model, see Box 9.2 and Problem 5 at the end of Chapter 9.

Omitted variables bias

We come now to the most important topic in all of econometric analysis: the problem of **omitted variables bias**. Suppose that the true model is as described by equation A.10 and related assumptions, and that we have a random cross-section sample, but we run a regression of Y only on X_1 through X_{k-1}. That is, we omit one of Y's potential determinants, X_k, from the regression. We might do this because our data set lacks a measure of X_k, or for other reasons. When we leave X_k out, we fail to hold it constant when estimating the effect of a change in X_1 on Y. If X_1 and X_k are correlated (when holding X_2 through X_{k-1} constant, as we do in our regression) then our OLS estimate $\widehat{b_1}$ may be biased.

More specifically, we can show that if b_1 is the true ceteris paribus effect of X_1 on Y, b_k is the true ceteris paribus effect of the omitted variable (X_k) on Y, and d is the hypothetical OLS estimate we would get for the slope coefficient on X_1 if we could run a regression of the omitted variable X_k on all the included variables X_1 through X_{k-1}, then when we omit X_k from the regression, our OLS estimate $\widehat{b_1}$ is an unbiased estimate not of b_1 but of

$$b_1 + b_k d \tag{A.15}$$

If the second term is not zero, then our OLS estimate of b_1 is a *biased* estimate of the causal effect of X_1 on Y. It provides an estimate that tends to be too high if the bias term $b_k d$ is positive and that tends to be too low if $b_k d$ is negative.

Careful thought about the two components in the bias term (b_k and d) helps us understand the nature of the bias, and of the socioeconomic circumstances in which the bias is likely to be large or small, positive or negative. The coefficient d is a measure of the correlation between X_1 and X_k that remains after holding X_2 through X_{k-1} constant. It answers the question: When we increase X_1 by 1 unit, while holding the other included variables constant, by how many units does the omitted variable X_k rise, on average, in our sample? The coefficient b_k answers the question: For each unit that we increase the omitted variable X_k, while holding all other regressors constant, by how much does Y increase? The product $b_k d$ therefore answers the question: When we increase X_1 by 1 unit, while holding X_2 through X_{k-1} constant, by how many units does Y increase or decrease *as a result of the accompanying change in the omitted variable* (which we are, unfortunately, not holding constant in this regression)? The formula implies that when we leave X_k out of the regression, the OLS estimate of the coefficient on X_1 might no longer reflect merely the ceteris paribus effect of X_1 on Y (b_1). It also incorporates the causal effect of the average change in X_k that is associated with a one-unit increase in X_1 in our data set. The bias may be positive or negative. If b_k and d are both positive or both negative, then the bias is positive. If one is positive and the other negative, the bias is negative. If either b_k or d is zero, there is no bias.

This important result—regarding the bias that can arise when possible determinants of Y are omitted from a regression—has two practical implications. First, even when researchers have no interest in studying the effects on Y of any determinants other than X_1, they must include measures of *all* determinants of Y in the regression of Y on X_1 if they wish to obtain unbiased estimates of the *causal effect* of X_1 on Y.[18] In most real-world applications, and with observational samples, X_1 is likely to be correlated with the other regressors; thus, leaving the other regressors out is likely to bias estimation of X_1's causal effect. Researchers must, therefore, take great care to work out (using social science reasoning, not necessarily mathematical equations) a comprehensive socioeconomic model of how Y is determined and then use that model to guide their selection of regressors.

Second, when researchers recognize that some potentially important determinants of Y are excluded from a regression, they can make educated guesses about the likely direction of the resulting bias, by making educated guesses about the likely signs of b_k and d. (We consider examples below.) Making such educated guesses is important when attempting to draw conclusions about causal effects from imperfect regressions. For example, if the magnitude of an estimate is a very small positive number, its confidence interval is narrow, and we suspect that it suffers from an *upward* omitted variables bias, then we can argue that "If we eliminated the bias, the estimate would likely fall. Thus our results give strong reason to rule out a large positive effect."

Unfortunately, we can almost always think of additional variables that *might* help determine Y and are not included in a regression. Thus the potential for omitted variables bias is a continual worry in econometric research. Later we provide an overview of ways researchers attempt to circumvent potential omitted variables biases. First, however, we consider an example that highlights the issues and techniques introduced thus far.

Program evaluation example

Suppose we wish to estimate the **impact**—or causal effect—of a government agricultural extension program on the incomes of participating farmers. The program pays extension agents to visit farmers and provide them with advice about how best to cultivate their farms, with the aim of raising farm productivity and income. We have an observational cross-section sample of farms, in which some farmers have received extension visits and some have not. The data are listed in Table A.2. With just 10 observations, the data set is much smaller than we would use in a real evaluation, but it is useful for exposition. The variable listed in the second column (P) is an example of a **participation indicator variable**, which takes the value 1 if the farmer participated in the program (i.e., received a visit) and 0 if not. The variable listed in the third column (Y) is the outcome variable of interest.

The simplest step we might take to estimate the program's impact is to compare average farm earnings for farmers who did and did not participate. When we do this, we find:

Mean earnings for participating farmers = $297.38

Mean earnings for nonparticipating farmers = $241.57

Difference in mean earnings = $55.81

---

[18] More precisely, they must include measures of any determinants of Y that vary across individuals in the sample and might be correlated with the included variable of interest.

Average farm earnings are \$55.81 per year higher for sample farmers who participated than for those who did not participate. This is a difference of 21 percent relative to the overall mean earnings of \$269.47. If this is a good estimate of average program impact, then the program looks successful (at least along this dimension of program performance).

But *is* this a good estimate of the program's ceteris paribus effect? Drawing on concepts introduced earlier, we see that this estimate may be misleading for three reasons: sampling error, failure to control for differences across farmer groups in variables for which we have measures in our dataset (e.g., the variable S in the final column of Table A.1), and failure to control for differences across farmer groups in variables for which we do not have measures.

The first reason the simple mean comparison may be misleading is sampling error. Even if the program has no impact, so that—in the population of farmers in this region—mean earnings are no different for farmers who did and did not receive extension visits, the means for the two types of farmers in our *sample* might look different as a result of sampling error. The smaller is our sample, and the more variable are farm incomes in the population (for reasons unrelated to extension visits), the more likely it is that at least one of the subsamples will be unusual, causing the sample averages of income to differ across the two groups of farmers (even though the population means are the same). To assess the confidence we should place in our estimate in the face of possible sampling error, we must estimate a 95 percent confidence interval for it. Statistical derivations provide us with formulas for calculating standard errors and confidence intervals for such differences in sample means.

It is useful to note, however, that we can use a specially formulated OLS regression to calculate the difference in sample means, and we may then easily calculate a 95 percent confidence interval for that difference using formulas presented earlier. More specifically, if we run an OLS regression of Y on the program participation indicator variable P, the estimate we obtain for the slope coefficient on P is an estimate of the difference in the population mean values of Y across participating and nonparticipating farmer groups. To see this, notice that when we run a regression of Y on P we are, by definition, estimating a population regression equation of the form

$$Y_i = a + bP_i + u_i \tag{A.16}$$

where u_i has mean zero in the population and is uncorrelated with P_i. This implies that the average of Y among farmers sharing a particular value for P is equal to $a+bP$. The average of Y among

■ TABLE A.2   **Data for Program Evaluation Example**

Farmer Identification Number (i)	Farmer Received an Agronomist Visit (P_i)? (1 = yes, 0 = no)	Farmer's Total Annual Earnings in Dollars (Y_i)	Years of Schooling Completed by the Farmer (S_i)
1	0	\$192.84	0
2	0	237.04	4
3	0	254.77	6
4	0	250.98	6
5	0	272.20	7
6	1	274.57	4
7	1	265.73	4
8	1	291.47	6
9	1	299.59	7
10	1	355.54	12

participating farmers (for whom $P=1$) is $a+b$, and the average of Y among nonparticipating farmers (for whom $P=0$) is a. The coefficient b is, therefore, the amount by which the average of Y among participating farmers exceeds the average of Y among nonparticipating farmers in the population. This is the same quantity we estimated earlier when we compared the sample average values of income (Y) across participating and nonparticipating farmers. We can show that the estimate of b derived by running an OLS regression of Y on P is, in fact, identical to the estimate of impact we derive by calculating the difference in sample means (as we did earlier). Calculating the difference in sample means this way allows us to use equations A.7 and A.9 to estimate the standard error and 95 percent confidence interval for this estimate.

When we regress Y on P using the data in Table A.2, we obtain the estimates (with standard errors in parentheses):

$$\widehat{Y}_i = 241.57 + 55.81 P_i$$
$$(14.61) \quad (20.66) \tag{A.17}$$

Our estimate of b equals 55.81, matching our earlier calculation of the difference in sample means. We obtain a standard error of 20.66, implying a 95 percent confidence interval of [8.16, 103.47]. Because the values 8.16 and 103.47 imply very different stories about the program's impact, we conclude that this confidence interval is wide and our estimate is imprecise. That is, we must conclude that sampling error may indeed be a significant problem, and we should not place great confidence in our estimated impact of \$55.81, even if we are confident that the assumptions underlying the regression of equation A.17 are true. (We will see, however, that this is not the end of the story.)

The second and third reasons why taking the simple difference in mean earnings for the two farmer groups may yield a misleading estimate of program impact are examples of omitted variables bias. Concern for both arises out of the possibility that the true model describing how Y is determined is best represented not by equation A.16 and related assumptions but by

$$Y_i = a + b_1 P_i + b_2 X_{2i} + \cdots + b_k X_{ki} + u_i \tag{A.18}$$

where u_i again has mean zero in the population, u_i is uncorrelated with P_i, and $X_2, \ldots, X_k$ may be correlated with P. The logic of omitted variables bias tells us that if additional variables $X_2, \ldots, X_k$ indeed help to determine Y, and if they are correlated with P, then running a regression of Y on P alone can yield biased estimates of program impact.

Unfortunately, when evaluating programs using observational data, we almost always have reason to suspect that the program participation indicator P is correlated with other determinants of Y, and thus that a simple regression of Y on P (or the equivalent comparison of average Y across participant and nonparticipant subsamples) would yield a biased estimate of the program's impact. We suspect bias because we know that individuals in the population were **selected** into participation or nonparticipation through some process that makes certain types of individuals (with certain typical values of $X_2, \ldots, X_k$) more likely to participate than others. (We discuss examples of such selection processes later.) This means that the values of $X_2, \ldots, X_k$ for participants tend to differ from those for nonparticipants. As a result, average Y might differ between participant and nonparticipant groups not only as a result of the program's impact but also as a result of these differences in other characteristics and circumstances. This potential for omitted variables bias arising out of selection into programs is often called the **program evaluation problem**.

Three types of selection might lead to omitted variables bias in the estimation of a program's impact. First, when a program offers a new opportunity to anyone who comes forward to claim it, individuals with certain characteristics are more likely to **self-select** into the program than others. For example, if a government sets up an agricultural extension program and invites interested farmers to request extension visits, then the farmers who ultimately participate will be the ones who heard about the program, anticipated that the benefits of participation would outweigh the costs, and took action. Participating farmers might, therefore, tend to listen more to the radio, be more entrepreneurial, or have larger and higher-quality farms (on which the switch to new crops and methods is likely to yield a higher payoff) relative to nonparticipating farmers. This implies that the participation indicator P is likely to be correlated with variables describing radio use, entrepreneurial tendencies, farm size, and farm quality. These same variables are also likely to belong in the Y equation, having their own ceteris paribus effects on farm earnings. Omitting them from a regression of Y on P, therefore, would bias the estimate of program impact. More specifically, we might worry that the farmers who self-select into the program would have characteristics that are conducive to *higher* incomes and therefore that our simple estimate would tend to *overstate* program impact. In the notation of equation A.15, this is a case in which d is positive, because the omitted variables are positively correlated with P, and b_k is positive, because the omitted variables have positive causal effects on Y.

A second type of selection arises when program personnel are given discretion over whom to invite or admit into a program. Depending on the nature of this **selection by program personnel**, the resulting bias might be upward or downward. If agricultural extension agents seek to maximize the poverty-reducing impact of their program, they might offer their limited time to the neediest farmers. In this case, participants might tend to be less literate, have fewer able-bodied adults in their households, have smaller farms, and lower-quality farmland relative to nonparticipants, and the coefficient on P in a simple regression of Y on P would tend to understate the program's impact. If instead, program personnel devote their time to the farmers most likely to succeed in using new techniques, then they might select better farmers with better farms, and the simple mean difference would tend to overstate the program's impact.

A final type of selection that might introduce bias into the simplest program-impact estimates is called **endogenous program placement**, and it has to do with policymakers' choices regarding *where* to roll programs out. If policymakers roll out an agricultural extension program in the communities where participating farms are likely to look most successful, or if they open the program to all communities and only communities with better farming conditions self-select into the program, then participants tend to live in communities with better farming conditions than nonparticipants, and simple mean comparisons tend to overstate impact. If policymakers roll out the program in communities where the need is greatest, by contrast, then participants tend to have inferior farming conditions and the simplest impact estimates tend to understate program impact.

All of these selection problems suggest that a simple regression of Y on P would suffer from omitted variables bias. When the omitted variables of concern are ones for which we have measures in our data set, the problem is one of **selection on observables**, and the solution is straightforward: We simply include the additional variables in our regression of Y on P, eliminating the associated omitted variables bias directly. We give the name **control variables** to the variables describing other determinants of Y that we include in the regression of Y on P, with the aim of preventing omitted variables bias. An alternative to OLS regression for eliminating the problem of selection on observables is the use of matching methods, as described in Gertler et al. (2011).

In the example described in Table A.2, we see that the average level of schooling S among participating farmers is higher than the average among nonparticipants. Because farmers with more schooling might achieve higher farm earnings, whether or not they participate, we must worry that omitting S from the regression of Y on P biases our impact estimate upward. To eliminate this problem, we run a regression of Y on P *and* S, and obtain the results (where numbers in parentheses are standard errors):

$$\widehat{Y}_i = 192.59 + 34.52P_i + 10.65S_i$$
$$(2.72) \quad (2.63) \quad (0.45)$$

$$(A.19)$$

Our estimate of the extension program's impact has fallen from \$55.81 in the simple mean comparison to \$34.52 in this comparison, which measures the difference in mean earnings between farmers who did and did not participate, *after accounting for any earnings differences across farmers that are the result of differences in schooling*. In this case, controlling for selection on observables reduces our estimate of the program's impact.

Again, we must acknowledge the potential for sampling error to render our estimate misleading, and we must assess this possibility by calculating a 95 percent confidence interval for $\widehat{b}_1$. When we do, we obtain the interval [28.30, 40.74]. This says that although the true difference between mean incomes for farmers who did and did not receive extension visits (after controlling for differences in their years of schooling) might not be exactly \$34.52, it is unlikely to be smaller than \$28.30 or greater than \$40.74. These values correspond to percentage increases relative to mean income of 10.5 and 15.1 percent. Both values therefore suggest significant but not enormous impacts. If we are confident that our estimate is unbiased, we have strong evidence of at least moderate success of the program.

Unfortunately, we almost always worry that selection causes a program's participants to differ from nonparticipants in the levels of variables for which we do not have measures and that help to determine Y. This is the problem of **selection on unobservables**, which is more difficult to solve than the problem of selection on observables. Researchers attempt to avoid this problem by collecting data on a comprehensive set of control variables to include in impact estimation regressions.[19] They can never be certain that they have eliminated this problem entirely, however, when using observational cross-section data on participants and nonparticipants. For example, even if we augmented the dataset of Table A.2 with measures of farmers' farm sizes and distances from agricultural extension offices and could thus control for these differences in our regression, we might still worry that participating farmers differ from nonparticipating farmers in entrepreneurial ability, which is very difficult to measure and is not measured in most data sets.

Approaches for circumventing omitted variables bias

In what follows, we describe five approaches used for eliminating (or at least reducing) the bias associated with omitting relevant variables. In cases of program evaluation, they constitute responses to the problem of selection on unobservables. Some of the methods are applied almost exclusively for program evaluation, while others are also applied to the study of more diverse research questions. No single method can be counted upon to deliver unbiased estimates in all circumstances. For each method, the reader should note what kinds of data are required for the approach to be feasible and what must be true about the omitted variables for the approach to yield unbiased estimates.

We use X_1 to indicate the variable whose causal effect we wish to estimate. In program evaluation examples, this stands for the participation indicator variable called P above. We use $X_2, \ldots, X_{k-1}$ to indicate observed determinants of Y other than X_1, and we use X_k as a shorthand reference to any omitted variables.

Randomized control trials

In a **randomized control trial** (RCT), researchers draw a sample from a population of interest, randomly divide that sample into two or more subsamples, and then set X_1 to different values for different subsamples. The most common application of the RCT approach is to program evaluation.

---

[19] When attempting to avoid omitted variables bias by including many control variables, researchers might include some variables that do not, in fact, help to determine Y. Fortunately, this inclusion of irrelevant variables does not introduce bias. It does reduce precision, suggesting that researchers should be somewhat cautious about adding variables of uncertain importance to regression equations, especially when samples are small.

In the simplest RCTs, researchers collaborate with program personnel to identify a set of individuals or communities that meet program eligibility criteria, select a sample from this population, and randomly divide the sample into a treatment group and a control group. Practitioners then roll out the program to members of the treatment group only, thereby setting the program participation indicator X_1 to 1 for members of that group and to 0 for the control group. After the program has had time to generate impact (e.g., after one year), researchers collect data on outcomes for all members of the treatment and control samples, and they estimate impact by running a regression of the outcome variable (Y) on the participation indicator (X_1), with or without additional regressors. (Often, program personnel then roll out the program to members of the control group.)

If an RCT is done well, this regression of Y on X_1, using the single cross section of data collected after treatment, yields an unbiased estimate of X_1's causal effect on Y, even if the regression omits controls for other Y determinants $X_2, \ldots, X_k$. The estimate of X_1's causal effect is unbiased, because randomized division of the overall sample into the treatment and control subsamples renders the distributions of all variables $X_2, \ldots, X_k$ virtually identical in the two subsamples, thereby rendering the variables *uncorrelated* with X_1. In the notation of equation A.15, RCTs eliminate omitted variables bias by creating a situation in which d equals zero (or is at least very close to zero).

The RCT method is considered by some to be the gold standard for estimating a program's causal effect because, unlike other methods described later, its efficacy does not depend on the omitted variables satisfying any restrictive assumptions. The results of RCTs are also easy to explain and interpret because they directly answer the question: "If we take two groups of people that are virtually identical and administer a treatment to one of them, what difference in outcomes emerges as a result of the treatment?"

The primary weakness of the RCT approach is its cost and difficulty. Often RCTs are feasible only if researchers find practitioners who are willing to collaborate and who have the power to determine how treatments are distributed across individuals or communities. For the simplest RCT designs, practitioners must agree to administer treatments only to randomly selected individuals or communities rather than using their usual criteria for determining which individuals or communities receive their scarce program resources. (For a description of other RCT designs, see Duflo et al., 2008.) Practitioners may be reluctant to do this for ethical and logistical reasons. Randomization prevents them from prioritizing delivery of a program's services to the neediest individuals or communities, and it can require them to roll their program out in many geographic locations simultaneously, rather than rolling it out more organically and cheaply over time.

As is true of any estimation method, RCTs can deliver misleading estimates for various reasons. Sampling error can render impact estimates misleading, especially if samples are small. Researchers attempt to rule this out by examining 95 percent confidence intervals for RCT impact estimates. Difficulties in rolling out a program or collecting data can also render RCT impact estimates biased. For example, practitioners might be reluctant to roll out a program to certain types of individuals or communities, and as a result they might treat only a selected subset of the treatment sample. Researchers often check that randomization has been implemented well by gathering **baseline data** on individuals' characteristics and outcomes before the program is rolled out and checking that the means and variances of the variables Y and $X_2, \ldots, X_k$ look similar in treatment and control samples.

Discontinuity designs

Sometimes even when a program has been rolled out to all eligible individuals (leaving no randomly selected control group), details of the program's eligibility rules allow researchers to identify two groups of individuals that are virtually identical in all respects, except that one group receives treatment by the program and the other does not.

Suppose eligibility is determined by observing each household's value of a continuous characteristic C and deeming as eligible only those with values of C above (or below) a well-defined threshold c. For example, a school-aged child may be eligible for a scholarship only if she scored over 50 percent on an academic achievement test, and a household may be eligible for a microcredit program only if it owns less than one-half acre of land. If researchers observe C for a large enough sample of households, then they may employ the **discontinuity design** approach in its simplest form to estimate program impact. To do this, they limit attention to subsamples of households with values of C just above and below threshold c, and they estimate the program's impact by comparing the average value of Y for households with C just above the threshold to the average value of Y for households with C just below the threshold.

For example, if households are eligible for a microcredit program only if they own less than 0.5 acres of land, then researchers might estimate the impact of the program on households' per capita consumption expenditure by comparing average per capita consumption expenditure for households owning 0.51 acres of land to the average for those owning 0.49 acres. Similarly, if children are eligible for a scholarship program only if they score at least 50 percent on an academic achievement test, then researchers might estimate the impact of scholarship receipt on the child's allocation of time to homework in the next year by comparing average homework time among children who scored 51 percent to the average for those who scored 49 percent. Even if C is itself a determinant of Y or is correlated with other determinants of Y, this simple comparison is unbiased because the values of C (and the distributions of other determinants that may be correlated with C) are nearly identical in the two groups. In the examples given, we would expect that households owning 0.49 acres are very similar to farmers owning 0.51 acres in every expect other than their program participation status and that children who earned scores of 51 percent are very similar to children who earned scores of 49 percent.

Researchers might instead employ a more elaborate version of the discontinuity design approach, in which they include in their samples observations with a wider range of C values. They estimate regression models that allow average Y to depend continuously on C below and above c, but they also allow Y to "jump" when C reaches the threshold c. That is, it allows the function relating Y to C to be discontinuous, rising or falling by a discrete amount at the value c. By allowing Y to depend continuously on C throughout its range, they acknowledge that C might have an independent effect on Y that is unrelated to the program's impact, and they might also pick up the effects of other Y determinants that are correlated with C. If, however, these effects cause Y to rise continuously as C increases, then the only reason for Y to jump as C crosses the threshold c is the associated abrupt change in program eligibility and participation. Researchers might therefore use the size of the jump as an estimate of the program's impact.

The discontinuity design approach is feasible only for evaluating programs with eligibility rules requiring a continuous variable to fall above or below a threshold, and only if researchers have a good measure of that continuous variable. It provides valid estimates only when eligibility rules are strictly enforced, so that the rate of participation in the program indeed rises sharply as C passes the threshold c. The method's primary weakness is that it provides a good estimate of average program impact only among individuals with values of C close to the eligibility limit. The average impact among *all* participants, including many with values of C far from the threshold c, may be quite different.

Instrumental variables estimation

When using RCTs, researchers circumvent omitted variables bias by *creating* variation in X_1 that is not correlated with any other determinants of Y. When using the **instrumental variables method**, as with the simple discontinuity design approach, researchers attempt to *find* variation in X_1 that is not correlated with any unobserved determinants of Y. More specifically, researchers look for some quirk in how X_1 is determined that causes an individual's value of X_1 to depend on a variable I that is *not* a determinant of Y and is not even correlated with any unobserved determinants of Y. If researchers have a measure of such a variable I—which is called an **instrument** for X_1 in the Y regression—then they may employ the instrumental variables (IV) regression method (also known as **two-stage least squares** regression) to obtain good impact estimates, even in a single observational cross-section data set. The estimate delivered by IV estimation is not (strictly speaking) unbiased, but it has the closely related good property of consistency, which means that as sample size becomes very large, the estimate becomes closer and closer to the true value. Thus we can think of it as a method with the potential to eliminate omitted variables bias.

A complete treatment of the instrumental variables method is beyond the scope of this appendix, but it is useful to sketch out the mechanics of how the method is performed and to suggest the intuition regarding how the method works. Suppose Y is determined according to equation A.10, but we lack data on X_k and must omit it from our regression. If we have data on one or more instrumental variables (having the characteristics described earlier), then we may obtain IV estimates in two steps or stages. For simplicity, let's assume that we have a single instrument I. In the first stage, we run a regression of X_1 on $X_2, \ldots, X_{k-1}$, and I. We then create a new variable, $\widehat{X}_1$, which contains the predicted values from this first stage regression. Note that $\widehat{X}_1$ is, by definition, just a linear function of $X_2, \ldots, X_{k-1}$ and I. In the second stage, we run a regression of Y on $\widehat{X}_1$ (rather than X_1) and X_2 through X_{k-1}. The coefficient on $\widehat{X}_1$ is the IV estimate of X_1's causal effect on Y.

To gain some insight into why this estimation method delivers an estimate of b free of omitted variables bias, recall that the OLS estimate of the coefficient on any one right-hand side variable is calculated using only the variation in that variable and Y that remains after holding all other right-hand side variables constant. This implies that the OLS estimate of the coefficient on $\widehat{X}_1$ in the second stage regression is calculated using only the variation in $\widehat{X}_1$ and Y that remains after holding $X_2, \ldots, X_{k-1}$ constant. Because $\widehat{X}_1$ contains the predicted values from the first-stage regression, we know that it varies only because of variation in $X_2, \ldots, X_{k-1}$ and I. After holding $X_2, \ldots, X_{k-1}$ constant, therefore, $\widehat{X}_1$ varies only as a result of variation in I. If I is truly uncorrelated with the omitted variable X_k, then the variation in $\widehat{X}_1$ that is driven by variation in I is variation in X_1 that is uncorrelated with the omitted variable. Because the second stage regression estimates the effect of X_1 on Y using only this good variation in X_1, it delivers an estimate free of omitted variables bias.

Instrumental variables estimation is feasible to perform, even with only a single observational cross-section dataset, as long as the dataset contains a variable that may serve as an instrument. The method yields a *good* estimate that is free of omitted variables bias, however, only if the instrument is valid. To be a **valid instrument**, I must satisfy two demanding conditions. First, it must have a statistically significant effect on X_1 in the first stage regression, so that $\widehat{X}_1$ indeed contains informative variation. Researchers can and should confirm that this is true. Second, I must *not* be a determinant of Y and must not be correlated with any omitted variable X_k. This means that the only channel through which I may be related to Y is through its effect on X_1. In most cases, it is impossible to confirm directly whether this second assumption holds. Researchers must offer good social science arguments as to why the instrument should affect X_1 but *not* Y. Development analysts must assess the plausibility of this argument before placing confidence in IV estimates.

For an example of what is involved in establishing the validity of an instrument, see Acemoğlu et al. (2001). These authors wish to estimate the impact on a country's GDP per capita of variables describing the quality of the country's institutions (a concept introduced in Chapter 2 and addressed more extensively in Chapters 12 and 13), using a cross section of country-level data. They recognize that GDP per capita may be determined by many country characteristics for which they cannot control directly in their regressions. They argue that variables describing historical mortality rates among European settlers during the colonial period are valid instruments for the institution variables in their current GDP per capita regressions. They argue, first, that historical mortality rates helped to determine current institutional conditions, because where mortality rates were high, few citizens of colonial powers settled and colonial powers made little effort to establish good institutions. Where mortality rates were low, by contrast, citizens of colonial powers did settle and colonial powers established good institutions. Because institutions tend to change only very slowly over time, countries where better institutions were established during the colonial period continue to have better institutions today. The authors demonstrate empirically that current institutional conditions are indeed correlated with historical mortality rates. The authors point out, second, that historical settler mortality rates should have no direct effect on current GDP per capita (and should, therefore, affect GDP per capita *only* through their effect on the quality of institutions), especially after including variables describing current health conditions in the second stage regression.

Fixed effects or first difference estimation

When researchers have access to panel data, and when they believe that any omitted variables are largely constant over time, they may employ the **fixed effects** approach. The fixed effects approach applies only when the true model generating the data looks like this:

$$Y_{it} = a + b_1 X_{1it} + \cdots + b_{k-1} X_{k-1,it} + b_k X_{ki} + u_{it} \tag{A.20}$$

where Y_{it} is the value of Y for individual i in time period t, X_{1it} is the value of X_1 for individual i in time period t, and X_k represents a determinant of Y that is omitted from the regression. u_{it} has mean zero and is uncorrelated with the Xs. This equation must be true in all time periods included in the panel, so that the coefficients a and b_1 through b_k are the same for all observations. Notice that X_{ki} has no t subscript, indicating that X_k takes the same value for all observations pertaining to individual i, regardless of time period. The term $b_k X_{ki}$, too, takes a single value for all observations pertaining to individual i in the panel, indicating that the omitted variable has an effect on Y that is fixed over time for each individual. It also indicates that if we could hold X_1 through X_{k-1} at the same levels for all individuals included in the sample, the average values of Y (averaged over time, separately for each individual in the panel) would vary across individuals as a result of variation in the omitted X_k.

Even though we do not observe the values of X_k directly, we can account for the variation in average Y across individuals resulting from variation in X_k by including in our regression (of Y on $X_1, \ldots, X_{k-1}$) a set of $n-1$ indicator variables that distinguish each individual in the panel from the other individuals (where n is the number of individuals in the sample.) The indicator variable relevant to individual j is a variable equal to 1 for observations that pertain to individual j and is equal to zero for all other observations in the data set. The indicator variables for individuals with relatively high values of the omitted variable will pick up relatively high estimated coefficients (assuming that the effect of the omitted variable is positive), and those for individuals with relatively low values of the omitted variable will pick up relatively low estimated coefficients. Including the indicator variables thus allows researchers to estimate the effect of the omitted variable on Y even without having data on the omitted variable itself. In so doing, it allows researchers to estimate the effect of X_1 on Y in a way that controls for variation in the omitted variable.

To gain further intuition into how the fixed effects method works, it is useful to consider a simple case in which our panel data set includes data on N individuals from only two time periods, 1 and 2. Substituting 1 and 2 in for t in equation A.20, we obtain

$$Y_{i1} = a + b_1 X_{1,i1} + \cdots + b_{k-1} X_{k-1,i1} + b_k X_{k,i} + u_{i1} \tag{A.21}$$

and

$$Y_{i2} = a + b_1 X_{1,i2} + \cdots + b_{k-1} X_{k-1,i2} + b_k X_{k,i} + u_{i2} \tag{A.22}$$

Subtracting the left- and right-hand sides of equation A.21 from the left- and right-hand sides of equation A.22, we obtain

$$\Delta Y_i = a + b\Delta X_{1i} + \cdots + b_{k-1}\Delta X_{k-1} + \Delta u_i \tag{A.23}$$

where ΔY_i may be read as "the change in Y_i from period 1 to period 2."

In deriving equation A.23, we have transformed the original statement of our model, which involves the *levels* of Y and $X_1, \ldots, X_k$, into a statement of the same model involving *changes* in Y and $X_1, \ldots, X_{k-1}$. Significantly, if X_k truly is constant over time for any individual i, then X_{ki} for period 2 is the same as X_{ki} for period 1, and ΔX_{ki} is exactly zero for every individual in the panel; thus no X_k term appears in the change equation A.23. Furthermore, equation A.23 describes a linear relationship between the left-hand side variable, ΔY, and the right-hand side variables $\Delta X_1, \ldots, \Delta X_{k-1}$, plus an error term that has mean zero and is not correlated with ΔX_1. This suggests that we can obtain unbiased estimates of the coefficients in equation A.23 by running an OLS regression of ΔY on $\Delta X_1, \ldots, \Delta X_{k-1}$. This is feasible, because our panel data set allows us to construct the variables ΔY and $\Delta X_1, \ldots, \Delta X_{k-1}$ and run this regression. We can also show that running this regression produces exactly the same estimates as the fixed effects method described above (in this simple case of a panel with only two time periods). This way of describing fixed effects estimation is useful because it emphasizes that the effect of X_1 on Y is estimated using only *variation over time* in Y, X_1 and $X_2, \ldots, X_{k-1}$. If X_k truly remains constant over time for every individual i, then by focusing only on changes in X_1 *over time* (rather than across individuals), we are focusing on changes in X_1 *while holding the omitted variable X_k constant.*

The fixed effects regression method is feasible as long as researchers have possession of panel data on Y, X_1, and any other determinants of Y that change over time. X_1 must also change over time, in differing amounts for different individuals in the sample, so that the sample contains variation in ΔX_1.

Fixed effects estimation produces estimates free of omitted variables bias only if all the omitted variables truly are constant over time. For example, if fixed effects estimation of an agricultural production function relating farm output Y to inputs X_1 and X_2 is to yield unbiased estimates of the causal effect of X_1 on Y, all inputs and other factors affecting farms' productivity that are omitted from the regression must truly be constant over time. Such an assumption may be plausible for omitted variables such as land quality (in panel data sets covering only a short time period, during which little land degradation takes place), but it might not be plausible for omitted variables describing weather conditions, which change from year to year. Unfortunately, it is impossible to test the validity of this assumption directly. Researchers must make plausible social science arguments as to why the important omitted variables should indeed be constant over time. If the omitted variables instead vary over time, then ΔX_1 may be correlated with ΔX_k, and even fixed effects estimates can suffer from omitted variables bias.

Researchers sometimes employ variants of the fixed effect approach to eliminate biases associated with omitted variables that are constant within subsets of cross section rather than panel datasets. For example, rather than creating a set of indicator variables that each take the value 1 for all observations pertaining to a particular individual in a panel data set, a researcher might create a set of indicator variables that each take the value 1 for all observations in a cross section of households that pertain to a particular community. Including such indicator variables controls for omitted variables that are the same for all households in the same community but vary across communities (e.g., omitted measures of local infrastructure quality). Once the community indicators are included, the regression uses only variation across households within communities to estimate the effect of household characteristics (e.g., income) on the outcome variable. When they include such community indicator variables, researchers say that they are controlling for *community fixed effects.* In similar fashion, they might construct indicator variables to control for *year fixed effects* in panel data or for *household fixed effects* in cross sections containing data on multiple children per household.

Difference-in-differences estimation

When using **difference-in-differences** estimation in its simplest form, researchers estimate the average effect of X_1 on Y by identifying a period of time during which the value of X_1 changed for some individuals but not for others. X_1 usually measures some feature of a policy, and the period involved is a period in which that policy feature changed for some people but not for others. In the case of program evaluation, X_1 is an indicator of program participation, and the period involved is a period during which some people became participants in the program and some remained nonparticipants. (Unlike in the case of a randomized control trial, participants might have self-selected or been selected into participation by program personnel.) Researchers gather data on Y from before and after the change and for samples from two groups: the treatment group, for whom X_1 changed during the study period, and the comparison group, for whom X_1 did not change. For each of the two groups, they calculate the change in average Y from before to after the policy change. Their estimate of the average effect of the policy change on Y is the difference between the before-to-after change in average Y for the treatment group ($\Delta \overline{Y}_t$) and the comparable before-to-after change in average Y for the comparison group ($\Delta \overline{Y}_c$). In the case of program evaluation, researchers compare the change over time in average Y (from before to after treatment by the program) for a group of program participants to the comparable change over time for a group of nonparticipants.

To grasp the assumptions that must be true for difference-in-differences estimation to yield unbiased estimates of the effect of X_1 on average Y, notice that we can think of the change in average Y for the treatment group ($\Delta \overline{Y}_t$) as containing two components: the change over time driven by the change in X_1 (i.e., the impact of the policy change, which we will call M) and the change driven by changes over time in any other factors (F). That is,

$$\Delta \overline{Y}_t = M + F \tag{A.24}$$

The change in average Y for the comparison group ($\Delta \overline{Y}_c$) contains no policy change impact, and thus it contains only change driven by changes in factors other than X_1. If both groups were affected by very similar changes over the study period in economic characteristics and conditions, it may be reasonable to assume that the change in Y driven by other factors experienced by the comparison group was the same as the change driven by other factors for the treatment group. In that case

$$\Delta \overline{Y}_c = F \tag{A.25}$$

and the change in average Y for the comparison group ($\Delta \overline{Y}_c$) provides a good estimate of the amount by which average Y in the treatment group would have changed had the treatment not happened. If this assumption is correct, then the difference between $\Delta \overline{Y}_t$ and $\Delta \overline{Y}_c$ should provide a good estimate of the policy change impact, because

$$\Delta \overline{Y}_t - \Delta \overline{Y}_c = (M + F) - F = M \tag{A.26}$$

The simple difference-in-differences estimation method just described is feasible when researchers possess repeated cross-section data from before and after a change in X_1, including subsamples drawn from groups that were and were not affected by the change in X_1.[20]

---

[20] The difference-in-differences method may also be employed when researchers have panel data, in which some individuals were affected by a change in X_1 and others were not. In such cases difference-in-differences estimates may be derived by running fixed effects regressions.

The method produces estimates that are free of omitted variables bias only if the somewhat subtle assumption underlying equation A.25 holds true. It must be the case that averages of Y would have changed over the study period by the same amount in the treatment and comparison groups (as a result of changes in factors other than X_1) had neither group experienced a change in X_1. This suggests that while the treatment and comparison groups need not be identical, they should be similar enough that we would expect them to be affected in much the same way by changes in general economic conditions over the sample period.

More elaborate applications of the difference-in-differences method allow Y to depend not only on X_1 and the other factors that drive identical changes in average Y for both groups but also on other determinants that can change over time in different ways for different individuals. In such cases, difference-in-differences estimates are derived using regressions rather than simple calculations of changes in average Y, but the intuition is largely the same.

Researchers sometimes use variants of the difference-in-differences approach to estimate the effects of policies that vary across geographic space, rather than over time. This is feasible when some feature of a policy's design varies across communities or districts, but it is relevant only to certain subpopulations within any community. It provides unbiased estimates of changes in policy design only if differences in Y across communities would be the same for the groups that are and are not affected by the policy variation, if the policy did not vary. For an example, see Field (2007).

Standard error adjustments

Several possible characteristics of the true error terms (u) can cause the estimates of standard errors and 95 percent confidence intervals to be misleading, sometimes leading researchers to think their estimates are more precise than they really are. These characteristics of the errors fall under labels of heteroskedasticity, clustering, and autocorrelation. Complete treatment of these econometric concerns is beyond the scope of this appendix, but readers should be aware that statistical derivations yield modified formulas for estimating standard errors and confidence intervals that are valid even in the presence of these problems. When researchers report that they have calculated "robust" and/or "clustered" standard errors, they are indicating that they have used these modified formulas to calculate standard errors that are valid even in the presence of heteroskedasticity and clustering. Analysts may use these standard errors to estimate confidence intervals and assess precision in the way described earlier.

Robustness

Often we do not know for sure which of several methods for estimating regression coefficients, or which of several methods for estimating standard errors, is likely to yield the best inferences. Good researchers brainstorm about all the possible econometric problems they might face and perform all the feasible estimation methods that might yield good inferences. When they find that diverse methods all yield the same inferences about the causal effect of primary interest, they demonstrate that their estimate is *robust* to changes in estimation method. Knowing that an estimate is robust in this way increases our confidence in it. When, instead, diverse estimation methods (which produce unbiased estimates under equally plausible but different assumptions) lead to quite different inferences about the causal effect of primary interest, then the estimate produced by any one method is said to be *fragile* to changes in the assumptions underlying estimation, and the estimate inspires less confidence.

Practical implications

When evaluating the quality of causal effect estimates, development analysts should ask the following questions:

- What is the causal effect of interest? That is, what is the outcome Y of primary interest and what is the determinant X_1 of primary interest?

- What list of possible determinants of Y is suggested by a reasonably general social science model of how Y is determined, and which of these possible determinants are likely to vary across observations in the relevant data set? For which of these possible determinants do the researchers control in their regressions?

- Which approaches do the researchers use to estimate the causal effect of X_1 on Y (i.e., OLS regression or matching methods with an observational cross section, OLS regression using data generated by an RCT, discontinuity design estimation, instrumental variables regression, fixed effects estimation, or difference-in-differences estimation)?

- If the researchers employ OLS regression with an observational cross section, for which possible determinants of Y that are likely to vary in the cross section do the authors fail to include controls? What educated guesses, if any, can be made regarding the likely sign of the biases resulting from this omission?

- If the researchers employ OLS regression with a randomized control trial, do baseline data suggest that the randomization succeeded in generating treatment and control samples in which the distributions of possible determinants of Y are very similar?

- If researchers employ a discontinuity design approach, do they demonstrate that program participation rates indeed increase sharply as the continuous measure on which participation is based crosses the critical threshold?

- If researchers employ instrumental variables estimation, which variables are employed as instruments for X_1, do first-stage regressions reveal that the instruments are indeed significant determinants of X_1, and do the authors provide compelling arguments as to why the instruments do not belong in the second-stage regression?

- If researchers employ fixed effects estimation, do the researchers provide compelling reasons to believe that any omitted variables that might induce bias in simple cross-section regressions are truly constant over time for each individual in the panel?

- If researchers employ difference-in-differences estimation, do the researchers provide compelling reasons to believe that the change over time in average Y experienced by the comparison group is very similar to the change over time in average Y that the treatment group would have experienced in the absence of the policy change?

- How well measured are all the variables involved? What educated guesses, if any, can be made regarding the likely sign of any biases introduced by measurement problems?

- Is the estimated effect large enough (in absolute value) to be considered economically important?

- Is the 95 percent confidence interval for the estimated impact of X_1 on Y narrow, indicating that it is a precise estimate, or is it wide, implying that we cannot draw strong conclusions about the size and economic importance of the effect from the current study?

REFERENCES

Acemoğlu, Daron, Simon Johnson, and James A. Robinson. "The Colonial Origins of Comparative Development: An Empirical Investigation." *American Economic Review* 91(5): 1369–1401, 2001. http://www.jstor.org/stable/2677930

Duflo, Esther, Rachel Glennerster, and Michael Kremer. "Using Randomization in Development Economics Research: A Toolkit." In T. Paul Schultz and John A. Strauss (eds.). *Handbook of Development Economics*, Volume 4. Amsterdam: Elsevier, 2008, pp. 3895–3962.

Field, E. "Entitled to Work: Urban Tenure Security and Labor Supply in Peru." *Quarterly Journal of Economics* 4(122): 1561–1602, 2007. doi:10.1162/qjec.2007.122.4.1561

Gertler, Paul J., Sebastian Martinez, Patrick Premand, Laura B. Rawlings, and Christel M. J. Vermeersch. *Impact Evaluation in Practice.* Washington, D.C.: World Bank, 2011.

Grosh, M. and P. Glewwe (eds.). *Designing Household Survey Questionnaires for Developing Countries: Lessons from 15 Years of the Living Standards Measurement Study.* Washington, D.C.: World Bank, 2000. http://external.worldbankimflib.org/uhtbin/cgisirsi/?ps=xeI6ekIGsA/JL/228640039/2/2#_

Wooldridge, J. *Introductory Econometrics: A Modern Approach. Fifth edition.* Mason, OH: South-Western Publishing, 2012.

Appendix B

Glossary

absolute poverty People are counted as living in absolute poverty when they cannot afford a minimally acceptable package of food, clothing, and shelter. See also *relative poverty*.

accountability mechanisms Accountability mechanisms are features of *governance structures* that reward policy-implementing agents for making high-quality *implementation choices* or punish them for making low-quality choices.

administrative targeting Administrative targeting is the use of *means tests* or *categorical restrictions* with the aim of directing a policy's benefits only to its *target groups*.

adverse selection Adverse selection arises in credit markets when potential borrowers differ in their inherent *default* probabilities, and when borrowers know these default probabilities but lenders do not. Under such conditions, lenders cannot distinguish safer from riskier borrowers, and they must consider how the loan terms they offer affect the mix of borrowers that select themselves into the market. More generally, a market is characterized by adverse selection when parties on one end of the market's transactions vary in quality and know their own qualities, while the parties on the other end cannot distinguish among trading partners of different qualities.

agglomeration economies Production technologies are characterized by agglomeration economies if producers' *total factor productivity* is higher when they are located near to one another than when they are spread out geographically, all else equal.

aggregate labor productivity Aggregate labor productivity is the average value of output produced per worker in an economy.

agricultural extension services Agricultural extension services are activities that help farmers acquire the skills and information necessary for using agricultural technologies profitably.

agricultural market intervention Policies of agricultural market intervention, also known as agricultural pricing policies, are policies that tax, subsidize, regulate, or involve the public sector directly in transactions involving agricultural inputs or outputs.

agricultural marketing boards The agricultural marketing boards examined in this text are state-owned entities that have exclusive rights to buy and sell specific crops and to provide the associated *marketing services*.

agricultural pricing policies See *agricultural market intervention*.

agricultural research Agricultural research encompasses purposeful efforts to develop new and better agricultural technologies, thereby making possible *technical change* in agriculture.

appreciate A country's currency appreciates when its *nominal exchange rate* falls, indicating that more units of foreign currency are now required to purchase one unit of the domestic currency.

appropriate An actor appropriates the full benefits generated by an action when she is able to make use of, and derive well-being from, all of those benefits. She fails to appropriate all the benefits when some benefits by their very nature are shared with others (as in the case of *public goods* investments or actions that generate positive *externalities*) or when some benefits are lost to others through theft, fraud, taxation, or expropriation.

asset An asset is any physical or mental resource or attribute that expands, in a long-lasting way, a household's capacity to achieve *well-being* and an economy's capacity to provide the goods, services, security, and opportunities from which people derive their well-being.

assurance game An assurance game is a *game theory* construct that illustrates how the coordination of people's expectations—regarding the actions that other members of a group will take—can catalyze *cooperation* that raises the well-being of all group members, and how *coordination failures* can prevent mutually beneficial cooperation.

autarky Autarky is a state of self-sufficiency in which an actor or set of actors engages in no trade with outside actors.

autarky equilibrium A local market for a particular good is in autarky equilibrium when local producers have no incentive to export and local consumers have no incentive to import.

autarky price In models of market equilibrium in the presence of *transfer costs*, the autarky price is the price associated with the intersection of the *local demand* and *local supply schedules*.

bargaining power In some *non-unitary models of household decision making*, a household member's bargaining power is her influence over the allocation of household resources. It rises as her *fallback position* improves.

behavioral conditions In programs that distribute services or benefits, behavioral conditions are stipulations that recipients may continue receiving benefits only if they achieve benchmark behaviors, such as sending their children to school regularly.

behavioral economics Behavioral economics is a subdiscipline of economics in which researchers test for specified departures from *neoclassical rationality* in the way people make decisions, using laboratory and field experiments.

capacity-building services Capacity-building services are efforts established by policymakers or high-level administrators to improve *policy implementation* by providing lower-level decision-making bodies and *frontline service providers* with information, training, management tools, or assistance in forming committees and achieving cooperation.

capitation grants Capitation grants are transfers of cash that provide *policy-implementing agents* with a fixed volume of financing per person in the population they serve.

cash transfer program A cash transfer program distributes cash grants to individuals or households meeting some combination of *eligibility rules* and *behavioral conditions*.

categorical restrictions Categorical restrictions are *eligibility rules* that limit the distribution of a program's benefits or services to people with certain characteristics that are relatively easy to observe, such as whether they have young children, own less than one hectare of land, or live in a particular community.

collateral Collateral is a name for assets that borrowers pledge to lenders, which lenders may claim as their own if borrowers fail to repay their loans in full.

common property resource A common property resource is a resource to which all members of a group have unimpeded access and for which use by one member reduces the value available for others. Examples include communal grazing lands, forests, fishing grounds, and canal-based irrigation systems.

community-based health insurance In community-based health insurance programs, members of communities or local organizations are asked to collaborate in designing, administering, and financing the provision of health insurance for members.

community participation Community participation refers to the involvement of community representatives in making local-level *policy implementation choices*.

competition Policymakers introduce competition into the governance of *policy implementation* when they require members of the policy's target population to choose from among multiple service-providing individuals or organizations and when they award contracts to firms or organizations that offer the best combination of quality and price.

complementary policies Two policies are complementary when having one policy in place improves the impact or reduces the budgetary cost of the other.

complements in consumption When two *normal goods* are complements in consumption, an increase in the price of one leads to a reduction in the consumption of both.

complements in production When two inputs are complements in production, an increase in the price of one reduces the use of both.

conditional cash transfer programs Conditional cash transfer programs are *cash transfer programs* in which recipients continue to receive benefits only if they satisfy specified *behavioral conditions*.

consumption expenditure A household's consumption expenditure is the total value of goods and services consumed by the household during a given period, including not only the goods and services the household purchases but also the value of the goods the household produces for its own consumption.

consumption smoothing Households engage in consumption smoothing when they undertake activities, such as borrowing, saving, or *income smoothing*, that cause their consumption expenditures to fluctuate less over time than their incomes.

contract enforcement institutions Contract enforcement institutions are *institutions* that encourage people to fulfill contractual promises, usually by attaching rewards to contract fulfillment or punishments to contract *default*.

cooperation Actors cooperate when they work together toward a common goal. In this text, more specifically, they cooperate when each undertakes an action for which she bears the entire cost, regardless of what others do, but which yields her substantial benefits only if others also cooperate.

coordination failure A coordination failure prevents a group from undertaking mutually beneficial investments when each actor would choose to invest if she expected all others to invest, but all actors instead choose not to invest because they do not expect others to invest.

corruption Corruption occurs when *policy-implementing agents* misuse for personal gain their policy-implementing authority or the public sector funding at their disposal. They might divert funds to personal use, accept bribes for ignoring their duties, or demand bribes before fulfilling their duties.

costs associated with risk In the general model of investment decisions of Chapter 10, the costs associated with risk include any premiums that would be paid for *insurance contracts* that protect against the investment's risks, as well as any reductions in *utility* associated with having to bear additional uninsured risk.

credit rationing Credit markets are characterized by rationing when less credit (of a certain type in a certain location) is forthcoming than is demanded at the going interest rate, implying that some potential borrowers who wish to borrow at the going rate obtain less credit than they would like or obtain no credit at all.

crop substitution An increase in the price of an agricultural output leads to crop substitution when it leads producers to reallocate land away from alternative crops and into the cultivation of the crop whose price increased.

crowding out A public sector activity crowds out a comparable private sector activity when the introduction of the public sector activity causes private actors (either directly or indirectly) to do less of the comparable activity.

decentralization A *governance reform* involves decentralization when it shifts the authority over some critical *policy implementation choices* from policymakers or high-level administrators to agents closer to the local level.

default A borrower defaults on a loan when she fails to comply with requirements for repayment of principal and interest. More generally, a party to a contract defaults when she fails to fulfill her contractual obligations.

demand-side financing   Demand-side financing for the distribution of government-subsidized goods or services involves the distribution to beneficiary households of the financial means to purchase the goods or services at subsidized prices from private sector providers (rather than supplying the subsidized goods or services directly to them through government distributors).

depreciate   A country's currency depreciates when *its nominal exchange rate* rises, indicating that fewer units of foreign currency are now required to purchase one unit of the domestic currency.

design change benefits   Design change benefits are any improvements in a policy's performance (e.g., increase in outreach among the poor, reduced *leakage*, increased impact, reduced cost) that would result from specified changes in *policy design details*.

design change costs   Design change costs are any deteriorating changes in a policy's performance (e.g., reduced outreach among the poor, increased *leakage*, reduced impact, increased cost) that would result from specified changes in *policy design details*.

determinants   In a theoretical model of how certain socioeconomic outcomes are determined, the determinants of the outcomes are any features of context or circumstance whose values are set outside the model and that help determine the outcomes, in the sense that changes in their values lead to changes in the outcomes.

development   As a subject of study, development encompasses the many ways material, physical, and social living conditions might improve and the processes and policies that help bring those improvements about. As an objective that guides policymakers, development is sustained improvement in the *well-being* of a country's many people, with special emphasis on improvements for the poor. As a process, development is the web of economic and social change through which widespread and sustained improvements in well-being come about.

development actors   Development actors are individuals and organizations that intervene in the socioeconomic system—by introducing *policies*—with the aim of improving development outcomes. They include governments and diverse *nongovernmental organizations*, as described in Box 1.1.

development indicators   Development indicators are measures of the speed and nature of socioeconomic change, including measures of *economic growth* and of changes in *poverty*, *inequality*, and *vulnerability*, that development actors use to assess development success.

diminishing marginal product of labor   A *production function* exhibits a diminishing marginal product of labor when the *marginal product of labor* falls as the level of labor employed is increased while holding other production inputs constant.

diminishing marginal utility   A *utility function* exhibits diminishing marginal utility when the *marginal utility* derived from consumption of a particular item falls as the quantity consumed of that item is increased while holding constant the quantities consumed of other items.

direct effects   In *policy analysis*, direct effects are changes in the *well-being* and behavior of the people who are directly affected by a policy. People are directly affected if they take advantage of new opportunities created by the policy or change their behavior in response to new constraints imposed by the policy.

disability-adjusted life years   The disability adjusted life years (DALYs) associated with a particular disease measure the future years of healthy life lost in part (through the onset of disability) or in full (through premature death) as a result of the onset of the disease in a given population and a given year.

discount   Human beings discount the future when they place less value on consuming some quantity in the future than they place on consuming the same quantity today.

discount factor   In models of choice involving the comparison of present and future consumption, a discount factor is a fraction between zero and one that converts units of *utility* enjoyed in a given future time period into (a smaller number of) units that are comparable to units of utility enjoyed one period sooner.

economic growth   A country's rate of economic growth is the rate of increase in its average income.

economic institutions   Economic institutions are economic policies; systems of contract law, property rights and law enforcement; and other *institutions* that help determine the rewards to participating in markets and to undertaking investment.

economics of institutions   The economics of institutions is a subdiscipline of economics in which researchers study the nature and impacts of institutional rules and norms, and the enforcement mechanisms that induce people to obey them.

education   Education refers to the acquisition of skills through primary and secondary schools, colleges, and universities, often by children and young adults before they enter the labor market.

efficient   A set of economic outcomes is efficient when there is no way to reallocate resources across uses in a way that makes one person better off without making anyone else worse off. In the provision of services, efficiency requires that services of given quantity and quality are produced at lowest possible cost.

efficiency wages   Employers pay efficiency wages when they pay wages above the market-clearing level for workers with certain skills because, by paying premium wages, they are able to reduce the total costs associated with the completion of labor tasks.

elasticity   The elasticity of one variable with respect to another is equal to the percentage change in the former that arises in response to a one percent increase in the other.

eligibility rules   Eligibility rules are statements of the criteria that potential beneficiaries must meet for official access to program benefits or services. Eligibility rules can take the form of *means tests* or *categorical restrictions*.

elite capture   Elite capture occurs when members of the local elite gain control over local governments or local committees that are involved in *policy implementation* and when they use that control to benefit the elite at the expense of other members of the community.

empirical questions   Empirical questions are questions that can be answered only through observation or experiment (rather than through the use of theory or other logic).

employer-specific skills Employer-specific skills are skills acquired through *job training* that raise a worker's productivity more in work for the employer who provided the training than in work for other employers.

endogenous variables In economic models, endogenous variables are quantities describing socioeconomic outcomes that are determined within the models (as functions of the *exogenous parameters*).

enforcement of institutional rules and norms Institutional rules and norms are enforced when mechanisms are in place to reward those who comply or punish those who do not comply. The mechanisms might involve penalties imposed by outside authorities, penalties that the parties subject to the institutions extract from one another, or psychological rewards and punishments that people experience in response to their own compliance or noncompliance.

Engel's law Engel's law is an empirical regularity that as income levels rise, the share of income spent on food falls.

ex ante responses to fluctuations Ex ante responses to fluctuations are activities that people undertake in anticipation of possible future *fluctuations and shocks* and that will help them avoid severe reductions in consumption when fluctuations and shocks cause their incomes to fall or their needs to rise. They include precautionary saving, purchase of *insurance contracts*, participation in *informal insurance institutions*, and *income-smoothing* activities.

ex post responses to fluctuations Ex post responses to fluctuations are activities that people undertake after experiencing *fluctuations and shocks* and that help them avoid severe reductions in consumption. They include borrowing, liquidating assets, and reallocating labor away from activities that have become less productive for generating income to other, more productive activities.

exogenous parameters In economic models, exogenous parameters are quantities describing features of socioeconomic circumstance that are taken as given from outside the model (and that help determine the value of the model's *endogenous variables*).

expected return The expected return on an *investment project* is the weighted average—across all possible *states of the world*—of the *returns to the investment*, where the weights are equal to the probabilities with which the various states occur.

expected utility The expected utility a decision maker associates with a particular risky choice is the weighted average—across all possible *states of the world*—of the *utility* she would experience in any state of the world after making the choice, where the weights are equal to the probabilities with which the various states occur. When the *utility function* relating the decision maker's utility in any state of the world to consumption in that state of the world is characterized by *diminishing marginal utility*, a decision maker who maximizes expected utility is *risk averse*.

exporting equilibrium In models of market equilibrium in the presence of *transfer costs*, a local market is in exporting

equilibrium when the *local export price* is greater than the *autarky price*, and local producers export some produce to external buyers.

external market price In models of market equilibrium in the presence of *transfer costs*, the external market price is the price at which the good may be bought or sold in the external market, which is the market outside the geographic scope of the local market that offers the best opportunities for longer-distance trade.

externality A private action produces an externality when it generates benefits or costs that are experienced by anyone other than the actor undertaking the action (and that this same actor does not come to *appropriate* or bear through market transactions).

factor accumulation Factor accumulation is growth in the quantities of physical or *human capital* per worker in an economy.

factor proportions model The factor proportions model is a model of international trade and *general equilibrium* in the domestic economy that treats all *factors of production* as perfectly mobile, or capable of being moved from one sector of production to another in pursuit of higher returns, and in which certain production sectors always use certain factors of production in higher proportions (relative to the quantities employed of other production factors) than other sectors.

factors of production In many economic models, the factors of production are labor, physical capital, and *human capital*, which are combined to produce output.

fallback position In some *non-unitary models of household decision making*, a household member's fallback position is the level of utility she would experience if household members failed to cooperate.

feedback effects In policy analysis, feedback effects are second-round effects on the well-being and behavior of the directly affected groups that come about as the first-round responses to the policy by the directly affected groups induce changes in markets, institutions, and the environment.

financial intermediaries Financial intermediaries in *loanable funds markets* and insurance markets perform all the services required to facilitate transactions and transfer funds between savers and borrowers or between participants in insurance transactions.

financial sustainability *Microfinance* institutions achieve financial sustainability when their revenue (from interest and fees on loans) exceeds their operating costs, which include the cost of funds, *supervision costs*, and costs associated with *default*.

financial transaction costs Financial transaction costs are the costs of carrying out financial transactions and include *supervision costs* and costs associated with *default*.

financing of investment An investor finances an investment when she musters the resources required to pay the up-front costs of the investment. She may finance immediate investment by *saving* out of current income, liquidating assets, or borrowing. An investor finds an investment infeasible if she cannot obtain adequate financing.

financing costs In the general model of investment decisions, financing costs are the costs of obtaining the financial means to cover the up-front costs. If an investor finances an investment by borrowing, the financing cost is the interest payment on the loan. If she finances by liquidating assets, the financing cost is the interest income forgone on the liquidated assets. If she finances by saving out of current income, the financing cost is the utility cost of delaying consumption.

fluctuations and shocks Fluctuations and shocks are variations over time in households' *income* or *needs*. Fluctuations are anticipated changes over time associated with seasons, life cycle stages, and the lumpiness of income receipts and purchases. Shocks are unanticipated changes associated with variation in agricultural growing conditions, prices, wages, employment status, health problems, theft, or other hazards.

food-based transfer program A food-based transfer program distributes free or low-cost food, or *voucher* documents that may be used to purchase food from the private sector, to individuals or households satisfying some combination of *eligibility rules* and *behavioral conditions*.

foreign aid Foreign aid, or official development assistance, includes grants and loans on concessionary terms from the governments of developed countries to developing countries or multilateral development agencies, distributed with the primary purpose of reducing poverty or promoting development.

formal sector In models of developing-country labor markets, workers in the formal sector are distinguished from workers in the *informal sector* on the basis of having one or more of the following: formal employment contracts, registration with payroll tax authorities, reasonably stable employment, or good working conditions in modern workplaces.

frontline service providers Frontline service providers are the teachers, nurses, agricultural extension agents, loan officers, water fee collectors, and other agents who are involved in delivering government or NGO services and who engage directly with clients on a daily basis.

functional distribution of income The functional distribution of income in an economy is the distribution of income across owners of different *factors of production*.

gains from trade When two economies enter into trade with each other, the gains from trade are the improvements in aggregate consumption opportunities that accrue to the populations of both economies.

game theory Game theory is a branch of applied mathematics used by economists and others to study how people make choices in strategic settings, which are settings in which decision makers are aware that the benefits they derive from their choices depend on the choices made by others.

general equilibrium General equilibrium models of market behavior (in contrast with *partial equilibrium* models) examine the simultaneous determination of prices and quantities exchanged in markets for all goods, services, and factors of production in an economy, taking into account the effects of price changes in any one market on supplies and demands in other markets.

general skills General skills are skills acquired through *education* or *job training* that raise workers' productivity the same amount in many jobs and are easily observed.

general subsidy A general subsidy on the purchase (sale) of a particular good (in contrast to a *targeted subsidy*) allows anyone to purchase (sell) as much as she wishes at the reduced (increased) price.

geographic targeting A program employs geographic targeting when it limits eligibility to people living only in specified geographic locations.

Gini coefficient The Gini coefficient is a measure of income inequality that ranges from zero (most equal) to one (most unequal) and that equals the ratio of two areas in a *Lorenz curve diagram*.

good governance Public sector institutions provide good governance for *policy* implementation when they lead *policy-implementing agents* to make high-quality *implementation choices*. This means that the agents avoid *corruption* and waste, provide services of high quality, and allocate resources across locations and uses in ways that balance policymakers' concerns for efficiency and equity.

governance reform A governance reform is a change in the design of the *governance structure* through which a policy is implemented. Important types of governance reform include *decentralization*, increased *community participation*, *privatization*, and increased use of *performance contracting*.

governance structure A governance structure is the set of institutional rules and norms that policymakers create to govern a policy's implementation.

governance structure design choices Governance structure design choices are critical features of *governance structures*, which influence the extent to which the various *inputs to high-quality implementation choices* are brought to bear on implementation choices. They include choices regarding how decision-making authority is allocated across *policy-implementing agents* of different types; rules regarding the allocation of expenditures and collection of revenue; criteria for selecting employees, contractors, and partners; capacity-building services provided to agents; and *accountability mechanisms*.

Green Revolution The Green Revolution is a name for the adoption of particular new agricultural technologies beginning in the 1960s. The relevant technologies involved the use of new varieties of wheat, rice, and corn that produced higher per-acre yields when cultivated using adequate fertilizer and water.

gross domestic product A country's gross domestic product (GDP) is the total value of goods and services produced within the country's borders in a given year, excluding the value of any raw materials or partially processed goods that are produced in the country and used up in the production of other goods and services. That is, it is the total *value added* produced within the country's borders in a given year.

gross enrollment rates   The gross enrollment rate (GER) in, say, primary education, is calculated by taking the number of children enrolled in primary school and dividing by the number of children of official primary school age in the population.

gross national product   A country's gross national product (GNP) or gross national income (GNI) is the total value of goods and services produced by the country's *factors of production* in a given year, excluding the value of any goods they produce that are used up in the production of other goods and services also produced by domestic factors of production. That is, it is the total *value added* produced by the country's factors of production in a given year.

group liability   *Microcredit* programs lend under group liability arrangements when they require borrowers to form groups within which the members are liable not only for repaying their own loans but also for repaying the loans of other group members who fail to repay on their own.

growth accounting studies   Growth accounting studies seek to identify the shares of historical *economic growth* that can be attributed to *factor accumulation* and *total factor productivity* growth.

headcount ratio   The headcount ratio is the fraction of a population for which an indicator of *well-being* (often *income* or *consumption expenditure* per capita within the individuals' households) falls below some *poverty line*.

health   A person's health is her multidimensional state of physical and psychological well-being or ill-being. A healthy person enjoys strength, vitality, comfort, and capacities for many physical and mental activities. The health a person can expect to experience in any year is a function of the health stock she brings into the year, the probabilities with which she is hit by various illnesses or injuries during the year, and the nature and quality of any health care she would receive.

health inputs   Health inputs are items that people may use to shield themselves from health risks in their environments, such as condoms and insecticide-treated bed nets.

home time   In economic models of time allocation, home time is a name for time spent in non–income-generating activities such as recreation, education, or child care.

household   A household is a group of people who share housing and meals.

human capital   Human capital encompasses the skills and abilities that workers bring into production as a result of past investments in *education*, *job training*, work experience, nutrition, and health care.

implementation choices   Implementation choices are choices made by *policy-implementing agents* that help determine a policy's *implementation outcomes*.

implementation outcomes   In this text, a policy's implementation outcomes are the details of how, in practice, the policy

alters people's opportunities and constraints and of what the policy costs. They include any policy design choices delegated by policymakers to decentralized decision makers, the nature and quality of any services provided by policy-implementing agents, the rigor with which the agents monitor and enforce compliance with rules, the extent to which associated public sector funds are wasted or stolen, the nature of any bureaucratic difficulties created by the policy, and the efficiency with which policy-implementation activities are carried out.

import-substituting industrialization   Import-substituting industrialization is a label given to development strategies centered on the use of *tariffs*, quantitative import restrictions, and overvalued *exchange rates* to encourage the development of domestic manufacturing sectors by protecting them from international competition.

import tariff   An import tariff is a tax on international import transactions.

importing equilibrium   In models of market equilibrium in the presence of *transfer costs*, a local market is in importing equilibrium when the *local import price* is less than the *autarky price*, and local consumers import some of the good from external producers.

incentive effects   In the study of policy impacts, incentive effects arise when a policy induces change in the behavior of directly affected groups by altering the marginal benefits or costs that members of the group associate with undertaking particular behaviors.

income   A household's income is the total value of resources the household earns in some period through the employment or rental of its human, physical, and financial assets. It is the total value of resources available for consumption or *saving* during the period, and it includes not only cash wages but also in-kind payments, bonuses, profits derived from the sale of goods or services produced by family enterprises, and the value of any food that the household consumes out of its own farm production.

income effects   In the study of policy impacts, the income effect on a particular household activity is the increase or decrease in that activity that comes about solely as the result of the associated increase or decrease in a household's *purchasing power* (or *utility*). More specifically, it is the change that would come about if the household experienced the same increase in purchasing power without experiencing any related changes in the marginal benefits and costs associated with particular behaviors (see *incentive effects*), intra-household distribution of decision-making authority (see *intrahousehold effects*), or liquidity (see *liquidity effects*).

income poverty   People live in income poverty when they live with per capita household *income* or *consumption expenditure* below some income-denominated *poverty line*.

income smoothing   Households engage in income smoothing when they choose income-generating strategies designed either to reduce the magnitude of seasonal fluctuations in income or to reduce the probability of being hit by devastating shocks to income.

increase in demand or supply   An increase in demand (supply) is a rightward shift in a demand (supply) schedule, indicating that while holding the price of the good constant at any level, the total quantity that market participants would wish to purchase (sell) has increased.

increase in the quantity demanded or supplied   An increase in the quantity demanded (quantity supplied) is an increase in the quantity of the good that market participants purchase (sell) as the result of a movement down and to the right (up and to the right) along a demand (supply) schedule, and represents a response to a price change.

indicator   In empirical studies, indicators are measures that are imperfectly correlated with, and used to draw inferences about, quantities of primary interest that cannot be measured directly.

indifference curve   An indifference curve connects all the combinations of the quantities consumed of two goods that would deliver the same level of *utility*. A complete set of indifference curves describes how a person's utility varies across the many possible combinations of quantities of the two goods that the person might consume.

indirect effect   In policy analysis, an indirect or spillover effect is a change—resulting from a policy—in the well-being or behavior of anyone who did not experience a direct effect of the policy. Indirect effects arise when the behavioral responses of the directly affected groups lead to changes in markets, institutions, or the environment.

industry-specific skills   Industry-specific skills are skills acquired through *job training* that raise workers' productivity by similar amounts in jobs for many employers, but only employers within a specific industry.

inequality   A society is characterized by inequality when some people experience lower levels of well-being than others.

inflation   An economy experiences inflation when its *price level* rises.

informal insurance institutions   Informal insurance institutions are rules and norms that require members of communities, ethnic groups, or extended families to give gifts or interest-free loans to other members of the group who have been hit by shocks, when they themselves are not suffering from such shocks.

informal sector   In models of developing-country labor markets, workers in the informal sector are distinguished from workers in the *formal sector* on the basis of having one or more of the following characteristics: self-employment or employment without a formal contract, no registration with payroll tax authorities, tenuous employment, or makeshift workplaces and poor working conditions.

infrastructure assets   Infrastructure assets are assets that provide drinking water, sanitation, irrigation, power, transportation, and communication services.

innovation   Innovation is the adoption of new ways of life and work.

inputs to high-quality implementation choices   In policy analysis, the inputs to high-quality implementation choices are elements that must be brought to bear on *policy implementation choices* to achieve good *implementation outcomes*. They include appropriate motivation (of the relevant policy-implementing agents); necessary resources, capacity, and local information (at the disposal of the relevant agents); and any necessary coordinating oversight (by policymakers or high-level administrators coordinating the work of multiple agents).

institution   An institution is a set of formal rules, informal norms, and related enforcement mechanisms that constrain people's choices regarding particular sets of actions.

insurance constraints   Potential investors are prevented from *investing* by insurance constraints when they would undertake an *investment project* if insurance markets were free of frictions and market failures, but they do not invest because insurance market imperfections prevent them from accessing appropriate insurance or allow them access to insurance only at unacceptably high premium rates.

insurance contract   Under an insurance contract, a buyer pays a fee, called a premium, to purchase the promise of specified payments, called indemnities, in specified bad states of the world.

integration of markets   Markets are integrated when trade takes place between them, and, as a result, prices in the markets rise and fall together as supply and demand conditions change.

intrahousehold effect   In the analysis of policy impacts, intrahousehold effects are changes in household choices that arise because a policy alters the relative influence of different household members in household decision making.

invest   Households invest when they undertake costly activities in the present with the hope of reaping rewards in the future. The costly activities create, upgrade or maintain *assets* or move assets into more productive uses.

investment project   In this text, an investment project is the creation of a particular *asset*, or a particular shift in how an asset is used, by a particular investor.

job training   Job training refers to workers' acquisition of skills after entering the labor market, usually through activities closely tied to specific lines of work or specific employers.

labor mobility   Labor mobility is workers' willingness and ability to move geographically, or to change employers or occupations, to take advantage of opportunities for higher earnings. Mobility is reduced when workers face significant *mobility costs*.

labor-using technical change   *Technical change* is (low-skill) labor using when it raises the *marginal product* of (low-skill) labor, thereby raising the demand for (low-skill) labor.

land rights institutions   Land rights institutions are *institutions* that protect *property rights* in land.

leakage   Leakage is a *targeting failure* that occurs when some benefits of a targeted policy are enjoyed by members of nontarget groups. Poverty-targeted programs suffer leakage when some benefits accrue to the nonpoor.

learning by doing   Producers learn by doing when they work out through trial and error how to operate more productively in a given environment, thereby increasing their *total factor productivity.*

liberalizing reforms   Liberalizing reforms are reforms that in some way reduce the degree of government intervention in markets by reducing the sizes of taxes and subsidies on transactions, relaxing regulations, reducing direct government involvement in production or marketing activities, or allowing greater private sector participation in those activities.

liquidity constraints   Potential investors are prevented from *investing* by liquidity constraints when they would undertake an *investment project* if credit markets were free of frictions and market failures, but they do not invest because credit market imperfections prevent them from accessing appropriate credit or allow them access to credit only at unacceptably high interest rates (and they also find it infeasible or unattractive to finance the investment by *saving* out of current income or by liquidating assets).

liquidity effects   In the analysis of policy impacts, liquidity effects are changes in household behaviors that arise because a policy relaxes or tightens a *liquidity constraint* on investment. A policy might relax a liquidity constraint, thereby spurring investment, by providing a household with credit, increasing the household's current income, or reducing the up-front cost of the investment.

living standards   Living standards are dimensions of a household's circumstances—such as the household's food consumption, the quality of its housing, or its fears regarding the future—that enter into household members' assessment of their *well-being.*

loanable funds market   The market for loanable funds is the market through which funds saved by savers are transferred to borrowers, who pay interest in exchange for the temporary use of the funds.

local demand schedule   In models of market equilibrium in the presence of *transfer costs*, the local demand schedule traces out, for each possible price that might be observed in the *local market*'s central marketplace, the total quantities of the good that would be purchased in that marketplace by anyone residing in the local market area, while holding constant all other determinants of the quantities demanded.

local export price   In models of market equilibrium in the presence of *transfer costs*, the local export price is the *external market price* minus the *transfer costs* associated with exporting the good from the local market to the external market.

local import price   In models of market equilibrium in the presence of *transfer costs*, the local import price is the *external market price* plus the *transfer costs* associated with importing the good from the external market to the local market.

local market   In models of market equilibrium in the presence of *transfer costs*, the local market encompasses the supplies and demands of all buyers and sellers who reside in a particular geographic region of interest, whether a small village, a larger region, or an entire country.

local supply schedule   In models of market equilibrium in the presence of *transfer costs*, the local supply schedule traces out, for each possible price that might be observed in the *local market*'s central marketplace, the total quantities of the good that would be sold in that market by anyone residing in the local market area, while holding constant all other determinants of the quantities supplied.

Lorenz curve   A Lorenz curve is a graph illustrating the nature and degree of income *inequality* in a society, which is derived by identifying the groups that constitute the poorest 1, 2, . . . 99, 100 percent of the population and plotting the percentages of the society's total income accruing to those groups. It is a curve with increasing slope connecting the points [0,0] and [100,100].

marginal product of labor   The marginal product of labor is (approximately) the amount by which output increases when a *technically efficient* producer increases her labor input by one unit while holding other input quantities constant.

marginal utility   The marginal utility of, say, food consumption is (approximately) the amount by which a consumer's utility would increase when food consumption is increased by one unit while holding constant the quantities consumed of other items.

market and institutional failures   Market and institutional failures are circumstances in which markets and private *institutions* alone fail to deliver socially optimal development outcomes. They constitute possible rationales for intervention by governments and other development actors.

market intermediaries   Market intermediaries are individuals specialized in producing one or more *marketing services.*

market power   Market power is a departure from perfect competition in markets, which allows producers to raise the price they charge above the competitive level without losing all customers or to reduce the wage they pay for labor below the competitive level without losing all workers.

marketing margin   The marketing margin is the difference between what *market intermediaries* charge for the goods they sell and what they pay for those same goods. It constitutes the pay they receive for the *marketing services* they provide.

marketing services   Marketing services are the activities that underlie *transfer costs* in market exchange, including transportation, storage, financing, wholesaling, and retailing activities.

means tests   Means tests are *eligibility rules* that limit the distribution of a program's benefits or services to people for whom specified measures of income or assets fall below specified thresholds.

mental accounts   In some non-neoclassical models of decision making, mental accounts are psychological constructs that constrain decision makers to use income from certain sources (or income saved under certain conditions) only for certain uses.

microcredit   Microcredit, one type of *microfinance* service, is the provision of small loans to clients poorer than are typically served by commercial banks.

microenterprises   Microenterprises are very small establishments producing goods or services using only the labor of the owner and her family and perhaps one or two employees.

microfinance   Microfinance is the provision of credit, savings-deposit, and other financial services to clients poorer than are typically served by commercial banks.

migrate   People migrate when they move their place of residence from one geographic location to another.

missing credit or insurance markets   A market for credit (insurance) is missing when credit (insurance) tailored to a specific loan use (risk) is unavailable for some types of clients in some locations.

mobility costs   Mobility costs are costs that workers incur when they move from one location or employer to another.

moral hazard   Credit markets are characterized by moral hazard when borrowers can improve their repayment probabilities by exerting more effort, but lenders and third parties cannot observe effort. Under such circumstances, lenders cannot enforce contractual requirements that borrowers exert effort and must consider how the loan terms they offer will affect borrowers' effort and repayment probabilities. More generally, a market is characterized by moral hazard when parties on one end of the market's transactions can, by exerting more effort, raise the benefits or reduce the costs of the transaction for parties on the other end, while parties on the other end cannot observe effort and cannot enforce effort requirements.

needs   A household's needs are the characteristics and circumstances—such as household size, disabilities of household members, customary demands for dowry or bride-price payments—that raise the quantity of *consumption expenditure* required for the household to achieve a given level of *well-being* and reduce the well-being the household derives from a given total quantity of *income*.

neoclassical rationality   The assumption of neoclassical rationality is the assumption that people make choices with the aim of maximizing their *utility* subject to the constraints they face, where utility is a function only of the goods, services, and experiences they would possess after making a choice. Neoclassical rationality encompasses additional, more specific assumptions about utility functions when applied to choices that involve comparisons between present and future consumption or between safer and riskier outcomes, as described in Chapter 10.

net buyer   A net buyer of a good, service, or input is a household that consumes more than it produces of the item in a given period and purchases the difference in the relevant market.

net enrollment rate   The net enrollment rate (NER) in, say, primary education, is calculated by taking the number of children who are enrolled in primary school and are of official primary school age and dividing by the number of children of official primary school age in the population.

net market labor supply   A household's net market labor supply is the difference between the total hours of labor the household devotes to any work activity—whether work for a wage, work on the family farm, or work in a family nonfarm enterprise—and the total hours of labor the household employs (on the family farm or in a family nonfarm enterprise) from any source—whether family members or workers hired from the market.

net marketed surplus   A farm household's net marketed surplus of a food crop is the difference between the total quantity of the crop the farm household produces and the total quantity it consumes.

net seller   A net seller of a good, service, or input is a household that produces more than it consumes of the item in a given period and sells the difference in the relevant market.

nominal exchange rate   A currency's nominal exchange rate (vis-à-vis a particular foreign currency) is the rate at which the foreign currency may be converted into this currency, denominated in units of domestic currency per unit of foreign currency.

nominal GDP growth   The rate of nominal GDP growth (in contrast to *real GDP growth*) is the rate of growth in a measure of *gross domestic product* that values goods and services produced in any time period using their prices in that same time period. Nominal GDP may grow either because the real quantity or quality of goods and services produced in the economy grows or because the *price level* rises.

nominal income measures   Measures of households' nominal incomes (in contrast to *real incomes*) are measures of income denominated in current local currency units.

noncoverage of target groups   Policies exhibit noncoverage of target groups (a *targeting failure*) when they fail to deliver benefits to some members of their *target groups*. For example, poverty-targeted transfer programs exhibit noncoverage when they fail to provide benefits to some poor households.

nongovernmental organizations (NGOs)   The nongovernmental organizations relevant to this text are not-for-profit organizations that are run without participating control by governments and that pursue development objectives.

nonlabor income   A household's nonlabor income is the *income* that it would earn even if it supplied no labor. It includes transfer payments received from governments, NGOs, or other households, as well as rental payments on properties the household owns and rents out.

nonmarket interactions   Nonmarket interactions are any interactions between people other than transactions in markets for goods, labor, or financial or nonfinancial services. They include such interactions as cooperating, giving gifts, sharing information, trusting, stealing, cheating, punishing, rewarding, and conveying approval or disapproval.

non-unitary models of household decision making   Nonunitary household models are models of household decision making that treat households as made up of multiple members, whose interests and power may differ, and who may engage in conflict as well as *cooperation* as they work out household decisions.

normal good   A normal good is a good whose consumption increases when a consumer's income increases while prices remain constant.

official development assistance   See *foreign aid*.

opportunity cost of time   The opportunity cost of time associated with undertaking a new activity is the value a decision maker would give up by shifting time out of other valuable activities into the new activity.

output   In *production functions*, when output is modeled as a function only of the *factors of production* (and not also as a function of raw materials and partially processed goods), output is synonymous with *value added*. When output is modeled as a function of raw materials and partially processed goods as well as the factors of production, it includes the entire value of all goods or services produced.

partial equilibrium   Partial equilibrium models of market behavior (in contrast to *general equilibrium* models) examine the determination of prices and quantities exchanged in just one or a small number of closely related markets, while taking prices in all other markets as given.

per capita income   Per capita *income* within a household or a country is the total of income earned by all members of that unit divided by the number of members.

performance contracting   Policymakers use performance contracting to improve the governance of policy implementation when they engage *policy-implementing agents* through contracts that tie their pay, benefits, continued employment, or promotions to measures of the agents' success in achieving measurable targets related to *policy objectives*.

policy   In this text, policy is a general term used to refer to any policy, program, or project implemented by any development actor. It represents an intervention in the socioeconomic system by a development actor.

policy analysis   Policy analysis involves the systematic use of logic and empirical evidence for identifying the facts to which policymakers must appeal when designing individual *policies* or deciding how to piece together packages of policies that are likely to maximize development success while satisfying practical constraints. The fundamental task in policy analysis is to set out a complete description of a policy's benefits and costs.

policy design details   A policy's design details are the details that describe how, in principle, the policy alters households' opportunities and constraints, for whom the policy alters those opportunities and constraints, and the *governance structure* for the public sector institutions through which the policy is to be implemented. For policies that offer benefits or services, they include the details of official *eligibility rules*, *behavioral conditions*, the nature and size of benefits or services offered, fees charged, and procedures for disseminating information and recruiting participants. For policies that impose regulations, they include the nature of the regulations, the rules determining who is liable for compliance, the provisions for monitoring compliance, and the penalties for noncompliance.

policy design question   A policy design question is a question regarding the benefits and costs of altering one or a small number of a *policy's design details*. See entries for *design change benefit* and *design change cost*, as well as the description of how to analyze the benefits and costs of policy design changes in section 15.4.

policy impacts   A policy's impacts are all the changes in well-being and behavior that are experienced by diverse groups throughout society and that result directly or indirectly from the policy's introduction.

policy implementation choices   Policy implementation choices are choices made by *policy-implementing agents* that help determine the policy's *implementation outcomes*.

policy-implementing agents   A policy's implementing agents are all the individuals and groups whose choices help determine the policy's *implementation outcomes*. For policies introduced by a central government, they may include central government bureaucrats working at central and lower levels, local government officials, community committees, partnering NGOs, and private-sector firms engaged either directly through government contracts or indirectly through demand-side financing.

policy objectives   A policy's objectives are the potential benefits (i.e., improvements in the well-being or behavior of specific target groups) that motivate policymakers to expend resources on the policy and that guide the policy's design.

political institutions   Political institutions are the rules and norms that determine who has *political power* in a society and how that power may be used.

political power   A group has political power when it is capable of influencing choices regarding the rules and norms that govern economic activity and daily life. A group's political power is a function of its economic power and the effectiveness of its organization.

poverty   People live in poverty when they experience *well-being* below some minimally acceptable level. Specific measures of poverty differ in how they measure well-being and how they define the minimally acceptable level of the chosen measure. Measures of poverty at the aggregate level differ also in the formulas they use to aggregate poverty measures across individuals.

poverty gap index   The poverty gap index is a measure of *poverty* at the aggregate level that is sensitive to differences in the prevalence of poverty and its average depth but not to differences in the prevalence of severe poverty among the poor.

poverty line   In the measurement of *poverty*, a poverty line defines the minimally acceptable level to which some *indicator* of a person's *well-being* must be compared for determining whether the person is poor and how poor she is.

poverty trap   An economy or group is stuck in a macro poverty trap when a *coordination problem* prevents investors from undertaking investments that would raise the economy or group out of poverty. A household is stuck in a micro poverty trap when the household has the mental and physical capacity to undertake *investments* that would raise it out of poverty, but it does not invest because—as a result of its very poverty—it lacks the financing or insurance that would make the investment feasible and attractive.

present bias   A decision maker exhibits present bias when she *discounts* the future more heavily when comparing consumption today to consumption one period from now than when she compares consumption in any future period to consumption in the subsequent period. Present bias represents a departure from *neoclassical rationality*.

price level   A country's current price level is the current cost, denominated in units of the country's currency, of purchasing a representative basket of goods and services.

principle of comparative advantage   The principle of comparative advantage states that new opportunities for market exchange between two parties leave both parties better off, even if one party can produce both goods at lower cost, as long as they differ in their relative aptitudes for producing different goods.

prisoner's dilemma   A prisoner's dilemma is a *game theory* construct illustrating why *cooperation* is very difficult, even when cooperation would leave everyone better off, when it is feasible for individuals to free ride. They free ride when they enjoy the benefits of other actors' cooperative behavior even while choosing not to cooperate themselves.

privatization   A *governance reform* involves privatization when it shifts authority for some *policy implementation choices* from the public sector to the private sector. This may be accomplished by shifting from direct government provision of subsidized services to the provision of subsidized services through private sector contractors or to the provision of subsidies through *demand-side financing*. It can also include reductions in direct government involvement in marketing activities and relaxation of prohibitions against private sector involvement in those activities.

production function   In economic models, a *production function* describes the maximum output that is technically feasible to produce when employing any given quantities of inputs.

production possibilities frontier   An economic unit's production possibilities frontier indicates all combinations of goods it can produce while engaging in *technically efficient* production and fully utilizing its *factors of production*.

profit   Profit is the difference between a producer's total revenue and total cost, where total cost includes the opportunity cost of the producer's own time and human capital.

property rights   People enjoy property rights over land or other assets when institutional rules and norms prevent others from expropriating or destroying the assets or appropriating the assets' returns.

pro-poor growth   During episodes of pro-poor growth, increases in a country's average income are accompanied by reductions in one or more aggregate *poverty* measures.

proximate sources of economic growth   The proximate sources of growth are the kinds of change in economic conditions that raise *aggregate labor productivity* and thus give rise to *economic growth*. They fall under the headings of *factor accumulation* and increases in *total factor productivity*.

public goods   Public goods are assets that generate services that are valuable to many people and that cannot be denied to anyone who wishes to use the services.

public goods problem   The public goods problem is the tendency for under-investment in *public goods* arising because potential investors cannot charge fees for the use of a public good's services and therefore cannot hope to recoup the cost of the investment. Sometimes the public goods problem is solved through *cooperation* among the individuals who stand to benefit from the investment.

public health policies   Public health policies seek to prevent illness and injury by encouraging health-protecting investments in infrastructure, the use of *health inputs*, or the undertaking of good *health behaviors*.

public sector   In this text, the public sector includes governments, *nongovernmental organizations*, and other development actors.

purchasing power   A household's purchasing power is its capacity to purchase the goods and services from which it derives its *utility*. Purchasing power rises when an increase in *income* or a reduction in a price allows the household to achieve a higher level of utility.

purchasing power parity exchange rates   Purchasing power parity exchange rates are exchange rates used to convert quantities measured in local currencies into U.S. dollar equivalents; they are determined by measuring the cost in local currency units of a basket of goods that costs $1 in the United States.

rationales for intervention   Rationales for intervention are reasons private actors, guided only by markets and private *institutions*, might make socially suboptimal choices, creating the potential for development-enhancing intervention by *development actors*.

rationing   A market is characterized by rationing when buyers are unable to buy as much as they would like at the going price.

real exchange rate   A country's real exchange rate (vis-à-vis a particular foreign country's currency) is equal to the *nominal exchange rate* of the country's currency vis-à-vis the foreign currency, multiplied by a measure of the foreign country's *price level* and divided by a measure of the country's own price level. When the real exchange rate rises, the price in domestic currency of purchasing a representative basket of goods in the foreign country rises relative to the comparable price of purchasing the same basket of goods locally.

real GDP growth   The rate of real GDP growth (in contrast to *nominal GDP growth*) is the rate of growth in a measure of *gross domestic product* that values goods and services at the same prices in the first and last periods of the interval over which growth is measured.

real income measures   Measures of households' real income (in contrast to *nominal income*) are measures of *income* denominated in current local currency units, divided by an index of current local *price levels*, and are intended to capture variation in households' *purchasing power*.

reciprocity   *In behavioral economics*, reciprocity refers to a particular departure from *neoclassical rationality* that renders people more willing to take costly actions that punish other people after they observe the others acting unfairly or renders them more willing to take costly actions that reward other people after they observe the others acting fairly.

reduction in demand or supply   A reduction in demand (supply) is a leftward shift in a demand (supply) schedule, indicating that while holding the price of the good constant at any level, the total quantity that market participants would wish to purchase (sell) has fallen.

reduction in the quantity demanded or supplied   A reduction in the quantity demanded (quantity supplied) is a reduction in the quantity of the good that market participants purchase (sell) as the result of a movement up and to the left (down and to the left) along a demand (supply) schedule, and represents a response to a price change.

relative poverty   People are counted as living in relative poverty when their incomes fall below a minimally acceptable fraction of the typical incomes in the economy. See also *absolute poverty*.

remittances   Remittances are private money transfers. In development discussions they are often transfers from or to family members who have migrated to other geographic locations.

rent seeking   Rent-seeking activities are activities through which individuals attempt to *appropriate* the returns to other people's production and investment activities rather than undertaking their own production and investment. They include theft, some forms of litigation, extraction of bribes, and lobbying for preferential treatment by government.

returns to an investment   An investment's returns are the improvements in the investor's life circumstances that flow from the creation or improved utilization of *assets*.

returns to scale   A *production function* exhibits increasing, constant, or decreasing returns to scale if, when the quantities of all inputs are doubled, output more than doubles, just doubles, or less than doubles, respectively.

risk   A decision involves risk when the benefits of taking a possible action depend on factors that are beyond the decision maker's control and are unknown at the time of the decision.

risk averse   Decision makers are risk averse when they are willing to accept a lower *expected return* in exchange for reduced *risk*.

risk pooling   A financial intermediary pools risks when it undertakes multiple risky investments with differing profiles of good and bad returns across *states of the world*, creating a portfolio of investments that together pay total returns that are much more similar across states of the world than are the returns to the individual investments.

saving   Decision makers engage in saving during a given period when they spend less than their *income* on consumption in that period.

savings-led microfinance   Savings-led microfinance is a branch of *microfinance* that encourages the formation of savings groups, which are groups of 5 to 50 members (all from the same community) that meet at frequent intervals to make small deposits to funds that are stored or loaned out by the group.

segmented labor markets   The market for a certain type of labor is segmented when some workers enjoy better wages and working conditions than other workers of the same type, because the employers paying the higher wages either cannot, or do not wish to, reduce their wages toward the market-clearing level.

self-targeting   A policy's benefits or subsidies are said to be self-targeting when *behavioral conditions*, logistical requirements, or other features of policy design render participation in the benefits particularly unattractive to nonpoor households, discouraging them from seeking participation.

service-level targeting   Policies employ service-level targeting when they attempt to render subsidies *self-targeting* by offering services at two or more levels of convenience or quality and attaching larger *subsidies* to the inferior services.

share tenancies   Share tenancies are arrangements under which landowners allow workers to cultivate plots of land in exchange for a share of the harvest.

shocks   Households are hit by (bad) shocks when they experience sudden reductions in income or sudden increases in needs.

social capital   Some social scientists use the term social capital to capture the advantages people enjoy as the results of membership in various groups. This text makes little use of the term, preferring instead to identify specifically the kinds of market and nonmarket interactions within groups that can raise and lower people's well-being and the *institutions* that govern these interactions.

specific factors model   The specific factors model is a model of international trade and *general equilibrium* in the domestic economy that treats some *factors of production* as perfectly immobile, or incapable of being moved from their current sectors of production to other sectors.

spheres of decision making   In some *non-unitary models of household decision making*, a household member's sphere of decision making is the set of choices over which the member exercises control.

spillover effects   See *indirect effects*.

squared proportional income gap index   The squared proportional income gap index, also known as the P2 Index, is a measure of *poverty* that is sensitive to differences in the prevalence of poverty, the average depth of poverty, and the prevalence of deep poverty among the poor.

standard economic assumptions   The standard economic assumptions about how people make choices are that people exhibit *neoclassical rationality*, that they have complete and accurate information, and that the only constraints they face are inescapable resource constraints such as budget constraints and technological constraints (in contrast to institutional constraints).

states of the world   In models of investment decisions in the presence of *risk*, different states of the world are different ways the world might evolve after an investment decision has been made that would lead to different *returns on the investment*.

structural change   Structural change is a shift in the distribution of workers across economic sectors and activities, usually associated with *economic growth*.

structuralism   Structuralism is a perspective on development based in part on the assumption that supply and demand *elasticities* of many sorts are low in developing countries, because the relevant actors have little ability or inclination to alter their behavior in response to changing economic incentives.

subsidy   The subsidy required for a development actor to provide a beneficiary household or community with a good, service, or asset through a particular policy is the total cost to the development actor of supplying the item less any revenue collected through fees or contributions.

substitutes in consumption   When two *normal goods* are substitutes in consumption, an increase in the price of one reduces the consumption of that good and increases the consumption of the other.

substitutes in production   When two inputs are substitutes in production, an increase in the price of one reduces the use of that one and increases the use of the other.

substitution effects   When examining the impact on household decision making of a change in a price, the substitution effect on a particular household activity is the increase or decrease in that activity that comes solely as a result of any associated change in relative prices (while holding the decision maker's *purchasing power* or *utility* constant).

supervision costs   In financial market transactions, supervision costs are the costs of information-gathering and trust-building activities undertaken with the aim of reducing *default* risks.

sustainability   In this text, a development program achieves sustainability if, after the relevant development actor has subsidized or catalyzed the creation of an asset or a service-providing firm or organization, the actor may leave the financing and execution of ongoing maintenance and service provision activities to households, community groups, firms, or organizations, thereby allowing the development actor's one-time intervention to generate benefits that are sustained for many years after the one-time intervention has ended.

target groups   A policy's target groups are the groups for which the policy aims to improve *well-being* in some way.

targeted subsidy   A targeted subsidy (in contrast to a *general subsidy*) is officially available only to individuals satisfying eligibility rules.

targeting failures   Targeted policies can exhibit two types of targeting failure: *leakage* to members of nontarget groups and *noncoverage of target groups*.

technical change   Technical change is change in the way goods and services are produced that enables producers to generate any given quantity of goods at lower cost or to produce higher-value goods at comparable cost.

technical efficiency   Producers are technically efficient when they produce the maximum output that is technologically possible from the inputs they employ.

terms of trade   A country's terms of trade is the ratio of the world market price of its exports to the world market price of its imports.

theory of the second best   The theory of the second best is an economic theory that reveals how an action that is socially desirable when all other actors in a system make socially optimal choices might not be socially desirable when other choices in the system are flawed. This implies that designing a policy to correct one *market and institutional failure* can do more harm than good when other failures remain uncorrected.

total factor productivity growth   Total factor productivity growth is the portion of the growth in the value of production (for a firm or a country) that is not explained by *factor accumulation*. At the country level it includes the effects of *technical change*, increases in *technical efficiency*, increases in *efficiency* in the allocation of resources across uses, reductions in *unemployment*, and reductions in wasteful uses of the factors of production.

trade liberalization   Trade liberalization is a *liberalizing reform* of policies toward a country's transactions in international markets.

tragedy of the commons   The tragedy of the commons is a prediction of simple *game theory* under assumptions of *neoclassical rationality* that people will overuse *common property resources*.

transaction costs   Buyers, sellers, and *market intermediaries* incur transaction costs when they undertake costly efforts to locate trading partners, reach agreements regarding transaction details or monitor compliance with agreements, and when they must bear the risk of losses to partners who *default* on contractual promises.

transfer costs   Transfer costs encompass all the transport, storage, financing, and *transaction costs* associated with the transfer of goods from their producers to their ultimate users.

underemployed   In some economic models of labor markets, people are underemployed when they work in jobs that make poor use of their skills or employ them for only a fraction of the hours they would like to work at the current wage.

unemployed   In economic models of labor markets, people are unemployed when they are not working and do not have a job but wish to work at the current market wage. In international labor statistics, people are treated as unemployed if they report that they are not working, do not have a job, are currently available for work, and have recently engaged in some job-seeking activity.

unitary models of household decision making   Unitary household models are models of household decision making that treat households as unified decision makers who seek simply and without conflict to maximize well-being as defined by a single *utility function*.

utility   Utility is a measure of how attractive a decision maker would find the results of a particular choice. It is usually assumed to be a function only of the quantities of goods and services she would consume after the choice has been made.

utility function   A utility function is a function describing the *utility* a decision maker would derive from consuming any given combination of quantities of various goods and services.

value added   For a production unit (whether a single firm or an entire country), the value added it produces in a given year is the difference between the total value of the goods and services the unit ultimately produces in the given year and the value of the raw materials and partially processed goods that it uses up in producing those goods.

value chain   A value chain is the sequence of activities required to facilitate production of a specific good and deliver it to its ultimate users according to whatever product or process standards they require. The chain of activities may include agricultural extension and financing for producers, quality certification, sorting, packaging, local and longer-distance transportation, wholesaling, customs clearance, and retailing services.

value of the marginal product of labor   The value of the marginal product of labor is the (approximate) increase in revenue associated with increasing labor by one unit while holding other inputs constant. For a competitive producer it equals the *marginal product of labor* times the price of one unit of output.

volume targeting   Policies distributing subsidized services employ volume targeting when they attempt to render the subsidies *self-targeting* by charging higher average fees to clients who use larger volumes of the services.

vouchers   Vouchers are documents that may be used to partially or fully cover the cost of purchasing specified goods or services from private providers.

vulnerability   People are vulnerable when they face significant risk of significant future reductions in well-being because they are exposed to *fluctuations and shocks* and they lack adequate opportunities for *ex ante* or *ex post responses to such fluctuations*. Development actors with different values might differ in how they define the "significant" risks and reductions that qualify people as meriting special policy attention because of their vulnerability.

well-being   A person's well-being is a summary assessment of how good or bad her life circumstances are, paying attention at a minimum to the quantities and qualities of the goods and services she consumes, the activities to which she allocates her time, and her hopes and fears regarding the future.

willingness to pay   A household's willingness to pay for an item is the highest price at which the household would choose to purchase the item.

workfare   Workfare programs provide opportunities for poor households to earn income by performing low-skill labor in public works projects.

Index

Note: Page numbers in **bold** refer to glossary terms